T0140231

Lecture Notes in Artificial Intelligence 13370

Subseries of Lecture Notes in Computer Science

More information about this subseries at https://link.springer.com/bookseries/1244

Gerard Memmi · Baijian Yang · Linghe Kong ·
Tianwei Zhang · Meikang Qiu (Eds.)

Knowledge Science, Engineering and Management

15th International Conference, KSEM 2022
Singapore, August 6–8, 2022
Proceedings, Part III

Editors
Gerard Memmi
Télécom Paris
Paris, France

Baijian Yang
Purdue University
West Lafayette, IN, USA

Linghe Kong
Shanghai Jiao Tong University
Shanghai, Shanghai, China

Tianwei Zhang
Nanyang Technological University
Singapore, Singapore

Meikang Qiu
Texas A&M University – Commerce
Commerce, TX, USA

ISSN 0302-9743 ISSN 1611-3349 (electronic)
Lecture Notes in Artificial Intelligence
ISBN 978-3-031-10988-1 ISBN 978-3-031-10989-8 (eBook)
https://doi.org/10.1007/978-3-031-10989-8

LNCS Sublibrary: SL7 – Artificial Intelligence

This Springer imprint is published by the registered company Springer Nature Switzerland AG
The registered company address is: Gewerbestrasse 11, 6330 Cham, Switzerland

Preface

This three-volume set contains the papers presented at the 15th International Conference on Knowledge Science, Engineering, and Management (KSEM 2022), held during August 6–8, 2022, in Singapore.

There were 498 submissions. Each submission was reviewed by at least 3, and on average 3.5, Program Committee members. The committee decided to accept 150 regular papers (30% acceptance rate) and 19 special track papers, giving a total of 169 papers. We have separated the proceedings into three volumes: LNCS 13368, 13369, and 13370.

KSEM 2022 was the fifteenth in this series of conferences which started in 2006. The aim of this interdisciplinary conference is to provide a forum for researchers in the broad areas of knowledge science, knowledge engineering, and knowledge management to exchange ideas and to report state-of-the-art research results. KSEM is in the list of CCF (China Computer Federation) recommended conferences (C series, Artificial Intelligence).

KSEM 2022 was held in Singapore, following the traditions of the 14 previous successful KSEM events in Guilin, China (KSEM 2006); Melbourne, Australia (KSEM 2007); Vienna, Austria (KSEM 2009); Belfast, UK (KSEM 2010); Irvine, USA (KSEM 2011); Dalian, China (KSEM 2013); Sibiu, Romania (KSEM 2014); Chongqing, China (KSEM 2015), Passau, Germany (KSEM 2016), Melbourne, Australia (KSEM 2017), Changchun, China (KSEM 2018); Athens, Greece (KSEM 2019), Hangzhou, China (KSEM 2020), and Tokyo, Japan (KSEM 2021).

The objective of KSEM 2022 was to bring together researchers and practitioners from academia, industry, and government to advance the theories and technologies in knowledge science, engineering, and management. KSEM 2022 focused on three broad areas: Knowledge Science with Learning and AI (KSLA), Knowledge Engineering Research and Applications (KERA), and Knowledge Management with Optimization and Security (KMOS).

We would like to thank the conference sponsors: Springer, Nanyang Technological University, Singapore, and Princeton University, USA. Moreover, we would like to express our gratitude to the honorary chairs and the KSEM Steering Committee chairs, Ruqian Lu (Chinese Academy of Sciences, China) and Dimitris Karagiannis (University of Vienna, Austria), and the members of the Steering Committee, who provided insight and guidance during all the stages of this effort. The KSEM 2022 general co-chairs, Ruby B. Lee (Princeton University, USA), Tianwei Zhang (Nanyang Technological University, Singapore), and Yaxin Bi (Ulster University, Jordanstown, UK), were extremely supportive in the conference organizing, call for papers, and paper review processes, and we thank them for the general success of the conference.

August 2022

Gerard Memmi
Baijian Yang
Linghe Kong
Tianwei Zhang
Meikang Qiu

Organizations

Honorary General Chairs

Ruqian Lu	Chinese Academy of Sciences, China
Dimitris Karagiannis	University of Vienna, Austria

General Co-chairs

Ruby B. Lee	Princeton University, USA
Tianwei Zhang	Nanyang Technological University, Singapore
Yaxin Bi	Ulster University, Jordanstown, UK

Program Chairs

Gerard Memmi	Telecom Paris, France
Baijian Yang	Purdue University, USA
Linghe Kong	Shanghai Jiao Tong University, China

Steering Committee

Ruqian Lu (Honorary Chair)	Chinese Academy of Sciences, China
Dimitris Karagiannis (Chair)	University of Vienna, Austria
Hui Xiong	Rutgers, The State University of New Jersey, USA
Yaxin Bi	Ulster University, Jordanstown, UK
Zhi Jin	Peking University, China
Claudiu Kifor	Sibiu University, Romania
Gang Li	Deakin University, Australia
Yoshiteru Nakamori	Japan Advanced Institute of Science and Technology, Japan
Jorg Siekmann	German Research Centre for Artificial Intelligence, Germany
Martin Wirsing	Ludwig-Maximilians-Universität München, Germany
Bo Yang	Jilin University, China
Chengqi Zhang	University of Technology Sydney, Australia
Zili Zhang	Southwest University, China
Christos Douligeris	University of Piraeus, Greece
Xiaoyang Wang	Zhejiang Gongshang University, China
Meikang Qiu	Texas A&M University–Commerce, USA

Publication Co-chairs

Meikang Qiu	Texas A&M University–Commerce, USA
Cheng Zhang	Waseda University, Japan

Publicity Chair

Shangwei Guo	Chongqing University, China

Technical Committee

Aniello Castiglione	University of Salerno, Italy
Beibei Li	Sichuan University, China
Bo Luo	University of Kansas, USA
Bowen Zhao	Singapore Management University, Singapore
Chaoshun Zuo	Ohio State University, USA
Cheng Huang	Sichuan University, China
Chunxia Zhang	Beijing Institute of Technology, China
Daniel Volovici	ULB Sibiu, Romania
Ding Wang	Peking University, China
Dongxiao Liu	University of Waterloo, Canada
Guangxia Xu	Chongqing University of Posts and Telecommunications, China
Guilin Qi	Southeast University, China
Guowen Xu	Nanyang Technological University, Singapore
Han Qiu	Tsinghua University, China
Hansi Jiang	SAS Institute Inc., USA
Hao Ren	The Hong Kong Polytechnic University, China
Hechang Chen	Jilin University, China
Jiahao Cao	Tsinghua University, China
Jianfei Sun	Nanyang Technological University, Singapore
Jianting Ning	Fujian Normal University, China
Jiaqi Zhu	Chinese Academy of Sciences, China
Jue Wang	SCCAS, China
Jun Zheng	New Mexico Tech, USA
Kewei Sha	University of Houston–Clear Lake, USA
Krzysztof Kluza	AGH University of Science and Technology, Poland
Leilei Sun	Beihang University, China
Man Zhou	Huazhong University of Science and Technology, China
Md Ali	Rider University, USA
Meng Li	Hefei University of Technology, China

Ming Li	Singapore Management University, Singapore
Neetesh Saxena	Bournemouth University, UK
Nhien An Le Khac	University College Dublin, Ireland
Pengfei Wu	National University of Singapore, Singapore
Pietro Ferrara	Università Ca' Foscari di Venezia, Italy
Qiang Gao	Southwestern University of Finance and Economics, China
Richard Hill	University of Huddersfield, UK
Robert Andrei Buchmann	Babeş-Bolyai University of Cluj Napoca, Romania
Salem Benferhat	University d'Artois, France
Serge Autexier	DFKI, Germany
Shangwei Guo	Chongqing University, China
Shaojing Fu	National University of Defense Technology, China
Shengmin Xu	Singapore Management University, Singapore
Shudong Huang	Sichuan University, China
Shuiqiao Yang	University of Technology Sydney, Australia
Songmao Zhang	Chinese Academy of Sciences, China
Ulrich Reimer	University of Applied Sciences St. Gallen, Switzerland
Wei Luo	Deakin University, Australia
Weipeng Cao	Shenzhen University, China
Wenyu Yang	Peking University, China
William de Souza	Royal Holloway, University of London, UK
Xiang Zhao	National University of Defense Technology, China
Xiangyu Wang	Xidian University, China
Xiaokuan Zhang	Georgia Institute of Technology, USA
Ximing Li	Jilin University, China
Xinyi Huang	Fujian Normal University, China
Yangguang Tian	Osaka University, Japan
Yaru Fu	Singapore University of Technology and Design, Singapore
Ye Zhu	Monash University, Australia
Yi Zheng	Virginia Tech, USA
Yiming Li	Tsinghua University, China
Yuan Xu	Nanyang Technological University, Singapore
Yuan Zhang	University of Electronic Science and Technology of China, China
Yueyue Dai	Nanyang Technological University, Singapore
Yunxia Liu	Huazhong University of Science and Technology, China

Zehua Guo	Beijing Institute of Technology, China
Zengpeng Li	Lancaster University, UK
Zheng Wang	Xi'an Jiaotong University, China
Zhisheng Huang	Vrije Universiteit Amsterdam, The Netherlands
Zhiyuan Tan	Edinburgh Napier University, UK
Zongming Fei	University of Kentucky, USA

Contents – Part III

Knowledge Management with Optimization and Security (KMOS)

Knowledge Management with Optimization and Security (KMOS)

Study on Chinese Named Entity Recognition Based on Dynamic Fusion and Adversarial Training

Fei Fan, Linnan Yang(✉), Xingyu Wu, Shengken Lin, Huijie Dong, and Changshan Yin

School of Big Data, Yunnan Agriculture University, Kunming, Yunnan, China
Feifan07@aliyun.com, lny5400@163.com, islsk@stu.xhsysu.edu.cn

Abstract. This paper aims at the Chinese Named Entity Recognition task, uses NEZHA Chinese pre-trained language model as the word embedding layer, then adopts the BiLSTM network architecture to encode it, and finally connects the CRF layer to optimize the output sequence. In order to enhance the fusion of semantic features of the NEZHA model in the upper, middle, and lower layers, an attention mechanism has been adopted to integrate the NEZHA coding layers. At first, weight was given to each representation generated by its 12 Transformer coding layers. Secondly, the weight value was dynamically adjusted through supervised training, and then the generated layer representation was weighted average to get the final word embedded representation. Finally, some noise was introduced to the input data, which is used for adversarial training to improve the generalization and robustness of the model. The results show that the F1 Score of the proposed model on Chinese Clinical Named Entity Recognition Dataset and people's daily corpus are respectively 98.52% and 96.84%, which are 2.36% and 4.21% respectively higher than the benchmark model Bert BiLSTM CRF.

Keywords: Natural language processing · Chinese named entity recognition · NEZHA · Dynamic fusion · Adversarial training

1 Introduction

Named Entity Recognition (NER) technology is one of the basic core tasks in natural language processing (NLP). It can identify entities in text and their corresponding types, such as human names, place names, institutional names, etc. It is an essential part of NLP downstream tasks such as Information Extraction, Q&A System, and Knowledge Graph.

Initially, rule and dictionary matching approaches were used in the research path of named entity recognition. For example, Liu et al. [1] recognized numeric and temporal expressions by designing and tuning optimal templates. Dictionary matching methods extract all matching strings from the target sequence utilizing entities built into the dictionary. These approaches may be successful in specific domains, but both fail to solve the OOV (Out-Of-Vocabulary) problem [2]. In addition, both methods rely heavily

G. Memmi et al. (Eds.): KSEM 2022, LNAI 13370, pp. 3–14, 2022.
https://doi.org/10.1007/978-3-031-10989-8_1

on time-consuming manual features. Later on, statistical machine learning approaches became popular, and CRF models [3] became the most commonly used method for named entity recognition. Li et al. [4] and Malarkodi et al. [5] used CRF models to identify agricultural named entities, such as crops, pests, and pesticides, on their self-constructed annotated corpus and obtained encouraging experimental results by selecting different combinations of features. The statistical-based machine learning approach effectively improves the accuracy of Chinese named entity recognition, but it is still time-consuming and tedious because it relies on feature engineering [6]. In addition, the CRF model is often unsatisfactory for the extraction of a large number of word-length entities in the text, and there are many breaks in the continuous entities.

Recurrent neural networks (RNNs) are widely applied to natural language processing tasks due to they maintain a memory based on historical information. They can be able to align with the text. Among RNNs, the Bi-directional long-short term memory network (BiLSTM) [7] is one of the most widely used RNN structures. Huang [8] was the first to apply BiLSTM and CRF to the sequence annotation task. Since BiLSTM has the powerful ability to learn word context representations, it has been adopted as an encoder by most NER models. Yue [9] proposed the Lattice LSTM network that encodes input character sequences and potential words for all matching dictionaries, making full use of word and word order information.

Recently, the pre-trained language model BERT [10] has been widely used on various NLP tasks, and some researchers have proposed to use the pre-trained language model BERT as a word embedding layer, and the acquired word representations have richer semantic and syntactic information because it has a more expressive bi-directional Transformer encoder [11]. Fabio [12] applied the BERT-CRF model to Portuguese NER to obtain the best F1 value on HAREM I; Jana [13] used the BERT pre-trained language model for entity recognition to achieve quite desirable results on CoNLL-2002 Dutch, Spanish and CoNLL-2003 English.

In recent years, the combination of deep learning and adversarial training has become popular in the field of natural language processing, and it has become an alternative path for text research as a regularization method. Miyato et al. [14] used deep learning techniques and proposed for the first time to add perturbations to the word vector layer for a semi-supervised text classification task. Bekoulis et al. [15] applied adversarial training to a joint model of entity recognition and relation extraction in a joint model, achieving excellent results across languages and multiple datasets. Zhou et al. [16], on the other hand, added perturbation to the word embedding layer to improve the generalization ability of named entity recognition models with low resources.

The remainder of the paper is organized as follows. Section 2 describes the basic network model for named entity recognition used in this article. Section 3 shows the principle of dynamic fusion and adversarial training algorithm. Section 4 discusses related research. Finally, Sect. 5 draws conclusions.

2 Methodology

2.1 Model Architecture

The primary model designed in this paper is the NEZHA (NEural contextualiZed representation for Chinese lAnguage understanding) [17] pre-trained language model of dynamic fusion, followed by the BiLSTM network architecture, and finally added to the CRF network layer. The model structure is shown in Fig. 1.

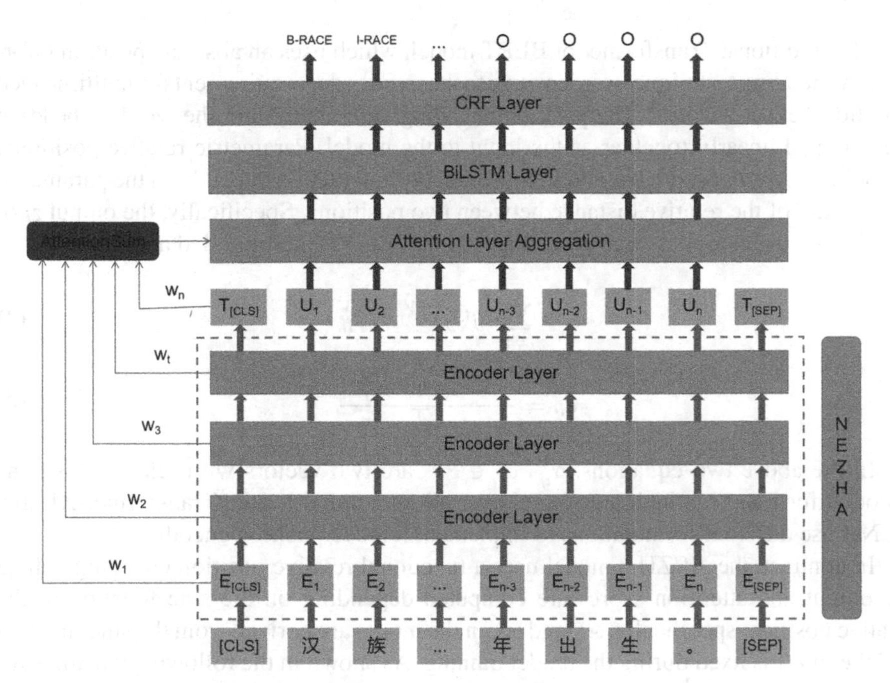

Fig. 1. Overall model architecture

2.2 Nezha Pre-trained Language Model

Huawei Noah's Ark Lab released the NEZHA pre-trained language model in 2019, based on the BERT model and trained on Chinese text. The main innovation is a functional relative position encoding technique, which encodes the relative position of the self-attentive layer by a predefined function without any trainable parameters.

In Transformer, each attention head processes a sequence of tokens $x = (x_1, x_2, \ldots, x_n)$, where $x_i \in R^{d_x}$, and outputs a sequence $z = (z_1, z_2, \ldots, z_n)$, where $z \in R^{d_z}$, and each attention head has three parameter matrices W^K, W^Q, $W^V \in R^{d_x \times d_z}$, to be learned, and the output z_i is computed as follows.

$$z_i = \sum_{j=1}^{n} \alpha_{ij}(x_j w^v) \tag{1}$$

The attention score α_{ij} between the hidden states at position i and position j is calculated using the softmax function.

$$\alpha_{ij} = \frac{exp e_{ij}}{\sum_k exp e_{jk}} \tag{2}$$

where e_{ij} is the scaled dot product between the linear transformations of the input elements.

$$e_{ij} = \frac{(x_i W^Q)(x_j W^k)^T}{\sqrt{d_z}} \tag{3}$$

The traditional Transformer or BERT model, which uses an absolute position information encoding technique, is insensitive to the word order requirement for multi-headed attention between words. The position encoding embedding and the word embedding are summed linearly together as the input to the model. Parametric relative positional encoding was proposed later, noting that the score calculation depends on the parametric embedding of the relative distance between two positions. Specifically, the output z_i of Eq. (1) and the computational procedure of e_{ij} of Eq. (3) are modified as follows.

$$z_i = \sum_{j=1}^{n} \alpha_{ij}(x_j W^V + \alpha_{ij}^V) \tag{4}$$

$$e_{ij} = \frac{(x_i W^Q)(x_j W^k + \alpha_{ij}^K)^T}{\sqrt{d_z}} \tag{5}$$

In the above two equations, α_{ij}^V, $\alpha_{ij}^K \in \mathbb{R}^{d_z}$ are two vectors with relative positions encoded for i and j, which are shared over all attentional heads. Transformer-XL and XLNet use different formulations to implement relative position encoding.

In contrast, the NEZHA model uses a functional relative position encoding, where the output and attention scores are computed depending on the sine function of the relative position, specifically, α_{ij}^V and α_{ij}^K in the model are derived from the sine function and the mode is fixed during the model training, As shown in the following equation, α_{ij} is used to represent α_{ij}^V, α_{ij}^K uniformly, and α_{ij} under dimension 2k and dimension 2k + 1 is considered respectively.

$$\alpha_{ij}[2k] = sin\left(\frac{j-i}{10000^{\frac{2 \cdot k}{d_z}}}\right) \tag{6}$$

$$\alpha_{ij}[2k+1] = cos\left(\frac{j-i}{10000^{\frac{2 \cdot k}{d_z}}}\right) \tag{7}$$

Each dimension of the location encoding corresponds to a sinusoidal function with different wavelengths for different dimensions. In the above equation, d_z is equal to the hidden dimension of each attention head in the NEZHA model (i.e., the hidden dimension divided by the number of attention heads). The wavelength is a geometric progression from 2π to $10000 \cdot 2\pi$. The fixed sine function was chosen because it allows the model to extrapolate to longer sequence lengths than those encountered in training. Techniques that have proven effective in BERT pre-trained models are also used, namely the full word mask technique, mixed-precision training, and LAMB optimizer, and the model performance is improved, and the training speed is significantly increased.

2.3 BiLSTM Network Layer

Traditional recurrent neural networks are usually characterized by a temporal structure and play an important role in tasks such as natural language processing and sequence prediction. LSTM is a recurrent neural network with memory units proposed by Schmidhuber in 1997, which is an improved version of the traditional recurrent neural network model.

LSTM is a typical operation of the popular RNN model that captures random sequence features and processes sequence data. The LSTM network mainly consists of three gating units and one memory unit, which will output two states to the next unit, the unit's state and the hidden state, respectively. The LSTM can capture remote dependencies through three gating mechanisms, namely, input gates, forgetting gates, and output gates. The input gate determines the percentage of the state saved from the current state to the cell state, the forgetting gate determines what information needs to be retained in the previous step, and the output gate is used to output the percentage of the state information from inside the memory cell at the current moment to determine the value of the next hidden state. The internal structure of an LSTM cell is shown in Fig. 2.

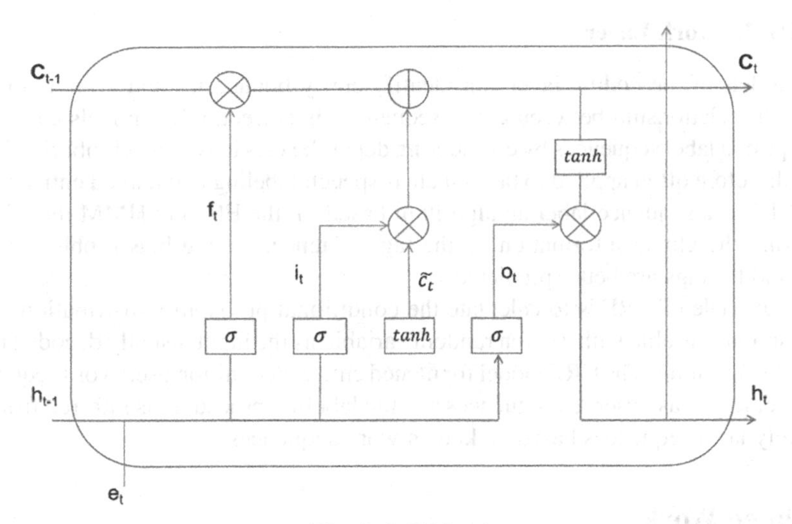

Fig. 2. LSTM unit

Since the one-way LSTM network can only capture the historical information of the acquired sequence, the category information of each word in the sequence is closely related to the context. Inspired by this, Graves et al. improved and proposed a bidirectional LSTM network (BiLSTM), which takes the model's ability to extract contextual information a step further, with applications in more domains such as speech recognition, lexical annotation, and named entity recognition.

First, we use the left and right contexts to identify named entities and then apply BiLSTM to mine the hidden expressions of characters from the global context, as shown in the following equation.

$$\left[\underset{h_1}{\rightarrow}, \underset{h_2}{\rightarrow}, \ldots, \underset{h_N}{\rightarrow}\right] = \underset{LSTM}{\rightarrow}([e_1, e_2, \ldots, e_N]) \tag{8}$$

$$\left[\underset{h_1}{\leftarrow}, \underset{h_2}{\leftarrow}, \ldots, \underset{h_N}{\leftarrow}\right] = \underset{LSTM}{\leftarrow}([e_1, e_2, \ldots, e_N]) \tag{9}$$

where e_i denotes the i-th character embedded after the word embedding layer, h_i denotes the output of the forward and reverse LSTM, and the hidden representation of the i-th character is concatenated by h_i.

$$h_i = \left[\underset{h_i}{\rightarrow}, \underset{h_i}{\leftarrow}\right] \tag{10}$$

Finally, the output of the BiLSTM layer is defined as $h = [h_1, h_2, \ldots, h_N]$, where $h_i \in R^{2s}$, S denotes the dimensionality of the LSTM hidden states.

2.4 CRF Network Layer

While models of the coding layer can identify entity boundaries and do not consider whether the relationship between entity sequences is correct, CRF models can obtain global optimal label sequences by considering dependencies between neighboring labels and are therefore often applied to tasks such as speech labeling and named entity recognition. CRF is a sequence labeling algorithm based on the EM and HMM models. By considering the global information on the tag sequence, the tag bias problem can be solved, and the tags are better predicted.

The rationale of CRF is to calculate the conditional probability distribution of the output random variable with a given random variable as the input, usually decoded using the Viterbi algorithm. The CRF model for named entity recognition used word sequences in input sentences as observed sequences and the labeling procedure is inferred from the most likely label sequences based on known word sequences.

3 Related Work

3.1 Dynamic Fusion

The paper published by Jawahar [18] in ACL 2019 states that low-level networks of BERT learn phrase-level information representations, middle networks of BERT learn rich linguistic features, while BERT's high-level network learns rich semantic information features. For entity recognition in the general domain, the model focuses on the top-level semantic features while ignoring the underlying features urgently needed by the entity recognition task. In addition, taking information directly from a high level can easily lead to over-fitting. Therefore, this study employs an attention-based multi-layer dynamic weight fusion approach to the BERT model.

Different BERT pre-trained language models also contain layer coding layers; generally, there are 12, 24, and 48 layers, recording the number of layers as L, as attention mechanism-based layer fusion, where both α and γ are trainable parameters. This is shown in Eqs. (11) and (12).

$$h = \gamma \sum_{i=1}^{N} w_i h_i \tag{11}$$

$$w_i = \frac{\exp(\alpha_i)}{\sum \exp(\alpha_j)} \tag{12}$$

where h is the output of the middle layer of the BERT model; w is the weight of each layer.

This paper weighs the representations generated by the 12-layer coding layer in the NEZHA pre-trained language model, then determines the weights dynamically through training. Each layer's weighted average gets the final feature representation and is then sent to the subsequent downstream network layer to obtain the prediction results.

3.2 Adversarial Training

The father of GAN Lan Goodfellow first proposed the concept of adversarial training [19] in 15 years of ICLR, simply adding a perturbation to the original input sample and being trained with it after obtaining the adversarial sample. That is, the problem can be abstracted into such a model:

$$\min_{\theta} - logP(y|x + r_{adv}; \theta) \tag{13}$$

Among these, y is the gold label, and θ is the model parameter. So how is the disturbance calculated? Goodfellow suggests that neural networks are vulnerable to linear perturbations due to their linear characteristics. So, he proposed the Fast Gradient Sign Method (FGSM) to calculate the perturbations of the input samples. Perturbation can be defined as:

$$r_{adv} = \epsilon \cdot sgn(\nabla_x L(\theta, x, y)) \tag{14}$$

where sgn is the symbolic function and L is the loss function. In summary, the two roles of adversarial training are improving the robustness of the model in response to malicious adversarial samples, providing a regularized supervised learning algorithm, reducing overfitting, and improving generalization ability.

At this point, the theoretical part of adversarial training is compared to intuitive, Madry's previous work in ICLR 2018 [20], and redefined the problem as a problem of finding a saddle point, the well-known Min-Max formula:

$$\min_{\theta} E_{(x,y)\in\mathcal{D}}\left[\max_{r_{adv}\in s} L(\theta, x + r_{adv}, y)\right] \tag{15}$$

The formula is divided into two parts, maximization of internal loss function and minimization of external empirical risk. The internal max is designed to find the perturbation of the worst-case, that is, the attack, where L is the loss function and S is the range space of the perturbation. The external min is designed to find the most robust model parameter, namely the defense, based on the attack mode, where the input samples are distributed. According to Madry, this formula simply and clearly defines two questions of the "spear and shield" of adversarial samples: how to construct strong enough adversarial samples? Moreover, how to make the model boring? The rest is the question of how to solve it.

We mentioned above that Goodfellow proposed FGSM in ICLR 2015 subsequently, and in ICLR 2017 [13], Goodfellow made a simple little modification to the portion of the computational perturbations in FGSM. Assuming that the embedding vectors of the input text sequence is [v1, v1, ..., vT], The perturbation for the x's embedding is:

$$r_{adv} = \epsilon \cdot g/||g||_2 \tag{16}$$

$$g = \nabla_x L(\theta, x, y) \tag{17}$$

where, G on behalf of the gradient, $||g||_2$ for L2 norm of the gradient, with the L2 norm made a scale, from the formula, L2 normalized more keep the direction of the gradient, and Max normalization is not necessarily in the same direction that the original gradient. Of course, they all have a common premise. That is, the loss function L must be linear or at least locally linear so as to ensure that the direction of gradient lifting is the optimal direction. Assuming that the number of rounds of mini-Batch is M and the number of the epoch is T, it can be seen from the code that the time complexity of FGSM and FGM is O(T*M).

In this study, two adversarial training algorithms, FGM and FGSM, found that the FGM effect was more applicable, so this method was used for adversarial training.

4 Experiment

4.1 Datasets

This paper selects CNER datasets from this paper [19], which are filtered and manually annotated according to the resume summary data of senior managers of listed companies. The datasets contain 1027 resume summaries with entity notation classified into eight categories, including human name, nationality, origin, race, major, degree, institution, and title.

This paper also performs statistics for text length, and considering the better capture of context information as well as the input sequence length limit of the BERT model, we tangent the text length by a 512-character length. To ensure the integrity of the sentence and reduce the absence of context semantics, the period as a tangent truncates the forward index of length 512, and the remaining sentences are added to the next subsequence, thus ensuring that a sentence is not cut into two parts.

4.2 Experimental Setup

This experiment uses a UTC 2021 x86_64 GNU/Linux server with a Quadro RTX 5000 graphics card and CUDA version 11.0. The neural network model is built in the PyTorch framework with PyTorch 1.7.1, and its corresponding Python version is 3.8. the following table lists the hyper-parameter values of the experimental model, with the word vector dimension set to 100 and the hidden layer dimension of the network model set to 128. In this paper, we introduce the Warm-up mechanism to mitigate the model over-fitting problem, with preheating learning rate set to 0.05, recession rate of 0.5, ADAM optimization algorithm, NEZHA fine-tuning learning rate of 1e-4, 5e-5, model training batch parameter of 16, and the number of iterations is set to 8. In addition, the accuracy P, recall R, and F1 values are used as the evaluation indicators of the experiment (Table 1).

Table 1. Hyper-parameters.

Hyper-parameters	Values
Warmup_proportion	0.05
decay_rate	0.5
train_epoch	8
learnig_rate	1e-4
embed_learning_rate	5e-5
sequence_length	512
lstm_hidden	128
batch_size	16

4.3 Results

The recognition effect of the model was tested on the annotated corpus without relying on artificial design features by constantly adjusting the model parameters. The training set in the corpus, the test set, divided by the validation set is 7:2:1 with no overlap between the three, so it is reasonable to take the output of the test set as an evaluation index of entity recognition effect.

To show the performance effect of the NEZHA-BiLSTM-CRF model proposed here in the Chinese named entity recognition task, we performed comparison experiments on other models, including BiLSTM-CRF, Bert-BiLSTM-CRF. We then compared the comprehensive effect of adding dynamic fusion and adversarial training. The specific comparison results are shown in the table below, and in the table, DF represents dynamic fusion, and AT represents adversarial training (Table 2).

Table 2. Experimental results.

Model	CNER			People's daily
	Precision (%)	Recall (%)	F1 (%)	F1 (%)
BiLSTM-CRF [8]	95.74	95.72	95.70	87.94
Bert-BiLSTM-CRF [12]	95.62	96.71	96.16	92.63
Nezha-BiLSTM-CRF	96.70	98.10	97.39	95.60
NEZHA-BiLSTM-CRF + DF	97.01	99.08	98.00	96.44
NEZHA-BiLSTM-CRF + DF + AT	97.60	99.50	98.52	96.84

From the results in the table, it can be seen that the F1 value of the proposed model and method in this paper improves by 2.82% in terms of comprehensive evaluation metrics when adding the comparison benchmark model BiLSTM-CRF, while based on the benchmark model BiLSTM-CRF, the large-scale pre-trained model BERT increased by only 0.46%, whereas the Chinese pre-trained language model NEZHA can improve by 1. 69%, which fully shows that the NEZHA pre-trained language model has more ability to extract features, is well-targeted for Chinese NER tasks, and can greatly improve the training speed of the model.

The addition of the NEZHA pre-trained language model can be improved by 0.61%, which shows the effectiveness of the dynamic fusion at all layers of NEZHA. Finally, the F1 value increases by 0.52% after adding countermeasure training, which shows that the countermeasure training algorithm can improve the generalization and robustness of the model.

In addition, we also selected the People's Daily corpus released by the Institute of Computational Language of Peking University for further validation of the experiment, which is one of the largest Chinese annotated corpora constructed in China, with information such as names of people, places, and organizations annotated in the corpus. The validation results also show the model's effectiveness and method proposed in this paper.

5 Conclusion

For the problems of text context-dependence and long entity type in the task of Chinese named entity recognition, this paper proposed a recognition method based on the Nezha pre-training model, which improves the performance of the model to a certain extent, and the hybrid precision training and lamb trainer also significantly improve the training speed. In this paper, we performed dynamic fusion for each layer of the NEZHA pre-trained model to obtain a better vector representation and verified the effectiveness of the semantic fusion mechanism. In addition, the input samples are trained in the way of adversarial training, which improves the robustness and generalization ability of the model to a certain extent, and improves the effect of Chinese named entity recognition.

The named entity recognition model proposed in this paper has achieved good recognition results in the open Chinese corpus. However, there are still some shortcomings that exist and need to be further improved and enhanced in future research work, which can be broadly focused on the following three aspects: first, potential word features will be incorporated into the model in this paper, combining BERT and Lattice LSTM to characterize the polysemy of words, while adding potential word features as a way to address the lack of contextual information. Second, introduce more advanced pre-trained language models, such as XLNET, RoFormer, etc., in order to further explore the model performance for better recognition effects. Third, some model compression methods, such as knowledge distillation [21], pruning, etc., are tried to reduce the training time, computational power, and spatial complexity.

Acknowledgement. This work has been supported by the Major Project of Science and Technology of Yunnan Province under Grant No. 202002AD080002.

References

1. Liu, W., Yu, B., Zhang, C., et al.: Chinese named entity recognition based on rules and conditional random field. In: Proceedings of the 2018 2nd International Conference on Computer Science and Artificial Intelligence, pp. 268–272 (2018)
2. Wang, X., Jiang, X., Liu, M., et al.: Bacterial named entity recognition based on dictionary and conditional random field. In: 2017 IEEE International Conference on Bioinformatics and Biomedicine (BIBM), pp. 439–444. IEEE (2017)
3. Wallach, H.M.: Conditional random fields: An introduction. Technical reports (CIS), p. 22 (2004)
4. Li, X., Wei, X.H., Jia, L., et al.: Recognition of crops, diseases and pesticides named entities in Chinese based in conditional random fields. Trans. Chin. Soc. Agric. Mach. **48**, 178–185 (2017)
5. Malarkodi, C.S., Lex, E., Devi, S.L.: Named entity recognition for the agricultural domain. Res. Comput. Sci. **117**, 121–132 (2016)
6. Zhou, G.D., Su, J.: Named entity recognition using an HMM-based chunk tagger. In: Proceedings of the 40th Annual Meeting of the Association for Computational Linguistics, pp. 473–480 (2002)
7. Hochreiter, S., Schmidhuber, J.: Long short-term memory. Neural Comput. **9**(8), 1735–1780 (1997)
8. Huang, Z., Xu, W., Yu, K.: Bidirectional LSTM-CRF models for sequence tagging. arXiv: 1508.01991 (2015)
9. Zhang, Y., Yang, J.: Chinese NER using lattice LSTM. arXiv:1805.02023 (2018)
10. Devlin, J., Chang, M.W., Lee, K., et al.: Bert: Pre-training of deep bidirectional transformers for language understanding. arXiv:1810.04805 (2018)
11. Vaswani, A., Shazeer, N., Parmar, N., et al.: Attention is all you need. In: Advances in Neural Information Processing Systems, pp. 5998–6008 (2017)
12. Souza, F., Nogueira, R., Lotufo, R.: Portuguese named entity recognition using BERT-CRF. arXiv:1909.10649 (2019)
13. Straková J., Straka M., Hajič J.: Neural architectures for nested NER through linearization. arXiv:1908.06926 (2019)
14. Wei, J., Ren, X., Li, X., et al.: NEZHA: neural contextualized representation for Chinese language understanding. arXiv:1909.00204 (2019)
15. Jawahar, G., Sagot, B., Seddah, D.: What does BERT learn about the structure of language? In: Proceedings of the 57rd Annual Meeting of the ACL (2019)

16. Goodfellow, I.J., Shlens, J., Szegedy, C.: Explaining and harnessing adversarial examples. arXiv:1412.6572 (2014)
17. Madry, A., Makelov, A., Schmidt, L., et al.: Towards deep learning models resistant to adversarial attacks. arXiv:1706.06083 (2017)
18. Miyato, T., Dai, A.M., Goodfellow, I.: Adversarial training methods for semi-supervised text classification. arXiv:1605.07725 (2016)
19. Miyato, T., Dai, A.M., Goodfellow, I.: Adversarial training methods for semi-supervised text classification. arXiv preprint arXiv:1605.07725 (2016)
20. Chen, X., Cardie, C.: Multinomial adversarial networks for multi-domain text classification. arXiv preprint arXiv:1802.05694 (2018)
21. Hinton, G., Vinyals, O., Dean, J.: Distilling the knowledge in a neural network. arXiv preprint arXiv:1503.02531 (2015) 2(7)

Spatial Semantic Learning for Travel Time Estimation

Yi Xu[1], Leilei Sun[1,2(✉)], Bowen Du[1,2], and Liangzhe Han[1]

[1] State Key Laboratory of Software Development Environment, Beihang University, Beijing 100191, China
{xuyee,leileisun,dubowen,liangzhehan}@buaa.edu.cn
[2] Peng Cheng Laboratory, Shenzhen 518055, China

Abstract. Travel time estimation is a crucial and fundamental problem in Intelligent Transportation Systems (ITS), which benefits multiple downstream applications such as route planning, ride-sharing and taxi dispatching. Most previous work mainly focuses on the spatial space of a single form, which are incomplete representations of trajectories thus leading to inaccurate estimation results because multi-semantic context information has not been fully extracted and only one form of spatial representations are exploited. Additionally, many researchers use recurrent neural networks to extract temporal dependencies inside trajectories, which leads to uneven allocation of weight and brings about time-consuming iterative propagation problems. In this paper, we propose a Spatial Semantic learning model for Travel time Estimation (SSTE), to generate multi-view spatial representations for trajectories. This model represents trajectories in Euclidean space and non-Euclidean space simultaneously to learn different spatial representations from the latent road networks. Furthermore, a self-supervised segment embedding module named Seg2Vec is designed to produce spatial semantic segment embeddings. Seg2Vec exploits edge-level semantic representations of segments in non-Euclidean space, which takes road type and co-occurrence into consideration simultaneously. A sequence learning component with high computational efficiency is utilized to aggregate spatiotemporal relations, multi-semantic segment embeddings, and external properties of the query trajectory. Extensive experiments are conducted on two real-world trajectory datasets. The experimental results demonstrate that our SSTE significantly outperforms existing models.

Keywords: Sequence learning · Segment embedding · Spatial semantic learning · Travel time estimation · Intelligent transportation system

1 Introduction

With the proliferation of GPS-enabled devices and the advances in location-aware mobile applications, enormous amounts of trajectory data are being

Supported by the National Natural Science Foundation of China (71901011, U1811463, 51991391, 51991395).

G. Memmi et al. (Eds.): KSEM 2022, LNAI 13370, pp. 15–26, 2022.
https://doi.org/10.1007/978-3-031-10989-8_2

generated at an unprecedented speed. A large amount of trajectory data provide opportunities to further enhance urban transportation systems and carry out various mining tasks, e.g., travel time estimation [8], destination prediction [5], and trajectory outlier detection [4]. Among these tasks, travel time estimation is fundamental to many urban transportation systems, e.g., bike-sharing [21,27], traffic monitoring, route planning, and real-time navigation.

Existing studies mainly build graphs in only one spatial space. However, just as Fig. 1 shows, the spatial space can be represented in different forms. Previous work with OD-based methods [22], GPS-based methods [15,21] and grid-based methods [1,27] mainly build graphs in Euclidean spatial space, ignoring the spatial semantic of trajectories in non-Euclidean space. To overcome the drawbacks of these path representation methods, segment-based methods [20,28] are employed to represent paths as sequences of segments in non-Euclidean space. They calculate the travel time of trajectories by summing up time of each segment, which overlooks the transition time between segments like waiting for traffic lights. Besides, complex multiple dynamics like the changing traffic conditions, external properties, and semantic information need to be taken into consideration. All these characteristics make the travel time of a certain trajectory at a certain departure time uncertain and hard to accurately predict.

To address these issues, we propose a Spatial Semantic learning model for Travel time Estimation (SSTE) to generate multi-view spatial representations. A segment embedding component with two self-supervised tasks named Seg2Vec is designed to learn spatial relationships in the non-Euclidean road networks. Segments that are closer in road networks have a higher frequency of co-occurrence and their embedding vectors have a closer distance in vector space. Then, spatial representations of different forms, time features and external properties are fused together through a sequence representation model with Convolution Neural Networks (CNN) to generate trajectory embeddings and output predicted travel time.

The main contributions of this paper are summarized as follows:

- We introduce a spatial semantic representation model for trajectories to learn the spatial representations in different spaces simultaneously. Besides, multiple semantic information and external properties are taken into consideration as well.
- A segment embedding framework Seg2Vec is specifically designed to generate segment embeddings. It ensures that road segments sharing co-occurrence of high frequency have similar embeddings. Seg2Vec is a general self-supervised framework for segment embeddings, which can be applied to multiple tasks in ITS.
- To the best of our knowledge, this article is the first to employ 1D CNN as a sequence learning model to extract temporal properties among segments for travel time estimation.

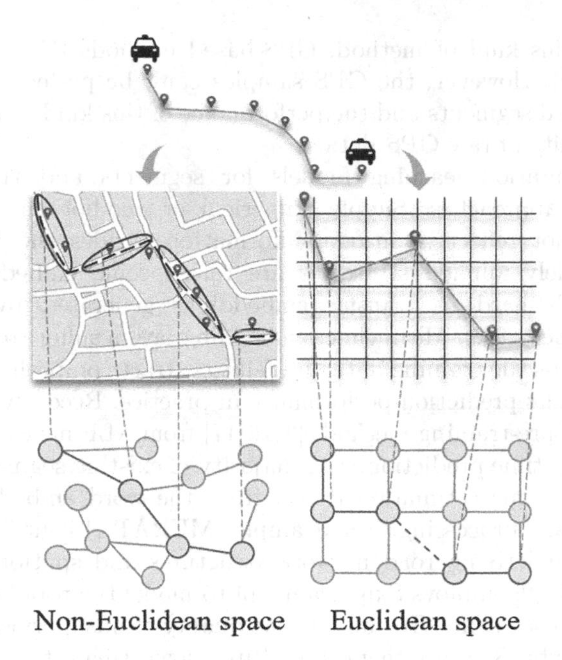

Fig. 1. Different spatial representations.

- Extensive experiments are conducted on two large-scale real-world datasets. The experimental results show that our model outperforms multiple existing travel time estimation methods significantly.

The rest of this paper is organized as follows: Sect. 2 summarizes previous research related to the studied problem. Section 3 presents the framework and introduces each component of our model. Section 4 evaluates the proposed model through experiments. Finally, Sect. 5 concludes the entire paper.

2 Related Work

Methods for travel time estimation can be divided into two categories: Origin-Destination-based (OD-based) methods and path-based methods. Under the framework of OD-based methods, it's only known where a trip will start and end [22]. Consequently, it's unavoidable to omit some information in the middle of a path. Instead of only using the origin and destination of a route, path-based methods try to make use of every part of a path. Path-based methods have 4 subdivides: segment-based methods, subpath-based methods, GPS-based methods and grid-based methods. Some segment-based methods [20,28] overlook transition time between segments like waiting time for the traffic lights. Others [6,10] just treat travel time estimation as a traffic speed prediction problem. Subpath-based methods [7,19,23] can ease transaction problems to some degree, but the requirement of fixed path length and locally aggregated information limits the performance of this kind of method. GPS-based methods [15,21] are comparatively convenient. However, the GPS samples can't be perfectly aligned with corresponding road segments and the performance of this kind of method highly relies on the quality of raw GPS data.

Most representation learning models for segments and trajectories are feature-designed approaches. Simple numerical or one-hot encoded categorical features cannot reflect additional information besides the index of locations. Other widely applied strategies are task-specific embedding methods [11,21,24,27]. It's hard to transfer embeddings generated by task-specific approaches to other tasks. Meanwhile, embedding layers suffer from over-fitting problems on small-scale training data and fail to extract comprehensive information, which will hurt prediction performance in practice. Recently, unsupervised or self-supervised pre-training methods [3,16,17] from NLP have attracted much attention in traffic time prediction. The majority of existing segment embedding models for traffic time estimation derive from the word embedding methods in natural language processing. For example, MURAT [13] utilizes DeepWalk [18] to capture underlying road network structures and spatiotemporal prior knowledge. CTTE [9] employs Skip-gram [16] to model the topological relationship between road segments. To validate the quality of unsupervised pre-trained embeddings, Trembr [8] apply them to multiple downstream tasks. Pre-training methods incorporate numerous universal information like neighbor information, relative position and functionalities through the process of training for segment embeddings, which can achieve better generalization and higher accuracy on downstream tasks. Meanwhile, unsupervised approaches only require unlabeled data for pre-training, which is more applicable in real life.

In this article, a new representation method is proposed. It divides trajectories into segments. However, instead of calculating segment time individually, it generates a uniform embedding vector for a trajectory. Besides, an unsupervised segment pre-training framework with two self-supervised tasks is designed, which can utilize unlabeled segment pairs derived from trajectories to generate general embeddings for segments.

3 Methodology

3.1 Definitions and Problem Formalization

Definition 1 (GPS Point). A GPS point g_i is defined as $g_i =< lat_i, lon_i, t_i >\in \mathbb{R}^3$, where $-90 \le lat_i \le 90, -180 \le lon_i \le 180$ are the coordinates of latitude and longitude in decimal degree. t_i is the timestamp of i_{th} GPS point. The set of GPS points $\mathbb{G} = \{g_1, g_2, ..., g_{|\mathbb{G}|}\}$, where $|\mathbb{G}|$ is the total number of GPS points.

Definition 2 (Road Network). A road network is a directed graph $\mathcal{G} = \{\mathbb{V}, \mathbb{E}\}$. $\mathbb{V} = \{v_1, v_2, ..., v_{|\mathbb{V}|}\}$ is a set of $|\mathbb{V}|$ intersections between road segments. $E = \{e_1, e_2, ..., e_{|\mathbb{E}|}\}$ is a set of $|\mathbb{E}|$ road segments after map-matching. A road segment takes road intersections as its start and end while it does not contain any crossing inside. $e_n = (v_{m_i}, v_{m_j})$ denotes that segment e_n takes intersection v_{m_i} and v_{m_j} as its start and end.

Definition 3 (Trajectory). The set of trajectories is $\mathbb{T} = \{T_1, T_2, ..., T_{|\mathbb{T}|}\}$, where $|\mathbb{T}|$ is the total number of trajectories. A GPS trajectory T_j comprises a sequence of GPS points, i.e., $T_j = \{g_1^j, g_2^j, ..., g_{l_j}^j\}$, where $g_k^j \in \mathbb{G}$ and l_j is the number of GPS points passed by T_i. Additionally, for each trajectory we record its external factors such as the starting time (timeID), the day of the week (weekID).

Travel Time Estimation. Given a query trajectory T_q and its departure time t_{begin}, our goal is to estimate the duration time t_{last} using the set of historical trajectories as well as the road network $\mathcal{G}$. Then, the arriving time will be calculated as $t_{end} = t_{begin} + t_{last}$.

3.2 Proposed SSTE Model

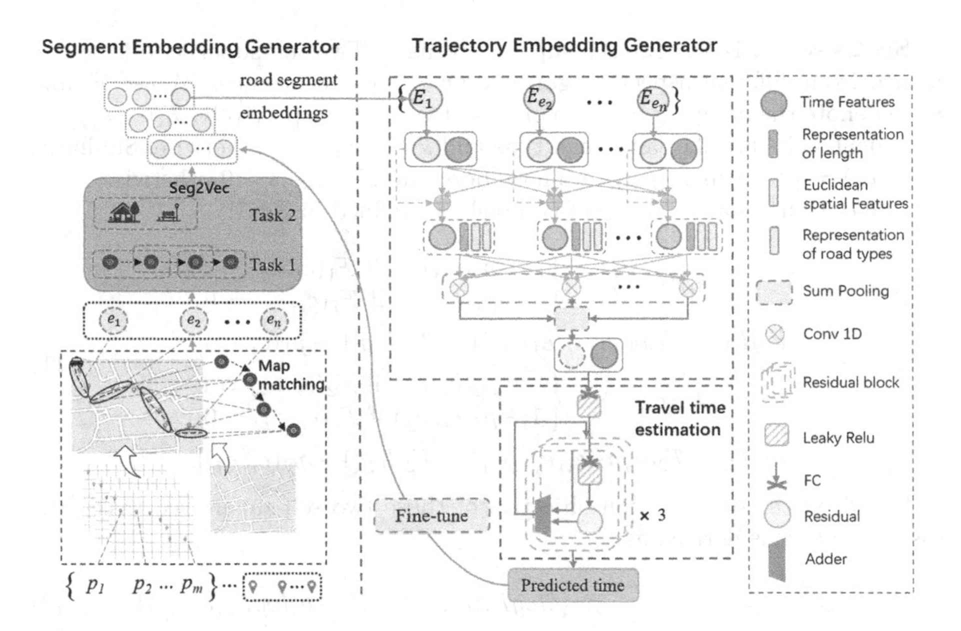

Fig. 2. The framework of proposed SSTE.

The framework of proposed model SSTE is shown in Fig. 2, which consists of 4 stages. The first stage is to transfer trajectories of GPS points to sequences of road segments. Corresponding map-matching algorithm is shown in Algorithm 1.

After map-matching for road segments, the second stage is to learn the segment embeddings. Then, a segment embedding method named Seg2Vec is specially designed to learn spatial semantic representations of road segments in non-Euclidean space.

Algorithm 1: Map-matching

Input: latent road network : $\mathcal{G} = \{\mathbb{V}, \mathbb{E}\}$:
set of trajectories : $\Gamma = \{T_1, T_2, ..., T_{n_t}\}$
Output: set of paths : $\Upsilon = \{P_1, P_2, ..., P_{n_p}\}$

```
1 for i = 1 to n_t do
2     matched_segment_list = Match(G, T_i)
3     foreach e in matched_segment_list do
4         if e != merged_segments_list.last() then
5             merged_segments_list = merged_segments_list + e
6     p_i = SPFFillPath(G, merged_segments_list)
7     Υ = Υ + p_i
8 return Υ
```

Seg2Vec consists of two self-supervised tasks. Two self-supervised tasks are defined from different aspects: segment type and co-occurrence. We use $\mathcal{F}_1$ and $\mathcal{F}_2$ to denote the mapping function of these two tasks respectively. $\mathcal{F}_1(e_i, e_j) = 1$ if segment pairs are the same road type and $\mathcal{F}_1(e_i, e_j) = 0$ otherwise. Similarly, $\mathcal{F}_2(e_i, e_j) = 1$ if segment pairs are neighbors and $\mathcal{F}_2(e_i, e_j) = 0$ otherwise.

The optimization objective of two tasks is defined in Eq. 1:

$$\begin{aligned} L_1(e_i, e_j) &= \begin{cases} p_1(e_i, e_j) \text{ if } \mathcal{F}_1(e_i, e_j) = 1 \\ 1 - p_1(e_i, e_j) \text{ if } \mathcal{F}_1(e_i, e_j) = 0, \end{cases} \\ logL_1 &= \mathcal{F}_1 logp_1(e_i, e_j) + [1 - \mathcal{F}_1] log[1 - p_1(e_i, e_j)], \\ L_2(e_i, e_j) &= \begin{cases} p_2(e_i, e_j) \text{ if } \mathcal{F}_2(e_i, e_j) = 1 \\ 1 - p_2(e_i, e_j) \text{ if } \mathcal{F}_2(e_i, e_j) = 0, \end{cases} \\ logL_2 &= \mathcal{F}_2 logp_2(e_i, e_j) + [1 - \mathcal{F}_2] log[1 - p_2(e_i, e_j)]. \end{aligned} \tag{1}$$

Based on the optimization objective of these two self-supervised tasks, the loss of Seg2Vec is derived as:

$$\mathcal{L}_{seg2vec} = - \sum_{(e_i, e_j) \in \mathbb{S}_{train}} \{\theta logL_1(e_i, e_j) + (1 - \theta) logL_2(e_i, e_j)\}, \tag{2}$$

where θ is used to parameterize the trade-off between two tasks.

During Seg2Vec, we maximize L_1 and L_2 through minimizing the overall Loss. For each training segment pair e_i and e_j in $\mathbb{S}_{train}$, stochastic gradient descent algorithm is applied during backpropagation training:

$$\begin{aligned} \mathbf{E}_i &= \mathbf{E}_i - \frac{\theta \sum_j \Delta logL_1(e_i, e_j) + (1 - \theta) \sum_j \Delta logL_2(e_i, e_j)}{\Delta \mathbf{E}_i}, \\ \mathbf{E}_j &= \mathbf{E}_j - \frac{\theta \sum_i \Delta logL_1(e_i, e_j) + (1 - \theta) \sum_i \Delta logL_2(e_i, e_j)}{\Delta \mathbf{E}_j}. \end{aligned} \tag{3}$$

After Seg2Vec, embedding vectors of road segments with the same road type and neighbor segments will have a close distance in the latent embedding space $\mathbf{E}$. Road segments embeddings will be fine-tuned during the process of travel time prediction. Non-Euclidean spatial semantic is extracted from real road network after Seg2Vec.

Trajectory embedding is the third stage of SSTE model. For each road segment e_i, segment embeddings generated by Seg2Vec $\mathbf{E}_i$, time features $\mathbf{H}_i^{period}$, static properties of roads $\mathbf{H}_i^E = [\mathbf{H}_i^{type}, H_i^{Length}]$ as well as Euclidean spatial features $\mathbf{H}^N$ are combined together to generate embeddings for trajectories in this phase:

$$\begin{aligned}\mathbf{H}_i^t &= Concat(\mathbf{E}_i, \mathbf{H}_i^{week}, \mathbf{H}_i^{date}, \mathbf{H}_i^{time}),\\ \mathbf{H}_i^T &= MLP(ReLU(MLP(\mathbf{H}_i^t))) + \mathbf{H}_i^t,\\ \mathbf{H}^N &= MLP([H_{begin}^{lat}, H_{begin}^{lon}, H_{end}^{lat}, H_{end}^{lon}]),\\ \mathbf{H}_i &= MLP(ReLU(MLP(Concat(\mathbf{H}_i^T, \mathbf{H}_i^E, \mathbf{H}^N)))),\end{aligned} \tag{4}$$

where H_i is the final segment embedding of segment e_i.

Then, 1D convolution is employed to capture the temporal information of trajectories and generate trajectory embeddings. 1D convolution over a discrete sequence of segment embeddings $\mathbf{H}_1, \mathbf{H}_2, ...\mathbf{H}_n$ is defined as:

$$(\mathbf{W} * \mathbf{H})_i = \sum_{j=1}^{k} \mathbf{W}_j \mathbf{H}_{i-j}, \tag{5}$$

where $\mathbf{W} \in \mathbb{R}^{k*d_h}$ is a kernel parameters. d_h is the dimension of the embedding of a single segment and k is kernel size of convolution. A sum pooling module is added after 1D convolution to aggregate the information of segments:

$$\mathbf{H}' = SumPooling(Concat((\mathbf{W} * \mathbf{H})_1, (\mathbf{W} * \mathbf{H})_2, ..., (\mathbf{W} * \mathbf{H})_n)), \tag{6}$$

where $\mathbf{H}' \in \mathbb{R}^{d_o}$ is the embedding vector of a trajectory with temporal information.

Finally, three residual fully connected layers are utilized to output the predicted travel time of the given trajectory based on the learned representation in the travel time estimation module:

$$\begin{aligned}\mathbf{X}_0 &= LeakyRelu(MLP(Concat(\mathbf{H}', \mathbf{H}_1^t))),\\ \mathbf{X}_{i+1} &= \mathbf{X}_i + MLP(\mathbf{X}_i), i = 0, 1, 2,\\ \widehat{t} &= MLP(\mathbf{X}_3).\end{aligned} \tag{7}$$

The loss function used for training the model is:

$$\mathcal{L} = \sum_{j=1}^{|\mathbb{P}|} (\widehat{t_j} - t_j)^2 + \lambda ||\mathbf{W}||^2, \tag{8}$$

where λ is a hyper-parameter to control the regularization strength and denotes all weights in the network. The Adam optimizer is utilized as the stochastic gradient descent optimization algorithm. Meanwhile, segment embeddings $\mathbf{E}$ are fine-tuned during this phase. The pre-trained segment embeddings from Seg2Vec are loaded as the initial weights of the model to generate the representation of trajectories. They will be updated through gradient descent.

4 Experiments

In this section, experimental results and detailed analysis are displayed to show the superiority of our model.

4.1 Data Description and Baselines

We evaluate our model on two large scale datasets: **Porto Taxi**[1] consists of 426023 trajectories generated by 442 taxis in Porto from July 1st, 2013 to Jun 30th, 2014. **Chengdu Taxi**[2] contains 434927 trajectories of 14864 taxis in Chengdu from August 3rd, 2014 to August 8th, 2014. The primitive form of a trajectory is a sequence of GPS points with longitude and latitude coordinates.

We compare our model with 10 baseline methods including statistic methods like TEMP [22], LR [25]; ensemble learning methods like Random Forest Regression (RF) [14], XGBoost [2], GBRegressor [12], DTRegressor [26]; deep learning methods like STNN [11], WDR [24], DeepTTE [21], CTTE [9]. Amongst deep learning methods, STNN is an OD-based method while DeepTTE is GPS-based, WDR and CTTE are segment-based methods.

4.2 Performance Evaluation

Prediction Accuracy on Porto. From Table 1 we can observe that the proposed SSTE model can significantly outperform all the baselines on Porto taxi dataset, including statistic methods (TEMP), simple regression methods (LR), ensemble learning methods (RF, GBRegressor, DTRegressor, XGBoost) and deep learning methods (STNN, WDR, DeepTTE, CTTE) in terms of MAE, MAPE, RMSE and PCC. Compared to the previous state-of-the-art models, SSTE achieves the lowest MAE 70.8339, the lowest MAPE 0.1531 and the lowest RMSE 98.0851. Meanwhile, SSTE achieves the highest PCC 0.9057 among all the models and the performance improvements are significant on all metrics.

[1] This is available at https://www.kaggle.com/crailtap/taxi-trajectory.
[2] This is available at https://challenge.datacastle.cn/v3/cmptDetail.html?id=175.

Table 1. Comparison results with baselines.

Dataset	Porto Taxi				Chengdu Taxi			
Metric	MAE	MAPE	RMSE	PCC	MAE	MAPE	RMSE	PCC
TEMP	115.1918	0.2915	159.5779	0.7282	136.8137	0.3868	299.4572	0.7376
LR	94.4094	0.2284	137.2526	0.8042	130.1079	0.3608	387.3377	0.7594
GBRegressor	125.1999	0.3384	168.6894	0.6933	209.9505	0.7204	357.6483	0.6062
DTRegressor	133.8035	0.3095	194.1654	0.6532	196.6894	0.4898	389.6364	0.5986
RF	94.3111	0.2281	137.2428	0.8042	130.2420	0.3616	286.8193	0.7705
XGBoost	140.0425	0.3605	286.3710	0.7594	132.9879	0.2942	289.8439	0.7533
STNN	141.3906	0.3054	197.1221	0.6740	191.4118	0.3420	365.4731	0.6683
WDR	80.9430	0.1744	110.1694	0.8790	125.6295	0.2538	284.9564	0.7675
DeepTTE	102.1990	0.2037	147.0077	0.8119	133.7677	**0.2210**	310.2036	0.7609
CTTE	79.0731	0.1708	109.0702	0.8820	133.3756	0.2662	290.5388	0.7655
SSTE	**70.8339**	**0.1531**	**98.0851**	**0.9057**	**107.1807**	0.2333	**263.6982**	**0.8035**

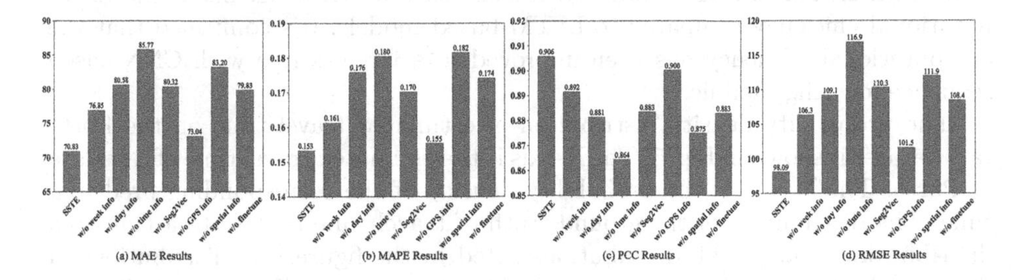

Fig. 3. Ablation study results.

Prediction Accuracy on Chengdu. As shown in Table 1, the proposed model SSTE has the best performance compared to other baselines including OD-based methods (Temp, LR, GBRegressor, DTRegressor, RF, XGBoost, STNN), GPS-based methods (DeepTTE) and segment-based methods (CTTE, WDR) over Chengdu taxi dataset on three metrics. SSTE reduces the MAE from 130.1079 to 107.1807, the RMSE from 284.9564 to 263.6982 and improves the PCC from 0.7675 to 0.8035.

4.3 Ablation Study

Figure 3 shows the performance of SSTE against its ablations on Porto Taxi Dataset. (a) It's observed that the experiment result is the worst when daily-period embedding vectors and weekly-period embedding vectors are removed at the same time, denoting that both daily-period components and weekly-period components are indispensable factors. (b) Segment embedding vectors generated by Seg2Vec are removed in SSTE w/o Seg2Vec; SSTE w/o GPS info excludes embedding vectors of GPS points. Both two spatial factors are removed in SSTE w/o spatial info; SSTE w/o GPS info has a better performance than SSTE w/o

Seg2Vec and there is no significant distinct difference between SSTE and SSTE w/o GPS. The experiment results of SSTE w/o GPS and SSTE w/o Seg2Vec show that segment embeddings are more pivotal than Euclidean spatial representations. And it confirms the superiority of segment-based methods compared to other approaches. (c) Segment embeddings generated by Seg2Vec keep unchanged during the inference period in SSTE w/o finetune. It's observed that the fine-tuning of segment embeddings generated by Seg2Vec in the inference phase will improve the representation ability of segment embeddings and model performance.

4.4 Computational Efficiency and Prediction Analysis

Experiments are conducted to confirm the computational efficiency of SSTE over models which use LSTM as trajectory embedding approaches. The average time cost of each epoch in different phases is shown in Fig. 4. We replace 1D CNN with LSTM in SSTE (LSTM). It's shown that 1D CNN has higher computational efficiency compared to LSTM-based models. It's confirmed that the computational efficiency has been improved to a large degree with CNN-based sequence learning module.

The probability density distribution of estimated travel time on the Porto taxi dataset is shown in Fig. 5. The X-axis is the estimated travel time of test data in Porto. The Y-axis is the probability density of the corresponding predicted time. The distribution of the ground truth of travel time is close to a Gaussian distribution. Amongst all distributions listed in the figure, the distributions of SSTE and ground truth are closest, showing that the predictions of SSTE are closest to the ground truth and SSTE achieves the best prediction results.

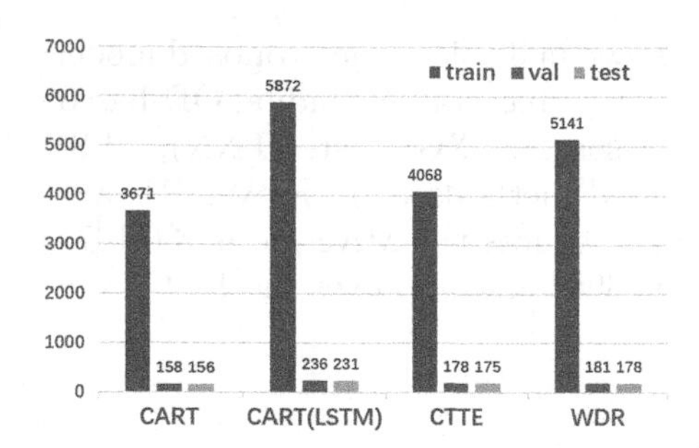

Fig. 4. Computational efficiency.

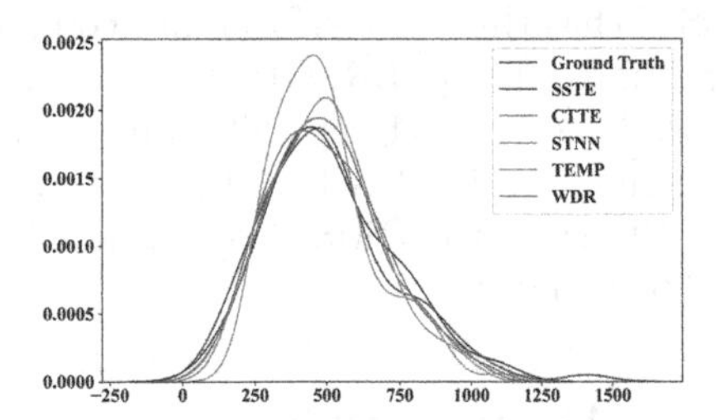

Fig. 5. The distribution of prediction.

5 Conclusion

In this paper, we proposed a novel spatial semantic learning model to generate multi-view spatial representations of trajectories for travel time estimation. Seg2vec can extract non-Euclidean spatial correlations, which benefits from the information of the road type and co-occurrence simultaneously. In the trajectory embedding module, Euclidean spatial information, multi-semantic contextual information, and external properties are fused with non-Euclidean spatial representations. Finally, 1D CNN is employed to extract temporal dependencies amongst segments. It's proved by experiments that 1D CNN can improve the computation efficiency compared to RNN-based methods. Additionally, Experimental results on two real-world benchmark datasets have shown our proposed model SSTE significantly improves the prediction accuracy compared to existing approaches.

References

1. Ayhan, S., Costas, P., Samet, H.: Predicting estimated time of arrival for commercial flights. In: Proceedings of the 24th ACM SIGKDD International Conference on Knowledge Discovery and Data Mining, pp. 33–42 (2018)
2. Chen, T., Guestrin, C.: XGBOOST: a scalable tree boosting system. In: Proceedings of the 22nd ACM SIGKDD International Conference on Knowledge Discovery and Data Mining, pp. 785–794 (2016)
3. Devlin, J., Chang, M.W., Lee, K., Toutanova, K.: Bert: Pre-training of deep bidirectional transformers for language understanding. arXiv preprint arXiv:1810.04805 (2018)
4. Du, B., Liu, C., Zhou, W., Hou, Z., Xiong, H.: Catch me if you can: detecting pickpocket suspects from large-scale transit records. In: Proceedings of the 22nd ACM SIGKDD International Conference on Knowledge Discovery and Data Mining, pp. 87–96 (2016)
5. Endo, Y., Nishida, K., Toda, H., Sawada, H.: Predicting destinations from partial trajectories using recurrent neural network. In: Kim, J., Shim, K., Cao, L., Lee, J.-G., Lin, X., Moon, Y.-S. (eds.) PAKDD 2017, Part I. LNCS (LNAI), vol. 10234, pp. 160–172. Springer, Cham (2017). https://doi.org/10.1007/978-3-319-57454-7_13
6. Fang, X., Huang, J., Wang, F., Zeng, L., Liang, H., Wang, H.: ConSTGAT: contextual spatial-temporal graph attention network for travel time estimation at Baidu maps. In: Proceedings of the 26th ACM SIGKDD International Conference on Knowledge Discovery and Data Mining, pp. 2697–2705 (2020)
7. Fu, T.y., Lee, W.C.: DeepIST: deep image-based spatio-temporal network for travel time estimation. In: Proceedings of the 28th ACM International Conference on Information and Knowledge Management, pp. 69–78 (2019)
8. Fu, T.Y., Lee, W.C.: TremBR: exploring road networks for trajectory representation learning. ACM Trans. Intell. Syst. Technol. (TIST) **11**(1), 1–25 (2020)
9. Gao, R., et al.: Aggressive driving saves more time? Multi-task learning for customized travel time estimation. In: IJCAI, pp. 1689–1696 (2019)
10. Hong, H., et al.: HetETA: heterogeneous information network embedding for estimating time of arrival. In: Proceedings of the 26th ACM SIGKDD International Conference on Knowledge Discovery and Data Mining, pp. 2444–2454 (2020)
11. Jindal, I., Chen, X., Nokleby, M., Ye, J., et al.: A unified neural network approach for estimating travel time and distance for a taxi trip. arXiv preprint arXiv:1710.04350 (2017)
12. Li, X., Li, W., Xu, Y.: Human age prediction based on DNA methylation using a gradient boosting regressor. Genes **9**(9), 424 (2018)

13. Li, Y., Fu, K., Wang, Z., Shahabi, C., Ye, J., Liu, Y.: Multi-task representation learning for travel time estimation. In: Proceedings of the 24th ACM SIGKDD International Conference on Knowledge Discovery and Data Mining, pp. 1695–1704 (2018)
14. Liaw, A., Wiener, M., et al.: Classification and regression by randomForest. R news **2**(3), 18–22 (2002)
15. Lin, X., Wang, Y., Xiao, X., Li, Z., Bhowmick, S.S.: Path travel time estimation using attribute-related hybrid trajectories network. In: Proceedings of the 28th ACM International Conference on Information and Knowledge Management, pp. 1973–1982 (2019)
16. Mikolov, T., Sutskever, I., Chen, K., Corrado, G., Dean, J.: Distributed representations of words and phrases and their compositionality. arXiv preprint arXiv:1310.4546 (2013)
17. Pennington, J., Socher, R., Manning, C.D.: GloVe: global vectors for word representation. In: Proceedings of the 2014 Conference on Empirical Methods in Natural Language Processing (EMNLP), pp. 1532–1543 (2014)
18. Perozzi, B., Al-Rfou, R., Skiena, S.: DeepWalk: online learning of social representations. In: Proceedings of the 20th ACM SIGKDD International Conference on Knowledge Discovery and Data Mining, pp. 701–710 (2014)
19. Rahmani, M., Jenelius, E., Koutsopoulos, H.N.: Route travel time estimation using low-frequency floating car data. In: 16th International IEEE Conference on Intelligent Transportation Systems (ITSC 2013), pp. 2292–2297. IEEE (2013)
20. Siripanpornchana, C., Panichpapiboon, S., Chaovalit, P.: Travel-time prediction with deep learning. In: 2016 IEEE Region 10 Conference (TENCON), pp. 1859–1862. IEEE (2016)
21. Wang, D., Zhang, J., Cao, W., Li, J., Zheng, Y.: When will you arrive? Estimating travel time based on deep neural networks. In: Proceedings of the AAAI Conference on Artificial Intelligence, vol. 32 (2018)
22. Wang, H., Tang, X., Kuo, Y.H., Kifer, D., Li, Z.: A simple baseline for travel time estimation using large-scale trip data. ACM Trans. Intell. Syst. Technol. (TIST) **10**(2), 1–22 (2019)
23. Wang, Y., Zheng, Y., Xue, Y.: Travel time estimation of a path using sparse trajectories. In: Proceedings of the 20th ACM SIGKDD International Conference on Knowledge Discovery and Data Mining, pp. 25–34 (2014)
24. Wang, Z., Fu, K., Ye, J.: Learning to estimate the travel time. In: Proceedings of the 24th ACM SIGKDD International Conference on Knowledge Discovery and Data Mining, pp. 858–866 (2018)
25. Weisberg, S.: Applied Linear Regression, vol. 528. Wiley, New York (2005)
26. Zhang, B., Wei, Z., Ren, J., Cheng, Y., Zheng, Z.: An empirical study on predicting blood pressure using classification and regression trees. IEEE Access **6**, 21758–21768 (2018)
27. Zhang, H., Wu, H., Sun, W., Zheng, B.: DeepTravel: a neural network based travel time estimation model with auxiliary supervision. arXiv preprint arXiv:1802.02147 (2018)
28. Zygouras, N., Panagiotou, N., Li, Y., Gunopulos, D., Guibas, L.: HTTE: a hybrid technique for travel time estimation in sparse data environments. In: Proceedings of the 27th ACM SIGSPATIAL International Conference on Advances in Geographic Information Systems, pp. 99–108 (2019)

A Fine-Grained Approach for Vulnerabilities Discovery Using Augmented Vulnerability Signatures

Xiaoxiao Zhou[1], Weina Niu[1](✉), Xiaosong Zhang[1], Ruidong Chen[1], and Yan Wang[2]

[1] School of Computer Science and Engineering, University of Electronic Science and Technology of China, Chengdu, China
202021080938@std.uestc.edu.cn, niuweina1@126.com

[2] School of Cyber Science and Engineering, Sichuan University, Chengdu 610065, China
yanwang@stu.scu.edu.cn

Abstract. Code similarity analysis quantitatively measures the similarity between two existing source codes by matching their signatures defined by code analyst. It is proven to be a promising way to discover hidden clone vulnerabilities when a vulnerability database is given. However, due to the slight differences between vulnerable code and patched code as well as the high modifications between original vulnerability and clone vulnerability, existing methods suffer from low accuracy, high false negative and coarse granularity. In this work, we present VCCD, a system focusing on discovering C/C++ clone vulnerabilities with fine granularity, which is more sensitive to code modification and keeps general to all kinds of vulnerability. We achieve this by presenting an augmented vulnerability signature comprising three components, i.e., contextual lines of code, vulnerable lines of code and fixed hunks of code. We propose a triplet matching algorithm to compare each target code signature as well as all vulnerability signatures to determine whether the target code is vulnerable or not. We compare VCCD with other state-of-the-art clone vulnerability discovery methods on eight popular real-world open-source projects. The evaluation result shows our approach discovers 21% more clone vulnerabilities compared with ReDeBug and 22% more clone vulnerabilities with VUDDY in acceptable time.

Keywords: Code similarity · Vulnerability discovery · Signature matching · Fine granularity

1 Introduction

Software security vulnerability (short for vulnerability) denotes a security related defect which is caused by an error in the configuration, design or development of system [1]. Hackers are able to exploit it to break some explicit or implicit

G. Memmi et al. (Eds.): KSEM 2022, LNAI 13370, pp. 27–38, 2022.
https://doi.org/10.1007/978-3-031-10989-8_3

security rules and threaten system security. Therefore, it is vital to discover and patch vulnerabilities in software systems as early as possible.

With rich open source code being more and more diverse and accessible, software developers are able to make use of existing code with ease instead of reproducing the wheels. It can save developers a lot of time, allowing them to focus on more challenging works. But it can also propagate hidden vulnerabilities, causing potential security risks. These vulnerabilities caused by code clones are also called clone vulnerabilities. A recent work [2] shows that clone vulnerabilities are much riskier than non-clone vulnerabilities. Therefore, many researchers have made the related works of clone vulnerability research [3–8], especially when this kind of vulnerability is more and more available.

Measuring the similarity of code is one promising approach to detect code clone. Code similarity is a kind of static analysis method, which has the advantages of small overhead and high efficiency. A lot of vulnerable code clone detection techniques [9–14] are proposed to discover clone vulnerabilities in many real-world programs. It firstly generates the target signatures and vulnerability signatures and then employs matching algorithms to judge whether target signature matches a vulnerability signature or not.

However, just like all static analysis methods, code similarity also has the big limitation of low accuracy. After careful analysis, we have come to the conclusion that there are two challenges: 1) the vulnerable function and the patched function have high similarity, which makes it easy for the code similarity method to mistake the fixed code as the vulnerable code and increases false positive; 2) there are a large number of codes that are highly modified on the original vulnerabilities but still contain vulnerabilities in real programs, and it is difficult for code similarity methods to identify such vulnerabilities, which increases false negative.

In this paper, we introduce a novel approach named VCCD (Vulnerable Code Clone Discover) to relieve above challenges. In detail, we combine both the vulnerable function and the patched function to distinguish specific lines of code that are strongly related to the contextual code, the vulnerable code and the fixed code hunk of a particular vulnerability. After dividing the vulnerability signature into three components, we design corresponding triplet matching algorithm to identify changes at different levels so that our approach is capable of discovering highly modified clone vulnerabilities. To sum up, we have made three contributions in our work. 1) A novel fine-grained code similarity technique by using our augmented vulnerability signature containing patch information to distinguish slight differences between vulnerable function and patched function. 2) A triplet matching algorithm based on our signatures consisting of three different comparing algorithms to detect clone vulnerabilities that are highly modified on the original vulnerability. 3) Implementation of our approach and a series of experiments to evaluate our approach.

Next, we will introduce the classification of code clone and summarize recent related works of code clone detection in Sect. 2, present the generation of code signature and describe the signature matching algorithm in Sect. 3, conduct a series of experiments and evaluate the performance of our approach in Sect. 4, and finally make a conclusion of our research in Sect. 5.

2 Related Works

In this section, we discuss the classification of code clone and summarize recent vulnerable code clone detection works.

2.1 Clone Type Taxonomy

Many code clone researchers divide the classification of code clone pair (X, Y) into four types [8,15]. Type-1: apart from possible differences of independent objects of execution such as comments, white spaces, line breaks, tabs and so on, X and Y are exactly identical. Type-2: apart from the differences of type-1 as well as possible differences of type names, identifier names, param names, and string literals, X and Y are structurally identical. Type-3: apart from the differences of type-2 as well as possible differences of some deleted or added statements compared to another segment, X and Y are syntactically identical. Type-4: X and Y are semantically identical code segments, but they have different syntax.

According to a recent study [2], there are 50% to 60% clone vulnerabilities are result from Type-3 vulnerable code clones. Our approach is focusing on Type-1 to Type-3 clone vulnerabilities detection at the granularity of line level.

2.2 Vulnerable Code Clone Detection

Many vulnerable code clone detection approaches have been proposed to discover clone vulnerabilities. For example, Zou et al. [13] proposed a semantics-based approach called SCVD, which presents a new code representation called program feature tree and then detects clone vulnerabilities by utilizing tree-based matching algorithm. Jang et al. [11] propose an unpatched code clone detection approach called ReDeBug, which leverages security patch files to extracts vulnerable lines and nearby textual lines, and then applys tokenization and normalization on each of them. Finally, it processes each token by adopting k hash functions and detects clone vulnerabilities based on comparison of the hash value between targets and security patches. Kim et al. [12] propose a precise and scalable approach called VUDDY, which discovers vulnerable code clones at granularity of function level.

3 Methodology

The architecture of our approach is displayed in Fig. 1, which consists of two stages, i.e., preprocessing stage and matching stage. Preprocessing stage can be further divided to two steps. The Generating Target Code Signatures step takes target code as input, and extracts signatures for all functions in the target code. The Generating Vulnerability Signatures step takes open source software as input for mining vulnerable and patched functions, and then extracts vulnerability signatures. Matching stage compares each target signature with all vulnerability signatures to predict whether the target function is vulnerable or not.

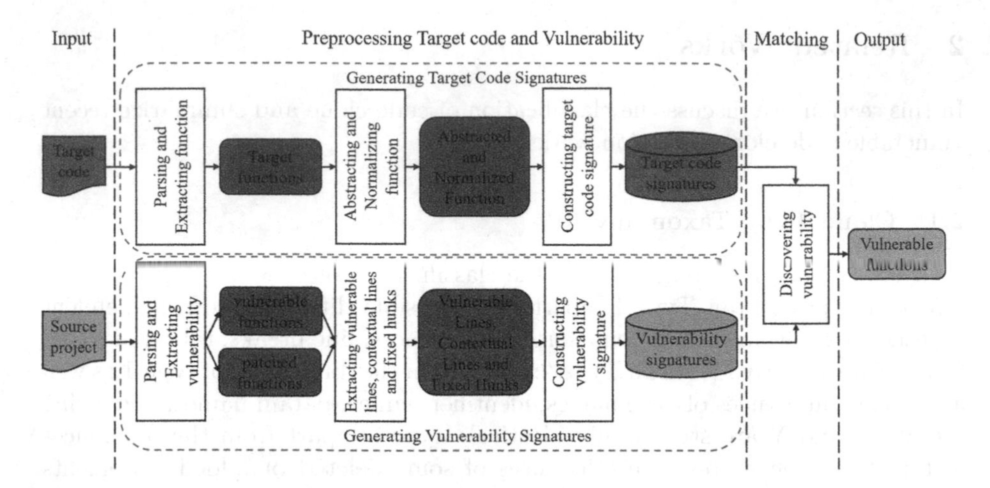

Fig. 1. Architecture of Our Approach (rounded rectangles represent intermediate results and rectangles represent sub-steps in VCCD)

3.1 Generating Target Code Signatures

Given the target system as input, we preprocess it and generate signature by three steps. 1) Extract functions: parse the system and find all C/C++ files. Then divide every C/C++ file into several parts so that each part contains only one function. 2) Abstract functions: employ normalized symbol **fparam**, **lvar** and **str** to replace all formal parameters, local variables and strings other than format strings in every function respectively. 3) Normalize functions: remove all white spaces, tabs, comments, and braces in every function and convert all letters to lowercase form. Abstraction and normalization enable our approach to become tolerant to modifications to some vulnerability independent objects, such as variables, parameters code formatting and comments in function.

3.2 Generating Vulnerability Signatures

We exploit both the vulnerable function and the corresponding security patch to extract vulnerability signature. The vulnerability signature consists of three components, which are defined as follows.

The first component is an ordered set of vulnerable lines (VLs) (i.e., the deleted lines of code when patch a vulnerability), which is strongly relative with the cause of a vulnerability and contributes much to the vulnerability. The second component is an ordered set of the contextual lines (CLs), which is the common line sequence of the vulnerable and patched function. Intuitively, CLs represent the contextual logic relationship of a function and will not be changed by a patch. But it still contributes much to a vulnerability because it contains the required context for a vulnerability and vulnerability is highly dependent on context [11]. We obtain them by removing deleted lines from the vulnerable function. The last component is a set of fixed hunks (FHs) in a patch. A fixed hunk consists of one code hunk containing a diff hunk in a patch only added lines as well as unchanged lines, which is related to the fixing process of a vulnerability. We employ it to exclude patched function especially when VLs only include few lines. Thus, a vulnerability signature can be represented by a triplet of the form (VLs, CLs, FHs). Finally, we apply the same abstraction and normalization process as Sect. 3.1 on each line in VLs, CLs and FHs.

For an instance, Table 1 displays the signature of vulnerability CVE-2021-28708. The red lines are deleted and the green lines are added lines by the patch.

Table 1. Signature of CVE-2021-28708

Vulnerable Lines (VLs)	casepage_order_1g:
	for(i=0;i<(1ul<<page_order_1g);i+=1ul<<page_order_2m)
	casepage_order_2m:
	page_list_add_tail(page,&p2m->pod.super);
	break;
	casepage_order_4k:
	page_list_add_tail(page,&p2m->pod.single);
Context Lines (CLs)	...
	switch(order)
	page_list_add_tail(page+i,&p2m->pod.super);
	break;
	break;
	default:
	bug();
	...
Fixed Hunks (FHs)	switch(order)
	casepage_order_2m...page_order_1g:
	for(i=0;i<(1ul<<order);i+=1ul<<page_order_2m)
	page_list_add_tail(page+i,&p2m->pod.super);
	break;
	casepage_order_4k...page_order_2m-1:
	for(i=0;i<(1ul<<order);i+=1ul<<page_order_4k)
	page_list_add_tail(page+i,&p2m->pod.single);
	break;
	default:
	bug();

3.3 Detecting Vulnerabilities Through Matching

Our goal is to provide an efficient matching algorithm to compare target signature with vulnerability signature to accurately discover clone vulnerabilities ranging from Type-1 to Type-3. Thus, the matching algorithm should be approximate and will not overwhelm the results with false positives.

Intuitively, codes are more likely unpatched clones of a particular vulnerability when it has the following characteristics: (1) share many lines of code with the CLs component of the vulnerability signature, (2) contain all lines of code in VLs of the vulnerability signature, (3) contain no fixed hunk in FHs of the vulnerability signature.

Algorithm 1. Signature Matching Algorithm

Input: $TSignature, VSignature.$
Output: matching result

1: $score = matchCL(TSignature, VSignature.CLs)$
2: **if** $score > threshold$ **then**
3:     **if** $isContain(TSignature, VSignature.VLs)$ **then**
4:         **for** FH in $VSignature.FHs$ **do**
5:             **if** $KMPmatch(TSignature, FH)$ **then**
6:                 **return** $True$
7:             **end if**
8:         **end for**
9:     **end if**
10: **end if**
11: **return** $False$

Algorithm 1 shows our signature matching algorithm. The algorithm receives a vulnerability signature as well as a target signature as input, and returns a result of True or False, which predicts whether the target function contains clone vulnerability of the vulnerable function represented by its signature or not.

The *matchCL* calculate the ratio of the length of common lines to the length of *VSignature.CLs*. In order to get length of common lines, we first leverage the python utility *difflib* to get unified diff file between *TSignature* as well as *VSignature.CLs* and then use the length of *TSignature* to subtract the length of lines prefixed with '-'. According to the official introduction of *difflib*, *matchCL* is quadratic time for the worst case and has expected-case behavior dependent in a complicated way on how many elements the sequences have in common; best case time is linear. The *score* measures the degree of matching between target signature and CLs in vulnerability signature.

The *isContain* function judges whether the target code contains the vulnerable lines with the same line order and returns a result of True or False. Obviously, it can be transformed into the problem of judging whether a subsequence exists and usually solved by greedy algorithm. We implement the function by employing a greedy-based matching algorithm with liner time complexity presented in [16]. It compares the lines in *TSignature* and *VSignature.VLs* sequentially, if the nth line in *TSignature* is the same as the mth line in *VSignature.VLs*, both n and m are incremented by one, otherwise only n is incremented by one.

When m is equal to the length of *VSignature.VLs*, it means that *TSignature* contains *VSignature.VLs*.

When the score exceeds threshold and the target code contains the vulnerable lines, we come to the last matching task. To ensure the target function is not patched, we need to confirm there is no hunk in fixed hunks contained in target function. There is a notation that a function containing a hunk means not only the function contains all lines of code in the hunk but also these lines are consequent in the function. So it an string matching problem. We employ the efficient KMP algorithm with time complexity of $O(m+n)$ to match target with each fixed hunk and determine whether the target function is vulnerable or not.

4 Experimental Evaluation

4.1 Experimental Setup

Evaluation Configuration. Our experiments were run on a machine with Windows 10, Intel(R) Core(TM) i5-8400 CPU @ 2.80 GHz and 16 GB RAM. The state-of-the-art methods ReDeBug and VUDDY compared in the experiments were configured with the same setting as reported in their original papers.

Table 2. Vulnerability database details

Project	#CVEs	#CWEs	#Functions
FFMpeg	72	14	84
LibAV	1	1	5
libtiff	33	12	42
Linux Kernel	258	59	360
OpenSSL	92	26	121
QEMU	121	35	212
tcpdump	93	5	130
Xen	117	29	182
Total	787	181	1,136

Dataset. We generate a vulnerability database including vulnerable functions and their corresponding patches from 8 popular open source projects that provide commit history messages on GitHub. The details of our vulnerability database are shown in Table 2.

For evaluation, we also require a test dataset that consists of code clones of both vulnerable and patched functions in our vulnerability database. In order to prove our approach is able to discover vulnerabilities of various clone types, it is necessary to obtain code clones covering Type-1 to Type-3. A typical solution is to extract the same function in multiple program versions. There is a intuitive assumption that different versions of a vulnerable function before the patch are still vulnerable, as long as those versions were released within one year of the patch. We regard them as vulnerable code clones. Similarly, the samples of the same function whose versions are behind to the patch are keep patched and we regard them as safe code clones. Thus, we extract six versions of the same function in our vulnerability database based on different time intervals related to patch date: soon ago, one month ago, six months ago, and soon later, one month later, six months later. Finally, the test dataset contains 1688 vulnerable clone functions and 1766 patched clone functions.

Evaluation Metrics. A common way to measure the performance is to count the TP (the number of vulnerable functions which are rightly reported), FP (the number of benign functions which are falsely reported as vulnerable), TN (The number of benign functions which are rightly reported) and FN (The number of vulnerable functions which are falsely reported as benign).

Then we calculate four widely used metrics, precision (P), recall (R), accuracy (A) and F1-measure (F1). Their meaning and calculation formula are shown in Table 3.

Table 3. Evaluation metrics

Metric	Formula	Meaning
Precision	$\frac{TP}{TP+FP}$	The accuracy of reported vulnerable functions
Recall	$\frac{TP}{TP+FN}$	The proportion of rightly reported vulnerable functions in the total vulnerable functions
Accuracy	$\frac{TP+TN}{TP+FP+TN+FN}$	The proportion of rightly reported functions in all functions
F1-measure	$\frac{2*P*R}{P+R}$	The comprehensive evaluation metric combining precision and recall

4.2 Accuracy Evaluation

We evaluate the performance of our approach by comparing its accuracy to two state-of-the-art approaches, i.e., ReDeBug and VUDDY, which are two common baselines of vulnerable code clone detection approaches. To compare with ReDeBug, as the author publish their implementation on Github, we are able to directly download the source code. To compare with VUDDY, as their source code is not available, we can only download the preprocessor on their open web service. And then we implement the rest detection stage of VUDDY for comparison with our approach.

Figure 2 Reports the accuracy comparison result of three approaches. From the bar chart, ReDeBug and VUDDY achieve higher precision than VCCD because both ReDeBug and VUDDY employ exact signature matching algorithm to maximize the precision.

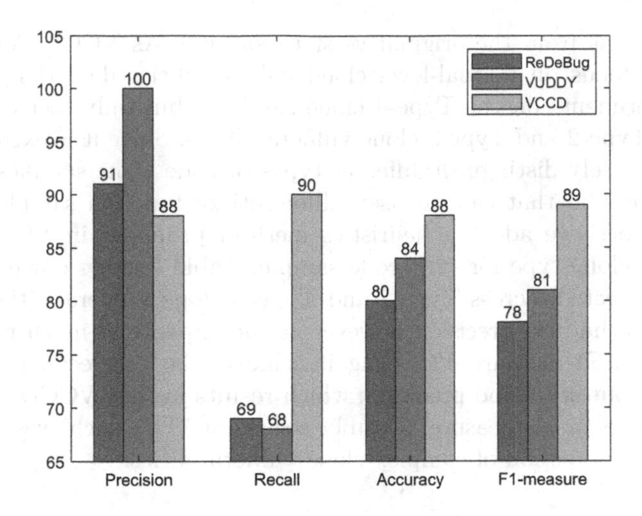

Fig. 2. Accuracy comparison

However, ReDeBug does not apply the step of abstraction to signatures, which makes it fails to detect Type-2 clone vulnerabilities. Besides, ReDeBug employs a sliding window mechanism and use changed hunk in vulnerable function to match target program. But in many cases, the contextual lines near the vulnerable lines are not related to the vulnerability, which leads to missing of a lot of Type-3 clone vulnerabilities in target system. VUDDY also employ exact signature matching algorithm and work at function level. It can only detect Type-1 and Type-2 clone vulnerabilities and fails to detect highly modified clone vulnerabilities. As a result, they both suffer from a large number of false negatives and lead to low recall, i.e., 69% and 68%.

In our work, we design a triplet signature matching algorithm consisting of one fuzzy matching algorithm and two exact matching algorithms, corresponding to the matching of the three components in our signature. It makes VCCD allow reasonable differences between target function and vulnerable function, and enables VCCD discover more complex clone vulnerabilities. Besides, VCCD works at granularity of line level and considers the fixing process from vulnerable function to patched function, which can limit the number of false positives to a low level. As a result, VCCD achieves best recall, i.e., 90%, and relatively low but still good precision, i.e., 88%, which enables it has best accuracy and F1-measure, respectively 88% and 89%. The result shows that VCCD is more effective to discover clone vulnerabilities.

4.3 Clone Type Sensitivity Analysis

To further evaluate the performance of our approach on complex clone vulnerability detection, we take both the vulnerable functions as well as the patched functions in our vulnerability database as original samples, and conduct experiments on only samples of modified functions in our test dataset, i.e., functions that are different from the original versions sample. As VCCD, VUDDY and ReDeBug all focus on textual-level clone vulnerabilities detection, we do not conduct experiments on the Type-4 clone samples, but only focus on the performance of Type-2 and Type-3 clone vulnerabilities. Since it is extremely challenging to precisely distinguish different types of code clone samples and so far there is no method that can precisely differentiate function samples based on code clone types, we adopt a heuristics method proposed in VGraph [17] to roughly label clone type for each code sample. Table 4 shows our experimental results. As expected, across Type-2 and Type-3 clone vulnerabilities, VUUDY again achieves the best precision however at the expense of much recall, which results in lowest F1-measure. VCCD again achieves the best recall and maintains relatively low but still good precision, which results in that VCCD outperforms other approaches in F1-measure. It can be seen that VCCD achieves better effectiveness on the detection of complex clone vulnerabilities.

Table 4. Performance of Type-2 and Type-3 clone detection

System	Type-2			Type-3		
	Precision	Recall	F1-measure	Precision	Recall	F1-measure
ReDeBug	88%	72%	79%	84%	61%	70%
VUDDY	**100%**	9%	16%	**100%**	2%	4%
VCCD	73%	**91%**	**81%**	73%	**76%**	**75%**

4.4 Parameter Sensitivity Analysis

In this section, we come to discuss the sensitivity of our method to the similarity threshold used in our matching algorithm. To that end, we perform experiment on the same dataset used in previous evaluation, but set the threshold from 0% to 100%, and compute four metrics used for performance evaluation for each configuration. Figure 3(a) shows line chart for Precision and Recall at each of different threshold configurations. From the line chart we can see that precision is getting higher and higher but recall is getting lower and lower as the threshold increases, which meets our expectation. Thus, we need to balance the precision and the recall to maximize overall performance. Then we come to the Fig. 3(b). According to Fig. 3(b), we can see our Accuracy and F1-measure keep the same change as the threshold increase. At threshold values of 0, our Accuracy and F1-measure are near zero. But they show significant growth when threshold increases from 0% to 30%, and maintain above 80% at large area of threshold values. Our Accuracy and F1-measure reach the maximum at the threshold of 80%, so we set 0.8 as default threshold of VCCD in our previous evaluation experiments.

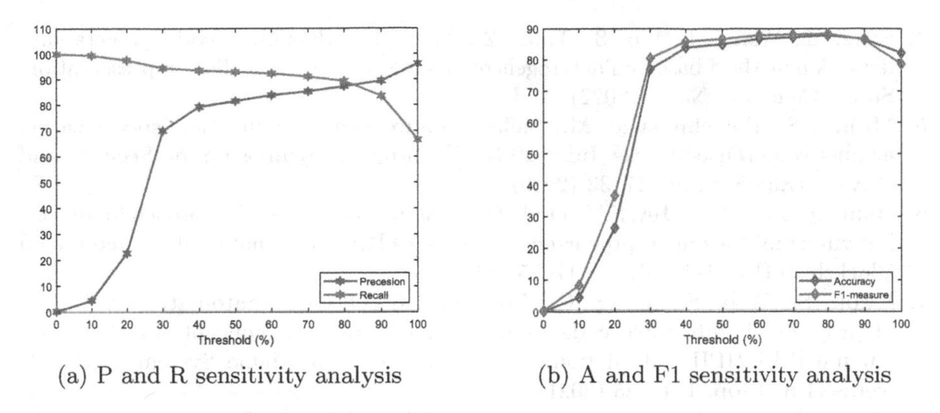

(a) P and R sensitivity analysis (b) A and F1 sensitivity analysis

Fig. 3. Performance at varying detection threshold.

5 Conclusion

In this work, we designed a fine-grained clone vulnerabilities discovery approach called VCCD focusing on Type-1 to Type-3 code vulnerabilities. Our approach introduced an augmented vulnerability signature comprising three components generating from the contextual lines of code, the vulnerable lines of code and the fixed hunks of code. Then we designed a triplet matching algorithm comprising one fuzzy matching algorithm and two exact matching algorithms to compare target signature with vulnerability signature and predict whether target function is vulnerable or not. The evaluation result showed that comparing to other state-of-the-art techniques, VCCD could detect complex clone vulnerabilities more effectively and achieve higher accuracy and F1-measure.

Acknowledgements. This work was supported in part by the National Science Foundation of China under Grant 61902262, in part by the National Key Research and Development Program of China under Grant 2018YFB0804103, Sichuan Science and Technology Program, Key Research and Development Projects (no. 2020YFG0461).

References

1. Ghaffarian, S.M., Shahriari, H.R.: Software vulnerability analysis and discovery using machine-learning and data-mining techniques: a survey. ACM Comput. Surv. **50**(4), 1–36 (2017)
2. Islam, M.R., Zibran, M.F., Nagpal, A.: Security vulnerabilities in categories of clones and non-cloned code: an empirical study. In: 2017 ACM/IEEE International Symposium on Empirical Software Engineering and Measurement (ESEM), pp. 20–29 (2017)
3. Wi, S., Woo, S., et al.: HiddenCPG: large-scale vulnerable clone detection using subgraph isomorphism of code property graphs. In: Proceedings of the ACM Web Conference 2022, WWW 2022, pp. 755–766 (2022)

4. Song, Z., Wang, J., Liu, S., Fang, Z., Yang, K.: HGVul: a code vulnerability detection method based on heterogeneous source-level intermediate representation. Secur. Commun. Netw. (2022)
5. Mishra, S., Polychronakis, M.: Saffire: context-sensitive function specialization against code reuse attacks. In: 2020 IEEE European Symposium on Security and Privacy (EuroSP), pp. 17–33 (2020)
6. Hum, Q., Tan, W.J., Tey, S.Y., et al.: Coinwatch: a clone-based approach for detecting vulnerabilities in cryptocurrencies. In: 2020 IEEE International Conference on Blockchain (Blockchain), pp. 17–25 (2020)
7. Kwon, S., Woo, S., Seong, G., Lee, H.: OCTOPOCS: automatic verification of propagated vulnerable code using reformed proofs of concept. In: 2021 51st Annual IEEE/IFIP International Conference on Dependable Systems and Networks (DSN), pp. 174–185 (2021)
8. Zhang, H., Sakurai, K.: A survey of software clone detection from security perspective. IEEE Access **9**, 48157–48173 (2021)
9. Li, J., Ernst, M.D.: CBCD: cloned buggy code detector. In: 2012 34th International Conference on Software Engineering (ICSE), pp. 310–320 (2012)
10. Li, Z., Shan, L., Myagmar, S., Zhou, Y.: CP-miner: finding copy-paste and related bugs in large-scale software code. IEEE Trans. Software Eng. **32**(3), 176–192 (2006)
11. Jang, J., Agrawal, A., Brumley, D.: ReDeBug: finding unpatched code clones in entire OS distributions. In: 2012 IEEE Symposium on Security and Privacy, pp. 48–62. IEEE (2012)
12. Kim, S., Woo, S., Lee, H., Oh, H.: VUDDY: a scalable approach for vulnerable code clone discovery. In: 2017 IEEE Symposium on Security and Privacy (SP), pp. 595–614 (2017)
13. Zou, D., et al.: SCVD: a new semantics-based approach for cloned vulnerable code detection. In: Polychronakis, M., Meier, M. (eds.) DIMVA 2017. LNCS, vol. 10327, pp. 325–344. Springer, Cham (2017). https://doi.org/10.1007/978-3-319-60876-1_15
14. Li, H., Kwon, H., Kwon, J., Lee, H.: CLORIFI: software vulnerability discovery using code clone verification. Concurr. Comput. Pract. Exp. **28**(6), 1900–1917 (2016)
15. Inoue, K., Roy, C.K.: Code Clone Analysis: Research, Tools, and Practices. Springer, Singapore (2021). https://doi.org/10.1007/978-981-16-1927-4
16. Jiang, W.P., Wu, B., Jiang, Z., Yang, S.B.: Cloning vulnerability detection in driver layer of IoT devices. In: Zhou, J., Luo, X., Shen, Q., Xu, Z. (eds.) ICICS 2019. LNCS, vol. 11999, pp. 89–104. Springer, Cham (2020). https://doi.org/10.1007/978-3-030-41579-2_6
17. Bowman, B., Huang, H.H.: VGRAPH: a robust vulnerable code clone detection system using code property triplets. In: 2020 IEEE European Symposium on Security and Privacy (EuroS&P), pp. 53–69. IEEE (2020)

PPBR-FL: A Privacy-Preserving and Byzantine-Robust Federated Learning System

Ying Lin[1,2](✉), Shengfu Ning[1], Jianpeng Hu[1], Jiansong Liu[1], Yifan Cao[1], Junyuan Zhang[1], and Huan Pi[1]

[1] School of Software, Yunnan University, Kunming, Yunnan, China
linying@ynu.edu.cn, {ningshengfu,12020219072}@mail.ynu.edu.cn
[2] Key Laboratory in Software Engineering of Yunnan Province, Kunming, China

Abstract. As a distributed machine learning framework, federated learning enables a multitude of participants to train a joint model privately by keeping training data locally. The federated learning is emerging as a promising alternative to solve data privacy protection, but it has been proven that federated learning is vulnerable to attacks from malicious clients, especially Byzantine attackers sending poisoned parameters during the training phase. To address this problem, several aggregation approaches against Byzantine failures have been proposed. However, these existing aggregation methods are only of limited utility in the setting of privacy protection. This paper proposes a privacy-preserving and Byzantine-robust federated learning framework (PPBR-FL) which achieves the objective to satisfy privacy and robustness simultaneously. We use the local differential privacy mechanism to realize privacy protection for the clients and propose a Byzantine-robust aggregation rule named as TPM (Trimmed Padding Mean) to realize robustness. Extensive experiments on two benchmark datasets demonstrate that the TPM outperforms the classical aggregation approaches in terms of robustness and privacy. When less than half of the workers are Byzantine attackers, the final global model not only achieves satisfactory performance against Byzantine attack, but also provide privacy protection on parameters to prevent privacy disclosure.

Keywords: Federal learning · Byzantine robustness · Differential privacy · Secure aggregation

1 Introduction

Federated Learning [11,12] (FL), which Google proposed in 2016, coordinates participants in a distributed way to conduct iterative training for a specific machine learning model. During the training process, as parameters need to be

This work is financed by "The project of Key Laboratory in Software Engineering of Yunnan Province (No. 2020SE305, 2020SE402)".

G. Memmi et al. (Eds.): KSEM 2022, LNAI 13370, pp. 39–50, 2022.
https://doi.org/10.1007/978-3-031-10989-8_4

uploaded to the server, so if no security protection is provided, malicious workers can reconstruct other users' training data by inference attacks [3,14]. Attackers can use model replacement to introduce a backdoor into the global model, thus learn other users' data [1]; Furthermore, an attacker can infer other participants' specific training data [13].

In order to protect data privacy in FL, various privacy protection approaches have been proposed [16,17]. Compared to encryption methods which need complex cryptographic operation, DP is regarded as a better privacy-preserving method. Parameters can be perturbed during the process of local training or global aggregation, thus making real parameters inaccessible to attackers. Among various differential privacy protection methods, the local differential privacy approach [2,7,24] does the privacy-preserving process on the client-side, which can achieve privacy protection without the need to trust the server.

In addition to privacy issues, the distributed nature also makes FL vulnerable to malicious attackers' adversarial manipulations. The goal of Byzantine-robust FL methods is to learn an accurate global model when there are a bounded number of malicious clients. For instance, a framework that can detect anomalous model updates was proposed in paper [9], leading to a targeted defense. However, accurate detection of attackers is almost impossible if there exist many participants. Secure aggregation methods, such as Median [22], Trimmed mean [23], and Krum algorithm [4] are another kind of methods to improve the Byzantine robustness of FL. These secure aggregation algorithms assume that the parameters computed by benign nodes are distributed around the true values, and the parameters computed by Byzantine nodes are mostly far from the true values, then aggregation can reduce the influence introduced by Byzantine nodes.

While there has been a lot of works studying how to protect the privacy or the robustness of FL [10], it still have problems to satisfy privacy and robustness simultaneously. Fortunately, some works have already attempted to achieve the two goals simultaneously. For example, paper [18] used weak differential privacy to enhance the robustness against backdoor attacks, however, weak differential privacy means adding a small amount of noise, which is insufficient to obtain reasonable privacy protection. In paper [15], authors used empirical evaluation to investigate whether the introduction of differential privacy can effectively defend against backdoor attacks with different levels of protection and utility. Although the paper [15] confirmed that we can use DP to mitigate backdoor attacks in FL, it is an empirical research and mainly focused on backdoor attacks.

To offer a promising solution to realize a FL system that are resistant to different types of adversaries and have privacy guarantees simultaneously, we deploy local differential privacy in the training process and propose a robust aggregation approach that is agnostic to DP noise to a certain extent. The main contributions of this paper are as follows:

(1) We propose a privacy-preserving and Byzantine-robust federated learning framework (PPBR-FL). It achieves competitive performance and are resistant to different types of adversaries investigated in this work.

(2) We propose a new Byzantine-robust aggregation rule TPM (Trimmed padding mean). We analyze and compare the aggregation effects of several classical Byzantine resilient aggregation rules, extensive experiments demonstrate that the TPM effectively distinguish benign clients and malicious clients in the presence of differential privacy protection, which significantly improves the robustness of the model even with the influence of differential privacy noise.
(3) We analyze how the privacy level and malicious nodes may influence the performance of the PPBR-FL, the experimental results show that although high-level privacy and more malicious nodes decrease the model's performance, the PPBR-FL still achieves the best performance in all settings.

The remaining parts of this paper are organized as follows. Section 2 surveys related work. Section 3 describes our method, Sect. 4 illustrates experimental results, and Sects. 5.6 analyzes the experimental results, Sect. 7 draws the conclusion and puts forward the direction of future improvement.

2 Related Works

2.1 Federated Learning

FL is a promising collaborative learning paradigm and parties in FL do not need to explicitly sharing their private data. The training process of FL involves multiple rounds R. Supposing there are N clients, each with a fixed number of data n_i, and $n = \sum_{i=1}^{N} n_i$. In the first round, the server generates a model with random parameter w^0, and sends it to all clients. Then at each round r, the server randomly selects K clients ($K \leq N$). Each selected client i iterates the local update $w_i^r = w_i^r - \eta g(w_i^r)$ with a fixed learning rate η multiple times. When those selected clients finish local training, they will send gradients $g(w_i^r)$ to the server. The server aggregates these gradients and applies the updates $w^{r+1} = w^r - \eta \sum_{i=1}^{K} \frac{n_k}{n} g(w_i^r)$ to compute the global parameter w^{r+1}. The server sends w^{r+1} to all participants to start a new round. After a certain number of rounds R,the training process is finished.

An equivalent update is given by Federated Averaging (FedAvg) [11]. The local model updates w_i^r from each client can be computed locally over several iterations of gradient descent to solve the optimization problem $w_i^r = w_i^r - \eta g(w_i^r)$, then the client uploads its local model parameter w_i^r to the server. The server computes a weighted average of the resulting models as $w^{r+1} = \sum_{i=1}^{K} \frac{n_k}{n} w_i^r$.

2.2 Differential Privacy

The DP protection method is generated to protect individual privacy information in a database when publishing data information, which can achieve a protection effect that does not significantly impact the output after inserting or deleting a particular record in the dataset.

If there are datasets D and D' with the same dimensions and attributes, and the two datasets differ by at most one record, then D and D' are called adjacent datasets.

Definition 1: ((ϵ,δ)-Local Differential Privacy) [5,6,19]. For any two adjacent datasets D and D', if there exists a randomized algorithm M if any output S of the algorithm M satisfies:

$$Pr[M(D) \in S] \leq e^{\epsilon} Pr[M(D') \in S] + \delta \tag{1}$$

then the algorithm M is said to satisfy (ϵ,δ)-DP, where δ is the privacy bias. If $\delta = 0$, we say that M is ϵ-differential privacy.The parameter ϵ is considered as a privacy budget. A lower ϵ means more noise and more robust privacy protection, and a higher ϵ means less noise and weaker privacy protection. The highest protection level is reached when ϵ is zero.

Definition 2: (global sensitivity) [6]: Given a function f: $D \rightarrow R^d$, for any two adjacent datasets D and D', the global sensitivity of f is defined as:

$$S_f = \max_{D,D'} \|f(D) - f(D')\|_2 \tag{2}$$

where R^d represents a d-dimensional real number vector, and $\|f(D) - f(D')\|_2$ is the L_2 distance between $f(D)$ and $f(D')$.

Definition 3: (Gaussian mechanism) [6]: The Gaussian mechanism with σ parameter is the addition of independent and identically distributed Gaussian noise to the true output of a function f. It is defined as follows:

$$M(D) = f(d) + Y \tag{3}$$

where $Y \sim N(0, \sigma^2 I)$ satisfies the Gaussian distribution.

3 Methodology

3.1 Privacy-Preserving and Byzantine-Robust Federated Learning Framework

Our proposed privacy-preserving and Byzantine-robust federated learning (PPBR-FL) framework mainly focus on two important objectives in FL: privacy and robustness. We aim to design an FL model that achieves Byzantine robustness against malicious nodes while providing privacy protection when clients upload their parameters to the server.

The PPBR-FL algorithm is shown in Algorithm 1. In each round, when clients finish local training, they need to perform a DP mechanism to compute perturbed local parameters before uploading to the server. Then, the server selects the optimal parameter by using our proposed Byzantine-robust aggregation rule named as TPM (Trimmed Padding Mean) and uses it as the global model parameters for the next round.

Algorithm 1: PPBR-FL

Input: The number of communication rounds R, the sampling ratio q, the LDP parameter (ϵ, δ)
Output: The learned PPBR-FL model;
1 Randomly initialize model parameters vector w^o; **for** $r = 0; r \leq R; r++$ **do**
2 Sever: Send w^r to all the clients, Randomly select K clients.
3 **for** *each clients* $i \in K$ **do**
4 Client: compute local parameter.
5 $w_i^r = w_i^r - \eta g(w_i^r)$
6 compute σ_i
7 add noise.
8 $w_i^{r*} = w_i^r + N(0, \sigma_i^2 I)$
9 send w_i^{r*} to sever.
10 **end**
11 Sever:
12 secure aggregation rule.
13 $w^r = TPM(w_1^{r*}, w_2^{r*}, ...w_K^{r*})$
14 update model parameter w^r
15 **end**

3.2 Calculation of Noise

In order to realize LDP protection, we use the Gaussian mechanism to add Gaussian noise into the computed local parameters. According to the **Theorem 1** in paper [20], to guarantee (ϵ,δ))-LDP for the i-th client, the standard deviation of Gaussian noise should satisfy:

$$\sigma_i = \frac{\Delta l \sqrt{2qR \ln\left(\frac{1}{\delta}\right)}}{\epsilon} \tag{4}$$

where q is the sampling ratio, R is the number of communication rounds,Δl denotes the sensitivity of the local training process and $l(.)$ denotes the local training process. As it has been proven in paper [20] that the sensitivity Δl satisfy:

$$\Delta l \leq \frac{2\gamma C}{n_i} \tag{5}$$

where C is the clipping threshold, and γ is a coefficient. In our experiments, we set $\gamma = 1$, so the calculation of σ_i can be rewritten as:

$$\sigma_i = \frac{2C \sqrt{2qR \ln\left(\frac{1}{\delta}\right)}}{\epsilon n_i} \tag{6}$$

Therefore, the addition of Gaussian noise $Y \sim N(0, \sigma^2 I)$ strictly ensures that each client meets (ϵ,δ))-LDP protection.

3.3 Secure Aggregation Rule: Trimmed Padding Mean

The proposed secure aggregation rule TPM is shown in Eq. 7

$$TPM(w_1, w_2, ...w_K) = \frac{\alpha K * median(w_1^r, w_2^r, ...w_K^r) + \sum_{i \in K(1-\alpha)} w_i^r}{K} \quad (7)$$

To get the optimal global model w^{r+1} , the server first calculates the median $\bar{w}$ for uploaded parameters $(w_i^r, i = 1...K)$ and uses the selected median $\bar{w}$ as the best local model. Assuming that the number of malicious or faulty clients is less than half of the clients, i.e. more than half of the clients are benign, then the median must close to the parameters values of good clients. Then, the server continues to perform the trimmed mean operation on all uploaded parameters $(w_i^r, i = 1...K)$ according to a certain ratio, and replaces those trimmed parameters as $\bar{w}$. At last, the global model w^{r+1} can be obtained by aggregating all the parameters using averaging method. In the Eq. 7, $\alpha = B/K$.

4 Experiments

4.1 Experiments Setup

In our experiments, we consider a typical FL scenario where a server coordinates 200 clients. We evaluate our solution against the baselines in two scenarios with having LDP-protection and no LDP-protection, respectively. In each communication round, we randomly select 20 clients ($K = 20$) for the learning tasks, among which a certain number of clients are malicious attackers. We set the Byzantine malicious clients to 4 ($B = 4$) and compare our solution under three Byzantine attacks: the Gaussian attack, the sign-flipping attack, and the zero-gradient attack [8,21].

Gaussian Attacks: The Gaussian attacks do not need any information from the workers. The Gaussian attacker $b \in B$ can replace some of the parameters with random noise sampled from a Gaussian distribution with mean u and variance m. In our experiments, we set variance m to 30 and mean u to $\frac{1}{K-B}\sum_{i \notin B} w_i$.

Sign-Flipping Attacks: The sign-flipping attacks flip the signs of parameters and enlarge the magnitudes. The sign-flipping attacker $b \in B$ sets its parameters $w_b = \frac{\beta}{K-B}\sum_{i \notin B} w_i$, where β is a negative constant. We set $\beta = -100$ in the experiments on the MNIST dataset and $\beta = -10$ in the experiments on the FashionMnist dataset.

Zero-Gradient Attacks: The Byzantine attacker $b \in B$ sends $w_b = -\frac{1}{B}\sum_{i \notin B} w_i$ to the server, so let that the sum of the parameters on the server-side is zero.

4.2 Datasets and Model

In this paper, we use two datasets MNIST and FashionMnist, both are classical datasets in the field of ML. MNIST is a handwritten digits dataset, and FashionMnist is a fashion product image dataset used as an alternative to MNIST.

These two datasets consist of 60,000 training samples and 10,000 test samples, and each sample is a $28 * 28$ pixel grayscale image.

We divide the dataset evenly among 200 clients. We train a CNN model over the two datasets respectively, The network architecture of CNN consists of two $5 * 5$ convolutional layers and two full connection layers. In our experiments, the learning rate is set to 0.01, the batch size is set to 32, and the maximum number of client-server communication rounds is set to 100.

4.3 Benchmark Byzantine-Robust Aggregation Rules

Krum [4]: The Krum algorithm selects a local model that is closest to other local models as the global model of the server as shown in Eq. 8, where $\sum_{i \to j} \|w_i - w_j\|^2$ runs over the $K - B - 2$ closest vectors to w_i. The final result of w_{i*} refers to the client, which has the minimum value of $\sum_{i \to j} \|w_i - w_j\|^2$ for all i. One advantage of Krum is that even if the selected client is malicious, its impact is minimal, because it is similar to the other normal clients.

$$Krum(w_1, w_2, ...w_K) = w_{i*} \min_{i \in K} \sum_{i \to j} \|w_i - w_j\|^2 \tag{8}$$

Median [22]: The median of $(w_1, w_2, ...w_K)$ is also defined as marginal median as the following Eq. 9.

$$MarMed(w_1, w_2, ...w_k) = v \tag{9}$$

where for any $j \in d$, the jth dimension of v is $v_j = median[(w_1)_j, (w_2)_j, ...(w_K)_j]$, $(w_i)_j$ is the jth dimension of w_i, $median(.)$ is the one-dimensional median.

Trimmed Mean [23]: The server first sorts values of the uploaded parameters $(w_1, w_2, ...w_k)$, then removes the head and tail parameters in proportion to respectively, and then calculates the average of the remaining $K(1 - 2\alpha)$ parameters as the value of the parameters for the next round. The calculation formula is shown in Eq. 10. In the Eq. 10, $\alpha = B/K$.

$$TrimmedMean(w_1, w_2, ...w_k) = \frac{\sum_{i \in K(1-2\alpha)} w_i}{K(1 - 2\alpha)} \tag{10}$$

5 Performance Evaluations

In this section, we evaluate the performance of our PPBR-FL in image classification with common ML model over two datasets. We demonstrate the effectiveness of our proposed TPM approach by comparing it with benchmark Byzantine-robust aggregation rules. Our experiments are implemented with Pytorch.

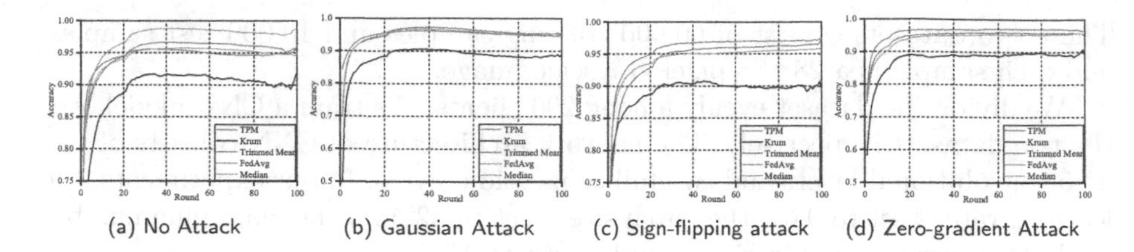

(a) No Attack (b) Gaussian Attack (c) Sign-flipping attack (d) Zero-gradient Attack

Fig. 1. Experimental results in MNIST dataset with no LDP protection

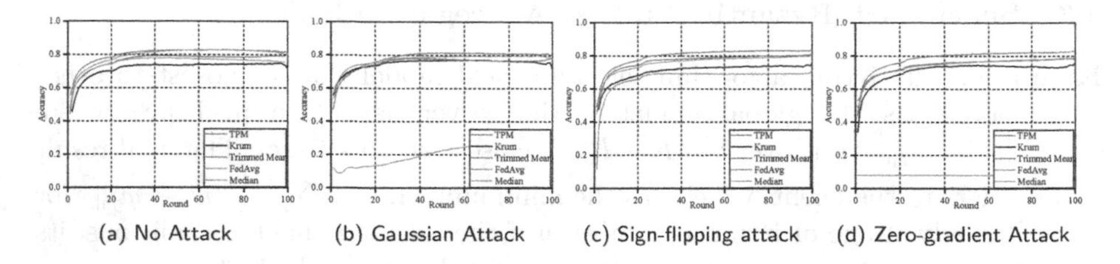

(a) No Attack (b) Gaussian Attack (c) Sign-flipping attack (d) Zero-gradient Attack

Fig. 2. Experimental results in FashionMnist dataset with no LDP protection

5.1 No LDP Protection

We first evaluate our proposed TPM in the case of no privacy protection, that is, the clients sends their parameters to the server directly.

As can be seen from Fig. 1 and Fig. 2, if there is no DP protection and no Byzantine attack, in the case of MNIST dataset, our proposed TMP aggregation rule is slightly lower than the FedAvg in model classification accuracy, but it is still better than other aggregation rules. In the case of FashionMnist dataset, our proposed TMP has similar classification accuracy to the FedAvg and is better than other aggregation rules. Furthermore, in the case of Byzantine attacks, the model's classification accuracy obtained by the FedAvg decreases significantly on both datasets. Compared with other aggregation rules, the classification accuracy of the model obtained by the TMP is the highest, and the accuracy maintains above 80% even under different attacks, which shows strong robustness.

5.2 With LDP Protection

We then evaluate our proposed TPM in the case of privacy protection, that is, the clients sends their perturbed parameters to the server for aggregation.

As can be seen from Fig. 3 and Fig. 4, in the case of no attack but with local differential privacy protection, the classification accuracy of the models obtained by Krum is all below 20%, which shows the Krum is most affected by noise. Although models obtained by other aggregation rules still maintain the average classification performance, they all slightly decrease compared with no LDP protection. When there are Byzantine attacks, we can see that the classification

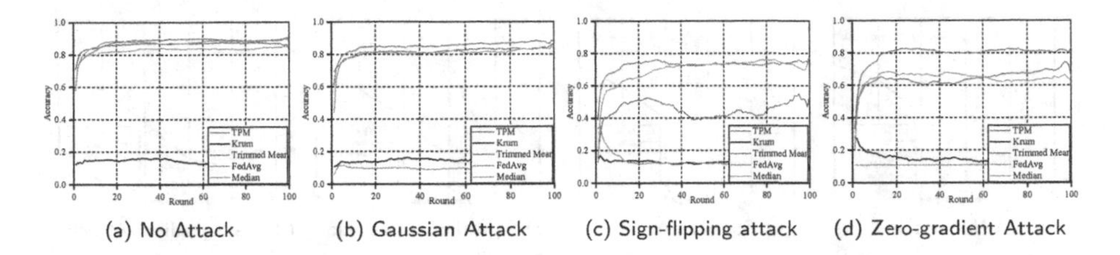

(a) No Attack (b) Gaussian Attack (c) Sign-flipping attack (d) Zero-gradient Attack

Fig. 3. Experimental results in MNIST dataset with LDP protection

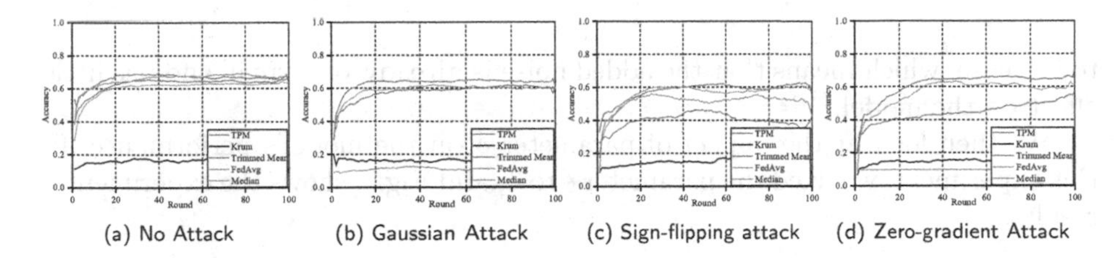

(a) No Attack (b) Gaussian Attack (c) Sign-flipping attack (d) Zero-gradient Attack

Fig. 4. Experimental results in FashionMnist dataset with LDP protection

accuracy of models obtained by different aggregation rules has been affected to vary degrees. However, the models obtained by our proposed TPM rules still maintain a higher classification accuracy than others, showing better robustness and privacy-preserving capability.

6 Discussions

High-level privacy protection means more noise needed, however, it will influence the final model's utility. Similarly, the number of malicious nodes influence the final model's performance. In this section, we demonstrate the performance of our proposed PPBR-FL under different noise level and malicious nodes. The dataset used here is the MNIST, and the case of FashionMnist is similar.

6.1 Impacts of Privacy Level

In this section, to evaluate how the privacy level may influence the classification performance of the model, we observe the impacts of different DP parameters on the accuracy of the model. We first look at the impact of parameter ϵ on the model. In order to better observe, we fixed the parameter δ to 0.01, and Fig. 5 shows the experimental results.

It can be seen that compared with several other aggregation rules, our proposed TPM maintains a higher model classification accuracy under different ϵ. Regardless of whether there is an attack, the classification accuracy of the model increases when ϵ becomes larger, but when ϵ increases to a certain value, the classification accuracy of the model does not change much although ϵ continues

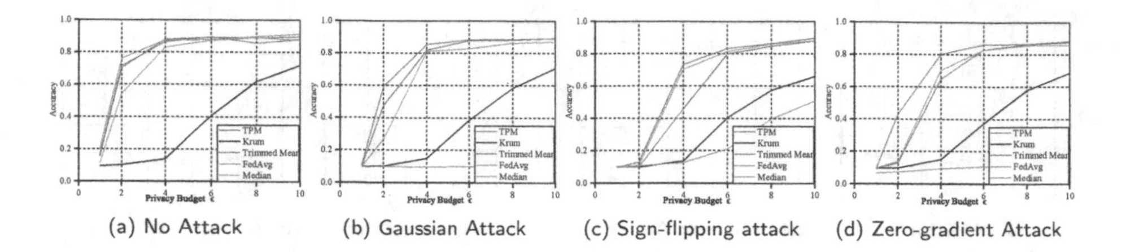

(a) No Attack (b) Gaussian Attack (c) Sign-flipping attack (d) Zero-gradient Attack

Fig. 5. Experimental results under different ϵ

to increase, which means that the added noise is already very small and has little effect on the model.

We then look at the impact of parameter δ on the model's performance. In this experiment, we fixed the parameter ϵ to 4, and Fig. 6 shows the experimental results.

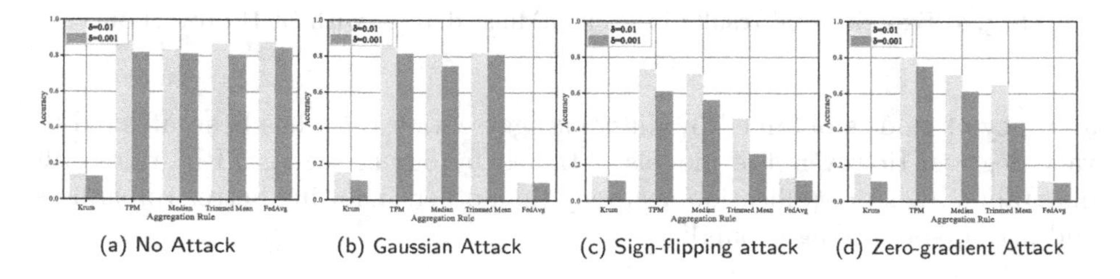

(a) No Attack (b) Gaussian Attack (c) Sign-flipping attack (d) Zero-gradient Attack

Fig. 6. Experimental results under different δ

It can be seen that the classification accuracy of the model increases when δ becomes larger. However, larger δ means lower privacy protection and little noise. If we want to improve the privacy protection level, we need to decrease δ. Regardless of whether there is attack, the proposed TMP still maintains a high accuracy and better ensures the robustness of the model.

6.2 Impacts of the Number of Malicious Clients

To understand how the number of malicious clients may harm the robustness of the model, we set the proportion of Byzantine nodes to all nodes from 5% to 30%. The experimental results on three attacks are illustrated in Fig. 7.

As can be seen from Fig. 7 that the classification performance of all the models obtained by different aggregation rules have been greatly affected, especially by the FedAvg and Krum. However, our proposed method achieves the best performance in all settings.

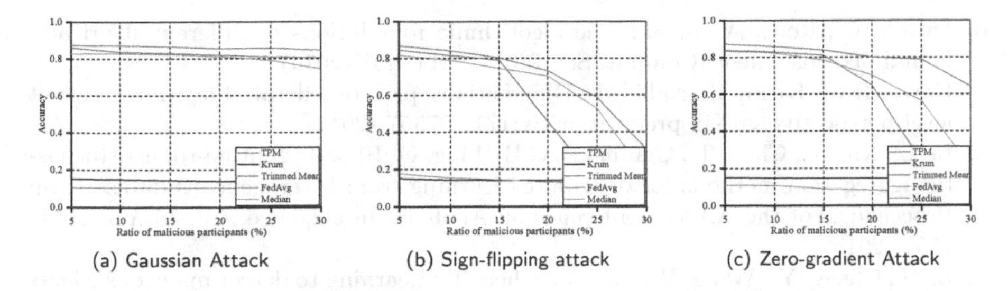

(a) Gaussian Attack (b) Sign-flipping attack (c) Zero-gradient Attack

Fig. 7. Experimental results of varying ratio of malicious participants under different attacks

7 Conclusion

In this paper, we proposed a privacy-preserving and Byzantine-robust Federated Learning framework. Exhaustive experiments show that in the case of local privacy protection, if there is no attack, the performance of the model obtained by the classic aggregation algorithm FedAvg is higher than our proposed TPM, but compared with other Byzantine robust aggregation algorithms, the classification performance of the model obtained by our proposed TPM is the highest. In the case of Byzantine attacks, whether with or without local differential privacy protection, TPM shows its superiority, and the performance of the model is better than other aggregation algorithms.

In general, our proposed PPBR-FL framework achieves the objective to satisfy privacy and robustness simultaneously. The superior performance of our method comes from the robust aggregation rules, which successfully separate benign and malicious clients' model updates. In the future, we will continue to study in depth how to maintain privacy and robustness simultaneously in the case of non-IID scenario.

References

1. Bagdasaryan, E., Veit, A., Hua, Y., Estrin, D., Shmatikov, V.: How to backdoor federated learning. In: International Conference on Artificial Intelligence and Statistics, pp. 2938–2948. PMLR (2020)
2. Bassily, R., Nissim, K., Stemmer, U., Thakurta, A.: Practical locally private heavy hitters. J. Mach. Learn. Res. **21**, 1–16 (2020)
3. Bhowmick, A., Duchi, J., Freudiger, J., Kapoor, G., Rogers, R.: Protection against reconstruction and its applications in private federated learning. arXiv preprint arXiv:1812.00984 (2018)
4. Blanchard, P., El Mhamdi, E.M., Guerraoui, R., Stainer, J.: Machine learning with adversaries: Byzantine tolerant gradient descent. In: Proceedings of the 31st International Conference on Neural Information Processing Systems, pp. 118–128 (2017)
5. Dwork, C., McSherry, F., Nissim, K., Smith, A.: Calibrating noise to sensitivity in private data analysis. In: Halevi, S., Rabin, T. (eds.) TCC 2006. LNCS, vol. 3876, pp. 265–284. Springer, Heidelberg (2006). https://doi.org/10.1007/11681878_14

6. Dwork, C., Roth, A., et al.: The algorithmic foundations of differential privacy. Found. Trends Theor. Comput. Sci. **9**(3–4), 211–407 (2014)
7. Geyer, R.C., Klein, T., Nabi, M.: Differentially private federated learning: a client level perspective. arXiv preprint arXiv:1712.07557 (2017)
8. Li, L., Xu, W., Chen, T., Giannakis, G.B., Ling, Q.:RSA: byzantine-robust stochastic aggregation methods for distributed learning from heterogeneous datasets. In: Proceedings of the AAAI Conference on Artificial Intelligence. vol. 33, pp. 1544–1551 (2019)
9. Li, S., Cheng, Y., Wang, W., Liu, Y., Chen, T.: Learning to detect malicious clients for robust federated learning. arXiv preprint arXiv:2002.00211 (2020)
10. Ma, C., et al.: On safeguarding privacy and security in the framework of federated learning. IEEE Netw. **34**(4), 242–248 (2020)
11. McMahan, B., Moore, E., Ramage, D., Hampson, S., y Arcas, B.A.: Communication-efficient learning of deep networks from decentralized data. In: Artificial Intelligence and Statistics, pp. 1273–1282. PMLR (2017)
12. McMahan, H.B., Moore, E., Ramage, D., y Arcas, B.A.: Federated learning of deep networks using model averaging. arXiv preprint arXiv:1602.05629 (2016)
13. Melis, L., Song, C., De Cristofaro, E., Shmatikov, V.: Inference attacks against collaborative learning. arXiv preprint arXiv:1805.04049 (2018)
14. Melis, L., Song, C., De Cristofaro, E., Shmatikov, V.: Exploiting unintended feature leakage in collaborative learning. In: 2019 IEEE Symposium on Security and Privacy (SP), pp. 691–706. IEEE (2019)
15. Naseri, M., Hayes, J., De Cristofaro, E.: Toward robustness and privacy in federated learning: experimenting with local and central differential privacy. arXiv preprint arXiv:2009.03561 (2020)
16. Qiu, H., Qiu, M., Lu, Z.: Selective encryption on ECG data in body sensor network based on supervised machine learning. Inf. Fusion **55**, 59–67 (2020)
17. Qiu, M., Gai, K., Xiong, Z.: Privacy-preserving wireless communications using bipartite matching in social big data. Fut. Gener. Comput. Syst. **87**, 772–781 (2018)
18. Sun, Z., Kairouz, P., Suresh, A.T., McMahan, H.B.: Can you really backdoor federated learning? arXiv preprint arXiv:1911.07963 (2019)
19. Wang, S., et al.: Local differential private data aggregation for discrete distribution estimation. IEEE Trans. Parallel Distrib. Syst. **30**(9), 2046–2059 (2019)
20. Wei, K., et al.: User-level privacy-preserving federated learning: analysis and performance optimization. IEEE Trans. Mob. Comput. **99**, 1-1 (2021)
21. Wu, Z., Ling, Q., Chen, T., Giannakis, G.B.: Federated variance-reduced stochastic gradient descent with robustness to byzantine attacks. IEEE Trans. Signal Process. **68**, 4583–4596 (2020)
22. Xie, C., Koyejo, O., Gupta, I.: Generalized byzantine-tolerant sgd. arXiv preprint arXiv:1802.10116 (2018)
23. Yin, D., Chen, Y., Kannan, R., Bartlett, P.: Byzantine-robust distributed learning: Towards optimal statistical rates. In: International Conference on Machine Learning, pp. 5650–5659. PMLR (2018)
24. Yu, L., Liu, L., Pu, C., Gursoy, M.E., Truex, S.: Differentially private model publishing for deep learning. In: 2019 IEEE Symposium on Security and Privacy (SP), pp. 332–349. IEEE (2019)

GAN-Based Fusion Adversarial Training

Yifan Cao[1], Ying Lin[1,2](✉), Shengfu Ning[1], Huan Pi[1], Junyuan Zhang[1], and Jianpeng Hu[1]

[1] School of Software, Yunnan University, Kunming, Yunnan, China
linying@ynu.edu.cn, ningshengfu@mail.ynu.edu.cn
[2] Key Laboratory in Software Engineering of Yunnan Province, Kunming, China

Abstract. In the field of artificial intelligence security, adversarial machine learning has made breakthroughs. However, it is still vulnerable to attacks under a wide variety of adversarial samples, and adversarial training is a very effective method against a wide variety of adversarial sample attacks. However, adversarial training tends to improve the accuracy of the adversarial samples while reducing the accuracy of the original samples. Thus, the robustness of adversarial training is greatly reduced. In order to improve the robustness of adversarial training, this paper proposes a fusion adversarial training model based on Generate adversarial network (GAN), which is applied to the adversarial training process, and this unsupervised learning framework can better learn the distribution of samples to generate high-quality samples. By controlling the proportion of different training losses, we improve the classification accuracy of the adversarial training model while maintaining the relatively high accuracy of the model for the original samples, thus greatly improving the robustness of the adversarial training model. In this paper, we conduct experiments based on the Fashion-MNIST and CIFAR10 datasets, and the results show that our model has high accuracy on both the original and adversarial samples for both grayscale and color maps.

Keywords: GAN · Adversarial attack · Adversarial training · Deep learning · Robustness

1 Introduction

With the rapid development and great success of deep learning [1], it is gradually being applied in many environments with strict security requirements, such as for malware detection [2], selective encryption [3], security-aware optimization [4], ad blockers, privacy protection [5] and speech recognition [6]. However, deep neural networks are vulnerable to some well-designed input samples [7, 8], which are formed in the dataset by intentionally adding subtle interference called adversarial samples [9], which are not well identified for humans, but it can cause the model to give a wrong output with high confidence in the testing or deployment phase. Therefore when applying deep neural networks to environments with strict security requirements, dealing with model vulnerability caused by adversarial samples becomes an important task. Although some results have been achieved in the defense research of adversarial samples, they face

G. Memmi et al. (Eds.): KSEM 2022, LNAI 13370, pp. 51–64, 2022.
https://doi.org/10.1007/978-3-031-10989-8_5

certain challenges as well. The biggest problem is that the models are less robust and vulnerable to adversarial attacks.

In this paper, we propose a GAN-based fusion adversarial training method. First, a generative adversarial network model is trained by GAN, which is used to generate adversarial samples by learning optimal perturbations and superimposing them to the original samples. Second, the fusion adversarial training optimizes the boundary distance between the original sample and the adversarial sample, and optimizes this part of the loss through continuous training, so that the boundary distance between the original sample and the adversarial sample is closer, which we accomplish in the fusion adversarial training by several iterations, and gradually find the balance of robustness and accuracy during the training process, by controlling the correlation coefficient between different optimization losses The correlation coefficients between the different optimization losses are controlled to improve the robustness of the adversarial training. Therefore, our work can be divided into two parts, the first part is to learn the perturbation and the second part is to optimize the bound. The main contributions of this paper are as follows:

(1) During the generation of adversarial samples, a generative adversarial network model is trained so that it can learn the perturbations in the input samples, and the adversarial samples are generated more realistically compared with the iteration-based adversarial sample generation method.
(2) Adversarial training is performed by adding GAN-generated adversarial samples, and the boundary between the original and adversarial samples is optimized while adversarial training. This enables the adversarial samples with higher classification accuracy under resisting different attack methods.
(3) During the fusion adversarial training, a balance between robustness and accuracy is found by controlling the correlation coefficients between different optimization losses, which further improves the classification accuracy of the model.

The remaining parts of this paper are organized as follows. Section 2 surveys related work. Section 3 describes our method, Sect. 4 illustrates experimental results, and Sect. 5 analyzes the experimental results, and some directions are given for future improvements.

2 Related Work

2.1 GAN

GAN is a new generative model proposed by Goodfellow [10] et al. in 2014. The unique adversarial idea of GAN makes it stand out among many generator models and is widely used in computer vision [11], natural language processing [12] and other fields. A typical GAN model contains two modules, a generator and a discriminator. The generator is used to learn the features of the real samples to generate samples that are close to the real samples, and the discriminator is used to distinguish the real samples from the generated samples, and in the process of continuous iteration, the discriminator discriminates better and better, and the generated samples generated by the generator become more and more realistic, so as to achieve a balance during repeated training. If the generator is denoted as $G(z)$ and the discriminator is denoted as $D(x)$, the optimization function of GAN can be defined as

$$\underset{G}{min}\underset{D}{max}\left\{\underset{x\sim\mathcal{D}_{tr}}{\mathbb{E}}\left[\log D(x)\right]+\underset{z\sim\mathcal{P}_z}{\mathbb{E}}\left[\log(1-D(G(z))\right]\right\} \tag{1}$$

2.2 Adversarial Attacks and Defense

An adversarial sample [13] is a new input sample x^{adv} formed by adding some very small but purposeful perturbations δ to sample x in the dataset, such that the perturbed sample input will result in a model output with high confidence in the wrong answer. The adversarial samples can be defined as

$$x^{adv}=\underset{\delta}{max}L(\mathbf{f},x,y)s.t.\|\delta\|_p\leq\epsilon\text{and}\,x+\delta\in[0,1]^D \tag{2}$$

Attacks launched using adversarial samples are called adversarial attacks, and common adversarial attack methods such as Fast gradient sign method (FGSM), momentum iterative gradient-based methods (MIFGSM), Projected gradient descent (PGD) and Basic Iterative Method (BIM). The fast gradient descent method, is used in a white-box setting to obtain the specific gradient direction by finding the derivative of the model with respect to the input, and multiplying it with the step size to obtain the perturbation added to the original image thus obtaining the adversarial sample, in the following way

$$x^{adv}=x+\varepsilon\cdot sign(\nabla_x J(x,y)) \tag{3}$$

The project gradient descent method [14], an iterative attack, can also be seen as an improvement on the FGSM attack algorithm, where the PGD attack does multiple iterations compared to one iteration of the FGSM attack, with each iteration cropping the perturbation to a certain range. The method is as follows

$$x_{t+1}=\Pi_{x+S}(x_t+\varepsilon\cdot sign(\nabla_x J(x_t,y))) \tag{4}$$

Since PGD has more iterations and adds some randomization operations, the attack using PGD is better than FGSM, but the computation of PGD attack is more time consuming.

Adversarial training is the current mainstream method for defending against adversarial attacks, and the robustness of the model can be improved by adversarial training. The maximum minimization formula of adversarial training is as follows

$$\underset{\theta}{min}\mathbb{E}_{(Z,y)\sim\mathcal{D}}\left[\underset{\|\delta\|\le\epsilon}{max}L(f_{\theta}(X+\delta),y)\right] \quad (5)$$

where X is denoted as the input of the sample, δ is the perturbation added to the input X, and y is the label of the input sample. max is achieved by making the perturbation δ obtained when the loss function is maximized so that the neural network can be misclassified as much as possible, while min is used to minimize the loss of the training data while the perturbation δ is determined so as to improve the robustness of the model.

3 Methodology

3.1 Overview

The network architecture of this paper is shown in Fig. 1, firstly a generative adversarial network model is trained which can be optimized to train a generator and discriminator according to a pre-trained classification model, the generator generates adversarial samples by learning the perturbations of the input samples and superimposing the perturbations on the input samples, and gradient cropping is used in the generative network model [15]. Thus, the phenomenon of gradient explosion is avoided. Under this model, the generator G receives the input data x. After training by the GAN model the generator G can learn the adversarial perturbation z. The data received by the discriminator G is the original sample x and the adversarial sample x' after superimposing the perturbation by the generator G. Using the idea of unsupervised learning [16] of GAN, the learning ability of the generator can be improved in the loop training through the continuous game between the generator and the discriminator, which can improve the authenticity of the adversarial samples.

In the adversarial training process, this paper uses fusion adversarial training, fusion adversarial training means that we generate more realistic adversarial samples by the generator on one side and get the model loss of the adversarial samples. The boundary distance between the original sample and the adversarial sample is optimized on the one hand. This adversarial sample can be generated iteratively, and we try to make the boundary distance between the original sample and the adversarial sample [17] as small as possible, so that the obtained model will be smoother and thus will not have much impact on the classification accuracy of the original sample, and by optimizing this process, we get the optimized loss of trade. Eventually we will get a more robust model.

3.2 Loss Function

adv loss: adv loss is the loss of the classification model f for the GAN generated adversarial samples $x + G(x)$, the purpose is to increase the accuracy of the classification model for identifying the adversarial samples, and its loss function is defined as follows:

$$L_{adv} = E_x f(x + G(x), y) \quad (6)$$

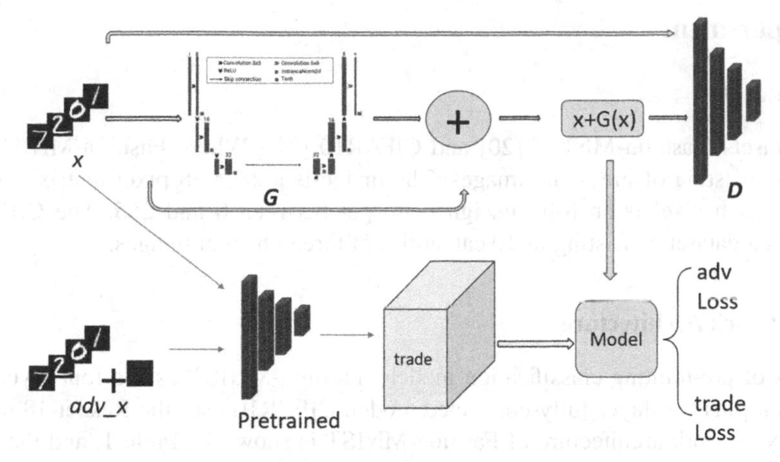

Fig. 1. Architecture of the fusion adversarial training

trade loss: trade loss [18] is to find a balance between accuracy and robustness [19], and the method used is to improve the robustness without affecting the accuracy by optimizing the decision boundary between the original and adversarial samples so that this distance is as small as possible, and its final optimized objective function is defined as follows:

$$L_{trade} = \underset{f}{min}E\left\{ \mathrm{E}(f(\boldsymbol{x})y) + \underset{x' \in \mathbb{B}(\boldsymbol{x},\epsilon)}{max} E\left(\frac{f(\boldsymbol{x})f\left(x'\right)}{\lambda} \right) \right\} \tag{7}$$

Therefore, the objective optimization function of the fusion training method proposed in this paper is:

$$L = \alpha L_{adv} + \beta L_{trade} \tag{8}$$

where α *and* β are hyperparameters intended to control the relative importance of the loss function.

3.3 Algorithm

The algorithm steps for fusion adversarial training are shown below, with Adam optimized loss used for the loss function, a training batch size of 16, and a training period of 10 rounds. The loss is optimized by calculating the relative entropy between the original samples and the adversarial samples, thus balancing the robustness and accuracy of the model. After different optimized losses are obtained, the weights between different losses are adjusted to the final robust model by dynamically. The pseudo code of our algorithm is shown in Algorithm 1.

4 Experiment

4.1 Datasets

Two datasets, Fashion-MNIST [20] and CIFAR10 [21]. Where Fashion-MNIST is a dataset consisting of grayscale images. The image is a 28 * 28 pixel matrix, and the value of each pixel is an 8-bit unsigned integer between 0 and 255. The CIFAR10 dataset is a dataset consisting of 10 categories of three-channel images.

4.2 Network Architecture

In terms of pre-training classification models, Fashion-MNIST uses a four-layer convolutional plus two-layer fully-connected model. CIFAR10 uses the Resnet-18 model. the GAN network architecture of Fashion-MNIST is shown in Table 1, and the GAN network architecture of CIFAR-10 is shown in Table 2.

Table 1. Fashion-MNIST GAN network architecture description.

Generator	Discriminator
3 * 3 conv 8 ReLU stride = 1	4 * 4 conv 8 stride = 2
InstanceNorm2d	LeakyReLU
3 * 3 conv 16 ReLU stride = 2	4 * 4 conv 16 stride = 2
InstanceNorm2d	BatchNorm2d LeakyReLU
3 * 3 conv 32 ReLU stride = 2	4 * 4 conv 32 stride = 2
InstanceNorm2d	BatchNorm2d LeakyReLU
3 * 3 convTranspose 16 ReLU stride = 2	1 * 1 conv 32 ReLU
InstanceNorm2d	Sigmoid
3 * 3 convTranspose 8 ReLU stride = 2	
InstanceNorm2d	
6 * 6 convTranspose 1	
Tanh	

Algorithm 1: Fusion Adversarial Training

Input: Training rounds Epoch, Number of iterations K, Batch size N,Training data set$\{(x_i, y_i)\}$,Step size η, Initialization Model $f(\theta)$, Model Parameters θ,Sample Perturbation ε,Correlation coefficient α , β
Initialization:Generator Model G
Output:Robust model after fusion adversarial training
Read data of batch size N from the training dataset
for i = 1 ; i < Epoch ; i++ **do**
    $x_i' \leftarrow G(x_i) + x_i$
    $x_i'' \leftarrow x_i + 0.001 \cdot \mathcal{N}(0, \mathrm{I})$
    For j = 1; j<K **do**
        $x_i'' \leftarrow \Pi_{\mathbb{B}(x_{i,\epsilon})}(\eta sign\left(\nabla_{x_i''} L(f_\theta(x_i), f_\theta(x_i''))\right) + x_i'')$
    end for
    $L_{trade} \leftarrow \theta - \eta \Sigma_{i=1}^{N} \nabla_\theta [L(f_\theta(x_i), y_i)) + L(f_\theta(x_i), f_\theta(x_i''))/\lambda]/N$
    $L(\theta) = \alpha L(x_i') + \beta L_{trade}$
    Update model parameter θ
end for

Table 2. CIFAR10 GAN network architecture description.

Generator	Discriminator
3 * 3 conv 8 ReLU stride = 1	4 * 4 conv 8 stride = 2
InstanceNorm2d	LeakyReLU
3 * 3 conv 16 ReLU stride = 2	4 * 4 conv 16 stride = 2
InstanceNorm2d	BatchNorm2d LeakyReLU
3 * 3 conv 32 ReLU stride = 2	4 * 4 conv 32 stride = 2
InstanceNorm2d	BatchNorm2d LeakyReLU
3 * 3 convTranspose 16 ReLU stride = 2	1 * 1 conv 32 ReLU
InstanceNorm2d	Sigmoid
3 * 3 convTranspose 8 ReLU stride = 2	
InstanceNorm2d	
6 * 6 convTranspose 3	
Tanh	

4.3 Experimental Setup

In this experiment, we take several different attacks of FGSM, MI-FGSM, PGD and BIM to test the robustness of the model. For different datasets, we set different attack perturbations, with perturbation $\varepsilon = 0.3$ on the Fashion-MNIST dataset and perturbation $\varepsilon = 0.03$ on the CIFAR10 dataset. in the training process of the GAN generative network model, the training batch size is 32, the loss function optimization uses the Adam optimizer, and the learning rate is initialized to 0.001, which decays gradually with the increase of training rounds during the training The learning rate is initialized to 0.001 and gradually decays with the increase of training rounds during the training process. In the fusion adversarial training process, our back propagation times are the same as PGD,the loss function is also optimized using Adam optimizer with a training batch size of 16, and the robustness and accuracy of the model are balanced by optimizing the boundary loss between the original samples and the adversarial samples.

4.4 Results

In this section we compare the experimental results on the Fashion-MNIST dataset and evaluate the robustness of the model by its accuracy rate under different attack methods. If the model can maintain a high accuracy rate under multiple attacks, then it indicates that the model is well defended and robust.

On the Fashion-MNIST, we first performed normal training, i.e., the training samples were normal samples, and obtained an accuracy of 92.34% for the normal training model. The model is used as a baseline for experimental comparison. From Table 3, we can see that the classification accuracy of the normal training model drops to almost 0 under different attack methods, and the model is less robust. Compared with the other three adversarial training methods, the classification accuracy of the method proposed in this paper is 86.02% for normal samples, which is slightly lower than the classification accuracy of other adversarial training methods for normal samples, but the robustness of the model is improved substantially, such as the classification accuracy of the adversarial samples can reach 62.10% under 10 iterations of PGD rounds of attacks.

Table 3. Fashion-MNIST adversarial training model accuracy.

Method	Normal	FGSM	BIM	PGD10	MIFGSM
Normal	92.34	23.76	0.01	0.50	0.07
GAN	91.05	38.13	46.7	53.62	28.37
FGSM	89.83	68.91	6.66	28.76	38.17
PGD	87.75	39.38	37.86	35.35	36.72
GWT (ours)	86.02	52.16	72.72	62.10	51.06

We also did comparison experiments on the CIFAR10, and first we used ResNet18 as a pre-trained model. Under different adversarial attacks, our model also has good recognition results. The specific experimental results are shown in Table 4 below.

Table 4. CIFAR10 adversarial training model accuracy.

Method	Normal	FGSM	BIM	PGD10	MIFGSM
Normal	92.10	0.01	0.01	0.01	0.01
GAN	90.84	54.20	13.1	1.12	23.56
FGSM	87.50	41.50	20.76	7.20	14.97
PGD	80.73	60.13	62.33	50.96	60.66
GWT (ours)	82.54	66.49	66.79	54.53	61.25

5 Discussion

5.1 Generating Network Modules

The role of the generator is to learn the perturbations of the original samples. In this paper, the generator G uses a self-encoder [22] structure, for both encoder and decoder with a three-layer convolutional architecture, while four residual blocks [23] are added in between the encoder and decoder, each residual block consisting of one 3 * 3 convolution. Discriminator is crucial because its discriminative effect directly determines the generative effect of the generator. The discriminator D is used to distinguish clean samples from generated samples and feeds the results to the generator G for the purpose of optimizing the GAN model in continuous iterations.

The loss of the Fashion-MNIST generative network model during training using a scatter plot, as shown in Fig. 2 below. We can see that the loss of the discriminator D decreases and gradually stabilizes as the number of training rounds increases, and the loss of the perturbation P learned by the generator and the loss of the generation of counteracting samples by the generator also gradually decreases and eventually converges to stability, while the optimization loss of the generator increases as the number of training rounds increases, but eventually also converges to stability, which means that the ability of the generator to generate counteracting perturbations is gradually enhanced.

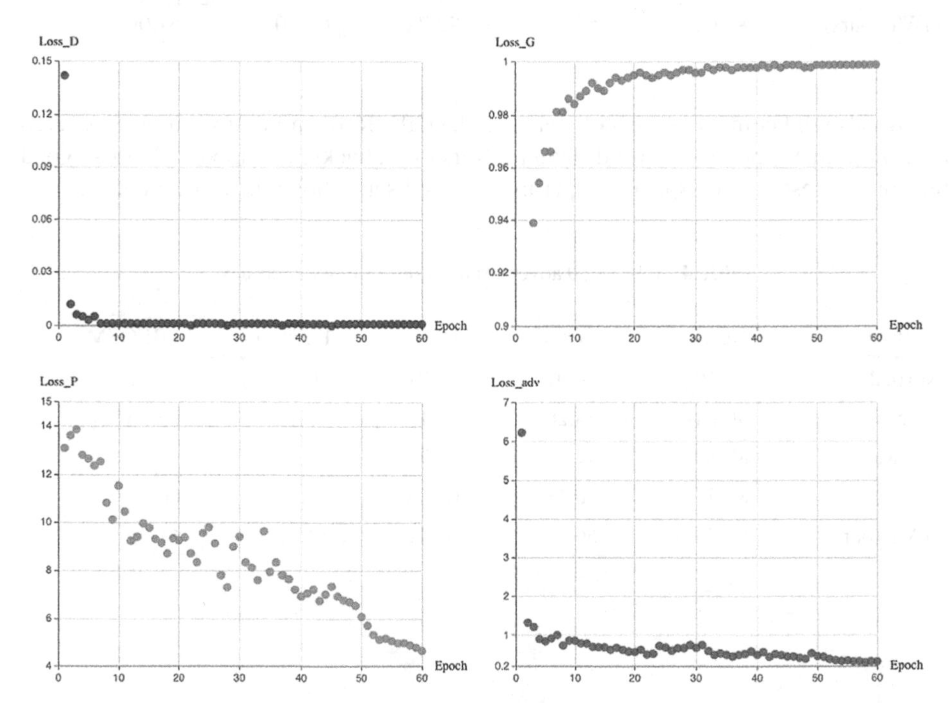

Fig. 2. The loss of the Fashion-MNIST generation model

The generative network model for the Cifar10 dataset is portrayed in a scatter plot as shown in Fig. 3 below.

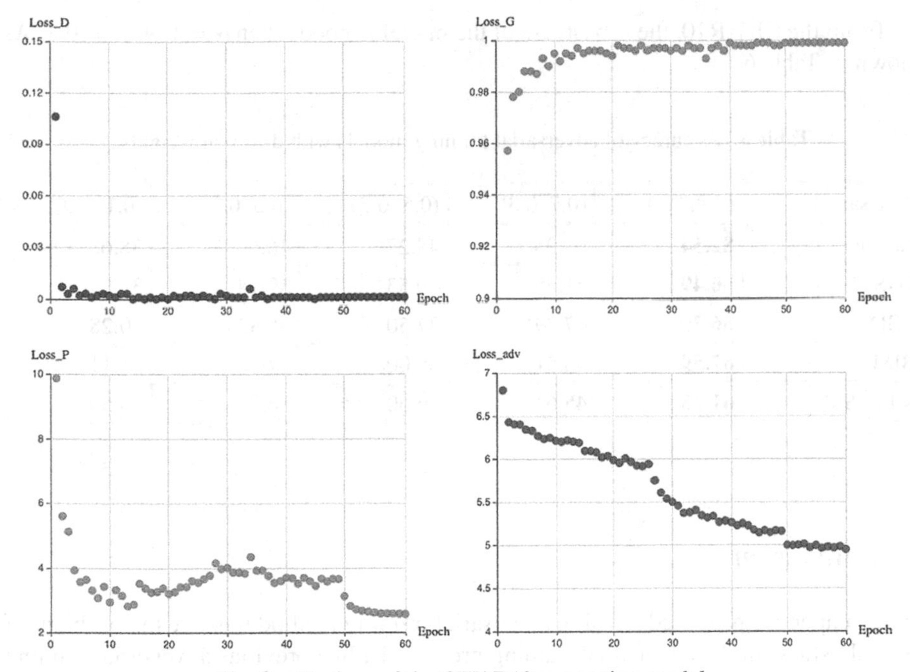

Fig. 3. The loss of the CIFAR10 generation model

5.2 Loss Function Weights

For different optimization losses, we used to find the best defense effect by assigning different weights [24]. In this section, comparative experiments are conducted for the weight selection of the loss function. There are two optimization losses, one is the loss of generating the adversarial network, and the other is the loss between the model for different outputs of the original and adversarial samples, the weight coefficient of the first loss is α, and the weight coefficient of the second loss is β. We assign different weights to each of these two losses for the experimental comparison.

For the FashionMNIST dataset, when $\alpha = 0.9$, $\beta = 0.1$, the defense of the model is relatively strong without losing too much of the normal sample accuracy. As shown in Table 5.

Table 5. Accuracy of adversarial training models with different weights.

Adv samples	(0.9, 0.1)	(0.7, 0.3)	(0.5, 0.5)	(0.3, 0.7)	(0.1, 0.9)
Normal	**86.02**	84.03	83.69	80.67	80.68
FGSM	52.16	51.65	53.83	57.96	57.94
PGD	**72.72**	67.62	72.36	72.38	72.14
BIM	**75.67**	65.02	69.63	70.93	70.41
MIFGSM	51.06	45.33	51.33	57.96	57.87

From the CIFAR10, the robustness of the model is good when $\alpha = 0.9, \beta = 0.1$. As shown in Table 6.

Table 6. Accuracy of adversarial training models with different weights.

Adv samples	(0.9, 0.1)	(0.7, 0.3)	(0.5, 0.5)	(0.3, 0.7)	(0.1, 0.9)
Normal	**82.54**	61.95	48.27	46.63	38.68
FGSM	**66.49**	51.65	40.53	39.14	33.09
PGD	**66.79**	47.79	37.50	36.82	30.28
BIM	**67.59**	48.51	38.00	37.32	31.11
MIFGSM	**61.25**	45.64	36.60	36.00	30.50

6 Conclusion

In this paper, we proposed a fusion adversarial training method to solve the problem of low robustness in the adversarial training process. Unlike previous adversarial training methods, this paper uses an adversarial generative network to process the original samples and generate scrambled adversarial samples, and the trained adversarial generative network is used to generate a certain range of attack perturbations during the adversarial training process. The robustness of the network model is improved overall. The effectiveness of our network architecture is also verified through relevant experiments on the Fashion-MNIST and CIFAR10 datasets. The method of this paper has some limitations at present, and the computational cost and defense performance of this paper still need to be improved for larger datasets. In addition, there are still many areas of concern in the correlation of different optimization losses of the model, and in future work, we will conduct research based on these aspects.

References

1. Zhang, Z., Cui, P., Zhu, W.: Deep learning on graphs: a survey. IEEE Trans. Knowl. Data Eng. (2020)
2. Grosse, K., Papernot, N., Manoharan, P., Backes, M., McDaniel, P.: Adversarial examples for malware detection. In: Foley, S.N., Gollmann, D., Snekkenes, E. (eds.) ESORICS 2017. LNCS, vol. 10493, pp. 62–79. Springer, Cham (2017). https://doi.org/10.1007/978-3-319-66399-9_4
3. Qiu, H., Qiu, M., Lu, Z.: Selective encryption on ecg data in body sensor network based on supervised machine learning. Inf. Fusion **55**, 59–67 (2020)
4. Qiu, M., Zhang, L., Ming, Z., Chen, Z., Qin, X., Yang, L.T.: Security-aware optimization for ubiquitous computing systems with seat graph approach. J. Comput. Syst. Sci. **79**(5), 518–529 (2013)
5. Qiu, M., Gai, K., Xiong, Z.: Privacy-preserving wireless communications using bipartite matching in social big data. Future Gener. Comput. Syst. **87**, 772–781 (2018)

6. Qin, Y., Carlini, N., Cottrell, G., Goodfellow, I., Raffel. C.: Imperceptible, robust, and targeted adversarial examples for automatic speech recognition. In: International Conference on Machine Learning, pp. 5231–5240. PMLR (2019)
7. Lu, J., Sibai, H., Fabry, E.: Adversarial examples that fool detectors. arXiv preprint arXiv: 1712.02494 (2017)
8. Sharif, M., Bhagavatula, S., Bauer, L., Reiter, M.K.: Accessorize to a crime: real and stealthy attacks on state-of-the-art face recognition. In: Proceedings of the 2016 ACM SIGSAC Conference on Computer and Communications Security, pp. 1528–1540 (2016)
9. Goodfellow, I.J., Shlens, J., Szegedy C.: Explaining and harnessing adversarial examples. arXiv preprint arXiv:1412.6572 (2014)
10. Goodfellow, I., et al.: Generative adversarial nets. In: Advances in Neural Information Processing Systems, vol. 27 (2014)
11. Deng, J., Dong, W., Socher, R., Li, L.J., Li, K., Fei-Fei, L.: ImageNet: a large-scale hierarchical image database. In: 2009 IEEE Conference on Computer Vision and Pattern Recognition, pp. 248–255. IEEE (2009)
12. Nadkarni, P.M., Ohno-Machado, L., Chapman, W.W.: Natural language processing: an introduction. J. Am. Med. Inform. Assoc. **18**(5), 544–551 (2011)
13. Szegedy, C., et al.: Intriguing properties of neural networks. arXiv preprint arXiv:1312.6199 (2013)
14. Dong, Y., et al.: Boosting adversarial attacks with momentum. In: Proceedings of the IEEE Conference on Computer Vision and Pattern Recognition, pp. 9185–9193 (2018)
15. Athalye, A., Engstrom, L., Ilyas, A., Kwok, K.: Synthesizing robust adversarial examples. In: International Conference on Machine Learning, pp. 284–293. PMLR (2018)
16. Ghahramani, Z.: Unsupervised learning. In: Bousquet, O., von Luxburg, U., Rätsch, G. (eds.) ML -2003. LNCS (LNAI), vol. 3176, pp. 72–112. Springer, Heidelberg (2004). https://doi.org/10.1007/978-3-540-28650-9_5
17. Xiao, C., Li, B., Zhu, J.Y., He, W., Liu, M., Song, D.: Generating adversarial examples with adversarial networks. arXiv preprint arXiv:1801.02610 (2018)
18. Zhang, H., Yu, Y., Jiao, J., Xing, E., El Ghaoui, L., Jordan, M.: Theoretically principled trade-off between robustness and accuracy. In: International Conference on Machine Learning, pp. 7472–7482. PMLR. (2019)
19. Carlini, N., et al.: On evaluating adversarial robustness. arXiv preprint arXiv:1902.06705 (2019)
20. Xiao, H., Rasul, K., Vollgraf, R.: Fashion-mnist: a novel image dataset for benchmarking machine learning algorithms. arXiv preprint arXiv:1708.07747 (2017)
21. Krizhevsky, A., Hinton, G., et al.: Learning multiple layers of features from tiny images (2009)
22. Louizos, C., Swersky, K., Li, Y., Welling, M., Zemel, R.: The variational fair autoencoder. arXiv preprint arXiv:1511.00830 (2015)

23. He, K., Zhang, X., Ren, S., Sun, J.: Deep residual learning for image recognition. In: Proceedings of the IEEE Conference on Computer Vision and Pattern Recognition, pp. 770–778 (2016)
24. Sudre, C.H., Li, W., Vercauteren, T., Ourselin, S., Jorge Cardoso, M.: Generalised dice overlap as a deep learning loss function for highly unbalanced segmentations. In: Cardoso, M.J., et al. (eds.) DLMIA/ML-CDS -2017. LNCS, vol. 10553, pp. 240–248. Springer, Cham (2017). https://doi.org/10.1007/978-3-319-67558-9_28

MAST-NER: A Low-Resource Named Entity Recognition Method Based on Trigger Pool

Juxiong Xu[1] and Minbo Li[1,2](✉)

[1] Software School, Fudan University, Shanghai 200438, China
{xujx19,limb}@fudan.edu.cn
[2] Shanghai Key Laboratory of Data Science, Shanghai 200438, China

Abstract. Named entity recognition (NER) is a basic knowledge extraction task. At present, many domains face a lack of labeled data, but current models for low-resource NER does not utilize the features of domain text. In this paper, we propose the MAST-NER model to improve the NER performance on domain-specific text. This model introduces multiple type pools based on entity triggers, and enhances sequence tagging through a multi-head attention mechanism, where the query matrix is jointly constructed by each type of triggers. MAST-NER can take full advantages of entity triggers on domain text with similar sentence patterns, and enable each type of entity recognition to be enhanced. The experimental results show that the model in this paper can achieve higher cost-effectiveness, especially for domain datasets (up to 3.33%). For general domain datasets, this model also has a certain performance improvement.

Keywords: Named entity recognition · Entity trigger · Attention mechanism · Deep learning · Natural language processing

1 Introduction

Named Entity Recognition (NER) aims to extract entities from a given text and classify them according to predefined categories (such as people, places, organization, etc.). NER is usually the first step in information extraction, and directly affects the accuracy of downstream applications. At present, deep learning based NER models represented by BiLSTM-CRF [1] have shown good performance in the general domain. However, these methods require a large amount of labeled data, which is scarce in many cases. For example, in the industrial field, many manufacturers have accumulated a large number of maintenance reports, which describes the equipment troubleshooting process. These reports contain a large number of domain entities, but labeling them is time-consuming and labor-intensive.

Recently, [2] proposed a named entity recognition method based on entity triggers, called TriggerNER. An entity trigger is a group of cue words or phrases that help us recognize an entity. For example, in sentence *"We had a fantastic lunch at Rumble Fish yesterday."*, we can infer that *"Rumble Fish"* is a

G. Memmi et al. (Eds.): KSEM 2022, LNAI 13370, pp. 65–76, 2022.
https://doi.org/10.1007/978-3-031-10989-8_6

restaurant name according to *"had ... lunch at"*, which is considered to be a entity trigger. Experiments show that TriggerNER achieves high cost-effective that using only 20% of the trigger-annotated sentences results in a comparable performance as using 70% of conventional annotated sentences.

The idea of TriggerNER is very suitable for domain-specific texts since many of them have similar sentence patterns. For example, the structure of an equipment maintenance report usually includes symptoms, causes and solutions. Similarly, a typical electronic medical record (EMR) contains symptoms, disease, time, and surgical items. These data have similar terminology, so entity triggers can work well. However, there are still some problems with applying TriggerNER to such these domain-specific texts:

1. Entity triggers of the same type may have similar representations. In sequence tagging, TriggerNER does not classify entity triggers, but only calculate the semantic distance between them and sentences, which easily leads to the obtained K entity triggers all belonging to the same type (such as symptoms or disease). However, there are usually multiple types of entities in one domain sentence (such as EMR), and getting only one type of triggers results in lower accuracy for other types of entities.
2. Some entity triggers are polysemous. For example, in a maintenance report, *"detect..."* may be followed by fault symptom or cause, which are essentially two types of triggers. Such cases cannot be distinguished in TriggerNER, which may weaken the effect of entity triggers.
3. A complete domain text usually has multiple types of entities. Ideally, a sentence should match multiple triggers to activate the corresponding types of entities. However, TriggerNER performs mean-pooling in these triggers, which does not distinguish the scope of different types of triggers. The effects of different triggers are diluted and not fully utilized.

To address these problems, we combine the multi-head attention mechanism and entity trigger type pool to propose MAST-NER, a Multi-head Attention and type-Specific pool-based Trigger NER model. Specifically, this method introduces entity triggers on the BiLSTM-CRF framework to improve the efficiency of entity annotation. Entity triggers are classified by type, and multiple binary classifiers are introduced to divide sentences. Various types of entity triggers jointly participate in sequence tagging. Besides, a multi-head attention mechanism is introduced to capture semantics in different subspaces, considering the relationship between hidden states and avoiding the interference between triggers. The main contributions of this paper are summarized as follows:

1. We propose Multi-head Attention and type-Specific pool-based Trigger NER (MAST-NER), an improved model based on TriggerNER [2]. This model significantly improves NER performance on domain-specific text.
2. We introduce trigger type pool. Sentence and entity types are classified and matched to maximize the effect of each type of trigger.
3. We introduce a multi-head attention mechanism to capture the semantics of different subspaces. Sentence-related triggers are concatenated into query

matrices through multiple pooling operations instead of mean-pooling. The introduction of multi-head attention mechanism and trigger type pool enables each type of entity to be enhanced.

The remainder of this paper is organized as follows: Sect. 2 presents previous works related to NER. Section 3 describes the overall architecture of our method as well as the model details. In Sect. 4, we present the experimental evaluation. Finally, Sect. 5 concludes the paper.

2 Related Work

At present, models based on deep learning have become the mainstream method for named entity recognition. A classic work is the BiLSTM-CRF model proposed by [1], which uses a bidirectional LSTM network to encode sequence context information followed by a conditional random field to restrict the label form of the sequence output. [3] regard NER as a machine reading comprehension task, propose a unified MRC framework and achieve SOTA. [4] proposed the BiFlaG model, which uses BiLSTM and graph convolutional networks to jointly learn planar entities and their internal dependencies. Chinese and English have completely different characteristics in linguistics, and many scholars have also conducted research on Chinese NER. [5] used Dilated Convolution to enhance the context encoding ability of the model and applied it to Chinese clinical NER. [6] proposed a weakly supervised method from the perspective of causality and achieved SOTA on Chinese NER datasets. [7] proposed the PLTE model, which is several times faster than the current SOTA model with comparable performance.

However, neural-based NER model usually requires a large amount of annotated training data, which is difficult to obtain in many domains. For low-resource NER, a common approach is to add auxiliary information. [8] used an additional entity dictionary for distantly supervision, which could benefit segmental neural NER models. [9] exploited sentence-level labels and proposed a joint model that enables multi-class classification equipped with a pre-training strategy, which can use sentence-level classifier to enhance NER main task. However, such valuable auxiliary information does not exist in all scenarios. And it may make the trained model biased. Another possible approach is transfer learning. [10] addressed zero-shot transfer for cross-lingual NER. However, in domain-specific scenarios, it is difficult to find source domains that are semantically similar and have a large amount of annotated data. There are also many researches related to low-resource or few-shot. [11] proposed a framework for training sequence tagging models with weak supervision consisting of multiple heuristic rules of unknown accuracy. [12] proposed an intelligent fault diagnosis method based on an improved domain adaptation method via ensemble learning. [13] proposed a novel dataset-specific feature extractor for zero-shot learning according to an attribute-based label tree, and further studied it in [14]. However, these methods are either not directly applicable to NER tasks or require additional information, which is not available in some domains. [2] introduced "entity triggers" and proposed a trigger matching network to jointly learn trigger representations and soft matching module, which could be more cost-effective than the traditional neural NER models. But as mentioned above, this method also has drawbacks when applied to domain-specific texts.

3 Methodology

In this paper, we propose Multi-head Attention and type-Specific pool-based Trigger NER (MAST-NER) to further improve the cost-effective of the trigger-based framework in domain text. The model includes two modules: Type Pool-based Trigger Matching Network (TPTMN) and Categorical Trigger Enhanced Sequence Tagging. The overall architecture is shown in Fig. 1.

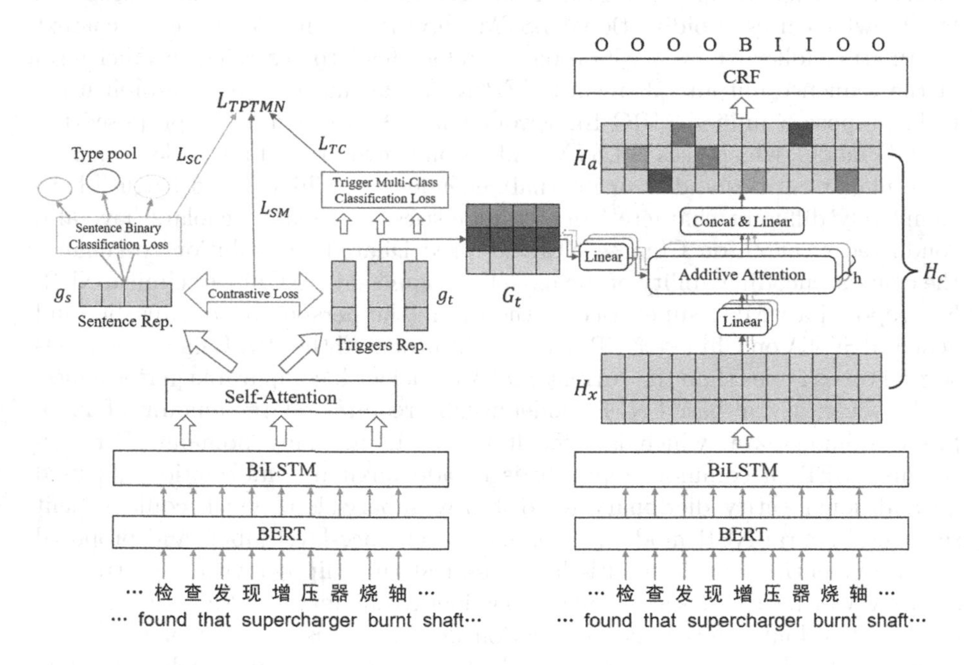

Fig. 1. The overall architecture of MAST-NER.

3.1 Type Pool-Based Trigger Matching Network

TPTMN is used to learn semantic representations of sentences and triggers in the same vector space, so that them can be matched by computing semantic similarity. First, a sentence is transformed into word vectors through a word embedding layer or a pre-trained model such as BERT [15].

After that, the word vector matrix of the sentence is passed through a bidirectional LSTM layer to obtain its hidden state sequence, and these sequences constitute the hidden state matrix H. The word vectors contained in the triggers form the hidden state matrix Z. A self-attention layer is used to jointly learn the attention-based vector representations of sentences and triggers, introduced by [16] as follows:

$$\overrightarrow{a_{\text{sent}}} = \operatorname{softmax}\left(W_2 \tanh\left(W_1 H^T\right)\right) \tag{1}$$

$$g_s = \overrightarrow{a_{\text{sent}}} H \tag{2}$$

$$\overrightarrow{a_{trig}} = \operatorname{softmax}\left(W_2 \tanh\left(W_1 Z^T\right)\right) \tag{3}$$

$$g_t = \overrightarrow{a_{trig}} Z \tag{4}$$

In order to distinguish different types of triggers, each entity type has its corresponding trigger pool, and a pool contains all the entity triggers and their representations. Assuming that the number of entity types is K. Usually one sentence contains multiple types of entities. In entity recognition, the first thing to consider is what types of entities are in the sentence to be predicted, so as to obtain the corresponding type of triggers. Therefore, K binary classifiers are trained to judge whether the sentence contains entities of this type, and the classifiers correspond 1-to-1 with the trigger type pool. The loss L_{SC} of the sentence classifier is defined as follows:

$$\begin{aligned} L_{SC} = -\sum_{K}\sum_{N} & \left[y_e \cdot \log\left(P\left(\hat{y}_e \mid g_s; \theta_{SC}\right)\right)\right. \\ & \left. + \left(1 - y_e\right) \cdot \log\left(1 - P\left(\hat{y}_e \mid g_s; \theta_{SC}\right)\right)\right] \end{aligned} \tag{5}$$

Where K and N represent the number of entity types and samples. y_e is the sample label. g_s is the sentence representation and θ_{SC} is the classifier parameter. Each classifier is a Multilayer Perceptron (MLP). During training, a sentence is used as a positive sample for t classifiers and a negative sample for other K-t classifiers if it contains t entities.

Trigger representation should be associated with entity types in order to activate the corresponding entities. Therefore, each trigger representation g_t will be input into a multi-classifier whose loss function L_{TC} is defined as follows:

$$L_{TC} = -\sum_{N}\sum_{k=1}^{K} y_k \cdot \log\left(P\left(\hat{y}_k \mid g_t; \theta_{TC}\right)\right) \tag{6}$$

Besides, sentences and associated triggers should have similar vector representations for matching via semantic similarity. The semantic similarity d is defined as the L2 norm of sentence representation g_s and trigger representation g_t. The contrastive loss function is used to calculate the matching loss L_{SM}:

$$L_{SM} = \sum_{N} y_m \frac{1}{2}\left(d\left(g_s, g_t\right)\right)^2 + \left(1 - y_m\right)\frac{1}{2}\left[m - d\left(g_s, g_t\right)\right]_+^2 \tag{7}$$

Where y_m is the pairwise label and m is the negative sample margin.

The form of L_{TC} and L_{SM} is the same as in TriggerNER. Finally, the loss function of TPTMN consists of these three parts:

$$L_{TPTMN} = L_{SC} + \lambda_1 L_{TC} + \lambda_2 L_{SM} \tag{8}$$

Where λ_1 and λ_2 are hyperparameters.

3.2 Categorical Trigger Enhanced Sequence Tagging

This module is used for final sequence labeling, and its architecture is similar to the regular NER model [1]. The difference is that an attention layer is added.

In training, the query matrix of the attention mechanism is constructed by triggers according to the type. Specifically, all triggers associated with sentence x are mean pooled by type. Triggers of the same type keep a mean vector $\hat{g}_t$. If the sentence lacks an entity of a certain type, the type is replaced by a negative large-valued vector. Finally, K (the number of entity types) vectors are obtained, and the query matrix G_t constructed by concatenating them, as shown in Fig. 2. The purpose of this step is to ensure that the query matrix dimension of different training sentence is the same, and be able to distinguish the semantics of different trigger type.

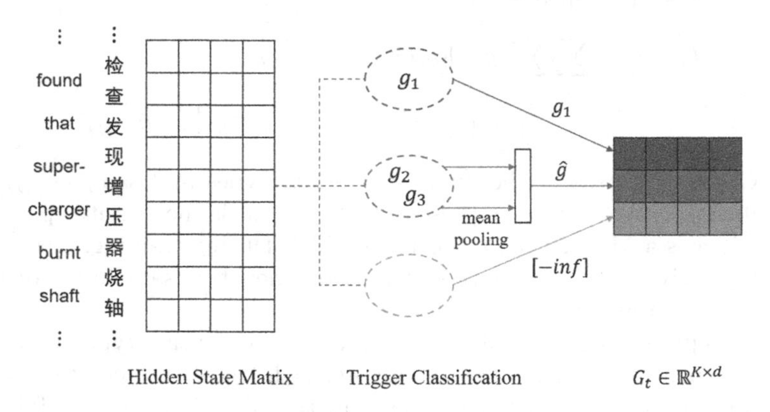

Fig. 2. Query matrix construction process.

The multi-head attention mechanism adopted in this paper is similar to Transformer [17], with the basic unit of additive attention:

$$\vec{a_i} = \text{softmax}(V_i^{\mathrm{T}} \tanh(W_i^H (H_x)^{\mathrm{T}} + W_i^G (G_t)^{\mathrm{T}})^{\mathrm{T}}) \tag{9}$$

$$H_i' = \vec{a_i} H_x \tag{10}$$

$$H_a = \text{Concat}\,(H_1', \ldots, H_h')\, W^o \tag{11}$$

Where H_x is the hidden state matrix of the sentence x through BiLSTM, G_t is the query matrix of attention, and W and V are the parameters of the attention mechanism.

The original matrix H_x and the attention-based matrix H_a are concatenated into H_c, which is input to the CRF layer for sequence tagging. The training purpose of this stage is the same as traditional NER task, the difference is that it's enhanced by attention-based trigger matrix.

3.3 Inference

For an unlabeled test sentence, after obtaining its hidden representation, K binary classifiers are used to determine whether it contains the corresponding type entity. If there is, select a trigger with the highest semantic similarity to the sentence from the trigger pool; otherwise, replace it with a negative large-valued vector. These trigger representations form an attention query matrix and enhance the sequence tagging, as shown in Fig. 3.

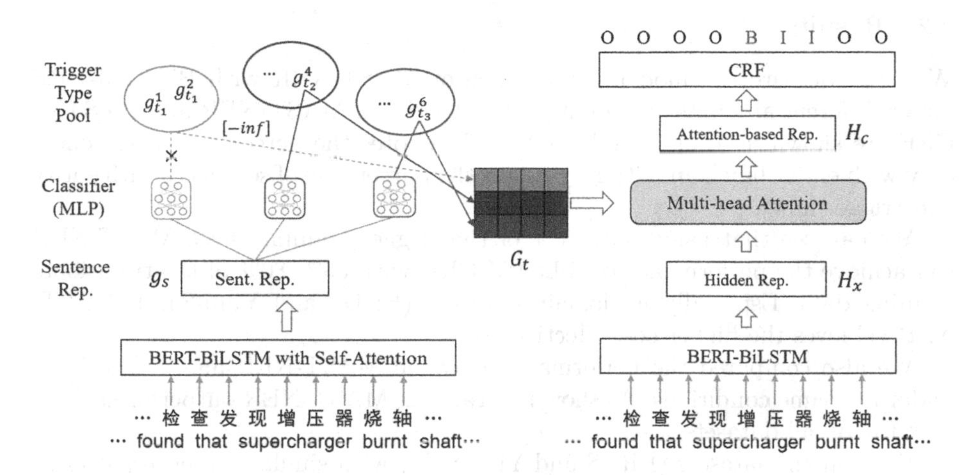

Fig. 3. Inference on unlabeled sentences.

4 Experiments

4.1 Experiments Setup

Four datasets are used for evaluation: two domain datasets and tow general datasets. Domain datasets include a Engine Repair Data Set (ERDS) and a Chinese electronic medical record NER dataset (Yidu-S4K) [18]. And general datasets are CoNLL2003 [19] and BC5CDR [20], which are commonly used in

NER task. The annotation schema of entities and triggers is the same as in TriggerNER, that is, each training data is labeled with an entity (labeled with "BIO") and its triggers (labeled with "T").

ERDS is a private dataset derived from a manufacturer's after-sales maintenance report. Its textual content involves the process of engine fault handing, including four entity types: Fault Phenomenon, Fault Location, Fault Status and Repair Method. As mentioned above, the patterns between sentences in ERDS are similar. It contains 5644 sentences, and 20% are labeled with entity triggers.

Yidu-S4K is published with the evaluation task of CCKS2019, "Medical Entity Recognition for Chinese EMR". This dataset is a plain text document of EMR labeled by professional teams. Six entity types are defined: disease, examination, inspection, surgery, drug and anatomical location, including 1379 sentences. Likewise, 20% of sentences are labeled with entity triggers.

We choose BiLSTM-CRF [1] and TriggerNER [2] as baselines. To ensure a fair comparison between these models, the settings of hyper-parameters are all the same.

4.2 Results

We first compare the model performance of MAST-NER with BiLSTM-CRF under different amounts of training data. Results of MAST-NER and BiLSTM-CRF are shown in Table 1. Where "sent." denotes the percentage of sentences only with entity label, and "trig." denotes the percentage of sentences with entity and trigger label.

We can see that using only 20% of the trigger training data, MAST-NER can achieve the performance of BiLSTM-CRF with 60%–80% of the traditional training data. Especially in domain datasets (ERDS and Yidu-S4K), MAST-NER achieves the higher cost-effectiveness.

We also compared the performance between MAST-NER and TriggerNER under the same conditions. As shown in Table 2, MAST-NER outperforms TriggerNER on all datasets.

For domain datasets (ERDS and Yidu-S4K) with similar sentence patterns, the TPTMN module of MAST-NER can classify the triggers into categories and enhanced recognition for each type of entity, so it achieves a large lead compared with TriggerNER. For general sentences (CoNLL2003 and BC5CDR), multiple binary classifiers in MAST-NER can determine the type of triggers that need to be used, while the KNN algorithm used in TriggerNER cannot be used for entities with changeable conditions, so it can also improve performance.

Table 1. Labor-efficiency study on MAST-NER and BiLSTM-CRF

	BiLSTM-CRF				MAST-NER		
sent.	Precision	Recall	F1	trig.	Precision	Recall	F1
ERDS							
10%	62.61	64.72	63.65	3%	65.77	62.56	64.13
20%	70.56	68.07	69.29	5%	69.62	63.64	66.49
30%	74.73	69.05	71.78	7%	70.91	69.32	70.11
40%	76.91	70.82	73.74	10%	73.15	71.47	72.3
50%	77.21	72.16	74.6	13%	75.42	72.86	74.11
60%	78.27	73.67	75.9	15%	77.92	74.16	75.99
70%	79.07	74.08	76.49	17%	78.35	75.59	76.95
80%	80.52	74.77	**77.54**	**20%**	79.6	76.19	**77.86**
Yidu-S4K							
10%	69.24	65.9	67.53	3%	70.11	66.52	68.27
20%	72.64	69.87	71.23	5%	72.25	69.25	70.72
30%	75.09	72.93	73.99	7%	74.01	73.62	73.86
40%	77.26	75.11	76.17	10%	75.11	74.48	74.79
50%	79.52	76.13	77.79	13%	77.73	76.22	76.97
60%	80.27	77.81	79.02	15%	78.32	76.96	77.63
70%	81.21	78.48	**79.82**	17%	78.86	78.06	78.45
80%	81.88	78.98	80.4	**20%**	80.66	79.5	**80.08**
CoNLL2003							
5%	70.85	67.32	69.04	3%	79.34	75.46	77.35
10%	76.57	77.09	76.83	5%	82.19	81.83	82.01
20%	82.17	80.35	81.3	7%	82.76	82.42	82.59
30%	83.71	82.76	83.23	10%	84.01	83.35	83.68
40%	85.31	83.1	84.18	13%	85.49	84.64	85.06
50%	85.07	83.49	84.27	15%	86.54	85.35	85.94
60%	85.58	84.54	85.24	17%	87.83	85.41	86.6
70%	86.87	85.3	**86.08**	**20%**	88.39	86.68	**87.53**
BC5CDR							
5%	63.37	43.23	51.39	3%	67.91	62.38	65.03
10%	68.83	60.37	64.32	5%	69.02	66.04	67.5
20%	79.09	62.66	69.92	7%	69.71	68.68	69.19
30%	80.13	65.3	71.87	10%	72.62	69.76	71.16
40%	82.05	65.5	72.71	13%	74.02	69.54	71.71
50%	82.56	66.58	73.71	15%	77.2	70.62	73.76
60%	81.73	70.74	**75.84**	17%	75.95	73.52	74.71
70%	81.16	75.29	76.12	**20%**	78.08	74.14	**76.06**

Table 2. Comparison results of MAST-NER and TriggerNER

	TriggerNER			MAST-NER		
trig.	Precision	Recall	F1	Precision	Recall	F1
ERDS						
3%	63.7	57.92	60.68	65.77	62.56	64.13
5%	66.92	59.02	62.72	69.62	63.64	66.49
7%	69.77	63.87	66.69	70.91	69.32	70.11
10%	73.32	66.76	69.89	73.15	71.47	72.3
13%	74.79	68.28	71.05	75.42	72.86	74.11
15%	75.95	69.95	72.83	77.92	74.26	76.05
17%	76.1	71.41	73.68	78.35	75.59	76.95
20%	76.92	72.28	**74.53**	79.6	76.19	**77.86**
Yidu-S4K						
3%	67.97	63.2	65.5	70.11	66.52	68.27
5%	70.81	67.93	69.34	72.25	69.25	70.72
7%	71.82	69.24	70.51	74.01	73.62	73.86
10%	73.39	70.4	71.87	75.11	74.48	74.79
13%	74.68	72.82	73.74	77.73	76.22	76.97
15%	75.31	73.51	74.4	78.32	76.96	77.63
17%	76.8	75.29	76.04	78.86	78.06	78.45
20%	78	76.35	**77.17**	80.66	79.5	**80.08**
CoNLL2003						
3%	76.36	74.33	75.33	79.34	75.46	77.35
5%	81.28	79.16	80.2	82.19	81.83	82.01
7%	82.93	81.13	82.02	82.76	82.42	82.59
10%	84.47	82.61	83.53	84.01	83.35	83.68
13%	84.76	83.69	84.22	85.49	84.64	85.06
15%	85.61	84.45	85.03	86.54	85.35	85.94
17%	85.25	85.46	85.36	87.83	85.41	86.6
20%	86.04	85.98	**86.01**	88.39	86.68	**87.53**
BC5CDR						
3%	66.47	57.11	61.44	67.91	62.38	65.03
5%	69.17	73.31	66.11	69.02	66.04	67.5
7%	64.81	69.82	67.22	69.71	68.68	69.19
10%	71.89	69.57	70.71	72.62	69.76	71.16
13%	73.36	70.44	71.87	74.02	69.54	71.71
15%	70.91	72.89	71.89	77.2	70.62	73.76
17%	75.67	70.6	73.05	75.95	73.52	74.71
20%	77.47	70.47	**73.97**	78.08	74.14	**76.06**

5 Conclusion

In this paper, we introduced MAST-NER to improve the NER performance for domain text in low-resource conditions. This method introduces entity triggers and type pools, and trained multiple classifiers accordingly for matching sentences and triggers. In sequence tagging, the NER process is enhanced by multi-head attention mechanism where the query matrix is directly constructed by different types of triggers. The experimental results showed that our method achieves a higher cost-effectiveness and outperforms TriggerNER. Especially on the domain datasets with similar sentence patterns, our method achieves the largest lead. In the future, we can explore trigger-based models based on more advanced sequence tagging mainframes instead of BiLSTM-CRF.

Acknowledgment. This paper is based on a research project supported by National Key Research and Development Project (Grant No. 2018YFB1703104) and National Natural Science Foundation of China (Grant No. 61671157).

References

1. Huang, Z., Xu, W., Yu, W.: Bidirectional LSTM-CRF models for sequence tagging. arXiv preprint arXiv:1508.01991 (2015)
2. Lin, B.Y., et al.: Triggerner: learning with entity triggers as explanations for named entity recognition. In: Proceedings of the 58th Annual Meeting of the Association for Computational Linguistics, pp. 8503–8511 (2020)
3. Li, X., Feng, J., Meng, Y., Han, Q., Wu, F., Li, J.: A unified MRC framework for named entity recognition. In: Proceedings of the 58th Annual Meeting of the Association for Computational Linguistics, pp. 5849–5859 (2020)
4. Luo, Y., Zhao, H.: Bipartite flat-graph network for nested named entity recognition. In: Proceedings of the 58th Annual Meeting of the Association for Computational Linguistics, pp. 6408–6418 (2020)
5. Qiu, J., Wang, Q., Zhou, Y., Ruan, T., Gao, J.: Fast and accurate recognition of Chinese clinical named entities with residual dilated convolutions. In: 2018 IEEE International Conference on Bioinformatics and Biomedicine (BIBM), pp. 935–942. IEEE (2018)
6. Zeng, X., Li, Y., Zhai, Y., Zhang, Y.: Counterfactual generator: a weakly-supervised method for named entity recognition. In: Proceedings of the 2020 Conference on Empirical Methods in Natural Language Processing (EMNLP), pp. 7270–7280 (2020)
7. Mengge, X., Yu, B., Liu, T., Zhang, Y., Meng, E., Wang, B.: Porous lattice transformer encoder for Chinese NER. In: Proceedings of the 28th International Conference on Computational Linguistics, pp. 3831–3841 (2020)
8. Liu, T., Yao, J.-G., Lin, C.-Y.: Towards improving neural named entity recognition with gazetteers. In: Proceedings of the 57th Annual Meeting of the Association for Computational Linguistics, pp. 5301–5307 (2019)
9. Kruengkrai, C., Hai Nguyen, T., Mahani Aljunied, S., Bing, L.: Improving low-resource named entity recognition using joint sentence and token labeling. In: Proceedings of the 58th Annual Meeting of the Association for Computational Linguistics, pp. 5898–5905 (2020)

10. Liu, L., Ding, B., Bing, L., Joty, S., Si, L., Mulda, C.M.: A multilingual data augmentation framework for low-resource cross-lingual NER. In: Proceedings of the 59th Annual Meeting of the Association for Computational Linguistics and the 11th International Joint Conference on Natural Language Processing, vol. 1: Long Papers, pp. 5834–5846 (2021)
11. Safranchik, E., Luo, S., Bach, S.: Weakly supervised sequence tagging from noisy rules. In: Proceedings of the AAAI Conference on Artificial Intelligence, pp. 5570–5578 (2020)
12. Li, Y., Song, Y., Jia, L., Gao, S., Li, Q., Qiu, M.: Intelligent fault diagnosis by fusing domain adversarial training and maximum mean discrepancy via ensemble learning. IEEE Trans. Indus. Informat. **17**(4), 2833–2841 (2020)
13. Luo, Y., Wang, X., Cao, W.: A novel dataset-specific feature extractor for zero-shot learning. Neurocomputing **391**, 74–82 (2020)
14. Xie, Z., Cao, W., Ming, Z.: A further study on biologically inspired feature enhancement in zero-shot learning. Int. J. Mach. Lear. Cybernet. **12**(1), 257–269 (2020). https://doi.org/10.1007/s13042-020-01170-y
15. Devlin, J., Chang Kenton, M.-W., Toutanova, L.K.: BERT: Pre-training of deep bidirectional transformers for language understanding. In: Proceedings of NAACL-HLT, pp. 4171–4186 (2019)
16. Lin, Z., Feng, M., Nogueira dos Santos, C., Yu, M., Xiang, B., Zhou, B., Bengio, Y.: A structured self-attentive sentence embedding. arXiv preprint arXiv:1703.03130 (2017)
17. Vaswani, A., et al.: Attention is all you need. In: Advances in Neural Information Processing Systems, vol. 30 (2017)
18. Han, X., et al. Overview of the CCKS 2019 knowledge graph evaluation track: entity, relation, event and QA. arXiv preprint arXiv:2003.03875 (2020)
19. Sang, E.T.K., De Meulder, F.: Introduction to the conll-2003 shared task: Language-independent named entity recognition. In: Proceedings of the Seventh Conference on Natural Language Learning at HLT-NAACL, pp. 142–147 (2003)
20. Li, J., et al.: Biocreative V CDR task corpus: a resource for chemical disease relation extraction. Database **2016** (2016)

Fuzzy Information Measures Feature Selection Using Descriptive Statistics Data

Omar A. M. Salem[1,2], Haowen Liu[1(✉)], Feng Liu[1(✉)], Yi-Ping Phoebe Chen[3], and Xi Chen[1(✉)]

[1] School of Computer Science, Wuhan University, Wuhan 430072, China
{omarsalem,hwenliu,fliuwhu,robertcx}@whu.edu.cn

[2] Faculty of Computers and Informatics, Suez Canal University, Ismailia 41522, Egypt
omarsalem@ci.suez.edu.eg

[3] Department of Computer Science and Information Technology, La Trobe University, Melbourne 3086, Australia
phoebe.chen@latrobe.edu.au

Abstract. Feature selection (FS) has proven its importance as a preprocessing for improving classification performance. The success of FS methods depends on extracting all the possible relations among features to estimate their informative amount well. Fuzzy information measures are powerful solutions that extract the different feature relations without information loss. However, estimating fuzzy information measures consumes high resources such as space and time. To reduce the high cost of these resources, this paper proposes a novel method to generate FS based on fuzzy information measures using descriptive statistics data (DS) instead of the original data (OD). The main assumption behind this is that the descriptive statistics of features can hold the same relations as the original features. Over 15 benchmark datasets, the effectiveness of using DS has been evaluated on five FS methods according to the classification performance and feature selection cost.

Keywords: Feature selection · Fuzzy information measures · Fuzzy sets · Descriptive statistics · Classification systems

1 Introduction

Nowadays, classification systems can be founded in many real-world problems of different domains such as medical, software engineering, and industrial domain [3,10]. In real-world problems, classification data may contain a lot of features, but not all the features are significant [22]. The bad effect of irrelevant and redundant features reduces the classification performance and increases the computational cost of classification systems [21]. FS is an effective preprocessing on classification data to select the most informative feature subset by keeping only the relevant features and filtering out the undesirable features [2].

G. Memmi et al. (Eds.): KSEM 2022, LNAI 13370, pp. 77–90, 2022.
https://doi.org/10.1007/978-3-031-10989-8_7

The existing FS methods can be defined as one of three types [1,6]: filter, wrapper, and embedded. Our study focus on the filter type due to its advantage over other types as simplicity of usage, efficiency in the computational cost, and independence of classifiers [1,15].

Information measures are popular and widely used in the filter type [21]. Estimating these measures requires discretizing the continuous features with the risk of information loss [23]. To avoid this risk, fuzzy information measures have been introduced as an extension of information measures, by mapping each feature into a fuzzy relation matrix (FRM). The matrix size expands with increasing the length of features. Thus, estimating the fuzzy information measures consumes high computational cost in the space and time resources [18]. To reduce the high cost of these resources, this paper proposes a novel method to generate FS based on fuzzy information measures using descriptive statistics data (DS) instead of the original data (OD). The main assumption behind this is that the descriptive statistics of features can hold the same relations as the original features.

In this paper, the remaining sections are designed as follows: Sect. 2 introduces the related work. Section 3 presents the proposed method. The design of the experiment is described in Sect. 4 while the results are analyzed in Sect. 5. Finally, Sect. 6 introduces the conclusion of this paper.

2 Related Work

According to the structure of FRM, FS methods based on fuzzy information measures can be divided into two categories: FS based on feature-vector relationship and FS based on feature-feature relationship. However, both categories require high computational cost for mapping the original features into a FRM to avoid the discretization process.

In the category of FS based on feature-vector, Luukka et al. introduced FS method based on fuzzy entropy, called FES, to estimate the informative amount of each feature [12]. FES depends on the relationship between the feature and its ideal vector to map the feature into a FRM. Ideal vector is a user-defined set of samples that represents the class information as possible [12,18]. The highest informative feature (lowest entropy) is suggested for selection while the lowest informative feature (highest entropy) is suggested for denying. An improved version of FES is proposed, called FSAE [11]. FSAE depends on an additional scaling factor to consider the distance among ideal vectors with the aim to adjust the informative level of each ideal vector. Shen et al. [19] conducted a comparison among the different components of FES method to study the effect of the combination among the different components. The main limitation of the previous methods is that no consideration for important feature relations such as redundancy and complementarity.

In the second category, Hu et al. proposed FS method based on fuzzy entropy to deal with the heterogeneous data [8]. In [7], Hu et al. used a positive region of data to improve the original method. However, these methods still suffer from denying important feature relations such as redundancy and complementarity.

To overcome this drawback, Yu et al. proposed FS methods based on fuzzy mutual information, called FMI-mRMR [23]. In [20], Tsai et al. conducted a detailed comparison between FS methods based on mutual and fuzzy mutual information. The experimental results confirm the outperformance of FS method based on fuzzy mutual information in terms of feature stability and classification accuracy. Salem et al., in [16], proposed an ensemble FS method, called FFS-RRD, which depends on fuzzy information and fuzzy rough measures to extract the different feature relations. In [17], Salem et al. proposed a new FS method based on fuzzy joint mutual information, called FJMI, to extract the different relations based on the joint discriminative ability, in contrast to the traditional methods which depend on the individual discriminative ability.

3 Proposed Method

Most of the current FS methods depend on the original features. In this paper, we propose using descriptive statistics to summarize the feature information and reduce the computational cost of FS methods.

3.1 Fuzzy Relation Matrix Based on the Original Data

In the following, we illustrate the FRM structure based on the original data according to the methods of feature-feature relationship and feature-vector relationship.

Feature-Feature Relationship: Suppose $F = \{x_1, x_2, ..., x_m\}$ is a feature of m samples. The FRM between the feature and itself will be as follows:

$$M(F) = \begin{bmatrix} s_{1*1} & s_{1*2} & \cdots & s_{1*m} \\ s_{2*1} & \cdots & \cdots & s_{2*m} \\ \cdots & \cdots & \cdots & \cdots \\ s_{m*1} & s_{m*2} & \cdots & s_{m*m} \end{bmatrix} \tag{1}$$

where $s_{i*j} \in [0, 1]$ is the similarity degree between x_i and x_j, where $i, j \in \{1, 2, \ldots, m\}$.

Feature-Vector Relationship: Suppose $F = \{x_1, x_2, ..., x_m\}$ is a feature of m samples and $V = \{y_1, y_2, ..., y_t\}$ is an ideal vector of t samples. The FRM between the feature and its ideal vector will be as follows:

$$M(F) = \begin{bmatrix} s_{1*1} & s_{1*2} & \cdots & s_{1*t} \\ s_{2*1} & \cdots & \cdots & s_{2*t} \\ \cdots & \cdots & \cdots & \cdots \\ s_{m*1} & s_{m*2} & \cdots & s_{m*t} \end{bmatrix} \tag{2}$$

where $s_{i*j} \in [0, 1]$ is the similarity degree between x_i and y_j, where $i \in \{1, 2, \ldots, m\}$ and $j \in \{1, 2, \ldots, t\}$.

3.2 Descriptive Statistics

Descriptive statistics (DS) is a set of measures that describe the structure of data [4,9]. DS has two main types of measures: central tendency and dispersion (variation). Central tendency is a single measurement that describes the set of samples via their average, midpoint, and most frequently sample. Measures of dispersion (variation) describe how much the samples vary or are close to the central tendency. In this study, we use well-known statistics measures such as minimum (min), maximum (max), mean, median, mode, and standard deviation (Std). The basic definitions of the six measures are as follows:

- **Mean (or arithmetic mean)** is the average value of a set of samples.
- **Median** is the midpoint value of an ordered set of samples.
- **Mode** is the most frequently occurring sample in the set of samples.
- **Minimum (Min)** is the lowest value in a set of samples.
- **Maximum (Max)** is the highest value in a set of samples.
- **Standard deviation (Std)** is a spread measure that describes how much each sample varies or is close to the mean of the set of samples.

3.3 FS Based on Descriptive Statistics

Traditional FS methods of fuzzy information measures depend on the FRM to represent the feature structure as possible. However, generating the FRM is expensive in the space and time cost. To overcome the cost limitations, we suggest generating the FRM by the descriptive statistics data instead of original data. Based on DS, the values of six statistics measures can represent the samples of feature with respect to the class label. In this way, we can reduce the size of FRM as well as cost. Figure 1 shows the main process of FS based on DS. Firstly, we calculate the descriptive statistics of the original data. Then, we apply the FS method on DS. The indexes of the selected features are used to return the selected features from the original data.

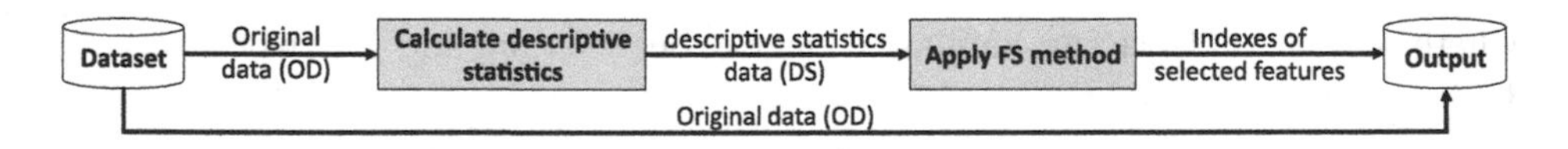

Fig. 1. The main process of FS based on descriptive statistics data.

The main procedure for generating a new dataset based on DS is described in Algorithm 1. The input of the algorithm is a dataset D, which consists of a set of features F and class label C. Firstly, we initialize the output dataset $Newdata$ as an empty list (line 1). Then, we divide the dataset into subsets of data $Fsubset$, according to the class label (lines 2–3). Line 4 defines an empty list $Fnew$ to store the descriptive statistics for each feature f_i in $Fsubset$. The descriptive statistics of f_i are calculated, stored in $Dstat$, and added to

Fnew list as shown in lines (5–9). After that, the class label is added to *Fnew* (line 10). Each *Fnew* of class c_i is appended to the final output *Newdata*. Finally, a *Newdata* is returned in line 13.

Algorithm 1. Dataset based on descriptive statistics

Input: A dataset $D = \langle F \cup C \rangle$, where F is a set of features and C is the class label.
Output: new data of descriptive statistics *Newdata*.

1: $Newdata \leftarrow [\,]$
2: **for each** $c_i \in C$ **do**
3: $\quad Fsubset \leftarrow F(c_i)$
4: $\quad Fnew \leftarrow [\,]$
5: $\quad$ **for each** $f_j \in Fsubset$ **do**
6: $\quad\quad Dstat \leftarrow [\,]$
7: $\quad\quad Dstat[] \leftarrow [mean(f_j), median(f_j), mode(f_j), min(f_j), max(f_j), std(f_j)]$
8: $\quad\quad Fnew \leftarrow Fnew \cup \{Dstatc\}$
9: $\quad$ **end for**
10: $\quad Fnew \leftarrow Fnew \cup \{c_i * ones(6, 1)\}$
11: $\quad Newdata \leftarrow append(Newdata, Fnew)$
12: **end for**
13: **return** *Newdata*

4 Experimental Design

The main phases of the experimental framework (data preparation, feature selection, and evaluation) are designed as shown in Fig. 2.

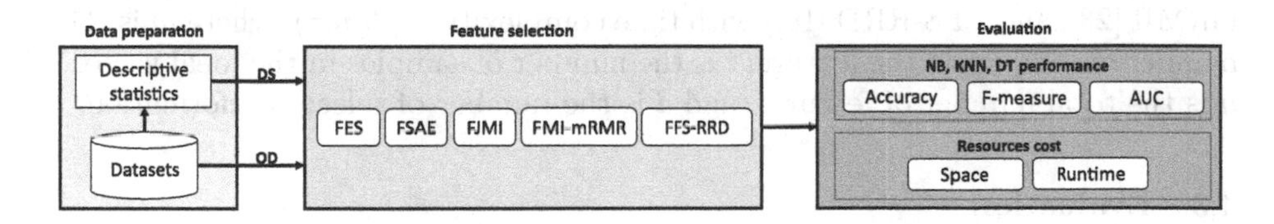

Fig. 2. The main phases of the experimental framework.

4.1 Data Preparation

To justify the effectiveness and efficiency of using DS, the experiment was conducted on 15 benchmark datasets collected from[1,2]. Table 1 shows the main properties of the used datasets. In this phase, the output is the original data (OD) and a new data of descriptive statistics (DS).

[1] https://archive.ics.uci.edu/ml/datasets.php.
[2] https://github.com/klainfo/NASADefectDataset.

Table 1. The main properties of the used datasets.

Dataset	Abbreviation	#Features	#instances	#classes
CM1	CM1	37	327	2
Credit approval	CAP	15	690	2
Glioma	GLO	4434	50	4
JMI	JMI	21	7720	2
KC1	KC1	21	1102	2
KC3	KC3	39	194	2
MC1	MC1	38	1952	2
MC2	MC2	39	124	2
MW1	MW1	37	250	2
SPECTF Heart	NHE	44	267	2
SPECT Heart	SHE	22	267	2
DNA	DNA	180	2000	3
Multiple features	MFE	649	2000	10
Ozone level detection	OLD	72	1848	2
seismic-bumps	SBU	18	2584	2

4.2 Feature Selection

To confirm the effectiveness of using DS, five FS methods (with 50% threshold of ranked features) have been used in the experimental comparison. FS methods is divided into two categories: feature-vector methods (FES [12] and FSAE [11]) with time complexity $O(mtn)$ and feature-feature methods (FJMI [17], FMI-mRMR [23], and FFS-RRD [16]) with time complexity $O(dnm^2)$, where m is the number of samples in the feature, t is the number of samples in the ideal vector, n is the total number of features, and d is the number of selected information.

4.3 Evaluation

The evaluation of our experiment depends on two parts: classification performance and feature selection cost.

Classification Performance: In the experiment, three well-known classifiers are used to verify the improvement of classification performance as Naive Bayes (NB) [5], k-Nearest Neighbors (KNN, K = 3) [13], and Decision Tree (DT) [13]. The main measures of classification performance are:

1- Accuracy: is the percentage of the correctly predicted instances.
2- F-measure: is the harmonic average of the classification precision and recall.

3- Area under the ROC curve (AUC): AUC is the size of the area under the ROC curve. ROC is a curve graph that represents the relation between the true positive rate and the false positive rate.

Feature Selection Cost: In this paper, the experiments were conducted in a computer system with Ryzen 7 4800H (2.9 GHz) CPU and 16 GB RAM.

4- Space cost: the space cost is defined by the size of the FRM. The matrix size of each feature with OD is $m * t$ for feature-vector methods while m^2 for feature-feature methods, where m is the number of samples in the feature and t is the number of samples in the ideal vector. For DS, the matrix size of each feature is $(6 * h) * t$ for feature-vector methods while $(6 * h)^2$ for feature-feature methods, where h is the number of classes. The reduced percentage of the FRM was also computed to show the reduction size that DS achieved compared to OD as [14]:

$$MR(\%) = 100 - \frac{w1}{w2} * 100 \tag{3}$$

where $w1$ is the relation matrix size of the feature with DS and $w2$ is the relation matrix size with OD.

5- Runtime cost: the execution time of the FS methods represents the runtime cost. The reduced percentage of time was also computed to show the reduction time that DS achieved compared to OD as [14]:

$$TR(\%) = 100 - \frac{r1}{r2} * 100 \tag{4}$$

where $r1$ is the runtime of DS and $r2$ is the runtime of OD.

5 Results and Analysis

5.1 Accuracy

The accuracy results of NB obtained by the different FS methods are shown in Table 2. Using DS improved the average accuracy of all FS methods with OD. FES with DS (for simplicity, FES (DS)) improved FES (OD) by 0.2%. Similarly, DS improved the average accuracy of FSAE, FJMI, FMI-mRMR, and FFS-RRD with OD by 0.5%, 5.9%, 0.3%, and 3.2%, respectively.

Table 3 shows the accuracy results of KNN obtained by the different FS methods. Among five methods, DS improved the average accuracy of three methods FJMI, FMI-mRMR, and FFS-RRD with OD by 2.8%, 1.2%, and 0.2%, respectively. For methods of FES and FSAE, OS improved the average accuracy of the used methods with DS by 0.6% and 0.3%, respectively.

The accuracy results of DT obtained by the different FS methods are shown in Table 4. DS improved the average accuracy of FES, FSAE, FJMI, FMI-mRMR, and FFS-RRD with OD by 0.3%, 0.1%, 2.3%, 0.4%, and 1.9%, respectively.

5.2 F-measure

Figure 3 shows the F-measure results of the three classifiers obtained by the FS methods. According to NB, DS improved the average F-measure of FES, FSAE, FJMI, FMI-mRMR, and FFS-RRD by 1.1%, 0.3%, 5%, 0.7%, and 1%. Using KNN, FES(OD), FSAE(OD), and FFS-RRD(OD) have more average F-measure than the same methods with DS by 0.8%, 0.1%, and 0.9%, respectively. FJMI(DS) and FMI-mRMR(DS) outperformed the original methods by 3.8% and 1.4%, respectively. For DT, DS improved the average F-measure of all used FS methods except FES. In FES, using OD has more F-measure by 0.5%. The remaining methods FSAE(DS), FJMI(DS), FMI-mRMR(DS), and FFS-RRD(DS) achieved more average F-measure compared to the original methods by 0.6%, 1.5%, 0.5%, and 1.9%, respectively.

Table 2. Classification accuracy derived by NB classifier among five FS methods using OD and DS. On average, DS outperformed OD in all FS methods.

Dataset	FES		FSAE		FJMI		FMI-mRMR		FFS-RRD	
	OD	DS	OD	DS	OD	DS	OD	DS	OD	DS
CM1	67.4	65.8	67.1	65.7	77.9	84.3	70.8	70.5	70.9	79.5
CAP	85	85	83.4	83.6	76.8	86.1	77	84.5	68.4	76.9
GLO	62.4	62	63.2	65.2	73.6	84.6	66.2	67.8	65.4	67.8
JMI	67.3	65.9	67.3	65.9	67	67.7	68.9	69.9	68.4	73.3
KC1	65.4	66	65.4	66.3	64.8	74.7	66.4	67.3	66.3	69.7
KC3	63	66.2	63	67.1	70.7	83.5	68.4	67	67.3	75.6
MC1	74.3	78.5	74.3	79.1	87	92.8	81.9	83.3	83	90.7
MC2	65.4	62.5	66	62.5	69.6	68.8	67.4	66.8	68.2	69.6
MW1	71.5	72.5	71.3	74	82	85.3	76.1	77	76.7	82.9
NHE	71.5	69.6	80.7	80.2	80.5	77.8	78.6	78.6	75.3	76.3
SHE	73.7	75.3	75.4	76.3	75.8	79.8	76.1	78.4	76.7	73.2
DNA	95.1	95.1	95.3	95.2	73.8	78.8	94.5	91.3	90.7	90.7
MFE	95.3	96.2	95.2	96	81.1	94	95.6	95.8	90.2	90.2
OLD	76.8	76.1	79	76.2	74.6	83.3	80.7	77.7	75.7	72
SBU	88.9	90	88.9	90.1	90.4	93.4	90.7	88.3	90	92.6
Average	74.9	75.1	75.7	76.2	76.4	82.3	77.3	77.6	75.5	78.7

Table 3. Classification accuracy derived by KNN classifier among five FS methods using OD and DS. On average, DS outperformed OD in three of five FS methods.

Dataset	FES		FSAE		FJMI		FMI-mRMR		FFS-RRD	
	OD	DS	OD	DS	OD	DS	OD	DS	OD	DS
CM1	85.6	82.7	83.9	82.5	84.2	82.9	82.3	82.7	82.8	84.3
CAP	85.4	85.4	87.5	85	76.3	85.5	73.8	82.4	63.5	74.5
GLO	77.8	72.8	78.4	74.4	78.4	84.6	77.8	79.8	78.2	74
JMI	76.5	77.2	76.5	77.2	76.3	76.8	75.8	76.1	76.1	77.9
KC1	73.5	74.1	73.5	73.7	75	76.9	74.7	74.2	75.4	72.8
KC3	82.1	81.6	82.1	80.9	77.5	79.9	79	81.6	78.3	84.4
MC1	98	97.9	98	97.9	98.1	97.9	97.9	97.9	98.2	98
MC2	70	65	68.2	67.7	58.7	64.7	71.4	70.1	70.8	65
MW1	88.6	89.1	88.2	88.4	90.4	89	90.1	90.2	89.9	89.3
NHE	78.7	77.9	79.9	79.3	79.9	81.1	79.5	79.5	78.5	79.4
SHE	75	78.2	72.1	75.6	75	76.7	72.6	78	76.5	72
DNA	69.8	69.8	73.4	73.7	73.8	78.2	73.7	74.3	60.5	60.5
MFE	97.4	97.6	97.4	97.6	86.9	96.5	97.9	97.6	95.8	95.8
OLD	96.1	96.5	96	96.4	96.1	96.4	96.2	96.5	96.2	96.8
SBU	92.2	92.4	92.2	92.6	92	93.4	93.3	93.2	92.4	92.2
Average	83.1	82.5	83.2	82.9	81.2	84.0	82.4	83.6	80.9	81.1

Table 4. Classification accuracy derived by DT classifier among five FS methods using OD and DS. On average, DS outperformed OD in all FS methods.

Dataset	FES		FSAE		FJMI		FMI-mRMR		FFS-RRD	
	OD	DS	OD	DS	OD	DS	OD	DS	OD	DS
CM1	84	82.4	84.3	82.5	87	87.2	81.8	82.8	82.3	86.9
CAP	85	85	85.4	87.2	75.4	84.7	75.7	84.4	67.9	75.8
GLO	55.2	54.8	47.6	49.4	56	56.6	43.4	41	44	49.2
JMI	78.5	79	78.5	79	78.3	78.8	78.7	78.6	78.6	79.2
KC1	76.9	76	76.9	75.1	74.6	76.9	76.1	75.6	75.5	74.1
KC3	81.8	82	81.8	81.7	79.6	81.4	82.4	79.9	78.8	81.6
MC1	98.2	98.2	98.2	98.2	98.2	98.2	98.2	98.2	98.2	98.2
MC2	64.7	66.6	67.8	71.4	67.8	70.6	65.6	68.8	68.3	71.1
MW1	88.4	88.6	90.4	88.7	89.2	87.9	88.8	89.4	88.6	89.8
NHE	79.4	79.4	80.8	78.6	77.5	78.5	79.1	78.9	76.7	79.4
SHE	73.3	75.4	74.4	75.3	75.1	80.3	73.8	75	76	77.6
DNA	92.5	92.5	92.9	92.8	73.8	78.7	92.9	88.6	87.3	87.3
MFE	93.3	95	93.5	94.8	84.6	92	94.2	94.3	88.5	88.5
OLD	96.1	96.1	96.1	96	96.7	96.9	95.9	96.2	95.7	96.9
SBU	93.4	93.4	93.4	93.4	93.4	93.4	93.4	93.4	93.4	93.4
Average	82.7	83.0	82.8	82.9	80.5	82.8	81.3	81.7	80.0	81.9

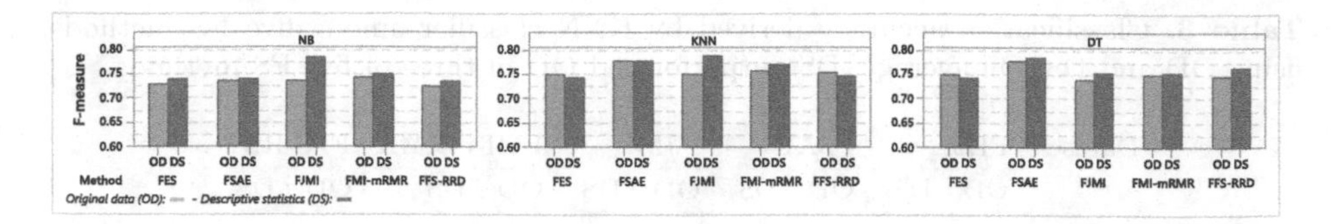

Fig. 3. Classification F-measure derived by the three classifiers among five FS methods using OD and DS. On average, DS outperformed OD in most FS methods using NB and DT. For KNN, OD outperformed DS in three FS methods

5.3 AUC

Figure 4 shows the AUC results of the used classifiers obtained by the FS methods. In FES, FS methods outperformed on NB with DS by 0.5% while outperformed on DT with OD by 0.2%. FES achieved the same result with DS and OD. Respectively, methods of FSAE, FJMI, and FMI-mRMR have been improved with DS by 1.5%, 1.9%, and 0.1% using NB, 0.1%, 4.1%, and 1.5% using KNN, and 1.9%, 2.8%, and 0.8% using DT. In FFS-RRD, the AUC was better with OD by 0.6%, 1.1%, and 0.9% using NB, KNN, and DT, respectively.

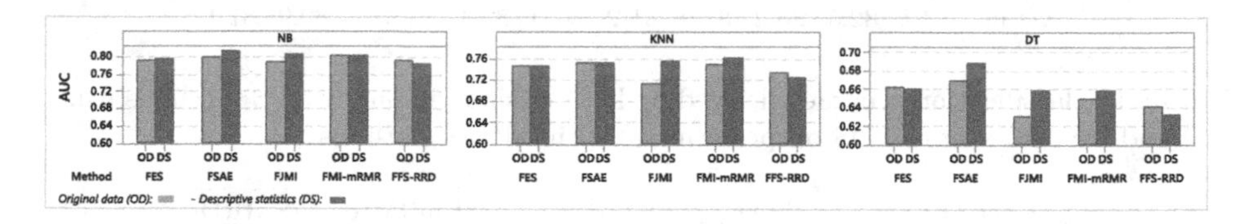

Fig. 4. Classification AUC derived by the three classifiers among five FS methods using OD and DS. On average, DS outperformed OD in most FS methods using.

5.4 Space Cost

Table 5 reports the relation matrix size of the feature in each dataset with OD and DS. It also shows the reduction percentage of matrix size (MR) induced by DS. It is obvious that FS methods with DS have a smaller matrix size than the same methods with OD. The reduction range induced by DS is from 52% to 99.84% using FES and FSAE while from 76.96% to around 100% using the remaining methods.

5.5 Runtime Cost

Table 6 reports the runtime efficiency on the FS methods with OD and DS. It also shows the reduction percentage of time (TR) induced by DS. It is obvious that FS methods with DS have a smaller runtime than the same methods with OD.

Table 5. Comparison of space cost on the FS methods between OD and DS. DS has the best space cost on all datasets

Dataset	FES/FSAE		MR(%)	FJMI/FMI-mRMR/FFS-RRD		MR(%)
	OD	DS		OD	DS	
CM1	327*2	(6*2)*2	96.330	327^2	$(6*2)^2$	99.865
CAP	690*2	(6*2)*2	98.261	690^2	$(6*2)^2$	99.970
GLO	50*4	(6*4)*4	52.000	50^2	$(6*4)^2$	76.960
JMI	7720*2	(6*2)*2	99.845	7720^2	$(6*2)^2$	≈100.00
KC1	1162*2	(6*2)*2	98.967	1162^2	$(6*2)^2$	99.989
KC3	194*2	(6*2)*2	93.814	194^2	$(6*2)^2$	99.617
MC1	1952*2	(6*2)*2	99.385	1952^2	$(6*2)^2$	99.996
MC2	124*2	(6*2)*2	90.323	124^2	$(6*2)^2$	99.063
MW1	250*2	(6*2)*2	95.200	250^2	$(6*2)^2$	99.770
NHE	267*2	(6*2)*2	95.506	267^2	$(6*2)^2$	99.798
SHE	267*2	(6*2)*2	95.506	267^2	$(6*2)^2$	99.798
DNA	2000*3	(6*3)*3	99.100	2000^2	$(6*3)^2$	99.992
MFE	2000*10	(6*10)*10	97.000	2000^2	$(6*10)^2$	99.910
OLD	1848*2	(6*2)*2	99.351	1848^2	$(6*2)^2$	99.996
SBU	2584*2	(6*2)*2	99.536	2584^2	$(6*2)^2$	99.998
Average	-	-	94.008	-	-	98.315

The reduction range induced by DS is from 83.9% to 99.99% using FES, 9.65% to 89.37% using FSAE, 1.36% to 76.22% using FJMI, 63.19% to 99.99% using FMI-mRMR, and 62.03% to 99.99% using FFS-RRD.

Table 6. Comparison of runtime cost on the FS methods between OD and DS. DS has the best runtime efficiency on all datasets.

Dataset	FES		FSAE		FJMI		FMI-mRMR		FFS-RRD	
	OD	DS	OD	DS	OD	DS	OD	DS	OD	DS
CM1	0.428742	0.02439	0.009218	0.008329	0.0096	0.006563	2.621383	0.067203	6.553457	0.08205
TR (%)	94.311		9.649		31.634		97.436		98.748	
CAP	1.214707	0.008385	0.00357	0.00146	0.003839	0.002375	1.914782	0.008474	4.786956	0.020408
TR (%)	99.310		59.105		38.116		99.557		99.574	
GLO	35.54285	5.721867	0.160168	0.066505	0.391724	0.35369	853.6609	314.2646	560.9826	213.0115
TR (%)	83.901		58.478		9.709		63.186		62.029	
JMI	373.4975	0.003991	0.038568	0.007782	0.022178	0.008228	495.8916	0.04638	1487.675	0.046238
TR (%)	99.990		79.822		62.901		99.991		99.990	
KC1	6.141769	0.002594	0.007138	0.002764	0.004871	0.002331	12.98244	0.011987	6.491221	0.027279
TR (%)	99.958		61.275		52.135		99.908		99.580	
KC3	0.130475	0.006057	0.003131	0.001104	0.002799	0.002429	1.661687	0.00957	4.154218	0.024887
TR (%)	95.358		64.747		13.218		99.424		99.401	

(*continued*)

Table 6. (*continued*)

Dataset	FES		FSAE		FJMI		FMI-mRMR		FFS-RRD	
	OD	DS	OD	DS	OD	DS	OD	DS	OD	DS
MC1	34.43672	0.0105	0.016591	0.003294	0.010812	0.005009	102.7852	0.023823	308.3556	0.036135
TR (%)	99.970		80.149		53.670		99.977		99.988	
MC2	0.059361	0.007061	0.002442	0.001036	0.002404	0.002371	0.309565	0.008864	0.681043	0.020617
TR (%)	88.105		57.575		1.361		97.137		96.973	
MW1	0.190526	0.006891	0.003237	0.001205	0.003057	0.002395	1.11319	0.009134	2.449017	0.024198
TR (%)	96.383		62.765		21.657		99.179		99.012	
NHE	0.101347	0.005195	0.002379	0.00081	0.002311	0.001595	0.360315	0.004761	0.792692	0.010015
TR (%)	94.874		65.951		30.968		98.679		98.737	
SHE	1.944846	0.004936	0.004029	0.001445	0.004111	0.002732	2.03347	0.01201	4.880328	0.031219
TR (%)	99.746		64.127		33.543		99.409		99.360	
DNA	39.75004	0.033494	0.109036	0.01316	0.071351	0.022158	1905.678	0.363506	622.712	0.485526
TR (%)	99.916		87.930		68.946		99.981		99.922	
MFE	482.2562	2.755366	0.708246	0.075309	0.794471	0.188911	29434.15	23.29409	8302.465	255.5522
TR (%)	99.429		89.367		76.222		99.921		96.922	
OLD	169.4312	0.017707	0.023083	0.006456	0.021521	0.008837	380.5805	0.068522	65.62529	0.083135
TR (%)	99.990		72.033		58.940		99.982		99.873	
SBU	13.17526	0.002211	0.005435	0.00181	0.005612	0.002438	40.37545	0.011567	113.0513	0.016277
TR (%)	99.983		66.699		56.563		99.971		99.986	
Average	77.220	0.574	0.073	0.013	0.090	0.041	2215.742	22.547	766.110	31.298
TR (%)	96.749		65.311		40.639		96.916		96.673	

Overall, It is obvious that FS methods with DS achieved the best classification performance in most cases. It justifies that summarizing the feature information by DS helps to define the feature information better. Moreover, DS reduced the size of FRM on each feature. This is because DS maps the feature into a smaller size of samples. As a result, the cardinal value of the feature based on DS is usually less than the cardinal value of the feature based on OD. This is also the same reason of why FS methods with DS have a smaller runtime than the same methods with OD.

6 Conclusion

Fuzzy information measures are powerful solutions for developing effective FS methods. However, the estimation cost of these measures is relative to the size of input data where increasing the former depends on increasing the latter. In this paper, we have introduced a novel method to reduce the high cost of FS methods based on fuzzy information measures. To achieve that, we generated descriptive statistics data (DS) from the original data (OD) to reduce the input data of FS methods. Consequently, the cost of FS methods based on fuzzy information measures has been reduced. The effectiveness of using DS has been evaluated on five FS methods. The experimental results confirm reducing the cost of FS methods and improving the classification performance in most cases. In future work, we plan to extend our study to cover more DS measures with the aim to highlight the importance of using DS for enhancing the FS process.

Acknowledgement. This research has been supported by the National Natural Science Foundation of China (62172309).

References

1. Bolón-Canedo, V., Sánchez-Maroño, N., Alonso-Betanzos, A.: Feature selection for high-dimensional data. Progr. Artif. Intell. **5**(2), 65–75 (2016). https://doi.org/10.1007/s13748-015-0080-y
2. Bommert, A., Sun, X., Bischl, B., Rahnenführer, J., Lang, M.: Benchmark for filter methods for feature selection in high-dimensional classification data. Comput. Stat. Data Anal. **143**, 106839 (2020)
3. Cateni, S., Colla, V., Vannucci, M.: A method for resampling imbalanced datasets in binary classification tasks for real-world problems. Neurocomputing **135**, 32–41 (2014)
4. Cavallaro, M., Fidell, L.: Basic descriptive statistics: commonly encountered terms and examples. Am. J. EEG Technol. **34**(3), 138–152 (1994)
5. Cheng, J., Greiner, R.: Comparing bayesian network classifiers. arXiv preprint arXiv:1301.6684 (2013)
6. Guyon, I., Gunn, S., Nikravesh, M., Zadeh, L.A.: Feature Extraction: Foundations and Applications, vol. 207. Springer, Heidelberg (2008). https://doi.org/10.1007/978-3-540-35488-8
7. Hu, Q., Xie, Z., Yu, D.: Hybrid attribute reduction based on a novel fuzzy-rough model and information granulation. Pattern Recogn. **40**(12), 3509–3521 (2007)
8. Hu, Q., Yu, D., Xie, Z.: Information-preserving hybrid data reduction based on fuzzy-rough techniques. Pattern Recogn. Lett. **27**(5), 414–423 (2006)
9. Kaur, P., Stoltzfus, J., Yellapu, V., et al.: Descriptive statistics. Int. J. Acad. Medi. **4**(1), 60 (2018)
10. Laradji, I.H., Alshayeb, M., Ghouti, L.: Software defect prediction using ensemble learning on selected features. Inf. Softw. Technol. **58**, 388–402 (2015)
11. Lohrmann, C., Luukka, P., Jablonska-Sabuka, M., Kauranne, T.: A combination of fuzzy similarity measures and fuzzy entropy measures for supervised feature selection. Exp. Syst. Appl. **110**, 216–236 (2018)
12. Luukka, P.: Feature selection using fuzzy entropy measures with similarity classifier. Exp. Syst. Appl. **38**(4), 4600–4607 (2011)
13. Patrick, E.A., Fischer, F.P.: A generalized k-nearest neighbor rule. Inf. Control **16**(2), 128–152 (1970)
14. Raza, M.S., Qamar, U.: Feature selection using rough set-based direct dependency calculation by avoiding the positive region. Int. J. Approx. Reason. **92**, 175–197 (2018)
15. Saeys, Y., Inza, I., Larrañaga, P.: A review of feature selection techniques in bioinformatics. bioinformatics **23**(19), 2507–2517 (2007)
16. Salem, O.A., Liu, F., Chen, Y.P.P., Chen, X.: Ensemble fuzzy feature selection based on relevancy, redundancy, and dependency criteria. Entropy **22**(7), 757 (2020)
17. Salem, O.A., Liu, F., Chen, Y.P.P., Chen, X.: Feature selection and threshold method based on fuzzy joint mutual information. Int. J. Approx. Reason. **132**, 107–126 (2021)
18. Salem, O.A., Liu, F., Chen, Y.P.P., Hamed, A., Chen, X.: Fuzzy joint mutual information feature selection based on ideal vector. Exp. Syst. Appl. **193**, 116453 (2022)

19. Shen, Z., Chen, X., Garibaldi, J.: Performance optimization of a fuzzy entropy based feature selection and classification framework. In: 2018 IEEE International Conference on Systems, Man, and Cybernetics (SMC), pp. 1361–1367. IEEE (2018)
20. Tsai, Y.S., Yang, U.C., Chung, I.F., Huang, C.D.: A comparison of mutual and fuzzy-mutual information-based feature selection strategies. In: 2013 IEEE International Conference on, Fuzzy Systems (FUZZ), pp. 1–6. IEEE (2013)
21. Vergara, J.R., Estévez, P.A.: A review of feature selection methods based on mutual information. Neural Comput. Appl. **24**(1), 175–186 (2013). https://doi.org/10.1007/s00521-013-1368-0
22. Xue, B., Zhang, M., Browne, W.N., Yao, X.: A survey on evolutionary computation approaches to feature selection. IEEE Trans. Evol. Comput. **20**(4), 606–626 (2015)
23. Yu, D., An, S., Hu, Q.: Fuzzy mutual information based min-redundancy and max-relevance heterogeneous feature selection. Int. J. Comput. Intell. Syst. **4**(4), 619–633 (2011)

Prompt-Based Self-training Framework for Few-Shot Named Entity Recognition

Ganghong Huang, Jiang Zhong(✉), Chen Wang, Qizhu Dai, and Rongzhen Li

College of Computer Science, Chongqing University, Chongqing 400044, China
{huangganghong,zhongjiang,wangchen,daiqizhu,lirongzhen}@cqu.edu.cn

Abstract. Exploiting unlabeled data is one of the plausible methods to improve few-shot named entity recognition (few-shot NER), where only a small number of labeled examples are given for each entity type. Existing works focus on learning deep NER models with self-training for few-shot NER. Self-training may induce incomplete and noisy labels which do not necessarily improve or even deteriorate the model performance. To address this challenge, we propose a prompt-based self-training framework. In the first stage, we introduce a self-training approach with prompt tuning to improve the model performance. Specially, we explore several label selection strategies in self-training to mitigate error propagation from noisy pseudo-labels. In the second stage, we fine-tune the BERT model over the high confidence pseudo-labels and original labels. We conduct experiments on two benchmark datasets. The results show that our method outperforms existing few-shot NER models by significant margins, demonstrating its effectiveness for the few-shot setting.

Keywords: Few-shot learning · Self-training · Prompt learning · Named entity recognition

1 Introduction

Named entity recognition (NER) is the task of detecting mentions of real-world entities from text and classifying them into predefined types (e.g., location, person and organization). It constitutes a core component in many NLP pipelines and is employed in a broad range of applications in knowledge extraction [8]. In recent years, deep learning models [4,10] have been proposed for NER and have shown strong performance. However, most deep learning methods require a large amount of annotated training data which is expensive and time-consuming [20]. The deep learning methods with a limited amount of labeled data usually lead to overfitting. This draws attention to a challenging but practical research problem: few-shot NER [9].

Recently, an increasing number of few-shot methods have been proposed to tackle the label scarcity issue, including supervised pre-training on noisy web data and self-training. Self-training uses a teacher model, trained using labeled

G. Memmi et al. (Eds.): KSEM 2022, LNAI 13370, pp. 91–103, 2022.
https://doi.org/10.1007/978-3-031-10989-8_8

data, to create synthetic labels for unlabeled examples [25]. In traditional self-training frameworks, the model labeling process inevitably introduces incomplete and noisy entity labels [30].

Moreover, the current methods train deep NER models over a simple or weighted combination of the strongly labeled and weakly labeled data, which may lose essential information about entities.

To tackle these challenges, we propose a prompt-based self-training framework with adaptive label selection. We refer to this framework as PBST. Our framework is composed of the following components: (i) Self-training: We adapt P-tuning v2 [16] as the initial teacher model for exploiting the few-shot learning potential of pre-trained language models to NER. The teacher model creates synthetic labels to train a student model. (ii) High confidence label selection: To suppress the noise and provide better stability, we propose to select tokens based on the three different confidence scores and remove mislabeled tokens. (iii) Fine-tuning: We finally fine-tune the model on the labeled data and high confidence data. Our method uses the high-confidence predictions of teacher model to improve generalization, where a pre-trained language model is used to initialize the NER model and generate entity embedding.

The contributions of this paper are as follows:

- We propose a prompt-based self-training framework for few-shot NER, comprised of a prompt tuning model, an adaptive label selection strategy and a fine-tuning step.
- We explore several pseudo label selection strategies that focus on entity information, and use an attention layer to assign weights to each selection strategy adaptively.
- Experimental results verify the effectiveness of the proposed method under the few-shot setting.

The rest of this paper is organized as follows. In Sect. 2 we introduce some related works on few-shot NER and prompting. In Sect. 3 we present the detailed descriptions of proposed model and approaches. In Sect. 4 we give the evaluation results and its analysis. Finally, we conclude this paper in Sect. 5.

2 Related Work

Few-Shot NER. Previous studies [19,23] of few-shot NER consider the setting that no strong label is available for training, but only weak labels generated by matching unlabeled sentences with external gazetteers or knowledge bases. The matching progress can be achieved by string matching [7], regular expressions [6], or heuristic rules. There has been some success with self-training using distant supervision [14]. In distant supervision, the labeling procedure is to match the tokens in the target corpus with concepts in knowledge bases [11]. Compared to their methods, our method does not rely on external knowledge, yet yields better results. Few-shot approaches [9] have also been explored to leverage very few labeled data for NER model training. Self-training [28] has been successfully applied to a variety of few-shot NER tasks.

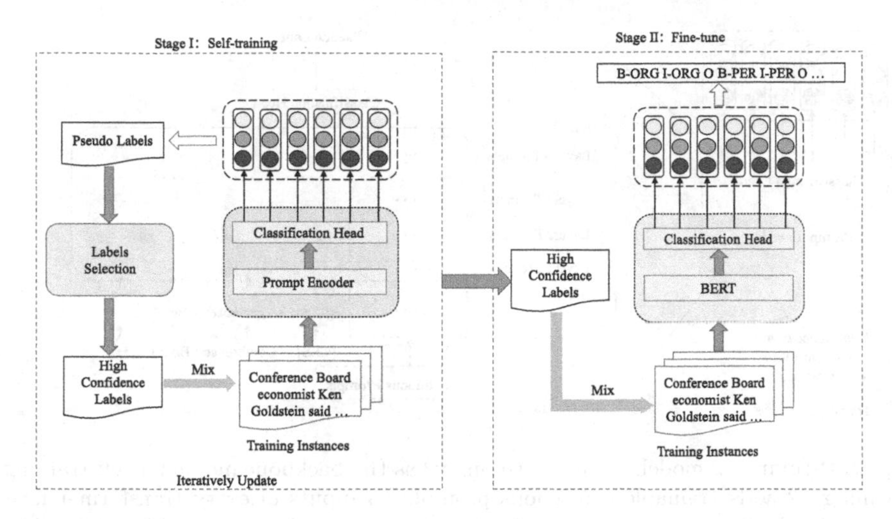

Fig. 1. Overview of our PBST framework. In Stage I, the pre-trained BERT as the initialized model is adapted to tune continuous prompts. Then the new model is trained using pseudo-labels generated by the previous model so that the model is iteratively updated. In Stage II, the BERT model is fine-tuned using high confidence labels generated by the model learned in Stage I.

Prompting. Prompting [15] refers to leveraging special templates in the input context to aid the language model (LM) prediction with respect to both understanding and generation. Since the emergence of GPT-3 [1], prompt-tuning has received considerable attention. It re-uses the masked LM objective to help alleviate the gap between different training objectives used at pre-training and fine-tuning. Therefore, the LMs can faster adapt to downstream tasks even with a few training samples. Liu et al. [17] proposed to add trainable continuous embedding to the original sequence of input word embedding. P-tuning v2 [16] leverages deep prompt tuning as in prefix-tuning [12] and uses the conventional classification paradigm with random-initialized linear heads. Therefore, P-tuning v2 can be applied to NER tasks as the base model for self-training. In this work, we scale prompting methods to few-shot settings.

3 Approach

To harness the power of few-shot labeled data and the pre-trained language model, we propose a prompt-based self-training method, PBST. We summarize the PBST framework in Fig. 1. In the first stage of PBST, we use a self-training approach to improve the BERT model fitting to the training data via prompt-tuning. Then, we propose three label selection strategies to analyze the confidence of entities from different perspectives and use an attention layer to adaptively assign weights to the three strategies. In the second stage, we fine-tune the BERT model with the labeled data and high-confidence data.

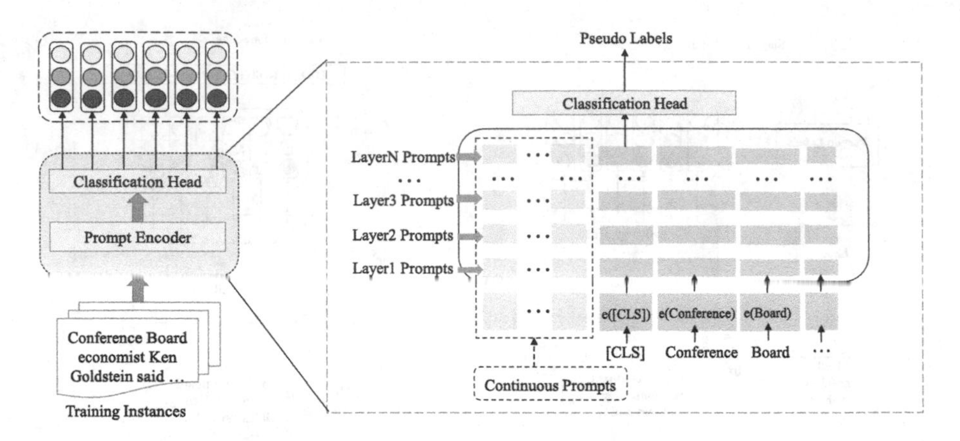

Fig. 2. P-tuning v2 model. We use P-tuning v2 as the backbone model for self-training. P-tuning v2 adds trainable continuous prompts to inputs of every transformer layer independently. The orange tokens refer to prompt embeddings we add and the blue tokens are embeddings stored or computed by frozen pre-trained language models. (Color figure online)

3.1 Prompt-Based Self-training Framework

In this section, we present our prompt-based self-training framework in detail. We use the P-tuning v2 model [16] which is initialized with a pre-trained BERT model as the base teacher model for self-training. As shown in Fig. 2, P-tuning v2 removes verbalizers with LM head and returns to the traditional class labels with ordinary linear head. The student model is trained using high confidence labels which are filtered by the label selection. Then, we assign the student model in the previous iteration as the new teacher model, which generates a new set of pseudo-labels for the next iteration to continue the training of the student model. The algorithm operates of stage I as follows:

1. Learn teacher model f_T via prompt tuning with labeled tokens D^L.
2. Generate soft labels using f_T on unlabeled tokens D^U:

$$\widetilde{\mathbf{y}}_i = f_{\mathbf{T}}\left(\widetilde{\mathbf{x}}_i\right), \forall \widetilde{\mathbf{x}}_i \in \mathcal{D}^{\mathrm{U}} \tag{1}$$

3. Generate high confidence labels using the label selection $\widetilde{\mathbf{y}}_i^*$. Our approach differs from previous work at this step, which we show is crucial for few-shot self-training.
4. Learn a student model f_S via prompt tuning on high confidence labels and true labels:

$$\mathcal{L}_{\mathrm{ST}} = \frac{1}{\left|\mathcal{D}^{\mathrm{L}}\right|} \sum_{\mathbf{x}_i \in \mathcal{D}^{\mathrm{L}}} \mathcal{L}\left(f_{\mathbf{S}}\left(\mathbf{x}_i\right), \mathbf{y}_i\right) + \frac{\lambda_{\mathrm{U}}}{\left|\mathcal{D}^{\mathrm{U}}\right|} \sum_{\widetilde{\mathbf{x}}_i \in \mathcal{D}^{\mathrm{U}}} \mathcal{L}\left(f_{\mathbf{S}}\left(\widetilde{\mathbf{x}}_i\right), \widetilde{\mathbf{y}}_i^*\right) \tag{2}$$

where λ^U is the weighting hyper-parameter.

It is optional to iterate from Step 1 to Step 4 multiple times, by initializing T in Step 1 with newly learned S in Step 4. We only perform self-training twice in our experiments, which has already shown excellent performance. In the next section, we will introduce how our framework selects high confidence labels.

3.2 High Confidence Label Selection

After applying the learned model to unlabeled data, some of the weakly generated labels may be incorrect [13]. These noisy labels will lead to poor performance of neural tagger in the next step. Inspired by Zhang et al. [29], we design a method to filter out noisy labels. We propose three label selection strategies to analyze the confidence of entities from different perspectives and propose to use an attention layer to adaptively assign weights to the three strategies.

Three Label Selections. In this module, we leverage three selecting strategies to mitigate error propagation from noisy pseudo-labeled sequences. We first introduce three entity confidence functions and then present an adaptive ensemble method for entity selection. To filter out noisy labels, we propose to maintain a high-precision entity set and compute thresholds for each entity type's confidence dynamically. The high-confidence selection essentially enforces the student model to better fit tokens with high confidence, thereby increasing the model's robustness to low-confidence tokens.

Entity Semantic Confidence. Each entity type has unified semantics. Therefore, entities with the same category are mapped to similar positions in the embedding space, and entities of different categories are far away from each other in the embedding space [5]. We focus on entity similarity by calculating whether two different texts are similar in a predefined category. We use this kind of semantic similarity as entity semantic confidence to judge whether the newly discovered entity is correct. Specifically, given an entity type t, its corresponding high-precision set H_t, and a pseudo entity e_p, we first compute a confidence score of e_p belonging to t by considering both its maximum pair similarity to the H_t (called local score) and its average similarity to H_t (called global score).

We introduce the cosin similarity to measure the similarity between a pseudo entity embedding e_p and a real entity embedding e_r. We query a pre-trained LM to obtain the set of token embeddings, denoted as x_p. Moreover, we use x_r to denote the set of all contextualized representations of the entity e_r in the given corpus. Then, we define the semantic similarity between e_p and e_r as:

$$R(e_p, e_r) = \cos(\mathbf{x}_p, \mathbf{x}_r) \tag{3}$$

We compute the pseudo entity's local score as:

$$\text{score}_i^{\text{loc}} = \max_{e_r \subseteq H_i} R(e_p, e_r) \tag{4}$$

The local score is estimated based on a single instance in the high-precision set. Although it helps explore new entities, it may be inaccurate in some cases. Therefore, we propose to compute a more reliable score to estimate the accuracy of an instance e_p belonging to an entity type t, which is called the global score. Specifically, we first sample a small set E_s from the high precision set H_t and then compute h^{sem}, which is the average of all instances' representations in E_s. In our work, we sample N times and compute the global score as:

$$\text{score}_i^{glb} = \frac{1}{N} \sum_{1 \leq j \leq N} R(e_p, e_r) \tag{5}$$

Entity semantic confidence of each pseudo label is calculated as:

$$S_i^{ESC} = \text{avg}\left(\text{score}_i^{\text{loc}}, \text{score}_i^{\text{glb}}\right) \tag{6}$$

Entropy Confidence. In general, entropy measures the uncertainty of things. We propose to select entities based on the entropy confidence. The function utilizes entropy of entity prediction probability:

$$S_i^{EC} = -\sum_{i=1}^{N} P_{\mathrm{T}}(e_p) \log P_{\mathrm{T}}(e_p) \tag{7}$$

Context-Based Consistency Confidence. According to the consistency criterion, the predicted results of the sample should be consistent with the results of its enhanced version. We use a generated entity to replace the entity from the sample. Then we obtain the enhanced samples and apply the model to predict the entity type of the generated entity. The consistency confidence of the new entity is estimated based on the predicted probability.

$$S_i^{CCC} = T\left(e_p\right), e_p \in s_a \tag{8}$$

Adaptive Weighting for Selection Strategies. Based on these representations of labels, we aggregate them and compute the attention scores to guide the final attention flow. The proposed attention can re-modulate the distribution of attention according to strategies. The attention layer adaptively assigns weights to each selection strategy. As shown in Fig. 3, this method allows a variety of confidence strategies to be considered. We also use a threshold θ of confidence to filter out noisy labels.

Adaptive Weighted Attention Layer. The attention layer can adaptively learn the importance from the input sequences with correlations between the pseudo labels and confidence scores. The attention mechanism calculates the weights corresponding to the different variables, where the weight values indicate the importance of the vectors. And the key feature information will be given a higher weight value. The attention layer consists of query matrix h_i, key matrix K_i and value matrix V_i. The process of computing the attention output can be described by the following formulas:

$$K_i = \text{concat}\left(h_i, h_i^{sem}, h_i^{aug}\right) \tag{9}$$

$$V_i = \text{concat}\left(S_i^{ESC}, S_i^{EC}, S_i^{CCC}\right) \tag{10}$$

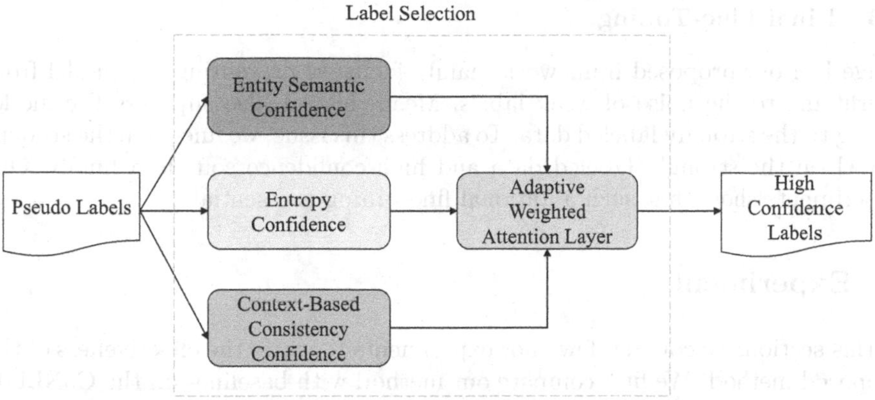

Fig. 3. Label selection. We use three selection strategies to select the pseudo labels from the teacher model separately, and then we use the attention layer to assign weights to different selection strategies to obtain adaptive labels. Finally, threshold filtering function is performed on the adaptive labels to generate high-confidence labels.

$$Att_i = \text{softmax}\left(\frac{h_i {K_i}^T}{\sqrt{d_q}}\right) V_i \tag{11}$$

where h_i is the original representation of the entity, h_i^{sem} is the average representation of entities in high precision, h_i^{aug} is the representation of the entity in the augmented sample and d_q refers to the dimension of attention.

Dynamic Threshold Estimation. We hypothesize that different categories of entities may have different thresholds for selecting high-quality labels. We may also need to use different thresholds at different iterations to dynamically balance exploration and reliability. We propose to use a dynamic threshold to select high-quality labels. Specifically, we hold out one entity instance in the high precision set and compute its confidence score with respect to the rest of the examples in the high-precision set. We randomly sample T times and use the minimum value as the threshold θ. For one of the entity types t, θ_t is calculated as:

$$\theta_{\mathrm{t}} = \min_{k \leq T, e_k \in H_i} \mathrm{S}_i\left(e_k\right) \tag{12}$$

In every iteration, we first predict the labels of all text spans using our neural tagging model. Then, we calculate the threshold of every entity type and select the confident token per category based on their prediction probabilities from the tagging model. The weakly labeled instance e_p will be selected into the high-precision set if its confidence score is larger than a threshold θ_t.

3.3 Final Fine-Tuning

Stage I of our proposed framework mainly focus on preventing the model from overfitting to the noise of weak labels. Meanwhile, it also suppress the model fitting to the strongly labeled data. To address this issue, we fine-tune the student model on the strongly labeled data and high-confidence soft data finally. Our experiments show that such additional fine-tuning is essential.

4 Experiments

In this section, we conduct few-shot experiments to verify the effectiveness of the proposed method. We first compare our method with baselines on the CoNLL03 dataset. We also report the performance of our method with different base models to verify the excellence of the P-tuning v2 model and the universality of the prompt-based self-training framework. Finally, we further analyze the importance of each component in an ablation study. We follow the few-shot setting, which supposes that only a small number of examples are used for training.

4.1 Experiment Settings

Evaluation Metrics and Datasets. To give an evaluation of models, we apply the F1 score as our evaluation metrics in the experiments. We consider two NER datasets as target tasks, CoNLL03 [21] and Ontonotes 5.0 [26]. CoNLL03 is a general domain NER dataset that has 22K sentences containing four types of general named entities: LOCATION, PERSON, ORGANIZATION, and MISCELLANEOUS. OntoNotes 5.0 English dataset which has 18 entity types, is a corpus that has roughly 1.7M words.

Pre-trained Models. Pre-trained language models have shown state-of-the-art performance for various tasks. In this work, we adopt the P-tuning v2 model as the base encoder by initializing the teacher with the pre-trained $BERT_{large}$ model and a randomly initialized token classification layer.

Few-shot Sampling. We simulate the few-shot data scenarios by sampling training instances from a training set as the training data. We conduct the greedy sampling strategy [27] to sample K (5, 10, 20, 100) labeled entities for each slot type from the train data, and add the remaining to the unlabeled set while ignoring their labels.

Table 1. Main results of PBST and compared baselines on CoNLL03 dataset under different few-shot settings.

Shots	K = 5	K = 10	K = 20	K = 100
Full-supervision				
BERT		92.4		
Few-shot supervision				
BERT	63.87	71.15	73.57	84.36
Few-shot supervision + unlabeled data				
CVT	51.15	54.31	66.11	81.99
SeqVAT	58.02	67.21	74.15	82.2
Mean Teacher	59.04	68.67	72.62	84.17
VAT	57.03	65.03	72.69	84.43
Classic ST	63.04	68.99	73.65	83.93
BOND	62.52	69.56	74.19	83.87
PBST (Ours)	**69.29**	**74.38**	**77.45**	**86.76**

4.2 Baselines

In our experiments, we compare the proposed method with competitive methods, involving both self-training based and distant supervision approaches. The first baseline we consider is the fully supervised BERT model trained on all available training data which provides the ceiling performance for the few-shot NER task. Each of the other models is trained on K training labels per slot type. We adopt several few-shot NER methods as baselines: (1) CVT [3] is a sequence labeling method based on cross-view training; (2) SeqVAT [2] incorporates adversarial training with conditional random field layer for sequence labeling; (3) Mean Teacher (MT) [24] averages model weights to obtain an aggregated teacher; (4) VAT [18] adopts virtual adversarial training to make the model robust to noise; (5) classic ST [22] is simple self-training method with hard pseudo-labels; (6) BOND [14] is the most recent work on self-training for sequence labeling with confidence-based sample selection and forms a strong baseline for our work.

4.3 Experimental Results

Table 1 shows the results of the proposed method and baselines for the few-shot setting. The fully supervised BERT provides the ceiling performance for the few-shot setting. We observe our method PBST to significantly outperform all methods including the models that also use the BERT encoder like MT, VAT, Classic ST, and BOND. Non BERT models like CVT and SeqVAT are consistently worse than other baselines. The experimental result on the CoNLL03 dataset shows that our model obtains 5.42 and 3.23 improvements over the few-shot BERT model for the 5-shot and 10-shot setting respectively.

Table 2. F1 scores of different models with 5 labeled samples for each task. PT-2: P-tuning v2. PBST(BERT): PBST uses BERT as base model.

Dataset	CoNLL03	OntoNotes 5.0
Full-supervision		
BERT	92.8	89.24
PT-2	90.2	86.46
Few-shot supervision (5 label per slot)		
BERT	63.87	66.35
PT-2	65.71	68.55
Few-shot supervision + unlabeled data		
PBST(BERT)	66.43	69.84
PBST	**69.29**	**73.46**

4.4 Validation of the Proposed Structure

The data volume with the best improvement (K = 5) in Table 1 is used to compare the BERT fine-tuning model and P-tuning v2 model on the two datasets. The results are reported in Table 2. We can observe that: (1) BERT fine-tuning method shows the poor ability of few-shot learning, and the P-tuning v2 method achieves improvement over BERT on CoNLL03 and OntoNotes 5.0. These results show the advantages of PT-2 as the base model. (2) The effects of the BERT model have also been improved under our prompt-based self-training framework and selection strategy, which proves the effectiveness of the framework.

4.5 Ablation Study

To gain insights of our two-stage framework, we investigate the effectiveness of several components of our method via ablation study. Table 3 shows the results on both CoNLL03 and OntoNotes 5.0 datasets. We perform an ablation study by removing self-training from PBST (denoted as "PBST w/o ST"). Removing this component leads to around 3.36 F1 performance drop on average demonstrating the impact of self-training.

To explore if pseudo-label confidence selection strategies are effective and complementary to each other, we compared using only one strategy with the ensemble strategy. We perform an ablation study by removing the adaptive weighted attention layer from PBST (denoted as "PBST w/o AWAL."). It means adopting an average method to ensemble these three results. We call it ensemble strategy for short. From the experimental results, it can be seen that the adaptive integration strategy compared to no strategy, the F1 score increases from 66.41 to 69.29 on CoNLL03. This verifies that the high-confidence labels help select data and yield more robust performance. Specifically, the integrated strategy has a higher F1 score than either strategy alone. Compared with using averaging ensemble strategy, our method improves 1.35 F1 score by leveraging

Table 3. Ablation study with 5 labeled samples. ST: Self-training. LS: Label Selection. LS1: Entropy Confidence. LS2: Entity Semantic Confidence. LS3: Context-Based Consistency Confidence. w/o AWAL: We replace the adaptive weighted attention layer with the averaging confidence. FT: Final fine-tuning on strongly labeled data.

Dataset	CoNLL03	OntoNotes 5.0
PBST w/o ST	65.93	69.29
PBST w/o LS	66.41	69.71
PBST w/ LS1	67.54	71.43
PBST w/ LS2	66.84	70.68
PBST w/ LS3	67.32	70.95
PBST w/o AWAL	67.94	72.62
PBST w/o FT	68.35	72.68
PBST	**69.29**	**73.46**

the adaptive weighted attention layer, which shows that different strategies may capture different types of knowledge and the layer combines the advantages of the strategies by assigning different weights. Moreover, the F1 score on OntoNotes 5.0 is also improved. This verifies that the adaptive weighted attention layer preserves more information and yield better-fitted models on both datasets.

Finally, we perform an ablation study by removing the fine tuning stage from PBST (denoted as"PBST w/o FT."). We observe that removing the fine-tuning step (Stage II) also hurts the overall performance.

5 Conclusion

In this work, we develop a prompt-based self-training framework PBST for few-shot NER tasks. PBST leverages self-training and P-tuning v2. We address the issue of error propagation from noisy pseudo-labels in the self-training framework by adaptive label selection and fine-tuning the BERT-NER model with high confidence labels. Our proposed method achieves outstanding performance on two benchmark datasets for few-shot settings. In addition, we discuss how to refine the self-training for better NER performance, including proposing an adaptive weighted attention layer to combine three confidence strategies that are used to select high-quality labels from pseudo labels. The entity semantic confidence strategy utilizes the semantic information of real entities and the semantic similarity between entities, which is very helpful for screening entities. The attention layer combines different selection strategies to identify entities from multiple dimensions, which leads to further improvements on self-training methods. We demonstrate their effectiveness in ablation experiments.

Acknowledgements. The authors would like to thank the Associate Editor and anonymous reviewers for their valuable comments and suggestions. This work is funded in part by the National Natural Science Foundation of China under Grants

No. 62176029, and in part by the graduate research and innovation foundation of Chongqing, China under Grants No. CYB21063. This work also is supported in part by the National Key Research, Development Program of China under Grants 2017YFB1402400, Major Project of Chongqing Higher Education Teaching Reform Research (191003), and the New Engineering Research and Practice Project of the Ministry of Education (E-JSJRJ20201335).

References

1. Brown, T., et al.: Language models are few-shot learners. Adv. Neural Inf. Process. Sys. **33**, 1877–1901 (2020)
2. Chen, L., Ruan, W., Liu, X., Lu, J.: SeqVAT: virtual adversarial training for semi-supervised sequence labeling. In: Proceedings of the 58th Annual Meeting of the Association for Computational Linguistics, pp. 8801–8811 (2020)
3. Clark, K., Luong, M.T., Manning, C.D., Le, Q.V.: Semi-supervised sequence modeling with cross-view training. arXiv preprint arXiv:1809.08370 (2018)
4. Devlin, J., Chang, M.W., Lee, K., Toutanova, K.: BERT: pre-training of deep bidirectional transformers for language understanding. arXiv preprint arXiv:1810.04805 (2018)
5. Ding, Z., Liu, K., Wang, W., Liu, B.: A semantic textual similarity calculation model based on pre-training model. In: Qiu, H., Zhang, C., Fei, Z., Qiu, M., Kung, S.-Y. (eds.) KSEM 2021. LNCS (LNAI), vol. 12816, pp. 3–15. Springer, Cham (2021). https://doi.org/10.1007/978-3-030-82147-0_1
6. Fries, J., Wu, S., Ratner, A., Ré, C.: SwellShark: a generative model for biomedical named entity recognition without labeled data. arXiv preprint arXiv:1704.06360 (2017)
7. Giannakopoulos, A., Musat, C., Hossmann, A., Baeriswyl, M.: Unsupervised aspect term extraction with B-LSTM & CRF using automatically labelled datasets. In: EMNLP , vol. 180 (2017)
8. Hu, F., Lakdawala, S., Hao, Q., Qiu, M.: Low-power, intelligent sensor hardware interface for medical data preprocessing. IEEE Trans. Inf. Technol. Biomed. **13**(4), 656–663 (2009)
9. Huang, J., et al.: Few-shot named entity recognition: an empirical baseline study. In: Proceedings of the 2021 Conference on Empirical Methods in Natural Language Processing, pp. 10408–10423 (2021)
10. Huang, Z., Xu, W., Yu, K.: Bidirectional LSTM-CRF models for sequence tagging. arXiv preprint arXiv:1508.01991 (2015)
11. Lee, S., Song, Y., Choi, M., Kim, H.: Bagging-based active learning model for named entity recognition with distant supervision. In: 2016 International Conference on Big Data and Smart Computing (BigComp), pp. 321–324. IEEE (2016)
12. Li, X.L., Liang, P.: Prefix-tuning: optimizing continuous prompts for generation. arXiv preprint arXiv:2101.00190 (2021)
13. Li, Y., Song, Y., Jia, L., Gao, S., Li, Q., Qiu, M.: Intelligent fault diagnosis by fusing domain adversarial training and maximum mean discrepancy via ensemble learning. IEEE Trans. Indus. Inform. **17**(4), 2833–2841 (2020)
14. Liang, C., et al.: BOND: BERT-assisted open-domain named entity recognition with distant supervision. In: Proceedings of the 26th ACM SIGKDD International Conference on Knowledge Discovery & Data Mining, pp. 1054–1064 (2020)

15. Liu, P., Yuan, W., Fu, J., Jiang, Z., Hayashi, H., Neubig, G.: Pre-train, prompt, and predict: a systematic survey of prompting methods in natural language processing. arXiv preprint arXiv:2107.13586 (2021)
16. Liu, X., Ji, K., Fu, Y., Du, Z., Yang, Z., Tang, J.: P-tuning v2: prompt tuning can be comparable to fine-tuning universally across scales and tasks. arXiv preprint arXiv:2110.07602 (2021)
17. Liu, X., et al.: GPT understands, too. arXiv preprint arXiv:2103.10385 (2021)
18. Miyato, T., Maeda, S.I., Koyama, M., Ishii, S.: Virtual adversarial training: a regularization method for supervised and semi-supervised learning. IEEE Trans. Pattern Anal. Mach. Intell. **41**(8), 1979–1993 (2018)
19. Peng, S., Zhang, Y., Yu, Y., Zuo, H., Zhang, K.: Named entity recognition based on reinforcement learning and adversarial training. In: Qiu, H., Zhang, C., Fei, Z., Qiu, M., Kung, S.-Y. (eds.) KSEM 2021. LNCS (LNAI), vol. 12815, pp. 191–202. Springer, Cham (2021). https://doi.org/10.1007/978-3-030-82136-4_16
20. Qiu, H., Zheng, Q., Msahli, M., Memmi, G., Qiu, M., Lu, J.: Topological graph convolutional network-based urban traffic flow and density prediction. IEEE Trans. Intell. Transp. Syst. **22**(7), 4560–4569 (2020)
21. Sang, E.T.K., De Meulder, F.: Introduction to the conll-2003 shared task: language-independent named entity recognition. In: Proceedings of the Seventh Conference on Natural Language Learning at HLT-NAACL 2003, pp. 142–147 (2003)
22. Scudder, H.: Probability of error of some adaptive pattern-recognition machines. IEEE Trans. Inf. Theory **11**(3), 363–371 (1965)
23. Shang, J., Liu, L., Ren, X., Gu, X., Ren, T., Han, J.: Learning named entity tagger using domain-specific dictionary. In: EMNLP (2018)
24. Tarvainen, A., Valpola, H.: Mean teachers are better role models: weight-averaged consistency targets improve semi-supervised deep learning results. In: 31st Conference on Neural Information Processing Systems (NIPS 2017), Long Beach, CA, USA (2017)
25. Wang, Y., et al.: Meta self-training for few-shot neural sequence labeling. In: Proceedings of the 27th ACM SIGKDD Conference on Knowledge Discovery & Data Mining, pp. 1737–1747 (2021)
26. Weischedel, R., et al.: Ontonotes release 5.0 ldc2013t19. Linguistic Data Consortium, p. 23. Philadelphia (2013)
27. Yang, Y., Katiyar, A.: Simple and effective few-shot named entity recognition with structured nearest neighbor learning. arXiv preprint arXiv:2010.02405 (2020)
28. Yarowsky, D.: Unsupervised word sense disambiguation rivaling supervised methods. In: 33rd Annual Meeting of the Association for Computational Linguistics, pp. 189–196 (1995)
29. Zhang, Y., Shen, J., Shang, J., Han, J.: Empower entity set expansion via language model probing. In: Proceedings of the 58th Annual Meeting of the Association for Computational Linguistics, pp. 8151–8160 (2020)
30. Zoph, B., et al.: Rethinking pre-training and self-training. Adv. Neural Inf. Process. Syst. **33**, 3833–3845 (2020)

Learning Advisor-Advisee Relationship from Multiplex Network Structure

Xiangchong Cui[1,2], Ting Bai[1,2], Bin Wu[1,2](✉), and Xinkai Meng[1,2]

[1] Beijing University of Posts and Telecommunications, Beijing, China
{cuixc,baiting,wubin,mengxinkai}@bupt.edu.cn
[2] Beijing Key Laboratory of Intelligent Telecommunications Software and Multimedia, Beijing, China

Abstract. The analysis of the advisor-advisor relationship can provide rich information for understanding the interactions among entities in academic network. Most of the existing methods mine the relationship in collaboration network. They focus on extracting deep relationships between attributes, but ignore the structure of nodes. Compared with the multiplex network, the collaboration network can only provide a single view, which describes whether the two nodes have co-authored publications. To tackle these problems, we propose an Attention-based Multiplex Network Structure Fusion (AMNSF) method for mining the advisor-advisee relationship. AMNSF takes the multiplex network as input composed of the acknowledgment network and the collaboration network where the acknowledgment network provides the social relationship between entities. We make full use of the network's structure information and design a novel network fusion mechanism to integrate the structure information from each layer. Finally, we conduct extensive experiments on a variety of datasets. The experimental results show that the proposed model outperforms the state-of-the-art methods.

Keywords: Advisor-advisee relationship · Graph neural network · Multiplex network · Scientific collaboration network

1 Introduction

Academic information has risen quickly in recent years as a result of a large amount of research work in academia and industry. Recent research into academic networks has also gotten a lot of interest. Researchers, conferences and other types of entities can be found in networks. Based on the analysis of the scientific networks, rich hidden information can be obtained. For example, the advisor-advisee relationship plays an important role in the research collaboration network. Previous literature [1] shows that both the advisor and the advisee benefit from the advisor-advisee relationship. Furthermore, the research on the advisor-advisee relationship can obtain a large amount of important information and apply it to scientific research-related applications, such as supervisor recommendation and research influence prediction.

G. Memmi et al. (Eds.): KSEM 2022, LNAI 13370, pp. 104–115, 2022.
https://doi.org/10.1007/978-3-031-10989-8_9

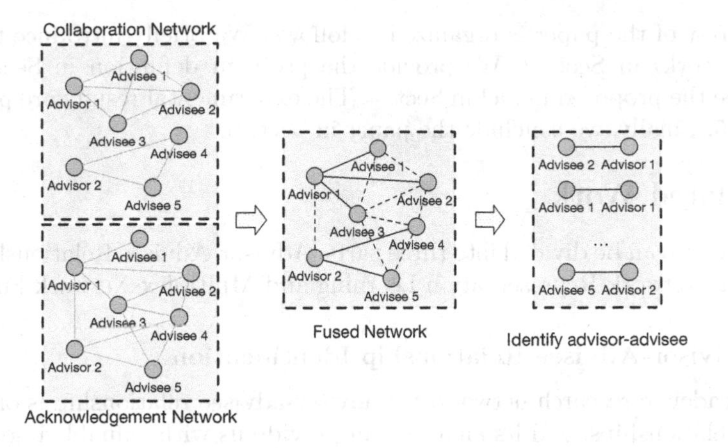

Fig. 1. An example of advisor-advisee relationship mining based on the fusion of collaboration network and acknowledgment network.

Recently, several studies proposed methods based on deep learning to mine advisor-advisee relationships in collaboration networks. However they do not make full use of the structure of nodes and rely on entity attributes. Thus different attribute choices have varying degrees of impact on the results. Besides, existing researches focus on the single-layer network, which can not provide a multi-view of the interaction between nodes.

To address the above challenges, we propose a novel model for advisor-advisee relationship mining, AMNSF, which makes full use of graph neural network and multiplex network information fusion technology. In order to describe the problem concisely, Fig. 1 presents an example of mining advisor-advisee relationship. Collaboration network can only provide collaborative relations, the acknowledgment network provides rich social relations. Besides, compared with the previous methods for mining advisor-advisee relationship, AMNSF focuses on learning the structural attributes of nodes. Finally, we conduct extensive experiments to evaluate the proposed model, and the results show the superiority of the proposed AMNSF model against the state-of-the-art models.

In summary, the contributions of this paper can be summarized as follows:

- We propose a novel method based on graph neural network and multiplex network fusion for mining advisor-advisee relationship, which uses attention mechanism to fuse structure information.
- We design an effective network fusion mechanism. We integrate the information of other layers in the process of learning each layer of the network.
- We introduce an acknowledgment network constructed from acknowledgment texts and conduct extensive evaluations combined with collaboration datasets. The experimental results proved the superiority of the proposed model.

The rest of the paper is organized as follows. We briefly introduce the most relevant works in Sect. 2. We provide the problem definition in Sect. 3. We introduce the proposed model in Sect. 4. The experimental results are presented in Sect. 5. Finally, we conclude the paper in Sect. 6.

2 Related Work

Related work can be divided into three parts: Advisor-Advisee Relationship Identification, Network Representation Learning and Multiplex Network Fusion.

2.1 Advisor-Advisee Relationship Identification

In the academic research network, the advisor-advisee relationship is one of the critical relationships, and its analysis can provide us with valuable information. Wang et al. [4] and Li et al. [7] propose probability model to extract advisor-advisee relationship. Besides, Zhao et al. [5] uses deep convolutional networks combined with improved recurrent neural network units. [3,6] use models based on stacked autoencoders. Most of the approaches discussed above are based on time-related hypotheses. As a result, these methods are vulnerable to the features of nodes.

2.2 Network Representation Learning

Node Embedding. Inspired by the skip-gram model, Perozzi et al. [8] was the first to introduce a node embedding representation learning method based on random walk. Tang et al. [9] and Cao et al. [10] design an algorithm to learn nodes' structure information. In addition, [14,15] propose methods of node embedding learning based on structural similarity.

Graph Neural Network. In this section, we briefly introduce graph neural networks. Defferrard et al. [16] and Kipf et al. [17] propose method based on graph signal processing. Hamilton et al. [18] proposes an inductive framework, which can learn a function that learns embeddings by sampling and aggregating the neighbor information of a given node. Velickovic et al. [19] proposes a masked self-attention layer, which gives different weights to neighbors. Based on the WL test, Xu et al. [20] proposes a simple and effective algorithm to capture the structure information of the network.

2.3 Multiplex Network Fusion

The goal of multiplex network embedding methods is to learn the low-dimensional representation of nodes by fusing the multiplex network. Jing et al. [12] designs a model based on high-order mutual information in a self-supervised way. Ning et al. [27] proposes an unsupervised node embedding model for multiplex networks, called HMNE. HMNE solves the problem of preserving the high-order neighbor information of nodes through the symmetric graph convolution-deconvolution component.

3 Problem Definition

A network can be denoted as $G = (V, E)$, where V represents the set of nodes in the graph, and E represents the set of edges between any two nodes. The important notations are summarized in Table 1.

Table 1. Notations.

Notation	Explanation
G	A multiplex network
G^l, A^l	A network/adjacency matrix of layer l respectively
V, E^l	The sets of nodes and edges in layer l, respectively
$\mathbf{X}^l$	The set of node features
i, $\mathbf{x}_i^l$	A node and its features, respectively
$\mathbf{h}_i^l$	The output of GCN
$\mathbf{h}_{sim}^l$, $\mathbf{h}_{diff}^l$	The similar/different information extracted from $\mathbf{h}^l$
$\tilde{\mathbf{h}}_{sim_i}^l$, $\tilde{\mathbf{h}}_{diff_i}^l$	The output of similar/different fusion
$\mathbf{z}_i^l$	The output of inter-layer fusion

Multiplex Network. Given an L-layer multiplex network, it can be denoted as $G = \{G^1, G^2, ..., G^L\}$, where $L >= 2$, $G^l = \{V, E^l\}$, E^L represents the set of edges in the L layer.

Advisor-Advisee Identification. Given the low-dimensional representation of the node and a pair of nodes, identify whether the relationship between the two node is advisor-advisee.

4 Method

In this part, we introduce detail of the AMNSF model, as shown in the Fig. 2.

4.1 Inter-layer Fusion

The inter-layer fusion includes GCN, Extract Sim and Diff and Attention-based Fusion.

Graph Convolution Network. Given a graph G, $\mathbf{D}$ is the degree matrix, and $\mathbf{A}$ is the adjacency matrix. Kipf et al. [17] considers spectral convolutions on graphs defined as:

$$\mathbf{g}_\theta \times \mathbf{x} = \mathbf{U}\mathbf{g}_\theta\mathbf{U}^T x \tag{1}$$

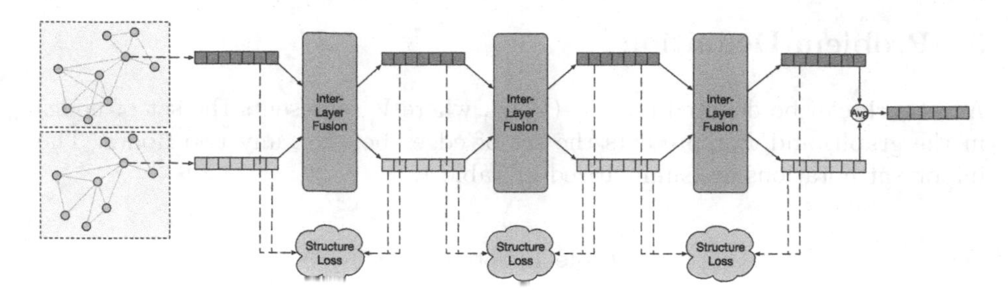

Fig. 2. The architecture of AMNSF Embedding, which is proposed to obtain node embedding containing structure information in each layer of network.

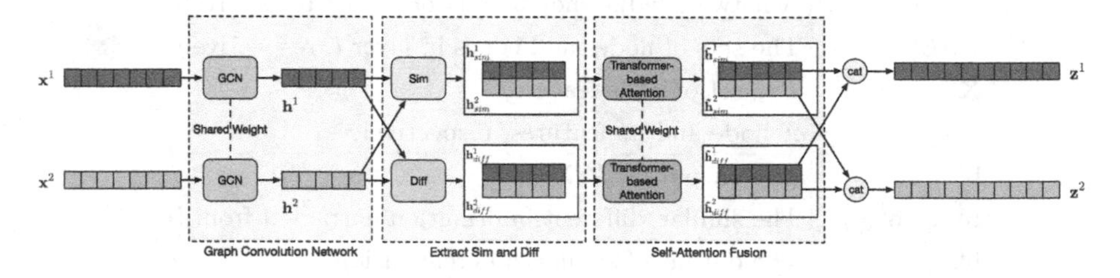

Fig. 3. The architecture of inter-layer fusion, which is composed of GCN, extract sim and diff and self-attention fusion.

where $\mathbf{U}$ is the matrix of eigenvectors of the normalized graph Laplacian. Kipf et al. [17] constrains the number of parameters to simplifies equation to:

$$\mathbf{H} = \tilde{\mathbf{D}}^{-\frac{1}{2}}\tilde{\mathbf{A}}\tilde{\mathbf{D}}^{-\frac{1}{2}}\mathbf{X}\mathbf{W} \tag{2}$$

where $\tilde{\mathbf{A}} = \mathbf{A} + \mathbf{I}$ and $\tilde{\mathbf{D}_{ii}} = \sum_{j=1}^{N} \tilde{\mathbf{A}}_{ij}$. The equation shows that the nodes' embedding are updated by aggregating neighbors which can capture local structure information. Therefore, we use GCN to generate nodes' embedding.

Extract Similarity and Difference. According to empirical analysis, if the output of GCN is directly fused, it will lead to the disorderly combination of similar information and unique information in the network. In order to solve the problem, we propose a distillation operation. The distillation operation uses a simple and effective linear transformation layer.

$$\mathbf{h}^{l}_{sim} = \sigma(\mathbf{W}_{sim} \cdot \mathbf{h} + \mathbf{b}_{sim}), l = 1, 2 \tag{3}$$

$\mathbf{h}^{l}_{diff}$ can be obtained in the same way. $\mathbf{W}$ and $\mathbf{b}$ are trainable parameters. Further We propose a loss function to make $\mathbf{h}^{l}_{sim}$ more similar, and $\mathbf{h}^{l}_{diff}$ more dissimilar.

$$L_{sd} = \frac{1}{N}\sum_{i=1}^{N}(||\mathbf{h}^{1}_{sim_i} - \mathbf{h}^{2}_{sim_i}||_2 - ||\mathbf{h}^{1}_{diff_i} - \mathbf{h}^{2}_{diff_i}||_2) \tag{4}$$

Self-attention Fusion. We propose a self-attention mechanism based on Transformer [24] to fuse the structure information of each layer. We use $\mathbf{h}_{sim}$ or $\mathbf{h}_{diff}$ as $\mathbf{v}$ directly, and we can obtain $\mathbf{q}^l = \mathbf{W}_Q \cdot \mathbf{v}^l$, $\mathbf{k}^l = \mathbf{W}_K \cdot \mathbf{v}^l$. Then the attention coefficient of a given node in the m-th layer network to the n-th layer network is

$$e_{mn} = \frac{exp(\mathbf{q}^m \cdot (\mathbf{k}^n)^T)}{\sum_{l=1}^{2} exp(\mathbf{q}^m \cdot (\mathbf{k}^l)^T)} \tag{5}$$

Finally, the fused similar information of each layer can be denoted as

$$\tilde{\mathbf{h}}^l_{sim} = \sum_{n=1}^{2} e_{ln} \cdot \mathbf{h}^n_{sim}, l = 1, 2 \tag{6}$$

$\tilde{\mathbf{h}}^l_{diff}$ can be obtained in the same way. The output of the l-th network after self-attention fusion is $\mathbf{z}^l = concat(\tilde{\mathbf{h}}^l_{sim}, \tilde{\mathbf{h}}^l_{diff})$.

4.2 Structure Loss

In this section, we propose an attention-based structural loss. Given a node i in the network, we denote the input of the Inter-Layer Fusion module as $\mathbf{x}_i^1$, $\mathbf{x}_i^2$ and the outputs are respectively $\mathbf{z}_i^1$, $\mathbf{z}_i^2$. First, we obtain attention vectors e_i^1, e_i^2 of node i which can be obtained by using cosine function. We then keep the first K largest values of $\mathbf{e}_i^1, \mathbf{e}_i^2$ respectively, and average them

$$\mathbf{e}_i = \frac{(TopK(\mathbf{e}_i^1) + TopK(\mathbf{e}_i^2))}{2} \tag{7}$$

We use $\mathbf{e}_i$ as a mask layer to obtain two fused attention vectors $\tilde{\mathbf{e}}_i^1$ and $\tilde{\mathbf{e}}_i^2$. Then the attention-based structural loss can be denoted as

$$L_{asl} = \frac{1}{2N} \sum_{j=1}^{N} (||\mathbf{e}_i - \tilde{\mathbf{e}}_i^1||_2 + ||\mathbf{e}_i - \tilde{\mathbf{e}}_i^2||_2) \tag{8}$$

The original network structure information can be maintained through this reconstructed loss function, and the structure information of other networks can also be learned. Besides, because only the K highest correlation strength with the central node are retained in Eq. 7, it can avoid introducing noise during the fusion process.

4.3 Prediction Layer

In order to apply the model to the task of mining the advisor-advisee relationship, we use a multi-layer perceptron as a classifier. Given the embeddings of two connected nodes i, j in the network $\mathbf{z}_i, \mathbf{z}_j$, the classifier can be denoted as:

$$y = MLP(concat(\mathbf{z}_i, \mathbf{z}_j)) \tag{9}$$

4.4 Model Optimization

In this section, we discuss how to train the training model. The supervised loss of the model is denoted as

$$L_{label} = \frac{1}{N}\sum_{i=1}^{N}[y_i \cdot log(\hat{y}_i) + (1 - y_i) \cdot (log(1 - \hat{y}_i))] \tag{10}$$

where y_i represents the true label, and $\hat{y}_i$ is the predicted value of the model. The unsupervised loss of the model learning node embedding is denoted as

$$L_{structure} = L_{sd} + L_{asl} \tag{11}$$

Finally, we sum all the loss functions as the loss of the entire model. The loss function of AMNSF is denoted as

$$L = L_{label} + L_{structure} + L_{\Theta} \tag{12}$$

where Θ represents the parameters of the model, and L_{Θ} is the $L2$ regularization loss of the model.

5 Experiments

We use the classification of advisor-advisee relationship as a downstream task to verify the performance of the model on several different datasets.

5.1 Datasets

Table 2. Statistics about different multiplex networks used in this study.

Dataset	Node	Edge_{ack}	Edge_{co}	AA
U1	1947	15183	6329	1839
U2	2541	27439	9893	2396
U3	2586	32574	10740	2450
U4	2822	28508	11048	2660
U5	2044	18750	7760	1927
U6	2599	25053	9715	2399
U7	1835	9887	7131	1745

We provide 7 datasets to verify the effectiveness of the model. Each dataset is a two-layer network constructed from two views, namely the acknowledgment network and the collaboration network. The detail of datasets shown in Table 2 where U1–U7 indicates that the datasets are obtained from 7 different universities, Edge_{ack}, Edge_{co} represents the number of edges in acknowledgment network and collaboration network respectively and Advisor-Advisee (AA) represents the number of advisor-advisee edges.

Acknowledgment Network. The acknowledgment network is composed of entities and relationships contained in the text of the acknowledgment chapter in the dissertation. In each acknowledgment chapter, the author of the paper is the central node, the named entities (including teachers, classmates, etc.) identified in text are neighbor nodes.

Collaboration Network. The construction of the scientific research collaboration network is based on the principle that scholars appear in the same paper. These papers include three sources from DBLP, AMiner, and MAG. In the previous work [3,6], there are fewer real labels in the dataset, but acknowledgment text contains a large number of real labels (in the dissertation, the author of each paper corresponds to his advisor). When constructing the collaboration network, to ensure the validity of the label, we filter the dataset of scientific research papers based on the advisors and advisees in the acknowledgment network.

5.2 Baselines

We compare our proposed method with four sets of baseline methods: AutoEncoder, Graph Embedding, Graph Neural Network and Multiplex Network Embedding methods.

AutoEncoder. Shifu [3] and Shifu2 [6] use autoencoder to mine the nonlinear relationship between attributes, and uses logistic regression as a classifier to identify the advisor-advisee relationships. So we use AutoEncoder to represents Shifu and Shifu2.

Node Embedding. DeepWalk [8], Node2Vec [23] and Role2Vec [15] are random-walk and skip-gram based embedding models. GraRep [10], NodeSketch [22], NetMF [21] and GraphWave [14] are matrix decomposition and local topology based embedding models.

Graph Neural Network. GCN [17], GAT [19], GIN [20] and GraphSAGE [18]. These four methods learn node embedding based on the local structure of the nodes.

Multiplex Network Embedding. HDMI [12] uses high-order mutual information to learn network embedding. HMNE [27] proposed a symmetric graph convolution-deconvolution neural network to learn node representations.

5.3 Implementation Details

As a binary classification task, we use accuracy as the criterion for judging the performance of the model. We use Adam optimizer with the learning rate of 0.001

and the weight decay of 0.009 to optimize the models and set the dimension of node embedding as 32. In addition, for the node embedding method based on random walk, we set the walk length to 20 and the number of walks to 10.

5.4 Results and Analysis

This section shows the experimental results of the downstream task to quantitatively prove the effectiveness of the model.

Table 3. Overall performance on advisor-advisee relationship identification.

Method	U1	U2	U3	U4	U5	U6	U7
AutoEncoder	0.769	0.835	0.892	0.866	0.809	0.855	0.817
DeepWalk	0.598	0.747	0.514	0.692	0.758	0.658	0.547
GraRep	0.796	0.692	0.837	0.834	0.769	0.786	0.557
Node2Vec	0.736	0.796	0.637	0.636	0.712	0.647	0.317
NodeSektch	0.722	0.807	0.837	0.794	0.773	0.757	0.433
NetMF	0.724	0.807	0.837	0.791	0.770	0.771	0.611
Role2Vec	0.722	0.807	0.837	0.793	0.769	0.786	0.589
GraphWave	0.722	0.807	0.837	0.793	0.769	0.786	0.567
GCN	0.733	0.865	0.870	0.837	0.906	0.906	0.904
GIN	0.668	0.840	0.818	0.936	0.907	0.906	0.931
GAT	0.923	0.807	0.864	0.875	0.892	0.786	0.876
GraphSAGE	0.798	0.867	0.907	0.893	0.799	0.866	0.886
HMNE	0.722	0.869	0.837	0.749	0.793	0.872	0.884
HDMI	0.890	0.857	0.861	0.905	0.923	0.901	0.918
AMNSF	**0.979**	**0.935**	**0.957**	**0.971**	**0.963**	**0.945**	**0.960**
Gain[%]	**6.07**	**7.59**	**5.51**	**3.74**	**4.33**	**4.30**	**3.11**

Overall Comparison. As shown in Table 3, experimental results show that AMNSF is superior to the most advanced models in the task of mining advisor-advisee relationships. (1) The autoencoder can mine the non-linear relationship between the features of input, the autoencoder-based method is superior than that node embedding method. (2) By aggregating neighbors' information to obtain structure information, GNN-based methods can achieve higher performance. Futhermore, AMNSF achieves more higher performance by introducing extra view information. (3) The high-order proximity of nodes and the inter-layer dependency of nodes are taken into account by HMNE. HDMI is designed to mine the dependency between node embedding and node attributes. However, they cannot be directly applied to mine the relationships between nodes.

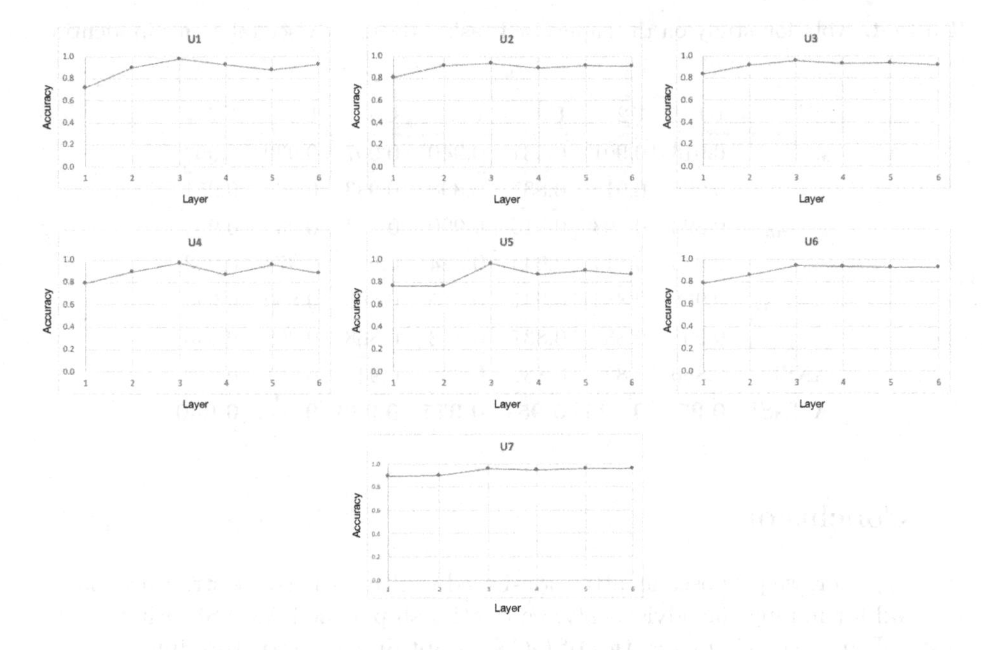

Fig. 4. AMNSF performance with different layers of inter-layer fusion in the model.

Effect of the Neural Layers' Number. Most of the existing GNN-based methods face the over-smoothing problem. In this paper, the attention-based structure loss can effectively mitigate this problem. The experimental results are shown in the Fig. 4, which clearly shows that the performance of the AMNSF model first increases with the increase of layers and then tends to be stable.

Ablation Study. In this section, we verify the effectiveness of several features proposed in this paper by removing the corresponding functional modules. (1)sl: Remove the structure loss to verify whether the model can learn and integrate the prominent structure information. (2)$saf(avg)$, $saf(max)$: The module based on self-attention fusion is removed, and Avg and Max are used to replace the module for node information fusion respectively. (3)esd, $esd(avg)$, $esd(max)$: By removing the extract sim and diff module, directly fuse the node representation obtained by GCN. Ablation analysis experimental results are shown in Table 4. (4) Attention-based Network Structure Embedding(ANSE): Taking only one-layer network as input to verify the impact of introducing extra view information.

Table 4. Ablation study on the supervised task: advisor-advisee relationship identification.

	U1	U2	U3	U4	U5	U6	U7
sl	0.918	0.901	0.931	0.940	0.907	0.939	0.953
$saf(avg)$	0.906	0.914	0.837	0.898	0.933	0.907	0.951
$saf(max)$	0.893	0.903	0.915	0.900	0.914	0.938	0.951
ssd	0.955	0.814	0.944	0.924	0.923	0.874	0.953
$esd(avg)$	0.958	0.884	0.947	0.915	0.865	0.880	0.948
$esd(max)$	0.961	0.837	0.837	0.873	0.868	0.909	0.946
ANSE	0.890	0.827	0.837	0.935	0.945	0.851	0.948
AMNSF	**0.979**	**0.935**	**0.957**	**0.971**	**0.963**	**0.945**	**0.960**

6 Conclusion

In this paper, we proposed an attention-based multiplex network structure fusion method for mining the advisor-advisee relationship, called AMNSF. First of all, AMNSF uses the characteristics of GCN to obtain local structure information. The distillation function combined with the loss function is capable of effectively separating the similar and different structure information of each layer. The novel fusion mechanism based on self-attention can fuse the interlayer's structure information. We evaluated the AMNSF on seven real-world datasets composed of acknowledgment network and collaboration network. The AMNSF's effectiveness is demonstrated by the results.

Acknowledgements. This work is supported by the National Natural Science Foundation of China under Grant (No. 61972047) and the NSFC-General Technology Basic Research Joint Funds under Grant (No. U1936220).

References

1. Malmgren, R.D., Ottino, J.M., Amara, L.A.N.: The role of mentorship in protege performance. Nature **41**(1), 622–626 (2010)
2. Wang, W., Liu, J., Xia, F., King, L., Tong, H.: Shifu: Deep learning based advisor-advisee relationship mining in scholarly big data. In: Proceedings of the 26th International Conference on World Wide Web, pp. 303–310 (2017)
3. Wang, C., et al.: Mining advisor-advisee relationships from research publication networks. In: ACM SIGKDD International Conference on Knowledge Discovery and Data Mining, pp. 203–212, July 2010
4. Zhao, Z., Liu, W., Qian, Y., Nie, L., Yin, Y., Zhang, Y.: Identifying advisor-advisee relationships from co-author networks via a novel deep model. Inf. Sci. **41**(1), 258–269 (2018)
5. Liu, J., et al.: Shifu2: a network representation learning based model for advisor-advisee relationship mining. IEEE Trans. Knowl. Data Eng. **33** (2019)

6. Li, Y., Liu, Z., Yu, H.: Advisor-advisee relationship identification based on maximum entropy model. Acta Phys. Sin. **62**(16), 581–586 (2013)
7. Perozzi, B., Al-Rfou, R., Skiena, S.: Deepwalk: Online learning of social representations. In: Proceedings the 20th ACM SIGKDD International Conference on Knowledge Discovery and Data Mining, pp. 701–710 (2014)
8. Tang, J., Qu, M., Wang, M., Zhang, M., Yan, J., Mei, Q.: Line: large-scale information network embedding. In; Proceedings of the 24th International Conference on World Wide Web, pp. 1067–1077 (2015)
9. Cao, S., Lu, W., Xu, Q.: GraRep: learning graph representations with global structure information. In: Proceedings of the 24th ACM International on Conference on Information and Knowledge Management, pp. 891–900 (2015)
10. Jing, B., Park, C., Tong, H.: HDMI: high-order deep multiplex Infomax. In: Proceedings of the 2021 IEEE/ACM International Conference on World Wide Web, pp, 2414–2424 (2021)
11. Donnat, C., Zitnik, M., Hallac, D., Leskovec, J.: Learning structural node embeddings via diffusion wavelets. In: Proceedings of the 24th ACM SIGKDD International Conference on Knowledge Discovery and Data Mining, pp. 1320–1329 (2018)
12. Ahmed, N.K., et al.: Learning role-based graph embeddings. arXiv:1802.02896 (2018). https://arxiv.org/abs/1802.02896
13. Defferrard, M., Bresson, X., Vandergheynst, P.: Convolutional neural networks on graphs with fast localized spectral filtering. In: Proceedings of the Advances in Neural Information Processing Systems, pp. 3844–3852 (2016)
14. Kipf, T.N., Welling, M.: Semi-supervised classification with graph convolutional networks. In: Proceedings of the International Conference on Learning Representations (2017)
15. Hamilton, W., Ying, Z., Leskovec, J.: Inductive representation learning on large graphs. In: Proceedings of the Advances in Neural Information Processing Systems, pp. 1024–1034 (2017)
16. Velickovic, P., Cucurull, G., Casanova, A., Romero, A., Lio, P., Bengio, Y.: Graph attention networks. In: Proceedings of the International Conference on Learning Representations (2018)
17. Xu, K., Hu, W., Leskovec, J., Jegelka, S.: How powerful are graph neural networks. In: Proceedings of the International Conference on Learning Representations (2019)
18. Qiu, J., Dong, Y., Ma, H., Li, J., Wang, K., Tang, J.: Network embedding as matrix factorization: unifying DeepWalk, LINE, PTE, and node2vec. In: Proceedings of the 10th ACM International Conference on Web Search and Data Mining, pp. 459–467 (2018)
19. Yang, D., Rosso, P., Li, B., Cudre-Mauroux, P.: NodeSketch: highly-efficient graph embeddings via recursive sketching. In: Proceedings of the 25th ACM SIGKDD International Conference on Knowledge Discovery and Data Mining, pp. 1162–1172 (2019)
20. Grover, A., Leskovec, J.: node2vec: scalable feature learning for networks. In: Proceedings of the 22nd ACM SIGKDD International Conference on Knowledge Discovery and Data Mining, pp. 855–864 (2016)
21. Vaswani, A., et al.: Attention is all you need. In: Proceedings of the Advances in Neural Information Processing Systems, pp. 6000–6010 (2017)
22. Hammond, D.K., Vandergheynst, P., Gribonval, R.: Wavelets on graphs via spectral graph theory. Appl. Comput. Harmon. Anal. **30**(2), 129–150 (2011)
23. Ning, N., Li, Q., Zhao, K., Wu, B.: Multiplex network embedding model with high-order node dependence. Complexity **2021** (2021)

CorefDRE: Coref-Aware Document-Level Relation Extraction

Zhongxuan Xue, Jiang Zhong(✉), Qizhu Dai, and Rongzhen Li

College of Computer Science, Chongqing University, Chongqing 400044, China
{xuezhongxuan,zhongjiang,daiqizhu,lirongzhen}@cqu.edu.cn

Abstract. Document-level Relation Extraction (Doc-level RE) aims to extract relations among entities from a document, which requires reasoning over multiple sentences. The pronouns are ubiquitous in the document, which can provide reasoning clues for Doc-level RE. However, previous works do not take the pronouns into account. In this paper, we propose **Coref**-aware **D**oc-level **RE** based on Graph Inference Network (CorefDRE) to infer relations. CorefDRE first dynamically constructs the heterogeneous **M**ention-**P**ronoun **A**ffinity **G**raph (MPAG) by integrating coreference information of pronouns. Then, **E**ntity **G**raph (EG) is aggregated from MPAG through the weight of mention-pronoun pairs, calculated by the noise suppression mechanism, and GCN. Finally, we infer relations between entities based the normalized EG. Moreover, We introduce the noise suppression mechanism via calculating affinity between pronouns and corresponding mentions to filter the noise caused by pronouns. Experimental results significantly outperform baselines by nearly 1.7–2.0 in F1 on three public datasets, DocRED, DialogRE, and MPDD. We further conduct ablation experiments to demonstrate the effectiveness of the proposed MPAG structure and the noise suppression mechanism.

Keywords: Document-level relation extraction · Mention-pronoun affinity graph · Noise suppression

1 Introduction

Relation Extraction (RE), a task that automatically extracts relational facts among entities from raw texts, is widely used in knowledge base construction [22] and question answering [18]. Previous researches mainly focus on sentence-level RE, which aims to identify relations between an entity pair in a single sentence. However, large amounts of relational facts are expressed by multiple sentences, which cannot be achieved by sentence-level RE. Therefore, researchers gradually pay more attention to document-level RE.

Doc-level RE not only handles the sentence-level RE but also captures complex interactions among cross-sentence entities in the document. Recent studies focus on graph-based reasoning skills [5,14,16], where coreference information,

G. Memmi et al. (Eds.): KSEM 2022, LNAI 13370, pp. 116–128, 2022.
https://doi.org/10.1007/978-3-031-10989-8_10

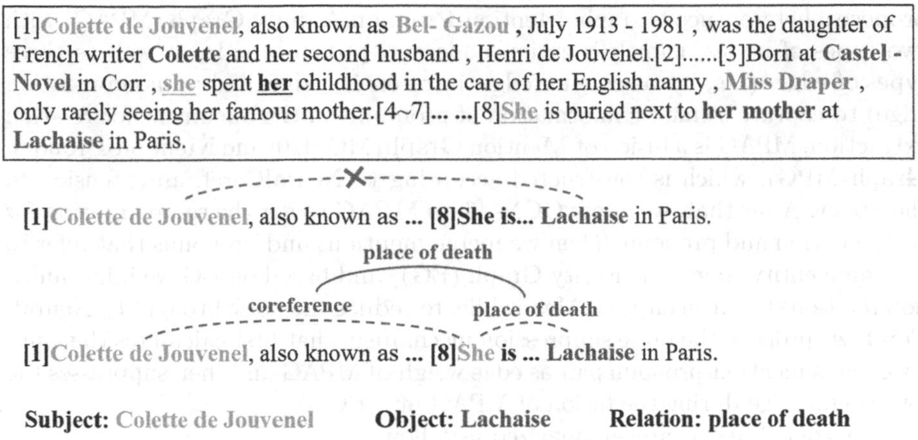

[1]Colette de Jouvenel, also known as Bel- Gazou , July 1913 - 1981 , was the daughter of French writer Colette and her second husband , Henri de Jouvenel.[2]......[3]Born at Castel - Novel in Corr , she spent her childhood in the care of her English nanny , Miss Draper , only rarely seeing her famous mother.[4~7]... ...[8]She is buried next to her mother at Lachaise in Paris.

[1]Colette de Jouvenel, also known as ... [8]She is... Lachaise in Paris.

place of death

coreference

place of death

[1]Colette de Jouvenel, also known as ... [8]She is ... Lachaise in Paris.

Subject: Colette de Jouvenel Object: Lachaise Relation: place of death

Fig. 1. An example document from DocRED. Entities are distinguished by color, with the reasoning clue and relation label listed offside.

especially produced by mentions, is extensively used for logical inference. However, the coreference information of pronouns, beneficial to obtaining interactive information across sentences [3] and multi-hop graph convolution, is ignored.

Figure 1 shows an example from the DocRED dataset [15]. As will be readily seen, only based on the fact that mention *Colette de Jouvebel* (in the 1*st* sentence) and pronouns *she* (in the 8*th* sentence) refer to the same entity, can we infer the relation of entity pair (*Colette de Jouvebel*, *Lachaise*) is the *place of death*. And the relational reasoning pattern of entity pairs (*Colette de Jouvebel*, *Castel−Novel*) and (*Colette*, *Lachaise*) is the same as above. Therefore, the pronouns in documents can produce rich semantic information, which is extremely vital to Doc-level RE. To verify the hypothesis, we randomly sample 100 documents from the DocRED training set and measure the number of pronouns and mention-pronoun pairs. Table 1 describes that each document has approximate 32 pronouns (*"he"*, *"him"*, *"his"*, *"she"*, *"her"*, etc.) and 14 mention-pronoun pairs. Obviously, pronouns can provide significant clues to Doc-level RE if some strategies are designed ingeniously.

Table 1. Statistics of pronouns and mention-pronoun pairs.

Type	Count
Pronouns	32
Mention-Pronoun pairs	14

To capture the feature produced by pronouns, we propose a novel Coref-aware Doc-level RE based on Graph Inference Network (CorefDRE). CorefDRE is a fine-tuned coreference-aware approach that instructs the model directly to learn the coreference information produced by mentions and pronouns. Specifically, we propose a heterogeneous graph, **M**ention-**P**ronoun **A**ffinity **G**raph (MPAG) with two types of nodes, namely mention node and pronoun node, as well as three types of edges (i.e., intra-sentence edge, intra-entity edge, and pronoun-mention edge) to capture semantic information of pronouns in the document for relation extraction. MPAG is a fusion of **M**ention **G**raph(MG) [20] and **M**ention-**P**ronoun **G**raph(MPG), which is constructed according to NeuralCoref, an extension to the Spacy. After that, we apply GCNs [6] to MPAG to get the representation for each mention and pronoun. Then we merge mentions and pronouns that refer to the same entity to get the Entity Graph (EG), and based on EG we infer multi-hop relations between entities. Meanwhile, to reduce the noise brought by NeuralCoref, we propose the noise suppression mechanism that first calculates the affinity of each mention-pronoun pair as edge weigh of MPAG and then suppresses the low weight edge during the fusion of MPAG into EG.

Our contributions are summarized as follows:

- We introduce a novel heterogeneous graph, Mention-Pronoun Affinity Graph (MPAG), which integrates the coreference information produced by mentions and pronouns to better adapt to Doc-level RE task.
- We propose a noise suppression mechanism to calculate the affinity between mention and corresponding pronoun for suppressing noise produced by false mention-pronoun pairs.
- We conduct experiments and the results outperform baseline by nearly 1.7–2.0 in F1 on the public datasets, DocRED, DialogRE, and MPDD, which demonstrate the effectiveness of our CorefDRE model.

This paper is organized as follows: Sect. 1 outlines the research on doc-level RE and the main contribution of this paper, Sect. 2 and section3 detail the proposed model and the experimental results, respectively. Section 4 describes the related work of graph-based doc-RE and Sect. 5 summarizes the advantages and disadvantages of this paper and provides the direction for future research.

2 Proposed Approach

We formulate the task of document-level RE (doc-level RE) in the following way: **Document** D: the document is the raw text containing multiple sentences, namely $D = \{\mathrm{s}_1, \mathrm{s}_2, \ldots, \mathrm{s}_\mathrm{n}\}$. **Entity** E: the entity set E consists of the entities that appear in the document. For each entity e_i, it is represented by a set of mentions in the document as well as an entity type: $e_i = (\{m_{i1}, m_{i2}, \ldots\}, t_i)$, where $t_i \in R_e$ (the set of predefined entity types in the datasets). **Mention** m: the mentions refer to the representation of entities in a document, and each mention refers to a span of words: $m = \{w_1, w_2, \ldots\}$. **Pronoun** p: pronouns are words that can refer to mention in a document (e.g., it, he, she, etc.).

Given the document D and entity set E, Doc-level RE is required to predict the relational facts between entities, namely $r_{s,o} = f(e_s, e_o)$, where e_s, e_o are subject entity and object entity in E, $r_{s,o}$ is a relational fact in pre-defined relation set R. In order to produce the above described output, our model, Coref-aware

Doc-level RE based on Graph Inference Network (CorefDRE), mainly consists of 3 modules: Mention-Pronoun Affinity Graph construction module (Subsect. 2.1), noise suppression mechanism (Subsect. 2.2), graph inference module (Subsect. 2.3), as is shown in Fig. 2.

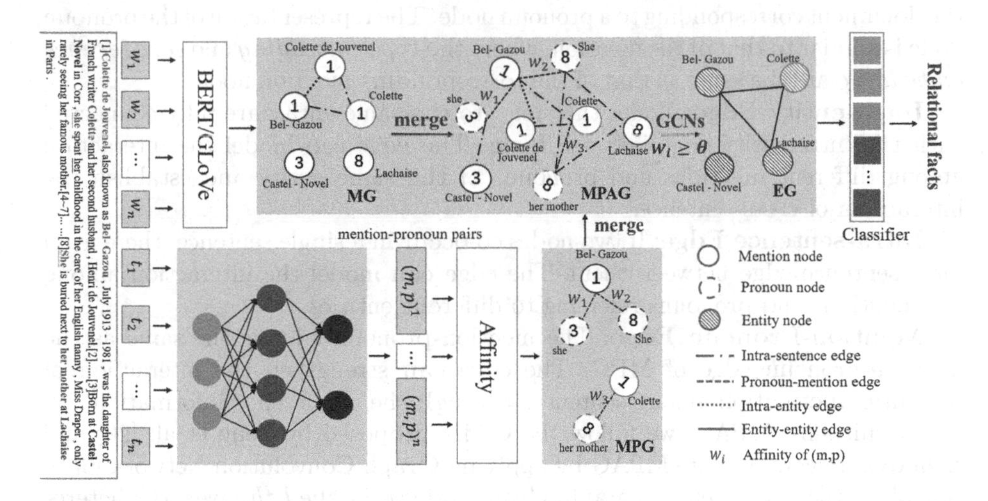

Fig. 2. The architecture of our CorefDRE. First, the document is fed into the encoder respectively, and then MG is constructed. Second, find the mention-pronoun pairs and use the noise suppression mechanism to calculates the affinity of mention-pronoun pairs as the weight of mention-pronoun edge, and then MPG is constructed. Third, merge MG and MPG to MPAG and mention-pronoun pairs with low affinity are inhibited when merging. Finally, after applying GCNs, MPAG is transformed into EG, where the paths between entities are identified for reasoning. Different entities are drawn with colors and the number i in each node denotes that it belongs to the i-th sentence.

2.1 Mention-Pronoun Affinity Graph Construction Module

To model the coreference relationships and enhanced the interactions between entities, Mention-Pronoun Affinity Graph (MPAG), a combination of MG and MPG, is constructed. MG is constructed according to Zeng et al. [20] but no document node here. MPG is constructed according to the mention-pronoun pairs generated by NeuralCoref. Specifically, the NeuralCoref first identify the pronouns that refer to the same mention and cluster the mention-pronoun pairs together as coreference clusters. For instance, we can obtain mention-pronoun pair clusters simply (e.g., [(*Bel Gazou*, *she*),(*Bel Gazou*, *She*),...,(*Colette*, *her mother*)]) from the sentences as shown in Fig. 2. And m and p in the pair (m, p) correspond a mention node m and a pronoun node p of MPG respectively, and there is a mention-pronoun edge between node m and node p.

There are two types of nodes and three types of edges in MPG:

Mention Node: each mention node in graph corresponds to a particular mention of an entity. The representation of the mention node m_i is defined by the concatenation of semantic embedding, coreference embedding and type embedding [15], namely $m_i = [avg_{w_k \in m_i}(h_k); t_m; c_m]$, where $t_m \in R_e$, c_m represents which entity it refers to, and $avg_{w_k \in m_i}(h_k)$ is the average representation of mention containing words encoded by encoder.

Pronoun Node: Each pronoun (e.g. *it*, *his*, *she*, etc.) refers to a mention in the document corresponding to a pronoun node. The representation of the pronoun node is similar to that of the mention, where the *type embedding* and *coreference embedding* are the same as that of the corresponding mention nodes.

Intra-entity Edge: Nodes that refer to the same entity are fully connected with the intra-entity edge between them. The edge can model the interaction among different mentions and pronouns of the same entity and establish the interaction of cross-sentence.

Intra-sentence Edge: If two nodes co-occur in a single sentence, there is an intra-sentence edge between them. The edge can model the interaction among the mentions and pronouns referring to different entities.

Mention-Pronoun Edge: The mention-pronoun edge is the same as the mention-pronoun edge of MPG. The edge can strengthen the interaction of semantic information among sentences through the coreference information.

To initialize MPAG, we follow the GAIN proposed by Zeng et al. [20] and then dynamically update MPAG by applying Graph Convolution Network [6] to convolute the heterogeneous graph. Given node n_i at the *l-th* layer, the heterogeneous graph convolutional operation is formed as follows:

$$n_i^{l+1} = \sigma\left(\sum_{e \in E}\sum_{j \in N}\frac{1}{|N|}W_e^l n_j^l + b_e^l\right) \tag{1}$$

where $\sigma(.)$ is the activation function. E denotes the set of different edges, N denotes the set of different neighbors of node n_i, and W_e^l, $b_e^l \in R^{d \times d}$ are trainable parameters.

To cover features of all levels, the node n_i is defined as the concatenation of hidden states of each layer:

$$n_i = \left[n_i^0; n_i^1; \ldots; n_i^N\right] \tag{2}$$

where n_i^l is the representation of node n_i at layer l, and n_i^0 is the initial representation of node n_i, which is formed by the document representation from encoder.

2.2 Noise Suppression Mechanism

Mention-pronoun pairs will produce noise because of the weak adaptability between the datasets and the NeuralCoref. Therefore, we propose the noise suppression mechanism to filter noise in the process of graph inferencing (Subsect. 2.3). In our framework, we adopt the BERT to measure the affinity of the mention-pronoun pairs as the weight of the mention-pronoun edge. For each pair $(mention, pronoun)$, we concatenate the context of *mention* and *pronoun* as input and produce a single affinity scalar for every pair when constructing MPAG. The input form of tokens is as follows:

$$\begin{aligned} &[CLS]\langle \text{ Mention } \rangle [SEP] \langle \text{ Pronoun } \rangle [SEP] \\ &where \, \langle \star \rangle := c_l [START] \star [END] c_r \end{aligned} \tag{3}$$

where $\star$ is mention tokens or pronoun tokens, c_l and c_r represent the text on left and right of "$\star$" respectively. The $[START]$ and $[END]$ are two special tokens fine-tuned that indicate the start and end of "$\star$" in the context respectively.

Inspired by Angell et al. [1], we make affinity symmetric by averaging the representation of $(mention, pronoun)$ and $(pronoun, mention)$ to improve the representation. And then the affinity of the mention-pronoun pair is calculated by passing the enhanced representation of pairs into a linear layer with sigmoid activation. For instance, the affinity between mention-pronoun pair $(mention, pronoun)$ is set 1, which is a strong signal for the fusion of MPAG. To calculate the affinity between the mention-pronoun pair accurately, we subtly design the positive sampling and negative sampling to train the affinity calculation. We screen out 300 positive samples D_p from the data D obtained by NeuralCoref and replace the mention m of the positive sample with other mentions m' randomly. To train the affinity module, we minimize the following triplet max-margin loss when training.

$$L_\varphi = \sum_{p_+, m \epsilon P^+} \sum_{p_-, m \epsilon P^-} l\left(m, p_+, p_-\right) \tag{4}$$

$$l(g, p, n) = \left[aff(g, n)^2 - (1 - aff(p, n))^2\right]_+ \tag{5}$$

where m and p are mention and pronoun in mention-pronoun pair (m, p) and $aff\,(m, p)$ is the affinity between m and p. The g, p, n in Eq. (5) are mention, negative pronoun, and positive pronoun referring to mention.

2.3 Graph Inference Module

Graph Merging. Inspired by Zeng et al. [20], we predict relational facts between entity pairs by reasoning on Entity Graph (EG), which is transformed from MPAG. Furthermore, the dynamic process of merging MPAG to EG is divided into three steps:

Step 1: Pronoun nodes that refer to the same mention are merged with the corresponding mention node to form a new mention node. Note that if the affinity between the mention-pronoun pair is less than the threshold θ, the pronoun does not participate in the merging process so that noise is depressed simply. For the *i-th* mention node merged from N pronoun nodes, it is represented by concatenating the mention and the average of its N pronoun node representations, and the representation of new mention node is defined as:

$$m_i = \bar{m}_i \oplus \frac{1}{N} \sum_n aff_n p_n \left(aff_n \geq \theta\right) \tag{6}$$

where $\bar{m}_i$ denotes the mention representation. p_n is the *n-th* pronoun referred to the mention m_i, aff_n is the affinity of $(\bar{m}_i, p_n)$ pair and $\oplus$ denotes concatenate operation.

Step 2: Mention nodes that refer to the same entity are merged to an entity node in EG. For the *i-th* entity node merged from N mention nodes, it is represented by the average of its N mention node representation:

$$e_i = \frac{1}{N} \sum_n m_n \tag{7}$$

Step 3: Intuitively, intra-sentence edges between the mentions, which refer to the two entities, are merged as the bi-directional edge in EG. The directed edge from entity node e_i to e_j in EG is defined as:

$$edge_{ij} = \sigma\left(W_q\left[e_i; e_j\right]\right) + b_q \tag{8}$$

where W_q and b_q are trainable parameters and σ is an activation function (e.g., ReLU).

We model the potential reasoning clue between the entity nodes in EG through the path between the entity nodes. Based on the representation of the edge, $two - hop$ path between entity nodes e_s and e_o is defined as:

$$\mathrm{P}^k_{s,o} = \left[edge_{s,i}; edge_{i,o}; edge_{o,i}; edge_{i,s}\right] \tag{9}$$

where i stands for the intermediate node. Since there are multiple paths between two entity nodes, an attention mechanism is introduced to fuse the path information and pay more attention to the strong path. Path information of the entity in EG is defined as:

$$s_i = \sigma\left(\left[e_s; e_o\right] \cdot W_l \cdot p^i_{s,o}\right) \tag{10}$$

$$\alpha_i = \frac{e^{s_i}}{\sum_j e^{s_j}} \tag{11}$$

$$p_{s,o} = \sum_i \alpha_i p^i_{s,o} \tag{12}$$

where α_i is the attention weight for i^{th} path and σ is an activation function (e.g., ReLU).

Relation Inference. According to the fusion of MPAG and noise suppression mechanism, The isomorphic graph EG is dynamically constructed, and the relationship between entity nodes can be predicted by the path inference. To identify the relationship of entity pair (e_s, e_o), we concatenate the following representations as $I_{s,o}$ and compute the probability of relation r from the pre-specified relation schema as Eq. (14):

$$I_{s,o} = \left[e_s; e_t; \left|e_s - e_o\right|; e_s \odot e_o; p_{s,o}\right] \tag{13}$$

$$P\left(r \mid \mathbf{e}_s, \mathbf{e}_o\right) = \operatorname{sigmoid}\left(W_b \sigma\left(W_a I_{s,o} + b_a\right) + b_b\right) \tag{14}$$

where e_s and e_o are the representation of subject and object entity in EG, and $p_{s,0}$ is the comprehensive inferential path information. W_a, W_b, b_a, b_b are trainable parameters and σ is an activation function (e.g., ReLU). We use binary cross entropy as the loss function to train our model.:

$$L = -\sum_{D\in S}\sum_{s\neq o}\sum_{r\in R} CrossEntropy\left(P\left(r \mid \mathbf{e}_s, \mathbf{e}_o\right), \overline{P}\left(r \mid \mathbf{e}_s, \mathbf{e}_o\right)\right) \tag{15}$$

where S denotes the whole corpus, and $\overline{P}\left(r \mid \mathbf{e}_s, \mathbf{e}_o\right)$ refers to ground truth.

3 Experiments

3.1 Dataset and Experimental Settings

DocRED [15]: DocRED consists of 3053 documents for training, 1000 for development and 1000 for test. And more than 40.7% of the relation facts require reasoning over multiple sentences. **DialogRE** [17]: DialogRE includes 1073 for training, 358 for development and 357 for test, and 95.6% of relational triples can be inferred through multiple sentences, where pronouns are extensively used. **MPDD** [2]: A publicly available Chinese dialogue dataset with the emotion and interpersonal relation labels and a mass of pronouns. To learn an effective representation for documents and capture the context of each mention, Following Yao et al. [15], for each word, we concatenate its word embedding, entity type embedding, and entity id embedding. And then we feed all the word representations into Glove/BERT to get the representation of the document. We extract the relation between pronoun and mention based on Huggingface's NeuralCoref and use BERT to pretrain the affinity for the mention-pronoun pair. We use 2 layers of GCN to encode the MPAG and EG. Our model is optimized with AdamW [9] and sets the dropout rate of GCN to 0.6, learning rate to 0.001.

3.2 Baseline Models

We use the following models as baselines.

CNN & BiLSTM: Yao et al. [15] proposed CNN and BiLSTM to encode the document into a sequence of the hidden state vectors. **Context-Aware**: Yao et al. [15] also proposed LSTM to encode the document and attention mechanism to fuse contextual information for predicting. **CorefBERT**: a pre-trained model was proposed by Ye et al. [16] for word embedding. **DocuNet-BERT**: Zhang et al. [21] proposed a U-shaped segmentation module to capture global information among relational triples.**GAIN-GloVe/GAIN-BERT**: Zeng et al. [20] proposed GAIN, which designed mention graph and entity graph to predict target relations, and make use of GloVe or BERT for word embedding, GCN for representation of the graph.

Table 2. Performance on DocRED. Models above the first double line do not use pre-trained models. Results with * are reported in their original papers. Ign F1 refers to excluding the relational facts shared by the training and dev/test sets.

Model	Dev		Test	
	Ign F1	F1	Ign F1	F1
CNN* [15]	41.58	43.45	40.33	42.46
BiLSTM* [15]	48.87	50.94	48.78	51.06
ConText-Aware* [15]	48.94	51.09	48.40	50.70
GAIN-GloVe [20]	53.12	55.37	52.71	55.18
CorefDRE-GloVe	**55.01**	**57.33**	**54.37**	**56.74**
$\text{BERT}_{\text{base}}$* [13]	-	54.16	-	53.20
$\text{CorefBERT}_{\text{base}}$* [16]	55.32	57.51	54.54	56.96
$\text{DocuNet-BERT}_{\text{base}}$* [21]	59.86	61.83	59.93	61.86
$\text{GAIN-BERT}_{\text{base}}$ [20]	59.21	61.25	59.03	59.12
CorefDRE-BERT$_{base}$	**60.85**	**63.06**	**60.78**	**60.82**

Table 3. Performance on the datasets DialogRE and MPDD.

Model	F1-DialogRE	Acc-MPDD
CNN [17]	46.1	-
BERT [8]	60.6	31.0
GAIN [8]	69.8	42.2
CoIn [8]	71.1	46.5
CorefDRE	**71.4**	**46.7**

3.3 Main Results

We compare our CorefDRE model with other baselines on the DocRED dataset. The results are shown in Table 2. We use F1 and Ign F1 as evaluation indicators to evaluate the effect of models. Compared with the models based on GloVe, CorefDRE outperforms strong baselines by 1.7–2.0 F1 scores on the development set and test set. Compared with the models on BERT-base, CorefDRE outperforms strong baselines by 1.6–1.9. These results suggest that MPAG can capture the interaction relationship of multi-sentences for better Doc-level RE. Although we only conduct the experiments on DocRED, DialogRE, and MDPP shown in Table 3, our model is fit to others since pronouns are the essential grammar and syntax of the natural language.

3.4 Ablation Study

To verify the effectiveness of different modules in CorefDRE, we further analyze our model and the results of the ablation study shown in Table 4.

First, we remove the noise suppression mechanism. We set the weight of the mention-pronoun edge directly to 1 and merge all the pronoun nodes with

Table 4. Performance of CorefDRE with different embeddings and submodules.

Model	Dev		Test	
	Ign F1	F1	Ign F1	F1
CorefDRE-GloVe	55.01	57.33	54.37	56.74
-noise suppression	53.57	55.85	53.02	55.26
-pronoun node	53.12	55.37	52.71	55.18
CorefDRE-BERT$_{base}$	60.85	63.06	60.78	60.82
-noise suppression	59.57	61.67	59.43	59.64
-pronoun node	59.21	61.25	59.03	59.12

the corresponding mention node when generating EG. Without the weight between pronoun node and mention node, the performance of CorefDRE-GloVe/CorefDRE-BERT$_{base}$ sharply drops by 1.39 F1 on the development set. This drop shows that the affinity between pronoun node and mention node plays a vital role in suppressing the noise caused by unsuitable mention-pronoun pairs.

Next, we remove the pronoun nodes. Specifically, we convert MPAG into MG proposed by Zeng et al. [20]. Without pronoun nodes, the result drops by an average of 1.88 F1 on the development set. This suggests that the pronoun nodes can capture richer information that mention node and document cannot capture effectively.

3.5 Case Study

Document Text	Model	Graph Inference	Prediction	Ground Truth
[0]... [2]Born in **Victoria** , Texas , **Conrad Johnson** was nine when his family moved to Houston. [3]Following studies at Yates High School , he attended Houston College for Negroes and graduated from **Wiley College**. ...	GAIN		(Conrad Johnson, Wiley College, NA) ×	(Conrad Johnson, Wiley College, Educated at)
	CorefDRE		(Conrad Johnson, Wiley College, Educated at) √	
[0]**Samuel C. Brightman** (1911 – 1992) was a journalist , war correspondent , freelance writer and adult educator. ... [3]He enlisted in the army in **World War II** and was assigned as a **Public Relations Officer** , responsible for transport, billeting , and general assistance for a group of newspaper reporters. ...	GAIN		(World War II, Public Relations Officer, NA) ×	(World War II, Public Relations Officer, Conflict)
	CorefDRE		(World War II, Public Relations Officer, Conflict) √	

Fig. 3. Case Study on our CorefDRE model and baseline model. The models take the document as input and predict relations among different entities in different colors. The *Graph Inference* is reasoning process on graphs and the *NA* stands for no relation.

Figure 3 illustrates the case study of our CorefDRE compared with baseline. As is shown, GAIN can not predict the relation of entity pairs (*Conrad Johnson*, *Wiley College*) and (*Samuel C. Brightman*, *World War II*), while CorefDRE can predict the relation between *Conrad Johnson* and *Wiley College* is *educated at* and the relation between *SamuelC. Brightman* and *World War II* is *conflict*, because pronoun nodes *he* and *He* can connect the entity pair (*Conrad Johnson*, *Wiley College*) and (*Samuel C. Brightman*, *World War II*) respectively. We observe that relation extraction among those entities needs pronouns to connect them across sentences. The observation indicates that the information introduced by pronouns is beneficial to relation extraction.

4 Related Work

Relation Extraction is to extract relation facts from a given text, while early researches mainly focus on predicting relation fact between two entities within a sentence [4,22]. These approaches include sequence-based methods, graph-based methods, and pre-training methods, which can tackle sentence-level RE effectively, and the dataset contains a fixed number of relation types and entity types. However, large amounts of real-world relational facts only can be extracted through multiple sentences.

Doc-Level Relation Extraction. Researchers extend sentence-level to Doc-level RE [12,21] and explore two trends. The first is the sequence-based method that uses the pre-trained model to get the contextual representation of each word in a document, which directly uses the pre-trained model to obtain the relationship between entities [7,10,16]. These methods adopt transformers to model long-distance dependencies implicitly and get the entities embedding, and feed them into a classifier to get relation labels. However the sequence-based methods cannot capture enough entity interactions when the document length is out of the capability of the encoder at a time. In order to model these interactions, the graph-based method are proposed to constructs graphs according to documents, which can model entity structure more intuitively [11,20,23]. These methods take advantage of LSTM or BERT to encode the input documents and obtain the representation of entities, then utilize the GCNs to update representation, and finally feed them into the classifier to get relation labels.

Coreference Dependency Relation Reasoning. Some previous efforts on Doc-level RE introducing coreference dependency for multi-hop inference are useful for solving multi-hop reasoning. Previous works [10,11,23] have shown that graph-based coreference resolution is obviously beneficial to construct dependencies among mentions for relation reasoning. [19] proposed intra-and-inter-sentential reasoning based on R-GCN to model multiple paths by covering all cases of logical reasoning chains in the graph. [14] introduced a reconstructor to rebuild the graph reasoning paths to guide the relation inference by multiple reasoning skills including coreference and entity bridge. However, none of the above methods model the influence of pronouns on relation extraction and reasoning directly. Our CorefDRE model deals with the problem by introducing a novel heterogeneous graph with mention-pronoun coreference resolution and noise suppression mechanism.

5 Conclusion and Future Work

This paper proposed CorefDRE which features two novel skills: the coref-aware heterogeneous graph, MPAG, and the noise suppression mechanism. Based on the proposed method, the model can extract document-level entity pair relation more effectively due to the richer semantic information brought by pronouns. Experiments demonstrated that our CorefDRE outperforms most previous models significantly and is orthogonal to pre-trained language models. However, there are still some problems not been completely solved. The noise generated by pronouns hinders the improvement of the performance of our model. In the future, we will explore other methods to construct less noisy mention-pronoun pairs to optimize CorefDRE.

Acknowledgements. The authors would like to thank the Associate Editor and anonymous reviewers for their valuable comments and suggestions. This work is funded in part by the National Natural Science Foundation of China under Grants No.62176029, and in part by the graduate research and innovation foundation of Chongqing, China under Grants No. CYB21063. This work also is supported in part by the National Key Research, Development Program of China under Grants 2017YFB1402400, Major Project of Chongqing Higher Education Teaching Reform Research (191003), and the New Engineering Research and Practice Project of the Ministry of Education (E-JSJRJ20201335).

References

1. Angell, R., Monath, N., Mohan, S., Yadav, N., Mccallum, A.: Clustering-based inference for biomedical entity linking. In: Proceedings of the 2021 Conference of the North American Chapter of the Association for Computational Linguistics: Human Language Technologies (2021)
2. Chen, Y.T., Huang, H.H., Chen, H.H.: MPDD: a multi-party dialogue dataset for analysis of emotions and interpersonal relationships. In: Proceedings of the 12th Language Resources and Evaluation Conference, pp. 610–614 (2020)
3. Dasigi, P., Liu, N.F., Marasovi, A., Smith, N.A., Gardner, M.: Quoref: a reading comprehension dataset with questions requiring coreferential reasoning. In: Proceedings of the 2019 Conference on Empirical Methods in Natural Language Processing and the 9th International Joint Conference on Natural Language Processing (EMNLP-IJCNLP) (2019)
4. Guo, Z., Nan, G., Lu, W., Cohen, S.B.: Learning latent forests for medical relation extraction. In: Proceedings of the Twenty-Ninth International Conference on International Joint Conferences on Artificial Intelligence, pp. 3651–3657 (2021)
5. Huang, H., Lei, M., Feng, C.: Graph-based reasoning model for multiple relation extraction. Neurocomputing **420**, 162–170 (2021)

6. Kipf, T.N., Welling, M.: Semi-supervised classification with graph convolutional networks. arXiv preprint arXiv:1609.02907 (2017)
7. Li, Y., Song, Y., Jia, L., Gao, S., Li, Q., Qiu, M.: Intelligent fault diagnosis by fusing domain adversarial training and maximum mean discrepancy via ensemble learning. IEEE Trans. Ind. Inform. **17**(4), 2833–2841 (2021)
8. Long, X., Niu, S., Li, Y.: Consistent inference for dialogue relation extraction. In: Proceedings of the Twenty-Ninth International Conference on International Joint Conferences on Artificial Intelligence (2021)
9. Loshchilov, I., Hutter, F.: Decoupled weight decay regularization. In: ICLR (2019)
10. Qiu, H., Zheng, Q., Msahli, M., Memmi, G., Qiu, M., Lu, J.: Topological graph convolutional network-based urban traffic flow and density prediction. IEEE Trans. Intell. Trans. Syst. **22**(7), 4560–4569 (2021)
11. Sahu, S.K., Christopoulou, F., Miwa, M., Ananiadou, S.: Inter-sentence relation extraction with document-level graph convolutional neural network. In: Proceedings of the 57th Annual Meeting of the Association for Computational Linguistics, pp. 4309–4316 (2019)
12. Wang, D., Hu, W., Cao, E., Sun, W.: Global-to-local neural networks for document-level relation extraction. In: Proceedings of the 2020 Conference on Empirical Methods in Natural Language Processing (EMNLP). pp. 3711–3721 (2020)
13. Wang, H., Focke, C., Sylvester, R., Mishra, N., Wang, W.: Fine-tune BERT for DocRED with two-step process. arXiv preprint arXiv:1909.11898 (2019)
14. Xu, W., Chen, K., Zhao, T.: Discriminative reasoning for document-level relation extraction. arXiv preprint arXiv:2106.01562 (2021)
15. Yao, Y., et al.: DocRED: a large-scale document-level relation extraction dataset. In: Proceedings of the 57th Annual Meeting of the Association for Computational Linguistics, pp. 764–777 (2019)
16. Ye, D., et al.: Coreferential reasoning learning for language representation. In: Proceedings of the 2020 Conference on Empirical Methods in Natural Language Processing (EMNLP), pp. 7170–7186 (2020)
17. Yu, D., Sun, K., Cardie, C., Yu, D.: Dialogue-based relation extraction. In: Proceedings of the 58th Annual Meeting of the Association for Computational Linguistics, pp. 4927–4940 (2020)
18. Yu, M., Yin, W., Hasan, K.S., dos Santos, C., Xiang, B., Zhou, B.: Improved neural relation detection for knowledge base question answering. In: Proceedings of the 55th Annual Meeting of the Association for Computational Linguistics (Volume 1: Long Papers), pp. 571–581 (2017)
19. Zeng, S., Wu, Y., Chang, B.: SIRE: Separate intra-and inter-sentential reasoning for document-level relation extraction. arXiv preprint arXiv:2106.01709 (2021)
20. Zeng, S., Xu, R., Chang, B., Li, L.: Double graph based reasoning for document-level relation extraction. In: Proceedings of the 2020 Conference on Empirical Methods in Natural Language Processing (EMNLP), pp. 1630–1640 (2020)
21. Zhang, N., et al.: Document-level relation extraction as semantic segmentation. arXiv preprint arXiv:2106.03618 (2021)
22. Zhang, Y., Zhong, V., Chen, D., Angeli, G., Manning, C.D.: Position-aware attention and supervised data improve slot filling. In: Proceedings of the 2017 Conference on Empirical Methods in Natural Language Processing, pp. 35–45 (2017)
23. Zhu, H., Lin, Y., Liu, Z., Fu, J., Chua, T.S., Sun, M.: Graph neural networks with generated parameters for relation extraction. In: Proceedings of the 57th Annual Meeting of the Association for Computational Linguistics, pp. 1331–1339 (2019)

Single Pollutant Prediction Approach by Fusing MLSTM and CNN

Ming Lian and Jing Liu(✉)

College of Computer Science, Inner Mongolia University, Hohhot 010021, China
32009082@mail.imu.edu.cn, liujing@imu.edu.cn

Abstract. Air pollution has a negative impact on people's health, and accurate prediction of future air pollutant concentrations is crucial for cities and individuals to take early warning and preventive measures against potential air pollution. In this paper, we propose an air pollutant prediction model, named CMLSTM, that well combines Mogrifier LSTM and CNN to predict a single pollutant for the next six hours using multi-site air pollutant data, meteorological data, and holiday information. Mogrifier LSTM can capture long-term air pollutant time-series features with richer contextual interactions, while CNN uses one-dimensional convolution to effectively model the spatial transport of air pollutants. We conduct experiments with four years of data from one city, and the results demonstrate CMLSTM has higher prediction accuracy than the baseline methods.

Keywords: Air pollutant forecast · Mogrifier LSTM · CNN · Spatio-temporal data mining

1 Introduction

With the continuous industrial development and urbanization, the air pollution problem is becoming more and more serious, and the effective management and protection of air pollution has become a key issue. The prediction of air pollutants plays a very important role in solving this problem, which can provide data support for the government to carry out protection and management work, and also provide guidance and suggestions for people lives.

For air pollution prediction, because air pollution has time variability and is highly correlated with historical data, it belongs to time series prediction. In recent years, most researchers have used Long Short-Term Memory(LSTM) for modeling and achieved good prediction results [1–3]. The accuracy of time series prediction partly relies on how to better learn the contextual relationships of the series. Although the LSTM is able to handle long-term dependencies of time-series data well, the current input and the previous output are fed into the LSTM layer completely independently. In other words, the current input and the previous output interact with each other in a unidirectional spatial-temporal state in the LSTM. As a result, the correlation between current input

G. Memmi et al. (Eds.): KSEM 2022, LNAI 13370, pp. 129–140, 2022.
https://doi.org/10.1007/978-3-031-10989-8_11

and context tends to disappear as the model becomes more complex. It is a challenge to better learn the context dependence of air pollution sequences.

Further, many models rely on local features from the target location for prediction without taking care of the spatial temporal correlation of air pollutants between neighboring regions. However, air pollution has not only high temporal variability but also high spatial variability, and the effect of spatial transmission has a facilitating effect on prediction, but at the same time faces the challenge of how to learn spatial features. The emergence of Convolutional Neural Networks (CNN) has provided a promising approach to spatial feature extraction. It differs from other methods that learn the spatial transmission of air pollution by separately predicting the data of each site to be weighted [4]. CNN can directly convolve the source data of various sites to learn the spatial interaction and improve the accuracy of prediction [5].

In solving the air pollution prediction problem, considering that air pollution has extremely high temporal and spatial variability, from the perspective of spatio-temporal integration, this paper proposes the CMLSTM model to predict the single pollutant concentration in the next six hours. Mogrifier LSTM [6] is used instead of traditional LSTM to model the time-series sequence of air pollutants and their associated factors. CNN is used to extract the spatial interaction feathers of air pollution at each station. Fusion of the output of the above two and then predict the next six hours of single contamination concentration. Experimentally demonstrate the higher accuracy of our model on real data.

2 Related Work

Initially, air pollution prediction was mainly based on numerical models. Frequently used models such as CMAQ [7]. Current air quality methods mainly develop air pollution prediction models from a data-driven perspective, without explicitly considering atmospheric processes, and learn air pollution patterns from historical air pollution data to predict future air pollution conditions. Traditional methods include the autoregressive model ARIMA [8], but ARIMA requires data to be stationary series and air quality is often influenced by many external factors, making it difficult to capture the patterns. In addition, SVM [9], random forest [10], and artificial neural network ANNS [11] in machine learning are also used to do air pollution prediction.

However, air pollution is affected by historical data and belongs to time series prediction, and traditional models are not designed for time series prediction and lose time correlation in prediction. The advent of recurrent neural network RNN has made a great progress in time series prediction, showing superior performance than other models in time series prediction tasks [12]. However, RNN suffers from the problem of gradient disappearance. To solve the problem of RNN gradient disappearance, Hochreiter et al. proposed the LSTM model [13]. LSTM can learn the long-term dependence of time series and has been applied to the prediction of various time series data [14]. It has also achieved good feasibility and excellent performance in air pollution prediction. Verma et al. [1]

used a bidirectional LSTM model to predict the severity of air pollutants in advance. Krishan et al. [2] evaluated the performance of the LSTM algorithm for hourly concentration prediction using five different combinations of factors and parameters such as vehicle emissions, meteorological conditions, traffic data and pollutant levels. The LSTM model was found to deal effectively with the complexity and to be very effective in ambient air quality prediction. Wang et al. [3] proposed a CT-LSTM approach based on a combination of chi-square test (CT) and LSTM to predict air quality.

In previous RNN and LSTM-based models, inputs and previous outputs were fed into the LSTM layer completely independently. By allowing rich interaction between the inputs and their contexts, contextual relationships can be further extracted. Extracting contextual correlations between state gates and enhancing the relationships between these gating units has been an important direction of improvement for LSTM. Qin et al. [15] introduced an input attention mechanism that adaptively extracts the relevant drive sequence (aka input features) at each time step by referring to the previous encoderhidden state. This approach allows the input of the LSTM unit to do an attentional interaction with the previous output, implementing an input feature selection function that improves the predictive capability of the model. Melis et al. proposed the Mogrifier LSTM (MLSTM for short) [6], which extends the LSTM in the form of mutual selection of the current input and previous output, interacts the sequence input with the upper context to maintain relevance, and extracts implicit features by iterative computation and demonstrates its effectiveness in various NLP tasks.

Because air pollution predictions have not only temporal variability but also extremely high spatial variability, researchers have begun to focus on the effects of spatial transport in recent years. Cheng et al. [17] proposed to use an attention mechanism to determine the contribution of surrounding stations to learn the spatial interaction of each station. Zhao et al. [4] predicted the pollutants of each station separately and then combined them through a fully connected layer as a way to learn the influence of other stations on the target station. Chang et al. [16] proposed to use an aggregated learning model to fuse the prediction results of neighborhood features with those of local features and other features through a fully connected layer to obtain the final prediction.

CNN has been successfully applied in image analysis, can be involved in the spatial distribution features [18]. Scholars began to try to combine LSTM models with convolutional neural networks for air pollution concentration forecasting. Conwg et al. [5] proposed a new spatio-temporal convolutional long short-term memory neural network to input PM2.5 concentration data from the current station and near-neighboring stations into the model after a one-dimensional convolutional operation. Yang Han et al. [19] used a 1×1 convolutional layer to enhance the learning of cross-featured spatial interactions between air pollution and important urban dynamic features, especially road density, building density/height, and street canyon effects.

In this paper, we will fuse MLSTM and CNN to do single air pollutant concentration prediction.

3 Method

We propose the prediction method of fusion of MLSTM and CNN. The model architecture is shown in Fig. 1. First, time-series data of air pollutants and their associated factors input to MLSTM. Then, the pollutant-related time series of each station are input to CNN. Finally, the output of these two parts are fused over the fusion prediction layer, and the fused data are sent to the fully-connected layer to obtain the single pollutant concentration for the next six hours.

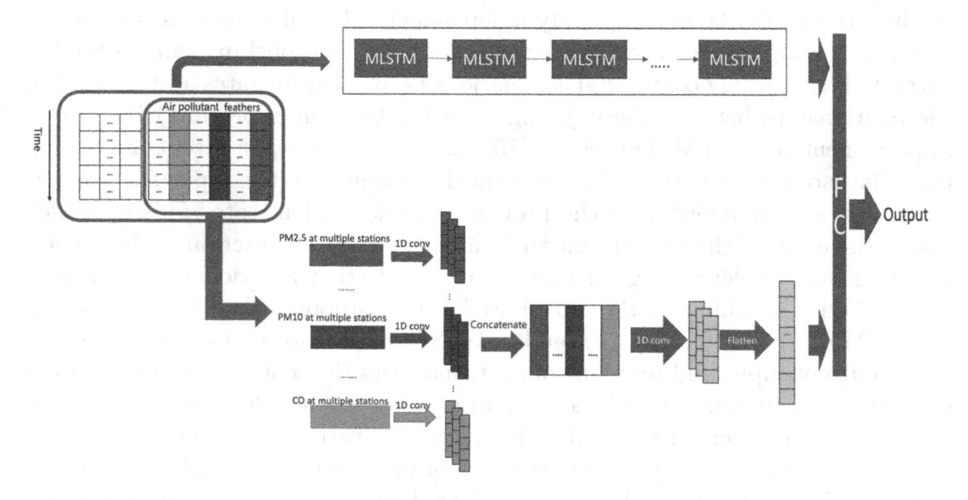

Fig. 1. Framework of proposed model

3.1 Timing Features of Pollutants Learned Using MLSTM

The Mogrifier LSTM is based on the standard LSTM and contains memory cells c with self-connections to store temporal states. Each memory cell is associated with an input gate i, a forget gate f and an output gate o to control the flow of sequential information. The various cell activations are calculated by using the following equations.

$$
\begin{aligned}
f &= \sigma(W^{fx}X + W^{fh}h_{prev} + b^f)\\
i &= \sigma(W^{ix}X + W^{ih}h_{prev} + b^i)\\
j &= \tanh(W^{jx}X + W^{jh}h_{prev} + b^j)\\
o &= \sigma(W^{ox}X + W^{oh}h_{prev} + b^o)\\
c &= f \odot c_{prev} + i \odot j\\
h &= o \odot \tanh(j)
\end{aligned}
\tag{1}
$$

where X and h are respectively an input element and the activation vector output by the corresponding memory unit. the W term represents the weight matrix, and the b term represents the bias vector. The $\odot$ is the elementwise product and σ is the logistic sigmoid function.

MLSTM is to allow input X and input $h_{prev}$to interact alternately before inputting the conventional LSTM. The interaction is shown in Fig. 2, and the interaction is performed according to the following operations.

$$X^i = 2\sigma(Q^i h_{prev}^{i-1}) \odot X^{i-2}, \qquad \text{for odd } i \in [1...r] \tag{2}$$

$$h_{prev}^i = 2\sigma(R^i X^{i-1}) \odot h_{prev}^{i-2}, \qquad \text{for even } i \in [1...r] \tag{3}$$

where $X^{-1} = X, h_{prev}^0 = h_{prev}$and the number of rounds $r \in N$ is a hyperparameter. If $r = 0$, the model is restored to a normal LSTM.

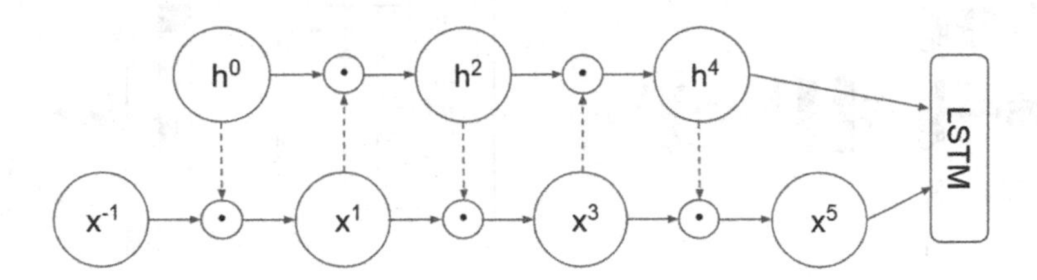

Fig. 2. Mogrifier with 5 rounds of updates.

In this paper, we concat the pollutant features of all stations, meteorological features and other features to obtain the features X. The feathers at time t is X_t and X_t is provided as an input element at time t to a memory unit of MLSTM. The features of each moment in the time period T constitute a time series feathers $\{X_i\}$,$\{X_i\} = X_1, X_2, ...X_T$, $X_i \in R^{D \times T}$. Where D represents the dimension of the features at each moment, and T represents the window size of the historical time series. The time series is encoded by MLSTM, and the h output from the last memory unit is used as the extracted time sequence features.

3.2 Spatial Features of Pollutants Learned Using CNN

The module consists of two 1D convolutional layers, as shown in Fig. 3. The first 1D convolutional layer is used to learn the spatial features of each pollutant at multiple stations, and the spatial features of each pollutant learned by the first 1D convolutional layer are concatenated and fed to the second 1D convolutional layer, and the second 1D convolutional layer is used to learn the interactions between pollutants.

Pollutants collected at time t from multiple air quality monitoring stations in a city to form a time-series vector of that pollutant at time t. The pollutant sequence vector is composed of a multi-site pollutant input matrix P in the order of time. Where $P \in R^{TXS}$,T is the time series window size, and S is the number of stations.

The multisite input matrix of each pollutant passes through the first one-dimensional convolution layer separately, and we take the multisite input matrix of PM2.5 as an example to describe this one-dimensional convolution process. This 1D convolutional layer consists of multiple convolutional kernels with time dimension w and variable dimension s. The convolutional kernels slide along the time axis and connect PM2.5 data from six stations at each moment by assigning different weights to them, and multiple 1D convolutional kernels can learn multiple feature vector representations from different aspects. Multiple feature vectors are combined along the data dimension to form multi-site PM2.5 spatial correlation features. The convolution process is shown in Fig. 4.

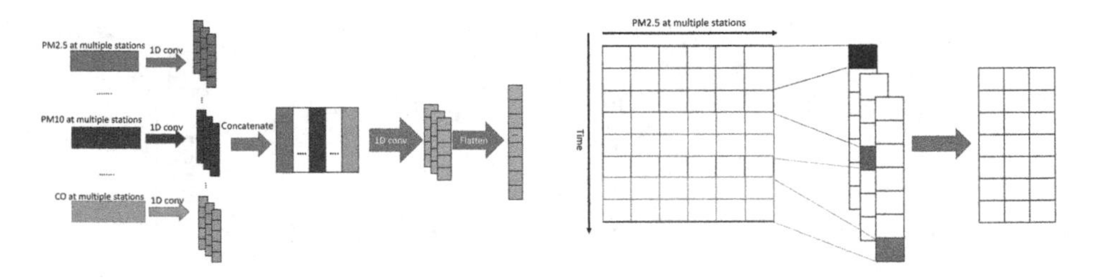

Fig. 3. Framework of CNN module

Fig. 4. The process of 1D conv

The operation of the i-th convolution filter can be expressed as following equation.

$$ki = relu(W_i \cdot P + b) \tag{4}$$

where W_i ($W_i \in R^{w \times s}$) is the weight matrix of the ith convolution kernel, and $\cdot$ is convolution operation. The output size of the convolution with a filter is $1 \times T_c$, $T_c = T - w + 1$, the output of k filters is $k \times T_c$.

The multi-site input matrices of various pollutants pass through the first one-dimensional convolutional layer respectively to form their respective spatial association features, and we connect the spatial association features of each pollutant along the data dimension and then send them to the second one-dimensional convolutional layer, which is a convolutional process that mainly learns the interaction relationships between different pollutants and finally obtains the spatial feature matrix for the fusion of multiple pollutants. The final output of our two-layer 1D convolution is flattened as the final output of this module.

3.3 Fusion and Forecasting

The last part is the output layer consisting of a fully connected network, which takes as input the MLSTM output vector and the output vector of the convolutional layer, connects the two components to learn all spatio-temporal shared features, combines these features in series, and uses a hidden layer to learn higher-order interactions. The final output is the predicted concentration of a single pollutant for the next six consecutive hours, and the network nodes in the output layer are calculated as following equation.

$$\hat{y} = W_p^t[h, c] + b_p \tag{5}$$

where W_p is the nerve weight vector of the prediction layer, b_p term is bias vector. h and c are the outputs of MLSTM module and CNN module respectively.

4 Experimental Scene Design

In this paper, we use the example of predicting PM2.5 in air pollutants, using historical 24-h data to predict PM2.5 concentrations for six consecutive hours in the future. We use data from a specific city in North China to conduct the experiment.

4.1 Data Sources

we uses three types of data related to air pollution in a city to make predictions, including multi-station air pollution data, urban meteorological data, and other features data.

Multi-station Air Pollution Data. The air pollution data used in this paper were obtained from the real-time national urban air quality release platform of the China National Environmental Monitoring Center, from which hourly data were extracted for six air quality monitoring stations in the city from 2017–2020, including air pollution index, PM2.5, PM10, SO2, NO2, O3, CO and their statistical features.

Urban Meteorological Data. The meteorological dataset comes from the meteorological data source of NCDC (National Climatic Data Center), which records the hourly meteorological data of the city 2017–2020 with meteorological elements: temperature, barometric pressure, dew point, wind direction and speed, cloudiness, and precipitation.

Other Features Data. In addition to the above two types of data, we also collected other data, including year, month, day, season, week, and holiday information.

4.2 Data Preprocessing

Before training the model, we need to perform some processing on the data to make it easier to use. First, missing data can lead to periodic misalignment of the time series, so we fill in the missing values for the small amount of missing values in the air pollutant data and meteorological data. Second, the magnitudes used for different feature data are different, and we will also normalize all data. Finally, in order to evaluate the model reasonably, we will also divide the training set data validation set data and test set data.

Missing Value Processing. For discrete data, we use the closest complement method to fill the missing values, for continuous data, if there are less than six consecutive missing values, we use the linear interpolation method to fill them, if there are more than six consecutive missing values, we use the random forest prediction to fill them, if there are still missing values after processing, then we use the closest complement method to fill the missing values.

Normalization. Since different variables are measured in different units, in order to make the model converge in the training process, the original data need to be dimensionless before building the model, and the approach taken in this paper is min-max normalization.

Data Set Division. Because the features of time series have time correlation, the order of data in the training set cannot be disrupted. Moreover, the changes of air pollutants vary drastically in different time periods each year, so we cannot simply take the data set of a certain time period as the test and validation. Therefore, in this paper, we use the first 75%, i.e., the first three years of data as the training set, and the data of the latter year are randomly divided into the validation and test sets in the ratio of measurement 1:1.

4.3 Implementation Details

In our model, a single-layer MLSTM is constructed with a hidden size of 128 and the number of interaction rounds in the MLSTM is set to 3. The CNN module contains two layers of one-dimensional convolution, each layer contains three convolutional kernels, the length of the convolutional kernel in the first layer and the convolutional kernel in the second layer are both 3 (time dimension), and the activation function is relu. Use droupout to reduce the occurrence of overfitting and set it to 0.5. The network is trained using Adam optimizer, MSELoss is chosen as the loss function, and early stop is used to end the training.

We compare our model with three baseline deep learning models, including the most basic recurrent network RNN, and two adaptations of the RNN, the LSTM and GRU [20]. RNN is an artificial neural network that takes sequential data as input and recurses in the direction of the sequence. The connections between nodes form a directed graph along the time series. LSTM is a special recurrent neural network based on a simple recurrent network with three gates, an input gate, an oblivion gate and an output gate. GRU is a specific recurrent neural network with a gate mechanism. GRU has two gates, a reset gate and an update gate. In order to compare the effect of adding CNN modules, our approach will also be compared with MLSTM without incorporating CNN modules.

In this paper, the baseline models and CMLSTM are constructed based on the deep learning framework of pytorch. All experiments are conducted on a PC server with AMD Ryzen 7 4800H with Radeon Graphics, 2.90 GHz and 16 GB of RAM.

4.4 Metrics

We use MAE, RMSE and R2 to evaluate the prediction accuracy of different models.

$$MAE = \frac{1}{n}\sum_{i=1}^{n}|y_i - \hat{y}_i|$$
$$RMSE = \sqrt{\frac{1}{n}\sum_{i=1}^{n}(y_i - \hat{y}_i)^2} \tag{6}$$
$$R2 = 1 - \frac{\sum_{i=1}^{n}(y_i - \hat{y}_i)^2}{\sum_{i=1}^{n}(y_i - \bar{y}_i)^2}$$

5 Results and Analysis

In this paper, we will analyze the experimental results from three aspects. First, we will compare the CMLSTM with the baseline models and then evaluate the prediction accuracy of the different models. Second, we will discuss the problems that appear in the test set. Finally, we will show the prediction effectiveness of CMLSTM by visualization and analyze it.

5.1 Evaluate Prediction Accuracy

Table 1 shows the performance of CMLSTM and other methods. It can be seen that CMLSTM has lower MAE, lower RMSE and higher R2 than the other models. Therefore, it can be inferred that CMLSTM has higher prediction accuracy than the other methods. Compared with LSTM, the MAE of the CMLSTM model proposed in this paper decreases by 24%, the RMSE decreases by 10%, and the R2 increases by 8%. We can see that the RNN with the gate mechanism performs better than the traditional RNN, because the gate mechanism effectively solves the problem of RNN gradient disappearance and has a better learning ability for long sequence data. The results show that the performance is slightly worse than that of the LSTM, but the difference is not significant. The reason is that GRU model is a partial simplification of the LSTM, and its ability to handle complex data may be slightly lower than that of the LSTM. The MLSTM proposed in this paper as a prediction method for air pollutants shows a lower error than other recurrent neural networks because it can better learn the contextual interaction of time series data. And we can infer that although features from other stations are added to the input MLSTM, the model does not learn spatial features sufficiently due to the complexity and diversity of the various input features, and the performance of the model is further improved by further fusion of CNN to extract spatial features.

Table 1. Average performance for six hours of continuous prediction

Method	MAE	RMSE	R2
RNN	20.397	35.51	0.666
GRU	16.818	34.095	0.692
LSTM	16.101	33.567	0.701
MLSTM	13.535	31.145	0.743
CMLSTM	12.298	30.171	0.756

5.2 Evaluate Prediction Accuracy After Removing Extreme Values

Because in the last year of data, there were 4 h on January 25 when PM2.5 exceeded 1000, which belonged to extreme haze weather. Due to the way the RMSE is calculated, the occurrence of such extreme values will have a large impact on the RMSE and also on other judging criteria. In order to compare each model more fully, we removed these extreme values and compared them again, and the results are shown in Table 2. The RMSE was found to have changed significantly. For each model, it remains certain that CMLSTM has the best performance. Compared with LSTM, the MAE of the CMLSTM model proposed in this paper decreases by 25%, the RMSE decreases by 17%, and the R2 increases by 12%.

Table 2. Performance after removal of extreme values

Method	MAE	RMSE	R2
RNN	19.939	30.678	0.672
GRU	16.282	27.618	0.734
LSTM	15.638	28.199	0.723
MLSTM	13.027	24.837	0.785
CMLSTM	11.747	23.469	0.808

5.3 Demonstrate Predicted Effects

From the most polluted winter season (from December to February of the following year), we selected 500 hours and compared the real and predicted curves with the data of the 1st, 3rd and 6th hours of the six consecutive predicted hours. As can be seen from Fig. 5, Fig. 6 and Fig. 7, the desired results were obtained for each hour of the forecast. Although the error in multi-step prediction increases with the prediction step, and the accuracy of the latter hours is significantly lower than that of the first hours, we see that the overall performance of the predictions for these hours is good, and even for the 6th hour, our model can accurately predict the trend.

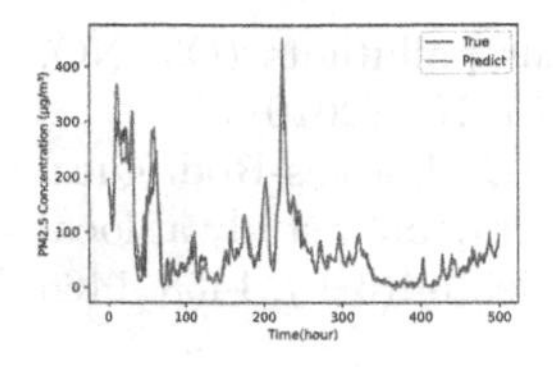

Fig. 5. 1st hour

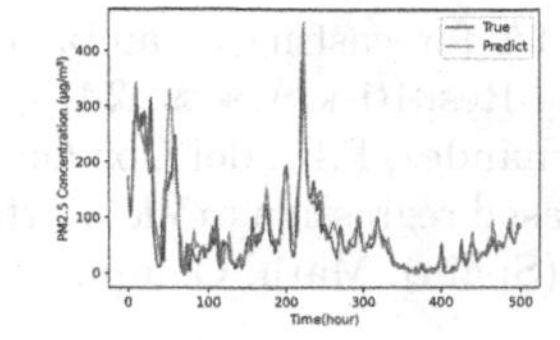

Fig. 6. 3rd hour

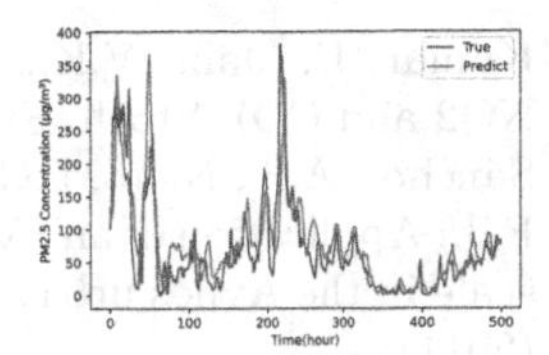

Fig. 7. 6th hour

6 Conclusion

In this paper, we proposed an air pollutant prediction model that fuses Mogrifier LSTM and CNN, i.e., CMLSTM model, to predict single air pollutant for the next six hours. We used MLSTM to extract the temporal features of the data. MLSTM is better able to learn the contextual interactions and is more capable of mining the data. We used CNN to extract the spatial interactions of air pollutants at each station, and the predictive power of the whole model is further enhanced by MLSTM after combining the spatial features extracted by CNN. We experimentally verified that our model has higher accuracy than the baseline models on real data.

Acknowledgement. This work was supported in part by the Inner Mongolia Science and Technology Plan Project (No. 2020GG0187), and Inner Mongolia Engineering Laboratory for Cloud Computing and Service Software, Inner Mongolia Key Laboratory of Social Computing and Data Processing.

References

1. Verma, I., Ahuja, R., Meisheri, H., Dey, L.: Air pollutant severity prediction using Bi-directional LSTM Network. In: 2018 IEEE/WIC/ACM International Conference on Web Intelligence (WI), pp. 651–654. IEEE (2018)
2. Krishan, M., Jha, S., Das, J., et al.: Air quality modelling using long short-term memory (LSTM) over NCT-Delhi. India. Air Qual. Atmos. Health **12**(8), 899–908 (2019)
3. Wang, J., Li, J., Wang, X., Wang, J., Huang, M.: Air quality prediction using CT-LSTM. Neural Comput. Appl. **33**(10), 4779–4792 (2020). https://doi.org/10.1007/s00521-020-05535-w
4. Zhao, J., Deng, F., Cai, Y., Chen, J.: Long short-term memory-Fully connected (LSTM-FC) neural network for PM2.5 concentration prediction. Chemosphere **220**, 486–492 (2019)
5. Wen, C., et al.: A novel spatiotemporal convolutional long short-term neural network for air pollution prediction. Sci. Total Environ. **654**, 1091–1099 (2019)
6. Melis, G., Ko čiský, T., Blunsom, P.: Mogrifier LSTM. In: International Conference on Learning Representations, pp. 1–13 (2020)
7. Binkowski, F.S., Roselle, S.J.: Models-3 Community Multiscale Air Quality (CMAQ) model aerosol component 1. Model description. J. Geophys. Res. Atmos. **108**(D6) (2003)

8. Kumar, U., Jain, V.K.: ARIMA forecasting of ambient air pollutants (O3, NO, NO2 and CO). Stoch. Environ. Res. Risk Assess. **24**(5), 751–760 (2010)
9. Sánchez, A.S., Nieto, P.G., Fernández, P.R., del Coz Díaz, J.J., Iglesias-Rodríguez, F.J.: Application of an SVM-based regression model to the air quality study at local scale in the Avilés urban area (Spain). Math. Comput. Model. **54**(5–6), 1453–1466 (2011)
10. Yu, R., Yang, Y., Yang, L., Han, G., Move, O.A.: RAQ-A random forest approach for predicting air quality in urban sensing systems. Sensors **16**(1), 86 (2016)
11. Xie, H., Ma, F., Bai, Q.: Prediction of indoor air quality using artificial neural networks. In: 2009 Fifth International Conference on Natural Computation, pp. 414–418 (2009)
12. Cui, R., Liu, M.: RNN-based longitudinal analysis for diagnosis of Alzheimer's disease. Comput. Med. Imaging Graph. **73**, 1–10 (2019)
13. Hochreiter, S., Schmidhuber, J.: Long short-term memory. Neural Comput. **9**(8), 1735–1780 (1997)
14. Chen, K., Zhou, Y., Dai, F.: A LSTM-based method for stock returns prediction: a case study of China stock market. In: 2015 IEEE International Conference on Big Data (Big Data), pp. 2823–2824. IEEE (2015)
15. Qin, Y., Song, D., Chen, H., Cheng, W., Jiang, G., Cottrell, G.: A dual-stage attention-based recurrent neural network for time series prediction. arXiv preprint arXiv:1704.02971 (2017)
16. Chang, Y.S., Chiao, H.T., Abimannan, S., Huang, Y.P., Tsai, Y.T., Lin, K.M.: An LSTM-based aggregated model for air pollution forecasting. Atmos. Pollut. Res. **11**(8), 1451–1463 (2020)
17. Cheng, W., Shen, Y., Zhu, Y., Huang, L.: A neural attention model for urban air quality inference: learning the weights of monitoring stations. In: Thirty-Second AAAI Conference on Artificial Intelligence, pp. 2151–2158 (2018)
18. Qiu, H., Zheng, Q., Msahli, M., Memmi, G., Qiu M., Lu, J.: Topological graph convolutional network-based urban traffic flow and density prediction. In: IEEE Transactions on Intelligent Transportation Systems, pp. 4560–4569 (2021)
19. Han, Y., Zhang, Q., Li, V.O., Lam, J.C.: Deep-AIR: a hybrid CNN-LSTM framework for air quality modeling in metropolitan cities. arXiv preprint arXiv:2103.14587 (2021)
20. Cho, K., et al.: Learning phrase representations using RNN encoder-decoder for statistical machine translation. In: Proceedings of the 2014 Conference on Empirical Methods in Natural Language Processing, pp. 1724–1734 (2014)

A Multi-objective Evolutionary Algorithm Based on Multi-layer Network Reduction for Community Detection

Xin Qi[1], Langzhou He[1], Jiaxin Wang[4], Zhanwei Du[3], Zheng Luo[1], and Xianghua Li[1,2](✉)

[1] College of Computer and Information Science, Southwest University, Chongqing 400715, China
li_xianghua@163.com
[2] School of Artificial Intelligence, Optics and Electronics (iOPEN), Northwestern Polytechnical University, Xi'an 710072, China
[3] School of Public Health, The University of Hong Kong, Hong Kong, China
zwdu@hku.hk
[4] State Grid Information and Telecommunication Group Co. Ltd., Beijing, China
wangjiaxin1@sgitg.sgcc.com.cn

Abstract. Community detection is an important method to reveal the characteristics of complex systems, which usually requires the system to meet the conditions of close connections within communities but sparse connections between communities. In view of this, community detection has been proven to be an NP-hard problem. Multi-objective evolutionary algorithm (MOEA) is an indispensable aspect of multi-layer network community detection. However, most MOEA-based multi-layer network detection algorithms only take the acquired prior information as the network preprocessing method and ignore its full utilization in optimization, resulting in the accuracy of network partition cannot be guaranteed. To this end, this paper proposes a multi-objective community detection algorithm based on multi-layer network reduction (MOEA-MR). Specifically, we use the non-negative matrix factorization method to generate the consistent prior information layer of multi-layer network. Based on this, a network reduction strategy based on node degree is constructed to recursively reduce the size of the prior information network. In addition, in the evolution process, we consider using the multi-layer network similarity to correct the mis-divided nodes in the local reduction community. Compared with other advanced community detection algorithms, the experimental results on the real-world and synthetic multi-layer networks proved the superiority of MOEA-MR.

Keywords: Multi-layer network reduction · Community detection · Multi-objective evolution · Consensus prior information · Dice similarity

1 Introduction

A variety of complex systems in the real world can be modeled as complex networks [1,2]. The traditional single-layer network can no longer meet the

G. Memmi et al. (Eds.): KSEM 2022, LNAI 13370, pp. 141–152, 2022.
https://doi.org/10.1007/978-3-031-10989-8_12

requirement of the existing research which focuses on diversified entities, so the multi-layer network with richer attributes has gradually become a research hotspot [3]. Community detection is essential to the understanding of the information and function of networks. Its overall goal is to divide a network into multiple clusters (communities). Many existing community detection algorithms focus on the topology of network, and require the sparse connections of intra-cluster but dense connections of inter-cluster. The current single-layer network clustering methods are relatively mature. For example, Girvan et al. propose the GN algorithm, which applies the concept of modularity function to network clustering for the first time [4]. Louvain algorithm obtains the network clustering results by optimizing the modularity repeatedly [5]. However, due to the complex characteristics of multi-layer networks, the single-layer network clustering methods applied on multi-layer networks have suboptimal performance.

Therefore, multi-layer network community detection algorithms based on different strategies were proposed in the past few years. Since the process of community detection is an NP-hard problem and Pareto optimal framework can provide a set of optimal compromise solutions based on optimization goals, the optimization algorithm has received great attention. According to the number of optimization goals, these algorithms can be divided into two types: single-objective optimization and multi-objective optimization. For single-objective optimization methods, only one objective function is selected for optimization in the iterative process. For example, GACD algorithm obtains good clustering results by optimizing modularity [6]. Pizzuti et al. implement network clustering by optimizing the fitness function [7]. For multi-objective methods that consider multiple objective functions simultaneously, the multi-objective evolution algorithm (MOEA) is strongly competitive in optimization calculations. For example, MOGA-Net algorithm introduces two functions (i.e., the community score and community fitness) for optimization calculation [8]. Moreover, Shi et al. use the concept of inter-objective correlation to develop a multi-objective optimization framework [9]. Furthermore, MOGA-@Net algorithm takes the structure of community and the similarity of nodes into consideration in order to obtain a high-quality solution [10]. Compared with single-objective optimization algorithms, multi-objective methods perform better because they focus on the links between the inter-community and intra-community simultaneously. However, the individual length of network code is proportional to the number of network nodes, which means that the search space of MOEA increases exponentially. What's more, they usually only take the topology information of network into full consideration without paying attention to the prior information.

To address the above problems, this paper proposes a multi-objective evolutionary algorithm based on multi-layer network reduction (MOEA-MR), which is used for community clustering in multi-layer networks. In the proposed MOEA-MR, a reduction strategy is used for network processing, which is based on the network consensus prior information layer, and the repairing strategy in the optimization process further improves the quality of network division. Specifically, the main contributions of this paper can be summarized as follows:

- The symmetric non-negative matrix factorization method is suggested for better applying the prior information of multi-layer networks. With this strategy, we obtain the non-negative low-dimensional representations of each network layer, and fuse them into a consensus prior information representation to enable clustering interpretation.
- A network reduction strategy based on the node degree is proposed for complex network clustering to reduce the computational complexity effectively. Specifically, local communities can be transformed into nodes of reduced network during the optimization, which is gainful for improving the scalability of large-scale multi-layer network.
- A network repairing strategy is proposed to correct the misidentified nodes after multi-layer network reduction, which helps improve the accuracy of clustering result.

The rest of the paper is organized as follows. Section 2 introduces the related work. The proposed MOEA-MR method is described in detail in Sect. 3. After that, Sect. 4 compares our proposed algorithm with several advanced network clustering methods. Finally, Sect. 5 gives a summary of this paper.

2 Related Work

The main goal of community detection is to divide a network into different subgraphs, among which the internal connections are maximized while the external links are minimized. In complex networks, these subgraphs are also called communities. Unlike single-layer networks, each layer of multi-layer network represents a kind of relationship. This means that we need to consider the information of different layers when clustering the network, and find a final partition that is most suitable for each layer of multi-layer network. An example of multi-layer network clustering is provided in Fig. 1.

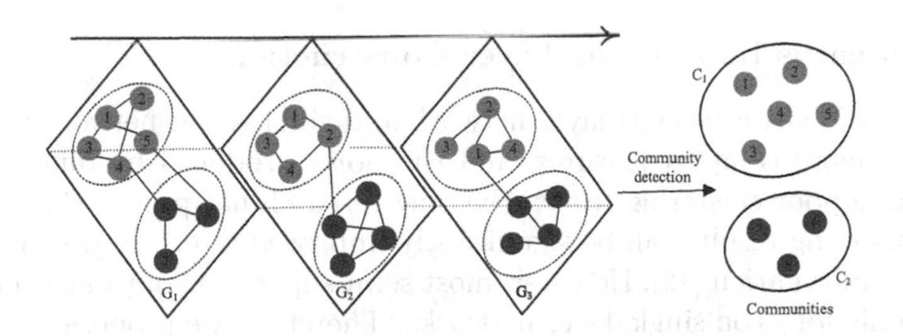

Fig. 1. Illustration of multi-layer networks with 8 nodes given in three different layers (i.e., G_1, G_2, and G_3). Two different color communities (i.e., C_1, C_2) can be identified in all layers.

For better multi-layer network clustering, several standard functions are proposed to measure the link density of inter-community and intra-community.

Here we formulate the multi-layer network clustering into a two-objective clustering optimization problem, utilizing ratio cut (RC) and kernel k-means (KKM) [11] as the objective function. Given a multi-layer network $G = (V, E_m)$ $(m = 1, ..., M)$, where M represents the total number layers of multi-layer network and E_m denotes the edge set of the mth layer. Moreover, $V = \{v_i\}_{i=1}^{N}$ indicates a set of nodes shared by all layers in G. The adjacency matrix of multilayer network is expressed as: $A^{(m)} \in R_+^{N*N}(m = 1, ..., M)$. The definition of bi-objective minimization problem is shown in Eq. (1).

$$\min \begin{cases} KKM = 2(N - c) - \sum_{i=1}^{c} \frac{L(V_i, V_i)}{|V_i|} \\ RC = \sum_{i=1}^{c} \frac{L(V_i, \overline{V}_i)}{|V_i|} \end{cases} \tag{1}$$

where c is the number of multi-layer network division. $L(V_i, V_i)$ and $L(V_i, \overline{V}_i)$ represent the internal and external connection density in the same community i, respectively. KKM means the density of intra-community, and RC denotes the density of inter-community. So far, KKM and RC have broad applications in MOEA algorithm and achieve a good performance. Therefore, we also adopt the same functions as optimization objectives.

3 Proposed Method

In this section, we present a detailed introduction of the proposed MOEA-MR. First, owing to the fact that the construction of multi-layer network consensus information and the network reduction method are essential to MOEA-MR, we describe them in Sect. 3.1 and 3.2 in detail respectively. After that, we explain the community repairing strategy based on the similarity information in Sect. 3.3, which is used to modify and simplify the dis-divided nodes in the local network. Section 3.4 demonstrates the genetic operators. Finally, the comprehensive framework of MOEA-MR is illustrated in Sect. 3.5.

3.1 Consensus Information Layer Construction

The difference between multi-layer network and single-layer network is that the former has more complex features, and the noise produced by different layers can lead to a poor clustering result. Existing research has proved that the accuracy of clustering results can be significantly improved after integrating the network prior information [12]. However, most semi-supervised optimized clustering methods only focus on single-layer networks. Therefore, we propose a concept of multi-layer network optimization clustering based on the prior information.

Up to now, the symmetric non-negative matrix factorization method has been successfully applied to network clustering problem [13], so our work also takes the idea into consideration to obtain the prior information of multi-layer networks. Firstly, each network layer is denoised by calculating its non-negative low-dimensional representation. After that, we fuse the low-dimensional representations of all layers into a common consensus information layer, which is applied to subsequent optimization process to improve the effectiveness of MOEA-MR algorithm. In particular, given a network represented by an N-layered adjacency matrix $(A_1, A_2, ..., A_n)$, Eq. (2) is utilized to get the consensus information layer of the multi-layer network.

$$A_{\text{cons}} = \frac{\sum_{i=1}^{n} A^{(i)} + \gamma H^{(i)} H^{(i)T}}{n(1+\gamma)} \tag{2}$$

where γ represents a constant. For each network layer i, we have the following constraints: $A^{(i)} \approx HH^T, H > 0$ and $H^T H = I$. We interpret A_{cons} as the consensus information matrix of extracting potential communities shared by the multilayer network and apply it to the clustering coding.

3.2 Network Reduction Strategy

To reduce the computational complexity of algorithm, a network reduction strategy is proposed to reduce the network scale during the process of optimization. Moreover, when the network topology is used for multi-objective network clustering based on genetic operations, some nodes are always in an indivisible group. Therefore, we can regard these indivisible nodes as a whole in the calculation, which will remain unchanged even in the later optimization.

The description of network reduction process proposed in this paper is given as follows. Considering that the network degree is an important feature of network adjacency matrix, our reduction strategy takes the node degree as an important division criterion. At first, the node with the largest degree is selected as an initial node after calculating degrees of all nodes in a network. Then we divide the initial node and its neighbors into a tentative community, and check all the nodes in it. Note that the node in the tentative community will be removed if the external connections number is more than half degree of itself. Finally, the tentative community after inspection can be guaranteed as a strong community, and all components in the tentative community are reduced to one node. Checking all remaining nodes of network until they have been completely represented as the reduced community.

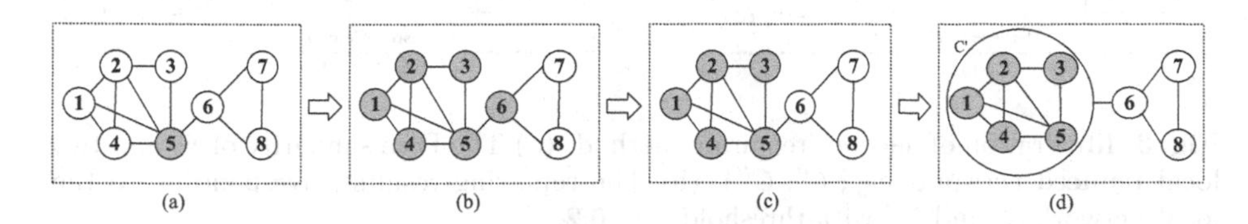

Fig. 2. Illustration of reduction strategies. (a) v_5 is selected due to its largest node degree. (b) The tentative community determined by v_5 contains $\{v_1, v_2, v_3, v_4, v_5, v_6\}$. (c) Delete v_6 from the subgraph. (d) The subgraph C' consists $\{v_1, v_2, v_3, v_4, v_5\}$ is compressed into one node based on the reduction strategy.

Figure 2 gives an example about representing the main idea of prereduction process, which considers a network with 8 nodes. First, the tentative community $\{v_1,v_2,v_3,v_4,v_5,v_6\}$ depicted in Fig. 2(b) is obtained based on v_5. Then, v_6 is eliminated because the links between this node and tentative subgraph $\{v_1,v_2,v_3,v_4,v_5,v_6\}$ are less than half of its degree, as shown in Fig. 2(c). Finally, by merging $\{v_1,v_2,v_3,v_4,v_5\}$ into one node, Fig. 2(d) shows the reduced network $\{C',v_6,v_7,v_8\}$.

3.3 Network Repairing Method

There are some reduced networks being found incorrect in the iterative evolution. To put it simply, the reduced network may find some nodes do not belong to itself, which is prone to lead to the poor performance of MOEA-MR. In order to settle this problem, we propose a reduced network repairing strategy based on the similarity prior information to correct the mis-divided nodes.

The similarity index of node is one of the most powerful indicators to evaluate the connectivity strength with node pairs. In order to preserve the structural characteristics of multi-layer networks, *Dice* index [14] based on the connections of all layers is determined to calculate the similarity prior information of multi-layer network, which can be depicted in Eq. (3).

$$D_s = \frac{2 \times Neighbours_{com}\left(v_i, v_j\right)}{Deg\left(v_i\right) + Deg\left(v_j\right)} \tag{3}$$

where $Neighbours_{\text{com}}\left(v_i, v_j\right)$ indicates the links of common neighbors of nodes v_i and v_j, and $Deg\left(v_i\right)$ means the degree of node v_i. It can be seen that the equation mentioned above considers the neighbors information of all layers when calculating the neighbor links of nodes.

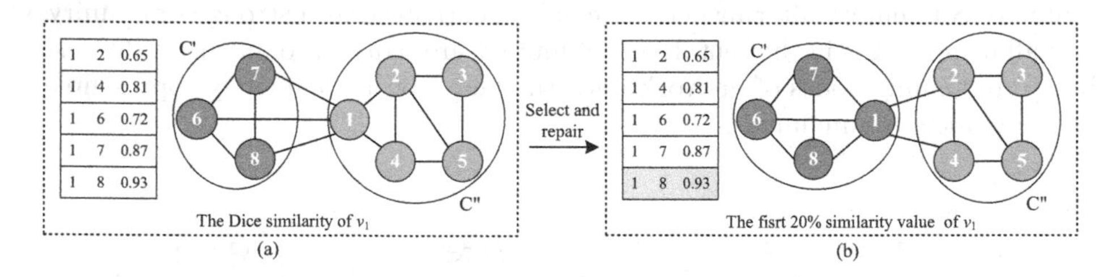

Fig. 3. Illustration of network repairing method. (a) The Dice similarity of v_1 and two local reduced network (e.g., C', C''). (b) The repairing results corresponding to the local network C' and C'' with threshold $\sigma = 0.2$.

After obtaining the similarity prior information of multi-layer network, the steps of the reduced network repairing strategy in this paper perform as follows. Specifically, for each community in the reduced network, checking whether the nodes it contains are selected in the same community with their most similar neighbor. If not, the nodes verified are mis-divided and need to be moved to other appropriate community. What's more, we give a threshold σ to judge the similarity of the node pairs, which means only the first σ% of node similarities are taken into consideration. In that case, we need to give up those smaller similarity value. Figure 3 shows the repairing strategy based on the reduced network with 8 nodes, and threshold σ is equal to 0.2. After repairing, the final reduced network changes to $\{v_1,v_6,v_7,v_8\}$ and $\{v_2,v_3,v_4,v_5\}$. By correcting the mis-divided nodes in reduction network, the quality of the final community division is greatly improved.

3.4 Encoding Method and Genetic Operators

This paper adopts the locus-based encoding method. In this coding method, each chromosome gene corresponds to a network node, and the gene value represents a neighbor of the node. In other words, there is a connection between nodes v_i and v_j if the ith gene value is j, and they are also in the same clustering. Figure 4(a) shows the locus-based encoding method with 7 network nodes, and Pop_1 represents the corresponding gene value. Different from the label-based coding, the method mentioned above does not need to define the number of communities beforehand, which greatly reduces the search space but also conducives to the genetic operator operation in the evolution.

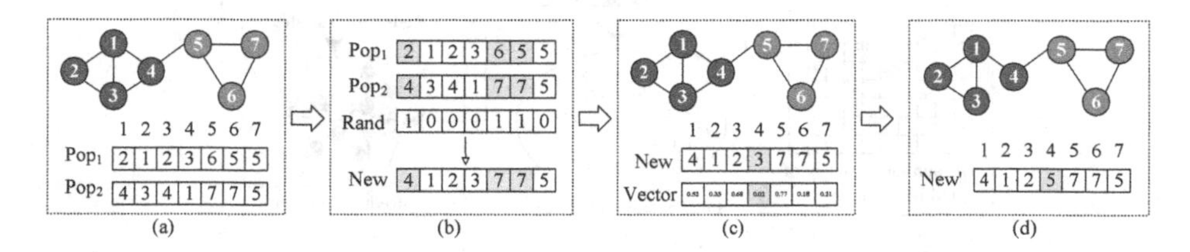

Fig. 4. Illustration of genetic operators. (a) The complex network used for the crossover operation and its two locus-based encoding individuals. (b) The value of offspring individual *New* is determined by *Rand*. If *Rand* = 1, the offspring chooses the value of Pop_2, otherwise Pop_1 will be taken into consideration. (c) The mutation operation adopts the *Vector* selected randomly in range of [0,1], in which the gene value of node is mutated to the index of its adjacent node if the value of corresponding vector is less than 0.1. (d) The newly mutated individual *New′* and its structure.

Genetic operators are important for exploration and exploitation of MOEA. In this paper, we use the uniform crossover and neighborhood-based mutation to improve the population diversity. The former is adopted because of its randomness. Specifically, we select parents to crossover and generate the offspring by randomly yielding a set of binary values, which own the same length with population. If the binary value is 0, the first parent is selected, otherwise, the second is selected. At the same time, the local information is taken into neighbor-based mutation, which selects the neighbors of parent-population for mutation according to the predefined mutation probability. The illustration of crossover and mutation operators is shown in Fig. 4.

3.5 General Framework of MOEA-MR

The proposed MOEA-MR utilizes a decomposition-based genetic algorithm framework (MOEA/D) [15], in which the multi-objective optimization problem is disassembled for a set of single-objective sub-problems according to the Tchebycheff definition in Eq. (4).

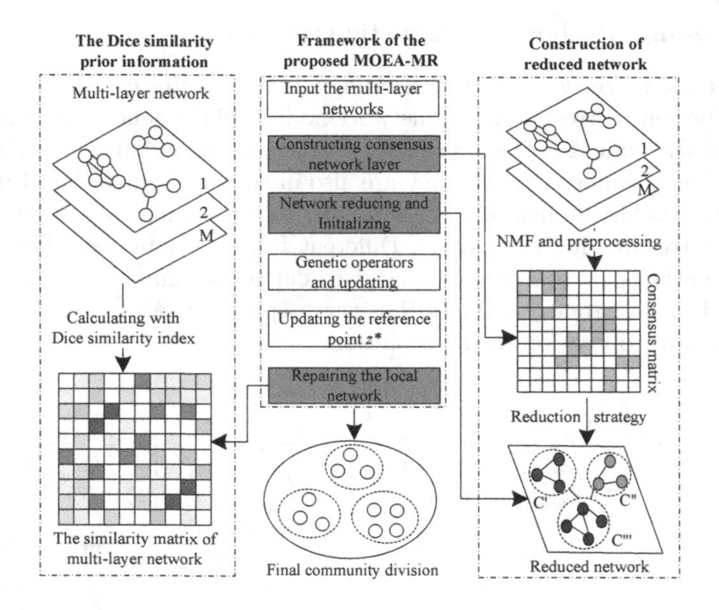

Fig. 5. The flow chart of the proposed MOEA-MR algorithm with four main steps.

$$\min g^{te}(x \mid w, z^*) = \max_{i=1}^{2} \{w_i \cdot (|F_i(x) - z_i^*|)\} \tag{4}$$

where $w = (w_1, w_2)$ with the constraints $\|w\|_2 = 1, w_1, w_2 > 0$. $z^* = (z_1^*, z_2^*)$ is a reference point and z_i^* is the minimal value of the ith objective function.

Figure 5 shows the overall flow of our proposed MOEA-MR algorithm with the following four main steps. At the beginning, the consensus information layer of a multilayer network is generated by exploiting the non-negative matrix factorization technology. Next, compressing the consensus information layer into a reduction network with the reduction strategy. At the third step, the population is initialized based on the locus-based encoding method. Meanwhile, the reference point z^* assigned by using the minimal values of KKM and RC is prepared for clustering. Finally, for each individual population, applying the uniform crossover and neighborhood-based mutation stagey to generate offspring chromosome. If the Tchebycheff value of offspring chromosome performs better than any existing chromosomes, the latter will be replaced. In particular, the repairing strategy suggested above is applied to correct misidentified nodes in the reduced network until reaching the maximal iteration of MOEA-MR.

4 Experiment

4.1 Experimental Design

Datasets and Comparison Algorithms. We test all algorithms on synthetic datasets and real-world datasets, where the former is produced based on the multilayer LFR benchmark (mLFR) [3]. Compared with other forms, the mLFR benchmark can control the community structure by adjusting the node degrees and the mixing parameters (μ) in multilayer networks. The value of μ ranges in $(0, 1)$, and the larger the μ value is, the more complex the community structure is. In addition to synthetic networks (e.g., Sdata1, Sdata2 and Sdata3), the real-world networks we consider include five different types and sizes (i.e., SND [16], MPD [16], WBN [16], CoRA [16], CiteSeer [16]). The basic description of datasets is listed in Table 1. What's more, the performance of MOEA-MR is compared with other classic community detection algorithms, namely, MOEA-MultiNet [17] (based on MOEA), GMC [19] (based on multi-view clustering), S2-jNMF [3], COMCLUS [18] and CSNMF [13] (based on matrix factorization).

Table 1. The description of synthetic networks and real-world networks.

Network	Layers	Nodes	Ground truth
SND	3	71	3
MPD	3	87	6
WBN	10	279	10
CoRA	2	1662	3
CiteSeer	2	3312	3
Sdata1	2	1000	6
Sdata2	3	5000	10
Sdata3	3	10000	16

Evaluation Metrics and Parameter Settings. To evaluate the quality of network clustering, this paper adopts two widely-used indicators, namely Normalized Mutual Information (NMI) [13] and Adjusted Rand Index (ARI) [13]. Both synthetic network and real-world networks can evaluate the similarity between the ground truth and division detected by algorithms. NMI and ARI use the value range from $[0, 1]$. If $NMI(A, B) = 0$, the division A and B are completely different; if $NMI(A, B) = 1$, the division A is the same with B, so ARI does. In the proposed MOEA-MR, the number of iterations is fixed as 200, which is the same as chromosomes, and σ value is set to 30%. It is worth remarking that all algorithms attain the mean value based on 10 dependent runs.

Table 2. Comparisons of several algorithms on real-world and synthetic networks. Note that * means that the algorithm failed to run on this network.

Network	Algorithms	MOEA-MR	MOEA-MultiNet	S2-jNMF	CSNMF	ComClus	GMC
SND	*NMI*	**0.727**	0.437	0.582	0.681	0.555	0.597
	ARI	**0.772**	0.201	0.452	0.493	0.481	0.428
MPD	*NMI*	**0.588**	0.494	0.516	0.504	0.421	0.451
	ARI	**0.499**	0.385	0.396	0.397	0.365	0.248
WBN	*NMI*	**0.457**	0.309	0.347	0.400	0.040	0.161
	ARI	**0.237**	0.142	0.191	0.225	0.167	0.048
CoRA	*NMI*	**0.723**	0.317	0.719	0.514	0.471	0.519
	ARI	**0.768**	0.243	0.626	0.491	0.447	0.526
CiteSeer	*NMI*	**0.301**	*	0.149	0.237	0.182	0.042
	ARI	**0.265**	*	0.147	0.207	0.119	0.012
Sdata1	*NMI*	**1**	*	0.924	0.962	0.943	0.954
	ARI	**1**	*	0.858	0.894	0.722	0.915
Sdata2	*NMI*	**1**	*	0.827	0.980	0.965	0.903
	ARI	**1**	*	0.716	0.991	0.748	0.999
Sdata3	*NMI*	**1**	*	0.452	0.946	0.894	0.999
	ARI	0.954	*	0.074	0.874	0.814	**0.963**

4.2 Experimental Result

In this section, the experiment results of all algorithms mentioned on real-world networks and synthetic networks are shown in Table 2. The experimental results demonstrate that the averaged NMI and ARI of MOEA-MR on Sdata1 and Sdata2 are 1, which means the real partition can be detected. Compared with other algorithms, the accuracy of MOEA-MR on the real-world network increased by nearly double on average. In addition, the performance of MOEA-MultiNet that uses the genetic algorithm framework is not good. This is because the traditional genetic algorithm is prone to fall into the local optimum and the search speed is very slow. Different from the framework mentioned above, the proposed MOEA-MR treats the local community as a node for calculating, which greatly reduces the search space in the large-scale networks, and the subsequent repairing strategy has further improved the accuracy of network division.

It is also shown that GMC has a better performance than MOEA-MR on Sdata3. That's probably due to the node degrees of mLFR network obey the power-law distribution, which makes it difficult to generate the dense local communities when the structure is fuzzy. Given that, we can conclude that for the most datasets, the proposed MOEA-MR is superior to other algorithms in terms of NMI and ARI, which also means that MOEA-MR is more competitive than other algorithms in detection performance.

4.3 Parameter Analysis

Figure 6 provides the experimental results of 10 independent runs based on 4 algorithms with varying similarity thresholds and mixing parameters. For synthetic networks, the larger the mixing parameter is, the fuzzier the network structure is. Figure 6 presents that MOEA-MultiNet algorithm is the most unstable, whereas the proposed MOEA-MR algorithm is completely opposite. In particular, when $\mu > 0.4$, the stability of MOEA-MR begins to decrease. What's more, compared with other options, the similarity threshold σ should also be relatively moderate like the μ value. It is obvious that $\sigma = 0.3$ has the best experimental effect on the algorithm. In short, the results mentioned above prove the influence of parameter settings on the experimental performance and MOEA-MR is superior to other methods on the synthetic dataset.

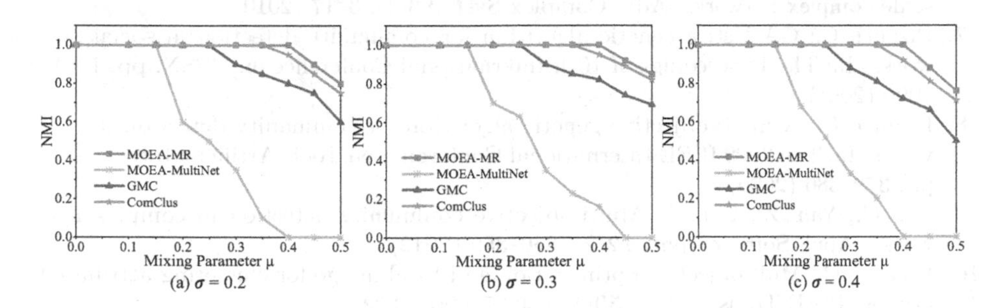

Fig. 6. The experimental result with different μ and σ values on synthetic networks implemented in 4 algorithms.

5 Conclusion

This paper proposed the MOEA-MR for community clustering in multi-layer complex networks. In MOEA-MR, the non-negative matrix factorization is used to generate the consensus prior information layer of multi-layer network. On this basis, a network reduction method based on the node degree is suggested to compress the size of common network in advance. After that, MOEA-MR adopts an algorithm framework based on MOEA/D, and formulates a repairing strategy based on the network similarity to correct the mis-divided nodes in the local network. The extensive results show the effectiveness of MOEA-MR on the network clustering problem based on the bi-objective optimization. In the future, it is desirable to consider extending the network reduction to cluster detection based on more targets owing to the multi-layer network structure is more complicated in reality.

Acknowledgements. This work was supported by the National Key R&D Program of China (2019YFB2102300), National Natural Science Foundation of China (61976181, 11931015), Natural Science Basic Research Plan in Shaanxi Province of China (2022JM-325) and Fundamental Research Funds for the Central Universities (D5000210738).

References

1. Gao, C., Su, Z., Liu, J., Kurths, J.: Even central users do not always drive information diffusion. Commun. ACM **62**(2), 61–67 (2019)
2. Gao, C., Fan, Y., Jiang, S., Deng, Y., Liu, J., Li, X.: Dynamic robustness analysis of a two-layer rail transit network model. IEEE Trans. Intel. Trans. Sys. (2021). https://doi.org/10.1109/TITS.2021.3058185
3. Ma, X., Dong, D.: Community detection in multi-layer networks using joint nonnegative matrix factorization. IEEE Trans. Knowl. Data Eng. **31**(2), 273–286 (2019)
4. Newman, M.E., Girvan, M.: Finding and evaluating community structure in networks. Phys. Rev. E **69**(2), 026113 (2004)
5. Blondel, V., Guillaume, J., Lambiotte, R., Lefebvre, E.: Fast unfolding of communities in large networks. J. Stat. Mech. **8**, P10008 (2008)
6. Shi, C., Yan, Z., Wang, Y.: A genetic algorithm for detecting communities in large-scale complex networks. Adv. Complex Syst. **13**(1), 3–17 (2010)
7. Pizzuti, C.: GA-Net: a genetic algorithm for community detection in social networks. In: The Proceedings of 10th International Conference on PPSN, pp. 1081–1090 (2008)
8. Pizzuti, C.: A multi-objective genetic algorithm for community detection in networks. In: The 2009 IEEE International Conference on Tools Artificial Intelligence, pp. 379–386 (2009)
9. Shi, C., Yan, Z., Cai, Y.: Multi-objective community detection in complex networks. Appl. Soft Comput. **12**(2), 850–859 (2012)
10. Pizzuti, C.: Multiobjective optimization and local merge for clustering attributed graphs. IEEE Trans. Cyber. **50**(12), 4997–5009 (2020)
11. Li, X., Qi, X., Liu, X.: A discrete moth-flame optimization with an l_2-norm constraint for network clustering. IEEE Trans. Net. Sci. Eng. **9**(3), 1776–1788 (2022)
12. Yang, L., Cao, X.: A unified semi-supervised community detection framework using latent space graph regularization. IEEE Trans. Cybern. **45**(11), 2585–2598 (2015)
13. Gligorijevic, V., Zafeiriou, S.: Non-negative matrix factorizations for multiplex network analysis. IEEE Trans. Pattern Anal. Mach. Intell. **41**(4), 928–940 (2019)
14. Xie, Y., Gong, M., Wang, S., Yu, B.: Community discovery in networks with deep sparse filtering. Pattern Recogn. **81**, 50–59 (2018)
15. Zhang, Q., Li, H.: MOEA/D: a multi-objective evolutionary algorithm based on decomposition. IEEE Trans. Evol. Comput. **11**(6), 712–731 (2007)
16. Bródka, P.: A method for group extraction and analysis in multilayer social networks. CoRR abs/1612.02377 (2016)
17. Liu, W., Wang, S.: An improved multiobjective evolutionary approach for community detection in multilayer networks. In: The 2017 IEEE Congress on Evolutionary Computation, Donostia, pp. 443–449 (2017)
18. Ni, J., Cheng, W., Fan, W., Zhang, X.: ComClus: a self-grouping framework for multi-network clustering. IEEE Trans. Knowl. Data Eng. **30**(3), 435–448 (2018)
19. Wang, H., Yang, Y., Liu, B.: GMC: graph-based multi-view clustering. IEEE Trans. Knowl. Data Eng. **32**(6), 1116–1129 (2020)

Detection DDoS of Attacks Based on Federated Learning with Digital Twin Network

Dingling Su and Zehui Qu(✉)

School of Computer and Information Science, Southwest University, Chongqing 400700, P.R. China
sdl19990405@email.swu.edu.cn, quzehui@swu.edu.cn

Abstract. With Intrusion detection algorithms based on deep learning becoming a hot research topic, most studies pay attention to improving detection accuracy but ignore the problem that can not train a high-precision model due to the limited data of each client. This paper proposes an intrusion detection method based on federated learning and the LSTM model to protect the privacy and improve the classification effect in limited data. As a result of the experiments carried out on the KDD CUP 1999 dataset containing the current DDoS attack types, it was observed that the attacks on network traffic were detected with up to 99.17% success. Furthermore, the federated learning model was constructed in the Digital Twin Network (DTN), an emerging network that utilizes digital twin (DT) technology to create the virtual twins of physical objects. It can real-time monitor the status of physical entities and feedback information to entities in time. Meanwhile, we propose a new optimization framework based on FedProx to tackle the system and statistical heterogeneity inherent in federated networks. This framework shows significantly more stable and accurate convergence behaviour and higher detection accuracy than FedProx and FedAvg.

Keywords: Intrusion detection · Distributed denial of service (DDoS) attack · Federated learning · Digital twin · LSTM model

1 Introduction

The Digital Twin (DT) [1–3] has been one of the most significant technology in timely monitoring dynamic situations of the physical model by building a simulation model. Here, DT is composed of a physical object, its virtual digital twin, and a mapping relationship that enables the co-evolution of both physical and virtual sides. The virtual digital twin continually adapts to operational changes based on the online collected data and predicts the state of the physical object. With the emergence of the internet of things, the development of communication modes, and the diversity of service types carried by the network, the network requires high flexibility and, as infrastructure, needs higher reliability. Therefore, digital twin technology is applied to the network to create the

G. Memmi et al. (Eds.): KSEM 2022, LNAI 13370, pp. 153–164, 2022.
https://doi.org/10.1007/978-3-031-10989-8_13

virtual image of the physical network facilities, that is, to build a digital network platform consistent with the physical network elements, topology, and data. The digital network platform can improve network safe and is an effective method for network anomaly detection, such as DDoS attacks mentioned below, which is the main work in this paper.

With the rapid development of computer and communications technology, the network has been the global information systems' most critical media facility. Thus, maintaining network security has become a prerequisite for ensuring the sustainable development of information work in various fields. Distributed Denial of Service (DDoS) attack [4,5] has been one of the most common and unable factors in the network and information environment. Attackers use many zombie machines to simultaneously send several normal or abnormal packets to the target. Ultimately, the target can not provide service due to the system resources or network bandwidth being exhausted or even collapsed [6–8].

In terms of the problem DDoS detection faced regarding the classification effect of variable small sample data, traditional methods, such as traffic cleaning technology based on monitoring and filtering of network traffic [4], signature-based and anomaly-based intrusion detection systems [9], do not have an excellent ability to process single and small data for the current data collection environment, which cause a significant degree of detection error. Artificial intelligence technology at this stage, such as deep learning, is highly dependent on the quantity and diversity of training data. However, due to the limited number of users, a sizeable sample of data is unavailable to a single device. Moreover, many internet privacy legal systems stipulate that raw data from users is not shared with others. Federal learning, a relatively novel machine, is highly suitable for solving the problem that data is stored in separate devices and can not be shared and protect privacy. Therefore, this paper will use it to distinguish abnormal traffic by distributed training.

In our study, there is a complex and efficient mapping relationship between the physical network and digital network platform by integrating the digital twin technology. Then it is aimed to detect DDoS attacks on the dataset by building an intrusion detection system with federated learning. The digital twin network platform can quickly find which client in the physical network is under attack by the detection system through real-time interactivity. Our study is focused on providing the following contributions:

- We construct the federated learning to detect DDoS attacks under the Digital Twin Networks. It does increase not only efficiency but also carries real-time monitoring of clients' status.
- We leverage the federated learning scheme to construct the Digital Twin Networks models, solving the data island problem and protecting data privacy.
- We propose an optimization framework based on FedProx [10] that deals with system and statistical heterogeneity inherent in federated networks and improves model accuracy. Moreover, we choose the LSTM model to detect DDoS attacks due to the correlation between features.

The paper is arranged as follows. In Sect. 2, studies in detecting DDoS attacks are included. In Sect. 3, the theorical background and structure of the proposed model are expressed. Section 4 contains the test environment, assessment criteria and test results. Finally, the general evaluation of the study has been made and future studies have been examined in Sect. 5.

2 Related Work

Under the background of Digital twin, the use of federated learning in DDoS attacks seems to be relatively less proposed than other machine learning. Other algorithms and models are used in many studies to detect DDoS attacks. In this section, the characteristics and shortcomings of these studies are summarized.

The paper [11] adopts the CAT (change-aggregation tree) mechanism to carry out a collaborative analysis of the router traffic flowing through the same ISP network and analyze the flow distribution of each interface to find some abnormalities. A similar flow distribution analysis solution is proposed in [12], but with the requirement that it implements constant or increasing speed flow detection on the backbone network by cross-correlation and weight vector analysis. They do not consider scenarios in which DDoS attacks and heavy traffic access cannot be distinguished. The paper [13] proposes a DDoS detecting method based on a random forest classification model with the classification standard of data flow information entropy. After extracting features from ordinary modes of DDoS attacks, they use their detecting model to distinguish normal or abnormal flow. However, it is only suitable for a single group; the detection accuracy is very low for multiple groups. To deal with the difficulty that traditional DDoS detection mechanism based on SDN controllers lacks network-wide monitoring information or exists serious communication overhead, a new cross-platform collaboration DDoS detection model is proposed in paper [14], called OverWatch. In the structure of OverWatch, they put forward a lightweight flow detection algorithm to capture fundamental eigenvalues of DDoS attack traffic by taking turns asking the values in the counter of the OpenFlow switch.

With the attack means becoming more and more complicated, the above DDoS attack detection has the shortcoming of low detection efficiency, hugely time-consuming, error report, etc. The anomaly detection algorithms based on machine learning can master some standard features by learning from existing intrusion behaviours and are used in many studies to distinguish abnormal traffic from regular traffic. Among these studies, the use of deep learning seems to be more successful than the use of shallow machine learning [15, 16]. The fight against DDoS is the most crucial factor in detecting and separating network traffic. The study [17] summarised the examination of some deep learning model [18–20], it showed that deep learning has a high level of accuracy in the detection of DDoS attacks. Moreover, it also suggested that a deep neural network (DNN) as a deep learning model can work quickly and with high accuracy because it includes feature extraction and classification processes in its structure and has layers that update itself as it is trained. In [21], they propose a DDoS attack detecting method based on a convolutional neural network (CNN), which includes the feature processing and detection model. Although there methods using deep learning in DDoS attacks show better performance, most of them ignore data distribution in real word, which is very unfavorable for their training. Therefore, Our method can solve this problem while ensuring accuracy.

3 Background and Proposed Model

3.1 The Framework of Federated Learning

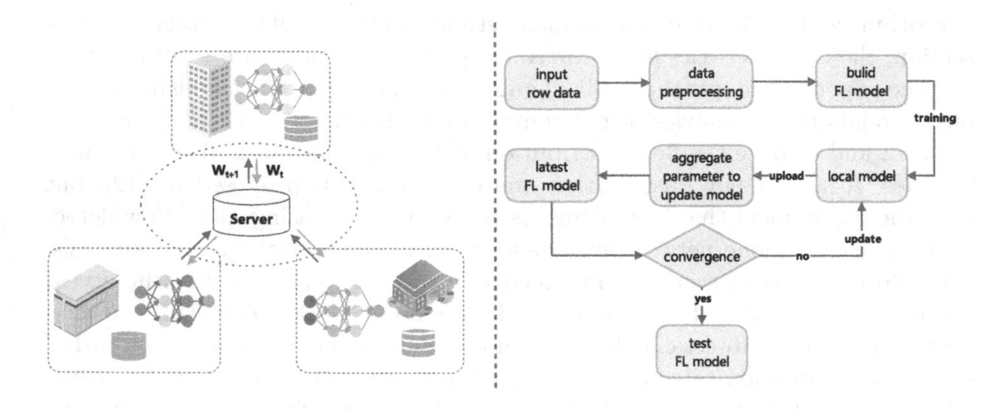

Fig. 1. The structure of federated learning

The DDoS attack detection model based on machine learning needs to extract features and carry out analytical learning on a massive of valid network packets, but whose number is highly few and data type is single for many organizations in many fields. Federated learning, which can leave the training data on a massive number of nodes (devices) and train a shared model by aggregating locally-computed updates, is adopted to solve the problem of data island. In federated learning, participants train their local model and send local weight to the centre unit, such as orchestrating a central server. Then the centre unit will send the global weight to the participant to update the local model. The training process of federated learning is shown in Fig. 1.

Considering the heterogeneity of data and the communication differences between devices in the network environment, the optimization algorithm was raised to reduce the inherent influence of federated learning. In the traditional setting of federated learning, such as the Federated Averaging (Fedavg) algorithm proposed by [22]. At each round, with the same learning rate and the number of local epochs, a subset $K \ll N$ of the total devices are selected and run stochastic gradient descent (SGD) locally for E number of epochs. Then the resulting model updates are averaged. The adjustment of local epochs plays a vital role in convergence. On the one hand, more local epochs can reduce communication, dramatically improving communication convergence speed in communication-constrained networks. On the other hand, a more significant number of local epochs may lead each client to deviate from the optima of the global objective. Moreover, in federated learning with training performance differences among clients and dissimilar systems resources, setting the fixed number of the local epochs may increase the risk that some clients do not complete training in time and therefore drop out of the procedure [23], seriously hurting the performance of convergence. In traditional federated learning methods (e.g., [24]; [22]), the aim of the global learning objective is to minimize:

$$\begin{array}{ll} \min_w f(w) = \sum_{k=1}^{N} p_k F_k(w) = \mathbb{E}_k\left[F_k(w)\right] \\ \text{s.t.} \quad p_k \geq 0, \sum_k p_k = 1, p_k = \frac{n_k}{n} \end{array} \tag{1}$$

To limit the impact of non-IID (identically and independently distributed) variable local updates and make each client towards the optima of the global objective as opposed to its local objective, instead of minimizing the local function $F_k(\cdot)$, the client k use its local solver of choice to minimize the following objective h_k:

$$\min_w h_k(w; w^t) = F_k(w) + \frac{\mu}{2}\left\|w - w^t\right\|^2 \tag{2}$$

Further, γ_k^t-inexact solution is introduced to dynamically adjust the number of local epoches through the imprecise solution of local function, which extremely ensures the tolerance for heterogeneous systems. If w^* satisfies the following Eq. 3, it is called $\min_w h_k\left(w; w_t\right)$ of γ_k^t-inexact solution.

$$\begin{array}{c} \left\|\nabla h_k\left(w^*; w^t\right)\right\| \leq \gamma_k^t \left\|\nabla h_k\left(w^t; w^t\right)\right\| \\ \nabla h_k\left(w; w^t\right) = \nabla F_k(w) + \mu\left(w - w^t\right) \\ \gamma \in [0, 1] \end{array} \tag{3}$$

We improve the algorithm according to FedProx Framework proposed by [10] in clients' processing strategy and as shown in Algorithm 1. Devices are divided into groups. The training process is divided into two stages: intra-group training and inter-group training, and different optimization strategies are adopted in different stages. Moreover, We select the top Z devices according to the gradient descending order instead of randomly selected clients, accelerating the convergence speed and improving accuracy through the same experimental setting results.

3.2 Federal Learning Integrated into Digital Twin Network

Digital twin (DT) can accurately substitute for a real-world object across multiple granularity levels, and this real-world object could be a robot, device, machine, complex physical system or an industrial process. With moving the definitions of DT technology to DTN (digital twin network) shown in Fig. 2(a), DTN is defined as a many-to-many mapping network constructed by multiple one-to-one DTs. DTN uses advanced communication technologies to realize real-time interaction between the physical object and its virtual twin, the physical object and other physical objects, and the virtual twin and other virtual twins. Meanwhile, the physical object and virtual twin can collaborate, share information, and complete tasks. The DTN, whose simple structure proposed by this paper is shown in Fig. 2(b), has been applied to detect DDoS attacks by using federated learning.

Algorithm 1: Our approach

Input: K, T, μ, γ, w^0, N, Z, M, E, k=1, $\cdots$, N
while $t = 0 < T - 1$ **do**
  Devices are divided into M groups
  for m=0,$\cdots$,M-1 **do**
    Each device k calculates gradient difference
      $\bigtriangledown grad_k^t = \sum(grad_{global}^t - grad_k^t)^2$
    Sort K devices in descending $\bigtriangledown grad_k^t$ order, and the server selects
      a subset S_t of K devices at the top Z devices
    The server sends w^t to all chosen devices
    Each chosen device $k \in S_t$ finds w_k^{t+1} which is a γ_k^t-inexact
      minimize of : $w_k^{t+1} \approx arg\min_w h_k(w; w^t) = F_k(w) + \frac{\mu}{2}\|w - w^t\|^2$
    Each chosen device $k \in S_t$ send w_k^{t+1}back to the server Server
      aggregates the w's as $w^{t+1} = \frac{1}{K}\sum_{k \in S_t} w_k^{t+1}$
  end
  t = t+1
  for D_t:*devices are choosen in the intra group training* **do**
    Server sends w^t to all chosen devices
    device $k \in D_t$ updates w^t for E epochs of SGD on F_k to obtain
      w_k^{t+1}
    device sends w_k^{t+1} back to the server Server aggregates the w's as
      $w^{t+1} = \frac{1}{K}\sum_{k \in D_t} w_k^{t+1}$
  end
  t = t+1
end

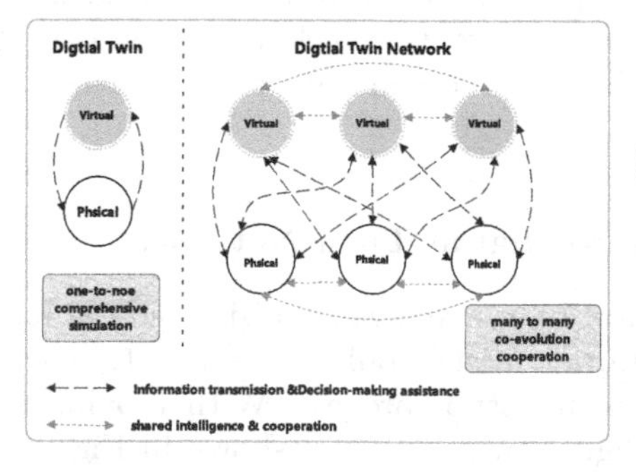

(a) The difference between DT and DTN

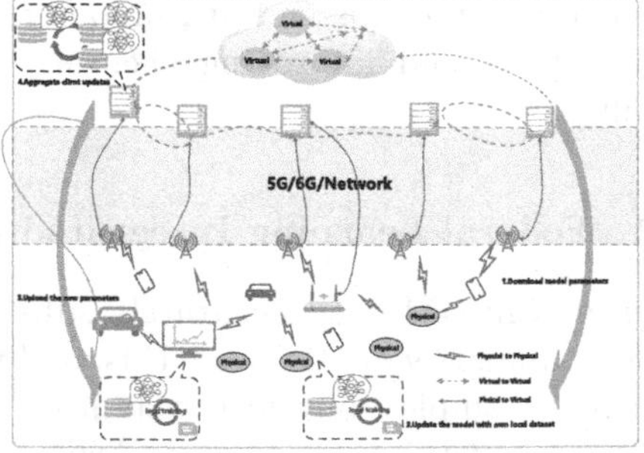

(b) The simple structure of DTN

Fig. 2. The DT and DTN

DTN provides a corresponding virtual network for the internet. The digital platform can artificially control clients through base stations and servers and use a federal learning model to detect abnormal traffic in advance. The actual physical node uses the information feedback from the virtualized network to improve network security.

3.3 The DDoS Attack Detection Model

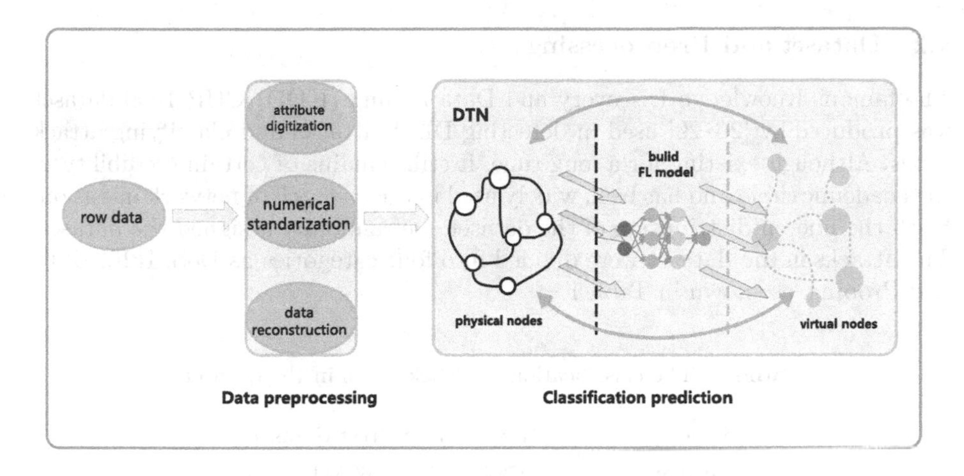

Fig. 3. The structure of DDoS attack detection model

The detection process mainly includes two steps: Data preprocessing and classification prediction. The structure of the DDoS attack detection model is shown in Fig. 3.

There are many non-numeric or unnecessary attributes on the DDoS dataset in data preprocessing, so these attributes need to be numeric, and all data should be normalized and reconstructed to obtain the *2D* standard dataset. The classification model will identify whether the network record belongs to normal or is attacked by distributed learning. Moreover, in the DTN construct, the federated model will be built on the digital twin platform, and the virtual digital platform can provide feedback to prepare actual physical nodes for prevention in advance. DTN can easily detect feedback, collect traffic information, and achieve real-time analysis on actual physical internet nodes with the detection model, computing, and communications technologies.

This paper divides each traffic sample into several parts. Furthermore, there is a strong or weak correlation among the features in the attack dataset, so each part is dependent on the other, which is regarded as a time step. LSTM (Long-short time memory) model [25] introduces a memory cell to replace each ordinary node in the hidden layers and can ensure that the gradients can pass through many times steps without vanishing and exploding. Therefore, the LSTM model is chosen to detect attacks.

4 Experiments and Results

4.1 Experiments Environment

The federated learning model training experiment is based on the hardware environment of Win 10 OS, Inter (R) Core (TM) i7-10700 CPU 2.90 GHz processor, 16 GB RAM, Netac 256 GB SSD, and NVIDIA K80 GPU, and the software environment of Python 3.7 programming language and libraries.

4.2 Dataset and Preprocessing

The famous Knowledge Discovery and Data mining (KDD) CUP 1999 dataset was produced by [26–29] used in detecting DDoS attacks and classifying attack types. Although existing for a long time, it still remains of certain credibility in the academic circle and has been widely used in the research of network intrusion. With the uneven distribution of the dataset, we randomly assigned the dataset. The attacks in the dataset were divided into four categories as DoS, R2L, U2R, and Probing, as shown in Table 1.

Table 1. The classification of attack types in the dataset

Type		Train dataset	Test dataset
Normal		97278	60541
Attack	DoS	395478	225833
	R2L	7222	10093
	Probing	5215	3058
	U2R	177	103

For data preprocessing, the specific steps were as follows:

(1) 41 features and one label of the network traffic packages in the dataset were needed for numerical conversion numerical standardization. The numerical conversion processing required three features (protocol_type, service, flag) and the string label for data type conversion. For example, the service feature contained 70 kinds of network service types, so they were coded from '1–70' one by one. "normal" was labelled '0' and other attacks were labelled '1–4' to detect attacks in the network traffic.

(2) The data type processed by LSTM in this paper was two-dimensional data, so converting the original data into a two-dimensional matrix is necessary. This paper adopted Gaussian distribution to randomly expand the length of each sample to 49 and then standardized the dataset. Lastly, turned the data into a 7 * 7 matrix.

4.3 Performance Metric

Confusion matrix [30] is used to determine the learning criteria of the model. The elements of the confusion matrix consist of True Positive (TP), False Positive (FP), True Negative (TN), False Negative (FN). TP indicates the number of records that correctly predict the attack traffic as an attack; TN indicates the number of records that correctly predict the normal flow records as normal; FP indicates the number of records that mistakenly predict the attack flow records as normal; FN indicates the number of records that mistakenly predict the normal traffic as an attack. The metrics obtained using these elements are described below as in [31]:
The accuracy obtained by Eq. 4 shows the model's correct prediction rate.

$$Accuracy = \frac{TP + TN}{TP + FP + TN + FN} \tag{4}$$

Precision obtained by Eq. 5 shows how much of the positive predictions are correctly predicted.

$$Precision = \frac{TP}{TP + FP} \tag{5}$$

Recall obtained by Eq. 6, shows how much of the true positives are predicted correctly.

$$Recall = \frac{TP}{TP + FN} \tag{6}$$

F score, obtained by Eq. 7, shows the stability between recall and sensitivity.

$$F1 = \frac{2 \times Precision \times Recall}{Precision + Recall} \tag{7}$$

4.4 Results

The experiment determined the global round and local epoch values to be 200 and 20 in training. On the one hand, to verify the accuracy of the detecting method, there was a set of controlled trials concerning the proposed model, Fedprox framework, and FedAvg framework (detailed in Sect. 3.1). On the other hand, it was also compared with federated learning with an original optimizer to verify the stability of the model dealing with data of non-IID.

The effect of data heterogeneity on convergence can be seen in Fig. 4, where the proposed model showed better convergence than federated learning based on Fedavg and Fedprox by several experiments. We have shown the training loss on the datasets, which were unevenly distributed to each node, modelling the data distribution in the real world. Increasing heterogeneity can lead to worse convergence, but setting the setting optimal value of u can help combat this.

The results of the three methods in performance metrics can be seen in Table 2, where the proposed model correctly detected DDoS attacks up to 99.17%, more than Fedprox and Fedavg. It showed that the accuracy improved in our proposed model. The results we obtained for the sample from the KDD Cup99 dataset show that federal learning based on LSTM and network traffic

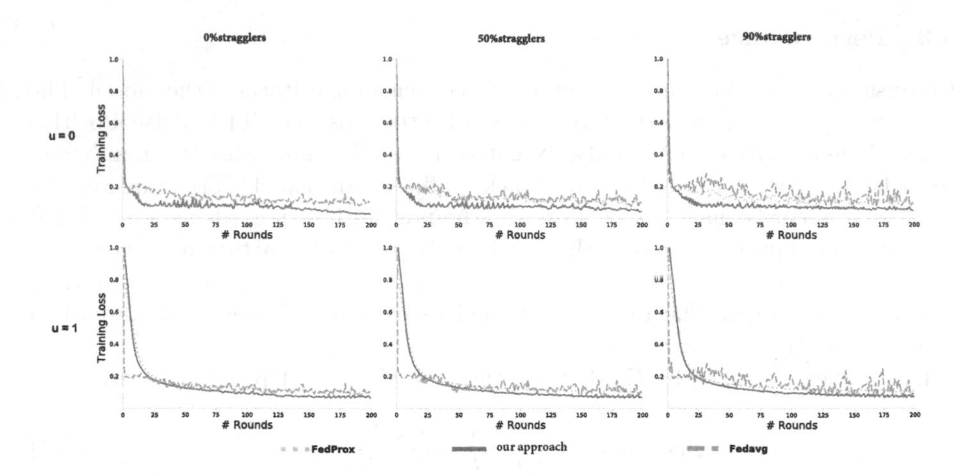

Fig. 4. Proposed approach results in significant convergence improvements relative to Fedprox and Fedavg. We simulate different levels of systems heterogeneity by forcing 0%, 50%, and 90% devices to be the stragglers (dropped by FedAvg). (1) Comparing these three optimization algorithms under the same experimental setting, we see that our algorithm's performance can help convergence in the presence of systems heterogeneity. (2) With the same levels of systems heterogeneity, we show that setting $u > 1$ can lead to more stable convergence. (3) Note that Fedprox with $u = 0$ and without systems heterogeneity (no stragglers) corresponds to Fedavg.

Table 2. The results of the three methods in performance metrics. With the experimental environment mentioned above, we show that the accuracy of our approach is higher relative to the Fedprox and Fedavg.

Methods	u and stragglers		Accuracy	Precision	Recall	F1
Fedavg	/	0%	97.76%	97.89%	99.45%	98.66%
		50%	98.01%	98.13%	99.58%	98.85%
		90%	97.42%	97.39%	99.10%	98.34%
Fedprox	$u = 0$	0%	97.76%	97.99%	99.31%	98.65%
		50%	97.29%	96.87%	99.72%	98.27%
		90%	97.21%	97.24%	99.46%	98.34%
	u=1	0%	97.01%	97.11%	99.67%	98.37%
		50%	96.99%	96.53%	99.77%	98.12%
		90%	96.98%	97.01%	99.54%	98.26%
Our approach	$u = 0$	0%	99.17%	99.03%	99.45%	99.24%
		50%	98.72%	97.91%	99.30%	98.60%
		90%	97.71%9	97.46%	99.32%	98.38%
	$u = 1$	0%	97.52%	97.61%	99.39%	98.49%
		50%	97.33%	97.23%	99.31%	98.26%
		90%	97.40%	97.29%	99.32%	98.28%

analysis has had great success in using small databases. Furthermore, through DTN technology, the physical node can defend quickly after receiving feedback information from the virtual platform.

5 Conclusion and Future Work

This paper proposes detecting DDoS attacks based on federated learning and the LSTM model under the Digital twin network. Federal learning, an innovative modelling mechanism, allows multi-party collaborative participation, which increases the number of the sample and protects the security of local data in each participant. Meanwhile, the digital twin network ensures the reliability of distributed training and cooperation among physical objects, which can respond quickly based on feedback from the virtual model. An improved optimization algorithm is introduced to solve heterogeneity inherent in federated networks. Our empirical evaluation across the KDD CUP 1999 dataset has achieved our expected effect and demonstrated that the optimization framework could significantly improve model accuracy and the convergence behaviour of federated learning in realistic heterogeneous networks.

References

1. Saracco, R.: Digital twins: bridging physical space and cyberspace. Computer **52**(12), 58–64 (2019). https://doi.org/10.1109/MC.2019.2942803
2. Pylianidis, C., Osinga, S., Athanasiadis, I.N.: Introducing digital twins to agriculture. Comput. Electron. Agric. **184**, 105942 (2021)
3. Lu, Y., Liu, C., Wang, K.I.K., Huang, H., Xu, X.: Digital Twin-driven smart manufacturing: connotation, reference model, applications and research issues. Robot. Comput. Integr. Manuf. **61**, 101837 (2020)
4. Jinhui, W.: The current main distributed denial of service and defence methods. In: 2019 12th International Conference on Intelligent Computation Technology and Automation (ICICTA), pp. 351–355 (2019)
5. Mahjabin, T., Xiao, Y., Sun, G., Jiang, W.: A survey of distributed denial-of-service attack, prevention, and mitigation techniques. Int. J. Distrib. Sens. Netw. **13**(12), 1550147717741463 (2017)
6. Wang, B., Zheng, Y., Lou, W., Hou, Y.T.: DDoS attack protection in the era of cloud computing and software-defined networking. Comput. Netw. **81**, 308–319 (2015)
7. Yan, Q., Yu, F.R.: Distributed denial of service attacks in software-defined networking with cloud computing. IEEE Commun. Mag. **53**(4), 52–59 (2015)
8. Prakash, A., Priyadarshini, R.: An intelligent software defined network controller for preventing distributed denial of service attack, pp. 585–589 (2018)
9. Rashid, A., Siddique, M.J., Ahmed, S.M.: Machine and deep learning based comparative analysis using hybrid approaches for intrusion detection system, pp. 1–9 (2020)
10. Li, T., Sahu, A.K., Zaheer, M., Sanjabi, M., Talwalkar, A., Smith, V.: Federated optimization in heterogeneous networks (2018)
11. Yu, C., Kai, H.: Collaborative change detection of DDoS attacks on community and ISP networks (2006)

12. Yuan, J., Mills, K.: Monitoring the macroscopic effect of DDoS flooding attacks. IEEE Trans. Depend. Sec. Comput. **2**(4), 324–335 (2005)
13. Singh, K.J., De, T.: An approach of DDOS attack detection using classifiers. In: Shetty, N.R., Prasad, N.H., Nalini, N. (eds.) Emerging Research in Computing, Information, Communication and Applications, pp. 429–437. Springer, New Delhi (2015). https://doi.org/10.1007/978-81-322-2550-8_41
14. Biao, H., Xiangrui, Y., Zhigang, S., Jinfeng, H., Jinshu, S.: OverWatch: a cross-plane DDoS attack defense framework with collaborative intelligence in SDN. Secur. Commun. Netw. **2018**, 1–15 (2018)
15. Roopak, M., Yun Tian, G., Chambers, J.: Deep learning models for cyber security in IoT networks, pp. 0452–0457 (2019)
16. Haider, S., Akhunzada, A., Ahmed, G., Raza, M.: Deep learning based ensemble convolutional neural network solution for distributed denial of service detection in SDNs (2019)
17. Cil, A.E., Yildiz, K., Buldu, A.: Detection of DDoS attacks with feed forward based deep neural network model. Expert Syst. App. **169**(4), 114520 (2020)
18. Srinivas, T., Manivannan, S.S.: Prevention of hello flood attack in IoT using combination of deep learning with improved rider optimization algorithm. Comput. Commun. **163**, 162–175 (2020)
19. Priyadarshini, R., Barik, R.K.: A deep learning based intelligent framework to mitigate DDoS attack in fog environment. J. King Saud Univ. Comput. Inf. Sci. **34**, 825–831 (2019)
20. Zhu, M., Ye, K., Xu, C.-Z.: Network anomaly detection and identification based on deep learning methods. In: Luo, M., Zhang, L.-J. (eds.) CLOUD 2018. LNCS, vol. 10967, pp. 219–234. Springer, Cham (2018). https://doi.org/10.1007/978-3-319-94295-7_15
21. Chuanhuan, L., Zhengjunl, S., Xiaoyon, Y., Xiaolin, L., Lian, G., Weimin, W.: Real-time DDoS attack detection based on deep learning. Telecommun. Sci. **33**(7), 13 (2017)
22. Mcmahan, H.B., Moore, E., Ramage, D., Hampson, S., Arcas, B.: Communication-efficient learning of deep networks from decentralized data (2016)
23. Bonawitz, K., et al.: Towards federated learning at scale: system design. Proc. Mach. Learn. Syst. **1**, 374–388 (2019)
24. Smith, V., Chiang, C.K., Sanjabi, M., Talwalkar, A.: Federated multi-task learning (2018)
25. Hochreiter, S., Schmidhuber, J.: Long short-term memory. Neural Comput. **9**, 1735–1740 (1997)
26. Mukkamala, S., Sung, A.H., Abraham, A.: Intrusion detection using an ensemble of intelligent paradigms. J. Netw. Comput. App. **28**(2), 167–182 (2005)
27. McHugh, J.: Testing intrusion detection systems: a critique of the 1998 and 1999 DARPA intrusion detection system evaluations as performed by Lincoln laboratory. ACM Trans. Inf. Syst. Secur. **3**(4), 262–294 (2000)
28. Lippmann, R., Haines, J.W., Fried, D.J., Korba, J., Das, K.: Analysis and results of the 1999 DARPA off-line intrusion detection evaluation (2000)
29. Stolfo, S.J., Fan, W., Lee, W., Prodromidis, A., Chan, P.K.: Cost-based modeling for fraud and intrusion detection: results from the JAM project (2000)
30. Guo, C., Zhou, Y., Ping, Y., Zhang, Z., Liu, G., Yang, Y.: A distance sum-based hybrid method for intrusion detection. Appl. Intell. **40**(1), 178–188 (2013). https://doi.org/10.1007/s10489-013-0452-6
31. Powers, D.M.W.: Evaluation: From precision, recall and F-Factor to ROC, informedness, markedness and correlation. J. Mach. Learn. Technol. **2**, 1–24 (2011)

A Privacy-Preserving Subgraph-Level Federated Graph Neural Network via Differential Privacy

Yeqing Qiu[1,2], Chenyu Huang[1], Jianzong Wang[1(✉)], Zhangcheng Huang[1], and Jing Xiao[1]

[1] Ping An Technology (Shenzhen) Co., Ltd., Shenzhen, China
jzwang@188.com, xiaojing661@pingan.com.cn
[2] Beijing Jiaotong University, Beijing, China
yeqing@bjtu.edu.cn

Abstract. Currently, the federated graph neural network (GNN) has attracted a lot of attention due to its wide applications in reality without violating the privacy regulations. Among all the privacy-preserving technologies, the differential privacy (DP) is the most promising one due to its effectiveness and light computational overhead. However, the DP-based federated GNN has not been well investigated, especially in the sub-graph-level setting, such as the scenario of recommendation system. The biggest challenge is how to guarantee the privacy and solve the non independent and identically distributed (non-IID) data in federated GNN simultaneously. In this paper, we propose DP-FedRec, a DP-based federated GNN to fill the gap. Private Set Intersection (PSI) is leveraged to extend the local graph for each client, and thus solve the non-IID problem. Most importantly, DP is applied not only on the weights but also on the edges of the intersection graph from PSI to fully protect the privacy of clients. The evaluation demonstrates DP-FedRec achieves better performance with the graph extension and DP only introduces little computations overhead.

Keywords: Recommendation system · Federated learning · Subgraph-level federated learning · Graph neural network · Differential privacy

1 Introduction

Graph neural network (GNN) has been applied to multiple scenarios such as molecule prediction [5,18], social network analysis [2,17], recommendation systems [8] and knowledge graph [20]. However, GNN approaches mainly rely on the centralized data, which is different from the real-world scenario where the source data may be stored at different organizations. For example, e-commerce platforms that sell different types of items have separate purchase and rating records of their users and items. In order to explore potential new users and provide better recommendation services to existing users, E-commerce platforms

G. Memmi et al. (Eds.): KSEM 2022, LNAI 13370, pp. 165–177, 2022.
https://doi.org/10.1007/978-3-031-10989-8_14

would build a better model jointly learned from multiple data resources. In the meantime, the user privacy should be protected for ethical concerns and compliance with government regulations.

As a result, approaches are presented to combine the well-known privacy-preserving framework, federated learning (FL), and GNN. Different technologies such as differential privacy (DP) [16,22,23,26], homomorphic encryption [22], secret sharing [26] are widely applied to dealing with risks of privacy leakage. Among the techniques mentioned above, DP is the most promising one due to its light computational overhead and high fidelity. DP perturbs the data with a small noise without lowering the accuracy of the entire model, *i.e.*, if the input signal changes, the distribution of the output only changes a little.

Currently, real-world scenarios of privacy-preserve graph learning mainly concentrates on three settings [7]: graph-level setting [26], sub-graph-level setting [14,22,23,25] and node-level setting [3]. Among these settings, sub-graph-level is the most attractive since it is a good fit to the most important/common application scenario such as recommendation system and knowledge graph. For example, in recommendation systems, every data holder will only own the part of graph that contains the relationship between user and item. The biggest challenge in this setting is preserving the privacy and solving the Non-IID problem in federated GNN simultaneously. However, these work either assume one party owns the global topology [7,26], which violate the basic assumption in general scenario where no one is allowed to own the whole typology, or do not consider the information from the neighbors [14,22], which do not solve the Non-IID problem and thus lead to low accuracy of the model. Therefore, these approaches cannot be directly applied in the general sub-graph level scenario.

In this paper, we propose a novel DP-based GNN that aims at the sub-graph level setting in Sect. 3. To solve the Non-IID problem, the FedRec that utilizes the K-hop extension to expand the sub-graph of each client is introduced. The privacy of the communication between clients is preserved via the Private Set Intersection (PSI). Furthermore, we propose DP-FedRec that leverages DP in FedRec. The core idea is to apply well-designed noises to both adjacency edges and weights of client's sub-graph. Specifically, the Laplacian noise is applied on the edges via Lapgraph algorithm and apply the Laplacian noise on the weights. The analysis and evaluation in Sect. 4 and 5 show the K-hop extension achieves better performance than previous schemes and the DP introduces limited computational overhead. We summarize the main contributions as follows:

- We propose a state-of-art learning paradigm on sub-graph setting based on DP, which is able to be applied to many link prediction tasks.
- We utilize K-hop extension for exchanged feature and adjacency information and preserve the privacy of both the feature and edge information via DP.
- We evaluate our algorithms on two recommendation datasets, and demonstrate the effectiveness of our approach.

2 Preliminaries

2.1 Problem Formulation

In this work, denote $\mathcal{U} = \{u_1, u_2, \cdots, u_n\}$ and $\mathcal{P} = \{p_1, p_2, \cdots, p_m\}$ as user and item respectively. The purchasing interaction of user and item relationship is represented by a bipartite graph $\mathcal{G} \in \mathbb{R}^{n \times m}$, in which the value of edges refers to the points the user rate the item. Since each client will only have a part of global graph, for client i, the user-item bipartite graph is denoted as $G^i = (V^i, E^i)$. In detail, the set of vertexes and edges are denoted as V^i, E^i respectively. The task is to predict the ratings of users and items based on user-item graph. Thus, client i will train a local model in round r, the parameters of which are denoted as θ_i^l. The global model parameter that aggregate from each client is θ^r. Additionally, define $\mathsf{dist}(x, y, \mathcal{G})$ as the shortest path of vertex x and y in graph $\mathcal{G}$. Define $\mathsf{dist}(v, \mathcal{S}, \mathcal{G}) = \min_{x \in \mathcal{S}} \mathsf{dist}(v, x, \mathcal{G})$. The notation is summarized in Table 1.

Table 1. Notations used in DP-FedRec.

l	Number of clients
n, m	Number of users and items in graph $\mathcal{G}$
u_i, p_i	User i, item i
G^i	User-item graph of client i
V^i, E^i	Vertex set and edge set in G^i
$\bar{G}^i$	Extended user-item graph of client i
$\bar{V}^i, \bar{E}^i$	Extended vertex set and edge set in $\bar{G}^i$
K	Parameter of K-hop extension
r	Communication round
θ^r	Parameters of global model in round r
θ_i^r	Parameters of client i's local model in round r
$\nabla\theta_i$	Gradient of parameters of local model

2.2 Local Differential Privacy

Local differential privacy guarantees the privacy of the user in the process of collecting information. Specifically, before the user uploads the data to an untrusted third party, a certain amount of noises is added to the uploaded data. This guarantees that the data collectors can hardly infer the specific information of any user, but are able to learn the statistical properties of the data by increasing the amount of data.

Different from the previous unweighted graph [23], the user-item graph in recommendation system is a weighted graph. Therefore, in order to protect information of user-item graph, the definition of DP in undirected weighted graph data is obtained by combining both unweighted undirected graph information and weight information. Consistent with prior work [23], we adapt the idea of edge differential privacy based on adjacency matrix.

Definition 1 (Neighbor Relation). *Two matrices are called neighbors if there is only one different node. Specifically, the graph corresponding to the two matrices can be obtained by adding or deleting an edge or modifying value of an edge.*

Definition 2 (ϵ-Weighted Edge Local Differential Privacy). *A mechanism M is called to satisfy ϵ-Weighted Edge Local Differential Privacy if for all neighbor matrix pairs X and X', and for any possible output $t \in Range(M)$:*

$$P[M(X) = t] \leq e^{\epsilon} P[M(X') = t] \tag{1}$$

2.3 Federated Graph Neural Network

Graph neural network is widely used in recent recommendation systems [24]. In this paper, we leverage the graph convectional network (GCN) [9] under the message passing neural network framework (MPNN). MPNN is a supervised learning framework which extracts information from the user-item graph by aggregating adjacency information into the latent space, and then generates the prediction from the latent space.

Furthermore, we extend GNN to the federated scenario which is the same as in [7]. Specifically, it is a sub-graph setting where each entity/company has a part of data/graph, such as users and rating information, and a model is jointly trained on the entire data for better prediction accuracy. Therefore, there are multiple clients and one centralized server. For communication round r in the training stage, client i will get the model parameter θ_i^r by training the local model for e epochs on the sub-graph G_r^i. The server will aggregates the parameters $\theta_r = \frac{\sum \theta_i^r}{l}$ and distribute them to all local clients, and each client updates its local model parameters as θ_i^r.

2.4 Private Set Intersection

Private Set Intersection (PSI) is a cryptographic protocol in multiparty computation. It allows two clients to get the intersection set of the data without revealing any information outside the intersected data. There are many different implementations of PSI, DP-FedRec instantiates the PSI the same as [10]. It leverages the programmable pseudo random function (OPPRF) which is fast and efficient.

3 Approach

3.1 Overview

The basic federated GNN framework does not use the graph information from others and could cause non-IID problem in the training data. We will first present FedRec which extends the sub-graph of each client without leaking the information of the edges. Then we will introduce DP-FedRec that combines FedRec and DP and jointly considers the privacy of both weights and connectivity of the edges simultaneously.

Specifically, DP-FedRec jointly trains a model via four steps as shown in Fig. 1: (i) All the clients add noises on the graph data including both weights and edges; (ii) The clients extend the local graph via K-hop extension; (iii) Each client trains the local model on the extended graph and submits the parameters to the server; (iv) The centralized server aggregates the parameters and distributes the updated parameters to all the clients. The process will continue until certain number of rounds is reached.

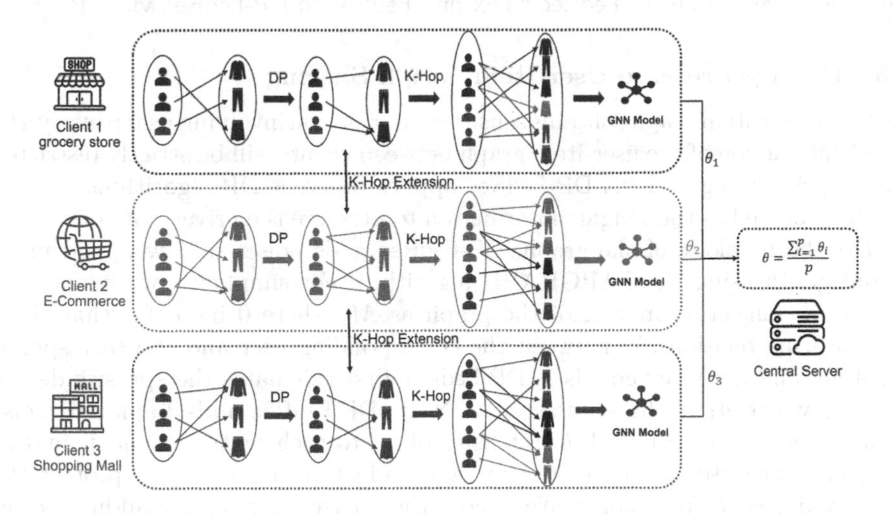

Fig. 1. Overall framework of DP-FedRec. Each bipartite graph refers to purchasing relationship between user and item in each platform and client. The purple ones are the users in the intersection set of clients' sub-graphs.

3.2 User-Item Graph K-Hop Expansion

To overcome the non-IID problem, FedRec privately exchanges the edges information between clients. The main idea is to expand the edges from the intersected users in different sub-graphs. In two-client setting, for example, the intersected users are the users appear in both sub-graphs. We integrate PSI to the K-hop extension, which avoid leaking the user-item information that is not in the intersection set.

Without loss of generality, suppose there are two clients, client i and client j, who exchange the edges information via K-hop extension and generate the extended sub-graph $\bar{G}^i$ and $\bar{G}^j$. The vertex set and edge set of user-item graph G^i are V^i and E^i respectively, and client j also records the $G^j = (V^j, E^j)$. Firstly, client i and client j will execute PSI protocol to get the intersection of V^i and V^j, denoted as $V^{i,j}$, *i.e.*, $V^{i,j} = \mathsf{PSI}(V^i, V^j)$ (Line 4 in Algorithm 1). Then, the K-hop extension is performed by extending the edges and vertexes on $V^{i,j}$. The extended vertex set $\bar{V}^{i,j}$ will cover the vertexes in V^j within K hops from $V^{i,j}$ (Line 5 in Algorithm 1). Similarly, the extended edge set $\bar{V}^{i,j}$ will cover the edges that both vertexes are in $\bar{V}^{i,j}$ (Line 6 in Algorithm 1). Next, the client

i and client j will exchange the extended vertex set and extended edge set (Line 7,10 in Algorithm 1). Lastly, the client i combines the extended vertexes and edges with G^i to form the new graph $\bar{G}^{(i)}$ (Line 11–14 in Algorithm 1). Through the exchange of edge information, the local model learns new information, and thus improves the accuracy of the global model.

However, the PSI only preserves the privacy of the edges the other clients do not own. It's not able to protect the privacy of the edges in the intersection set. Thus, we leverage DP to FedRec to extend FedRec to DP-FedRec via DP.

3.3 Privacy-Preserve User-Item Graph Sharing

Since the user-item graph contains sensitive information involving user privacy, the direct interaction of the user-item graph between clients will be strictly restricted due to privacy regulations. DP-FedRec applies different DP algorithms in both topology as well as the weights information to preserve the privacy of both.

For the topology of the graph, DP-FedRec adds noises to a weighted undirected graph using the LAPGRAPH algorithm. For simplicity, we denote the user-item connection matrix of the graph as M, where 0 indicates that there is no scoring relationship between the corresponding user and the corresponding item, and the vice versa is 1. DP-FedRec first calculates the sparsity degree $T = n_1$ where n_1 is the number of 1. Next, DP-FedRec adds Laplacian noise with a mean value of 0 and an intensity of λ_1 to each matrix element, and at the same time uses a part of the privacy budget (usually 1%) to protect the sparsity degree T from noise. We denote the sparse degree after adding noises is T'. Finally, DP-FedRec leaves the top T' large elements of the matrix after adding noise as 1, and others as 0.

For the protection of the edge weights information of the user-item graph, a Laplace noise with a mean value of 0 and an intensity of λ_2 is added directly to the new graph formed by the above algorithms.

4 Analysis

4.1 Privacy Analysis

The privacy of DP-FedRec is protected by the following aspects: (i) The vertexes outside of the intersection set during K-hop extension. The privacy of this part is guaranteed by PSI. (ii) The vertexes within the intersection set during K-hop extension. The privacy of this part is guaranteed by DP. The protection of privacy is divided into protection of the topology structure and protection of the weights of the edges. For preservation of topology, the Laplace noise is added to its adjacency matrix using the Lapgraph algorithm so that the information is perturbed. For protection of edge weights, the values of edge weights are disturbed by adding noises directly to the edge weights. It has been demonstrated in [23] that when the noise added satisfies $Lap(0, \frac{\Delta f_1}{\epsilon_1})$, the Lapgraph algorithm satisfies $\epsilon_1 - DP$. At the same time, due to the characteristics of Laplace mechanism [4], the noise added to the edge weights satisfies $Lap(0, \frac{\Delta f_2}{\epsilon_2})$, which is $\epsilon_2 - DP$. By Composition theorem [4], DP-FedRec satisfies $\epsilon_1 + \epsilon_2$-DP.

Algorithm 1. K-hop extension of client i

Input: K, the parameter of K-hop; the graph G^i
Output: the extended graph $\bar{G}^i$
1: **procedure** K-HOP EXTENSION(K, i)
2: $\bar{V}^i = V^i$, $\bar{E}^i = E^i$
3: **for** $u_j \in \mathcal{U} \backslash \{u_i\}$ **do**
4: $V^{i,j} = \mathsf{PSI}(V^i, V^j)$
5: $\bar{V}^{i,j} = \bar{V}^{i,j} \cup \{v | \mathsf{dist}(v, V^{i,j}, G^i) \leq k \wedge v \in V^i\}$
6: $\bar{E}^{i,j} = \bar{E}^{i,j} \cup \{< x, y > | x, y \in \bar{V}^{(i,j)}\}$
7: Send $(\bar{V}^{i,j}, \bar{E}^{i,j})$ to client j
8: **end for**
9: **for** $u_j \in \mathcal{U} \backslash \{u_i\}$ **do**
10: Receive $(\bar{V}^{j,i}, \bar{E}^{j,i})$ from client j
11: $\bar{V}^i = \bar{V}^i \cup \bar{V}^{j,i}$
12: $\bar{E}^i = \bar{E}^i \cup \bar{E}^{j,i}$
13: **end for**
14: **return** $\bar{G}^i = (\bar{V}^i, \bar{E}^i)$
15: **end procedure**

4.2 Performance Analysis

First, consider the time complexity of DP-FedRec for one client. Since a certain amount of noise needs to be added to each element of the adjacency matrix, the time for single addition of noise is $\mathcal{O}(|V^i|^2)$. Then analysis is performed on the communication complexity of DP-FedRec for client i. Since DP-FedRec requires interaction between two clients, communication cost of such interaction between clients is $\mathcal{O}(l^2)$. Each interaction contains PSI, K-hop extension, and adding noise towards expanded graph data. Correspondingly, the time complexity of PSI is $\mathcal{O}(|V^i|)$, the time complexity of K-hop extension is $O(|V^i|)$. The time for single addition of noise, as analyzed above, is $\mathcal{O}(|V^i|^2)$. So the communication cost of DP-FedRec is $\mathcal{O}(l^2 \cdot |V^i|^2)$.

5 Evaluation

5.1 Evaluation Setup

Implementation. We implement both FedRec and DP-FedRec via Python based code of FedGraphNN [7]. We conduct the evaluation on a computation instance equipped with 2.1 GHz 64 Intel(R) Xeon(R) Gold 6130 CPU, 512 GB memory and 8 Tesla V100 GPU with 12 GB.

Dataset. We conduct evaluation on two datasets: Epinions [19] and MovieLens [6]. The Epinions dataset contains consumers' ratings on items from the Epinions website. The MovieLens dataset contains the users' rating of different movies from the MovieLens website. For both datasets, we divide the graph to different clients via the item category, *i.e.*, the items with same category and their relevant users will be assigned to the same client. In particular, due to the large number of points in the epinions dataset and the limitation of memory, we only select 12 categories for experiments. Table 2 shows the average number of users, items and edges after separation.

Table 2. Dataset description. The K is the parameter of K-hop, n is the number of users, the m is the number of items and #edges is the number of edges. For centralized, the number of user, items and edges is the total number.

Dataset	Number of clients	K	Average n for each client	Average n for each client	Average #edges for each client
Epinions	Centralized	/	21296	163874	870838
	8	2	21052	117641	754303
		10	21172	163588	870266
	12	2	21007	105897	720281
		10	21165	163539	870227
MovieLens 1M	Centralized	/	6040	3706	1000209
	8	1	5894	3704	995298
		5	6040	3706	1000209
	12	1	5409	3699	972759
		5	6040	3706	1000209

Setting of Experiments. Our evaluation goal is to prove two claim: the K-hop extension improves the accuracy of the federated GNN and the leverage of DP in DP-FedRec do not reduce the accuracy too much. The experiments is conducts under two client settings: 8 and 12 clients. Five experiments were performed in each setting: (i) Centralized training, the central server owns the full graph for training; (ii) FedGraphNN with FedAvg, the structure proposed in [7], which is also the baseline we compared. For simplicity we denote it as FedGraphNN in the remaining sections; (iii) FedRec, where we only perform K-hop extension without adding noise to the interactive content. The purpose of this experiment is to demonstrate that the K-hop extension helps to increase the accuracy of link prediction; (iv) DP-FedGraphNN, we add Laplace(0, 1) noise to the edge weights of the user-item graph based on FedGraphNN as a baseline to compare with DP-FedRec. (v) DP-FedRec with different K, which is realized by adding noise to the interactive content on the basis of the third group of FedRec. For evaluation metrics, we adopt mean absolute error (MAE), mean square error (MSE) and root mean square error (RMSE) to evaluate the accuracy of edge weights prediction and record the average time it takes to add noise to a single client in each experiment.

5.2 Performance of K-Hop Extension

Table 3 and Table 4 show the performance of centralized server, FedRec and FedGraphNN. It indicates that FedRec performed better than FedGraphNN in all metrics. The result proves the K-hop extension does really help to handle the non-IID problem in federated learning and thus improve the link prediction accuracy.

The effect of DP-FedRec is also better than FedGraphNN, which proves that the K-hop extension algorithm based on local differential privacy improves the performance of the model while protecting privacy. Meanwhile The K-Hop extension is very robust even with adding noise to the graph data.

Table 3. Performance of different systems with 8 clients. Noising time refers to the time of adding noise per client.

Dataset/8 clients	Model type	System	MAE	MSE	RMSE	Noising time (s)
Epinions	W/O DP	Centralized	0.8377	1.2464	1.1164	/
		FedGraphNN	0.8719	1.3424	1.1559	
		FedRec	0.8643	1.3303	1.1505	
	W/ DP	DP-FedGraphNN	0.8724	1.3484	1.1584	/
		DP-FedRec (K=2)	0.8689	1.3415	1.1560	328
		DP-FedRec (K=10)	0.8658	1.3278	1.1523	517
MovieLens1M	W/O DP	Centralized	0.8812	1.1782	1.0855	/
		FedGraphNN	0.8832	1.1850	1.0884	
		FedRec	0.8793	1.1786	1.0884	
	W/ DP	DP-FedGraphNN	0.8912	1.2057	1.0980	/
		DP-FedRec (K=1)	0.8820	1.1798	1.0862	4
		DP-FedRec (K=5)	0.8813	1.1783	1.0875	4

5.3 Performance of Differential Privacy

From the results, the performance of DP-FedRec does not decrease much than FedRec. However, after adding noise to FedGraphNN, accuracy drops a lot.

Table 4. Performance of different systems with 12 clients. Noising time refers to the time of adding noise per client.

Dataset/12 clients	Model type	System	MAE	MSE	RMSE	Noising time (s)
Epinions	W/O DP	Centralized	0.8377	1.2464	1.1164	/
		FedGraphNN	0.8674	1.3279	1.1502	
		FedRec ($K = 10$)	0.8635	1.3270	1.1496	
	W/ DP	DP-FedGraphNN	0.8716	1.3298	1.1513	/
		DP-FedRec ($K = 2$)	0.8625	1.3261	1.1493	314
		DP-FedRec ($K = 10$)	0.8585	1.3258	1.1493	501
MovieLens1M	W/O DP	Centralized	0.8812	1.1782	1.0855	/
		FedGraphNN	0.8931	1.2454	1.1152	
		FedRec ($K = 5$)	0.8874	1.1850	1.0883	
	W/ DP	DP-FedGraphNN	0.8989	1.2669	1.1247	/
		DP-FedRec ($K = 1$)	0.8936	1.2257	1.1063	3
		DP-FedRec ($K = 5$)	0.8907	1.1991	1.0948	4

When the number of clients in the Epinions dataset is 12, the effect of DP-FedRec is better than that of FedRec, which to a certain extent shows that the noise added in the experiment not only protects the privacy of the data from being leaked, but also ensures the data availability is not compromised, reflecting the balance between data privacy and availability.

We also recorded the average time for each client to add noise. According to our analysis, the time for adding noise is positively correlated with the number of points in the graph, *i.e.*, the number of points increases, the time it takes to add noise will increase, while the increase in the number of edges does not significantly increases the time it takes to add noise.

In the Epinions dataset and MovieLens1M dataset, the number of points of Epinions is significantly larger than that of MovieLens1M, and the number of edges of MovieLens1M is significantly larger than the number of points of Epinions. Summarizing the average time to add noise per client in the experiments, we found that the time required to add noise to the Epinions dataset is much greater than that required for Movielens which is consistent with our analysis.

6 Related Work

6.1 Federated Recommendation System

Federated Learning is being applied in lots of field [11,21]. And as the laws and regulations of data and privacy become stricter, recommendation systems based on federated learning with privacy-preserving features have become a hot research trend. FCF [1], a classic federated recommendation system, is the first collaborative filtering framework based on the federated learning paradigm. They build a joint model by using user implicit feedback. [14] is a privacy-preserving method which leverages the behavior data of massive users and meanwhile don't require centralized storage to protect user privacy to train news recommendation model with accuracy. FedFast [13] achieves high accuracy for each user during the federated learning training phase as quickly as possible. In each training round, They sample from a set of participating clients and apply an active aggregation method that propagates the updated model to the other clients.

6.2 Differential Privacy Graph Neural Network

Several literature leverage DP to preserve the privacy of GNN. Solitude [12] is a privacy-preserving learning framework based on GNN, with formal privacy guarantees based on edge local differential privacy. The crux of Solitude is a set of new delicate mechanisms that calibrate the introduced noise in the decentralized graph collected from the users. LDPGen [15] is a multi-phase technique that incrementally clusters users based on their connections to different partitions of the whole population. LDPGen carefully injects noise to ensure local differential privacy whenever a user reports information. There are only few works that combine the DP with the GNN federated learning. [22] applies differential privacy techniques to the local gradients of GNN model to protect user privacy in federated learning setting. But it need a third-party server to store embedding of users besides training server. So FedGNN is a two-server model. In [26], They propose (VFGNN), a federated GNN learning model for privacy-preserving node classification task under data vertically partitioned setting. They leave the private data related computations on data holders, and delegate the rest of computations to a semi-honest server. However, their work has an strong assumption that every data holders have the same nodes, which is far different from real scenario.

7 Conclusion and Future Work

In this paper, we proposed DP-FedRec a privacy-preserving federated GNN framework for recommendation system. To overcome the challenge of the Non-IID problem under the privacy regulation, DP-FedRec integrates the PSI and the DP technique with the federated GNN. The PSI-based K-hop extension helps to extend the sub-graph of each client without leaking any non-intersection information to solve the non-IID problem. Moreover, DP preserves not only the privacy of weights but also the privacy of edges/topology in the intersection information to guarantee the privacy. We implemented the prototype of DP-FedRec and tests it on different datasets. Compared with other works, the evaluation shows DP-FedRec achieves high performance and only induces little computations overhead. In the future, we would like to investigate a universal DP for both weights and edges in graph data for better performance.

Acknowledgement. This paper is supported by the Key Research and Development Program of Guangdong Province under grant No. 2021B0101400003.

References

1. Ammad-Ud-Din, M., et al.: Federated collaborative filtering for privacy-preserving personalized recommendation system (2019)
2. Chen, J., Ma, T., Xiao, C.: FastGCN: fast learning with graph convolutional networks via importance sampling. In: 6th International Conference on Learning Representations, ICLR 2018 (2018)
3. Cheung, T.H., Dai, W., Li, S.: FedSGC: federated simple graph convolution for node classification. In: International Workshop on Federated and Transfer Learning for Data Sparsity and Confidentiality in Conjuncation with IJCAI 2021, FTL-IJCAI 2021 (2021)
4. Dwork, C., Roth, A.: The algorithmic foundations of differential privacy. Found. Trends Theor. Comput. Sci. **9**(3–4), 211–407 (2013)
5. Fout, A., Byrd, J., Shariat, B., Ben-Hur, A.: Protein interface prediction using graph convolutional networks. In: 31st Conference on Neural Information Processing Systems, NeurIPS 2017 (2017)
6. Harper, F.M., Konstan, J.A.: The movielens datasets: history and context. ACM Trans. Interact. Intell. Syst. (TiiS) **5**(4), 1–19 (2015)
7. He, C., et al.: FedGraphNN: a federated learning benchmark system for graph neural networks. In: ICLR 2021 Workshop on Distributed and Private Machine Learning (DPML) (2021)
8. Jin, B., Gao, C., He, X., Jin, D., Li, Y.: Multi-behavior recommendation with graph convolutional networks. In: Proceedings of the 43rd International ACM SIGIR Conference on Research and Development in Information Retrieval (2020)
9. Kipf, T.N., Welling, M.: Semi-supervised classification with graph convolutional networks. In: 5th International Conference on Learning Representations, ICLR 2017 (2017)
10. Kolesnikov, V., Matania, N., Pinkas, B., Rosulek, M., Trieu, N.: Practical multi-party private set intersection from symmetric-key techniques. In: Proceedings of the 2017 ACM SIGSAC Conference on Computer and Communications Security (2017)
11. Kong, L., Tao, H., Wang, J., Huang, Z., Xiao, J.: Network coding for federated learning systems. In: Neural Information Processing - 27th International Conference, ICONIP 2020 (2020)
12. Lin, W., Li, B., Wang, C.: Towards private learning on decentralized graphs with local differential privacy. CoRR abs/2201.09398 (2022)
13. Muhammad, K., Wang, Q., O'Reilly-Morgan, D., Tragos, E., Lawlor, A.: FedFast: going beyond average for faster training of federated recommender systems. In: The 26th ACM SIGKDD Conference on Knowledge Discovery and Data Mining, KDD 2020 (2020)
14. Qi, T., Wu, F., Wu, C., Huang, Y., Xie, X.: Privacy-preserving news recommendation model learning. In: Proceedings of the 2020 Conference on Empirical Methods in Natural Language Processing: Findings (2020)
15. Qin, Z., Yu, T., Yang, Y., Khalil, I., Xiao, X., Ren, K.: Generating synthetic decentralized social graphs with local differential privacy. In: ACM SIGSAC Conference on Computer and Communications Security (2017)
16. Qiu, H., Qiu, M., Zhihui, L.U.: Selective encryption on ECG data in body sensor network based on supervised machine learning. Inf. Fusion **55**, 59–67 (2020)
17. Qiu, M., Gai, K., Xiong, Z.: Privacy-preserving wireless communications using bipartite matching in social big data. Future Gener. Comput. Syst. **87**, 772–781 (2017)

18. Qiu, M., Zhang, L., Ming, Z., Chen, Z., Qin, X., Yang, L.T.: Security-aware optimization for ubiquitous computing systems with seat graph approach. J. Comput. Syst. Sci. **79**(5), 518–529 (2013)
19. Richardson, M., Agrawal, R., Domingos, P.: Trust management for the semantic web. In: International Semantic Web Conference (2003)
20. Schlichtkrull, M., Kipf, T.N., Bloem, P., van den Berg, R., Titov, I., Welling, M.: Modeling relational data with graph convolutional networks. In: Gangemi, A., et al. (eds.) ESWC 2018. LNCS, vol. 10843, pp. 593–607. Springer, Cham (2018). https://doi.org/10.1007/978-3-319-93417-4_38
21. Wang, J., Huang, Z., Kong, L., Li, D., Xiao, J.: Modeling without sharing privacy: federated neural machine translation. In: International Conference on Web Information Systems Engineering (2021)
22. Wu, C., Wu, F., Cao, Y., Huang, Y., Xie, X.: FedGNN: federated graph neural network for privacy-preserving recommendation. In: International Workshop on Federated Learning for User Privacy and Data Confidentiality in Conjunction with ICML 2021, FL-ICML 2021 (2021)
23. Wu, F., Long, Y., Zhang, C., Li, B.: Linkteller: recovering private edges from graph neural networks via influence analysis. In: Proceedings of the Symposium on Security and Privacy (2021)
24. Wu, Z., Pan, S., Chen, F., Long, G., Zhang, C., Philip, S.Y.: A comprehensive survey on graph neural networks. IEEE Trans. Neural Netw. Learn. Syst. **32**(1), 4–24 (2020)
25. Yang, C., Wang, H., Zhang, K., Chen, L., Sun, L.: Secure deep graph generation with link differential privacy. In: The 30th International Joint Conference on Artificial Intelligence, IJCAI 2021 (2021)
26. Zhou, J., et al.: Vertically federated graph neural network for privacy-preserving node classification. In: The 31st International Joint Conference on Artificial Intelligence, IJCAI 2022 (2022)

ε−MC Nets: A Compact Representation Scheme for Large Cooperative Game Settings

Errikos Streviniotis[1](✉), Athina Georgara[2], and Georgios Chalkiadakis[1]

[1] Technical University of Crete, Chania, Greece
{estreviniotis,gehalk}@intelligence.tuc.gr
[2] Artificial Intelligence Research Institute, CSIC, Barcelona, Spain
ageorg@iiia.csic.es

Abstract. In this paper we put forward ε-MC nets, a novel succinct rule-based representation scheme for large cooperative games. First, we provide a polynomial algorithm that reaches the proposed representation by exploiting the agents' estimates over marginal contributions, along with their acceptable information loss, ε, regarding these estimates. Then we introduce the notion of *equivalence classes* of agents, and exploit it to *(i)* obtain an even more compact representation; and *(ii)* derive *new*, previously unheld, beliefs over the value of unobserved agent collaboration patterns. Moreover, we present theoretical and empirical results on the information loss arising from this "representational compression", and on the degree of succinctness achieved. Notably, we show that an arbitrary number of merges to reach the compressed representation, exhibits an information loss that does not exceed ε. Finally, we provide theoretical guarantees for the coalitional relative error and the Shapley value in the ε-MC net with respect to the initial representation.

Keywords: Knowledge representation · Large coalitional games · MC nets · Rule-based representation · Equivalent agents

1 Introduction

Coalitional games [2] capture settings where individuals need to form coalitions in order to fulfil some complicated task, which they would not be able to accomplish on their own or to achieve better outcomes. As the number of individuals scales up, the number of different possible coalitions one may participate in rises exponentially. Thus, it is essential to find schemes for representing large coalitional games in an efficient way. Moreover, in large open multiagent systems, we may have hundreds or thousands of agents which form coalitions in order to perform complex tasks. In such large settings, it is unrealistic to assume that we can have complete knowledge over every possible collaboration pattern between the agents. As such, it is natural to assume that we have *estimates* over the value of potential collaboration patterns. Fully representing such multiagent systems can be extremely inefficient as the number of agents rises.

G. Memmi et al. (Eds.): KSEM 2022, LNAI 13370, pp. 178–190, 2022.
https://doi.org/10.1007/978-3-031-10989-8_15

In this light, we provide a novel representation that encodes the prior information of the agents over the value of some observed collaboration patterns in a succinct way. Specifically, we build on the celebrated MC-nets representation [3,6–8], and enhance it with the ability to exploit similarities among agent collaboration patterns. To do so, we equip our scheme with an $\varepsilon \in \mathbb{R}^+$ signifying how far away from our perceived value of a collaboration pattern we are willing to deviate in order to compress an original rule. Acknowledging that the environment is not fully observable (i.e., the values of the rules of the initial representation may be different than the true ones), allowing a deviation of at most ε in order to compress the representation is a reasonable trade-off. The $\varepsilon-$MC nets representation captures collaboration patterns with similar values among similar agents; encodes them into compact rules; and retains the highly attractive *full expressiveness* and *conciseness* properties of the MC net representation.[1]

As such, our contributions in this paper are as follows. First, we propose a novel succinct representation scheme for (large) cooperative games. Then, we provide an algorithm that compresses the original game to reach the $\varepsilon-$MC nets representation; study its complexity; and provide theoretical results regarding: *(i)* the information loss of the perceived value of agent collaboration patterns; *(ii)* the relative error on the coalitional values; and *(iii)* the (estimated) *Shapley value* [11] of the game after the representation's compression, showing that they are bounded by ε, and a value proportional to ε, respectively. We extend our algorithm so that it exploits "equivalence classes" of agents in order to produce an even more compact representation of the game, inspired by the original work of [8]. This variant can also *produce* new, previously unknown, collaboration patterns among agents. Finally, we conduct a systematic evaluation of our algorithm, studying its behaviour in various realistic settings, and reporting on the degree of succinctness achieved and other measures of interest. Our experimental results confirm the effectiveness of our approach.

2 Preliminaries

Let $N = \{1, \ldots, n\}$ be a finite non-empty set of agents, with $|N| = n$. A coalitional game with transferable utility, also referred to as *characteristic function game (CFG)*, is given by a pair $\langle N, v\rangle$, where N is a set of agents, and $v : 2^N \rightarrow \mathbb{R}$ a characteristic function that maps each coalition $S \subseteq N$ to a real number [2]. The *Marginal Contribution Networks* representation [8] for a CFG $G = \langle N, v\rangle$ is given by a set of rules of the form: *Pattern* $\rightarrow$ *value.* A pattern consists of positive and negative literals, where each literal corresponds to some agent. The "positiveness" or "negativeness" of the literal indicates that agent's presence or absence in the pattern, respectively. A rule $r : p_1 \wedge p_2 \wedge \cdots \wedge p_x \wedge \neg n_1 \wedge \neg n_2 \wedge \cdots \wedge \neg n_y \rightarrow val_r$ applies on a coalition $S \subseteq N$, denoted by $S \models r$, *iff* each positive literal p_i exists in S, i.e., $p_i \in S$ for $i = 1, \ldots, x$, and no negative literal n_j exists in S, i.e., $n_j \notin S$ for $j = 1, \ldots, y$. Given a coalition S, we can compute its utility by summing up the values of all

[1] This work is an improved version of our earlier work presented in [13].

the rules that apply to S: $v(S) \equiv \sum_{S \models r} val_r$. [8] shows that *(i)* any CFG can be represented by a set of such rules [8], and *(ii)* computing the Shapley values [11] in an MC-net representation is easy.

3 The ε-MC Net Representation

Here we describe the $\varepsilon-$MC nets representation scheme. An ε-MC net constitutes a compact set of rules based on an initial MC-net representation. The compactness is achieved by merging patterns and regulating the rule-values accordingly. Let $N = \{a_1, \cdots, a_n\}$ be a set of agents ($|N| = n$) and $L = \{i, \neg i \; \forall a_i \in N\}$ be the set of literals corresponding to agents in N ($|L| = 2 \cdot n$). Formally,

Definition 1 ($\varepsilon-$*MC net Rule*). An $\varepsilon-$MC net rule is of the form $i \wedge \text{CG} \rightarrow val$. Here $i \in L$ is called the *common literal* and CG, the i's *collaborations group*, is of the form $\{\{\bigwedge_{j \in L, j \neq i} j\}, \{\bigwedge_{k \in L, k \neq i} k\}, \cdots\}$, and represents a set of distinct collaboration patterns among agents in $N \setminus \{a_i\}$. Each pattern $p = \{\bigwedge_{j \in L, j \neq i} j\}$ is a conjunction among a subset of literals in L; while an agent's positive and negative literals cannot both appear in the same p. $val \in \mathbb{R}$ expresses the estimated value of the collaboration pattern between literal i and any pattern of literals $p \in \text{CG}$. $\varepsilon \in \mathbb{R}^+$ is a parameter denoting how far from the rule's value we are willing to depart in order to compress the representation.

Intuitively, the $\varepsilon-$MC net rule denotes that a collaboration between i and *any* pattern of literals p in CG, has an expected value val. (Thus, in reality CG is a disjunction $\vee$ of patterns.) Then, ε represents the margin of information loss we are willing to accept in order to compress the representation; specifically, it denotes the acceptable information loss for merging an MC-net rule with some other rule (be that an MC-net or an ε-MC net one; this will be clarified in what follows). Naturally, the larger the ε, the wider these margins are, and the more compact the representation we obtain. Notice that any MC-net rule can be trivially written as an ε-MC net rule (with one pattern $p \in \text{CG}$ and an arbitrary i as the common literal); while any ε-MC net rule can be rewritten as a collection of MC-net rules (see e.g., Sect. 3.2 below).

The process of compressing an initial MC-net set of rules to a final set of $\varepsilon-$MC nets rules works by progressively building the collaborations group around some common literal, via merging rules. We distinguish two types of merging: *(a)* the full-merge, and *(b)* the half-merge. The *full-merge* describes the merge of two MC-net rules that produces a new $\varepsilon-$MC net rule. A full-merge can occur if the rules share a *common literal* (indicating the presence or absence of mutual agent) between the rules, and if the values of the two rules differ by at most ε, where ε is the margin of information loss that we are willing to accept. Formally, two MC-net rules $r_1 : Pattern_1 \rightarrow val_1$ and $r_2 : Pattern_2 \rightarrow val_2$, where $Pattern_1$ and $Pattern_2$ are a conjunction of literals,[2] can be full-merged (CanFullMerge(r_1, r_2)) *iff*:

[2] Note that a pattern may consist of only one literal, representing singletons, thus we can assume that $i \rightarrow val \equiv i \wedge \bot \rightarrow val$, where $\bot$ is the empty clause.

Algorithm 1. Merging MC-net Rules

```
1: R ← initial set of MC-net rules of size m
2: R' ← ∅
3: for r ∈ R do
4:    CG ← ∅
5:    V_CG, min, max, avg ← val_r
6:    Remove r from R
7:    for r' ∈ R do
8:       if CanFullMerge(r, r') OR CanHalfMerge(r, r') then
9:          Insert val_r' in V_CG
10:         Insert non common literals in CG
11:         Update min, max, avg variables
12:         Rule r becomes: {common literal} ∧ CG → avg{V_CG}
13:         Remove r' from R
14:      end if
15:   end for
16:   Insert r in R'
17: end for
18: return R'
```

(I) $i \equiv j$, where $i \in Pattern_1$ and $j \in Pattern_2$. The two literals are identical if they refer to the same agent, and they are both positive or both negative;
(II) $|val_1 - val_2| \leq \varepsilon$, i.e., the values of the two rules are at most ε away.

The resulting ε–MC net rule is $r_{merged} : l_{common} \wedge \text{CG} \rightarrow \frac{val_1+val_2}{2}$, where l_{common} is the common literal, and $\text{CG} = \{Pattern_1', Pattern_2'\}$, where $Pattern_1' = Pattern_1 \backslash \{i\}$ and $Pattern_2' = Pattern_2 \backslash \{j\}$. Similarly, given an ε-MC net rule $r : i \wedge \text{CG} \rightarrow avg\{V_{CG}\}$, where CG is a set of patterns and V_{CG} is the set containing all the values of the rules merged so far to produce r, and their average value $avg\{V_{CG}\}$ is the value of r; and an MC-net rule $r_3 : Pattern_3 \rightarrow val_3$, we say that r_3 can be half-merged with r (CanHalfMerge(r, r_3)) *iff*:

(III) $i \equiv j$, where $j \in Pattern_3$. The two literals are identical if they refer to the same agent, and they are both positive or both negative; and
(IV) $avg\{V_{\text{CG}}\} - \varepsilon \leq val_3 \leq avg\{V_{\text{CG}}\} + \varepsilon$; and
(V) $\max_{v \in V_{\text{CG}}} v - \varepsilon \leq avg\{V_{\text{CG}} \cup \{val_3\}\} \leq \min_{v \in V_{\text{CG}}} v + \varepsilon$.

The resulting rule after the half-merge is: $r_{merged} : i \wedge \text{CG}' \rightarrow avg\{V_{\text{CG}} \cup \{val_3\}\}$, where $\text{CG}' \equiv \text{CG} \cup \{Pattern_3'\}$, and $Pattern_3' = Pattern_3 \backslash \{j\}$. (We discern two sets of merging conditions, since we use different kind of rules in each case.)

Algorithm 1 illustrates a quadratic (in the number of rules) algorithm that performs a series of full- and half-merges, compressing the initial set of MC-net rules R to a succinct representation captured via R' of ε–MC nets rules, with $|R'| \leq |R| = m$. Going through Algorithm 1, we see that the outer loop in line 3 needs exactly m iterations, where m is the size of the initial set of MC-net rules. The inner loop in lines 7–15 needs at most m iterations; while the condition in line 8 is trivial. As such the complexity of the algorithm is $\mathcal{O}(m^2)$.

In a nutshell, the ε-MC net representation has a number of desired properties. First of all, it retains the fully expressiveness and the conciseness of the classic MC nets representation, but is also able to form even more compact rules by performing a series of merges between rules with similar values that contain common literals. Moreover, note that the proposed representation applies to settings with uncertainty by simply "paying" an additional information loss, which in any case never exceeds ε, as we show in the next section. Another beneficial property of the ε-MC net representation is that it allows us to exploit the common literal to prune the initial rule space while computing the coalitional values by disregarding rules where their common literal is not part of the coalition of interest. Finally, our scheme easily adopts a notion of equivalent classes of agents to not only further compress the representation, but also to *learn* new rules from previously unheld information that emerges through the compression process.

3.1 A Bound on the Values of $\varepsilon-$MC Nets Rules

Here we provide a bound that our representation guarantees on the maximum information loss of any $\varepsilon-$MC nets rule with respect to its initial MC-net rule. We show that due to the necessary conditions for full- and half-merge, the information loss on the initial values is at most ε. Obviously this bound is tight.

Lemma 1. *For any full-merge between two MC-net rules r_x and r_y producing a new $\varepsilon-$MC net rule r_z, it holds that: $|val_z - val| \leq \frac{\varepsilon}{2}$, where $val = \{val_x, val_y\}$.*

Proof. It is straightforward following condition (II).

Theorem 1. *For any MC-net rule $\tilde{r} : i \wedge Pattern_j \rightarrow val$ that is merged (either full- or half-merged) in the process of reaching an ε-MC net rule $r_{merged} : i \wedge CG_{merged} \rightarrow v_{merged}$, with $CG_{merged} = \{Pattern_j, Pattern_k, \cdots, Pattern_x\}$ and $v_{merged} = avg\{V_{CG_{merged}}\}$, it holds that: $|v_{merged} - val| \leq \varepsilon$.*

Proof. All proofs can be found in https://rb.gy/aexgbt.

Note that since the coalitional utility is derived by *summing* the rules applying in the coalition at hand, a direct consequence of Theorem 1 is that the utility of a coalition S is computed via the ε-MC nets rules, exhibits an information loss *equal at most to* $\sum_{S \models r} \varepsilon$, where r is any ε-MC net rule that applies to S.

3.2 Decompression of the ε-MC Net Representation

Given an initial MC-net representation described by a set of rules R, we achieve a compressed $\varepsilon-$MC net representation described by a set of rules R' following the merging rules detailed in the previous section. We can always decompress R' into a set $\hat{R}$ of classic MC-net rules (with $|\hat{R}| \geq |R'|$ and $|\hat{R}| = |R|$): $R \overset{\text{compress}}{\longrightarrow} R' \overset{\text{decompress}}{\longrightarrow} \hat{R}$.

We present the process in order to be comprehensive and provide clarity. Let an ε-MC net rule $r' : i \wedge CG \rightarrow v_{r'}$ where $CG = \{\text{pattern}_1,$

$\text{pattern}_2, \cdots, \text{pattern}_k\}$, which has been reached by the merges (both full- and half-) over the rules in R. Any such ε−MC net rule r' can then always be substituted by the rules in $\hat{R}$:

$$R = \left.\begin{matrix} r_1 : i \wedge \text{pattern}_1 \to val_1 \\ r_2 : i \wedge \text{pattern}_2 \to val_2 \\ \vdots \\ r_k : i \wedge \text{pattern}_k \to val_k \end{matrix}\right\} k \quad ; \quad \hat{R} = \left.\begin{matrix} \hat{r}_1 : i \wedge \text{pattern}_1 \to v_{r'} \\ \hat{r}_2 : i \wedge \text{pattern}_2 \to v_{r'} \\ \vdots \\ \hat{r}_k : i \wedge \text{pattern}_k \to v_{r'} \end{matrix}\right\} k$$

Hence $\hat{R}$ is a decompressed set of rules such that $|R| = |\hat{R}|$. Note that there is exact correspondence between R and $\hat{R}$, i.e., for each rule in R there is exactly one rule in $\hat{R}$ describing the same collaboration. We remind the reader that according to Theorem 1 for any initial rule $r_j : i \wedge \text{pattern}_j \to val_j$ in R and its corresponding decompressed rule $\hat{r}_j : i \wedge \text{pattern}_j \to v$ in $\hat{R}$ it holds that $|v - val_j| \leq \varepsilon$. Finally, notice that the decompressed representation is a classic MC-net representation. A similar procedure can be applied in the variant with equivalent classes, however, in this case we have that $|\hat{R}| \geq |R|$.

3.3 Relative Error Guarantees

Earlier we presented a theoretical bound on the *absolute* error, ε, between the merged value and the value of an initial MC-net rule. However, this suggests an *a priori knowledge* over the magnitude of the rule values, which may not be always the case, especially in large cooperative environments. Instead, one may find more beneficial to express a *relative* error, $\tilde{\varepsilon}$, on the coalitional values. Thus, we now explore the relation between relative and absolute errors in order to exploit the useful results previously obtained.

Assume we want to compress the initial MC-net representation into an ε-MC net one, while the relative error of the coalitional values does not exceed $\tilde{\varepsilon}$. The value of some S in the initial MC-net R is given by $v(S) = \sum_{i=1}^{\mu_S} val_{r_i}$ where μ_S is the number of rules that apply on S; similarly, in a decompressed ε-MC net R' the value of S is $v'(S) = \sum_{i=1}^{\mu_S} v_{r'_i}$. Thus, for any S we demand that $\left|\frac{v(S)-v'(S)}{v(S)}\right| \leq \tilde{\varepsilon}$. Following Theorem 1, the absolute error between the two coalitional values is: $|v(S) - v'(S)| \leq \mu_S \cdot \varepsilon$, and thus for the relative error it holds that $\left|\frac{v(S)-v'(S)}{v(S)}\right| \leq \frac{\mu_S}{v(S)} \cdot \varepsilon$, which does not exceed $\tilde{\varepsilon}$ if and only if $\varepsilon \leq \frac{v(S)}{\mu_S} \cdot \tilde{\varepsilon}$. Thus, we need to find an acceptable information loss ε such that for any coalition S it holds $\varepsilon \leq \frac{v(S)}{\mu_S} \cdot \tilde{\varepsilon}$; in other words any absolute error $\varepsilon \leq \tilde{\varepsilon} \cdot \min_{S \subseteq N} \frac{v(S)}{\mu_S}$.

3.4 Equivalence Classes of Agents

Here we discuss a variant of our representation that exploits not only (the presence or absence of) *mutual* agents (indicated via common literals), but also *equivalence classes* of agents: agents in the same class may have similar behaviour, preferences or properties. Such a variant can be very useful in partially observable environments, where we are aware of a subset of collaboration patterns, or in settings where new agents arrive over time. Considering equivalences among agents we manage to: *(a) compress even more* the representation compared to the initial version; *(b) extract underlying collaboration patterns that are "new"*, as they could not have been observed in the initial set of MC-net rules.

Definition 2 (Equivalent Agents). *Given a set of agents N, and a similarity metric $s : N \times N \rightarrow [0, 1]$, two agents i and j are equivalent iff $s(i, j) \geq T$, with T a threshold in $[0, 1]$.*[3]

In this version, the rules take the form $\Omega_{\text{equiv}} \wedge \text{CG} \rightarrow val$, where Ω_{equiv} is a set of equivalent agents (all as positive or all as negative literals) and it substitutes the *common literal* of the initial representation. In words, a rule $\Omega_{\text{equiv}} \wedge \text{CG} \rightarrow val$ is interpreted as: *Our estimate of the collaboration between any literal $i \in \Omega_{\text{equiv}}$ with any pattern $p \in \text{CG}$ is equal to val.* We can easily obtain the variant with the equivalence classes by slightly changing Algorithm 1. That is, we simply need to check whether the rules r and r' have agents in the same *equivalence class* instead of just mutual agents (i.e., common literals). In other words, we need to check if there exists a literal i in Ω_{equiv} on rule r such that any of the literals in rule r' belongs in the same equivalence class. Such a modification results to an increase in the computational complexity to $\mathcal{O}(n^2 \cdot m^2)$, where n is the number of agents, and m is the size of the initial set of rules.[4]

Intuitively, in this version agents belonging in the same class are expected to have similar behaviour, preferences or properties—for example, in a search & rescue mission all firefighters comprise one equivalence class, while all nurses another. We are thus able to obtain an estimate over the utility of a previously unseen collaborative pattern based on our expectations that equivalent agents behave similarly. Of course, there is a trade-off: to extract new patterns, we drop our guarantees provided by our theoretical results.

Now, this variation may result in *ambiguous* $\varepsilon-$MC nets rules: depending on the way agents' equivalence is determined, we may end up producing overlapping rules, i.e., multiple $\varepsilon-$MC nets rules may apply to the very same collaborative pair. To overcome this ambiguity we set the *post-merge estimate* for a collaboration pattern p to the average value of the rules that apply to p.

4 Shapley Values for ε-MC Nets

In this section we explore the concept of *Shapley value* in the ε-MC net representation, and provide theoretical guarantees on the error incurred. The Shapley value [11] is a celebrated solution concept designed to capture the notion of

[3] The threshold denotes the minimum similarity degree for two agents in order for them to be equivalent, and depends on the problem at hand. In our experimental evaluation we demonstrate how to employ specific correlation metrics to this purpose.

[4] To ensure the practicality of the algorithm for large n and m, we note that our implementation *samples* an agent in Ω_{equiv}, and checks the conditions for mutual *or* equivalent agents. Thus the complexity of our *implementation*, is $\mathcal{O}(n \cdot m^2)$.

fairness in CFGs. Intuitively, it grants each player i a payment ϕ_i that is proportional to her expected marginal contribution in the game. Given an MC-net representation, we can compute the Shapley values of the agents.

Proposition 1 ([8]). *The Shapley value of an agent in a marginal contribution network is equal to the sum of the Shapley values of that agent over each rule.*

Proposition 2. *Proposition 1 holds for the ε-MC nets as well.*

Next we compute the *Shapley values* of the agents over the rules in the ε-MC net representation. Following [8], we distinguish two cases, considering (a) *positive literals* and (b) *mixed literals* (both positive and negative).

Only Positive Literals. The Shapley value of any MC-net rule $r : i \wedge Pattern \rightarrow val_r$ that contains only positive literals, is equal to $\frac{val}{m}$, where val is the value of the rule and m is the number of literals in the pattern [8]. In a ε-MC net rule r', the Shapley value of an agent i depends on whether the agents is the common literal in the rule. That is, in case i is the common literal in r' then: $\phi_{\varepsilon,i,r'} = \sum_{c \in CG_{r'}} \frac{val_{r'}}{|c|+1}$, while if i is in a pattern c within the collaborations group, then: $\phi_{\varepsilon,i,r'} = \frac{val_{r'}}{|c|+1}$.

Theorem 2. *Given an ε-MC nets representation R' with only positive literals, for any agent i, we obtain an estimate $\phi_{\varepsilon,i} = \sum_{r \in R'_i} \phi_{\varepsilon,i,r}$ of the actual Shapley value ϕ_i s.t.: $|\phi_i - \phi_{\varepsilon,i}| \leq \sum_{r \in R_i} \frac{\varepsilon}{m_r}$, where R_i and R'_i are the subsets of rules regarding agent i in the initial and the ε-MC net representation, respectively.*

Mixed Literals. Inspired by [8], for rules that have mixed literals, we can consider the positive and the negative literals separately. According to [8] in a classic MC-net representation, if i is a positive literal, a rule r will apply *iff* i occurs in a given permutation after the rest of the positive literals but before any of the negative literals. Formally, let $\phi_{i,r}$ denote the Shapley value of i, p_r denote the cardinality of the positive set, and n_r denote the cardinality of the negative set, then: $\phi_{i,r} = \frac{(p_r-1)!n_r!}{(p_r+n_r)!} \cdot val_r = \frac{val_r}{p_r \cdot \binom{p_r+n_r}{n_r}}$.

Similarly to the case with only positive literals, the Shapley value of an agent i as positive literal in an ε-MC net rule depends on whether i is the common literal. That is, if i is the common literal in ε-MC net rule r' then $\phi_{\varepsilon,i,r'} = \sum_{c \in CG_{r'}} \frac{val_{r'}}{p_c \cdot \binom{p_c+n_c}{n_c}}$ where p_c denote the cardinality of the positive set in pattern $c \in CG_{r'}$, and n_c denote the cardinality of the negative set in $c \in CG_{r'}$.[5] Now if i is in pattern c within the collaborations group, then $\phi_{\varepsilon,i,r'} = \frac{val_{r'}}{p_c \cdot \binom{p_c+n_c}{n_c}}$.

For a given negative literal $\neg i$, the appearance of i in some pattern will be responsible for cancelling the application of the rule if all positive literals come before the negative literals in the ordering, and $\neg i$ is the first among the negative

[5] The cardinality of positive/negative sets in pattern c also considers the common literal.

literals. That is, let rule $r : a \wedge b \wedge \neg i \wedge \neg j \rightarrow val$, i is responsible for canceling the application of r in any permutation of some pattern where literals a and b proceed the appearance of i, while j either appears after i or not at all. Therefore: $\phi_{\neg i,r} = \frac{p_r!(n_r-1)!}{(p_r+n_r)!} \cdot (-val_r) = \frac{-val_r}{n_r \cdot \binom{p_r+n_r}{p_r}}$.

Again, the Shapley value of an agent i as negative literal in an ε-MC net rule depends on whether i is the common literal. That is, if i is the common literal in ε-MC net rule r' then $\phi_{\varepsilon,\neg i,r'} = \sum_{c \in CG_{r'}} \frac{-val_{r'}}{n_c \cdot \binom{p_c+n_c}{p_c}}$; while if i is in pattern c within the collaborations group, then $\phi_{\varepsilon,\neg i,r'} = \frac{val_{r'}}{n_c \cdot \binom{p_c+n_c}{p_c}}$.

Theorem 3. *Given an ε-MC nets representation R' (with mixed literals), for any agent i (appearing as a positive literal i, a negative literal $\neg i$, or both) we can provide an estimate $\phi_{\varepsilon,i} = \sum_{r \in R_i'^+} \phi_{\varepsilon,i,r} + \sum_{r \in R_i'^-} \phi_{\varepsilon,\neg i,r}$ of the actual Shapley value ϕ_i such that:*

$$|\phi_i - \phi_{\varepsilon,i}| \leq \varepsilon \cdot \Big(\sum_{r \in R_i^+} \frac{1}{p_r \cdot \binom{p_r+n_r}{n_r}} + \sum_{r \in R_i^-} \frac{1}{n_r \cdot \binom{p_r+n_r}{p_r}} \Big)$$

where $R_i'^+ \subseteq R'$ and $R_i'^- \subseteq R'$ are subsets of rules regarding agent i as positive or negative literal in the ε-MC net representation R'. Respectively, $R_i^+ \subseteq R$ and $R_i^- \subseteq R$ are subsets of rules regarding agent i as positive or negative literal in the initial MC net representation R.

5 Experimental Evaluation

Here we evaluate the performance of our algorithms via simulations. All experiments ran on a PC with i5@2.2 GHz and 8 GB of RAM. The framework was coded in Python 3.8. We used synthetic data, and the presented results are the average values over 5 sets of experiments on settings with same properties *wrt.* ε, and number of agents and rules used, as we explain immediately below.

5.1 ε-MC Nets with Mutual Agents

First we present experiments performed to evaluate our approach with mutual agents (i.e., common literals), using synthetic data. We generated synthetic data with varying number of agents $n = \{100, 200, 300\}$ and rules $m = \{\frac{n\cdot(n-1)}{2}, \frac{n\cdot(n-1)}{3}, \frac{n\cdot(n-1)}{4}\}$. In each dataset, every rule consists of a pair of agents, (either as positive or negative literals, i.e. we have in total $2 \cdot n$ literals) randomly selected out of $\binom{n}{2}$ possible unordered pairs; and the rule's value is drawn from $\mathcal{U}(1, 200)$. For each $\langle n, m \rangle$ we generated 5 datasets, to a total of 45 datasets.

We ran our algorithm for each setting using different values of ε. We use the *reduction percentage (RP)* to measure the compactness achieved in the ε−MC nets representation by computing the number of rules comprising the new representation compared to the initial MC-net one. Formally,

$$RP = \Big(1 - \frac{\#\varepsilon\text{-MC nets rules} + \#\text{un-merged rules}}{\#\text{initial MC-net-like rules}}\Big) \cdot 100\%$$

Figure 1a illustrates the results of applying Algorithm 1 on this set of experiments. We can see that for ε fixed across different settings, the RP achieved by our algorithm increases as the number of rules increases. Such a result is expected, since when we have more rules it is more likely to find MC-net rules that satisfy the conditions for merging, and thus the algorithm produces more compact representations. Also, for the same number of MC-net rules, as ε increases, we observe that the achieved reduction increases as well. This is due to the fact that for greater values of ε, the conditions for merging are more relaxed, and thus easier to be met. Indicatively, in settings with $n = 300$, $m = 44850$ and $\varepsilon = 2$ we get $RP = 66.5\%$, while for $n = 300, m = 44850, \varepsilon = 8$ we achieve $RP = 85.1\%$. Note that for m $= \frac{n\cdot(n-1)}{2}$ our algorithm always achieves RP greater than 46%.

5.2 Mutual vs Equivalent Agents

We now compare the performance of our approach using only mutual agents against its variant that considers equivalent agents, in terms of RP. Here we generated 75 synthetic datasets, 5 for each $\langle n, m\rangle$ combination, following the process described in the previous section; now $n = 50, 100, 200, 300$ and 400, while $m = \frac{n\cdot(n-1)}{2}, \frac{n\cdot(n-1)}{3}$, and $\frac{n\cdot(n-1)}{4}$; and again rule values are drawn from $\mathcal{U}(1, 200)$. In order to determine equivalence among agents we adopted the following scenario: agents participate in a *ridesharing setting* as drivers or commuters. First, to determine the agents' payoffs, we ran the "PK Algorithm" from [1], which computes *kernel-stable* [2,12] payments for such scenarios. Specifically, for each dataset we run the PK algorithm for a number of partitions depending on the number of agents in the dataset. Each such partition consists of a randomly sampled coalition S containing one driver (20% of agents are drivers) and 1 to 4 commuters, along with a set of singletons corresponding to the remaining agents.

In order to determine equivalent classes of agents, as soon as we have the agents payoffs received in different sampled partitions, for every i, j pair we build two ranking lists M_i and M_j respectively, as follows: *For the kth sampled partition π (with $S \in \pi$): (1) if $\{i, j\} \subseteq S$, then add i's payoff according π in the kth position of M_i and add j's payoff according π in the kth position of M_j; otherwise (2) $i \in S$ and $\exists\ \pi'$ such that $j \in S'$ and $S \setminus \{i\} \equiv S' \setminus \{j\}$ with $S' \in \pi'$, then add i's payoff according π in the kth position of M_i and add j's payoff according π' in the kth position of M_j.* We then use the lists above by applying the Kendall's τ distance [9] and the Pearson Correlation Coefficient (PCC) [4], and we consider agents i and j to be equivalent[6] if it holds that $K(M_i, M_j) \geq 0.97$ *and* $r_{M_i,M_j} \geq 0.97$. Figure 1b shows the results (average over 5 datasets with the same combination $\langle n, m\rangle$). We see that the algorithm that takes advantage of equivalences consistently achieves *manyfold greater reduction* than the algorithm with the mutual agents. Indicatively, for $n = 300$, $m = 44850$ and $\varepsilon = 2$ we achieve an $RP = 81.45\%$ compared to ∼66.5% for solely mutual agents. Finally, the variant with equivalence classes achieves an RP up to 87.5%

[6] We consider equivalences only on positive literals.

for $n = 400$, $m = 79800$, $\varepsilon = 3$. This improvement is expected, since equivalences allows us to exploit information not considered with mutual agents only.

Finally, our experiments confirm that the extra information on equivalences among agents allows us to not only produce more succinct representations, but to also learn new collaboration patterns. We show this through the NCP ratio:

$$NCP = \frac{\text{New collaboration patterns}}{\text{Total number of collaboration patterns}} \cdot 100\%,$$

		ε = 2	ε = 4	ε = 6	ε = 8
n = 100	m = 2475	33.35%	44.60%	51.88%	56.90%
	m = 3300	38.32%	49.60%	57.10%	62.27%
	m = 4950	46.50%	57.75%	64.74%	69.49%
n = 200	m = 9950	46.62%	57.87%	64.77%	69.46%
	m = 13267	51.97%	63.18%	69.70%	74.15%
	m = 19900	59.50%	70.26%	76.26%	80.04%
n = 300	m = 22425	54.12%	65.40%	71.85%	76.11%
	m = 29900	59.56%	70.31%	76.24%	80.01%
	m = 44850	66.56%	76.57%	81.82%	85.10%

(a)

		ε = 1	ε = 2	ε = 3
n = 50	m = 613	18.95%	25.00%	28.20%
	m = 817	19.92%	27.23%	30.61%
	m = 1225	21.52%	27.73%	30.37%
n = 100	m = 2475	47.20%	56.65%	60.76%
	m = 3300	48.12%	56.24%	60.05%
	m = 4950	47.95%	54.29%	56.51%
n = 200	m = 9950	67.91%	73.57%	75.63%
	m = 13267	66.86%	71.01%	72.38%
	m = 19900	61.68%	63.41%	64.26%
n = 300	m = 22425	76.47%	79.00%	79.77%
	m = 29900	73.35%	74.75%	75.13%
	m = 44850	64.75%	65.16%	65.28%
n = 400	m = 39900	79.58%	80.66%	80.95%
	m = 53200	75.08%	75.61%	75.71%
	m = 79800	65.48%	65.68%	65.76%

(c)

			ε = 1	ε = 2	ε = 3
n = 50	m = 613	ε-MCMut	14.70%	21.98%	27.20%
		ε-MCEq	23.77%	32.13%	37.64%
	m = 817	ε-MCMut	18.74%	26.87%	32.45%
		ε-MCEq	28.29%	37.59%	43.47%
	m = 1225	ε-MCMut	23.08%	32.81%	39.04%
		ε-MCEq	33.09%	43.18%	49.43%
n = 100	m = 2475	ε-MCMut	24.06%	33.35%	39.65%
		ε-MCEq	43.77%	53.25%	58.77%
	m = 3300	ε-MCMut	28.99%	38.70%	45.40%
		ε-MCEq	48.41%	57.44%	62.97%
	m = 4950	ε-MCMut	35.85%	46.41%	52.88%
		ε-MCEq	54.99%	63.93%	68.79%
n = 200	m = 9950	ε-MCMut	36.09%	46.58%	52.92%
		ε-MCEq	60.28%	67.72%	72.49%
	m = 13267	ε-MCMut	41.39%	51.93%	58.27%
		ε-MCEq	63.84%	71.33%	75.58%
	m = 19900	ε-MCMut	48.78%	59.51%	65.68%
		ε-MCEq	69.20%	76.19%	80.07%
n = 300	m = 22425	ε-MCMut	43.60%	54.18%	60.46%
		ε-MCEq	67.98%	74.59%	78.19%
	m = 29900	ε-MCMut	48.74%	59.51%	65.68%
		ε-MCEq	71.29%	77.59%	80.93%
	m = 44850	ε-MCMut	55.98%	66.48%	72.46%
		ε-MCEq	75.50%	81.45%	84.52%
n = 400	m = 39900	ε-MCMut	48.89%	59.41%	65.68%
		ε-MCEq	72.53%	78.54%	81.81%
	m = 53200	ε-MCMut	54.01%	65.70%	70.65%
		ε-MCEq	75.60%	81.36%	84.40%
	m = 79800	ε-MCMut	60.92%	71.29%	76.88%
		ε-MCEq	79.49%	84.73%	87.50%

(b)

Fig. 1. (a) *RP* for Algorithm 1 with only Mutual Agents. (b) *RP* per setting of "Mutual vs Equivalent Agents". (c) *NCP* per setting of "Mutual vs Equivalent Agents".

where the denominator corresponds to the number of initial MC-net rules plus the new collaborative pairs of agents that our algorithm produced, exploiting equivalences among agents.[7] Figure 1c shows the *NCP*s for every setting when we employ the algorithm using equivalence classes of agents (averages are over the 5 different datasets for each combination $\langle n, m \rangle$). As the results show, for a given n, the *NCP* is rising as ε rises. Intuitively, since for larger ε our algorithm achieves more merges, and new collaboration patterns are discovered. Indicatively, in settings with n = 400, m = 39900 and $\varepsilon = 3$, we achieve an NCP ∼80.95%.

6 Conclusions and Future Work

In this work we introduced a novel succinct representation for cooperative games. This extends the work of [8] to have rules that include sets of agents, instead of

[7] In case of ambiguities, we count the collaboration pattern once.

just individuals. We formally defined the $\varepsilon-$MC nets rules, merging conditions, and we proposed a polynomial algorithm for constructing such a representation. Moreover, we provided theoretical bounds regarding the Shapley value, and the absolute and relative error of the compressed representation *wrt* the initial one. Then, as envisaged by [8], we considered equivalence classes of agents, and put forward a variant of our algorithm which takes these into account, and which can generate values for collaboration patterns that were initially unknown.

Future work will extend our algorithm to perform a *backtracking* technique. That is, merges rejected at some point may become feasible due to equivalent agents. One could also devise techniques to exploit the initial order of rules, in the spirit of heuristics used in constraint satisfaction problems; explore *machine learning* to extract the equivalent classes of agents, in terms of agents' behaviour [10] or preferences [5].

Acknowledgements. E. Streviniotis has been supported by the Onassis Foundation - Scholarship ID: G ZR 012-1/2021-2022. A. Georgara has been supported by TAILOR (H2020-952215), 2019DI17, Crowd4SDG (H2020-872944), CI-SUSTAIN (PID2019-104156GB-I00) and Enzyme Advising Group.

References

1. Bistaffa, F., Farinelli, A., Chalkiadakis, G., Ramchurn, S.: A cooperative game-theoretic approach to the social ridesharing problem. Artif. Intell. **246**, 86–117 (2017)
2. Chalkiadakis, G., Elkind, E., Wooldridge, M.: Computational Aspects of Cooperative Game Theory. Morgan & Claypool Publishers, San Rafael (2011)
3. Elkind, E., Goldberg, L.A., Goldberg, P.W., Wooldridge, M.: A tractable and expressive class of marginal contribution nets and its applications. Math. Log. Q. **55**(4), 362–376 (2009)
4. Freedman, D., Pisani, R., Purves, R.: Statistics (International Student Edition), 4th edn. WW Norton & Company, New York (2007)
5. Georgara, A., Troullinos, D., Chalkiadakis, G.: Extracting hidden preferences over partitions in hedonic cooperative games. In: Douligeris, C., Karagiannis, D., Apostolou, D. (eds.) KSEM 2019. LNCS (LNAI), vol. 11775, pp. 829–841. Springer, Cham (2019). https://doi.org/10.1007/978-3-030-29551-6_73
6. Greco, G., Malizia, E., Palopoli, L., Scarcello, F.: On the complexity of core, kernel, and bargaining set. Artif. Intell. **175**(12), 1877–1910 (2011)
7. Hirayama, K., Hanada, K., Ueda, S., Yokoo, M., Iwasaki, A.: Computing a payoff division in the least core for MC-nets coalitional games. In: Principles and Practice of Multi-Agent Systems (PRIMA 2014), pp. 319–332 (2014)
8. Ieong, S., Shoham, Y.: Marginal contribution nets: a compact representation scheme for coalitional games. In: Proceedings of the 6th ACM Conference on Electronic Commerce (EC 2005), pp. 193–202 (2005)
9. Kendall, M.: Rank Correlation Methods. Griffin, London (1948)
10. Ogston, E., Overeinder, B., van Steen, M., Brazier, F.: A method for decentralized clustering in large multi-agent systems. In: Proceedings of the 2nd International Joint Conference on Autonomous Agents and Multiagent Systems, AAMAS 2003, pp. 789–796. Association for Computing Machinery, New York (2003)

11. Shapley, L.: A value for n-person games. In: Contributions to the Theory of Games II, pp. 307–317. Princeton University Press, Princeton (1953)
12. Stearns, R.E.: Convergent transfer schemes for n-person games. Trans. Am. Math. Soc. **134**(3), 449–459 (1968)
13. Streviniotis, E., Georgara, A., Chalkiadakis, G.: A succinct representation scheme for cooperative games under uncertainty. In: Proceedings of the 20th International Conference on Autonomous Agents and MultiAgent Systems, AAMAS 2021, pp. 1661–1663. International Foundation for Autonomous Agents and Multiagent Systems, Richland (2021)

An Incentive-Compatible and Efficient Mechanism for Matching and Pricing in Ride-Sharing

Bing Shi[1,2](✉), Xizi Huang[1], and Zhi Cao[1]

[1] School of Computer Science and Artificial Intelligence, Wuhan University of Technology, Wuhan, China
{bingshi,hxizi,caozhi}@whut.edu.cn

[2] Shenzhen Research Institute of Wuhan University of Technology, Shenzhen, China

Abstract. As a novel and economic transportation way, ride-sharing has attracted more and more passengers and drivers to participate. How to match passengers with drivers efficiently has become a key issue. Specifically, drivers are usually heterogeneous with different costs, and they may behave strategically (e.g. reveal their private cost information untruthfully) in order to make more profits. Drivers' strategic behavior may lead to inefficient matching, and thus result in the loss of social welfare of ride-sharing platform and drivers. In this paper, we intend to solve this issue by designing an incentive-compatible and efficient mechanism, which can match passengers with drivers and determine the payments to drivers in order to maximize the social welfare while ensuring drivers reveal their cost information truthfully. Specifically, we design an order matching algorithm with a branch and bound based route planning algorithm to accelerate the matching process. Meanwhile, we compute the payments to drivers based on the second pricing mechanism. In so doing, we propose a second pricing based ride-sharing mechanism (SPRM), which satisfies incentive compatibility, individual rationality, budget balance and computational efficiency. We further run extensive experiments to evaluate our mechanism based on the real Manhattan taxi order data and vehicle fuel consumption data. The experimental results show that SPRM can guarantee drivers' profits and improve the ratio of drivers' participation and the ratio of served orders, and eventually achieve greater social welfare than two typical benchmark approaches, GPri and ND.

Keywords: Ride-sharing · Mechanism design · Incentive compatibility · Order matching · Pricing

1 Introduction

The increased amount of vehicles results in serious traffic congestion in the urban transportation system [4]. However, these vehicles are not utilized well when providing riding service. Actually, a vehicle usually carries only 1.6 passengers on average [5]. To relieve the traffic pressure, crowdsourcing based ride-sharing

G. Memmi et al. (Eds.): KSEM 2022, LNAI 13370, pp. 191–204, 2022.
https://doi.org/10.1007/978-3-031-10989-8_16

methods are proposed, and more and more companies (e.g. Didi Chuxing and Uber) have entered this market to increase vehicle seat usage. As more and more passengers and drivers participate in such a business, the ride-sharing platform needs to match riding orders with drivers efficiently and determine the payments to drivers to incentivize them to provide the riding service.

In this paper, we assume that the platform charges up-front fares to passengers when they submit the riding orders. Note that it could be problematic to require passengers to bid for vehicles and this kind of mechanism may not work well in the practical application [10]. Therefore, we adopt the up-front fares and do not consider the strategic bidding behavior of passengers. The platform determines the up-front fares according to the pick-up and drop-off locations, current demand and supply and so on. Passengers then determine whether to accept the up-front fares or not. Then the same as some existing works [14,17], we assume that the ride-sharing platform adopts an auction mechanism to determine the matching between the orders and drivers. Specifically, the platform publishes the orders to available drivers, and then drivers compete with each other by bidding their costs for serving orders. The cost depends on several factors, such as fuel cost, vehicle wear, maintenance cost and so on. The platform then matches orders with drivers and makes the payments to drivers. However, drivers are usually self-interested, and they may untruthfully report their costs to make more profits. Drivers untruthfully revealing their cost information may lead to inefficient order matching, and then reduce the overall social welfare of drivers and the platform. Moreover, the mechanism may need to match a large number of incoming orders with thousands of feasible vehicles. Therefore, the mechanism should be computationally efficient, Therefore, we need to design an efficient mechanism that incentivizes drivers to bid truthfully to maximize the social welfare.

In more detail, we design an efficient mechanism to match orders with drivers to maximize the social welfare of the platform and drivers. This paper advances the state of art in the following ways. We design an approximated order matching algorithm with a branch and bound based route planning algorithm to accelerate the matching process, and then compute the payments to the drivers based on the second pricing mechanism. In so doing, we design a second pricing based ride-sharing mechanism, which is named SPRM. We prove that this mechanism can satisfy incentive compatibility, individual rationality, budget balance[1] and computational efficiency. We run extensive experiments to evaluate our mechanism based on the real Manhattan taxi order data and vehicle fuel consumption data. We find that SPRM can make greater social welfare than two typical benchmark approaches, GPri [17] and Nearest Dispatching (ND). The experimental results also show that SPRM can guarantee the drivers' profits and improve the ratio of drivers' participation and the ratio of served orders.

[1] Incentive compatibility means that drivers have no incentive to strategically manipulate their costs to increase their profits. Individual rationality means that the driver's profits are not negative. Budget balance means that the profits of the platform are not negative.

The rest of the paper is structured as follows. In Sect. 2, we introduce the related work. In Sect. 3, we describe the basic settings of this paper. In Sect. 4, we introduce the proposed mechanism in detail, and in Sect. 5, we experimentally evaluate the proposed mechanism. Finally, we conclude in Sect. 6.

2 Related Work

There exist plenty of works on investigating the issues of the crowdsourcing based ride-sharing systems, such as minimizing the total traveling distance [3,8], maximizing the ratio of served orders [13,15], maximizing the platform's profits [16] and so on. Furthermore, there exist some works using auction based methods to match orders with drivers. In [1], the ride-sharing platform proposes an auction-based mechanism to maximize its own profits. In [6], the authors propose a heuristic algorithm to determine ride-sharing travel plan dynamically and use VCG mechanism to determine the payments of participants. In [7], a second-price sealed auction mechanism is proposed to do the order matching to increase the ratio of served orders and minimize the traveling distance. In [17], an auction-based method is proposed to balance the supply and demand of drivers and passengers. Furthermore, there exist some works on investigating travel expenses of passengers [2], such as that in [10], a pricing algorithm is proposed for passengers based on their riding demands, and an online mechanism is proposed to encourage passengers to report information truthfully.

However, to the best of our knowledge, existing works usually ignore the profits of vehicle drivers, which may result in drivers refusing to provide the ride-sharing service if they make a loss in this business. Therefore in this paper, we propose an incentive-compatible mechanism to maximize the social welfare of the platform and the drivers, in order to ensure that both sides are willing to participate in the ride-sharing business.

3 Basic Settings

In this section, we first describe how the ride-sharing system works in this paper, and then give the relevant symbols and definitions. Finally, we provide a formal definition of the problem.

We first introduce how the online ride-hailing system works. When a passenger sends the riding orders to the platform, the platform computes the up-front fare charged to the passenger. Then the platform puts the orders where the passengers have accepted the fares into the order pool and publish these orders to the online drivers. The driver will bid on the feasible orders, and then the platform matches the orders according to the drivers' bids and compute the payments to drivers.

3.1 Symbols and Definitions

We model the order matching process as a one-side reverse auction which runs in a set of time slot $\mathcal{T} = \{1, 2, \cdots, T\}$. Drivers will run on a road network to serve orders following travel plans. The related concepts are defined as follows.

Definition 1 (Order). *Order $o \in \mathcal{O}$ is defined as a tuple $(l_o^s, l_o^e, t_o^s, \overline{wt}_o, \overline{dr}_o, n_o, f_o)$, where $\mathcal{O}$ represents the set of orders. l_o^s and l_o^e represent the departure and destination of order o respectively, t_o^s is the earliest time when order o leaves l_o^s, $\overline{wt}_o$ is the maximum time that order o is willing to wait after t_o^s, and $\overline{dr}_o$ indicates the maximum detour ratio that passengers can tolerate for order o, n_o is the number of passengers in order o, f_o is the up-front fare charged to passengers by the platform.*

We use $dis(l_o^s, l_o^e)$ to represent the shortest distance between l_o^s and l_o^e. Note that passengers will withdraw their orders if the actual departure time $\overline{t_o^s}$ is more than $t_o^s + \overline{wt}_o$. Furthermore, order o has a certain detour tolerance where passengers hope that the trip distance cannot exceed $(1 + \overline{dr_o}) \cdot dis(l_o^s, l_o^e)$.

Definition 2 (Driver). *Driver $d \in \mathcal{D}$ is defined as a tuple $(\theta_d, \mathcal{O}_d)$, where $\theta_d = (l_d^s, l_d^e, [t_d^s, t_d^e], c_d, n_d)$ is the driver's type, which is the private information known by himself. In more detail, l_d^s and l_d^e represent the driver's origin and destination respectively. $[t_d^s, t_d^e]$ is the driving time interval, where t_d^s and t_d^e represent the earliest time to leave l_d^s and the latest time to reach l_d^e. c_d is the unit cost, and n_d is the maximum number of passengers that the vehicle can carry, $\mathcal{O}_d$ represents the set of orders allocated by the platform to driver d, where $\mathcal{O}_d \subseteq \mathcal{O}$. Furthermore, we use $\Theta = \{\theta_1, \theta_2, \cdots, \theta_{|D|}\}$ to denote the set of private types of all drivers, and use Θ_{-d} to denote the set of private types of all drivers excluding driver d. We use $\overline{V}$ to represent the average driving speed.*

Definition 3 (Travel Plan). *tp_d is defined as the travel plan of driver d, which is a sorted sequence of nodes $l_d^1 \to l_d^2 \to \cdots \to l_d^{|tp_d|}$, where $l_d^k (k = 1, 2, 3, ..., |tp_d|)$ is the origin or destination of the order allocated to driver d (that is $l_d^k \in \{l_o^s \mid o \in \mathcal{O}_d\} \cup \{l_o^e \mid o \in \mathcal{O}_d\}$).*

Note that the travel plan is dynamically changed when a new order is inserted. We use $dis_{tp_d}(l_u, l_v)$ to represent the actual traveling distance between l_u and l_v on the travel plan t_p, and $dis_d(tp_d)$ is the traveling distance of driver d at location l_d following travel plan tp_d:

$$dis_d(tp_d) = dis(l_d, l_d^1) + \sum_{k=1}^{|tp_d|-1} dis(l_d^k, l_d^{k+1}) \tag{1}$$

Now $dr_{tp_d}(o)$ is the actual detour ratio of order o under travel plan tp_d:

$$dr_{tp_d}(o) = dis_{tp_d}(l_o^s, l_o^e)/dis(l_o^s, l_o^e) - 1 \tag{2}$$

According to the above definition, if the driver's travel plan is feasible, the following conditions should be satisfied:

(1) $\forall o \in \mathcal{O}_d$, we have $l_o^s \prec l_o^e$ for l_o^s and l_o^e in tp_d.
(2) $\forall o \in \mathcal{O}_d$, we have $dis_{tp_d}(l_d^s, l_o^s) \leq (\overline{t_o}^s - t_d^s) \cdot \overline{V}$.
(3) $\forall o \in \mathcal{O}_d$, we have $dr_{tp_d}(o) \leq \overline{dr}_o$.
(4) $\forall o \in \mathcal{O}_d$, we have $dis_{tp_d}(l_d^s, l_d^e) \leq (t_d^e - t_d^s) \cdot \overline{V}$.
(5) The number of passengers in the vehicle does not exceed n_d.

The above condition 1 means that the driver needs to pick up and drop off passengers according to the origin and destination of the order. Condition 2 and 3 mean that the travel plan should satisfy the order's detour ratio and waiting time. Condition 4 means that the driver must arrive at the destination on time. Condition 5 means that the number of passengers in the vehicle must meet the seat limit. The travel plan that satisfies the above five conditions is called a feasible plan. We use $\mathcal{F}_d$ to represent the set of all feasible plans of the driver.

3.2 Social Welfare

In the ride-sharing system, driver d may not strategically report the type information such as departure l_d^s, destination l_d^e, travel time $[t_d^s, t_d^e]$, and vehicle seat number n_d since the platform can use some technical manners to prevent such misreporting (e.g. acquiring vehicle's location using GPS, computing the remaining available seat capacity according to vehicle type and current served orders). However, the driver can misreport the unit cost c_d to make more profits since the ride-sharing platform cannot verify the driver's cost information.

According to Eq. 1, the cost of driver d following travel plan tp_d is $cost_d(tp_d) = c_d \cdot dis_d(tp_d)$, and its profit is:

$$u_d = p_d - cost_d(tp_d) \tag{3}$$

where p_d is the payment received from the platform. The platform makes profits through the difference between the passengers' up-front fares and the payments to drivers:

$$\mathcal{U}^P = \sum_{d \in \mathcal{W}} \left(\sum_{o \in \mathcal{O}_d} f_o - p_d \right) \tag{4}$$

where $\mathcal{W} \subseteq \mathcal{D}$ is the set of drivers serving orders. Now, the social welfare of the platform and the drivers is:

$$SW = \mathcal{U}^P + \sum_{d \in \mathcal{W}} u_d = \sum_{d \in \mathcal{W}} \left(\sum_{o \in \mathcal{O}_d} f_o - cost_d(tp_d) \right) \tag{5}$$

3.3 Problem Formulation

Based on the above description, we give the problem formulation of this paper.

Definition 4 (Order Matching for Maximizing Social Welfare). *Given the set of orders $\mathcal{O}$ and the set of drivers $\mathcal{D}$, the platform determines the order matching to maximize the social welfare SW, while ensuring that the driver $d \in \mathcal{W}$ who gets the order can successfully serve the order, i.e. the travel plan of each driver is feasible ($tp_d \in \mathcal{F}_d \neq \varnothing$).*

Definition 5 (Driver Pricing). *The platform needs to determine the payment to driver $d \in \mathcal{W}$ according to the order matching result, the set of orders $\mathcal{O}$ and the set of private types $\hat{\Theta}$ submitted by all drivers, satisfying incentive compatibility, individual rationality and budget balance.*

4 Mechanism Design

We now design a Second-Pricing based Ride-sharing Mechanism (SPRM) to do the order matching and pricing, which is shown in Algorithm 1. Line 2 in Algorithm 1 uses the order matching algorithm to allocate the orders to drivers. For each matched pair (o, d^*) in $\mathcal{M}$, SPRM uses the second price pricing algorithm to compute the payments to driver d^* in line 3 to 5. In the following, we will introduce the order matching algorithm and driver pricing algorithm in detail.

4.1 Order Matching Algorithm

The order matching algorithm of SPRM mechanism is shown in Algorithm 2. Specifically, line 2 sorts the orders according to the descending up-front charged fares, and in lines 3 to 6, the sorted orders are matched one by one. In the matching process, the driver with the lowest additional travel cost is selected to ensure the maximum social welfare.

Algorithm 1. Second-Pricing based Ride-sharing Mechanism

Input:

the set of orders $\mathcal{O}$, the set of drivers $\mathcal{D}$

Output:

the set of drivers $\mathcal{W}$ who obtain the orders, and the corresponding set of payments $\mathcal{P}$

1: **Initialize:** $\mathcal{W} \leftarrow \varnothing, \mathcal{P} \leftarrow \varnothing$;
2: $\mathcal{M}$ =Order_Matching$(\mathcal{O}, \mathcal{D})$;
3: **foreach** matched pair $(o, d^*) \in \mathcal{M}$ **do**
4: Second_pricing$((o, d^*), \mathcal{D}, \mathcal{W}, \mathcal{P})$;
5: **end**
6: **return:** $\mathcal{W}, \mathcal{P}$;

Algorithm 2. Order Matching Algorithm: Order_Matching$(\mathcal{O}, \mathcal{D})$

Input:

the set of orders $\mathcal{O}$, the set of drivers $\mathcal{D}$

Output:

the set of matched pairs $\mathcal{M}$

1: **Initialize:** $\mathcal{M} \leftarrow \varnothing$;
2: Sort the orders in $\mathcal{O}$ in descending up-front fares to get $\mathcal{O}'$;
3: **foreach** $o \in \mathcal{O}'$ **do**
4: $d^*, \Delta cost_{o,d^*} \leftarrow$ Select_Best_Driver $(o, \mathcal{D})$;
5: $\mathcal{M} \leftarrow \mathcal{M} \cup \{(o, d^*)\}$;
6: **return:** $\mathcal{M}$;

Driver Selection Algorithm. In the order matching, we select the driver with the lowest additional travel cost from the feasible set of drivers to server the order. For serving order o, the additional travel cost for driver d is:

$$\Delta \cos t_{o,d} = \hat{c}_d \cdot (dis_d(tp_d \cup \{l_o^s, l_o^e\}) - dis_d(tp_d)) \tag{6}$$

where $tp_d \cup \{l_o^S, l_o^e\}$ is the new travel plan after adding the departure and destination of order o into the original travel plan of driver d.

The driver selection algorithm is shown in Algorithm 3. For a certain order $o \in \mathcal{O}$, line 3 will determine whether driver $d \in \mathcal{D}$ can pick up the passengers on time and whether the driver can arrive at the destination on time. Then line 5 will reschedule the route according to the departure and destination of order o and the driver's current travel plan tp_d. The route planning algorithm adopts a branch and bound based method, which will be introduced in the below. Lines 6 and 7 can find the best driver d^* matched with order o.

In the above route planning problem, we design a branch and bound based route planning algorithm to reschedule the travel plan. The algorithm will recurse all possible travel plans, and we will use pruning to eliminate nonviable branches. There are pruning operations at each recursion step to ensure that the current travel plan is feasible to reduce the searching cost and accelerate the route planning. The travel cost pruning is used to eliminate the recursive branch whose current cost has exceeded the optimal cost. The travel plan feasibility pruning use the five conditions of a feasible plan to prun the current travel plan by selecting the branches that can form a feasible plan. The time complexity is equivalent to the time complexity of recursive searching, with $O(\ell^2)$ in the worst case, where $\ell = \max_{d \in \mathcal{D}_t}\{|tp_d|\}$.

Algorithm 3. Driver Selection Algorithm: Select_Best_Driver$(o, \mathcal{D})$

Input:
order o, the set of orders $\mathcal{D}$

Output:
driver d^* with the lowest additional travel cost $\Delta cost^*$

1: $d^* \leftarrow NULL, \Delta cost^* \leftarrow \infty$;
2: **foreach** $d \in \mathcal{D}$ **do**
3: if $dis(l_d^s, l_o^s) \leq (\bar{t}_o^s - t_d^s) \cdot \overline{V}$ **and** $dis(l_d^s, l_o^s) + dis(l_o^s, l_o^e) + dis(l_o^e, l_d^e) \leq (t_d^e - t_d^s) \cdot \overline{V}$ **then**
4: $tp^* \leftarrow \varnothing, cost^* \leftarrow \infty$, $S \leftarrow (\varnothing, tp_d, \{l_o^s, l_o^e\}, l_d, t, n_d, 0)$;
5: Use the Branch and Bound based Route Planning Algorithm to reschedule the travel plan;
6: **if** $tp_d^* \neq \varnothing$ **and** $\Delta cost^* > cost_d(tp_d^*) - cost_d(tp_d)$ **then**
7: $d^* \leftarrow d, \Delta cost^* \leftarrow cost_d(tp_d^*) - cost_d(tp_d)$;
8: **end**
9: **end**
10: **end**
11: **return:** $d^*, \Delta cost^*$;

4.2 Driver Pricing Algorithm

After matching orders with drivers, the platform needs to compute the payments to drivers, which is based on second pricing, as shown in Algorithm 4.

For a matching pair (o, d^*), the platform will temporarily delete the driver d^* with the lowest additional travel cost, and find driver d' with the lowest additional travel cost from the remaining drivers in line 1 of Algorithm 4, and then the platform will use $\Delta cost_{o,d^*} \leq f_o$ to determine whether the driver exists (line 2). If it exists, $\Delta cost_{o,d^*}$ is taken as the payment to driver d^*. Furthermore, the platform will allocate order o to driver d^*. Finally we update the driver's travel plan tp_{d^*} and the current number of passengers n_{d^*}.

4.3 Theoretical Analysis

SPRM mechanism can satisfy the typical economic properties: incentive compatibility, individual rationality and budget balance, and can guarantee computational efficiency.

Theorem 1. *SPRM can guarantee incentive compatibility.*

Proof. We use Myerson theorem [9] to prove that SPRM can guarantee incentive compatibility. According to Myerson's theorem, a mechanism is incentive compatible if and only if the mechanism can satisfy the following two conditions:

1) The order matching algorithm is monotonic: If the private cost information $\hat{c}_d$ revealed by driver d can help him to get the order, driver d can get the order with the lower cost information $\hat{c}'_d$ (i.e. $\hat{c}'_d \leq \hat{c}_d$).

Algorithm 4. Pricing Algorithm: Second_pricing($(o, d^*), \mathcal{D}, \mathcal{W}, \mathcal{P}$)

Input:
a matched pair $(o, d^*) \in \mathcal{O} \times \mathcal{D}$, the set of drivers $\mathcal{D}$, the set of drivers $\mathcal{W}$ who obtain orders, and the set of payments $\mathcal{P}$

Output:
the updated set of drivers $\mathcal{W}$ who obtain orders, and the updated set of payments $\mathcal{P}$

1: $d', \Delta cost_{o,d'} \leftarrow Select\_Best\_Driver(o, \mathcal{D} \backslash \{d^*\})$;
2: **if** $\Delta cost_{o,d^*} \leq f_o$ and $\Delta cost_{o,d'} \leq f_o$ **then**
3:     **if** $d^* \in \mathcal{W}$ **then**
4:         $p_{d^*} \leftarrow p_{d^*} + \Delta cost_{o,d'}$;
5:     **else**
6:         $p_{d^*} \leftarrow \Delta cost_{o,d'}$;
7:         $\mathcal{W} \leftarrow \mathcal{W} \cup \{d^*\}, \mathcal{P} \leftarrow \mathcal{P} \cup \{p_{d^*}\}$;
8:     **end**
9:     $\mathcal{O}_{d^*} \leftarrow \mathcal{O}_{d^*} \cup \{o\}, n_{d^*} \leftarrow n_{d^*} - n_o$, update tp_{d^*};
10: **end**
11: **return:** $\mathcal{W}$, $\mathcal{P}$;

---

2) The payments to driver is critical price: The payment to the driver is the maximum payment. In other words, if driver d reveals the private cost information $\hat{c}_d$ untruthfully, and his additional travel cost is more than p_d, he will not obtain the order.

We now prove that our mechanism can satisfy the above two conditions. Obviously, the order matching algorithm is monotonic since the driver selection algorithm chooses the driver with the lowest additional travel cost. When driver d reveals lower cost information, driver d will be the optimal driver again. Then the payment to the driver calculated by the second-price pricing is the critical price. When the cost $\hat{c}_d$ revealed by the driver is too high to make $\Delta cost_{o,d'} < \Delta cost_{o,d^*}$, the driver selection algorithm will choose driver d' instead of driver d, which causes driver d to be unmatched with order o. According to Myerson's theorem, SPRM can guarantee incentive compatibility. Theorem 1 is proved.

Theorem 2. *SPRM can guarantee individual rationality.*

Proof. We need to prove that the profit of driver d is non-negative. Due to the monotonicity of the driver selection algorithm, there is $\Delta cost_{o,d'} \geq \Delta cost_{o,d^*}$ in each round of order matching, where the driver's profit is $u_{d^*} = p_{d^*} - cost_{d^*}(tp_{d^*}) = \sum_{o \in \mathcal{O}_d} (\Delta cost_{o,d'} - \Delta cost_{o,d^*}) \geq 0$. Theorem 2 is proved.

Theorem 3. *SPRM can ensure the budget balance of the platform.*

Proof. We now prove that the profit of the platform is non-negative. In line 6 of Algorithm 4, we have $\Delta cost_{o,d'} \leq f_o$, and the platform's profit is $\mathcal{U}^p = \sum_{d \in \mathcal{W}} (\sum_{o \in \mathcal{O}_d} f_o - p_d) = \sum_{d \in \mathcal{W}} \sum_{o \in \mathcal{O}_d} (f_o - \Delta cost_{o,d'}) \geq 0$. Theorem 3 is proved.

Theorem 4. *SPRM satisfies computational efficiency.*

Proof. We now prove SPRM can be executed within a polynomial time. During each round of order matching, the worst time complexity of the driver selection algorithm for a single order is $O(|\mathcal{D}| \cdot \ell^2)$. Then the total time complexity is $O(|\mathcal{O}| \cdot |\mathcal{D}| \cdot \ell^3)$. Theorem 4 is proved.

5 Experimental Analysis

In this section, we evaluate our mechanism based on the Manhattan taxi order data set, which has been widely used by related works [1,11–13].

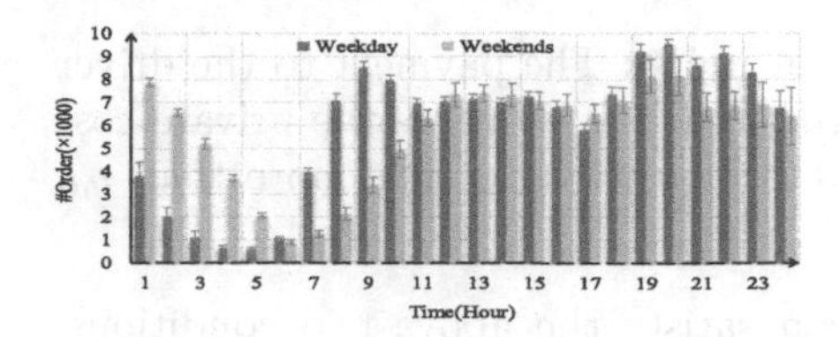

Fig. 1. Orders on weekdays and weekends

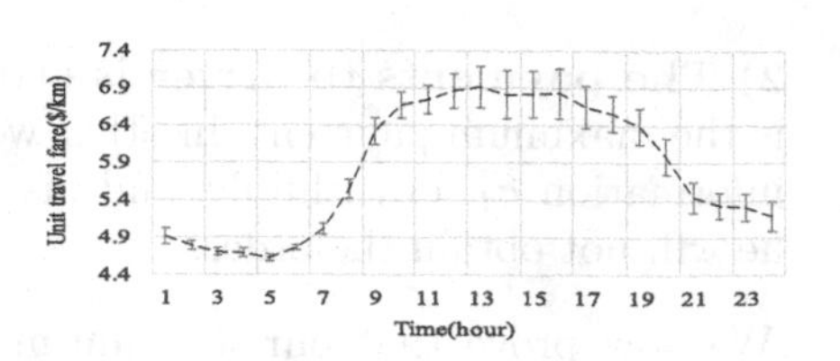

Fig. 2. Unit travel fare

5.1 Data Set and Characteristics

In this section, we introduce the data set and describe how to extract the characteristics of the data, which will be used to generate data for running experiments.

Order Data Set. We collect a data set of taxi orders on Manhattan Island in June 2016 from New York City Taxi and Limousine Commission.[2] Each order data includes the latitude and longitude of the departure and the destination, the departure time, the travel time, the fare and the travel distance.

Fuel Consumption Data Set. We collect the urban vehicle fuel consumption data of type M1 and M2 from China Automobile Fuel Consumption Query System[3] of the Ministry of Public Information of China.

Order Data Cleaning. We find that the number of orders on weekdays and weekends varies greatly over time, as shown in Fig. 1. For consistency, we use the order data of weekdays to extract the traveling characteristics.

Extracting Passenger Pricing Rules. We compute the average unit travel fare per hour, where $\overline{f}^k$ is the average unit travel fare in k-th hour. The dynamics of unit travel fare is shown in Fig. 2.

Clustering Road Network Nodes. We use K-Means algorithm to cluster 4573 nodes on Manhattan network into 40 regions according to the frequency of departure and destination in the order data set. We use $R^s = \{R_1^s, R_2^s, \cdots, R_{40}^s\}$ to represent 40 regions of the origin of the order data, and $R^e = \{R_1^e, R_2^e, \cdots, R_{40}^e\}$ to represent 40 regions of the destination of the order data.

5.2 Experiment Settings

Data Generation and Experimental Parameters. We select the peak period from 19:00 to 20:00 on weekdays as the time period We use time slot $\Delta t = 5$ min to divide one hour into 12 time slots, and each order contains only one passenger. We set the average vehicle speed to be 7.2 mph. We randomly selects a node from R_u^s and R_v^e respectively as the departure node l_o^s and destination node l_e^s of order o, and then uses $f_o = \overline{f}^{20} \cdot dis(l_o^s, l_o^e)$ to calculate the trip

[2] http://www.nyc.gov/html/tlc/html/about/trip_record_data.shtml.
[3] http://chaxun.miit.gov.cn/asopCmsSearch.

fare of order o. In addition, the maximum waiting time $\overline{wt_o}$ is randomly selected from {5 min, 10 min, 15 min, 20 min}, and the detour ratio $\overline{dr_o}$ is randomly selected from {0.25, 0.50, 0.75, 1.00}. Since the unit cost and fuel consumption data are not in the same magnitude, we use a factor 2.5/6.8/1.6[4] to scale the fuel consumption data to the taxi rate in New York City. Besides, we randomly select the time slot as the driver's departure time, randomly select a value from [10 min, 60 min] as the length of the travel time interval, and randomly select the node as the driver's departure point. The capacity of vehicle seats is set to 4.

Benchmark Approaches and Metrics. In this paper, we choose two typical benchmark approaches, which are GPri [17] and Nearest Dispating (ND). GPri uses a greedy algorithm to match orders and uses a uniform pricing rule for drivers. The nearest dispatching (ND) algorithm is adopted by major ride-sharing platforms such as Uber, which selects the nearest available driver to serve the new order. We run experiments to evaluate our mechanism against these two approaches in terms of the following metrics.

- **Ratio of participated drivers** which refers to the ratio of the number of drivers who serve orders to the total number of drivers.
- **Average profits of participated drivers** which refer to the ratio of the cumulative profits of drivers serving orders to the total number of such drivers.
- **Ratio of served orders** which refers to the ratio of the number of served orders to the total number of orders.
- **Average order payments** which refer to the ratio of the total payments of the matched orders to the number of orders.
- **Average random travel distance** which refers to the ratio of the total driving distance of drivers who are currently not serving any orders to the total number of drivers.
- **Social welfare** which refers to total profits of the platform and drivers.

5.3 Experimental Results

The experiments are run on a machine with AMD Ryzen7 4800H processor. The experiment increases the number of drivers from 500 to 2500. For each number of drivers, the experiment is repeated 10 times and we compute the average results.

We first analyze the ratio of participated drivers. According to Fig. 3, we find that the pricing rules of GPri and ND will cause a large number of drivers to refuse to provide services. Compared with SPRM, the participation ratio is reduced by about 20% and 11% respectively. When the total number of vehicles increases, the number of drivers serving orders has increased from 450 to 1000, and then become saturated. Because more vehicles are involved in the business, but with limited incoming orders, the driver maybe not willing to participate since it cannot get enough orders. From Figs. 4 and 5, we find that the average

[4] The reason of 2.5/6.8/1.6 being used is because (1) The basic unit rate in New York City is 2.5 dollars per mile; (2) The average fuel consumption of New York City taxis is 6.8 liters/100 km; (3) 1.6 is the factor converting from miles to kilometers.

profits and ratio of served orders who provide ride-sharing services under GPri and ND are also lower than SPRM, where the average profits are only about 27% and 45% of SPRM and the ratio of served orders is only about 44% and 57% of SPRM.

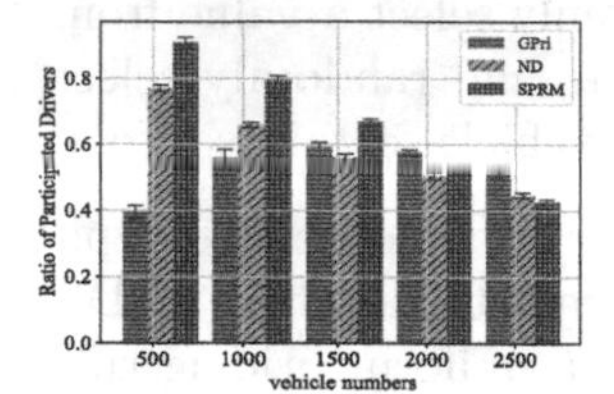

Fig. 3. Ratio of participated drivers

Fig. 4. Average profits of participated drivers

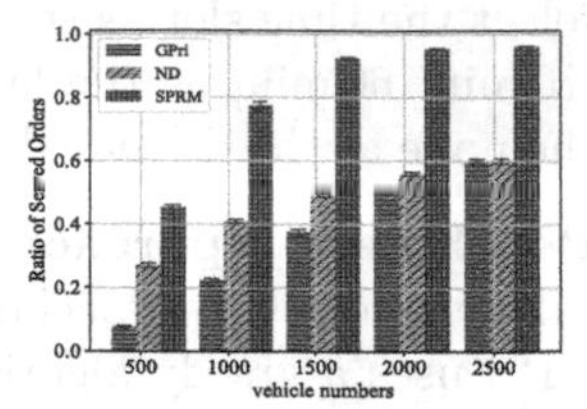

Fig. 5. Ratio of served orders

From Fig. 6, we can see that compared with SPRM, the average order payments of GPri and ND has been reduced by about 43% and 29% respectively. SPRM can make drivers obtain more orders, which can improve the average profits of drivers. From Fig. 7, we can find that as the number of vehicles increases, the average random travel distance of SPRM and ND vehicles gradually increases, and GPri does not increase or decrease monotonously. We believe this is caused by the drivers' participation. Comparing Fig. 3 with Fig. 7, we can see that as the number of vehicles increases, the drivers' participation ratio and the average random travel distance is opposite. The decreased participation ratio of drivers leads more drivers to travel randomly on the road, resulting in increased average random travel distance.

From Fig. 8, we can find that as the number of vehicles increases, the social welfare of three mechanisms increases. SPRM can make about 70% and 65% higher welfare than GPri and ND mechanisms. Furthermore, the social welfare of SPRM increases significantly until the number of drivers is saturated. This is because when the number of vehicles increases until 1500, more orders are matched, and thus the social welfare grows faster.

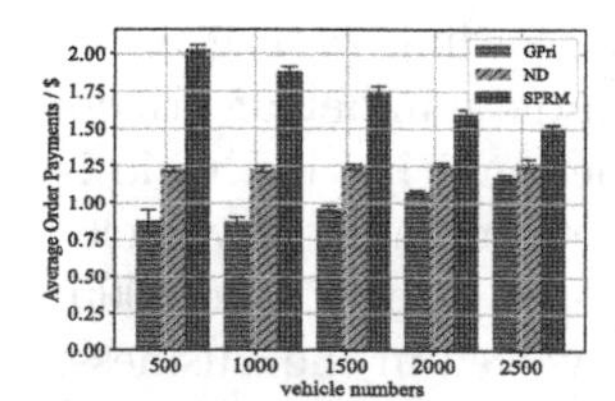

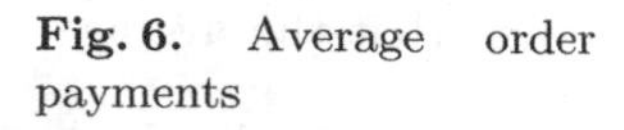

Fig. 6. Average order payments

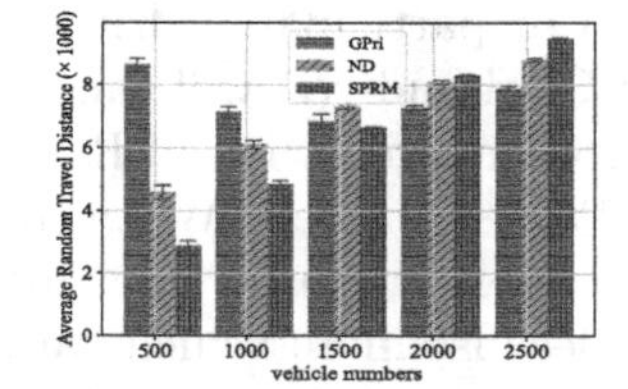

Fig. 7. Average random travel distance

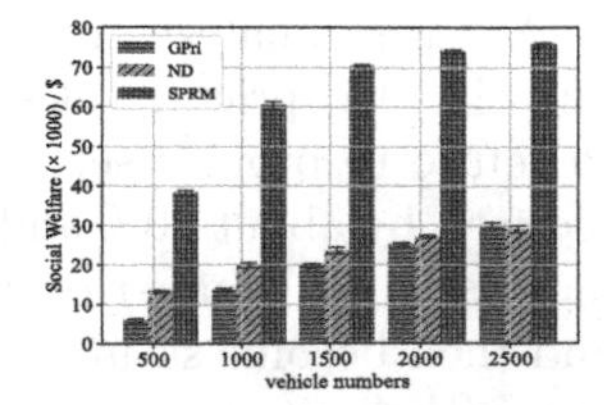

Fig. 8. Social welfare

6 Conclusion

In this paper, we designed an order matching and pricing mechanism which is incentive compatible, to maximize the social welfare of the platform and drivers. Specifically, we designed a second pricing based ride-sharing mechanism (SPRM), where we implemented an efficient order matching algorithm including branch and bound based route planning algorithm to accelerate the matching process and compute the payments to drivers based on second pricing rule. We proved that SPRM can satisfy incentive compatibility, individual rationality, budget balance and computational efficiency. Furthermore, we run extensive experiments to evaluate our mechanism based on the real Manhattan taxi order data. We found that SPRM can guarantee the driver's profits, achieve a better ratio of participated drivers and the ratio of served orders, and eventually achieve greater social welfare than two typical benchmark approaches, GPri and ND.

Acknowledgement. This paper was funded by the Shenzhen Fundamental Research Program (Grant No. JCYJ20190809175613332), the Humanity and Social Science Youth Research Foundation of Ministry of Education (Grant No. 19YJC790111), the Philosophy and Social Science Post-Foundation of Ministry of Education (Grant No. 18JHQ060) and the Fundamental Research Funds for the Central Universities (WUT:2022IVB004).

References

1. Asghari, M., Deng, D., Shahabi, C., Demiryurek, U., Li, Y.: Price-aware real-time ride-sharing at scale: an auction-based approach. In: The 24th ACM SIGSPATIAL International Conference on Advances in Geographic Information Systems, pp. 1–10 (2016)
2. Babaioff, M., Dughmi, S., Kleinberg, R., Slivkins, A.: Dynamic pricing with limited supply. ACM Trans. Econ. Comput. **3**(1), 1–26 (2015)
3. Bei, X., Zhang, S.: Algorithms for trip-vehicle assignment in ride-sharing. In: The 32nd AAAI Conference on Artificial Intelligence, pp. 3–9 (2018)
4. Cao, B., Alarabi, L., Mokbel, M.F., Basalamah, A.: SHAREK: a scalable dynamic ride sharing system. In: The 16th IEEE International Conference on Mobile Data Management. vol. 1, pp. 4–13 (2015)
5. Jeanes, P.: Can total car emissions be reduced enough by 2020? Traffic Eng. Control **51**(1), 6–8 (2010)
6. Kamar, E., Horvitz, E.: Collaboration and shared plans in the open world: studies of ridesharing. In: The 21st International Joint Conference on Artificial Intelligence, p. 187 (2009)
7. Kleiner, A., Nebel, B., Ziparo, V.: A mechanism for dynamic ride sharing based on parallel auctions. In: The 22nd International Joint Conference on Artificial Intelligence, pp. 266–272 (2011)
8. Ma, S., Zheng, Y., Wolfson, O.: T-share: a large-scale dynamic taxi ridesharing service. In: The 29th International Conference on Data Engineering, pp. 410–421 (2013)
9. Myerson, R.B.: Optimal auction design. Math. Oper. Res. **6**(1), 58–73 (1981)

10. Shen, W., Lopes, C.V., Crandall, J.W.: An online mechanism for ridesharing in autonomous mobility-on-demand systems. In: The 25th International Joint Conference on Artificial Intelligence, pp. 475–481 (2016)
11. Tong, Y., Zeng, Y., Zhou, Z., Chen, L., Ye, J., Xu, K.: A unified approach to route planning for shared mobility. Proc. VLDB Endow. **11**(11), 1633 (2018)
12. Xu, Y., Tong, Y., Shi, Y., Tao, Q., Xu, K., Li, W.: An efficient insertion operator in dynamic ridesharing services. In: The 35th International Conference on Data Engineering, pp. 1022–1033 (2019)
13. Yuen, C.F., Singh, A.P., Goyal, S., Ranu, S., Bagchi, A.: Beyond shortest paths: Route recommendations for ride-sharing. In: The World Wide Web Conference, pp. 2258–2269 (2019)
14. Zhang, C., Wu, F., Gao, X., Chen, G.: Online auctions with dynamic costs for ridesharing. In: The 23rd International Conference on Parallel and Distributed Systems, pp. 127–134 (2017)
15. Zhang, L., et al.: A taxi order dispatch model based on combinatorial optimization. In: The 23rd ACM SIGKDD International Conference on Knowledge Discovery and Data Mining, pp. 2151–2159 (2017)
16. Zheng, L., Chen, L., Ye, J.: Order dispatch in price-aware ridesharing. Proc. VLDB Endow. **11**(8), 853–865 (2018)
17. Zheng, L., Cheng, P., Chen, L.: Auction-based order dispatch and pricing in ridesharing. In: The 35th International Conference on Data Engineering, pp. 1034–1045 (2019)

MEOD: A Robust Multi-stage Ensemble Model Based on Rank Aggregation and Stacking for Outlier Detection

Zhengchao Jiang, Fan Zhang, Hao Xu, Li Tao(✉), and Zili Zhang

College of Computer and Information Science, Southwest University, Chongqing 400715, China
xhiimp@email.swu.edu.cn, {tli,zhangzl}@swu.edu.cn

Abstract. In ensemble-based unsupervised outlier detection, the lack of ground truth makes the combination of basic outlier detectors a challenging task. The existing outlier ensembles usually use certain fusion rules (majority voting, averaging) to aggregate base detectors, which results in relatively low model accuracy and robustness. To overcome this problem, in this research, we propose a robust Multi-stage Ensemble model based on rank aggregation and stacking for Outlier Detection (MEOD). The proposed model uses multiple unsupervised outlier detection algorithms to form a base detector pool. Such a pool can be utilized for extracting useful representations from the train set and integrating base detector results using a ranking aggregation-based approach. To further optimize the proposed model, a stacking-based dynamic classifier selection ensemble model is also proposed, and the best-behaved classifier is adaptively selected as the base learner in the stacking stage on different datasets. Some extensive experiments are also committed to prove that MEOD outperforms the other seven state-of-the-art benchmarks in most cases.

Keywords: Outlier detection · Anomaly detection · Ensemble model · Representation learning · Rank aggregation · Stacking approach

1 Introduction

Outliers, also known as anomalies, are data points that do not fit well with the general data distribution [17]. Since the existence of outliers can remarkably affect the results of statistical analyses, it becomes pivotal to identify and remove anomalous data objects from the general data distribution so that the integrity of data models can be preserved [21]. So far, outlier detection techniques have been widely used in the real world [4], such as intrusion detection in cybersecurity, fraud detection in financial transactions data, and health diagnosis. However, one shortcoming stands out that the ground truth is difficult to obtain in outlier mining. Thus, unsupervised detection methods are commonly used to accomplish the above tasks [1]. Some classic outlier detection algorithms include

G. Memmi et al. (Eds.): KSEM 2022, LNAI 13370, pp. 205–218, 2022.
https://doi.org/10.1007/978-3-031-10989-8_17

the Isolation Forest (IF) [19], Local Outlier Factor (LOF) [6], K-Nearest Neighbors (KNN) [3] and One-class Support Vector Machine (OCSVM) [20]. However, these single algorithms have limited generalization ability and can only achieve good performance when the data satisfy certain assumptions. Moreover, only using a single unsupervised outlier detection algorithm tends to generate low true positive and true negative rates [1].

In recent years, the ensemble learning method has shown strong capability in data mining, and machine learning [18]. Specifically, the ensemble approach achieves stronger performance than its counterparts by combining multiple base detectors. Numerous ensemble methods have been proposed, such as bagging, boosting, and stacking [1]. Although ensemble learning has been attached great attention in machine learning, the exploration of outlier ensemble techniques still lacks. On one hand, the unsupervised property and ground truth lack makes their construction difficult [1]. On the other hand, existing parallel outlier ensembles lack a reliable selection for base detectors. Usually, all base detectors are merged directly, thus limiting the benefits of model fusion. Since each base detector may not be suitable for identifying outliers in all datasets, if an inappropriate base detector is added in the model combination process, it will directly affect the stability and accuracy of the model [2].

To address the limitations above, this paper proposes a fully unsupervised model called the robust Multi-stage Ensemble model based on rank aggregation and stacking for Outlier Detection (MEOD). Outlier scores are obtained by applying various unsupervised outlier detection methods to the original feature space and then aggregated robustly to generate pseudo-labels. The motivation behind this research is that unsupervised outlier detection algorithms are better at learning complex patterns in extremely imbalanced datasets than supervised methods [4]. And we treat the output of unsupervised methods as input to supervised classifiers as unsupervised feature engineering or representation learning. Finally, the improved ensemble method stacking is used as the final output classifier. Overall, the MEOD application is intuitive, efficient and robust in unsupervised outlier detection. The main contributions can be summarized as follows:

- We propose a robust multi-stage outlier detection model (MEOD). The model explores fully unsupervised representation learning techniques, combining the strengths of both unsupervised and supervised machine learning approaches by making a multi-stage approach that exploits each of their individual performance capabilities in outlier detection, making the model more efficient and stable.
- We employ two approaches to improve the interpretability of MEOD. First, the theoretical explanation is provided based on the bias-variance tradeoff. Second, when MEOD uses it and why it works is explained in detail through visualization.

The rest of the paper is organized as follows. Section 2 introduces related work on this model. In Sect. 3, the proposed MEOD model is analyzed in detail.

Section 4 presents the corresponding experimental results. Finally, we conclude this paper and discuss the future outlooks in Sect. 5.

2 Related Work

2.1 Unsupervised Outlier Detection Methods

Unsupervised methods can identify hidden patterns or intrinsic structures in datasets without pre-learning parameters or labels. In this paper, we divide our unsupervised outlier detection methods into seven categories [4]: (i) Density-based approaches such as Local Outlier Factor (LOF); (ii) Statistical-based approaches such as Gaussian Mixture Model (GMM); (iii) Distance-based approaches such as K-Nearest Neighbor (KNN); (iv) Clustering-based approaches such as k-Means; (v) Linear-based approaches such as Principal Component Analysis (PCA); (vi) Ensemble-based approaches such as Isolation Forest (IF); (vii) Graph-based approaches such as Connectivity-based Outlier Factor (COF). These methods are based on different assumptions and can achieve better results on certain datasets when the corresponding assumptions are satisfied [1]. In view of this, this study uses diverse types of unsupervised outlier detection methods as base detectors to build an effective ensemble.

2.2 Representation Learning with Rank Aggregation

In recent years, representation learning has gained great popularity [25]. Due to the remarkable ability to learn semantically rich features, deep neural networks have become a widely used technique to support many machine learning tasks. However, a prominent problem with these deep learning techniques is that large amounts of labelled data are often required to learn these expressive features effectively [10]. Their transformation ability suffers when dealing with unsupervised tasks in the real world, such as clustering and outlier detection. Therefore, we explore unsupervised representation learning techniques to enable downstream unsupervised learning to bridge this gap in these critical domains. Unsupervised representation learning can automatically extract expressive feature representations from data without ground truth. We leverage this idea by viewing unsupervised outlier detection methods as tools for extracting richer representations from limited data and combining the scores of these unsupervised outlier detection methods using Rank Aggregation Outlier Scores (RAOS) which works as the input to a supervised learning problem. Rank-based methods use outlier scores to rank data points into a list. Such ranking makes algorithms more comparable and then combined by facilitates. Combining multiple ranking lists into a single ranking is called ranking aggregation, and it has a rich history in social choice and information retrieval theory [15]. Previous work has demonstrated that the method effectively optimises supervised learning and enriches data representations [10].

2.3 Outlier Ensemble

The ensemble methods have been shown to be an effective way to enhance the performance of outlier detection model [1]. It aims to enhance model performance by training multiple single-base detectors and combining their decisions using an ensemble strategy. Bagging, boosting, and stacking are the mainstream ensemble strategies for outlier detection [1]. In particular, the stacking [23] strategy is often used in outlier detection models due to its excellent performance and high robustness. For example, Fangyi Wan et al. (2019) proposed an outlier detection method stacked autoencoder (SAE) [22]. Yongliang Cheng et al. (2019) proposed a model HS-TCN based on stacking for anomaly detection [8]. The previous works have demonstrated the superiority of the stacking strategies in building ensemble models. Moreover, the effects of the stacking strategy also depend on the performance of base classifiers. Thus, this study proposes a stacking-based dynamic classifier selection ensemble model, which dynamically selects the most appropriate classifier as the basic learner in the stacking stage according to different datasets, which enhances the predictive performance and robustness of the ensemble model.

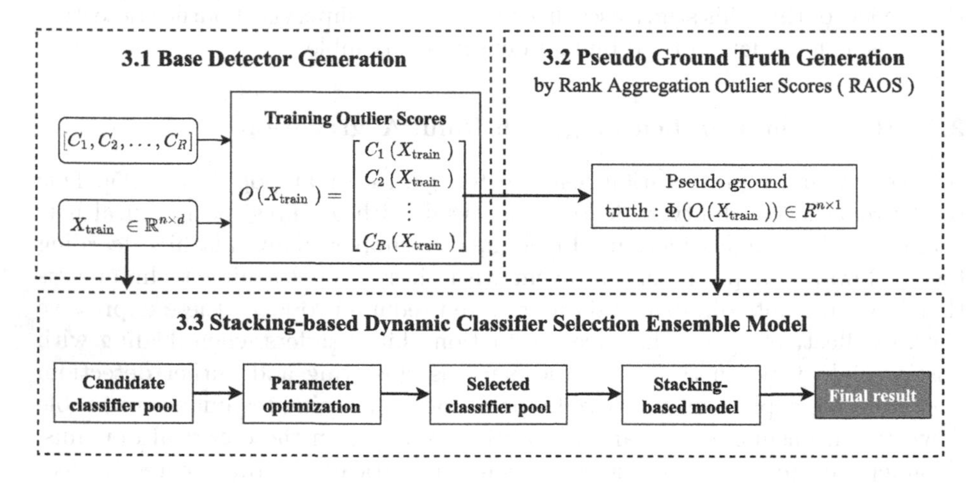

Fig. 1. The overall flow chart of MEOD.

3 Algorithm Design

This work proposes a robust multi-stage ensemble model based on rank aggregation and stacking for outlier detection (MEOD). As shown in Fig. 1, the proposed model mainly consists of three stages. First, a new data representation is generated. In detail, we apply various unsupervised outlier detection methods to the training data to obtain transformed outlier scores, which can act as new data representations. Then we ensemble the newly generated outliers to generate pseudo-labels through ranking aggregations. Finally, we input the newly generated training set into the stacking-based dynamic classifier selection ensemble model for training an outlier detection model. In the rest of this paper, the following subsections describe the detailed implementation of the three stages and theoretically analyze the proposed model.

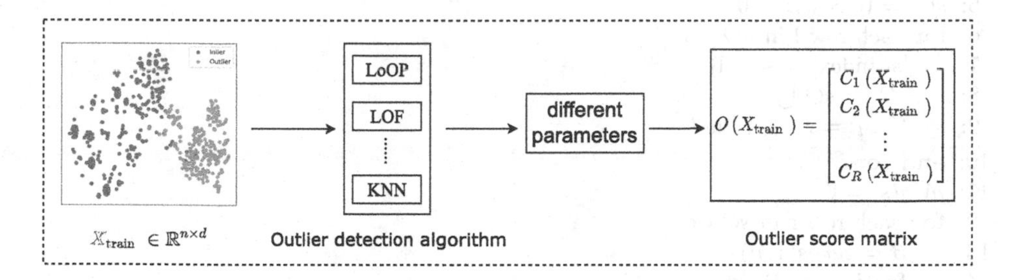

Fig. 2. Base detector generation.

3.1 Base Detector Generation

To better extract useful data representations from the training set, diverse base detectors should be used to build an effective ensemble [1]. Six classic outlier detection algorithms, namely, LoOP [16], LOF [6], KNN [3], Avg-kNN, IF [19] and OCSVM [20], have been widely employed to clean outlier in data. The outlier scores of the training set can be obtained by these six classical outlier detection methods (i.e., LoOP scores, LOF scores, KNN scores, Avg-kNN scores, IF scores, and OCSVM scores). After that, the scores are normalized and standardized to the same order magnitude respectively. It is worth noting that the diversity may suffer since each outlier detection algorithm subsamples the training set and feature space or changes model hyperparameters. In this stage (Fig. 2), each algorithm builds multiple base detectors using different hyperparameters to enhance the outlier adaptability of base detectors.

Specifically, $X_{\text{train}} \in R^{n \times d}$ denotes training set with n points and d features. The model first selects the six outlier detection algorithms mentioned above and initializes it with a series of hyperparameters to generate a base detection pool $[C_1, C_2, \ldots, C_R]$. Then X_{train} is input to the base detector pool for training. Finally, the results are combined into an outlier score matrix $O(X_{\text{train}})$, which is formalized in Eq. (1), where $C_r(\cdot)$ denotes the score vector from the γth base detector.

$$O(X_{\text{train}}) = [C_1(X_{\text{train}}), \ldots, C_r(X_{\text{train}})] \in R^{n \times R} \tag{1}$$

Algorithm 1. Rank Aggregation Outlier Scores (RAOS)

Input: O: = outlier score matrix
Output: fR: = aggregated final rank list
1: nO: = $\emptyset$, n = length(O)
2: **for** each column l in O **do**
3: nO: = $nO \bigcup$ Rank(l)/n
4: **end for**
5: sO: = $\emptyset$, S_{sort}: = $\emptyset$
6: **for** each row l in nO **do**
7: [sl,index] = sort(l)
8: sO: = $sO \bigcup sl$
9: S_{sort}: = $S_{sort} \bigcup$ index
10: **end for**
11: $pVals$: = $\emptyset$
12: **for** each row r in sO **do**
13: $\beta = zeros(1, n)$
14: **for** j: = 1...R **do**
15: $p_{j,R}(\mathbf{r}) := \sum_{t=j}^{R} \binom{R}{t} r_{(j)}^{t} \left(1 - r_{(j)}\right)^{R-t}$
16: $\beta(1, j) := \beta(1, j) + p_{j,R}(\mathbf{r})$
17: **end for**
18: $\rho(\mathbf{r}) = \min(\beta)$
19: **end for**
20: $fR = sort(\rho)$
21: **return** fR

3.2 Pseudo Ground Truth Generation by RAOS

In this stage, we integrate outlier scores using Rank Aggregation Outlier Scores (RAOS) and define the outlier scoring function as the mapping function $\Phi(\cdot)$. The $\Phi(\cdot)$ is then applied in the outlier matrix $O\left(X_{\text{train}}\right)$ and then the outlier score matrix $\Phi\left(O\left(X_{\text{train}}\right)\right)$ is acquired, which can better describe the degree of outliers in Eq. (2).

$$\text{target } = \Phi\left(O\left(X_{\text{train}}\right)\right) = \Phi\left(\left[C_1\left(X_{\text{train}}\right), \ldots, C_r\left(X_{\text{train}}\right)\right]\right) \in R^{n \times 1} \tag{2}$$

Algorithm 1 demonstrates the concrete steps of RAOS. The first step is normalization. Specifically, we input an $n \times R$ matrix of outliers (n is the number of samples and R is the number of base detectors). For each column of outlier scores we divide its rank by the length of the rank list to calculate the normalized rank for each sample point. For each sample point, we get a normalized ranking vector $\boldsymbol{r} = (r_1, r_2, \ldots, r_R)$, where r_j represents the normalized ranking of the sample in the jth base detector. Then, for any normalized rank vector r_i, it is reordered to obtain $\boldsymbol{r} = (r_{i1}, r_{i2}, \ldots, r_{iR})$ such that $r_{i1} \leq \cdots \leq r_{iR}$. Finally, we compute the final aggregated outlier score based on the rearranged ranking vector. Specifically, for the ranking vector r of each sample point, we compute the probability that $\hat{r}_{(j)} \leq r_{(j)}$, with $\hat{r}_{(j)}$ generated by the uniform null model, and this probability can be expressed as a binomial probability in Eq. (3).

$$P_{j,R}(r) := \sum_{t=j}^{R} \binom{R}{t} r^t (1-r)^{R-t} \tag{3}$$

Since the number of informative ranks is unknown, we define the final score of the rank vector r as the minimum of $P_{j,R}(\boldsymbol{r})$ in Eq. (4), and order all rank vectors according to their corresponding ρ scores to generate pseudo-labels.

$$\rho(\boldsymbol{r}) = \min_{j=1,\ldots,R} P_{j,R}(\boldsymbol{r}) \tag{4}$$

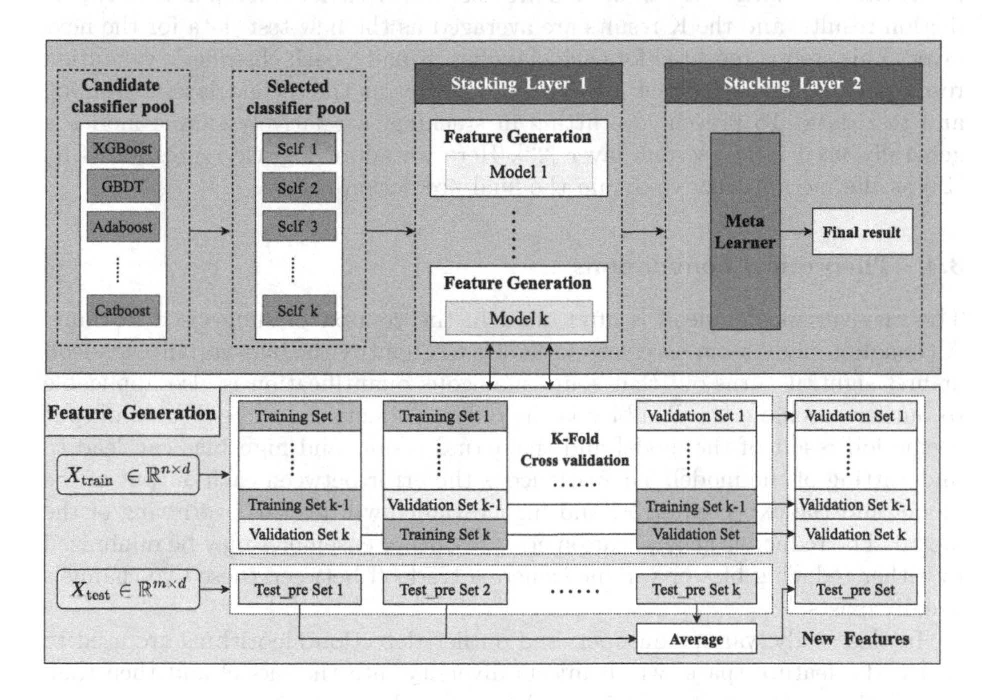

Fig. 3. Stacking-based dynamic classifier selection ensemble model.

3.3 Stacking-Based Dynamic Classifier Selection Ensemble Model

In this stage, we propose a stacking-based dynamic classifier selection ensemble model, which automatically optimizes the parameters of the base classifier and dynamically selects the top m base classifiers with the best performance as the basic learner, thereby improving the performance of the ensemble model.

As shown in Fig. 3, XGBoost [7], GBDT [12], Adaboost [11], RF [5], LightGBM [14] and Catboost [9] are used as candidate base classifiers.

Firstly, the hyperparameter optimization framework selects the best parameters for n candidate base classifiers. After that, we leverage the test set to verify the performance of each candidate base classifier separately. Among those n base classifiers, m optimal base classifiers are selected according to the ROC-AUC evaluation metric. The selected m base learners predict the training samples respectively and then use the prediction results as the training samples of the next layer. The specific training process is shown in the "Feature Generation" module in Fig. 3. The training data is divided into K folds, and K training times are carried out. For each training, one part of the K samples is reserved for testing, and the K test results are combined as the new training data for the next layer. After training, the test data is predicted, a classifier corresponds to K prediction results, and the K results are averaged as the new test data for the next layer. This step is repeated for each classifier. Finally, each classifier's validation result set and test result set are spliced together as the second layer's training and test data. To prevent overfitting in stacking, a relatively simple model is generally used in the second layer [23]. Here we adopt logistic regression (LR) [13] as the meta-learner to obtain the final prediction result.

3.4 Theoretical Foundations

The bias-variance tradeoff is often used in the context of supervised learning. Although it might seem necessary for labels to quantify the bias-variance tradeoff at first sight, it turns out that some analogous quantification is also applicable to outlier ensemble [2]. The bias is the difference between the expected output prediction result of the model and the actual result, and high bias can lead to underfitting of the model. The variance is the error between each output of the model and the expected error, and high variance will lead to overfitting of the model. The reducible generalization error in outlier ensembles may be minimized by either reducing bias or variance where a tradeoff between these two channels usually exists.

In this study, various unsupervised outlier detection algorithms are used to enrich the feature space, which injects diversity into the model and then rank aggregation outlier scores. This can be regarded as a variance reduction approach, since a diverse base detector combination reduces the variance of the outlier ensemble. However, such a combination causes an inaccurate base detector to be included in the ensemble, thus generating higher model bias. This also explains why averaging all base detector scores doesn't work well. Moreover, the stacking-based dynamic classifier selection ensemble model can achieve low variance without introducing too much bias. In conclusion, MEOD reduces bias and variance through multi-stage modeling and has the potential to improve generalization ability at different stages.

4 Experiments Design

4.1 Datasets and Evaluation Metrics

Table 1 summarizes 17 real-world outlier detection datasets used in this study from ODDS[1]. In each experiment, 70% of the total data work as the training set, and the remaining 30% serve as the test set. This study employs two evaluation indicators widely used for outlier detection: Receiver Operating Characteristic (ROC-AUC) and Precision [24]. The evaluation indicators are determined by true positive (TP), true negative (TN), false positive (FP), and false negative (FN) values. And the predictive precision is defined in Eq. (5).

$$\text{Precision} = \frac{TP}{TP + FP} \tag{5}$$

AUC is a commonly used evaluation index in binary classification tasks, which is defined as the area enclosed by the ROC curve and the coordinate axis. The value of this area is between 0 and 1. Generally speaking, the larger the AUC value of the classification model, the better the model performance.

Table 1. Real-world outlier detection datasets used for experiments.

Dataset	#Samp.(n)	#Dims.(d)	%Outlier
Annthyroid	7200	6	534 (7.42%)
Arrhythmia	7200	274	66 (15%)
Breastw	683	9	239 (35%)
Cardio	1831	21	176 (9.6%)
Letter	1600	32	100 (6.25%)
Mammography	11183	6	260 (2.32%)
Mnist	7603	100	700 (9.2%)
Musk	3062	166	97 (3.2%)
Optdigits	5216	64	150 (3%)
Pendigits	6870	16	156 (2.27%)
Pima	768	8	268 (35%)
Satellite	6435	36	2036 (32%)
Satimage-2	5803	36	71 (1.2%)
Shuttle	49097	9	3511 (7%)
Speech	3686	400	61 (1.65%)
Thyroid	3772	6	93 (2.5%)
Vowels	1456	12	50 (3.4%)

[1] http://odds.cs.stonybrook.edu/.

4.2 Parameter Settings

In this research, the effectiveness of the proposed model depends on the diversity and accuracy of the base detector generation. Therefore, in the base detector construction stage, six classical unsupervised outlier detection approaches are used: i) LoOP ii) LOF iii) KNN iv) Avg-kNN v) IF and vi) OCSVM. They are all imported from the Python module "PyOD" [24]. And we further induce diversity by tuning the hyperparameters of these approaches. Specifically, for nearest neighbour based algorithms, including kNN, Avg kNN, LOF, and LoOP, the range of parameter k is defined as [5, 10, 15, 20, ..., 100]. Considering the high time complexity of the LoOP algorithm, a narrower k range of [3, 5, 10, 15, 20] is utilized. For OCSVM, the kernel is fixed to "rbf", and a different upper bound is used on the training error score. For isolation forest, the number of estimators can be in the range [20, 50, 70, 100, 150, 200, 300]. In the stage of dynamic classifier selection based on stacking, the parameters are optimized through the Hyperopt framework. The three best-behaved classifiers are selected from the six-candidate classifiers as the base learner of the stacked model (using the AUC evaluation metric). The training set is divided into five folds for training the base learner. Finally, the Logistic Regression (default parameters) is used as the meta-learner.

Table 2. ROC-AUC scores of MEOD (average of 10 independent experiments).

Data	LOF	OCSVM	IF	LSCP	COPOD	SUOD	ECOD	MEOD (ours)
Annthyroid	0.7469	0.5523	0.8539	0.744	0.7737	0.79	0.7569	**0.9048(1)**
Arrhythmia	0.8024	0.6106	0.8099	0.7778	0.7359	0.8177	0.7867	**0.8357(1)**
Breastw	0.5961	0.9789	0.9639	0.933	0.9827	0.8625	0.9838	**0.9894(1)**
Cardio	0.5196	0.9385	0.9214	0.88	0.9103	0.9087	**0.9485**	0.8643(7)
Letter	0.8413	0.8916	0.5963	**0.9051**	0.5377	0.7017	0.5376	0.6859(5)
Mammography	0.7122	0.8537	0.8515	0.721	0.8774	0.8961	**0.9234**	0.8821(3)
Mnist	0.6966	0.5213	0.7777	0.7343	0.7892	0.8213	0.8454	**0.8623(1)**
Musk	0.5451	0.8472	**0.9951**	0.6558	0.9442	0.9315	0.9565	0.9663(2)
Optdigits	0.655	0.5587	0.7207	0.586	0.6816	0.6872	0.6356	**0.8437(1)**
Pendigits	0.5103	0.9281	**0.9488**	0.5198	0.8941	0.9315	0.9166	0.9362(2)
Pima	0.554	0.6098	0.7248	0.6001	0.6254	0.705	0.5261	**0.7714(1)**
Satellite	0.5566	**0.8512**	0.7367	0.5601	0.6561	0.6931	0.7659	0.7891(2)
Satimage-2	0.5618	0.7626	**0.9964**	0.5776	0.9612	0.9854	0.9435	0.9178(5)
Shuttle	0.5432	0.7175	0.9962	0.5334	0.9942	0.9921	**0.9973**	0.9323(5)
Speech	0.5551	0.529	0.5463	0.5487	0.539	0.5506	0.5197	**0.6973(1)**
Thyroid	0.8755	0.8537	**0.9798**	0.832	0.9185	0.9679	0.9579	0.8914(5)
Vowels	**0.9237**	0.7802	0.7735	0.9289	0.5165	0.8052	0.3732	0.8878(3)
Average	0.6586	0.7521	0.8349	0.7081	0.7846	0.8263	0.7867	**0.8622**

4.3 Performance Comparison with Baselines

In this subsection, we compare the performance of MEOD with seven other outlier detection models. Our goal is to include a variety of models to make comparison more convincing. Specifically, the seven competitors are Local Outlier

Factor (LOF), One-Class Support Vector Machines (OCSVM), Isolation Forest (IF), Locally Selective Combination of Parallel (LSCP), Copula-Based Outlier Detection (COPOD), Large-scale Unsupervised Outlier Detection (SUOD) and Empirical Cumulative Outlier Detection (ECOD). Their implementations can all be found in PyOD [24]. The experimental results in this section are obtained through 10 independent experiments, and the highest score is highlighted in bold.

Table 3. Precision of MEOD (average of 10 independent experiments).

Data	LOF	OCSVM	IF	LSCP	COPOD	SUOD	ECOD	MEOD (ours)
Annthyroid	0.3237	0.104	**0.3804**	0.2428	0.236	0.2338	0.2963	0.2727(4)
Arrhythmia	0.5385	0.2238	0.4375	0.3846	0.375	0.5714	0.5	**0.5833(1)**
Breastw	0.1507	0.8904	0.9506	0.2603	0.9437	0.6857	0.9306	**0.9863(1)**
Cardio	0.1915	0.5319	0.4561	0.234	0.4651	0.4483	**0.6429**	0.3012(6)
Letter	0.3793	0.4167	0.1094	**0.4516**	0.0357	0.1111	0.069	0.4324(2)
Mammography	0.1781	0.274	0.1594	0.2192	0.3836	0.32	**0.4189**	0.3711(3)
Mnist	0.2593	0.1665	0.2512	0.3194	0.2406	0.3781	**0.3894**	0.2947(4)
Musk	0.0556	0.2267	**0.7857**	0.3714	0.2857	0.3226	0.4595	0.7333(2)
Optdigits	**0.18**	0.02	0.0182	0.02	0.0263	0.0384	0.0244	0.0989(2)
Pendigits	0.0556	**0.3148**	0.2826	0.0741	0.2195	0.2791	0.1923	0.2892(2)
Pima	0.4052	0.4937	0.6024	0.4304	0.4568	0.5513	0.3333	**0.6939(1)**
Satellite	0.4159	0.4595	0.62	0.3997	0.5008	0.5484	0.5622	**0.8847(1)**
Satimage-2	0.1808	0.012	**0.7947**	0.1909	0.7778	0.4444	0.619	0.7399(3)
Shuttle	0.1244	0.2129	**0.9656**	0.1264	0.9573	0.8469	0.9218	0.8704(4)
Speech	0.0909	0.0455	0.044	0.0909	0.1048	0.019	0.0667	**0.137(1)**
Thyroid	0.1852	0.2222	**0.4643**	0.1852	0.2727	0.4348	0.36	0.3011(4)
Vowels	0.3125	0.1667	0.25	0.3158	0.0912	0.4	0.1026	**0.4848(1)**
Average	0.2369	0.2813	0.4454	0.2539	0.3749	0.3902	0.4052	**0.4985**

Overall Result. MEOD consistently performs better at both ROC and Precision. Among the 17 datasets in Table 1, MEOD has the highest average ROC score of 0.8622 (see Table 2), which is about 3% higher than the second-best alternative, iForest. Notably, iForest has been the SOTA method in many large-scale outlier detections. Additionally, MEOD ranked first in 7 out of 17 experiments and the top three in 12 out of 17 experiments.

Likewise, Table 3 shows that MEOD also outperforms the baseline on Precision. Among the eight outlier detection methods, MEOD achieved an average precision of 0.4985, a 5% improvement over the second-place iForest. MEOD ranks first in 6 out of 17 datasets and in the top three in 12 datasets.

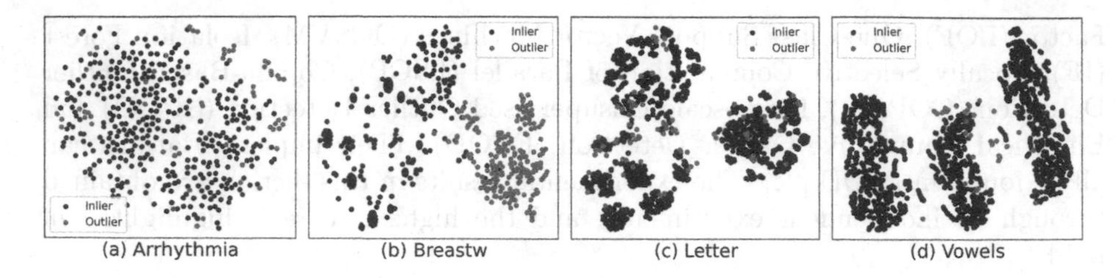

Fig. 4. 2-D visualization of selected datasets. Blue represents inliers, and orange represents outliers. In both Arrhythmia and Breastw datasets, where outliers are in the tail of at least one dimension, MEOD is the best model compared to the baseline. In both the letter and vowels datasets, the outliers are not in the tails of any dimension but are mixed with inliers, so the performance of MEOD degrades.

Case Study. Although MEOD performs well on most datasets, we notice that its performance drops significantly on some datasets, as shown in Table 2 and 3. In the case study, we have a deeper insight in this by visualizing the selected dataset in 2-D.

In Fig. 4, We first show that MEOD outperforms all baselines on two datasets, Arrhythmia and Breastw. It also presents Letter and Vowels, two datasets that do not achieve optimal performance. The visualization shows that MEOD accurately captures outliers when they are tailed in at least some dimensions (Fig. 3(a) and Fig. 3(b)). However, its performance degrades when outliers are well mixed with normal points or hidden in the middle of normal points in all dimensions (Fig. 3(c) and Fig. 3(d)). But outliers are unlikely to be similar to normal points in all dimensions in the real world, which also explains why MEOD can always be applied to most datasets.

5 Conclusion

This paper presented MEOD, a robust multi-stage ensemble model based on rank aggregation and stacking for outlier detection. The model was first applied to the test data through various unsupervised anomaly detection methods to obtain transformed outlier scores as new data representation. Then, our model used ranking aggregation to integrate the newly generated outliers and thresholds to generate pseudo-labels. Finally, the stacking-based ensemble learning method was combined with dynamic classifier selection to achieve good results. Some extensive experiments were committed to demonstrate that MEOD outperforms all other seven state-of-the-art benchmarks.

In future research, the need for outlier detection will be seriously considered to reduce the complexity of the models which are selected for obtaining predictive results in a short period. Owing to this, our future research focus will be an efficient outlier detection model combining high performance and low complexity.

References

1. Aggarwal, C.C.: Outlier ensembles: position paper. ACM SIGKDD Explor. Newsl. **14**(2), 49–58 (2013)
2. Aggarwal, C.C., Sathe, S.: Theoretical foundations and algorithms for outlier ensembles. ACM SIGKDD Explor. Newsl. **17**(1), 24–47 (2015)
3. Akoglu, L., Tong, H., Vreeken, J., Faloutsos, C.: Fast and reliable anomaly detection in categorical data. In: Proceedings of the 21st ACM International Conference on Information and Knowledge Management, pp. 415–424 (2012)
4. Boukerche, A., Zheng, L., Alfandi, O.: Outlier detection: methods, models, and classification. ACM Comput. Surv. (CSUR) **53**(3), 1–37 (2020)
5. Breiman, L.: Random forests. Mach. Learn. **45**(1), 5–32 (2001)
6. Breunig, M.M., Kriegel, H.P., Ng, R.T., Sander, J.: LOF: identifying density-based local outliers. In: Proceedings of the 2000 ACM SIGMOD International Conference on Management of Data, pp. 93–104 (2000)
7. Chen, T., Guestrin, C.: XGBoost: a scalable tree boosting system. In: Proceedings of the 22nd ACM SIGKDD International Conference on Knowledge Discovery and Data Mining, pp. 785–794 (2016)
8. Cheng, Y., Xu, Y., Zhong, H., Liu, Y.: HS-TCN: a semi-supervised hierarchical stacking temporal convolutional network for anomaly detection in IoT. In: 2019 IEEE 38th International Performance Computing and Communications Conference (IPCCC), pp. 1–7. IEEE (2019)
9. Dorogush, A.V., Ershov, V., Gulin, A.: Catboost: gradient boosting with categorical features support. arXiv preprint arXiv:1810.11363 (2018)
10. Forestier, G., Wemmert, C.: Semi-supervised learning using multiple clusterings with limited labeled data. Inf. Sci. **361**, 48–65 (2016)
11. Freund, Y., Schapire, R.E., et al.: Experiments with a new boosting algorithm. In: ICML, vol. 96, pp. 148–156. Citeseer (1996)
12. Friedman, J.H.: Greedy function approximation: a gradient boosting machine. Ann. Stat. 1189–1232 (2001)
13. Hosmer, D.W., Jr., Lemeshow, S., Sturdivant, R.X.: Applied Logistic Regression, vol. 398. Wiley, Hoboken (2013)
14. Ke, G., et al.: Lightgbm: a highly efficient gradient boosting decision tree. In: Advances in Neural Information Processing Systems 30 (2017)
15. Kolde, R., Laur, S., Adler, P., Vilo, J.: Robust rank aggregation for gene list integration and meta-analysis. Bioinformatics **28**(4), 573–580 (2012)
16. Kriegel, H.P., Kröger, P., Schubert, E., Zimek, A.: Loop: local outlier probabilities. In: Proceedings of the 18th ACM Conference on Information and Knowledge Management, pp. 1649–1652 (2009)
17. Lai, K.H., Zha, D., Xu, J., Zhao, Y., Wang, G., Hu, X.: Revisiting time series outlier detection: definitions and benchmarks. In: Thirty-fifth Conference on Neural Information Processing Systems Datasets and Benchmarks Track (Round 1) (2021)
18. Li, Y., Song, Y., Jia, L., Gao, S., Li, Q., Qiu, M.: Intelligent fault diagnosis by fusing domain adversarial training and maximum mean discrepancy via ensemble learning. IEEE Trans. Industr. Inf. **17**(4), 2833–2841 (2020)
19. Liu, F.T., Ting, K.M., Zhou, Z.H.: Isolation-based anomaly detection. ACM Trans. Knowl. Discov. Data (TKDD) **6**(1), 1–39 (2012)
20. Ma, J., Perkins, S.: Time-series novelty detection using one-class support vector machines. In: Proceedings of the International Joint Conference on Neural Networks, vol. 3, pp. 1741–1745. IEEE (2003)

21. Najafi, M., He, L., Philip, S.Y.: Outlier-robust multi-aspect streaming tensor completion and factorization. In: IJCAI, pp. 3187–3194 (2019)
22. Wan, F., Guo, G., Zhang, C., Guo, Q., Liu, J.: Outlier detection for monitoring data using stacked autoencoder. IEEE Access **7**, 173827–173837 (2019)
23. Wolpert, D.H.: Stacked generalization. Neural Netw. **5**(2), 241–259 (1992)
24. Zhao, Y., Nasrullah, Z., Li, Z.: PyOD: a python toolbox for scalable outlier detection. arXiv preprint arXiv:1901.01588 (2019)
25. Zhu, J., Li, X., Gao, C., Wang, Z., Kurths, J.: Unsupervised community detection in attributed networks based on mutual information maximization. New J. Phys. **23**(11), 113016 (2021)

MTN-Net: A Multi-Task Network for Detection and Segmentation of Thyroid Nodules in Ultrasound Images

Leyao Chen, Wei Zheng, and Wenxin Hu(✉)

School of Data Science and Engineering, East China Normal University, Shanghai, China
wzheng@admin.ecnu.edu.cn, wxhu@cc.ecnu.edu.cn

Abstract. Automatic detection and segmentation of thyroid nodules is crucial for the identification of benign and malignant nodules in computer-aided diagnosis (CAD) systems. However, the diverse sizes of thyroid nodules in ultrasound images, nodules with complex internal textures, and multiple nodules pose many challenges for automatic detection and segmentation of thyroid nodules in ultrasound images. In this paper we propose a multi-task network based on Trident network, called MTN-Net, to accurately detect and segment the thyroid nodules in ultrasound images. The backbone of MTN-Net can generate scale-specific feature maps through trident blocks with different receptive fields to detect thyroid nodules with different sizes. In addition, a novel semantic segmentation branch is embedded into the detection network for the task of segmenting thyroid nodules, which is also valid for the complete segmentation of nodules with complex textures. Furthermore, we propose an improved NMS method, named TN-NMS, for combining thyroid detection results from multiple branches, which can effectively suppress falsely detected internal nodules. The experimental results show that MTN-Net outperforms the State-of-the-Arts methods in terms of detection and segmentation accuracy on both the public TN3K dataset and the public DDTI dataset, which indicates that our method can be applied to CAD systems with practical clinical significance.

Keywords: Ultrasound image · Thyroid nodule · Detection · Segmentation · Multi-task network

1 Introduction

Thyroid nodule is a common clinical problem [1] and its incidence rate has risen rapidly worldwide. Ultrasound imaging technology has the characteristics of non-invasive, non-radioactive, convenient and inexpensive [2]. It is the primary tool for the diagnosis of thyroid nodule diseases. The diagnosis of thyroid nodules in ultrasound images depends on experienced clinicians [3]. However, due to the low contrast and low signal-to-noise ratio of ultrasound images, it hinders

G. Memmi et al. (Eds.): KSEM 2022, LNAI 13370, pp. 219–232, 2022.
https://doi.org/10.1007/978-3-031-10989-8_18

clinicians from making effective diagnosis. In order to solve this problem, more and more computer-aided diagnosis(CAD) systems are developed to assist in the diagnosis of thyroid diseases. In traditional CAD systems, the Region of Interest (ROI) of nodules is first defined manually by the clinicians, which is very time consuming and highly dependent on the clinicians' experience, and then the nodules are segmented based on the ROI. Therefore, automatic detection and segmentation of thyroid nodules is essential for CAD systems. The detection of thyroid nodules is used to predict the bounding boxes of nodules, and then automatic segmentation of nodules is performed based on the bounding boxes, which can effectively reduce the workload of clinicians.

In recent years, many deep learning methods have been proposed and applied to the detection and segmentation of thyroid nodules in ultrasound images.

Thyroid Nodule Detection Methods. Thyroid nodule detection models in ultrasound images can be divided into two types: two-stage models and one-stage models. In order to obtain higher detection precision, the two-stage models are usually applied to the detection of thyroid nodules. Li et al. [4] proposed an improved Faster R-CNN [12] for thyroid papillary carcinoma detection. By using the strategy of layer concatenation, the detector can extract the features of surrounding region around the cancer regions, which improves the detection performance. Liu et al. [5] replaced the layer concatenation strategy with Feature Pyramid Network(FPN) [13] and added it to Faster R-CNN [12] to construct a multi-scale detection network, which can extract the features of nodules with different scales. Abdolali et al. [6] replaced the network backbone from Faster R-CNN [12] to Mask R-CNN [14] with higher performance, using a well-designed loss function and transfer learning strategy to achieve high accuracy on a small dataset. These two-stage detection models mentioned above can obtain high precision in thyroid nodule detection, but the detection speed is lower than the one-stage models. In order to detect thyroid nodules with different scales, Song et al. [7] utilized a multi-scale SSD [15] model with spatial pyramid module to achieve high detection accuracy. To fully extract multi-scale features from feature maps, shahroudnejad et al. [8] constructed a one-stage model with FPN for detecting and classifying pyramid nodules, which can extract global and local information from feature maps. The above detection methods fully extracted thyroid nodule features at different scales by adding modules that extract multi-scale features, such as the connection between low-level and high-level layers, and FPN, thereby improving the accuracy of detecting thyroid nodules.

Thyroid Nodule Segmentation Methods. Ying et al. [9] proposed a cascaded convolutional neural network that first segmented the Region of Interest(RoI) containing thyroid nodules, and then used a VGG network to accurately segment thyroid nodules on the basis of RoI. Wang et al. [10] constructed a cascade segmentation network based on DeepLabv3plus [16]. The rough location of nodules was first obtained, and then the nodules were segmented accurately based on the rough location, which eliminated the influence of the area around the nodules on the segmentation results, and thus obtained more accurate segmentation results.

To remove the mistake recognition of non-thyroid areas as nodules, Gong et al. [11] embedded a priori guided feature module of thyroid region into the nodule segmentation model for the first time, which improved the accuracy of nodule localization and enhanced the segmentation performance of thyroid nodules. The above-mentioned thyroid nodule segmentation methods first remove the influence of irrelevant regions, and then perform further segmentation on the Region of Interest(RoI), thus reducing the false recognition of non-nodular regions as nodules.

Although many deep learning methods have been applied to the detection and segmentation tasks of thyroid nodules, most of them only complete one of the two tasks. Only a few methods can detect and segment thyroid nodules simultaneously. Among them, thyroid nodule detection methods achieve high accuracy while maintaining high efficiency, but there are still many problems in detecting thyroid nodules with extreme sizes, nodules with complex internal texture, and multiple nodules. It leads to missed detection of small nodules, false detection of intermediate nodules, and false detection of tissue similar to nodules as nodules. In addition, thyroid nodule segmentation method achieves high accuracy while there are still many challenges to be solved in becoming a real-time system.

To address the above problems, we propose a multi-task thyroid nodule detection and segmentation model based on Trident network [17], called MTN-Net. It is embedded with a novel semantic segmentation branch for accurate segmentation of thyroid nodules, and it includes an improved NMS algorithm, called TN-NMS, for combining the thyroid nodule detection results from multiple branches. Therefore, MTN-Net achieves significant effects on the detection of thyroid nodules with different sizes and thyroid nodules with complex internal texture, and effectively suppresses the false detection of intermediate nodules in large nodules.

The main contributions of this paper can be summarized as follows:

- We propose a multi-task network based on Trident network [17] for the detection and segmentation of thyroid nodules in ultrasound images, which can generate specific scale feature maps through trident block [17] with different receptive fields. So it is effective in detecting thyroid nodules with different sizes.
- A novel semantic segmentation branch based on FCN [18] is embedded into the detection network to complete the segmentation task of thyroid nodules, which is valid for completely segmenting the thyroid nodules with complex texture.
- We propose an improved NMS algorithm called TN-NMS to fuse the detection results from multiple branches, which can successfully suppress the false detection results of internal nodules in large nodules.

The rest of this paper is as follows: we first describe the details of our proposed model and the feature generation in Sect. 2. We then introduce the experimental setup and results in Sect. 3. Finally, we conclude our work and indicate future directions in Sect. 4.

2 Method

2.1 Overall Architecture

The proposed MTN-Net is a multi-branch two-stage thyroid nodule detection and segmentation model based on Trident network [17]. Figure 1 illustrates the overall architecture of our proposed MTN-Net. The network is composed of backbone, extended Faster R-CNN head, and TN-NMS algorithm. We adopt ResNet-101 with trident blocks as the backbone, in which the conv4_x stage consists of trident blocks containing three branches. It can fully extract the multi-scale features of thyroid nodules in ultrasound images, and thus contributing to the detection of thyroid nodules with different sizes. Additionally, we add a novel semantic segmentation branch to the extended Faster R-CNN head to accomplish the thyroid nodule segmentation task. Finally, an improved NMS algorithm called TN-NMS is used to combine the detection results of thyroid nodules from multiple branches.

Ultrasound images of thyroid nodules are input to the backbone to generate feature maps with different receptive fields. They are then fed into the extended Faster R-CNN head to produce the corresponding detection and segmentation results, which are eventually combined by the TN-NMS algorithm to generate the output results.

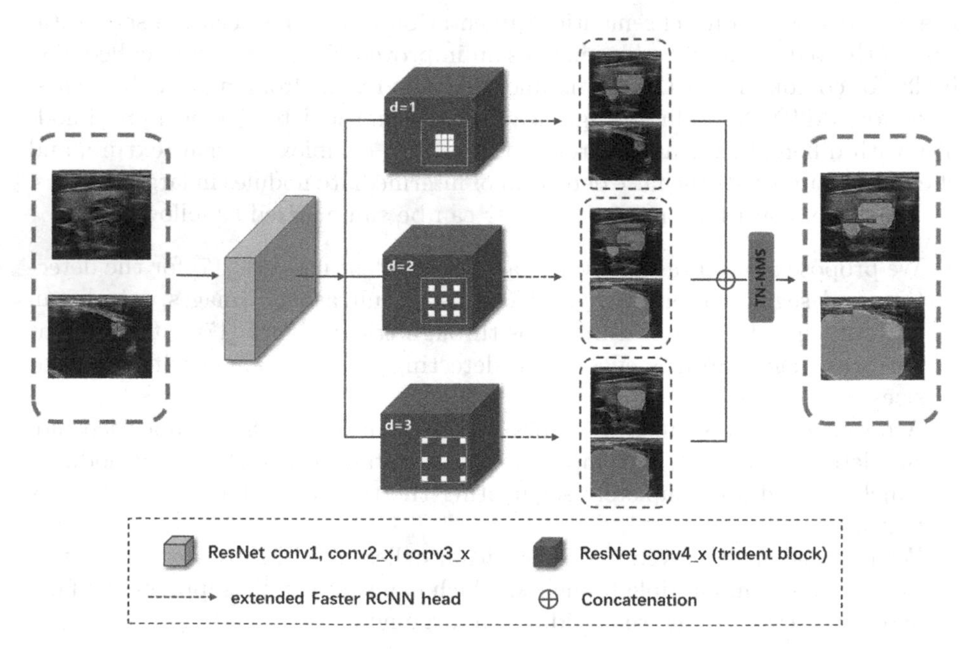

Fig. 1. The architecture of proposed MTN-Net. MTN-Net is comprised of backbone (ResNet-101 with trident blocks), extended Faster R-CNN head, and TN-NMS algorithm.

2.2 Semantic Segmentation Branch

We use a novel semantic segmentation branch based on FCN [18] to segment thyroid nodules. This semantic segmentation branch is embedded into the Faster R-CNN detection head and parallel to the bounding-box classification and regression. In addition, we add an RoIAlign [14] layer in Faster R-CNN head to remove the rough space quantization of RoIPool [19], which can improve the accuracy of mask prediction at pixel level. The extended Faster R-CNN head is displayed in Fig. 2. Different from the existing extended Faster R-CNN heads mentioned in [14], our extended Faster R-CNN head has a novel semantic segmentation branch capable of segmenting thyroid nodules with complex textures more completely. We add four convolution layers before the deconvolution layer of the semantic segmentation branch to fully obtain the features in the Region-of-Interest(RoI), so as to completely segment the nodules with complex internal texture. Meanwhile, we add L_{mask} to the loss function. For some predicted boxes that do not contain thyroid nodules, the proposed semantic segmentation branch can suppress some incorrectly detected boxes through L_{mask}.

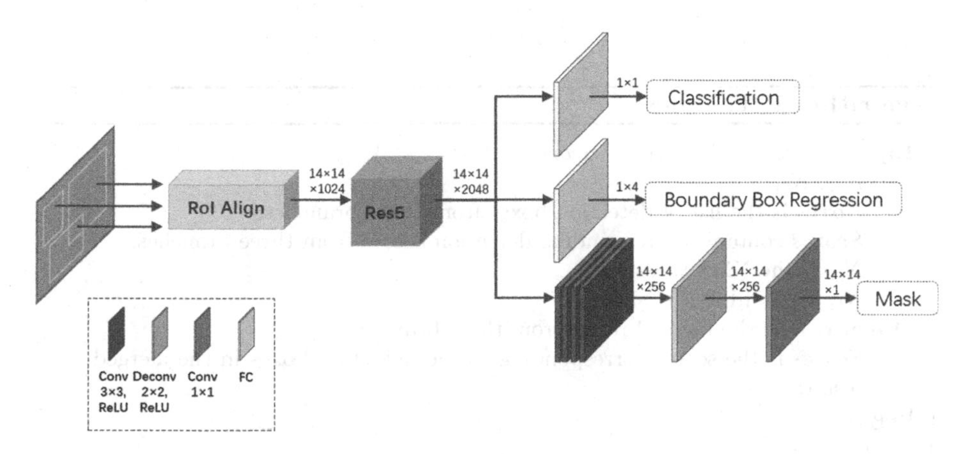

Fig. 2. The architecture of our extended Faster R-CNN head, in which a novel semantic segmentation branch is embedded to complete the segmentation task of thyroid nodules.

2.3 TN-NMS

NMS is utilized to merge the detection results from multiple branches in Trident network [17]. It is described as [20]:

$$S_i = \begin{cases} S_i, & iou\left(\mathcal{M}, b_i\right) < N_t \\ 0, & iou\left(\mathcal{M}, b_i\right) \geq N_t \end{cases} \tag{1}$$

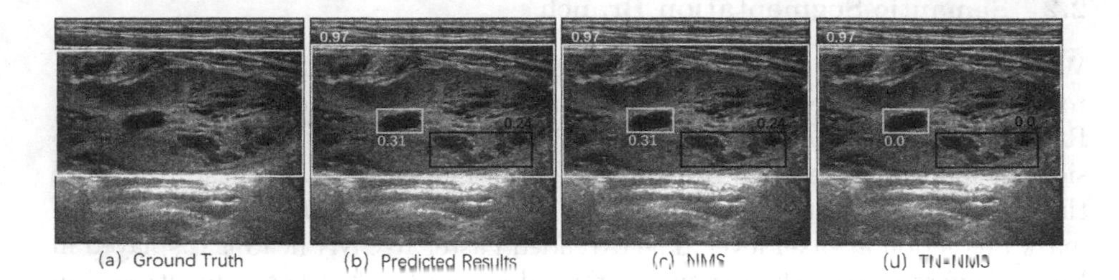

Fig. 3. The results of a thyroid nodule with complex internal texture being correctly detected (yellow) and incorrectly detected (red and green) along with their confidence scores. Since the *iou* (0.03) of the red and yellow boxes, as well as the *iou* (0.11) of the green and yellow boxes, are much smaller than the threshold 0.5, the results of incorrect detections cannot be suppressed using the NMS algorithm (as shown in (c)). In contrast, the *niou* (1.0) of the red box and the yellow box, as well as the *niou* (1.0) of the green box and the yellow box exceed the threshold 0.9, so the TN-NMS algorithm can successfully suppress the bounding boxes of these false detections (as shown in (d)) (Color figure online)

Algorithm 1: TN-NMS

Input: $Boxes = \{b_1, ..., b_N\}$, $Scores = \{s_1, ..., s_N\}$, N_{t_1}, N_{t_2};
Boxes is the list of detection boxes from three branches;
Scores contains corresponding detection scores from three branches;
N_{t_1} is the NMS threshold;
N_{t_2} is the nIoU threshold;
Output: $\mathcal{R}$ is the merged result from three branches;
Scores is the scores corresponding to the detection boxes in the merged result;

1 **begin**
2 $\quad \mathcal{R} \leftarrow \{\}$
3 $\quad$ **while** $Boxes \neq empty$ **do**
4 $\quad\quad m \leftarrow \text{argmax}\{Scores\}$
5 $\quad\quad \mathcal{M} \leftarrow b_m$
6 $\quad\quad \mathcal{R} \leftarrow \mathcal{R} \bigcup \mathcal{M}$; $Boxes \leftarrow Boxes - \mathcal{M}$
7 $\quad\quad$ **for** b_i *in Boxes* **do**
8 $\quad\quad\quad$ **if** $iou\,(\mathcal{M}, b_i) \geq N_{t_1}$ *or* $niou\,(\mathcal{M}, b_i) \geq N_{t_2}$ **then**
9 $\quad\quad\quad\quad Boxes \leftarrow Boxes - b_i$
10 $\quad\quad\quad\quad Scores \leftarrow Scores - s_i$
11 $\quad\quad\quad$ **end**
12 $\quad\quad$ **end**
13 $\quad$ **end**
14 $\quad$ **return** $\mathcal{R}, Scores$
15 **end**

The input data in Eq. 1 consists of an ordered list of detection boxes *Boxes* with scores *Scores* and a threshold N_t. S_i represents a re-scoring function, $\mathcal{M}$ is the box with the highest score in *Boxes*, b_i indicates the currently selected box in *Boxes*, *iou* denotes the intersection area divided by the union area of two boxes, N_t is a threshold indicating whether the currently selected box b_i should be removed. NMS starts by selecting the bounding box $\mathcal{M}$ with the highest score in *Boxes*, calculates the *iou* of the remaining bounding boxes b_i in *Boxes* and $\mathcal{M}$, then deletes the bounding box b_i whose *iou* is greater than the threshold N_t, which is usually set to 0.5. However, the area of intermediate nodules detected by mistake is usually much smaller than that of large nodules, resulting in the *iou* of their corresponding bounding boxes less than 0.5, and thus the NMS algorithm is unable to suppress the results of these false detections, as shown in Fig. 3(c). Therefore, in order to suppress the bounding box of these intermediate nodules, we propose a new calculation method for thyroid nodule detection, named *niou*, which represents the intersection region of b_i and $\mathcal{M}$ divided by the region of b_i. It is described as:

$$niou\left(\mathcal{M}, b_i\right) = \frac{\mathcal{M} \cap b_i}{b_i} \tag{2}$$

The *niou* calculated by the bounding box of incorrectly detected nodules and correctly detected nodules is usually equal to or close to 1.0, so that the results of incorrect detection above the threshold 0.9 are successfully suppressed, as shown in Fig. 3(d). Meanwhile, we add *niou* to the NMS algorithm and propose an improved NMS algorithm, named TN-NMS, which is used to combine the detection results of three branches and is described as:

$$S_i = \begin{cases} S_i, & iou\left(\mathcal{M}, b_i\right) < N_{t_1} \text{ and } niou\left(\mathcal{M}, b_i\right) < N_{t_2} \\ 0, & iou\left(\mathcal{M}, b_i\right) \geq N_{t_1} \text{ or } niou\left(\mathcal{M}, b_i\right) \geq N_{t_2} \end{cases} \tag{3}$$

where N_{t_1} and N_{t_2} are thresholds that determine whether the currently selected bounding box b_i should be removed from *Boxes*. The detailed process of TN-NMS is shown in Algorithm 1. In each step of TN-NMS, the scores of all detection boxes that overlap with $\mathcal{M}$ are updated, then the detection boxes with a score of 0 are removed from *Boxes*, hence the computational complexity of each step of TN-NMS is $\mathcal{O}(N)$, where N is the number of detection boxes in Boxes. Therefore, for N detection boxes in *Boxes*, the computational complexity of the TN-NMS algorithm is $\mathcal{O}(N^2)$, which is the same as that of the NMS algorithm.

2.4 Loss Function

As shown in Fig. 1, the proposed network is a multi-task network, whose loss function combines the loss of classification, bounding box regression and segmentation. In order to improve performance, we add weighting factors to the loss function of each task. Therefore, the total loss function on each Region of Interest(RoI) is defined as follows:

$$L_{\text{total}} = \lambda_{cls} * L_{\text{cls}} + \lambda_{\text{box}} * L_{\text{box}} + \lambda_{\text{mask}} * L_{\text{mask}} \tag{4}$$

where L_{cls}, L_{box}, L_{mask} indicate classification loss, bounding box regression loss and mask segmentation loss respectively. λ_{cls}, λ_{box}, λ_{mask} are weighting factors of each component. We use the cross entropy loss function to calculate the classification loss of thyroid nodules, and utilize the smooth L1 loss for boundary box regression. The definitions of these two tasks are the same as those defined in [19]. Besides, we adopt the binary cross entropy loss to calculate the mask segmentation loss defined on the foreground proposals. Therefore, the loss of mask segmentation task is defined as follows:

$$L_{\text{mask}} = -\frac{1}{n^2} \sum_{0 \leq i,j \leq n} BCE\left(y_{ij}, y_{ij}^*\right) \tag{5}$$

where n is the length and width of each mask, y_{ij} is the predicted value and y_{ij}^* is the growth truth of each class. Furthermore, weighting factors can help optimize the performance of classification, detection and segmentation tasks.

3 Experiments

3.1 Dataset and Preprocessing

We evaluated the proposed architecture on the public thyroid nodule region segmentation dataset called TN3K provided in [11], which contains 3493 ultrasound images obtained from 2421 patients. In addition, we compare the performance of our proposed method with State-of-the-Arts methods on the public DDTI dataset [21]. It contains 347 thyroid ultrasound images from 299 patients with thyroid disease, annotated by radiologists for thyroid nodule segmentation results. All the cases in the DDTI dataset are from the IDIME Ultrasound Department, one of the largest imaging centers in Colombia.

In order to adopt these two datasets to thyroid nodule detection and segmentation, we add the bounding box annotation for object detection. Besides, we use the operation of adaptive histogram equalization for each image to transform the gray level of the image, so as to improve the contrast of the image. In addition, we perform data augmentation operations on the preprocessed images used for training, including random mirror flip, random left-right flip, random clipping, random sharpening, random increase or decrease of image contrast.

3.2 Implementation Details

The proposed network is implemented in PyTorch 1.8.1. The experimental codes are modified on the basis of Detectron2 [22], and many default configuration parameters are used for model training and inference. The model is trained on two NVIDIA Tesla P100 GPUs with a batch size of 16, and the backbone of the network is pre-trained on MS-COCO [23]. In our experiments, N_{t_1} and N_{t_2} in TN-NMS are set to 0.5 and 0.9 respectively, and λ_{cls}, λ_{box}, λ_{mask} of loss function are set to 2, 5 and 2 respectively. Moreover, the model is trained with the stochastic gradient descent optimizer and the learning rate of warmup and cosine annealing for 50 epochs, whose learning rate increases linearly to 0.05 in the first 1000 iterations, then decreases gradually in the form of cosine annealing. The total time of model training is 20 h, and the inference time of each image is 0.85 s.

3.3 Evaluation Metrics

For the evaluation, in order to accurately quantify the performance of our model, standard COCO metrics including AP (Average Precision), AP_{50} and metrics for evaluating the Average Precision of objects with different size, including AP_S (less than 32×32), AP_M (from 32×32 to 96×96), AP_L (greater than 96×96) are used as evaluation metrics. Since the smallest thyroid nodule contained in the DDTI dataset are larger than 32×32 pixels in size, AP_S cannot be used as an evaluation metric for the DDTI dataset. Therefore, we measure the thyroid nodule detection and segmentation performance of AP, AP_{50}, AP_M, AP_L on the DDTI dataset.

3.4 Ablation Study

In order to validate the performance of our proposed architecture, the evaluation metrics of detection and segmentation are used to quantify the comparison between our proposed model and baseline model. The baseline is Trident network with a mask prediction branch proposed in [14], which includes a 2×2 deconvolution layer with stride 2 and a 1×1 convolution layer for predicting mask. Baseline/ResNet-101 backbone refers to the baseline network with ResNet-101 as the backbone. Then we respectively add semantic segmentation branches and TN-NMS algorithm on baseline, which is denoted as bNet+S and bNet+T.

Table 1. Ablation studies on the detection of thyroid nodules.

Model	TN3K					DDTI			
	AP	AP_{50}	AP_S	AP_M	AP_L	AP	AP_{50}	AP_M	AP_L
Baseline/ResNet-101 backbone	54.7	85.7	32.8	47.3	61.1	49.0	85.1	42.0	57.2
bNet+S	54.9	86.6	30.6	47.2	62.5	49.8	87.2	43.7	57.5
bNet+T	54.7	86.6	**36.7**	48.0	61.6	49.7	85.5	43.0	57.4
Ours	**55.2**	**87.1**	34.4	**48.2**	**62.8**	**51.3**	**88.7**	**45.4**	**57.8**

As shown in Table 2, bNet+S improves 1.2% and 1.0% on AP_L for nodule segmentation on TN3K and DDTI, respectively, which indicates that semantic segmentation branche has high performance in segmenting large nodules. From Table 1, we can see that bNet+T has a 3.9% and 0.4% improvement on AP_S and AP_L for TN3K and 0.2% improvement on AP_L for DDTI, respectively, which demonstrates that the TN-NMS algorithm improves the detection performance of large and small nodules by suppressing the internal nodules in large nodules.

Table 2. Ablation studies on the segmentation of thyroid nodules.

Model	TN3K					DDTI			
	AP	AP_{50}	AP_S	AP_M	AP_L	AP	AP_{50}	AP_M	AP_L
Baseline/ResNet-101 backbone	56.2	84.6	32.0	50.1	61.7	46.7	84.3	41.1	53.2
bNet+S	56.5	85.6	31.4	50.0	**62.9**	47.7	85.5	43.4	54.2
bNet+T	56.3	85.4	**36.0**	50.6	62.5	47.0	84.4	41.3	53.6
Ours	**56.8**	**86.9**	35.5	**50.8**	**62.9**	**49.0**	**86.6**	**44.7**	**54.4**

When both are added into baseline, MTN-Net greatly enhances in all evaluation metrics compared to baseline. However, the AP_S of MTN-Net is lower than that of bNet+T. We consider that the semantic segmentation branch focuses too much on large nodules, and thus has lower performance on the detecting and segmenting small nodules, there by leading to the lower performance of MTN-Net than that of bNet+T.

3.5 Comparisons Against State-of-the-Arts Methods

We compared our framework MTN-Net with several state-of-the-art approaches, including Mask R-CNN [14], Cascade Mask R-CNN [24], Mask Scoring R-CNN [25], PointRend [26]. Mask R-CNN is a commonly used two-stage detection and segmentation model. And Cascade Mask R-CNN is a multi-head model based on Cascade R-CNN, which has higher detection accuracy than Mask R-CNN. Besides, Mask Scoring R-CNN adds a branch for scoring masks on the basis of Mask R-CNN, which enhances the accuracy of segmentation. Furthermore, PointRend is optimized for image segmentation at the edges of objects, resulting in better performance at the hard-to-segment edges of objects.

Table 3. Performance comparison of thyroid nodule detection on TN3K and DDTI.

Model	TN3K					DDTI			
	AP	AP_{50}	AP_S	AP_M	AP_L	AP	AP_{50}	AP_M	AP_L
Mask R-CNN	52.1	84.5	28.3	45.2	59.5	45.1	82.8	38.2	53.5
Cascade Mask R-CNN	53.9	84.8	31.0	47.1	61.3	47.5	84.3	43.0	54.0
Mask Scoring R-CNN	53.1	84.4	**37.3**	45.6	62.0	47.6	83.4	39.4	57.1
PointRend	54.5	85.0	37.1	47.3	61.3	47.4	82.0	40.0	56.1
Ours	**55.2**	**87.1**	34.4	**48.2**	**62.8**	**51.3**	**88.7**	**45.4**	**57.8**

Quantitative Analysis on TN3K. Tables 3 and 4 demonstrate the quantitative comparison results between our MTN-Net and other SOTA models on the public TN3K dataset. MTN-Net greatly improves AP, AP_{50}, AP_M, and AP_L against other SOTA models. However, the performance in detecting and segmenting

Table 4. Performance comparison of thyroid nodule segmentation on TN3K and DDTI.

Model	TN3K					DDTI			
	AP	AP_{50}	AP_S	AP_M	AP_L	AP	AP_{50}	AP_M	AP_L
Mask R-CNN	54.4	84.5	30.0	48.3	60.7	42.6	80.2	36.4	49.7
Cascade Mask R-CNN	55.5	84.7	31.6	49.8	62.0	45.6	84.4	41.0	51.0
Mask Scoring R-CNN	55.1	84.6	**37.5**	49.5	61.1	46.1	82.9	41.5	51.9
PointRend	56.2	85.8	36.5	50.3	62.3	46.4	81.0	39.5	53.2
Ours	**56.8**	**86.9**	35.5	**50.8**	**62.9**	**49.0**	**86.6**	**44.7**	**54.4**

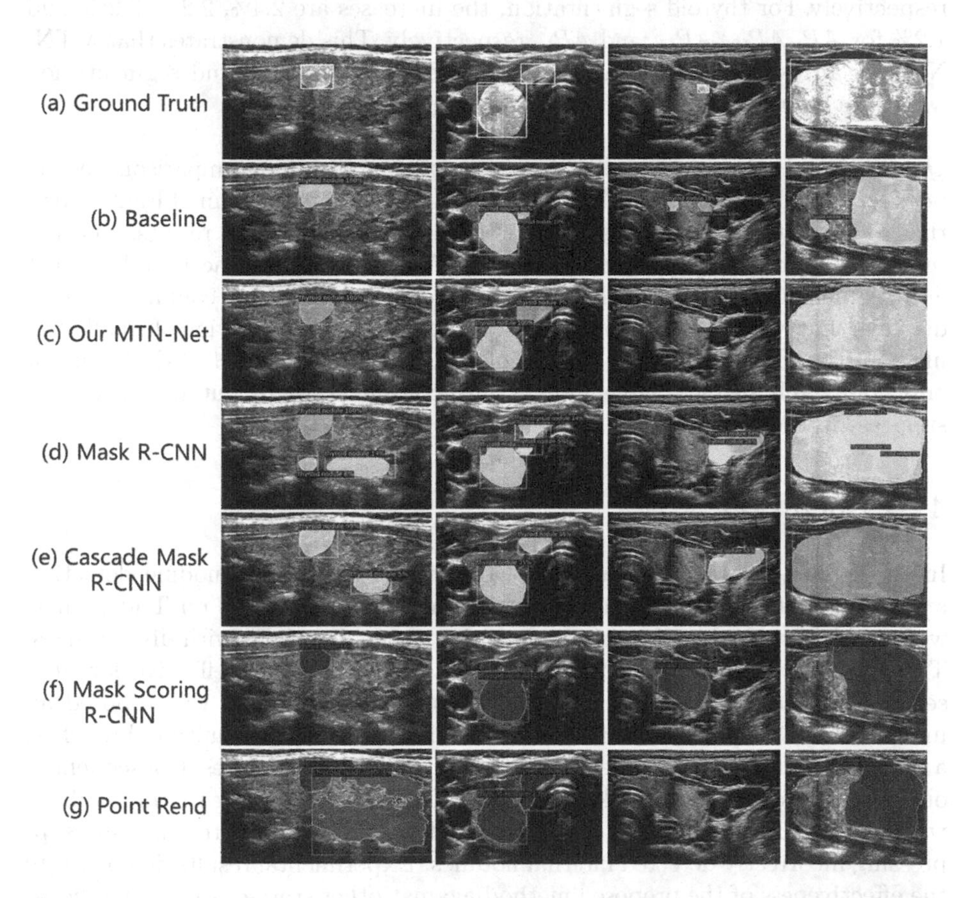

Fig. 4. Qualitative comparison of our MTN-Net and SOTA models. Among them, Baseline, Our MTN-Net, Mask R-CNN, Cascade Mask R-CNN (yellow) are implemented based on Detectron2, and Mask Scoring R-CNN and Point Rend (green) are implemented based on MMDetection [27] (Color figure online)

small nodules (less than 32 × 32 pixels) is inferior to Mask Scoring R-CNN and Point Rend. Since the appearance and texture of some small nodules are extremely similar to the surrounding tissues, MTN-Net is prone to mis-detect other tissues and organs as small nodules. Nevertheless, MTN-Net has high accuracy on both AP_M, and AP_L, which indicates its remarkable competitiveness in detecting and segmenting medium and large nodules.

Quantitative Analysis on DDTI. As shown in Tables 3 and 4, MTN-Net exceeds other SOTA models in the above metrics on the DDTI dataset. For thyroid detection, it increases 3.8%, 4.4%, 2.4%, and 0.7% for AP, AP_{50}, AP_M, and AP_L, respectively. For thyroid segmentation, the increases are 2.4%, 2.2%, 3.2%, and 1.2% for AP, AP_{50}, AP_M, and AP_L, respectively. This demonstrates that MTN-Net has an excellent performance in both nodule detection and segmentation when the nodule size is larger than 32 × 32 pixels.

Qualitative Analysis. Figure 4 illustrates the qualitative comparison results between our MTN-Net and other SOTA models. The first column of Fig. 4 shows that MTN-Net can successfully exclude false-positive detection results. And the second column of Fig. 4 illustrates that MTN-Net is able to accurately detect and segment multiple thyroid nodules. In addition, the third column of Fig. 4 displays that MTN-Net is significantly competitive in the detection of small nodules. Furthermore, the fourth column of Fig. 4 indicates that MTN-Net can not only completely segment large nodules with complex texture, but also effectively suppress internal nodules.

4 Conclusion

In this paper, we proposed a two-stage network for thyroid nodule detection and segmentation in ultrasound images. Our network is built on Trident network, which is capable of precisely detecting thyroid nodules with diverse sizes. The semantic segmentation branch added to the network is effective for fully segmenting large nodules with complex textures. In addition, we proposed an improved NMS algorithm to fuse the detection results from multiple branches, and it is useful to suppress the false detection of internal nodules. Consequently, our network achieves a remarkable competitiveness in detecting thyroid nodules with diverse sizes, segmenting completely nodules with internal texture, and suppressing incorrectly detected internal nodules. Experimental results demonstrate the effectiveness of the proposed method against other state-of-the-art methods. In the future, we will utilize self-supervision methods to further reduce the false positive rate of our model for thyroid nodule detection and segmentation in ultrasound images.

Acknowledgements. This research is funded by East China Normal University-Qiniu Intelligent Learning Joint Laboratory. The computation is supported by ECNU Multifunctional Platform for Innovation (001).

References

1. Haugen, B.R., et al.: 2015 American thyroid association management guidelines for adult patients with thyroid nodules and differentiated thyroid cancer: the American thyroid association guidelines task force on thyroid nodules and differentiated thyroid cancer. Thyroid **26**(1), 1–133 (2016)
2. Savelonas, M.A., Iakovidis, D.K., Legakis, I., Maroulis, D.: Active contours guided by echogenicity and texture for delineation of thyroid nodules in ultrasound images. IEEE Trans. Inf. Technol. Biomed. **13**(4), 519–527 (2008)
3. Chen, J., You, H., Li, K.: A review of thyroid gland segmentation and thyroid nodule segmentation methods for medical ultrasound images. Comput. Methods Progr. Biomed. **185**, 105329 (2020)
4. Li, H., et al.: An improved deep learning approach for detection of thyroid papillary cancer in ultrasound images. Sci. Rep. **8**(1), 1–12 (2018)
5. Liu, R., Zhou, S., Guo, Y., Wang, Y., Chang, C.: Nodule localization in thyroid ultrasound images with a joint-training convolutional neural network. J. Digital Imaging **33**(5), 1266–1279 (2020)
6. Abdolali, F., Kapur, J., Jaremko, J.L., Noga, M., Hareendranathan, A.R., Punithakumar, K.: Automated thyroid nodule detection from ultrasound imaging using deep convolutional neural networks. Comput. Biol. Med. **122**, 103871 (2020)
7. Song, W., et al.: Multitask cascade convolution neural networks for automatic thyroid nodule detection and recognition. IEEE J. Biomed. Health Inform. **23**(3), 1215–1224 (2018)
8. Shahroudnejad, A., et al.: TUN-Det: a novel network for thyroid ultrasound nodule detection. In: de Bruijne, M., et al. (eds.) MICCAI 2021. LNCS, vol. 12901, pp. 656–667. Springer, Cham (2021). https://doi.org/10.1007/978-3-030-87193-2_62
9. Ying, X., et al.: Thyroid nodule segmentation in ultrasound images based on cascaded convolutional neural network. In: Cheng, L., Leung, A.C.S., Ozawa, S. (eds.) ICONIP 2018. LNCS, vol. 11306, pp. 373–384. Springer, Cham (2018). https://doi.org/10.1007/978-3-030-04224-0_32
10. Wang, M., et al.: Automatic segmentation and classification of thyroid nodules in ultrasound images with convolutional neural networks. In: Shusharina, N., Heinrich, M.P., Huang, R. (eds.) MICCAI 2020. LNCS, vol. 12587, pp. 109–115. Springer, Cham (2021). https://doi.org/10.1007/978-3-030-71827-5_14
11. Gong, H., et al.: Multi-task learning for thyroid nodule segmentation with thyroid region prior. In: 2021 IEEE 18th International Symposium on Biomedical Imaging (ISBI), pp. 257–261. IEEE (2021) https://doi.org/10.1109/ISBI48211.2021.9434087
12. Ren, S., He, K., Girshick, R., Sun, J.: Faster R-CNN: towards real-time object detection with region proposal networks. Adv. Neural Inf. Process. Syst. **28**, 1–9 (2015)
13. Lin, T.Y., Dollár, P., Girshick, R., He, K., Hariharan, B., Belongie, S.: Feature pyramid networks for object detection. In: Proceedings of the IEEE Conference on Computer Vision and Pattern Recognition, pp. 2117–2125 (2017). https://doi.org/10.48550/arXiv.1612.03144
14. He, K., Gkioxari, G., Dollár, P., Girshick, R.: Mask R-CNN. In: Proceedings of the IEEE International Conference on Computer Vision, pp. 2961–2969 (2017). https://doi.org/10.48550/arXiv.1703.06870

15. Liu, W., et al.: SSD: single shot multibox detector. In: Leibe, B., Matas, J., Sebe, N., Welling, M. (eds.) ECCV 2016. LNCS, vol. 9905, pp. 21–37. Springer, Cham (2016). https://doi.org/10.1007/978-3-319-46448-0_2
16. Chen, L.C., Zhu, Y., Papandreou, G., Schroff, F., Adam, H.: Encoder-decoder with atrous separable convolution for semantic image segmentation. In: Proceedings of the European Conference on Computer Vision (ECCV), pp. 801–818 (2018). https://doi.org/10.48550/arXiv.1802.02611
17. Li, Y., Chen, Y., Wang, N., Zhang, Z.: Scale-aware trident networks for object detection. In: Proceedings of the IEEE/CVF International Conference on Computer Vision, pp. 6054–6063 (2019). https://doi.org/10.1109/ICCV.2019.00615
18. Long, J., Shelhamer, E., Darrell, T.: Fully convolutional networks for semantic segmentation. In: Proceedings of the IEEE Conference on Computer Vision and Pattern Recognition, pp. 3431–3440 (2015). https://doi.org/10.1109/CVPR.2015.7298965
19. Girshick, R.: Fast R-CNN. In: Proceedings of the IEEE International Conference on Computer Vision, pp. 1440–1448 (2015). https://doi.org/10.1109/ICCV.2015.169
20. Bodla, N., Singh, B., Chellappa, R., Davis, L.S.: Soft-NMS-improving object detection with one line of code. In: Proceedings of the IEEE International Conference on Computer Vision, pp. 5561–5569 (2017). https://doi.org/10.1109/ICCV.2017.593
21. Pedraza, L., Vargas, C., Narváez, F., Durán, O., Muñoz, E., Romero, E.: An open access thyroid ultrasound image database. In: 10th International Symposium on Medical Information Processing and Analysis. vol. 9287, p. 92870W. International Society for Optics and Photonics (2015). https://doi.org/10.1117/12.2073532
22. Wu, Y., Kirillov, A., Massa, F., Lo, W.Y., Girshick, R.: Detectron2 (2019). https://github.com/facebookresearch/detectron2
23. Lin, T.-Y., et al.: Microsoft COCO: common objects in context. In: Fleet, D., Pajdla, T., Schiele, B., Tuytelaars, T. (eds.) ECCV 2014. LNCS, vol. 8693, pp. 740–755. Springer, Cham (2014). https://doi.org/10.1007/978-3-319-10602-1_48
24. Cai, Z., Vasconcelos, N.: Cascade R-CNN: high quality object detection and instance segmentation. IEEE Trans. Pattern Anal. Mach. Intell. **43**(5), 1483–1498 (2019)
25. Huang, Z., Huang, L., Gong, Y., Huang, C., Wang, X.: Mask scoring R-CNN. In: Proceedings of the IEEE/CVF Conference on Computer Vision and Pattern Recognition, pp. 6409–6418 (2019). https://doi.org/10.1109/CVPR.2019.00657
26. Kirillov, A., Wu, Y., He, K., Girshick, R.: Pointrend: image segmentation as rendering. In: Proceedings of the IEEE/CVF Conference on Computer Vision and Pattern Recognition, pp. 9799–9808 (2020). https://doi.org/10.1109/CVPR42600.2020.00982
27. Chen, K., et al.: MMDetection: Open MMLab detection toolbox and benchmark. arXiv preprint arXiv:1906.07155 (2019)

Dual Adversarial Federated Learning on Non-IID Data

Tao Zhang, Shaojing Yang, Anxiao Song(✉), Guangxia Li, and Xuewen Dong

School of Computer Science and Technology, Xidian University, Xi'an 710071, China
{taozhang,gxli,xwdong}@xidian.edu.cn, songanxiao2019@163.com

Abstract. Federated Learning (FL) enables multiple distributed local clients to coordinate with a central server to train a global model without sharing their private data. However, the data owned by different clients, even with the same label, may induce conflicts in the latent feature maps, especially under the non-IID FL scenarios. This would fatally impair the performance of the global model. To this end, we propose a novel approach, DAFL, for Dual Adversarial Federated Learning, to mitigate the divergence on latent feature maps among different clients on non-IID data. In particular, a local dual adversarial training is designed to identify the origins of latent feature maps, and then transforms the conflicting latent feature maps to reach a consensus between global and local models in each client. Besides, the latent feature maps of the two models become closer to each other adaptively by reducing their Kullback Leibler divergence. Extensive experiments on benchmark datasets validate the effectiveness of DAFL and also demonstrate that DAFL outperforms the state-of-the-art approaches in terms of test accuracy under different non-IID settings.

Keywords: Federated learning · Non-IID data · Latent feature map · Dual adversarial training · Kullback Leibler divergence

1 Introduction

Federated Learning (FL) is an emerging distributed learning framework where multiple local clients coordinate with a central server to train a global model without sharing their private data [16,24], which is superior to traditional centralized learning paradigms in data privacy [2,17,19] and communication efficiency [6]. Its effectiveness highly depends on the data distribution. FL works well on independent and identically distributed (IID) data, that is, clients are similar to each other in their private data distribution. However, in many real-world scenarios, data are typically non-identically distributed among clients. The non-IID data still poses severe challenges for existing FL to train an effective global model [7,14]. Recent studies [11,12,26] have shown that the non-IID data can result in a significant performance drop of the global model in terms of convergence and accuracy since it can deflect the direction of local optimum and deviate global model updates.

G. Memmi et al. (Eds.): KSEM 2022, LNAI 13370, pp. 233–246, 2022.
https://doi.org/10.1007/978-3-031-10989-8_19

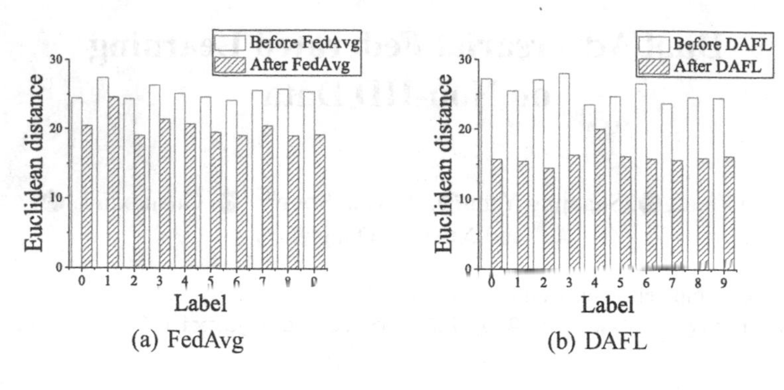

Fig. 1. The Euclidean distance of latent feature maps extracted by two clients on FashionMnist dataset.

There have been many efforts to improve the performance of FL on non-IID data. Some attempts pull the local models closer to the global model, thus limiting the variety of local updates. For example, Wu et al. [21] proposed a heterogeneous model reuse method to decrease the weight divergence of local training models by sharing a subset of public data among clients. Li et al. [11] added the local weight regularization term to restrict the directions of local updates. And, Karimireddy et al. [8] achieved linear speedup by reducing client-variance during the updates. However, they cannot solve the clients' inherent data distribution diversity and fully leverage the underlying latent feature information. Thus, some approaches personalize the global model to deliver good performance for each client in the federation. For instance, Fallah et al. [3] derived a proper initial shared model over all clients from the Model-Agnostic Meta Learning (MAML) problem formulation [4]. Then, personalized models can be quickly adapted to the local data of different clients after training a few steps on this shared model. Smith et al. [20] considered fitting separate but related models simultaneously to learn personalized models. However, in most real-world situations, a well-trained and high-quality global model is required to provide unbiased decisions and precise predictions [18,23], rather than some personalized ones.

Different from existing studies, we observe that the data from different clients may induce conflicting latent feature maps, which would fatally degrade the performance of FL. As shown in Fig. 1, by measuring the Euclidean Distance of latent feature maps extracted by two clients for the data with the same label on FashionMnist dataset [22], it can be observed that before the global training, the latent feature maps of each label among clients have great diversity.

If the average strategy is simply adopted to aggregate the local models, the generalization of the global model will be degraded as a result of conflicting representations of latent feature maps. Thus, we try to tackle the problem based on an intuitive idea: the server transforms the conflicting latent feature maps among clients to reach a consensus rather than just synchronizing the global and local models. Compared with FedAvg [16], the results in Fig. 1 show that the conflicting latent feature maps can be effectively mitigated after adopting our proposed DAFL.

Motivated by the idea above, we propose a novel dual adversarial federated learning (DAFL) approach on non-IID data, which implicitly deals with the conflicting latent feature maps of the data with the same label among clients to mitigate the inherent data distribution diversity. Specifically, each model structure in DAFL is divided into two components: a classifier and a latent feature map extractor. The classifier is the fully connected (FC) layers of the original model, while the latent feature map extractor is the rest layers to extract latent feature maps of data. Furthermore, we introduce an auxiliary discriminator to the global model and the local model to recognize which model the input latent feature map belongs to. Moreover, in the local training process, a dual adversarial training consists of both the forward and the backward training is designed. By making the feature extractors generate approximate latent feature maps, the training transforms the conflicting latent feature maps to reach a consensus between global and local models in each client. And in the forward training process, the global model gains various personalized latent feature information from clients. The inherent data distribution diversity can then be mitigated through the generalization feature information of the global model in the backward training. Besides, the latent feature maps of the two models become closer to each other adaptively by reducing their Kullback Leibler (KL) divergence [13, 15]. The contributions of this paper are as follows:

- We observe that the latent feature maps of the data with the same label are in conflict on non-IID data and analyze the reason for the suboptimal performance of the global model from the perspective of the latent feature map.
- We propose a dual adversarial federated learning approach on non-IID data. Our approach takes full advantage of latent feature maps information to effectively implement the global aggregation and implicitly mitigate the conflicting latent feature maps among clients.
- We design a local dual adversarial training consisting of both the forward and the backward training. The local training can identify the origins of latent feature maps and make the global and local models reach a consensus on the latent feature map.
- Extensive experiments are conducted on benchmark datasets. Compared with the state-of-the-art approaches, the results confirm the effectiveness of DAFL on non-IID data.

The remainder of this paper is organized as follows. Preliminaries are given in Sect. 2. Section 3 presents the details of the proposed DAFL. In Sect. 4, we conduct a series of experiments to evaluate the superiority of our DAFL. Finally, we conclude this paper in Sect. 5.

2 Preliminaries

2.1 Federated Learning

Federated Learning (FL) aims to train a generalized global model which performs well on the dataset of each local client. FL consists of K clients, defined as $[K]$, and a central server S. The client k owns a local private dataset $\mathcal{D}_k = \{\mathcal{X}_k, \mathcal{Y}_k\}$, where $\mathcal{X}_k$ is the input space and $\mathcal{Y}_k$ is the label space. And $\mathcal{D}_k = \{\mathcal{X}_k, \mathcal{Y}_k\}$ cannot be accessed by the central server and other clients due to privacy concerns. Suppose n_k is the number of samples on $\mathcal{D}_k$, and N is the total number of samples on $\mathcal{D} = \cup_{k\in[K]}\mathcal{D}_k$. The objective of FL is to solve the following empirical risk minimization (ERM) problem:

$$\min_{w} F(w) := \min_{w} \sum_{k=1}^{K} \frac{n_k}{N} F_k(w) \tag{1}$$

$$F_k(w) := E_{(x_k,y_k)\sim p_k} \mathcal{L}_k(w; x_k, y_k) \tag{2}$$

where $\mathcal{L}_k(w; x_k, y_k)$ represents the loss function associated with the sample $(x_k, y_k) \in (\mathcal{X}_k, \mathcal{Y}_k)$ and the parameter vector $w \in \mathcal{R}^d$, and p_k is the distribution over $\mathcal{X}_k \times \mathcal{Y}_k$. The focus of this paper is on non-IID data and the probability distribution p_k of local clients are not identical.

At each round t in the training process of typical FL [16], S randomly samples a subset $K_t \subseteq [K]$ of all clients at ratio r and aggregates the local model parameters w_k^t to generate the global model parameters w^t, which are exchanged with each client in K_t. Then the local model parameters w_k^t of all clients are replaced directly by the global model parameters w^t at the next round $t+1$. Instead, in our approach, both w_k^t and w^t learn the latent feature map information from each other to reach a consensus via local dual adversarial training, where w_k^t is stored to one cache unit in client k and w^t is only exchanged with the server S.

2.2 Generative Adversarial Network

Generative Adversarial Network (GAN) [1,5] is a generative modeling approach that consists of two components: a generator G enables random vector $z \sim P_Z$ to generate approximate data samples $G(z)$, and a discriminator D distinguishes between generated samples $G(z)$ and real samples drawn from a distribution P_X. G is trained to confuse D. The objective of GAN can be formulated as a two-player game, and G and D can be trained jointly by solving

$$\min_{G} \max_{D} E_{x\sim P_X}[logD(x)] + E_{z\sim P_Z}[log(1 - D(G(z)))] \tag{3}$$

In our approach, the generator is removed, and only the discriminator is adopted to distinguish the source of the latent feature maps. The input of the discriminator is the output of the latent feature map extractor. Inspired by the Nash equilibrium of GAN in the local training process, the conflict in the latent feature maps between global and local models is mitigated to reach a consensus.

3 Proposed Approach

3.1 Local Training Structure

As depicted in Fig. 2, each local trained model structure (e.g., ResNet model, AlexNet model.) is divided into two components: a feature extractor and a classifier. For the

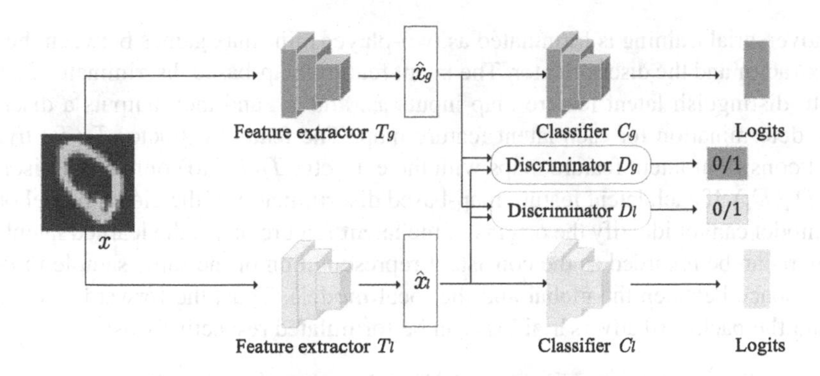

Fig. 2. Local training structure.

ease of presentation, we use subscripts g or l to represent the corresponding components of the global model or the local model, respectively. Take the global model as an example. With model weight w_g, we use $w_{g,e}$ to represent the weight of the feature extractor and $w_{g,c}$ to represent the weight of the classifier. The latent feature map extractor $T_g(w_{g,e}; x) : \mathcal{X} \to \mathcal{R}^m$ can map an input example $x \subseteq \mathcal{X}$ from the input space $\mathcal{X}$ into a latent feature map $\hat{x}_g = T_g(x) \in \mathcal{R}^m$. Without losing generality, we use the classifier $C_g(w_{g,c}; \hat{x}_g)$ to transform $\hat{x}_g$ to the label space $\mathcal{Y}$. Besides, an auxiliary latent feature map-based discriminator $D_g(\theta_g; \hat{x})$ is added to the global model, which tries to distinguish the local latent feature map $\hat{x}_l$ and the global latent feature map $\hat{x}_g$ via a scalar output $\hat{y} = D_g(\hat{x})$.

In each round of the model update process, the local model parameters w_l and the local discriminator's model parameters θ_l are stored in local cache units, and the global model parameters w_g and the global discriminator's model parameters θ_g are only exchanged with the server S.

3.2 Local Dual Adversarial Training

DAFL retains the principle of traditional federated learning that it does not share private data and assigns the training tasks to the local clients. Inspired by the Nash equilibrium of GAN, we expect to make the global and local models in each client reach a consensus in latent feature maps. Thus, the auxiliary discriminator is applied to identify the origins of the latent feature maps and learn a consistent representation of the same sample between them in latent feature map space. Specifically, the latent feature map extractors T_g and T_l extract latent feature maps $\hat{x}_g$ and $\hat{x}_l$ of the same sample x from local data, respectively. The discriminators D_g and D_l take both $\hat{x}_g$ and $\hat{x}_l$ as inputs, and their outputs are denoted as the binary variable $d \in \{1, 0\}$, which indicates whether the latent feature map input comes from the global model or the local model.

In the local training process, we design an efficient dual adversarial training that consists of both the forward and the backward adversarial training. The objective of dual adversarial training is formulated as two-player mini-max games between the feature extractor and the discriminator. The latent feature map-based discriminator $D_g(D_l)$ aims to distinguish latent feature map inputs $\hat{x}_g$ and $\hat{x}_l$, and then outputs a discriminating determination for each latent feature map. The feature extractor $T_g(T_l)$ tries to extract consistent latent feature maps with the extractor $T_l(T_g)$ to confuse the discriminator $D_g(D_l)$. If each latent feature map-based discriminator of the global model or the local model cannot identify the origins of the latent feature maps, the learned latent feature map can be regarded as the consistent representation of the same sample in latent feature space between the global and the local models. Thus, the forward adversarial loss and the backward adversarial loss can be formulated respectively as:

$$\mathcal{L}_{D_g} = -E_{\hat{x}_l \sim p(\hat{x}_l)}[log(D_g(\hat{x}_l))] - E_{\hat{x}_g \sim p(\hat{x}_g)}[log(1 - D_g(\hat{x}_g))]$$

$$\mathcal{L}_{T_g} = E_{\hat{x}_g \sim p(\hat{x}_g)}[log(1 - D_g(\hat{x}_g))] \tag{4}$$

$$\mathcal{L}_{D_l} = -E_{\hat{x}_g \sim p(\hat{x}_g)}[log(D_l(\hat{x}_g))] - E_{\hat{x}_l \sim p(\hat{x}_l)}[log(1 - D_l(\hat{x}_l))]$$

$$\mathcal{L}_{T_l} = E_{\hat{x}_l \sim p(\hat{x}_l)}[log(1 - D_l(\hat{x}_l))] \tag{5}$$

where $p(\hat{x}_l)$ and $p(\hat{x}_g)$ are distributions of the latent feature maps $\hat{x}_l$ and $\hat{x}_g$. The discriminator D_g is trained to output $d = 1$ when the latent feature input is from the local model and yields $d = 0$ if the latent feature input came from the global model and the D_l is trained by exchanging only the binary variable output for different origins of latent feature maps.

3.3 Latent Feature Map Classification

We use two terms for the loss of latent feature map classification. The first is the cross-entropy (CE) loss of classification to measure the prediction accuracy, and the second is the distribution difference of latent feature maps between global and local models in each client based on Kullback Leibler (KL) divergence. These two loss terms can be formulated respectively as:

$$\mathcal{L}_g = \mathcal{L}_{kl}(\hat{x}_g, \hat{x}_l) + \mathcal{L}_{ce}(y, C_g(\hat{x}_g)) \tag{6}$$

$$\mathcal{L}_l = \mathcal{L}_{kl}(\hat{x}_l, \hat{x}_g) + \mathcal{L}_{ce}(y, C_l(\hat{x}_l)) \tag{7}$$

where $C_g(\cdot)$ and $C_l(\cdot)$ refer to the classification function of global model and local model. $\mathcal{L}_{ce}$ is the CE loss between the ground-truth label y and softmax output of the classifier C_g or C_l that is generally used in classification tasks. And $\mathcal{L}_{kl}$ is the KL loss, which tries to match latent feature map outputs, enabling proximity latent feature maps of the two models in each client to share the learned feature information.

Furthermore, we optimize the models based on the above two losses in the same local mini-batch by combining both the local dual adversarial training-based loss and latent feature map classification-based loss. Thus, the complete loss for w_g and w_l are rewritten as:

$$\mathcal{L}_{w_g} = \mathcal{L}_{T_g} + \mathcal{L}_g \tag{8}$$

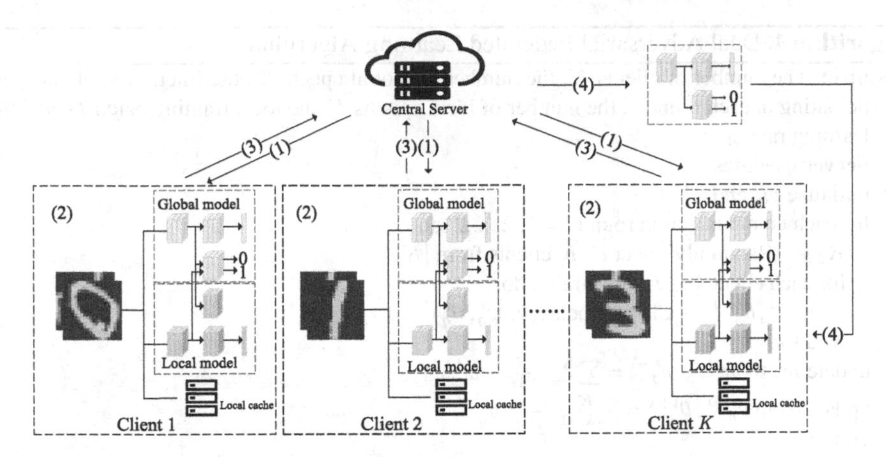

Fig. 3. Overall framework of DAFL. Step 1 shows that the central server broadcasts a new global model and a new auxiliary discriminator to the clients. Step 2 stands for that each local client employs our dual adversarial training to update the global model and its local model. Step 3 indicates that the clients upload the updated global model and the discriminator to the central server. Step 4 represents that the central server aggregates the updated global models and the discriminators, respectively.

$$\mathcal{L}_{w_l} = \mathcal{L}_{T_l} + \mathcal{L}_l \tag{9}$$

In each iteration, we fix the parameters of the discriminators D_g and D_l and train the global and local models using $\mathcal{L}_{w_g}$ and $\mathcal{L}_{w_l}$ in Eq. 8 and Eq. 9. Then parameters of the two models are fixed and the discriminators are trained using $\mathcal{L}_{D_g}$ and $\mathcal{L}_{D_l}$ in Eq. 4 and Eq. 5.

3.4 Algorithm of DAFL

We provide the overall framework of DAFL in Fig. 3. The dual adversarial training is applied to deal with the non-IID problem. The training process of DAFL can be summarized as algorithm 1. DAFL starts with initial global model parameters w_g^0 and auxiliary discriminator's parameters θ_g^0, controlled by the central server S. At the same time, all clients start with initial local model parameters w_l^0 and auxiliary discriminator's parameters θ_l^0 stored in local cache units. At each round t in the training process, S uniformly selects a subset of the clients $K_t \subseteq [K]$ in the fraction c. Then, S broadcasts the latest w_g^t and the θ_g^t to each client $k \in K_t$.

Instead of directly training on the copy of the global model, the client k employs our local dual adversarial training between the $w_{g,k}^t$ and the $w_{l,k}^t$ on its local data $\mathcal{D}_k$. Due to the different data distributions, the local model of each client will focus on different data features. In the forward adversarial training, the $w_{g,k}^t$ can be trained to learn the personalized latent feature information from $w_{l,k}^t$, keeping the generalization ability in the mean time to reach a forward consensus. In the backward adversarial

Algorithm 1. Dual Adversarial Federated Learning Algorithm

Require: The number of clients K, the number of global epochs T, the fraction of clients participating in each round c, the number of local epochs E, the local training batch B, and the learning rate η_t.

1: **Server executes:**
2: initialize w_g^0 and θ_g^0
3: for each communication round t = 1, 2,....,T do
4: $K_t \leftarrow$ (Randomly select $c \cdot K$ clients from $[K]$)
5: for each client $k \in K_t$ in parallel do:
6: $w_{g,k}^{t+1}, \theta_{g,k}^{t+1} \leftarrow$ Client-Update(k, w_g^t, θ_g^t)
7: end for
8: update w_g^t to w_g^{t+1}, $w_g^{t+1} = \sum_{k=1}^{K} \frac{|D_k|}{|D|} w_{g,k}^{t+1}$
9: update θ_g^t to θ_g^{t+1}, $\theta_g^{t+1} = \sum_{k=1}^{K} \frac{|D_k|}{|D|} \theta_{g,k}^{t+1}$
10: end for

11: **function** Client-Update(k, w_g^t, θ_g^t)
12: $w_{g,k}^t = w_g^t$, $\theta_{g,k}^t = \theta_g^t$, get $w_{l,k}^t$, $\theta_{l,k}^t$ from local cache
13: for each local training epoch from 1 to E do
14: for B in local training batches do
15: $w_{g,k}^{t+1} = w_{g,k}^t - \eta_t \nabla \mathcal{L}_{w_g} (w_{g,k}^t, B)$
16: $\theta_{g,k}^{t+1} = \theta_{g,k}^t - \eta_t \nabla \mathcal{L}_{D_g} (\theta_{g,k}^t, B)$
17: $w_{l,k}^{t+1} = w_{l,k}^t - \eta_t \nabla \mathcal{L}_{w_l} (w_{l,k}^t, B)$
18: $\theta_{l,k}^{t+1} = \theta_{l,k}^t - \eta_t \nabla \mathcal{L}_{D_l} (\theta_{l,k}^t, B)$
19: end for
20: end for
21: store $w_{l,k}^{t+1}$, $\theta_{l,k}^{t+1}$ in cache units
22: return $w_{g,k}^{t+1}$, $\theta_{g,k}^{t+1}$

training, $w_{l,k}^t$ can be trained to learn the generalization latent feature information from $w_{g,k}^t$. The inherent data distribution diversity among clients can be mitigated through a backward consensus because the personalized latent feature map representation can be suppressed, and the $w_{l,k}^t$ can generate latent feature maps with more general information. Thus, the divergence on latent feature maps among clients will be mitigated, and the clients will reach a consensus on latent feature maps of the data with the same label implicitly through the FL training. After the local update, the client k rewrites its cache to the new local model parameters $w_{l,k}^{t+1}$ and the new local discriminator's parameters $\theta_{l,k}^{t+1}$. And it sends $w_{g,k}^{t+1}$ and $\theta_{g,k}^{t+1}$ back to the server S. Then, S performs the efficient aggregation through model averaging to generate the new global model parameters w_g^{t+1} and the new discriminator's parameters θ_g^{t+1} according to the local data size.

4 Experiments

4.1 Setup

Baselines: We compare DAFL with three state-of-the-art approaches, FedAvg [16], FedProx [11] and Scaffold [8]. FedAvg is a traditional federated learning approach that aggregates the local models according to the data size. FedProx is a generalization of FedAvg to tackle the non-IID problem and regularize the local training by adding a proximal term in the objective function of the local model. And Scaffold is an algorithm that utilizes the control variates to correct for the client-drift.

Datasets and Models: We conduct experiments on three datasets including MNIST [10], FashionMnist [22], and CIFAR-10 [9]. Among them, MNIST dataset is for digit image classification. It is composed of 60,000 training images and 10,000 test images. Each of them is a 28×28 pixel gray handwritten image. FashionMnist covers the front pictures of 70,000 different products from 10 categories. The image size, number of training and test samples, and number of categories of FashionMnist are exactly the same as those of classic MNIST. And CIFAR-10 contains 50,000 training images and 10,000 test images. Each of them is a 32×32 pixel color image, related with a label from ten categories.

We train different models for these datasets. For MNIST, we employ a CNN model with two 5×5 convolutional layers (the first with 32 channels, the second with 64 channels, each followed with 2×2 max pooling) and two fully connected (FC) layers. For FashionMmnist, we employ a CNN model with four conventional layers (each followed with 2×2 max pooling and ReLU activation) and two FC layers. For CIFAR-10, the model is a convolutional neural network with two 3×3 convolutional layers (the first with 6 channels, the second with 16 channels, each followed with 2×2 max pooling and ReLU activation) and two FC layers.

Client Heterogeneity: To generate the non-IID data partition among clients, we sort all data samples based on their labels and then split them into numbers of shards allocated to each client randomly and uniformly. The shard size can determine the degree of non-IID, in which the larger shard size indicates the higher data distribution diversity. We use α to denote three different degree of non-IID problem. And $\alpha = 0.1(0.2, 0.3)$ indicates that data on each client belong to one (two, three) label(s), respectively.

Configurations: We use PyTorch to implement DAFL and the other baselines. The code is implemented via FedLab [25]. For MNIST, we run 50 global communication rounds when $\alpha = 0.3$ or $\alpha = 0.2$, and 100 global communication rounds when $\alpha = 0.1$. Besides, we run 100 and 200 rounds for FashionMnist and CIFAR-10, respectively, with 100 clients in total and a ratio $r = 10\%$ of sampling clients. We adopt a local updating step $T = 16$ and a mini-batch size $B = 16$. The learning rate η is fixed with 0.01, and the scale of the proximal term is set to $\mu = 0.2$ for FedProx.

4.2 Results and Analysis

Effectiveness of Local Dual Adversarial Training. Firstly, to assess the efficiency of our local dual adversarial training scheme, we compare the latent feature maps

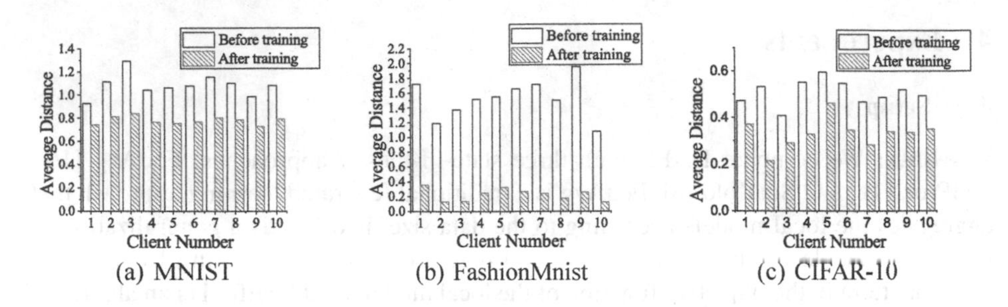

Fig. 4. Average distance of latent feature maps between global and local model.

difference between the global and local models based on the Euclidean distance before and after the local training process. Figure 4 shows the results the average distance of the latent feature maps has decreased significantly after the local dual adversarial training. Thus, our local training scheme can work well in transforming the conflicting latent feature maps of the same sample to reach a consensus between the global and local models.

Secondly, the single adversarial federated learning (SAFL) only has the forward adversarial learning where the global model can learn the latent feature distribution of local models in the local training process. Unlike SAFL, DAFL retains the forward adversarial training and introduces extra backward adversarial training to weaken the influence of inherent feature distribution difference, promoting the training process of the global model. As shown in Fig. 5, the effectiveness of the local dual adversarial training is remarkable. When the global epochs are fixed, it is demonstrated that DAFL can achieve higher accuracy of the global model compared with SAFL and outperforms SAFL on the convergence speed and stability of the global model. The results validate the efficiency of the backward adversarial training, which hinders the convergence of the global model by generating latent feature maps with more general representation.

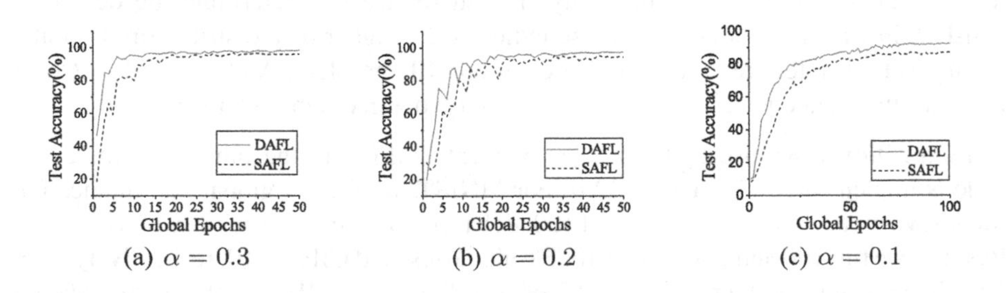

Fig. 5. The test accuracy of DAFL and SAFL with different degree of non-IID data.

Finally, we compare the local dual adversarial training with the direct alignment approach Fed-L_1. Based on L_1 distance, Fed-L_1 aligns the latent feature maps between the global and local models directly by adding the L_1 distance loss to the local loss function. From Table 1, we can see that the local dual adversarial training can enhance the performance of the global model more effectively and reach a better consensus between the global and local models than Fed-L_1. Thus, the effectiveness of our local dual adversarial training has been well validated.

Table 1. The test accuracy (%) of the global model in different FL approaches with different non-IID settings.

Settings	Approaches	MNIST	FashionMnist	CIFAR-10
IID	FedAvg	98.76	86.73	56.67
	FedProx	98.90	87.15	57.18
	Scaffold	98.91	86.92	56.82
	Fed-L_1	98.79	**88.06**	55.71
	DAFL	**98.99**	88.03	**62.13**
non-IID ($\alpha = 0.3$)	FedAvg	97.53	85.91	53.49
	FedProx	98.27	87.75	53.34
	Scaffold	98.25	87.14	57.55
	Fed-L_1	98.20	86.62	57.97
	DAFL	**98.54**	**88.23**	**58.04**
non-IID ($\alpha = 0.2$)	FedAvg	96.69	84.52	52.29
	FedProx	96.32	83.62	51.27
	Scaffold	96.59	85.14	**56.85**
	Fed-L_1	96.14	85.84	55.41
	DAFL	**97.54**	**86.04**	56.56
non-IID ($\alpha = 0.1$)	FedAvg	88.15	66.13	(-)
	FedProx	92.22	64.47	(-)
	Scaffold	91.32	62.95	(-)
	Fed-L_1	91.80	62.32	(-)
	DAFL	**92.46**	**66.77**	(-)

Effectiveness on Different α Settings. To assess the impact of the non-IID on the accuracy, we run the experiments on the MNIST dataset with different degree of non-IID data. As shown in Fig. 6, the gain and the trajectory of DAFL are more notable and steady with different settings of α on MNIST. Furthermore, the distance between two curves increases as α decreases. In addition, although DAFL consumes more time on the local training, it performs better on the convergence speed. These results verify our motivations that DAFL is induced from mitigating the conflicting latent feature maps of the data with the same class among clients, which is otherwise not accessible by FedAvg. Thus, DAFL is robust against non-IID degree so that it is effective enough to confront the non-IID problem.

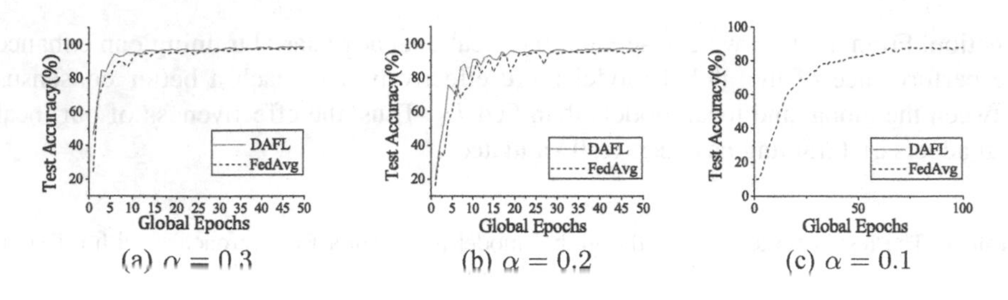

Fig. 6. The test accuracy of DAFL and FedAvg with different degree of non-IID data.

Top-performance of DAFL. We show the test accuracy of the global model for all of the baseline approaches on three real-world datasets. With IID data setting and a variety of non-IID data settings in Table 1, DAFL is the top-performing approach and outperforms the other state-of-the-art approaches with a considerable margin in most cases. The reason is that other approaches cannot make full use of the latent feature maps to handle the inherent latent feature distribution differences among clients, which would lead to the suboptimal performance of the global model on those non-IID clients. On the contrary, DAFL has an advantage in mitigating conflicting latent feature maps.

5 Conclusion

In this paper, we focused on the non-IID problem, and proposed a novel dual adversarial federated learning approach to eliminate the notable conflicting latent feature maps among clients. A local dual adversarial training that consists of the forward and the backward training was proposed to implicitly generate the consensus latent feature map of the data with the same label, achieving higher accuracy of the global model and mitigating the divergence on latent feature maps among clients. Extensive experiments demonstrated that our DAFL achieves superior performance to the state-of-the-art works on non-IID data. In future work, we will conduct rigorous convergence analyses of DAFL. And we plan to optimize our algorithm to reduce the time complexity of local training for broader applications.

Acknowledgements. This work was supported in part by the National Key R&D Program of China (Grant No. 2018YFE0207600), the Key Research and Development Program of Shaanxi (Grant No. 2021ZDLGY07-05, 2019ZDLGY13-03-01), the Innovation Capability Support Program of Shaanxi(Grant No. 2020CGXNG-002), and the Fundamental Research Funds for the Central Universities (Grant No. JB210306).

References

1. Arora, S., Ge, R., Liang, Y., Ma, T., Zhang, Y.: Generalization and equilibrium in generative adversarial nets (GANs). In: Precup, D., Teh, Y.W. (eds.) Proceedings of the 34th International Conference on Machine Learning, ICML, vol. 70, pp. 224–232. PMLR (2017)

2. Bonawitz, K.A., et al.: Practical secure aggregation for privacy-preserving machine learning. In: Proceedings of the 2017 ACM SIGSAC Conference on Computer and Communications Security, CCS, pp. 1175–1191. ACM (2017)
3. Fallah, A., Mokhtari, A., Ozdaglar, A.E.: Personalized federated learning with theoretical guarantees: a model-agnostic meta-learning approach (2020)
4. Finn, C., Abbeel, P., Levine, S.: Model-agnostic meta-learning for fast adaptation of deep networks. In: Precup, D., Teh, Y.W. (eds.) Proceedings of the 34th International Conference on Machine Learning, ICML, vol. 70, pp. 1126–1135. PMLR (2017)
5. Goodfellow, I.J., et al.: Generative adversarial nets. In: Ghahramani, Z., Welling, M., Cortes, C., Lawrence, N.D., Weinberger, K.Q. (eds.) Advances in Neural Information Processing Systems, vol. 27, pp. 2672–2680 (2014)
6. Guo, X., Liu, Z., Li, J., et al.: VeriFL: communication-efficient and fast verifiable aggregation for federated learning. IEEE Trans. Inf. Forensics Secur. **16**, 1736–1751 (2021)
7. Kaissis, G., Makowski, M.R., Rueckert, D., Braren, R.: Secure, privacy-preserving and federated machine learning in medical imaging. Nat. Mach. Intell. **2**(6), 305–311 (2020)
8. Karimireddy, S.P., et al.: SCAFFOLD: stochastic controlled averaging for federated learning. In: Proceedings of the 37th International Conference on Machine Learning, ICML, vol. 119, pp. 5132–5143. PMLR (2020)
9. Krizhevsky, A., Hinton, G.: Learning multiple layers of features from tiny images. Handbook Syst. Autoimmune Dis. **1**(4), 7 (2009)
10. LeCun, Y., Bottou, L., Bengio, Y., Haffner, P.: Gradient-based learning applied to document recognition. Proc. IEEE **86**(11), 2278–2324 (1998)
11. Li, T., Sahu, A.K., Zaheer, M., Sanjabi, M., Talwalkar, A., Smith, V.: Federated optimization in heterogeneous networks. In: Dhillon, I.S., Papailiopoulos, D.S., Sze, V. (eds.) Proceedings of Machine Learning and Systems 2020, MLSys. mlsys.org (2020)
12. Li, X., Huang, K., Yang, W., Wang, S., Zhang, Z.: On the convergence of FedAvg on Non-IID data. In: 8th International Conference on Learning Representations, ICLR. OpenReview.net (2020)
13. Liu, C., Shum, H.: Kullback-Leibler boosting. In: 2003 IEEE Computer Society Conference on Computer Vision and Pattern Recognition, pp. 587–594. IEEE Computer Society (2003)
14. Liu, Y., et al.: FedVision: an online visual object detection platform powered by federated learning. In: The Thirty-Fourth AAAI Conference on Artificial Intelligence, AAAI. pp. 13172–13179. AAAI Press (2020)
15. Mathiassen, J.R., Skavhaug, A., Bø, K.: Texture similarity measure using Kullback-Leibler divergence between gamma distributions. In: Heyden, A., Sparr, G., Nielsen, M., Johansen, P. (eds.) ECCV 2002. LNCS, vol. 2352, pp. 133–147. Springer, Heidelberg (2002). https://doi.org/10.1007/3-540-47977-5_9
16. McMahan, B., et al.: Communication-efficient learning of deep networks from decentralized data. In: Proceedings of the 20th International Conference on Artificial Intelligence and Statistics, AISTAT, vol. 54, pp. 1273–1282. PMLR (2017)
17. Qiu, H., Qiu, M., Lu, Z.: Selective encryption on ECG data in body sensor network based on supervised machine learning. Inf. Fusion **55**, 59–67 (2020)
18. Qiu, M., Gai, K., Xiong, Z.: Privacy-preserving wireless communications using bipartite matching in social big data. Future Gener. Comput. Syst. **87**, 772–781 (2018)
19. Qiu, M., Zhang, L., Ming, Z., Chen, Z., Qin, X., Yang, L.T.: Security-aware optimization for ubiquitous computing systems with SEAT graph approach. J. Comput. Syst. Sci. **79**(5), 518–529 (2013)
20. Smith, V., et al.: Federated multi-task learning. In: Advances in Neural Information Processing Systems, vol. 30, pp. 4424–4434 (2017)

21. Wu, X., Liu, S., Zhou, Z.: Heterogeneous model reuse via optimizing multiparty multiclass margin. In: Chaudhuri, K., Salakhutdinov, R. (eds.) Proceedings of the 36th International Conference on Machine Learning, ICML, vol. 97, pp. 6840–6849. PMLR (2019)
22. Xiao, H., Rasul, K., Vollgraf, R.: Fashion-MNIST: a novel image dataset for benchmarking machine learning algorithms. CoRR abs/1708.07747 (2017)
23. Yang, Q., et al.: FLOP: federated learning on medical datasets using partial networks. In: KDD 2021: The 27th ACM SIGKDD Conference on Knowledge Discovery and Data Mining, Virtual Event, pp. 3845–3853. ACM (2021)
24. Yang, Q., Liu, Y., Chen, T., Tong, Y.: Federated machine learning: concept and applications. ACM Trans. Intell. Syst. Technol. **10**(2), 12:1–12:19 (2019)
25. Zeng, D., Liang, S., Hu, X., Xu, Z.: FedLab: a flexible federated learning framework. CoRR abs/2107.11621 (2021)
26. Zhao, Y., Li, M., Lai, L., Suda, N., Civin, D., Chandra, V.: Federated learning with Non-IID data. CoRR abs/1806.00582 (2018)

Low-Quality *DanMu* Detection via Eye-Tracking Patterns

Xiangyang Liu, Weidong He, Tong Xu(✉), and Enhong Chen

School of Data Science, University of Science and Technology of China, Hefei, China
{liuxiangyang,hwd}@mail.ustc.edu.cn,{tongxu,cheneh}@ustc.edu.cn

Abstract. With the development of online video platforms, a comment visualization system that inserts dynamic and contextualized comments on a video has become popular in Japan and China, known as *DanMu*, which provides a feeling of "virtual liveness". However, at the same time, it also brings some bad influences such as goal impediment and information overload, distraction problems, impolite and irrelevant comments. To solve this problem, there are several studies utilizing textual content for low-quality *DanMu* detection. However, they leave out the visual context and do not consider users' watching behavior. To this end, in this paper, we propose an end-to-end multimodal classification framework for low-quality *DanMu* detection. Specifically, we first design a lab-based user study to investigate users' watching patterns. Based on the discovered fixation patterns, we propose a new fusion method to fuse them with textual context. Moreover, visual content is also considered with a further fusion mechanism. Our model outperforms other baselines in almost all classification metrics in the real-world dataset.

Keywords: Datasets · Neural networks · Eye-Tracking pattern · Text tagging

1 Introduction

In the process of booming development of video market, one emerging type of user-generated comment named *DanMu* [10] has become more and more popular at many online video platforms, e.g., *niconico*[1] in Japan and *Bilibili*[2] in China. Unlike traditional online reviews displayed in a separate space outside the video, *DanMu* is overlaid directly on the top of videos by synchronizing the comment with specific playback time, somewhat similar in appearance to the film subtitles. Previous research has indicated that *DanMu* creates a feeling of "virtual liveness" [16] as well as an experience of co-viewing [17], which largely increases users' watching experience. However, *DanMu* technology also brings some bad influences, e.g., goal impediment and information overload [15], distraction problem [13], impolite and irrelevant comments (quarrels between fans, or spoilers)

[1] http://www.nicovideo.jp/.
[2] http://www.bilibili.com/.

G. Memmi et al. (Eds.): KSEM 2022, LNAI 13370, pp. 247–259, 2022.
https://doi.org/10.1007/978-3-031-10989-8_20

[4,22], etc. Some typical instances are illustrated in Fig. 1. The audience had a dispute over the food price mentioned in the video.

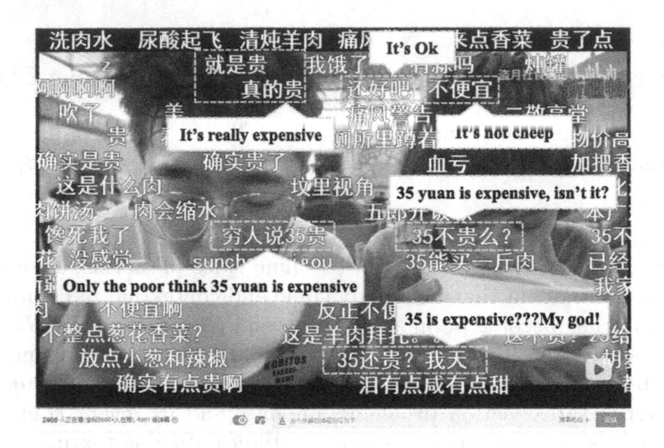

Fig. 1. A screenshot from a video which is introducing local food. *DanMu* in Dotted box are impolite and irrelevant comments that affect users' watching experience.

To alleviate this problem, some video platforms allowed users to filter *DanMu* utilizing pre-defined rules or regular expressions, which was not flexible. In academia, [23] proposed a Similarity-Base Network with Interactive Variance Attention to detect spoilers from *DanMu*. To better utilize the context information of *DanMu*, a graph convolutional encoder and a contextual encoder were used to capture the semantic feature of *DanMu* by [12]. At the application level, [18] designed and implemented a cloud-assisted *DanMu* filtering framework, including a CNN-based *DanMu* quality classifier that runs on the cloud server and a front-end Google Chrome browser extension. However, they usually only leveraged the textual context information, i.e., the surrounding *DanMu*, to judge whether a *DanMu* should be filtered. We argue that the visual context is necessary for low-quality *DanMu* detection, especially for irrelevant comments detection. Moreover, users usually exhibit specific patterns when watching videos with *DanMu*. For example, people tend to link textual descriptions to visual depictions in a simple manner and often become confused if the link is not clear [8]. However, how to utilize these patterns to improve performance is still largely underexplored.

Along this line, we collect a user-generated video dataset[3] and conduct a series of dedicated experiments to explore users' watching behavior with an eye-tracker. The eye-tracker could collect users' eye movements during the video watching process. Through analyzing users' eye movements, we found that users tend to pay attention to *DanMu* that have similar semantics when watching videos. In addition, we also discover several fixation patterns. We propose an

[3] We will publish the dataset after the acceptance of this paper.

end-to-end multimodal classification framework for low-quality *DanMu* detection based on these observations. To be specific, we first utilize a convolutional neural network (CNN) to encode visual context. Then, we leverage BERT [6] to obtain the embeddings of *DanMu*. To combine users' watching behavior, we design a pattern encoder to extract related features about defined eye-tracking patterns. Thereafter, we propose a new fusion method based on the bilinear model to fuse eye-tracking features and text representation. Finally, representations from different modalities are combined for *DanMu* classification.

In general, the contribution of this paper can be summarized as follows:

- We conduct a lab-based user study to collect various user behavior data when watching videos with *DanMu*, which will be released to the research community.
- We propose an end-to-end multimodal classification framework for low-quality *DanMu* detection with several discovered fixation patterns.
- We conduct extensive experiments to evaluate the proposed model, and the results show the effectiveness compared with several state-of-the-art baselines.

2 Eye-Tracking Pattern Mining

This section will introduce our dataset and make some preliminary analyses of eye-tracking data to explore the human eye-tracking patterns.

2.1 Data Preparation

We collect a user-generated videos dataset from *Bilibili*, one of the largest video-sharing platforms in China, which focuses on animation, movies, etc. To be specific, this dataset contains 62 videos, each lasting around 5 min long and containing about 1000 *DanMu*. All videos are divided into 12 groups. Each group includes 5 or 6 videos, and the total time is no more than 30 min.

We recruit 14 participants to take our tasks. There are eight males and six females with ages ranging from 21 to 24. All of them are undergraduate, or graduate students and their majors vary from natural science and engineering to humanities and sociology. All participants are familiar with *DanMu* and usually browse the online video platforms. In addition, we screen all applicants according to their visual acuity to ensure that the collected eye-tracking data are correct. Each group of videos is watched by 6 participants at least to eliminate random factors.

To obtain eye-tracking data, we use a *Tobii Pro*[4] eye tracker to record the eye-tracking of participants during watching videos whose deviation is within the character level. Before taking tasks, there is a calibration process for each participant to ensure that the data of eye movements can be recorded accurately. After that, they need to rate the correlation between the *DanMu* and the video scene where the *DanMu* appears, with 1 being related and −1 not. Considering

[4] www.tobiipro.com.

that we aim to filter out the worst *DanMu*, samples with labels mean larger than 0.8 are considered positive, and the remaining are negative samples. Finally, we get 11,000 positive samples and 27,039 negative samples to help us construct a binary classification problem.

Table 1. Toy example of eye-tracking data

Time(s)	x	y	Type	Duration(ms)	Fixation_x	Fixation_y*	Focus_type	Focus_text**
19.642	1229	335	Fixation	183	1229	351	*DanMu*	Not really
19.658	1219	337	Fixation	183	1229	351	Image	
19.675	1212	338	Fixation	183	1229	351	Image	
19.692	1212	325	Fixation	183	1229	351	*DanMu*	Not really
19.708	1220	365	Fixation	183	1229	351	Image	
19.725	1235	369	Fixation	183	1229	351	*DanMu*	I have 6 years

*Fixation_x and Fixation_y stand for coordinates of gazed position.
**Tranlated from Chinese.

2.2 Eye-Tracking Pattern Generalisation

Some examples of eye-tracking data in our dataset are presented in Table 1. Before processing the collected eye-tracking data, we first need to understand how it reveals our watching behavior. From previous work, we can learn that the eye reads a frame of videos in discrete chunks by making a series of fixations and saccades. A fixation is a brief moment, around 250 ms, where the eye is paused on a *DanMu* or an area of this frame, and the brain processes the visual information. A saccade is a fast eye movement to take in the subsequent fixation. In other words, a fixation means the participant is concentrating on reading, and a saccade is a bond that connects two fixations.

Preliminary statistical results show that gazing at *DanMu* is a sparse behavior while watching a video, which naturally raises our question: does this sparse behavior include more information, or in other words, is the gazed *DanMu* significantly different from other *DanMu*? We attempt to analyze this issue from a semantic perspective. To be specific, we select a Chinese image caption dataset, calculate the BLEU score, and compare it with the *DanMu*' BLEU score, as shown in Fig. 2. We have found that the semantics of the overall *DanMu* is more diverse than that of the image caption dataset. But the gazed *DanMu* has a lower diversity, which means people tend to pay attention to *DanMu* with similar semantics when watching videos. However, a gazed *DanMu* by participants does not always mean that the *DanMu* is related to the video content. For example, [7] note that fixations focused on two points mean that participants got confused with elements on the screen. To distinguish between different types of fixations, inspired by [7] we have defined three fixation patterns as Table 2 shows. In practice, each *DanMu* corresponds to one or more patterns because different participants have differences in cognitive behavior.

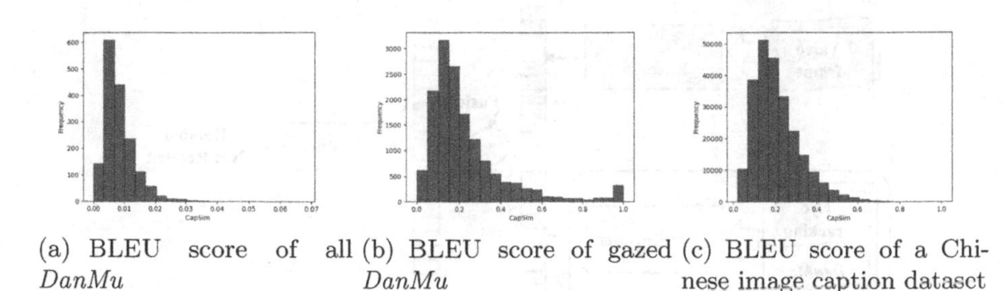

(a) BLEU score of all *DanMu* (b) BLEU score of gazed *DanMu* (c) BLEU score of a Chinese image caption dataset

Fig. 2. Semantic analysis

Table 2. Definition to eye-tracking patterns (with ratio of occurrences of patterns)

Patterns id	Occurred ratio	Eye-tracking pattern generalisation
Pattern #1	36.45%	Many short fixations across several *DanMu*
Pattern #2	51.91%	Short fixations on specific *DanMu* followed by some regressions
Pattern #3	11.64%	Long fixations on specific *DanMu*

3 Technical Framework

Previous research [2,3,5] on multimodal tasks has provided a helpful paradigm that takes output vectors of independent network models of different modalities as input. Then the fusion module will combine the output vectors into a single vector as the multimodal joint representation.

We follow this paradigm to define the structure of the framework as having three components, a vision encoder, a joint *DanMu*-eyetracking encoder, and a classifier that predict the joint two prior components' embedding (Fig. 3). We opt for the "early fusion" scheme for joining predictions. The modular nature of this structure allows us to analyze the joint *DanMu*-eyetracking encoder quantitatively.

3.1 Vision Encoder

We utilize a standard CNN architecture ResNet50 [9] for the vision encoder. And we'll replace the last full connection layer of ResNet with a new full connection layer that maps pooling out to the d-dimension. Then we resize the input video frame to 480 * 270 and rescale the pixel values to lie within the range $[-1, 1]$ and get the visual representation $\mathbf{v}_i \in \mathbb{R}^{batch \times d_t}$.

3.2 Joint *DanMu*-Eyetracking Encoder

As Fig. 3 shows, the joint *DanMu* eye-tracking encoder consists of two parts. One is used to represent the text with Bert [6] directly. Here we use Bert's pooled

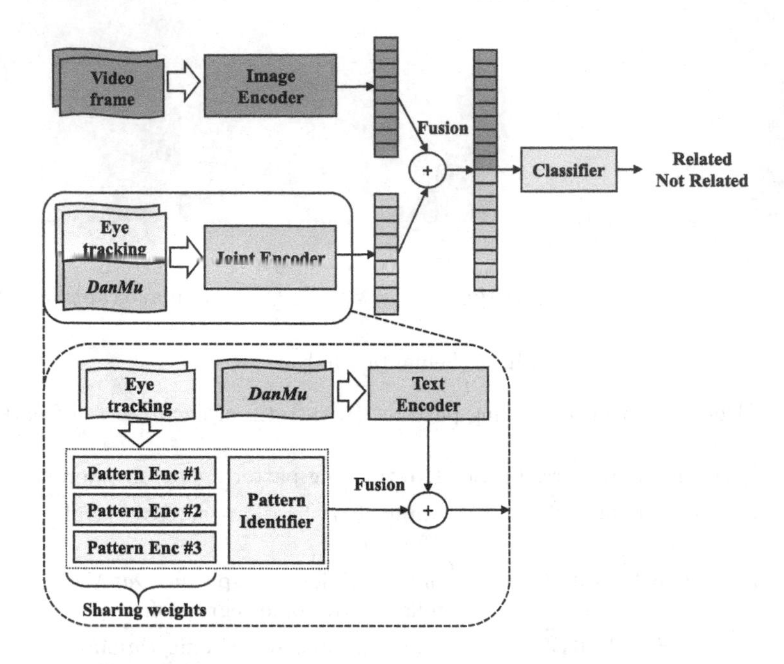

Fig. 3. End-to-end multimodal classification framework.

out vector as the direct text embedding. The other part is the eye-tracking pattern encoding module to extract eye-tracking pattern features to enhance text representation.

3.3 Eyetracking Pattern Encoder

As we discussed in Sect. 2, the eye-tracking data of a *DanMu* can be represented as

$$v_{raw} = [\chi(g), p_g, \bar{t}_{g/s}] \tag{1}$$

where $\chi(g)$ is a 0–1 variable used to indicate whether the *DanMu* is gazed at by more than one subject. p_g represents the probability of the subject gaze at the *DanMu*; $\bar{t}_{g/s}$ represents the average time for all participants to stare at this *DanMu*. We can calculate these features as follows:

$$p_g = \frac{N_s}{N}, \bar{t}_{g/s} = \frac{T_g}{N} \tag{2}$$

where N is the number of participants, N_s is the number of participants who gazed at a specific *DanMu*, T_g represents the total time for all participants to gaze at a specific *DanMu*.

After feature engineering, we get three synthetic features. Further encoding will be achieved through a linear affine transformation, where we use a diagonal matrix as the invertible matrix. This diagonal matrix can adjust the weight of each synthetic feature and provide interpretability for the eye-tracking pattern encoder. As discussed above, each *DanMu* may correspond to multiple fixation patterns, so we use three eye-tracking pattern encoders with shared parameters to encode each pattern of a *DanMu* separately. After encoding, a pattern identifier module is used to sum the above vectors. To be specific, this part is calculated as follows:

$$\mathbf{v}_{et} = \sum_{p}^{\mathbb{P}} w_p(\mathbf{D} \cdot \mathbf{v}_{raw}) \in \mathbb{R}^{|\mathbf{v}_{raw}|} \tag{3}$$

where w_p is the weight of the pattern p given by pattern identifier, $\mathbf{D}$ is the parameter diagonal matrix.

3.4 Fusion Method

Most fusion methods can only be used for two input modalities. Some particular fusion method suitable for multimodalities fusion needs to convert each vector to a dockable vector. As the length of an eye-tracking vector is too short compared to the length of a vision or a text vector, forcibly mapping the eye-tracking vector into a much higher dimension space will bring unnecessary redundancy and make it hard to train. As we discussed in Sect. 2, eye-tracking data can be easily matched with *DanMu* text. Therefore, our fusion approach is divided into two steps. The first step is to integrate the eye-tracking vector with the text vector to obtain joint representation and then fuse it with the vision vector. To accomplish this fusion task, we apply convolution as the linearizing operation in the bilinear model [20] as our text-eye-tracking fusion method.

More specifically, we first extract text embedding $\mathbf{v}_t \in \mathbb{R}^{batch \times d_t}$ from Bert and eye-tracking pattern encoder $\mathbf{v}_{et} \in \mathbb{R}^{batch \times d_e}$ for tensor product operation: $\mathbf{v}_{et} \otimes \mathbf{v}_t \in \mathbb{R}^{batch \times d_e \times d_t}$. Before this step, to avoid possible null eye-tracking vectors that could adversely affect the final embedding, we replace the 0–1 variable $\chi(g)$ with its one-hot encoding in the eye-tracking representation. Then a convolution operation is applied to linearize the result of the tensor product. Defining $f_c(*)$ as a convolution operation and W as a linear transform, the joint *DanMu*-eyetracking representation can be calculated as follow:

$$v_{joint} = W \cdot f(\mathbf{v}_{et} \otimes \mathbf{v}_t) \in \mathbb{R}^{|\mathbf{v}_i|} \tag{4}$$

Finally, we obtain the multimodal representation:

$$v_{mm} = Concat(W \cdot f_c((\sum_{p}^{\mathbb{P}} w_p \mathbf{D}[\chi(g), p_g, \bar{t}_{g/s}]) \otimes \mathbf{v}_t), \mathbf{v}_i) \tag{5}$$

4 Experiments

This section will evaluate our method in a real-world dataset and compare it with the baselines we selected.

4.1 Experimental Setup

For a fair comparison with other methods, we use the same image encoder and text encoder as the backbone. In all experiments, we use an AdamW solver with a learning rate = 0.00002 and a schedule with a learning rate that decreases linearly from the initial learning rate set in the optimizer to 0.

As our dataset labels are imbalanced, we sample 1000 positive and negative samples as the validation and test sets, respectively. Accuracy and F1 score are our model criteria, while the loss function during the training stage is the cross-entropy loss function.

4.2 Comparison of Baseline Methods

To evaluate the performance of our proposed model, we compare it with the following methods as baselines:

- **fastText.** This is a lightweight library for efficient learning of word representations and sentence classification developed by [11]. FastText is often on par with deep learning classifiers in terms of accuracy and many orders of magnitude faster for training and evaluation.
- **Smartbullets.** TextCNN is introduced to tackle sentence-level classification tasks with convolutional neural networks. [18] construct a user-centered *DanMu* filter with this method named Smartbullets.
- **Multimodal classifier(Text+Image).** This is our model without eye-tracking data. We replace the joint encoder with a Bert text encoder.

We choose the model with the lowest validating loss during the training phase to test on the test set. The experimental results are shown in Table 3.

From the result of the experiments, we discover that both multimodal context and eye-tracking data can effectively improve model performance. Our model is better than the baselines we selected, of course.

Table 3. Overall performance

Methods	Accuracy	F1-score
fastText	0.6375	0.7180
Smartbullets	0.6540	0.7232
Bert classifier	0.6520	0.7240
MM classifer(Text+Image)	0.6975	0.7389
MM classifer(Text+Image+eye-tracking)	**0.7375**	**0.7552**

4.3 Fusion Method Experiment

To verify the effectiveness of the fusion module we have designed for this task, we have selected some typical fusion methods as the baselines to compare with our methods, which are as follows:

- **Concatenation.** This is the most basic multimodal fusion method with strong applicability and wide application. This method directly concatenates the two vectors together to get the target vector [19].
- **Co-attention.** This is a method proposed by [14] for image-text fusion. The specific fusion process is as follow:

$$C^P = [H^q; H^p softmax(H^p(H^q)^T)]softmax(H^q(H^p)^T) \quad (6)$$

  Then the LSTM model is used to map C^P into a given output space.
- **Bilinear pooling with linearizing.** Bilinear pooling take the outer product of two vectors $p \in \mathbb{R}^{d_p}$ and $q \in \mathbb{R}^{d_q}$ and learn a linear transform W [21], the result vector z can be calculated as follow:

$$z = W \cdot Vec(p \otimes q) \quad (7)$$

  where $\otimes$ denotes the outer product and $Vec(*)$ denotes linearizing the outer product matrix in a vector.

We chose the model with the lowest validating loss during the training phase to test on the test set, and the experiment results are shown in Table 4. We also draw the loss curve and the accuracy curve of the validation set when different fusion methods are used during the training process, as shown in Fig. 4. The results prove that our proposed fusion method is superior to the given baseline in prediction accuracy and convergence performance.

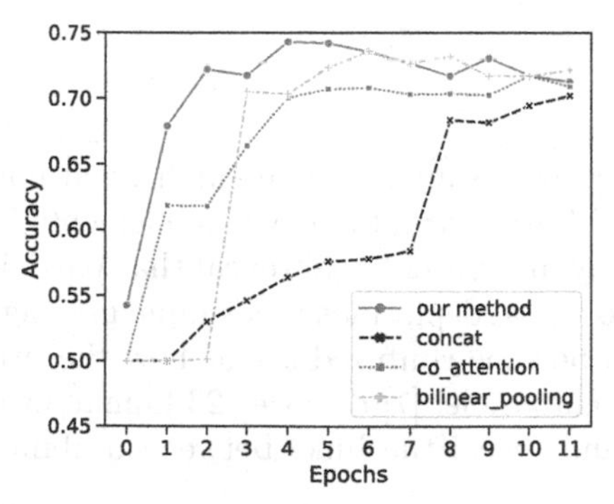

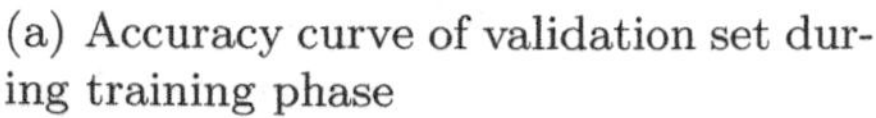
(a) Accuracy curve of validation set during training phase

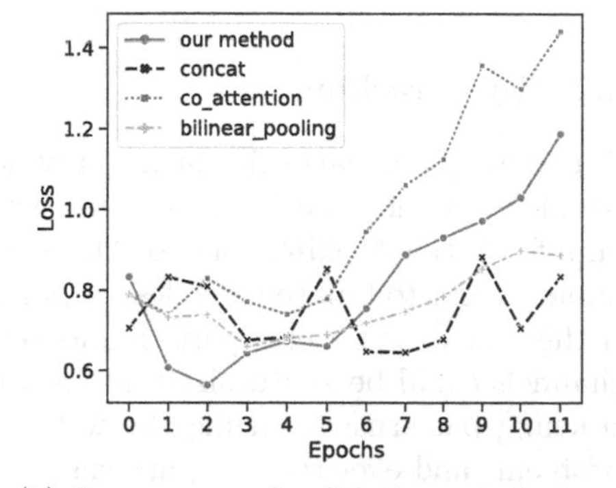

(b) Loss curve of validation set during training phase

Fig. 4. Performance of given fusion methods during training phase

Table 4. Fusion methods performance

Method	Accuracy	F1-score
Concatenation	0.5770	0.6887
Co-attention	0.7025	0.7403
Bilinear pooling with linearizing	0.7015	0.7326
Bilinear pooling with convolution (Ours)	**0.7375**	**0.7552**

5 Related Works

5.1 Low-Quality *DanMu* Detection

Recent studies of low-quality *DanMu* detection mainly focus on keyword matching and deep learning methods. Keyword matching methods are based on predefined keywords widely used in famous video platforms. However, the keyword matching methods require human-fixed input and have high recall and low precision performance since they treat many positive comments as low-quality *DanMu*. The other domain of research is machine learning methods. [23] propose a Similarity-Based Network with Interactive Variance Attention to detect spoilers from *DanMu*. They construct a word-level attentive encoder and a sentence-level interactive variance attention network to embedding *DanMu* text with their contextual information. To better utilize the context information of *DanMu*, a graph convolutional encoder and a contextual encoder are used to capture the semantic feature of *DanMu* by [12]. At the application level, [18] design and implement a cloud-assisted *DanMu* filtering framework, including a CNN-based *DanMu* quality classifier that runs on the cloud server and a front-end Google Chrome browser extension. However, they leave out the multimodal context as well as the human watching behavior.

5.2 Eye-Tracking

A review of the early literature provides a few examples of research regarding people's eye movements as they integrated both textual and visual elements in an information-seeking context [20]. Faraday and Sutcliffe [8] reveal that participants sought to link textual descriptions to visual depictions in a simple manner. If the link wasn't clear, participants often become confused about how the two channels could be synthesized into a coherent whole. [7] discover 23 human eye-tracking patterns of surfing the website and reveal the links between usability problems and eye-tracking patterns.

5.3 Fusion Methods

Fusion is a crucial research topic in multimodal studies, which integrates information extracted from different unimodal data sources into a single compact multimodal representation. Three types of fusion methods are mainly used for the multimodal task, namely, simple operation-based, attention-based, and bilinear pooling-based methods.

A widely used operation-based fusion method is concatenation [24] which is not required the same number of elements arranged in an order. However, this simple fusion method is not ideal enough. To get a better fusion performance, some more complex but better methods are proposed. A typical method is attention fusion which utilizes attention mechanisms in modal fusion. Attention mechanisms often refer to the weighted sum of a set of vectors with scalar weights [1]. Among these attention fusion methods, co-attention is a representative method. In the original paper, the authors use co-attention to fuse the image modal and text modal in VQA. This method uses symmetric attention structures to generate attended not only image feature vectors but also language vectors[14]. Based on the bilinear model, [21] proposes a fusion method that facilitates multiplicative interactions between all elements in both input vectors via computing their outer product.

6 Conclusion

In this work, we tackled the problem of low-quality *DanMu* detection using the image, text contents, and eye-tracking data. Our main idea is human visual cognitive patterns imply the emotional tendency of the viewed object. To understand human cognitive processes, we collect an eye-tracking dataset to mine human cognitive patterns during watching behavior. Then a weight-shared pattern encoder is applied to adaptively represent different patterns. It is clear from the experiments that introducing human eye-tracking patterns and visual information can efficiently improve the quality and accuracy of predictions.

However, the eye-tracking patterns we defined do not fully utilize sequence features of the eye-tracking data. In further studies, we will try to extract features from eye-tracking sequences with a more efficient method.

Acknowledgements. This work was partially supported by the grants from the National Natural Science Foundation of China (No.62072423)

References

1. Bahdanau, D., Cho, K., Bengio, Y.: Neural machine translation by jointly learning to align and translate. arXiv preprint arXiv:1409.0473 (2014)
2. Chen, L., Li, Z., He, W., Cheng, G., Xu, T., Yuan, N.J., Chen, E.: Entity summarization via exploiting description complementarity and salience. IEEE Trans. Neural Netw. Learn. Syst. (2022)
3. Chen, L., Li, Z., Wang, Y., Xu, T., Wang, Z., Chen, E.: MMEA: entity alignment for multi-modal knowledge graph. In: Li, G., Shen, H.T., Yuan, Y., Wang, X., Liu, H., Zhao, X. (eds.) KSEM 2020. LNCS (LNAI), vol. 12274, pp. 134–147. Springer, Cham (2020). https://doi.org/10.1007/978-3-030-55130-8_12

4. Chen, Y., Gao, Q., Rau, P.L.P.: Watching a movie alone yet together: understanding reasons for watching Danmaku videos. Int. J. Human-Comput. Interact. **33**(9), 731–743 (2017)
5. Choi, J.H., Lee, J.S.: EmbraceNet: a robust deep learning architecture for multimodal classification. Inf. Fusion **51**, 259–270 (2019)
6. Devlin, J., Chang, M.W., Lee, K., Toutanova, K.: BERT: pre-training of deep bidirectional transformers for language understanding. arXiv preprint arXiv:1810.04805 (2018)
7. Ehmke, C., Wilson, S.: Identifying web usability problems from eyetracking data (2007)
8. Faraday, P., Sutcliffe, A.: Making contact points between text and images. In: Proceedings of the Sixth ACM International Conference on Multimedia, pp. 29–37 (1998)
9. He, K., Zhang, X., Ren, S., Sun, J.: Deep residual learning for image recognition. In: Proceedings of the IEEE Conference on Computer Vision and Pattern Recognition, pp. 770–778 (2016)
10. He, M., Ge, Y., Chen, E., Liu, Q., Wang, X.: Exploring the emerging type of comment for online videos: DanMU. ACM Trans. Web (TWEB) **12**(1), 1–33 (2017)
11. Joulin, A., Grave, E., Bojanowski, P., Mikolov, T.: Bag of tricks for efficient text classification. In: Proceedings of the 15th Conference of the European Chapter of the Association for Computational Linguistics, vol. 2, Short Papers, pp. 427–431. Association for Computational Linguistics, April 2017
12. Liao, Z., Xian, Y., Li, J., Zhang, C., Zhao, S.: Time-sync comments denoising via graph convolutional and contextual encoding. Pattern Recogn. Lett. **135**, 256–263 (2020)
13. Liu, L., Suh, A., Wagner, C.: Who is with you? Integrating a play experience into online video watching via Danmaku technology. In: Kurosu, M. (ed.) HCI 2017. LNCS, vol. 10272, pp. 63–73. Springer, Cham (2017). https://doi.org/10.1007/978-3-319-58077-7_6
14. Lu, J., Yang, J., Batra, D., Parikh, D.: Hierarchical question-image co-attention for visual question answering. In: Lee, D., Sugiyama, M., Luxburg, U., Guyon, I., Garnett, R. (eds.) Advances in Neural Information Processing Systems, vol. 29. Curran Associates, Inc. (2016)
15. Lv, G., Xu, T., Chen, E., Liu, Q., Zheng, Y.: Reading the videos: temporal labeling for crowdsourced time-sync videos based on semantic embedding. In: Proceedings of the AAAI Conference on Artificial Intelligence, vol. 30 (2016)
16. Lv, G., et al.: Gossiping the videos: an embedding-based generative adversarial framework for time-sync comments generation. In: Yang, Q., Zhou, Z.-H., Gong, Z., Zhang, M.-L., Huang, S.-J. (eds.) PAKDD 2019. LNCS (LNAI), vol. 11441, pp. 412–424. Springer, Cham (2019). https://doi.org/10.1007/978-3-030-16142-2_32
17. Lv, G., et al.: Understanding the users and videos by mining a novel DanMU dataset. IEEE Trans. Big Data. **8**, 535–551 (2019)
18. Niu, H., Li, J., Zhao, Y.: Smartbullets: a cloud-assisted bullet screen filter based on deep learning. In: 2020 29th International Conference on Computer Communications and Networks (ICCCN), pp. 1–2. IEEE (2020)
19. Nojavanasghari, B., Gopinath, D., Koushik, J., Baltrušaitis, T., Morency, L.P.: Deep multimodal fusion for persuasiveness prediction. In: Proceedings of the 18th ACM International Conference on Multimodal Interaction, pp. 284–288 (2016)
20. Rayner, K., Rotello, C.M., Stewart, A.J., Keir, J., Duffy, S.A.: Integrating text and pictorial information: eye movements when looking at print advertisements. J. Exp. Psychol. Appl. **7**(3), 219 (2001)

21. Tenenbaum, J.B., Freeman, W.T.: Separating style and content with bilinear models. Neural Comput. **12**(6), 1247–1283 (2000)
22. Wang, J.: How and why people are impolite in DanMU? Internet Pragmat. **4**, 295–322 (2021)
23. Yang, W., Jia, W., Gao, W., Zhou, X., Luo, Y.: Interactive variance attention based online spoiler detection for time-sync comments. In: Proceedings of the 28th ACM International Conference on Information and Knowledge Management, pp. 1241–1250 (2019)
24. Zhou, B., Tian, Y., Sukhbaatar, S., Szlam, A., Fergus, R.: Simple baseline for visual question answering. arXiv preprint arXiv:1512.02167 (2015)

TSC-GCN: A Face Clustering Method Based on GCN

Jinmin Xue[1], Shengdong Qu[1], Jingxian Li[1], Yan Chu[1](✉), and Zhengkui Wang[2]

[1] Harbin Engineering University, Harbin 150001, China
{xuejinmin,lijingxian,chuyan}@hrbeu.edu.cn
[2] Singapore Institute of Technology, Singapore, Singapore
zhengkui.wang@singaporetech.edu.sg

Abstract. For face clustering, the density of each cluster distribution in the feature space is different. Too high similarity pruning will lead to the sparse clustering not being divided and reducing the recall ratio, while too low similarity pruning will lead to the decline of clustering accuracy. We propose the Two-Stage Clustering Method Based on Graph Convolutional Neural Network (TSC-GCN), in which the clustering size are set to measure the sparse degree of clustering and pruning with a low similarity degree. The clustering with sparse distribution is screened out, then the requirements for nodes similarity are improved. At the same time, the number of neighbor nodes is set to prevent the clustering core from deviating from the aggregation of nodes, and the clustering with dense distribution is screened out. The experimental results show that TSC-GCN can give a good consideration of the accuracy and recall ratio both, and achieve better clustering effectiveness than the state-of-the-art methods.

Keywords: Graph convolutional network · Facial clustering · Pruning screening

1 Introduction

Recently, there have been a large amount of face images generated daily due to the popularity of the cameras. This has unfortunately incurred big challenges for the face image management systems. Face clustering has become a very common approach to manage the face images for the purpose of face recognition or face labelling, etc. [1–4]. Traditional clustering methods rely on specific assumptions. For example, K-Means [5] requires the data set to be convex-shaped, and spectral clustering [6] requires different clusters with similar sizes. They all lack of the capability to deal with face images with complex data distributions. In order

Supported by Fundamental Research Funds for the Central Universities under Grant No. 3072022TS0601 and National Key Laboratory Foundation of Underwater Measurement and Control Technology.

G. Memmi et al. (Eds.): KSEM 2022, LNAI 13370, pp. 260–271, 2022.
https://doi.org/10.1007/978-3-031-10989-8_21

to improve the adaptability of complex data distributions, recent research has proposed clustering methods to learn cluster patterns based on GCN link prediction, and show great performance improvement over traditional methods in terms of accuracy [2,7]. These link prediction-based methods improve the performance of face clustering and have fewer requirements on the data distribution. They all share some common operations, including generation of the subgraph for each instance as central node first followed by predicting the linkage probability between the central node and its neighbors. In the end, they organize the instance into clusters by the linkage. However, though these approaches are effective enough to identify more accurate clusters, they have resulted in high computation overheads. The main computation bottleneck of the approaches is the need to get individual subgraphs or sub-networks from its local context for each image instance. This has unfortunately resulted in a huge number of subgraphs generations and led to further heavy learning tasks as well. We have observed that the generated subgraphs are usually highly overlapping. A central node could be a neighbor node in other subgraphs which results in excessive redundant calculation costs, and at the same time, the inference speed is reduced.

The contributions of our paper are summarized as follows:

(1) We propose a new GCN-based face clustering TSC-GCN, which is both time-efficient and effective.
(2) We conducted extensive experiments to evaluate TSC-GCN against existing methods in IJB-B face datasets.

Section 2 shows the related work about the graph convolutional neural networks and face clustering. Section 3 introduces the details of the proposed TSC-GCN. Section 4 and 5 provide the experimental evaluations and conclusions respectively.

2 Related Work

Graph Convolutional Neural Network has an excellent performance in processing graph data without regular spatial structure, so it is widely used in classification and link prediction tasks. Yao et al. [9] used an entire corpus to manually construct large heterogeneous graphs and learned them by GCNs to greatly improve text classification performance. Chu et al. [10] used Bilinear Convolutional Neural Network to fuse the high and low dimensional features. We use GCN to mine the complex relationships embedded between nodes and infer connectivity.

Unsupervised face clustering is to make face images similar within the class, and mutually exclusive between the classes. Traditional face clustering algorithms do not rely on machine learning and are implemented by manually designing clustering rules, such as K-means [5] and DBSCAN [11]. Vidal et al. [12] proposed Sparse Subspace Clustering, which utilized the bottom line subspace structure in data. Lin et al. [13] used linear support vector machines to design the nearest neighbor similarity measure based on data samples. Shi et al. [14]

proposed Conditional Pairwise Clustering, which defines the Clustering problem as a Conditional random field and uses Pairwise similarity between faces to complete Clustering.

In supervised face clustering, Tapaswi et al. [15] proposed ball cluster learning, which divided feature space into balls with equal radii, and each ball represents a cluster. Meanwhile, the relationship between balls is constrained. Wang et al. [2] proposed a graph convolution face clustering algorithm based on link prediction, which used GCN to capture the local context of face data and accurately judge the link possibility of face pairs. Lei et al. [7] designed two GCN modules, which were respectively used to detect high-quality cluster proposals and eliminate noise in them to obtain high-quality clustering results.

Though supervised face clustering has been proven to be more effective, it suffers from high computation overhead, as they all need to generate a lot of subgraphs for connectivity learning. In contrast, our proposed method divides face data by density and only predicts the connectivity of the low-density part. The high-density part is naturally connected, which speeds up the operation with good accuracy.

3 TSC-GCN

3.1 Problem Description

Due to the development of neural networks, feature extraction has been able to extract high-dimensional features. However, the clustering results are unsatisfactory in calculating the difference between the feature vectors of two face images. Thus, the similarity between face images is calculated by constructing subgraphs. In the node subgraph, the connection relationship between connected nodes is represented by an adjacency matrix. GCN can aggregate neighborhood information to obtain embeddings. Furthermore, the embeddings of the node subgraph are obtained and are used to obtain the similarity between nodes through the classification function. The larger similarity value means that they are more likely to belong to the same cluster.

When the similarity between two nodes is greater than or equal to a threshold, the two nodes are in the same cluster, and an edge can be added in. We evaluate algorithm results by using pseudo labels, which are not the real identity labels of nodes, but are temporarily assigned to nodes in the same cluster. As shown in Fig. 1, face images with the same pseudo-label are in the same cluster, and y_i is pseudo labels, where i represents the i-th cluster. When evaluating the clustering, the pseudo labels are compared with the real labels, and the PRECISION, RECALL, PAIRWISE F-score, and NMI are calculated.

3.2 Framework Overview

This method calculates the similarity through GCN and completes clustering in two stages, which is named as Two-Stage Clustering Method Based on Graph Convolutional Neural Network (TSC-GCN). The framework is shown in Fig. 2.

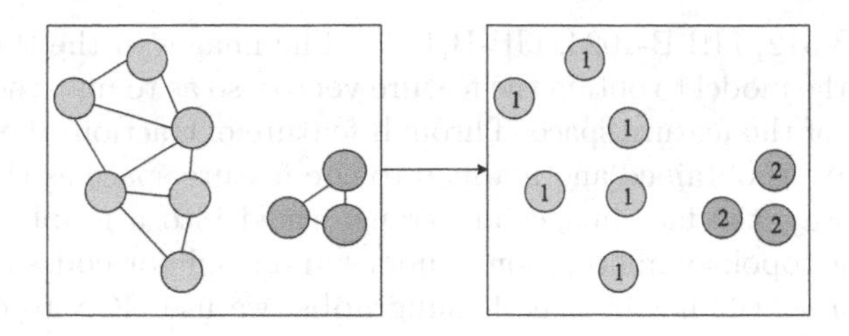

Fig. 1. Pseudo labels as the substitutions of the original labels

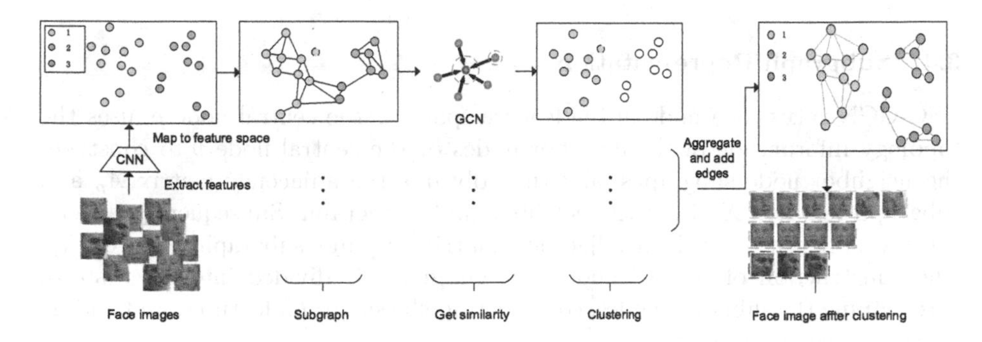

Fig. 2. The framework of TSC-GCN

Firstly, the features of the face images are extracted by the convolutional neural network, the embeddings of the face images are obtained, and then the obtained feature vector is mapped to the feature space. The face images in the feature space are regarded as nodes, and each node in the feature space is regarded as the center node. In order to use the topology of neighbor nodes to represent the center node, a subgraph corresponding to the center node is constructed according to the topology information of the neighbor nodes of the center node. Secondly, the node subgraph is used as the local data to be processed by the graph convolutional neural network, the embeddings of the node subgraph is implemented, and the similarity between the nodes is obtained through the classification. Using the similarity, we can get clusters in two stages. Finally, all the clustering results are merged and the nodes in a cluster are edged to obtain the classified face images.

3.3 Face Image Feature Representation

TSC-GCN uses the method provided in the ArcFaces face recognition model [20] to extract the features of the image. In the face alignment, the five key points of the face are detected by MTCNN, and the cropped 112 × 112-dimensional face images are obtained after normalization. The features of the face images are extracted by the resnet50 model, and we can get the 512-dimensional embeddings through the fully connected layer. The training set of the model is the joint dataset of MS-Celeb-1M [21] and VGGFace2 [22]. IJB-B [8] is divided into three datasets IJB-B-512, IJB-B-1024, IJB-B-1845. The images in the three data sets are input into the model to obtain the feature vector, so as to map the face images into the nodes of the feature space. Through feature extraction, the embeddings of the face image is obtained and mapped to the feature space as the face image node. In this way, the face images are transformed into a graph structure. In order to use the topology information of nodes and neighbor nodes in the feature space to construct the neighbor node subgraphs, we use GCN to calculate the embeddings of the node subgraphs. After classification, the prediction is done according to the similarity between nodes, so as to obtain the clusters.

3.4 Subgraph Representation

TSC-GCN takes each node in the feature space as the central node p, uses the topology information of the neighbor nodes of the central node p to construct the neighbor node subgraphs, and then obtains the adjacency matrix A_p and subgraph features X_p from the neighbor node subgraph. Subsequently we can get the similarity based on adjacency matrix A_p and subgraph features X_p. The construction of the neighbor node subgraph is divided into three steps: determining the subgraph nodes, constructing the subgraph features, and adding edges between the nodes.

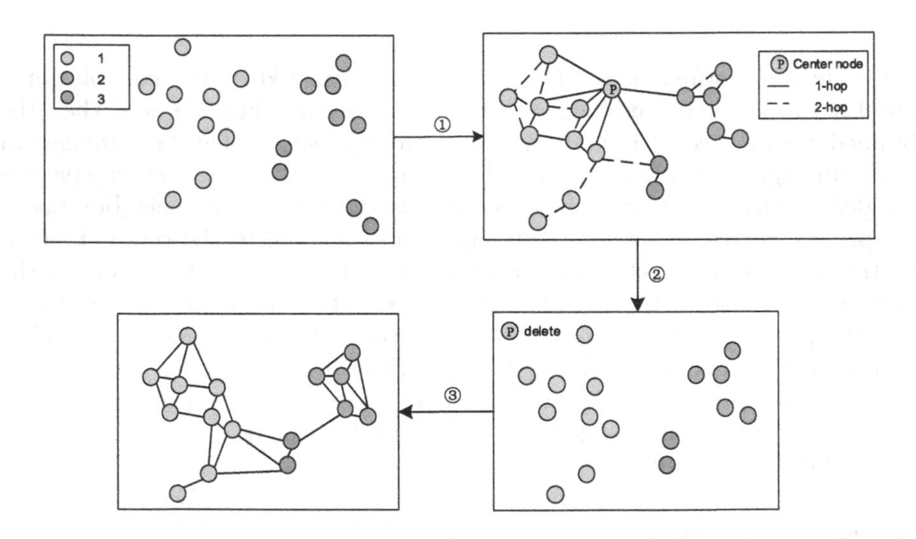

Fig. 3. The process of subgraph construction

Step 1: Identify subgraph nodes. Find the neighbor nodes of h-hop and less than h-hop of the center node p, and use all the neighbor nodes as subgraph nodes. Note that the center node p is not included in the subgraph node set. Figure 3 shows the search of 2-hop subgraph nodes. The solid lines are edges between the 1-hop neighbor nodes and the dotted lines are edges between the 2-hop neighbor nodes.

Step 2: Build subgraph features. The subgraph features are constructed according to the face image features of the central node and the subgraph nodes. Concretely, the feature vectors of each subgraph node are subtracted from the feature vectors of the central node, and then these new feature vectors are formed as a row vector, which is the subgraph feature X_p corresponding to the central node p. The subgraph feature X_p is defined as:

$$X_p = [..., x_i - x_p, ...]^T, \ i \in V_p \tag{1}$$

where X_p is the subgraph feature, x_i is the feature of ith subgraph node, and x_p is the feature of the center node.

Step 3: Add edges between two nodes. In order to avoid large differences of each node in the subgraph. For a node a in the subgraph node set V_p, we record the U neighbor nodes closest to this node a which form a new node set V_u. If $b \in V_u \cap V_P$, we add a edge between node a and node b. Take the nodes in the subgraph node set V_p as the central node respectively, repeat the above process to add edges, and finally get the topology of the neighbor node subgraph. This topology is represented by an adjacency matrix A_p. The value of u is 3 in Fig. 3.

3.5 Similarity Estimator

Using the adjacency matrix A_p and subgraph features X_p, we can get the similarity on the graph convolution network. The input of the convolution layer is the adjacency matrix A_p and subgraph feature X_p, and the output is a transformed subgraph feature Y_p. The GCN is described as:

$$Y = \sigma([X||GX] \, W) \tag{2}$$

where $X \in R^{N \times d_{in}}$, $Y \in R^{N \times d_{out}}$, d_{in}, d_{out} are the input and output dimensions of the node feature respectively. $G = g(X, A)$ is a $N \times N$ dimensional aggregation matrix, where each row adds to 1. W is the weight matrix of the convolutional layer. $\sigma()$ is a nonlinear activation function. $G = g(X, A)$ adopts mean value aggregation, where $G = \Lambda^{-\frac{1}{2}} \mathrm{A} \Lambda^{-\frac{1}{2}}$, A is the adjacency matrix, Λ is a diagonal matrix and $\Lambda_{ii} = \sum_j \mathrm{A}_{ij}$.

3.6 Form Clusters

Pruning with too high similarity will cause sparse clusters to be unable to be divided, reducing RECALL while pruning with too low similarity will lead to the decline of clustering accuracy. TSC-GCN improves the division of dense clusters by pruning and aggregating nodes with a higher degree of similarity. In addition, aggregated nodes are filtered by setting nc (neighbor count) to prevent deviation from the cluster core when aggregating nodes. If the number of neighbor nodes is greater than or equal to nc, the node does not deviate from the clustering core, and the node and its neighbor nodes are aggregated. TSC-GCN has two states, one is to limiting the size of clusters,and the other is to limit the number of neighbor nodes. The similarity inferred by GCN is used as the input, and the threshold of limiting the cluster size is firstly obtained to get a part of the final cluster that is relatively sparse and a part of the remaining node sets to enter the stage of limiting the number of neighbor nodes. After the stage of limiting the number of neighbor nodes, all nodes are assigned to the cluster, and the face image clustering is completed.

Limit the Cluster Size. We can set a threshold to prune the cluster. All nodes are in the same cluster are connected together. However, simply using the similarity method will lead to mistakenly deleting a node that actually is in the same cluster during the pruning process, which will ultimately affect the clustering effect. Therefore, in the first stage, the pruning strategy based on the cluster set size threshold is adopted. At the same time, the similarity threshold of the nodes is gradually increased during the iterative clustering of the remaining nodes. In this way, the large set of clusters is pruned, and some clusters with less than optimal similarity representation ability are iteratively filtered out. For the remaining nodes, the value of similarity is higher, and we can take them to the stage of limiting the number of neighbor nodes for further screening.

Limiting the Number of Neighbor Nodes. In order to further distinguish which of these high similarity neighbor nodes are actually the same cluster as the given node. The remaining nodes after screening have a high similarity with the given node. In order to further distinguish between those neighbors with high similarity, which are actually in the same cluster as the given node, it is possible to introduce a variable: the number of neighbor nodes whose similarity with the given node is greater than or equal to Th2. The more neighbor nodes is, the higher the probability that a given node represents this cluster is. Add these qualified neighbor nodes and the given node to the cluster, store these neighbor nodes with a queue, which means check whether the number of neighbor nodes meet the requirements. If so, the neighbor nodes are added to the cluster, and these neighbor nodes are inserted into the tail of the queue. The above process is repeated for the nodes in the node queue until the queue is empty. At this time, a cluster will be obtained. Update the remaining node set and find the next cluster according to the above method. When the remaining node set is empty, the clustering ends.

The algorithm is described as Algorithm 1.

4 Experiments and Analysis

4.1 Dataset and Metrics

TSC-GCN is tested on the public face clustering benchmarks: IJB-B [8], which consists of seven different subtasks. The three subtasks with the largest number

Algorithm 1. Face Clustering Methods Based on GCN

```
Data: ImagedatasetV
Result: ThefinalClusteringResults
 Extract face image feature x;
 Build neighbor node subgraphs,and get subgraph node set V_p;
 Get subgraph features X_p using equation (1);
 Build adjacency matrix A_p, and add an edge between node a and node b, which
 b ∈ V_u ∩ V_P, A_ab = A_ba = 1;
 Calculate the similarity;
 th1 ← q;               /* q is a predefined value */
 while The number of nodes in set remain ≤ p × the total number of nodes do
     Put the nodes whose similarity ≥ th1 into set S;
     if the number of nodes in S ≤ MAX_SIZE then
         Put set S into Result;
         Delete nodes in set S from set remain;
     else
         Clear set S;
         Increase the value of th1 with a step;
     end
 end
 th2 ← r;               /* r is a predefined value */
 Build a remaining node queue using the nodes in set remain;
 while remaining node queue is not empty do
     Take the nodes in the remaining node queue as the queue head of the node
       queue and add it to the set Q;
     while node queue is empty do
         Record the number of the neighbor nodes of the node whose similarity ≥
           th2;
         if the number of the nodes ≥ nc then
             /* nc is a constant value */
             Add the neighbor nodes to the node queue;
             Add the neighbor nodes to set Q;
         end
         Get the next node in the node queue;
         Add Q to set result;
         Delete nodes which is in Q from the remaining node queue;
     end
 end
 return result;
```

are selected. The numbers of identities included in the three subtasks are 512, 1024, and 1845 respectively, and the numbers of samples included are 18171, 36575, and 68195 respectively. We use the model trained on a random subset of CASIA [16] dataset for testing clustering. We use the most mainstream face clustering evaluation metrics [17]: Bcubed F-score (denoted as F_B) and Pairwise F-score (denoted as F_P).

4.2 Parameter Setting

For the density selection threshold is determined to be 0.4 after many experiments. The initial learning rate of momentum and SGD is 0.1, and the weight decay value is $1e^{-5}$. The infrastructure/hardware (GPU/CPU/RAM) set up is (Tesla P100/Intel Xeon/16 GB).

4.3 Results and Analysis

Table 1 shows the comparison results of TSC-GCN and other base methods. The best results are shown in bold. The results in Table 1 show that our method is much better than traditional clustering methods in IJB-B compared to traditional methods. Specifically, TSC-GCN's Pairwise F-score is about 4% higher than the existing method.

Table 1. Comparison on IJB-B data set.

Method	IJB-B-512		IJB-B-1024		IJB-B-1845	
	F_B	F_P	F_B	F_P	F_B	F_P
K-Means [5]	0.612	0.436	0.603	0.413	0.600	0.301
Spectral [6]	0.517	0.310	0.508	0.217	0.516	0.246
AHC [23]	0.795	–	0.797	–	0.739	–
AP [18]	0.494	–	0.484	–	0.477	–
DBSCAN [11]	0.753	–	0.725	–	0.695	–
ARO [19]	0.763	–	0.758	–	0.755	–
PAHC [13]	–	–	0.639	–	0.755	–
ConPAC [14]	0.656	–	0.641	–	0.755	–
DDC [24]	0.802	–	0.805	–	0.800	–
L-GCN [2]	0.833	0.843	0.833	0.853	0.814	0.677
TSC-GCN	**0.834**	**0.913**	**0.835**	**0.890**	**0.811**	**0.712**

4.4 Hyperparameter Analysis

We analyzed the hyperparametric similarity th1, th2, and neighbor count nc in both phases. We chose the Pairwise F-score as the evaluation metric for clustering effectiveness. Also, a comparison with L-GCN was made for reference and analysis.

The First Stage. In the first stage, i.e. the limiting clustering size stage, the value of the hyperparameter th1 affects the effect of clustering. As can be seen in Fig. 4, the TSC-GCN shows an overall upward trend in Pairwise F-score as the value of th1 increases. Once th1 is too high, some similar images will be excluded from the clusters.

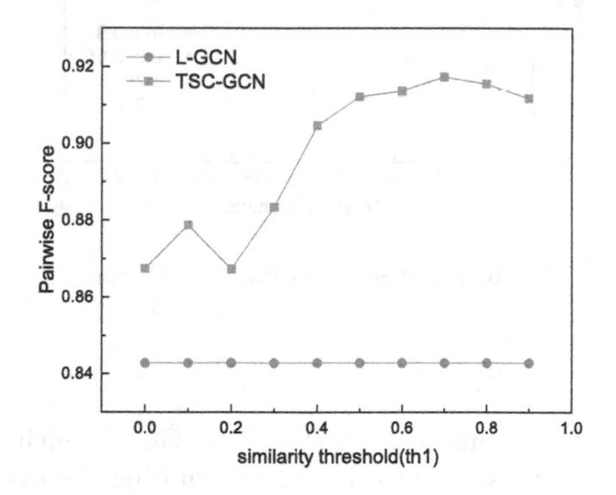

Fig. 4. Effect of th1 on Pairwise F-score

The Second Stage. The second stage is the combination of the two hyperparameters th2 and nc, which then filter the clusters. To address the shortcomings of th1, we exclude the interference of high similarity node pairs by setting a threshold for the number of neighboring nodes nc. Theoretically, the higher the number of surrounding neighboring nodes, the higher the confidence that the node can represent the cluster it is in. As can be seen from Fig. 5 and Fig. 6, the clustering results are relatively sensitive to the choice of the similarity threshold th2.

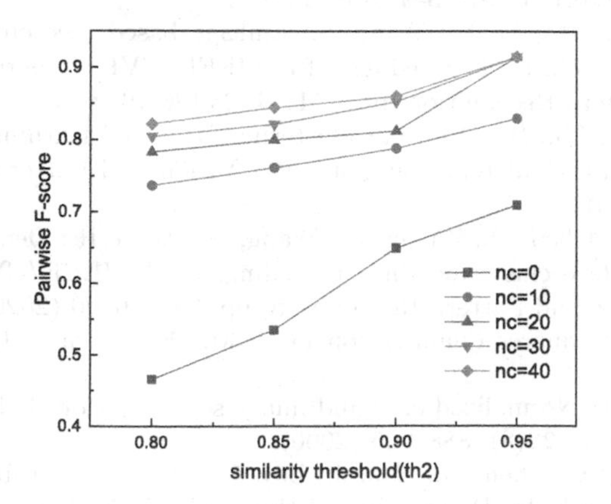

Fig. 5. Effect of th2 on Pairwise F-score

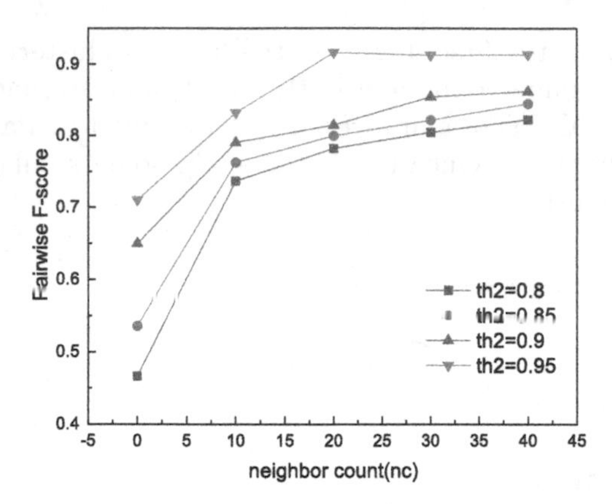

Fig. 6. Effect of nc on Pairwise F-score

5 Conclusions

We proposed a novel face clustering method TSC-GCN, which divided the process of obtained cluster results into two stages, limiting the size of clusters and the number of neighboring nodes. The purpose was to filter out the clusters that were more dispersed and were densely distributed in the feature space respectively. It was experimentally verified that the TSC-GCN could well balance precision and recall both, and achieved better clustering results when the runtime was at the same level as the existing methods.

References

1. Yang, L., Huang, Q., Huang, H., Xu, L., Lin, D.: Learn to propagate reliably on noisy affinity graphs. In: Vedaldi, A., Bischof, H., Brox, T., Frahm, J.-M. (eds.) ECCV 2020, Part XV. LNCS, vol. 12360, pp. 447–464. Springer, Cham (2020). https://doi.org/10.1007/978-3-030-58555-6_27
2. Wang, Z., Zheng, L., Li, Y., Wang, S.: Linkage based face clustering via graph convolution network. In: Proceedings of the IEEE/CVF Conference on Computer Vision and Pattern Recognition, pp. 1117–1125 (2019)
3. Li, P., Zhao, H., Liu, H.: Deep fair clustering for visual learning. In: Proceedings of the IEEE/CVF Conference on Computer Vision and Pattern Recognition, pp. 9070–9079 (2020)
4. Guo, S., Xu, J., Chen, D., Zhang, C., Wang, X., Zhao, R.: Density-aware feature embedding for face clustering. In: Proceedings of the IEEE/CVF Conference on Computer Vision and Pattern Recognition, pp. 6698–6706 (2020)
5. Lloyd, S.: Least squares quantization in PCM. IEEE Trans. Inf. Theory **28**(2), 129–137 (1982)
6. Shi, J., Malik, J.: Normalized cuts and image segmentation. IEEE Trans. Pattern Anal. Mach. Intell. **22**(8), 888–905 (2000)
7. Yang, L., Zhan, X., Chen, D., Yan, J., Loy, C., Lin, D.: Learning to cluster faces on an affinity graph. In: Proceedings of the IEEE/CVF Conference on Computer Vision and Pattern Recognition, pp. 2298–2306 (2019)

8. Whitelam, C., et al.: IARPA Janus benchmark-b face dataset. In: Proceedings of the IEEE Conference on Computer Vision and Pattern Recognition Workshops, pp. 90–98 (2017)
9. Yao, L., Mao, C., Luo, Y.: Graph convolutional networks for text classification. In: Proceedings of the AAAI Conference on Artificial Intelligence, vol. 33, pp. 7370–7377 (2019)
10. Chu, Y., Wang, Z., Wang, L., Zhao, Q., Shan, W.: Fine-grained image classification based on target acquisition and feature fusion. In: Qiu, H., Zhang, C., Fei, Z., Qiu, M., Kung, S.-Y. (eds.) KSEM 2021, Part III. LNCS (LNAI), vol. 12817, pp. 209–221. Springer, Cham (2021). https://doi.org/10.1007/978-3-030-82153-1_18
11. Ester, M., Kriegel, H., Sander, J., Xu, X., et al.: A density-based algorithm for discovering clusters in large spatial databases with noise. In: KDD, pp. 226–231(1996)
12. Elhamifar, E., Vidal, R.: Sparse subspace clustering: algorithm, theory, and applications. IEEE Trans. Pattern Anal. Mach. Intell. **35**(11), 2765–2781 (2013)
13. Lin, W., Chen, J., Chellappa, R.: A proximity-aware hierarchical clustering of faces. In: The 12th IEEE International Conference on Automatic Face and Gesture Recognition, pp. 294–301. IEEE (2017)
14. Shi, Y., Otto, C., Jain, A.K.: Face clustering: representation and pairwise constraints. IEEE Trans. Inf. Forensics Secur. **13**(7), 1626–1640 (2018)
15. Tapaswi, M., Law, M., Fidler, S.: Video face clustering with unknown number of clusters. In: Proceedings of the IEEE/CVF International Conference on Computer Vision, pp. 5027–5036 (2019)
16. Yi, D., M., Lei, Z., Liao, S., Li, S.Z.: Learning face representation from scratch. arXiv preprint arXiv:1411.7923 (2014)
17. Amigó, E., Gonzalo, J., Artiles, J., Verdejo, F.: A comparison of extrinsic clustering evaluation metrics based on formal constraints. Inf. Retr. **12**(4), 461–486 (2009)
18. Frey, B.J., Dueck, D.: Clustering by passing messages between data points. Science **315**(5814), 972–976 (2007)
19. Otto, C., Wang, D., Jain, A.: Clustering millions of faces by identity. IEEE Trans. Pattern Anal. Mach. Intell. **40**(2), 289–303 (2017)
20. Deng, J., Guo, J., Zafeiriou, S.: ArcFace: Additive angular margin loss for deep face recognition. arXiv reprint arXiv:1801.07698 (2018)
21. Guo, Y., Zhang, L., Hu, Y., He, X., Gao, J.: MS-Celeb-1M: a dataset and benchmark for large-scale face recognition. In: Leibe, B., Matas, J., Sebe, N., Welling, M. (eds.) ECCV 2016, Part III. LNCS, vol. 9907, pp. 87–102. Springer, Cham (2016). https://doi.org/10.1007/978-3-319-46487-9_6
22. Cao, Q., Shen, L., Xie, W., Parkhi, O.M., Zisserman, A.: VGGFace2: a dataset for recognising faces across pose and age. In: IEEE International Conference on Automatic Face and Gesture Recognition (FG) (2018)
23. Jain, A.K., Dubes, R.C.: Algorithms for Clustering Data. Prentice Hall Inc., Englewood Cliffs, New Jersey (1988)
24. Lin, W., Chen, J., Castillo, C., Chellappa, R.: Deep density clustering of unconstrained faces. In: Proceedings of the IEEE Conference on Computer Vision and Pattern Recognition, pp. 8128–8137 (2018)

Spotlight on Video Piracy Websites: Familial Analysis Based on Multidimensional Features

Chenlin Wang[1], Yonghao Yu[1], Ao Pu[1], Fan Shi[2,3](✉), and Cheng Huang[1,3]

[1] School of Cyber Science and Engineering, Sichuan University, Chengdu, China
{wangchenlin,yuyonghao,puao}@stu.scu.edu.cn,
codesec@scu.edu.cn

[2] College of Electronic Engineering, National University of Defense Technology, Hefei, China
shifan17@nudt.edu.cn

[3] Anhui Province Key Laboratory of Cyberspace Security Situation Awareness and Evaluation, Hefei, China

Abstract. With the gradual increase in awareness of intellectual property protection in recent years, it has become imperative to strengthen the monitoring and regulation of digital piracy. The previous countermeasures suffer from low accuracy or passive data collection. Furthermore, the commonly adopted website clustering methods focus exclusively on a few attributes. The results obtained do not draw a comprehensive picture of the connections between websites within a family. In this paper, we aim to address the issue of digital piracy being challenging to identify, trace, monitor, and regulate in the current situation, utilizing video piracy websites targeting Chinese consumers as an example. The present architecture enables proactive discovery and detection of suspicious websites with a 96.2% accuracy, compensating for traditional digital piracy detection inadequacies. The proposed novel feature extraction method for clustering video piracy websites can synthesize multiple aspects in terms of layout, content, and infrastructure. The clustering results indicate that the websites belonging to the same family obtained by the proposed method show a more comprehensive similarity.

Keywords: Proactive discovery · Piracy detection · Multidimensional features · Feature serialization · Website clustering

1 Introduction

Along with the flourishing development of the Internet and the continuous improvement of network infrastructure, the number of Chinese Internet users is booming. According to The 48th Statistical Report on China's Internet Development [6], the amount of China's online video (including short video) users had reached 944 million by June 2021, accounting for 93.4% of all Internet users. At

G. Memmi et al. (Eds.): KSEM 2022, LNAI 13370, pp. 272–288, 2022.
https://doi.org/10.1007/978-3-031-10989-8_22

the same time, the black market of pirated videos is overgrowing. According to iResearch's [11] definition, video piracy refers to the free or paid distribution of video resources on the Internet without the authorization of copyright owners and purchasers. Video Piracy Website (VPW) provides a staggering amount of pirated videos to Internet users. Operators of VPW continue to reach a high level of profitability by setting up VIPs, placing advertisements, and selling pirated videos. The operation mode of VPW is already well developed after going through stages of development such as the server storage model, P2P model, hotlink model, and cloud storage model. Currently, the development trend of VPW is from centralization to decentralization, bringing significant challenges to the fight against piracy.

Nowadays, several websites allow users to download pirated videos from streaming cyberlockers directly. Streaming cyberlockers have several things in common: first, they have no copyright checking policy; second, these websites often use circumvention tactics, such as additional settings on the homepage to make the website appear compliant and legitimate; and finally, they mostly disable search functions to prevent visitors from finding the resources they store. Streaming cyberlockers rely on third-party indexing websites to provide a searchable directory of video links and maintain a query function. The blocking of third-party indexing websites does not affect the streaming cyberlockers, ultimately creating a scenario in which streaming cyberlockers and third-party indexing websites operate in a symbiotic relationship.

As of now, there have been several studies on video piracy. Lyu et al. [15] investigated Chinese Internet users' attitudes toward video piracy and examined the factors affecting their attitudes. AliCloud [2] extracted the copyright information in the video DNA and uploaded it for deposition. They realized the integration and data exchange to build a blockchain-based copyright protection solution. Ibosiola et al. [10] analyzed the links to cloud storage on the websites and studied these links' characteristics and potential relationships. The above work suffers from the issue that they can only perform passive defense or detect a single category of VPW. We need the ability to fight against piracy more proactively and to analyze the characteristics of particular VPW families more comprehensively.

In summary, the primary contributions of this paper are listed as follows:

- We combine the incremental crawler and the BERT model to build a VPW detection model, which achieves timely proactive discovery and high detection accuracy of 96.2%.
- We design an encoding method to store multidimensional features in sequences. Combined with the string comparison algorithm, we can use each feature to divide VPWs into different groups efficiently.
- We cluster websites using layout, content, and infrastructure features. The websites belonging to the same cluster obtained by the presented method possess a more comprehensive similarity.

The rest of this paper is structured as follows: Sect. 2 discusses the related work. Section 3 shows the overall architecture and details the methods we used to detect and cluster VPW. Section 4 provides the experiments and analysis related to this work. Section 5 concludes the paper and proposes future works.

2 Related Work

2.1 Features Extraction

Content. Babapour et al. [3] used natural language processing and text mining techniques such as TF-IDF and SVD to extract the content feature from webpage text. Maktabar et al. [16] employed the Bag-of-Words technique and Part-of-Speech tags to construct the content feature vector and segregate the fraudulent websites.

Layout. Bozkir et al. [5] proposed a ranking approach that considers visual similarities among webpages by using layout-based and vision-based features. Experimental results showed that their approach promisingly simulates the average human similarity judgment. Balogun et al. [4] proposed a meta-learning model based on the functional tree for detecting phishing websites. Experimental results showed that the functional tree and its variants are superior to some existing phishing websites detection models. Mao et al. [18] focused on extracting features from CSS layout files. To extract and quantify CSS features, they transferred their property values into computable types by doing some simplified encoding.

Website Infrastructure. The technology of Cyberspace Surveying and Mapping (CSM) detects, analyses, and visualizes all kinds of cyberspace resources and their relationships [27]. By building a map of cyberspace resources, we can comprehensively describe and display cyberspace information. Cyberspace search engines adopt CSM technology. Unlike Web search engines, cyberspace search engines can obtain the critical information of the target and conduct a comprehensive analysis and display [14]. Many cyberspace search engines have been well developed, such as Shodan, Zoomeye, Censys and FOFA.

2.2 Website Detection

The main approaches to detecting websites can be broadly divided into two categories, traditional machine learning approaches [13,17,24,25] and deep learning approaches [9,20,21,28]. Researchers do not need to extract features manually or have extensive knowledge while using deep learning methods. The latest studies in website detection have focused on deep learning models in recent years. Du et al. [9] proposed an intelligent classification schema based on the deep neural network using mixed featured extractors consisting of Text-CNN Feature Extractor and Bidirectional GRU Feature Extractor. Patil et al. [20] proposed a deep neural network to predict structural similarity between 2D layouts using

Graph Matching Networks (GMN). Their network's retrieval results are more consistent with human judgment of layout similarity. Yang et al. [28] proposed a multidimensional feature phishing detection approach. Under the control of a dynamic category decision algorithm, the speed and accuracy are all improved. Rajaram et al. [21] proposed a Convolutional Neural Network framework with 18 layers and transfer learning to classify websites using screenshots and URLs of phishing websites and legitimate websites. They achieved the integration of the visual-similarity-based and the character-based approach.

2.3 Websites Clustering

Jie et al. [12] proposed a label to class clustering analysis method and label category similarity attribute to compare the relevance of different types of website addresses. The clustering results showed that darknet sites can be gathered together unsupervised. Nagai et al. [19] proposed a new malicious website identification technique by clustering the WS-trees. Experiment results verified that the proposed approach identifies malicious websites with reasonable accuracy. Rentea et al. [22] proposed a clustering algorithm to cluster an extensive collection of URLs and selected centroids from each cluster, such that each URL in the cluster is similar with at least a centroid. The proposed algorithm is fast and scales well on large datasets. Drew et al. [8] proposed an optimized combined clustering method by extracting key website features, including text, HTML structure, file structure, and screenshots of websites. The results showed that their method more accurately groups similar websites together than existing general-purpose consensus clustering methods.

3 Methodology

In this section, we provide a detailed description of the methods we used. We divide our research into four parts: proactive discovery, VPW detection, VPW feature extraction, and familial clustering. The overall architecture is shown in Fig. 1.

3.1 Proactive Discovery

We employ incremental crawlers in conjunction with automatic keyword and external link extraction. By observing the layouts of VPWs, we found that the majority of them would include external links at the bottom of the webpages. Since developers typically index the links pointing to the resources inside the website with relative paths, another characteristic of the external links is that the links start with "http(s)". Our crawler can locate and extract the external links more efficiently based on the above findings. We use a record table to avoid duplicate crawling of an existing one.

The encoding on a portion of webpages does not perfectly match how it claims to be encoded. We replace these garbled characters with spaces since

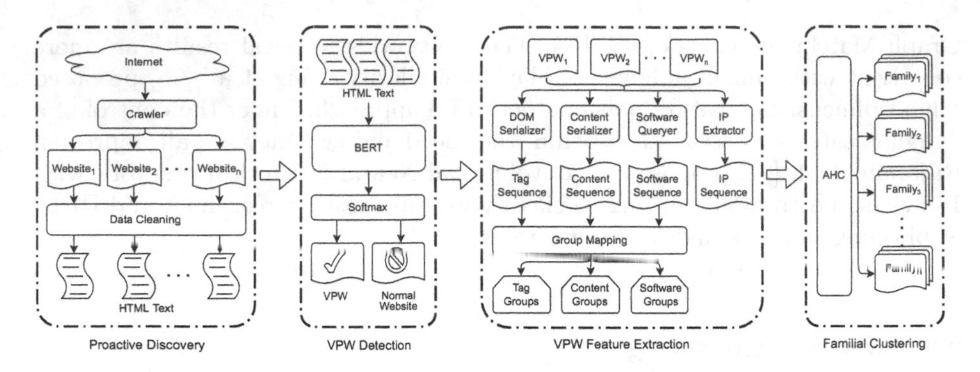

Fig. 1. Overall architecture.

they usually do not contribute to the characterization of the page. Additionally, the comments on websites are also meaningless, and we eliminate this part in the same manner. Then we extract the text from HTML files of all website homepages and record the mapping relations.

3.2 VPW Detection

The detection model in this paper is implemented based on the BERT model. BERT [7] stands for bidirectional encoder representations from transformers. Transformers can handle sequential input data and do not need to process the data in order based on the self-attention mechanism [26]. Self-attention can calculate interrelations between all words in a sentence. These interrelations then adjust the weight of each word to obtain their new expressions. These new expressions contain semantic meanings and interrelations. Therefore, the vector obtained by the self-attention mechanism has a more global expression than the traditional mechanism.

To further enhance the semantic representation of the model, we select the Chinese Wikipedia corpus as a pre-training task and then input HTML text into the model for targeted training.

3.3 VPW Feature Extraction

Layout Sequence. Researchers have conducted many studies on the layout similarity of webpages, primarily focusing on image-based comparisons. For example, in the research of phishing webpages, Abdelnabi et al. [1] proposed a method for comparing visual similarity using screenshots. Unfortunately, the image-based layout comparison method is too computationally expensive. To reduce the overhead while accurately recording the layout features of webpages, we serialize the layout into a one-dimensional sequence. Since some HTML tags can only uniquely represent the nested relationships when the start and end positions are determined, we need to record them entirety. We selectively serialize tags frequently found in VPWs, further reducing the overhead. The encoding table is shown in Table 1.

Table 1. Encoding table.

Tag	Code	Tag	Code
a	A	li	G
div	B	input	H
link	C	form	I
img	D	p	J
script	E	table	K
ul	F	span	L

Here we give an example of webpage layout serialization. There are two simple webpages in Fig. 2, Page 1 will be encoded as "EEFGGGGGGFLLC", and Page 2 will be encoded as "FGGGGGGFCLL". It is worth noting that we only encode the tags in the encoding table.

```
<html>
<head>
    <title>page 1</title>
    <script>some code</script>
</head>
<body>
    <ul type="some type">
        <li>some text</li>
        <li>some text</li>
        <li>some text</li>
    </ul>
    <span>some text</span>
    <link rel="xxx" href="a link"/>
</body>
<html>
```

(a) Page 1

```
<html>
<head>
    <title>page 2</title>

</head>
<body>
    <ul type="some type">
        <li>some text</li>
        <li>some text</li>
        <li>some text</li>
    </ul>
    <link rel="xxx" href="a link"/>
    <span>some text</span>
</body>
<html>
```

(b) Page 2

Fig. 2. Example of HTML code for two similar webpages.

Content Sequence. Term Frequency-Inverse Document Frequency (TF-IDF) is a statistical method to assess the importance of a word for one of the documents.

Term Frequency (TF) represents the number of times a word appears in a document. The importance of the word w in a document can be expressed as:

$$TF_{w,d} = \frac{n_{w,d}}{\sum_i n_{i,d}} \tag{1}$$

This formula calculates the importance of word w to the document d. $n_{w,d}$ indicates the number of times word w appears in document d. $\sum_i n_{i,d}$ is the sum of the occurrences for all words in document d.

Inverse Document Frequency (IDF) measures the ability of words to distinguish between categories. The ability of word w can be expressed as:

$$IDF_w = log\frac{|D|}{|\{d : n_w \in d_i\}|} \tag{2}$$

$|D|$ is the number of all documents. $|\{d : n_w \in d_i\}|$ is the number of documents containing word w.

TF-IDF represents the weight of words. The weight of word w in document d can be expressed as:

$$TF\text{-}IDF_{w,d} = TF_{w,d} \times IDF_w \tag{3}$$

We first extract all the Chinese corpus in HTML and train the TF-IDF model. Since the TF-IDF score's decile is the most significant number in this score, we take all the TF-IDF scores' deciles of a particular website and join them into a sequence. We give a few simple examples, as shown in Table 2.

Table 2. Example of content sequences for three websites.

Website	TF-IDF scores	Content sequence
1	0.21, 0.33, 0.00, 0.10, 0.56	23015
2	0.23, 0.37, 0.10, 0.17, 0.51	23115
3	0.42, 0.33, 0.00, 0.00, 0.22	43002

Website Infrastructure. We aggregate data from various cyberspace search engines, maximizing the combination of each search engine to make our statistics more comprehensive and reliable. We gather information about the server software to determine the habits of the operating entity building the website and IP address to determine the network segment in which the server is located. We also serialize the two features acquired above to evaluate the similarity of the infrastructure between websites in the subsequent step. We stitch together all the server software for the website into a sequence so that the sequences between websites with similar software is also alike. An example is shown in Table 3.

Table 3. Example of three websites using similar server software.

Website	Software
1	Nginx, jQuery-3.3.1, Bootstrap
2	CNZZ, Nginx, jQuery-3.2, Bootstrap
3	Swiper Slider, Nginx, jQuery-1.11.3, Bootstrap

We intercept the first three segments for the website's IP address, make up each segment into three digits, and then join the three parts into a nine-digit number. These nine-digit sequences can be used later in the clustering step to indicate the distance between network segments in which different websites are located. An example of the process is shown in Fig. 3.

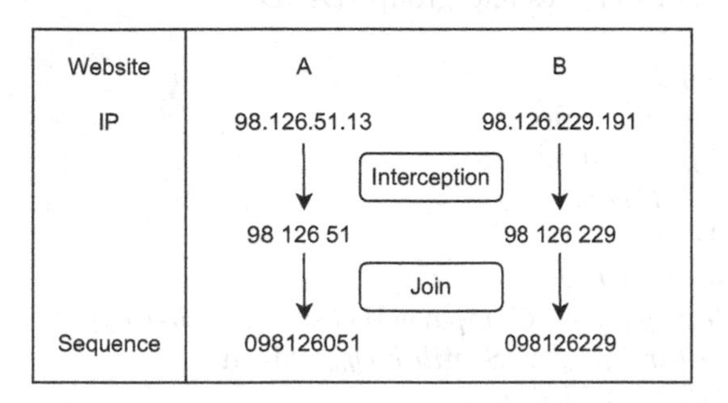

Fig. 3. Example of IP sequence processing.

Group Mapping. After the above extraction and encoding, we can obtain sequences of each webpage's layout, content, and software. We use a sequence comparison algorithm to calculate the similarity between two webpages in the above three aspects. The core formula of the algorithm is as follows.

$$similarity = \frac{Lsum - Ldist}{Lsum} \tag{4}$$

Lsum is the sum of the lengths of two sequences. *Ldist* is the edit distance, i.e., the minimum number of edit operations required to convert from one to the other between two sequences. Both insert and delete operations add 1 to the value of *Ldist* and replace operations add 2. The edit distance of two sequences a and b is denoted as $Ldist_{a,b}(|a|, |b|)$, which can be calculated as follows.

$$Ldist_{a,b}(i,j) = \begin{cases} max(i,j) & \text{if } min(i,j) = 0 \\ min \begin{cases} Ldist_{a,b}(i-1,j) + 1 \\ Ldist_{a,b}(i,j-1) + 1 \\ Ldist_{a,b}(i-1,j-1) + 2_{(a_i \neq b_j)} \end{cases} & \text{otherwise} \end{cases} \tag{5}$$

$|a|$ and $|b|$ denote the lengths of sequences a and b respectively. $2_{(a_i \neq b_j)}$ is a characteristic function with the value of 2 when $a_i \neq b_j$ and 0 otherwise. $Ldist_{a,b}(i,j)$ denotes the distance between the first i characters of a and the first j characters of b. After obtaining the edit distances of two sequences, we perform a similarity calculation. Here we take the sequences obtained from the two webpages shown in Fig. 2 as an example. The edit distance between the sequence of Page 1 and Page 2 is 4 and further get the similarity as 0.83. The comparison between software sequences or content sequences goes the same way.

The IP sequence can be standardized and fed directly to the clustering algorithm. However, layout, content, and software sequences must be mapped first. The specific implementation is shown in Algorithm 1.

Algorithm 1: Group mapping using sequence similarity.

```
Input: List of websites, L
Output: Dict of websites and group IDs, D
1  D ← empty dict
2  GID ← new GID
3  while L is not empty do
4      Similarity_old ← 0
5      Website_1 ← L.pop()
6      Mate ← Website_1
7      for Website_2 in L do
8          Similarity_new ← Compare(Website_1, Website_2)
9          if Similarity_new > Similarity_old then
10             Mate ← Website_2
11             Similarity_old ← Similarity_new
12         end
13     end
14     if D.get(Mate) is not None then
15         D[Website_1] ← D.get(Mate)
16     else
17         D[Website_1] ← GID
18         D[Mate] ← GID
19         GID ← new GID
20     end
21 end
```

Algorithm 1 first initializes an empty dictionary D, generates a random *GID*. Then the following operations are performed for each website in the list L. The algorithm first pops up a website, assigns it to $Website_1$, and initializes the *Mate* of $Website_1$ to itself and $Similarity_{old}$ to 0. Then, $Website_1$ compares with each remaining $Website_2$ in list L. If the $Similarity_{new}$ between $Website_1$ and $Website_2$ is higher than the $Similarity_{old}$, the algorithm sets the *Mate* of $Website_1$ to $Website_2$ and assigns the $Similarity_{new}$ to $Similarity_{old}$. After $Website_1$ finishes comparing with all the websites in list L, the algorithm then tries to find out if the *Mate* is already grouped in the dictionary. If yes, the algorithm then assigns the *Mate*'s group ID to $Website_1$. Otherwise, the algorithm assigns *GID* to both $Website_1$ and *Mate*, generating a new *GID*. Finally, Algorithm 1 divides two websites corresponding to the highest sequence similarity into a group. After the algorithm execution, each website is assigned three group IDs according to its layout, content, and software.

3.4 Familial Clustering

Clustering is the task of dividing a dataset into different clusters according to specific criteria. The data object is more similar to other data objects in the same cluster and dissimilar to data objects in other clusters. Hierarchical clustering is a method that decomposes a dataset hierarchically until certain conditions are met. Traditional hierarchical clustering algorithms are divided into two main algorithms: divisive clustering and agglomerative clustering. Divisive clustering uses a top-down strategy. This algorithm splits a cluster that contains the whole data and proceeds by splitting clusters recursively until individual data is split into singleton clusters. Agglomerative clustering uses a bottom-up strategy. This algorithm treats each data as a singleton cluster at the outset. It then successively agglomerates pairs of clusters until all clusters have been merged into a single cluster that contains all data.

We use the three group IDs and IP sequences as input features to cluster the VPWs. We choose Agglomerative Hierarchical Clustering (AHC) as our clustering method. And we use StandardScaler to standardize features by removing the mean and scaling to unit variance.

4 Experiment

In this section, we use collected data to train the BERT model and perform VPW detection. We then conduct a familial clustering and visualize the results. We analyze two cases to illustrate the superiority of using multidimensional features for clustering.

4.1 Dataset

The experimental dataset are collected by the methods mentioned in Sect. 3.1 which contain 22363 pieces of data. To train the BERT model, we label some data with 1, meaning the VPW (blacklist) and 0, meaning the normal websites (whitelist). After the manual screening, the training dataset has 1752 whitelist data and 1336 blacklist data. Each piece of data includes the URL, domain name, title, update time, Etc. Then we download all websites' HTML files and extract the text using the methods mentioned in Sect. 3.1.

4.2 Evaluation Metrics

We use weighted Accuracy, Precision, Recall, and F1-score to evaluate the performance of the BERT model. Accuracy represents the percentage of correct predictions. The Precision represents the accuracy of predicting positive samples. The Recall represents the probability of predicting positive samples in the actual positive samples. The F1-score comprehensively reflects Precision and Accuracy.

We use the silhouette coefficient [23] to evaluate the performance of AHC. The silhouette coefficient is a measure of clustering validity, and its core formula is as follows.

$$SilhouetteCoefficient_i = \frac{(b_i - a_i)}{max(a_i, b_i)} \tag{6}$$

In the formula, i denotes object i. a_i is the average intra-cluster distance, i.e., the average distance between i and the other objects within a cluster. b_i is the average inter-cluster distance, i.e., the average distance between i and all objects in other clusters. The silhouette coefficient ranges from –1 to 1. A large positive value indicates that the cluster's intra-dissimilarity a_i is much smaller than the smallest inter-dissimilarity b_i, and thus object i is well-clustered.

4.3 Experimental Settings

VPW Detection. The experiment uses the BERT model, choosing the Voting Ensemble model (consisting of Logistic Regression, Random Forest, Gradient Boosting, and Xgboost) and RNN model as a comparison. We randomly split our dataset into train and validation sets using a 90/10 cut and take HTML text as model input. The size of the BERT embedding vector is set to 768. The learning rate is $5e^{-5}$, and the batch size is 8.

Familial Clustering. We divide this subsection into two parts: pre-processing and parameter setting.

Pre-processing. The layout sequence preserves the layout information of webpages well and makes it possible to compare a large number of webpages. We divide the tag sequence into four segments of 250 characters each and compare the similarity of the characters in each of the four segments between every two webpages. The stacked histogram of statistical results is shown in Fig. 4.

Four colors indicate the similarity distribution in the four segments shown in the stacked histogram. The heights of the bars in different colors represent the number of a certain similarity in each segment. The trend of the similarity distribution of layout sequences for different segments is about the same. It is noteworthy that many samples with similarities of 0 and 1 appear in the statistics for characters 500–750 and 750–1000. This situation occurs because some websites have layout sequences less than or equal to 500 in length. If we compare an empty sequence with a non-empty sequence, the similarity is 0. If we

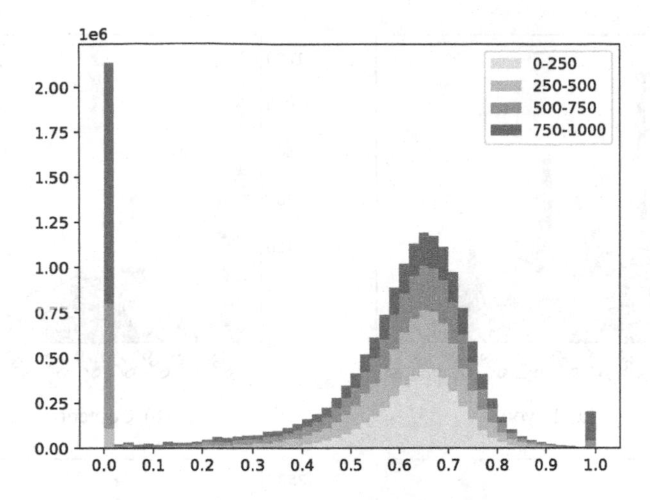

Fig. 4. Similarity distribution calculated using different segments of the layout sequence.

compare two empty sequences, the similarity is 1. To reduce the effect of extreme values on the detection results, we take the first 500 characters of each webpage's layout sequence to compare. In addition, sequence truncation emphasizes the top of the webpage, which significantly impacts the webpage's layout. It reduces the effect of the bottom of the webpage on the similarity calculation, which generally only affects the number of resources provided by the webpage.

The processing of content and software sequences does not need to be as complex as layout sequences. We can easily obtain these two sequences and use Algorithm 1 to process them into different groups, respectively. We obtain the IP sequence of each website with the process shown in Fig. 3. IP sequences do not need to be mapped to groups but only standardized. The standardized mapping results of the four aspects mentioned above are shown in Fig. 5.

Hyperparameter Tuning. In order to select a suitable hyperparameter, We use the silhouette coefficient for evaluation. The variation of the silhouette coefficient and the number of clusters with the distance threshold is shown in Fig. 6. The line indicates the silhouette coefficient, and the bars are the number of clusters. We chose 0.10 as the distance threshold for clustering, and the silhouette coefficient is 0.712.

4.4 Results

Detection Results. The results of the VPW detection are shown in Table 4.

The experimental results show that the BERT model used in this article can improve the detection effect of VPW. With the BERT model, we automatically classify the remaining unlabelled websites collected in Sect. 4.1. Finally, the model classifies 10978 VPWs and 11385 normal websites for our subsequent familial clustering.

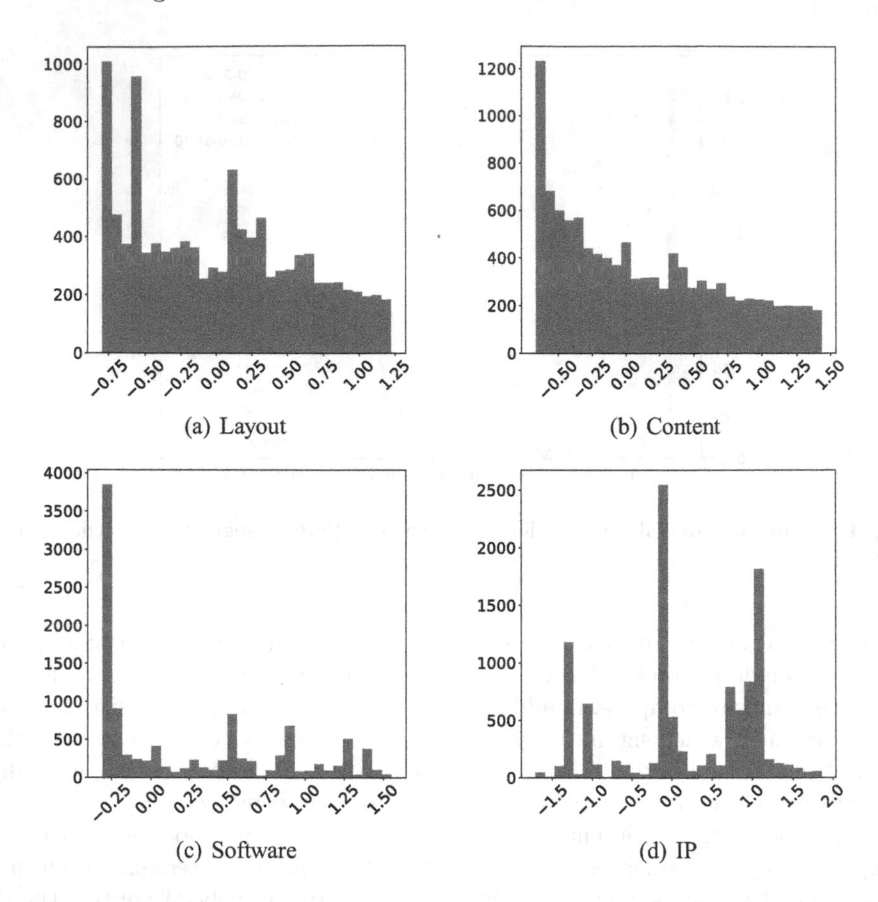

Fig. 5. The number of samples corresponding to different groups of each feature.

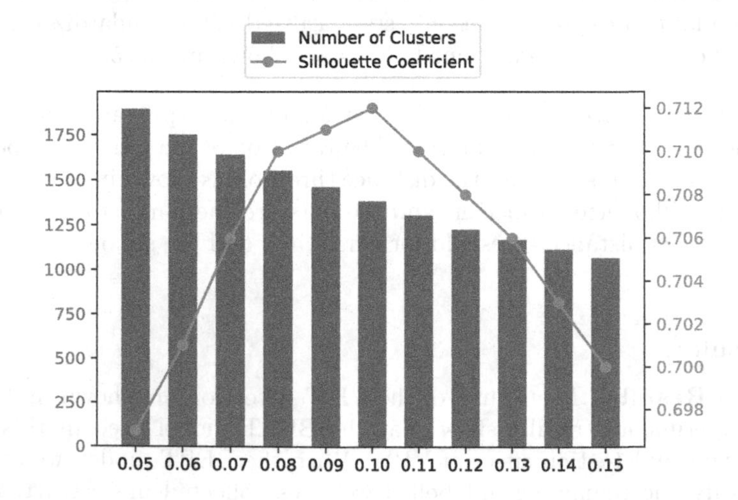

Fig. 6. Variation of silhouette coefficient and the number of clusters with distance threshold.

Table 4. Comparison of Voting Ensemble, RNN and BERT.

Model	Accuracy	Precision	Recall	F1-score
Voting Ensemble	87.97%	88.20%	87.97%	88.03%
RNN	92.78%	92.86%	92.78%	92.80%
BERT	**96.20%**	**96.21%**	**96.20%**	**96.20%**

Clustering Results. After the familial clustering, we visualize the clustering results as a graph. The graph of partial clustering results is shown in Fig. 7. The large nodes represent cluster labels. The small nodes associated with the large node represent the VPWs belonging to the cluster.

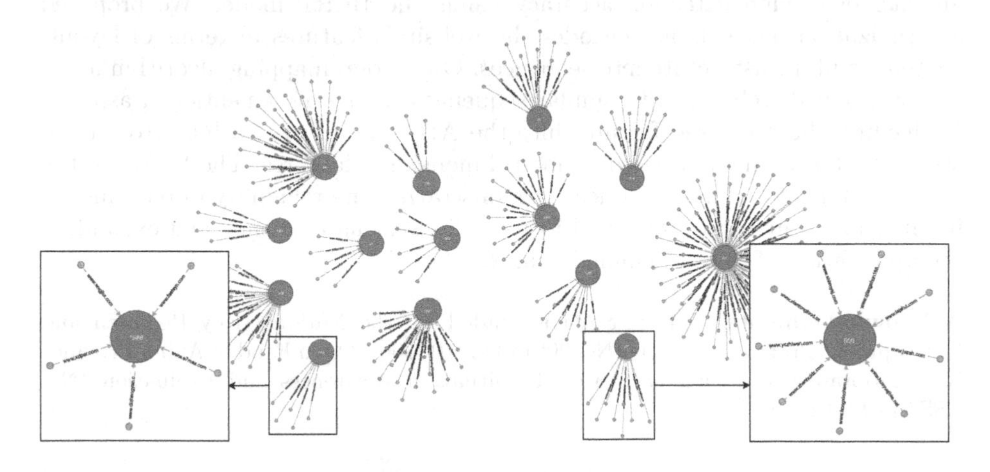

Fig. 7. Partial clustering results.

4.5 Case Study

We provide two cases to illustrate the clustering results. We call the group corresponding to the largest proportion of a feature in a cluster the dominant group. We further show the percentage of the dominant group within the cluster for each feature. For the cluster labeled 590 in Fig. 7, the statistical results are shown in Table 5. For the cluster labeled 1688 in Fig. 7, the statistical results are shown in Table 6. The same cluster of websites obtained by our method is more similar in layout, content, and infrastructure. Our clustering results allow a more comprehensive familial analysis of VPWs.

Table 5. VPWs labeled 590.

Feature	Percentage
Layout	88.89%
Cotent	77.78%
Software	100.00%
IP	66.67%

Table 6. VPWs labeled 1688.

Feature	Percentage
Layout	100.00%
Cotent	60.00%
Software	100.00%
IP	80.00%

5 Conclusion and Future Work

In this paper, we collected video piracy websites through proactive discovery and achieved high detection accuracy using the BERT model. We proposed a serialization method that encodes the website's features in terms of layout, content, and infrastructure into sequences. Our group mapping algorithm accurately grouped websites with similar sequences in the aforementioned aspects. By feeding the processed features into the AHC, we created a hitherto unseen VPW clustering method based on multidimensional features. The VPWs in the same cluster were almost identical, demonstrating the reliability of our clustering method. Our future work will focus on increasing efficiency and expanding the application of website familial analysis.

Acknowledgements. This research is funded by the National Key Research and Development Program of China (No. 2021YFB3100500), Open Fund of Anhui Province Key Laboratory of Cyberspace Security Situation Awareness and Evaluation (No. CSSAE-2021-001).

References

1. Abdelnabi, S., Krombholz, K., Fritz, M.: Visualphishnet: zero-day phishing website detection by visual similarity. In: Proceedings of the 2020 ACM SIGSAC Conference on Computer and Communications Security, pp. 1681–1698 (2020)
2. Alicloud (2022). https://www.aliyun.com/solution/blockchain/bcpp
3. Babapour, S.M., Roostaee, M.: Web pages classification: an effective approach based on text mining techniques. In: 2017 IEEE 4th International Conference on Knowledge-Based Engineering and Innovation (KBEI), pp. 0320–0323. IEEE (2017)
4. Balogun, A.O., et al.: Improving the phishing website detection using empirical analysis of function tree and its variants. Heliyon **7**(7), e07437 (2021)
5. Bozkir, A.S., Sezer, E.A.: Layout-based computation of web page similarity ranks. Int. J. Hum. Comput. Stud. **110**, 95–114 (2018)
6. CNNIC: The 48th statistical report on China's internet development. Technical report, China Internet Network Information Center (2021)
7. Devlin, J., Chang, M.W., Lee, K., Toutanova, K.: Bert: pre-training of deep bidirectional transformers for language understanding. arXiv preprint arXiv:1810.04805 (2018)

8. Drew, J.M., Moore, T.: Optimized combined-clustering methods for finding replicated criminal websites. EURASIP J. Inf. Secur. **2014**(1), 1–13 (2014). https://doi.org/10.1186/s13635-014-0014-4
9. Du, M., Han, Y., Zhao, L.: A heuristic approach for website classification with mixed feature extractors. In: 2018 IEEE 24th International Conference on Parallel and Distributed Systems (ICPADS), pp. 134–141. IEEE (2018)
10. Ibosiola, D., Steer, B., Garcia-Recuero, A., Stringhini, G., Uhlig, S., Tyson, G.: Movie pirates of the caribbean: exploring illegal streaming cyberlockers. In: Twelfth International AAAI Conference on Web and Social Media (2018)
11. iResearch: 2018 report of copyright protection in China's pan-entertainment industry. Technical report, iResearch (2018)
12. Jie, X., Haoliang, L., Ao, J.: A new model for simultaneous detection of phishing and darknet websites. In: 2021 7th International Conference on Computer and Communications (ICCC), pp. 2002–2006. IEEE (2021)
13. Kumar, J., Santhanavijayan, A., Janet, B., Rajendran, B., Bindhumadhava, B.: Phishing website classification and detection using machine learning. In: 2020 International Conference on Computer Communication and Informatics (ICCCI), pp. 1–6. IEEE (2020)
14. Li, R., Shen, M., Yu, H., Li, C., Duan, P., Zhu, L.: A survey on cyberspace search engines. In: Lu, W., et al. (eds.) CNCERT 2020. CCIS, vol. 1299, pp. 206–214. Springer, Singapore (2020). https://doi.org/10.1007/978-981-33-4922-3_15
15. Lyu, Y., Xie, J., Xie, B.: The attitudes of Chinese online users towards movie piracy: a content analysis. In: Sundqvist, A., Berget, G., Nolin, J., Skjerdingstad, K.I. (eds.) iConference 2020. LNCS, vol. 12051, pp. 169–185. Springer, Cham (2020). https://doi.org/10.1007/978-3-030-43687-2_13
16. Maktabar, M., Zainal, A., Maarof, M.A., Kassim, M.N.: Content based fraudulent website detection using supervised machine learning techniques. In: Abraham, A., Muhuri, P.K., Muda, A.K., Gandhi, N. (eds.) HIS 2017. AISC, vol. 734, pp. 294–304. Springer, Cham (2018). https://doi.org/10.1007/978-3-319-76351-4_30
17. Malhotra, R., Sharma, A.: An empirical study to classify website using thresholds from data characteristics. In: Hu, Y.-C., Tiwari, S., Mishra, K.K., Trivedi, M.C. (eds.) Ambient Communications and Computer Systems. AISC, vol. 904, pp. 433–446. Springer, Singapore (2019). https://doi.org/10.1007/978-981-13-5934-7_39
18. Mao, J., et al.: Phishing page detection via learning classifiers from page layout feature. EURASIP J. Wirel. Commun. Netw. **2019**(1), 1–14 (2019). https://doi.org/10.1186/s13638-019-1361-0
19. Nagai, T., et al.: A malicious web site identification technique using web structure clustering. IEICE Trans. Inf. Syst. **102**(9), 1665–1672 (2019)
20. Patil, A.G., Li, M., Fisher, M., Savva, M., Zhang, H.: Layoutgmn: neural graph matching for structural layout similarity. In: Proceedings of the IEEE/CVF Conference on Computer Vision and Pattern Recognition, pp. 11048–11057 (2021)
21. Rajaram, J., Dhasaratham, M.: Scope of visual-based similarity approach using convolutional neural network on phishing website detection. In: Satapathy, S.C., Bhateja, V., Janakiramaiah, B., Chen, Y.-W. (eds.) Intelligent System Design. AISC, vol. 1171, pp. 435–452. Springer, Singapore (2021). https://doi.org/10.1007/978-981-15-5400-1_45
22. Rentea, R., Oprişa, C.: Fast clustering for massive collections of malicious URLs. In: 2021 IEEE 17th International Conference on Intelligent Computer Communication and Processing (ICCP), pp. 11–18. IEEE (2021)
23. Rousseeuw, P.J.: Silhouettes: a graphical aid to the interpretation and validation of cluster analysis. J. Comput. Appl. Math. **20**, 53–65 (1987)

24. Shabudin, S., Sani, N.S., Ariffin, K.A.Z., Aliff, M.: Feature selection for phishing website classification. Int. J. Adv. Comput. Sci. Appl. **11**(4), 587–595 (2020)
25. Ubing, A.A., Jasmi, S.K.B., Abdullah, A., Jhanjhi, N., Supramaniam, M.: Phishing website detection: an improved accuracy through feature selection and ensemble learning. Int. J. Adv. Comput. Sci. Appl. **10**(1), 252–257 (2019)
26. Vaswani, A., et al.: Attention is all you need. In: Advances in Neural Information Processing Systems 30 (2017)
27. Xu, R., et al.: Cyberspace surveying and mapping: Hierarchical model and resource formalization. In: IEEE INFOCOM 2019-IEEE Conference on Computer Communications Workshops (INFOCOM WKSHPS), pp. 68–72. IEEE (2019)
28. Yang, P., Zhao, G., Zeng, P.: Phishing website detection based on multidimensional features driven by deep learning. IEEE Access **7**, 15196–15209 (2019)

A Vehicle Value Based Ride-Hailing Order Matching and Dispatching Algorithm

Shuai Xu[1], Zeheng Zhong[1], Yikai Luo[1], and Bing Shi[1,2](✉)

[1] School of Computer Science and Artificial Intelligence,
Wuhan University of Technology, Wuhan, China
{xushuai,lyk,bingshi}@whut.edu.cn

[2] Shenzhen Research Institute of Wuhan University of Technology, Shenzhen, China

Abstract. Online ride-hailing has become one of the most important transportation ways in the modern city. In the ride-hailing system, how to efficiently match passengers (orders) with vehicles and how to dispatch idle vehicles are key issues. In the online ride-hailing system, the ride-hailing platform needs to match riding orders with vehicles and dispatches the idle vehicles efficiently to maximize the social welfare. However, the matching and dispatching decisions at the current round may affect the supply and demand of ride-hailing in the future rounds since they will affect the future vehicle distributions in different geographical zones. In fact, vehicles in different zones at different times may have different values for the matching and dispatching results. In this paper, we use the vehicle value function to characterize the spatio-temporal value of vehicles in each zone and then use it to design the order matching and idle vehicle dispatching algorithm to improve the long-term social welfare. We further run experiments to evaluate the proposed algorithm. The experimental results show that our algorithm can outperform benchmark approaches in terms of the social welfare, and can also achieve effective utilization of idle vehicles and thus improve the service ratio.

Keywords: Ride-hailing · Order matching · Idle vehicle dispatching · Social welfare

1 Introduction

As the quick development of ride-hailing business, various online ride-hailing platforms have emerged, such as DiDi and Uber. In fact, the annual volume of passengers transported by DiDi has exceeded 10 billion.[1] The market value of the global online ride-hailing business is expected to grow to $285 billion by 2030. In such a business, the ride-hailing platform needs to match riding orders with vehicles and dispatch idle vehicles efficiently in order to improve the profit.

Specifically, the ride-hailing platform needs to match vehicles with orders while dispatching idle vehicles to the potential high-demanding zones to avoid

[1] http://news.cctv.com/2020/10/26/ARTIRbGKnKHCeLzgSAltRgwJ201026.shtml.

G. Memmi et al. (Eds.): KSEM 2022, LNAI 13370, pp. 289–301, 2022.
https://doi.org/10.1007/978-3-031-10989-8_23

randomly exploring potential riding orders periodically (i.e., over multiple rounds). The ride-hailing platform should maximize the long-term social welfare[2] (i.e., the sum of social welfare of all rounds), instead of maximizing the social welfare of one round. However, the current matching and dispatching decisions may affect the future vehicle distributions, and thus affect the future matching and dispatching, which may affect the overall social welfare. Therefore, we need to consider the decision of current round on the future impacts when designing the order matching and idle vehicle dispatching algorithm to maximize the long-term social welfare. In more detail, historical information about matching and the corresponding social welfare can provide the implicit information about how much value the vehicle can provide in the spatial-temporal state, which can provide some insights for designing the matching and dispatching algorithm. Therefore, we design a vehicle value function to characterize the future value the vehicle can provide in the spatial-temporal state, and then use this value function to design the order matching and idle vehicle dispatching algorithm. In so doing, our algorithm can take into account the impacts of current decisions on the future rounds, and thus can improve the long-term social welfare.

In more detail, this paper advances the state of the art in the following ways. Firstly, we design a vehicle value function to characterize the future value the vehicle can provide. Then we consider the dispatching of idle vehicle to a zone as a virtual order. In so doing, we combine the order matching problem and idle vehicle dispatching problem as a whole order matching problem. We then convert the order matching problem to a bipartite graph maximum weight matching problem with the vehicle values as the edge weights. In so doing, we can complete the matching and dispatching quickly, and can avoid the issue that vehicles are concentrated in some zones. We run experiments to evaluate the proposed algorithm. The experimental results show that the proposed algorithm can outperform benchmark approaches in terms of the long-term social welfare. It can also improve the service ratio and achieve an effective utilization of idle vehicles.

The rest of this paper is organized as follows. We introduce the related work in Sect. 2. We then describe basic settings in Sect. 3, and introduce the proposed algorithms in Sect. 4. We provide experimental analysis in Sect. 5 and conclude the paper in Sect. 6.

2 Related Work

There exist many works about ride-hailing, especially in the order matching and idle vehicle dispatching issues [9,14]. For the order matching problem, the ride-hailing platform usually matches vehicles with orders to maximize profit, maximize order service ratio or minimize the travel distance. For maximizing profit, Cheng et al. [2] proposed a queueing theory-based order matching framework, while combining demand forecasts with predicted idle time slots to maximize the expected profits of the platform for each round. For maximizing the order

[2] In this paper, we assume that vehicles belong to the ride-hailing platform, and thus the social welfare consists of the profits of the ride-hailing platform and passengers.

service ratio, Garaix et al. [3] proposed an iterative algorithm to solve the order matching problem to maximize the order service ratio. For minimizing vehicle travel distance, Cao et al. [1] proposed a large-scale many-to-many matching algorithm based on spatial pruning techniques in the shared mobility environment to minimize the detour distance of vehicles.

There also exist some works about dispatching idle vehicles. Holler et al. [5] proposed a deep reinforcement learning based approach for solving the order matching and idle vehicle dispatching problems to maximize the profits of all vehicles. Haliem et al. [4] proposed a route planning framework based on demand forecasting and reinforcement learning to dynamically generate optimal routes. Liang et al. [6] integrated both real-time order matching and idle vehicle dispatching within a Markov decision process framework to increase drivers' profits while reducing the waiting time of passengers. Shou et al. [10] used Markov decision process to model an idle vehicle finding passengers and used inverse reinforcement learning to solve the reward function of the model.

However, to the best of our knowledge, existing works usually did not consider the impacts of current decision of order matching and idle vehicle dispatching on the future rounds, and did not maximize the long-term social welfare. Furthermore, existing works usually analyzed the order matching and dispatching problems separately. In this paper, we address the above issues by taking the spatio-temporal value of vehicles into account, and consider the order matching and idle vehicle dispatching as a whole to maximize the long-term social welfare.

3 Basic Settings

In this paper, we assume that all vehicles are managed by the online ride-hailing platform. In the ride-hailing system, firstly, passengers submit riding orders to the platform. Then the platform matches orders with available vehicles, and provide dispatching suggestions for idle vehicles.

Furthermore, we divide the entire time into T time steps (i.e., rounds) $\mathcal{T} = \{1, 2, \cdots T\}$. The geographical zone where passengers and vehicles are located is constructed as a road network, which is defined as follows:

Definition 1. ***Road Network.*** *The road network is defined as a weighted graph $G = (L, E)$ where L is the set of nodes and E is the set of edges on the road network. We use $dis\,(l_i, l_j)$ to represent the shortest path from node l_i to l_j. $dis\,(l_i, l_j)$ is also used to denote the weight of edge $\langle l_i, l_j \rangle$.*

The riding order is defined as follows:

Definition 2. ***Order.*** *An order $o \in \mathcal{O}$ is defined as a tuple $(l_o^p, l_o^d, t_o^r, t_o^w, val_o)$, where l_o^p, l_o^d is the pick-up and drop-off locations of order o respectively, t_o^r is the time when the order o is raised, t_o^w is the maximum time that a passenger in order o is willing to wait for the riding service, val_o is the highest price the passenger is willing to pay for the service, which can be regarded as the real value of this order for the passenger.*

Noted that in the realistic scenarios, passengers do not need to express the above value information when submitting orders. However, such information will be used to maximize social welfare. Therefore, similar to existing work [15,16], we assume that the passenger is required to submit this value for the riding service. Note that passengers may not reveal this information truthfully in order to obtain more profits. How to prevent passengers from dishonestly revealing their values is beyond the scope of this paper. In addition, we assume that when the order o is not matched within t_o^w time, the passenger is not willing to wait and the order will be cancelled.

Definition 3. ***Vehicle.*** *A vehicle $v \in \mathcal{V}$ is defined as a tuple (l_v, c_v), where l_v is the current position and c_v is the unit travel cost.*

Note that different types of vehicles may have different unit travel costs. When the platform matches orders with vehicles, it can only match the order with feasible vehicle, which is defined as follows.

Definition 4. ***Feasible Vehicle.*** *For an order o, a feasible vehicle v must serve a passenger before the maximum waiting time t_o^w, that is, $dis(l_v, l_o^p) \leq V_{avg} \cdot t_o^w$, where $dis\,(l_v, l_o^p)$ is the distance from the current position l_v of the vehicle to the pick-up position l_o^p of order o, and V_{avg} is the average speed of the vehicle.*

We now introduce the social welfare of the ride-hailing system, which consists of the profits of the passengers and the platform. The passenger's profit u_o is the passenger's true value for order o minus its payment for the riding service:

$$u_o = \begin{cases} val_o - p_o, & o \in O^w \\ 0, & o \notin O^w \end{cases} \tag{1}$$

where p_o is the price paid to the platform and $\mathcal{O}^w$ is the set of matched orders. When order o is not matched, the passenger's profit $u_o = 0$. The platform's profit is the sum of passengers' payments for the matched orders minus the costs of the corresponding vehicles to complete these orders over all time steps: $U_p = \sum_{t=1}^{T} \sum_{o \in \mathcal{O}_t^w} \left(p_o - C_{\Theta_t(o)}^o\right)$, where $\mathcal{O}_t^w$ is the set of matched orders at time step t, Θ_t denotes the matching results at time step t, and $\Theta_t(o) = v$ means that order o is matched with vehicle v. $C_{\Theta_t(o)}$ is the cost of vehicle $\Theta_t(o)$ completing order o, which is:$C_{\Theta_t(o)}^o = \left(dis\left(l_{\Theta_t(o)}, l_o^p\right) + dis\left(l_o^p, l_o^d\right)\right) \cdot c_{\Theta_t(o)}$.

We now give the definition of social welfare. Note that in this paper, we consider the long-term social welfare, which is the sum of the profits of all participants over the whole time steps, i.e., the summary profits of the platform and passengers, which is:

$$\begin{aligned} SW &= \sum_{t=1}^{T} \left(\sum_{o \in \mathcal{O}_t^w} (val_o - p_o) + \sum_{o \in \mathcal{O}_t^w} \left(p_o - C_{\theta_t(o)}^o\right) \right) \\ &= \sum_{t=1}^{T} \sum_{o \in \mathcal{O}_t^w} \left(val_o - C_{\Theta_t(o)}^o\right) \end{aligned} \tag{2}$$

4 The Algorithm

In this paper, we intend to maximize the long-term social welfare over all time steps. Therefore, we need to consider the impacts of current decision on the future matching. We design a vehicle state value function, which implies the ability of vehicles to make social welfare in different spatio-temporal states. Then based on the vehicle value function, we design the order matching and idle vehicle dispatching algorithm.

4.1 Vehicle Value Function

The vehicle value function shows the potential social welfare the vehicle can make in the future in the current spatial-temporal state, which is:

Definition 5. ***Vehicle Value Function.*** *The vehicle value function is $V(t, g, c)$, where $t \in T$ is the time step, $g \in G$ is the zone index at which the vehicle is located, and c is the vehicle unit travel cost.*

At each time step, the platform collects order information and makes decisions based on the current vehicle states, including whether the vehicle is matched with the order, whether the vehicle is stationary, or whether the vehicle is idle and dispatched to some place. Then the platform computes the social welfare of the current time step and enter into the next step. In such a multi-round matching process, we can capture how the current vehicle state can affect the future social welfare, i.e., the vehicle value function. This process is a sequential decision process, and thus we can model it as a Markov Decision Process (MDP) [11], and then compute the state value function by value iteration.

In the following, we give the description of MDP $M = \langle S, A, P, r, \gamma \rangle$.

State: The state of each vehicle is defined as a tuple $s = (t, g, c) \in S$, which is the vehicle value function.

Action: The action is $a \in A = \{a_1, a_2, a_3\}$, where a_1 means that the platform matches an order with a vehicle, a_2 means that the vehicle is stationary, and a_3 means that the platform dispatches an idle vehicle to an adjacent zone.

Reward: The reward r is the profit of the passengers and the platform when the action is taken. Note that the reward is 0 when the vehicle's action is stationary and negative (caused by the vehicle's travel cost) when the vehicle's action is dispatched. The reward value r is calculated as: $r = val_o - C_{\Theta(o)}$, where val_o is the passenger's value for an order o and $C_{\Theta(o)}$ is the cost required for the vehicle $\Theta(o)$ to complete the order o. For an order which lasts for T time steps, the cumulative reward R_γ is: $R_\gamma = \sum_{t=0}^{T-1} \gamma^t \frac{r}{T}$, where γ is a discount factor that decreases the impact of the past rewards, and is set to 0.9.

In this paper, we solve the MDP by using value iteration. The platform collects historical matching data to construct a historical state transition tuple $D = \{(s_i, a_i, r_i, s_i')\}$, which means that the agent acts a_i in the state s_i to obtain an instant reward r_i and transfer to the next state s_i'. Since different types of vehicles may have different unit travel cost, we use cost c to represent the type information of the vehicle, and therefore the state transition information of the same type of vehicle constitutes a value function data set. Referring to existing work [13], we assume that the online policy generating the state transfer data remains constant during the phase of learning the value function. In the following, we will omit the policy parameter π. State transition involves three actions, which are matching orders, stationery and idle vehicle dispatching.

When the action is to match an order, the vehicle receives an immediate reward R_γ and makes a state transfer. The Temporal difference (TD) update rule is:

$$V(s) = V(s) + \alpha\left[R_\gamma + \gamma V(s') - V(s)\right] \tag{3}$$

where $s = (t_0, g, c)$ is the state of the vehicle at the current time step, $s' = (t_3, g_{ld}, c)$ is the state of the vehicle after completing the matching order, in which t_3 is the time step when the passenger reaches the destination and g_{ld} is the index of the order destination zone.

When the action is being stationary, the immediate reward of the agent is 0. The TD update rule is:

$$V(s) = V(s) + \alpha\left[0 + \gamma V(s'') - V(s)\right] \tag{4}$$

Since the vehicle takes a stationary action, the position of the vehicle does not change, i.e., $s'' = (t_1, g, c)$.

When the action is to dispatch idle vehicle, we construct a virtual order where the value is 0, the origin of the order is g, and the destination of the order is one of the neighboring zones of g. The TD update rule is:

$$V(s) = V(s) + \alpha\left[{R_\gamma}' + \gamma V(s''') - V(s)\right] \tag{5}$$

where $s''' = (t_2, g''', c)$ is the state of the vehicle after the dispatching is completed, in which t_2 is the time step when the idle vehicle is dispatched to the destination, $g''' \in g_{near}$ is a neighboring zone of g.

Next, we describe how to compute the vehicle value function V. The platform first collects historical state transfer data, and then uses a dynamic programming based value iteration algorithm to backward recursively calculate value $V(s_i)$ in each state to obtain the vehicle value function $V(s)$. The details are shown in Algorithm 1.

4.2 Order Matching and Idle Vehicle Dispatching Algorithm Based on Value Function

After obtaining the vehicle value function, we now describe how to use this function to design the order matching and idle vehicle dispatching algorithm. The order matching and idle vehicle dispatching problem to maximize the social welfare is actually a bipartite graph maximum weight matching problem. At each time step t, the set of orders O_t and the set of vehicles V_t are two disjoint sets

Algorithm 1: Dynamic Programming based Value Iteration Algorithm(DPVI).

Input: History state transfer tuple $D = \{(s_i, a_i, r_i, s_i')\}$, where each state $s_i = (t_i, g_i, c)$ consists of the current time step, geographic zone index and cost of the vehicle.

Output: Vehicle value function V

1 **Initialize:** $\forall s, V(s) \leftarrow 0, N(s) \leftarrow 0$;
2 **for** $t = T - 1$ *to* 0 **do**
3 $\quad D_t \leftarrow \{(s_i, a_i, r_i, s_i') | \forall s_i = (t_i, g_i, c),\ t_i = t\}$;
4 $\quad$ **foreach** $(s_i, a_i, r_i, s_i') \in D_t$ **do**
5 $\quad\quad N(s_i) \leftarrow N(s_i) + 1$;
6 $\quad\quad V(s_i) \leftarrow V(s_i) + \frac{1}{N(s_i)} \left(\gamma^{\Delta t(a_i)} V(s_i') + R_\gamma(a_i) - V(s_i)\right)$
7 $\quad$ **end**
8 **end**
9 **return** V

of vertices of the bipartite graph. The weight of edge $\langle o, v \rangle$ is the difference ΔV of the value of vehicle v after completing order o, which is: $\Delta V = \gamma^{\Delta t_{o,v}} V(s') - V(s) + R_\gamma$, where s is the state when the vehicle v is matched with the order o and s' is the state when the vehicle v delivers the passenger corresponding to the order o to the destination, $\Delta t_{o,v}$ is the time required for vehicle v to complete this trip, and R_γ is the cumulative reward. The details of the value function-based order matching and idle vehicle dispatching algorithm are shown in Algorithm 2, which is named VFOMIVD for short.

In Algorithm 2, line 1 initializes the set of matched orders $\mathcal{O}^w$, the matching result Θ, the social welfare SW. For each time step of order matching and idle vehicle dispatching, lines 3 and 4 initialize the set of orders $\mathcal{O}_t$ and vehicle set $\mathcal{V}_t$. The order collection $\mathcal{O}_t$ contains orders submitted by passengers at the current time step and orders that have not been matched in previous steps and are still within the maximum waiting time. The vehicle set $\mathcal{V}_t$ includes vehicles that are not serving orders at the current step, i.e., idle vehicles. Lines 5 to 17 construct the bipartite graph. For each matching pair $\langle o, v \rangle$, the platform calculates the difference ΔV and use it as the weights of the edges of the bipartite graph.

Note that only the matching pair $\langle o, v \rangle$ with $\Delta V > 0$ is inserted into the bipartite graph, while if vehicle v cannot serve the passenger corresponding to order o within the maximum waiting time, its corresponding $\Delta V = 0$. For each idle vehicle v, the platform fictitiously creates several virtual orders o' from the current location of vehicle v to its neighboring zone $g \in g_{near}$. In so doing, the algorithm combines the order matching and idle vehicle dispatching as a whole. In the order matching, the platform calculates the difference $\Delta V'$ of its corresponding state value and insert it into the bipartite diagram. In lines 18, the platform solves the bipartite graph using the Kuhn-Munkres algorithm [8]. Line 19 calculates the social welfare for the current time step, and lines 20 to 22 record the results for the current time step. Finally, the platform updates the

Algorithm 2: Value Function based Order Matching and Idle Vehicle Dispatching Algorithm(VFOMIVD).

Input: Iterate through the set of orders $\mathcal{O}$, the set of vehicles $\mathcal{V}$, and the vehicle state value function V.
Output: The set of matched orders $\mathcal{O}^w$, matching result Θ, social welfare SW.

```
1  Initialize: O^w ← ∅, Θ ← ∅, SW = 0 ;
2  for t = 0 to T do
3      O_t ← {o ∈ O | t_o^r + t_o^w ≤ t + Δt};
4      V_t ← select_empty_vehicles (V, t);
5      Initialize the bipartite graph G = (O_t, V_t, E);
6      foreach ⟨o, v⟩ ∈ O_t × V_t do
7          calculate the state value difference ΔV corresponding to ⟨o, v⟩;
8          if ΔV > 0 then
9              assign the weights of edges ⟨o, v⟩ to ΔV and insert them into the
                bipartite graph;
10     end
11     foreach v ∈ V_t do
12         foreach g ∈ g_near do
13             calculate the difference ΔV' of the state value of the vehicle v from
                the current position to the neighboring zone g ;
14             if ΔV' > 0 then
15                 assign the weights of edges ⟨o', v⟩ to ΔV' and insert them into
                    the bipartite graph G;
16         end
17     end
18     O_t^w, Θ_t, V_t ← KM (G);
19     SW_t ← calculate_social_welfare (O_t^w, Θ_t);
20     O^w ← O^w ∪ O_t^w;
21     Θ ← Θ ∪ Θ_t;
22     SW ← SW + SW_t;
23     Update vehicle trip information in Θ_t;
24     O ← O \ O_t^w;
25 end
26 return O^w, Θ, SW
```

trips of the vehicles that have been matched with orders and eliminates the set of orders $\mathcal{O}_t^w$ that have been matched from the set of orders $\mathcal{O}$.

5 Experimental Analysis

In this section, we run experiments to evaluate the proposed algorithm based on the real taxi order data in New York city, which has been used by a large number of related works [9,13,15].

(1) Order Data. We collect taxi order data on Manhattan Island in June 2019 from New York City Taxi and Limousine Commission (TLC).[3] Each taxi order data contains departure and destination locations, order starting time, trip fare and trip mileage.
(2) Map Data: We use Manhattan taxi zone map provided by TLC as the map data, and we number each zone.
(3) Fuel Consumption Data. We cannot find the travel cost data of New York taxis. Instead, we collect the urban vehicle fuel consumption data of type M1 and M2 from China Automobile Fuel Consumption Query System[4] of the Ministry of Public Information of China to compute the vehicle cost in the below.
(4) The Shortest Path Cache. To ensure that the distance between any two nodes can be quickly queried during experiments, we pre-build the cache of the shortest path matrix and the shortest path distance matrix.
(5) Order Data Processing. We remove some orders with noises (i.e. orders with invalid fares, zero trip milage and so on). We eliminate the order data in those isolated zones. We count the number of orders per hour each day and we find that the number of orders on weekdays and weekends varies greatly over time. For consistency, we use the order data of weekdays (20 days in total) in the evaluation.

5.1 Experimental Settings

The number of orders for each hour of a weekday is also significantly different, and the performance of the algorithm in the peak period is more important. Furthermore, a large number of order data in the peak time period is also helpful to generate the vehicle value function. Therefore, we choose the time period (19:00 to 21:00) in the weekday for the evaluation. We now compute the average number of order data from 19:00 to 21:00 in these 20 days, and randomly choose the average number of one day as the order input. For other parameters, we set the length of each time step as 60 s. The maximum waiting time for passengers is chosen randomly from $\{3\,\text{min}, 4\,\text{min}, 5\,\text{min}, 6\,\text{min}, 7\,\text{min}, 8\,\text{min}\}$. The average vehicle travel speed V_{avg} is set to 7.2 mph. For each vehicle, the unit travel cost is randomly selected from $\{6, 8, 10\} \times 2.5/6.8/1.6\$/\text{km}$.[5] The initial location of the vehicle is randomly selected in Manhattan taxi zone map. In the experiments, we try different numbers of vehicles, which is increased from 1500 to 3000. For each experiment, we repeat it for 10 times and compute the average result.

[3] https://www1.nyc.gov/site/tlc/about/tlc-trip-record-data.page.
[4] https://yhgscx.miit.gov.cn/fuel-consumption-web/mainPage.
[5] The basic fare of New York taxi is 2.5$ per mile, the average fuel consumption is 6.8 L per one-hundred kilometres according to the above fuel consumption data, and 1.6 is the converting factor between mile and kilometre.

5.2 Evaluation of Order Matching and Idle Vehicle Dispatching Algorithm

In this section, we evaluate the proposed VFOMIVD algorithm against some benchmark algorithms.

Benchmark Algorithms and Metrics

(1) **mdp** [13]. The mdp algorithm also utilizes the vehicle value function to guide the order matching, but its vehicle state does not consider the variability of vehicles in terms of cost and also does not consider the dispatching of idle vehicles.
(2) **mT-Share** [7]. The mT-Share algorithm intends to minimize the vehicle travel cost. The order matching in the mT-Share algorithm uses a greedy algorithm to match orders with vehicles with the least extra cost.
(3) **Nearest-Matching**. The Nearest-Matching algorithm is widely used in industry (i.e., Uber), where the platform matches orders with the nearest vehicles.
(4) **Greedy&GPri** [16]. The Greedy&GPri algorithm greedily matches orders with vehicles with the highest social welfare iteratively and adopts a critical value-based pricing algorithm. The reason of choosing this greedy method is that existing research has showed that greedy method can perform well in the crowdsourcing tasks [12].

In terms of the evaluation metrics, in addition to the social welfare, we also investigate service ratio, which is the ratio of the number of matched orders to the total number of orders submitted by passengers.

Analysis of Experimental Results

The experimental results are shown in Fig. 1(a). We find that as the number of vehicles increases, the social welfare increases since more orders are served. We find that VFOMIVD algorithm achieves the highest social welfare. We also find that greedy based method Greedy&Gpri can perform well. We also look into the service ratio in Fig. 1(b). We find that the VFOMIVD algorithm achieves the maximum service ratio. Although the service ratio of algorithms such as mdp is close to that of the VFOMIVD algorithm when the number of vehicles increases, the social welfare of the VFOMIVD algorithm is still the largest. This may imply in our algorithm, vehicles are more likely to converge to zones where more social welfare is generated.

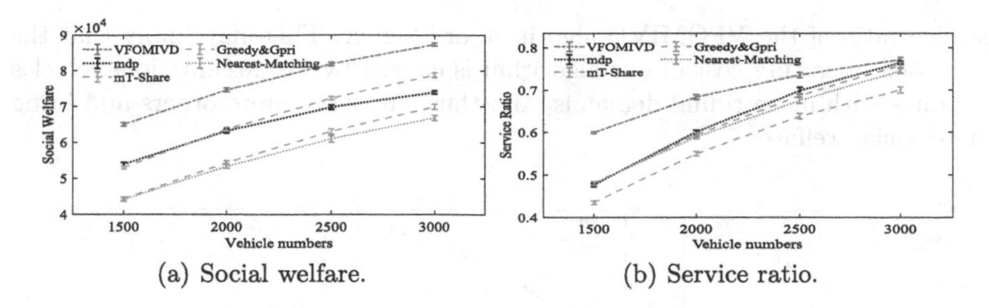

(a) Social welfare. (b) Service ratio.

Fig. 1. Experiments of order matching and idle vehicle dispatching algorithm.

5.3 Evaluation of Idle Vehicle Dispatching

In this section we further analyze the effectiveness of the idle vehicle dispatching algorithm. In order to evaluate the performance of the idle vehicle dispatching algorithm, we combine different benchmark dispatching algorithms with the order matching module of VFOMIVD to generate the benchmark algorithms.

Benchmark Algorithms and Metrics

1. **VFOM**. We remove the idle vehicle dispatching module of VFOMIVD algorithm (lines 12 to 19 in Algorithm 2) and keep the order matching module.
2. **VFOM-RD**. This algorithm adds random dispatching into VFOM algorithm, which randomly dispatches idle vehicles to their neighboring zones. Random dispatching has been used in related works [16].
3. **VFOM-ND**. It adds the nearest dispatching to the VFOM algorithm, which is a common dispatching algorithm used by companies (e.g., Uber) to dispatch idle vehicles to the nearest neighboring zone [3].

In addition to evaluating the performance on social welfare and service ratio, we consider one more metric to evaluate the idle vehicle dispatching algorithm, which is the platform operating cost, consisting of the costs of all served orders and idle vehicles travelling to dispatched zones over the whole time steps.

Analysis of Experimental Results

The experimental results are shown in Fig. 2(a). We find that VFOMIVD algorithm achieves the largest social welfare. As the number of vehicles increases, the social welfare obtained by all algorithms increases. We also find that the social welfare of VFOM algorithm (where no dispatching algorithm is used) and VFOM-RD is similar. This may imply that random dispatching is not beneficial for the utilization of idle vehicles. From Fig. 2(b), we find that the VFOMIVD algorithm achieves the maximum service ratio. This means that after using the proposed dispatching algorithm, the platform can serve more orders, and thus can achieve the maximum social welfare. From Fig. 2(c), we find that the platform operating cost of the VFOMIVD algorithm is higher than the VFOM algorithm. However, from Figs. 2(a) and 2(b) we find that the social welfare and service ratio of the VFOMIVD algorithm are higher. This may imply that the increased operating cost of our algorithm is caused by dispatching idle vehicles to zones with more riding demands, and thus can serve more orders and bring more social welfare.

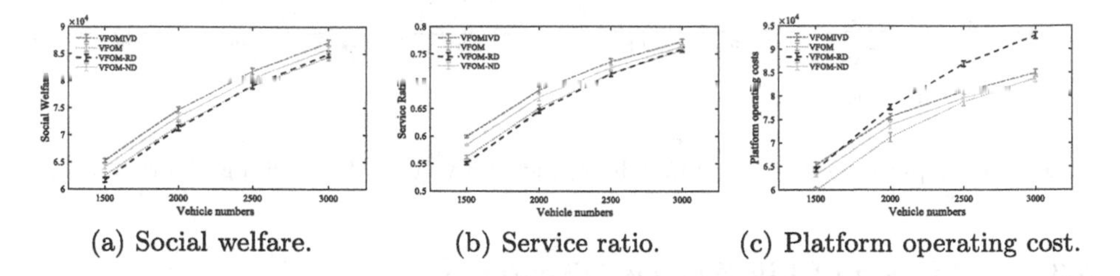

(a) Social welfare. (b) Service ratio. (c) Platform operating cost.

Fig. 2. Experiments of idle vehicle dispatching.

In summary, we find that because VFOMIVD algorithm takes into account the spatio-temporal value of vehicles and dispatches vehicles to zones where more vehicles are needed, it can utilize idle vehicles to serve more riding orders, and thus can increase social welfare.

6 Conclusion

In this paper, we proposed an order matching and idle vehicle dispatching algorithm to maximize the long-term social welfare in the ride-hailing system. By considering the impacts of current order matching and idle vehicle dispatching decisions on the future rounds, we design a vehicle value function, which can characterize the ability of the vehicle to make social welfare in the future spatio-temporal state. Based on the vehicle value function, we design the order matching and idle vehicle dispatching algorithm. Finally, we run extensive experiments to evaluate the proposed algorithm. The experimental results show that our algorithm can help online ride-hailing platforms to dispatch idle vehicles efficiently to improve the utilization of idle vehicles, and thus can increase the service ratio and social welfare.

Acknowledgement. This paper was funded by the Shenzhen Fundamental Research Program (Grant No. JCYJ20190809175613332), the Humanity and Social Science Youth Research Foundation of Ministry of Education (Grant No. 19YJC790111), the Philosophy and Social Science Post-Foundation of Ministry of Education (Grant No. 18JHQ060) and the Fundamental Research Funds for the Central Universities (WUT:2022IVB004).

References

1. Cao, B., Hong, F., Wang, K., Xu, J., Zhao, L., Fan, J.: Uroad: an efficient method for large-scale many to many ride sharing matching. J. Comput. Res. Dev. **56**(4), 866 (2019)

2. Cheng, P., Feng, C., Chen, L., Wang, Z.: A queueing-theoretic framework for vehicle dispatching in dynamic car-hailing. In: 35th International Conference on Data Engineering, pp. 1622–1625 (2019)
3. Garaix, T., Artigues, C., Feillet, D., Josselin, D.: Optimization of occupancy rate in dial-a-ride problems via linear fractional column generation. Comput. Oper. Res. **38**(10), 1435–1442 (2011)
4. Haliem, M., Mani, G., Aggarwal, V., Bhargava, B.: A distributed model-free ride-sharing approach for joint matching, pricing, and dispatching using deep reinforcement learning. IEEE Trans. Intell. Transp. Syst. **22**, 1–12 (2021)
5. Holler, J., et al.: Deep reinforcement learning for multi-driver vehicle dispatching and repositioning problem. In: 2019 IEEE International Conference on Data Mining, pp. 1090–1095 (2019)
6. Liang, E., Wen, K., Lam, W.H., Sumalee, A., Zhong, R.: An integrated reinforcement learning and centralized programming approach for online taxi dispatching. IEEE Trans. Neural Netw. Learn. Syst. 1 (2021)
7. Liu, Z., Gong, Z., Li, J., Wu, K.: Mobility-aware dynamic taxi ridesharing. In: 36th International Conference on Data Engineering, pp. 961–972 (2020)
8. Munkres, J.: Algorithms for the assignment and transportation problems. J. Soc. Ind. Appl. Math. **5**(1), 32–38 (1957)
9. Sharma, S.K., Routroy, S., Yadav, U.: Vehicle routing problem: recent literature review of its variants. Int. J. Oper. Res. **33**(1), 1–31 (2018)
10. Shou, Z., Di, X., Ye, J., Zhu, H., Zhang, H., Hampshire, R.: Optimal passenger-seeking policies on e-hailing platforms using Markov decision process and imitation learning. Transp. Res. Part C Emerg. Technol. **111**, 91–113 (2020)
11. Sutton, R.S., Barto, A.G.: Reinforcement Learning: An Introduction. MIT Press, Cambridge (2018)
12. Tong, Y., She, J., Ding, B., Chen, L., Wo, T., Xu, K.: Online minimum matching in real-time spatial data: experiments and analysis. Proc. VLDB Endow. **9**(12), 1053–1064 (2016)
13. Xu, Z., et al.: Large-scale order dispatch in on-demand ride-hailing platforms: a learning and planning approach. In: 24th ACM SIGKDD International Conference on Knowledge Discovery and Data Mining, pp. 905–913 (2018)
14. Yi, X., Yongxin, T., Wei, L.: Recent progress in large-scale ridesharing algorithms. J. Comput. Res. Dev. **57**(1), 32 (2020)
15. Zhao, H., Xiao, M., Wu, J., Liu, A., An, B.: Reverse-auction-based competitive order assignment for mobile taxi-hailing systems. In: 2019 Database Systems for Advanced Applications, pp. 660–677 (2019)
16. Zheng, L., Cheng, P., Chen, L.: Auction-based order dispatch and pricing in ridesharing. In: 35th International Conference on Data Engineering, pp. 1034–1045 (2019)

Privacy-Preserving Deep Learning in Internet of Healthcare Things with Blockchain-Based Incentive

Wenyuan Zhang[1,2], Peng Li[3], Guangjun Wu[1,2](✉), and Jun Li[1,2]

[1] Institute of Information Engineering, Chinese Academy of Sciences, Beijing 100093, China
{zhangwenyuan,wuguangjun,lijun}@iie.ac.cn

[2] School of Cyber Security, University of Chinese Academy of Sciences, Beijing 100049, China

[3] National Computer Network Emergency Response Technical Team/Coordination Center of China, CNCERT/CC, Beijing 100029, China
lipeng@cert.org.cn

Abstract. Privacy-preserving deep learning has drawn tremendous attention recently, especially in the IoHT-enabled medical field. As a representative, federated learning can guarantee the privacy of training data and training models, but there are still many security issues that are ignored. During the training process, the content of parameters may be tampered with to affect the overall accuracy, and the parameter server may also be malicious. In this paper, we propose a blockchain architecture to solve these problems, which uses blockchain-based payment incentive method to force miners and medical institutions to behave honestly, thereby speeding up convergence. In addition, considering that the miners are disconnected in the real network environment, which leads to the interruption of the consensus protocol and affects the convergence speed, we design the Robust Proof-of-Stake (RPoS) consensus based on PVSS to solve this problem. Experiments show that the incentive mechanism we design can improve the accuracy of predictions and reduce the possibility of dishonesty among participants.

Keywords: Blockchain · Federated learning · Internet of Healthcare Things (IoHT) · Proof of Stake (PoS) · Incentives · Privacy protection

1 Introduction

Internet of Healthcare Things (IoHT) devices [2] have become the focus of attention in the healthcare field. The booming development of the Internet of Things provides a new paradigm for the acquisition of medical data [8]. The medical data can be obtained by the lightweight medical physical devices, such as wearable medical device, bracelets, and smart chest patches. Usually, the process relays on the dedicated sensor systems [9], embedded microprocessors (e.g., MCU, and SoC), and mature wireless network standards (e.g., 5G, ZigBee, and NB-IoT)

G. Memmi et al. (Eds.): KSEM 2022, LNAI 13370, pp. 302–315, 2022.
https://doi.org/10.1007/978-3-031-10989-8_24

to achieve real-time collection, calculation, and sharing of health information, such as blood oxygen level, blood pressure, weight, and heart rate. Moreover, the medical data capture systems would generate massive and accurate EHRs [1], and the EHRs contains a large of amount of high-quality valuable data for medical institutions.

Machine learning tasks aimed at analyzing user health status, predicting diseases, etc. have made significant progress in recent years [4,18], and their training process requires a large amount of high-quality data as training samples, which often come from the own data centers of hospitals. The rise of IoHT has provided more accurate data for the prediction of medical institutions [21]. However, there is a problem of data silos among medical institutions, and the privacy of medical data makes institutions reluctant to share their data directly. Federal learning was proposed to solve this problem [10]. Medical institutions do not need to share data, but can make more accurate predictions or classifications only by providing model parameters.

However, traditional federated learning relies on a centralized parameter server for parameter aggregation. Once a physical failure or Byzantine attack occurs, federated learning will face the risk of single-point failure. In addition, in the process of sharing parameters, federated learning can infer the original data distribution [13], which is intolerable in the medical field due to the importance of personal medical data privacy. To address the above two problems, many works have introduced blockchain as a decentralized solution [6,12]. In the blockchain-based method, the miners can aggregate parameters in distributed ways, and the systems ensure the correctness of aggregated content and the honesty of miners through consensus protocol. However, most of the existing schemes adopt the PoW consensus [3,19]. The PoW consensus will conduct the meaningless hash operations and consume a lot of energy with the poor performance. Although PoS consensus can solve the high energy consumption and low throughput problems of PoW, it cannot tolerate nodes offline when generating random seeds negotiated by all participants. If the miner nodes go offline during the consensus execution process, it will not only bring the blockchain system to a halt, but also significantly slow down the rate of federal learning convergence. Therefore, we design a robust consensus based on PoS improvement, Robust Proof of Stake (RPoS), which allows nodes participating in the consensus to go offline or enter during the execution of the consensus.

Incentive mechanisms for federated learning include reputation mechanisms [20], optimal pricing strategies [17], and game theoretical model [5]. However, in a federated learning system that has not yet involved a buyer's market, the above incentive mechanisms-based works lose their underlying assumptions. We hope that medical institutions can be motivated enough to participate in the federated learning before training. Therefore, based on the above two points, we design a blockchain-based payment incentive method. On the one hand, it provides token incentives for medical institutions that join a training *Epoch*. On the other hand, miners can point out parameters that tend to be malicious, and the miners will be rewarded with tokens after multi-party verification. Furthermore, in order to prevent frequent or malicious designations, miners will be punished more than rewards when attacked the system. The punishment mechanism will greatly reduce the possibility of malicious miners participating in RPoS, and gradually lose their own tokens as malicious behavior accumulates.

The contributions of the paper are summarized as follows:

- We propose a novel blockchain-enabled secure federated learning architecture for IoHT, which guarantees the security of the federated learning parameters transfer process and the robustness of the overall architecture, preventing the single point of failure of the system. In addition, we introduce differential privacy (DP) integration in the architecture to protect the security of parameters transfer process.
- We propose robust consensus RPoS, which can tolerate nodes being offline during the consensus process to improve the system availability. The number of miner tokens relied on in RPoS can be dynamically adjusted according to the incentive mechanism we design.
- We design a blockchain-based payment incentive method, which includes two parts: Participate Incentive Mechanism (PIM) and Aggregation Incentives Mechanism (AIM). PIM realizes incentives for medical institutions to participate in the training process and provides continuous payment incentives. AIM allows miners to actively check for potential privacy leaks risk and provide payment incentives for well-behaved miners.

The rest of the paper is organized as follows. Section 2 illustrates our system architecture and the RPoS consensus algorithm. Section 3 introduces the designed federated learning incentive algorithm. Experiments and Analysis are elaborated in Sect. 4. Finally, we summarize our work and present a future outlook in Sect. 5.

2 Proposed Method

2.1 System Overview

As a distributed trusted architecture, blockchain has been widely used in different fields such as privacy protection [16], access control [15] etc. For federated learning in the IoHT-enabled medical data sharing field, we design a blockchain-based payment incentive architecture based on the good performance of blockchain in terms of privacy, incentives and fairness. The architecture consists the following components:

Medical Institutions: Medical institutions refer to the local servers of major hospitals or medical research units, which own local heterogeneous medical data belonging to the medical institutions. Using $S = \{S_1, S_2, \ldots, S_N\}$ to denote a set of servers with a total number of N. Medical institutions act as local training nodes for federated learning.

IoHT Devices: IoHT devices are mobile medical devices used to collect different modalities of medical data from different patients. They communicate with designated medical institution servers various network protocols, and in order to protect the privacy of patients, differential privacy (DP) is used to process patient data. Assuming that there are p IoHT devices in total, we denote the set of IoHT devices as $E = \{E^1, E^2, \ldots, E^p\}$, and the IoHT devices set whose ownership belongs to the medical institution server D_i as $E_i = \{E_i^1, E_i^2, \ldots, E_i^{x_i}\}$, x_i represents the total number of IoHT devices owned by institution i, where $p = \sum_{i=1}^{N} x_i$.

Parameter Server: Parameter server is a server used for parameters release for system initialization and distribution of authentication keys for all parties. Generally, it is held by credible institutions, such as government supervision agencies, market functional departments, etc.

Miners: Miners are full-node servers participating in the consensus of the public blockchain. They can be the server devices with strong computing and storage capabilities. There are m miners total, which are represented as $M = \{M_1, M_2, \ldots, M_m\}$. Miners form a set of accounting committees, all miner nodes will initially receive the random seed ρ sent by the parameter server. Miners need to correctly perform model parameter aggregation tasks by competing for the right to produce blocks in each *Epoch*. Miners also serve as the communication relay task for IoHT devices, so that medical institutions can collect medical data belonging to their own devices more quickly.

Blockchain: Blockchain is an immutable data structure. Its full nodes are stored in the Miner servers, and the light nodes are stored in the IoHT devices. The block data of the full nodes contain information such as timestamp, transaction Merkle tree, hash value of the previous block, and smart contracts. It is a secure distributed ledger that records the federated learning process.

Healthcare Coin (HCoin): *HCoin* is the token circulating within the system. The *HCoin* is used to incentivize honest participants and punish evil adversaries. After all participants are authenticated, the initial *HCoin* is provided by the parameter server.

Epoch: *Epoch* is the round of stake change of the blockchain system, and it is also a round of model aggregation of federated learning. Each *Epoch* will generate the random seed ρ of the next round and the list of participating miners. During this period, the consensus protocol supports dynamic entry and exit of miners.

Before starting the introduction of the whole process, we formally define the process of federated learning. The medical institution server S_i saves its local data $\mathbb{D}_i$, and the model parameter trained by the local training set (x_i, y_i) from *Epoch* t as ω_i^t, which is calculated by local training process $\omega_i^t \leftarrow \omega_i^{t-1} - \eta \nabla l(\omega_i^{t-1}, b)$, where $l(\cdot, \cdot)$ is loss function, k is the number of training samples, where $n = \sum_{i \in N} n_i$, $n_i = |\mathbb{D}_i|$, n is the number of training data. In each *Epoch* t, medical institutions add noise to ω_i^t through differential privacy technology based on *Laplace* random noise to protect the data privacy of federated learning parameters in the blockchain network. Medical institutions need to train a classifier $f(\omega^t)$, where ω^t is the globally aggregated parameter. The parameter aggregation function is

$$\omega^t = \sum_{i=1}^{N} \frac{n_i}{n} \omega_i^t. \tag{1}$$

The parameters ω^t obtained by training are packaged into transactions by miners. After miners compete for the right to produce block, the leader sets the results to the blockchain, and each medical institution downloads the aggregated parameters as the initialization parameters for the next *Epoch* of training.

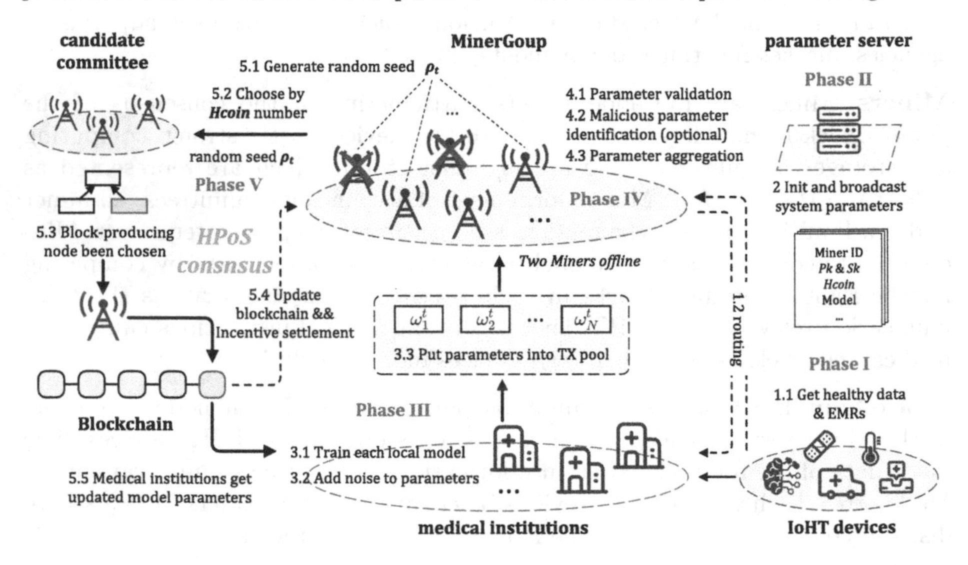

Fig. 1. Architecture of blockchain-enabled secure federated learning for IoHT.

2.2 Model Design

In this section, we discuss the architecture's workflow of the architecture shown in Fig. 1.

Phase I: Medical Data Collection. Medical data comes from IoHT devices in different medical institutions and static medical devices within institutions. The ownership of different IoHT devices belongs to their respective medical institutions, and medical institutions have their private keys Sk_i^s. When the IoHT devices collect a certain amount of data, it will actively decide whether to directly transmit the data encrypted by the public key Pk_i^s to the medical institution according to its location. The miner servers act as relay nodes. The IoHT devices will store all the block headers as light nodes, simply sort according to the miner asset field of the block header, and sort according to the distance of the miner server, and select the appropriate miner group server for forwarding. After forwarding the encrypted data of the IoHT device, each time it is correctly forwarded, it will get additional *HCoin* incentives for the IoHT device.

Phase II: Parameter Initialization of All Parties. The parameter server obtains the needs of all parties and formulates the training objectives of federated learning. After specifying the list of participants in this training, the server requests the identity public key Pk_I^s from all parties. After comparing and verifying the identity private key Sk_I^s stored locally on the parameter server, the parameter server will initialize the parameter set, model and start *HCoin* and send it to the medical institutions of all parties through the blockchain smart contract. In addition, the parameter server broadcasts the public key set of medical institutions participating in the training to the blockchain miner participants, and confirms the unique ID of each miner node.

Phase III: Local Training of Medical Institutions. The medical institutions that obtain the initialization parameters start local training, and encapsulate the training result of an *Epoch* and the result ω_i^t signed with the private key Sk_i^s into a transaction and put it into the blockchain transaction pool. The training results need to be processed with differential privacy (DP) to prevent the parameters from being stolen by adversaries during the transmission process and revealing user privacy:

$$D' = D + Laplace(\Delta f/\varepsilon), \tag{2}$$

where $\Delta f = \max_{D,D'} \|f(D) - F(D')\|_1$, D is the parameter ω_i^t that needs to be shared, and $f(\cdot)$ represents the query function. Each correct submission of the medical institution will accumulate incentives and receive rich *HCoin* rewards after the training.

Phase IV: Distributed Aggregation of Parameters. After miners receive the transactions in the transaction pool, they first verify the collected transactions through the public key set obtained from the parameter server, and then check whether they are repeatedly obtained after the verification is passed. During this time, miners can use publicly available methods to test shared parameters for malicious tendencies. A correct identification will make the miner get a high profit, otherwise a large amount of *HCoin* will be deducted if it is verified as false. After the pre-specified parameter collection time is reached, the miners execute the parameter aggregation algorithm to obtain ω^t, and package the aggregated parameters, timestamps, the number of miners' *HCoin*, and the identification proof into a block for broadcasting.

Phase V: Execution of Consensus. By executing the RPoS consensus, a random seed ρ_t is obtained, and a block-producing node selection algorithm based on the number of miners' *HCoin* is performed, and block-producing node is selected from the miner committee. Miners who have obtained the right to produce blocks will broadcast the results of this *Epoch* of training and broadcast the blocks to the entire network. After the global blockchain generates a new block, it triggers the requests contract of the medical institutions, jumps to **Phase III**, and performs the next training until the model converges.

2.3 RPoS Consensus

The consensus protocol is the core of the blockchain system and determines the security of the federated learning architecture. A robust consensus protocol can have dynamic joinability, which can prevent the system from being shut down due to node offline, and greatly improve the training time of federated learning. Compared with PoS, RPoS extends its block-producing node selection algorithm, guarantees the robustness of candidate nodes in generating globally consistent random numbers. The specific process of this consensus protocol is described below.

When the parameter server initializes the system, the initial random seed ρ_0 and the miner's initial *HCoin* are hard-coded for the blockchain system. Miner nodes generate their own public and private key pairs. The number of *HCoin* of each miner is represented as $minerstake_i$, and this *HCoin* holding determines the probability of the block-producing node becoming the block-producing node in each *Epoch*.

RPoS block-producing node selection algorithm is divided into two parts: (1) all miners cooperate to generate an uncontrollable random seed ρ according to the initial value, (2) randomly select the block-producing node based on the random number ρ and the number of *HCoin* held by miners $minerstake_i$.

Generate Random Seed ρ: PoS needs to randomly determine a block-producing node based on a globally known random seed before each *Epoch* of block production according to the stake of the participating miners. But unfortunately, the random seed cannot be obtained by direct sharing. The adversary can infer the next largest possible block-producing node according to the rights and interests held by all parties, and attack the miner node centrally, which will cause the blockchain system to face huge risk. We want to obtain a pre-agnostic random seed that is known to the block candidate committee before each block production starts. In addition, during the generation of the random seed, if the miner node goes offline due to network problems or hostile behavior, it will not adversely affect the generation of the random seed. Therefore, we designed a random seed generation algorithm based on publicly verifiable secret sharing (PVSS [11]), which can tolerate k-m-1 nodes offline during the random seed generation process for k miner participants. It should be noted that we do not modify PVSS, only use it. The algorithm details can refer to Algorithm 1.

All k miner nodes that are expected to participate in the next block competition form a node committee, which is represented as $MinerGroup = \{M_1, M_2, \ldots, M_k\}$, and M_i will generate a random string s_i and a random number $nonce_i$. Then use $share(k, s_i)$ from PVSS to generate shares $\sigma_1^i, \sigma_2^i, \ldots, \sigma_k^i$, each *share* σ_k^i is signed by private key of M_i. M_i broadcasts the signed $share(k, s_i)$ and *commitment* $com(nonce_i, s_i)$ to the blockchain.

Algorithm 1: Generate random seed ρ_t

Input: $MinerGroup = \{M_1, M_2, \ldots, M_k\}$, threshold m, the public-private key pair set $\{(Pk_1, Sk_1), (Pk_2, Sk_2), \ldots, (Pk_k, Sk_k)\}$ for $MinerGroup$, initialization $\rho_t \leftarrow 0$, *Epoch* t;

Output: random seed ρ_t;

```
1  for each Miner_i, i = 1 to k do
2      s_i ← M_i;
3      nonce_i ← M_i;
4      {σ_1^i, σ_2^i, ..., σ_k^i} ← share(k, s_i);
5      {C(σ_1^i), C(σ_2^i), ..., C(σ_k^i)} ← Sk_i;
6      Broadcast com(nonce_i, s_i), {C(σ_1^i), C(σ_2^i), ..., C(σ_k^i)};
7  end
8  for each Miner_j, j = 1 to k do
9      if M_j finished its broadcast then
10         open(nonce_j, s_j) ← M_j;
11         Broadcast open(nonce_j, s_j);
12     end
13 end
14 wait until time.spend > 4/5 |t|;
15 for each Miner_i, i = 1 to k do
16     for x = 1 to k − 1 do
17         if open(nonce_x, s_x) don't exist after check then
18             M_i submits σ_i^x;
19         end
20     end
21     for unchecked s_x do
22         wait m − 1 σ_1^x to m−1;
23         {σ_1^x, σ_2^x, ..., σ_{m−1}^x} ← Pk_x;
24         s_x ← rec(σ_1^x, σ_2^x, ..., σ_m^x);
25     end
26     wait until all s_x have been checked or recovered;
27     for v = 1 to k do
28         ρ_t ← s_v ⊕ ρ_t;
29     end
30 end
31 return ρ_t;
```

After generating cryptographic primitives, M_i generates an *open* for its *commitment*, and broadcasts $open(nonce_i, s_i)$ to the blockchain to expose its *commitment*.

After a time threshold ($4/5\,|t|$ is taken in this article), if $MinerGroup$ has not yet received the *open* of x, it means that M_x failed to broadcast $open(nonce_x, s_x)$, and all M_i submit σ_i^x at this time. When m *shares* $\sigma_1^x, \sigma_2^x, \ldots, \sigma_m^x$ are received, each M_i can restore s_x through $rec(\sigma_1^x, \sigma_2^x, \ldots, \sigma_m^x)$, that is, through the process tolerates k-m-1 miners going offline after generating a shared local cryptographic random string. After *MinerGroup* has collected all random strings, it can uniformly generate an unpredictable random seed ρ_t within the *Epoch* t.

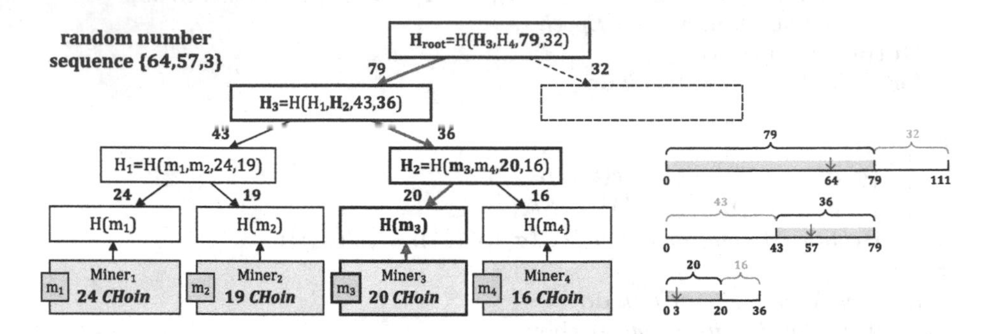

Fig. 2. Selection of block-producing node.

Randomly Select the Block-Producing Node: In order to incentivize honest miner nodes, we select the top 30% miners with *HCoin* as the candidate committee, and sort by referring to the unique ID of miner nodes. Miners are leaf nodes of the merkle tree. As shown in Fig. 2, the miner and the *HCoin* it owns form a merkle tree. Different from the merkle tree in the transaction, this data structure is only used to select miners and does not store transaction information. All miners use the random seed ρ_t to generate a same *random number sequence* (because of the same random seed ρ_t), the number of random numbers contained in it is the number of layers of the merkle tree. The number of *HCoin* of each miner is stored in the leaf node. The parent node of the two nodes stores the *hash* of the sum of the *hash* of the child nodes and the sum of the equity values of the two child nodes. Choosing between left and right subtrees based on weights as the next goal.

The random seed generates a random number within the range of the sum of the stakes of the left and right subtrees of the node. We stipulate that when the random number is smaller than the larger equity value, the child node corresponding to the larger equity is selected. This method ensures that the block-producing node is selected according to the probability of the stake size. As shown in the Fig. 2, *random number sequence* $\{64, 57, 3\}$ is generated according to the stake, miners choose left, right, and left subtrees, respectively, and finally decides that the block-producing node is $Miner_3$.

3 Algorithm

The incentive mechanism makes the participants of various medical institutions more willing to participate in the federated learning process, which makes the training data sources more abundant, and the model classification or prediction is more accurate. The participation incentive mechanism (PIM) is set up to motivate all parties to participate. Use blockchain to perform distributed processing of federated learning aggregation to prevent the risk of single-point failure of the parameter aggregation server, which depends on the honest behavior of miners. In order to motivate miners to complete the aggregation task faster and prevent miners from performing wrong aggregation, set Aggregated Incentive Mechanism (AIM).

Participation Incentive Mechanism (PIM): The parameter server provides a market platform for training budgets and training results for medical institutions. After setting the training target, the parameter server will formulate the expected market profit W of this training, and set the start-up capital budget SC accordingly. The establishment of the SC is fair, so the SC of the parties are equal. In order to prevent the participants from arbitrage through SC and withdraw in the middle of training, a certain amount of deposit DC is set for each party, and a decay factor is provided to represent the contribution of each party in the training process. We use π to denote the amount returned to each participant after completing a federated learning

$$\pi = SC + DC + \sum_{t=1}^{T} att(t) * \delta - pun(t) * \delta, \tag{3}$$

where T denotes the total number of training *Epoch*, and δ represents the incentive unit price, which is determined by the expected market profit and is defined by the parameter server in the initial process of a *Epoch* of training. $att(t)$ is the revenue decay factor function, t represents the training *Epoch*, the function obeys the Log-logistic distribution, denoted as

$$att(t) = 1 - \frac{(\gamma * t)^{\beta}}{\alpha^{\beta} + (\gamma * t)^{\beta}}, \tag{4}$$

where α is the model convergence rate factor, β is the convergence decay threshold factor, and γ is the time gain factor.

$pun(t)$ is the penalty decay factor function, denoted as

$$pun(t) = \frac{\beta * (\frac{\alpha}{\gamma})^{\beta} * t^{\beta-1}}{(b + t^{\beta})^{2}}, \tag{5}$$

where b is the penalty factor, $b = (\alpha/\gamma)^{\beta}$.

Aggregation Incentives Mechanism (AIM): The blockchain miners provide a decentralized and secure model aggregation and depository platform for federated learning. The miners play full nodes of the blockchain, which need to verify the parameters of the parameter pool and aggregate according to the rules. Then They implement the consensus protocol honestly. The AIM is divided into two parts, miners' verification revenue and the aggregated *HCoin* incentives from the RPoS.

After receiving the local parameters trained by medical institutions, miners need to check the parameters, including whether there are risks such as abnormal parameter content and poisoning attack [7]. As long as a problem is found during inspection [14], the miner activates the contract to record the problem of the server, and forms a transaction to compete with the aggregation parameters for the right to produce a block. After the transaction content is agreed by most miners in the blockchain consensus stage, the miner can get the check reward *CHR*. At the same time, if the content is verified as wrong and the miner competes to obtain the block right, the parameter content of the server will be missing in this aggregation, which will affect the convergence of the training set and slow down the training speed. Therefore, The miner will be deducted the same value of *HCoin*. *CHR* is calculated as follows:

$$CHR(t) = \lambda * att(t) * \delta, \tag{6}$$

where λ is the test excitation gain factor.

The correct model parameter aggregation of miners is critical to the security of the entire architecture. After miners complete the parameter content verification, model parameter aggregation begins. Correct aggregation will give miners the right to correctly participate in RPoS. When miners obtain the right to produce block, they will receive the block reward *BLR* given by the blockchain system. Because the RPoS consensus calculates the random seed based on the reward and determines the block generation probability of the block, and the income of the miners' work are related to the expected market profit W, which is expressed as:

$$BLR = \vartheta * W, \tag{7}$$

where ϑ is the price influence factor determined by the parameter server based on the current expected market profit dynamics.

4 Experiment Evaluations

We use the MNIST dataset to verify the plausibility of the proposed incentive mechanism. The MNIST dataset is a well-known multi-class image dataset that is often used to test the accuracy of algorithms. We set up 20 medical institutions to jointly perform a classification task.

We verify the rationality of the PIM algorithm firstly. As shown in Fig. 3, in the process of improving the accuracy of the model, the accuracy of the model rises rapidly in the previous *Epoch*, and then rises steadily with little room for improvement. We compress the *HCoin* incentive amount into the range [0, 1]. Experiments show that in the fast-rising part, the system has greater incentives for medical institutions. As the model tends to be stable, the incentive *HCoin* also decreases. Similarly, the penalty *HCoin* peak at the stage where the accuracy rate rose the fastest. At this time, if the medical institution do evil, such as withdrawing or publishing malicious parameters, it will be punished much higher than other *Epoch*. This also reflects that the training parties contribute more to the model accuracy in the early stages of training.

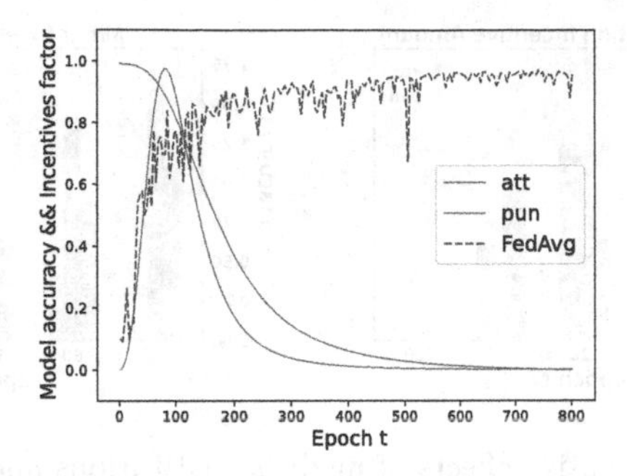

Fig. 3. Incentive curve for medical institutions.

Next we simulate a situation where a medical institution continuously publishes malicious parameters during training. As shown in Fig. 4, we simulated 5% and 10% of medical institutions doing evil respectively. The experimental results show that the larger the proportion of evil medical institutions, the overall accuracy and convergence speed will be greatly reduced. Later, because of the introduction of the AIM algorithm, the simulated miners are willing to verify the parameters of the medical institution after obtaining the parameters, and can find the real problems of the parameters. Experiments have shown that by incentivizing miners to discover malicious parameters, the accuracy of the model will be greatly improved, and it will converge quickly.

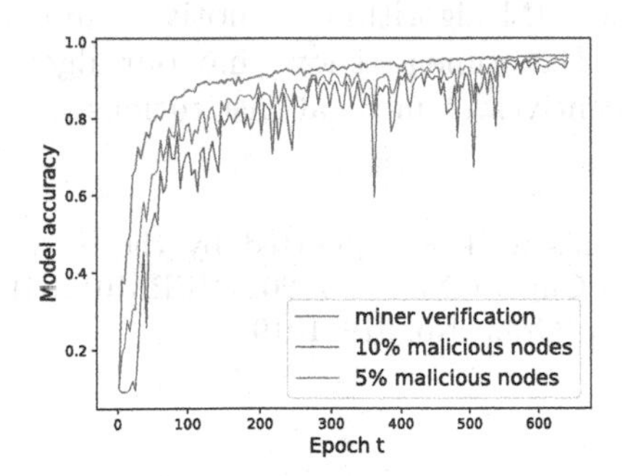

Fig. 4. Incentive curve for medical institutions.

Figure 5 can reflect the average profit and punishment *HCoin* of medical institution nodes in different *Epoch*. The experiment reflects that in the middle and early stages of training, the punishment will be greater than the profit. The gap between the two is narrowed in the later stage of training. The figure on the right shows the expected relationship between the incentive *HCoin* that Miners can obtain in the face of different proportions of malicious medical institutions. Experiments show that in the presence of malicious medical institutions, Miners' incentives will be far greater than when the medical institutions are all honest.

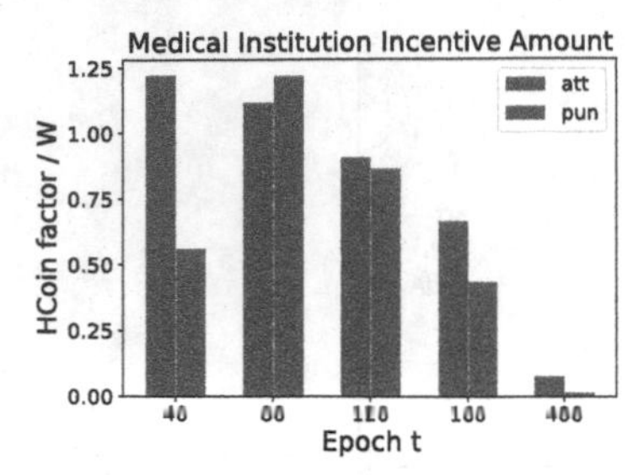

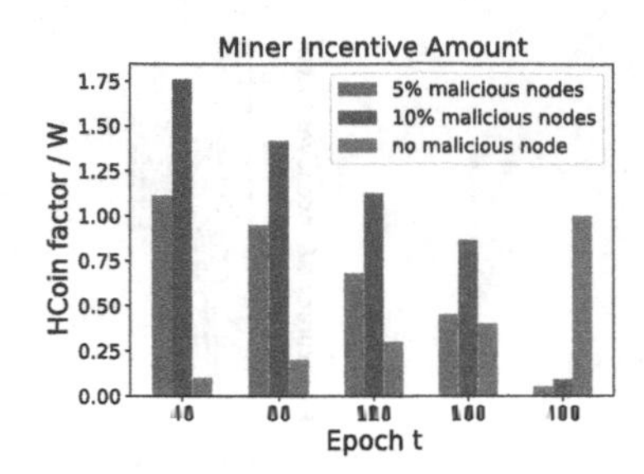

Fig. 5. Incentive effects of medical institutions and miners.

So Miners tend to find problematic parameters. In addition, Miners can get more benefits from discovering malicious parameters in the early stage of training, and can get more block rewards in the later stage. This incentivizes Miners to be honest throughout the training period with a token-incentive approach.

5 Conclusions

In this paper, we propose an architecture of blockchain-enabled secure federated learning for IoHT, it ensures the security of shared parameters of medical institutions in federated learning. We design the RPoS consensus, using the PVSS method to tolerate miners offline during the consensus process. In addition, we design the PIM algorithm to motivate medical institutions to participate in training and design the AIM algorithm to motivate miners to discover parameter security problems. Experiments show that our algorithms have significant advantages for the incentives of medical institutions and the improvement of training accuracy.

Acknowledgements. This work is supported by the National Key Research and Development Program of China (Grant No. 2021YFB3101305), National Natural Science Foundation of China (Grant No. 61931019).

References

1. Acampora, G., Cook, D.J., Rashidi, P., Vasilakos, A.V.: A survey on ambient intelligence in healthcare. Proc. IEEE **101**(12), 2470–2494 (2013)
2. Asif-Ur-Rahman, M., et al.: Toward a heterogeneous mist, fog, and cloud-based framework for the internet of healthcare things. IEEE Internet Things J. **6**(3), 4049–4062 (2018)
3. Bao, X., Su, C., Xiong, Y., Huang, W., Hu, Y.: FLchain: a blockchain for auditable federated learning with trust and incentive. In: 2019 5th International Conference on Big Data Computing and Communications (BIGCOM), pp. 151–159. IEEE (2019)
4. Cai, C., Niu, M., Liu, B., Tao, J., Liu, X.: TDCA-NET: time-domain channel attention network for depression detection. In: Proceedings of Interspeech, pp. 2511–2515 (2021)

5. Hu, Q., Wang, S., Xiong, Z., Cheng, X.: Nothing wasted: full contribution enforcement in federated edge learning. IEEE Trans. Mob. Comput. (2021)
6. Li, J., et al.: Blockchain assisted decentralized federated learning (BLADE-FL): performance analysis and resource allocation. IEEE Trans. Parallel Distrib. Syst. **33**(10), 2401–2415 (2021)
7. Li, X., Qu, Z., Zhao, S., Tang, B., Lu, Z., Liu, Y.: Lomar: a local defense against poisoning attack on federated learning. IEEE Trans. Dependable Secure Comput. (2021)
8. Madushanka, A., Dissanayake, U., Ramanayake, K., Hemali, S., Kathriarachchi, R.: The internet of things for health care (2020)
9. Mills, J., Hu, J., Min, G.: Communication-efficient federated learning for wireless edge intelligence in IoT. IEEE Internet Things J. **7**(7), 5986–5994 (2019)
10. Rieke, N., et al.: The future of digital health with federated learning. NPJ Digit. Med. **3**(1), 1–7 (2020)
11. Schoenmakers, B.: A simple publicly verifiable secret sharing scheme and its application to electronic voting. In: Wiener, M. (ed.) CRYPTO 1999. LNCS, vol. 1666, pp. 148–164. Springer, Heidelberg (1999). https://doi.org/10.1007/3-540-48405-1_10
12. Shayan, M., Fung, C., Yoon, C.J., Beschastnikh, I.: Biscotti: a blockchain system for private and secure federated learning. IEEE Trans. Parallel Distrib. Syst. **32**(7), 1513–1525 (2020)
13. Song, C., Ristenpart, T., Shmatikov, V.: Machine learning models that remember too much. In: Proceedings of the 2017 ACM SIGSAC Conference on Computer and Communications Security, pp. 587–601 (2017)
14. Tolpegin, V., Truex, S., Gursoy, M.E., Liu, L.: Data poisoning attacks against federated learning systems. In: Chen, L., Li, N., Liang, K., Schneider, S. (eds.) ESORICS 2020. LNCS, vol. 12308, pp. 480–501. Springer, Cham (2020). https://doi.org/10.1007/978-3-030-58951-6_24
15. Wang, S., Wu, G., Ning, Z., Li, J.: Blockchain enabled privacy preserving access control for data publishing and sharing in the internet of medical things. IEEE Internet Things J. **9**(11), 8091–8104 (2021)
16. Wu, G., Wang, S., Ning, Z., Zhu, B.: Privacy-preserved EMR information publishing and sharing: a blockchain-enabled smart healthcare system. IEEE J. Biomed. Health Inform. (2021)
17. Zhan, Y., Li, P., Qu, Z., Zeng, D., Guo, S.: A learning-based incentive mechanism for federated learning. IEEE Internet Things J. **7**(7), 6360–6368 (2020)
18. Zhang, C., Gao, X., Ma, L., Wang, Y., Wang, J., Tang, W.: GRASP: generic framework for health status representation learning based on incorporating knowledge from similar patients. In: Proceedings of the AAAI Conference on Artificial Intelligence, vol. 35, pp. 715–723 (2021)
19. Zhang, H., Li, G., Zhang, Y., Gai, K., Qiu, M.: Blockchain-based privacy-preserving medical data sharing scheme using federated learning. In: Qiu, H., Zhang, C., Fei, Z., Qiu, M., Kung, S.-Y. (eds.) KSEM 2021. LNCS (LNAI), vol. 12817, pp. 634–646. Springer, Cham (2021). https://doi.org/10.1007/978-3-030-82153-1_52
20. Zhang, J., Wu, Y., Pan, R.: Incentive mechanism for horizontal federated learning based on reputation and reverse auction. In: Proceedings of the Web Conference 2021, pp. 947–956 (2021)
21. Zhou, X., et al.: Deep-learning-enhanced human activity recognition for internet of healthcare things. IEEE Internet Things J. **7**(7), 6429–6438 (2020)

A Novel Spectral Ensemble Clustering Algorithm Based on Social Group Migratory Behavior and Emotional Preference

Mingzhi Dai[1,2], Xiang Feng[1,2(✉)], Huiqun Yu[1,2], and Weibin Guo[1]

[1] Department of Computer Science and Engineering, East China University of Science and Technology, Shanghai 200237, China
{Y30180707,xfeng,yhq,gweibin}@ecust.edu.cn

[2] Shanghai Engineering Research Center of Smart Energy, Shanghai 200237, China

Abstract. Clustering is an unsupervised machine learning technique for data mining to find objects with similar characteristics in a group. However, due to the lack of relevant prior information on the data, numerous single models or methods cannot identify the shape and size of the clusters. Therefore, an ensemble of multiple weak models is required to further mine the implicit information of the data and improve the clustering accuracy. LSMC-EPMC is an evolutionary clustering algorithm that consists of three parts, the emotional preference and migration behavior clustering (EPMC) model, the Laplacian spectral clustering model, and the Monte Carlo statistical data simulation model. This paper mainly integrates the spectral clustering model and the Monte Carlo statistical data simulation method into the EPMC algorithm by mapping the individual in EPMC and the optimized center point in the other two methods. Through numerous experiments, LSMC-EPMC shows a significantly increased performance to EPMC and is highly competitive with the other seven clustering algorithms on several standard datasets.

Keywords: Evolutionary optimization algorithm · Laplacian spectral-domain · Monte Carlo simulation · Ensemble learning · Data clustering

1 Introduction

With the continuous growth and evolution of artificial intelligence, natural heuristic algorithms are becoming more and more popular among scholars. They can solve many complex optimization problems due to their intelligence, such as clustering tasks. These heuristic algorithms utilize principles similar to bionics to simulate the evolution, cooperation, or foraging process of animals or plants. For instance, as a well-known heuristic algorithm based on the foraging behavior of birds swarm system, particle swarm algorithm (PSO) [1] is widely used by scholars due to its fast convergence speed and easy implementation. The simulated

G. Memmi et al. (Eds.): KSEM 2022, LNAI 13370, pp. 316–328, 2022.
https://doi.org/10.1007/978-3-031-10989-8_25

annealing (SA) algorithm [2] is a classic heuristic algorithm, which is a probability-based algorithm derived from the principle of solid annealing and has the characteristics of random iterative approximate asymptotic convergence. The ant colony optimization (ACO) algorithm [3] is inspired by the path planning behavior of ants in the process of foraging cooperation. Li et al. [4] propose a new heuristic optimization method which is an experience by the animal migration behavior (AMO), it mimics the process of animals transfer from one habitat to another. Inspired by natural biogeography and its mathematics, Simon et al. [5] proposed a biogeography-based optimization (BBO) algorithm to solve high-dimension optimization and real-world sensor selection problems.

Spectral clustering represents a bunch of clustering algorithms based on different graph cut theories. One of the classic graph cut algorithms is Cheeger cut. Its optimal segmentation is also an NP problem [6]. Szlam et al. [7] describe the process of Cheeger cuts balanced subgraphs. Therefore, the eigenvectors of the Laplacian matrix eigendecomposition can be used to settle the graph cut problem [8], so as to approximate the best partition mode of the clustering problem. As shown in Fig. 1(a), all data points can be considered fully connected. After the operation of graph cut, the optimal cutting mode can divide the whole graph into several partitions, which represent the most appropriate clustering mode.

In addition, as a classic numerical calculation method guided by probability and statistics theory [9] and the law of large numbers [10], the Monte Carlo method [11] utilizes an information-intensive and high-speed computing computer as a platform to transform complex research objects or calculation problems into simulations of random numbers and their digital characteristics. In machine learning [12,13], especially in reinforcement learning, a relatively fuzzy model is generally created for the obtained sample data set, and the parameters in the model are selected by the Monte Carlo method to make the residual error of the original data smaller.

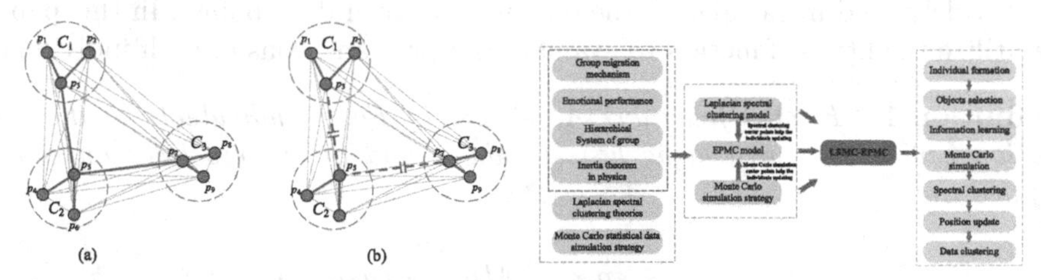

(a) A graph with all data points are fully connected and the clustering mode C_1, C_2, C_3 by cutting two edges

(b) The sub-model structure of LSMC-EPMC

Fig. 1. Basic theory and sub-model structure of the LSMC-EPMC

In order to further efficient the clustering performance of emotion preference and migration behavior model, we integrated several learners and methods for learning, then proposed an ensemble algorithm called LSMC-EPMC in this paper. The LSMC-EPMC contains three parts of the emotional preference and migration behavior model (EPMC) [14], the Laplacian spectral clustering model, and the Monte Carlo statistical data simulation model. The basic theory and sub-model structure of the LSMC-EPMC algorithm are shown in Fig. 1(b). The red frame represents the partition of the emotional preference and migration behavior model. The main contributions of this paper are as follows:

1. The manifold spectral clustering mode based on Laplacian eigenmaps is introduced to help update the position of the individual in the emotional preference and migration behavior model, and attempt to promote the performance when dealing with clustering tasks.
2. A Monte Carlo statistical data theory is designed to simulate the cluster center point to help the emotional preference and migration behavior model approaching the optimal individual, and endeavor to benefit the efficiency of clustering.
3. Numerous experiments were performed to compare the proposed ensemble model LSMC-EPMC with the other seven clustering algorithms on solving data clustering problems through testing on several standard datasets.

The rest content of this paper is organized as follows: The related models and theories of LSMC-EPMC are introduced in Sect. 2. Section 3 give the calculation steps and algorithm details of the proposed LSMC-EPMC. Section 4 shows the work of the experiment. Finally, Sect. 5 concludes the paper.

2 Mathematical and Physical Models

2.1 Emotional Preference and Migration Behavior Model

As a commonly used distance measurement criterion, Euclidean distance has been widely used in calculating the distance between data points. In this paper, we utilize the fitness function to evaluate the pros and cons of each individual.

Definition 1. *(Fitness function) As shown in Eq. 1, individuals in the population can be measured using fitness values, and the fitness function can be defined as:*

$$fit(p, M) = \frac{p \times \sum_{i=1}^{n} \left\| Ins_i - Ins_{label} \right\|^2}{\min \left\| x_a - x_b \right\|} \quad (1)$$

where p and M represent the number of the clusters and the individual matrix, respectively. And Ins_i and Ins_{label} represent an instance in the dataset and the label class it belongs to, x_a and x_b represent two clustering centers in individual matrix M. The smaller the numerator, the smaller value of the function. Therefore, the goal of the optimizing is to minimize the fitness function Eq. 1 and find the individual M_{op}.

This section briefly introduce the emotional preference and migration behavior (EPMC) model proposed by Feng et al. [14]. It consists of four sub-parts: the migration model, the emotional preference model, the social group model, and the inertial learning model. The first two models can help individuals find the global optimal learning object and the best learning object nearby. The third model divides the population into two groups to improve learning ability, and the last model can help individuals explore more solution space.

2.2 Manifold Laplacian Spectral Clustering Model

Let $G = (V, E)$ be an undirected graph with vertex set $V = v_1, ..., v_n$. Supposing that the graph G is weighted, w_{ij} represents the non-negative weight between the two vertices v_i and v_j. For any two vertices in V, there can be an edge connection or no edge connection. Since it is an undirected graph, $w_{ij} = w_{ji}$. The similarity matrix S of the sample point distance measurement is used to obtain the weighted adjacency matrix $W = (w_{ij})_{i,j=1,2,...,n}$ of the graph. For any point v_i in the graph, its degree d_i is defined as the sum of the weights of all edges connected to it.

According to the definition of the degree of each point, we can get a nn degree matrix D, which is a diagonal matrix, as defined in Eq. 2:

$$D = \begin{pmatrix} deg(v_1) & \cdots & \cdots \\ \vdots & \ddots & \vdots \\ \cdots & \cdots & deg(v_n) \end{pmatrix} \tag{2}$$

For the cut graph of the undirected graph G, our proposal is to cut the graph $G = (V, E)$ into k subgraphs that are not connected. A subgraph $G^S = (S, E^S)$ of $G = (V, E)$ is composed of a set of vertices $S \subseteq V$ and a set of edges $E^S \subseteq E$. The set of each subgraph point is: $G_1^S, G_2^S, \ldots G_k^S$, they satisfy $G_i^S \cap G_j^S = \emptyset$, and $G_1^S \cup G_2^S \cup \ldots \cup G_k^S = G$. For the set of any two subgraph points $A, B \subset V$, $A \cap B = \emptyset$, the weight of the cut between A and B is $W(A, B) = \sum_{i \in A, j \in B} w_{ij}$. Then for the set of k subgraph points $G_1^S, G_2^S, \ldots G_k^S$, the NCut is donated as Eq. 3,

$$NCut\left(G_1^S, G_2^S, \ldots G_k^S\right) = \frac{1}{2} \sum_{i=1}^{k} \frac{W\left(G_i^S, \bar{G}_i^S\right)}{vol\left(G_i^S\right)} \tag{3}$$

where $vol\left(G^S\right) = \sum_{i \in A} d_i$. The unnormalized graph Laplacian matrix is defined as:

$$L = D - W \tag{4}$$

In this way, we can continue to follow the idea of *Ratio*Cut to find the smallest first k eigenvalues of $L_{sym} = D^{-\frac{1}{2}} L D^{-\frac{1}{2}}$, then find the corresponding eigenvectors, and standardize them to get the final eigenmatrix F. Finally, it is sufficient to perform traditional clustering on the matrix F.

2.3 Determining Parameters for the Model Using the Monte Carlo Method

The *Naive* Monte Carlo method is the most popular and frequently used method to settle multi-dimensional MC problems. Supposing an approximate computation of the integral $Q[f] = \int_{\Omega} f(\mathbf{x})p(\mathbf{x})d\mathbf{x}$, and the expectation the random variable $\phi = f(\delta)$ is that $\mathbf{E}\phi = \int_{\Omega} f(\mathbf{x})p(\mathbf{x})d\mathbf{x}$. Among them, δ is a random point in the probability density function $p(x)$, and all variables $\delta_1, \delta_2, \ldots, \delta_N$ are independent with $\phi_1 = f(\delta_1), \ldots, \phi_N = f(\delta_N)$. Common Monte Carlo estimation is based on the N repeated simulations and simulate the dataset through the minimum cut set. Given the simulation set $\tau_i = f_s\left(x_1^{(i)}, \ldots, x_n^{(i)}\right)$, the common Monte Carlo estimate can be expressed as the following form: $\widehat{T}_s = \frac{1}{N}\sum_{i=1}^{N} f_s\left(x_1^{(i)}, \ldots, x_n^{(i)}\right)$. The variance estimated by the Monte Carlo algorithm is proportional to N^{-1}, and $Var\left(\hat{T}_s\right) = Var\left(\frac{1}{N}\sum_{i=1}^{N}\tau_i\right) = \frac{1}{N^2}Var\left(\sum_{i=1}^{N}\tau_i\right) = \frac{1}{N}Var\left(\tau_i\right)$. More generally, the central limit of Monte Carlo can be expressed as:

$$P\left(\left|T_s - E\left(T_s\right)\right|\right) > z\frac{\sqrt{\mathrm{Var}\left(\tau_i\right)}}{\sqrt{n}} \approx P(|Z| > z) \tag{5}$$

where $Z \sim N(0,1)$. Therefore, for the expected accuracy $\varepsilon > 0$ with a confidence level of $1-\alpha$, Monte Carlo simulation with $n = z_{\frac{\delta}{2}}^2 \mathrm{Var}\left(\tau_i\right)\varepsilon^{-2}$ is required, where the quantile $z_{\frac{\alpha}{2}}$ is selected to ensure $P\left(Z > z_{\frac{\alpha}{2}}\right) = \frac{\alpha}{2}$. Naturally, $z_{\frac{\alpha}{2}}$ is a constant for any regular confidence level.

3 The Proposed LSMC-EPMC Optimization Algorithm

3.1 Main Framework of LSMC-EPMC Algorithm

The LSMC framework consists of 3 main components and 6 sub-parts. First, the emotional preference and migration behavior model initializes the population and other parameters, and evaluates and ranks the individuals in the population. Then individuals update their position based on the best individuals in the population and the excellent neighbor around them, and the model uses a certain strategy to eliminate inferior individuals in the population. Second, by matching individual cluster centers with a similar class of spectral cluster centers, Laplacian spectral cluster solutions can help individuals update their positions. Finally, the Monte Carlo method can simulate similar center points to assist individual's update according to the law of large numbers.

3.2 Calculation Steps of LSMC-EPMC Algorithm

The optimization steps of the proposed LSMC-EPMC algorithm can be listed as follows:

Step 1: Data preprocessing and initialization
During the preprocessing, the upper and lower bounds of the dataset are calculated. The parameter initialization contains the scale of the population (NP), the number the elite individuals($elite$), the initial number of clusters(k), the maximum number of iterations($iteration$), the maximum number of running rounds(run), and so on.

Step 2: Evaluation and grouping
All individuals evaluate their fitness values according to Eq. 1 and sort the NP individuals in the population from small to large. Among them, the top $elitenum$ individuals are considered as *elite*, and the remaining individuals are considered as ordinary individuals. Besides, all data points are assigned to the nearest centroid (a row of the individual matrix M_i). When a centroid has no data point or only one data point, the centroid will be ignored and the data point will be reassigned.

Step 3: Selection of learning objects
As depicted in Sect. 2.1 [14], the individual selects the best individual in the population.

Step 4: Laplacian spectral cluster centers learning

Hypothesis 1. Supposing that the emotional preference and migration behavior model contains p central points at the t-th iteration, the *elite* are selected to be updated. When considering using the center point of spectral clustering to update the centroid in an individual, the mode combined with spectral clustering is recorded as SpectClus-p, that is, there are p spectral clustering center points that assist the base model to update the individual.

Hypothesis 2. Supposing that the classes with the largest number of temporary labels in the current iteration on the Laplacian learning are the actual classes of the dataset.

Hypothesis 3. In the current iteration, if the Euclidean distance between a certain spectral cluster center point and a certain centroid of the individual is the smallest, the spectral cluster center-point can be identified as the same class as the centroid.

After matching the actual centroid of the individual with the same class of the spectral clustering center point one by one, then the SpectClus-p method can utilize to update the individual. The SpectClus-p method acts on *elite*, and ordinary individuals follow the elite individuals in the population to learn and update to reach the optimal more properly.

Step 5: Individual learning and updating
After selecting the ideal learning object, the individual updates the position. If the individual's fitness becomes better, go to **Step 6**, otherwise, The model will determine whether to accept this update.

Step 6: Replace of emotional preference matrix

After the individual updates the position, the corresponding emotional preference matrix $feel_{i,j}$ is updated simultaneously. The elements in the emotional preference matrix are set to 1 initially.

Step 7: Elimination of inferior individuals
In each iteration, the LSMC-EPMC algorithm eliminates individuals with poor fitness values in the second half of the population with a certain probability P_e, and adds new individuals to the population.

Step 8: Monte Carlo simulate cluster centers learning

Hypothesis 1. Supposing that the classes with the largest number of temporary labels in the current iteration on the Monte Carlo simulate are the actual classes of the dataset.

Hypothesis 2. After using the Monte Carlo method to expand and filter the data features of several classes in the current iteration, the mean value of the expanded data is selected as the current better center point $Center_{mc}$.

Hypothesis 3. In the current iteration, if the Euclidean distance between a certain Monte Carlo simulation center and a certain centroid of the individual is the smallest, the Monte Carlo simulation center can be identified as the same class as the centroid.

After matching the actual centroid of the individual with the same class of the Monte Carlo simulation center one by one, then the Monte Carlo simulation center is utilized to update the individual. The Monte Carlo simulation method acts on *elite*, and ordinary individuals are updated synchronously in social group to reach the optimal.

Step 9: Termination
The algorithm repeats **Step 2** to **Step 8** until met the termination condition or reached the maximum number of iterations. Finally, the optimal solution is obtained, and the algorithm ends.

Suppose that the computational complexity of choosing a learning object is O_c in the LSMC-EPMC. Moreover, O_e and O_o represent the computational complexity of position updating rule for elite and ordinary, respectively. The computational complexity of spectral and Monte Carlo operator are represented by O_s and O_m, respectively. In addition, the size of elite and ordinary (N_e and N_o) of LSMC-EPMC. So the computation complexity of LSMC-EPMC is $N_e \cdot (O_c + O_e) + N_o \cdot (O_c + O_o) + O_s + O_m$.

4 Experiment and Results

This section discusses the computational experiments performed with the proposed LSMC-EPMC algorithm. And 11 *UCI* standard datasets were used in the experiment, including the Iris, Soybean, Glass, Seeds, Vowel, Car Evaluation (CE), User Knowledge (UK), Wine, BLOOD, Hagerman's Survival (HK) and Banknote. Authentication (BA).

The operating environment of all experiments is running on Lenovo Shenteng 1800 HPCC, which has 8 computing nodes and 1 console node. Each compute node is a high-performance server with two 2.4 GHz quad-core CPUs and 24 GB of memory. The operating system of all servers is Red Hat Enterprise Linux 7, and the experimental computing platform is MATLAB R2021b.

Table 1. Parameter settings details on eight algorithms

Algorithm	Parameter setting
EPMC	As depicted in [14]
K-Means	k is set to be equal to the real $ClusNum$ of the dataset
Cop-kmeans	k is set to be equal to the real $ClusNum$ of the dataset, the indices of the pairs that must be in the same cluster nML is set to 8, the indices of the pairs that cannot be in the same cluster nCL is set to 8
Graph-SSC	The certainty of each observed label is set to 10, the number of initial labels in each class is set to 10, the number of nearest neighbors is set to 29, and set the hyperparameter $\alpha = 100$, $\beta = e^{-3}$
PSO	The weight factor w reduces from 0.9 to 0.4 and c_1, c_2 are set to 2
AMO	The range of critical interval is set to 5
BBO	The number of *elite* is set to $elitenum = 2$, and the mutation rate is set to $P_e = 0.05$
LSMC-EPMC	The number of *elitenum* is set to 2, the number of iterations T is set to 100, the initial number of clusters k is set to 10 (Vowel is 15), the number of *runs* is set to 25, set $\alpha = 0.8$ and $\beta = 0.2$, the scale of Monte Carlo simulation data is set to 5000, the hyperparameter of Gaussian similarity in spectral clustering is set to 0.9, and the max mutation rate $P_{e,max}$ is set to 0.05

The computational result is compared with the other seven algorithms, including a machine learning algorithm: K-means algorithm, two semi-supervised algorithms: Cop-kmeans algorithm, Graph-SSC algorithm, and four optimization algorithms: PSO algorithm, BBO algorithm, AMO algorithm and EPMC algorithm. In all experiments, the population size of the eight algorithms is set to 15, and the maximum number of iterations is set to 100. The initial number of clusters is set to 15 for Vowel and 10 for the rest of the datasets. All algorithms run 25 times independently, and we take the average value as the final result for comparison. The parameter setting details of the remaining algorithms are shown in Table 1.

The clustering performance of the eight algorithms is evaluated according to four criteria. The first one is the internal quality ($fitness$) measure, which is defined in Eq. 1. The smaller the $fitness$, the better the performance. The second one is the Jaccard coefficient ($JacIndex$). Kou et al. [15] use the Jaccard coefficient to test the quality of clustering results, which measure the similarity between instances properly. The larger the $JacIndex$, the better the algorithm. The third one is the Average number of clusters ($ClusNum$), which is calculated by Eq. 6. The closer the result is to the actual classes of the dataset, the better the algorithm. The last one is the $Time$, which records the speed of the eight algorithms on clustering. The smaller the $Time$, the better the algorithm.

$$ClusNum = \frac{\sum_{i=1}^{run} clusnum_i}{run} \tag{6}$$

where $clusnum_i$ represents the final number of clusters in each round, and run represents the execute round of the algorithm.

The results of the $fitness$, $JacIndex$, $ClusNum$ and $Time$ executed by the eight optimization algorithms are listed in Tables 2 and 3, respectively. In Table 2, the data shows the Average Best-so-far (*Avg*), Best-so-far (*Best*), Worst-so-far (*Worst*), and the standard deviation of Best-so-far-solution (*Std*) of all execution results. The best *Avg* of the eight algorithms are shown in bold.

In order to analyze the performance of all algorithms more intuitively, a summary of Friedman test is used. The smaller the rank of the test result, the better the algorithm. Figure 2(a) describes the Friedman ranking results on the $fitness$ of eight algorithms. From Fig. 2(a) we can conclude that the LSMC-EPMC algorithm gets the ten best results among 11 datasets, and is only slightly

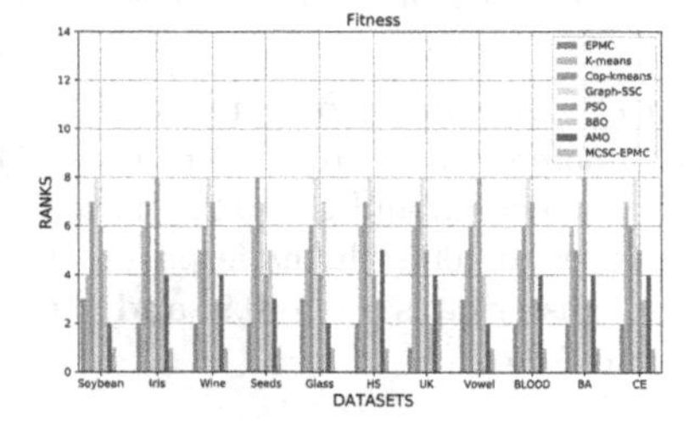

(a) Friedman ranking results on the $fitness$

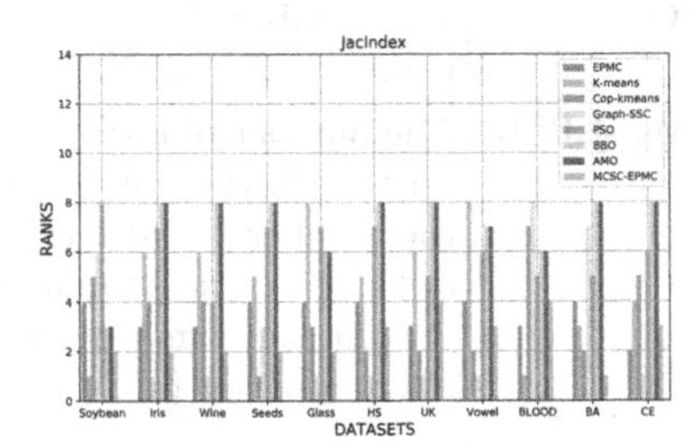

(b) Friedman ranking results on the $JacIndex$

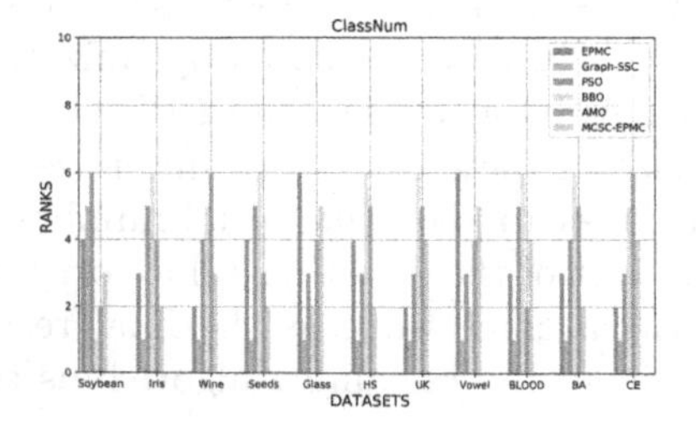

(c) Friedman ranking results on the $ClusNum$

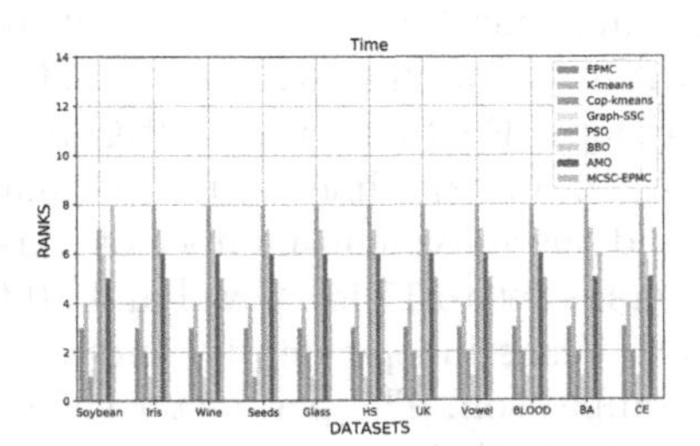

(d) Friedman ranking results on the $Time$

Fig. 2. The Friedman ranking results on the $fitness$, $JacIndex$, $ClusNum$ and $Time$ of eight algorithms

Table 2. Fitness results on eight algorithms

Dataset	Indices	EPMC	K-means	Cop-kmeans	Graph-SSC	PSO	BBO	AMO	LSMC-EPMC
Iris	Avg	25.95	33.68	34.59	29.38	41.48	32.29	30.87	**20.46**
	Best	20.83	28.72	25.86	28.43	30.16	27.05	24.67	18.89
	Worst	34.60	42.28	46.39	31.26	49.38	35.78	38.18	23.18
	Std	2.85	5.83	5.69	0.96	5.71	2.45	3.46	0.998
Soybean	Avg	7.63	21.72	30.01	49.67	28.76	26.13	7.32	**6.11**
	Best	6.64	18.65	18.95	29.74	21.33	23.50	6.44	5.26
	Worst	9.54	31.09	40.47	54.00	34.86	28.72	7.97	7.38
	Std	0.75	5.04	4.27	7.29	3.11	1.24	0.40	0.543
Wine	Avg	16.21	33.86	57.78	109.74	61.57	17.90	18.15	**15.41**
	Best	17.69	36.52	51.52	68.63	49.01	18.74	18.77	16.69
	Worst	21.74	37.95	68.89	168.7	91.23	23.05	23.32	22.83
	Std	1.11	0.47	4.16	24.58	8.89	1.24	1.34	1.404
Seeds	Avg	20.48	60.16	67.60	62.66	35.46	49.7	23.94	**16.99**
	Best	17.20	58.59	63.66	59.65	30.52	43.35	18.02	16.24
	Worst	24.65	85.94	77.59	65.88	41.94	58.65	28.95	19.43
	Std	1.94	5.38	3.00	1.93	3.01	3.33	3.47	0.772
Glass	Avg	6.88	49.44	52.47	88.26	8.41	55.25	6.47	**5.69**
	Best	5.11	34.72	42.80	62.43	7.62	41.15	4.67	4.51
	Worst	9.42	84.34	64.71	104.1	9.21	72.76	8.12	6.85
	Std	1.16	11.01	6.11	9.25	0.37	7.54	0.89	0.774
HS	Avg	55.36	151.06	155.21	255.5	59.92	55.64	70.36	**54.36**
	Best	49.05	147.2	150.9	156.7	53.43	47.76	59.40	48.63
	Worst	63.35	187.8	159.7	722.6	63.02	60.90	80.26	58.98
	Std	3.97	8.04	2.38	115.7	2.71	2.98	5.85	3.44
UK	Avg	**163.73**	287.51	290.06	325.18	271.13	165.9	241.34	187.34
	Best	126.6	275.2	278.08	291.7	235.1	153.9	213.7	137.01
	Worst	217.8	293.7	308.85	372.6	307.1	169.8	253.1	212.41
	Std	30.80	7.26	9.49	25.37	17.19	4.69	10.98	20.57
Vowel	Avg	259.08	508.72	511.88	773.86	811.39	390.9	249.13	**221.0**
	Best	213.3	472.5	494.36	681.0	682.9	354.6	181.9	174.1
	Worst	364.9	528.3	540.54	875.5	907.9	420.9	347.6	282.8
	Std	47.00	13.28	10.19	46.12	55.09	17.76	48.03	31.80
BLOOD	Avg	27.47	154.33	172.48	5937	454.85	28.83	39.18	**26.09**
	Best	24.30	154.33	167.27	399.1	380.1	22.89	32.69	22.28
	Worst	33.66	154.33	177.06	48762	612.0	31.41	44.44	30.58
	Std	2.02	0	2.71	9915	62.39	2.20	3.35	1.81
BA	Avg	375.82	639.24	608.40	1281.85	1681.60	381.7	503.19	**367.04**
	Best	348.6	629.5	600.03	974.3	1123	289.6	409.2	342.31
	Worst	445.4	643.75	617.24	2399	2374	406.5	514.9	387.55
	Std	24.19	3.48	4.45	269.3	313.4	28.16	27.52	13.50
CE	Avg	1093.5	1622.9	1561.44	2002.45	1492.4	1371	1417.7	**1063.5**
	Best	730.2	1353	1506.6	1854	930	893.4	1173	1106.0
	Worst	1263	1587	1665.4	2304.6	1122	996.9	1268	1268.0
	Std	161.7	66.75	48.08	110.7	46.82	23.17	22.52	35.08

inferior to EPMC and BBO algorithm on the UK dataset during the *fitness* criterion. Specifically, the proposed LSMC-EPMC algorithm and three classic algorithms (PSO, BBO, AMO) are superior to the two semi-supervised learning methods (Cop-kmeans, Graph-SSC) on the *fitness* criterion. This may be due to the defective algorithm design, which leads to individuals escaping the optimal

Table 3. Results of *JacIndex*, *ClusNum* and *Time* on eight algorithms

Dataset	Measure	EPMC	K-means	Cop-kmeans	Graph-SSC	PSO	BBO	AMO	LSMC-EPMC
Iris	JacIndex	0.62	0.27	0.34	0.74	0.23	0.19	0.28	0.68
	ClusNum	2.56	–	–	3.00	3.88	6.32	3.84	3.08
	Time	9.74	10.88	0.72	0.05	45.20	37.20	25.80	13.23
Soybean	JacIndex	0.40	0.56	0.39	0.34	0.26	0.45	0.33	0.52
	ClusNum	2.16	–	–	2.08	6.36	4.36	3.00	2.8
	Time	4.84	5.29	0.04	0.06	15.40	13.00	9.99	53.66
Wine	JacIndex	0.30	0.20	0.26	0.34	0.21	0.12	0.12	0.31
	ClusNum	3.08	–	–	3.00	4.28	9.15	9.20	3.24
	Time	12.22	14.35	0.09	0.06	54.40	48.40	32.60	32.08
Seeds	JacIndex	0.51	0.27	0.60	0.51	0.23	0.16	0.26	0.57
	ClusNum	2.20	–	–	3.00	5.48	10.0	3.44	2.72
	Time	11.93	15.38	0.11	0.15	63.80	52.60	36.20	23.7
Glass	JacIndex	0.26	0.11	0.26	0.34	0.15	0.21	0.24	0.30
	ClusNum	2.00	–	–	6.00	4.60	5.72	3.00	2.56
	Time	11.84	19.88	0.12	0.09	65.10	56.90	37.20	25.14
HS	JacIndex	0.32	0.31	0.38	0.51	0.27	0.15	0.29	0.32
	ClusNum	4.76	–	–	2.00	4.76	8.40	6.00	4.76
	Time	16.45	18.45	0.07	0.06	91.60	53.80	51.30	22.05
UK	JacIndex	0.26	0.12	0.27	0.36	0.13	0.08	0.08	0.24
	ClusNum	3.32	–	–	4.00	5.76	10.0	9.20	6.6
	Time	20.75	27.97	0.36	0.08	121.0	99.40	68.20	38.14
Vowel	JacIndex	0.10	0.03	0.16	0.28	0.05	0.04	0.08	0.10
	ClusNum	2.20	–	–	11.0	6.32	8.04	3.32	2.52
	Time	73.4	90.13	0.84	0.25	393.0	391.0	272.0	147.8
BLOOD	JacIndex	0.40	0.55	0.20	0.20	0.39	0.22	0.46	0.39
	ClusNum	9.52	–	–	2.00	9.76	9.80	8.96	9.64
	Time	36.95	41.44	0.12	0.09	222.9	159.8	113.2	84.53
BA	JacIndex	0.36	0.36	0.38	0.30	0.33	0.25	0.32	0.38
	ClusNum	5.04	–	–	2.00	5.08	7.00	5.84	4.84
	Time	66.11	73.22	0.41	0.14	417.7	333.1	208.7	210.64
CE	JacIndex	0.32	0.25	0.24	0.42	0.19	0.11	0.12	0.30
	ClusNum	2.84	–	–	4.00	8.36	10.0	10.00	9.36
	Time	37.3	63.39	1.13	0.15	526.8	365.4	283.8	391.22

solution prematurely. In general, except the User Knowledge dataset, LSMC-EPMC can obtain superior results among eight algorithms include the EPMC optimization algorithm on the *fitness* criterion.

Then, Fig. 2(b), Fig. 2(c) and Fig. 2(d) indicate the Friedman ranking results on the *JacIndex*, *ClusNum* and *Time* of eight algorithms, respectively. As can be seen from Fig. 2(b), the semi-supervised learning method Graph-SSC is superior to other algorithms on most datasets during the *JacIndex* criterion, which possibly rely on the thorough consideration of the data by the graph structure. And the LSMC-EPMC can get the superior results among most datasets on the *JacIndex* criterion. Since K-means and Cop-kmeans have determined the initial number of clusters, Fig. 2(c) only shows the Friedman ranking results of the LSMC-EPMC algorithm and other six algorithms on the *ClusNum* criterion. As can be concluded from Fig. 2(c), the LSMC-EPMC algorithm is slightly inferior to the semi-supervised learning method Graph-SSC, but is higher than the other five algorithms including EPMC on most datasets during the $ClusNum$ criterion. Besides, Fig. 2(d) describes the running time Friedman ranking of the eight algorithms. We can be seen from Fig. 2(d) that the LSMC-EPMC algorithm shows worse speed than two semi-supervised learning methods, but its Friedman ranking is higher than the other three classic algorithms and EPMC on most datasets during the $Time$ criterion. In addition, the Friedman ranking of the proposed LSMC-EPMC algorithm is superior to all other seven algorithms on the $fitness$ criterion.

5 Conclusion

Based on the emotional preference and transfer behavior model, an ensemble algorithm called LSMC-EPMC which merged several learners and methods was proposed in the paper. First, we incorporate the spectral clustering based on Laplacian eigenmaps to update the individual position in optimization. Second, a Monte Carlo statistical data theory is used to simulate the cluster center point and help to approach the optimal. Third, the proposed LSMC-EPMC is applied to settle the data clustering tasks.

Then, numerous experiments were performed to compare the proposed LSMC-EPMC with the other seven clustering algorithms on several standard datasets. The paper utilized four criteria to measure the clustering performance of the eight algorithms. In addition, the Friedman test was used to analyze the ranking of the eight algorithms. Through the Friedman ranking results, we can conclude that the clustering performance of the proposed LSMC-EPMC is better than the other seven algorithms including the EPMC.

However, there are still many flaws that need to be settled. For instance, on the high-dimensional dataset (Vowel dataset) or the large-scale dataset (BA dataset), the number of centers searched by the LSMC-EPMC is still far from the actual number of classes. Furthermore, time consumption also requires more attention. In the future, we will focus on the application of LSMC-EPMC to real-world unmanned system mixed precision problems, and further improve the biophysical and mathematical models of LSMC-EPMC to realize the parallelism.

Acknowledgements. This work was supported in part by the National Natural Science Foundation of China under Grant NOs. 61772200, Shanghai Pujiang Talent Program (17PJ1401900), the Information Development Special Funds of Shanghai Economic and Information Commission under Grant NO. XX-XXFZ-02-20-2463, and the Key Program of National Natural Science Foundation of China (62136003).

References

1. Lv, J., Shi, X.: Particle swarm optimization algorithm based on factor selection strategy, pp. 1606–1611 (2019)
2. Xin, X., Li, K.-J., Sun, K., Liu, Z., Wang, Z.-D.: A simulated annealing genetic algorithm for urban power grid partitioning based on load characteristics, pp. 1–5 (2019)

3. Guan, B., Zhao, Y., Li, Y.: An improved ant colony optimization with an automatic updating mechanism for constraint satisfaction problems. Expert Syst. Appl. **164**, 114021 (2021)
4. Li, X., Zhang, J., Yin, M.: Animal migration optimization: an optimization algorithm inspired by animal migration behavior. Neural Comput. Appl. **24**, 1867–1877 (2014)
5. Simon, D.: Biogeography-based optimization. IEEE Trans. Evol. Comput. **12**, 702–713 (2008)
6. Qiu, H., Zheng, Q., Msahli, M., Memmi, G., Qiu, M., Jialiang, L.: Topological graph convolutional network-based urban traffic flow and density prediction. IEEE Trans. Intell. Transp. Syst. **22**(7), 4560–4569 (2021)
7. Szlam, A., Bresson, X.: Total variation and cheeger cuts, pp. 1039–1046 (2010)
8. Dai, M., Guo, W., Feng, X.: Over-smoothing algorithm and its application to GCN semi-supervised classification. In: Qin, P., Wang, H., Sun, G., Lu, Z. (eds.) ICPCSEE 2020. CCIS, vol. 1258, pp. 197–215. Springer, Singapore (2020). https://doi.org/10.1007/978-981-15-7984-4_16
9. Qin, W.: A study on real estate price by using probability statistics theory and grey theory, pp. 153–156 (2019)
10. Ma, H., Sun, Y., Miao, Yu.: Some extensions of the classical law of large numbers. Commun. Stat. Theory Methods **49**, 3228–3237 (2020)
11. Mikhov, R., et al.: A two-stage Monte Carlo approach for optimization of bimetallic nanostructures, pp. 285–288 (2020)
12. Mohamed, S., Rosca, M., Figurnov, M., Mnih, A.: Monte Carlo gradient estimation in machine learning. J. Mach. Learn. Res. **21**, 1–62 (2020)
13. Kimmel, R., Li, T., Winston, D.: An enhanced machine learning model for adaptive Monte Carlo yield analysis, pp. 89–94 (2020)
14. Feng, X., Zhong, D., Yu, H.: A clustering algorithm based on emotional preference and migratory behavior. Soft. Comput. **24**(10), 7163–7179 (2019). https://doi.org/10.1007/s00500-019-04333-4
15. Kou, G., Peng, Y., Wang, G.: Evaluation of clustering algorithms for financial risk analysis using MCDM methods. Inf. Sci. **275**, 1–12 (2014)

An Improved Semantic Link Based Cyber Community Discovery Model on Social Network

Weiran Liu, Qiyu Ruan, Liang Zhang, and Wei Ren(✉)

Southwest University, Chongqing 400715, China
adventure@email.swu.edu.cn, oicq@swu.edu.cn

Abstract. Online communities emerge as a major way of delivering and sharing resources. Yet communities in social networks cannot be accurately classified due to the randomness of clustering and the insufficient use of semantics of links. In this paper, a semantic inference based community discovery model is proposed to extract multiple layers of semantics from the topological structure of node relationships and semantic connections between nodes to search and discover communities. The ego-Twitter dataset was used, which contains 81306 nodes (accounts) and 1768149 edges, to test the proposed model. Experiments show that our model is suitable for sparse networks and nodes that contain rich semantics. Especially, in terms of modularity, our model outperforms the Latent Factor Model (LFW) and K-means algorithm. Our model outperforms LFW by achieved faster speed when the scale of online community is expanded to more than 1000, which demonstrates that our model has higher efficiency with network that has abundant semantics.

Keywords: Community discovery · Semantic link · Semantic inference

1 Introduction

The study of community discovery is aim to decompose complex network topology into meaningful node clusters [1–3]. The mainstream community discovery methods now are based on cluster calculations. These algorithms conduct unsupervised learning by observing the attributes of network nodes; However, when these algorithms are applied to node classification of social networks, accurate classifications cannot be achieved [4].The reasons may lie in the different attributes of existing network nodes, various definitions of online community, unsatisfied initializations for cluster algorithms, which will affect the calculation accuracy and the clustering results may ends in randomness. Meanwhile, the existing partition algorithms focus solely on nodes' data such as in and out degree but do not pay much attention to the semantics of individual node and links' attribute information [5, 6]. The current community discovery algorithms are mainly used on undirected graph, whereas community nodes often show its directivity. In order to accurately describe the node relationships, directivity is added to the analysis of community network [7]. We can simulate real-world networks such as social networks

G. Memmi et al. (Eds.): KSEM 2022, LNAI 13370, pp. 329–338, 2022.
https://doi.org/10.1007/978-3-031-10989-8_26

with high accuracy by pay attention to different kinds of links and explain the attributes of them.

The algorithm Satuluri [8] proposed of symmetrizing directed graph in 2011, and the LSW-OCD [9] proposed by Haiyan Zhang in 2015, all transformed the directed graph into undirected graph with directional weight according to the vector of nodes. Yet the node semantics and the relationship between semantics haven't been extracted and been studied. Semantics can not only demonstrate the meaning of objects, but also the relationship between objects. Particularly, in social networks, users' behaviors are closely connected to their own characteristics, hobbies and habits; the application of semantics in online community discovery makes it possible of mining non-data information and to better understand the attributes of users (nodes), so as to achieve a more accurate results of communities' discovery. This paper proposes a semantic link based cyber community discovery model for online community discover in social network considering the great potential of semantics to community discovery.

The rest of the paper is structured as follows. Section 2 prepares readers with the basis of semantic network and semantic search. Section 3 presents the semantic link based online community discovery model. Section 4 presents experimental analysis. Finally, the conclusion is given in Sect. 5.

2 Semantic Network and Semantic Search

Semantic network is the extension of current network so that people and machines can understand each other better [10]. The concept nodes in the semantic network are organized in levels, which can represent the plane relationship between individual nodes and the vertical relationship of different nodes in different levels [11]. Semantic search is the core of semantic network. According to the difference of ontology processing principle, semantic search process can be classified into three types: enhanced semantic search, knowledge-based semantic search and rest [12, 13]. The enhanced semantic search is based on the traditional search engine and adds the ontology library in the traditional database. The ontology library supplements the abstract concept of keywords. Therefore, the semantic search can map the keywords used for input to one or a group of entities or concepts in the semantic network, and use the "point" and "edge" in the semantic network to analyze and reason the graphical expression of entities, concepts, values, attributes and relationships, End users will get rich relevant knowledge from semantic search. However, methods based on keywords cannot support formal query. The search based on semantic annotation is only used as the enhancement of search engine, and the accuracy has not been significantly improved. Therefore, we propose a spatial community discovery model based on semantic relationship. By paying attention to the semantic characteristics between nodes (Equal, Similar, Reference, etc.), we use semantic link for enhanced reasoning, hoping to get community discovery results closer to the real situation.

3 Semantic Link Based Online Community Discovery Model

This paper proposes a spatial model of semantic reasoning for network community discovery and resource tracking. The spatial model divides the complex network topology into a multi-layer model with semantic relations between nodes. The proposed model can be divided into plan topology and vertical tree topology. The vertical elevation of the model is a forest with tree structure, which reflects the hierarchical relationship of the model and represents all the relationships between the nodes of the *n-th* layer and the semantics (data, resources and services) of each node on the $n + 1$ and *n-th* planes. The semantic relationships of layer n, $n + 1$ are shown in Fig. 1.

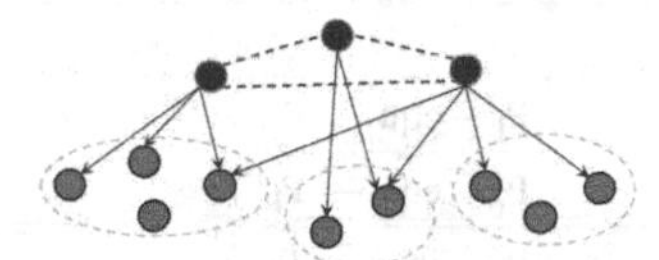

(a)The *n-th* layer, *n*+1layers have tree semantic relations

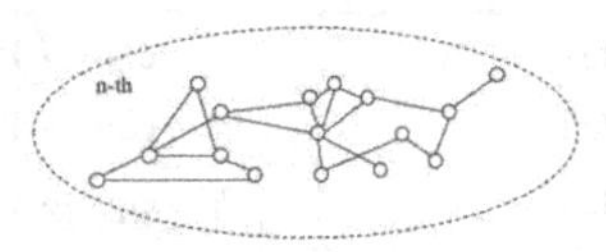

(b) *n-th* plane semantic relationship

Fig. 1. The semantic relationship of layers

In order to reduce semantic fuzziness, nodes supporting similar concepts are calculated by similarity and replaced by subclasses or equivalence relations respectively. The semantic query and community discovery can be quickly forwarded to the appropriate semantic level, which can improve the search speed.

3.1 Model Description

Six semantic link types (Equal, Similar, Reference, etc.) are divided into two categories according to their characteristics.

Equality, Reference and Sequence. On the horizontal plane, the relationship between language nodes is represented by a directed graph. In the definition space model, the graph on the *n-th* plane is $G_n = <V_n, Equ_n, Ref_n, Seq_n>$, where V_n is the set of all points in the *n-th* plane, Equ_n represents the set of nodes with "equal" semantic link type in the *n-th* plane, the same goes for Ref_n and Seq_n.

This paper defines similarity as: suppose the semantic similarity of two nodes A and B is α. When α is greater than 0.6, the type of semantic link is classified as equal, if α is less than 0.6, it is considered that the semantics of A and B are irrelevant.

Reference is defined as: *Ref* refers to the node relationship set of all semantic links in the figure with the type of "reference", $Ref_n = <r_{n1}, r_{n2} \ldots r_{nm}>$, and r_{ni} refers to the *i-th* "reference" semantic link in the figure on the *n-th* plane. *Seq* is the set of all nodes whose semantic link type is "sequence", $Seq_n = <s_{n1}, s_{n2} \ldots r_{nm}>$, and s_{ni} is the *i-th* sequence.

Implication and Subclass. The structure on the vertical plane can be expressed as a set of semantic nodes and "subclass" semantic links and "implication" semantic links, $T = (V_n, Sub, Imp)$. The semantic link of "subclass" is expressed as $sub = \cap < v_i, \ldots .v_n >$, where each $<v_i, \ldots .v_n>$ is a "subclass" semantic link from node v_i to v_n. By definition, the "subclass" semantic link has a transitive relationship. "Implication" usually does not simply refer to a simple and clear inclusion relationship.

In order to measure and correct the similarity between node objects, a semantic reasoning table is proposed according to the definition of semantic link relationship in literature [11] and the needs of community discovery, as shown in Table 1.

Table 1. Reasoning rules of semantic link network

No	Rules	Summarization
Rule1	$P_i - equ \rightarrow P_i$	-
Rule2	$P_i - equ \rightarrow P_j$	$P_j - equ \rightarrow P_j$
Rule3	$P_i - equ \rightarrow P_j, P_j - equ \rightarrow P_k$	$P_i - equ \rightarrow P_k$
Rule4	$P_i - imp \rightarrow P_j, P_j - imp \rightarrow P_k$	$P_j - imp \rightarrow P_k$
Rule5	$P_i - st \rightarrow P_j, P_j - st \rightarrow P_k$	$P_j - st \rightarrow P_k$
Rule6	$P_i - imp \rightarrow P_j, P_j - st \rightarrow P_k$	$P_j - imp \rightarrow P_k$
Rule7	$P_i - imp \rightarrow P_j, P_j - ref \rightarrow P_k$	$P_j - ref \rightarrow P_k$
Rule8	$P_i - st \rightarrow P_j, P_j - ref \rightarrow P_k$	$P_j - ref \rightarrow P_k$
Rule9	$P_i - N \rightarrow P_j, P_j - sim \rightarrow P_k$	$P_j - N \rightarrow P_k$
Rule10	$P_i - \varnothing \rightarrow P_j, P_j - sim \rightarrow P_k$	$P_j - N \rightarrow P_k$

Among them, $imp = \cap < v_i, \ldots .v_n >$ represents the set of semantic nodes that may generate reasoning. *equ* stands for equality relation, *sim* stands for similarity relation, *ref* stands for reference relation and *st* stands for subclass relation.

Similarity Calculation. In this paper, each entity e defined is represented as a *vector(e)* of a word space, and each dimension corresponds to a word. The value of the dimension indicates the relative importance or representativeness of the word in describing *e*. A keyword query *q* is also expressed as a *vector(q)* in a word space. Finally, the correlation between *e* and *q* can be expressed as the cosine of the angle between *vector(e)* and *vector(q)*.

The similarity of semantic structure depends on two basic elements: 1. Semantic nodes constitute the leaf nodes of the community, and the query is also composed of leaf nodes, so it is related to the semantic structure of the community. 2. The similarity degree of the ancestor node of the node.

Table 2 defines the functions called to implement the similarity algorithm and their explanations.

The similarity of N_i and N_j semantic structures of different nodes in the semantic network is calculated as follows:

Table 2. Notations and explanations

Notation	Explanation
Peer (N_i)	Semantic mapping node of semantic node N_i
Length (N_i, N_j)	Number of nodes on the path from semantic node N_i to N_j
Max-Semantic-Clique (N_i)	Maximum semantic group including semantic node N_i
Min-Common-Sub-Tree (N_i)	Minimum common subtree including semantic node N_i
Semantic-Node-Similarity-Degrees (N_i, N_j)	Similarity between semantic nodes N_i and N_j

Algorithm 1.Semantic-Structure-Similarity-Degrees (N_i, N_j)

1: IF $N_i \in$ One of the largest semantic groups in the community
THEN T = Max-Semantic-Clique (N_i)
ELSE T = Min-Common-Sub-Tree (N_i)
END IF

2 : Root (N_i) = T
IF Length(N_i, N_j) = 1
THEN Semantic-Structure-Similarity-Degrees(N_i, N_j)=Semantic-Node-Similarity-Degrees (N_i, N_j)
ELSE NodeSet = {N_i, ..., Root (N_i)} //All nodes from node N_i to the root node of N_i
$\overrightarrow{FV} = (fv_{N_i}, \dots, fv_{Root(N_i)})$ //Contains the similarity vector from root node to node N_i

$$fv_{N_k} = \begin{cases} 0 \text{ //The mapping node corresponding to } N_k \text{ does not belong to the mapping path of } N_k \\ \text{Semantic} - \text{Node} - \text{Similarity} - \text{Degrees}\left(N_k, \text{Peer}(N_k)\right) \text{ //other} \end{cases} \quad (1)$$

// $\vec{w}$ is the weight vector, which indicates the importance of nodes in the NodeSet, and W_{N_k} indicates the importance between nodes.

$$W_{N_k} = \begin{cases} \frac{1}{2}, N_k = N_i \\ \frac{1}{2}^k, k = \text{length}\left(N_i, N_k\right), \text{and } N_k \neq N_i \\ 1 - \sum_{l=1}^{n-1} W_{N_L} = \frac{1}{2}^{n-1}, n = \text{length}\left(N_i, \text{Root}(N_i)\right), N_k = \text{Root}\left(N_i\right) \end{cases}$$

(2)

$$\text{Semantic} - \text{Structure} - \text{Similarity} - \text{Degrees}\left(N_i, N_j\right) = \frac{\overrightarrow{W} \cdot \overrightarrow{FV}}{|\overrightarrow{W}||\overrightarrow{FV}|}$$

(3)

Among that

$$\overrightarrow{W} \cdot \overrightarrow{FV} = W_{N_i} fv_{N_i} + \dots + W_{Root_{(i)}} fv_{Root_{(i)}}$$

(4)

$$|\vec{X}| = \|\vec{X}\|_2 = \sqrt{x_1^2 + \dots + x_k^2}$$

(5)

END IF

Algorithm 1 describes the similarity of semantic structure between different nodes.

Reconstructing the Semantic Link Network. Algorithm 2 describes how to build a spatial network model by constructing the community spatial structure in the community space, and then divide the community structure by calculating and modifying the semantic similarity.

Algorithm 2. Constructing the Spatial model of semantic link network

---

1 : The data captured by the web page is filtered through the ontology set, and the output set *S* is initialized.

2 : Traverse the whole community set and determine *Vn, Eqa, Ref, Seq, Sub, Imp* of some nodes by using the relationship between ontologies,the reasoning table is used to traverse the constructed map to accelerate the convergence of the relationship between nodes.

3 : Take the id of the user's speech as the subject primary key, and construct the spatial model *M* = (*G, T*) through semantic group mapping, semantic node mapping and semantic path mapping, where *G* = <*Vn, Eqa, Ref, Seq*>, *T* = (*Vn, Sub, Imp*);

4 : Calculate the word *vector(V)* entered by the user and the semantic structure similarity (*Sim*) between each node.

5 : Normalize the semantic structure similarity of each node (N)$N_{Sim_i} = \frac{Sim_i - Sim_{min}}{Sim_{max} - Sim_{min}}$. (7)

6 : Sort them.Sort(NodeSet$\{N_{Sim_1}, \ldots, N_{Sim_n}\}$). (8)

7 : Let the matrix Mark = 0 //Mark nodes that have been calculated

IF $N_{Sim_i} == 1$

THEN FOR Ni in G.Eqa set or T.Sub set ∈ N_{Sim_i}

Ni⊂S

Mark[i] = 1

IF $N_{Sim_i} =< 0.2$

THEN FOR Ni in T.Sub set or G.Eqa set ∈ N_{sss}

Ni ⊄ S

Mark[i] = 1

8 : FOR Mark[i] == 0 and SimNi > 0.6 //Correction of similarity by correlation degree between nodes

ImportantNi = 1

ImportantNj = 0.7

FOR Nj in Imp set

ImportantNj = ImportantNj + SimNi *(1-α) ImportantNi

FOR Nj in Seq set

ImportantNj = ImportantNj + SimNi * (1-β) ImportantNi

FOR Nj in Ref set

ImportantNj = ImportantNj + SimNi * (1-γ) ImportantNi

FOR Mark[j] == 0

SimNj = Important * SimNj

IF SimNj > 0.6

Nj ⊂ S

Mark[j] = 1

Return S

The algorithm is divided into three parts:

First the algorithm adopts the idea of P2P to construct mutual mapping of community space nodes. Then the algorithm normalizes the semantic structure similarity in order to preprocess the similarity correction, and also to obtain standardized output and avoid the influence of extreme outliers. The algorithm quickly forwards to the Equal set and Null/Unknown set of the node. Finally the importance of vertices can be propagated to adjacent vertices along the associated edge. During initialization, the importance of entities with high query relevance is set to 1 and the importance of other entities is set to 0.7. Continuously select the most important entity from the unprocessed entities (Mark == 0) for processing, and add its importance to the importance of implication, sequence and reference entities in the graph.

4 Experiment and Analysis

In experiment, we use the ego-Twitter data set provided by Stanford University. The density of its social network graph is 0.00053494, which can well represent the friend relationship in the real world. The experimental environment of this paper is running on a computer with AMD Ryzen 7 4800HS CPU, 16 GB memory and Win10 system.

4.1 Experimental Results and Analysis of Community Discovery Model

Effectiveness of Community Discovery Model. First we randomly selects a user in ego-Twitter, then established a two-tier social network relationship diagram, which contains 274 nodes and a total of 5183 sides. We constructs an original directed graph without weight, and the dense matrix is obtained by reasoning. The number of edges is 12476, which contains all semantic relations. The dense matrix is used as the input of similarity calculation to obtain the undirected graph. We divides the community nodes in the undirected graph and obtains the community discovery results. The results of friend directed graph (original), friend directed graph (transformation), friend undirected graph, and friend community discovery are shown in Fig. 2.

In Fig. 2, (a) Friend directed graph (original data) is inferred based on semantic relationship, and (b) Friend directed graph (transformation) is obtained through six semantic link types (Equal, Similar, Reference, etc.). Then, the directed graph is transformed into undirected graph (c) by calculating node semantic similarity. Finally, reasoning based on semantics to obtain the final discovery result.

(a) Friend directed graph (original data)

(b) Friend directed graph (transformed)

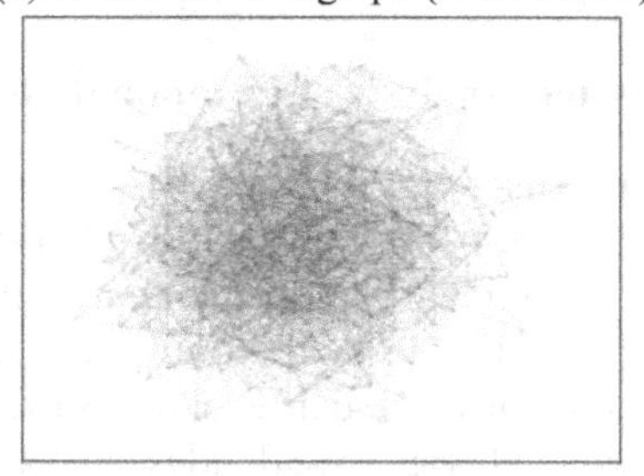

(c) Friend undirected graph

Fig. 2. Results of community discovery

Algorithm Performance Comparison. In order to compare the relationship between community size and modularity faced by different algorithms, we choose K-means and Late Factor Model (LFM), which are the mainstream algorithms of community discovery. In the experiment, network starts from 0 nodes, 40 new Twitter user nodes were randomly selected from the database each time and added to the original network. Through simulation, it is found that all algorithms grow linearly under fitting. With the increase of network nodes, the result of K-means algorithm is unstable and fluctuates greatly, so it is not suitable for community discovery of directed graph. The comparison results of the three algorithms are shown in Fig. 3.

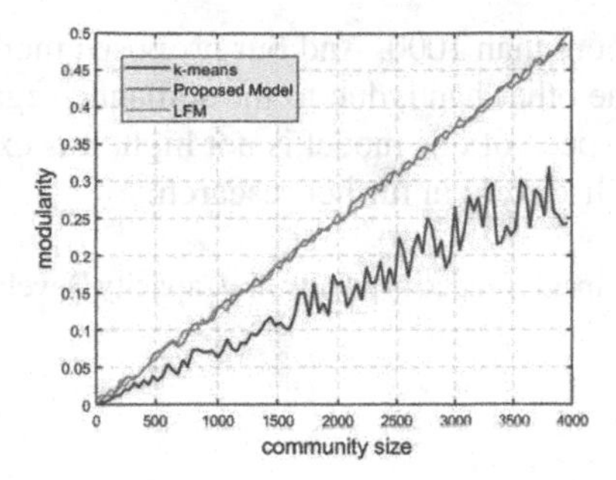

Fig. 3. Results of algorithm comparisons

The results of LFM and the proposed model are similar in terms of community division. Yet, when the community size increases to 1000, the modularity of our pro-posed model shows its advantages.

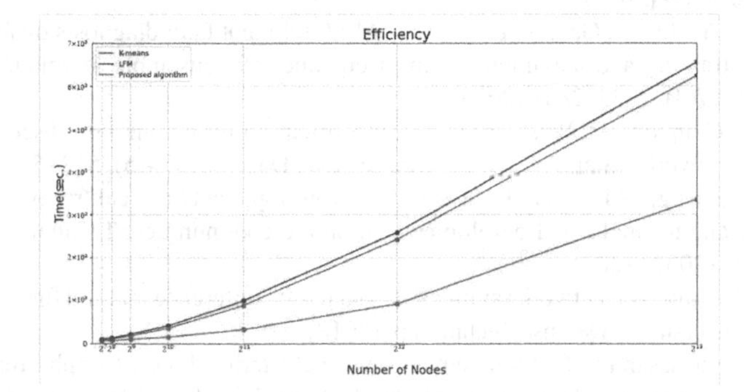

Fig. 4. The proposed model compares with K-means and LFM in efficiency

Figure 4 shows that as the number of nodes increases, our proposed algorithm takes less time than LFM and more time than K-means. The efficiency of our algorithm is better than that of LFM. The efficiency of K-means algorithm is the best. The reason may lies in that K-means uses simple clustering of nodes attributes while the other two algorithms applied reasoning rules in the process.

5 Conclusion

This paper proposed a network community discovery model based on semantic reasoning, and creatively discusses the composition and segmentation of network community from the perspective of semantic network. Based on the horizontal and vertical characteristics of nodes' semantics, the model uses both the tree topology and the spatial network structure to classify nodes into groups based on semantic reasoning. The experiment results show that the proposed model outperforms LFW and k-means algorithms in terms of modularity. Our model per-form even better when the node scale of online community expands to more than 1000. And our proposed model has higher efficiency in grouping nodes. On the other hand, due to the semantic segmentation and the complexity of reasoning, the speed of this model is not high. It is expected that we improve the speed of community discovery in further research.

Acknowledgement. This paper is funded in part by the Capacity Development Grant of Southwest University (SWU116007).

References

1. Rossetti, G.: ANGEL: efficient, and effective, node-centric community discovery in static and dynamic networks. Appl. Netw. Sci. **5**(1), 1–23 (2020). https://doi.org/10.1007/s41109-020-00270-6
2. Qiu, H., Zheng, Q., Msahli, M., Memmi, G., Qiu, M., Lu, J.: Topological graph convolutional network-based urban traffic flow and density prediction. IEEE Trans. Intell. Transp. Syst. **22**(7), 4560–4569 (2020)
3. Li, Y., Song, Y., Jia, L., Gao, S., Li, Q., Qiu, M.: Intelligent fault diagnosis by fusing domain adversarial training and maximum mean discrepancy via ensemble learning. IEEE Trans. Industr. Inf. **17**(4), 2833–2841 (2020)
4. Coscia, M., Giannotti, F., Pedreschi, D.: A classification for community discovery methods in complex networks. Stat. Anal. Data Mining ASA Data Sci. J. **4**(5), 512–546 (2011)
5. Yang, Z.L., Zhang, W.J., Yuan, F., et al.: Measuring topic network centrality for identifying technology and technological development in online communities. Technol. Forecast. Soc. Chang. **167**, 120673 (2021)
6. Ransa, C.: Research on network sampling and statistical inference method for social network. National University of Defense Technology (2018)
7. Satuluri, V., Parthasarathy, S.: Symmetrizations for clustering directed graphs. In: Proceedings of the 14th International Conference on Extending Database Technology, pp. 343–354. ACM (2011)
8. Zhang, H., Liang, X., Zhou, X.: Overlapping community discovery algorithm for local extension of directed graph. Data Acquisition Process. (003), 683–693 (2015)
9. Berners-Lee, T., Hendler, J., Lassila, O.: The semantic web. Sci. Am. **284**(5), 34–43 (2001)
10. Tan, Y., Zhang, J., Xia, X.: Research on the development process and current situation of semantic network. Libr. Inf. Knowl. (06), 102–110 (2019)
11. Principles of semantic networks: Explorations in the representation of knowledge. Morgan Kaufmann, San Francisco (2014)
12. Weikum, G., Dong, X.L., Razniewski, S., et al.: Machine knowledge: creation and curation of comprehensive knowledge bases. Found. Trends® Databases **10**(2–4), 108–490 (2021)
13. Hu, F., Lakdawala, S., Hao, Q., Qiu, M.: Low-power, intelligent sensor hardware interface for medical data preprocessing. IEEE Trans. Inf. Technol. Biomed. **13**(4), 656–663 (2009)

NNDF: A New Neural Detection Network for Aspect-Category Sentiment Analysis

Lijian Li[1,2], Yuanpeng He[1,3(✉)], and Li Li[1]

[1] College of Computer and Information Science College of Software, Southwest University, Chongqing 400715, China
{lljllj,hyppyh010403}@email.swu.edu.cn, lily@swu.edu.cn
[2] School of Engineering, The Hong Kong University of Science and Technology, Hong Kong 999077, China
[3] School of Computer Science, Peking University, Peking 100871, China

Abstract. Aspect-category sentiment analysis (ACSA) is crucial for capturing and understanding sentiment polarities of aspect categories hidden behind in sentences or documents automatically. Nevertheless, existing methods have not modeled semantic dependencies of aspect terms and specified entity's aspect category in sentences. In this paper, we propose a New Neural Detection Network, named NNDF in short, to enhance the ACSA performance. Specifically, representations of input sentences and aspect categories contained in our method are generated by a CNN-pooling-BiLSTM structure respectively, where sentences are represented based on their contextual words and aspect categories are represented based on word embeddings of entities category-specific. Then, a Transformer-based encoder is used to model implicit dependency of sentence contexts and aspect categories of entities in sentences. Finally, the embedding of aspect-category is learned by the novel bidirectional attention mechanism for the sentiment classification. Besides, experiments conducted on Restaurant and MAMS benchmark datasets for the task demonstrate that NNDF achieves more accurate prediction results as compared to several state-of-the-art baselines.

Keywords: Aspect-category sentiment analysis · Transformer-based encoder · Bidirectional attention mechanism

1 Introduction

Aspect-based sentiment analysis (ABSA) is a fine-grained sentiment analysis task which has attracted increasing attention in industry and academia. Other than traditional sentiment analysis tasks which predict sentiment polarity of a sentence or document, ABSA mainly focuses on identifying emotional polarities of multiple aspects contained in a sentence. Besides, it mainly consists of two tasks, i.e., aspect term sentiment analysis (ATSA) and aspect category sentiment analysis (ACSA). ATSA aims to predict emotional polarities towards aspect terms contained in a sentence. Contrast to the ATSA, ACSA is intended to analyze the sentiment polarity of a set of predefined aspect categories which are possibly not existing in sentences. A typical example of

G. Memmi et al. (Eds.): KSEM 2022, LNAI 13370, pp. 339–355, 2022.
https://doi.org/10.1007/978-3-031-10989-8_27

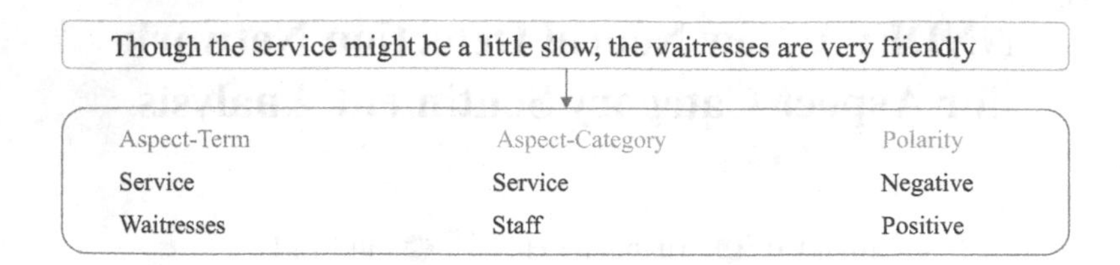

Fig. 1. An example of the sentence manifesting multi aspect emotions

the comparison ATSA and ACSA, based on the sentence "Though the service might be a little slow, the waitresses are very friendly" is in Fig. 1. In the ATSA, "service" and "waitresses" are aspect terms, which are visible in the sentence denoting the positive and negative emotions, respectively. In the ACSA, two aspect categories are "staff" and "service" which also express the same emotions, but the "staff" category doesn't appear in the sentence. In this paper, the focus of our research is mainly on ACSA. Therefore, how to accurately identify aspect categories and their contexts in sentences and obtain their relations is the main challenge we face.

Previous sentiment analysis works are almost sentence-based, which only focus on prediction of the emotional orientation of a whole sentence. Therefore, if we still apply the traditional models in ACSA, the outputs will possess some biases with respect to practical conditions. Recently, since neural network models were introduced into ACSA task, the performance of related models has been greatly improved. Based on Convolutional Neural Networks (CNN) and Recurrent Neural Networks (RNN), most early models achieved good performance. By employing convolutional windows-fixed filters, CNN and its derived models can effectively acquire semantic features and dependencies between words of sentences. Nevertheless, complex syntactic information contained in sentences still can not be obtained. e.g., for RNN [1] and its derivations, they are very sufficient for data with sequence characteristics and can mine temporal and semantic information in data. Hence, compared with other models, these sequence models based on RNN achieve better performance in ACSA. However, as the number of aspect categories with different sentiment polarities in sentences increases, they can not accurately obtain semantic features of aspect categories and their dependencies. Then, as the attention mechanism was proposed [2], combining it with RNN or CNN allows these models [3–5] to concentrate on key features for aspect terms which play great roles in sentiment prediction. However, because a sentence may contain various aspect categories, simply employing a single attention module is not enough to adequately obtain semantic features and associations between aspect categories and contexts. In general, these pre-existing models have following problems: (1) Noise data from other aspect categories will interfere with sentiment prediction. (2) These models can not fully acquire aspect-specific features and semantic dependencies of sentences because they contain multiple aspect categories.

To alleviate the aforementioned issues, in this paper, we propose a New Neural Detection Network, named NNDF in short, which applies the Pre-trained Bidirectional Encoder Representations from Transformers (BERT) to encode context words and aspect categories respectively to word embedding and utilizes a global feature extraction layer to capture both local and long-term feature information of sentences. Then, with the Transformer module [6], NNDF can better acquire semantic dependencies and emotional information and obtain connections between contexts and aspect categories. Finally, we utilize the bidirectional attention mechanism [7] to synchronously learn multi-aspect categories and their relations, which also avoids interference from sentiment information of other aspect categories.

All in all, our contributions can be summarized as follows:

- We propose a novel framework called NNDF for the aspect-category sentiment analysis.
- Our method leverages the Transformer-based encoder to capture implicit dependency of the sentence context and aspect categories of entities simultaneously, followed by the novel bidirectional attention mechanism is used to learn the aspect-category embedding.
- We conduct extensive experiments on two benchmark datasets, namely Restaurant and MAMS, and compare our results against several state-of-the-art baselines across on the ACSA task. The experimental results have verified the effectiveness of NNDF.

Organization: The remainder of this paper is organized as follows. We review related research in this area in Sect. 2. In Sect. 3, we formalize the problem and give an overview of the framework of our proposed NNDF model. Section 4 provides the details of the proposed NNDF model. In Sect. 5 and Sect. 6, we conduct extensive experimental evaluations and provide an analysis of the effectiveness of NNDF in terms of the ACSA task. Meanwhile, we also conduct the results of node embeddings for quantitative evaluations. Finally, the conclusion and future work are described in Sect. 7.

2 Related Work

This section briefly reviews related works from different semantic analysis granularity, i.e., sentence-level sentiment analysis methods and aspect-level sentiment analysis methods.

2.1 Sentence-Level Sentiment Analysis Methods

Machine Learning-Based Methods. Bhoi [8] compared the performances of various machine learning methods, including Naive Bayes, Decision Tree, Random Forest, Extra Trees, Extreme Gradient Boosting (XGBoost) and Support Vector Machine (SVM) [9]. Among of them, SVM gets the best classification results. However, these methods need to pre-construct abundant features and do lots of pre-processing for input sentences. The performance of these models greatly depends on the features of artificial construction and sufficient prior knowledge, which will cost more human resources.

Deep Neural Network-Based Methods. Since deep neural networks were applied widely to the field of sentiment classification, some models benefiting from them have obtained great performances. Compared with machine learning based models, deep neural networks are more powerful in capturing complex high-order features with non-linear activation functions, which usually yields better performance. For example, RNNs and CNNs [10–12] are capable of flexibly acquiring features of sentences. Account for positive conditions discussed before, some derived models have been proposed. Tang *et al.* [13] first proposed the idea of considering the semantic relatedness between target aspect term and its context word who also put forward two target-dependent LSTM modules to automatically capture features of aspect terms and contexts. Besides, some researchers combined CNN and LSTM to obtain both local and long-term semantic dependent information. Further, Yoon *et al.* [14] proposed a Multi-Channel Lexicon Integrated CNN-BiLSTM model, which utilized a multi-channel method on lexicon to improve lexicon feature and CNN and BiLSTM to obtain the n-gram features as well as long-term dependent information respectively. Besides, Wang *el al.* [15] put forward a novel CNN-LSTM model, which is composed of a regional CNN (R-CNN) and LSTM. Different from traditional CNN which regards a whole input text as input text, the regional CNN splits sentences into different regions whose useful local features will be effectively extracted. Moreover, by integrating R-CNN and LSTM, both local features and long-term dependent information can be utilized in the prediction process. Inspired by Wang's work, we designed a global feature extraction layer which is composed of CNN and RNN and inherits main advantages of Wang's work.

2.2 Aspect-Level Sentiment Analysis Methods

Deep Neural Network-Based Methods. All above models do not successfully take aspect-aware information into consideration and establish correlations between aspect terms and their emotional information in training completely. Then, researchers applied the attention mechanism to address the problem, which achieved good performance so that more and more attention-based models were raised. In view of this, some researchers combined LSTM with the attention mechanism, and also provided some valuable solutions in correlation construction. Wang *et al.* [3] applied the attention mechanism to establish semantic dependencies between contexts and aspect terms by appending aspect term embedding into word vectors as the input vectors. Besides, to generate more comprehensive representations, Ma *et al.* [16] designed more complicated network structures, including two separate attention modules which were used to learn attention weight of aspect terms and sentences. Inspired by Wang, some studies tried to apply the attention mechanism to other network structures. For instance, Tang *et al.* [17] employed the deep memory network and attention mechanism to generate deeper text representation. And Gu *et al.* [18] adopted a bidirectional attention mechanism to mutually establish relationships between sentences and aspect terms. In the last, Xue *et al.* [19] made computations parallel and effectively decreased training time by using CNN and gating units, but accuracy of the proposed model had not been improved significantly.

Transformer-Based Methods. Transformer [6] based methods make great progress in comparison to CNN and RNN in ACSA tasks. Jiang *et al.* [20] combined capsule networks with BERT to compute the deeper representations of sentences and aspect terms. Moreover, Wu *et al.* [21] adopted the pre-trained RoBERTa as backbone network to predict sentiment polarities of multi-aspect terms. And Wu *et al.* [22] put forward the quasi-attention to enable their model to learn both additive and subtractive attention, which effectively calculates the context-aware attention representations. All these works have achieved excellent performances, so we employ BERT as our backbone network to ensure accuracy of downstream classification task of our model.

Graph Neural Network-Based Methods. The prevalence of graph neural network based models, typically GCN [23–25], has led to excellent performance gains on sentiment analysis tasks. Liu *et al.* [7] utilized GCN to obtain sentence structure information and employed the bidirectional attention mechanism to acquire useful interactive information between aspect terms and contexts. By building a dependency tree of sentence, Zhang *et al.* [26] used a GCN module to better acquire semantic dependencies and syntactic information. In addition, Li *et al.* [27] integrated syntactic information and semantic dependencies through the SynGCN and SemGCN module simultaneously and employed two regularizers to model correlations among words.

3 Preliminary

In this section, we first formulate our task. Then, we introduce the framework of our proposed NNDF model.

3.1 Task Definition

The ACSA task aims to predict emotional polarity of designated aspect categories. Given a sentence $S = \{W_1, W_2, \cdots, W_n\}$ and we pre-defined special aspect categories $C = \{C_1, C_2, \cdots, C_m\}$ which may be a word or a phrase. The purpose of this paper is to predict the emotional polarities $y \in \{1, ..., P\}$. P is the number of sentiment categories, and the lengths of sentence S and aspect categories C are n and m. In the following, we take a sentence "The bar area was fairly crowded but service remained friendly and efficient" as an example shown in Fig. 2. Two aspect categories in the sentence are "place" and "service", and the emotional polarities towards them are negative and positive.

3.2 Solution Framework

The whole framework of NNDF can be illustrated in Fig. 3. The framework is divided into two key components:

- Embedding layer, it is used for forming the unified representations for encoding feature vectors of input nodes with different dimensions.
- Global Feature Extraction layer, Transformer Encoder Layer, Bidirectional Attention Layer, and Classification Layer.

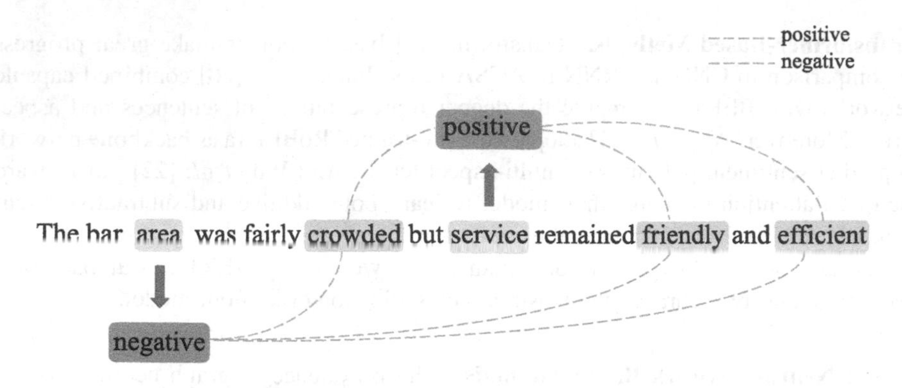

Fig. 2. A sentence from MAMS dataset. The categories "place" and "service" show negative and positive. And "place" is not presented in the sentence.

4 The Proposed Method

In this section, we first formulate our task, and then introduce the framework of our proposed NNDF model.

4.1 Input Representation Layer

We apply the GloVe embedding or BERT embedding in embedding layer to transform the sentence S into word embedding $\boldsymbol{E} = \{E_1, E_2, \cdots, E_n\}$. Then, we will briefly introduce the two embedding methods.

GloVe Embedding [28]**:** The GloVe model has high computational efficiency, and its scale of calculation is proportional to the corpus. When the corpus is small, the GloVe model still works well enough. Therefore, we use the pre-trained GloVe to convert sentence S into word embedding E. The context embedding is presented as $\boldsymbol{E}^s \in R^{d_e \times n}$ and d_e is the dimension of word vector. And the categories embedding is represented as $\boldsymbol{E}^c \in R^{d_e \times m}$. After the sentence passes through the embedding layer, we concatenate categories embedding and sentence embedding into the categories-aware sentence embedding $\mathbf{E}^{sc} = [\mathbf{E}^s; \mathbf{E}^c]$.

BERT Embedding [29]**:** Compared with traditional embedding methods, BERT has obtained obvious improvement since it was introduced into NLP tasks. The input of BERT consists of a token, segmentation, and position embedding. Therefore, to utilize pre-trained BERT, the sentence and categories are denoted as $\{[CLS], S_1, S_2, \cdots, [SEP]\}$ and $\{[CLS], C_1, C_2, \cdots, [SEP]\}$. Then, the input will be transformed to the presentation $\{H_{[CLS]}, H_{[S_1]}, \cdots, H_{[S_n]}, H_{[SEP]}\}$ and $\{H_{[CLS]}, H_{[C_1]}, \cdots, H_{[C_m]}, H_{[SEP]}\}$ respectively.

4.2 Global Feature Extraction

We will introduce the global feature extraction layer (GFE), which is composed of CNN and BiLSTM.

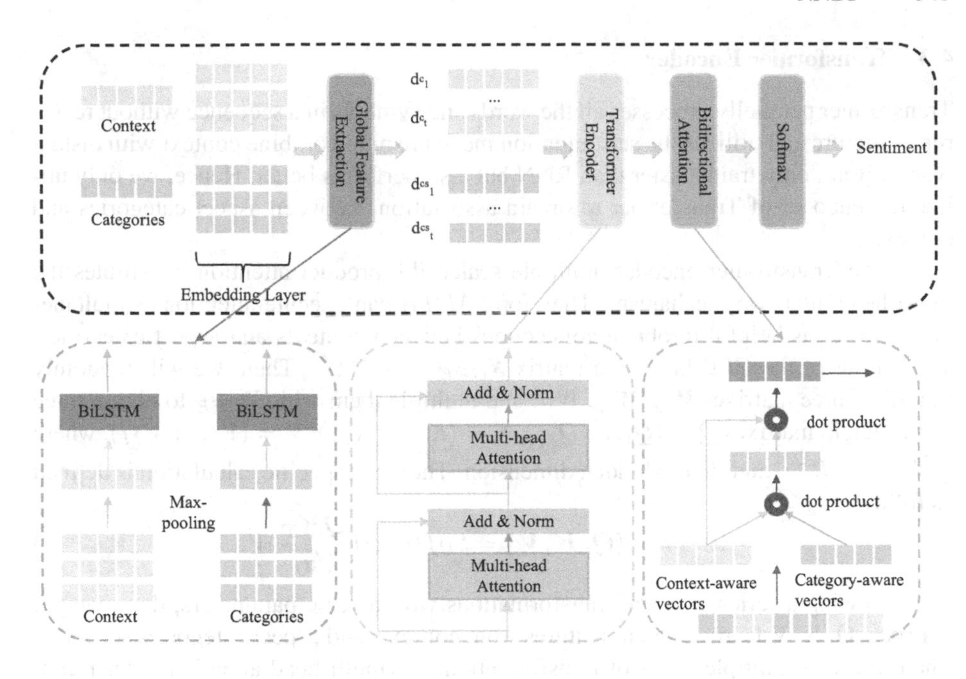

Fig. 3. The overall architecture of NNDF

CNN: We utilize the convolutional layer to extract local features and reduce dimensions of input. Convolving the window vectors, each filter can generate different features at separate positions. And as filter moves, numerous local features of sentences are captured. In this paper, we set the number and length of filter to be 150 and 3. Besides, we select ReLU which is easy to calculate and speed up convergence of the network as our non-linear transformation function in the convolution process. Then, we applied K-Max pooling to output of convolutional layer, because max-pooling layer not only reduces the amount of computations but also preserves the most significant information. And output of all max-pooling layers will be fused to produce input of BiLSTM.

BiLSTM: Due to weak ability of CNN to capture long-term features, we put BiLSTM over CNN to acquire long-term semantic information, which deals with the problems of gradient explosion as well as gradient vanishing and utilizes gating units and memory cells to selectively capture useful semantic information in both directions. The update of hidden states and memory cells contents, which includes current input and past state, is determined by gate units, consisting of input, output and forget gate. In this case, we set the dimension of all hidden layers in BiLSTM to be 150. Then, we regard the last hidden state of BiLSTM as the final representation. Therefore, output of GFE will contain local features and long-term semantic information, which will help Transformer module to establish better connections between contexts and aspect categories.

4.3 Transformer Encoder

Transformer parallelly processes all the words and symbols in a sequence without recurrent structure and utilizes the self-attention mechanism to combine context with distant words. It not only trains faster than RNN but also performs better. Hence, we only utilize the encoder of Transformer to obtain associations between aspect categories and contexts.

In the Transformer encoder, multiple scaled dot-product attention constitutes the multi-head attention mechanism. Therefore, MHA can execute attentions simultaneously, which is helpful to obtain connections between contexts and aspect categories. The output of the GFE layer is a matrix $\boldsymbol{X_{GFE}} \in R^{M \times d_e}$. Then, we will randomly initialize three matrixes $\boldsymbol{W_Q}$, $\boldsymbol{W_K}$, $\boldsymbol{W_V}$, and multiple them with X_{GFE} to obtain three same weight matrixes $\boldsymbol{Q} = (\boldsymbol{Q}_1, ..., \boldsymbol{Q}_M), \boldsymbol{K} = (\boldsymbol{K}_1, ..., \boldsymbol{K}_M), \boldsymbol{V} = (\boldsymbol{V}_1, ..., \boldsymbol{V}_M)$, where $q_i, k_i, v_i \in R^{\frac{d_h}{h}}$, and d_h is a hidden dimension. Then, the specific calculation is defined as follows:

$$Attention(\boldsymbol{Q}, \boldsymbol{K}, \boldsymbol{V}) = Softmax(\frac{\boldsymbol{Q}\boldsymbol{K_T}}{\sqrt{\boldsymbol{d_k}}})\boldsymbol{V} \tag{1}$$

Following a series of linear transformations with diverse parameters, three weight matrixes **Q, K, V** learn different features from contexts and aspect categories severally. Then, through multiple times of transformation, the multi-head attention further captures degrees of associations between aspect categories and its semantic words. The summing of all outputs of scaled dot-product attention will be output of multi-head attention:

$$MHA(\mathbf{Q}, \mathbf{K}, \mathbf{V}) = Concat(head_1, ..., head_h)\boldsymbol{W}^O \tag{2}$$

$$head_i = Attention(\boldsymbol{Q}\boldsymbol{W}_i^Q, \boldsymbol{K}\boldsymbol{W}_i^K, \boldsymbol{V}\boldsymbol{W}_i^V) \tag{3}$$

where $\boldsymbol{W}_i^Q \in R^{d_h \times d_k}, \boldsymbol{W}_i^K \in R^{d_h \times d_k}, \boldsymbol{W}_i^V \in R^{d_h \times d_v}, \boldsymbol{W}^O \in R^{d_h}$, and $d_k = d_v = d_h/h$. In this paper, we set $h = 8$ which is the number of attention layers. And output of GFE layer will be used as input of Transformer encoder and aspect categories representation $MHA^{ca} = [h_1^{ca}, h_2^{ca}, \cdots, h_m^{ca}]$ and context representation $MHA^c = [h_1^c, h_2^c, \cdots, h_m^c]$ will be calculated, where $\boldsymbol{h}_i^{ca}, \boldsymbol{h}_i^c \in R^{d_h}$.

4.4 Bidirectional Attention

We utilize bidirectional attention to further fuse the feature information of contexts and aspect categories. During the process of calculation, attention vectors go into the modeling layer with embedding vectors from the previous layer for each time step, which contributes to decreasing loss of information. And we will fuse semantic dependencies by categories-aware attention and context-aware attention mechanism.

Categories-Aware Attention: Assume the output matrices of contexts and aspect categories are $\boldsymbol{h}^c = [h_1^c, h_2^c, \ldots, h_t^c, \cdots, h_n^c]$ and $\boldsymbol{h}^{ca} = [h_1^{ca}, h_2^{ca}, \cdots, h_t^{ca}, \cdots, h_m^{ca}]$. The calculation is defined as follows:

$$\alpha = \sum_{i=1}^{m} \frac{\exp(e\boldsymbol{h}^{\bar{c}\mathrm{T}} \cdot \boldsymbol{W}_{ca} \cdot \boldsymbol{h}_{ca_i}^{ca})}{\sum_{i=1}^{m} \exp(\boldsymbol{h}^{\bar{c}\mathrm{T}} \cdot \boldsymbol{W}_{ca} \cdot \boldsymbol{h}_{ca_i}^{ca})} \cdot h_{ca_i}^{ca} \tag{4}$$

$$r^{ca} = \sum_{i=1}^{M} \alpha \cdot h_{ca_i}^{ca} \tag{5}$$

where r^{ca} is representation of categories, which has learned lots of emotional information from contexts. $\bar{h^c}$ is obtained by average pooling context vectors. $h_{ca_i}^{ca}$ represents aspect category vectors and W_{ca} denotes the attention weight matrix.

Contexts-Aware Attention: Similarly, we will utilize the new categories-aware representation for the same calculation. Then, the new context representation will be calculated as $\mathbf{r}^{ca}$. The expression of calculation is:

$$\beta = \frac{\exp\left(\bar{r^{ca}}^{\mathrm{T}} \cdot W_c \cdot h_i^c\right)}{\sum_{i=1}^{m} \exp(\bar{r^{ca}}^{\mathrm{T}} \cdot W_c \cdot h_i^c)} \tag{6}$$

$$r^c = \sum_{i=1}^{M} \beta \cdot h^c \tag{7}$$

where $\mathbf{r}^c$, which contains the semantic relevance of aspect categories and contexts, is the final representation for the sentiment prediction.

4.5 Loss Function and Training

We will input the final representation r^c into the classification layer to predict the emotional polarities towards aspect categories given.

$$p = Softmax(W_p r^c + b_p), \tag{8}$$

where p is sentiment polarities towards aspect categories, W_p, b_p are learnable parameters. And to constrain randomness dropout brings, we apply the Regularized Dropout (R-Drop) [30] to put a regular constraint on prediction, which reduces inconsistency between training and testing. Compared with the traditional training methods, R-Drop only adds a KL-divergence loss function.

$$L_i^{CE} = -\log P_\theta^{(1)}(y_i|x_i) - \log P_\theta^{(2)}(y_i|x_i), \tag{9}$$

$$L_i^{(KL)} = \frac{1}{2}[KL(P_\theta^{(2)}(y|x_i))||P_\theta^{(1)}(y|x_i) + KL(P_\theta^{(1)}(y|x_i))||P_\theta^{(2)}(y|x_i)], \tag{10}$$

$$L_i = L_i^{CE} + \alpha L_i^{KL}. \tag{11}$$

where x_i, y_i are results of two predictions with the same parameters, L_i^{CE} is the sum of two original cross-entropy functions. L_i^{KL} is KL divergence between two models, α is weight of KL loss. In this paper, α will be set to 3, which is different from the optimal solution proposed in the original paper.

5 Experiments

In this section, we compare the performance of our proposed NNDF model with several state-of-the-art baselines, and a few variants of NNDF itself, using two benchmark datasets.

5.1 Experiment Settings

Datasets: We select two benchmark datasets to conduct a series of experiments to evaluate the performance of NNDF, which includes Restaurant [31][1] and MAMS datasets [32][2]. Then, we will briefly introduce the two datasets. Compared with the Restaurant dataset, MAMS adopts five aspect categories from the Restaurant dataset and adds two more aspect categories to deal with some chaotic cases. Different from other datasets, every sentence from MAMS expresses multiple emotional polarities. The release of MAMS pushes forward the development of the ABSA task and prevents it from degenerating to sentence-level sentiment analysis. Table 1 provides specific quantitative information of two datasets.

Table 1. The statistics of both Restaurant and MAMS datasets in the experiments

Dataset		Pos.	Neg.	Neu.	Total.
Restaurant	Train	2164	807	637	3608
	Test	728	196	196	1120
MAMS	Train	1929	2084	3077	7090
	Validation	241	259	388	888
	Test	245	263	393	901

Baselines: In order to evaluate NNDF more comprehensively, we exploit a series of state-of-the-art models as baselines for comparison, including variations of RNN models, CNN with gate units, capsule network, heterogeneous GCN-based models, and Transformer-based models.

- LSTM [1] is a basic RNN network, which utilizes output of the last layer as final sentence representation to conduct emotional categorization.
- TD-LSTM [13] integrates the aspect terms into LSTM to establish correlations between aspects and contexts.
- ATAE-LSTM [3] adds input aspect terms embedding into vector of each word and utilizes the attention mechanism to better establish dependencies between aspect terms and input vector.
- BiLSTM+Attn, based on AT-LSTM, replaces LSTM with BiLSTM to enable the model to take information from both directions of semantic features into accounts.
- IAN [16] uses two same parts which are composed of LSTM and an attention mechanism to learn representations of aspect terms and contexts interactively. Then, concatenate two representations as final representation for emotion prediction.
- MemNet [13] uses multiple computational layers to calculate text representation and representation of the last layer will be used for emotional categorization.
- GCAE [19] utilizes the convolutional layer and gate units to parallelly generate and capture aspect-related sentiment features, which is more efficient than RNN-based models.

[1] The Restaurant dataset of SemEval-2014 Task 4: https://alt.qcri.org/semeval2014/task4.
[2] The MAMS dataset: http://tcci.ccf.org.cn/conference/2020.

- PBAN [18] appends positional vectors into input vectors, which can distill aspect-aware information better, and employs bidirectional attention mechanism to establish semantic dependencies between aspect terms and their emotional information.
- BRET [29] utilizes the multi-layer bidirectional transformer encoder to compute more comprehensive representation.
- RoBERTa [33] pre-trains with eight times larger batches and corpora and employs dynamic masking to take place of static masking in BERT, compared with BERT.
- RoBERTa-TMM [34] adopts the pre-trained RoBERTa as backbone network, then fine-tune it on the MAMS dataset.
- CapsNet [20] uses bidirectional gated recurrent unit (BiGRU) to obtain contextualized representation and feeds them into capsule network whose outputs are used to predict emotional polarities.
- CapsNet-BERT combines strength of the capsule network and BERT. The pre-trained BERT is used to compute deep representations of sentences and aspect terms, which will be fed into a capsule network to predict sentiment polarities.
- ASGCN [26] employs Bidirectional LSTM to capture contextual information regarding aspect terms and uses GCN to obtain edge information of syntactical dependencies, which enables the model to capture dependencies among aspect terms.
- QACG-BERT [22] improves the structure of BERT to be context-aware and appends a quasi-attention mechanism. By learning quasi-attention weights which could be negative, the model could learn compositional attention that supports subtractive attention.
- DualGCN [27] obtains syntactic information and semantic dependencies by the SynGCN and SemGCN module. Then, usage of regularizers with semantic constraints is to solve the overlapping problem of semantic information, which makes emotion prediction more accurate.

Implementation Details: We choose 300-dimension Glove vectors to generate word embedding for non-Transformer-based models. For Transformer-based models, we utilize pre-trained BERT as the backbone network whose embedding dimension and hidden state dimensions are set to 768. For MAMS dataset and Restaurant dataset, we set the size of mini-batch to be 64 and 32 respectively. Then, we employ Adam [35] as our optimization function to update models parameters in iterations. And for non-Transformer-based models and Transformer-based models, we set the initial learning rates to be 0.0003 and 0.00003. The initial dropout rate will be set to 0.5. Finally, we obtain final results by averaging the outputs of 5 round of running.

6 Experimental Results and Analyses

We utilize accuracy and macro-averaged F1-score as our assessment metrics to assess performance of NNDF. The experimental results are shown in Table 2. Obviously, NNDF achieves the best performance in comparison to other baseline methods on two datasets. Then, we will make some discussions and analyses based on the experimental results.

Table 2. The performance results (%) of different methods on the two datasets for the aspect-category Sentiment task. The best and second best results in each column is boldfaced and underlined respectively (the higher, the better). Improvements over the best baseline are shown in the last row

Method	MAMS		Restaurant	
	Acc	F1	Acc	F1
LSTM	47.37	0.432	72.77	0.554
TD-LSTM	**62.37**	**0.497**	**75.09**	**0.587**
ATAE-LSTM	70.63	0.584	77.58	0.66
BiLSTM+Attn	66.3	0.553	76.36	0.645
IAN	-	-	78.6	0.689
MemNet	63.29	0.541	76.54	0.653
GCAE	72.11	0.613	77.84	0.675
PBAN	-	-	81.16	0.716
CapsNet	73.99	0.629	83.55	0.735
ASGCN	-	-	80.77	0.722
DualGCN	-	-	**84.27**	**0.781**
BERT	78.29	0.697	90.44	0.806
RoBERTa	77.44	0.683	-	-
QACG-BERT	-	-	90.67	0.813
RoBERTa-TMM	78.03	0.686	-	-
CapsNet-BERT	**79.46**	**0.698**	**91.38**	**0.824**
NNDF	76.42	0.672	83.76	0.728
NNDF-BERT	**81.53**	**0.713**	**92.26**	**0.835**

The performance of all models on the Restaurant dataset is much higher than the one on the MAMS dataset. The result remains consistent with our intuition that the sentences in the MAMS dataset involve more aspect categories, which makes it more difficult for those models to accurately detect emotional information and establish correlations of different aspect categories. The performance of TD-LSTM has made great progress compared with the original LSTM, because TD-LSTM utilizes LSTM to separately capture features of aspect terms and contexts and model their relationships. But one thing needs to be pointed out is that it cannot judge which one of contextual features contributes more to the determination of emotional polarity. To generate a more comprehensive representation, ATAE-LSTM integrates embedding of aspect term into vector of each word. Different from ATAE-LSTM, IAN pays more attention to establishing the relationship between aspect terms and contexts which not only calculates the weight of each word in contexts but also learns weight of each word in corresponding aspect terms. Besides, PBAN achieves outstanding performance by appending positional vectors to input vectors to enable the model to find aspect terms and related information more accurately and utilizing bidirectional attention to model correlations between aspect terms and contexts. The experimental results proved that adding position information is vital for finding the location of aspect categories in ACSA task.

For GCN-based models, the performance of DualGCN on Restaurant dataset is better than ASGCN. In the process of extracting feature information, problem of overlapping semantic dependencies exists, which means that one category will match some semantic information of another category. For DualGCN model, it uses orthogonal and differential regularizers to learn an semantic attention matrix and features respectively, which solves interference of semantic information of other aspect terms. Previous experimental results have proved that LSTM is not skilled in aspect-specific feature extraction. It is not enough to use a BiLSTM in obtaining aspect-specific features, or it will result in unapparent improvement. For ASGCN model, due to the excellent ability of GCN to employ semantic dependencies and syntactic information despite the usage of LSTM, ASGCN still achieves great performance.

Obviously, compared with non-Transformer-based models, Transformer-based models have made great progress in performance improvement on two datasets, which proves the strong ability of BERT. But at the same time, it also costs generous time. To calculate representations of each layer, the theoretical time complexity of NNDF is $\mathcal{O}(n^2 \cdot d)$, where n is the length of input sequence, d is the dimension of representation. For our model, in comparison with non-Transformer-based models, NNDF achieves the second performance, second only to DualGCN. Compared with Transformer-based methods, NNDF-BERT achieves the best performance on both datasets. The performance of NNDF-BERT on MAMS datasets exceeds CapsNet-BERT by 2.07%. In general, NNDF-BERT accurately extracts feature information and models relationships between aspect categories and contexts, and the relationships enable aspect categories to better match corresponding emotional information.

6.1 Case Study

To further explore how our model outperforms other ones, we use our model, CapsNet-BERT, ASGCN to predict a sentence from MAMS dataset, which has two aspect categories named "food" and "service". Figure 4 and Table 3 provides the experimental results, where the underline indicates that the weight of the word is the largest, followed by the wavy underline and the overline is the lowest. Based on the results of experiment, NNDF performs better than the other two models. Through the visual analysis above, when NNDF accurately locates words representing aspect categories in sentences, they are distributed the highest weight. And different with the other two models, it finds out words or phrases that represent emotional information of specific aspect categories and reduces influences brought by other interfering words. Besides, another point which should be pointed out is that NNDF assigns some weight to conjunction word "but", which sets up a symbol of differentiation of semantic orientation and helps distinguish sentiment information of two aspect categories named "space" and "service" well. Thus, the above analysis proves that NNDF has a better ability to identify emotional information of each category than pre-existing models.

Table 3. The weight visualization of a sentence for CapsNet, DualGCN and NNDF

Model	Category	Attention visualization	Prediction	Label
CapsNet	Place	The bar area was fairly crowded but service remained friendly	Neu.	Neg.
	Service	The bar area was fairly crowded but service remained friendly	Pos.	Pos.
DualGCN	Place	The bar area was fairly crowded but service remained friendly	Neg.	Neg.
	Service	The bar area was fairly crowded but service remained friendly	Pos.	Pos.
NNDF	Place	The bar area was fairly crowded but service remained friendly	Neg.	Neg.
	Service	The bar area was fairly crowded but service remained friendly	Pos.	Pos.

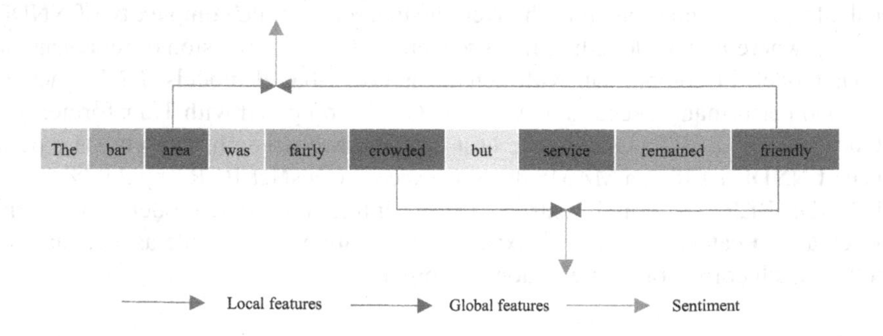

Fig. 4. The weight visualization of a sentence for NNDF

6.2 Ablation Study

We conduct some ablation studies to further explore the function of each part of NNDF in this section. And the experimental results of the ablation study are provided in Table 4.

Table 4. The experimental results of the ablation study

Model	MAMS (ACSA)		Restaurant (ACSA)	
	Acc	F1	Acc	F1
NNDF	76.42	0.672	83.76	0.728
NNDF w/o GFE	75.37	0.665	81.14	0.701
NNDF w/o BA	73.76	0.641	82.37	0.713
NNDF w/o TE	73.45	0.637	**82.69**	**0.716**
NNDF w/o R	**75.67**	**0.669**	82.57	0.715

where NNDF w/o BA denotes that NNDF removes the bidirectional attention layer and uses the original attention mechanism. NNDF w/o GFE denotes NNDF without the global feature extraction layer. And NNDF w/o TE represents Transformer encoder layer-removed NNDF. Besides, NNDF w/o R symbolizes NNDF without R-Drop and using the original cross-entropy function. According to Table 3, it is interesting to see that the experimental results of NNDF w/o BA are similar to NNDF w/o TE. It implies that both Transformer encoder and bidirectional attention are significant to establish relationships between aspect categories and their emotional information. Obviously, NNDF w/o GFE performs worse on both datasets, which suggests that the GFE layer helps to locate multiple aspect categories and capture their corresponding features. Finally, without R-Drop, the performance of NNDF w/o R receives the same percentage of deterioration on both datasets, which indicates that R-Drop can improve the generalization ability of NNDF.

7 Conclusion

In this paper, we proposed a new Transformer-based model with bidirectional attention mechanism. NNDF mainly focuses on establishing connections between aspect categories and their emotional information and filtering noise information during prediction. And except for the GloVe embeddings, we employ a pre-trained BERT to encode our sentences and categories to further enhance the performance of NNDF. We conduct a series of experiments on Restaurant and MAMS datasets. The experimental results indicate that NNDF-BERT achieves the best performance in comparison to some strong baseline models. Our future work will concentrate on two aspects:

- the time cost of our model is large for the abundant RNNs. Therefore, we will focus on using the GCN to obtain semantic dependencies to decrease the training time.
- we will strengthen associations between semantic dependencies. We tend to remould the structure of the Transformer to further capture the syntactic dependencies and incorporate syntactic and semantic information.

Acknowledgement. We greatly appreciate the valuable suggestions and encouragement from anonymous reviewers and the editor.

References

1. Sepp, H., Jürgen, S.: Long short-term memory. Neural Comput. **9**(8), 1735–1780 (1997)
2. Bahdanau, D., Cho, K., Bengio, Y.: Neural machine translation by jointly learning to align and translate (2015)
3. Wang, Y., Huang, M., Zhu, X., Zhao, L.: Attention-based LSTM for aspect-level sentiment classification. In: EMNLP, pp. 606–615 (2016)
4. Chen, P., Sun, Z., Bing, L., Yang, W.: Recurrent attention network on memory for aspect sentiment analysis. In: EMNLP, pp. 452–461 (2017)
5. Huang, B., Ou, Y., Carley, K.M.: Aspect level sentiment classification with attention-over-attention neural networks. In: SBP-BRiMS, pp. 197–206 (2018)
6. Vaswani, A., et al.: Attention is all you need. In: NIPS, pp. 5998–6008 (2017)

7. Liu, J., Liu, P., Zhu, Z., Li, X., Xu, G.: Graph convolutional networks with bidirectional attention for aspect-based sentiment classification. Appl. Sci. **11**(4), 1528 (2021)
8. Bhoi, A., Joshi, S.: Various approaches to aspect-based sentiment analysis. CoRR, abs/1805.01984 (2018)
9. Vicente, I.S., Saralegi, X., Agerri, R.: EliXa: a modular and flexible ABSA platform. CoRR, abs/1702.01944 (2017)
10. Castellucci, G., Filice, S., Croce, D., Basili, R.: UNITOR: aspect based sentiment analysis with structured learning. In: SemEval, pp. 761–767 (2014)
11. Johnson, R., Zhang, T.: Semi-supervised convolutional neural networks for text categorization via region embedding. In: NIPS, pp. 919–927 (2015)
12. Kim, Y.: Convolutional neural networks for sentence classification. CoRR, abs/1408.5882 (2014)
13. Tang, D., Qin, B., Feng, X., Liu, T.: Effective LSTMS for target-dependent sentiment classification. In: COLING, pp. 3298–3307 (2016)
14. Yoon, J., Kim, H.: Multi-channel lexicon integrated CNN-BILSTM models for sentiment analysis. In: ROCLING, pp. 244–253. The Association for Computational Linguistics and Chinese Language Processing (ACLCLP) (2017)
15. Wang, J., Yu, L., Lai, K.R., Zhang, X.: Dimensional sentiment analysis using a regional CNN-LSTM model. In: ACL (2016)
16. Ma, D., Li, S., Zhang, X., Wang, H.: Interactive attention networks for aspect-level sentiment classification. In: IJCAI, pp. 4068–4074 (2017)
17. Tang, D., Qin, B., Liu, T.: Aspect level sentiment classification with deep memory network. In: EMNLP, pp. 214–224 (2016)
18. Gu, S., Zhang, L., Hou, Y., Song, Y.: A position-aware bidirectional attention network for aspect-level sentiment analysis. In: COLING, pp. 774–784 (2018)
19. Xue, W., Li, T.: Aspect based sentiment analysis with gated convolutional networks. In: ACL, pp. 2514–2523 (2018)
20. Jiang, Q., Chen, L., Xu, R., Ao, X., Yang, M.: A challenge dataset and effective models for aspect-based sentiment analysis. In: EMNLP-IJCNLP, pp. 6279–6284 (2019)
21. Wu, Z., Ying, C., Dai, X., Huang, S., Chen, J.: Transformer-based multi-aspect modeling for multi-aspect multi-sentiment analysis. In: NLPCC, pp. 546–557 (2020)
22. Wu, Z., Ong, D.C.: Context-guided BERT for targeted aspect-based sentiment analysis. In: AAAI/EAAI, pp. 14094–14102 (2021)
23. Msahli, M., Qiu, H., Zheng, Q., Memmi, G., Lu, J.: Topological graph convolutional network-based urban traffic flow and density prediction. IEEE TITS **22**(7), 4560–4569 (2020)
24. Li, Y., Song, Y., Jia, L., Gao, S., Qiu, M.: Intelligent fault diagnosis by fusing domain adversarial training and maximum mean discrepancy via ensemble learning. IEEE TII **17**(4), 2833–2841 (2020)
25. Fei, H., Lakdawala, S., Qi, H., Qiu, M.: Low-power, intelligent sensor hardware interface for medical data preprocessing. IEEE Trans. Inf. Technol. Biomed. **13**(4), 656–663 (2009)
26. Zhang, C., Li, Q., Song, D.: Aspect-based sentiment classification with aspect-specific graph convolutional networks. In: EMNLP-IJCNLP, pp. 4567–4577 (2019)
27. Li, R., Chen, H., Feng, F., Ma, Z., Wang, X., Hovy, E.H.: Dual graph convolutional networks for aspect-based sentiment analysis. In: ACL/IJCNLP, pp. 6319–6329 (2021)
28. Pennington, J., Socher, R., Manning, C.D.: Glove: global vectors for word representation. In: EMNLP, pp. 1532–1543 (2014)
29. Devlin, J., Chang, M., Lee, K., Toutanova, K.: BERT: pre-training of deep bidirectional transformers for language understanding. In: NAACL-HLT, pp. 4171–4186 (2019)
30. Liang, X., et al.: R-drop: regularized dropout for neural networks. CoRR, abs/2106.14448 (2021)

31. Kirange, D.K., Deshmukh, R.R., Kirange, M.D.K.: Aspect based sentiment analysis SemEval-2014 task 4. AJCSIT **4**, 72–75 (2014)
32. Chen, L., Xu, R., Yang, M.: Overview of the NLPCC 2020 shared task: multi-aspect-based multi-sentiment analysis (MAMS). In: Zhu, X., Zhang, M., Hong, Yu., He, R. (eds.) NLPCC 2020. LNCS (LNAI), vol. 12431, pp. 579–585. Springer, Cham (2020). https://doi.org/10.1007/978-3-030-60457-8_48
33. Liu, Y., et al.: Roberta: a robustly optimized BERT pretraining approach. CoRR, abs/1907.11692 (2019)
34. Wu, Z., Ying, C., Dai, X., Huang, S., Chen, J.: Transformer-based multi-aspect modeling for multi-aspect multi-sentiment analysis. In: Zhu, X., Zhang, M., Hong, Yu., He, R. (eds.) NLPCC 2020. LNCS (LNAI), vol. 12431, pp. 546–557. Springer, Cham (2020). https://doi.org/10.1007/978-3-030-60457-8_45
35. Kingma, D.P., Ba, J.: Adam: a method for stochastic optimization. In: ICLR (2015)

Fourier Enhanced MLP with Adaptive Model Pruning for Efficient Federated Recommendation

Zhongyang Ai[1,2], Guangjun Wu[1(✉)], Binbin Li[1], Yong Wang[1], and Chuantong Chen[3]

[1] Institute of Information Engineering, Chinese Academy of Sciences, Beijing, China
{aizhengyang,wuguangjun,libinbin,wangyong}@iie.ac.cn
[2] School of Cyber Security, University of Chinese Academy of Sciences, Beijing, China
[3] Jinan Cigarette Factory, China Tobacco Shandong Industrial Co., Ltd., Jinan, China
chenchuantongnb@163.com

Abstract. Federated learning (FL) is gradually gaining traction as the de facto standard for distributed recommendation model training that takes advantage of on-device user data while reducing server costs. However, the computation resources of user devices in FL are usually much more limited compared to servers in a datacenter, which hinders the application of some advanced recommendation models (*e.g.*, Transformer-based models) in FL. In addition, models with better recommendation performance tend to have more parameters, which increases the cost of communication between servers and user devices. Therefore, it is difficult for existing federated recommendation methods to achieve a good trade-off between recommendation accuracy and computation and communication costs. As a response, we propose a novel federated recommendation framework for efficient recommendations. First, we propose an all-MLP model by replacing the self-attention sublayer in a Transformer encoder with a Fourier sublayer, in which the noise information in the user interaction data is effectively attenuated using Fast Fourier Transform and learnable filters. Second, we adopt an adaptive model pruning technique in the FL framework, which can significantly reduce the model size without affecting the recommendation performance. Extensive experiments on four real-world datasets demonstrate that our method outperforms existing federated recommendation methods and strikes a good trade-off between recommendation performance and model size.

Keywords: Recommender system · Sequential recommendation · Federated recommendation · Federated learning · All-MLP model

G. Memmi et al. (Eds.): KSEM 2022, LNAI 13370, pp. 356–368, 2022.
https://doi.org/10.1007/978-3-031-10989-8_28

1 Introduction

Recommender systems (RSs) are widely deployed in online platforms because they can predict users' potential interests in items based on their historical behavior. Early studies of traditional RSs usually use collaborative filtering to model user's preferences, based on historical feedback [8,19]. On this basis, matrix factorization technology is proposed [8,9] to enhance the generalization ability of the model. Furthermore, deep learning-based models [11,23] have gradually become the mainstream solution for recommendation task due to their flexibility and expressivity. More recently, Transformer-based methods [16,20] have shown remarkable performance in this task by stacking multi-head self-attention layers. These methods require collecting local data from user devices and then training a large-scale recommendation model in a central server. However, some of the policies and legislation implemented to regulate the use of users' private data, such as the General Data Protection Regulation (GDPR)[1] and the California Consumer Privacy Act (CCPA)[2], may make such centrally trained recommendation models no longer work.

Fortunately, Federated Learning (FL) [7,13] addresses this specific challenge by facilitating decentralized training of RSs. In such federated RSs [1,2,14], first, a subset of users is assigned by the central server to train a shared recommendation model using their local data. The server then aggregates all local models into a global model that is sent to the devices to provide recommendations. During the whole process, the users' private data does not leave their local devices to maximize privacy protection. Client devices in FL are typically resource-constrained in terms of computing power, communication bandwidth, memory and storage size, while existing advanced recommendation models (*e.g.*, Transformer-based models) usually have complex network structures and a large number of parameters. Therefore, training a well-performing recommendation model locally on a resource-limited client can take prohibitively long and consume a large amount of energy. In addition, the recommendation model needs to be transmitted many rounds between the user clients and the server during the FL process, so a large model size can induce a huge communication overhead.

To address these above challenges, we propose a novel framework named MPERec to implement efficient federated recommendations, which can achieve a good balance between recommendation accuracy and model size. In order to reduce the model size without compromising recommendation accuracy, an intuitive idea is to discard components of the model that do not contribute to model performance. We refer to such components as *noise components* and define them at both data and parameter levels. At the data level, we consider items in a user's interaction sequence that are unrelated to the user's real interests and have no impact on the user's subsequent behaviors as noise components of the data. To counteract their effects, we borrow the idea of employing filtering algorithms to attenuate noise in the frequency domain from the field of signal processing

[1] https://gdpr-info.eu.
[2] https://oag.ca.gov/privacy/ccpa.

[15]. Specifically, we implement a lightweight all-MLP network by replacing the self-attention sublayer in a Transformer encoder with a Fourier sublayer, in which Fast Fourier Transform and learnable filters are utilized to reduce the potential impact of noise components. At the model parameter level, we consider those parameters that have little impact on the model update as the noise components of the parameters. In response, we propose an adaptive model pruning technique that finds an optimal set of remaining (*i.e.*, not pruned) model parameters for the most efficient training in the near future. In this way, the size of the model and the number of parameters are effectively reduced without compromising the future potential of the model. To verify the effectiveness of our method, we conduct extensive experiments on four real-world datasets. Experimental results indicate that MPERec consistently outperforms centrally training methods and FL-based methods, where the all-MLP network results in better recommendation performance and lower time complexity, and adaptive model pruning further reduces the model size and significantly accelerates the model convergence. The major contributions of this paper are summarized as follows:

- We propose a lightweight all-MLP recommendation model in which a Fourier sublayer is utilized to reduce the time complexity of the model and the potential influence of noise.
- We propose an adaptive model pruning technique in the federated setting that can significantly reduce the model size without compromising the recommendation performance of the model.
- We conduct extensive experiments on four benchmark datasets. The experimental results show that our method consistently outperforms centrally trained methods and FL-based methods while effectively reducing computational and communication consumption.

2 Proposed Method

2.1 Problem Statement

Let $\mathcal{U} = \{u_1, u_2, \ldots, u_{|\mathcal{U}|}\}$ denote a set of users and $\mathcal{V} = \{v_1, v_2, \ldots, v_{|\mathcal{V}|}\}$ denote a set of items. For user $u \in \mathcal{U}$, the list $\mathcal{S}^u = (v_1^u, v_2^u, \ldots, v_{n_u}^u)$ denote the user's interaction sequence in chronological order, where $v_t^u \in \mathcal{V}$ is the item that u has interacted with at time step t and n_u is the length of interaction sequence for u. During the training process, at time step t, the recommendation model predicts the next item depending on the previous t items. Formally, given the contextual item sequence $\mathcal{S}^u$, the task of our recommendation model is to predict the next item that u is likely to interact with at time step $n_u + 1$, which can be denoted as $P(v_{n_u+1}^u = v| \ \mathcal{S}^u)$.

2.2 Fourier Enhanced MLP Recommendation Model

Background on the Fourier Transform. The Fourier Transform decomposes a function into its constituent frequencies. Given a sequence of numbers $\{x_l\}$ with $l \in [0, L-1]$, the 1D discrete Fourier Transform (DFT) is defined by the formula:

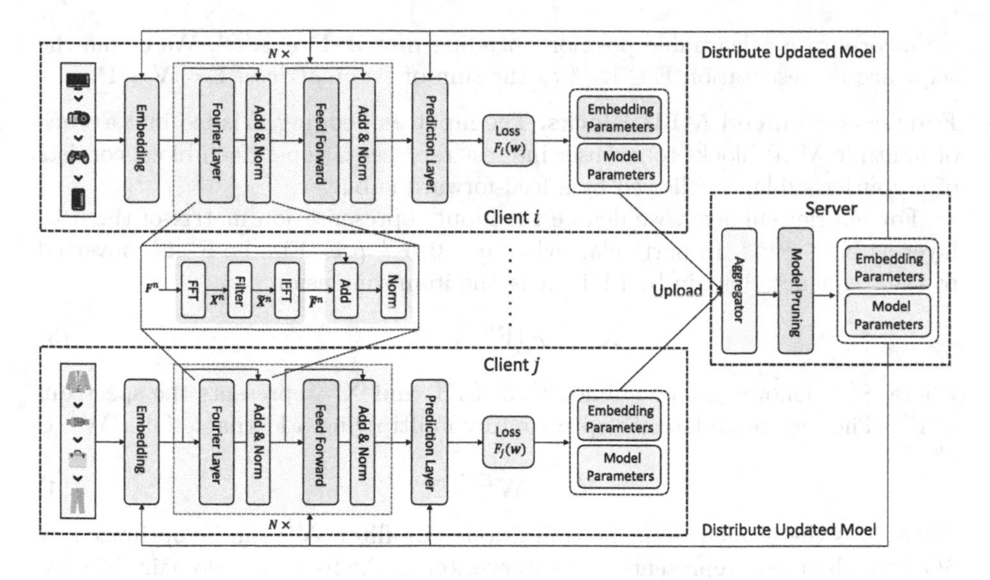

Fig. 1. The overview framework of MPERec.

$$X_k = \sum_{l=0}^{L-1} x_l e^{-\frac{2\pi i}{L} lk}, \quad 0 \leq k \leq L-1. \tag{1}$$

For each k, the DFT generates a new representation X_k as a sum of all of the original input tokens x_l, with so-called "twiddle factors". In this way, X_k represents the spectrum of the sequence $\{x_l\}$ at the frequency $\omega_k = 2\pi k/L$. The DFT X_k can be converted to the original sequence by the inverse DFT (IDFT) as:

$$x_l = \frac{1}{L} \sum_{k=0}^{L-1} X_k e^{\frac{2\pi i}{L} lk}. \tag{2}$$

The Fast Fourier Transform (FFT) is a widely used approach for computing the DFT [4]. The standard FFT algorithm is the Cooley–Tukey algorithm [3], which recursively re-expresses the DFT of a sequence of length L and reduce the time complexity to $\mathcal{O}(LlogL)$. Correspondingly, the inverse DFT can also be computed efficiently by the inverse FFT (IFFT). FFT and IFFT, together with filters of different frequencies, are widely used to filter noise signals in the digital signal processing area [21]. In this work, we draw on this idea to reduce the effect of the noise components in user data.

Embedding Layer. We create an item embedding matrix $\mathbf{M}_I \in \mathbb{R}^{|\mathcal{V}| \times d}$, where d is the latent dimension. The embedding look-up operation retrieves the previous l items' embeddings and stacks them together into a matrix $\mathbf{V} \in \mathbb{R}^{l \times d}$. To let our model be aware of the relative position of the items in a sequence, we incorporate a learnable position encoding matrix $\mathbf{P} \in \mathbb{R}^{l \times d}$. We define the sequence representation $\mathbf{E} \in \mathbb{R}^{l \times d}$ as the sum of two matrices: $\mathbf{E} = \mathbf{V} + \mathbf{P}$.

Fourier-Enhanced MLP Blocks. The input embedding $\mathbf{E}$ is fed into a stack of multiple MLP blocks to get user interest representations. Each block consists of a Fourier sublayer followed by a feed-forward sublayer.

For Fourier sublayer, we denote the input representation matrix of the n-th layer as $\mathbf{F}^n \in \mathbb{R}^{l \times d}$. In particular, when $n = 0$, $\mathbf{F}^0 = \mathbf{E}$. Firstly, $\mathbf{F}^n$ is converted to the frequency domain by FFT along the item dimension:

$$\mathbf{X}^n = \mathcal{F}(\mathbf{F}^n) \in \mathbb{C}^{l \times d}, \tag{3}$$

where $\mathcal{F}(\cdot)$ denotes the one-dimensional FFT and $\mathbf{X}^n$ represents the spectrum of $\mathbf{F}^n$. Then we modulate the spectrum by multiplying a learnable filter $\mathbf{W}^F \in \mathbb{C}^{l \times d}$:

$$\widetilde{\mathbf{X}}^n = \mathbf{W}^F \odot \mathbf{X}^n, \tag{4}$$

where $\odot$ is the element-wise multiplication. The filter $\mathbf{W}^F$ can be optimized by SGD to adaptively represent an arbitrary filter in the frequency domain. Finally, we adopt the IFFT to transform $\widetilde{\mathbf{X}}^n$ back to the time domain:

$$\widetilde{\mathbf{F}}^n = \mathcal{F}^{-1}(\widetilde{\mathbf{X}}^n) \in \mathbb{R}^{l \times d}, \tag{5}$$

where $\mathcal{F}^{-1}(\cdot)$ denotes the inverse one-dimensional FFT. With the operations of FFT and IFFT, the noise components in the input representations are effectively attenuated. Following [6], we utilize layer normalization, residual connections and dropout to alleviate the gradient vanishing and unstable training problems:

$$\widetilde{\mathbf{F}}^n = \mathrm{LayerNorm}(\widetilde{\mathbf{F}}^n + \mathrm{Dropout}(\widetilde{\mathbf{F}}^n)). \tag{6}$$

For feed-forward sublayer, we adopt a two-layer feed-forward network with ReLU activation in between to endow the model with the nonlinearity and consider interactions between different latent dimensions:

$$\mathrm{FFN}(\widetilde{\mathbf{F}}^n) = \mathrm{ReLU}(\widetilde{\mathbf{F}}^n \mathbf{W}^{(1)} + \mathbf{b}^{(1)})\mathbf{W}^{(2)} + \mathbf{b}^{(2)} \tag{7}$$

where $\mathbf{W}^{(1)}, \mathbf{W}^{(2)} \in \mathbb{R}^{d \times d}$ and $\mathbf{b}^{(1)}, \mathbf{b}^{(2)} \in \mathbb{R}^d$.

Prediction Layer. After N stacked Fourier-enhanced MLP blocks, we have the user's preference representation $\mathbf{F}_t^N$ adaptively and hierarchically extracted from the previous t items. We calculate the user's preference score for the item v at time step $(t+1)$ by employing a latent factor model:

$$P(v) = \mathbf{V}_i \mathbf{F}_t^N, \tag{8}$$

where $\mathbf{V}_i \in \mathbb{R}^d$ is the embedding vector of item v.

Complexity Analysis. Transformer-based models such as SASRec [6] and BERT4Rec [22] typically stack multi-head self-attention blocks to learn sequential representations and achieve state-of-the-art performance on sequential recommendation tasks. However, there is a severe issue with the Transformer-based model that prevents it from being directly applicable to the FL framework, namely, quadratic time complexity and high memory usage. As a comparison, our model is solely based on MLP-based structures, which can significantly reduce both the space and time complexity for modeling sequence data and largely reduces the number of involved parameters.

Specifically, we compare the complexity of the two types of models when the sequence length is l. In Transformer-based models, the atom operation of self-attention mechanism, namely canonical dot-product, causes the time complexity and memory usage per layer to be $\mathcal{O}(l^2)$. In contrast, our MLP-based model consists of FFT and IFFT operations with the cost of $\mathcal{O}(l \cdot log\ l)$, and feed-forward networks with the cost of $\mathcal{O}(l)$, which means the total complexity is $\mathcal{O}(l \cdot log\ l)$. We will make a further numerical comparison of the recommendation performance and efficiency in Sect. 3.

2.3 Federated Framework with Model Pruning

Federating the Recommendation Model. We implement the recommendation model in the FL framework proposed in [13] to achieve federated recommendations. We treat each user $u \in \mathcal{U}$ as a client in the FL system. For each client u with a fixed local dataset $\mathcal{S}^u$, its local empirical risk is defined as $F_u(\mathbf{w}) := \frac{1}{|\mathcal{S}^u|} \sum_{i \in \mathcal{S}^u} f_i(\mathbf{w})$, where $f_i(\mathbf{w})$ is the loss function with model parameter vector $\mathbf{w}$. The goal of the system is to minimize the global empirical risk:

$$\min_{\mathbf{w}} F(\mathbf{w}) := \frac{1}{|\mathcal{U}|} \sum_{u \in \mathcal{U}} F_u(\mathbf{w}). \tag{9}$$

In the FL process, client u performs multiple SGD steps on its local empirical risk $F_u(\mathbf{w})$ to update the model parameter vector $\mathbf{w}$. The server then performs a parameter fusion step, which involves gathering local parameters from clients and computing an aggregated parameter. In the following, we call this procedure of multiple local SGD steps followed by a fusion step a *round*.

As mentioned in Sect. 1, the above FL process is severely challenged when the model size is large in mobile computing scenarios where clients' computation and communication resources are limited. To address this challenge, we propose a adaptive model pruning technique in our framework.

Adaptive Model Pruning. As illustrated in Fig. 1, the pruning is done at the server after receiving parameter updates from clients. In each step, adaptive model pruning finds the best set of *remaining* (*i.e.*, are not pruned) model parameters for the most efficient training in the near future, where "efficient" refers to high model performance and fast training speed. To achieve this, we estimate the empirical risk reduction divided by the time required for an FL round, for any given subset of the parameters being pruned.

Empirical Risk Reduction. After the parameter fusion step in the server, all clients start model training based on the same parameter vector $\mathbf{w}$. Therefore, we study the change of the empirical risk after one SGD step at k iteration. Let $\mathbf{g}_{\mathbf{w}}(k)$ denote the stochastic gradient of parameter $\mathbf{w}$ computed on the full parameter space at k iteration, in which case $\mathbb{E}[\mathbf{g}_{\mathbf{w}}(k)] = \nabla F(\mathbf{w}(k))$. Then, a mask vector $\mathbf{m}_{\mathbf{w}}(k)$ is defined that is zero if the corresponding component in $\mathbf{w}(k)$ is pruned and one if not. The pruned parameter vector is denoted by $\mathbf{w}'(k)$, and the SGD step in the next iteration will be calculated based on $\mathbf{w}'(k)$:

$$\mathbf{w}(k+1) = \mathbf{w}'(k) - \alpha \mathbf{g}_{\mathbf{w}'}(k) \odot \mathbf{m}_{\mathbf{w}'}(k), \tag{10}$$

where α is the stepsize. For simplicity, we omit the subscripts $\mathbf{w}'$ of $\mathbf{g}$ and $\mathbf{m}$ below. Now we have:

$$\begin{aligned} F(\mathbf{w}(k+1)) &\approx F\left(\mathbf{w}'(k)\right) + \left\langle \nabla F\left(\mathbf{w}'(k)\right), \mathbf{w}(k+1) - \mathbf{w}'(k) \right\rangle & (11) \\ &= F\left(\mathbf{w}'(k)\right) - \alpha \left\langle \nabla F\left(\mathbf{w}'(k)\right), \mathbf{g}(k) \odot \mathbf{m}(k) \right\rangle & (12) \\ &\approx F(\mathbf{w}'(k)) - \alpha \|\mathbf{g}(k) \odot \mathbf{m}(k)\|^2 & (13) \end{aligned}$$

where $\langle \cdot, \cdot \rangle$ is inner product, (11) is from Taylor expansion, (12) is because of (10), and (13) is obtained by using the gradient to approximate its expectation, *i.e.*, $\mathbf{g}(k) \approx \nabla F\left(\mathbf{w}'(k)\right)$. Let $\mathcal{M}$ denote the index set of the parameters that are not pruned, which corresponds to the indices of the non-zero values of the mask vector $\mathbf{m}(k)$. Then, the approximate empirical risk reduction after the SGD step (10) is calculated as:

$$\begin{aligned} F\left(\mathbf{w}'(k)\right) - F(\mathbf{w}(k+1)) &\approx \alpha \|\mathbf{g}(k) \odot \mathbf{m}(k)\|^2 \\ &\propto \|\mathbf{g}(k) \odot \mathbf{m}(k)\|^2 \\ &= \sum_{j \in \mathcal{M}} g_j^2 =: \varDelta(\mathcal{M}) \end{aligned} \tag{14}$$

where g_j is the j-th component of $\mathbf{g}(k)$ and the sef function $\varDelta(\mathcal{M})$ is defined in (14). We use $\varDelta(\mathcal{M})$ as the approximate risk reduction.

Time of One FL Round. When the remaining parameters of the recommendation model is $\mathcal{M}$, the time of a round of FL is defined as a set function $T(\mathcal{M}) := \mu + \sum_{j \in \mathcal{M}} t_j$, where μ is a constant representing a fixed system overhead, and t_j is the time corresponding to the j-th parameter component. According to our experimental results, t_j for all j that of the same neural network remains the same. As such, before the pruning starts, we can estimate the quantities $\{t_j\}$ and μ by measuring the time of one FL round for a small subset of different model sizes.

Optimization Objective. Our goal is to find an optimal set of remaining parameters $\mathcal{M}$ that can maximize the empirical risk reduction per unit training time, which can be expressed by: $\varGamma(\mathcal{M}) := \frac{\varDelta(\mathcal{M})}{T(\mathcal{M})}$.

The adaptive pruning approach can reduce the model size continuously as long as such reduction has no negative impact on future training. Intuitively, the model that emerges from this procedure has a small size while still retaining full "trainability" in subsequent iterations. Parameter components for which the corresponding gradient components remain zero or close to zero will be pruned.

3 Experiments

3.1 Experimental Setup

Dataset. We evaluate the proposed method on four real-world representative datasets, which are very different in domains, size and sparsity:

- **Amazon**[3]**:** This is a series of product review datasets, composed of product reviews and metadata crawled from *Amazon.com* by McAuley et al. [12]. We select two subcategories: "Beauty" and "Sports & Outdoors".
- **MovieLens**[4]**:** This is a popular movie rating data used to evaluate recommendation algorithms. In this work, we adopt a well-established version, ML-1m, which includes 1 million ratings.
- **Steam**[5]**:** This is a dataset collected by Kang and McAuley [6] from Steam, a major online video game distribution platform.

For dataset preprocessing, we follow the common procedure in [6,17]. For all datasets, we transform the presence of a review or rating to implicit feedback (*i.e.*, the user interacted with the item). To ensure the quality of the dataset, following the common practice in [6,10,22], we discard users and items with fewer than 5 related actions. In all experiments, we randomly select 80% of the clients as training clients, 10% as validation clients, and the rest as test clients.

Evaluation Metrics. To evaluate the ranking list of all the methods, we employ two widely adopted Top-N metrics including Hit@10 and NDCG@10. Hit@10 indicates the percentage of the ground-truth items that appear in the top 10 recommended items. NDCG@10 is the normalized discounted cumulative gain at 10, assigning larger weights on higher positions. To simplify the computation, we follow the common strategy in [6,10,22]. For each user, we randomly sample 100 negative items and rank these items against the ground-truth item to evaluate the metrics. The average scores of test clients in terms of two metrics are calculated and reported.

Baselines. To fully demonstrate the effectiveness of our proposed MPERec solution, we include three groups of recommendation baselines:

- Early classical methods. Including a matrix factorization-based method, **BPR** [18], and two sequential recommendation methods, **FPMC** [17] and **GRU4Rec** [5], based on Markov chain and RNN, respectively.
- Transformer-based methods. A line of work that employs the self-attention mechanism to model users' behaviour sequences, including **SASRec** [6], **BERT4Rec** [22] and **TiSASRec** [10].
- Federated recommendation methods. A line of work that implements a recommendation model in an FL framework to achieve privacy-preserving recommendations, including **FCF** [1], **FedMF** [2] and **FedFast** [14].

[3] http://jmcauley.ucsd.edu/data/amazon/.
[4] https://grouplens.org/datasets/movielens/.
[5] https://cseweb.ucsd.edu/~jmcauley/datasets.html#steam_data.

3.2 Recommendation Performance

Table 1 shows the recommendation performance of all methods on the four datasets. It can be observed that:

Table 1. The performance of MPERec with other baseline methods over four datasets. The best performance and second best performance for each column are indicated in bold and underlined fonts, respectively.

Method	Beauty		Sports		ML-1m		Steam	
	Hit	NDCG	Hit	NDCG	Hit	NDCG	Hit	NDCG
BPR	0.2412	0.1453	0.2698	0.1879	0.5813	0.3249	0.5912	0.3415
FPMC	0.2595	0.1591	0.4761	0.2512	0.6898	0.5135	0.6019	0.4171
GRU4Rec	0.2911	0.1817	0.4467	0.2414	0.7138	0.5346	0.5714	0.3891
SASRec	0.4826	0.3143	0.4912	0.2911	0.8093	0.5751	0.8281	0.6012
BERT4Rec	0.4916	0.3244	0.4998	0.2860	0.8119	0.5878	0.8114	0.5987
TiSASRec	0.4986	0.3318	0.4818	0.2814	0.8214	0.5897	0.8402	0.6094
FCF	0.2312	0.1381	0.2312	0.1817	0.5513	0.3041	0.5512	0.3156
FedMF	0.2513	0.1534	0.2379	0.1701	0.5789	0.3261	0.5413	0.3313
FedFast	0.2536	0.1514	0.2790	0.2092	0.5849	0.3354	0.5880	0.3425
MPERec	**0.5124**	**0.3510**	**0.5091**	**0.2965**	**0.8412**	**0.6008**	**0.8604**	**0.6164**

Transformer-based methods consistently outperform methods from the other two groups by a large margin on all datasets. This may be due to the fact that Transformer-based architectures have more complex structures and more learnable parameters, corresponding to their stronger capacity to model user behavior. Among the early classical methods, the non-sequential method BPR has the worst recommendation performance. This illustrates that capturing the sequential patterns of user behaviors help effectively improve the expressivity of the model. The overall recommendation performance of the federated recommendation methods is comparable to that of BPR since they all apply a relatively simple recommendation model in the FL framework.

MPERec improves over all the baseline methods on four datasets with respect to the two metrics. On the one hand, we apply a all-MLP architecture and learnable filters in the recommendation model, enabling the model to have better recommendation performance than Transformer-based models with lower time complexity and memory usage. On the other hand, we apply an adaptive model pruning technique to enable relatively complex recommendation models to be easily deployed in an FL framework, which allows our method to achieve a substantial lead over other federated recommendation methods.

3.3 Ablation Study

There are several key components in MPERec, including learnable filters (Filter), adaptive model pruning (Pruning), point-wise feed-forward network (PFFN),

Table 2. NDCG@10 on four datasets. Bold score indicates performance better than the default version, while ↓ indicates performance drop more than 10%.

Architecture	Dataset			
	Beauty	Sports	ML-1m	Steam
MPERec	0.3510	0.2965	0.6008	0.6164
w/o Filter	0.2865↓	0.2313↓	0.5404↓	0.5579
w/o Pruning	**0.3542**	0.2961	0.5996	0.6096
w/o PFFN	0.3360	0.2788	0.5590	0.5817
w/o RC	0.3011↓	0.2549↓	0.5689	0.5909
1 block ($N = 1$)	0.3470	0.2867	0.5871	0.6098
3 blocks ($N = 3$)	**0.3570**	0.2956	**0.6121**	**0.6248**
4 blocks ($N = 4$)	0.3506	0.2914	**0.6182**	**0.6279**

residual connection (RC), and the block number N of the MLP layer. To further understand their impact on recommendation performance, we conduct ablation experiments over them on four datasets. Table 2 shows the results of our default version ($N = 2$) and its seven variants on all four datasets. We introduce the variants and analyze their effects respectively:

(1) **Filter.** Without the filter layer attenuating the effect of noise, the performance of the model drops dramatically on all datasets. This indicates that the learnable filter is a very critical component in our all-MLP model.
(2) **Pruning.** Removing adaptive model pruning did not result in a significant improvement in recommendation performance. This is because the pruning technique we applied prunes those parameters that have little impact on the future training of the model, ensuring that the model performance is not affected to the maximum extent possible while reducing the model size.
(3) **PFFN.** Without PFFN, the results show a significant declinc, especially on dense datasets (*e.g.*, ML-1m). This is because PFFN can endow the model with nonlinearity as well as integrate the information contained in different latent dimensions, which is more important for long sequence data.
(4) **RC.** The results show that RC has a greater impact on the performance on sparse datasets (*e.g.*, Beauty). Presumably this is because information in lower layers is difficult to propagate to the final layer, and this information is highly useful for making recommendations on sparse datasets.
(5) **Number of blocks N.** We observe that increasing the number of blocks significantly boosts the performance on dense datasets (*e.g.*, ML-1m). The declines in Beauty and Sports with $N = 4$ are primarily due to overfitting.

3.4 Training Time Reduction

MPERec enables efficient federated recommendations owing to its inclusion of two important components, Fourier-enhanced MLP and adaptive model pruning.

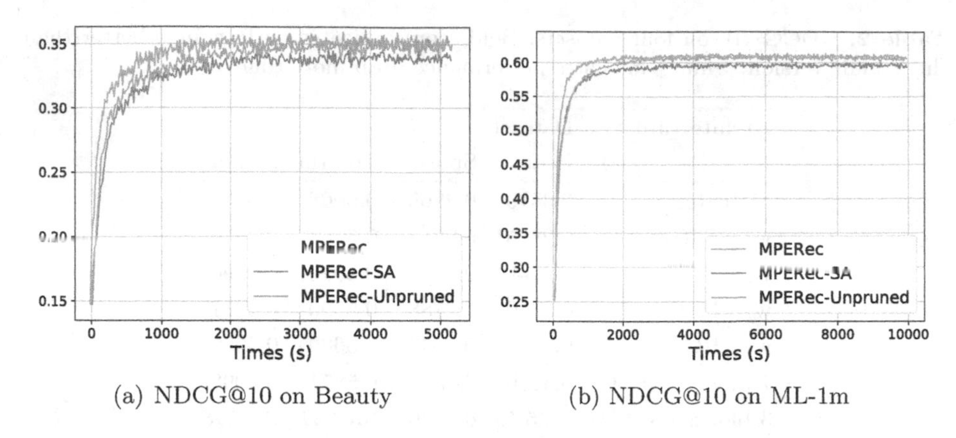

(a) NDCG@10 on Beauty

(b) NDCG@10 on ML-1m

Fig. 2. Performance (NDCG@10) vs. time results of 2 datasets.

To fully illustrate the role of these two components in improving training efficiency, we conduct experiments on the test performance of MPERec and its two variants over training time. We removed the model pruning module in MPERec to obtain the variant MPERec-Unpruned. Additionally, we replace the Fourier layer in MPERec with a standard self-attention layer and name it MPERec-SA. Figure 2 shows the test performance (NDCG@10) vs. time results on ML-1m and Beauty, and we have the following observations:

First, the fluctuations of the performance curve on ML-1m are significantly smaller than those on Beauty, which indicates that the model will perform more consistently and stably on dense datasets. Second, without the model pruning module, MPERec-Unpruned converges to similar performance achieved by MPERec on both datasets, but with significantly lower convergence speed. This suggests that the adaptive model pruning technique can effectively improve the model training efficiency. Third, the convergence point of the MPERec-SA curve is lower than the other two curves, which indicates that the model with the all-MLP structure in our method has better recommendation performance compared to the more complex Transformer structure instead.

3.5 Impact of Latent Dimensionality

The latent dimensionality d is a key hyperparameter of recommendation models, which is important for both recommendation performance and training efficiency. A larger d tends to help increase the expressiveness of the model, but also introduces more computational effort. To investigate the effect of d on different methods, we conduct comparative experiments on our proposed MPERec and three Transformer-based methods. Figure 3 shows the NDCG@10 for these methods on two datasets with d varying between 10 and 100.

One of the most obvious observations is that the performance of each method tends to converge with increasing dimensionality. A larger latent dimension does not necessarily improve model performance, especially on sparse dataset Beauty.

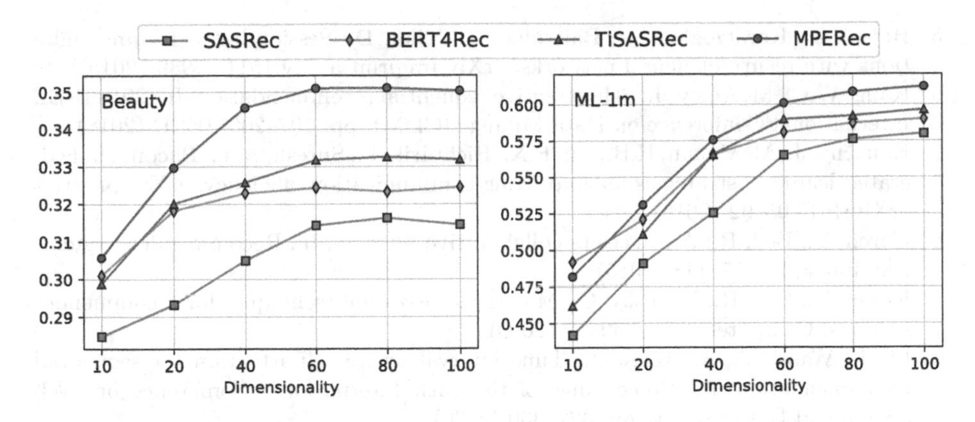

Fig. 3. Effect of the latent dimensionality d on NDCG@10.

This may be due to overfitting. In terms of details, the performance of TiSASRec has a slight advantage over BERT4Rec, both of which are significantly better than SASRec. Finally, our method consistently outperforms all other methods on both datasets, especially in the case of relatively large latent dimensionality.

4 Conclusion

In this work, we propose an efficient federated recommendation framework, in which a recommendation model with an all-MLP structure is implemented to effectively reduce the time complexity, and an adaptive model pruning technique is applied to further reduce the model size and the number of parameters. Extensive experimental results on four real-world datasets show that our proposed method consistently outperforms other methods in terms of recommendation performance, while reducing computational complexity and training time significantly.

Acknowledgements. This work is supported by the National Key Research and Development Program of China under Grant 2021YFB3101503; by the National Natural Science Foundation of China under Grant 61931019.

References

1. Ammad-Ud-Din, M., et al.: Federated collaborative filtering for privacy-preserving personalized recommendation system. arXiv preprint arXiv:1901.09888 (2019)
2. Chai, D., Wang, L., Chen, K., Yang, Q.: Secure federated matrix factorization. IEEE Intell. Syst. **36**(5), 11–20 (2020)
3. Frigo, M., Johnson, S.G.: The design and implementation of FFTW3. Proc. IEEE **93**(2), 216–231 (2005)
4. Heideman, M.T., Johnson, D.H., Burrus, C.S.: Gauss and the history of the fast Fourier transform. Archive for History of Exact Sciences, pp. 265–277 (1985)

5. Hidasi, B., Karatzoglou, A., Baltrunas, L., Tikk, D.: Session-based recommendations with recurrent neural networks. arXiv preprint arXiv:1511.06939 (2015)
6. Kang, W.C., McAuley, J.: Self-attentive sequential recommendation. In: 2018 IEEE International Conference on Data Mining (ICDM), pp. 197–206. IEEE (2018)
7. Konečný, J., McMahan, H.B., Yu, F.X., Richtárik, P., Suresh, A.T., Bacon, D.: Federated learning: strategies for improving communication efficiency. arXiv preprint arXiv:1610.05492 (2016)
8. Koren, Y., Bell, R.: Advances in collaborative filtering. In: Recommender Systems Handbook, pp. 77–118 (2015)
9. Koren, Y., Bell, R., Volinsky, C.: Matrix factorization techniques for recommender systems. Computer **42**(8), 30–37 (2009)
10. Li, J., Wang, Y., McAuley, J.: Time interval aware self-attention for sequential recommendation. In: Proceedings of the 13th International Conference on Web Search and Data Mining, pp. 322–330 (2020)
11. Lian, J., Zhou, X., Zhang, F., Chen, Z., Xie, X., Sun, G.: xDeepFM: combining explicit and implicit feature interactions for recommender systems. In: Proceedings of the 24th ACM SIGKDD International Conference on Knowledge Discovery & Data Mining, pp. 1754–1763 (2018)
12. McAuley, J., Targett, C., Shi, Q., Van Den Hengel, A.: Image-based recommendations on styles and substitutes. In: SIGIR, pp. 43–52 (2015)
13. McMahan, B., Moore, E., Ramage, D., Hampson, S., Aguera y Arcas, B.: Communication-efficient learning of deep networks from decentralized data. In: Artificial Intelligence and Statistics, pp. 1273–1282 (2017)
14. Muhammad, K., et al.: FedFast: going beyond average for faster training of federated recommender systems. In: Proceedings of the 26th ACM SIGKDD International Conference on Knowledge Discovery & Data Mining, pp. 1234–1242 (2020)
15. Rabiner, L.R., Gold, B.: Theory and Application of Digital Signal Processing. Prentice-Hall, Englewood Cliffs (1975)
16. Radford, A., Narasimhan, K., Salimans, T., Sutskever, I.: Improving language understanding by generative pre-training (2018)
17. Rendle, S., Freudenthaler, C., Schmidt-Thieme, L.: Factorizing personalized Markov chains for next-basket recommendation. In: WWW (2010)
18. Rendle, S., Freudenthaler, C., Gantner, Z., Schmidt-Thieme, L.: BPR: Bayesian personalized ranking from implicit feedback. arXiv preprint arXiv:1205.2618 (2012)
19. Sarwar, B., Karypis, G., Konstan, J., Riedl, J.: Item-based collaborative filtering recommendation algorithms. In: Proceedings of the 10th International Conference on World Wide Web, pp. 285–295 (2001)
20. Shaw, P., Uszkoreit, J., Vaswani, A.: Self-attention with relative position representations. arXiv preprint arXiv:1803.02155 (2018)
21. Soliman, S.S., Srinath, M.D.: Continuous and discrete signals and systems, Englewood Cliffs (1990)
22. Sun, F., et al.: BERT4Rec: sequential recommendation with bidirectional encoder representations from transformer. In: CIKM, pp. 1441–1450 (2019)
23. Xue, H.J., Dai, X., Zhang, J., Huang, S., Chen, J.: Deep matrix factorization models for recommender systems. In: IJCAI, vol. 17, pp. 3203–3209 (2017)

Empowering Graduate Students' Service Delivery by Using an Agile Chatbot: A Conceptual Framework

Songlak Sakulwichitsintu(✉)

Sukhothai Thammathirat Open University, Nonthaburi 11120, Thailand
songlak.sak@stou.ac.th

Abstract. Today advances in information and communication technology are providing information services to answer students' questions. Innovative ways to support teaching and learning in higher education institutions are welcome in today's competitive environment. They will enable students to stay engaged in their studies and finish their studies on time. In this paper, I have outlined how chatbots are developed by applying Agile principles to enable chatbots that fully meet the needs of service providers and service users. For instance, there is chatbot development based on the software development life cycle. Let's start with the collection of user requirements from all concerned stakeholders. This is done in order to draw up a chatbot model and assess its suitability. Then the development of the first version of the chatbot with Agile principles was undertaken. After testing and receiving user feedback, a new version of the chatbot was designed. This study covers the development of chatbots, including monitoring the needs of both service providers and service users. This process enables chatbots to provide information services efficiently.

Keywords: Agile · Chatbot · Service delivery · Graduate students · Information service

1 Introduction

Technology continues to improve and expand support services for the convenience of users. The services include education, health, government and private sector clients. To ensure the quality of service and response to the needs of customers or service users is important [1–3].

The development of chatbot capabilities starts with studying users' problems and collecting all users' requirements. Therefore, careful and thorough data collection of requirements in these areas is of the utmost importance, even before system analysis and design commences. If comprehensive information is not collected from all relevant parties, this might render the developed chatbots effectively inoperable, or may not meet the actual needs.

To store the initial data only once, may result in the user providing only partial information. This may be because there is still no detailed enough concept of how the

G. Memmi et al. (Eds.): KSEM 2022, LNAI 13370, pp. 369–377, 2022.
https://doi.org/10.1007/978-3-031-10989-8_29

chatbot can help in providing information. As a consequence, the agile principle is used in the development of the system so that chatbot developments are periodically modified. This process of asking and confirming the user's needs more than once leads to a wider range of options. Therefore, by scheduling group meetings with those involved, the chatbot's functionality is as comprehensive as possible in all aspects of information services [4, 5].

Focusing on service users or customers involves narrowing the development cycle, so that the results of work are more reliable and the risk of system failure is less. Innovation plays an important role in Agile development. New technology is applied based on knowledge, experience and teamwork [6, 7].

Graduate Studies Offices maintain important resources that support teaching and learning for graduate students, in both master's and doctoral programs. Providing answers to questions is important for students to be able to solve problems related to teaching and learning. This helps provide students with the confidence they need to overcome problems which may affect the progress of their studies. It should be noted that the information service of the staff can only be done during business hours. Therefore, the convenience of receiving services is quite limited for students. The introduction of technology as a service tool is an attractive solution, which meets the needs of providing services anywhere and anytime.

Chatbot is an alternative that can be used as a service tool for students. This tool is designed to manage the exchange of frequently asked questions and answers. Questions and answers are collected by personnel in the graduate studies department. Then, as a service, they organize the data into appropriate groupings of questions and answers. Chatbots can display a user interface with menus and fields to enter the text that users want to know. Responses can be designated as relevant; or recommendations can be made based on information imported into the chatbot system.

Chatbots are able to create awareness and transparent communication with one another. They also in a wider range of provide non-technical team members with the means to participate in collaborative project operations, such as the use of chatbots for deployment [8, 9]. Service problems are caused by not giving service users the opportunity to participate in the process of service providers. This includes considering the possible advantages of using technology to assist in the provision of services [10, 11]. The objective here would be to provide knowledge, as well as a variety of academic information that can be published as instructive material. This would benefit users in a growing number of practical ways. This might include, for example, how Agile chatbots could be developed as part of the software development life cycle [5, 12].

The rest of the paper will be structured as follows. Part Two will provide the background information of Agile software development. Part Three will thereafter present the chatbot development that has been used in the research, which is followed by a presentation of the information service and service delivery in Part Four. Thereafter, Part Five presents the conceptual framework of Agile chatbot, and lastly, a discussion and a conclusion are made in Part Six.

2 Agile Software Development

The Agile development method is known as the Test Driven Development method (TDD). This method involves a limited reiteration of automated testing. After the initial testing phase, it is revised and re-tested to achieve the optimal result. This is in contrast to traditional software development methods, which are tested after all programming has been completed. Compliance with TDD minimizes anomalies and improves program quality. TDD has two main rules: 1) If the test fails, a program is written to solve the problem. 2) Steps are taken to ensure mistakes are not duplicated in the program [13–15].

Agile supports in-house project management. It is a way to improve service efficiency with governance that responds to the needs of the public. Everyone is equal and has a shared social responsibility. In addition, Agile helps organization determine ways to integrate changing user needs in order to achieve maximum service efficiency [16, 17].

The Agile system, or program development, is characterized by rapid interaction and the capacity to modify or change parts of the work that are not yet complete. The focus is on project work facilitated by internal teamwork. However, the coordination mechanisms used in Agile projects have not received the necessary attention, which affects the integrity of the data and the ability to support coordination [18, 19].

To transform a traditional university into a digital university (e.g. university 4.0), takes some time for careful planning, probably not less than 10 years. Some universities have already created models for the structure, including details related to budgets and organizational cultures. It is has been found that the adoption of Agile methods to accommodate rapid and easily adaptable changes is reasonably feasible. The Agile-based model covers process definitions by taking into account the culture of the organization. Increasingly, modern universities place greater importance on student-centered learning. More and more, students are required to be able to exchange knowledge and be able to apply knowledge in practice for sustainable self-development [20, 21].

Many organizations are now taking advantage of the potential of Agile concepts to be put to significantly greater use. In particular, a challenge has arisen to change corporate culture in order to accelerate the development cycle and the measurement of customer value [22, 23].

3 Chatbot Development

Artificial Intelligence (AI) is increasingly involved in our daily lives. It perceptively creates and analyzes software and hardware. It could be called an intelligence agent. Such intelligence agents approach projects differently, from simple tasks to complex functions. Chatbots can be said to be typical examples of AI adoption, as well as one of the most advanced examples of intelligent human-computer interaction (HCI). Versatile chatbots are able to retain domain knowledge, provide various services and objectives, process inputs and methods to generate responses, evaluate human-aid alternatives, and design methods of creation [24, 25].

Chatbots have extraordinary ability to use language to communicate with users. For instance chatbots can be designed to inform students' decision-making in choosing elective courses. Other chatbot features include conversation management components, conversational interaction design, collecting and analyzing student opinions, and data management of various courses. Chatbots have generated positive feedback in terms of their functionality and features that provide academic advice [26, 27].

Chatbots are also being used in universities to provide educational information to students. Students do not have to waste time waiting to contact the staff directly. By organizing academic content gathered by chatbots, a knowledge base can be created. The data collection may include questions and answers received by the university's service office. In addition, related educational work processes are available according to the dialog flow and ontology. It is also designed to meet special needs for appropriate and accurate information, particularly for new students [28, 29].

Research on the use of chatbots for education and enhanced learning opportunities for university students is ongoing. There are still problems concerning the use of chatbots in education for improved learning. A technology adoption model was employed to gain a greater understanding of established methods before the introduction of chatbots. This study is very important for researchers, people in charge of policy making, and system designers for e-learning platforms. Teachers and students stand to benefit substantially by these efforts to make learning more efficient [30, 31].

One the foremost benefits of using a chatbot is that can act as a smart tutor in an interactive environment. This includes the ability to respond to course information and content, documentation involving additional courses, and answering in-depth questions. Learning can vary according to the needs of each individual. Similarly, there are features that offer support to students seeking to improve their particular living conditions. Chatbots can also help disadvantaged students, and those who have unique family responsibilities. Pupils who have different approaches to learning, or who respond to unconventional methods, have access to comprehensive resources assembled from multiple campuses. Chatbots can mitigate potential technical limitations, and accommodate differing timelines required for training and a lack of interpersonal emotional understanding [32, 33].

4 Information Service and Service Delivery

The level of satisfaction among students with access to services, provided within the university, depends on the type of service [34, 35]. The study concluded that high quality technology-based time management methods can improve service delivery and the performance of service personnel. It is recommended that technology should be integrated with service to enhance time management skills. Moreover, the policies of employee management should be enforced to improve service delivery and work efficiency [36, 37].

Delivery of services processes are related to the use of technology in providing services. It was found that the delivery of service on the basis of users' centricity will directly affect the success of the service delivery and the technology used [38, 39]. Technology plays an integral role in the delivery of information services. It allows students to access a wide range of resources, as well as benefiting from the latest academic developments. Distance learning students find these high-tech assets especially helpful [40, 41].

5 Conceptual Framework for Agile Chatbot

When developing a chatbot, it is important to take into account three key components. The first part is the overall objective, the scope of chatbots, and the common needs of service users and service providers. The second part is the target audience, or those who have inquiries. And the third part comprises major features of Agile principles and User Participation: these include the planning of the chatbot development project, and the development of chatbot functionality (see Fig. 1).

The first component – defining thc objectives and scope of the chatbot development – should come from a study of the problems and needs of the service provider encounters when trying to provide information services to users conveniently and quickly. The basic features of this element should reflect the needs of the service users when addressing the problems and needs of all stakeholders. The questionnaire, or search query information, may be collected from relevant sources to support further improvement of the chatbot. Furthermore, it should specify additional elements concerning the method of study.

The second one – regarding the chatbot's target audience – should consist of both the service provider and the subscriber. This should respond to those who wish to make inquiries. They may be members of the general public who need to know detailed information to make decisions and so forth. Other interested parties, in service industries and their customer base, require information about people and entities associated with important routine transactions.

There are two parts to the third and final section. The first part focuses on chatbot development planning. This consists of three main areas: utilization, content, and usability. In terms of utilization, problem solving is emphasized. The objective here is providing accurate results based on user preferences, questions and answers. The content section covers correspondence containing questions and answers, recommendations and messages used in communication. The content is comprehensively structured to fulfill the specified objectives and scope. The goal of the third aspect, usability, is to maximize ease of use. This is accomplished by using radio buttons instead of answers, using text to clearly communicate interactions with users, selection of varying response times in alternative media, and thc similarity to conversations with officials. The second part deals with the development of chatbot functionality using Agile principles. This involves periodic testing and the collection of feedback from service providers and user representatives. It has the ability to go back and edit revisions mutually agreed upon. This will enable the development of faster and more responsive chatbots to boost service to users. Moreover, upgraded data collection in chatbots is directly beneficial to the service users. It displays frequently asked questions for users to see. With the application of Agile principles, the development of chatbots becomes faster. Now with periodic testing and the collection of all varieties of feedback, efforts to modify and improve performance to meet the needs of the service users will yield stronger and quicker results. Along with these fundamental technical advances, the principle of user engagement is likely to be expanded further and empowered.

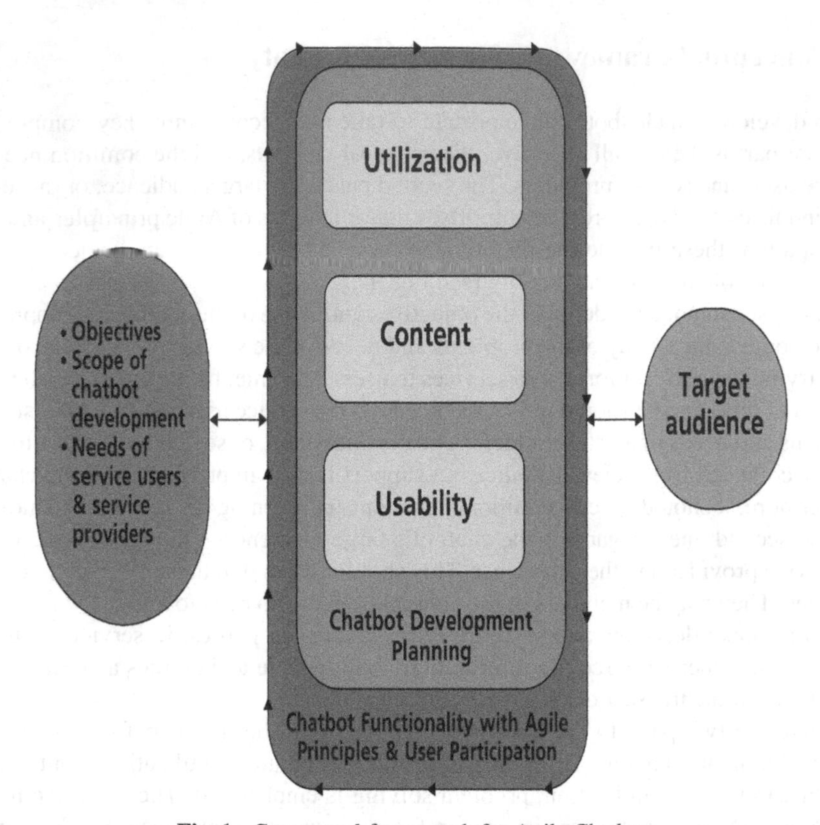

Fig. 1. Conceptual framework for Agile Chatbot.

6 Discussion and Conclusion

This paper outlines a conceptual framework for how Agile Chatbot supports service delivery for graduate students. This framework aims to guide chatbot systems developers in making informed decisions about which elements or activities should be considered for user centered engagement.

The proposed framework explains how the chatbot will be tested for the first time. After Graduate Studies Office staff, experts and students take part in test, they will give the feedback on how chatbots might be modified further based on agile principles. Chatbot development issues discussed here concentrate on how the needs of related users could be met. The emphasis is on working as much as possible for the purpose of providing increasingly comprehensive information.

In the development of chatbot with the traditional software development life cycle (SDLC), it was found that the first step was to collect the requirements until the last step of the implementation. This took a long time and when users used it, it may not meet the needs of 100% of users' requirements. Consequently, the chatbot was not used at full capacity. Unlike the development of Agile chatbot that can review users' needs in a shorter period of time to ensure that the chatbot was used at full efficiency and effectiveness.

Comparisons of the service providers' and service users' chatbot usage with the first and second version of the chatbot showed that the information service of the second version of the chatbot was of higher quality and faster through an user interface with an understandable menu. The feedback from users of the second version of the chatbot has been satisfactory that the bugs found in the first version of the chatbot have been fixed, and that it is in line with the users' needs. This allows users to use the information received for real use.

Some universities have begun to introduce chatbots to help provide information to students. However, in order to provide as much information as possible that responds to students' needs, both technical and non-technical stakeholders should be involved in the process of collecting and organizing data requirements. In summary, this is the first important stage in examining how all interested parties might ultimately benefit in the most efficient way.

References

1. Djelassi, S., Diallo, M.F., Zielke, S.: How self-service technology experience evaluation affects waiting time and customer satisfaction? A moderated mediation model. Decis. Support Syst. **111**, 38–47 (2018)
2. Grossman, G., Platas, M.R., Rodden, J.: Crowdsourcing accountability: ICT for service delivery. World Dev. **112**, 74–87 (2018)
3. Heikkinen, S., Jäntti, M.: Studying continual service improvement and monitoring the quality of ITSM. In: Piattini, M., Rupino da Cunha, P., García Rodríguez de Guzmán, I., Pérez-Castillo, R. (eds.) QUATIC 2019. CCIS, vol. 1010, pp. 193–206. Springer, Cham (2019). https://doi.org/10.1007/978-3-030-29238-6_14
4. Muhyidin, A., Setiawan, M.A.F.: Developing UNYSA Chatbot as information services about Yogyakarta State University. In: Journal of Physics: Conference Series. IOP Publishing (2021)
5. Matthies, C., Dobrigkeit, F., Hesse, G.: An additional set of (automated) eyes: Chatbots for Agile retrospectives. In: 2019 IEEE/ACM 1st International Workshop on Bots in Software Engineering (BotSE) (2019). IEEE
6. Abrahamsson, P., Salo, O., Ronkainen, J., Warsta, J.: Agile software development methods: Review and analysis (2017)
7. Ju, X., Ferreira, F.A., Wang, M.: Innovation, agile project management and firm performance in a public sector-dominated economy: empirical evidence from high-tech small and medium-sized enterprises in China. Socioecon. Plann. Sci. **72**, 100779 (2020)
8. Lebeuf, C., Storey, M.-A., Zagalsky, A.: Software bots. IEEE Softw. **35**(1), 18–23 (2017)
9. Zafar, A., Ahola, M.: Human-artificial systems collaboration in service innovation and social inclusion. In: Russo, D., Ahram, T., Karwowski Di Bucchianico, W., Di, G., Taiar, R. (eds.) IHSI 2021. AISC, vol. 1322, pp. 527–532. Springer, Cham (2021). https://doi.org/10.1007/978-3-030-68017-6_78
10. Pedersen, H., Kermit, P.S., Söderström, S.: "You have to argue the right way": user involvement in the service delivery process for assistive activity technology. Disabil. Rehabil. Assist. Technol. **16**(8), 840–850 (2021)
11. Lim, C., Kim, K.-J.: Experience design board: a tool for visualizing and designing experience-centric service delivery processes. J. Retail. Consum. Serv. **45**, 142–151 (2018)
12. Stoeckli, E., Dremel, C., Uebernickel, F., Brenner, W.: How affordances of Chatbots cross the chasm between social and traditional enterprise systems. Electron. Mark. **30**(2), 369–403 (2019). https://doi.org/10.1007/s12525-019-00359-6

13. Al-Saqqa, S., Sawalha, S., AbdelNabi, H.: Agile software development: methodologies and trends. Int. J. Interact. Mob. Technol. **14**(11), 246–270 (2020)
14. Moe, M.M.: Comparative study of test-driven development (TDD), behavior-driven development (BDD) and acceptance test–driven development (ATDD). Int. J. Trend Sci. Res. Dev. **3**, 231–234 (2019)
15. Choma, J., Guerra, E.M., da Silva, T.S.: Developers' initial perceptions on TDD practice: a thematic analysis with distinct domains and languages. In: Garbajosa, J., Wang, X., Aguiar, A. (eds.) XP 2018. LNBIP, vol. 314, pp. 68–85. Springer, Cham (2018). https://doi.org/10.1007/978-3-319-91602-6_5
16. Beck, K., Beedle, M., Van Bennekum, A., Cockburn, A., Cunningham, W., Fowler, M., et al.: The agile manifesto. Agile Alliance (2001). http://agilemanifesto.org/
17. Mergel, I., Ganapati, S., Whitford, A.B.: Agile: a new way of governing. Public Adm. Rev. **81**(1), 161–165 (2021)
18. Zaitsev, A., Gal, U., Tan, B.: Coordination artifacts in Agile software development. Inf. Organ. **30**(2), 100288 (2020)
19. Zaitsev, A., Gal, U., Tan, B.: Coordination artifacts in agile software development. Inf. Organ. **30**(2), 100288 (2020)
20. Kerroum, K., Khiat, A., Bahnasse, A., Aoula, E.-S.: The proposal of an agile model for the digital transformation of the University Hassan II of Casablanca 4.0. Procedia Comput. Sci. **175**, 403–410 (2020)
21. Smite, D., Moe, N.B., Levinta, G., Floryan, M.: Spotify guilds: how to succeed with knowledge sharing in large-scale agile organizations. IEEE Softw. **36**(2), 51–57 (2019)
22. Dingsøyr, T., Lassenius, C.: Emerging themes in agile software development: introduction to the special section on continuous value delivery. Inf. Softw. Technol. **77**, 56–60 (2016)
23. Bambauer-Sachse, S., Helbling, T.: Customer satisfaction with business services: is agile better? J. Bus. Ind. Mark. **26**(8), 1389–1402 (2021)
24. Albayrak, N., Özdemir, A., Zeydan, E.: An overview of artificial intelligence based Chatbots and an example Chatbot application. In: 2018 26th Signal processing and communications applications conference (SIU). IEEE (2018)
25. Chen, J.-S., Tran-Thien, Y.L., Florence, D.: Usability and responsiveness of artificial intelligence Chatbot on online customer experience in e-retailing. Int. J. Retail Distrib. Manage. **49**, 1512–1531 (2021)
26. Ho, C.C., Lee, H.L., Lo, W.K., Lui, K.F.A.: Developing a Chatbot for college student programme advisement. In: 2018 International Symposium on Educational Technology (ISET). IEEE (2018)
27. Ismail, H., Hussein, N., Elabyad, R., Said, S.: A serverless academic adviser Chatbot. In: The 7th Annual International Conference on Arab Women in Computing in Conjunction with the 2nd Forum of Women in Research (2021)
28. Santoso, H.A., Winarsih, N.A,S., Mulyanto, E., Sukmana, S.E., Rustad, S., Rohman, M.S., et al.: Dinus Intelligent Assistance (DINA) Chatbot for university admission services. In: 2018 International Seminar on Application for Technology of Information and Communication. IEEE (2018)
29. Susanna, M.C.L., Pratyusha, R., Swathi, P., Krishna, P.R., Pradeep, V.S.: College Enquiry Chatbot. Int. Res. J. Eng. Technol. (IRJET) **7**, 784–788 (2020)
30. Malik, R., Sharma, A., Trivedi, S., Mishra, R.: Adoption of Chatbots for learning among university students: role of perceived convenience and enhanced performance. Int. J. Emerg. Technol. Learn. **16**(18), 200–212 (2021)
31. Fryer, L.K., Nakao, K., Thompson, A.: Chatbot learning partners: connecting learning experiences, interest and competence. Comput. Hum. Behav. **93**, 279–289 (2019)
32. Gupta, S., Yu, C.: Supporting inclusive learning using Chatbots? A Chatbot-led interview study. J. Inf. Syst. Educ. **33**(1), 99–109 (2022)

33. Chang, C.Y., Hwang, G.J., Gau, M.L.: Promoting students' learning achievement and self-efficacy: a mobile Chatbot approach for nursing training. Br. J. Edu. Technol. **53**(1), 171–188 (2022)
34. Ekpoh, U.I.: Assessing university students' satisfaction with service delivery: implications for educational management. Glob J Arts Human Soc Sci. **6**(6), 48–60 (2018)
35. Hwang, Y.-S., Choi, Y.K.: Higher education service quality and student satisfaction, institutional image, and behavioral intention. Soc. Behav. Personal. Int. J. **47**(2), 1–12 (2019)
36. Bagah, J., Asante, J., Abdulai, M.-E.: Is time management a panacea for effective service delivery and staff performance? University for development studies in perspective. ADRRI J. Arts Soc. Sci. **16**(9), 20–44 (2019)
37. Kim, C., Lee, H.: A patent-based approach for the identification of technology-based service opportunities. Comput. Ind. Eng. **144**, 106464 (2020)
38. Larsson Ranada, Å., Lidström, H.: Satisfaction with assistive technology device in relation to the service delivery process—a systematic review. Assist. Technol. **31**(2), 82–97 (2019)
39. Taherdoost, H.: Development of an adoption model to assess user acceptance of e-service technology: E-service technology acceptance model. Behav. Inf. Technol. **37**(2), 173–197 (2018)
40. Ndhlovu, D., Simui, F., Mwewa, G., Chota, A., Kakana, F., Mundende, K., et al.: "WhatsApp" as a Learner Support tool for distance education: Implications for Policy and Practice at University of Zambia. (2018)
41. Fujs, D., Vrhovec, S., Žvanut, B., Vavpotič, D.: Improving the efficiency of remote conference tool use for distance learning in higher education: a kano based approach. Comput. Educ. **181**, 104448(2022)

Event Detection Based on Multilingual Information Enhanced Syntactic Dependency GCN

Zechen Wang[1], Binbin Li[2(✉)], and Yong Wang[2(✉)]

[1] School of Cyber Security, University of Chinese Academy of Sciences, Beijing, China
wangzechen@iie.ac.cn
[2] Institute of Information Engineering, CAS, Beijing, China
{libinbin,wangyong}@iie.ac.cn

Abstract. Event detection is a hot and difficult problem in information extraction. It is widely used in automatic news extraction, financial event analysis and other fields. However, most of the existing event detection methods only focus on a single language, ignoring the event information provided by other languages, and can not solve the problem of polysemy in a single language, which makes it difficult to improve the performance of event detection methods. To solve these problems, this paper proposes a new Event Detection based on Multilingual Information Enhanced Syntactic Dependency GCN. Specifically, the model translates the original language and aligns words, takes multilingual data as input, and constructs syntactic dependency diagrams for initial language sentences. Then, a graph neural network is constructed based on the syntactic dependency graph, and combined with the attention mechanism, the nodes of the syntactic dependency graph are enhanced by the translated language. Finally, the classifier finds the trigger and judges the event type. The model effectively improves the recognition efficiency of polysemous words by using multilingual information, and makes full use of sentence structure information by using syntactic dependency graph. Experiments on ace2005 benchmark data set show that the model can detect events effectively and is obviously superior to the existing event detection methods.

Keywords: Event detection · Multilingual information · Semantic dependency graph · GCN · Attention mechanism

1 Introduction

Event detection belongs to information extraction task, which is an important natural language processing task. The purpose is to identify the event reference from the text and determine the category of the event [2]. Specifically, for a given sentence, it is necessary to detect whether there are triggers in the sentence and classify the triggers. [7] at present, there are still many problems in event detection. This paper mainly solves the following two problems:

G. Memmi et al. (Eds.): KSEM 2022, LNAI 13370, pp. 378–390, 2022.
https://doi.org/10.1007/978-3-031-10989-8_30

First, in the event extraction corpus similar to ace2005 data set [5], the single language corpus often lacks effective information to distinguish the ambiguity of polysemy. For example, for the sentence "an American tank fired on the abandoned hotel". It is necessary to detect and extract "fire" as the trigger of the event contained in the marking sentence, and classify the event according to the content described by the event. Obviously, since the trigger "fire" means "shot", this sentence expresses an attack event. According to the classification of events in ACE2005 guidance document, the event should be classified as "attack". However, in the process of automatic extraction, the word "fire" may be incorrectly recognized. For example, in sentence 2, "he has fired his air defense chief", "fire" means "dismissal", so it will be wrongly classified as "end position" according to ace2005 guidance document. Fortunately, a polysemy in a given language often corresponds to multiple monosemy in another language. With the development of machine translation tasks in recent years, the method of machine translation can translate polysemy more accurately by combining context and other information.

Second, the existing event detection methods often do not fully analyze the syntactic structure. A sentence is a sequence of words. It is generally believed that the closer the distance between words, the greater the relevance. Verbs, nouns and adjectives are more likely to appear in sentences as triggers. However, compared with the distance and part of speech between words, the direct or indirect relationship of words in sentence structure is more important to identify triggers. For the sentence "an American tank fired on the abandoned hotel". In the process of automatic extraction, the word "abandoned", as a verb, may also be mistakenly regarded as a trigger, resulting in the error of trigger recognition and event type judgment. In order to correctly distinguish the relationship between different verbs and nouns in sentences, dependency parsing is often used. In recent years, the types of dependency parsing methods have gradually increased. Each has its own advantages and disadvantages. It can label sentences with simple or complex structures, and gradually expand its application in a variety of natural language processing tasks.

Based on the existing research, this paper proposes an event detection method based on multilingual information enhanced syntactic dependency GCN, which can make good use of syntactic structure and multilingual information. The model translates the original language, constructs a graph convolution network based on syntactic dependency graph, solves the ambiguity of monolingual words, fully extracts the relationship between words, and finally finds the trigger accurately through the classifier to judge the event type. Finally, by comparing with baseline experiment, the superiority of this method in accuracy and F1 value can be reflected.

2 Related Works

Previously, there have been some research on event detection based on multilingual enhancement and dependency parsing.

For multilingual enhancement, Zhu et al. [21] Proposed a Chinese English event extraction model. However, the model uses traditional machine learning methods to extract features, and can not deeply analyze the structure of structured sentences. Liu et al. [14]. Proposed a cross language event detection method. This method shows high operation efficiency when dealing with articles containing multiple languages, but the latest and most effective translation tools are not fully utilized, and only achieve general results when allowing longer operation time. Chen et al. [15] Proposed to realize the event detection task based on multilingual gated attention mechanism and LSTM. This method also uses multilingual information to solve the problem of polysemy at one time. However, LSTM focuses more on the sequence information of context and lacks the semantic association information between words.

Some natural language processing models have used various features such as vocabulary, grammar and semantics as input for event detection. For example, Liu et al. [16] believed that triggers and arguments should be paid more attention than other words in the process of event detection, so they constructed an attention vector to encode each trigger, argument and context word. EDEEI model [20] constructs a part of speech based attention map, which uses the correlation between part of speech and trigger text to capture events. These methods only use part of speech and location to construct the network, and do not really use dependency syntax to analyze the relationship between words. Dependency parsing based methods are widely used in the field of biology. Kilicoglu proposed heuristic [8] and trigger based [9] methods. These methods need to construct grammatical rules for biological events, which are difficult to be widely used in news and other texts. Lai et al. [11] Constructed a graph neural network for biological texts based on dependency parsing. The generality of the model is greater than that of previous studies. However, in order to increase the computational efficiency, the node information is simplified by scoring, and the node information is over compressed.

To sum up, there are still many problems to be solved in the research of event extraction based on multilingual enhancement and dependency parsing.

3 Contribution

The following contributions differentiate our method from previous work.

1. A graph neural network structure based on dependency syntactic graph is designed. By constructing syntactic graph, we can better capture the dependencies between words, and capture the relationship between these relationships and triggers through GCN.
2. Based on the constructed graph neural network, a multi language node enhancement method based on word alignment and attention mechanism is proposed to solve the problem of word ambiguity through multi language comparison
3. The evaluation of the proposed method on the ace2005 benchmark data set shows that the proposed method has better performance than other latest methods.

4 Method

In this section, we present our framework for the proposed Event Detection based on Multilingual Information Enhanced Syntactic Dependency GCN (MS-GCN) model. We first describe the hierarchy of the model, and then show the details of the algorithm along with the key intuition underlying it.

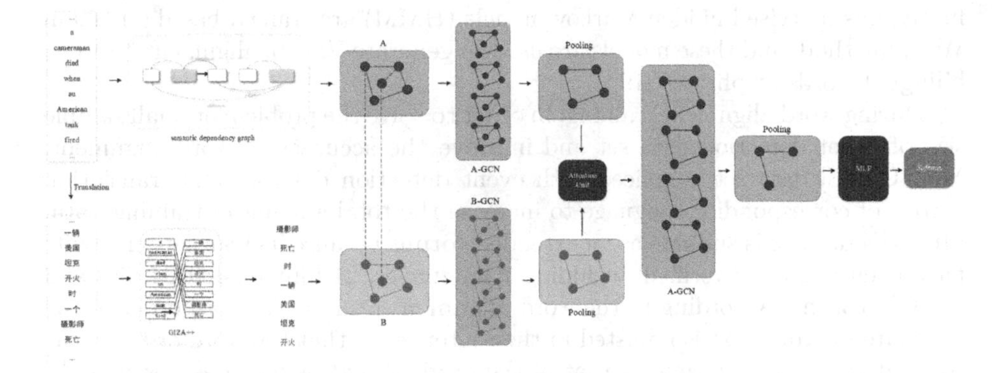

Fig. 1. The framework of MS-GCN model.

The proposed framework is illustrated in Fig. 1. The event detection can be treated as a classification problem in the proposed model which detects events and event types by identifying triggers and trigger types. This section will introduce the framework of the model, first describe the hierarchy of the model, and then show the details of the algorithm. The framework of MS-GCN model is shown in Fig. 1. Similar to the existing research methods, MS-GCN model also solves the problem of event detection as a word classification problem. The model traverses each word in the sentence to determine whether it is a trigger. If so, it further determines which event type the word represents. MS-GCN model includes the following parts: Translation, Multilingual word alignment, dependency syntax graph generation, GCN construction, pooling, node attention calculation, secondary pooling, classification.

Text translation obtains the multilingual text corpus corresponding to the original event detection corpus through the method of machine translation, and uses the word alignment tool to establish a one-to-one mapping relationship for the words in the translated corpus. Connecting these vectors can generate a new word vector. The newly generated word vector is used for feature extraction, node enhancement and feature selection. Node enhancement extracts original features from feature extraction, and provides processed features for feature selection to obtain high-quality features. Finally, the feature is input into the classifier to get the trigger and its classification. Each part of the model is described in detail below.

4.1 Multilingual Alignment

MS-GCN model calls the existing Baidu machine translation service for text translation. Take ace2005 English text as input and output the corresponding Chinese translation text. The translated Chinese text is segmented, and Giza + + [17] is used to align the text before and after translation. Giza + + is a widely used word alignment program, which is generally applied to phrase based translation systems. In the process of word alignment using Giza + +, firstly, unsupervised hidden Markov models (HMM) are trained based on Baum Welch method, and these models are used to generate Viterbi alignment between bilingual words or phrases [19].

During word alignment training, in order to solve the problem of small sample size of event detection data set and improve the accuracy of word alignment, MultiUN [3] data set is spliced with event detection data set and translation corpus of corresponding language to increase the total amount of training data. MultiUN dataset is suitable as an extended corpus because its translation results have been manually verified, including 7 languages, 21 bitexts, 489334 files and 1.99Gb Tokens. According to the word alignment results, the word order of the translated corpus text is adjusted in the sentence, so that the word order of the translated text is the same as that of the original text as much as possible. As shown in the example in Fig. 1, the original English text is "cameraman died when an American tank fired", the translated text is " 一辆美国坦克开火时摄影师死亡 ", and the text after word segmentation and word alignment is "摄影师 死亡 时 一辆 美国 坦克 开火".

4.2 Dependency Parsing Feature

See Fig. 2.

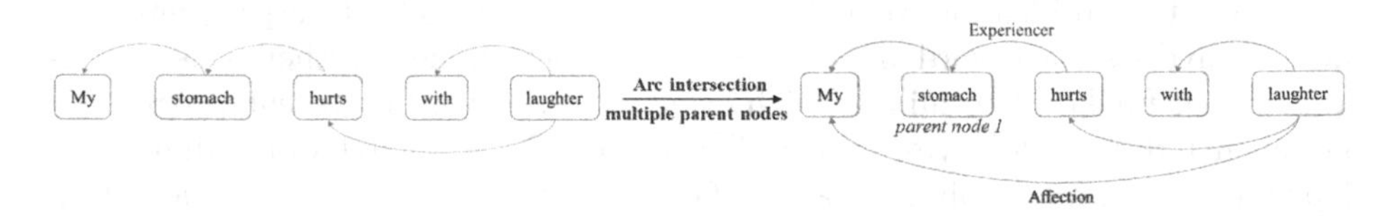

Fig. 2. Comparison of dependency tree (left) and dependency graph (right).

Dependency parsing (DP) reveals its syntactic structure by analyzing the dependency between components in a language unit. [] intuitively speaking, dependency parsing identifies the grammatical components of "subject predicate object" and "definite complement" in the sentence, and analyzes the relationship between each component. At present, dependency semantic tree is widely used for dependency syntactic analysis. However, the form of dependency tree often omits some important semantic relationships. Semantic dependency graph parsing allows arc intersection and multiple parent nodes on the basis of semantic dependency tree, which makes the analysis of grammatical structures such as conjunction, concurrent language and conceptual transposition more comprehensive (Table 1).

Table 1. 16 dependency semantic relations.

Tag	SBV	VOB	IOB	FOB
Description	Subject-verb	Verb-object	Indirect-object	Fronting-object
Tag	COO	POB	LAD	RAD
Description	Coordinate	Preposition-object	Left adjunct	Right adjunct
Tag	DBL	ATT	ADV	CMP
Description	Double	Attribute	Adverbial	Complement
Tag	IS	WP	HED	NONE
Description	Independent structure	Punctuation	Head	None

We select 16 dependency semantic relations for annotation, including 14 kinds of relevance and header (HED) and non relevance (none) (Fig. 3).

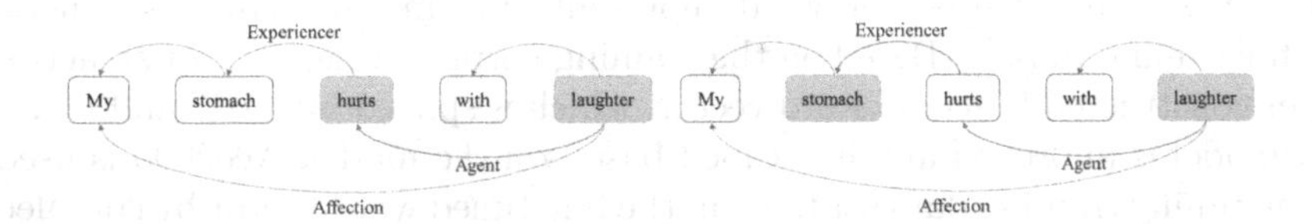

Fig. 3. Direct relationship (left) and indirect relationship (right).

The main structure of a general sentence contains one or two subjects and is associated with a trigger. Therefore, direct correlation and indirect correlation are selected for corpus statistics. There are 15 * 15 possible relationships between the two words. Generate a dependency syntax matrix with a size of 225 * n (n is the maximum sentence length), and statistically generate an association representation matrix by counting the relationship between the semantic dependency graphs corresponding to each sentence. Then the matrix is compressed by SVD and normalized to obtain the vector representation of each relationship. The resulting semantic dependency feature vector can be expressed as a combination of dependency vector and numerical representation of the relative position of relational words, which is represented as SDF (Fig. 4).

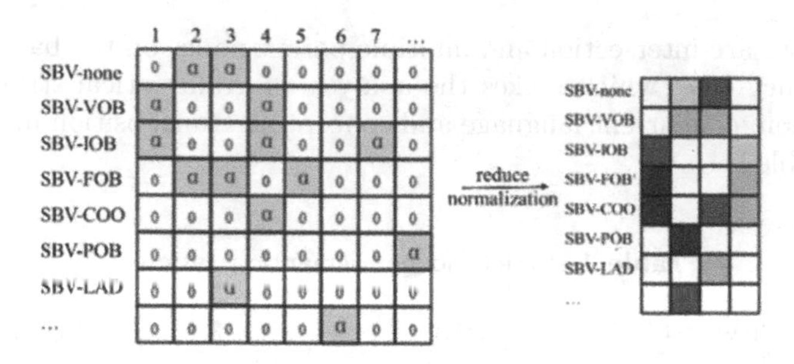

Fig. 4. Generation of SDF.

4.3 Node Vector Representations

In this paper, node vector of GCN is composed of three feature vectors: content word feature vector (CWF), position feature vector (PF) and dependent syntactic feature vector (DPF). Among them, CWF is a word vector, and each word corresponds to a CWF vector, which can distinguish the meaning of the same word in different contexts. Pf reflects the position of triggers, counting from the first word of each sentence. The position information is expressed as an integer and further transformed into a unique heat vector. DPF is the dependency syntactic feature vector introduced in the previous section.

The word vector used for word representation in this paper is generated after fine tuning Bert [8] Based on the training corpus. A new vector structure is further constructed based on word vector, which is spliced by CWF and PF. MS-GCN model is improved and fine tuned based on the model. Ace2005 is used as the fine tuning training data set to train the fine tuned word vector by completing the sentence classification task. Through this fine-tuning training, the produced word vectors generate different word vectors for the same word corresponding to different contexts, which can distinguish the different meanings of words with the same spelling in different contexts, so as to solve the problem of polysemy. At the same time, through the pre-training of large corpus, a large amount of external information is introduced to supplement the information not contained in the context of event detection task corpus, which effectively solves the problem of insufficient information caused by the small event detection corpus.

Position vectors are used to represent the position information of words in sentences. In the process of event detection, it is necessary to classify the words in the input sentence. In order to express the trigger information in a sentence, it is necessary to establish the relationship between each word in the sentence and the candidate trigger. To construct this relationship, PF is defined as the relative distance between the current word and the candidate trigger. PF is encoded, and each distance value is represented by an embedded vector. When training the distance vector, we need to construct the matrix to generate the distance vector, initialize and optimize it.

Let the size of CWF be d_{CWF}, the size of SF be d_{SF}, the size of SDF be d_{SDF}, the size of location code be d_{PF}. Represent word vector of the i-th word in the sentence as $x_i \in R^d$, $d = d_{\text{CWF}} + d_{\text{SF}} + d_{\text{SDF}} + d_{\text{PF}}{}^*2$.

4.4 GCN Construction

We construct this graph convolutional network models as an undirected connected graph [10] $\mathcal{G} = \{\mathcal{V}, \mathcal{E}, \mathbf{A}\}$. Which consists of a set of nodes $|\mathcal{V}$ with $|\mathcal{V}| = n$, a set of edges $|\mathcal{E}$ with $|\mathcal{E}| = n$ and the adjacency matrix $|\mathcal{A}$. If there is an edge between node $|\rangle$ and node $||$, the entry $\mathbf{A}(i, j)$ denotes the weight of the edge; otherwise, $\mathbf{A}(i, j) = 0$. We denote the degree matrix of $\mathbf{A}$ as a diagonal matrix $\mathbf{D}$, where $\mathbf{D}(i, i) = \sum_{j=1}^{n} \mathbf{A}(i, j)$. Then, the Laplacian matrix of $\mathbf{A}$ is denoted as $\mathbf{L} = \mathbf{D} - \mathbf{A}$. The corresponding symmetrically normalized Laplacian matrix is $\tilde{\mathbf{L}} = \mathbf{I} - \mathbf{D}^{-\frac{1}{2}}\mathbf{A}\mathbf{D}^{-\frac{1}{2}}$, where $\mathbf{I}$ is an identity matrix.

The adjacency matrix corresponding to the source language is represented as $\mathbf{A}$, and the adjacency matrix represented by the translated language is $\mathbf{B}$. When calculating the graph convolution for the first time, steps $\mathbf{A}$ and $\mathbf{B}$ are the same. For the second time, we just calculate on $\mathbf{A}$. Here, take $\mathbf{A}$ as an example. This deep model on graphs contains several spectral convolutional layers that take a vector $\mathbf{X}^p$ of size $n \times d_p$ as the input map of the **p**th layer and output a map $\mathbf{X}^{p+1}$ of size $n \times d_{p+1}$ by:

$$\mathbf{X}^{p+1}(:, j) = \sigma\left(\sum_{i=1}^{d_p} \mathbf{V} \begin{bmatrix} \left(\boldsymbol{\theta}_{i,j}^{p}\right)(1) & & 0 \\ & \ddots & \\ 0 & & \left(\boldsymbol{\theta}_{i,j}^{p}\right)(n) \end{bmatrix} \mathbf{V}^T \mathbf{X}^p(:, i)\right), \quad \forall j = 1, \cdots, d_{p+1}$$

where $\mathbf{X}^p(:, i)$ $\left(\mathbf{X}^{p+1}(:, j)\right)$ is the$i$ th (jth) dimension of the input (output) map, respectively; $\boldsymbol{\theta}_{i,j}^{P}$ denotes a vector of learnable parameters of the filter at the p th layers. Each column of V is the eigenvector of L and $\sigma(\cdot)$ is the activation function.

4.5 Node Enhancement

The node enhancement contains an attention unit mainly contains the attention node enhancement module. Attention mechanism is usually used to reweight and encode vector sequences. In the MS-GCN model, the bilingual logical unit uses the attention mechanism to emphasize the relationship between different words expressing the same meaning in the two languages. The node enhancement module pairs the maps corresponding to Chinese and English sentences as the input of attention mechanism. The word meaning of each candidate trigger is directly represented by word vectors from two different languages, so as to emphasize the word meaning of the trigger to be extracted and realize the disambiguation of polysemy.

Each map generated in feature extraction module is a nX. The maps represented as K are taken as the inputs of attention mechanism. The attention calculation process is as follows. A new random matrix WQ of length w is computed. The product of two vectors is calculated to obtain a new matrix Q.

The random matrix WK whose width is w and the length is k_1 is acquired, and the product of the random matrix WK and WQ produces the matrix WV. Calculate the product of WV and map to gain the matrix V.

Based on the three generated K, Q, V matrices, an attention matrix Z is calculated by using the following formula:

$$Z = \mathrm{softmax}\left(\frac{Q \times K^T}{\sqrt{X}}\right) V$$

Train Wk, WQ, WV matrices. The scoring function is as follows:

$$f_{\text{score}} = \frac{Q \cdot K^T}{\sqrt{X}}$$

Then the Z matrix is compressed with max pooling to generate a vector z. Based on the updated $WK, WQandWV$, the product of z and K constructs a new attention map.

4.6 Classifier

This module concatenates the CWFs of the current word and the words on the left and right of the current one, to obtain the vector P of length $3 * CWF$. The learned sentence level features and word features are connected into a vector $\mathrm{F} = [\mathrm{L}, \mathrm{P}]$. In order to calculate the confidence of the event type of each trigger, the feature vector is inputted into the classifier $O = W_s F + b_s$. W_s is the transformation matrix of the classifier, b_s is the bias, and O is the final output of the network, where the output type is equal to the total number of event types plus one to include the "not a trigger" tag that does not play any role in the event.

5 Experiment

In this section, we design three different scenarios based on ACE 2005 benchmark dataset for event detection. We investigate the empirical performances of our model and compare it to the existing state-of-the-art models. The ACE 2005 dataset is utilized as the benchmark experimental dataset. The test set used in the experiment contains 40 Newswire articles and 30 other documents randomly selected from different genres. The remaining 529 documents are used as the training set.

5.1 Experimental Settings

On Wikipedia and bookcorpus, BERT is trained to generate the word content vector. The dimension of the CWF is set as 128. WordNet 3.0 is utilized to generate SF, the number of words used in training is 6 thousand and the dimension of word vector structure is 488.

In trigger classification, the window size is 3. We set the number of convolution kernel to 200, batch size to 170, and position vector dimension to 5.

Random gradient descent is used to train the neural network. It mainly includes two parameters p and α. Set $p = 0.95$ and $\alpha = 1E\text{-}6$. For drop out operations, set the rate to 0.5. The optimizer is Adam.

Similar to the previous work, we use the following criteria to judge the correctness of each predicted event. The trigger recognition is correct if the extracted trigger matches the reference trigger. The recognition and classification of the trigger are correct if the event subtype of the extracted trigger matches the event subtype of the reference trigger.

Based on the above criteria, the effect of event detection is judged, and Precision (P), Recall (R) and F value (F1) are used as evaluation indexes.

5.2 Evaluation of Event Detection Methods

To demonstrate how the proposed algorithm improves the performance over the state-of-the-art event detection methods, we compare the following representative methods from the literature:

(1) Li's baseline [12]: Li et al. proposed a feature-based system which used artificially designed lexical features, basic features and syntactic features.
(2) Liao's cross-event [13]: The cross-event detection method proposed by Liao and Grishman used document level information to improve the performance of ACE event detection.
(3) Hong's cross-entity [6]: Hong et al. exploited a method to extract events through cross-entity reasoning.
(4) Li's joint model [12]: Li et al. also developed an event extraction method based on event structure prediction.
(5) DMCNN method [1]: A word representation model was established to capture the semantic rules of words, and adopted a framework based on dynamic multi pool convolutional neural network.
(6) EDEEI method [20]: an event detection method based on external information and semantic network adopts the neural network framework including part of speech and attention map (Table 2).

Table 2. Overall performance on the ACE 2005 blind test data

Methods	Trigger identification			Trigger classification		
	P	R	F	P	R	F
Li's baseline	76.2	60.5	67.4	74.5	59.1	65.9
Liao's cross-event	N/A			68.7	68.9	68.8
Hong's cross-entity	N/A			72.9	64.3	68.3
Li's joint model	76.9	65	70.4	73.7	62.3	67.5
DMCNN model	80.4	67.7	73.5	75.6	63.6	69.1
EDEEI model	**77.0**	**72.9**	**74.9**	**77.3**	**62.2**	**69.9**
MS-GCN model	**78.5**	**71.8**	**75.0**	**78.2**	**63.7**	**70.2**

Among all methods, MS-GCN model has the best performance. Compared with the existing methods, the accuracy and F value of trigger recognition are significantly improved. Compared with Li, Liao and Hong's methods, it can be found that only relying on vocabulary, syntax and features is not enough to accurately extract triggers. The comparison with DMCNN shows that the semantic rules that can be captured only by the word representation model are relatively limited. The comparison with EDEEI model shows that the attention mechanism constructed only by part of speech information is lower than MS-GCN model in distinguishing ambiguous words. The introduction of multilingual knowledge can effectively improve the accuracy of event detection.

5.3 Analysis of Different Languages

This section presents a detailed comparison of the translation attention between en-de, en-fr and en-cn respectively. The purpose is to test for advantages and disadvantages of each language pair.

The advantages of using en+cn can be observed visually and quantitatively in Table 3. It can be seen that the combination of English and Chinese achieves the best performance on both trigger identification and trigger classification. It may because that Chinese has more different syntax than french and Germany.

Table 3. Performance with different languages.

Methods	Trigger identification F (%)	Trigger identification + classification F (%)
en+de	66.2	56.9
en+fr	71.7	66.7
en+cn	**75.0**	**70.2**

5.4 Effectiveness of Semantic Dependency Graph Features

In order to verify the effectiveness of attention mechanism, similar to the method used in literature [4,18], this paper conducted a comparative experiment with and without dependent syntactic features. It can be seen from Table 4 that the model with dependent syntactic features is better than the model without dependent syntactic features in event detection.

Table 4. Performance with and without semantic dependency graph features

Methods	Trigger identification F (%)	Trigger identification + classification F (%)
Without SDF	73.2	65.9
With SDF	**75.0**	**70.2**

Experimental results show that dependency syntactic features improve the efficiency of event detection. It shows that the syntactic map successfully establishes the deep relationship between words, and the characteristics of this relationship are successfully extracted. This relationship is helpful to improve the effect of trigger recognition and classification.

6 Conclusion

This paper proposes an event detection method based on multilingual information enhancement and syntactic dependency graph. This paper designs a GCN model based on syntactic dependency graph, constructs an attention mechanism based on multilingual information, and makes the syntactic features related to triggers easier to capture. Experiments on the widely used ace2005 benchmark data set show that this method is obviously superior to the existing event detection methods. In addition, the experimental results are fully analyzed in this paper. By showing the performance of the algorithm, it is proved that MS-GCN is a very effective event detection model

Acknowledgments. This work was supported by National Natural Science Foundation of China (No. 61931019).

References

1. Chen, Y., Xu, L., Liu, K., Zeng, D., Zhao, J.: Event extraction via dynamic multi-pooling convolutional neural networks. In: ACL, pp. 167–176 (2015)
2. Cheng, D., Yang, F., Wang, X., Zhang, Y., Zhang, L.: Knowledge graph-based event embedding framework for financial quantitative investments. In: SIGIR 2020: The 43rd International ACM SIGIR Conference on Research and Development in Information Retrieval (2020)
3. Eisele, A., Yu, C.: Multiun: a multilingual corpus from united nation documents. In: Proceedings of the International Conference on Language Resources and Evaluation, LREC 2010, 17–23 May 2010, Valletta, Malta (2010)
4. Ferguson, J., Lockard, C.: Semi-supervised event extraction with paraphrase clusters. In: Proceedings of the 2018 Conference of the North American Chapter of the Association for Computational Linguistics: Human Language Technologies, vol. 2 (2018)
5. Grishman, R., Westbrook, D., Meyers, A.: NYU's English ACE 2005 system description. J. Satisfiability (2005)
6. Hong, Y., Zhang, J., Ma, B., Yao, J., Zhou, G., Zhu, Q.: Using cross-entity inference to improve event extraction. In: ACL, pp. 1127–1136 (2011)
7. Ji, H., Grishman, R.: Refining event extraction through cross-document inference. In: ACL 2008, Proceedings of the 46th Annual Meeting of the Association for Computational Linguistics, 15–20 June 2008, Columbus, Ohio, USA (2008)
8. Kilicoglu, H., Bergler, S.: Syntactic dependency based heuristics for biological event extraction. In: Proceedings of the BioNLP 2009 Workshop Companion Volume for Shared Task, pp. 119–127. Association for Computational Linguistics, Boulder, Colorado, June 2009

9. Kilicoglu, H., Bergler, S.: Effective bio-event extraction using trigger words and syntactic dependencies. Comput. Intell. **27**(4), 583–609 (2011)
10. Kipf, T.N., Welling, M.: Semi-supervised classification with graph convolutional networks (2016)
11. Lai, V.D., Nguyen, T.N., Nguyen, T.H.: Event detection: gate diversity and syntactic importance scores for graph convolution neural networks (2020)
12. Li, Q., Ji, H., Huang, L.: Joint event extraction via structured prediction with global features. In: ACL, pp. 73–82 (2013)
13. Liao, S., Grishman, R.: Using document level cross-event inference to improve event extraction. In: ACL, pp. 789–797 (2010)
14. Liu, J., Chen, Y., Liu, K., Zhao, J.: Neural cross-lingual event detection with minimal parallel resources. In: EMNLP-IJCNLP (2019)
15. Liu, J., Chen, Y., Liu, K., Zhao, J.: Event detection via gated multilingual attention mechanism. In: Proceedings of the AAAI Conference on Artificial Intelligence, vol. 32 (2018)
16. Liu, S., Chen, Y., Liu, K., Zhao, J.: Exploiting argument information to improve event detection via supervised attention mechanisms. In: Proceedings of the 55th Annual Meeting of the Association for Computational Linguistics (Volume 1: Long Papers) (2017)
17. Och, F.J.: Giza++: training of statistical translation models (2000)
18. Saedi, C., Branco, A., Rodrigues, J.A., Silva, J.: Wordnet embeddings. In: Proceedings of the Third Workshop on Representation Learning for NLP, ACL 2018 (2018)
19. Tomeh, N., Allauzen, A., Yvon, F.: Maximum-entropy word alignment and posterior-based phrase extraction for machine translation. Mach. Transl. **28**(1), 19–56 (2013). https://doi.org/10.1007/s10590-013-9146-4
20. Wang, Z., Wang, S., Zhang, L., Wang, Y.: Exploiting extensive external information for event detection through semantic networks word representation and attention map. In: Paszynski, M., Kranzlmüller, D., Krzhizhanovskaya, V.V., Dongarra, J.J., Sloot, P.M.A. (eds.) ICCS 2021. LNCS, vol. 12742, pp. 707–714. Springer, Cham (2021). https://doi.org/10.1007/978-3-030-77961-0_56
21. Zhu, Z., Li, S., Zhou, G., Rui, X.: Bilingual event extraction: a case study on trigger type determination. In: Proceedings of the 52nd Annual Meeting of the Association for Computational Linguistics (Volume 2: Short Papers) (2014)

Semantic Annotation of Videos Based on Mask RCNN for a Study of Animal Behavior

Nourelhouda Hammouda[1(✉)], Mariem Mahfoudh[1,2], and Mohamed Cherif[3]

[1] University of Kairouan, Kairouan, Tunisia
hamouda.nourelhouda@gmail.com
[2] MIRACL Laboratory, University of Sfax, Route de Tunis Km 10, B.P. 242, 3021 Sfax, Tunisia
[3] INRAT Animal and Forage Production Laboratory, Ariana, Tunisia

Abstract. Detection and tracking of object video are of great interest in various fields like security, traffic, and public places... In this article, we are interested in agriculture and animal husbandry. The majority of existing video object tracking applications aim to extract the object's trajectory based on the detection results and then correlate the obtained coordinates in most frames. But to build knowledge about animal behavior in open pasture, and how long it takes for each behavior, we need the coordinates of each object in all the video's frames. Therefore, in our paper, we aim in the first step to extract all the information about each animal (sheep) from the video. Our research is not limited to knowing behaviors only, but we also seek in the second step to collect the information extracted using specific rules to build knowledge about the effects of animal behavior on themselves, on the pastures, and to know the status of the pastures. This knowledge subsequently contributes to making the best decisions to preserve the vegetation cover and the quality of animal production. We use the Mask R-CNN detector and MS COCO dataset to detect and extract the location of the animal in each frame. We use the Hungarian algorithm to associate similar objects in all video frames. Then we correct the detection and association mistakes. Our approach was able to achieve 100% tracking of all sheep if the sheep not moving very fast. Finally, we use ontologies OWL to represent and extract Knowledge and we express in SWRL the semantic rules which help us to study animals behavior.

Keywords: Video annotation · Deep learning · Mask RCNN · Semantic annotation · Ontology · Animal behavior · Making decision · SWRL

1 Introduction

The vegetation cover of the natural pastures is characterized by the diversity and richness of its components that can improve the quality of animal production. This subject has received great attention from the National Institute of Agricultural Research in Tunisia (INRAT), to take advantage of these characteristics

G. Memmi et al. (Eds.): KSEM 2022, LNAI 13370, pp. 391–402, 2022.
https://doi.org/10.1007/978-3-031-10989-8_31

while maintaining its permanent presence. Therefore, they suggest studying the behavior of animals in pastures with a smartly and accurately method that helps them in making good use of this wealth. On the one hand, the study of the behaviors helps to know the type of plant compatible with each animals breed and the effect of these behaviors on itself. On the other hand, animal behavior helps us to know the effect of grazing on the pastures. Thus, we can control it to preserve the vegetation cover from desertification.

Many studies have already started using automatic surveillance techniques to monitor animal behavior and to analyze human behavior. [9] and [5] surveyed lots of research contributions in this domain. They mentioned that improving the accuracy and quality of the detector played a very important role in correctly tracking objects in the video. The most notable are deep learning-based detection methods such as Faster R-CNN, Mask R-CNN, YOLO, SSD... In this context, [1] carried out a full survey of most work interested to solve the mission of tracking multiple MOT (Multiple Object Tracking) objects on single-camera videos, these algorithms consist of four main steps, the detection step is the first step.

Annotation of visual data is important as it provides ground truth labels of real-world objects, scenes, and events... But the manual annotation is a complex, time-consuming, and laborious task that can only be performed by one expert to ensure the accuracy of the annotation and use the same criteria. Recently, [15] noted that ontology is of paramount importance in facilitating semantic communication between different metadata to provide a semantic description of images. We also find that the ontologies and their backing technologies like OWL, construct more complex semantic classes by combining and intersecting existing concepts [14].

In our paper, we are interested in extracting knowledge from a video with a high-resolution and fixed camera. This phase requires the detection and recognition of the animals (sheep) based on Mask RCNN detector, using MS COCO dataset. Then the tracking of each animal throughout the video sequence using Hungarian algorithm to facilitate the association process. To determine the behavior of each animal later.

Our paper is organized as follows: in the next section, we will describe related work on detection, tracking, extraction, and analysis knowledge. In Sect. 3, we will explain our approach, the methods in which we build our work, and the contributions we have made to improve the tracking process and to study the knowledge extracted. Then, we will evaluate and discuss our approach results.

2 Related Works

This section reviews previous techniques for detecting and tracking multiple objects in video and the contributions of ontology to the study of behavior and decision support.

2.1 Video Annotation

"A video is the result of a sequence of frames displayed with a sufficiently fast frequency" [12]. Detecting and recognizing objects in all video frames, then associating each object with all its images throughout the video poses many challenges (occlusion, shadow, no-rigid object deformation...) [19].

Recently, deeper CNNs (DCNNs) have led to unprecedented improvements in the detection of more general categories of objects [10,20]. CNN's successful applications to image classification have been transferred to object detection, resulting in a region-based CNN detector (RCNN) [2]. Since then, much object detection research has drawn on the rapidly evolving area of RCNN work. Since 2013, in an attempt to improve performance, many detectors have been proposed. Additionally, [9] presented a survey on the properties and performance of infrastructures for generic object detection.

They presented two main categories of detectors: Region-based (Two-Stage Framework) and Unified Pipeline (One-Stage Pipeline). In the first category, there are RCNN, which were among the first to explore CNN for generic object detection and developed RCNN, This approach has seen several improvements, including the SPPNet, Fast RCNN, Faster RCNN, RFCN until it reached then proposed the Mask RCNN to tackle the segmentation of object instances at the pixel level by extending Faster RCNN. Mask RCNN adds a branch that generates a binary mask for each RoI. The new branch is a fully convolutional network (FCN) located on top of a CNN feature map. To avoid misalignment caused by the original RoI Pooling (RoIPool) layer, a RoIAlign layer was proposed to preserve spatial correspondence at the pixel level. With a ResNeXt101-FPN backbone [8], Mask RCNN achieved the best results in terms of COCO object instance segmentation and bounding object detection. And the second category, among the algorithms, includes the YOLOv2 and YOLO9000: proposed YOLOv2, an improved version of YOLO. It reached the state of the art in standard detection tasks such as PASCAL VOC and MS COCO. SSD (Single-shot detector): To preserve real-time speed without sacrificing excessive detection accuracy. SSD effectively combines RPN ideas in Faster RCNN, YOLO, and multi-scale CONV functions to achieve fast detection speed while maintaining high detection quality.

Detection has been used for several purposes, the most important is to track objects which have made significant progress in the last decade. [18] noted recently, that some researchers used online and offline CNN method processing to segment and track at one time and it showed fast and accurate tracking results and segmentation. In addition, a full investigation has been done by [1], the authors reported that online algorithms are too slow compared to batch tracking algorithms, especially when using algorithms that often require a lot of computation like deep learning algorithms. Most of the MOT algorithms share some of their steps. We mention, for example, some of the proposed approaches: [21] suggested a tracking method consisting of four stages: Detection, extraction of appearance characteristics, and the association then tracking of moving objects. And the approach of [6] consists of only two phases: online tracker and then association.

We noticed in most of these works that they use the appearance features, applied and evaluated on humans only, also they use the center of the detection frame or a small part of the object to track the movement of the object. [1] reported that methods that do not exploit appearance are less efficient. They also showed that the most efficient detectors currently are the Faster R-CNN and its variants. [10] points out that the tracking-by-detection model is widely used, but it still faces some difficulties, and there are several reform attempts recently.

2.2 Behavior Study

We need now to analyze the data extracted from the first stage like the duration of each activity, the indicator of each activity duration, the season during which these activities take place, etc.

According to [16], ontology is a discipline of philosophy, it is the study of being as an entity, of what is? what type, what structure? their properties? Among these works, we cite: [4] went further than the formal definition of the various management behavior specifications integrated into the management information definitions, they focused on the definition of the rules of behavior in the management information with SWRL, a rules language defined to complete the OWL functionality. [3] used the ontology to present a semantic classification method based on objects in high-resolution satellite imagery. [13] also used the ontology to model human behavior. [17] used it to build a Semantic Ship Behavior Model (SMSB) to analyze potential ship behaviors.

3 Proposed Methodology

Our study is composed of two phases, as shown in the Fig. 1. The first consists of video annotation; extracting from the video, all information about each target object. The second step is to make the annotations semantic by studying and analyzing the knowledge constructed based on the data extracted. In phase 1, we aim to extract information from the video that could help us to analyze the behavior of animals. So in the first step, we will detect all the animals and then track them throughout the video. To track the animals, we chose the method closest to our needs because most of the existing solutions are applied to objects that can be easily distinguished, such as pedestrians and cars... However, in our case, the sheep are almost very similar. And in each step, we will try to identify all the errors and possible gaps that could affect the quality of the tracking and check all the results before recording. In phase 2, we convert all the given rules to ontology models to help us make decisions when defining and analyzing behavior.

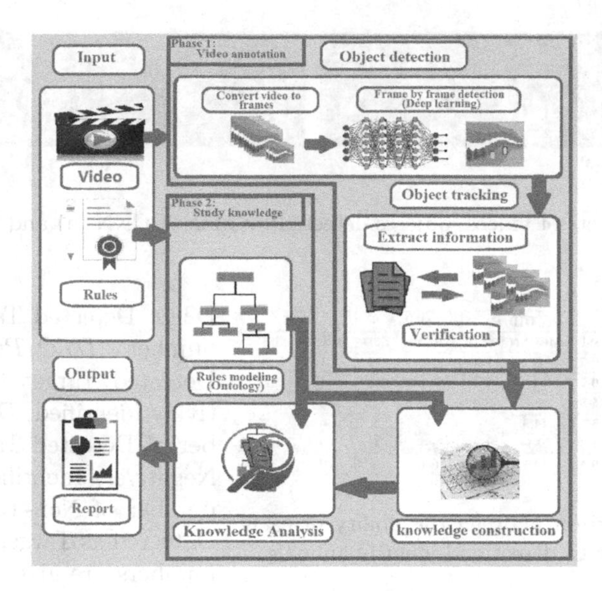

Fig. 1. Our proposed approach.

3.1 Video Annotation

Detection Step. To choose the appropriate detector, we make a comparison between the two detectors, SSD and Mask R-CNN. We test the accuracy and reliability of object identification according to each detector. We used six videos: two videos each contain a single animal, one video contains six animals, two videos contain more than six animals, and one video contains a very large number of animals.

Figure 2(a) shows the Mask RCNN detector result. It could detect all animals even if there is an occlusion. But, he rarely fails to spot certain animals. It can detect a large number of animals. From time to time, it detects part of the animal and/or part of the background as a single object or as two objects. Moreover, sometimes he considers the same animal, whether the whole body or part of it, as two animals. These faults appear frequently, especially when animals are very close to the camera or their colors are similar to the color of grass.

Figure 2(b) shows one of the SSD detector results. It could detect the animal most of the time, even if there is an occlusion when we have a little number of sheep. While it can only detect 4 to 7 animals in other videos. In a few moments, it detects the same animal as two animals. But, for several moments, he was unable to detect anything despite the 'Sheep' being very conspicuous. From time to time, the size of the box is slightly larger compared to the detected object. Also, it was remarkable that some of the chests were in the wrong location.

Based on these tests, we can easily compare the performance of each detector. Using Table 3, we can make a decision about which detector will be used in our project. We have in this table V_i with i = [1..6]: Video number, nb: Number of sheep per video, DON: Detected Objects Number,

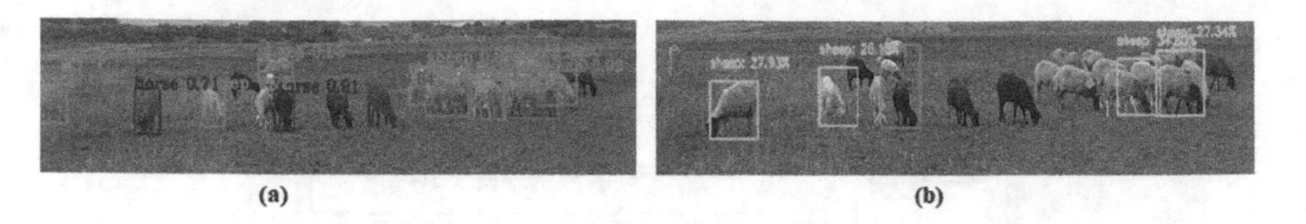

Fig. 2. Extracts of videos, objects detected by Mask RCNN (a) and by SSD (b).

DON/Video	OTD		$OTD_I P$		$OTD_I N$		$NTOD_T$	
Detector	MRCNN	SSD	MRCNN	SSD	MRCNN	SSD	MRCNN	SSD
$v_1(nb = 1)$	1-2	0-2	1	0-1	0-1	0-1	1	0
$v_2(nb = 1)$	1-2	0-2	1	0-1	0-1	0-1	1	0
$v_3(nb = 6)$	6-2	5-8	4-3	3-6	1-0	1-2	0	0
$v_4(nb \gg 15)$	18-14	3-5	14-3	4-3	3	1	0	1-2
$v_5(nb \gg 15)$	24-17	1-3	20-14	1-3	3-4	1	0	0-2
$v_6(nb \gg 20)$	20-7	0-4	19-1	4-0	6-1	0	0	0

Fig. 3. Comparison between the ability of each detection device to detect and identify animals.

DTO: Detected Target Objects number, $DTO_I P$: number of Detected Target Objects Positively Identified, $DTO_I N$: number of Detected Target Objects Negatively Identified, $NTOD_T$: number of Non-Target Objects Detected as Target objects. The numbers are given here present in all moments of the videos.

Videos	V_1		V_2		V_3		V_4		V_5		V_6	
Errors	Mask	SSD	Mask	SSD	Mask	SSD	Mask	SSD	Mask	SSD	Mask	SSD
$Error_1$	No	Yes	No	Yes	Yes	Yes	No	Yes	No	Yes	No	Yes
$Error_2$	Yes	Yes	Yes	No	No	No	No	Yes	No	Yes	No	No
$Error_3$	Yes	Yes	Yes	Yes	Yes	Yes	No	No	No	No	No	No
$Error_4$	Yes	Yes	Yes	Yes	Yes	Yes	Yes	Yes	Yes	Yes	Yes	No

Fig. 4. Errors occurred in each test.

Video number i, Yes: the $error_j$ exists, No: the $error_j$ does not exist step, j = [1..4].

We notice, using this table, that the Mask RCNN detector is the least likely to make the errors in the V4 and V5 videos, while they are equal in the V6 video. But in the V6 video, the only error that the SSD detector makes is $error_1$, but we can't rely on his performance, because he could only detect four of more than twenty creatures.

Four types of errors we observed during these tests that they are: The failure to detect all the animals throughout the video ($error_1$), to detect non-target objects as objects targets ($error_2$), detect a single target object as two different objects ($error_3$) and poorly recognizing objects ($error_4$). We simplify the existence of errors in all videos with Table 4. We have in this table V_i with i = [1..6]:

After these results, we choose the Mask RCNN detector to use in our project. Although the results are acceptable under conditions similar to those of the V4 and V5 videos, the possibility of errors remains probable. Certainly, this will affect the proper tracking of each object. Therefore, we will do our best to avoid as many errors as possible and ensure good tracking.

Tracking Step. After important searches, we found that almost all searches depend on the box object detected, their center or the contour of mask object detected ... etc. to associate the pairs of the objects. But in our case, these methods can make false associations. As we show in Fig. 5(a), we cannot specify the true center of each object during an occlusion. Therefore, we propose another method for a good selection of the center that gives the true object position.

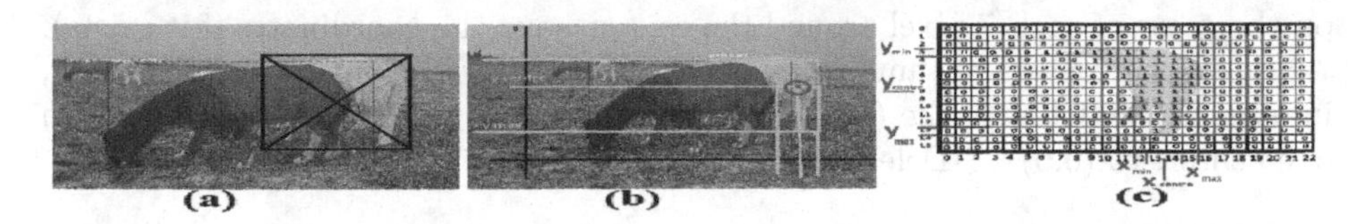

Fig. 5. Solution proposed to improve position selection.

The Mask R-CNN detector gives us a matrix of 0 and 1, as shown Fig. 5(c), for each object mask, it has the same image Fig. 5(b) dimension. Our proposal is:

$$Y_{centre} = (Y_{min} + Y_{max})/2$$
$$X_{centre} = (X_{min} + X_{max})/2(\text{of line } Y_{centre})$$

y_{min} is the first-row index and y_{max} is the last row index, which contain one or more columns with "1". X_{min} is the first column index and X_{max} the last column index in the line y_{center} which have "1". With this method, we can associate the centers of objects in the image (i-1) and in the image (i), using the Hungarian algorithm. The next position of the object S is the position of the center (i) closest to its center (i-1).

Now, we cite some errors that can hinder the tracking process, we will propose for each type a solution to reduce its incidence as much as possible. We have four potential errors cases to appear, that can negatively affect tracking quality.

Case (1): The number of objects in the frame (i-1) is greater than the number of objects in the frame (i). Case (2): The number of objects in the frame (i-1), is less than the number of objects in the frame (i). Case (3): The number of objects in the frame (i-1) is equal to the number of objects in the frame (i). Case (4): Detection of a target object "Sheep" as a non-target object like "Cow". It is often caused by occlusion or detection of the object more than once.

We proposed solutions for almost all detection errors, that give a better annotation video (by detecting objects, identifying target objects, then tracking them through the video). The steps for phase 1, then, are as follows:

1-Detection using Mask R-CNN (Save each image, Extract classification, center coordinates (x, y) and mask matrix of each object). 2-Eliminate double masks: (Compare all mask arrays for single image, Eliminate duplicated object). 3-Propose associations and verify them (Propose an association using the Hungarian algorithm [7], Compare the matrices of each proposed pair, Give each verified pair the same name, Save the pairs have the same name, Search for each odd object, a partner among all previously recorded objects, Give). 4-Eliminate non-target objects: (Compare the classification of each object in all images, Eliminate objects which most of the time were classified as objects other than sheep). 5-Eliminate objects that never move: (Compare the coordinates of each object in all frames, Eliminate objects that never move throughout the video). 6-Find undetected objects: (Extract the image where the object was not detected and the nearest image from which the object was detected, Predict possible coordinates for the new center, Find the coordinates the closer based on the color of each 7 pixel around the center, save the coordinates if it exists). 7-Empty the centers of same mask:(Count the centers belonging to each mask, in each frame, Change the (x, y) of all the centers of each mask has more than one center, to (0,0)). 8-Delete empty tables.

3.2 Study Knowledge

Ontology plays a central role in our methodology. The ontology serves as a pivot to combine the classification of results and the formalization of knowledge. With a set of individual class instances, the ontology can constitute a knowledge base [11]. In our study, we will express in Web Ontology Language (OWL) the information that helps to specify the behaviors and analyze them, while the semantic rules are expressed in Semantic Web Rule (SWRL).

Knowledge Construction: Specify Animal Behavior. We mean, by the behavior of animals the activities that they perform in the pasture: movement, ingestion, or rest. Given the importance of the results of these activities, we will create an ontology model (Fig. 6) that will help us achieve the best and most accurate results.

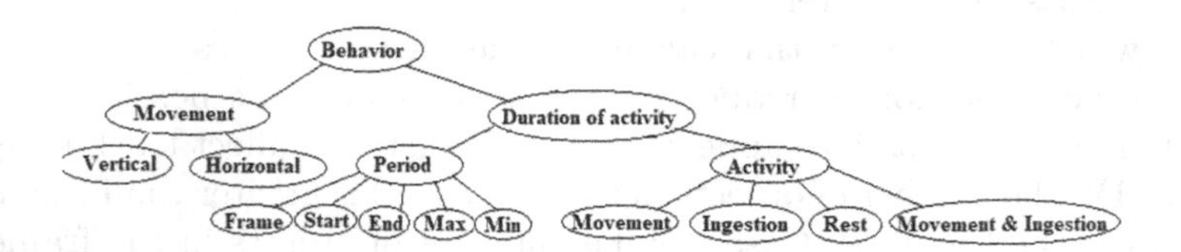

Fig. 6. An extract from animal behavior ontology model.

The semantic rule modeling process includes building Mark rules and decision rules. The construction of Mark rules is based on a semantic concept, and the process moves from low-level features to semantic concepts. Then, decision rules are obtained based on Mark rules and prior knowledge. The process moves from advanced features to identifying trends, period features (frame, start, end, minimum, maximum), and activities. The ontology model of Mark rules represents the different states of motion on the X and Y axes, with each subclass representing a state of the parent class.

Mark rules are expressed in SWRL and semantic relationships between object features and classes are constructed. For example, the case where $Y_D > Y_F$ and $X_D > X_F$ is expressed in SWRL as follows:

- periode(?I,$?Y_D$,$?Y_F$,$?Y_{min}$,$?Y_{max}$), greaterThan($?Y_D$,$?Y_F$)→ $Y_D > Y_F$
- periode(?I,$?X_D$,$?X_F$,$?X_{min}$,$?X_{max}$), greaterThan($?X_D$,$?X_F$)→ $X_D > X_F$

This means that the characteristic Y_D of an object > their Y_F designates the case we called "$Y_D > Y_F$", the same for the characteristic X_D of an object > their X_F denotes the case we called "$X_D > X_F$". With, period(? X), X is an individual of period, greaterThan(?X, ?Y) represents attributes, and x and y are variables.

The decision rules for four types of activities are acquired from a priori knowledge and the technical regulations of the project. We have formalized these decision rules using OWL as follows:

- Movement $\equiv X_D > X_F \sqcup X_D < X_F$
- Ingestion $\equiv Y_D > Y_F \sqcup Y_{min} > Y_D \sqcup Y_i > Y_{max}$
- Rest $\equiv \neg$ Movement $\sqcap \neg$ Ingestion
- Movement&Ingestion $\equiv$ Movement $\sqcap$ Ingestion

Decision rules are expressed in SWRL, and semantic relationships between mark rules and classes are constructed. For example, Movement&Ingestion is expressed in SWRL as follows:

$X_D > X_F$(?period), $Y_D > Y_F$(?period) → Displacement&Ingestion(?period). This means that an activity with characteristics (movement on the X axis and movement on the Y axis) $X_D > X_F$ and $Y_D > Y_F$ is Movement&Ingest.

Knowledge Analysis: Study Animal Behavior. The objectives of our study of animal behavior in pastures are to know (1) the effect of grazing on natural rangelands and (2) the role of rational grazing in animal self-sufficiency. Using the results of the "Specify Behaviors" process and set of rules we can build an ontology that allows us to achieve our goals. We explain here one of these extraction knowledge processes.

Use of Pasture: Three main criteria to know the state of pastures degradation, whether it is very poor, poor, moderately rich, rich, or satisfactory. The ontology mark rules model presents the TRM rate of restoration of the natural vegetation cycle, the season, and the animal behavior (mainly represented by the consumption rate of pastoral species; ingestion rate).

Mark rules are expressed in SWRL and semantic relationships between object features and classes are constructed. For example, the case where the TRM rate is class [0.20], the season is "summer" and the ingestion rate is]40.50] are expressed in SWRL as follows:

- TRM(?rate), greaterThan(?rate, 0), lessThanOrEqual(?rate, 20) → [0,20]
- Tingestion($?rate_{ing}$), greaterThan($?rate_{ing}$, 40), lessThanOrEqual ($?rate_{ing}$, 50) →]40,50]
- Season(?S), Equal (?S, summer) → summer

This means that the "rate" characteristic of an object > at 0 and < at 20 denotes the case we called "[0,20]", and the characteristic "$rate_{ing}$ " of an object > at 40 and < at 50 designates the case that we called "]40,50]", the same for the characteristic "S" of an object = summer designates the case that we called "summer" With, P(? X), X is an individual of period, lessThanOrEqual(?x, ?y) represents attributes, and x and y are variables. Decision rules for pasture use states are acquired from a priori knowledge and technical regulations of the project. We formalized the decision rule from the previous example, using OWL as follows:

- Massive ≡ summer ⊓ [0.20] ⊓]40.50]

Decision rules are expressed in SWRL, and semantic relationships between brand rules and classes are constructed. For example, Rich usage is expressed in SWRL as follows: summer(?S), [0.20] (?rate),]40.50] ($?rate_{ing}$) → Massive(?state).

This means that a use state with summer characteristics, [0.20](TRM) and]40.50] (ingestion rate) is Heavy use.

4 Evaluation and Discussion

Our approach has resolved many issues, both in detection and tracking. Here we present the challenges we discussed earlier and the results obtained.

Detection. Our approach manages to detect and recognize all target objects well. It overcame the challenges caused by occlusion, and the variance of objects number throughout the video.

Association. Since our approach has overcome the challenge of varying the number of objects in the video, it can track every object well. In addition, the deleting of object coordinates when it has a large percentage of mask intersection with another helps to avoid calculating the object more than once in each frame and thus it provides good and accurate tracking

Tracking. To test the effectiveness of our approach, we used two videos, one (video 1) of 28 s, contains 5 sheep present since the beginning of the video sequence, and another sheep has been entered at the end of the video (Fig. 7(a). The second (video 2) is 5 s long, and contains more than 25 sheep present from the beginning of the video sequence to the end, as shown in the Fig. 7(b). The first video was converted to 571 frames, Fig. 8V(1).(a) shows the results of detection and association steps. The number of sheep detected is greater than the actual number of sheep. Figure 8V(1).(b) shows our proposed approach results to find the missing coordinates while deleting the repeated ones, so the alleged objects were deleted. It contained the coordinates of several sheep, and this happened because of occlusion between the sheep. Our approach here was able to track all the six sheep by 100%.

Fig. 7. One of video_1 (a) and video_2 (b) frames.

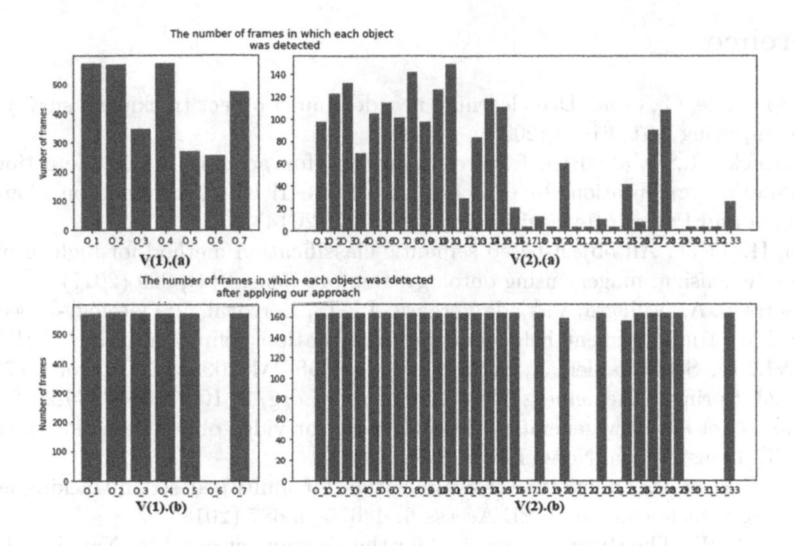

Fig. 8. Object detection results using Mask RCNN.

The video (2) was converted to 163 frames, the detection and the association result was shown in Fig. 8V(2).(a). 33 sheep were found, this number is higher than the actual number of sheep. The sheep that did not move their coordinates throughout the detection period were removed, Fig. 8V(2).(b) shows the result of our optimization.

We noticed in this case (video 2), that there was great confusion in the association between certain objects because they confused their coordinates with the other's coordinates. This happened when there was a large occlusion in addition to the rapid movement of these sheep.

5 Conclusion

In this article, we introduced our two-stages approach. The first is the semantic annotations of a video sequence to extract all the information needed to build and study the knowledge in the second stage. We clarified all the steps that guarantee us a 100% tracking based on a 100% detection using the Mask RCNN detector and a true association by pressing the Hungarian algorithm to reduce the process of looking for associations. In each step, we mentioned the problems that could be hindering our work and the appropriate solutions to remove them as much as possible.

Although object detection had a lot of attention in the past decade, the best detectors are still far from saturated in performance, it also remains an open challenge. In this paper, we presented a new method for video object tracking based on the Mask R-CNN detector. The result of this approach helps us to assure a good annotation of the video. Based on it, in the second stage, we will study the behavior of each animal and determine the effects of the behavior on the animal itself, and the pasture.

References

1. Ciaparrone, G., et al.: Deep learning in video multi-object tracking: a survey. Neurocomputing **381**, 61–88 (2020)
2. Girshick, R., et al.: Rich feature hierarchies for accurate object detection and semantic segmentation. In: Proceedings of the IEEE Conference on Computer Vision and Pattern Recognition, pp. 580–587 (2014)
3. Gu, H., et al.: An object-based semantic classification method for high resolution remote sensing imagery using ontology. Remote Sens. **9**(4), 329 (2017)
4. Guerrero, A., Villagrá, V.A., de Vergara, J.E.L., Berrocal, J.: Ontology-based integration of management behaviour and information definitions using SWRL and OWL. In: Schönwälder, J., Serrat, J. (eds.) DSOM 2005. LNCS, vol. 3775, pp. 12–23. Springer, Heidelberg (2005). https://doi.org/10.1007/11568285_2
5. Jiao, L., et al.: New generation deep learning for video object detection: a survey. IEEE Trans. Neural Netw. Learn. Syst. (2021)
6. Kim, S.J., et al.: Online tracker optimization for multi-pedestrian tracking using a moving vehicle camera. IEEE Access **6**, 48675–48687 (2018)
7. Kuhn, H.W.: The Hungarian method for the assignment problem. Nav. Res. Logist. Q. **2**(1–2), 83–97 (1955)
8. Lin, T.Y., et al.: Feature pyramid networks for object detection. In: Proceedings of the IEEE Conference on Computer Vision and Pattern Recognition, pp. 2117–2125 (2017)
9. Liu, L., et al.: Deep learning for generic object detection: a survey. Int. J. Comput. Vision **128**(2), 261–318 (2020)
10. Luo, W., et al.: Multiple object tracking: a literature review. Artif. Intell. **293**, 103448 (2021)
11. Noy, N.F., et al.: Ontology development 101: a guide to creating your first ontology (2001)
12. Parekh, H.S., et al.: A survey on object detection and tracking methods. Int. J. Innov. Res. Comput. Commun. Eng. **2**(2), 2970–2979 (2014)
13. Phan, N., et al.: Ontology-based deep learning for human behavior prediction with explanations in health social networks. Inf. Sci. **384**, 298–313 (2017)
14. Sasse, J., et al.: Semantic metadata annotation services in the biomedical domain-a literature review. Appl. Sci. **12**(2), 796 (2022)
15. Wang, X., et al.: Data modeling and evaluation of deep semantic annotation for cultural heritage images. J. Doc. (2021)
16. Welty, C., Guarino, N.: Supporting ontological analysis of taxonomic relationships. Data Know. Eng. **39**(1), 51–74 (2001)
17. Wen, Y., et al.: Semantic modelling of ship behavior in harbor based on ontology and dynamic Bayesian network. ISPRS Int. J. Geo Inf. **8**(3), 107 (2019)
18. Yao, R., et al.: Video object segmentation and tracking: a survey. arXiv preprint arXiv:1904.09172 (2019)
19. Yazdi, M., Bouwmans, T.: New trends on moving object detection in video images captured by a moving camera: a survey. Comput. Sci. Rev. **28**, 157–177 (2018)
20. Zaidi, S.S.A., et al.: A survey of modern deep learning based object detection models. Digit. Signal. Process. 103514 (2022)
21. Zhou, Z., et al.: Online multi-target tracking with tensor-based high-order graph matching. In: 2018 24th International Conference on Pattern Recognition (ICPR), pp. 1809–1814. IEEE (2018)

Modeling Empathy Episodes with ARD and DMN

Weronika T. Adrian(✉), Julia Ignacyk, Krzysztof Kluza,
Mirosława M. Długosz, and Antoni Ligęza

AGH University of Science and Technology, al. A. Mickiewicza 30,
30-059 Krakow, Poland
{wta,kluza,mmd,ligeza}@agh.edu.pl

Abstract. Empathy, the ability to emotionally understand other people's feelings, might be modeled in various ways. In this paper, we try to look at the empathy episodes from the knowledge engineering perspective. We present the possibility of modeling the empathy episodes using the Attribute Relationship Diagrams (ARD) and Decision Model and Notation (DMN) modeling notations and methods.

Keywords: Empathy episodes · Attribute Relationship Diagrams · Decision Model and Notation · Empathy modeling

1 Introduction

Feelings might be a powerful tool and a key component of human perception. They help to separate the important things from the unimportant. Something that evokes a strong emotional response is not likely to be ignored – it will "stick" in the mind and feed into the decision-making process. Moreover, emotional skills are a fundamental component of intelligence, especially in the areas of preference learning and adaptation. Under the term empathy, there is a very wide range of experiences. According to Merriam Webster's dictionary [10], empathy is the act of understanding, becoming aware of, being sensitive to, and vicariously experiencing the feelings, thoughts, and experiences of someone from the past or present without fully communicating the feelings, thoughts, and experience in an objectively explicit way. Emotion researchers [1] define empathy as the ability to sense other people's emotions, combined with the ability to imagine what someone else might be thinking or feeling. Our recognition of emotions depend on various properties. Moreover, some issues might also negatively influence recognition of emotions [4].

Knowledge about empathy, represented in a formal way, may significantly improve the affective computing systems that take into consideration the analysis of the emotional states of people. In this paper, we describe a concept of modeling and representing empathy using the existing knowledge representation methods which can be suitable for such modeling. Attribute Relationship Diagrams (ARD) provide a suitable way to grasp the dependencies between empathy

G. Memmi et al. (Eds.): KSEM 2022, LNAI 13370, pp. 403–413, 2022.
https://doi.org/10.1007/978-3-031-10989-8_32

properties while Decision Model and Notation (DMN) can illustrate the decision process for the empathy episodes.

The paper is structured as follows. Section 2 provides the background concerning the empathy. Section 3 provides the overview of the cognitive schema model of empathy. In Sect. 4, we present the decision model of the empathy phenomenon. The final section discusses our results and concludes the paper.

2 Preliminaries

The concept of empathy covers a broad spectrum of phenomena. Therefore, an accurate definition requires an equally broad theoretical concept. The word empathy is derived from the late 19th century German word Einfühlung. In the exact translation it means "into feelings". Based on this term, Lipps defined empathy as "objectified self-enjoyment" referring to the internal mechanism of imitation of an observed person or object [3]. Titchener understood empathy as the process of humanizing objects and reading into them [16]. Lipps stated that by observing another person's emotional state, humans are able to mimic the signs of that state and thus experience similar reactions. Empathy began to be seen as an active process in which people try to "get into the skin" of another person, understand and feel the situation in which someone is [5]. Köhler [8] in defining empathy paid more attention to observing the other person's states than understanding them. George [9] saw the empathy as the concepts of assuming the role of another person and, consequently, understanding how they perceive the world. Piaget [13] studied children's development with a particular focus on critical cognitive abilities by basing empathy as a concept of decentration. According to his assumptions, children would increase their ability to distinguish between their own and others' experiences through development. At the beginning of life, a person does not have this ability, looking at the world egocentrically, only with the passage of time they develop and change perspective.

2.1 Empathy Cognitive Schema

Davis attempted to create an approach to the topic by presenting a research scheme of empathy [1]. His definition states that it is a set of theoretical constructs that pertain to an individual's response to the experiences of others; chief among these constructs are the processes that occur in the observer and the affective and non-affective effects that occur as a result of such processes [1]. Additionally, he defined what an empathic episode is as a situation in which the person of the observer comes into contact with the observed in some way and some type of response (cognitive, affective, and/or behavioral) occurs on the part of the observer [2]. The episode consists of four parts:

1. antecedent conditions, which characterize the observer, the observed, and the situation,
2. process, which is the individual mechanisms,

3. intrapersonal outcomes (cognitive and affective responses of the observer),
4. interpersonal outcomes (behavioral reactions oriented toward the observer).

Psychologist have identified the links between the above areas (Fig. 1). The closer the constructs are to each other, the more they influence each other.

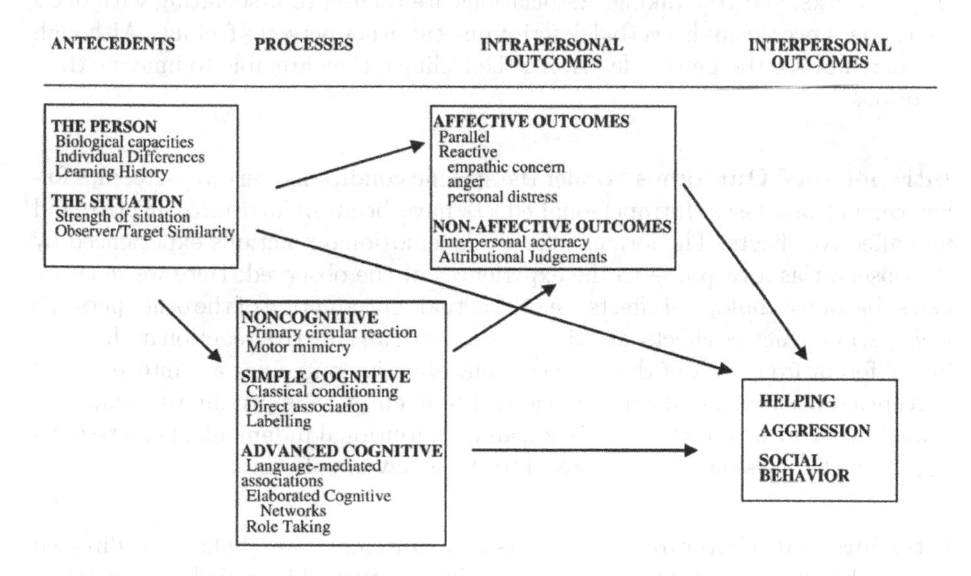

Fig. 1. Davis empathy cognitive model [1]

Antecedent Conditions. When analyzing an empathic episode, one must pay attention to the initial states of those involved, as well as the situation itself. The ability to empathize is primarily influenced by biological abilities. Equally important are individual abilities to tend to engage in processes related to the concept. There are many methods and tools for measuring such predispositions. Another aspect that counts is an individual's history of learning empathic values and behaviors. The situation in which individuals find themselves cannot be overlooked. The greatest influence is the intensity of the event. At the moment of a very powerful event, when our emotions are running high, the other characteristics listed lose their importance. In an empathic episode, the more the individuals involved are similar, the more the intensity of the observer's affective and non-affective response increases.

Processes. Empathic processes can be divided into three classes. They can be grouped on the basis of the degree of cognitive effort and observer experience. The non-cognitive group does not include cognitive activity, such as unconscious or automatic behaviours. The second class are simple cognitive processes, which involve eliciting basic cognitive processes from the observer. These include classical conditioning, direct association, and labeling, They correlate directly with the experience of perceiving an emotion evoked by a particular stimulus in the past. In a future in a similar emotional situation, an affective response will occur. But also associations of emotional states, stereotypes, and suppositions of emotions that might be experienced at a particular time. The third class constitute advanced cognitive processes, which include language mediated associations, formed cognitive networks, and role taking. Associations are related to associating with one's own experience through a verbal description of another person's feelings. Although one may not see the person describing the feelings, they are able to imagine their emotions.

Intrapersonal Outcomes. Under the specific conditions, certain outcomes follow certain processes. Intrapersonal effects have been divided into affective and non-affective effects. The former refer to the emotional reactions experienced by the observer as a response to the experiences of the observed. Here we separate two subgroups: analogical effects, i.e., the actual reproduction of the other person's feelings, and reactive effects, i.e., the occurrence of an affective reaction in the man, but different from that of the observer. The affective outcomes are interpersonal perceptual accuracy, defined as a successful attempt to approximate someone's thoughts, feelings, and characteristics, and attributional judgments, i.e., attributing causes to one's own behaviors and to the behaviors of others.

Interpersonal Outcomes. Interpersonal Outcomes are behaviors directed at the observer that result from pre-existing contact. These include behaviors toward the other person in this group.

3 Modeling the Empathy Cognitive Schema

For creating the model of the empathy cognitive schema, we propose to use two notations, namely. Attribute Relationship Diagrams for modeling dependencies between empathy properties and Decision Model and Notation for the decision process for the empathy episodes.

3.1 Attribute Relationship Diagrams

Attribute Relationship Diagrams (ARD) aims at capturing relations between "attributes" of a specific system. Such "attributes" denote the system's properties or variables considered in decision logic. ARD was originally introduced in [11] as a method for prototyping a knowledge base structure, similarly to the relational database structure from ERD diagrams. ARD models can be created in an iterative and hierarchical process. In this process, the models become detailed and more specific, and keep the functional dependencies between the system elements. Below, we use the ARD formalization from [7].

Definition 1. *A* ***property*** $p \in P$ *is a non-empty set of attributes describing the property and representing a piece of knowledge about a certain part of the system being designed. A* ***simple property*** $p \in P^s$ *is a property consisting of a single attribute* ($|p| = 1$)*. A* ***complex property*** $p \in P^c$ *is a property consisting of multiple attributes* ($|p| > 1$)*. Note that* $P = P^s \cup P^c$.

Definition 2. *A* ***dependency*** $d \in D$ *is an ordered pair of properties* (f, t)*, where* $f \in P$ *is the* ***independent property*** *and* $t \in P$ *is the* ***dependent property*** *that depends on* f*. If* $f = t$ *the property is called* ***self-dependent****. For notational convention* $d = (f, t), d \in D, D \subseteq P \times P$ *will be presented as:* $d(f, t)$[1].

A (functional) dependency is a relation between two properties that shows that in order to determine the dependent property attribute values, values of the attributes of the independent property are needed.

Definition 3. *A* ***derivation*** $q \in Q$ *is an ordered pair of properties* (f, t)*, where* $t \in P$ *is derived from* $f \in P$ *upon a transformation. Similarly to dependency* $Q \subseteq P \times P$*, however* $D \cap Q = \emptyset$.

Definition 4. *A* ***Design Process Diagram*** G_D *is a triple* (P, D, Q)*, where:*

- P *is a set of properties,*
- D *is a set of dependencies,*
- Q *is a set of derivations.*

The DPD diagram is a directed graph with properties as nodes and both dependencies and derivations as edges.

Definition 5. *An* ***Attribute Relationship Diagram*** G_A *is a pair* (P_{ARD}, D)*, where:*

- $G_D = (P, D, Q)$,
- P_{ARD} *is a subset of* G_D *properties* ($P_{ARD} \subseteq P$) *such that* $P_{ARD} = \{p_i \in P \colon \forall_{p_j \in P}\, (p_i, p_j) \notin Q\}$,
- *and* D *is a set of dependencies.*

ARD diagrams are usually depicted as graphs with the properties represented as nodes and dependencies represented as edges.

A fragment of an ARD diagram with two properties and the dependency between them is presented in Fig. 2 to illustrate the ARD concepts.

[1] $d(f, t)$ denotes a dependency d from a property f to a property t.

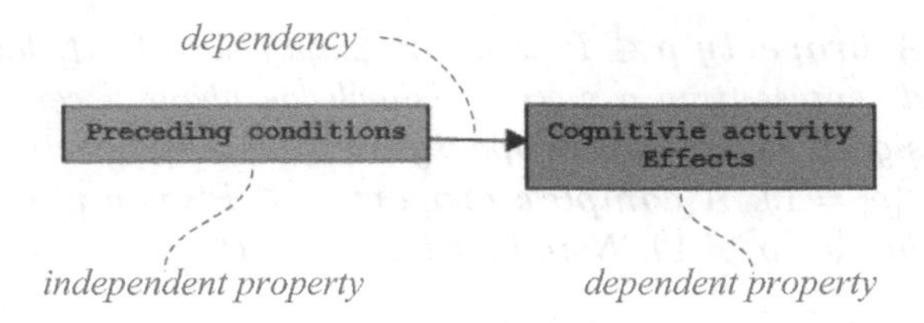

Fig. 2. An example of a simple ARD diagram

The diagram should be interpreted in the following way: `Cognitive activity` and `Effects` depend on some `Preceding conditions`. Note that in other modeling languages, the dependency is often modeled inversely, i.e. as an arrow pointing from a dependent object to an independent one, e.g. in UML [15].

3.2 ARD Design Process

Specification of ARD is an iterative process that serves as a tool for diagram specification. The diagram transformations constitute the core aspects of the ARD method. They transform a property into one or more properties, specifying new derivations and dependencies into a G_D model. These transformations are also required in order to introduce new attributes. For the transformation of properties from the diagram G_A^1 into the properties in diagram G_A^2, the properties in the G_A^2 diagram are more specific than in the G_A^1. During the design process, the ARD model becomes more and more specific.

The process consists in finalizing the properties into more detailed attributes and splitting more complex properties into simple ones and gradually adding the dependencies between them [12]. Such splitting might be of a various form:

- Split all to single – splits an element into elements containing only single attributes,
- Split selected to single – splits an element into two elements, but only one of them needs to be of single attribute,
- Split to left – splits an element into two and adds a single dependency relation. The first element will be of type independent and the second element will be of type dependent.
- Split to right – works similarly to "Split to left", but the direction of the single relationship changes. The first element will be of dependent type, while the second will be of independent type.
- Split to left as middle – similar to the above, but the element before splitting must be a dependency relation as independent. In this situation, the first element will be split and the new element will be a single attribute between the pre-existing elements.
- Split to right as middle – similar to the above, but the element before splitting must be in one dependency relationship as dependent.

3.3 Modeling the Cognitive Schema of Empathy

Based on Davis' description, an empathy cognitive schema diagram was created using the ARD method. The prepared concept will be used during prototyping of decision rules and simulation of empathic episode. We start with the root "Empathy" element (Fig. 3). According to the theory, an empathetic episode occurs on the basis of initial conditions, with the existence of cognitive activity, leading to effects. In Davis' schema, the greatest relationship is between adjacent constructs (Fig. 4).

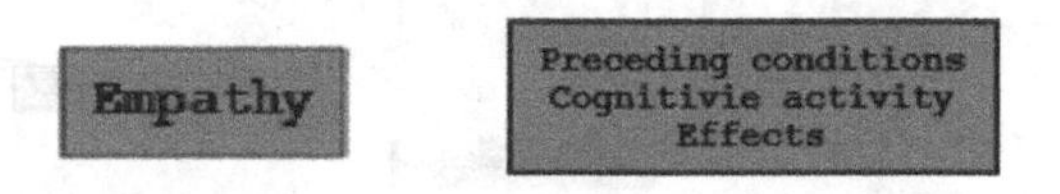

Fig. 3. Root Empathy element

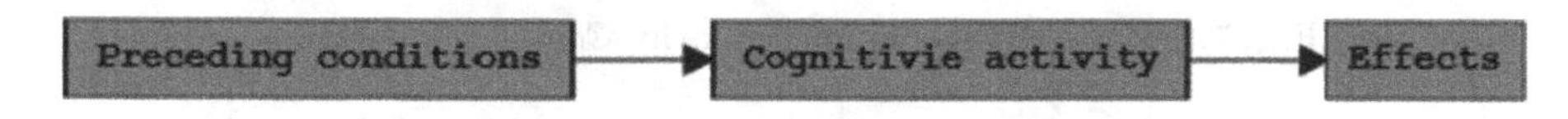

Fig. 4. Split to right

Effects can be divided into Processes and Outcomes (Fig. 5). The processes that occur directly affect the person's results and performance.

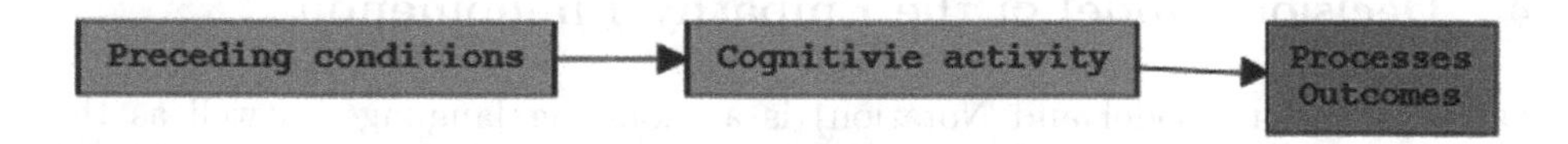

Fig. 5. Finalization

Outcomes can be divided into interpersonal and intrapersonal effects. The former relate to our feelings and behaviors towards ourselves (intrapersonal) and the latter towards other people (interpersonal).

The procesing conditions consist of information regarding the Person (observer) and the Situation they are in. The Person attribute can be further decomposed into biological abilities, individual differences, and history of experience (Fig. 6). The description of the situation, on the other hand, consists of its intensity and its similarity to the observer.

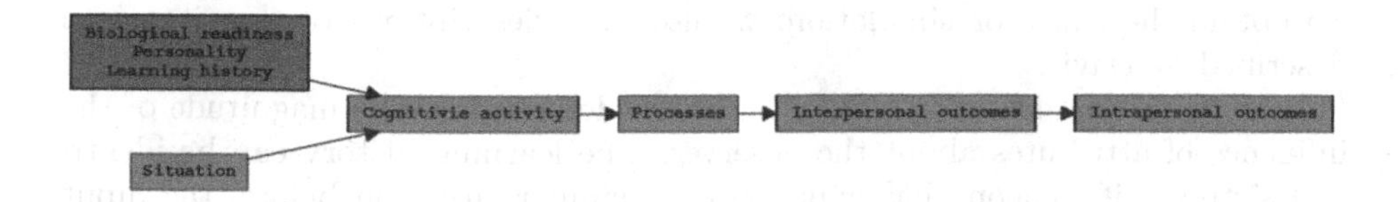

Fig. 6. Introducing more attributes

Processes depend on cognitive activity. Based on it, processes can be divided into three groups: non-cognitive (low level), post cognitive (medium level), and advanced cognitive (high level). Finally, the intrapersonal effects occurring within a person can be affective as well as non-affective (Fig. 7).

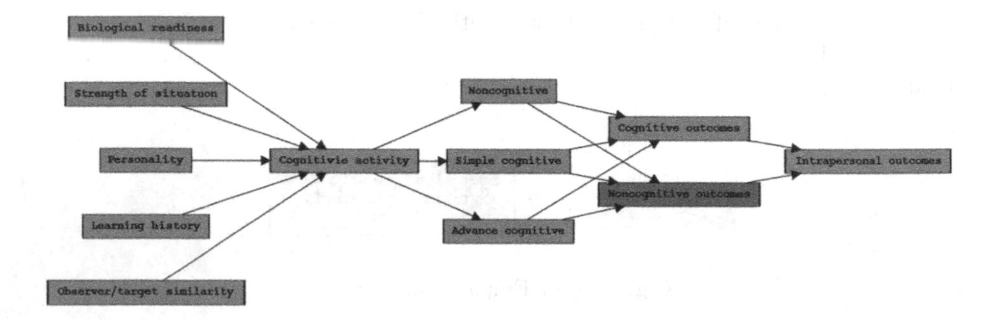

Fig. 7. Final ARD model for Empathy Cognitive Schema

The final version of the ARD model illustrates the importance of attributes describing the person and the situation in which the observer finds themselves. On this basis, further parts of the empathetic episode occur, during which different processes take place but with similar types of effects.

4 Decision Model of the Empathy Phenomenon

DMN (Decision Model and Notation) is a modeling language as well as the notation for specifying business decisions and rules. DMN is easily readable by different types of people involved in decision management [14]. It uses Decision Requirements Diagrams (DRGs) and decision tables. A DRD is a graph that describes the dependencies of a decision on other supporting decisions and sources of information. Decision tables represent a set of related input and output expressions what allows for inferring the decision based on the specific conditions.

The created empathy schema model (Fig. 8) is the starting point along with a description of a real life situation for the empathy simulation. An obstacle was encountered during rule development. The real-life situations were not described in enough detail, making it impossible to prototype rules at such an advanced level. The knowledge that was available allowed the creation of decision tables and a DMN model based on the schema from Fig. 1.

Our DMN model contains 5 attributes with input data and 4 decision tables. To obtain the rules for simulation, we used the descriptions of the situations described by Davis.

During the modeling, a problem arose in determining the magnitude of the influence of attributes about the observer. The learning history can be identified simply – if someone has experienced a similar situation before, the input value can be determined as true. In order to describe the magnitudes and rules for biological propensities and individual differences, additional measurement methods would need to be introduced, as well as an analysis of their effect on the empathic episode. Without such information, it is not possible to create relationships arising from these two attributes.

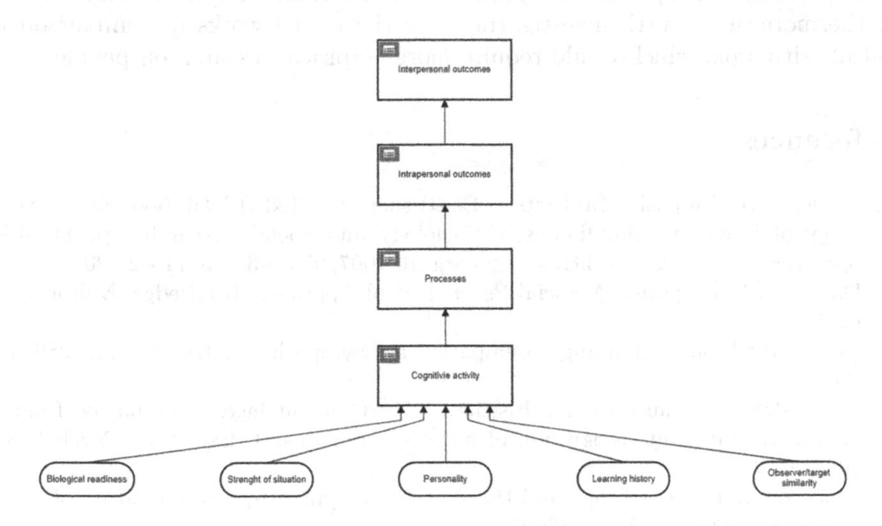

Fig. 8. Decision requirements diagram for the empathy schema model

Based on Davis's considerations [1], it can be inferred that the more intense the event, the greater the cognitive activity. If it is really high, other factors have no effect on the episode. The similarity between the observer and the observed enhances the cognitive activity, so the presence of commonalities between the participants in the episode increases the level of activity.

Processes are directly derived from cognitive activity. The higher its level, the more advanced processes will occur. If it is low, non-cognitive events can be expected. Based on the processes occurring, intrapersonal effects can be determined at a very high level. For low-level cognitive processes, there will be affective effects, for higher-level non-affective effects, and for advanced processes, both sets of results. Based on previous results, interpersonal outcomes occur only in an event with affective and non-affective intrapersonal outcomes.

5 Conclusions

In this paper, we presented a novel way of modeling empathy episodes. For representing the lower level knowledge about the particular properties of the empathy cognitive process and their functional dependencies, we took advantage of the Attribute Relationship Diagrams. For the decision part of the empathy cognitive process, we used Decision Model and Notation. Using such models, it is possible not only to illustrate the process of the empathy episodes from the knowledge engineering perspective, but also simulate the empathy episodes using the existing DMN simulators[2]. Although simple, our model might be helpful for validating or generating more empathetic behavior of agents, for example in computer games industry. In our future works, we would like to extend the model with more properties and parameters, especially in a more fuzzy way [6]. Furthermore, it is worth investigating how the model works in comparison to real life situation, which would require more empirical research on people.

References

1. Davis, M.H.: Empathy. In: Stets, J.E., Turner, J.H. (eds.) Handbook of the Sociology of Emotions. Handbooks of Sociology and Social Research, pp. 443–466. Springer, Boston (2006). https://doi.org/10.1007/978-0-387-30715-2_20
2. Davis, M.H.: Empathy: A Social Psychological Approach. Routledge, Milton Park (2018)
3. Debes, R.: From einfühlung to empathy. In: Sympathy: A History, pp. 286–322 (2015)
4. Israelashvili, J., Sauter, D.A., Fischer, A.H.: Different faces of empathy: feelings of similarity disrupt recognition of negative emotions. J. Exp. Soc. Psychol. **87**, 103912 (2020)
5. Jahoda, G.: Theodor Lipps and the shift from "sympathy" to "empathy". J. Hist. Behav. Sci. **41**(2), 151–163 (2005)
6. Jobczyk, K., Ligęza, A.: A fuzzy multi-agent problem in a conceptual and operational depiction. In: Rutkowski, L., Scherer, R., Korytkowski, M., Pedrycz, W., Tadeusiewicz, R., Zurada, J.M. (eds.) ICAISC 2020. LNCS (LNAI), vol. 12416, pp. 346–356. Springer, Cham (2020). https://doi.org/10.1007/978-3-030-61534-5_31
7. Kluza, K., Nalepa, G.J.: Towards rule-oriented business process model generation. In: Ganzha, M., Maciaszek, L.A., Paprzycki, M. (eds.) Proceedings of the Federated Conference on Computer Science and Information Systems - FedCSIS 2013, Krakow, Poland, 8–11 September 2013, pp. 959–966. IEEE (2013)
8. Köhler, W.: Gestalt Psychology: An Introduction to New Concepts in Modern Psychology, vol. 18. WW Norton & Company, New York (1970)
9. Mead, G.H.: The Works of George Herbert Mead: Mind, Self and Society from the Stand Point of a Social Behaviorist. University of Chicago Press, Chicago (1934)
10. Merriam-Webster: Empathy. https://www.merriam-webster.com/dictionary/empathy
11. Nalepa, G.J., Ligęza, A.: Conceptual modelling and automated implementation of rule-based systems. In: Software Engineering: Evolution and Emerging Technologies. Frontiers in Artificial Intelligence and Applications, vol. 130, pp. 330–340. IOS Press, Amsterdam (2005)
12. Nalepa, G.J., Wojnicki, I.: The ARD+ knowledge representation. https://ai.ia.agh.edu.pl/hekate:ardplus
13. Piaget, J.: The Moral Judgment of the Child. Routledge, Milton Park (2013)
14. Silver, B.: DMN Method & Style. Cody-Cassidy Press (2016)

[2] E.g. Camunda Simulator https://consulting.camunda.com/dmn-simulator/.

15. Suchenia, A., Łopata, P., Wiśniewski, P., Stachura-Terlecka, B.: Towards UML representation for BPMN and DMN models. In: MATEC Web of Conferences, vol. 252, p. 02007. EDP Sciences (2019)
16. Titchener, E.B.: The schema of introspection. Am. J. Psychol. **23**(4), 485–508 (1912)

A Novel RVFL-Based Algorithm Selection Approach for Software Model Checking

Weipeng Cao[1,2], Yuhao Wu[2], Qiang Wang[3(✉)], Jiyong Zhang[4], Xingjian Zhang[1], and Meikang Qiu[5]

[1] CAAC Key Laboratory of Civil Aviation Wide Surveillance and Safety Operation Management and Control Technology, Civil Aviation University of China, Tianjin, China

[2] College of Computer Science and Software Engineering, Shenzhen University, Shenzhen, China
caoweipeng@szu.edu.cn

[3] Institute of System Engineering, Chinese Academy of Military Science, Beijing, China
18513688908@163.com

[4] School of Automation, Hangzhou Dianzi University, Hangzhou, China
jzhang@hdu.edu.cn

[5] Department of Computer Science, Texas A&M University-Commerce, Commerce, TX, USA

Abstract. Software model checking is the technique that automatically verifies whether software meets the given correctness properties. In the past decades, a large number of model checking techniques and tools have been developed, reaching a point where modern model checkers are sophisticated enough to handle large-scale software systems. However, due to the fact that the software model checkering techniques are diverse and each of them is designed and optimized for a specific type of software system, it remains a hard problem for engineers to efficiently combine them to verify the complex software systems in practice. To alleviate this problem, we propose a novel algorithm selection approach based on Random Vector Functional Link net (RVFL) for software model checking, namely Kaleidoscopic RVFL (K-RVFL). The novel design of feature hybridization and fusion enables K-RVFL to extract more diverse and multi-level features. We have also carried out a thorough experimental evaluation on a publicly available data set and compared K-RVFL with a number of neural networks, including RVFL, Extreme Learning Machine (ELM), Stochastic Configuration Network (SCN), Back Propagation algorithm (BP), and Supporting Vector Machine (SVM). The experimental results demonstrate the usefulness and effectiveness of K-RVFL.

Keywords: Software verification · Software model checking · Algorithm selection · Random vector functional link · Neural networks

G. Memmi et al. (Eds.): KSEM 2022, LNAI 13370, pp. 414–425, 2022.
https://doi.org/10.1007/978-3-031-10989-8_33

1 Introduction

Software model checking is a prevailing technique that aims at automatically verifying whether a software satisfies the given correctness properties [6]. In the past decades, a large amount of model checking techniques have been developed and successfully applied to many fields. However, given a number of software model checking tools, the engineers are still facing the problem of 'which is the most suitable one for verifying my software?'. This question arises since the underlying model checking techniques are diverse and there is no single solution that works well for all kinds of software systems. Each model checking technique has its individual characteristics and thus strengthens on a specific type of software. Moreover, there has been a growing awareness of the need to understand how each model checking tool performs and which one is most suitable for a specific type of software, in order to promote software model checking to a larger industrial scope [2,7,13].

Previously the machine learning based algorithm prediction problem has been investigated in some related work [9,12,13]. Instead of selecting the most suitable software model checking tool, their work aims to predict the ranking in terms of the verification performance. All the prediction models are constructed by using Supporting Vector Machine (SVM). In our previous work [14], we view the above problem as an instance of the algorithm selection problem and propose to build the selection model by using neural network techniques [4]. To boost the capability of neural networks, we also define a set of software features that are precise enough to represent the key structural characteristics of the software on the source code level, such as the variable role usage, control flow metrics and loop patterns. Compared with SVM, neural network techniques have several advantages. For example, neural networks are more efficient in handling large data sets than SVM, due to the fact that SVM suffers from the difficulty of parallelizing the learning process.

In this work, we go one step further and propose a novel Kaleidoscopic RVFL algorithm (K-RVFL) with a feature hybridization and fusion mechanism. The network structure of K-RVFL still maintains the direct links from the input layer to the output layer, such that the model's feature extraction ability is enhanced and a regularization for the randomization is provided. Different from RVFL, K-RVFL uses multiple types of bounded non-linear functions such as *Sigmoid* and *Sin* function as its activation function. The input data first undergoes the non-linear mapping through each activation function, and then the output matrix corresponding to each activation function is used as the input of other activation functions for secondary mapping. This process of feature hybridization provides the capability of extracting much more diverse features from the training data. Then, in the feature fusion step, we linearly fuse multi-level features (including the original ones) to get the final feature matrix. The output weights are computed by using the least square method. Last but not the least, K-RVFL maintains the non-iterative training mechanism of RVFL, which enables the ability of fast learning.

To this end, the following contributions have been made in this work.

(1) We present a general formalization of the algorithm selection problem for software model checking. Our work shows that the neural network techniques, in particular, the randomized learning algorithms can solve this problem efficiently and achieve state-of-the-art results. The proposed approach can be extraordinarily helpful for applying software model checking techniques to complex industrial software systems.
(2) We have proposed a novel RVFL algorithm named K-RVFL. Multiple types of activation functions, two-time non-linear mappings, and the fusion of multi-level features can bring rich features to K-RVFL, which enables the model to produce more accurate decisions. It is worth mentioning that the idea of K-RVFL can also be applied to other randomized algorithms such as ELM and SCN.
(3) We have carried out a thorough experimental evaluation, which shows that our proposed K-RVFL algorithm can achieve higher prediction accuracy than ELM, RVFL, SCN, BP, and SVM algorithms. Moreover, compared with BP and SVM algorithms, the training speed of K-RVFL is increased by more than 100 times and 300 times, respectively.

2 Related Works

The work in [13] proposes a SVM based technique to construct a strategy selector for the verification of different programs. The selector takes as input a set of program features and outputs a strategy for verification. A strategy defines the algorithm or parameter that can be useful for verifying the given program. The primary aim of the work in [8,9] is to empirically evaluate and explain the performance differences of the various model checkers in the annual software verification competition (SV-COMP). A portfolio solver based on support vector machine has also been proposed, which essentially chooses the most performant tool for a given model checking task based on the evaluations. In their work, they show that the overall performance of the portfolio solver outperforms all the other tools, which in our opinion demonstrates a strong viability and usefulness of algorithm selection for software verification The work in [7] studies the ranking prediction problem for software model checking. A ranking of the candidate model checkers can indicate which is the most suitable one for the give software at hand. However, their prediction model is also based on SVM.

The authors in [2] present a specific strategy selector for the model checker CPAChecker[1]. However, the selector only works for CAPChecker, because the strategies are merely different parameter specifications or model checking algorithm configurations integrated in CPAChecker. Moreover, the selection model is explicitly defined and implemented in CPAChecker. No machine learning techniques are applied. The experimental evaluation shows that the performance of their strategy selector is much better than any single algorithm configuration of CPAChecker. Similarly in [12], a technique called PeSCo has been proposed

[1] https://cpachecker.sosy-lab.org/.

to predict the likely best sequential combination of algorithm configurations in CPAChecker. The approach is also based on support vector machine.

In our previous work [14], we have proposed for the first time to employ the randomized learning algorithm to solve the algorithm selection problem for software verification. Later in [15] a novel algorithm based on the long-short term memory network (LSTM) has been proposed, which uses word2vec to obtain a representation of the software. For more preliminaries, please refer to [14,15].

3 Algorithm Selection Based on Neural Network with Random Weights

3.1 Extracting Features for Software Model Checking Tasks

In order to solve the algorithm selection problem using the framework of machine learning, we need to represent the software model checking tasks. For this purpose, we define a set of features and the corresponding metrics that can precisely characterize the software on the source code level, leveraging on the related works [8–10].

The first set of features are based on variable roles. Basically, a variable role indicates the usage pattern of the variable in the source code. The choice of roles is inspired by the standard concepts in programming, such as counter, bit-vector and file descriptor etc. In total, we have defined 27 variable roles. For a given software source code f and the set of variable roles $Roles$, we compute a mapping $Res : Roles \to Vars$ from variable roles to the program variables. The variable role metric m_R that represents the relative occurrence of each variable role $R \in Roles$ is defined as $m_R = |Res(R)|/|Vars|$, where $|Vars|$ represents the total number of variables.

The second set of features are based on loop patterns. In total, we define four different loop patterns including syntactically bounded loops, syntactically terminating loops, simple loops, and hard loops. The corresponding metric is called loop pattern based metric. For a given software source code f, we compute the set of syntactically bounded loops L^{SB}, the set of syntactically terminating loops L^{ST}, the set of simple loops L^{simple}, the set of hard loops L^{hard}. The loop pattern based metrics m_{lp} represents the relative occurrence of each loop pattern $lp \in \{ST, SB, simple, hard\}$ and it is computed as $m_{lp} = |L^{lp}|/|Loops|$, where $|Loops|$ represents the set of all loops.

Both variable role based metrics and loop pattern based metrics can be efficiently computed from the software source code by using static analysis techniques [11]. We omit the elaboration since it is out of the scope of this paper.

We denote a software model checking task by $v = (f, p, type)$, where f, p, and $type$ are the software source file, property, and the property type, respectively. We use $Tasks$ to represent the set of software model checking tasks. Each task serves as a sample of the data set for model training. The corresponding feature vector for a task v is defined by $\mathbf{x}(v) = (\mathbf{m}_R, \mathbf{m}_{lp}, type)$, where $type \in \{0, 1, 2, 3\}$ encodes the verification property type, i.e., reachability, memory safety, overflow and termination.

3.2 Formalizing the Algorithm Selection Problem

In this subsection we present how to encode the algorithm selection problem as a multi-classification problem. For each task $v = (f, p, type) \in Tasks$, the function $ExpAns : Tasks \rightarrow \{true, false\}$ defines the expected answer of whether software f satisfies property p. In other words, this function defines the ground truth for each task, which is regardless of the model checking tool being used.

Given a model checking tool $t \in Tools$ and a task $v = (f, p, type) \in Tasks$, applying tool t to verify task v in limited time and resources would produce an answer $PracAns(t, v) = (ans_{t,v}, time_{t,v})$, where $ans_{t,v} \in \{true, false, unknown\}$, and $time_{t,v}$ is the amount of computing time. We remark that the answer $ans_{t,v}$ could be *unknown*, meaning that the tool t is unable to check whether the property holds or not. due to the fact that the software model checking problem generally is undecidable [6].

In neural networks based machine learning techniques, we need labeled data for model training. In our case, the label of a task is the (likely) best tool that is able to verify this task correctly. We denote by $L : Tasks \rightarrow Tools$ the labeling function. Given a task $v \in Tasks$ and a tool $t \in Tools$, we set $L(v) = t$ if the following two conditions are satisfied:

1 the tool t provides the correct answer on v, i.e., $ans_{t,v} = ExpAns(v) \wedge ans_{t,v} \neq unknown$;
2 the tool t costs the least time among $Tools$ that can provide the correct answer, i.e., $\forall t' \in \{t' \mid t' \neq t \wedge (ans_{t',v} = ExpAns(v)) \wedge (ans_{t',v} \neq unknown)\}$, $time_{t',v} > time_{t,v}$.

Finally, the algorithm selection problem studied in this work can be formalized as follows. Given a set of software model checking tasks $Tasks$ and a set of model checking tools $Tools$, the algorithm selection problem for software model checking is to find a selection model $M : Tasks \rightarrow Tools$, such that $M(v)$ gives the best possible tool for solving v, i.e., $M(v) = L(v)$.

3.3 Our Proposed Kaleidoscopic RVFL Algorithm

In classical RVFL, only one type of activation function is used to perform the non-linear feature mapping, however, in K-RVFL three different non-linear functions are defined and used as the activation functions. In this work, we have chosen the Sigmoid function, Sin function, and Triangular basis transfer function as the three activation functions. Note that any arbitrary bounded non-linear function can be chosen as the activation function in K-RVFL.

The network structure of the K-RVFL algorithm is shown in Fig. 1, where X, O, d, m, ω, b, and β refer to the input of the model, the output of the model, the node number of the input layer, the node number of the output layer, input weights, hidden biases, and output weights, respectively. K-RVFL also has only one hidden layer and its input layer and output layer are directly connected. The difference between the RVFL and K-RVFL is that the single hidden layer of the RVFL only makes one-time non-linear feature mapping based on a single type of

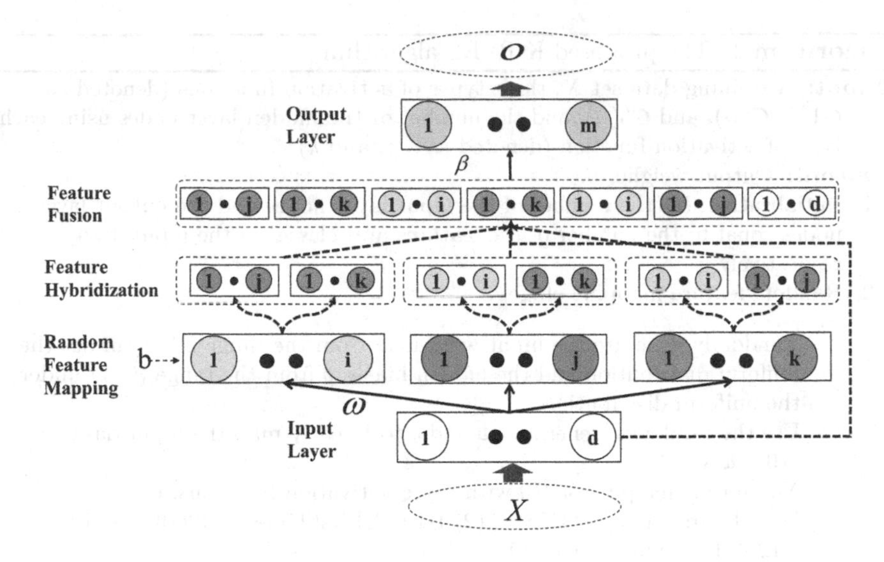

Fig. 1. The K-RVFL network structure.

activation function, while the hidden layer of the K-RVFL consists of multiple types of activation functions and makes two-time non-linear feature mapping, so that the K-RVFL can extract more diverse and multi-level features from the input data.

Specifically, In K-RVFL the input data first undergoes the non-linear mapping of each specific activation function (i.e., the random feature mapping layer). Then the corresponding output matrix will be used as the input of the other two activation functions for feature mapping for the second time. For example, if the input matrix first passes through the non-linear mapping of the Sigmoid function in the hidden layer, it will then be mapped by the Sin function and the Trigonometric basis function in the feature hybrid stage. This step is called the feature hybridization. After this two-stage nonlinear mapping, it is the feature fusion step, where we fuse the extracted features with the original features to get the final feature matrix of the hidden layer. Finally, the output weights are obtained by solving a system of linear matrix equations.

K-RVFL algorithm is summarized and depicted in Algorithm 1. For machine learning algorithms, the diversity of data features is very useful for the correct decision of the model. For example, one of the most important reasons for the success of deep learning is that it can achieve the features hybridization through the layer by layer processing of multiple hidden layers and then obtain the diverse and multi-level features. The basic idea behind the K-RVFL is to improve the diversity of features through multiple types of activation functions and multiple non-linear mappings without adding too many hidden layers. The advantage of this method is that the shallow network structure can make the K-RVFL maintain fast training speed and the feature hybridization and fusion strategy can make the model obtain better feature information. Fast and high accuracy

Algorithm 1: The proposed K-RVFL algorithm

Input: A training data set X, three types of activation functions (denoted as $G1(\cdot)$, $G2(\cdot)$, and $G3(\cdot)$), and the number of the hidden layer nodes using each type of activation function (denoted as i, j, and k).

Output: Output weights β.

1: Initialization: set the number of the input layer nodes and the output layer nodes equal to the number of the features and classes of the input data, respectively;

2: Random feature mapping stage:

- Randomly generate the input weights ω from the range (-1, 1) under the uniform distribution and the hidden biases b from the range (0, 1) under the uniform distribution.
- Use the randomly generated ω and b to linearly map the input data: $H0 = \omega X + b$
- Non-linear mapping of $H0$ with three activation functions: (1) H1_G1_FirstTime = G1(H0), (2) H1_G2_FirstTime = G2(H0), and (3) H1_G3_FirstTime = G3(H0)

3: Feature hybridization stage: The nonlinear mapping matrix corresponding to each activation function is used as the input of the other two activation functions for the second-time nonlinear feature mapping.

- For $G1$'s output matrix:

$$H2\_G1\_SecondTime = [G2(H1\_G1\_FirstTime), G3(H1\_G1\_FirstTime)].$$

- For $G2$'s output matrix:

$$H2\_G2\_SecondTime = [G1(H1\_G2\_FirstTime), G3(H1\_G2\_FirstTime)].$$

- For $G3$'s output matrix:

$$H2\_G3\_SecondTime = [G1(H1\_G3\_FirstTime), G2(H1\_G3\_FirstTime)].$$

4: Feature fusion stage: Linearly fuse the non-linear mapping feature matrix with the original feature matrix.

$$\mathbf{H3} = [H2\_G1\_SecondTime, H2\_G2\_SecondTime, H2\_G3\_SecondTime, X].$$

5: Solve the output weights: $\beta = \mathbf{H3}^{+}T$, where T and $\mathbf{H3}^{+}$ refer to the samples' real labels and **H3**'Moore-Penrose generalized inverse, respectively.

are both very important for the application of the software model checking tools recommendation system in practical engineering.

4 Experimental Evaluation

4.1 Preparation of the Data-Set

We collect the raw data for the verification tasks in the annual competition on software verification [1], in order to compare with the previous results in the related work [9]. We remark that each year the competition tasks are mostly the same, with only minor additions and changes in the category structure.

We extract the features of the tasks and compute the vector representations. Each dimension of the vector corresponds to a specific feature introduced in Sect. 3. In total, the data set has 31371 samples. For each sample, there are 46 attributes. Then for each task, we add a label to its vector representation to indicate the most suitable tool according to the competition results. We artificially create 3 classes for the classification.

In our experiments, the training set and testing set are divided according to 8:2. Similarly, we divide the original training set into pure training set and corresponding validation set according to 8:2 to select the best model for each method.

4.2 Parameters Settings

In our experiment, we choose the most commonly used randomization strategy for ELM and RVFL. That is, for their input weights, we generate them from (-1, 1) randomly and keep them unchanged throughout the subsequent training process. For the input weights of SCN, we generate them according to a supervisory strategy [5]. We set the number of hidden layer nodes in all comparison algorithms to the same and choose *Sigmoid* function as their activation function.

4.3 Experimental Results

In the experimental evaluations, we compare the accuracy and learning time of all the six relevant algorithms on the above dataset, including ELM, RVFL, SCN, BP, SVM, and K-RVFL. The number of hidden layer nodes in these algorithms is selected from {50, 100, 150, 200, 250, 300, 350, 400, 450, 500} one by one. The experiments are conducted with MATLAB R2016b software. Each experiment results are the average of 50 independently experiments. Figures 2–3 and Table 1 show our experimental results.

In Fig. 2, we compare the testing performance of five related algorithms with our proposed K-RVFL algorithm. According to these experimental results, one can infer that ELM, RVFL, SCN, and K-RVFL models can get better performance with the number increase of the hidden nodes. However, the performance of the BP model fluctuates greatly due to the difficulty of setting best values for its hyper-parameters and the instability of the gradient descent method. Therefore, compared with the traditional neural network BP algorithm, NNRW based algorithms always enjoy a higher accuracy and better stability. Compared with the SVM algorithm, all NNRW based algorithms except ELM can achieve better

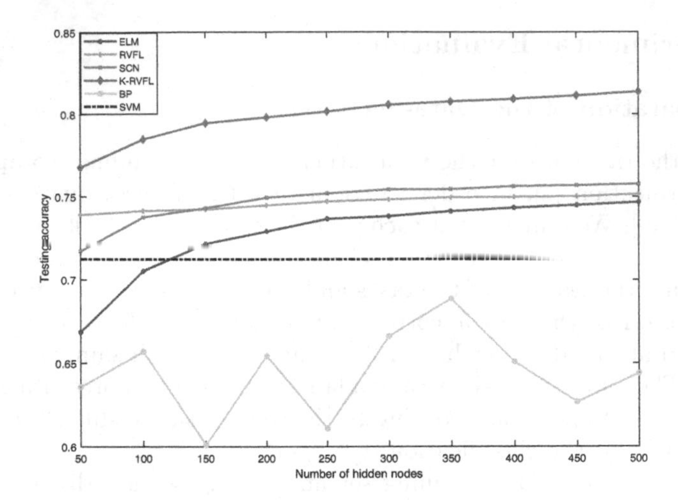

Fig. 2. Comparison of testing accuracy between the relevant algorithms.

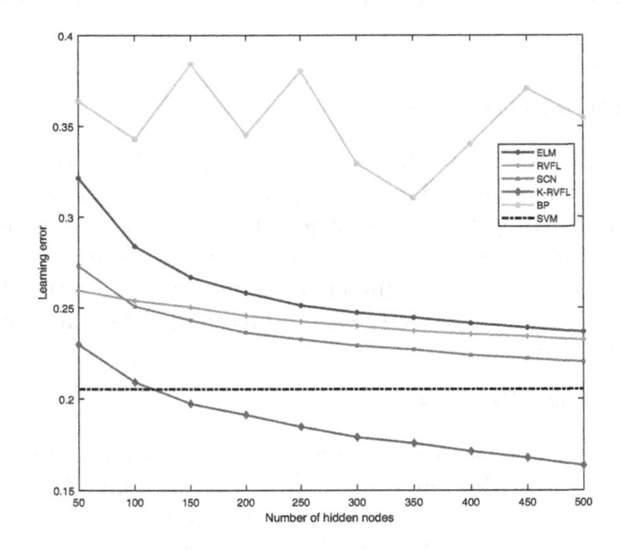

Fig. 3. Comparison of learning error between the relevant algorithms.

generalization performance, and they all have higher prediction accuracy when the hidden nodes are over 150. For the original NNRW algorithms (i.e., RVFL, ELM, and SCN), we can see that RVFL and SCN have better prediction performance than ELM regardless of the number of hidden layers. This is due to the special architecture design of RVFL and the supervised random method of SCN, which play a positive role in the model training. However, when the number of hidden layers increases, the differences between their performances decrease to a comparable level. Compared with the above algorithms, our proposed K-RVFL achieves the highest prediction accuracy in all cases. The margin shows that the improvement is substantial. It is worth mentioning that this is also the current SOTA result in the model checking algorithm selection task. Previous SOTA results are based on the SVM algorithm [9].

Figure 3 shows the learning error changing curves of ELM, RVFL, SCN, BP, SVM, and our proposed algorithm K-RVFL. In general, one can observe that the learning errors of the NNRW based models will gradually decrease with the increase of the hidden nodes, and they all have lower learning errors than the BP algorithm. Moreover, we can find that our proposed K-RVFL model Moreover, e can find that our proposed K-RVFL algorithm can achieve faster error reduction than other NNRW based algorithms (i.e., ELM, RVFL, and SCN) in the training process. This phenomenon implies that K-RVFL can approach the lower bound of error at the fastest speed. This also implies that compared with other algorithms, the proposed K-RVFL has faster convergence speed. And under the same network complexity, K-RVFL is expected to have better prediction performance than other models.

Table 1. Comparison of training time between ELM, RVFL, SCN, BP, SVM, and K-RVFL. The best results are in bold.

Hidden nodes	ELM	RVFL	SCN	KRVFL	BP	SVM
50	**0.1962**	0.4056	29.1138	0.8218	74.7245	5854.6707
100	**0.5014**	0.6767	73.1227	1.7042	114.2707	*
150	**0.7441**	1.0349	180.7078	2.9453	155.1274	*
200	**1.0371**	1.5728	278.0518	4.3165	185.7504	*
250	**1.5382**	1.8062	389.2362	5.6323	229.2435	*
300	**1.7697**	2.2901	432.3528	8.0344	267.0893	*
350	**2.2885**	2.8411	551.4656	10.4330	314.0300	*
400	**2.7827**	3.3347	719.3612	12.2311	334.8561	*
450	**3.2261**	4.1006	970.5653	14.3265	357.9287	*
500	**3.8875**	4.6264	1170.5231	17.1579	383.6377	*

In Table 1, we compare the training time of the proposed K-RVFL algorithm with other algorithms. From the experimental results, we can conclude that compared with the traditional neural network BP and SVM, the NNRW based algorithms have absolute advantages in the training speed of the model. Taking the proposed K-RVFL algorithm as an example, its model training speed is more than 100 times faster than BP and more than 300 times faster than SVM.

One can also find that the ELM algorithm can achieve faster learning time than other algorithms. The main reason is that compared with ELM, RVFL and K-RVFL have a relatively complex network structure, which may result in higher computational complexity. For SCN, it uses a supervised mechanism to initialize its input weights, so its training time is also longer than ELM.

We believe that the design of feature hybridization and fusion is a useful means, which can enable K-RVFL to extract more diverse and multi-level features and thus provide much better performance. This advantage also makes it great potential in time-critical applications [3].

5 Conclusion and Future Work

In this work, we propose to use neural network techniques to solve the algorithm selection problem for software model checking. We also propose an improved RVFL algorithm named K-RVFL to train the selection model. K-RVFL uses multiple types of activation functions to improve the diversity of features and uses feature hybridization to extract multi-level features, which have a positive impact on the correct decision-making of the model. K-RVFL inherits the non-iterative training mechanism of the RVFL and maintains the advantage of extremely fast training speed. Moreover, we conduct extensive experiments which demonstrate the effectiveness of neural network techniques for this problem. Our results show that K-RVFL has obvious advantages over the existing state-of-the-art algorithm (i.e., SVM) in both the prediction accuracy (81.37% vs 71.24%) and the training speed (17.16 s vs 5854.67 s). K-RVFL also outperforms the other randomized learning algorithms, including ELM, RVFL, and SCN and traditional neural network BP.

Acknowledgements. This work was supported by National Natural Science Foundation of China (Grant No. 62106150), CAAC Key Laboratory of Civil Aviation Wide Surveillance and Safety Operation Management and Control Technology (Grant No. 202102), and CCF-NSFOCUS (Grant No. 2021001).

References

1. Beyer, D.: Reliable and reproducible competition results with BenchExec and witnesses (report on SV-COMP 2016). In: Chechik, M., Raskin, J.-F. (eds.) TACAS 2016. LNCS, vol. 9636, pp. 887–904. Springer, Heidelberg (2016). https://doi.org/10.1007/978-3-662-49674-9_55
2. Beyer, D., Dangl, M.: Strategy selection for software verification based on Boolean features. In: Margaria, T., Steffen, B. (eds.) ISoLA 2018. LNCS, vol. 11245, pp. 144–159. Springer, Cham (2018). https://doi.org/10.1007/978-3-030-03421-4_11
3. Cao, W., Gao, J., Ming, Z., Cai, S., Shan, Z.: Fuzziness-based online sequential extreme learning machine for classification problems. Soft Comput. **22**(11), 3487–3494 (2018). https://doi.org/10.1007/s00500-018-3021-4
4. Cao, W., Wang, X.-Z., Ming, Z., Gao, J.: A review on neural networks with random weights. Neurocomputing **275**, 09 (2017)
5. Cao, W., Xie, Z., Li, J., Xu, Z., Ming, Z., Wang, X.: Bidirectional stochastic configuration network for regression problems. Neural Netw. **140**, 237–246 (2021)
6. Clarke, E.M., Henzinger, T.A., Veith, H., Bloem, R.: Handbook of Model Checking, vol. 10. Springer, Cham (2018). https://doi.org/10.1007/978-3-319-10575-8

7. Czech, M., Hüllermeier, E., Jakobs, M.-C., Wehrheim, H.: Predicting rankings of software verification tools. In: Proceedings of the 3rd ACM SIGSOFT International Workshop on Software Analytics, SWAN 2017, pp. 23–26 (2017)
8. Demyanova, Y., Pani, T., Veith, H., Zuleger, F.: Empirical software metrics for benchmarking of verification tools. In: Kroening, D., Păsăreanu, C.S. (eds.) CAV 2015. LNCS, vol. 9206, pp. 561–579. Springer, Cham (2015). https://doi.org/10.1007/978-3-319-21690-4_39
9. Demyanova, Y., Pani, T., Veith, H., Zuleger, F.: Empirical software metrics for benchmarking of verification tools. Formal Methods Syst. Des. **11**, 289–316 (2017). https://doi.org/10.1007/s10703-016-0264-5
10. Demyanova, Y., Veith, H., Zuleger, F.: On the concept of variable roles and its use in software analysis. In: FMCAD, pp. 226–229 (2013)
11. Nielson, F., Nielson, H.R., Hankin, C.: Principles of Program Analysis. Springer, Cham (2015). https://doi.org/10.1007/978-3-662-03811-
12. Richter, C., Wehrheim, H.: PeSCo: predicting sequential combinations of verifiers. In: Beyer, D., Huisman, M., Kordon, F., Steffen, B. (eds.) TACAS 2019. LNCS, vol. 11429, pp. 229–233. Springer, Cham (2019). https://doi.org/10.1007/978-3-030-17502-3_19
13. Tulsian, V., Kanade, A., Kumar, R., Lal, A., Nori, A.V.: MUX: algorithm selection for software model checkers. In Proceedings of the 11th Working Conference on Mining Software Repositories, MSR 2014, pp. 132–141 (2014)
14. Wang, Q., Cao, W., Jiang, J., Zhao, Y., Ming, Z.: NNRW-based algorithm selection for software model checking. In: International Conference on Extreme Learning Machine (ELM) (2019)
15. Wang, Q., Jiang, J., Zhao, Y., Cao, W., Wang, C., Li, S.: Algorithm selection for software verification based on adversarial LSTM. In: 2021 7th IEEE International Conference on Big Data Security on Cloud (BigDataSecurity), High Performance and Smart Computing, (HPSC) and Intelligent Data and Security (IDS), pp. 87–92 (2021)

Named Entity Recognition in Biology Literature Based on Unsupervised Domain Adaptation Method

Xingjian Xu[1](✉), Fang Liu[2], and Fanjun Meng[2]

[1] Inner Mongolia Normal University, Hohhot 010000, China
xingjian@imnu.edu.cn
[2] Century College, Beijing University of Posts and Telecommunications, Beijing 100010, China
ciecmfj@imnu.edu.cn

Abstract. By the careful rearrangement and analysis, various meaningful information could be extracted from the published biological literature, which is of great significance for the related follow-up research. Since the rapid accumulation of literature publications, manual-based curation method is too inefficient to cope with the massive biological literature data. Knowledge extraction methods in computer science seem to be able to process the biology literature more efficiently, however, most of them are based on supervised learning and greatly limited by the annotation quality of the species corpora. Here we present a new named entity recognition algorithm named biolitNER, which features unsupervised domain adaptation and accordingly has the capability to recognize named entities on biomedical literature across domains. Considering the lack of well-annotated corpora of many species, biolitNER is of great utility for named entity recognition and bears critical significance for biomedical literature curation in various species. Experimental verification shows that, compared with traditional programs, biolitNER produces higher quality results and has a satisfactory runtime performance.

Keywords: Domain adaptation method · Name entity recognition · Literature mining · Unsupervised learning · Biology big data

1 Introduction

Extensive knowledge could be mined out from the published biology literature, including the functions of biology entities (e.g., gene, protein, species) and interactions between them [1, 2]. Many widely used biomedical databases are constructed by literature mining and have become the indispensable tools when conducting biomedical research, such as PubMed [3], PDB [4], lncRNA wiki [5], IC4R [6]. Since biology publications are generated at an ever-growing pace and many of them are rarely accessed once after published in journals nowadays, extraction of useful information from a huge quantity of biology literature has become increasingly challenging. Although automatic methods may not fully replace humans on this task, they have been shown to be able to improve our productivity [7, 8]. Among them, named entity recognition (NER), involving identification

G. Memmi et al. (Eds.): KSEM 2022, LNAI 13370, pp. 426–437, 2022.
https://doi.org/10.1007/978-3-031-10989-8_34

of named entities in biology literature, is of critical significance in literature curation and has become a necessary supplement to human curation. NER is a subtask of information extraction, which is also a kind of classic task in the field of natural language processing [9, 10].

When the applied text material migrating from natural language to the more specific biology literature, numerous new difficulties have been arisen, for example the relatively casual abbreviation for some terminologies, the entity mapping between its Latin formal name and English conventional name, newly named entity identified in related biology experiments [11–13]. Since the traditional NER algorithms can't provide a good solution addressing problems above, several special methods have been proposed for facilitating recognition of biology named entities, such as BioCreative [8], BioBERT [14], OGER++ [15], MetaMap [16], Bio-NER [17].

However, in practical applications, they may not work as well as intended, especially when there is lack of high-quality annotated corpora with required types of entities in target domains of interest [18–20], which is very common for many species. This is because most of these existing methods mainly take supervised learning method as their implementation approach. A lot of studies [21] have reported that a model trained on the data in one domain (e.g., text about plant) usually performs much worse when applied into another domain (e.g., text about animal). Therefore, it is desirable to apply domain adaptation methods [22, 23] in NER to transfer the model from the source domain (e.g., plant) to the target domain (e.g., animal).

Considering that in practice there is often no annotated data available for the target domain, we present a NER program, biolitNER, that is based on conditional random fields and powered by three unsupervised domain adaptation methods, viz., structural correspondence learning, feature subletting and bootstrapping. Through the validation under different datasets, biolitNER is proven to be able to produce results with higher quality and have a better runtime efficiency.

2 Methods

The overall of biolitNER program is illustrated in Fig. 1. In this section, we will describe the detailed implementation of "Joint Training and Prediction" module. Let D_s and D_t be the data sets from the source and target domains, respectively, and D_s is labeled while D_t is not. The objective is to use D_s and D_t to build a model that predicts a label sequence given a token sequence. A labeled data set consists of tokenized sentences (token sequences) with a label assigned to each token. The label can be B-* (B- GENE), I-* (I-GENE), or O, which represents the beginning, inside and outside of a named entity (gene), respectively. An unlabeled data set consists of token sequences without labels.

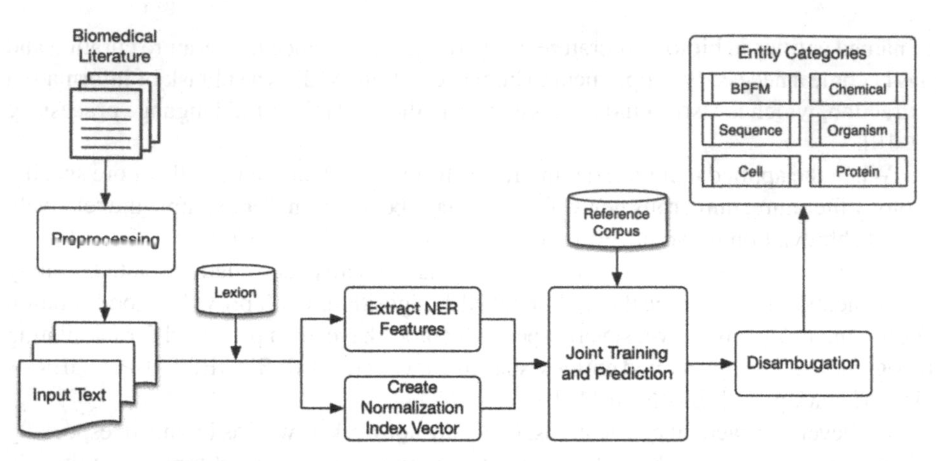

Fig. 1. Overview of biolitNER program

2.1 Conditional Random Fields

For supervised NER, conditional random fields (CRFs) [24], specifically linear chain CRFs, have shown promising results [25]. CRFs model the conditional probability of the label sequence y given the token sequence x as:

$$P(y|x) = \frac{1}{Z(x)}\exp\left\{\sum_k w_k f_k(x, y)\right\} \tag{1}$$

$$Z(x) = \sum_y \exp\left\{\sum_k w_k f_k(x, y)\right\} \tag{2}$$

where f_k, called a feature, is a (typically binary) function on the token sequence x and the label sequence y, w_k is a feature weight and obtained by maximum likelihood estimation on the training set. For inference, a Viterbi-like dynamic programming algorithm is employed to find the label sequence with the highest conditional probability. We use a typical feature set for NER [25], including word, word class, brief word class, prefixes, suffixes, and the features of previous and next two words.

2.2 Structural Correspondence Learning

Structural correspondence learning (SCL) assumes there are some common features in the source and target domains (pivot features) and estimates the correspondence between other features that are domain specific. Pivot features are usually frequent enough in both domains and highly correlated with labels [21]. SCL trains a linear classifier for each pivot feature. Then it builds a matrix $W = [w_1 w_2 ... w_m]$, where w_i is the coefficients of the i-th classifier and stacks the first h left-singular vectors of W as rows into a matrix θ. Finally, it augments the original feature vector x with θ_x. We propose a modified version of SCL ($\mathrm{SCL_m}$), which forces CRFs to learn only on the overlapping features of the source and target domains.

2.3 Feature Subsetting

Feature subsetting (FS) trains a regularized model such that the weights of features with bigger differences in distributions between the source and target domains are penalized more. The log-likelihood of the model is:

$$L(w) = \sum_{(x,y)\in D_s} \log P(y|x) - \lambda \sum_{k} |w_k|^{\gamma} d(E_{D_s}(f_k), E_{D_t}(f_k)) \tag{3}$$

$$E_{D_s}(f_k) = \frac{1}{N_s} \sum_{(x,y)\in D_s} f_k(x, y) \tag{4}$$

$$E_{D_t}(f_k) = \frac{1}{N_t} \sum_{x\in D_t} \sum_{y} f_k(x, y) p_w(y|x) \tag{5}$$

where $E_{D_s}(f_k)$ and $E_{D_t}(f_k)$ is the estimated expectation of f_k on the source and target domains, respectively. λ and γ are parameters to control the model. $d(x, y)$ is a function as the measure of the difference. We use Eq. (6) as distance measure function, which shows better performance in previous experiments [22].

$$d(x, y) = (\log x - \log y)^2 \tag{6}$$

2.4 Bootstrapping

Bootstrapping (BS) trains a model on D_s at first. Then it uses this model to label and score instances in D_t, and adds K instances with highest scores from D_t into D_s. It repeats the previous steps until meeting some stopping criterion. We follow the method in Wu et al., 2009 [26] with some modifications. The score of instance i is $(H_s(i) - H_t(i))P(i)$ where $H_s(i)$ and $H_t(i)$ are the entropy of instance i on the source and target domains, respectively, and $P(i)$ is the probability of the predicted label sequence given the input sequence. The stopping criterion is that at least one instance exists in the selected K instances such that either its entropy on the source domain is lower than on the target domain, or its maximum likelihood with respect to y on the source domain is higher than on the target domain.

3 Results

3.1 Datasets

We developed a named entity recognition program based on conditional random fields powered with unsupervised domain adaptation methods, including SCL, FS, and BS (see Methods). We implemented the baseline algorithm (linear chain CRFs) and domain adaptation methods in Java based on MALLET [27] and evaluated all the methods on three different annotated datasets (see Table 1), namely, GENETAG(GT) [28], GENIA(GN) [29] and Fly [30]. A example prediction output of biolitNER is described in Fig. 2 (the input raw text of this example is token from part of the abstract of PMID 25979172).

To investigate the prediction quality more carefully, all entities are divided into six categories, including biological process and molecular function (BPMF), sequence (DNS and RNA), cells, chemicals, organisms, proteins. The detailed token distribution among different data sets are described in Table 2. All the experiments in this paper are conducted in a Linux server with the CPU of AMD 5950x and 128 GB memory.

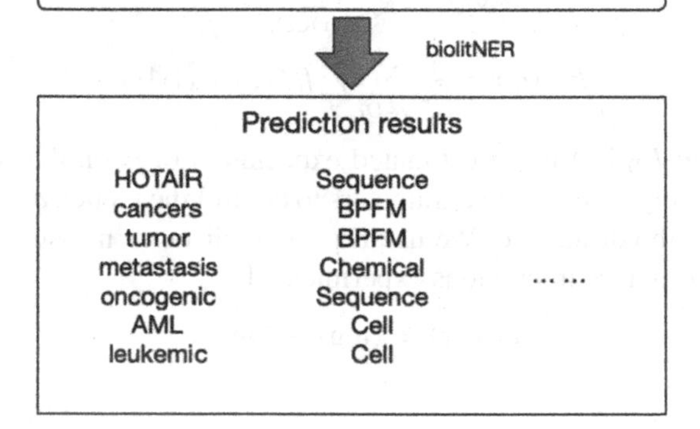

Fig. 2. Example prediction results of biolitNER

Table 1. Data sets

Name	Training		Test	
	# Sentences	# Tokens	# Sentences	# Tokens
GENETAG (GT)	7500	212808	2500	70820
GENIA (GN)	18546	560864	3856	114709
Fly	420	11549	180	5265

Table 2. Token distribution among different data sets

Entity category	GENETAG (GT)	GENIA (GN)	FLY
BPMF	6774	11472	2854
Sequence	21561	36951	6851
Cell	2058	4578	1066
Chemical	7588	10084	768
Organism	302	361	161
Protein	11256	20074	2558

3.2 Evaluation of Different Domain Adaptation Algorithm

By using one data set as the source and another as the target, we formulated six different NER tasks (see Table 3). For comparison, we trained the baseline algorithm on the labeled target domain training set as "golden standards". Macro-averaged F1 scores (see Eq. 10) for different labels (such as B, I, O) were used as the measure of performance.

$$P = \frac{TP}{TP+FP} \tag{7}$$

$$R = \frac{TP}{TP+FN} \tag{8}$$

$$F1 = \frac{2PR}{P+R} \tag{9}$$

$$Macro\_F1 = \frac{1}{n}\sum_{i=1}^{n} F1_i \tag{10}$$

In Eqs. 7–10, TP means the true positive samples count, FP means the false positive samples count, FN means the false negative sample counts, P is the precision, R is the recall, $Macro\_F1$ is the macro-averaged F1 score and F_{1i} is the F1 score of the i-th category. The remaining five algorithms and their parameter settings are described in Table 3.

Table 3. Tested algorithms and their parameter settings

Algorithm	Parameters
FS_1	Feature subsetting with $\lambda = 1, \gamma = 1$
FS_2	Feature subsetting with $\lambda = 1, \gamma = 2$
SCL	Structural correspondence learning with h = 25
SCL_m	Structural correspondence learning with overlapping features with h = 25
BS	Bootstrapping with K = 10

Comparative results (see Table 4 and Fig. 3) show that the most stable algorithms are FS ($\gamma = 1$) and SCL, as they outperform the baseline algorithm in all six tasks, and in five of them, FS outperforms SCL. FS_2 ($\gamma = 2$) performs comparably with FS_1 ($\gamma = 1$), suggesting that γ does not have a significant influence on FS. As noted, GENETAG represents a comprehensive data set containing abstracts from multiple different species, whereas GENIA and Fly are restricted to a specific species collecting abstracts exclusively from human and fly, respectively. SCL_m performs better than SCL in four tasks when the source domain training set is restricted.

Table 4. Macro-averged F1 scores of the algorithms on different tasks. The task name "GT-GN" means taking GENETAG as source against GENIA as target, and so on to the remaining five other tasks.

Algorithm	Task					
	GT-GN	GT-Fly	GN-GT	GN-Fly	Fly-GT	Fly-GN
Golden	0.85	0.65	0.84	0.65	0.84	0.85
Baseline	0.79	0.57	0.74	0.52	0.49	0.46
FS_1	0.79	0.58	**0.75**	**0.55**	0.53	0.48
FS_2	0.78	0.59	0.74	0.54	**0.54**	**0.50**
SCL	**0.79**	0.57	0.74	0.52	0.50	0.47
SCL_m	0.78	0.56	0.75	0.52	0.52	0.49
BS	0.79	**0.59**	0.74	0.53	0.31	0.30

Conversely, when it is comprehensive, SCL outperforms SCL_m. The performance of BS deteriorates as the source domain training set changes from GENETAG through GENIA to Fly. This result indicates that BS is sensitive to whether the source domain training set is comprehensive or restricted; when it is restricted, BS is more likely to make mistakes in labeling unlabeled instances in D_t, and once adding an incorrectly labeled instance into D_s, it is prone to add more and finally yield a wrong model. Taken together, FS_1, FS_2, SCL, SCL_m are all reasonable choices for general application, because they are superior to others even when the source domain data set is not comprehensive.

3.3 Comparison with Other NER Programs

We validate the NER prediction quality and runtime performance of biolitNER (FS1 algorithm) with five other commonly used biomedical NER programs, including BioCreative [8], OGER++ [15], MetaMap [16], Bio-NER [17]. In this experiment, the dataset of GENETAG is used as source, and GENIA is used as target. Statistics for each dataset above are also described in Table 1.

Here we use the macro-averaged F1 score to evaluate the NER prediction quality of different programs and the result is shown in Table 4. As we can see in the Table 5, the F1 score of biolitNER outperforms all other programs for all entity categories. Except biolitNER proposed in this paper, the second best is OGER++, and these scores are basically consistent with reports in other publications [8, 15].

CPU time is used to measure the program runtime performance and the corresponding result of comparison conducted within the datasets of GENETAG, GENIA, Fly is shown in Fig. 4.

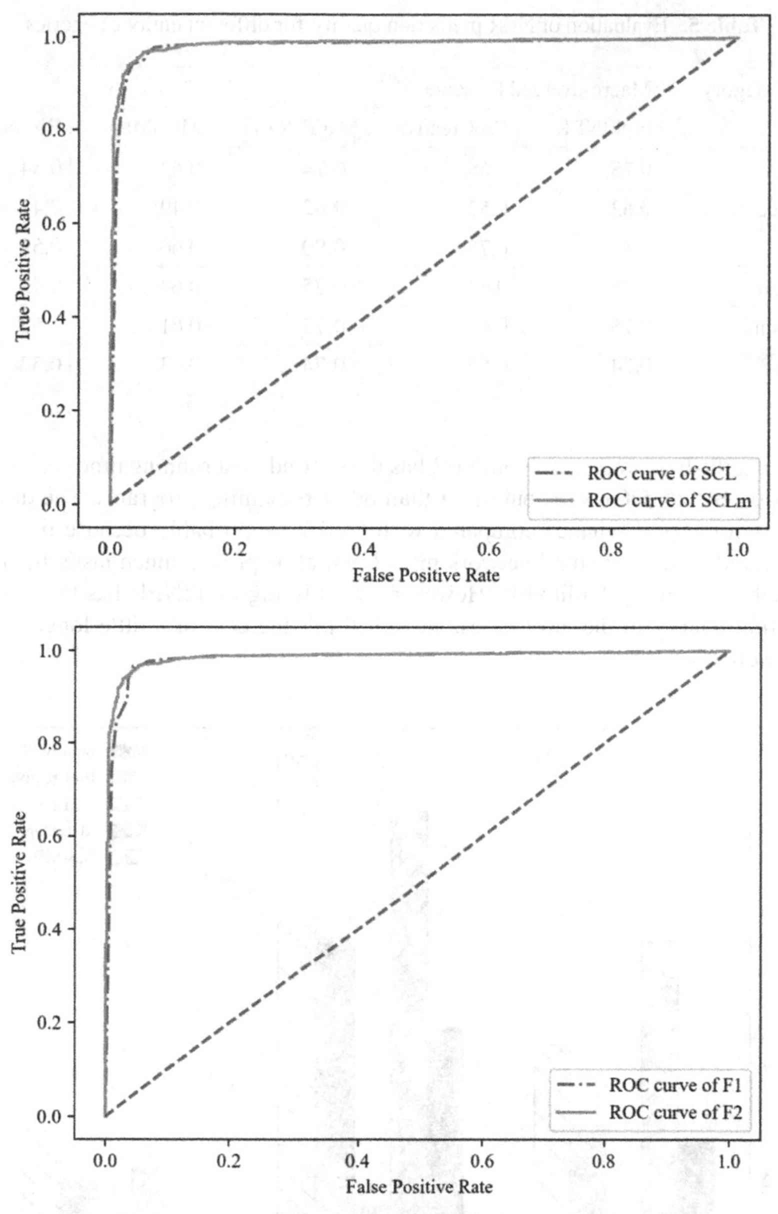

Fig. 3. ROC curve of FS1, FS2, SCL and SCL_m (GT-GN dataset)

Table 5. Evaluation of NER prediction quality for different entity categories

Entity category	Macro-averged F1 score				
	biolitNER	BioCreative	OGER++	MetaMap	Bio-NER
BPMF	**0.75**	0.68	0.74	0.63	0.54
Sequence	**0.62**	0.52	**0.62**	0.49	0.41
Cell	**0.81**	0.75	0.80	0.66	0.59
Chemical	**0.77**	0.62	0.75	0.64	0.49
Organism	**0.75**	0.64	0.72	0.61	0.52
Protein	**0.74**	0.63	0.74	0.63	0.52

Among the five programs, biolitNER has the second-best running time performance, barely slower than OGER++, but faster than other remaining programs. The disadvantage of runtime performance compared with OGER++ probably because the latter is implemented by using natural network model, which is proven much faster than statistical methods used by biolitNER. However, considering biolitNER has the best NER predication quality in the most cases, we still think the cost of a little longer running time is well worth paying.

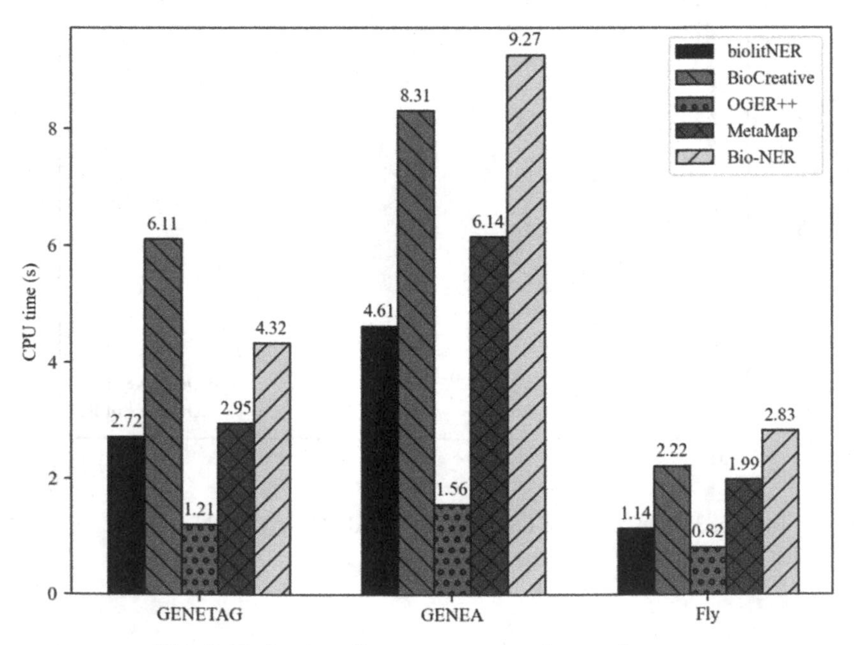

Fig. 4. Evaluation of program running time performance

4 Conclusion

Unlike existing programs, our program features unsupervised domain adaptation and accordingly has the capability to perform named entity recognition on biomedical literature in any species. Considering the lack of annotated biomedical corpora in many species, our program is of great utility for named entity recognition and bears critical significance for biomedical literature curation in various species. We carefully evaluate the output quality and performance of biolitNER with four other commonly used NER program, the experiment results show that biolitNER has the ability to produce the best quality NER predictions with a gratifying performance.

Acknowledgments. This work is supported by grants from the Talent Project of Inner Mongolia Natural Science Foundation (No. 2019BS06001), Talent Project of Inner Mongolia University (No. 2017YJRC020), Inner Mongolia Natural Science Foundation (No. 2019MS06014) and Inner Mongolia Education Department Sociology and Philosophy Special Project (ZSZX21088).

Data Availability. The project code of biolitNER and the datasets used in this paper to produce the experimental results are publicly available at GitHub (https://github.com/xingjianxu/biolitNER). All the code of biolitNER is also open sourced and accessible at GitHub under MIT license.

Conflicts of Interest. The authors declare that there are no conflicts of interest regarding the publication of this paper.

References

1. Holzinger, A., Jurisica, I.: Knowledge discovery and data mining in bio-medical informatics. In: Holzinger, A., Jurisica, I. (eds.) Interactive Knowledge Discovery and Data Mining in Biomedical Informatics: State-of-the-Art and Future Challenges, pp. 1–18. Springer, Heidelberg (2014). https://doi.org/10.1007/978-3-662-43968-5_1
2. Lyu, H., Wan, M., Han, J., Liu, R., Wang, C.: A filter feature selection method based on the maximal information coefficient and Gram-Schmidt Orthogonalization for biomedical data mining. Comput. Biol. Med. **89**, 264–274 (2017)
3. PubMed 2.0: Medical Reference Services Quarterly, vol. 39, No. 4. https://www.tandfonline.com/doi/abs/10.1080/02763869.2020.1826228. Accessed 18 Apr 2022
4. Berman, H., Henrick, K., Nakamura, H., Markley, J.L.: The worldwide Protein Data Bank (wwPDB): ensuring a single, uniform archive of PDB data. Nucleic Acids Res. **35**, D301–D303 (2007)
5. Ma, L., et al.: LncRNAWiki: harnessing community knowledge in collaborative curation of human long non-coding RNAs. Nucleic Acids Res. **43**, D187–D192 (2015)
6. Sang, J., et al.: IC4R-2.0: rice genome reannotation using massive RNA-seq data. Genomics, Proteomics Bioinf. **18**, 161–172 (2020)
7. Wei, C.-H., Harris, B.R., Li, D., Berardini, T.Z., Huala, E., Kao, H.-Y., Lu, Z.: Accelerating literature curation with text-mining tools: a case study of using PubTator to curate genes in PubMed abstracts. Database (Oxford) 2012:bas041 (2012)
8. Lu, Z., Hirschman, L.: Biocuration workflows and text mining: overview of the BioCreative 2012 Workshop Track II. Database 2012:bas043 (2012)

9. Lample, G., Ballesteros, M., Subramanian, S., Kawakami, K., Dyer, C.: Neural Architectures for Named Entity Recognition. arXiv:160301360 [cs] (2016)
10. Yadav, V., Bethard, S.: A Survey on Recent Advances in Named Entity Recognition from Deep Learning models. arXiv:191011470 [cs] (2019)
11. Tang, B., Cao, H., Wang, X., Chen, Q., Xu, H.: Evaluating word representation features in biomedical named entity recognition tasks. BioMed Res. Int. **2014**, e240403 (2014)
12. Habibi, M., Weber, L., Neves, M., Wiegandt, D.L., Leser, U.: Deep learning with word embeddings improves biomedical named entity recognition. Bioinformatics **33**, i37–i48 (2017)
13. Gridach, M.: Character-level neural network for biomedical named entity recognition. J. Biomed. Inform. **70**, 85–91 (2017)
14. Lee, J., et al.: BioBERT: a pre-trained biomedical language representation model for biomedical text mining. Bioinformatics **36**, 1234–1240 (2020)
15. Furrer, L., Jancso, A., Colic, N., Rinaldi, F.: OGER++: hybrid multi-type entity recognition. J. Cheminformatics **11**(1), 1 (2019). https://doi.org/10.1186/s13321-018-0326-3
16. Aronson, A.R., Lang, F.-M.: An overview of MetaMap: historical perspective and recent advances. J. Am. Med. Inf. Assoc. **17**, 229–236 (2010)
17. Soomro, P.D., Kumar, S., Banbhrani, S.A.A., Raj, H.: Bio-NER: bio-medical named entity recognition using rule-based and statistical learners. Int. J. Adv. Comput. Sci. Appl. (IJACSA) **8**, 12 (2017)
18. Thompson, P., Nawaz, R., McNaught, J., Ananiadou, S.: Enriching a biomedical event corpus with meta-knowledge annotation. BMC Bioinf. **12**, 393 (2011). https://doi.org/10.1186/1471-2105-12-393
19. Mohan, S., Li, D.: MedMentions: A Large Biomedical Corpus Annotated with UMLS Concepts. arXiv:190209476 [cs] (2019)
20. Vincze, V., Szarvas, G., Farkas, R., Móra, G., Csirik, J.: The BioScope corpus: biomedical texts annotated for uncertainty, negation and their scopes. BMC Bioinf. **9**, S9 (2008). https://doi.org/10.1186/1471-2105-9-S11-S9
21. Blitzer, J., Dredze, M., Pereira, F.: Biographies, bollywood, boom-boxes and blenders: domain adaptation for sentiment classification. In: Proceedings of the 45th Annual Meeting of the Association of Computational Linguistics. Association for Computational Linguistics, Prague, Czech Republic, pp. 440–447 (2007)
22. Satpal, S., Sarawagi, S.: Domain adaptation of conditional probability models via feature subsetting. In: Kok, J.N., Koronacki, J., Lopez de Mantaras, R., Matwin, S., Mladenič, D., Skowron, A. (eds.) PKDD 2007. LNCS (LNAI), vol. 4702, pp. 224–235. Springer, Heidelberg (2007). https://doi.org/10.1007/978-3-540-74976-9_23
23. Wu, D., Lee, W.S., Ye, N., Chieu, H.L.: Domain adaptive bootstrapping for named entity recognition. In: Proceedings of the 2009 Conference on Empirical Methods in Natural Language Processing. Association for Computational Linguistics, Singapore, pp. 1523–1532 (2009)
24. Lafferty, J.D., McCallum, A., Pereira, F.C.N.: Conditional random fields: probabilistic models for segmenting and labeling sequence data. In: Proceedings of the Eighteenth International Conference on Machine Learning, pp. 282–289 (2001)
25. Leaman, R., Gonzalez, G.: BANNER: an executable survey of advances in biomedical named entity recognition. In: Pacific Symposium on Biocomputing, vol. 663, pp. 652–663 (2008)
26. Wu, D., Lee, W.S., Ye, N., Chieu, H.L.: Domain adaptive bootstrapping for named entity recognition. In: Proceedings of the 2009 Conference on Empirical Methods in Natural Language Processing, pp. 1523–1532 (2009)
27. McCallum, A.K.: MALLET: A Machine Learning for Language Toolkit (2002)

28. Tanabe, L., Xie, N., Thom, L.H., Matten, W., Wilbur, W.J.: GENETAG: a tagged corpus for gene/protein named entity recognition. BMC Bioinf. **6**, S3 (2005). https://doi.org/10.1186/1471-2105-6-S1-S3
29. Kim, J.-D., Ohta, T., Tateisi, Y., Tsujii, J.: GENIA corpus–a semantically annotated corpus for bio-text mining. Bioinformatics **19**, i180–i182 (2003)
30. Vlachos, A., Gasperin, C.: Bootstrapping and evaluating named entity recognition in the biomedical domain. In: Proceedings of BioNLP at HLT-NAACL 2006 (2006)

A Lightweight Target Detection Algorithm Based on Improved MobileNetv3-YOLOv3

Tong Fang, Baoshuai Du, Yunjia Xue, Guang Yang, and Jingbo Zhao(✉)

School of Information and Control Engineering, Qingdao University of Technology, Qingdao, Shandong, China
zhaoyancheng2021@163.com

Abstract. To solve the problems of complex model structure, large number of parameters, and high resource consumption that make it difficult to meet the real-time requirements of embedded target detection tasks, this paper proposed a lightweight target detection algorithm based on improved MobileNetv3-YOLOv3. This algorithm uses MobileNetv3 network to replace the backbone of the original YOLOv3 network, and the reduction of network parameters greatly improves the detection speed of the algorithm; the loss function is modified to CIoU to improve the accuracy and detection speed of the network. The experimental results showed that the improved lightweight detection algorithm on the VOC07 + 12 dataset has a 1.55% improvement in mAP and a 2.47 times improvement in FPS on CPU compared to the original YOLOv3 algorithm. This improved algorithm ensures the detection accuracy based on a significant increase in detection speed, which reflects the theoretical and application value of the research.

Keywords: MobileNetv3 · Object detection · YOLOv3 · Lightweight target detection algorithm · CIoU

1 Introduction

Currently SLAM (simultaneous localization and map building) algorithms have an important position in robot motion estimation and map building applications. Semantic perception of unknown environments by mobile robots is a frontier of current research in robotics and computer vision, and target detection can be used to achieve the perception of semantic information in the environment.

With the development of deep learning and the improvement of GPU computing power, deep learning based target detection algorithms have become mainstream [1]. The current target detection algorithms can be broadly divided into two categories with the development of deep learning [2]: Two-stage target detection algorithms and one-stage target detection algorithms [3, 4]. Two-stage target detection algorithms are far superior to traditional detection algorithms in terms of accuracy, but it is difficult to apply to mobile devices such as mobile robots with poor computing power due to their large computing power. The regression-based One-stage target detection algorithm, on the other hand, can achieve real-time operation with little loss of accuracy, and thus is

G. Memmi et al. (Eds.): KSEM 2022, LNAI 13370, pp. 438–448, 2022.
https://doi.org/10.1007/978-3-031-10989-8_35

widely used in mobile. Also deep learning based target detection is widely used in urban traffic flow monitoring [5], intelligent fault diagnosis [6] and other fields.

The classical YOLOv3 has a better detection effect [8, 9], but its complex model and the number of ten million parameters have great drawbacks in both debugging, training and deployment stages. Considering the limited computing power of mobile platforms, this paper replaces the feature extraction network Darknet53 of YOLOv3 with MobileNetv3 to reduce the number of parameters of the network and modifies the regression loss function of the grasping frame with the CIoU method. In this way, the speed of the algorithm in mobile platform detection is improved on the basis of ensuring the detection accuracy. Finally, the effectiveness of the proposed model is verified on the VOC07 + 12 dataset.

The paper is organized as follows. Section 2 describes the innovative nature of the algorithms in this paper and introduces the improvement of the backbone network part and the improvement of the loss function based on CIoU. Section 3 presents the ablation experiments, which demonstrate the effectiveness of the proposed algorithm and understand the contributions of different elements. Section 4 contains conclusions and future work.

2 Algorithm of this Paper

2.1 Lightweight Feature Extraction Network Improvement Based on MobileNetv3

To be able to achieve low latency high frequency real-time target detection on an embedded platform with limited computing power, this paper proposes a backbone feature extraction network using the lightweight network MobileNetv3 to replace YOLOv3 [10].

In this paper, MobileNetv3-large is used. This version combines MobileNetv1's Deep Separable Convolution, MobileNetv2's Inverted Residuals and Linear Bottleneck, and SE modules [11], uses neural structure search to search the configuration and parameters of the network. Although the number of parameters is increased in the large version compared to MobileNetv3-small, the small increase in the number of parameters can be exchanged for an increase in the detection accuracy, which guarantees the detection accuracy for the lightweight detection algorithm proposed in this paper (Fig. 1).

In MobileNetv3, the number of parameters can be greatly reduced by using depth-separable convolution instead of normal convolution.

In the model where the input feature map size is $D_I \times D_I$ and the number of channels is M. When a convolution kernel of size $D_K \times D_K$ is used to output the feature map of size $D_I \times D_I$ and the number of channels is N, the number of parameters P_C and the amount of computation C_C required for one ordinary convolution are shown in Eqs. (1) and (2).

$$P_C = D_K \times D_K \times M \times N \quad (1)$$

$$C_C = D_K \times D_K \times M \times N \times D_I \times D_I \quad (2)$$

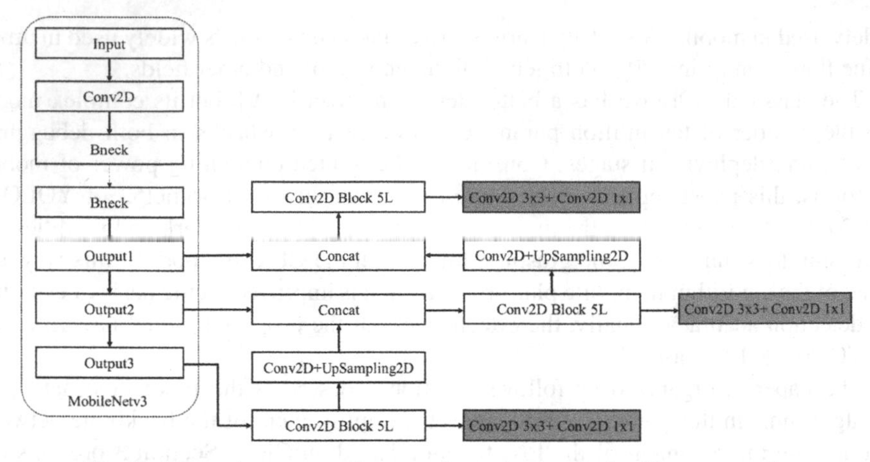

Fig. 1. Network structure diagram after replacing the backbone network.

And in the depth-separable convolution, the number of parameters P_W and the amount of computation C_W required are shown in Eqs. (3) and (4).

$$P_W = D_K \times D_K \times M + M \times N \tag{3}$$

$$C_W = D_K \times D_K \times M \times D_I \times D_I + M \times N \times D_I \times D_I \tag{4}$$

So for the same feature map and convolution kernel, the ratio of the number of parameters to the amount of computation required for a depth-separable convolution versus an ordinary convolution is.

$$P = \frac{D_K \times D_K \times M + M \times N}{D_K \times D_K \times M \times N} = \frac{1}{N} + \frac{1}{D_K^2} \tag{5}$$

$$C = \frac{D_K \times D_K \times M \times D_I \times D_I + M \times N \times D_I \times D_I}{D_K \times D_K \times M \times N \times D_I \times D_I} = \frac{1}{N} + \frac{1}{D_K^2} \tag{6}$$

It can be seen that the use of depth-separable convolution instead of normal convolution can reduce a significant portion of the number of parameters and computation, which lays the foundation for the implementation of porting the target detection algorithm to the mobile platform side where the arithmetic power is much less.

The special block of MobileNetv3 introduces the inverse residual structure with linear bottleneck. The residual structure can significantly improve the training effect of the network without adding additional parameters and with only less computation, and the inverse residual mechanism is to first use 1 × 1 convolution in the residual block to boost the number of channels before subsequent operations with residual edges; and the weight of each channel is adjusted by introducing a lightweight attention mechanism (Fig. 2).

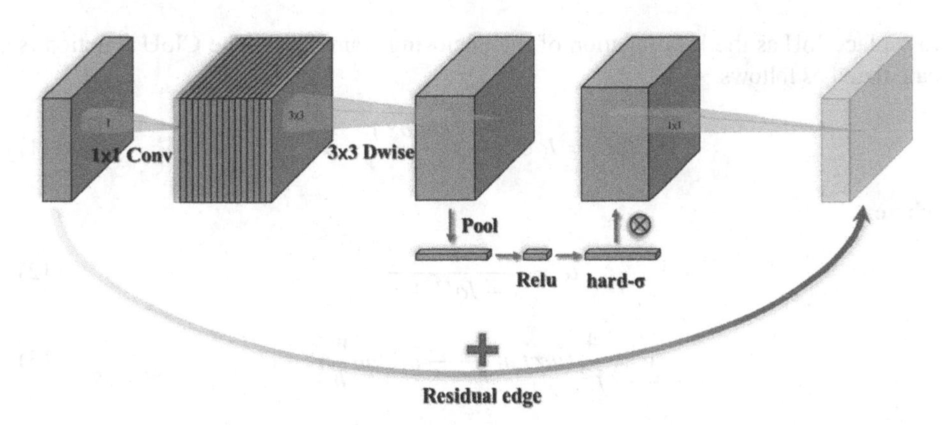

Fig. 2. MobileNetv3 block.

In the use of activation function, swish function can effectively improve the network accuracy, but the computation is too large and time consuming, especially in the mobile end of the time consuming embodiment will be more obvious, which is not conducive to the algorithm to reduce the detection time.

$$swish\, x = x \cdot \sigma(x) \tag{7}$$

where $\sigma(x)$ is the Sigmoid function:

$$\sigma(x) = \frac{1}{1 + e^{-x}} \tag{8}$$

So ReLU6(x + 3)/6 is used to approximate the replacement of the sigmoid function in order to achieve a fast computation that can be performed on any hardware or software platform. The algorithm uses the h-swish activation function instead of the original swish function.

$$h - swish[x] = s\frac{ReLU6(x + 6)}{6} \tag{9}$$

2.2 CIoU-Based Loss Function Improvement

In YOLOv3, the performance of target detection is evaluated by IoU. IoU is defined as the intersection and merging ratio between the true frame and the predicted frame, as shown in Eq. (10). Where P is the prediction frame and R is the real frame.

$$IoU = \frac{P \cap R}{P \cup R} \tag{10}$$

However, there is a problem with using IoU, when there is no intersection between the prediction frame and the real frame, IoU is 0, and there is no gradient nor can the parameters be updated. To solve this problem, this algorithm uses the CIoU function to replace IoU as the loss function of the enclosing frame [12]. The CIoU function is calculated as follows.

$$CIoU = IoU - \frac{\rho^2(b, b^{gt})}{c^2} - \alpha v \tag{11}$$

where:

$$\alpha = \frac{v}{1 - IoU + v} \tag{12}$$

$$v = \frac{4}{\rho^2}(arctan\frac{w^{gt}}{h^{gt}} - arctan\frac{w}{h})^2 \tag{13}$$

where $\rho^2(b, b^{gt})$ represents the Euclidean distance d between the center points of the prediction frame and the real frame, c represents the diagonal distance of the smallest closed region that can contain both the prediction frame and the real frame, α and v are penalty factors, and w^{gt}, h^{gt} and w, h are the width and height of the real frame and the prediction frame, respectively (Fig. 3).

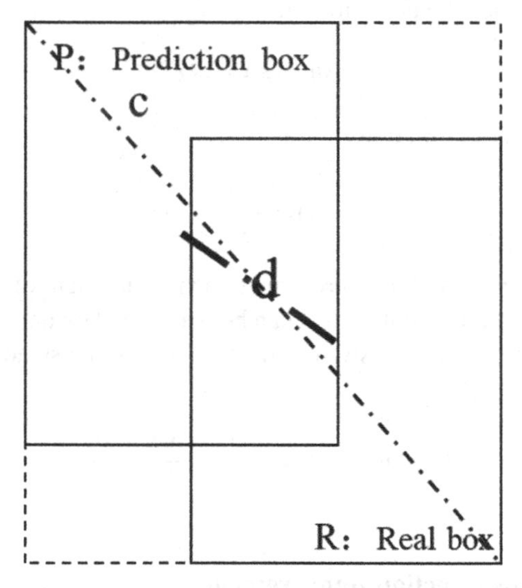

Fig. 3. Geometric relationship between the prediction box and the real box.

3 Experimental Results and Analysis

3.1 Experimental Environment and Model Training

The experiments in this paper are based on the Pytorch 1.7.1 framework, the programming language is Python 3.8, the experimental OS is Windows 10, the processor is

Intel(R) Core(TM) i7-10750H CPU @ 2.60 GHz, the GPU model is NVIDIA GeForce RTX 2060, the CUDA version is 11.0, and Cudnn version 8.0.5.39.

In the selection of dataset, this paper uses the classical dataset of target detection, VOC07 + 12. The VOC07 + 12 dataset is divided into a total of 4 major categories and 20 minor categories, with 21504 labeled images. The dataset is divided according to the ratio of 9:1, with 19354 images as the training set and 2150 images as the test set. The experiments use the average precision (AP) to respond to the detection results of targets in each category, use the mean average precision (mAP) as a measure of detection accuracy, the higher the mAP, the better the comprehensive performance of the model in all categories, and use the time consumed to detect each image as a measure of detection speed.

In order to verify the effect of the proposed algorithm in this paper, influenced by the arithmetic power, during the training process, only the pre-training weights of the backbone network are loaded, the optimizer for training is chosen as Adam, the initial learning rate is 1e−3, and the learning rate decay strategy is cosine annealing. In order to improve the robustness of the proposed algorithm, Mosaic data augmentation [13] was performed on the first 70% of the training set during the algorithm training process, and the specific implementation idea is as follows: firstly, four images are read at a time; then these four images are scaled, rotated, and color-field transformed, respectively, and placed well according to the four directions; finally, the combination of images and the combination of frames is performed.

3.2 MobileNetv3 Detection Effect After Replacing Backbone

The original YOLOv3 algorithm is set to A, and the algorithm after replacing backbone with MobileNetv3 is set to B. The experimental results of the two algorithms in terms of accuracy and speed are shown in Table 1.

Table 1. Comparison of detection effect after replacing backbone.

Detection algorithm	Training set	mAP/%	FPS (GPU)	FPS (CPU)
A	VOC07 + 12	67.56	27.24	2.10
B	VOC07 + 12	63.78	22.78	4.97

Compared with the original YOLOv3 network, the detection accuracy decreases after using MobileNetv3 to replace backbone, and the detection speed on CPU is greatly improved because the number of parameters is greatly reduced after replacing the backbone feature extraction network with MobileNetv3, which can reduce the time needed for algorithm detection, but the reduction in the number of parameters also makes the network less effective and the detection accuracy decreases.

3.3 Improved Detection Effect of CIoU-Based Loss Function

The original YOLOv3 algorithm is set as A, and the improved algorithm based on the loss function of CIoU is set as B. The experimental results of the two algorithms in terms of accuracy and speed are shown in Table 2.

Table 2. Comparison of detection results after using CIoU loss function.

Detection algorithm	Training set	mAP/%	FPS (GPU)	FPS (CPU)
A	VOC07 + 12	67.56	27.24	2.10
B	VOC07 + 12	69.50	27.67	2.35

Compared with the original YOLOv3 network, the detection effect of the network is improved after modifying the loss function, and the detection time is also slightly accelerated. The experiment proves that by improving the loss function of the original YOLOv3 algorithm, it can be more beneficial for the model to achieve better results.

3.4 Analysis of Experimental Results of Light-Weight Target Detection Algorithm

In this paper, we compare the detection effect of the improved YOLOv3 algorithm with the original YOLOv3 algorithm. It is shown in Fig. 4.

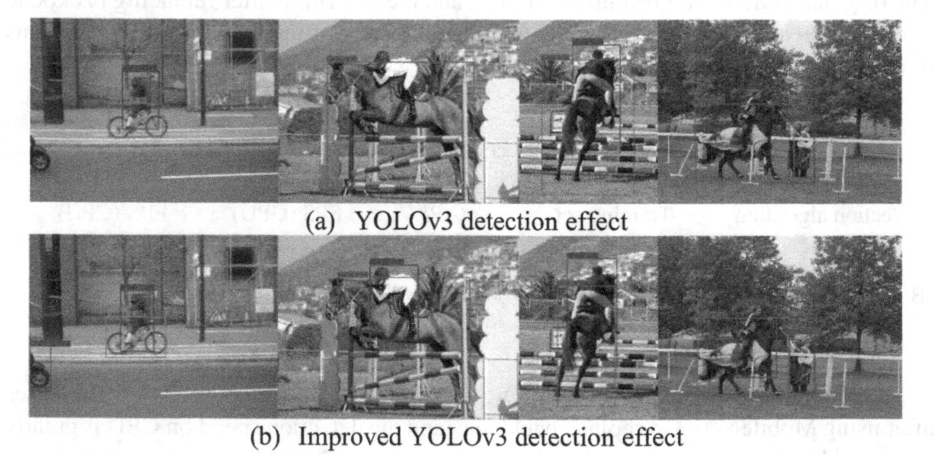

(a) YOLOv3 detection effect

(b) Improved YOLOv3 detection effect

Fig. 4. Comparison of detection effects on VOC07 + 12 dataset.

The improved algorithm in this paper was compared with the original YOLOv3 algorithm and the current mainstream Two-stage detection algorithm Faster-RCNN in terms of performance. The results of mAP and AP comparison for various types of targets on the test set are shown in Fig. 5 and Table 3.

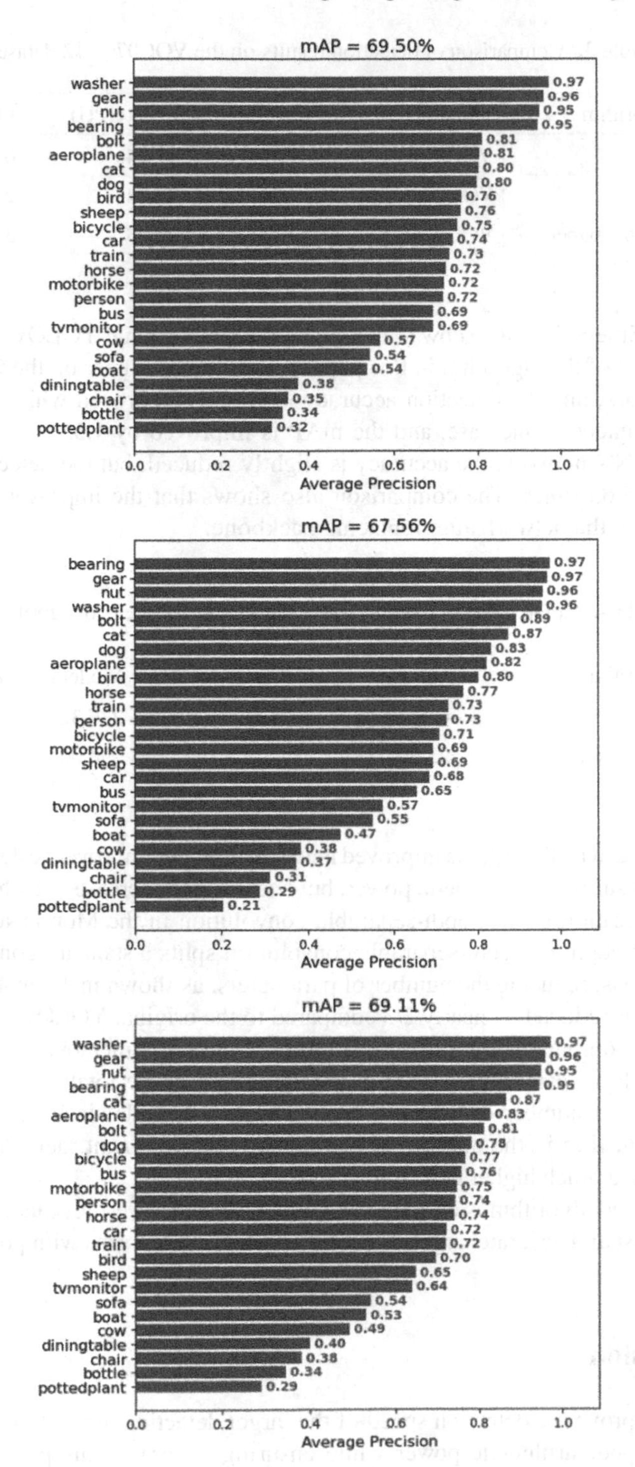

Fig. 5. Comparison of AP and mAP of different algorithms on VOC07 + 12 dataset.

Table 3. Comparison of detection results on the VOC07 + 12 dataset.

Detection algorithm	Training set	mAP/%	FPS (GPU)	FPS (CPU)
Faster-RCNN	VOC07 + 12	69.50	17.24	0.93
YOLOv3	VOC07 + 12	67.56	27.24	2.10
Algorithm of this paper	VOC07 + 12	69.11	23.93	5.24

The experimental results show that compared to the original YOLOv3 network, the detection speed of the algorithm in this paper is 2.47 times higher on the CPU than the original network, and the detection accuracy is slightly improved while the detection speed is guaranteed to increase, and the mAP is improved by 1.55%, compared with the Faster-RCNN network, the accuracy is slightly reduced, but the detection speed is improved by 5.63 times. The comparison also shows that the improvement of CIoU works better for the network after replacing backbone.

Table 4. Comparison of the number of parameters of the two algorithms.

Detection algorithm	Number of participants	Model file size/M
YOLOv3	61,949,149	236.32
Algorithm of this paper	23,608,237	90.06

As can be seen in Table 3, the improved network does not improve the detection speed on GPUs with sufficient arithmetic power, but has a slight decrease, which is due to the general optimization of the depth-separable convolution in the MobileNetv3 network on GPUs. Although the depth-separable convolution splits a standard convolution into two convolutions, reducing the number of parameters, as shown in Table 4, the number of parameters is reduced by nearly 2/3 compared to the original YOLOv3 network. The CPU tends to compute data serially. Therefore, if the GPU memory is large enough, because each layer can be processed in parallel at once, the total computing time is dominated by the number of layers of the network. For CPUs lacking parallelism, a significant reduction in the number of parameters, the dominant factor in computing time, results in a much higher detection speed.

The proposed algorithm is effective on CPU, which also verifies that this algorithm can achieve fast and accurate target detection on mobile platforms with poor arithmetic power.

4 Conclusion

In order to improve the detection speed of the target detection algorithm on embedded devices with poor arithmetic power while ensuring accuracy, this paper proposed a lightweight target detection algorithm based on improved MobileNetv3-YOLOv3, which greatly reduced the number of parameters in the network by introducing MobileNetv3 as the backbone feature extraction network of the algorithm, and the loss function is also improved based on CIoU The loss function is also improved based on CIoU. Compared with the original YOLOv3 network, the mAP of the algorithm in this paper is improved by 1.55%, and the detection speed on CPU is improved by 2.47 times. The algorithm proposed in this paper is able to meet the task of real-time accurate target detection by embedded devices using limited on-board processor computing resources in terms of comprehensive evaluation of detection accuracy and detection speed.

In the subsequent research work, we will continue to compress the model, including channel pruning and other operations to continue to reduce the parameters, and further improve the detection speed of the model on the mobile device side with lower performance on the basis of ensuring the detection accuracy, the proposed algorithm will also be applied to more areas to prove the potential impact of the algorithm.

Acknowledgment. This work is supported in part by the National Natural Science Foundation of China under Grant 51475251, the Natural Science Foundation of Shandong Province under Grant ZR2013FM014 and in part by the Qingdao Municipality Livelihood Plan Project under Grant 22-3-7-xdny-18-nsh.

References

1. Lin, T.Y., Dollar, P., Girshick, R., et al.: Feature pyramid networks for object detection. In: IEEE Conference on Computer vision and Pattern Recognition (CVPR), pp. 936–944. Las Vegas, USA (2017)
2. Qin, P., Tang, C.M., Liu, Y.F., et al.: Infrared target detection method based on improved YOLOv3. Comput. Eng. **48**(3), 211–219 (2022)
3. Li, G.J., Hu, J., Ai, J.Y.: Vehicle detection based on improved SSD algorithm. Comput. Eng. **48**(1), 266–274 (2022)
4. Redmon, J., Divvala, S., Girshick, R., et al.: You only look once: unified, real-time object detection. In: IEEE Conference on Computer vision and Pattern Recognition (CVPR), pp. 779–788. Las Vegas, USA (2016)
5. Msahli, M., Qiu, H., Zheng, Q., et al.: Topological graph convolutional network-based urban traffic flow and density prediction. IEEE Trans. Intell. Transp. Syst. **22**(7), 4560–4569 (2021)
6. Li, Y., Song, Y., Jia, L., et al.: Intelligent fault diagnosis by fusing domain adversarial training and maximum mean discrepancy via ensemble learning. IEEE Trans. Industr. Inf. **17**(4), 2833–2841 (2020)
7. Redmon, J., Farhadi, A.: YOLO9000: better, faster, stronger. In: Proceedings of the IEEE Conference on Computer Vision and Pattern Recognition (CVPR), pp. 6517–6525. New York, USA (2017)
8. Redmon, J., Farhadi, A.: YOLOv3: An Incremental Improvement. arXiv e-prints, (2018)
9. Zhao, Z.Q., Zheng, P., Xu, S.T., et al.: Object detection with deep learning: a review. IEEE Trans. Neural Netw. Learn. Syst. **30**(11), 3212–3232 (2019)
10. Woo, S., Park, J., Lee, J.-Y., Kweon, I.S.: CBAM: convolutional block attention module. In: Ferrari, V., Hebert, M., Sminchisescu, C., Weiss, Y. (eds.) ECCV 2018. LNCS, vol. 11211, pp. 3–19. Springer, Cham (2018). https://doi.org/10.1007/978-3-030-01234-2_1
11. Howard, A., Sandler, M., Chen, B., et al.: Searching for MobileNetV3. 2019 IEEE/CVF International Conference on Computer Vision (ICCV), pp. 1314–1324. Seoul, Korea (2020)

12. Zheng, Z., Wang, P., Ren, D., et al.: Enhancing geometric factors in model learning and inference for object detection and instance segmentation, In: 9th International Proceedings on Proceedings, IEEE Transactions on Cybernetics, pp. 1–13 (2020)
13. Bochkovskiy, A., Wang, C.Y., Liao, H. YOLOv4: Optimal speed and accuracy of object detection. arXiv:2004.10934 (2020)

Hypergraph-Based Academic Paper Recommendation

Jie Yu, Junchen He, and Lingyu Xu(✉)

School of Computer Engineering and Science, Shanghai University, Shanghai 200444, People's Republic of China
{jieyu,junchenhe,xly}@shu.edu.cn

Abstract. Academic paper recommendation aims to provide personalized recommendation services for scholars from massive academic papers. Deep Learning-based Collaborative Filtering plays an important role in it, and most of existing method are based on bipartite graph, which causes it fail to realize multi-features fusion, and the over-smooth property of GCN limits the generation of embedding with high-order similarity, resulting in the decline of recommendation quality. In this paper, we propose a hypergraph-based academic paper recommendation method. Based on hypergraph, APRHG (Academic Paper Relation HyperGraph) is constructed to not only model the complex academic relationship between users and papers, but also realize the multi-features fusion. In addition, the L-HGCF (Light HyperGraph based Collaborative Filtering) algorithm, which could mine high-order similarity between papers, is proposed to provide trusted recommendations. We conduct experiments on the public dataset, and compare the performance with several deep learning based Collaborative Filtering to confirm the superiority of our method.

Keywords: Hypergraph · Collaborative filtering · Academic paper recommendation

1 Introduction

Academic papers are considered to be important indicators of advances in a field. They are also important mediums for researchers to communicate with each other. Due to the rapid emergence of big academic data recently, the cognitive burden of scholars to search for the academic knowledge they want has increased. In the construction of digital library, Information Retrieval (IR) technology [13] are used to alleviate this problem to some extent, but sometimes junior researchers may have no idea on how to choose appropriate queries fed into the search box. In such an environment, there is an urgent requirement for an effective academic paper recommendation technology, by which researchers can be freed from tedious and time-consuming paper screening.

Collaborative Filtering (CF) has become one of the most popular and widely used algorithms for academic paper recommendation, which is based on the

G. Memmi et al. (Eds.): KSEM 2022, LNAI 13370, pp. 449–462, 2022.
https://doi.org/10.1007/978-3-031-10989-8_36

assumption that users with similar behaviors have similar preferences for papers. However, except for the users' historical preference for papers, the co-citation and co-keyword relationship between papers are two other key features by which academic paper recommendation differentiates from general recommendation tasks. When the emerging CF algorithms, especially some GCN-based CF algorithms [2,6], are applied to academic paper recommendation, the absence of these two key features will lead to unsatisfactory recommendation results. These GCN-based CF algorithms are generally based on bipartite graph which uses two kinds of vertices to represent users and papers respectively, and use edges represent users' preferences for papers. However, bipartite graph has insufficient ability of fusing co-citation and co-keyword relationship between papers. In addition, the preferences of the current user and similar users are represented in form of third-order neighbors. And at least three layers of GCN are needed to be stacked to complete embedded propagation between them. The over-smooth property of GCN [9] limits the generation of embedding with high-order similarity, resulting in the decline of recommendation quality.

To tackle this challenging issue, in this paper, we propose a hypergraph-based academic paper recommendation method. According to users' historical preference and academic relation between papers, we present APRHG (Academic Paper Relation HyperGraph) which meets the requirements complex relationship description and multi-features fusion. Academic relations including co-citation and co-keyword relationship between papers, they are fused by extending the semantic of hyperedges (i.e., regard co-citation relationship as a hyperedge). In addition, we propose the L-HGCF (Light HyperGraph based Collaborative Filtering) algorithm based on the simplified hypergraph convolution network (HGCN) to provide trusted recommendations. Compared with GCN, L-HGCF algorithm has a clearer logic and has advantages in embedding propagation, and extensive experiments show the whole recommendation method achieves great performance in the task of academic paper recommendation.

The main contributions of our work are summarized as follows:

(1) Based on hypergraph, we proposed the APRHG which takes full advantage of co-citation and co-keyword relationship between papers, and because user vertices are not introduced into the graph, we avoid stacking multi-layers GCN for mining high-order similarity, as with bipartite graph.
(2) Based on the constructed APRHG, we proposed an L-HGCF algorithm to learn latent vectors which represent relationship between papers and then provide trusted recommendations.
(3) We conducted experiments compared with four deep learning algorithms on the public dataset CiteUlike-A [15]. At the same time, we conducted detailed ablation experiments to verify the rationality of the components. Experimental results demonstrate the effectiveness of our method.

The rest of this paper is organized as follows. In the next section we review related work. Section 3 illustrates the overall framework of our recommendation method. Section 4 evaluates the experimental results compared with baseline models and Sect. 5 presents ablation studies. Finally in Sect. 6, we provide a conclusion and discuss prominent future research directions.

2 Related Work

Collaborative Filtering (CF) is a prevalent recommendation technique and has been successfully applied in multiple domains including e-commerce [3], movies [8] and so on. The early CF methods [8] worked by establishing a database of users' preferences for items.

With the development of intelligent technology [4,10], especially the application of graph convolution neural network (GCN) [11], researchers began to explore GCN-based CF problems, they applied deep learning to CF problems and made good progress. GCMC [2] represented interaction data such as movie ratings as bipartite user-item graph with labeled edges, and then applied a graph-based auto-encoder on it. In order to learn embeddings such as e-commerce item embedding, NGCF [17] propagated embedding of users and items on the bipartite graph, which effectively inject the collaborative signal into the embedding process. Based on NGCF, LightGCN [6] simplified the GCN operation for collaborative filtering, so that the model only contains the most important components in GCN, neighborhood aggregation.

The traditional CF algorithms have been widely used in academic paper recommendation system. Yang *et al.* [19] presented an academic paper recommendation system which uses a ranking-oriented CF method based on users' access logs. Sugiyama *et al.* [14] developed an academic paper recommendation system, which incorporate the associated papers information when building the user profile according to the citation network. Xia *et al.* [18] proposed to establish the additional relationship between papers according to the co-author information. They constructed the tripartite graph which contains user, papers and authors to combine the co-author relationship between papers with users' historical preferences for papers.

However, limited by structure of bipartite graph, GCN-based CF deep learning algorithms cannot fuse multi-features provided by the academic papers. Meanwhile, the over-smooth property of GCN [9] limits the generation of embedding with high-order similarity, resulting in the decline of recommendation quality. Based on these problems, we propose to build our academic paper recommendation method based on hypergraph, which will be described in detail later.

3 HyperGraph-Based Academic Paper Recommendation

3.1 Architecture of Recommendation Method

Figure 1 sketches the overall framework of our proposed academic paper recommendation method. The method is divided into two stages: APRHG construction and L-HGCF algorithm. APRHG is used to describe the complex academic

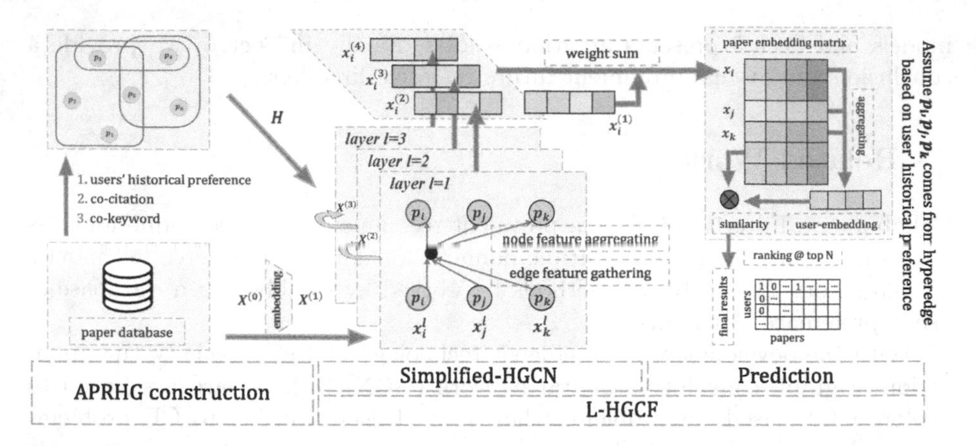

Fig. 1. The overall framework of our proposed academic paper recommendation method.

relationship between users and papers, and L-HGCF algorithm is proposed to provide trusted recommendations based on the constructed hypergraph.

Section 3.2 and Sect. 3.3 will introduce the detail of APRHG construction and L-HGCF algorithm, respectively.

3.2 Academic Paper Relation Hypergraph

Hypergraph is a special graph whose edge connect two or more vertices [1]. Based on Hypergraph, we propose an APRHG (Academic Paper Relation Hypergraph) which is defined as follows:

Definition 1. *APRHG (Academic Paper Relation HyperGraph) is defined by* $G = (P, E, W)$, *where*

- $P = \{p_1, p_2, ..., p_n\}$ *is the vertex set,* p_i *represent academic paper i;*
- $E = \{e_i^r = (p_{i1}^r, p_{i2}^r, ..., p_{ik}^r) | r \in R\}$ *is the hyperedge set, where* R *denote different kinds of hyperedge. Each hyperedge* e_i^r *is the subset of the paper set, they have academic relation r with each other;*
- W *is a diagonal matrix assign weight to each hyperedge.*

From the definition of APRHG, it can be seen that academic papers that have academic relation can be gathered by hyperedge. If some vertices are surrounded by more same hyperedges, it indicates that they have higher correlation and the corresponding papers have more similarity.

An APRHG can be denoted by a $|P| \times |E|$ incidence matrix H, with entries defined as Eq. (1)

$$h(p, e) = \begin{cases} 1, p \in e \\ 0, p \notin e \end{cases} \quad (1)$$

Considering the academic relationship including relation between users and papers, as well as papers, we define three types of hyperedges:

1) Hyperedges based on users' historical preference for papers. Each user in the record is regarded as a hyperedge, by which the user's preferred papers are connected with each other.
2) Hyperedges based on co-citation relationship between papers. Given the original citation network, each time one vertex in the citation network is selected as the center point and its connected vertices including the center point itself are used to generate one hyperedge.
3) Hyperedges based on co-keyword relationship between papers. Considering that the keywords of title has rich semantics, the semantic information of the title will be diluted if the title and abstract are processed into bag of word together, so we treat keywords in the title as hyperedges, and papers whose title contain this keyword are treated as vertices which are connected by these hyperedges.

In this paper, we adopt the stack strategy to obtain the complete hypergraph structure, which can be formulated as $H = H^{(0)} \| H^{(1)} \| H^{(2)} \| ... \| H^{(n)}$, where $\|$ denotes concatenation operation, $H^{(0)}$ to $H^{(n)}$ denote hyperedges constructed by different features, respectively.

3.3 Light Hypergraph Algorithm Based Collaborative Filtering

Inspired by the work of Feng *et al.* [5] and Jiang *et al.* [7], we propose L-HGCF algorithm in this paper.

Firstly, The title, abstract, and keywords of papers are processed into the bag of words as papers attribution $X^{(0)}$. Based on $X^{(0)}$, the embedding matrix $X^{(1)}$ is obtained through an embedding component. The paper embedding matrix $X^{(1)}$, together with the constructed incidence matrix H of ARPHG, are then transferred into the simplified HGCN (HyperGraph Convolution Network) layer [5].

For the target paper p_i, messaging happens between p_j connected by the common hyperedges, and then follows an aggregation process which is weighted according to weight of hyperedges. It can be represented in a matrix form as Eq. (2)

$$X^{(l+1)} = \sigma(D_p^{-\frac{1}{2}} H W D_e^{-1} H^T D_p^{-\frac{1}{2}} X^{(l)} \theta^{(l)}) \tag{2}$$

where $X^{(l)}$ is the input of (l)-th layer. D_p and D_e are the diagonal matrices of the paper degree defined as $d(p) = \sum_{e \in E} W(e) h(p, e)$ and hyperedge degree defined as $\delta(e) = \sum_{p \in P} h(p, e)$, respectively. W is a diagonal matrix store all the positive weight of hyperedges. $\theta^{(l)}$ is the learnable weight matrix and $\sigma(.)$ is non-linear activation function like eLU and LeakyReLU.

In order to light the burden of model, we abandon the use of feature transformation $\theta^{(l)}$ and nonlinear activation $\sigma(.)$, and retain only the most important component in HGCN, neighborhood aggregation, in our model. As shown in Eq. (3).

$$X^{(l+1)} = D_p^{-\frac{1}{2}} H W D_e^{-1} H^T D_p^{-\frac{1}{2}} X^{(l)} \tag{3}$$

The input of the first layer HGCN $X^{(1)}$, is the embedding from the attribute values of the original papers $X^{(0)}$. Once $X^{(1)}$ are given, the embeddings at higher layers are computed via our Simplified HGCN layer which is defined in Eq. (3). After K-layer calculation, we further combine the embeddings which are obtained at each layer to form the final representation of a paper, show in Eq. (4):

$$X = \sum_{k=1}^{K+1} \alpha_k X^{(k)} \tag{4}$$

where $\alpha_k > 0$ denotes the importance of the k-th layer embedding in constituting the final embedding. In our experiment, we set α_k uniformly as $1/(1+k)$.

In our proposed academic paper recommendation method we regard only papers as vertices. Therefore, a strategy is needed to aggregate user embedding. In this paper, user embedding is obtained by averaging embedding of historical preferred papers, show as Eq. (5).

$$x_u = \frac{1}{N} \sum_{i=1}^{N} x_i \tag{5}$$

And then the similarity between users and papers is defined as the inner product of their final representations, show as Eq. (6):

$$y_{ui} = x_u^T x_i \tag{6}$$

The final recommendation results to user u are decided according to the descending order of similarity y_{ui}.

The only trainable parameters in our algorithm come from the embedding component which outputs $X^{(1)}$, i.e., $\theta = \{X^{(1)}\}$. We design a tuple-wise loss function which satisfies the hyperedge property as show in Eq. (7).

$$L = -\sum_{u=1}^{M} \sum_{i \in u} \Big(\sum_{j \in u, j \neq i} ln\sigma(x_i^T x_j) - \sum_{k \notin u} ln\sigma(x_i^T x_k) \Big) + \lambda \|X^{(1)}\|^2 \tag{7}$$

where λ controls the L2 regularization strength. $\sigma(.)$ is the sigmoid function. M includes only hyperedges which are based on users' historical preference for papers. We see papers connected by these hyperedges as positive examples, and sample the negative samples to be 10 times the amount of the positive samples. This loss function encourages the prediction of positive entry to be higher than its negative counterparts. We employ the Adam optimizer and use it in a mini-batch manner.

The computational cost of our approach to generate paper recommendations for users mainly comes from three steps: paper similarity computation - Eq. (3) (4). User embedding computation - Eq. (5) and recommendation list generation - Eq. (6). In order to avoid repeat computing, we calculate the matrix of $D_p^{-\frac{1}{2}} H W D_e^{-1} H^T D_p^{-\frac{1}{2}}$ and store it beforehand, so that time complexity of the first step is $O(n^2d)$, the second step is $O(mn)$, and last one is $O(mn)$. Where we assume the number of user and paper is m and n, the dimension of paper attribution is d.

4 Experimental Analysis

4.1 Experimental Settings

Table 1. Statistics of the preprocessed experimented data.

Dataset	#User	#Paper	#Interaction	#Citation	#Key word
CiteUlike-A	4880	11845	172267	31517	582

We select dataset collected on the famous academic literature sharing website CiteULike[1], named CiteUlike-A [15]. The dataset contains users' historical preference for papers, the citation network of papers and raw data of title and abstract, for which the statistics are shown in Table 1. For this dataset, we filter out the papers and their records with damaged title or abstract, and filter out users less than 10 records and papers less than 5 records. And then we randomly divide the dataset into two subsets, in which 80% of the historical preference records constitute the training set and the other 20% of the preference records constitute the test set.

For performance evaluation, we adopt three widely-used metrics, including precision@K, recall@K, and normalized discounted cumulative gain (ndcg@K). The metrics are computed by the Eq. (8), Eq. (9), and Eq. (10), respectively. In our experiments, K is set as 20.

$$precision@k = \frac{\sum_u |R(u) \cap T(u)|}{\sum_u |R(u)|} \tag{8}$$

$$recall@k = \frac{\sum_u |R(u) \cap T(u)|}{\sum_u |T(u)|} \tag{9}$$

where $R(u)$ is the list of recommendations to user u and $T(u)$ is the list of true selections of user u.

$$ndcg@k = Z_K \sum_{i=1}^{K} \frac{2^{r_i} - 1}{log_2(1+i)} \tag{10}$$

where Z_K is the normalization factor, the value of r_i is 0 or 1, indicating the predictive correlation of paper i, and $1/log_2(1+i)$ represents the importance coefficient at i position.

[1] https://citeulike.org/.

The proposed L-HGCF algorithm is implemented in PyTorch. The hidden dimension, i.e., the embedding size for papers, are fixed as 64 and the embedding parameters are initialized with the Xavier method. The batch size is set as 32. For all compared methods, we opt for the Adam optimizer and use the default learning rate of 0.001 and the random seed of all models is set to 1024. The L2 regularization coefficient λ is searched in the range of $\{0, 1e{-}5, 1e{-}4, 1e{-}3, 1e{-}2, 1e{-}1\}$. The layer combination coefficient α_k is uniformly set to $1/(1+k)$, where K is the number of layers. We test K in the range of 1 to 4, and satisfactory performance can be achieved when K equals to 2.

4.2 Performance Comparison with Baseline Models

Four recent competitive methods are selected for performance comparison. They are representatives of three graph structures, namely graph free structure (BPR-MF [12]), simple graph structure (SNDE [16]) and Bipartite graph structure (LightGCN [6], MCMC [2]), respectively.

(1) BPR-MF [12]: a classic matrix factorization method using the BPR as loss function, which optimizes the embedding of users and items through pairwise ranking between the positive instances and sampled negative items.
(2) SDNE [16]: a graph representation learning frame-work which jointly exploits the first-order and second-order proximity to preserve the network structure.
(3) GCMC [2]: a graph auto-encoder framework for recommendation system from the perspective of matrix completion, in which a graph convolution layer is introduced to generate user and item embeddings through message passing.
(4) LightGCN [6]: a simplified GCN-based recommendation framework which integrates the user-item interactions into the embedding process. For this method, we construct two bipartite graphs. One is the general model namely LightGCN-1 as Eq. (11). In the other one namely LightGCN-2, extra citation network is introduced to build the graph as Eq. (12).

$$A = \begin{pmatrix} 0 & R \\ R^T & 0 \end{pmatrix} \tag{11}$$

$$A = \begin{pmatrix} 0 & R \\ R^T & C \end{pmatrix} \tag{12}$$

where R is the Rating matrix, C is Citation network between papers.

Meanwhile, according to the different types of hyperedge. Four hypergraphs for L-HGCF algorithm are designed. They are:

1) APRHG-1 contains hyperedges based on users' historical preference for papers;
2) APRHG-2 adds additional hyperedges based on co-citation relationship;
3) APRHG-3 adds additional hyperedges based on co-keyword relationship;

4) APRHG-4 combines all the three hyperedges.

And corresponding algorithms are named as L-HGCF-1, L-HGCF-2, L-HGCF-3 and L-HGCF-4, respectively.

Table 2. Overall performance comparison of all baselines and L-HGCF algorithm.

Method	Recall	Precision	ndcg	Historical preference	Co-citation	Co-keyword
BPR-MF	0.02248	0.00768	0.06669	✓		
SDNE	0.00629	0.00215	0.02145	✓		
GCMC	0.02413	0.00824	0.07120	✓		
LightGCN-1	0.03446	0.01177	0.10485	✓		
LightGCN-2	0.01949	0.00665	0.05835	✓	✓	
L-HGCF-1	0.03491	0.01192	0.10776	✓		
L-HGCF-2	0.03507	0.01198	0.11197	✓	✓	
L-HGCF-3	0.03491	0.01192	0.11136	✓		✓
L-HGCF-4	0.03507	0.01198	0.11197	✓	✓	✓

The experimental results are shown in Table 2. From these results we can have the following observations.

1) BPR-MF: BPR-MF is the only model that does not rely on graph structure for information transmission in our experiment. It's simple and effective design brings good performance. The recall@20 of BPR-MF achieves 0.02248.
2) SDNE: The performance of SDNE is poor, and its recall@20 is only 0.00629. The reason is that in SDNE every two papers marked by the same user are connected as neighbors, and the large number of generation of edges blur the relation between papers, which result in the decline of the quality of recommendation.
3) GCMC: GCMC achieved similar performance with BPR-MF (the recall@20 of GCMC is 0.02413). From the perspective of features used, both of them use only users' historical preference for papers. Structurally, GCMC uses only one-layer GCN, which failed to mine the high-order relationships between papers.
4) LightGCN-1 and LightGCN-2: The bipartite graph structure and three-layers GCN operation of LightGCN-1 lead to good results. The recall@20 of LightGCN-1 achieves 0.03446. However, when it comes to LightGCN-2, in which extra citation network is introduced to build the graph, the recall@20 achieves only 0.01949. Integrating extra citation network results in poor performance. It can be seen that the effect of bipartite graph structure in multi-feature fusion is not satisfactory.
5) L-HGCF: Due to the flexible modeling of APRHG and well-crafted L-HGCF algorithm, our method of attribute combination for hyperedge all have achieved excellent performance. APRHG modeling meets the requirements complex relationship description and multi-features fusion. The L-HGCF algorithm has a clear logic and an advantage in embedding propagation compared with GCN.

5 Ablation and Effectiveness Analysis

5.1 On the Number of Layers

Simplified-HGCN plays an important role in our L-HGCF algorithm. To explore how the number of layers of Simplified-HGCN affects the performance of our L-HGCF algorithm, we vary the depth of Simplified-HGCN in the range of $\{1, 2, 3, 4\}$. At the same time, we design two variant components to verify the beneficial of Simplified-HGCN and layer combination in our L-HGCF algorithm:

1) Complete-HGCN that use complete HGCN defined by Eq. (2) instead of simplified HGCN as Eq. (3), and we applied layer combination in this variant component.
2) Single-HGCN that use only the output of the last layer of simplified HGCN and does not use layer combination.

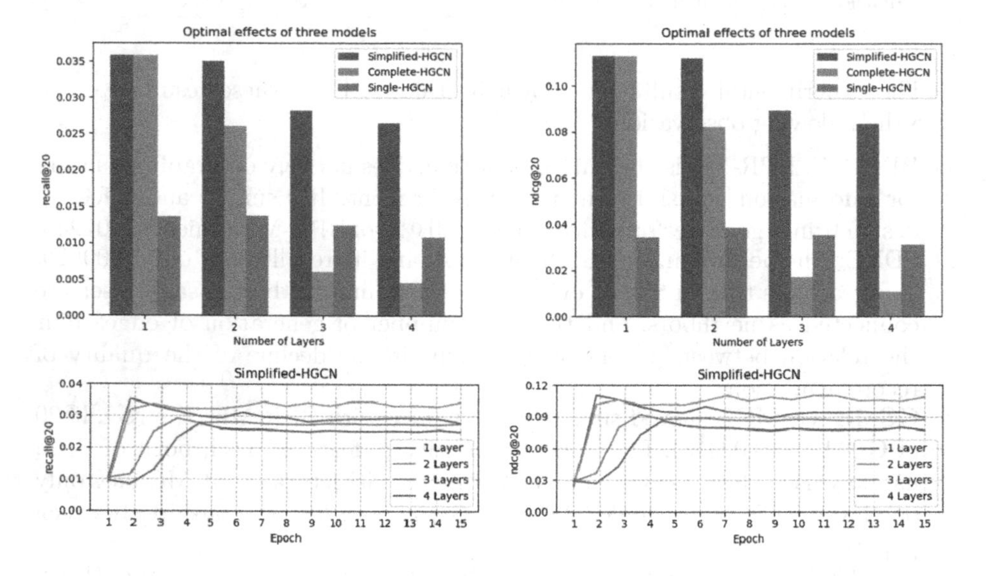

Fig. 2. (up) Optimal performance of recall@20 and ndcg@20 at different layers of Simplified-HGCN, the variant Complete-HGCN and Single-HGCN. (down) Convergence performance of recall@20 and ndcg@20 w.r.t. epoch of Simplified-HGCN at different layers

Figure 2(up) shows optimal performance of recall@20 and ndcg@20 at different layers of Simplified-HGCN, Complete-HGCN and Single-HGCN, respectively.

Focusing on Complete-HGCN, whose recall@20 declines from 0.03581 of layer 1 to 0.00450 of layer 4. With the increase of network layers, its performance continues to decline. The reason is that the increasing number of learnable parameters causes the over-fitting problem in the model.

Focusing on Single-HGCN, we find that when the number of layers increases from 1 to 4, its performance improves at the beginning, the peak point is located at layer 2 and the recall@20 is 0.01379. And after that, it decreases and drops to the worst point of layer 4, where the recall@20 is only 0.01078. This shows that the embedding of smoothing vertices using first-order and second-order neighbors is useful for recommendation, but it will suffer from over-smoothing problems when using higher-order neighbors.

Focusing on Simplified-HGCN whose recall@20 varies from 0.03581 of layer 1 to 0.02652 of layer 4, its performance is significantly better than Single-HGCN. Compared with quickly drop of Complete-HGCN, Simplified-HGCN has a much more stable and nice performance. This shows the effectiveness of layer combination for addressing over-smoothing and simplified HGCN for addressing overfitting problem.

Figure 2(down) shows the convergence curve of Simplified-HGCN at different layers. Although 1-layer Simplified-HGCN obtains an optimal performance with recall@20 is 0.03581 at the second epoch, it couldn't maintain this advantage later. In comparison, 2-layer Simplified HGCN has a much more robust and stable performance whose best recall@20 is 0.03507 at the 11th epoch. Therefore, the final number of layers of Simplified-HGCN is determined as 2.

5.2 On the Aggregation Schemes of User Embedding

In our proposed academic paper recommendation method, we regard only papers as vertices, and an extra strategy is needed to generate user embedding. To explore how the aggregation schemes of user embedding affects the performance, we design three strategies to generate user embedding.

1) Mean-strategy: All the papers are assigned by the same weights, which is applied in our method;
2) Norm-strategy: Different papers are assigned by different weights. Suppose the weight matrix is denoted by M, paper weight can be computed by Eq. (13):

$$M = D^{-\frac{1}{2}} R B^{-\frac{1}{2}} \tag{13}$$

   where R is the rating matrix, D and B are the diagonal matrices indicate degree of the users and papers, respectively.
3) Net-strategy: We take users as vertices and construct the other hypergraph model. The generated users embedding then be transferred to the L-HGCF algorithm for training together with papers embedding.

Figure 3 shows the convergence curves of recall@20 and ndcg@20 of three strategies. Since the high similarity of curves of mean-strategy and norm-strategy, the details of them at epoch 4 to 15 are show in the figure in the right. It can be seen that compared with Norm-strategy, Mean-strategy has subtle advantages, and they both achieve convergence from the 3th epoch. The net-strategy has the slowest convergence speed and insufficient performance of

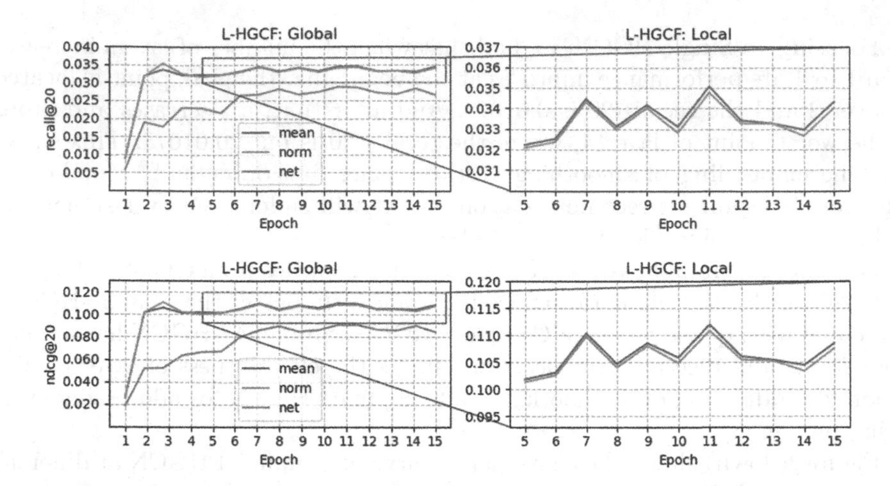

Fig. 3. Convergence performance of recall@20 and ndcg@20 w.r.t. epoch of the 2-layer L-HGCF with different choices of user aggregation schemes. the details of the mean and norm at epoch 5 to 15 are show in the figure right

recommendation. The convergence curves show that mean-strategy is effective, therefore we adopted the mean-strategy in our L-HGCF algorithm.

6 Conclusions

In this work, we proposed a hypergraph-based academic paper recommendation method. The method is divided into two stages: APRHG construction and L-HGCF algorithm. Specifically, it allows explicitly modeling complex academic relationship and realizing multi-features fusion, and thus can yield more informative embeddings using the proposed L-HGCF algorithm, which can provide trusted recommendations. Extensive experiments on public dataset demonstrate significant improvements over competitive baselines. As shown in the experimental results, we can conclude that the hypergraph modeling and multi-features information are useful for papers representation.

Digital libraries are on the rise, and online research social platforms such as ScholarMate[2] are more and more popular, we believe that academic paper recommendation model is instructive for the future development of them. Hypergraph naturally has the ability of modeling complex relationships and multi-features fusion. Future work will focus on the construction of user portrait that can mine high-order similarity between users and improve the recommendation ability of our academic paper recommendation method.

[2] www.scholarmate.com.

References

1. Bai, S., Zhang, F., Torr, P.H.: Hypergraph convolution and hypergraph attention. Pattern Recogn. **110**, 107637 (2021)
2. Berg, R.V.D., Kipf, T.N., Welling, M.: Graph convolutional matrix completion. arXiv preprint arXiv:1706.02263 (2017)
3. Cheng, H.T., et al.: Wide & deep learning for recommender systems. In: Proceedings of the 1st Workshop on Deep Learning for Recommender Systems, pp. 7–10 (2016)
4. Fei, H., Lakdawala, S., Qi, H., Qiu, M.: Low-power, intelligent sensor hardware interface for medical data preprocessing. IEEE Trans. Inf. Technol. Biomed. **13**(4), 656–663 (2009)
5. Feng, Y., You, H., Zhang, Z., Ji, R., Gao, Y.: Hypergraph neural networks. In: Proceedings of the AAAI Conference on Artificial Intelligence, vol. 33, pp. 3558–3565 (2019)
6. He, X., Deng, K., Wang, X., Li, Y., Zhang, Y., Wang, M.: LightGCN: simplifying and powering graph convolution network for recommendation. In: Proceedings of the 43rd International ACM SIGIR Conference on Research and Development in Information Retrieval, pp. 639–648 (2020)
7. Jiang, J., Wei, Y., Feng, Y., Cao, J., Gao, Y.: Dynamic hypergraph neural networks. In: IJCAI, pp. 2635–2641 (2019)
8. Kabbur, S., Ning, X., Karypis, G.: FISM: factored item similarity models for top-n recommender systems. In: Proceedings of the 19th ACM SIGKDD International Conference on Knowledge Discovery and Data Mining, pp. 659–667 (2013)
9. Li, Q., Han, Z., Wu, X.M.: Deeper insights into graph convolutional networks for semi-supervised learning. In: Thirty-Second AAAI Conference on Artificial Intelligence (2018)
10. Li, Y., Song, Y., Jia, L., Gao, S., Li, Q., Qiu, M.: Intelligent fault diagnosis by fusing domain adversarial training and maximum mean discrepancy via ensemble learning. IEEE Trans. Industr. Inf. **17**(4), 2833–2841 (2020)
11. Qiu, H., Zheng, Q., Msahli, M., Memmi, G., Qiu, M., Lu, J.: Topological graph convolutional network-based urban traffic flow and density prediction. IEEE Trans. Intell. Transp. Syst. **22**(7), 4560–4569 (2020)
12. Rendle, S., Freudenthaler, C., Gantner, Z., Schmidt-Thieme, L.: BPR: Bayesian personalized ranking from implicit feedback. arXiv preprint arXiv:1205.2618 (2012)
13. Samatha, B.: A novel ontological domain model for information retrieval within digital library (2018)
14. Sugiyama, K., Kan, M.Y.: Scholarly paper recommendation via user's recent research interests. In: Proceedings of the 10th Annual Joint Conference on Digital Libraries, pp. 29–38 (2010)
15. Wang, C., Blei, D.M.: Collaborative topic modeling for recommending scientific articles. In: Proceedings of the 17th ACM SIGKDD International Conference on Knowledge Discovery and Data Mining, pp. 448–456 (2011)
16. Wang, D., Cui, P., Zhu, W.: Structural deep network embedding. In: Proceedings of the 22nd ACM SIGKDD International Conference on Knowledge Discovery and Data Mining, pp. 1225–1234 (2016)
17. Wang, X., He, X., Wang, M., Feng, F., Chua, T.S.: Neural graph collaborative filtering. In: Proceedings of the 42nd International ACM SIGIR Conference on Research and Development in Information Retrieval, pp. 165–174 (2019)

18. Xia, F., Liu, H., Lee, I., Cao, L.: Scientific article recommendation: exploiting common author relations and historical preferences. IEEE Trans. Big Data **2**(2), 101–112 (2016)
19. Yang, C., Wei, B., Wu, J., Zhang, Y., Zhang, L.: Cares: a ranking-oriented CADAL recommender system. In: Proceedings of the 9th ACM/IEEE-CS Joint Conference on Digital Libraries, pp. 203–212 (2009)

Automated Reliability Analysis of Redundancy Architectures Using Statistical Model Checking

Hongbin He[1], Hongyu Kuang[1], Lin Yang[1], Feng Yang[1], Qiang Wang[1(✉)], and Weipeng Cao[2]

[1] National Key Laboratory of Science and Technology on Information System Security, Systems Engineering Institute, Academy of Military Sciences, Beijing, China
18513688908@163.com

[2] College of Computer Science and Software Engineering, Shenzhen University, Shenzhen, China
caoweipeng@szu.edu.cn

Abstract. Reliability is a fundamental property for mission and safety-critical systems, and adopting redundancy architectures is a common and prominent practice to increase system reliability. This paper proposes a novel approach for the modeling and quantitative reliability analysis of redundancy architectures based on the SBIP framework. Our approach supports modeling the nominal system behavior and the system faults in a unified formal model, which can be further integrated into the rigorous component-based system design paradigm advocated by BIP. We also propose two categories of metrics for formal reliability evaluation of redundancy architectures in terms of whether the system can operate correctly or provide reduced functionalities in the presence of faults. We take a computation unit as the running example and apply the proposed approach to analyze static redundancy and dynamic redundancy, which are Triple Module Redundancy architecture and Cold Standby architecture respectively. The experimental results show that our approach can accurately model various redundancy architectures and provide a comprehensive analysis of reliability and related properties in an automated manner. Moreover, our approach can be easily extended to a wide range of fault types and behaviors.

Keywords: Model based system design · Model based reliability analysis · Statistical model checking · Redundancy architecture

1 Introduction

Reliability is the desired ability for mission and safety-critical systems, which generally speaking characterizes the ability of the system to continue to operate the intended functions correctly even in the presence of faults [2,18]. Among all the possible approaches to increase the system reliability, a common and prominent practice in reliability engineering is to replicate the components carrying out critical functions and encapsulate them in architectural redundancy patterns so that the single point of failure can

H. He and H. Kuang—Contribute equally to this work.

G. Memmi et al. (Eds.): KSEM 2022, LNAI 13370, pp. 463–476, 2022.
https://doi.org/10.1007/978-3-031-10989-8_37

be avoided and when faults occur in a limited number of critical components, they can be identified and excluded upon reconfiguration without compromising the overall functionality of the system. The most well-known redundancy architectural patterns are static Triple Modular Redundancy (TMR) and dynamic Cold Standby, which have been widely used in the practical development of mission and safety-critical systems [23].

Despite the practical needs of designing and analyzing safety-critical systems, the reliability analysis of systems built with redundancy architectures, in general, is a difficult task due to the lack of specific techniques addressing both modeling and automated analysis. Previous works mostly use fault tree analysis (FTA) [16] and rely on a substantial amount of labor effort for the reliability verification and analysis. In [15] the authors analyze the reliability of cascaded TMR with "paper-and-pencil" techniques. However, such approaches cannot be generalized to cover a wide range of architectural patterns. Some other works [9,10] propose to use SMT techniques to perform automated analysis of redundancy architectures and it improves the overall scalability concerning the monolithic case, obtaining speed-ups of various orders of magnitude. However, they do not consider the system's dynamic behavior or integrate it with the process of model-based system design.

In order to automate the reliability evaluation of different redundancy architectures, we follow the methodology of model-based design and safety analysis [21], which has been promoted as an increasingly prominent approach for the development of safety-critical systems. In model-based design, various development activities such as simulation, verification, testing, and code generation are based on a unified model, describing system behavior and architectures. In the model-based safety analysis, the model of the system behavior is further extended and augmented by taking into account the faulty behavior of software and hardware components. We then can analyze the reliability properties based on the extended system in the presence of faults. The main advantage of this methodology is that the system and safety engineers work off a common, unambiguous model of the system leading to tighter integration between the systems and safety engineering processes. The common model ensures that reliability analysis results are relevant and up-to-date as the system architecture evolves and allows reliability assessment early in the system design process. Additionally, it supports the exploration of different architectures and design choices by automatically determining which choices will increase reliability. Ideally, computational tools such as model checkers can automate many reliability analysis activities, leading to more accurate and complete reliability analyses while reducing manual effort.

In this work, we leverage the SBIP framework. SBIP [22] is a stochastic extension of BIP (Behavior-Interaction-Priority) [3,4,7,17] with an emphasis on formal modeling and statistical analysis of safety-critical systems exhibiting stochastic behaviors. BIP is a component-based system design framework advocating the rigorous design methodology for complex hardware/software mixed system design [3,24]. The concept of rigorous system design can be understood as a formal, accountable and coherent process for deriving correct-by-construct system implementations from high-level specifications. The essential safety properties of the design are guaranteed at the earliest possible design phase by applying algorithmic verification to the system model. Then the system implementation is automatically generated by a sequence of property preserving model transformations, progressively refining the model with details specific to the target platforms. The BIP framework provides a well-defined modeling language and an associated toolbox to realize the rigorous system design flow. The modeling language allows the construction of composite components from atomic components through the layered application of interactions and priorities. The BIP toolbox supports both verifications of high-level system designs [5] and automatic model transformation and code generation of low-level implementations from high-level system designs. In practice, BIP has been actively used in several applications [1,19].

To this end, the contributions of this work can be summarized as follows.

(1) We propose a novel approach for the modeling and quantitative reliability analysis of redundancy architectures based on the SBIP framework. Our approach supports modeling the nominal system behavior and the system faults in a unified formal model, which can be further integrated into the rigorous component-based system design paradigm.
(2) We propose two categories of metrics to evaluate the reliability and related properties of redundancy architectures, in terms of whether the system is able to operate correctly or provide reduced functionalities in the presence of faults. All the properties are specified as formulas in bounded LTL and automatically analyzed using the statistical model checker for BIP [22].
(3) We further take a computation unit as the running example and apply the proposed approach to the analysis of two widely used redundancy architectures, i.e., the static triple duplication redundancy and the dynamic cold standby redundancy. The experimental results show that our approach can accurately model various redundancy architectures and provide a comprehensive analysis of reliability and related properties in an automated manner.

The remainder of this paper is organized as follows. Section 2 describes the related works. In Sect. 3, we carry out a study with the computation unit and build a formal model of CU including both nominal and faulty behavior within the SBIP framework. Then we develop the formal model of TMR and Cold Standby architectures and analyze their reliability using SBIP. Finally, Sect. 4 concludes the paper and points out our future work.

2 Related Work

COMPASS (Correctness, Modeling, and Performance of Aerospace Systems) [8] is an international research effort aiming to ensure system-level correctness, safety, dependability, and performability of onboard computer-based aerospace systems. COMPASS uses a System-Level Integrated Modeling (SLIM) language for modeling and specifying hardware/software systems, and the COMPASS toolset supports for timed failure propagation graphs, non-deterministic models, the newly developed statistical model checking and requirement formalization approaches.

The Altarica language [6] can also formally specify the behavior of systems when faults occur. An Altarica model can be assessed be employing complementary tools such as fault tree generator and model-checker. FSAP/NuSMV-SA [11,12] is a toolset for safety and reliability analysis. FSAP/NuSMV-SA supports failure mode definition and model extension through automatic failure injection.

The work in [14] proposes a model-based approach using dynamic fault trees for the safety analysis of vehicle guidance systems. Its flexibility could support new partitions and architectural changes being accommodated automatically. The fault tree analysis in [9,10] aims at evaluating characteristics of redundancy architectures without considering the behaviors of components. The work in [20] proposes an intelligent fault diagnosis method based on an improved domain adaptation method. In [25], a module based on redundancy is designed within the formalism of timed automata and formally analyzed using the UPPAAL model checker. The work in [13] presents an approach based BIP framework for the rigorous design of FDIR components. It leverages the statistical model checking to check the requirement satisfaction and the code generation feature of the BIP compiler. Our work differs from the previous work in that we mainly focus on the reliability analysis of redundancy architectures. The work in [15] presents an ad-hoc algorithm that can analyze the reliability of computational chains based on Triple Modular Redundancy with one voter. Differently, we provide ways to make quantitative analyses reliability of redundancy architectures in full automation.

3 Formal Modeling and Reliability Analysis in SBIP

This section introduces a simple computation unit (CU) that will be used as a running example to illustrate the concepts and our approach throughout. Firstly, we build a formal model of CU including both nominal and faulty behavior within the SBIP framework. Then we build the formal model of TMR and Cold Standby architectures.

3.1 A Computation Unit Example

The computation unit is a common module in many embedded systems, for instance, the detection system in the space field. Its function is to receive the instructions of the upper main control system, then obtain the data from the lower sensor, process the data, and return the processing results to the main control system.

We consider an abstract model of CU, which receives data from some components as its input and computes an output to the other components. Let `cu_input` be the input and `cu_output` be the output of the CU. To simplify the model, we assume that the value of `cu_output` ranges from -1 to 1, where 1 indicates the correct computation, -1 indicates the incorrect computation and 0 is the cleared output. Initially, the value of `cu_output` is 1. An impulse generator is used to first issue an edge impulse xms every T time unit to force the CU to read its input, compute and place the result in `cu_output`, and then clear the output. Figure 1 displays a system with one fault-free CU, one Impulse generator and their connector modeled in SBIP. In the Impulse generator model, the Impulse generator automaton models the impulse generator periodically produces edge impulses. A clock x is declared to record the time between sending of two edge impulses. Starting from the initial state `S0`, it generates a signal through port xms in each T time unit that synchronizes with the port xms of the CU automaton, then generates a signal through port $clear$ that synchronizes with the port $clear$ of the CU automaton. In the CU model, a variable `cu_output` is declared to represent the computing result of CU. Starting from the initial state `Good`, it receives a signal through

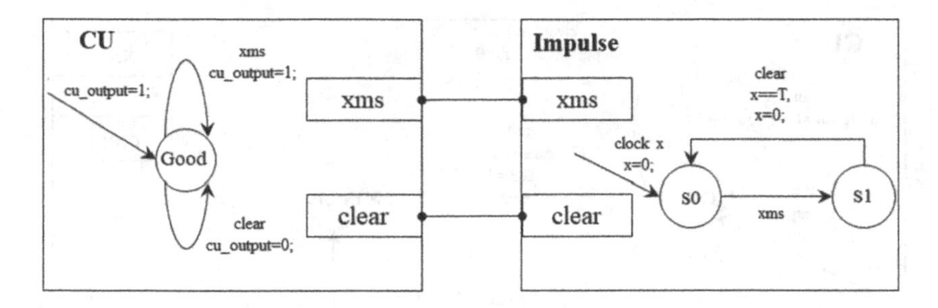

Fig. 1. Fault-free CU model

port xms that computes an output and receives a signal through port $clear$ that clears an output.

We consider that following three kinds of faults that may occur in a CU.

- $FAULT_0$: CU enters a deadlock state.
- $FAULT_1$: CU enters an error state in which it computes incorrect results.
- $FAULT_2$: CU enters a livelock state and executes only internal actions without any outputs.

The fault-affected CU model is shown in Fig. 2. Initially, CU works well and stays in location *Good*. The self-loop in fault-free location *Good* models the scenario when a synchronization impulse xms occurs, and the CU outputs a correct result. From location *Good*, the CU automaton selects which fault may occur in a stochastic manner. We use exponential distribution to approximate the failure occurrence model for the faults mentioned above in this work. In SBIP, we define a stochastic port with a gamma density function, i.e., its scheduling time is sampled with respect to a gamma function with alpha 1 and beta 100 to indicate the probability of the occurring fault. If $FAULT_0$ occurs, it moves to the error location $Error0$ and the automaton deadlocks. Since the xms is defined as a broadcast channel, the Impulse automaton can still execute it when the CU stays in location $Error0$. The Impulse automaton can still execute the xms. The location $Error1$ is reached from location *Good* when $FAULT_1$ occurs. The model outputs incorrect data when the signal xms is issued in this location. Similarly, if $FAULT_2$ occurs, the CU goes to location $Error2$, in which it fails to output data when the signal xms is issued. We also add fault transitions from location $Error1$ to $Error0$ and $Error2$, because a $FAULT_1$ may be followed by one of the other faults.

An auxiliary variable `cu_fault` indicates whether the CU is faulty. It is initially 0, representing that the CU is in location *Good*. When a fault occurs in the CU, the value of `cu_fault` becomes 1.

3.2 Formal Model of Triple Modular Redundancy Architecture

The **TMR** model consists of three replicated CUs, one Impulse generator and one Voter (see Fig. 3). Since the Impulse generator and Voter are not redundant in this architecture, it is prone to single-point failures. However, its complexity is usually significantly lower than that of the three modules, and this safety gap is tolerated. So we assume that no faults occur in the Impulse generator or the Voter.

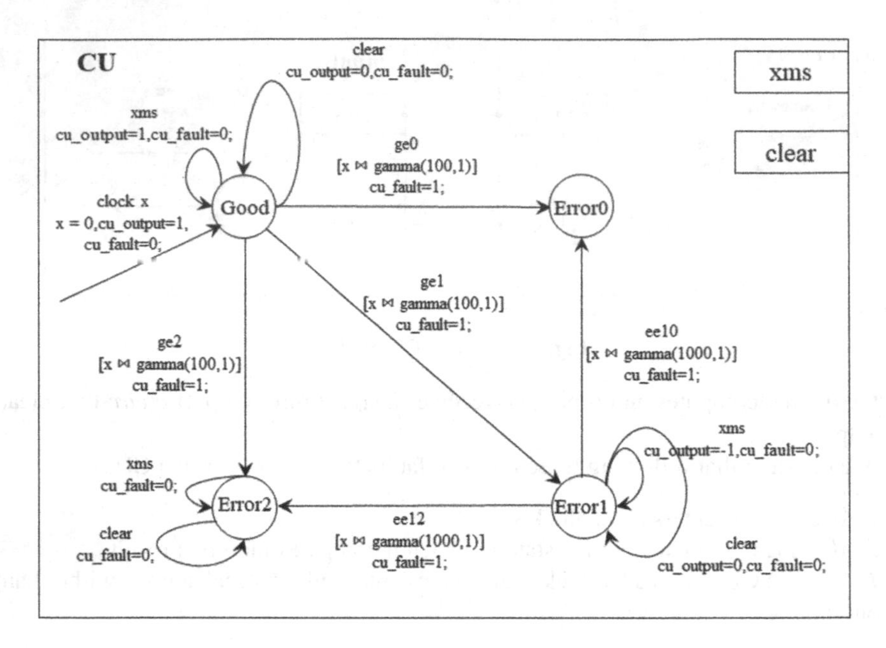

Fig. 2. A SBIP model of fault-effected CU

In the Impulse generator model (see Fig. 4), the automaton generates a synchronization signal through port xms to trigger the three CUs to process their inputs and start the computation. Then it generates a signal through port $x5ms$ to trigger the Voter to check on the outputs of CUs after CU_PERIOD time units. Finally, a $clear$ is sent after $VOTER\_PERIOD$ time units to trigger the three CUs to clear their outputs.

In **TMR**, the CU model (see Fig. 5) is similar to fault-effected CU, but it has two additional ports. The port $fault$ of `CUi` synchronizes with the port $faulti$ of the Voter automaton, and the port *output* of `CUi` synchronizes with the port *outputi* of the Voter automaton. In **TMR**, we define the system as in a degraded state when one CU is faulty and the other two CUs are fault-free.

In this model, a Voter is used to detect the faults (see Fig. 6). When it receives the $x5ms$ signal, it calls two functions: `fault_check()` and `vote()`. Function `fault_check()` evaluates whether any CU is faulty. It gets the value of variable cu_fault of `CUi` through port $faulti$. If it is 1, then Voter treats `CUi` as faulty. Otherwise, it is fault-free. Function `vote()` computes the voting algorithm. It compares results from the three CUs and outputs the majority value to the buffer `voter_output`. If the results of the three CUs are different, it computes the value of `CU0`.

3.3 Formal Model of Dynamic Cold Standby Redundancy Architecture

We build the cold standby redundancy architecture model (see Fig. 7), which contains one Impulse generator, one Primary CU, one Backup CU, and one Switch. The Impulse generator and Primary CU are similar to that of the **TMR** model, but all ports of Primary CU are connected to the port $primary$ of Switch.

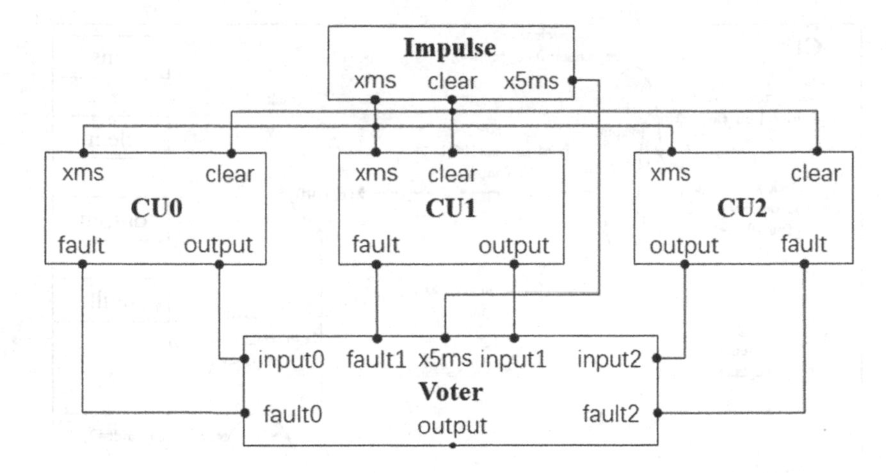

Fig. 3. Triple Modular Redundancy model

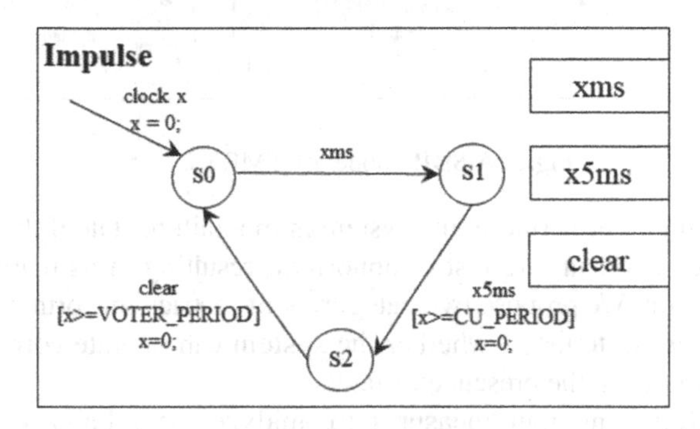

Fig. 4. A SBIP model of Impulse generator

The Switch automaton is shown in Fig. 9. The Switch initiates in the state `S0` and sets variable `is_fault` to 0, which means the Primary CU is fault-free. Moreover, the Switch only interacts with the Primary CU in state `S0`. The port *isswitch* connects with the port *fault* of the Primary CU. The port *isswitch* is active and the state `S0` transfers to state `S1` when the condition `is_faulty` == `1` holds. Then the Switch interacts with the Backup CU in the state `S1`.

The Backup CU automaton is shown in Fig. 8. The initial state is in `Start`, and it transfers to state `Good` when the port *backup* is active. Moreover, the function of Backup CU is similar to Primary CU after it locates the state `Good`. It may still locate in state `Good` in the next state, or transfer to state `Errori`. All ports of the Backup CU except port *backup* are connected to the port *backup* of Switch.

3.4 Formal Reliability Analysis Using SBIP

As stated above, reliability refers to the capability of the system to operate correctly in the presence of faults. The system is in a fault-free state if the system safely operates, and the system is in a degraded state if the system still safely operates but provides

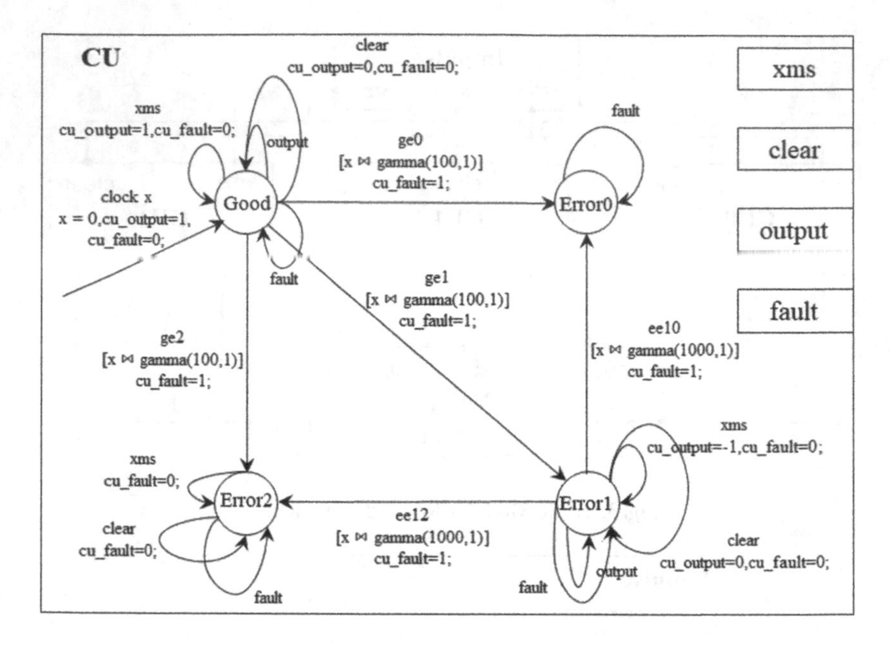

Fig. 5. A SBIP model of TMR's CU

reduced functionality. Furthermore, the system is in a failure state if the function of the system, parts or components are lost or abnormal, resulting in its inability to perform the expected function. We propose two categories of metrics for formal reliability evaluation of the system in terms of whether the system can operate correctly or provide reduced functionalities in the presence of faults.

We use the following four measures to analyze the reliability of the system. `Reliability` means the probability of the system being in a fault-free state. `Failures In Time` (`FIT`) means the average probability of the system being in a fault-free state during the considered operational lifetime. `Degraded Availability` (`DA`) means the probability of the system being in a degraded state. Moreover, `Full Function Availability` (`FFA`) means the probability of the system being in a fault-free and degraded state.

`Reliability` is obtained by first computing the time-bounded probability to reach a state where the system has failed and then complementing this value. To obtain the average failure-probability, the complement of the reliability is scaled with the lifetime (to determine the failures in time, `FIT`). `DA` is obtained by computing the time-bounded reachability probability for reaching a degraded state. `FFA` is obtained by computing the complement of the time-bounded reachability probability for reaching a failed or degraded state.

The formal definition of the measures is given in Table 1. The detailed BLTL specifications of the measures estimated on the Triple Modular Redundancy model and dynamic redundancy model are followed.

In order to simplify writing, we assume that the cf_i represents that the i-th CU is faulty, i.e., variable `cu_fault` of the i-th CU equals to 1, and $\overline{cf_i}$ represents the i-th CU is fault-free, i.e., variable `cu_fault` of the i-th CU equals to 0. The ϕ_T represents

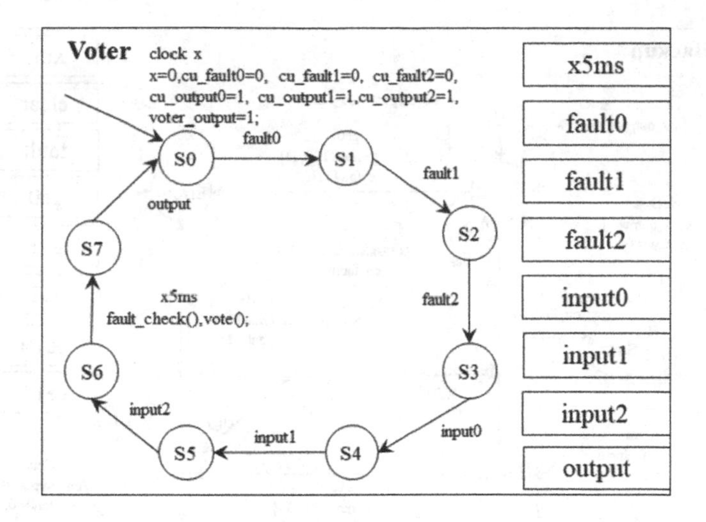

Fig. 6. A SBIP model of TMR's Voter

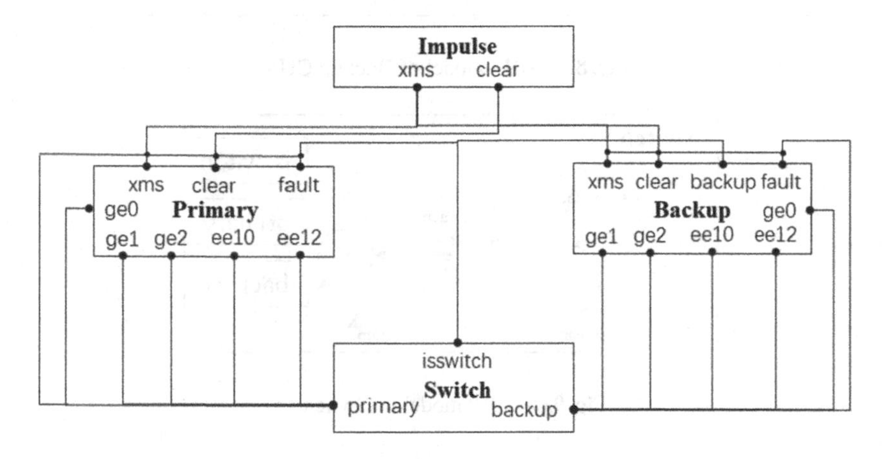

Fig. 7. Cold Standby model

the detailed BLTL specification of the Triple Modular Redundancy model, and the ϕ_D represents the detailed BLTL specification of the dynamic redundancy model.

- For `Reliability`:

$$\phi_T(t) = 1 - \mathbf{F}[0,t]((cf_0 \wedge cf_1 \wedge cf_2) \vee (\overline{cf_0} \wedge cf_1 \wedge cf_2) \vee (cf_0 \wedge \overline{cf_1} \wedge cf_2) \vee (cf_0 \wedge cf_1 \wedge \overline{cf_2})) \quad (1)$$

$$\phi_D(t) = 1 - \mathbf{F}[0,t](cf_0 \wedge cf_1) \quad (2)$$

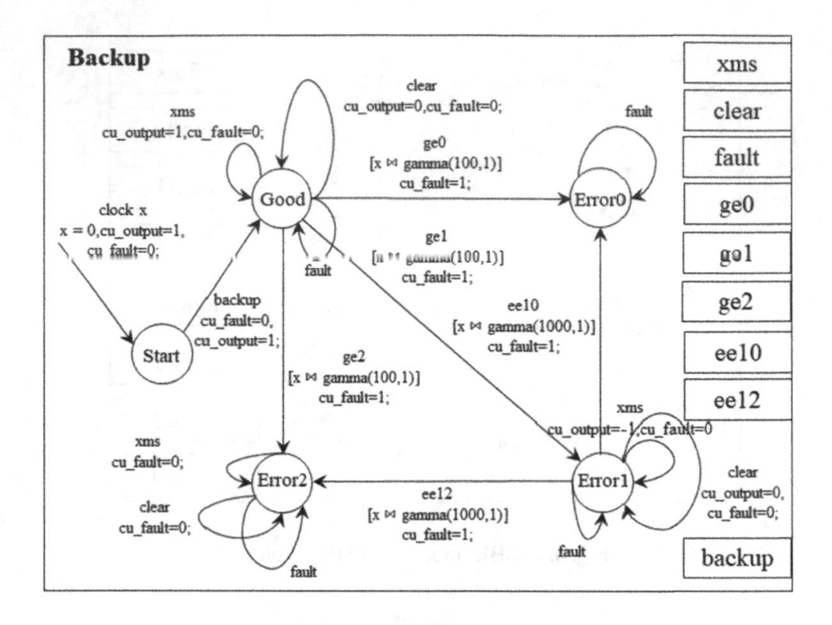

Fig. 8. A SBIP model of Backup CU

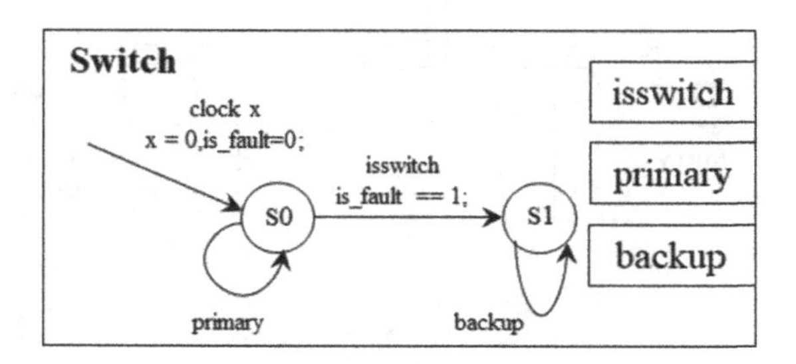

Fig. 9. A SBIP model of Switch

- For FIT:

$$\phi_T(t) = \frac{1}{lifetime}(1 - \mathbf{F}[0, lifetime]((cf_0 \wedge cf_1 \wedge cf_2) \vee(\overline{cf_0} \wedge cf_1 \wedge cf_2) \vee (cf_0 \wedge \overline{cf_1} \wedge cf_2) \vee (cf_0 \wedge cf_1 \wedge \overline{cf_2}))) \tag{3}$$

$$\phi_D(t) =) = \frac{1}{lifetime}(1 - \mathbf{F}[0, lifetime](cf_0 \wedge cf_1)) \tag{4}$$

- For DA:

$$\phi_T(t) = \mathbf{F}[0, t]((\overline{cf_0} \wedge \overline{cf_1} \wedge cf_2) \vee (\overline{cf_0} \wedge cf_1 \wedge \overline{cf_2}) \vee(cf_0 \wedge \overline{cf_1} \wedge \overline{cf_2})) \tag{5}$$

$$\phi_D(t) = \mathbf{F}[0, t](cf_0 \wedge \overline{cf_1}) \tag{6}$$

Table 1. Definition of measures

	Measure	Model checking queries
System	Reliability	$1 - P(\mathbf{F}^t\ \texttt{failed})$
	FIT	$\frac{1}{lifetime} \cdot (1 - P(\mathbf{F}^{lifetime}\ \texttt{failed}))$
Degradation	DA	$P(\mathbf{F}^t\ \texttt{degraded})$
	FFA	$1 - P(\mathbf{F}^t\ (\texttt{failed} \vee \texttt{degraded}))$

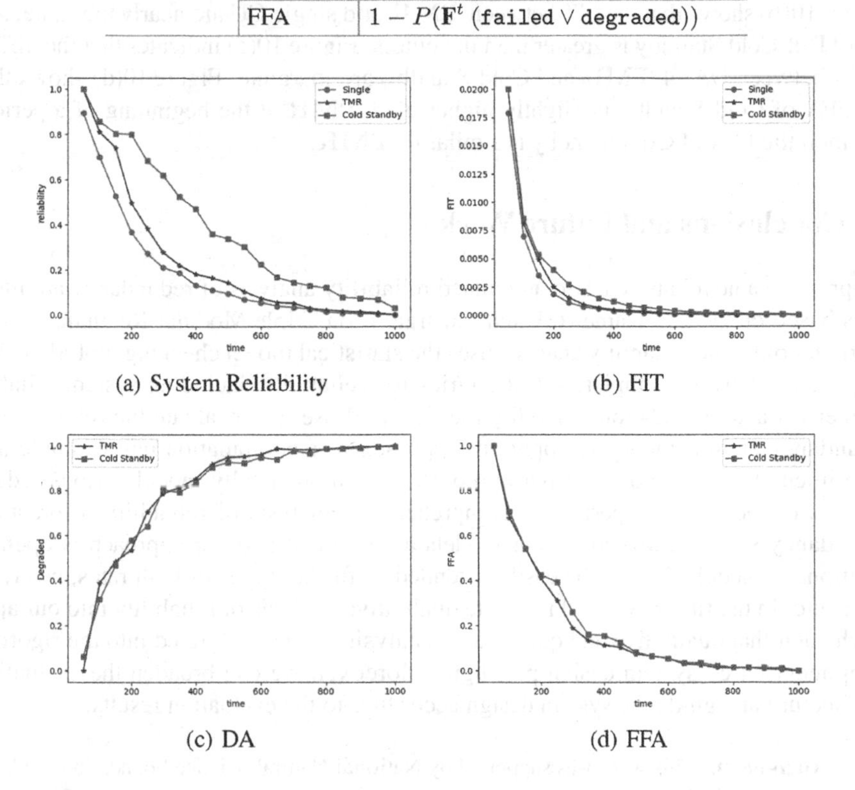

(a) System Reliability

(b) FIT

(c) DA

(d) FFA

Fig. 10. Results of experimental evaluations using statistical model checking

- For FFA:

$$\begin{aligned} \phi_T(t) = 1 - \mathbf{F}[0,t]((cf_0 \wedge cf_1 \wedge cf_2) \vee (\overline{cf_0} \wedge cf_1 \wedge cf_2) \\ \vee(cf_0 \wedge \overline{cf_1} \wedge cf_2) \vee (cf_0 \wedge cf_1 \wedge \overline{cf_2}) \vee (\overline{cf_0} \wedge \overline{cf_1} \wedge cf_2) \\ \vee(\overline{cf_0} \wedge cf_1 \wedge \overline{cf_2}) \vee (cf_0 \wedge \overline{cf_1} \wedge \overline{cf_2})) \end{aligned} \quad (7)$$

$$\phi_D(t) = 1 - \mathbf{F}[0,t]((cf_0 \wedge cf_1) \vee (cf_0 \wedge \overline{cf_1})) \quad (8)$$

In the experimental evaluations, probability estimation algorithm is utilized. It enables to compute the probability p for S to satisfy ϕ. Give a *precision* δ, this algorithm computes a value for p' such that $|p' - p| \leq \delta$ with confidence $1 - \alpha$. We use probability estimation with (α = 0.2, δ = 0.2) for all the analyses and rely on the parametric exploration to analyze specifications ϕ_T(t) and ϕ_D(t).

Figure 10(a) shows a comparison of the reliability of a single CU, **TMR**, and Cold Standby model. The x-axis represents the time steps and the y-axis represents the probability of property. We observe that **TMR** is slightly more reliable than single CU and Cold Standby is more reliable than single CU and **TMR**. Because three CUs in **TMR** are executed concurrently and the backup CU is activated after the primary CU is faulty, the reliability of Cold Standby is higher at the beginning of a period. The result of Fig. 10(b) shows that the FIT between **TMR** and single CU are nearly the same, and the FIT of Cold Standby is greater than the others. Figure 10(c) indicates that the differences between DA of **TMR** and Cold Standby are marginal. Figure 10(d) shows that the FFA of Cold Standby is Slightly higher than **TMR** at the beginning of a period, and then the FFA of Cold Standby is similar to **TMR**.

4 Conclusions and Future Work

We propose a novel approach to automated reliability analysis of redundancy architectures based on the BIP framework and illustrate it on Triple Modular Redundancy and Cold Standby. The reliability analysis uses the statistical model checking tool SBIP. We propose a relatively complete set of metrics for reliability, including system reliability metrics and degradation reliability metrics, and use it to evaluate the reliability of redundancy architectures. We apply our approach to a computation unit example and experimental results show that our approach can automatically model various redundancy architectures and perform a comprehensive analysis of reliability in practical redundancy systems. Moreover, our models are scalable and our approach is open to additional - models that can be easily extended to further types of fault rates, behavior types, etc. In the future, we will integrate qualitative analysis of reliability into our approach such that qualitative and quantitative analysis can be integrated into the rigorous component-based system design paradigm. Moreover, we can broaden the evaluation architecture and guide the system design according to the evaluation results.

Acknowledgment. This work was supported by National Natural Science Foundation of China (Grant No. 62106150).

References

1. Abdellatif, T., Bensalem, S., Combaz, J., De Silva, L., Ingrand, F.: Rigorous design of robot software: a formal component-based approach. Robot. Auton. Syst. **60**(12), 1563–1578 (2012)
2. Avizienis, A., Laprie, J.C., Randell, B., Landwehr, C.: Basic concepts and taxonomy of dependable and secure computing. IEEE Trans. Dependable Secure Comput. **1**(1), 11–33 (2004)
3. Basu, A., et al.: Rigorous component-based system design using the BIP framework. IEEE Softw. **28**(3), 41–48 (2011)
4. Basu, A., Bensalem, S., Bozga, M., Bourgos, P., Sifakis, J.: Rigorous system design: the BIP approach. In: Kotásek, Z., Bouda, J., Černá, I., Sekanina, L., Vojnar, T., Antoš, D. (eds.) MEMICS 2011. LNCS, vol. 7119, pp. 1–19. Springer, Heidelberg (2012). https://doi.org/10.1007/978-3-642-25929-6_1

5. Bensalem, S., Bozga, M., Nguyen, T., Sifakis, J.: Compositional verification for component-based systems and application. IET Softw. **4**(3), 181–193 (2010)
6. Bieber, P., Bougnol, C., Castel, C., Christophe Kehren, J.-P.H., Metge, S., Seguin, C.: Safety assessment with Altarica. In: Jacquart, R. (ed.) Building the Information Society. IIFIP, vol. 156, pp. 505–510. Springer, Boston, MA (2004). https://doi.org/10.1007/978-1-4020-8157-6_45
7. Bliudze, S., et al.: Formal verification of infinite-state BIP models. In: Finkbeiner, B., Pu, G., Zhang, L. (eds.) ATVA 2015. LNCS, vol. 9364, pp. 326–343. Springer, Cham (2015). https://doi.org/10.1007/978-3-319-24953-7_25
8. Bozzano, M., Bruintjes, H., Cimatti, A., Katoen, J.-P., Noll, T., Tonetta, S.: COMPASS 3.0. In: Vojnar, T., Zhang, L. (eds.) TACAS 2019. LNCS, vol. 11427, pp. 379–385. Springer, Cham (2019). https://doi.org/10.1007/978-3-030-17462-0_25
9. Bozzano, M., Cimatti, A., Mattarei, C.: Efficient analysis of reliability architectures via predicate abstraction. In: Bertacco, V., Legay, A. (eds.) HVC 2013. LNCS, vol. 8244, pp. 279–294. Springer, Cham (2013). https://doi.org/10.1007/978-3-319-03077-7_19
10. Bozzano, M., Cimatti, A., Mattarei, C.: Formal reliability analysis of redundancy architectures. Formal Aspects Comput. **31**(1), 59–94 (2019). https://doi.org/10.1007/s00165-018-0475-1
11. Bozzano, M., Villafiorita, A.: Improving system reliability via model checking: the FSAP/NuSMV-SA safety analysis platform. In: Anderson, S., Felici, M., Littlewood, B. (eds.) SAFECOMP 2003. LNCS, vol. 2788, pp. 49–62. Springer, Heidelberg (2003). https://doi.org/10.1007/978-3-540-39878-3_5
12. Bozzano, M., Villafiorita, A.: The FSAP/NuSMV-SA safety analysis platform. Int. J. Softw. Tools Technol. Transf. **9**(1), 5–24 (2007). https://doi.org/10.1007/s10009-006-0001-2
13. Dragomir, I., Bensalem, S.: Rigorous design of FDIR systems with BIP. Electron. Commun. Eur. Assoc. Softw. Sci. Technol. (ECEASST) **77** (2019). https://doi.org/10.14279/tuj.eceasst.77.1107, https://researchr.org/publication/DragomirB19
14. Ghadhab, M., Junges, S., Katoen, J.P., Kuntz, M., Volk, M.: Safety analysis for vehicle guidance systems with dynamic fault trees. Reliab. Eng. Syst. Saf. **186**, 37–50 (2019)
15. Hamamatsu, M., Tsuchiya, T., Kikuno, T.: On the reliability of cascaded TMR systems. In: 2010 IEEE 16th Pacific Rim International Symposium on Dependable Computing, pp. 184–190 (2010)
16. Hiraoka, Y., Murakami, T., Yamamoto, K., Furukawa, Y., Sawada, H.: Method of computer-aided fault tree analysis for high-reliable and safety design. IEEE Trans. Reliab. **65**(2), 687–703 (2016)
17. Konnov, I., Kotek, T., Wang, Q., Veith, H., Bliudze, S., Sifakis, J.: Parameterized systems in BIP: design and model checking. In: Proceedings of the 27th International Conference on Concurrency Theory (CONCUR 2016), p. 30-1. Schloss Dagstuhl-Leibniz-Zentrum fuer Informatik (2016)
18. Laprie, J.: Dependable computing and fault tolerance: concepts and terminology. In: Twenty-Fifth International Symposium on Fault-Tolerant Computing 1995, 'Highlights from Twenty-Five Years', p. 2 (1995)
19. Lekidis, A., Stachtiari, E., Katsaros, P., Bozga, M., Georgiadis, C.K.: Model-based design of IoT systems with the BIP component framework. Softw. Pract. Exp. **48**(6), 1167–1194 (2018)
20. Li, Y., Song, Y., Jia, L., Gao, S., Li, Q., Qiu, M.: Intelligent fault diagnosis by fusing domain adversarial training and maximum mean discrepancy via ensemble learning. IEEE Trans. Ind. Inf. **17**(4), 2833–2841 (2021)
21. Lu, K.L., Chen, Y.Y.: Model-based design, analysis and assessment framework for safety-critical systems, Virtual, Taipei, Taiwan, pp. 25–26 (2021)

22. Mediouni, B.L., Nouri, A., Bozga, M., Dellabani, M., Legay, A., Bensalem, S.: $\mathcal{S}$BIP 2.0: statistical model checking stochastic real-time systems. In: Lahiri, S.K., Wang, C. (eds.) ATVA 2018. LNCS, vol. 11138, pp. 536–542. Springer, Cham (2018). https://doi.org/10.1007/978-3-030-01090-4_33
23. Schnellbach, A.: Fail-operational automotive systems. Ph.D. thesis, Graz University of Technology (2016)
24. Sifakis, J.: System design automation: challenges and limitations. Proc. IEEE **103**(11), 2093–2103 (2015)
25. Zhang, M., Liu, Z., Morisset, C., Ravn, A.P.: Design and verification of fault-tolerant components. In: Butler, M., Jones, C., Romanovsky, A., Troubitsyna, E. (eds.) Methods, Models and Tools for Fault Tolerance. LNCS, vol. 5454, pp. 57–84. Springer, Heidelberg (2009). https://doi.org/10.1007/978-3-642-00867-2_4

Research on Fabric Defect Detection Technology Based on EDSR and Improved Faster RCNN

Li Yao, Naigang Zhang, Ao Gao, and Yan Wan(✉)

School of Computer Science and Technology, Donghua University, Shanghai, China
{yaoli,winniewan}@dhu.edu.cn

Abstract. In order to solve the problems of various kinds of defects, defect ratio varies greatly, imbalanced defect aspect ratio and high integration degree with background in fabric defect detection, a method combining super-resolution reconstruction technology and deep learning detection was proposed. Firstly, the enhanced deep residual networks for single image super-resolution is used to enrich the defect feature information, reduce the fusion degree of defect and background texture, and enhance the extraction ability of various defect features. Then, the defect features are analyzed according to K-means clustering algorithm. Based on the three default anchor frame ratios provided by Faster RCNN, six new types of anchor ratios are added. Then, FPN module and DCNv2 module were introduced in Faster RCNN to improve the ability to identify defects with different areas and shapes. Finally, the pooling mode of ROI layer was modified to eliminate the error caused by quantization operation. The results of the three kinds of comparative experiments show that the method based on EDSR and improved Faster RCNN has a better overall recognition rate for multiple kinds of fabric defects than other current methods, and can be used in the production and operation of textile enterprises.

Keywords: Fabric defect detection · EDSR · Faster RCNN

1 Introduction

Fabric defect detection is an important part of improving product quality and reducing product cost in textile enterprises. Some common defects (as shown in Fig. 1 below) are elongated and have a high degree of integration between defects and background. So it will not only affect the appearance and wearing comfort of cloth, but also lead to an average reduction of 45%–65% of the price of cloth [1]. However, the current manual detection method used by enterprises has problems such as fatigue of workers, high cost, slow speed, missed detection, false detection. Therefore, it is very necessary to study automatic and accurate detection methods.

At present, automatic fabric defect detection methods can be divided into two categories. The first type is based on traditional machine learning technology, mainly using statistical analysis, spectrum and model-based methods. The second category is the method based on deep learning.

G. Memmi et al. (Eds.): KSEM 2022, LNAI 13370, pp. 477–488, 2022.
https://doi.org/10.1007/978-3-031-10989-8_38

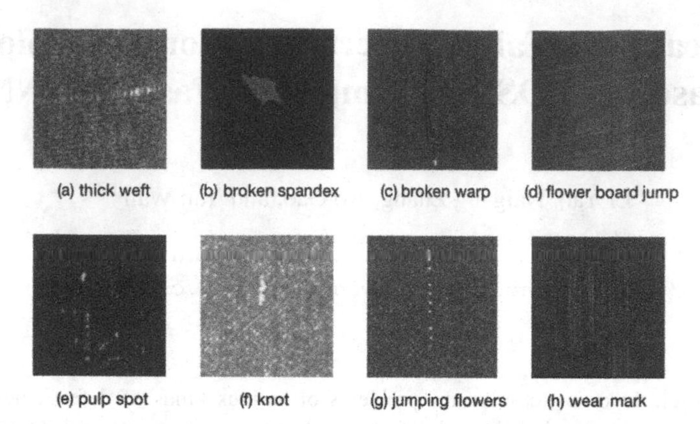

Fig. 1. Figure of some enlarged defects

Among the methods based on statistical analysis, Banumathi proposed a method based on gray level co-occurrence matrix combined with artificial neural network to detect six kinds of defects [2]. Sourav Tola et al. used Haralick parameters related from distance and direction and sparse autoencoder with appropriate sparsity for detection [3]. The biggest problem of the method based on statistical analysis is that the defects need to be large enough.

In the method based on spectrum, Gabor filter has good locality in both spatial domain and frequency domain. Tang et al. proposed a method combining Gabor filter and Histogram of Oriented Gradient (HOG), which used HOG to eliminate the influence of background texture and noise on defect detection [4]. Tong et al. used compound differential evolution to optimize the parameters of Gabor filter and realized feature extraction of fabric defects [5]. However, the detection performance of the spectral based method depends on the selection of filter, which requires large manual intervention and is not strong generalization.

In the model-based approach, the commonly used strategy is Gaussian Markov random field (GMRF). Xu et al. proposed a model based on GMRF, which can obtain the parameter distribution of GMRF model from defect-free fabric image for subsequent defect detection [6]. However, this methods also require a large enough texture region.

Among the method based on deep learning, Wang et al. proposed an RFB model to fuse shallow features and then extract features through the attention mechanism module [7]. Xie analyzed the influence of YOLOv3 using different backbone networks on the detection efficiency and accuracy of defects [8]. In addition, Liu et al. detected defective fabric through SSD network and had a good effect on small defect detection [9]. Wei et al. used VGG16 as the backbone network to complete the detection of four defects by reducing the number of anchor and the complexity of the model [10]. By adding feature fusion network and deformable convolution into Cascade RCNN, An achieved the detection of 20 defects [11]. Although the detection accuracy of these method have been improved, it is still difficult to detect defects with high integration degree with the background, such as hundred feet, which often plays a crucial role in the quality assurance of modern fabric defects detection.

All of the above methods failed to put forward general solutions to the problems of multiple types of defects, high coincidence degree with background, large difference in proportion area and extreme aspect ratio. Therefore, this paper proposes a method combining EDSR [12] and improved Faster RCNN. First, the EDSR network is used to reconstruct the image, extract the overall features of flaws and reduce the influence of background texture. Then, the reconstructed image is input into the detection network for defect classification. The detection network is based on Faster RCNN. FPN module [13] is introduced to deal with defects with small proportion area, DCNv2 module [14] is introduced to deal with defects with extreme aspect ratio. In the RPN module, K-means clustering algorithm is used to set the ratio of anchor. In the ROI module, ROIPooling is replaced by ROIAlign [15] to eliminate the errors caused by the two quantization operations. Finally, the obtained feature images were sent to the full connection layer for defect regression and classification. Subsequently, this paper studies 20 kinds of defects that have a great impact on fabric quality in the production process of enterprises, and verifies the accuracy of the model by setting three kinds of comparative experiments. The results show that the proposed method achieves an average detection accuracy of 85.0%, and the overall recognition rate is significantly higher than other methods, which can be put into production.

2 Model Structure Based on EDSR and Improved Faster RCNN

Based on the above analysis, this paper proposes a detection method combining EDSR and improved Faster RCNN, as shown in Fig. 2 below.

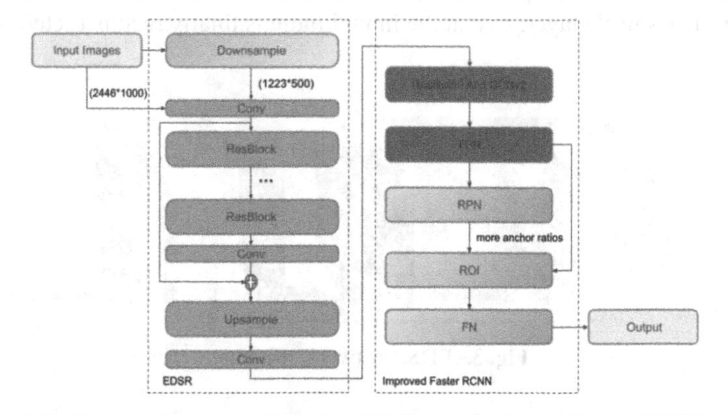

Fig. 2. Model structure based on EDSR and improved Faster RCNN

First, a $2\times$ downsampling is performed on the input image to obtain a low resolution data set, and then the image is fed into the EDSR network. Then defect types were classified and identified based on Faster RCNN. The basic characteristics of flaws were analyzed by clustering to find out the similarity of each flaw type in size, so as to improve the anchor frame ratio of the original Faster RCNN. FPN module can effectively improve the multi-scale capability of the network, and DCNv2 module can enable the network to independently learn the size of deformable convolution kernel. By introducing the above two modules into the Faster RCNN network, the network's ability to identify small flaws and defects with misadjusted aspect ratio can be enhanced. Considering that ROIPooling is used in the ROI module of the original Faster RCNN network, which adopts double quantization rounding, affecting the accuracy of the final classification, this paper improves it into ROIAlign to increase the accuracy of the final classification by replacing the rounding operation and finally completing the defect detection.

2.1 EDSR Network

Super resolution (SR) technology refers to the technology of reconstructing corresponding high resolution (HR) images from low resolution (LR) images. Among them, the enhanced Deep Super Resolution Network (EDSR) was the champion solution in the NTIRE2017 Super Resolution Challenge. As shown in Fig. 3 below, EDSR mainly includes ResBlock module and Upsample module. The ResBlock module is used to learn the mapping between LR and HR. Considering that the information of LR and HR is similar, ResBlock no need to learn the high-frequency information in LR and HR, but only learn the difference between them. ResBlock consists of convolution layer (Conv), activation layer (Relu), and residual-scaling layer (Mult). The Conv layer and Relu layer are mainly used to extract image features and increase the non-linear transformation capability. The Mult layer multiplies the convolution processed data by the scaling number before adding residual blocks, so as to prevent too many ResBlocks from leading to unstable training. Upsample module is used to enlarge image pixels, including Conv layer and Shuffle layer. In the Conv layer, the channels of the input feature graph are doubled, and then feature maps of the two channels are inserted into each other to double the size through Shuffle layer, so that the input image is finally reconstructed with super resolution.

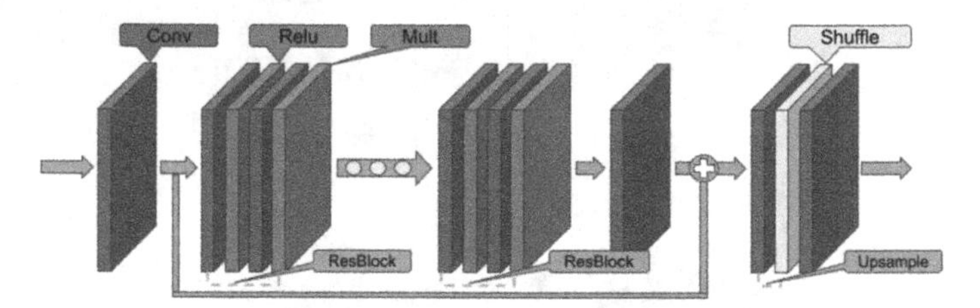

Fig. 3. EDSR network structure

Peak Signal to Noise Ratio (PSNR) is an important evaluation index of EDSR reconstruction effect. The key point of using EDSR network to improve the accuracy of defect detection is to reduce noise and improve PSNR. Considering the complexity of defects, the PSNR threshold is set at 43.27 in this paper to ensure that the image reconstructed by EDSR has enough clear defects in less time. After the PSNR threshold is reached, the reconstructed image is obtained and sent to the deep learning detection network for defect recognition and detection. At the same time, the model proposed in this paper will add a sub-sampling module before EDSR, which will acquire LR images corresponding to data sets through Bicubic algorithm, and then transform LR images and original data sets into DIV2K data sets by changing image names, so as to facilitate training in EDSR network.

2.2 Initial Network of Faster RCNN

Faster RCNN proposed in 2016 is a typical representative of the two-stage detection model. It puts target classification and location in the same network model.Schematic diagram of the Faster RCNN network structure model is shown in Fig. 4.

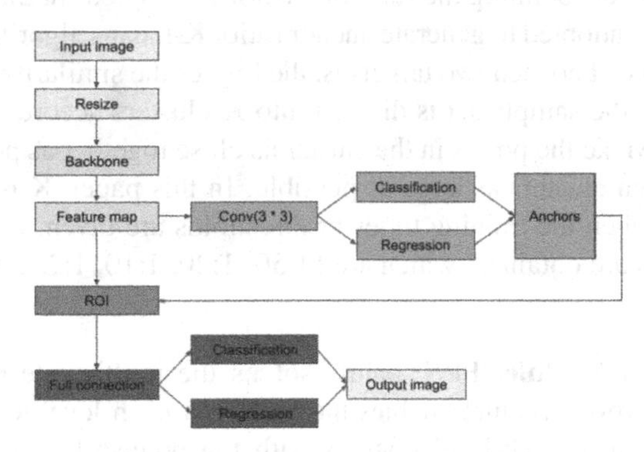

Fig. 4. Schematic diagram of Faster RCNN network

First, all images entered into the network are adjusted in length and width. Then the feature extraction network carries out feature extraction on the input image. Faster RCNN uses VGG16 as the trunk feature extraction network. Although simple, its detection accuracy is too low, and it has problems of gradient disappearance and gradient explosion. In recent years, Faster RCNN uses ResNet50 as a feature extraction network. ResNet50 introduces residual wiring and Batch Normalization while increasing the number of network layers to address poor detection accuracy and gradient-related issues. The final feature map is then fed into the Region Proposal Network (RPN). RPN first carries out 3×3 convolution for the input feature graph, and then carries out two 1×1 convolution. The obtained results are respectively classified and predicted by regression. Softmax function and linear regression are used for coordinate adjustment during classification, and then the sliding window mechanism is used to generate candidate boxes to extract feature information. The main process of sliding window is to use a 3×3 convolution kernel to slide on the feature graph. During each sliding process of the convolution kernel, each center point of the sliding window will generate 9 anchors, namely candidate boxes. The candidate box has three scales $\{1{:}1, 1{:}2, 2{:}1\}$ and three scales $\{128^2, 256^2, 512^2\}$. Finally, As the size of candidate boxes is not uniform, the prospective suggestion boxes judged by RPN will be sent into the ROI Pooling layer for adjustment, and then intercepted on the shared feature map, and then predicted through classification prediction and regression prediction network.

2.3 Improved Faster RCNN

In this paper, four main improvements are made to Faster RCNN, namely, resetting the anchor ratio, introducing FPN module and DCNv2 module, and adjusting ROIAlign to ROIPooling.

Adjust Anchor Frame Proportion. The original Faster RCNN anchors have a total of nine styles. However, these patterns are obtained from standard VOC datasets and are not applicable to the fabric defect detection data set in this paper. Considering the different shapes of defects, large differences in length-width ratio and large variation in proportion area, the method of self-defining the ratio of anchor is adopted. In this paper, K-means clustering method is adopted to generate anchor ratio. K-means algorithm considers that the closer the distance between two targets is, the higher the similarity is. Therefore, for a given sample set, the sample set is divided into K clusters according to the distance between samples. Make the points in the cluster as close together as possible, and make the distance between clusters as large as possible. In this paper, K is set as 9, and the training will stop when the training times or thresholds are given. Finally, a total of 9 anchor frame ratios are obtained, which are {1:50, 1:20, 1:10, 1:2, 1:1, 2:1, 10:1, 20:1, 50:1} respectively.

Introduce the FPN Module. FPN mainly solves the multi-scale problem in target detection. This network structure enables the output of each level to combine the rich semantic information of high-level features with the precise location information of low-level features, so the model can detect objects of different sizes and scales, and the pyramid feature graph at the bottom can better detect small defects. In this paper, FPN is placed after ResNet50. It consists of three paths: bottom-up, top-down, and lateral connections. Figure 5 shows the implementation of FPN. In bottom-up path, the scaling multiple of the last four residual blocks generated by the previous network relative to the original image is {4, 8, 16, 32}, and the 32-fold feature graph is obtained by 1 * 1 convolution. In the top-down path, M4, M3, M2 and M1 are successively obtained by M5 through 2 times up-sampling (using Nearest Neighbor algorithm). In lateral connections, 1 * 1 convolution operation is performed on C5 first to change the channel number to 256D, and then the corresponding positions of C5 and M5 are combined to fuse features. Finally, P5 is obtained by 3 * 3 convolution to reduce the alibration effect caused by the Nearest Neighbor algorithm. In turn, feature maps P4, P3 and P2 of different scales after fusion are obtained, which all contain rich multi-scale feature information of defects.

Introduce the DCNv2 Module. In Faster RCNN backbone network, the convolution operation every time just for computing the pixels and the pixels around (the number depends on the size of the convolution kernels, the shape of rectangular) convolution operation, mainly including sampling and weighted sum of two steps, used by the formula below formula 1, which R is the size of the receptive field, p_n is all pixels in R, w is the weight, p_0 is each position of the input to x, and y is the output.

$$y(p_0) = \sum_{p_0 \in R} w(p_n) \cdot x(p_0 + p_n) \tag{1}$$

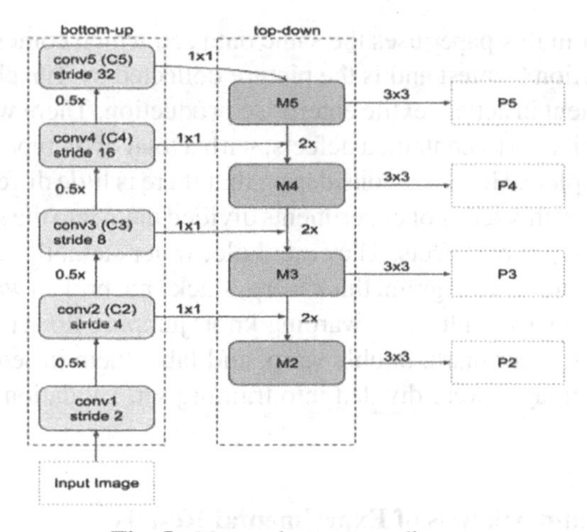

Fig. 5. Network structure diagram

As can be seen from Formula (1), no matter how deep the network is, the receptive field is always rectangular and of fixed size, which cannot adapt to the characteristic of special shape of defects. In particular, traditional convolution operation cannot achieve a good detection effect for defects with extremely mismatched aspect ratios such as thick warp, slack end and thin and dense paths. Therefore, in this paper, deformable convolutional network is introduced into Faster RCNN, see Formula (2) below. DCNv2 enhances the dynamic sampling capability of the module by using additional offset (Δ_{p_k}), which can dynamically learn the size of the convolution kernel and better adapt to the irregular shape of defects.

$$y(p) = \sum_{k=1}^{K} w_k \cdot x\left(p + p_k + \Delta_{p_k}\right) \cdot \Delta_{m_k} \tag{2}$$

Adjust the ROI Layer Pooling Method. In ROI module, ROIPooling is improved to ROIAlign. This is because in the process of ROI pooling, there will be two quantization and round operations, which are respectively to map the original area marked by candidate boxes to the feature graph and then divide the feature graph with a size of 7 × 7 from the feature graph for subsequent full connection. Two round operation will bring slight network deviation, ROIAlign can eliminate the deviation caused by quantization round through bilinear interpolation.

3 Experiments and Results

3.1 Experimental Setting and Datasets

The experimental environment of this paper is unified. All experiments were based on Ubuntu20.04 LTS operating system with 32 GB memory, two RTX 2080Ti graphics cards, MMDetection deep learning framework, PyTorch 1.8 and Python 3.7. The learning rate of all experiments was set to 0.0025, and each experiment was trained for 24 epochs.

The experiment in this paper uses the same data set, which comes from Ali Tianchi Fabric defect Detection Contest and is the picture collected by Tianchi and Guangdong Provincial government in actual textile enterprise production. There were a total of 9576 samples, among which 5913 contained defects, with a total of 34 types of defects, which were relatively complete. However, considering that there is little difference between the types of some defects, this series of experiments divided them into the same category, and finally obtained 20 types of defects. They are: hole, water stain, three silk, knot, flower board jump, hundred feet, wool grain, thick warp, slack end, broken warp, hanging warp, thick weft, weft shrinkage, pulp spot, warping knot, jumping flowers, broken spandex, thin and dense paths, wear mark, double warp, and label them in sequence as 1–20. In addition, all defect images were divided into training set, validation set and test set in 8:1:1 ratio.

3.2 Comparison and Analysis of Experimental Results

Experimental Results and Analysis Before and After Improvement of Faster RCNN. The first type of experiment is mainly to verify the improvement of detection effect by different improvement points of Faster RCNN. There are four groups of experiments, which respectively train the original Faster RCNN model, the Faster RCNN model integrating FPN, the Faster RCNN model integrating FPN and re-setting anchor for defects, and the DCNv2 integrated Faster RCNN model. Finally, the experimental model is used to verify the test set. Table 1 below shows the final results.

Table 1. Results of Experiment 1

Object detection algorithm	mAP@[IoU = 0.5]
(a) Faster RCNN baseline	41.2%
(b) Faster RCNN + FPN	45.3%
(c) Faster RCNN + FPN + Anchor ratio setting	59.0%
(d) Improved Faster RCNN proposed in this paper	64.2%

In Fig. 6, the pictures labeled (a), (b), (c) and (d) are generated by the model labeled in Table 1 above. It can be seen from the figure that before and after FPN fusion, the knot recognition rate of the model has been greatly improved, but the subsequent improvement of the anchor frame proportion and the newly added DCNv2 do not greatly improve the detection accuracy, because the original anchor ratios has been able to adapt to the changes of knot defects.

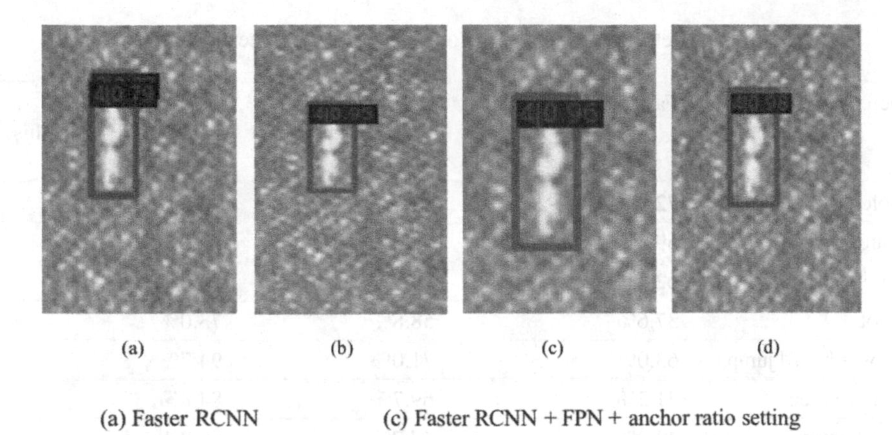

(a) Faster RCNN (c) Faster RCNN + FPN + anchor ratio setting
(b) Faster RCNN + FPN (d) Improved Faster RCNN proposed in this paper

Fig. 6. Test results of knot defect detection using each model

The results of the first type of experiment show that the improved model can improve the detection accuracy of small and slender defects. However, due to its high degree of integration with the background, the detection accuracy of defects such as thin and dense paths is only 45.8%, which proves that it is not enough to rely only on the improvement of Faster RCNN. Therefore, this paper continues to verify EDSR's detection of defects.

Experimental Results and Analysis Before and After Introducing EDSR Network. In order to improve the recognition rate of the whole defect and the defect with higher impurity with the background texture, an EDSR module was added to the above model to conduct the second type of experiment. Table 2 shows the experimental results.

Table 2. Results of Experiment 2

Object detection algorithm	mAP@[IoU = 0.5]
Improved faster RCNN proposed in this paper	64.2%
Improved faster RCNN + EDSR proposed in this paper	85.0

Table 3 makes statistics on the increase and decrease of detection rate of each type of defects, and Fig. 7 shows the test results of thin and dense paths.

As can be seen from the above two tables, the detection ability of all categories has been improved after the introduction of EDSR module. Among them, broken warp, weft shrinkage and thin and dense paths have been greatly improved after the application of EDSR because the defects are slender and have a high degree of integration with the background.

Table 3. Detection results of various defects in the three algorithms

Defect	Faster RCNN baseline	Improved Faster RCNN (this paper)	Improved Faster RCNN + EDSR (this paper)
Hole	72.9%	93.5%	93.6%
Water stains	59.5%	58.4%	88.0%
Three silks	62.3%	73.9%	91.0%
Knot	37.6%	58.8%	73.0%
Flower board jump	63.0%	71.0%	94.7%
Hundred feet	31.2%	69.7%	84.8%
Wool grain	42.9%	47.7%	60.8%
Thick warp	0%	84.8%	94.8%
Slack end	31.5%	68.8%	93.6%
Broken warp	40.5%	51.3%	88.3%
Hanging warp	13.1%	52.1%	87.7%
Thick weft	50.2%	66.2%	80.6%
Weft shrinkage	31.5%	37.9%	65.9%
Pulp spot	57.7%	79.5%	95.9%
Warping knot	65.2%	70.2%	89.7%
Jumping flowers	38.8%	79.0%	94.9%
Broken spandex	57.3%	60.0%	66.5%
Thin and dense paths	6.7%	45.8%	72.1%
Wear mark	38.9%	56.2%	92.6%
Double warps	24.1%	59.2%	90.4%

Fig. 7. Test results of thin and dense paths

Figure 7 above shows the detection results of thin and dense paths. (c) shows the test results of the final model after incorporating EDSR. It can be seen from the naked eye that the defect characteristics of fine files are significantly strengthened.

Compare the Experimental Results and Analysis of Other Methods. Cascade RCNN is also a common model in two-stage detection network, while Yolo is a common model in one-stage detection network. In order to compare the difference between the algorithm and other algorithms, Cascade RCNN is used in this paper to set up 6 groups of comparison experiments. The backbone network of Cascade RCNN uses ResNet50 and ResNetX101 respectively. Table 4 shows the final result.

Table 4. Results of Experiment 3

Object detection algorithm	mAP@[IoU = 0.5]
Cascade RCNN (ResNet50) + FPN	52.4%
Cascade RCNN (ResNet50) + FPN + anchor setting	64.2%
Cascade RCNN (ResNet50) + FPN + anchor setting + DCNv2	66%
Improved Cascade RCNN (ResNet50) + EDSR	67.4%
Cascade RCNN (ResNetX101) FPN	57.9%
Cascade RCNN (ResNetX101) + FPN + anchor setting	68.7%
Cascade RCNN (ResNetX101) + FPN + anchor setting + DCNv2	68.2%
Improved Cascade RCNN (ResNetX101) + EDSR	69.6%
Yolov3 [8]	32.54%
EDSR + Improved Faster RCNN (this paper)	84.9%

Experimental results show that the proposed algorithm based on EDSR and improved Faster RCNN has obvious advantages over networks such as Cascade RCNN and Yolov3 in detecting multiple kinds of defects.

4 Conclusion

This paper mainly made relevant improvements based on EDSR and Faster RCNN. Firstly, the EDSR module is introduced to reconstruct the super-resolution image, and the defect and background information are separated. Then, FPN and DCNv2 network modules are integrated based on Faster RCNN, and the ratio of anchor is reset by K-means, and the network accuracy of ROIAlign is increased by replacing ROIPooling, so as to deal with the problem of large difference in defect area and extreme aspect ratio of defects. In order to verify the usability and precision of the model, three kinds of comparison experiments were conducted on 5913 high-resolution images. The final experiment proves that the proposed method can effectively improve the accuracy of defect recognition compared with other current methods. However, the method in this paper still has some problems, such as unsatisfactory detection of defects such as wool grain and weft shrinkage, and slow detection due to the complicated network structure of the model, which need to be further improved in the future.

References

1. Stojanovic, R., Mitropulos, P., Koulamas, C., Karayiannis, Y., Koubias, S., Papadopoulos, G.: Real-time vision-based system for textile fabric inspection. Real-Time Imaging **7**, 507–518 (2001)
2. Banumathi, P., Nasira, G.M.: Artificial neural network techniques in identifying plain woven fabric defects. Res. J. Appl. Sci. Eng. Technol. **9**(4), 272–276 (2015)
3. Tola, S., Sarkar, S., Chandra, J.K., Sarkar, G.: Sparse auto-encoder improvised texture-based statistical feature estimation for the detection of defects in woven fabric. In: Chakraborty, M., Jha, R.K., Balas, V.E., Sur, S.N., Kandar, D. (eds.) Trends in Wireless Communication and Information Security. LNEE, vol. 740, pp. 143–151. Springer, Singapore (2021). https://doi.org/10.1007/978-981-33-6393-9_16
4. Tang, X., Huang, K., Qin, Y.: Fabric defect detection based on Gabor Filter and HOG. Comput. Measur. Control **26**(9), 39–42 (2018)
5. Tong, L., Wong, W.K., Kwong, C.K.: Differential evolution-based optimal Gabor filter model for fabric inspection. Neurocomputing **173**, 1386–1401 (2016)
6. Xu, Y., Meng, F., Wang, L.: Fabric surface defect detection based on GMRF Model. In: International Conference on Artificial Intelligence and Information Systems, pp. 1–4 (2021)
7. Wang, Y., Hao, Z., Zuo, F., Su, Z.: Fabric defect target detection algorithm based on YOLOv4 improvement. In: Xing, C., Fu, X., Zhang, Y., Zhang, G., Borjigin, C. (eds.) WISA 2021. LNCS, vol. 12999, pp. 647–658. Springer, Cham (2021). https://doi.org/10.1007/978-3-030-87571-8_56
8. Xie, J., Wang, W., Liu, T.: Fabric surface defect detection based on YOLO v3 with different backbone networks. Measur. Control Technol. **40**(3), 61–66 (2021)
9. Liu, Z., Liu, S., Li, C., Ding, S., Dong, Y.: Fabric defects detection based on SSD. In: Proceedings of the 2nd International Conference on Graphics and Signal Processing, pp. 74–78 (2018)
10. Wei, B., Hao, K., Tang, X.-S., Ren, L.: Fabric defect detection based on faster RCNN. In: Wong, W.K. (ed.) AITA 2018. AISC, vol. 849, pp. 45–51. Springer, Cham (2019). https://doi.org/10.1007/978-3-319-99695-0_6
11. An, J., Tang, Y., Ma, X.: Defect detection algorithm of plain cloth based on deep neural network. Packag. Eng. **42**(3), 246–251 (2021)
12. Lim, B., Son, S., Kim, H., Nah, S., Mu Lee, K.: Enhanced deep residual networks for single image super-resolution. In: The IEEE Conference on Computer Vision and Pattern Recognition Workshops, pp. 136–144 (2017)
13. Lin, T.Y., Dollár, P., Girshick, R., He, K., Hariharan, B., Belongie, S.: Feature pyramid networks for object detection. In: Proceedings of the IEEE Conference on Computer Vision and Pattern Recognition, pp. 2117–2125 (2017)
14. Zhu, X., Hu, H., Lin, S., Dai, J.: Deformable ConvNets v2: more deformable, better results. In: Proceedings of the IEEE/CVF Conference on Computer Vision and Pattern Recognition, pp. 9308–9316 (2019)
15. Cai, Z., Vasconcelos, N.: Cascade R-CNN: delving into high quality object detection. In: Proceedings of the IEEE Conference on Computer Vision and Pattern Recognition, pp. 6154–6162 (2018)

GM-Attack: Improving the Transferability of Adversarial Attacks

Jinbang Hong[1,2], Keke Tang[3], Chao Gao[2], Songxin Wang[4], Sensen Guo[5], and Peican Zhu[2(✉)]

[1] School of Computer Science, Northwestern Polytechnical University, Xi'an 710072, China
[2] School of Artificial Intelligence, Optics, and Electronics (iOPEN), Northwestern Polytechnical University, Xi'an 710072, China
{cgao,ericcan}@nwpu.edu.cn
[3] Cyberspace Institute of Advanced Technology, Guangzhou University, Guangzhou 510006, China
[4] School of Information Management and Engineering, Shanghai University of Finance and Economics, Shanghai 200433, China
sxwang@mail.shufe.edu.cn
[5] School of Cybersecurity, Northwestern Polytechnical University, Xi'an 710072, China
guosensen@mail.nwpu.edu.cn

Abstract. In the real world, blackbox attacks seem to be widely existed due to the lack of detailed information of models to be attacked. Hence, it is desirable to obtain adversarial examples with high transferability which will facilitate practical adversarial attacks. Instead of adopting traditional input transformation approaches, we propose a mechanism to derive masked images through removing some regions from the initial input images. In this manuscript, the removed regions are spatially uniformly distributed squares. For comparison, several transferable attack methods are adopted as the baselines. Eventually, extensive empirical evaluations are conducted on the standard ImageNet dataset to validate the effectiveness of GM-Attack. As indicated, our GM-Attack can craft more transferable adversarial examples compared with other input transformation methods and attack success rate on Inc-v4 has been improved by 6.5% over state-of-the-art methods.

Keywords: Deep neural networks · Adversarial attack · Adversarial examples · Data augmentation · White-box/black-box attack · Transferability

1 Introduction

With the prosperous of modern technology, we have witnessed the impressive prosperous of vision-related tasks [5], including autonomous driving, image classification, and face recognition, particularly after the coming forth of deep neural

G. Memmi et al. (Eds.): KSEM 2022, LNAI 13370, pp. 489–500, 2022.
https://doi.org/10.1007/978-3-031-10989-8_39

networks (DNNs). Nevertheless, as reflected by recent studies, adversarial examples [1] can be crafted through incorporating carefully designed perturbations; with these examples, DNNs can be fooled easily. Thus, conceivable threats will be incurred to safety- and security-sensitive applications; numerous scholars devote their endless efforts to study adversarial attacks for DNN-based applications. Furthermore, for different neural network models, adversarial examples that are crafted on certain model might mislead others with a relatively high probability, being referred to as transferability [11]. Given adversarial examples with high transferabilities, it is feasible for hackers to attack practical DNN-based applications even if no information is collected regarding target model.

According to the extent of information obtained for the considered models, there mainly exists two types of adversarial attacking methods, i.e., white-box attack and black-box one. We are anticipated to possess complete knowledge regarding the target model for white-box attack, while corresponding attack performance through existing methods is nearly perfect; however, when facing target models with incomplete knowledge or unclear defense mechanisms, the attack performance is likely to be reduced by a large extent, i.e., corresponding adversarial examples are of weak transferability [6]. Usually, adversarial examples are crafted on white-box model with a single input; thus, the obtained adversarial examples may overfit the discriminative region of the white-box model. However, for models with different structures or defense mechanisms, corresponding discriminative regions are not identical, which increases the difficulty of attack these neural network models effectively with the obtained adversarial examples.

In practice, it is usually difficult or economic-cost to obtain the knowledge of the target model to be attacked; thus, it is highly preferable to improve the transferability of adversarial examples, especially facing practical scenarios. To solve this dilemma, a series of technologies have been developed by numerous scholars, which are mainly classified into three categories, being listed as gradient optimization [3,10], input transformations [4,15,17,18] and ensemble-model attacks [9,11]. Furthermore, scholars have also proposed some methods aiming to defend against adversarial attacks. Among these methods, adversarial training [21] is an effective method through incorporating adversarial examples into the training set during the train process. Input modification (such as denoising, image compression, random smoothing) can be incorporated to further improve the efficiency of defense methods.

As revealed by existed studies, the input transformation is effective in improving the transferability of adversarial examples while different input transformation approaches are widely adopted, such as randomly resizing and padding, translation, scale and etc. Through adopting these approaches, we can take the information from other categories into consideration which is beneficial to improve the probability of misleading DNNs to category the adversary into other categories. However, for majority of the existing input transformation methods, there exists a drawback, i.e., they are largely limited to conventional spatial transformation approaches. Inspired by recent development of data augmentation strategies (such as image blending, information removal [20]), we proposes a novel information deletion based attack method, that is **G**rid **M**ask-Attack (named as GM-Attack). The main idea of our proposed approach is given as: Firstly, we derive a set of images by removing some regions from the input images. The removed regions are a set of spatially uniformly distributed squares. Due to the lack of information, the model discriminates regions of these images which are different from the input ones. Then, we calculate the gradient of these pictures simultaneously, the obtained adversarial examples seem to be less correlated with the discriminative regions of the white-box model; thus, when attacking other black-box models, they are more transferable which indicates a better attacking performance. Contributions of our work are listed as:

- Instead of adopting traditional input transformation approaches, we propose a mechanism to derive masked images through removing some regions from the initial input images. Here, the removed regions are spatially uniformly distributed squares.
- To further obtain more transferable adversarial examples, our proposed method can be linearly integrated with existing works, i.e., DIM, TIM.
- Through conducting experiments on different classification models, our proposed model is proved to be superior compared with the studied SAT attacking methods.

The rest of the manuscript is organized as: Sect. 2 introduces some related works. The proposed GM-Attack approach is provided in Sect. 3 in detail. Later, we conduct extensive experiments and the analysis of obtained simulation results are also elucidated in Sect. 4. Eventually, Sect. 5 concludes this manuscript.

2 Related Works

For different models, corresponding decision boundaries seem to be similar; hence, based on those known models, we can generate adversarial examples which can then be utilized to attack unknown models. The efficiency of such attacks depends on the transferability of the obtained adversarial samples. Thus, numerous scholars devote to improving the transferability of adversarial samples. A series of related methods are proposed, being roughly classified into three types, i.e., gradient optimization attacks, input transformation attacks and ensemble-model attacks.

Gradient Optimization Attacks. Goodfellow *et al.* proposed the earliest gradient-based attack approach, i.e., Fast Gradient Sign Method (FGSM), which generates adversarial examples by introducing perturbations into the input image [6]. In order to increase the success rate of white-box attack, Kurakin *et al.* try to use the FGSM iteratively, being referred to as I-FGSM. Nevertheless, such method is likely to stuck in local optimization, which reduces the transferability of adversarial samples [8]. Later, Dong *et al.* combine the momentum method with I-FGSM (i.e., MI-FGSM), which is shown to be effective in improving the transferability of adversarial samples [3]. Then, Lin *et al.* incorporate Nesterov's accelerated gradient (NAG) to I-FGSM; because of the forward-looking property of NAG, corresponding transferability of gradient-based adversarial attacks can be further improved [10]. From the perspective of path optimization, Wang *et al.* take advantage of gradient changes near past data points to additionally adjust current gradient; thus, a more stable perturbation direction can be derived [16].

Input Transformation Attacks. Through randomly transforming the input with a certain probability, Xie *et al.* propose an improved attack method, namely DI-FGSM, which is capable of alleviating the tendency of over-fitting. The transferability of adversarial samples can be inherently improved through the adoption of diversified inputs [17]. Later, Dong *et al.* conduct the translation operation through translating the input to generate a set of images, i.e., TI-FGSM; by taking the gradient of these images simultaneously, the crafted adversarial examples are less sensitive to white-box model [4]. According to the scale invariance of the deep learning model, Lin *et al.* proposed an improved method named as SI-FGSM; the authors try to scale the input to derive a higher success rate under black-box attack [10]. Inspired by the potential improvement of adopting data augmentation, Zhang *et al.* propose Admix which is capable of creating more transferable adversarial examples [15].

Ensemble Model Attacks. For certain model, corresponding generated adversarial examples might have the disadvantage of over-fitting problems; thus, it might be useful to attack multiple models simultaneously with existing gradient attack methods (such as FGSM), and comprehensively consider different loss function gradients of multiple models [11].

3 Methodology

3.1 Gradient-Based Attacks

Before further discussion, some notations are provided in advance. Here, we assume that x indicates an input example and y^{real} denotes the true label, while x^{adv} represents the adversarial example of the input x. For a classifier with a loss function $J\left(x, y^{real}\right)$, the overall goal of attacks is to craft adversarial examples to maximize $J\left(x^{adv}, y^{real}\right)$. To be consistent with other attack methods, the difference of x^{adv} and x is anticipated to be restricted with in a provided threshold ϵ, i.e., $\left\|x^{adv} - x\right\|_{\infty} \leq \epsilon$. There are a bunch of Gradient-based Attack methods while some of them are listed for an illustration. The meanings of these notations remain unless otherwise stated.

Fast Gradient Sign Method (FGSM) [6]: Goodfellow *et al.* first proposed FGSM in 2015, and this is the earliest pioneering work for gradient-based attack. The FGSM is implemented through adding perturbation once, which is given by:

$$x^{adv} = x + \epsilon \cdot \operatorname{sign}\left(\nabla_x J(x, y^{real})\right) \tag{1}$$

where $\nabla_x J(x, y^{real})$ represents the gradient of loss function.

Iterative Fast Gradient Sign Method (I-FGSM) [8]: Kurakin *et al.* iteratively uses FGSM to create adversarial examples, while the perturbation size of each iteration depends on a step size factor α. The formula is:

$$x_0^{adv} = x, \quad x_{t+1}^{adv} = \text{Clip}_x^{\epsilon}\left\{x_t^{adv} + \alpha \cdot \text{sign}\left(\nabla_x J\left(x_t^{adv}, y^{\text{real}}\right)\right)\right\} \tag{2}$$

where Clip_x^{ϵ} denotes a function aiming to restrict the size of x^{adv}.

Momentum Iterative Fast Gradient Sign Method (MI-FGSM) [3]: Dong *et al.* try to integrate the momentum method into I-FGSM, which ensures the gradient direction to be more stable. The updating rule is given by:

$$\begin{aligned} g_{t+1} &= \mu \cdot g_t + \frac{\nabla_x J\left(x_t^{adv}, y^{\text{real}}\right)}{\left\|\nabla_x J\left(x_t^{adv}, y^{\text{real}}\right)\right\|_1} \\ x_{t+1}^{adv} &= \text{Clip}_x^{\epsilon}\left\{x_t^{adv} + \alpha \cdot \text{sign}\left(g_{t+1}\right)\right\} \end{aligned} \tag{3}$$

where $x_0^{adv} = x$ and $g_0 = 0$, μ indicates the decay factor.

Diverse Inputs Method (DIM) [17]: Xie *et al.* randomly transform the input with probability *p*. While *T*() denotes a stochastic transformation function, including random resizing and random padding. Corresponding formula is:

$$\begin{aligned} x_{t+1}^{adv} &= \text{Clip}_x^{\epsilon}\left\{x_t^{adv} + \alpha \cdot \text{sign}\left(\nabla_x L\left(T\left(x_t^{adv}, p\right), y^{real}, \theta\right)\right)\right\} \\ T\left(x_t^{adv}, p\right) &= \begin{cases} T\left(x_t^{adv}\right) & \text{with probability } p \\ x_t^{adv} & \text{with probability } 1-p \end{cases} \end{aligned} \tag{4}$$

Translation-Invariant Method (TIM) [4]: Dong *et al.* utilizes a set of translated images in order to optimize the adversarial perturbations. Aiming to reduce the calculation of gradients, authors in [4] propose to convolve gradients of untranslated images with predefined kernels for efficient computation.

Scale-Invariant Method (SIM) [10]: Lin *et al.* considers the scale-invariant properties of deep learning. For the same model, the losses of the original images and the scaled ones are close. Hence, Lin *et al.* utilize the average gradient of the scaled image to replace the currently gradient that is necessary to be calculated:

$$\begin{aligned} \bar{g}_{t+1} &= \frac{1}{m}\sum_{i=0}^{m-1} \nabla_{x_t^{adv}}\left(J\left(x_t^{adv}/2^i, y^{real}, \theta\right)\right) \\ g_{t+1} &= \mu \cdot g_t + \frac{\bar{g}_{t+1}}{\|\bar{g}_{t+1}\|_1} \end{aligned} \tag{5}$$

Admix Attack Method [19] is first proposed to utilize the information of other labels which is anticipated to handle the over-fitting problem. Wang *et al.* provide an hint to mix two types of images whereas the labels remain to be unchanged. Then, adversarial examples can be derived through deriving average gradient of the mixed image set.

3.2 Proposed Model

The discriminant region the known model used in training is highly likely to be different from the black box model to be attacked; this incurs the difficulty of attacking the black box model with generated adversarial examples. As reflected by previous studies, data augmentation plays an important and effective role in mitigating adversarial examples from over-fitting known models. While information deletion based data augmentation methods are capable of improving the training effect of deep learning models by a large extent. For these information deletion based data augmentation methods, information can be deleted from the input images with the adoption of various strategies. If too much information is deleted; this might incur the scenario of assigning a new label to the initial image. Whereas if too much information is retained, then the effect on the training process might be largely limited. Thus, it is highly necessary to specify a good balance; among those proposed algorithms to strike such balance, GridMask [2] seems to be a good choice which is implemented by removing a set of spatially uniformly distributed grids.

Inspired by above discussions, we present an efficient adversarial attack method through integrating the information deletion based data augmentation strategies with gradient-based adversarial attack methods, named as Grid Mask-Attack (GM-Attack for short). The masked image $\tilde{x}$ is generated randomly according to Eq. 6. While the mask is controlled by four parameters being provided as r, d, ψ_x, and ψ_y.

$$\tilde{x} = x \times Mask(r, d, \psi_x, \psi_y) \tag{6}$$

where r indicates the keep ratio which determines the proportion of information of the image to be retained, d denotes the length of each grid, ψ_x and ψ_y represent the randomly generated values varying in [0, d-1], which are used to shift the grid mask. For the Mask, if $Mask_{i,j} = 0$, the pixel(i, j) of image x will be discarded while the remaining parts will be reserved. An overall schematic of GM-Attack is provided in Fig. 1. When combining with the momentum method, the integrated attack method (i.e., GM-MI-FGSM) is shown in Algorithm 1.

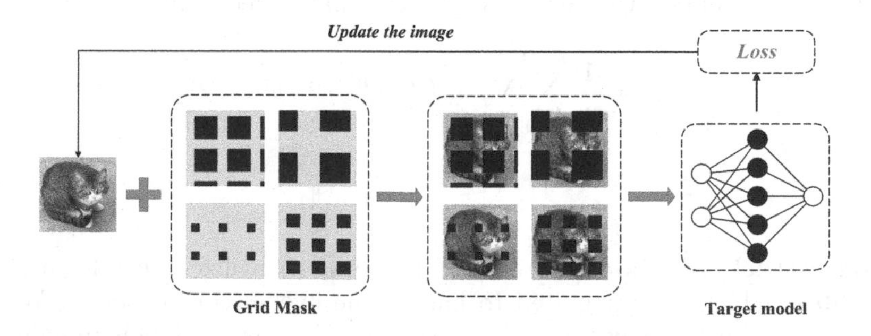

Fig. 1. An overall schematic of our proposed attack strategy (GM-Attack).

Similar as the gradient based attacks afore-mentioned, we will update the input image iteratively. However, we generate a set of masked images by adding random grid mask into the input image before calculating the gradient in each iteration. Instead of taking the gradient of the input image, we compute the average gradient of the set of masked images as:

$$\widetilde{g}_{t+1} = \frac{1}{m_1 \cdot m_2} \sum_{j=0}^{m_1-1} \sum_{i=0}^{m_2-1} \nabla_{x_t^{adv}} J\left((x_t^{adv} \cdot Mask_j)/2^i, y^{real}\right) \tag{7}$$

where m_1 and m_2 indicates the numbers of masked images and scaled copies respectively, and $Mask_j$ denotes a randomly generated grid mask.

Algorithm 1. The GM-MI-FGSM Algorithm.

Input:
An input image x and the true label y^{real}, a classifier f with loss function J ;
Perturbation size ϵ, number of iterations T and the decay factor μ;
The keep ratio of the input image r, length of the grid d, number of masks m_1, and number of scaled copies m_2;
Output:
An adversarial example x^{adv};
1: Initialization $\alpha = \epsilon/T$; $x_0^{adv} = x$; $g_0 = 0$; $\widetilde{g}_0 = 0$
2: **for** $t = 0 \to T-1$ **do**
3: Calculate the gradient $\widetilde{g}_t$ by Eq. 7.
4: Update g_t:

$$g_{t+1} = \mu \cdot g_t + \frac{\widetilde{g}_{t+1}}{\|\widetilde{g}_{t+1}\|_1}$$

5: Update x_{t+1}^{adv}:

$$x_{t+1}^{adv} = x_t^{adv} + \alpha \cdot \text{sign}\left(g_{t+1}\right)$$

6: **end for**
7: **return** $x^{adv} = x_T^{adv}$;

---

4 Experiments

4.1 Experimental Setup

Dataset. For the considered dataset, we utilize 1,000 images belonging to 1,000 categories which are randomly chosen from a widely adopted validation set, i.e., ILSVRC 2012 validation set [12]. The accuracies of classification for all the adopted models are perfect here.

Models. Aiming to illustrate the transferability, a bunch of normally trained models are selected as the target ones which will be attacked by the adversarial examples obtained through different approaches. Four normally trained models are incorporated as target models, i.e., Inception-v3 [13], Inception-v4 [14],

Resnet-v2-101 [7], Inception-Resnet-v2 [14], denoted as Inc-v3, Inc-v4,Res-101 and IncRes-v2 respectively for short. Furthermore, some adversarially trained models are also incorporated, being listed as Inc-v3$_{ens3}$, Inc-v3$_{ens4}$ and IncRes-v2$_{ens}$ [21].

Baselines. For comparison, four input transformations (DIM, TIM, SIM and Admix) are adopted as the baselines. Aiming to further reflect the superiority of GM-Attack, our proposed method is also integrated with two other input transformations (DIM and TIM); the obtained attack method is denoted as GM-DI-TI-FGSM.

Hyper-Parameters. To be in consistent, attack parameter settings in [15] are utilized; maximum perturbation ϵ equals to 16, number of iteration T is assigned to 10, step size α equals to 1.6. For TIM, the adopted Gaussian kernel is 7×7. For MI-FGSM, we set the decay factor μ to 1.0. The transformation probability p for DIM is set to 0.5, while for SIM, m equals to 5 which denotes the number of copies. For Admix, we assign the number of samples m_2 and blend image ratio η to 3 and 0.2 respectively as in [15]. For GM-Attack, we set $r = 0.7$, $d = [96, 200]$, $m_2 = 5$ and $m_1 = 26, 26, 22, 20$ for the Incorporated normally trained models.

4.2 Attack with Single Input Transformation

In this subsection, experiments are performed aiming to indicate the capability of our approach in crafting more transferable adversarial examples compared with other existing input transformation methods. Four normally trained models are utilized as the target models while seven models as the testing ones, the attack success rate is the criterion used to assess performance of different attacking strategies. Corresponding obtained attack success rates are listed as in Table 1.

As indicated, with obtained adversarial examples, GM-Attack is of the best transferability on the considered models for most of the scenarios. Specially, for white-box attacks (with a * behind the success rate), there seems to be no loss in the success rate. When crafting adversarial examples on Inc-v4, the success rate for our proposed GM-Attack is 5.8% higher than the Admix attacks on average which is the best existing approach. Under the black-box setting, attack success rate through GM-Attack is the highest compared with the other attack approaches which arrives at 94.9%. Furthermore, we find that adversarial examples crafted on Inc-v4 and IncRes-v2 have better transferability compared with the others which might be affected by network structures.

4.3 Attack with Combined Input Transformation

Linear combinations of input transformation methods have been shown to be effective [15]. Furthermore, we combine GM-Attack, Admix and Sim with DI-TIM [4], being denoted as GM-DI-TIM, Admix-DI-TIM and SIM-DI-TIM respectively to demonstrate the effectiveness of our method. Similarly, all the

Table 1. Performance (indicated by attack success rate) for scenarios with single input transformations. Here, adversarial examples are crafted under single model (four models are incorporated) and used to attack seven models. * represents the values obtained for white-box attacks.

Model	Method	$Inc-v3$	$Inc-v4$	Res-101	$IncRes-v2$	$Inc-v3_{ens3}$	$Inc-v3_{ens4}$	$IncRes-v2_{ens}$
$Inc-v3$	DIM	0.999*	0.643	0.532	0.609	0.199	0.183	0.093
	TIM	**1.000***	0.488	0.395	0.436	0.248	0.213	0.132
	SIM	**1.000***	0.694	0.627	0.673	0.325	0.307	0.173
	Admix	**1.000***	0.826	0.752	0.809	0.390	0.392	0.192
	GM-Attack	**1.000***	**0.868**	**0.792**	**0.838**	**0.422**	**0.417**	**0.211**
$Inc-v4$	DIM	0.729	0.974*	0.565	0.651	0.202	0.211	0.116
	TIM	0.586	0.996*	0.423	0.465	0.262	0.234	0.172
	SIM	0.806	0.996*	0.688	0.742	0.478	0.448	0.291
	Admix	0.878	0.994*	0.780	0.832	0.559	0.504	0.337
	GM-Attack	**0.931**	**1.000***	**0.839**	**0.893**	**0.628**	**0.577**	**0.367**
$Res-101$	DIM	0.758	0.695	0.980*	0.700	0.357	0.316	0.199
	TIM	0.593	0.521	0.993*	0.518	0.354	0.313	0.231
	SIM	0.752	0.689	0.997*	0.690	0.437	0.385	0.263
	Admix	0.854	0.808	0.997*	0.796	0.510	0.453	0.309
	GM-Attack	**0.862**	**0.821**	**1.000***	**0.820**	**0.515**	**0.476**	**0.310**
$IncRes-v2$	DIM	0.701	0.634	0.587	0.935*	0.309	0.239	0.177
	TIM	0.622	0.554	0.505	0.974*	0.328	0.276	0.233
	SIM	0.847	0.811	0.764	0.990*	0.563	0.483	0.428
	Admix	0.899	0.875	0.819	0.991*	0.642	0.567	**0.500**
	GM-Attack	**0.949**	**0.922**	**0.877**	**0.997***	**0.674**	**0.592**	0.490

Table 2. Performance (indicated by attack success rate) with combined methods input. Here, adversarial examples are crafted under single model (four models are considered) and used to attack seven models. * represents the values obtained for white-box attacks.

Model	Method	$Inc-v3$	$Inc-v4$	Res-101	$IncRes-v2$	$Inc-v3_{ens3}$	$Inc-v3_{ens4}$	$IncRes-v2_{ens}$
$Inc-v3$	SI-DI-TIM	0.991*	0.836	0.767	0.808	0.652	0.633	0.465
	Admix-DI-TIM	0.999*	0.890	0.831	0.870	0.753	0.719	**0.616**
	GM-DI-TIM	**1.000***	**0.940**	**0.898**	**0.918**	**0.788**	**0.776**	0.590
$Inc-v4$	SI-DI-TIM	0.879	0.987*	0.777	0.830	0.724	0.682	0.575
	Admix-DI-TIM	0.904	0.990*	0.820	0.873	0.753	0.719	0.616
	GM-DI-TIM	**0.950**	**0.998***	**0.886**	**0.922**	**0.840**	**0.805**	**0.694**
$Res-101$	SI-DI-TIM	0.847	0.822	0.990*	0.848	0.758	0.735	0.634
	Admix-DI-TIM	0.910	0.877	0.999*	0.892	0.811	0.774	**0.701**
	GM-DI-TIM	**0.928**	**0.894**	**1.000***	**0.896**	**0.836**	**0.787**	**0.701**
$IncRes-v2$	SI-DI-TIM	0.888	0.868	0.839	0.978*	0.787	0.742	0.723
	Admix-DI-TIM	0.910	0.877	0.859	0.977*	0.820	0.780	0.763
	GM-DI-TIM	**0.960**	**0.944**	**0.924**	**0.996***	**0.896**	**0.860**	**0.813**

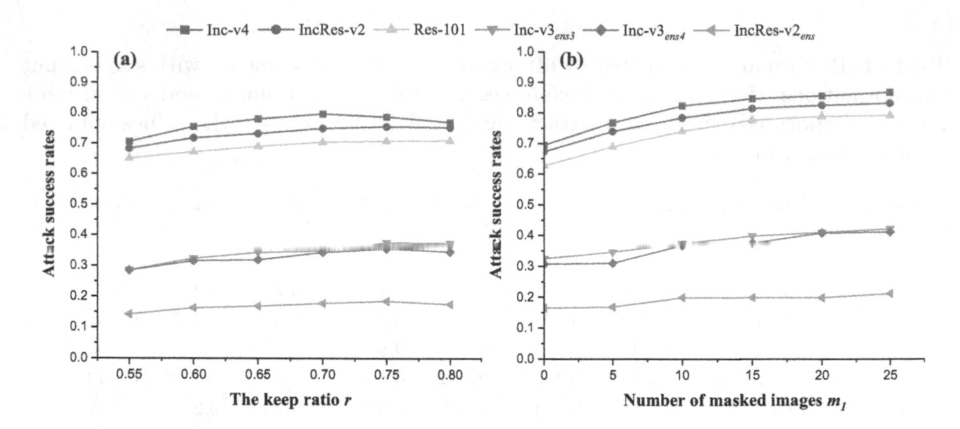

Fig. 2. Attack success rates on six target models for black-box attack. Adversarial examples crafted on Inc-v3 are utilized for scenarios with different parameters, i.e., keep ratio r and number of masked images m_1.

seven models are adopted here to test the performance of attack with the adversarial examples crafted on four normally trained models. Corresponding obtained attack success rates are listed as in Table 2.

As indicated, our proposed method is superior compared with the others for majority of the scenarios. Given black-box setting, GM-Attack is able to achieve a good attack success rate on average which is above 90% when attacking a normally trained model. After complex input transformation, the success rates of SIM and Admix for white-box attack are reduced to 97.8% and 97.7% respectively, while the success rate of GM-Attack for white-box attack remains to be above 99%. When attacking the adversarially trained models, the success rate of GM-Attack reaches 89.6%, while corresponding values for existed methods are all less than 82%. Furthermore, the average attack success rates of GM-Attack on Inc-v4 has been improved by 6.5% over state-of-the-art methods.

4.4 Parameter Analysis

Furthermore, we also conduct extensive experiments to explore the effects of two parameters (r and m_1) on attack success rate; obtained results are provided in Fig. 2. For simplicity, we only consider adversarial examples crafted on Inc-v3, while experiments using adversarial examples crafted on other models can be performed accordingly.

As in Fig. 2(a), there exists an optimal value of r, i.e., r_{opt}, for different target models. When $r < r_{opt}$, the transferability increases gradually if larger r is adopted indicated by a higher attack success rate; otherwise, corresponding transferability decreases instead. Interestingly, for the considered two target models, i.e., the normally trained one and the adversarially trained one, r_{opt} varies. For the normally trained one, r peaks around 0.7, whereas r peaks around 0.75 on the adversarially trained model. As in Fig. 2(b), for adversarial examples, the transferability increases gradually with the increase of m_1. However, we find that the growth rate becomes smaller with the increase of m_1. It is worth mentioning that even if we increase m_1 to 25, the attack success rate is still improving. Due to the huge amount of memory required when m_1 is larger, we only consider scenarios for $m_1 < 25$ here.

5 Conclusion

This paper proposes an information deletion based attack method, i.e., GM-Attack, to enhance the transferability of adversarial examples. Specially, the proposed method generates a set of masked images by randomly removing some regions of the input images. The regions are a set of spatially uniformly distributed grids. Then, we calculate the average gradient of masked images to update the input image. Extensive experiments are performed and corresponding results obtained by our proposed model are compared with those for other state-of-the-art algorithms. As indicated, the performance of our proposed model is superior with regarding to the others. The proposed method is capable of crafting more transferable adversarial examples compared with other input transformation methods. We hope our proposed GM-Attack that removes information from input image will elucidate potential directions for adversarial attacks.

Acknowledgement. This work was supported by the National Key R&D Program of China (No. 2020AAA0107704), National Natural Science Foundation of China (Nos. 62073263, 62102105, 61976181, 62025602), Guangdong Basic and Applied Basic Research Foundation (Nos. 2020A1515110997, 2022A1515011501), Science and Technology Program of Guangzhou (Nos. 202002030263, 202102010419), Technological Innovation Team of Shaanxi Province (No. 2020TD-013).

References

1. Szegedy, C., et al.: Intriguing properties of neural networks. In: International Conference on Learning Representations (ICLR), Banff (2014)
2. Chen, P., Liu, S., Zhao, H., and Jia, J.: Gridmask data augmentation. arXiv preprint arXiv:2001.04086 (2020)
3. Dong, Y., et al.: Boosting adversarial attacks with momentum. In: Proceedings of the IEEE Conference on Computer Vision and Pattern Recognition (CVPR), Salt Lake City, pp. 9185–9193 (2018)
4. Dong, Y., Pang, T., Su, H., Zhu, J.: Evading defenses to transferable adversarial examples by translation-invariant attacks. In: Proceedings of the IEEE Conference on Computer Vision and Pattern Recognition (CVPR), Long Beach, pp. 4312–4321. IEEE (2019)
5. Girshick, R.B.: Fast R-CNN. In: Proceedings of IEEE International Conference on Computer Vision (ICCV), Santiago, pp. 1440–1448. IEEE (2015)
6. Goodfellow, I.J., Shlens, J., Szegedy, C.: Explaining and harnessing adversarial examples. In: Proceedings of International Conference on Learning Representations (ICLR), San Diego (2015)

7. He, K., Zhang, X., Ren, S., Sun, J.: Deep residual learning for image recognition. In: Proceedings of the IEEE Conference on Computer Vision and Pattern Recognition (CVPR), Las Vegas, pp. 770–778. IEEE (2016)
8. Kurakin, A., Goodfellow, I., Bengio, S.: Adversarial examples in the physical world. arXiv preprint arXiv:1607.02533 (2016)
9. Li, Y., Bai, S., Zhou, Y., Xie, C., Zhang, Z., Yuille, A.L.: Learning transferable adversarial examples via ghost networks. In: The Thirty-Fourth AAAI Conference on Artificial Intelligence, New York City, pp. 11458–11465 (2020)
10. Lin, J., Song, C., He, K., Wang, L., Hopcroft, J.E.: Nesterov accelerated gradient and scale invariance for adversarial attacks. In: International Conference on Learning Representations (ICLR), New Orleans (2019)
11. Liu, Y., Chen, X., Liu, C., Song, D.: Delving into transferable adversarial examples and blackbox attacks. In: International Conference on Learning Representations (ICLR). Palais des Congrès Neptune (2017)
12. Russakovsky, O., et al.: ImageNet large scale visual recognition challenge. Int. J. Comput. Vision (IJCV) **115**(3), 211–252 (2015)
13. Szegedy, C., Vanhoucke, V., Ioffe, S., Shlens, J., Wojna, Z.: Rethinking the inception architecture for computer vision. In: Proceedings of IEEE Conference on Computer Vision and Pattern Recognition (CVPR), Las Vegas, pp. 2818–2826. IEEE (2016)
14. Szegedy, C., Ioffe, S., Vanhoucke, V., Alemi, A.A.: Inception-v4, Inception-Resnet and the impact of residual connections on learning. In: Proceedings of AAAI Conference on Artificial Intelligence, San Francisco, pp. 4278–4284 (2017)
15. Wang, X., He, X., Wang, J., He, K.: Admix: enhancing the transferability of adversarial attacks. In: Proceedings of the IEEE International Conference on Computer Vision, Montreal, pp. 16158–16167. IEEE (2021)
16. Wang, X., He, K.: Enhancing the transferability of adversarial attacks through variance tuning. In: Proceedings of the IEEE Conference on Computer Vision and Pattern Recognition, Montreal, pp. 1924–1933. IEEE (2021)
17. Xie, C., et al.: Improving transferability of adversarial examples with input diversity. In: Proceedings of the IEEE Conference on Computer Vision and Pattern Recognition (CVPR), Long Beach, pp. 2730–2739. IEEE (2019)
18. Zou, J., Pan, Z., Qiu, J., Liu, X., Rui, T., Li, W.: Improving the transferability of adversarial examples with resized-diverse-inputs, diversity-ensemble and region fitting. In: Vedaldi, A., Bischof, H., Brox, T., Frahm, J.-M. (eds.) ECCV 2020. LNCS, vol. 12367, pp. 563–579. Springer, Cham (2020). https://doi.org/10.1007/978-3-030-58542-6_34
19. Zhang, H., Moustapha, C., Dauphin, Y.N., Lopez-Paz, D.: Mixup: beyond empirical risk minimization. In: International Conference on Learning Representations (ICLR), Vancouver (2018)
20. Zhong, Z., Zheng, L., Kang, G., Li, S., Yang, Y.: Random erasing data augmentation. In: Proceedings of the AAAI Conference on Artificial Intelligence, New York City, pp. 13001–13008 (2020)
21. Tramèr, F., Kurakin, A., Papernot, N., Goodfellow, I., Boneh, D., McDaniel, P.: Ensemble adversarial training: attacks and defenses. In: International Conference on Learning Representations (ICLR), Vancouver (2018)

Adversarial Cycle-Consistent Autoencoder for Category-Aware Out-of-Town Recommendation

Lijiao Qin[1,2,3] and Defu Lian[1,2,3](✉)

[1] School of Data Science, University of Science and Technology of China, 230027 Hefei, China
qinlijiao@mail.ustc.edu.cn, liandefu@ustc.edu.cn
[2] State Key Laboratory of Cognitive Intelligence, 230027 Hefei, China
[3] Yangtze River Delta Information Intelligence Innovation Research Institute, 241000 Wuhu, China

Abstract. Out-of-town recommendation aims to provide Point-of-Interest (POI) recommendation when users leave their hometown and arrive in a new city. To infer the out-of-town preferences of cold-start users based on their hometown preferences, some recent methods directly train a mapping function between users' hometown preferences and out-of-town preferences. Unfortunately, they depend on a large number of overlapping users who left check-in histories in both the home city and the out-of-town city to build the mapping relationships. Also, they don't fully explore the category hierarchy knowledge of POIs, which can help with robust POI representations. To this end, in this paper, we propose Adversarial Cycle-Consistent Autoencoder for Category-Aware Out-of-Town Recommendation named ACCAC, which effectively learns the mapping function even in the case that the number of overlapping users is limited. Specifically, we first utilize denoising autoencoders to learn pre-trained POI embeddings augmented with category hierarchy knowledge. Then we introduce a cycle-consistent generative adversarial network to explore potential mapping relationships. Extensive experiments on real-world out-of-town recommendation datasets demonstrate the effectiveness of ACCAC.

Keywords: Recommender systems · Out-of-town recommendation · Autoencoder · Category hierarchy · Cycle consistency

1 Introduction

In the past decade, various location-based software services such as Foursquare, Yelp, Google places have played an essential role in our daily life. The goal of a personalized location-based recommender system is to provide POIs which can satisfy users' preferences according to the history of their check-in activities and information of POIs. As a specific scenario of POI recommendation, out-of-town

G. Memmi et al. (Eds.): KSEM 2022, LNAI 13370, pp. 501–515, 2022.
https://doi.org/10.1007/978-3-031-10989-8_40

recommendation has attracted more and more attention. It is able to make POI recommendation when users leave their home city and arrive in a new city for the purpose of travel or business. When users live in cities they are familiar with, such as their home city or working city, it does not require much effort for them to find places which are related to their interests. However, POI recommendation is of vital importance when users reach unfamiliar cities and have not acquired enough knowledge about them. In this case, they need an effective out-of-town recommender system that helps find suitable POIs.

Some location-aware models [4,7,14,19] considering geographical proximity are proposed for out-of-town POI recommendation. However, they haven't considered the phenomenon of user interest drift. Interest drift refers to that users tend to change their inherent interests when they travel in different cities owing to the varieties of characteristics in culture, landscape, and so on among cities. Some works based on probability [17,21,22] or deep learning [16] are developed to address such challenge. They fuse users' hometown preferences with crowd preferences of the target city to model interest drift. Recently, TrainOR [20] has been proposed to directly train a mapping function between users' hometown preferences and out-of-town preferences. It captures the pattern of interest drift in a more complicated way via the users who left check-in histories in both the home city and target city, also known as overlapping users.

However, many existing methods suffer from some of the following disadvantages and limitations. 1) It requires collecting the data of a large number of overlapping users before training if utilizing overlapping users as a bridge between the home city and target city. Nevertheless, the acquisition of a large amount of such kind of data is not a simple task due to users' privacy concerns. It will result in a sharp decline in model performance when the overlapping data is scarce. 2) They ignore the category hierarchy knowledge graph of POIs which helps learn richer POI embeddings even facing the data sparsity challenge. We should leverage categorical hierarchy information to obtain more robust representations of the POIs rarely appearing in the users' check-ins. 3) They apply an end-to-end manner to jointly train the data of both the home city and target city. However, this end-to-end manner will exacerbate the instability of the model, especially when lacking overlapping users. They haven't considered pre-training, which is more effective in many cases to integrate knowledge from another source to facilitate various scenarios in recommender systems [10,13].

To fully consider these key factors, we propose Adversarial Cycle-Consistent Autoencoder for Category-aware out-of-town recommendation named ACCAC which effectively learns users' cross-city check-in relationships. Specifically, we first devise a special autoencoder augmented with the hierarchical category information of POIs to obtain the pre-trained POI embeddings for both the home city and target city. The category augment mechanism enriches POI embeddings and facilitates building relationships between POIs from different cities. After obtaining pre-trained POI embeddings, we adopt a dual autoencoder structure to build the mapping relationships between users' hometown preferences and out-of-town preferences. Inspired by cycle-consistent generative adversarial network (CycleGAN), which can relate data from different domains without any mapping labels [6,25], we also build pseudo pair mapping pairs to establish more potential mapping relationships between users' check-in behaviors in the home city and target city. In this way, the mapping relationships are capable of being built more precisely. To sum up, the main contributions of this paper are as follows:

- We devise a special autoencoder augmented with hierarchical category information to learn the pre-trained robust POI embeddings for both the home city and target city.
- We adopt a dual autoencoder structure to learn the mapping relationships between users' hometown preferences and out-of-town preferences and utilize CycleGAN to further optimize the mapping procedure.
- We conduct comprehensive experiments on real-world datasets. Experimental results demonstrate that our proposed model outperforms several state-of-the-art models significantly.

2 Related Work

Out-of-town recommendation. Out-of-town POI recommendation aims to make POI recommendations for users who come to a new city [17]. Some works leveraged auxiliary information like POI reviews [18,23] or social relationships [7] to solve the cold-start issue in out-of-town recommendation. However, they didn't consider the phenomenon of interest drift. The core task to tackle the phenomenon is to correlate users' preferences in the home city and target city. CKNN [1] modeled user preferences via a weighted category hierarchy and provided recommendations for travellers following social opinions extracted from the local experts who could share similar category interests to capture the interest drift. In addition, BPTFSLR [24] grouped both users in the home city and target city into communities according to user preferences extracted from reviews and generated POI recommendations to tourists via community matching. This method learned the interest drift at the granularity of the community. Some methods based on LDA (Latent Dirichlet Allocation) [17,21,22] employed the topic model to build interest drift between the home city and target city. For instance, LSARS [21] split the city topics into the city-independent topics and the shared ones. It recommended POIs from the target city which were distributed in the same common topics as the target user's topics in the home city. Recently, advanced deep neural models have played a more important role in out-of-town recommendation [16,20]. We can find that most of the methods capture interest drift via fusing the users' hometown preferences and crowd preferences of the target city. Different from other works, TrainOR [20] directly built a non-linear mapping between users' hometown preferences and out-of-town preferences, which could establish more complicated and reasonable interest drift patterns. Compared with TrainOR, the key of our proposed model is to build more robust mapping relationships in the case that a few mapping pair labels are available. To achieve this goal, we fully utilize the features of POIs' category hierarchy to connect the POIs from different cities more closely. Also, we introduce CycleGAN to explore potential mapping relationships.

3 Methodology

In this section, we first introduce several definitions correlated to our work and then detail our proposed model.

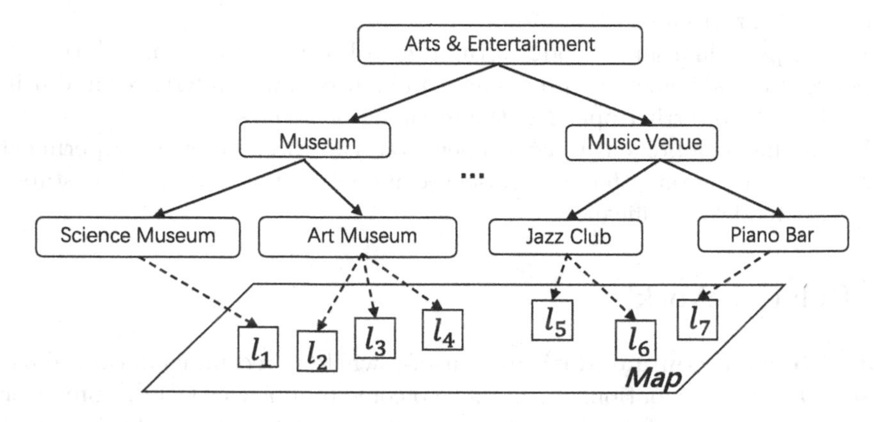

Fig. 1. An example of a multi-layer category hierarchy.

3.1 Preliminaries and Technical Framework

Definition 1: User Hometown. Since the attribute of hometown isn't available in our datasets, we choose the city where a user has the largest number of check-ins as the user's hometown following [5].

Definition 2: Hierarchy of Categories. In a location-based social network, a user can mark a POI (e.g., a park) and write reviews or tips about it, also known as a check-in in an LBSN. As shown in Fig. 1, we depict the squares on the map as POIs. Each POI is associated with a set of categories denoting its functionalities. The categories of POIs have different granularities, which are usually represented by a category hierarchy. For example, in Fig. 1, "Arts & Entertainment" category includes "Museum", "Music Venue" and etc. "Museum" includes sub-categories such as "Science & Museum", "Art & Museum" and so on. The hierarchy of categories is a tree $\mathcal{T}$ in which an edge describes a parent-child relationship. Intuitively, the deeper sub-category a POI is located in the tree, the more specific category information it has. The category hierarchy is available from Foursquare and Yelp.

When users leave their hometown and arrive in a new city for travelling or business, we aim to select the POIs in the new city that maybe interest them before they have any check-ins in the new city. Typically, we have the following problem statement:

Problem 1: Out-of-town Recommendation. POI recommendation is widely explored on a user-POI checkin matrix $\mathbf{R} \in \mathbb{R}^{M \times N}$, where there are M users and N POIs, each entry $r_{u,i}$ represents the frequency of user u visit POI i. We binarize the matrix where each entry $r_{u,i} \in \{0, 1\}$ denotes whether user u has visited POI i. For out-of-town recommendation, we denote the user set, POI set and binarized implicit feedback matrix as $\mathcal{U}_x, \mathcal{V}_x$ and $\mathbb{R}_x$ for the home city. Similarly, we have $\mathcal{U}_y, \mathcal{V}_y$ and $\mathbb{R}_y$ for the target new city. In addition, each POI in the home city or target city has an attribute of category hierarchy as mentioned above. On the other hand, there are a set of users who travel from the home city to the target new city called overlapping users, we denote this set as $\mathcal{U}_o$. Given a target user's check-ins in the hometown, the overall goal is to recommend a list of POIs located in the target city which are in line with the user's interests (Fig. 2).

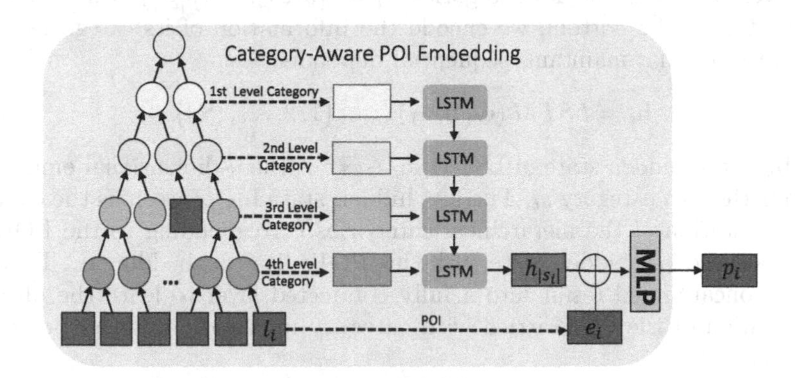

(a) Category-Aware POI Embedding Component

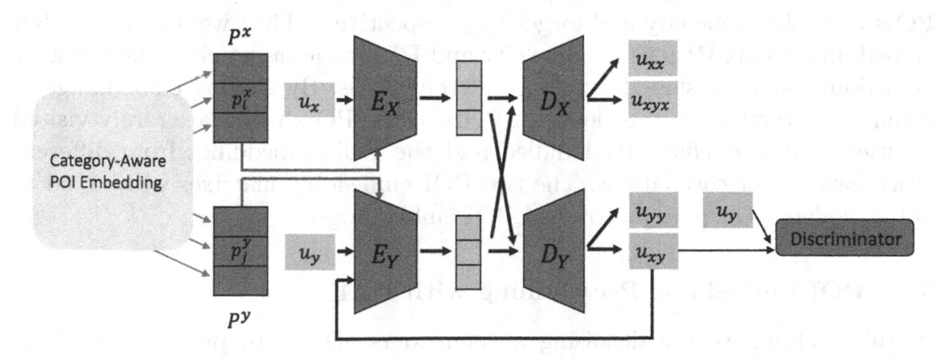

(b) Overall Framework

Fig. 2. The framework overview of ACCAC.

3.2 Category-Aware POI Embedding

A POI is labeled as multi-layer hierarchical categories from the bottom to the top in $\mathcal{T}$ where the top category is the most general category and the bottom category is the most fine-grained category. Intuitively, categories at deeper layers express more specific concepts than upper layers. This characteristic motivates us to use Long Short-Term Memory (LSTM) [2,8] to characterize a POI's related categories at different levels. LSTM is an artificial neural network that's able to deal with sequential data and is trained to memorize valuable history knowledge and forget non-relevant knowledge. We can treat the categories from upper to lower as sequential data and feed them into LSTM, then LSTM can pass relevant information down the chain of the category hierarchy.

We project each POI node in $\mathcal{T}$ to an embedding vector $\mathbf{e}_i \in \mathbb{R}^d$ and each category node to an embedding vector $\mathbf{c}_j \in \mathbb{R}^d$, where d is the embedding dimension. Given a POI l_i and its categories $S_i = \{s_1, s_2, \ldots, s_{|S_i|}\}$ which is sorted from the top to the bottom, we encode the information of its categories using an LSTM layer that maintains sequential dependencies:

$$\mathbf{h}_t = LSTM\left(\mathbf{c}_t, \mathbf{h}_{t-1}\right), t \in \{1, 2, \ldots, |S_i|\}, \tag{1}$$

where $\mathbf{h}_t$ is the hidden state of LSTM, $\mathbf{c}_t \in \mathbb{R}^d$ is the d-dimensional embedding vector for the t-th category s_t. The last hidden state $\mathbf{h}_{|S_i|}$ is seen as the composite representation of the hierarchical categories corresponding to the POI. We concatenate the last hidden state with this POI's basic embedding $\mathbf{e}_i$. Then, we feed the concatenated result into a fully connected layer to learn the ultimate representation of the POI carried with category information. It can be defined as follows:

$$\mathbf{p}_i = MLP\left(\mathbf{h}_{|S_i|} \oplus \mathbf{e}_i\right), \tag{2}$$

where MLP denotes Multi-layer perceptron. We concatenate embeddings of all POIs from the home city and target city respectively. Then we obtain the POI embedding matrix $\mathbf{P}^x$ for the home city and $\mathbf{P}^y$ for the target city. The category embedding space is shared between different cities. By sharing embeddings of common hierarchical categories with POIs, those POIs which are rarely visited by users could be efficiently handled and the POI embeddings from different cities have larger correlations. The two POI embedding matrixes will be fed to autoencoders to acquire pre-trained POI embeddings.

3.3 POI Embedding Pre-training with DAE

In this section, we use denoising autoencoders (DAE) to pre-train the POI embeddings for both the home city and target city. A DAE has two main parts: an encoder that maps the input into a lower-dimensional representation and a decoder that maps the representation to a reconstruction of the original input. The DAE to learn the POI embeddings for each city can be formulated as:

$$\begin{aligned} \mathbf{z} &= Encoder(\mathbf{u}), \\ \hat{\mathbf{u}} &= Decoder(\mathbf{z}), \end{aligned} \tag{3}$$

where the input $\mathbf{u}$ is a multi-hot vector describing the user's preferences to POIs and $\mathbf{1}$ in the vector denotes that the user has checked in a certain POI. *Encoder* and *Decoder* are typically fully connected networks, $\mathbf{z}$ denotes a compression of the input into a lower-dimensional space. $\hat{\mathbf{u}}$ is the re-constructed representation of the original representation.

To integrate the POI embedding matrix into DAE, the first hidden layer is expressed as follows:

$$\mathbf{m}^{(0)} = \mathbf{P}^T \mathbf{u}, \tag{4}$$

where $\mathbf{P}$ is the POI embedding matrix and $\mathbf{m}^{(0)}$ is the first hidden layer of DAE. The other hidden layers in DAE adopt normal fully connected networks formulated as follows:

$$\mathbf{m}^{(i)} = f(\mathbf{W}^{(i)}\mathbf{m}^{(i-1)} + \mathbf{b}^{(i)}), \tag{5}$$

where $\mathbf{W}^{(i)}$ and $\mathbf{b}^{(i)}$ denote the weight matrix and bias of a fully connected layer, and $f(\cdot)$ is the activation function. We also utilize the POI embedding matrix in the output layer of DAE:

$$\hat{\mathbf{u}} = \mathbf{P}\mathbf{m}^{(k)}, \tag{6}$$

where $\mathbf{m}^{(k)}$ is the last hidden layer of DAE.

In our out-of-town recommendation scenario, we have two DAEs for the home city and the target city respectively. We denote the multi-hot vector describing the preferences of a certain user who left check-in activities in the home city as $\mathbf{u}_x$. The encoder and decoder for the home city is denoted as $E_x(\cdot)$ and $D_x(\cdot)$. Similarly, we have $\mathbf{u}_y$, $E_y(\cdot)$ and $D_y(\cdot)$ for the target city. We denote the reconstruction procedure as follows:

$$\begin{aligned} \mathbf{u}_{xx} &= D_x E_x(\mathbf{u}_x), \\ \mathbf{u}_{yy} &= D_y E_y(\mathbf{u}_y). \end{aligned} \tag{7}$$

The POI embeddings in the home city and the target city are learned by minimizing the following re-construction loss:

$$\mathcal{L}_{REC} = \sum_{u \in \mathcal{U}_x} \ell_1(\mathbf{u}_x, \mathbf{u}_{xx}) + \sum_{u \in \mathcal{U}_y} \ell_1(\mathbf{u}_y, \mathbf{u}_{yy}), \tag{8}$$

while for the loss function ℓ_1, we adopt multinomial log loss defined as follows:

$$\begin{aligned} \ell_1(y, \hat{y}) &= -\frac{1}{N}\left(\sum_{i=1}^{N} y_i \cdot \log(p_i)\right), \\ p_i &= \frac{\exp(\hat{y}_i)}{\sum_{j=1}^{N} \exp(\hat{y}_j)}. \end{aligned} \tag{9}$$

The reconstruction design of DAEs makes the POI embeddings comprehensive and interpretable. In the next step of building mapping relationships between users' hometown and out-of-town preferences, the POI embeddings will be frozen, i.e., the parameters of the first hidden layer and the last hidden layer of the two DAEs will not be updated during the mapping stage.

3.4 Latent Space Mapping

In this section, we capture the cross-city check-in relationships between users' preferences in the home city and target city by utilizing the overlapping users as a bridge. The learning procedure is formalized as follows:

$$\mathbf{u}_{xy} = D_y E_x(\mathbf{u}_x), \tag{10}$$

where $\mathbf{u}_x$ is a multi-hot vector describing a certain user's hometown preferences, while $\mathbf{u}_{xy}$ is the predicted out-of-town preference vector. The mapping loss is defined as follows:

$$\mathcal{L}_{map} = \sum_{u \in \mathcal{U}_o} \ell_1(\mathbf{u}_y, \mathbf{u}_{xy}), \tag{11}$$

where $\mathbf{u}_y$ is this user's ground-truth out-of-town preferences. The mapping loss can directly build the relationships between users' hometown preferences and out-of-town preferences.

3.5 GAN with Cycle Consistency

GAN with cycle consistency loss works in an unsupervised manner using a collection of data from the source and target domain that do not need to be related in any way. In our out-of-town recommendation scenario, we introduce it to further explore the data from non-overlapping users and then encourage generating richer mapping relationships between the user preferences in the home city and target city. To be specific, we build pseudo pair mapping of preferences between the users' hometown preferences and out-of-town preferences and leverage cycle consistency loss to constrain the procedure. First, we denote the cross-city encoding-decoding operator as follows:

$$\begin{aligned} T_{xy} &= D_y \circ E_x, \\ T_{yx} &= D_x \circ E_y, \end{aligned} \tag{12}$$

$T_{xy}(\cdot)$ employs the encoder of the home city and the decoder of the target city while $T_{yx}(\cdot)$ employs the encoder of the target city and the decoder of the home city. $T_{xy}(\cdot)$ aims to transform user preferences from the home city to the target city while $T_{yx}(\cdot)$ has the opposite functionality. Then we implement the cycle-mapping procedure:

$$\mathbf{u}_{xyx} = T_{yx} \circ T_{xy}(\mathbf{u}_x), \tag{13}$$

where the operator $T_{yx} \circ T_{xy}(\cdot)$ first transforms user preferences from the home city to the target city and then in turn transforms user preferences from the target city to the home city. The one way cycle consistency loss to constraint the cycle-mapping procedure is formulated as:

$$\mathcal{L}_{cycle} = \sum_{u \in \mathcal{U}_x} \ell_1(\mathbf{u}_x, \mathbf{u}_{xyx}). \tag{14}$$

In addition to the two DAEs, an adversarial discriminator $Dis(\cdot)$ is trained. GAN works as a competition among the generator and discriminator. The generator wants to make the generated vector $\mathbf{u}_{xy}$ resemble a real vector. The discriminator $Dis(\cdot)$ needs to do a binary classification task, in which it aims to identify the $\mathbf{u}_y$ as true but $\mathbf{u}_{xy}$ as false. The following losses are used:

$$\begin{aligned}\mathcal{L}_{\mathrm{GAN}_{xy}} &= \sum_{u \in \mathcal{U}_x} \ell_2\left(Dis\left(\mathbf{u}_{xy}\right), 1\right), \\ \mathcal{L}_{\mathrm{DIS}_{xy}} &= \sum_{u \in \mathcal{U}_x} \ell_2\left(Dis\left(\mathbf{u}_{xy}\right), 0\right) + \sum_{u \in \mathcal{U}_y} \ell_2\left(Dis\left(\mathbf{u}_{y}\right), 1\right),\end{aligned} \tag{15}$$

namely, the generator and discriminator losses of GAN. As for the loss function ℓ_2, we adopt binary cross entropy loss.

3.6 Model Learning

We optimize the generative adversarial model in an alternate mode. During the stage of generation, we try to minimize $\mathcal{L}$ defined as follows:

$$\mathcal{L} = \mathcal{L}_{map} + \lambda_1 \mathcal{L}_{cycle} + \lambda_2 \mathcal{L}_{\mathrm{GAN}_{xy}}, \tag{16}$$

while during the stage of discrimination, the goal of the model is to minimize $\mathcal{L}_{\mathrm{DIS}_{xy}}$. We repeat the two-stage procedure until convergence.

4 Experiments

In this section, we compare our model with numbers of out-of-town baselines on four real-world datasets. The ablation experiments will also be discussed.

4.1 Experiment Settings

Table 1. Statistics of the datasets

Dataset		# Users	# POIs	# Check-ins	# travellers
PL→AU	Portland	45001	12059	621446	468
	Austin	55978	15237	804985	
AU→BO	Austin	55978	15237	804985	381
	Boston	36253	8805	489005	
NY→LA	New York	24343	10907	394540	415
	Los Angeles	9850	5894	141728	
NY→CH	New York	24343	10907	394540	299
	Chicago	7244	3739	108692	

Datasets. To explore users' cross-city POI visiting behaviors, we build four real-world out-of-town recommendation tasks including PL→AU, AU→BO from Yelp [11], and NY→LA, NY→CH from Foursquare [11] to evaluate our model. PL→AU stands for traveling from Portland to Austin, AU→BO stands for Austin to Boston, NY→LA stands for New York to Los Angeles and NY→CH stands for New York to Chicago. To ensure the data quality, in each dataset, we filter out users with less than five interactions and POIs with less than ten interactions. As the details listed in Table 1 illustrates, there are a large number of check-ins in the home city and target city. However, the number of users who travel from the home city to the target city is no more than one thousand. This requires us to seek an effective way to build cross-city check-in relationships. For each task, we divide overlapping users following 25% for training, 25% for validating to optimize hyperparameters, and 50% for testing.

Baselines. To evaluate the performance of our model for out-of-town recommendation, we compare it with the following baselines:

- **TOP-All**: it is a very simple method that recommends the POIs most frequently visited by all users, including locals and travellers in the target city.
- **TOP-Traveller**: this method recommends POIs according to the popularity among travellers.
- **UCF**: this method utilizes the check-in histories of overlapping users and implements the traditional user-based CF method to recommend POIs for a target user according to the check-in behaviors of similar users. The cosine similarity between two users' location vectors in the home city is leveraged as the similarity between two users.
- **BPR-MF** [15]: this model leverages MF to factorize the user-POI matrix into the latent factors and optimizes the MF training by the pairwise ranking loss. To be applied to the out-of-town scenario, it constructs a unified matrix that all users and POIs from the home city and target city are taken as rows and columns respectively.
- **EMCDR-BPR** [12]: this method is a state-of-the-art cross-domain recommendation framework for cold-start users. In out-of-town recommendation scenario, it first obtains the user and POI embeddings for the home city and target city via the pre-training with Matrix Factorization. Then it leverages a multi-layer perceptron to capture the nonlinear mapping relationship across cities by using overlapping users between different cities as a bridge.
- **UIDT** [5]: UIDT utilizes novel user and POI embedding design to incorporate knowledge from travellers' visit records in their hometown and local people's visit records in the target city, so as to supplement insufficient information about drifting interests. It's designed for the scenario of making out-of-town recommendation for the target user who has left some check-ins in the target new city. To make the method adaptive to our totally cold-start scenario, i.e., the target user hasn't left any check-ins in the target new city, we design the user embedding for the traveller as a transformation from the user embedding of hometown. We use an MLP as the transformation function.

Table 2. Performance comparison

Methods	PL→AU				AU→BO			
	R@10	R@20	R@30	N@30	R@10	R@20	R@30	N@30
BPR-MF	0.0233	0.0424	0.0545	0.0788	0.0214	0.0347	0.0446	0.0854
TrainOR	0.0600	0.1129	0.1661	0.1612	0.0837	0.1024	0.1250	0.2174
TOP-All	0.0663	0.1153	0.1490	0.1643	0.0579	0.1056	0.1291	0.2608
UCF	0.0698	0.1204	0.1524	0.2295	0.0689	0.0945	0.1162	0.2450
TOP-Traveller	0.0767	0.1360	0.1820	0.2315	0.0760	0.0996	0.1407	0.2789
UIDT	0.0656	0.1394	0.1850	0.2130	0.0830	0.1204	0.1415	0.2643
HOPE	0.0764	0.1331	0.1881	0.2128	0.0719	0.1087	0.1464	0.2732
EMCDR-BPR	0.0749	0.1267	0.1644	0.2084	0.0814	0.1224	0.1569	0.2874
ACCAC	**0.1019**	**0.1695**	**0.2180**	**0.2925**	**0.1030**	**0.1521**	**0.1908**	**0.2971**
Methods	NY→LA				NY→CH			
	R@10	R@20	R@30	N@30	R@10	R@20	R@30	N@30
BPR-MF	0.0579	0.0701	0.0808	0.2660	0.0270	0.0355	0.0447	0.1274
TrainOR	0.1544	0.1862	0.1986	0.6833	0.1152	0.1768	0.2062	0.5881
TOP-All	0.1376	0.1634	0.1777	0.6823	0.1219	0.1475	0.1716	0.5723
UCF	0.1537	0.1772	0.1894	0.6910	0.1408	0.1856	0.2244	0.6048
TOP-Traveller	0.1539	0.1832	0.2010	0.6984	0.1290	0.1662	0.1920	0.5727
UIDT	0.1497	0.1803	0.1959	0.6977	0.1411	0.1684	0.1979	0.5729
HOPE	0.1403	0.1715	0.1941	0.6637	0.1335	0.1743	0.2064	0.5443
EMCDR-BPR	0.1434	0.1839	0.2103	0.6807	0.1562	0.2033	0.2293	0.6050
ACCAC	**0.1578**	**0.2031**	**0.2277**	**0.7074**	**0.1647**	**0.2304**	**0.2650**	**0.6402**

- **HOPE** [16]: this deep neural model incorporates the information of hometown preferences, out-of-town preferences and region-based out-of-town pattern of visitors together for out-of-town recommendation. In our cold-start out-of-town recommendation scenario, we remove the out-of-town preferences module.
- **TrainOR** [20]: TrainOR adopts an MLP as the nonlinear mapping function between users' hometown preferences and out-of-town check-in behavior and integrates this mapping function with travel intention building to make out-of-town recommendation.

Evaluation Metrics. We adopt Recall@k (R@k) and NDCG@k (N@k) to evaluate the performance of different methods. These metrics are commonly used in top-N recommendations.

Implementation Details. We implement all the models using pytorch, and run the codes on GPU machines of Nvidia GeForce RTX 2080 Ti. All models based on MF or deep learning are trained using Adam[9] optimizer and the mini-batch size is set to 512. As for MF-based baselines, i.e., BPR-MF, EMCDR-BPR and UIDT, we tune the dimension of embeddings in [32, 64, 128, 256]. For the mapping function of EMCDR-BPR, we use a two-layer network with hidden units $2 \times k$ where k denotes the embedding dimension.

The details of implementing our proposed method are as follows. The overall structure for denoising autoencoders is [200, 100, 50, 100, 200], where [200, 100, 50] is the encoder part and [50, 100, 200] is the decoder part. 50 represents the dimension of the latent vector output from the encoder. The dimension of the LSTM hidden layer is set to 200. As for the discriminator network, we adopt the structure [200, 100, 1] for all tasks. In addition, Dropout is used in the input layer and we set the Dropout probability 0.5. The activation function f is set as the tanh function. λ_1 and λ_2 are tuned in the range of [0.01, 0.05, 0.1, 0.5, 1, 5, 10]. The learning rate for the pre-training stage is set to 0.001 while the learning rate for the mapping stage is set to 0.0001.

4.2 Comparison with Baselines

The performance of all methods over the four out-of-town recommendation tasks are reported in Table 2. We can obtain the following findings by analyzing the results.

- *Finding 1 - Our proposed model consistently outperforms all baselines in all four tasks.* It is clear that our proposed model outperforms other competitor models significantly when facing the practical challenge that a small portion of users overlap between the home city and target city.
- *Finding 2 - TOP-based methods are surprisingly very competitive baselines and outperform some well-designed approaches.* Though TOP-based methods are non-personalized, they show relatively good performance. Meanwhile, TOP-Traveller performs better than TOP-All in all four tasks, we can explain these phenomena for that users usually go to an unfamiliar city for the purpose of tourism and they prefer to visit attractions that have high popularity among other travellers.
- *Finding 3 - EMCDR-BPR shows comparable performance to many baselines but even drops behind TOP-Traveller in some tasks.* This suggests that the pre-training and mapping structure is a good choice to learn interest drift patterns [3]. However, it performs worse than TOP-Traveller in **NY→CH** task. This justifies its mechanism sometimes isn't able to leverage the beneficial knowledge obtained from hometown for out-of-town recommendation when the number of overlapping users is very limited. We can speculate it is because EMCDR-BPR recommends POIs which are strongly biased to the out-of-town preferences of the overlapping users used for training.
- *Finding 4 - UIDT and HOPE drop behind TOP-Traveller in some tasks.* Though they incorporate knowledge from travellers' visit records in their hometown and local people's visit records in the target city, they still perform worse than TOP-Traveller in some tasks, which is probably due to the following reasons. On the one hand, they discard the useful data of non-overlapping users' check-in activities in the home city. On the other hand, they both adopt an end-to-end manner to train the models, the joint training for the two cities is very unstable that not only causes the failure of learning POI embeddings but also greatly influences the effectiveness of learning interest drift patterns.

- *Finding 5 - The methods which merely use the data of overlapping users perform poorly.* UCF and TrainOR perform poorly since they merely utilize the data from overlapping users. These observations suggest that it's impracticable to neglect the check-in behaviours of non-overlapping users in our tasks.
- *Finding 6 - BPR-MF performs the worst in all tasks.* The very poor performance of BPR-MF verifies that mixing the data of two cities together isn't feasible, especially when the overlapping users occupy a very small proportion.

4.3 Ablation Study

To evaluate the effect of the hierarchical category feature and the CycleGAN, we compare ACCAC with its different variants respectively. These variants of ACCAC are listed as follows:

- **ACCAC-CYCLE_GAN-CAT**, which doesn't use the feature of category hierarchy and removes GAN with cycle consistency loss.
- **ACCAC-CYCLE_GAN**, which removes GAN with cycle consistency loss. This version doesn't build pseudo pair mapping relationships.
- **ACCAC-CAT**, a simplified version of ACCAC that doesn't use the feature of category hierarchy.

Table 3. Ablation study on all four tasks.

Methods	PL→AU				AU→BO			
	R@10	R@20	R@30	N@30	R@10	R@20	R@30	N@30
CCAC-CYCLE_GAN-CAT	0.0940	0.1452	0.2015	0.2491	0.0932	0.1393	0.1736	0.2849
CCAC-CYCLE_GAN	0.0971	0.1571	0.2028	0.2854	0.0937	0.1404	0.1790	0.2878
CCAC-CAT	0.0973	0.1635	0.2111	0.2854	0.0928	0.1439	0.1857	0.2846
CCAC	**0.1019**	**0.1695**	**0.2180**	**0.2925**	**0.1030**	**0.1521**	**0.1908**	**0.2971**
Methods	NY→LA				NY→CH			
	R@10	R@20	R@30	N@30	R@10	R@20	R@30	N@30
CCAC-CYCLE_GAN-CAT	0.1494	0.1889	0.2106	0.6875	0.1587	0.2195	0.2516	0.6295
CCAC-CYCLE_GAN	0.1535	0.1932	0.2207	0.6888	0.1602	0.2198	0.2571	0.6387
CCAC-CAT	0.1562	0.1950	0.2216	0.6928	0.1600	0.2221	0.2594	0.6382
CCAC	**0.1578**	**0.2031**	**0.2277**	**0.7074**	**0.1647**	**0.2304**	**0.2650**	**0.6402**

The results of the variants are shown in Table 3, from which we can have the following observations. First, ACCAC-CYCLE_GAN performs better than ACCAC-CYCLE_GAN-CAT. Such results validate the effectiveness of category hierarchy knowledge, which is carried with rich semantic information. Second, ACCAC-CAT has better performance than ACCAC-CYCLE_GAN-CAT, demonstrating that GAN with cycle consistency loss is able to capture more potential mapping relationships between users' hometown preferences and out-of-town preferences. Third, ACCAC performs the best among them, which verifies that the combination of the extraction of hierarchical category feature knowledge and GAN with cycle consistency loss can further improve the performance in our out-of-town recommendation tasks.

5 Conclusion

In this paper, we propose a novel model to resolve out-of-town recommendation problem. First, we extract useful information from the hierarchical categories of POIs and utilize denoising autoencoders to obtain representative pre-trained POI embeddings. Then, we adopt adversarial cycle-consistent dual autoencoder model to learn the non-linear mapping function between users' hometown preferences and out-of-town preferences. This enables to alleviate the challenge that the number of overlapping users between the home city and target city is very limited. By evaluating our model on four real-world out-of-town recommendation datasets, our approach is proved to outperform the compared baseline models. In future work, we will attempt to use more auxiliary information like user reviews to further improve the performance of our model.

References

1. Bao, J., Zheng, Y., Mokbel, M.F.: Location-based and preference-aware recommendation using sparse geo-social networking data. In: Proceedings of the 20th International Conference on Advances in Geographic Information Systems, pp. 199–208 (2012)
2. Chen, L., et al.: Entity summarization via exploiting description complementarity and salience. IEEE Trans. Neural Netw. Learn. Syst. **2022**, 1–13 (2022)
3. Chen, L., Li, Z., Wang, Y., Xu, T., Wang, Z., Chen, E.: MMEA: entity alignment for multi-modal knowledge graph. In: Li, G., Shen, H.T., Yuan, Y., Wang, X., Liu, H., Zhao, X. (eds.) KSEM 2020. LNCS (LNAI), vol. 12274, pp. 134–147. Springer, Cham (2020). https://doi.org/10.1007/978-3-030-55130-8_12
4. Ding, D., Zhang, M., Pan, X., Yang, M., He, X.: Modeling personalized out-of-town distances in location recommendation. In: 2020 IEEE International Conference on Data Mining (ICDM), pp. 112–121. IEEE (2020)
5. Ding, J., Yu, G., Li, Y., Jin, D., Gao, H.: Learning from hometown and current city: cross-city poi recommendation via interest drift and transfer learning. Proc. ACM Interact. Mobile Wear. Ubiquit. Technol. **3**(4), 1–28 (2019)
6. Dwibedi, D., Aytar, Y., Tompson, J., Sermanet, P., Zisserman, A.: Temporal cycle-consistency learning. In: Proceedings of the IEEE/CVF Conference on Computer Vision and Pattern Recognition, pp. 1801–1810 (2019)
7. Ference, G., Ye, M., Lee, W.C.: Location recommendation for out-of-town users in location-based social networks. In: Proceedings of the 22nd ACM International Conference on Information and Knowledge Management, pp. 721–726 (2013)
8. Hochreiter, S., Schmidhuber, J.: Long short-term memory. Neural Comput. **9**(8), 1735–1780 (1997)

9. Kingsma, D., Ba, J.: Adam: a method for stochastic optimization. In: Proceedings of 2th International Conference on Learning Representations. New York, NY, USA (2014). https://arxiv.org/abs/1412.6980v1
10. Liu, J., et al.: Exploiting aesthetic preference in deep cross networks for cross-domain recommendation. In: Proceedings of the Web Conference 2020, pp. 2768–2774 (2020)
11. Liu, Y., Pham, T.A.N., Cong, G., Yuan, Q.: An experimental evaluation of point-of-interest recommendation in location-based social networks. Proc. VLDB Endow. **10**(10), 1010–1021 (2017)
12. Man, T., Shen, H., Jin, X., Cheng, X.: Cross-domain recommendation: an embedding and mapping approach. In: IJCAI, vol. 17, pp. 2464–2470 (2017)
13. Ouyang, Y., Liu, W., Rong, W., Xiong, Z.: Autoencoder-based collaborative filtering. In: Loo, C.K., Yap, K.S., Wong, K.W., Beng Jin, A.T., Huang, K. (eds.) ICONIP 2014. LNCS, vol. 8836, pp. 284–291. Springer, Cham (2014). https://doi.org/10.1007/978-3-319-12643-2_35
14. Pham, T.A.N., Li, X., Cong, G.: A general model for out-of-town region recommendation. In: Proceedings of the 26th International Conference on World Wide Web, pp. 401–410 (2017)
15. Rendle, S., Freudenthaler, C., Gantner, Z., Schmidt-Thieme, L.: BPR: Bayesian personalized ranking from implicit feedback. arXiv preprint arXiv:1205.2618 (2012)
16. Sun, H., Xu, J., Zhou, R., Chen, W., Zhao, L., Liu, C.: Hope: a hybrid deep neural model for out-of-town next poi recommendation. In: World Wide Web, pp. 1–20 (2021)
17. Wang, H., Fu, Y., Wang, Q., Yin, H., Du, C., Xiong, H.: A location-sentiment-aware recommender system for both home-town and out-of-town users. In: Proceedings of the 23rd ACM SIGKDD International Conference on Knowledge Discovery and Data Mining, pp. 1135–1143 (2017)
18. Xiao, L., Min, Z., Yongfeng, Z.: Joint factorizational topic models for cross-city recommendation. In: Chen, L., Jensen, C.S., Shahabi, C., Yang, X., Lian, X. (eds.) APWeb-WAIM 2017. LNCS, vol. 10366, pp. 591–609. Springer, Cham (2017). https://doi.org/10.1007/978-3-319-63579-8_45
19. Xie, M., Yin, H., Wang, H., Xu, F., Chen, W., Wang, S.: Learning graph-based poi embedding for location-based recommendation. In: Proceedings of the 25th ACM International on Conference on Information and Knowledge Management, pp. 15–24 (2016)
20. Xin, H., et al.: Out-of-town recommendation with travel intention modeling. In: Proceedings of the AAAI Conference on Artificial Intelligence, vol. 35, pp. 4529–4536 (2021)
21. Yin, H., Cui, B., Sun, Y., Hu, Z., Chen, L.: LCARS: a spatial item recommender system. ACM Trans. Inf. Syst. (TOIS) **32**(3), 1–37 (2014)
22. Yin, H., Cui, B., Zhou, X., Wang, W., Huang, Z., Sadiq, S.: Joint modeling of user check-in behaviors for real-time point-of-interest recommendation. ACM Trans. Inf. Syst. (TOIS) **35**(2), 1–44 (2016)
23. Zhang, C., Wang, K.: Poi recommendation through cross-region collaborative filtering. Knowl. Inf. Syst. **46**(2), 369–387 (2016)
24. Zhao, Y.L., Nie, L., Wang, X., Chua, T.S.: Personalized recommendations of locally interesting venues to tourists via cross-region community matching. ACM Trans. Intell. Syst. Technol. (TIST) **5**(3), 1–26 (2014)
25. Zhu, J.Y., et al.: Multimodal image-to-image translation by enforcing bi-cycle consistency. In: Advances in Neural Information Processing Systems, pp. 465–476 (2017)

Prompt as a Knowledge Probe for Chinese Spelling Check

Kun Peng[1,2], Nannan Sun[1(✉)], Jiahao Cao[1,2], Rui Liu[1,2], Jiaqian Ren[1,2], and Lei Jiang[1]

[1] Institute of Information Engineering, Chinese Academy of Sciences, Beijing, China
{pengkun,sunnannan,caojiahao,liurui,renjiaqian,jianglei}@iie.ac.cn
[2] School of Cyber Security, University of Chinese Academy of Sciences, Beijing, China

Abstract. Chinese Spelling Check (CSC) is a challenging task to detect and correct wrong characters in Chinese sentences. Since most Chinese spelling mistakes are caused by visual or pronunciation similarities of characters, recent researches tend to utilize external phonological and morphological resources for this task. However, their works rely heavily on hand-constructed confusion sets and multimodal data, causing high labor costs. To this end, we propose an end-to-end generative model called PromptCSC. First, we notice that the misspelling of characters causes unnatural semantic incoherence in sentences. By using the prompt template as a knowledge probe, PromptCSC detects and outputs the error probability of each character in the sentence. The error locations are then corrected using BERT's soft mask mechanism. Experimental results on the SIGHAN benchmarks show that our approach achieves excellent performance without external resources.

Keywords: Chinese Spelling Check · Prompt-tuning · Natural language processing · Pre-training model · BERT

1 Introduce

Chinese is an ideographic language, and each Chinese character is an independent and basic unit in the dictionary. Most Chinese spelling mistakes are caused by characters' visual and phonological similarities. These mistakes include human writing mistakes and machine recognition mistakes, such as Optical Character Recognition (OCR) [1] and Automatic Speech Recognition (ASR) [2].

The purpose of Chinese Spelling Correction (CSC) is to detect and correct typos in sentences, which is challenging and crucial for many downstream applications, such as OCR, search query correction [3], essay scoring [4]. The CSC task only considers misspellings, not redundancies or missing characters. It means that the input and output sentences of the model are the same length. Spelling mistakes in English often result in a problem that the word is not in the dictionary [5], making it easy to detect. But in Chinese, every character that

G. Memmi et al. (Eds.): KSEM 2022, LNAI 13370, pp. 516–527, 2022.
https://doi.org/10.1007/978-3-031-10989-8_41

Table 1. Two cases of Chinese spelling mistakes.

Cases	Example
Wrong	企鹅生活在南极州
Translation	Penguins live in the southernmost state
Truth	企鹅生活在南极洲
Translation	Penguins live in Antarctica
Wrong	如果中了大奖，你姓福吗?
Translation	If you win the jackpot, is your surname Fu?
Truth	如果中了大奖，你幸福吗?
Translation	Are you happy if you win the jackpot?

can be read on a computer system is a basic unit in a dictionary. Since there are no clear word boundaries between Chinese characters, we can only judge the correctness by contacting the context. Table 1 shows two cases of Chinese spelling mistakes. The first misspelling 州/洲 is caused by visual similarity, and the second misspelling 姓/幸 is caused by pronunciation similarity. In Table 1 case 1, 洲 means continent but 州 means state. To correct spelling, we need not only phonology but also world knowledge. In Table 1 case 2, 幸福 means happiness but 姓福 means surname Fu, and we can only judge it by referring to morphology and the semantics of the entire sentence span. Therefore, the ability of the model to learn world knowledge and contextual semantics is critical for CSC.

Pre-trained language models like BERT [6] have made great progress on the CSC task. Recent researches attempt to use knowledge of the phonetics and morphology of Chinese characters. They construct confusion sets containing a series of similar character pairs. In the work of SpellGCN [7], they used a GCN network [8] to incorporate pre-extracted similarity knowledge into BERT, but such work heavily relies on hand-constructed confusion sets and has limited coverage of characters. More recently, Both ReaLise [9] and PHMOSpell [10] used a multimodal model to integrate phonetic, glyph, and semantic information. They achieved new success, but their models require an extra-large amount of data to pre-train the model.

In this paper, we observe that spelling mistakes can corrupt the semantics of Chinese sentences. In order not to rely on external resources, we hope to further activate the semantic understanding ability of the pre-training language models. Prompt-tuning [11] is a new fine-tuning paradigm. By selecting appropriate prompt templates and fine-tuning targets, prompt-tuning forces the model to be more adaptive to downstream tasks. The task-related knowledge is further activated to improve the model performance.

Motivated by the above observations, we propose an end-to-end model called PromptCSC. PromptCSC uses the prompt method to activate semantic knowledge related to spell checking from BERT, and we design a pointer network to find the locations of spelling errors. Specifically, PromptCSC consists of a prompt-based detector and a softmask-based corrector. Both of them are based on BERT. In the detector, we use a designed prompt template as a knowledge probe to detect the semantic incoherence of the input sentence, then output the error probability for each token position. Next, inspired by the work of Softmask Bert [12], in the corrector, we mask each token according to its error probability. Using this dynamic masking mechanism, the character with a higher error probability will be masked more thoroughly. At last, we input the soft masked tokens sequence into BERT and output the corrected sentence.

The contributions of our work are as follows: (1) We are the first to use the prompts method on the CSC task. Compared with previous methods, PromptCSC does not require extensive multimodal data or hand-crafted confusion sets. (2) Experiments on the SIGHAN benchmarks demonstrate that PromptCSC outperforms most baseline methods. (3) Benefit from prompts learning, it is easy to migrate PromptCSC to industrial scenarios with fewer data.

The following sections of this paper are as follows: Sect. 2 presents the related works. Section 3 describes task formulation and architecture of our model. Section 4 shows experimental results. Section 5 gives conclusion.

2 Related Works

2.1 Chinese Spelling Correction

CSC is an important task. Early works [13,14] devised different system rules to regulate spelling and handle erroneous Chinese characters. In Xiong's [15] work, they use the Hidden Markov Model and a rule-based ranking model. After that, the neural network methods brought great progress to CSC, such as the sequence labeling method [16] and the sequence-to-sequence model [17].

Pre-trained language models have achieved great success in many NLP tasks. Faspell [18] trained a BERT-based Deep Noise Reduction Encoder (DAE) and a Confidence-Phonetic-Shape-Similarity-based Decoder (CSD) to dynamically select the Chinese character candidates. However, due to the completely random mask method, the model cannot comprehensively learn the rules of misspellings. Softmask-Bert [12], which inspired our work, uses a GRU network to predict the error positions of a sentence, and uses a soft mask mechanism to mask tokens with error probability. DCN [19] proposes a Dynamic Connected Networks (DCN), which can build dependencies between adjacent characters, to make full use of context information.

Recent works consider incorporating more external knowledge to improve model performance. SpellGCN [7] pre-designed two glyph and phonetic similarity maps, and then used a GCN network [8] to incorporate the similarity information into the BERT model. However, since the similarity map is handcrafted and covers limited Chinese characters, the model performance will drop when the target is not in the candidates. PLOME [20] designs a masking strategy based on semantic confusion sets, using pinyin and stroke as input for model pre-training and fine-tuning. REALISE [9] and PHMOSpell [10] use a multimodal approach to fuse glyph visual and phonological information. However, these works rely heavily on manually constructed confusion sets and external multimodal resources.

2.2 Prompt Tuning

Prompt tuning [21] is a new fine-tuning paradigm. It makes the model more suitable for downstream tasks by selecting appropriate templates, while avoiding adding additional parameters. Prompt tuning achieves great success in Few-shot and Zero-shot scenes. Due to the difficulty of hand-crafting the best template [22], works by PET [23] and AutoPrompt [24] attempt to automatically select the most appropriate template for downstream tasks. Other works [22,25,26] go further and try to build parameterized templates, these works achieve new success. However, manually selecting the appropriate prompt templates is a challenging task, and automatically constructing prompt templates incurs additional computational overhead.

3 Method

3.1 Task Formulation

CSC can be regarded as a special sequence-to-sequence task, because only the misspelled characters need to be modified, so the input and output lengths are the same. Given a Chinese sentence $X = \{x_1, x_2 ... x_n\}$, n is the sentence length. In the sentence-level CSC task, the model needs to detect and correct all misspelled Chinese characters in the sentence, and output its corresponding corrected sentence $Y = \{y_1, y_2 ... y_n\}$.

3.2 Model

Our model is shown in Fig. 1, which consists of a detector and a corrector, both of which are implemented with BERT's encoder. Given a sentence, first, we combine it with the designed template, then feed it into the BERT-encoder detector and output a representation. The representation is used as a misspelling probe in a pointer network, and outputs the error probability at each token position. After that, we use the soft mask method to mask each token with its error probability, then input it into the corrector, and finally output the corrected sentence. In the following subsections, we will introduce the specific implementation of the detector and corrector respectively.

Prompt-Based Detector. As a new paradigm for knowledge mining in pre-trained language models [21], prompts can be regarded as a probe to activate specific knowledge [27]. We observe that the semantics of misspelling locations are incoherent in a Chinese sentence. So we can construct a prompt template as

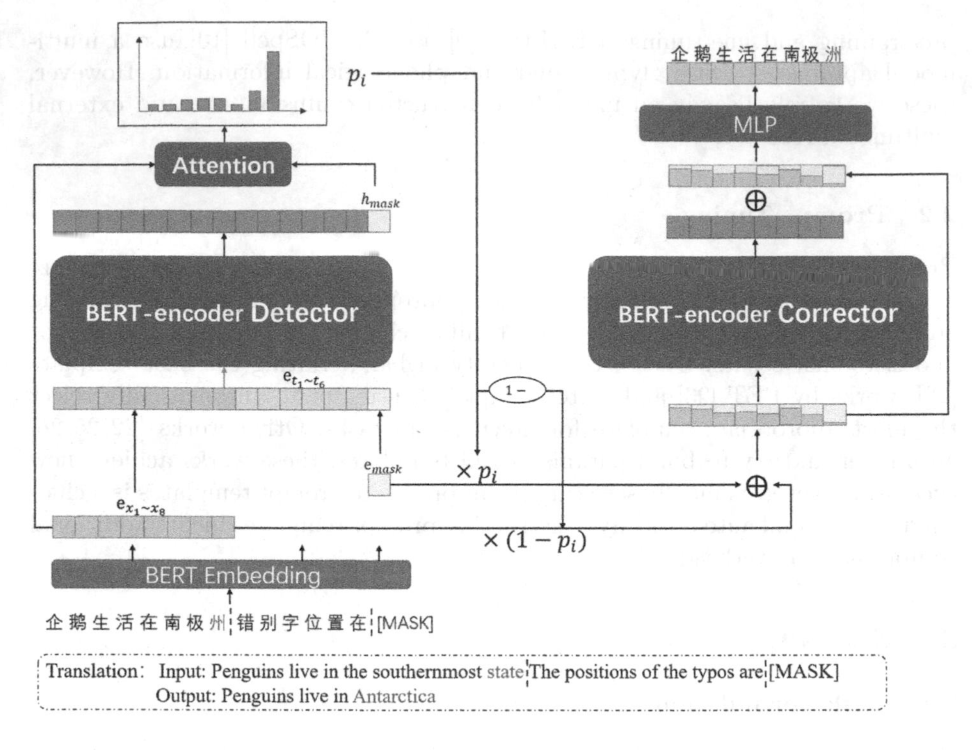

Fig. 1. Architecture of PromptCSC.

a semantic probe to detect semantic incoherences in the sentence. It also forces the model to activate relevant knowledge.

The prompt-based detector is shown on the left in Fig. 1. First, we manually or automatically build a prompt template $T = \{t_1, t_2 ... t_m\}$, m is the template length. Such as '错别字位置是' (The location of the type is).

After that, we concatenate the embedding of original sentence X, template T and [MASK] together as follows:

$$L = (E_{x_1:x_n}, E_{t_1:t_m}, E_{mask})$$

where $E_{x_1:x_n}$, $E_{t_1:t_m}$, E_{mask} are the embedding of X, T, $[MASK]$ respectively. L is the input embedding of detector, the length of L is $n + m + 1$. Inputting L into the BERT-encoder detector and outputting the representation H of the last layer.

$$H = (H^x_{1:n}, H^t_{1:m}, h_{mask})$$

where H^x,H^t and h_{mask} is the corresponding representations of X, T and $[MASK]$. h_{mask} is the key output of prompt learning, it can be used as a knowledge probe in a pointer network to indicate where spelling mistakes are. We use the attention mechanism to calculate the error probability for each token x_i:

$$p_i = \sigma(h^T_{mask} e_{x_i})$$

where i is the position, e_{x_i} is the embedding of x_i, σ is a sigmoid activation function. The sequence of character error probabilities are as follows:

$$P_{det} = \{p_1, p_2...p_n\}, p_i \in [0, 1]$$

Figure 2 shows an example of P_{det}, we can see that the error probability is higher near the error location. The detector's loss function is defined as follows:

$$\mathcal{L}_{det} = -\sum_{i=1}^{n} l_i \log p_i$$

where $l_i \in \{0, 1\}$ is the label of characters in original sentence, 1 means wrong and 0 means right.

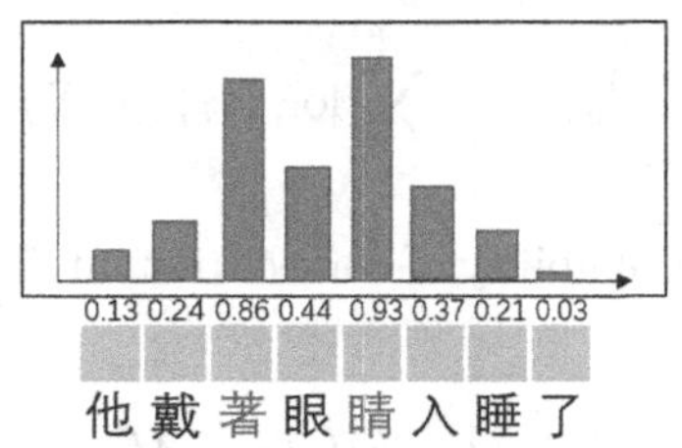
0.13 0.24 0.86 0.44 0.93 0.37 0.21 0.03
他戴著眼睛入睡了
False: he fell asleep wearing writing eye
Truth: he fell asleep with glasses on

Fig. 2. An example of error probability distribution

Softmask-Based Corrector. BERT's default hard mask mechanism randomly masks 15% of the original characters. Since the masking process is not associated with the wrong characters, it is hard to learn the relevant knowledge that caused the misspelling, resulting in a low error detection rate. The soft mask mechanism is an extension of the hard mask, which uses the error probability to mask the characters, effectively improving the correction ability of the model.

As shown on the right in Fig. 1, our softmask-based corrector is a sequential multi-class labeling model. The input is the original sentence embedding: $E_X = (e_{x_1}, e_{x_2}...e_{x_n})$, and output is the corrected character sequence: $Y = \{y_1, y_2...y_n\}$. Inspired by Softmask-bert [12], for each e_{x_i} in E_X, we soft mask it with its corresponding error probability p_i:

$$e'_{x_i} = (1 - p_i) \times e_{x_i} + p_i \times e_{mask}$$

where e_{mask} is the embedding of [MASK], e'_{x_i} is the soft masked embedding of e_{x_i}. The soft masked embedding sequence is $E' = (e'_{x_1}, e'_{x_2}...e'_{x_n})$.

When the error probability p_i is close to 1, e'_{x_i} is close to e_{mask}; when the error probability p_i is close to 0, e'_{x_i} is close to original e_{x_i}. This means that misspelled tokens have a high probability of being masked and predicted, forcing the model to learn knowledge about misspellings.

Inputting E' into Bert-encoder corrector and outputting the representations of the last hidden layer: $H^c = (h_1^c, h_2^c...h_n^c)$. Then we feed H^c into a residual connection:

$$\tilde{H}^c = H^c + E'$$

For each token of the sequence, the correction probability is calculated as follows:

$$P_{cor}(y_i = \tilde{y_i}|X) = softmax(W\tilde{h}_i^c + b) \times \tilde{y_i}$$

where $\tilde{y_i}$ is the candidate token, $P_{cor}(y_i = \tilde{y_i}|X)$ is the probability that the predicted value is $\tilde{y_i}$. $\tilde{h}_i^c \in \tilde{H}^c$, W and b are parameters of a linear layer. Take the token with the highest probability as the output of the final model prediction.

Corrector's loss function can be defined as follows:

$$\mathcal{L}_{cor} = -\sum_{i=1}^{n} \log P_{cor}(y_i|X)$$

where $P_{cor}(y_i|X)$ is the probability of correct output. The final total loss function of the model is defined as:

$$\mathcal{L} = (1-\lambda)\mathcal{L}_{det} + \lambda\mathcal{L}_{cor}$$

where $\lambda \in [0, 1]$ is a coefficient.

4 Experiments

4.1 Datasets

We used SIGHAN benchmarks [1,17,28], which contains 7476 samples. Following previous work [9,10,19], we also included 271329 dummy data made by OCR and ASR methods [16]. We split a total of 277801 samples into train sets and validation sets. In this paper, we assume that the maximum length of sentences is 128, and we prune sentences larger than this length in the dataset. In fact, only a few sentences exceed this length. We evaluate our model on three standard test datasets: SIGHAN13, SIGHAN14, and SIGHAN15, which have 1000, 1062, and 1100 examples, respectively. The detailed statistic of the data is presented in Table 2.

Table 2. Statistics of datasets

Training data	Erroneous sent/Sent	Avg. length
SIGHAN13	683/1700	43.6
SIGHAN14	3358/3437	49.6
SIGHAN15	2273/2339	31.3
Wang-271k	271009/271329	42.5
Total	277323/278805	42.7
Test data	Erroneous sent/Sent	Avg. length
SIGHAN13	971/1000	74.3
SIGHAN14	520/1062	50.0
SIGHAN15	541/1100	30.6
Total	2032/3162	50.9

4.2 Baselines

We compare our model with recent advanced works to evaluate the performance of our method. These baselines are listed below:

- **FASpell** [18]. This method designs a BERT-based Deep Noise Reduction Encoder to dynamically generate candidate words.
- **Softmask-BERT** [12]. This method designs a GRU detector to identify the error probability and predict the correct character using a soft-mask BERT.
- **SpellGCN** [7]. This method integrates hand-crafted phonological and morphological knowledge graphs using GCN.
- **DCN** [19]. This method proposes a Dynamic Connected Networks (DCN) that can build dependencies between adjacent characters.
- **ReaLise** [9] and **PHMOSpell** [10]. These two methods use a multimodal approach to integrate glyph visual and phonological information.

4.3 Experimental Setup

Our model is implemented based on pytorch[1], and the code is based on the work of Cai [29]. We use Chinese-BERT [30] to initialize our model parameters. Our model is trained with a batch size of 32 and is tested with a batch size of 16. We use the AdamW optimizer to train the model with a learning rate of $1e^{-4}$ for 10 epochs, and then gradually decrease the learning rate for another 10 epochs. All experiments are performed on a GeForce RTX 3090 with 16G memory.

Our experiments use a sentence-level evaluation metric, which requires that all misspellings in a sentence are fully detected or corrected. Therefore, it is more rigorous than the character-level evaluation method. We select the optimal λ, which is 0.8 for all the datasets.

[1] https://pytorch.org/.

4.4 Main Results

We compare our model with baseline methods on three test datasets. The results are shown in Table 3. Previous methods first detect and then give the corrected results. But PromptCSC directly outputs the corrected result, so the detection-level and correction-level accuracy/F1 are the same.

Table 3. Main results on different test datasets.

Method	SIGHAN13				SIGHAN14				SIGHAN15			
	Det		Cor		Det		Cor		Det		Cor	
	Acc.	F1	Acc.	F1	Acc.	F1	Acc.	F1	Acc.	F1	Acc.	F1
Faspell	-	69.1	-	66.2	-	57.0	-	55.4	-	63.5	-	62.6
Spell-GCN	-	77.2	-	75.4	-	67.2	-	65.3	-	77.7	-	75.9
DCN	-	83.0	-	81.0	-	68.9	-	67.2	-	79.0	-	76.3
ReaLise	**82.7**	85.4	**81.4**	84.1	78.4	69.6	77.7	68.1	**84.7**	79.3	**84.0**	77.8
PHMOSpell	77.1	86.7	75.4	85.6	**78.5**	**75.5**	76.9	73.1	82.6	80.5	80.9	78.1
Softmask-BERT[a]	60.1	75.1	60.1	75.1	73.8	70.2	73.8	70.2	81.7	80.2	81.7	80.2
Our model	78.8	**87.8**	78.8	**87.8**	77.8	75.4	**77.8**	**75.4**	83.1	**81.8**	83.1	**81.8**

[a]Means unofficial implementation. Det means detection-level and Cor means correction-level. Acc means accuracy.

As shown in Table 3, PromptCSC achieves the highest F1 at both detection-level and correction-level. Specifically, compared with the highest F1 method (PHMOSpell), at the detection-level, PromptCSC outperforms PHMOSpell 1.1% on SIGHAN13, −0.1% on SIGHAN14, 1.3% on SIGHAN15. At the correction-level, the improvements are 2.2% on SIGHAN13, 2.3% on SIGHAN14, and 2.7% on SIGHAN15. For accuracy, at the detection-level, PromptCSC outperforms PHMOSpell 1.7%, −0.7%, 0.5% respectively. At the correction-level, PromptCSC outperforms PHMOSpell 3.4%, 0.9%, 2.2% respectively. The above results prove that our model is much better than PHMOSpell in both accuracy and f1.

As for the highest accuracy baseline method (ReaLise). On detection-level accuracy, PromptCSC is 3.9%, 0.7%, 1.6% lower than ReaLise, respectively. On correction-level accuracy, PromptCSC is 2.6%, −0.1%, 0.9% lower than ReaLise, respectively. However, on detection-level F1, PromptCSC is 2.4%, 5.8%, 2.5% higher than ReaLise. On correction-level F1, PromptCSC is 3.7%, 7.3%, 4.0% higher than ReaLise. Besides, our model does not use multimodal data and achieves good performance.

The results of Softmask BERT† in Table 3 were unofficially implemented by Cai [29]. Compared with Softmask BERT, PromptCSC has average improved accuracy by 7.8% and F1 by 6.3%. This suggests that the prompt-based detector is a very effective component.

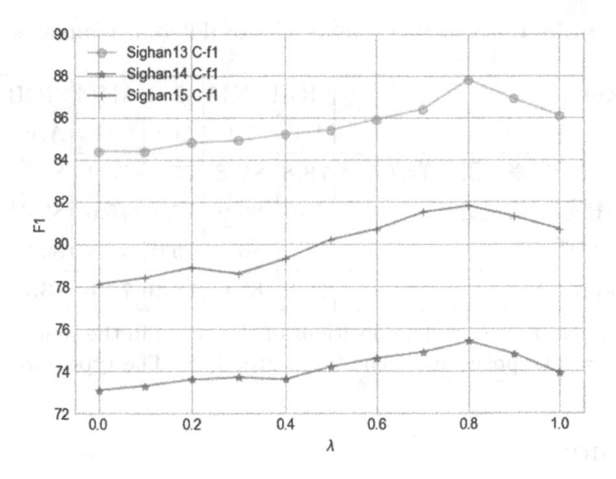

Fig. 3. Effects of different λ

4.5 Effect of Hyper Parameter

In the loss function, the coefficient λ has a very important impact on the result. Figure 3 shows the effects of different λ on the correction-level F1 of different datasets. As shown in Fig. 3, the best value of λ is 0.8. Such a result means that the corrector (0.8) is more important than the detector (0.2). Because the corrector can correct errors that are not clearly pointed out by the detector. For example, the error probability of the sentence "埃及金子/字塔" (Egyptian Gold Tower/Pyramids) is (0.11,0.13,0.19,0.34,0.23). The probability of the wrong location is not high, but since the model contains sufficient world knowledge, it can be corrected correctly.

4.6 Effect of Auto Prompt

Previous works [22,25,26] have demonstrated that by constructing parameterized templates, better results can be achieved than manually constructing templates. In this paper, we also explore the impact of parameterized templates. We used 8 consecutive undefined tokens as an initialization template: [unuesd1]-[unuesd8], and before inputting it into the detector, we used an LSTM to make it semantically relevant. Table 4 shows the correction-level results of the parameterized template and three handcrafted templates. The best λ is 0.8. Compared with the best hand-constructed templates, parameterized template improves the accuracy and F1 by 0.1% on average. This shows that the improvement of the auto-prompt method on the CSC task is limited. There is still a need for research.

Table 4. Correction-level results of different templates

Prompt	SIGHAN13		SIGHAN14		SIGHAN15	
	Acc.	F1	Acc.	F1	Acc.	F1
T_1 = 句子中错误汉字的位置是	**78.8**	**87.8**	77.8	75.4	83.1	81.8
T_2 = 错别字位置是	77.6	86.9	77.3	75.0	82.6	81.4
T_3 = 错别字在	77.1	86.1	76.0	74.4	80.9	79.4
Auto-prompt	78.5	87.6	**78.9**	**75.6**	**83.4**	**81.9**

Translation: T_1 = The positions of the typos in the sentence are. T_2 = The positions of the typos are. T_3 = The typos are.

5 Conclusion

In this paper, we proposed an end-to-end model called PromptCSC for Chinese spelling check. PromptCSC uses a prompt-based detector to find the unnatural locations in sentence semantics, and outputs error probabilities. Besides, a softmask-based corrector is used to better incorporate error probability distribution. Compared with previous works, the proposed PromptCSC achieves the highest F1 score and outperforms most baseline methods in accuracy. Benefit from prompt-tuning, PromptCSC does not require extensive additional multimodal data or hand-crafted confusion sets. PromptCSC can be easily migrated to industrial scenarios with fewer data. In future work, we will further explore the effectiveness of the prompt-tuning method on Chinese grammatical error correction, which is a more difficult task.

References

1. Yu, L.C., Lee, L.H, Tseng, Y.H., Chen, H.H.: Overview of SIGHAN 2014 bake-off for Chinese spelling check. In: CIPS-SIGHAN Joint Conference on Chinese Language Processing (2014)
2. Liu, C.-L., et al.: Visually and phonologically similar characters in incorrect Chinese words: analyses, identification, and applications. ACM Trans. Asian Lang. Inf. Process. **10**(2), 1–39 (2011)
3. Gao, J., Li, X., Micol, D., Quirk, C., Sun, X.: A large scale ranker-based system for search query spelling correction. In: International Conference on Computational Linguistics (2010)
4. Burstein, J., Chodorow, M.: Automated essay scoring for nonnative English speakers. Association for Computational Linguistics (2002)
5. Tachibana, R., Komachi, M.: Analysis of English spelling errors in a word-typing game
6. Devlin, J., Chang, M.W., Lee, K., Toutanova, K.: BERT: pre-training of deep bidirectional transformers for language understanding (2018)
7. Cheng, X, Xu, W., Chen, K., Jiang, S., Qi, Y.: SpellGCN: incorporating phonological and visual similarities into language models for Chinese spelling check (2020)
8. Kipf, T.N., Welling, M.: Semi-supervised classification with graph convolutional networks (2016)

9. Xu, H.D, Li, Z., Zhou, Q., Li, C., Mao, X.L.: Read, listen, and see: leveraging multimodal information helps Chinese spell checking (2021)
10. Huang, L., Li, J., Jiang, W., Zhang, Z., Xiao, J.: PHMOSpell: phonological and morphological knowledge guided Chinese spelling check. In Proceedings of the 59th Annual Meeting of the Association for Computational Linguistics and the 11th International Joint Conference on Natural Language Processing, vol. 1, Long Papers (2021)
11. Jiang, Z., Xu, F.F., Araki, J., Neubig, G.: How can we know what language models know? (2019)
12. Zhang, S., Huang, H., Liu, J., Li, H.: Spelling error correction with soft-masked BERT (2020)
13. Mangu, E.L.: Automatic rule acquisition for spelling correction (1997)
14. Ying, J., Tong, W., Tao, L., Wang, F., Zhang, W.: A rule based Chinese spelling and grammar detection system utility. In: 2012 International Conference on System Science and Engineering (ICSSE) (2012)
15. Zhang, S., Xiong, J, Hou, J., Zhang, Q., Cheng, X.: HANSpeller++: a unified framework for Chinese spelling correction. In: Proceedings of the Eighth SIGHAN Workshop on Chinese Language Processing (2015)
16. Wang, D., Song, Y., Li, J., Han, J., Zhang, H.: A hybrid approach to automatic corpus generation for Chinese spelling check. In: Proceedings of the 2018 Conference on Empirical Methods in Natural Language Processing (2018)
17. Tseng, Y.H., Lee, L.H., Chang, L.P., Chen, H.H.: Introduction to SIGHAN 2015 bake-off for Chinese spelling check. In: Proceedings of the 8th SIGHAN Workshop on Chinese Language Processing (SIGHAN 2015) (2015)
18. Hong, Y., Yu, X., He, N., Liu, N., Liu, J.: Faspell: a fast, adaptable, simple, powerful Chinese spell checker based on DAE-decoder paradigm. In: Proceedings of the 5th Workshop on Noisy User-generated Text (W-NUT 2019), 2019
19. Wang, B., Che, W., Wu, D., Wang, S., Liu, T.: Dynamic connected networks for Chinese spelling check. In: Findings of the Association for Computational Linguistics: ACL-IJCNLP 2021 (2021)
20. Wang, B., Che, W., Wu, D., Wang, S., Liu, T.: Dynamic connected networks for Chinese spelling check. In: Findings of the Association for Computational Linguistics, ACL-IJCNLP 2021 (2021)
21. Brown, T.B., Mann, B., Ryder, N., Subbiah, M., Amodei, D.: Language models are few-shot learners (2020)
22. Liu, X., Zheng, Y., Du, Z., Ding, M., Tang, J.: GPT understands, too (2021)
23. Schick, T., Schütze, H.: Exploiting cloze questions for few shot text classification and natural language inference (2020)
24. Shin, T., Razeghi, Y., Logan, I., Wallace, E., Singh, S.: Autoprompt: eliciting knowledge from language models with automatically generated prompts (2020)
25. Li, X.L., Liang, P.: Prefix-tuning: optimizing continuous prompts for generation (2021)
26. Lester, B., Al-Rfou, R., Constant, N.: The power of scale for parameter-efficient prompt tuning (2021)
27. Petroni, F., et al.: Language models as knowledge bases? (2019)
28. Wu, S., Liu, C., Lee, L.: Chinese spelling check evaluation at SIGHAN bake-off 2013. In: SIGHAN Workshop on Chinese Language Processing (2014)
29. Cai, H., Chen, D.: Bert based correction models. GitHub (2020). https://github.com/gitabtion/BertBasedCorrectionModels
30. Cui, Y., et al.: Pre-training with whole word masking for Chinese BERT (2019)

W-Hash: A Novel Word Hash Clustering Algorithm for Large-Scale Chinese Short Text Analysis

Yaofeng Chen[1], Chunyang Zhang[2], Long Ye[1], Xiaogang Peng[1], Meikang Qiu[3], and Weipeng Cao[1](✉)

[1] College of Computer Science and Software Engineering, Shenzhen University, Shenzhen 518060, China
chenyaofeng@email.szu.edu.cn, {pengxg,caoweipeng}@szu.edu.cn
[2] Information Systems, Technical University of Munich, Munich, Germany
[3] Department of Computer Science, Texas A&M University-Commerce, Commerce, TX 75428, USA

Abstract. Short text clustering is an unsupervised learning technique for pattern discovery and analysis of short text datasets, which has been applied to many scenarios such as business risk control and audit. With the development of digitalization over the last few years, the data scale in various scenarios has increased rapidly. Traditional short text clustering methods such as K-means face many challenges in large-scale data analysis, such as difficult to preset hyperparameters and high computational complexity. To alleviate this problem, we propose a novel clustering algorithm called Word Hash clustering algorithm (W-Hash) for Chinese short text analysis. Specifically, W-Hash does not require a pre-specified number of clusters, and it has much lower computational complexity than the traditional clustering approaches. To verify the effectiveness of W-Hash, we apply it to solve a real-life business audit problem. The corresponding experimental results show that W-Hash outperforms traditional clustering algorithms in both training time and result rationality.

Keywords: Short text clustering · Clustering · K-means · Business audit

1 Introduction

Cluster analysis is an unsupervised learning technique that can split a given dataset into several clusters [1]. Within the same cluster, data objects are more similar to each other than to those in other clusters. Thus, we may discover the underlying patterns in the raw data and exploit them. In recent decades, various clustering algorithms have been proposed and widely used in many scenarios, such as bioinformatics analysis [2].

Currently the most commonly used clustering algorithms can be divided into the following categories [3]: clustering algorithms based on partition, hierarchy, density, grid, model, and fuzzy theory. These algorithms have their specific strengths and weaknesses and are fit for different problems. For example, text knowledge mining requires

G. Memmi et al. (Eds.): KSEM 2022, LNAI 13370, pp. 528–539, 2022.
https://doi.org/10.1007/978-3-031-10989-8_42

clustering algorithms can support natural language processing or can be combined with natural language processing algorithms.

This study focuses on the analysis of short Chinese texts. Specifically, we apply this technique to solve the relevant company identification problem, which is one of the key technologies for follow-up gang risk analysis in business audits. To deal with the challenge of too much data in practice, we proposed a novel Chinese short text clustering algorithm based on word hash in this study, namely Word Hash clustering algorithm (W-Hash). W-Hash first segments the Chinese short text into words and hashes them by converting the raw text into the hash string. Then the clusters satisfying the similarity threshold can be identified by hash string matching. This approach has the following advantages: First, there is no need to preset the number of clusters. Second, the computational complexity of W-Hash is theoretically much lower than that of traditional clustering algorithms such as K-means [4] and DBSCAN [5]. Finally, the clusters output by W-Hash can contain the same samples, which makes it can identify potential reasonable clusters more comprehensively. The contributions of this study are as follows:

- We have proposed a novel clustering algorithm W-Hash, which can deal with large-scale Chinese short text analysis effectively.
- We have verified the effectiveness of W-Hash from both theory and practice. In our experiment, W-Hash not only reduces the training time by more than 90% compared with traditional clustering algorithms such as K-means and DBSCAN, but also gives more reasonable clustering results.
- We have applied the proposed W-Hash to solve a real-life relevant company identification problem in business audits and also verified its effectiveness.

2 Related Work

The authors in [6] designed a concept decomposition method to estimate the cluster memberships of short texts. In [7], the authors proposed a convolution neural network (CNN) based short text clustering method. In their method, the word2vec technique was used to extract vector representation from the original Chinese text data. Then, the authors used CNN to extract the high-level representation of word vectors and then used some traditional clustering methods to cluster them. The work of improving the features expression of short text through CNN can also be found in [8, 9]. Microblogs topic detection is one of the most common scenarios for Chinese short text analysis. The authors of [10] developed a three-layer hybrid algorithm to deal with the microblog data mining problem. By iteratively splitting large-sized clusters and merging small-sized clusters, their algorithm can achieve better clustering effects than traditional clustering algorithms such as K-means. To handle the topic drift problem in the short text analysis, Chen et al. [11] developed a Dirichlet process bi-term-based mixture model, which can mine the word co-occurrence pattern by word-pairs information.

Many of the above works focus on the preprocessing of short text data, but there are not many innovations in clustering algorithms. When traditional clustering algorithms such as K-means and DBSCAN are used to solve large-scale short text analysis problems in real life, sometimes they cannot be processed because the data size is too large. Hashing-based clustering algorithms show high computational efficiency in some specific large-scale data processing problems, such as MinHash and SimHash [12]. However, the existing methods still suffer from some defects in solving the business audit problem to be solved in this study. For example, SimHash can only convert each sample into a unique hash string, and then find the relevant text through nearest neighbor retrieval to form a cluster. Although SimHash improves the computational efficiency of this process by indexing, it still needs to calculate the pairwise similarity between all text pairs. Because the hash string corresponding to each text is unique, this process is still time-consuming in large-scale data clustering scenarios. To alleviate this problem, we propose a new clustering algorithm named W-Hash, which can greatly improve the clustering efficiency and diversity of large-scale short texts.

3 Details of W-Hash

3.1 Overview

The workflow of the proposed W-Hash is as follows:

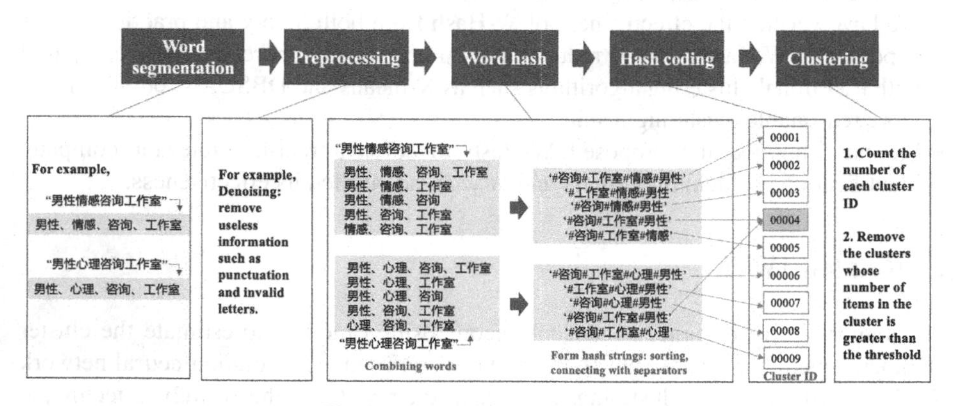

Fig. 1. The workflow of W-Hash

As Fig. 1 shows, W-Hash is composed of five steps: word segmentation, word denoising, word hashing, hash string encoding, and cluster (with denoising). Word segmentation and word denoising are preprocessing steps before clustering. The last three steps are the process of clustering. The details of each step are explained as follows:

1) **Word segmentation:** Divide the sentences in the original text into their corresponding component words.
2) **Word denoising:** Remove meaningless words after the word segmentation step, including punctuation marks, invalid letters, etc. If necessary, only keywords can be extracted and all other words can be removed.
3) **Word hashing:** This is the core of W-Hash. There are two steps: first, select the word combinations for hashing; second, form the word hash string. The details are given as follows.

Select the word combinations for hashing: the combinations are selected according to the requirement of clustering similarity. Assume that the input text has w words after word segmentation and denoising. We also assume that the texts to be aggregated are required to have at least w-m words that are the same as the input text. Then the number of combinations can be calculated as:

$$\text{Number of word combinations} = \sum\nolimits_{i=0}^{m} C_w^i \tag{1}$$

The value of m can bc calculated as follows:

$$m \le \frac{n1*(1-\mathrm{f})}{1+f} \tag{2}$$

where f means the Jaccard similarity threshold. That is, the similarity between texts must be greater than the threshold f to be grouped into one cluster. In (2), if $n1$ is the minimum word count of all input texts in the dataset, then m guarantees that the Jaccard similarity between all texts in the same cluster is greater than the threshold. If $n1$ is the mean word count of all input texts in the dataset, then m still ensures that the Jaccard similarity between most texts in the same cluster is greater than the threshold.

As shown in Fig. 1, the input text is "男性情感咨询工作室". After word segmentation and denoising, we obtain a set of 4 words {男性, 情感, 咨询, 工作室}. If the minimum word count of other input texts is also 4, and the Jaccard similarity threshold is set to 0.6, we can obtain that $m = 1$ from the above formula. Then the text "男性情感咨询工作室" can have $C_4^1 + 1 = 5$ word combinations, which are [男性, 情感, 咨询, 工作室], [男性, 情感, 工作室], [男性, 情感, 咨询], [男性, 咨询, 工作室], [情感, 咨询, 工作室]. Similarly, the word combinations of "男性心理咨询工作室" can be obtained as [男性, 心理, 咨询, 工作室], [男性, 心理, 工作室], [男性, 心理, 咨询], [男性, 咨询, 工作室], [心理, 咨询, 工作室].

4) **Form the word hash string:** After selecting the word combinations, the words in each combination are sorted and then concatenated by a fixed separator (e.g., #), thus forming the word hash string. For example, the word combination [男性, 心理, 咨询, 工作室] can be sorted to [咨询, 工作室, 心理, 男性] and concatenated to '# 咨询#工作室#心理#男性' using the separator #.
5) **Form the word hash string:** After selecting the word combinations, the words in each combination are sorted and then concatenated by a fixed separator (e.g., #), thus forming the word hash string. For example, the word combination [男性, 心理, 咨询, 工作室] can be sorted to [咨询, 工作室, 心理, 男性] and concatenated to '# 咨询#工作室#心理#男性' using the separator #.

3.2 Pseudo-Code of W-Hash

The pseudo-code of W-Hash is shown in Algorithm 1, and the word hashing process involved in it is shown in Algorithm 2.

Algorithm 1: W-Hash algorithm

Input: A Chinese short text dataset ***X = [x_1, x_2, …, x_n]***, Jaccard similarity threshold *f*, the threshold *mx* for the number of items in each cluster, and the word difference threshold *m*.

Output: The clustering result: *{x_1: cluster_id_1, x_2: cluster_id_2, ..., x_n: cluster_id_n}*, where *cluster_id_n* is the cluster id of each input text *x_i*.

Initialization:

n1=0 //mean of word segmentations

n2= Integer.MAX_VALUE //minimum of word segmentations

m=0 // the word difference threshold

start_clusterid=10000000 //starting index of cluster

cluster_id_map ={} //dictionary mapping from hash string to *cluster_id*

For *x_i* in ***X***:

Step 1. Word segmentation: segment the input text *x_i* using word segmentation tools (e.g., Hanlp, Jieba) and obtain the corresponding *word_list_i* = [*w_1, w_2,..., w_k1*], which means *x_i* is divided into *k1* words.

Step 2. Word denoising: remove meaningless characters from *word_list_i*, including punctuations. Keywords can also be extracted from *word_list_i* using a pre-defined keyword dictionary. After denoising, we obtain *f_word_list_i* = [*w_1, w_2, ..., w_k2*], where *k2* is the word count after denoising. Note that *k2<=k1*.

n1=n1+ k2

n2=min([n2, k2])

Set *n1 = n1/length(X)*

Set *n2 = n2*

If model==*mean_estimation*:

Set *m=min([0, n1*(1-f)/(1+f)])*

If model== *min_estimation*:

Set *m=min([0, n2*(1-f)/(1+f)])*

For *x_i* in ***X***:

Repeat **Step 1.**

Repeat **Step 2.**

Step 3. Word hashing: *res* = **split_hash**(*f_word_list_i, m*)

Step 4. Hash string encoding:

For *cluster_str* in *res*:

cluster_id = *start_clusterid*

If *cluster_str* not in *cluster_id_map*:

Save(*x_i, cluster_id*) //save the short text *x_i* with corresponding cluster id

start_clusterid = *start_clusterid*+1

Else:

cluster_id= *cluster_id_map[cluster_str]* //extract the corresponding cluster_id

Save(*x_i, cluster_id*) //save the short text *x_i* with corresponding cluster id

Step 5. Cluster denoising:

Sum up the number of items under each cluster id: the values are {*cluster_id_1: n_1, cluster_id_2: n_2, ..., cluster_id_n: n_n*}, where each entry indicates that there are *n_n* items in the *n*-th cluster id.

Remove the clusters whose number of items exceeds the defined threshold *mx*.

Return the remaining clusters.

Algorithm 2: Word Hashing

Input: A short text word segmentation list *f_word_list* = [*w_1, w_2, ..., w_k*] and the word difference threshold *m*.

Output: The clustering result: *res* = [*cluster_str_1, cluster_str_2, ..., cluster_str_k*], which represents all cluster strings to which the short text belongs.

split_hash(*f_word_list, m*):

f_word_list.sort() //sort the short text word segmentation list

res = [] //represents all cluster strings to which the short text belongs

//Obtain all the word hashing results when the number of different words varies from 0 to *m*+1

for *i* in range(0, *m*+1):

res.extend(sub_split_hash(*arry,i,0,[]*))

return *res*

```
sub_split_hash(arry,m, start_select_idex,not_select_idexs):
    l = len(arry) //get the number of words; arry: short text word segmentation list
    if l <= m or m < 0:
        return []
  if m==0:
        tem = []
    for i in range(0, l):
        if i not in not_select_idexs:
            tem.append(arry[i])
        return ['#'.join(tem)]
    res=[]
    for i in range(start_select_idex, l): //iterate over the index from start_select_idex to l, and
choose a word to remove
        not_select_idexs.append(i) //word with index=i will be removed
        res.extend(sub_split_hash(arry,m-1,i+1,not_select_idexs)) //recursive call to obtain the
next word to be removed
        not_select_idexs.remove(i) //backtrack and reset not_select_idexs
    return res
```

3.3 Computational Complexity Analysis of W-Hash

From the above details of W-Hash, it can be seen that the proposed W-Hash avoids the steps of similarity calculation and comparison in the clustering process of traditional clustering algorithms, so as to implement efficient clustering with approximate linear-time complexity. To compare the performance specifically, we demonstrate the theoretical calculation below (Table 1):

Table 1. Time complexity comparison of clustering algorithms

Algorithm	Time complexity
W-Hash	$O\left(\left(\sum_{i=0}^{m} C_w^i\right) * n\right)$
K-means	$O(t * k * n)$
DBSCAN	$O(n * n)$

where n is the scale of input data, w is the number of words to proceed in word hashing, and m is the word difference threshold, which is calculated by (2). In addition, k is the number of formed clusters and t is the number of iterations in the K-means algorithm.

4 Experiments

To verify the effectiveness of the proposed algorithm in solving large-scale short text clustering problems, this section shows its application to a real-life relevant company identification problem in business audits.

4.1 Datasets

The experimental data source is the desensitized dataset provided by a commercial company, with each sample describing information such as the name and business scope. The information can be used to conduct gang risk prevention and control analysis in practice. According to statistics of related investigated cases, there is a high correlation between the names of the companies in gangs. This feature makes it possible for us to identify them using clustering methods. This experiment will verify the effectiveness of the proposed algorithm based on this problem.

Statistics of the dataset used in this paper are shown in Table 2, and some sample examples are shown in Table 3. We can see from Table 3 that each sample is a company name. We can use a word segmentation tool (e.g., Jieba) to split each sample into several keywords. For example: "临澧县富旺装饰材料经营部" will become: {临澧县, 富旺, 装饰, 材料, 经营部} after word segmentation. Table 2 shows the statistical characteristics of word segmentation in this dataset. Next, we test the clustering effect of the proposed algorithm and other traditional clustering algorithms on this dataset.

Table 2. Summary of the dataset

Number of samples	30000
Maximum of word segmentation	10
Minimum of word segmentation	1
Mean of word segmentation	4.2819

4.2 Experimental Setup

This experiment compares the clustering performance of the proposed W-Hash algorithm with K-means and DBSCAN on the above-mentioned dataset. K-means and DBSCAN are implemented based on Scikit-Learn. The hyperparameters of K-means are set as follows: {k = 6000, max_iter = 50, n_init = 10, init = k-means++, n_jobs = 1}. The hyperparameters of DBSCAN are set as follows: {min_samples = 2, eps = 1.5, algorithm

Table 3. Example of samples in the dataset

Samples in the dataset	
	临澧县富旺装饰材料经营部
	临澧县广嘉装饰材料经营部
	临澧县橙紫装饰材料经营部
	临澧县天金装饰材料经营部

= kd_tree}. The hyperparameters of our proposed W-Hash algorithm are set as follows: {m = 1, cluster_max_num = 1000}.

In addition, K-means and DBSCAN involve the similarity calculation of word vectors. In the experiment, we first convert the segmentation combinations of each sample to word vectors and then store them in the form of the sparse matrix. Therefore, the dataset used in our experiment will be transformed into a matrix of *row*col*, with *row* is the number of samples and *col* is the word count of each sample. The i-th row represents the word vector corresponding to the i-th sample.

4.3 Results Analysis

According to the above settings, K-means, DBSCAN, and the proposed W-Hash algorithm are used to perform clustering operations, and their training time is shown below (Table 4):

Table 4. Clustering time comparison

Algorithm	Clustering time (s)
K-means	2290.9
DBSCAN	41.03
Ours	2.08

We can observe from the above table that the training time of our proposed W-Hash algorithm is significantly less than that of the other two algorithms, which shows that our proposed algorithm is far more efficient than the others in large-scale Chinese short text analysis.

Below, we take "四川悦顺商贸有限公司" as the query term to show the relevant clustering results of these three algorithms (i.e., Table 5).

We can observe from Table 5 that results from both K-means and DBSCAN have only one cluster that contains the given query term, among which the cluster from K-means contains 8 samples, while the cluster from DBSCAN has 6809 samples. Our proposed W-Hash algorithm resulted in two clusters containing the query term, with each cluster containing 5 samples. Through analyzing the samples within clusters, it can be found that intuitively, the results given by K-means and W-Hash algorithm are consistent with human cognition. In other words, these two algorithms give more reasonable results. The semantic correlation between samples in the two clusters output by W-Hash is high. Specifically, the samples in one cluster correspond to similar contextual meanings, and the other correspond to the same entity words. However, in this case, the result of DBSCAN seems not to be logical. In other words, it is hard to understand the correlation between samples in clusters from the perspective of human.

Table 5. Example of clustering results

Algorithm	Clustering results		
	Company name	Cluster id	Number of items within the cluster
K-means	四川悦顺商贸有限公司	371	8
	四川一品晟宴商贸有限公司	371	
	四川优创一品商贸有限公司	371	
	四川汇樽商贸有限公司	371	
	四川亚格商贸有限公司	371	
	四川美皇商贸有限公司	371	
	四川一品优购商贸有限公司	371	
	四川蓉城一品商贸有限公司	371	
DBSCAN	四川悦顺商贸有限公司	8	6809 (To save space, only 8 randomly selected samples are listed as examples)
	马鞍山市花山区司法局	8	
	南京三森网络科技有限公司	8	
	深圳市思拓软件有限公司	8	
	徐州沙城网络科技有限公司	8	
	文安县拓普科技有限公司	8	
	河南清阳电力设备有限公司	8	
	武汉快点广告有限公司	8	
Ours	四川悦顺商贸有限公司	10001948	5
	济宁悦顺商贸有限公司	10001948	
	固始县悦顺商贸有限公司	10001948	
	东海县悦顺商贸有限公司	10001948	
	洛阳悦顺商贸有限公司	10001948	
	四川悦顺商贸有限公司	10001949	5
	四川汇樽商贸有限公司	10001949	
	四川亚格商贸有限公司	10001949	
	四川美皇商贸有限公司	10001949	
	四川火烈鸟商贸有限公司	10001949	

We conducted statistical analysis on the clustering results of these three algorithms, and the experimental results are as follows (Table 6):

Table 6. Summary of the clustering results

Algorithm	No. of clusters	Mean number of items within each cluster	Maximum number of items within each cluster	Minimum number of items within each cluster	No. of items within each isolated cluster
K-means	6000	5	512	1	0
DBSCAN	4923	6.09	6832	2	1544
Ours	9812	3.75	70	2	0

It can be observed from the above table that our algorithm results in the largest number of clusters, but the average number and the maximum number of samples in clusters are both smaller than that of other algorithms. This is because there is some sample overlap between clusters in the results given by our method, as shown in Table 5. Neither K-means nor our method has isolated clusters.

After completely analyzing the output results of the above algorithm, we found that most of the clusters output by DBSCAN are in line with expectations, but there are huge clusters in the results. In other words, in the clustering results of DBSCAN, when the number of samples in the cluster is small, the correlation between samples in the cluster is relatively high. However, when the number of samples in the cluster is large, the correlation between samples in the cluster is low. In addition, it is hard to set the hyperparameters of DBSCAN. For example, setting the threshold value of the nearest neighbor range to a value that is too large or too small will lead to obvious non-cognitive clusters in the clustering results. In addition, DBSCAN also faces the problem of different clusters having different densities, and it is difficult to set the min_samples parameter uniformly. The disadvantage of k-means is that the hyperparameter K is difficult to preset and it is also sensitive to outliners. Compared with these two clustering methods, the W-Hash algorithm proposed by us has the advantages of significant ease of use and high computational efficiency.

5 Conclusions and Future Work

In this paper, we proposed a novel clustering algorithm (i.e., W-Hash) for large-scale Chinese short text analysis. In comparison with commonly used clustering algorithms, such as K-means and DBSCAN, W-Hash has extremely high computational efficiency. To prove the effectiveness of W-Hash, we applied it to solve a real-life relevant company identification problem in business audits. The experimental results show that W-Hash not only reduces the training time by more than 90% compared with K-means and DBSCAN, but also gives more reasonable clustering results. In the future, we will consider applying the proposed algorithm to other related scenarios, such as disease detection [13, 14], and software vulnerability detection [15].

Acknowledgment. This work was supported by National Natural Science Foundation of China (Grant No. 62106150), CAAC Key Laboratory of Civil Aviation Wide Surveillance and Safety Operation Management and Control Technology (Grant No. 202102), and CCF-NSFOCUS (Grant No. 2021001).

References

1. Sharma, K.K., Seal, A.: Clustering analysis using an adaptive fused distance. Eng. Appl. Artif. Intell. **96**, 103928 (2020)
2. Tian, T., Zhang, J., Lin, X., Wei, Z., Hakonarson, H.: Model-based deep embedding for constrained clustering analysis of single cell RNA-seq data. Nat. Commun. **12**(1), 1–12 (2021)
3. Xu, D., Tian, Y.: A comprehensive survey of clustering algorithms. Ann. Data Sci. **2**(2), 165–193 (2015). https://doi.org/10.1007/s40745-015-0040-1
4. Ahmed, M., Seraj, R., Islam, S.M.S.: The k-means algorithm: a comprehensive survey and performance evaluation. Electronics **9**(8), 1295 (2020)
5. Khan, K., Rehman, S.U., Aziz, K., Fong, S., Sarasvady, S.: DBSCAN: past, present and future. In: The Fifth International Conference on the Applications of Digital Information and Web Technologies (ICADIWT 2014), pp. 232–238, February 2014
6. Jia, C., Carson, M.B., Wang, X., Yu, J.: Concept decompositions for short text clustering by identifying word communities. Pattern Recogn. **76**, 691–703 (2018)
7. Wan, H., Ning, B., Tao, X., Long, J.: Research on Chinese short text clustering ensemble via convolutional neural networks. In: Liang, Q., Wang, W., Jiasong, Mu., Liu, X., Na, Z., Chen, B. (eds.) Artificial Intelligence in China. LNEE, vol. 572, pp. 622–628. Springer, Singapore (2020). https://doi.org/10.1007/978-981-15-0187-6_74
8. Hao, M., Xu, B., Liang, J.Y., Zhang, B.W., Yin, X.C.: Chinese short text classification with mutual-attention convolutional neural networks. ACM Trans. Asian Low-Resour. Lang. Inf. Process. (TALLIP) **19**(5), 1–13 (2020)
9. Dai, D., et al.: An inception convolutional autoencoder model for Chinese healthcare question clustering. IEEE Trans. Cybern. **51**(4), 2019–2031 (2019)
10. Geng, X., Zhang, Y., Jiao, Y., Mei, Y.: A novel hybrid clustering algorithm for topic detection on Chinese microblogging. IEEE Trans. Comput. Soc. Syst. **6**(2), 289–300 (2019)
11. Chen, J., Gong, Z., Liu, W.: A Dirichlet process biterm-based mixture model for short text stream clustering. Appl. Intell. **50**(5), 1609–1619 (2020). https://doi.org/10.1007/s10489-019-01606-1
12. Zamora, J., Mendoza, M., Allende, H.: Hashing-based clustering in high dimensional data. Expert Syst. Appl. **62**, 202–211 (2016)
13. Cao, W., Yang, P., Ming, Z., Cai, S., Zhang, J.: An improved fuzziness based random vector functional link network for liver disease detection. In: 2020 IEEE 6th International Conference on Big Data Security on Cloud (BigDataSecurity), pp. 42–48, May 2020
14. Patwary, M.J., Cao, W., Wang, X.Z., Haque, M.A.: Fuzziness based semi-supervised multimodal learning for patient's activity recognition using RGBDT videos. Appl. Soft Comput. **120**, 108655 (2022)
15. Tang, G., et al.: A comparative study of neural network techniques for automatic software vulnerability detection. In: 2020 International Symposium on Theoretical Aspects of Software Engineering (TASE), pp. 1–8, December 2020

HLB-ConvMLP- Rapid Identification of Citrus Leaf Diseases

Shuang Peng[1], Xianshu Peng[1], Zhuochen Dai[2], and Li Tao[3](✉)

[1] Hanhong College, Southwest University, Chongqing City, China
[2] College of Engineering and Technology, Southwest University, Chongqing City, China
[3] College of Computer and Information Science, Southwest University, Chongqing City, China
tli@swu.edu.cn

Abstract. Citrus is an important economic product, but the occurrence of citrus HuangLongBing (HLB) has brought great losses to the citrus industry, so how to effectively control this disease has become a focus of current researches. Based on the hyperspectral imaging technology and lightweight neural network technology, this study is to provide a basis for improving the accuracy of detection and end edge deployment for HLB disease. A hybrid model of convolutional neural network and Convolutional multilayer perceptron (MLP) is proposed to recognize HLB leaves and normal leaves through sample learning (HLB-ConvMLP), and the accuracy and complexity of the model are also analysed. The test indexes of the proposed model on the dataset are 96.69% Sensitivity, 94.56% Specificity, 95.18% Accuracy, and 92.11% F1 -Score respectively. The parameter size is 194.67 KB, and the inference speed on i5 CPU is 0.013 ms per image. The result shows that our proposed model has higher accuracy, fewer weight parameters and faster inference speed compared with traditional convolutional neural networks like ResNet. Hence our proposed model can better meet the requirements of end edge model deployment and provide a reference for real-time detection of HLB disease.

Keywords: Convolutional neural network · Multiple neural network · Hyperspectral imaging technology · HuangLongBing

1 Introduction

Citrus industry is one of the most important agricultural cash crop industries and also the pillar industry of agricultural economy in many areas. However, currently there is no cure for the citrus disease (HLB), a devastating disease in the citrus industry which can severely infect all known citrus species [1] and cause great losses to the citrus industry. Therefore, it is urgent to develop a rapid and effective identification method for the HLB disease.

In traditional methods, field diagnosis is an early identification method of HLB, but this method is subjective, depending on the judgment of professionals, so its accuracy is not high. Later, with the development of biochemical

G. Memmi et al. (Eds.): KSEM 2022, LNAI 13370, pp. 540–549, 2022.
https://doi.org/10.1007/978-3-031-10989-8_43

technology, Polymerase chain reaction (PCR) has become a mainstream method to detect HLB. But this method relies on DNA sequences, and is costly and time-consuming. Nowadays, with the development of machine learning and chip technology, many machine learning algorithms are applied in practical industrial applications. For example, a Topological Graph Convolutional Network (ToGCN) followed with a Sequence-to-sequence (Seq2Seq) framework was proposed to predict future traffic flow and density with temporal correlations [2], an intelligent fault diagnosis method based on an improved domain adaptation method was proposed to solve the problem of data domain mismatch in smart manufacturing [3] and an interface of a low-power programmable system on chip was designed to reduce the overall power consumption of the heart disease monitoring system [4]. As for the filed of agriculture, machine learning and deep learning become a leading tool in predicting and controlling the occurrence of various plant diseases. Especially the Convolutional Neural Networks (CNNs) such as VGG [12] becomes the most common networks in recognizing diseased plant because of its high performance.

In this paper, we take a deep forward step in exploiting the function of lighted hybrid neural network(CNNs and MLPs) combined with hyperspectral imaging technology in controlling the occurrence of HLB disease. In particular, we compare the performance of proposed model with traditional neural networks, ResNet [13], MobieNetV3 [14] and Vision-Transformer [15] specifically. The results show the great potential of the proposed models in detection HLB diseased leaf and we will deploy it into phone or with hyperspectral camera in the future work and hope to provide a reference for real-time detection of HLB disease.

The remainder of this paper is organized as follows. Section 2 discusses the Technical challenges and related work. Section 3 describes our methodology in total, which includes the data preparation and data preprocessing. Also, the detail of the proposed model will be described explicitly in Sect. 3. Section 4 shows the experiment results of the proposed model and the comparison details with traditional neural networks. In Sect. 5, the ablation study is carried out, and the function of each block of proposed model and numbers of channels will be displayed. Finally, Sect. 6 concludes the paper and our future work.

2 Related Work

In recent years, some related scholars have combined the spectral imaging technology with the machine learning method to detect HLB in citrus agricultural production. For example, Xiao Huaichun [5] used hyperspectral camera to collect data of citrus leaves and combined the data with the characteristic wavelength of sensitive spectrum and the texture characteristics of leaves at that wavelength, which contributed to his visual discrimination model of infected leaves by integrating atlas. The identification accuracy of this method reached about 96.7%. And Deng Xiaoling et al. [6] combined modulated fluorescence technology with probabilistic neural network algorithm to detect the citrus diseases, and the experimental results showed that this method achieved favorable results in the detection of healthy citrus leaves and zinc-deficient leaves. However, most of the above researches are based on traditional machine learning methods to classify and learn the extracted citrus leaf features such as wavelength, while there are a few related researches in the field of image.

In actual production, real-time monitoring of HLB through video equipment can better meet the actual needs of the majority of fruit farmers, so it has become the focus of this study. Dai Zehan [7] collected a large number of citrus leaf images as datasets-including HLB-diseased leaves, healthy leaves and nutrition-deficient leaves. Then he used the lightweight depth convolutional neural network model to train and evaluate the datasets, and finally deployed the model on smart phones. The model assessment result accuracy is about 93.1%. The results show that convolutional neural network can be used in the recognition of HLB disease. Su Hong et al. [8] adopted R-CNN (Region with Convolutional Neural Network Features) model algorithm to identify leaf symptoms such as citrus HLB disease, canker disease and red spider infection. And its average accuracy rate of HLB disease identification reached 95.31%.

However, because the spectral bands of the visible light camera are close to the spectral bands of the image perceived by human eyes, misjudgment will occur if citrus leaves show similar symptoms of nutritional deficiency to HLB disease. Based on this, we use hyperspectral imaging technology and convolutional neural network to analyze the symptoms of citrus HLB disease. In this paper, Convolution layer and Multi-layer perceptron (MLP) are used to build a recognition model of HLB disease with high accuracy, fast recognition speed and few weight parameters, providing reference for end edge equipment.

3 Methods

3.1 Data Preparation

When HLB disease occurs in citrus, the phenotype of characters is complex, and there are three general manifestations, namely mottled yellow, uniform yellow and lack of element yellow [9]. The method that analyzes the color and texture of diseased leaf through the imaging by a visible light camera will result in problems such as indistinguishable misjudgment between common element-lacking yellow and HLB diseased yellow leaf. While Hyperspectral imaging technology uses a hyperspectral camera to form leaf image of the tested plants in the vision-near-infrared band (400–1000 nm). Within the band range of imaging, the spectral characteristics presented can better reflect the information of pigment, moisture and dry matter in the plant [10].

Therefore, in this paper, the healthy and diseased plants provided by the Guangxi Characteristic crop Research Institute, Guilin, Guangxi, China were selected as the research objects. A hyperspectral camera was used to sample citrus leaves and establish corresponding datasets. The datasets obtained included 199 normal leaf hyperspectral data and 423 diseased leaf hyperspectral data. Then, black-and-white correction and important band screening are carried out for hyperspectral data. Finally, the single channel image under the important band is extracted as the image data set. Image data as shown in the Fig. 1.

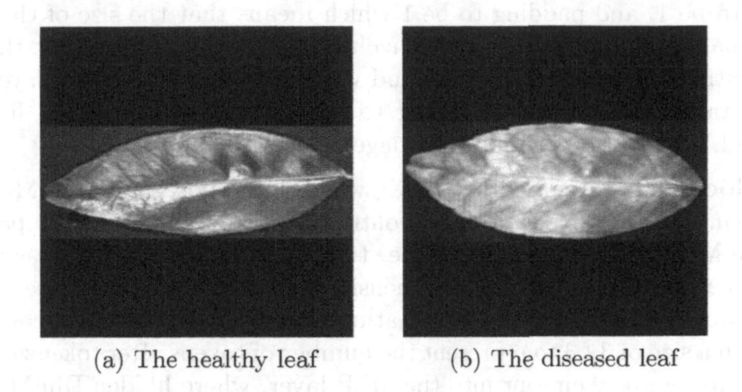

(a) The healthy leaf (b) The diseased leaf

Fig. 1. The training detail of proposed model.

3.2 HLB-ConvMLP

With the development of convolutional networks, many researchers use convolutional neural networks to perform auxiliary screening of agricultural diseases. However, most of these models focus on the recognition accuracy of the model, and do not pay much attention to the weight reduction of the model. Therefore, inspired by UneXt [11], we proposed a light and fast recognization network (HLB-ConvMLP) for Citrus greening disease. On the premise of maintaining high accuracy, the model weight parameters are reduced to improve the model reasoning speed and provides the basis for the edge deployment of the model.

NetWork Design: The proposed model is consist of three parts, namely, convolutional block, MLP Block, and Classifier Head. After the feature extraction of the convolutional block, the feature map is shifted and mapped by MLP block, and the image is classified and recognized by Classifier Head. Its specific structure is shown in the Fig. 2.

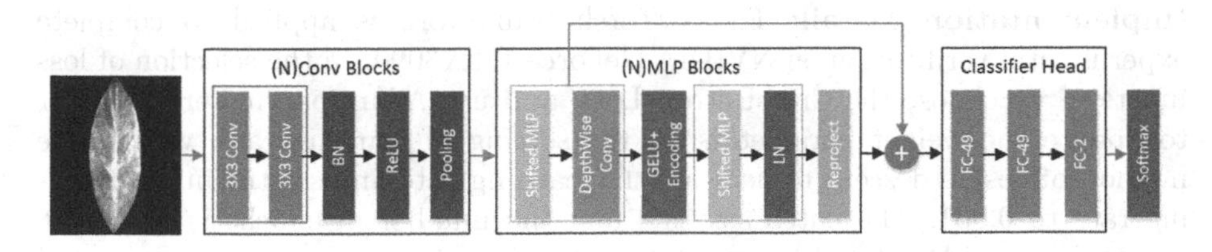

Fig. 2. The whole illustrate of the proposed model

Convlutional Block is consist of the convolutional layer, Batch Normalization layer, pooling layer, and activation function. Image features are first extracted through two convolutional layers. Here, we set the convolution layer to be 3 by 3, strdie to be 1, and padding to be 1 which means that the size of the feature image remains unchanged after the convolutional layer. Subsequently, the Batch Normalization layer keeps the mean and variance of inputs of each layer of the network stable, and maxpooling layer to downsample feature map, finally we choose ReLU activation to map the image feature nonlinear.

MLP Block here is inspired by UneXt which is proposed by Jeya Maria Jose Valanarasu. etc. and makes a great contribution in UneXt. In this paper, we follow the MLP Block structure in UneXt. In an MLP Block, the image feature graph first moves along the width dimension and is tokenized. Before tokenization, the number of channels in the feature graph is adjusted by a convolution kernel with a size of $3 * 3$ to represent the number of tokens after tokenize. Tokens after tokenizing are then sent into the MLP layer, where hidden DimMention is the hyperparameter that can be set. Then, the mapped features were transformed into feature maps after Depthwise convolution position coding and GELU activation function nonlinear mapping, and the movement along the height direction and MLP mapping were carried out.

Classifier Head is inspired by the VGG [12]. After being processed by Convolutional Blocks and MLP Blocks, the feature graph is flattened (flatten), passes through three fully connected layers, and finally achieves the classification effect by softmax function. In each full connection layer (FC), we used the ReLU activation function and the Drop out operation.

4 Experiments and Results

Dataset: In terms of data preprocessing, we collected the data set of leaves processed by hyperspectral camera, and scaled them to $224 * 224$ for the convenience of subsequent model training. Meanwhile, fixed random number seeds divided the training set and verification set in the ratio of 8:2, through which the performance of the model proposed by us was verified. Meanwhile, in the training set, we expand the data set by random rotation and random vertical flip.

Implementation Detail: The PyTorch framework is applied to complete experimental verification on NVIDIA GeForce RTX3090. In the selection of loss function, we choose the CrossEntropyLoss, and use Adam parameter optimizer to update the weight parameters. In the setting of learning rate, we use the method of cosine descent to decrease the learning rate and set the initial learning rate to 0.001. The batch size is 4 and the number of epochs is set to 20. Accuracy rate (ACC) and loss value (Loss) are used to measure the accuracy of the model. Noting that the inference speed is measured through Intel i5-8265U CPU and the time of data reading and preprocessing is excluded unless otherwise specified. The performance of the trained and validated model is shown in the Fig. 3.

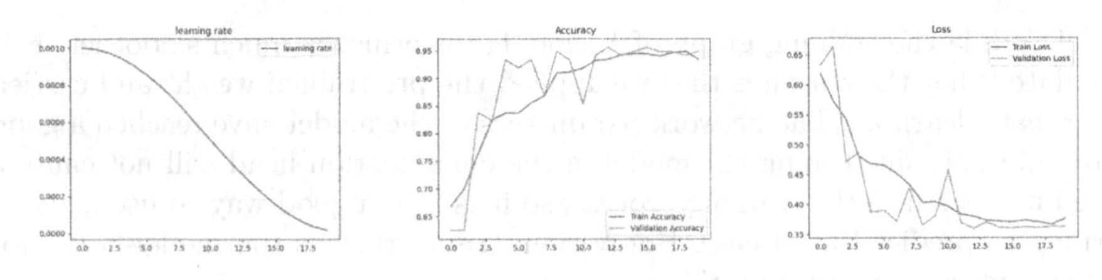

(a) The illustrate of Cosine learning rate (b) The accuracy of proposed model (c) The loss of proposed model

Fig. 3. The training detail of proposed model

Performance Comparision: We compared the proposed model with common classification network model baselines. In terms of convolutional networks, we compared the proposed model with ResNet [14] and MobileNetV3 [12] in terms of accuracy and loss rate to measure the accuracy of the model, and in terms of model size and reasoning speed to measure the efficiency of the model. At the same time, we also compare the performance of VisionTransformer [15], the recently excellent attentional model network, as the baseline of attentional model network. When comparing VisionTransfromer networks, we choose Vit-base-Patch16-224 model as the baseline network, and in order to ensure its performance SOTA, we introduce training weights on imageNet21K for transfer learning. The final comparison results are shown in the Table 1.

Table 1. The comparison detail of proposed model and traditional baselines.

Method	Performance metrics (%)		Computation complex	
	Acc	Loss.	Params (MB)	Inference speed (ms)
MobileNetV3	94.85	0.388	5.92	0.019
ResNet34	92.65	0.413	81.33	0.154
Vision transformer	94.71	0.201	327.35	0.896
Proposed	**96.32**	**0.351**	**0.194**	**0.013**

As can be seen from Table 1, under the same hyper-parameter setting, the accuracy of the model proposed by us is relatively higher, and the model has been greatly improved in terms of parameter size and reasoning speed. MobileNetV3 has the smallest size among traditional convolutional neural networks, and it takes the least time to reason a picture than other traditional networks. Noting that the we applied MobileNetV3-small in this paper. And the training details of the other networks are as in the Fig. 4.

As can be seen, most networks show great fluctuation during training period. Taking ResNet34 as an example, during the initial training of the model, a large training loss occurs, which may be caused by poor initialization of the model. While the training graph of Vision Transformer is much smoother, it is speculated that the reason is that we applied the pre-trained weight and carried out transfer learning. The network parameters of the model have reached a good state, and only fine-tuning the model in the classification head will not cause a large fluctuation in the training process, so it is also a good way to use transfer learning to predict leaf disease. But Vision Transformer is too model-heavy for deployment, so is rejected in this paper.

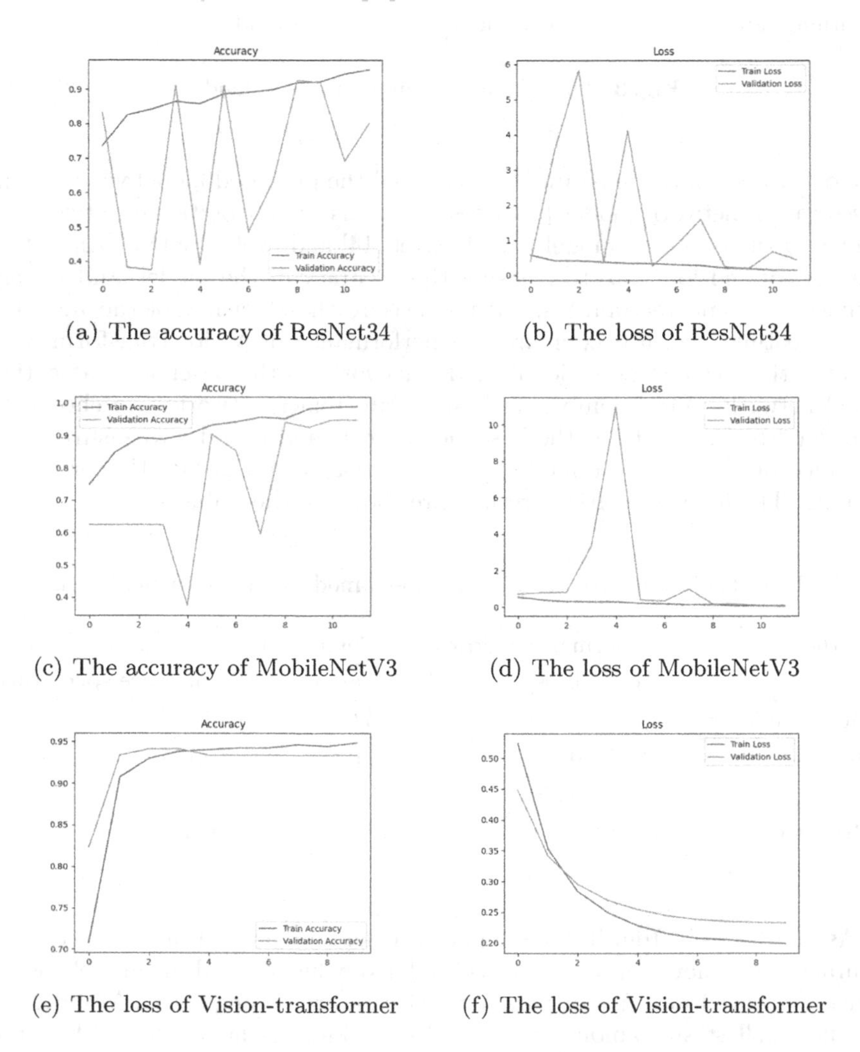

(a) The accuracy of ResNet34 (b) The loss of ResNet34

(c) The accuracy of MobileNetV3 (d) The loss of MobileNetV3

(e) The loss of Vision-transformer (f) The loss of Vision-transformer

Fig. 4. The training detail of proposed model.

Implementation with trained model: To verify the actual effects of the proposed model, we load the trained model weights on local computers for effect verification. The CPU used in the experiment was I5-8265U @ 1.60ghz 1.80ghz.

A total of 622 images were tested, including 199 normal images and 423 sick images. To verify the performance of proposed model, sensitivity (Sen.), specificity (Spe.), accuracy (Acc.), and F1-score were used to measure the accuracy of the model, as shown in the following formula.

$$Sensitive(Sen.) = \frac{\mathrm{TP}}{\mathrm{TP} + \mathrm{FN}} \tag{1}$$

$$Specificity(Spe.) = \frac{\mathrm{TN}}{\mathrm{TN} + \mathrm{FP}} \tag{2}$$

$$Accuracy(Acc) = \frac{\mathrm{TP} + \mathrm{TN}}{\mathrm{TP} + \mathrm{FP} + \mathrm{TN} + \mathrm{fN}} \tag{3}$$

$$F1 - score = \frac{2 \times \mathrm{TP}}{2 \times \mathrm{TP} + \mathrm{FP} + \mathrm{FN}} \tag{4}$$

where TP, TN, FP and FN represents True Positive, True Negative, False Positive and False Negative, respectively. Sen is used to measure the ratio of predicted positive to actual positive, and Spe measures the ratio of predicted negative to actual negative. ACC is the mean of Sen. Spe and F1-Score is the weighted sum of Sen and Spe. In the same condition, we use the average time of the predicted images to represent the reasoning time of the model, the test result is shown in the Table 2:

Table 2. The detail of implementation with trained model.

Device	Sen (%)	Spe (%)	ACC (%)	F1-score (%)	Inference speed (ms)
i5 -8265u	96.69	94.56	95.18	92.11	0.013

5 Discussion

In this section, we explore the performance impact of each module on the proposed model. Similarly, the ACC and Loss mentioned above are used to measure the accuracy of the model, and Params Size and Inference Time are used to measure the practicality of the model. Starting from MLP Block, we replace the last two MLP Blocks with two convolutional Blocks and one MLP Block after one Convolutional Block respectively, which is shown as Full Conv and Single MLP Conv in table 3.

Then we explore the influence of the number of feature channels on model performance, We increase the number of channels for each Block in HLB-ConvMLP in the order of the number of channels in VGG16, namely, we changed the number of channels of five modules in HLB-ConvMLP from [8, 16, 32, 16, 8] to [8, 16, 32, 64, 64] and [64, 128, 256, 512, 512], that is, the effect comparison is shown in Table 4.

Table 3. The comparison detail of changing MLP Blocks.

Method	Performance metrics (%)		Computation complex	
	Acc	Loss.	Params (MB)	Inference speed (ms)
Full Conv	95.58	0.365	198.82	0.034
Single MLP Conv	96.31	0.354	197.18	0.018
Proposed model	96.32	0.351	194.67	0.013

Table 4. The comparison detail after the number of channels changing.

C1	C2	C3	C4	C5	Acc.	loss.	Params (MB)	Inference speed (ms)
64	128	256	512	512	62.50	0.688	26.70	0.26
8	16	32	64	64	75.00	0.559	0.99	0.022
8	16	32	16	8	96.32	0.351	0.194	0.013

As can be seen from Table 3 above, replacing the Convlutional Block with the MLP Block can not only increases the accuracy of the model, but also can improve the inference speed. Besides, it can be seen from Table 4 that number of channel has a great influence on the accuracy of the model. Increasing the number of channels will inevitably increase the parameter size and the inference speed of the model. Therefore, selecting the number of channels is very important.

6 Conclusion

Citrus HLB disease is a devastating disease in citrus industry, and there is no effective treatment at present. Inspired by the traditional VGG model and UneXt, this paper designs a lightweight model suitable for citrus HLB detection. The hyperspectral citrus leaf datasets are applied as research objects. The results show that the model is effective, and it is expected to provide reference for the deployment of end edge equipment for citrus HLB disease detection. In the future work, we are devoted into deploying the lightweight model on an Android phone or embedding it in a hyperspectral camera. To achieve effectively control of HLB disease is our ultimate goal.

References

1. Sun, X., et al.: Rapid diagnosis of normal, deficiency and HuangLongbing disease citrus leaves by hyperspectral imaging. Spectros. Spect. Anal. **37**(2), 551–556 (2017)
2. Qiu, H., Zheng, Q., Msahli, M., Memmi, G., Qiu, M., Lu, J.: Topological graph convolutional network-based urban traffic flow and density prediction. IEEE Trans. Intell. Transp. Syst. **22**(7), 4560–4569 (2021)

3. Li, Y., Song, Y., Jia, L., Gao, S., Li, Q., Qiu, M.: Intelligent fault diagnosis by fusing domain adversarial training and maximum mean discrepancy via ensemble learning. IEEE Trans. Indus. Inform. **17**(4), 2833–2841 (2021)
4. Hu, F., Lakdawala, S., Hao, Q., Qiu, M.: Low-power, intelligent sensor hardware interface for medical data preprocessing. IEEE Trans. Inf. Technol. Biomed. **13**(4), 656–663 (2009)
5. Xiao, H.: Study on diagnostic method of Citrus HuangLongbing disease based on hyperspectral imaging. East China Jiaotong University, Jiangxi (2019). (in Chinese)
6. Deng, X., Lin, L., Lan, Y.: Diagnosis of citrus Huanglongbing disease based on modulated fluorescence detection. J. South China Agric. Univ. **37**(2), 113–116 (2016). (in Chinese)
7. Zehan, D., Zheng, Z., Lishu, H., et al.: Symptom recognition of Citrus Huanglongbing disease based on deep convolutional neural network. J. South China Agric. Univ. **41**(4), 111–119 (2020). (in Chinese)
8. Su, H., et al.: Recognition of Citrus diseases and insect pests based on regional convolutional neural network model. Southwest China J. Agric. **33**(4), 805–810 (2020). (in Chinese)
9. Xuefeng, W.: Field symptoms, occurrence regularity and control measures of citrus Huanglongbing disease. China Fruit Indus. Inf. **33**(5), 21–22 (2016). (in Chinese)
10. Haiyong, W.: Rapid detection of Citrus Huanglongbing disease based on optical imaging technology. Zhejiang University, Zhejiang (2018). (in Chinese)
11. Valanarasu, J.M.J., Patel, V.M: UNeXt: MLP-based Rapid Medical Image Segmentation Network." arXiv preprint arXiv:2203.04967 (2022)
12. Simonyan, K., Zisserman, A.: Very deep convolutional networks for large-scale image recognition (2014). arXiv preprint arXiv:1409.1556
13. He, K., Zhang, X., Ren, S., Sun, J.: Deep residual learning for image recognition. In: Proceedings of the IEEE Conference on Computer Vision and Pattern Recognition, pp. 770–778 (2016)
14. Howard, A., et al.: Searching for mobilenetv3. In: Proceedings of the IEEE/CVF International Conference on Computer Vision, pp. 1314–1324 (2019)
15. Dosovitskiy, A., et al.: An image is worth 16x16 words: Transformers for image recognition at scale (2020). arXiv preprint arXiv:2010.11929

Natural Image Matting with Low-Level Feature Attention Guidance

Hang Jiang, Song Wu, Dehong He, and Guoqiang Xiao(✉)

College of Computer and Information Science, Southwest University, Chongqing, China
{jianghang,swu20201514}@email.swu.edu.cn, {songwuswu,gqxiao}@swu.edu.cn

Abstract. Previous natural image matting algorithms have difficulties with transition regions in the foreground and background, such as tiny and detailed structures like hair. This paper argues that more efficient low-level features can help the network recover details with minor increases in network capacity and computational complexity. The proposed method, termed low-level feature channel guidance net LFCGN, has two advantages: 1) it introduces a low-level feature channel attention module designed to make the model parameters more efficient and can even lead to high-level feature map generation. 2) a dynamic upsampling is used in the decoder stage, making the detail part recover more efficiently. Experiments are evaluated on the Composition-1k dataset, and the experimental results show that our method obtained competitive performance compared to the state-of-the-art on task of image matting.

Keywords: Image matting · Computer vision · Deep learning · Attentional mechanisms · Feature mining

1 Introduction

With the rapid development of deep learning and computer vision [10,17,20], natural image matting has shown a wide range of applications in the real world. Natural image matting is a vision task of obtaining high-quality alpha matting, i.e., to predict the transparency of each pixel point of the foreground from the given original image. Natural image matting is a challenging and versatile technique, which has been widely used in various photo and video editing applications, including film production, photo compositing, and more.

Mathematically, for the given digital image I, it can be represented as a linear combination of foreground and background information as follows:

$$I_p = \alpha_p F_p + (1 - \alpha_p) B_p, \qquad \alpha_p \in [0, 1] \tag{1}$$

where F_p and B_p denote the RGB values of foreground and the background at pixel p, respectively, and α_p is the desired alpha matte value. Image matting problem is a kind of ill-posed problem because it targets to solve seven values (α_p, F_p and B_p) with only three known RGB values of (I_p), as shown in Eq. (1). Most

G. Memmi et al. (Eds.): KSEM 2022, LNAI 13370, pp. 550–561, 2022.
https://doi.org/10.1007/978-3-031-10989-8_44

of the existing methods [9,19,28] define a Trimap to simplify the task of image matting. The Trimap consists of a pure foreground, a pure background, and unknown regions for the given image. Benefiting the use of Trimap, the solution space for image matting is reduced to the unknown regions; meanwhile, the Trimap implicitly indicates the foreground of the images, which is very effective when there are multiple foreground objects in the image.

However, natural image matting is still challenging for the existing methods. Firstly, the background could be very complex in the image, resulting in the color distribution of the foreground and the color distribution of the background being very similar. Thus, it could seriously affect the performance of traditional color-based matting methods. Secondly, images could contain tiny structures such as hair and animal fur or even fine structures such as spider webs, which could further increase the difficulty for the matting algorithms. Generally speaking, the first challenge is more related to high-level contextual semantic features of images. In contrast, the second challenge is more related to low-level textural detail features of images. The current deep learning-based natural image matting methods have considerably improved the performance. This is mainly because these methods exploit the color and texture detailed information and the contextual semantic information of the original image, which is beneficial for the first challenge. However, for the second challenge, which requires that the deep model can accurately compute the matting values at the tiny or fine structure of the image, this remains a problem to be further optimized.

Most of the current deep learning-based image matting methods, such as [1,9,28], are based on the encoder-decoder architecture. The encoder-decoder architecture can well extract the high-level contextual features of the image, which has already demonstrated its high performance on the task of image segmentation. However, in the field of natural image matting, due to the introduction of Trimap, image matting is transformed into the problem of solving the matting values of unknown regions. Therefore, natural image matting relies more on low-level features extracted by deep models, unlike the image segmentation task. Moreover, learning-based methods treat the feature maps with the same weights, and this processing wastes unnecessary computations on low-level features and even affects the effectiveness of the extracted high-level semantic features.

From this perspective, this paper proposes an image matting method to focus more on the details of images, which could learn more powerful low-level structural features of the image, meanwhile guiding the learning accuracy of high-level semantic features. Following the previous deep image matting methods, we use encoder-decoder as the backbone for the image matting.

The main contribution of our paper can be summarized as follows:

1. A new perspective on natural image matting is proposed, arguing that the shallowest low-level features affect the accuracy of deep models more effectively than high-level features;

2. Based on this point of view, we introduce a low-level feature channel guidance module (LFCG) to explicitly assign weights to low-level feature maps at the early stage of the network learning;
3. Our proposed method achieves competitive performance compared to the state-of-the-art on the challenging Adobe Composition-1k dataset based on the same lightweight network.

2 Related Work

Current image matting methods can be divided into non-learning-based methods and learning-based methods.

Non-learning-Based Methods. Sampling-based methods [4,7,8,26,27] mainly use statistical methods to sample and model the color of known foreground and background regions and determine the best color pair of each unknown pixel as well as calculate the alpha mattes. Propagation-based methods [2,14] propagate the alpha values of known regions to unknown regions according to the affinities among adjacent pixels. Nevertheless, traditional methods utilize color information and location information instead of semantic and context information, which may lead to the loss of essential detail.

Learning-Based Methods. Trimap-based learning matting methods require manually labeled Trimap as an additional input. Xu *et al.* [28] first proposed an encoder-decoder structure to estimate alpha mattes. The refinement stage of their work produces obvious bounds. They also released the Adobe Deep image Mattring dataset, a large dataset for deep learning-based matting. Hou*et al.* [9] used two encoder-decoder structures to extract local and global contextual information and perform matting. Lu *et al.* [19] argue that the parameter indexes in the un-pooling layers in the upsampling decoder can influence the matting performance, and a learnable plug-in structure is introduced, namely IndexNet, to improve the pooling and upsampling process.

Automatic matting does not require an additional Trimap as an auxiliary input, thus avoiding the need to create the Trimap itself. Still, generally, such methods limit the class of foreground or need to introduce other kinds of inputs. Ke *et al.* [12] proposes MODnet to obtain alpha matting of images or videos of people automatically. Sengupta *et al.* [24] uses a hand-shot background image and human segmentation result image as additional input to replace the Trimap. Chen *et al.* [3] constructed a large portrait dataset that can automatically generate Trimap and get alpha matting. Li *et al.* [15] proposed an end-to-end network that can be used to automatically matting in animals, and a BG-20k dataset has been released, which can be used to expand the synthetic matting dataset.

The above automatic matting methods are implicitly limited to a single foreground subject, while Trimap-based natural image matting mostly requires high memory requirements and computing complexity. Therefore it motivates us to construct a more effective and efficient natural image matting algorithm.

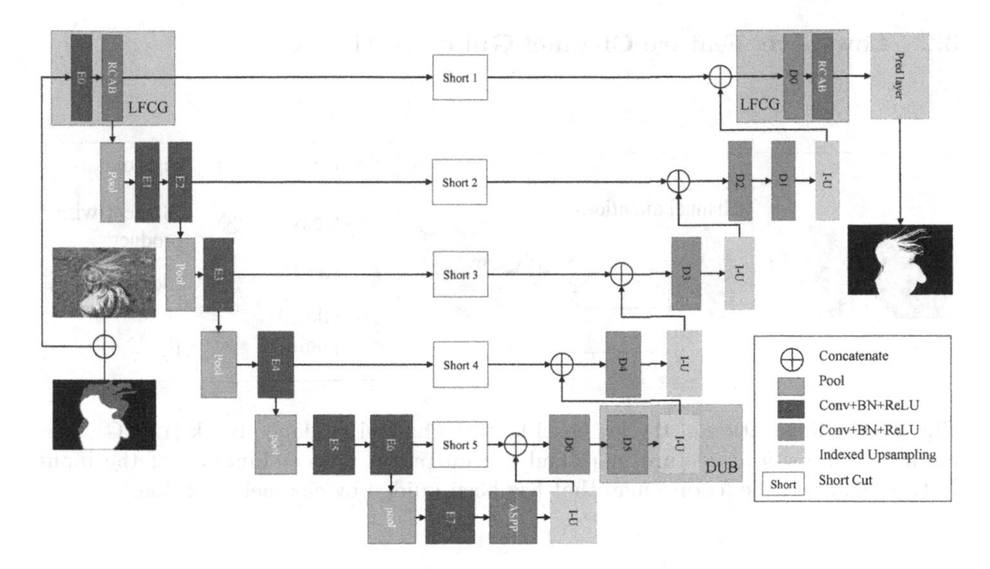

Fig. 1. Overview of our proposed matting framework. The baseline model shares the same architecture without LFCG blocks and DUB block. The inputs to the model are the original image and its corresponding trimap. The black arrows denote feature flow. The feature flows of the encoder stage used in the DUB module are not shown in this figure to keep neat.

3 The Proposed Method

Our proposed model is based on MobileNetv2 [23], which means that unlike networks with a large number of parameters, our model can be trained and inferred more efficiently on a single GPU with high-resolution images. A U-net [22] like encoder-decoder structure is firstly employed to serve as an image matting backbone. Then a Low-level Feature Attention Guidance module is designed for the high performance of image matting.

3.1 Baseline Structure

The U-Net-based architecture [22] is the dominant structure in the natural image matting task. Our backbone is also based on the U-Net architecture, as shown in Fig. 1. Unlike the traditional U-Net, MobileNetv2 pre-trained on ImageNet [5] is employed as the encoder and decoder, with the advantages of low computational complexity. Batch Normalization and ReLU6 are used following each convolutional layer to accelerate the convergence of the network. The network's input is a synthetic image and its corresponding Trimap, which are concatenated together as the input for the deep model by cropping them on the fly. The output is the alpha matte of the corresponding image.

3.2 Low-Level Feature Channel Guidance (LFCG)

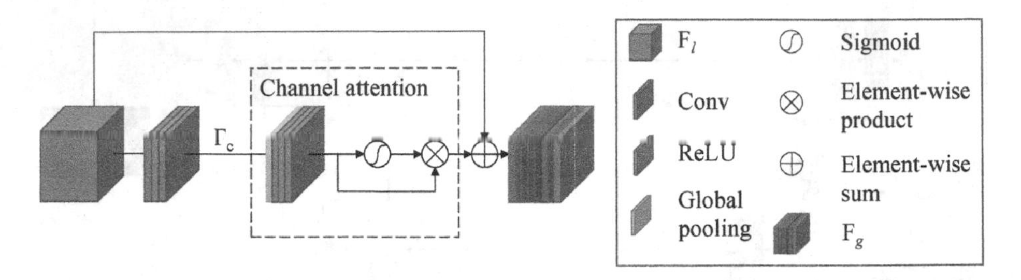

Fig. 2. The illustration of the low-level feature channel guidance block (LFCG). The input is the low-level feature map, and the output is the combination of the input feature map and the feature map that has been guided by channel attention.

Since natural image matting is a computer vision task focused on low-level features, one way to improve matting accuracy is to extract more powerful low-level feature representations. The channel attention mechanism [11] has demonstrated its capability on feature representations learning. Therefore, Residual Channel Attention Block (RCAB) [29] is proposed to focus on multi low-level layers to improve the performance of the deep model with almost no additional parameters. RCAB is an integrator of channel attention and residual network. Since it keeps both the information before channel attention and after channel attention, it could further guide the extraction of subsequent high-level features and improve the effectiveness of feature fusion in the decoder stage, which ultimately enhances the network performance. Moreover, the proposed LCFG is additionally integrated to make it more effective for image matting.

For our LFCG, we can formalize it as:

$$F_g = F_l + F_c * (CA(F_c)), \tag{2}$$

where F_g is the low-level feature map after the guidance from the LFCG module, F_l is the input low-level feature map, CA is the channel attention module, and F_c is the feature map of F_l after a simple convolution operation. The overall structure is shown in Fig. 2.

3.3 Dynamic Upsampling Block (DUB)

Inspired by [19] and [25], we argue that simply using a pooling layer with a fixed kernel in natural image matting tasks affects the detail recovery of the image. Therefore Dynamic Upsampling Block (DUB) is employed. Specifically, we use a learning-based method to combine the upsampling layers of the decoder stage and the feature maps corresponding to the encoder stage. First, for the feature map F_e in the encoder stage, we perform four convolution operations with a

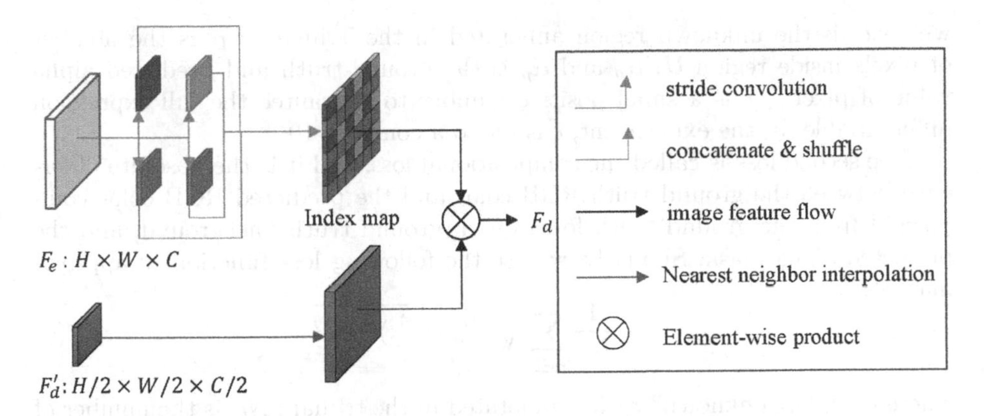

Fig. 3. The illustration of the dynamic upsampling block (DUB). The shuffle order of the Index map is not fixed and is shown in the figure for visual purposes.

stride of 2, and then concatenate them together to obtain the index map, which records the spatial information of the feature map in the encoder stage. In the decoder stage, the feature map F_d' is upsampled and then multiplied with the index map pixel by pixel, thus realizing a dynamic upsampling method.

Formally, the designed dynamic upsampling can be expressed as:

$$F_d = IM * U(F_d'), \tag{3}$$

where F_d is the dynamic upsampled feature map with the size of $H \times W \times C$, U is the nearest neighbor interpolation upsampling operation, F_d' is the feature map of the upper decoder stage with the size of $H/2 \times W/2 \times C$, IM is an index map with different spatial information, which can be represented as:

$$IM = Shuffle(Cat(SC(F_e))) \tag{4}$$

where F_e is the feature map of the encoder stage with the size of $H \times W \times C$, SC is the convolution with a stride of 2, Cat is doing concatenate operations on pixels, $Shuffle$ is a shuffling operation on pixels. The overall structure of DUB is shown in the Fig. 3.

3.4 Loss Function

The loss functions used in our network are alpha prediction loss and compositional loss introduced by Xu *et al.* [28]. Alpha loss is the absolute difference between the grand truth in each pixel and the predicted alpha map. The loss value of the whole image is formulated as:

$$L_\alpha = \frac{1}{N_U} \sum_{p \in U} \sqrt{(\alpha_p - \hat{\alpha_p})^2 + \epsilon^2} \tag{5}$$

where U is the unknown region annotated in the Trimap, N_U is the number of pixels inside region U. α_p and $\hat{\alpha_p}$ is the ground-truth and predicted alpha value of pixel p. ϵ is a small positive number to guarantee the full expression differentiable. In the experiment, ϵ is set to a constant 10^{-6}.

The second loss is called the compositional loss, and it is the absolute difference between the ground truth RGB color and the predicted RGB color composited from the ground truth foreground, ground truth background, and the predicted alpha mask. Similarly, we use the following loss function to approximate it:

$$L_c = \frac{1}{N_U} \sum_{p \in U} \sqrt{(C_p - \hat{C_p})^2 + \epsilon^2} \tag{6}$$

where U is the "unknown" region annotated in the trimap, N_U is the number of pixels inside region U. C_p and $\hat{C_p}$ is the RGB channels obtained by composing the grand truth and predicted alpha values of pixel p with the foreground image.

The full loss of our network is then a weighted sum of the two loss terms: $L = w_1 \cdot L_\alpha + w_2 \cdot L_c$. In our experiments, we fix $w_1 = 0.5, w_2 = 0.5$.

4 Experiments

4.1 Implementation Details

The encoder of our model is first initialized with the MobileNetv2 [23] pre-trained on ImageNet [5] and then trained in end-to-end on the Adobe Deep Image Matting Dataset [28]. The network was trained for a total of 31 epochs and approximately 133,610 iterations. We used the Adam [13] optimizer, setting its parameters $\beta_1 = 0.9$ and $\beta_2 = 0.999$, with an initial learning rate $\lambda = 0.01$. We scaled down the learning rate by 10× at 15-th and 25-th epochs. To compare with [28], we use the same training method as [28]. We also use the same strategy for data augmentation, cropping the RGB images and their corresponding Trimap by 320 × 320, random flipping, random scaling, and random dilation of the Trimap. All training data are created on the fly.

4.2 Dataset and Evaluation Metrics

Dataset. We use the Adobe Image Matting dataset [28] to train and test the performance of our model. This dataset contains 431 foreground images for training and 50 foreground images for testing and all with high-quality alpha annotations. Following the [28], for the training set, each foreground image is combined with 100 background images from the COCO dataset [18], and for the testing set, each image is combined with 20 background images from the PASCAL VOC2012 dataset [6]. Thus we used a total of 43100 training images and 1000 test images.

Evaluation Metrics. We use four common metrics in natural image matting to evaluate the predicted alpha mattes, namely absolute differences (SAD), mean squared error (MSE), gradient error (Grad), and connectivity error (Conn). SAD

Table 1. Quantitative comparisons to the baseline on Composition-1k dataset. $LFCG_E$ and $LFCG_D$ refer to the use of LFCG in the encoder and decoder stages, respectively.

Baseline	DUB	$LFCG_D$	$LFCG_E$	SAD	MSE	Grad	Conn
✓	×	×	×	49.46	0.014	28.66	49.07
✓	✓	×	×	48.44	0.013	29.52	47.90
✓	✓	✓	×	48.01	0.013	27.80	47.16
✓	✓	×	✓	45.92	0.012	26.56	44.12
✓	✓	✓	✓	**44.57**	**0.012**	**26.03**	**43.24**

and MSE focus more on numerical absolute differences, while Grad and Coon [21] focus more on visual differences. In addition, to illustrate the effectiveness of the models, we list the number of model parameters as evaluation metrics, which can visually show the effectiveness of the parameters of different models and also indirectly indicate the time and memory consumption required for model inference.

4.3 Ablation Study

Table 2. Testing results on the Composition-1k Dataset. The best performance is in boldface. For all metrics, smaller is better.

Methods	SAD	MSE	Grad	Conn	Params
Global Matting [8]	133.6	0.068	97.6	133.3	–
Closed-Form [14]	168.1	0.091	126.9	167.9	–
KNN Matting [2]	175.4	0.103	124.1	176.4	–
Deep Matting [28]	50.4	0.014	31.0	50.8	130545K
IndexNet [19]	45.8	0.013	25.9	43.7	5953K
Ours	**44.6**	**0.012**	**25.4**	**43.0**	**5490K**

In this section, we report the results of ablation experiments to demonstrate the effectiveness of the modules introduced by our network. The results of the experiments are listed in the Table 1. We use the four metrics mentioned in the previous section to evaluate our model. As can be seen in the Table 1, the performance of the model with our LFCG has improved in terms of metrics compared to the baselines, which indicates that LFCG successfully extracts more effective feature maps. In addition, we further investigate the effect of LFCG blocks on the model at different stages. We can see that the introduction of LFCG at the primary stage in the encoder brings more improvement than introducing LFCG at the decoder stage. Thus, we argue that extracting more effective feature maps at the encoder stage could guide the model to generate more effective high-level feature maps in the decoder stage. The introduction of LFCG in the decoder stage can only tell the model which features are valid in the model prediction, but there are already redundant feature maps before that. In other words, with the same model capacity, introducing LFCG first will allow the model to have more accurate feature maps.

4.4 Experiment Results

We compare the performance of our model with other state-of-the-art models. We also compare our results with non-deep learning methods and deep learning-based methods. The results are reported in Table 2. For more experimental results, please see Fig. 4.

As shown in the Fig. 4, the visual performance of our model improves on difficult samples like light bulbs, and our experimental results outperform other methods on fine structures like spider webs and small balls with holes, which is the result of the combination of the introduction of LFCG in the encoder stage

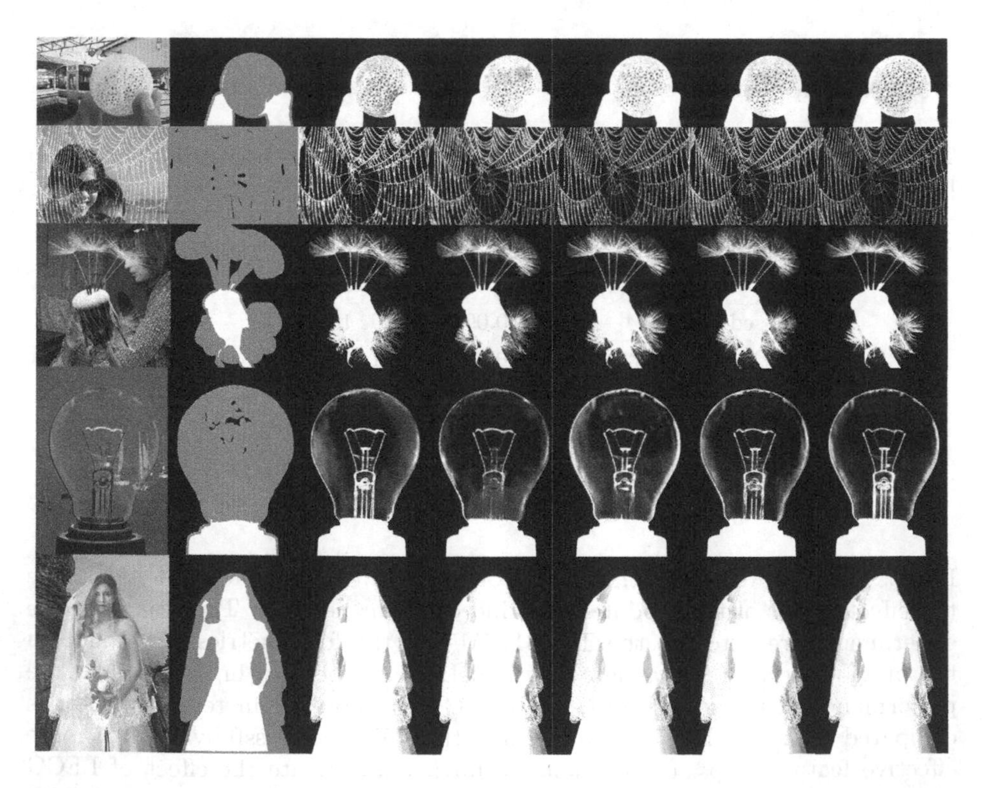

Fig. 4. The visual results on the Adobe testing dataset. For each row of images, from left to right: original image, trimap, Deep Image Matting [28], IndexNet [19], GCA [16], ours, ground-truth. Please zoom in for more details.

to better utilize the low-level feature maps and the use of DUB in the decoder stage.

With the same number of parameters, our model outperforms the other models in all four evaluation metrics. Although our model is lower than the GCA [16] method in terms of metrics, the network capacity and training time of the GCA model itself is far superior to our model. Compared with the original GCA paper, our model uses less than 4% of its training resources and training time. Therefore, it is worthwhile for us to greatly reduce the number of model parameters and speed up inference by sacrificing a small amount of model accuracy.

5 Conclusion

In this work, we proposed a new natural image matting structure in which different low-level feature maps are given different weights at the early stage of the network. Thus, it could guide the model to extract features more efficiently without increasing the network capacity, making it more accurate in alpha prediction at details. Moreover, a low-level feature-guided module is also designed. Extensive experiments demonstrate the effect of different stages of low-level feature maps on the accuracy of the model. Experimental results also show that the proposed module improves the performance compared to the baselines and the composition-1k dataset in terms of SAD, MSE, and Conn metrics.

References

1. Cai, S., et al.: Disentangled image matting. In: Proceedings of the IEEE/CVF International Conference on Computer Vision, pp. 8819–8828 (2019)
2. Chen, Q., Li, D., Tang, C.K.: KNN matting. IEEE Trans. Pattern Anal. Mach. Intell. **35**(9), 2175–2188 (2013)
3. Chen, Q., Ge, T., Xu, Y., Zhang, Z., Yang, X., Gai, K.: Semantic human matting. In: Proceedings of the 26th ACM international conference on Multimedia, pp. 618–626 (2018)
4. Chuang, Y.Y., Curless, B., Salesin, D.H., Szeliski, R.: A Bayesian approach to digital matting. In: Proceedings of the 2001 IEEE Computer Society Conference on Computer Vision and Pattern Recognition, CVPR 2001, vol. 2, pp. II-II. IEEE (2001)
5. Deng, J., Dong, W., Socher, R., Li, L.J., Li, K., Fei-Fei, L.: ImageNet: a large-scale hierarchical image database. In: 2009 IEEE Conference on Computer Vision and Pattern Recognition, pp. 248–255. IEEE (2009)
6. Everingham, M., Van Gool, L., Williams, C.K., Winn, J., Zisserman, A.: The pascal visual object classes (VOC) challenge. Int. J. Comput. Vis. **88**(2), 303–338 (2010)
7. He, B., Wang, G., Shi, C., Yin, X., Liu, B., Lin, X.: Iterative transductive learning for alpha matting. In: 2013 IEEE International Conference on Image Processing, pp. 4282–4286. IEEE (2013)
8. He, K., Rhemann, C., Rother, C., Tang, X., Sun, J.: A global sampling method for alpha matting. In: CVPR 2011, pp. 2049–2056. IEEE (2011)

9. Hou, Q., Liu, F.: Context-aware image matting for simultaneous foreground and alpha estimation. In: Proceedings of the IEEE/CVF International Conference on Computer Vision, pp. 4130–4139 (2019)
10. Hu, F., Lakdawala, S., Hao, Q., Qiu, M.: Low-power, intelligent sensor hardware interface for medical data preprocessing. IEEE Trans. Inf. Technol. Biomed. **13**(4), 656–663 (2009)
11. Hu, J., Shen, L., Sun, G.: Squeeze-and-excitation networks. In: Proceedings of the IEEE Conference on Computer Vision and Pattern Recognition, pp. 7132–7141 (2018)
12. Ke, Z., et al.: Is a green screen really necessary for real-time portrait matting? arXiv preprint arXiv:2011.11961 (2020)
13. Kingma, D.P., Ba, J.: Adam: A method for stochastic optimization. arXiv preprint arXiv:1412.6980 (2014)
14. Levin, A., Lischinski, D., Weiss, Y.: A closed-form solution to natural image matting. IEEE Trans. Pattern Anal. Mach. Intell. **30**(2), 228–242 (2007)
15. Li, J., Zhang, J., Maybank, S.J., Tao, D.: End-to-end animal image matting. arXiv e-prints pp. arXiv-2010 (2020)
16. Li, Y., Lu, H.: Natural image matting via guided contextual attention. In: Proceedings of the AAAI Conference on Artificial Intelligence, vol. 34, pp. 11450–11457 (2020)
17. Li, Y., Song, Y., Jia, L., Gao, S., Li, Q., Qiu, M.: Intelligent fault diagnosis by fusing domain adversarial training and maximum mean discrepancy via ensemble learning. IEEE Trans. Ind. Inf. **17**(4), 2833–2841 (2020)
18. Lin, T.-Y., et al.: Microsoft COCO: common objects in context. In: Fleet, D., Pajdla, T., Schiele, B., Tuytelaars, T. (eds.) ECCV 2014, Part V. LNCS, vol. 8693, pp. 740–755. Springer, Cham (2014). https://doi.org/10.1007/978-3-319-10602-1_48
19. Lu, H., Dai, Y., Shen, C., Xu, S.: Indices matter: learning to index for deep image matting. In: Proceedings of the IEEE/CVF International Conference on Computer Vision, pp. 3266–3275 (2019)
20. Qiu, H., Zheng, Q., Msahli, M., Memmi, G., Qiu, M., Lu, J.: Topological graph convolutional network-based urban traffic flow and density prediction. IEEE Trans. Intell. Transp. Syst. **22**(7), 4560–4569 (2020)
21. Rhemann, C., Rother, C., Wang, J., Gelautz, M., Kohli, P., Rott, P.: A perceptually motivated online benchmark for image matting. In: 2009 IEEE Conference on Computer Vision and Pattern Recognition, pp. 1826–1833. IEEE (2009)
22. Ronneberger, O., Fischer, P., Brox, T.: U-Net: convolutional networks for biomedical image segmentation. In: Navab, N., Hornegger, J., Wells, W.M., Frangi, A.F. (eds.) MICCAI 2015 Part III. LNCS, vol. 9351, pp. 234–241. Springer, Cham (2015). https://doi.org/10.1007/978-3-319-24574-4_28
23. Sandler, M., Howard, A., Zhu, M., Zhmoginov, A., Chen, L.C.: MobileNetV2: inverted residuals and linear bottlenecks. In: Proceedings of the IEEE Conference on Computer Vision and Pattern Recognition, pp. 4510–4520 (2018)
24. Sengupta, S., Jayaram, V., Curless, B., Seitz, S.M., Kemelmacher-Shlizerman, I.: Background matting: the world is your green screen. In: Proceedings of the IEEE/CVF Conference on Computer Vision and Pattern Recognition, pp. 2291–2300 (2020)
25. Shi, W., et al.: Real-time single image and video super-resolution using an efficient sub-pixel convolutional neural network. In: Proceedings of the IEEE Conference on Computer Vision and Pattern Recognition, pp. 1874–1883 (2016)

26. Wang, J., Cohen, M.F.: An iterative optimization approach for unified image segmentation and matting. In: Tenth IEEE International Conference on Computer Vision (ICCV 2005) Volume 1, vol. 2, pp. 936–943. IEEE (2005)
27. Wang, J., Cohen, M.F.: Optimized color sampling for robust matting. In: 2007 IEEE Conference on Computer Vision and Pattern Recognition, pp. 1–8. IEEE (2007)
28. Xu, N., Price, B., Cohen, S., Huang, T.: Deep image matting. In: Proceedings of the IEEE Conference on Computer Vision and Pattern Recognition, pp. 2970–2979 (2017)
29. Zhang, Y., Li, K., Li, K., Wang, L., Zhong, B., Fu, Y.: Image super-resolution using very deep residual channel attention networks. In: Proceedings of the European Conference on Computer Vision (ECCV), pp. 286–301 (2018)

Identifying Taxi Commuting Traffic Analysis Zones Using Massive GPS Data

Yang Qin[1], Linjiang Zheng[1,2(✉)], Li Chen[1,2], and Weining Liu[1,2]

[1] College of Computer Science, Chongqing University, Chongqing, China
{zlj_cqu,qy_cqu,lwn}@cqu.edu.cn

[2] Key Laboratory of Dependable Service Computing in Cyber Physical Society of Ministry of Education, Chongqing University, Chongqing, China

Abstract. The rapid urbanization process leads to the spatial separation of residence and workplace, which further complicates the commuting pattern of urban residents. Commuting travel by taxi between residence and workplace is convenient and common, while few studies focus on mining commuting pattern using taxi GPS data. In this paper, we propose a taxi commuting traffic analysis zones (TAZs) identification method to identify the regional-level commuting patterns of taxis. The method mainly includes three steps: dividing TAZs considering Point of interest (POI) information, obtaining flow transfer matrix, and identifying commuting TAZs using K-means algorithm. Extensive experiments are conducted on taxi GPS dataset from Chongqing, China. The results show that the method is efficient. 52 pairs of TAZs with commuting relationship are successfully identified, and some typical commuting features are analyzed. The analysis results provide valuable reference for relevant departments and companies, for example, designing custom buses.

Keywords: Taxi GPS data · Regional-level commuting pattern · TAZs · POI

1 Introduction

With the rapid development of China urbanization process, great changes have taken place in the urban spatial structure, resulting in the separation of residence and workplace. This brings about some problems, such as longer commuting time and longer commuting distance, which further complicates the commuting needs of urban residents [1]. As an important mode of transportation, taxi plays an important role in reflecting the patterns of residents travel activities. Taxi GPS data has been used in taxi driver behavior analysis [2], trajectory mining [3], flow forecasting [4, 5], time forecasting [6] and other studies. Commuting travel by taxi between residence and workplace is convenient and common. However, few studies focus on using taxi GPS data to discover the taxi regional-level commuting pattern.

Many experts have conducted in-depth research on the commuting pattern using smart card data and private car data. Mining commuting pattern based on smart card data mainly includes three processes: generation of travel chain, identification of departure

G. Memmi et al. (Eds.): KSEM 2022, LNAI 13370, pp. 562–578, 2022.
https://doi.org/10.1007/978-3-031-10989-8_45

and destination and comparison of travel modes [7, 8]. Some studies also find that the hot spots of potential commuter bus passengers can be regarded as candidate locations of customized buses stops and can be used to set customized buses candidate routes [9, 10]. Identifying commuters based on private car data mainly focuses on describing time similarity and spatial similarity [11]. There are three main processes: extracting travel OD, commuting definition based on time similarity and spatial similarity, identifying commuter vehicles. In terms of identification methods, some scholars use hierarchical clustering [12], density peak clustering [13] and other algorithms. Yaw [14] et al. use the iterative self-organizing data analysis algorithm (ISODATA) to identify commuter vehicles. In the research of identifying commuter individuals, most scholars use machine learning methods, such as various clustering methods, and the effect is remarkable.

In the commuting behavior study of urban residents, Fu [15] et al. propose a commuting passenger flow identification model using taxi GPS data, and identify the distribution of residence and workplace. Statistics method are mainly used in the research. Traditional statistical methods are time-consuming and inefficient, and their limitations are prominent when facing the data set with complex data structure and huge volume. Machine learning method overcomes these difficulties and it is very efficient for data mining. K-means algorithm had achieved remarkable achievements in the research of identifying commuter individuals, because it has low computational complexity and fast convergence speed.

In view of this, we propose a commuting TAZs identification method to discover the regional-level commuting patterns of taxis, where GPS data, urban road network and POI information are fully explored. The method mainly includes three steps: dividing TAZs considering POI information, obtaining flow transfer matrix, and identifying commuting TAZs using K-means algorithm. The main contributions in this paper are as follows:

(1) We propose a bottom-up TAZs division method based on fine-grained meta cells. This method employs road network data to build a TAZs network that meets the needs of personalized analysis. This method is suitable for all cities, especially those with complex road network.
(2) We propose a commuting TAZs identification method based on K-means clustering. The method directly identify pairs of commuting TAZs using flow and its stability factor in the morning and evening peaks between pairs of TAZs, so it has high accuracy. The effect is remarkable, especially in the case of massive dataset.
(3) Extensive experiments are conducted on taxi GPS dataset from Chongqing, China. We have identified 52 pairs of TAZs with commuting relationship and analyzed spatio-temporal characteristics of commuting TAZs. The analysis results provide valuable reference for relevant departments and companies, for example, designing custom buses.

The remainder of this paper is organized as follows. Section 2 introduces the proposed method. Section 3 uses Chongqing real-world datasets as a case study and analyzes the spatio-temporal characteristics of commuting TAZs. Section 4 summarizes this paper.

2 Methodology

Different from individual-level commuting pattern, regional-level commuting pattern reflects the characteristics of TAZs. Focusing on urban regional-level commuting pattern, we propose a new commuting TAZs identification method, which mainly includes three steps: dividing TAZs, obtaining flow transfer matrix and identifying commuting TAZs. Firstly, we divide TAZs based on road network data and build a TAZs network. And then, combining with the POI information, we analyze the POI of TAZs, which is helpful to improve the rationality and accuracy of aggregating zones in Dividing TAZs. Secondly, we obtain flow transfer matrix, and the difficulty lies in allocate OD to TAZs. Thus, we propose a frequency-based allocation method. Thirdly, we identify commuting TAZs using the K-means clustering method. In which, an important feature coefficient of dispersion (COD) is employed to portrait the commuting pattern. Figure 1 shows the overview of framework.

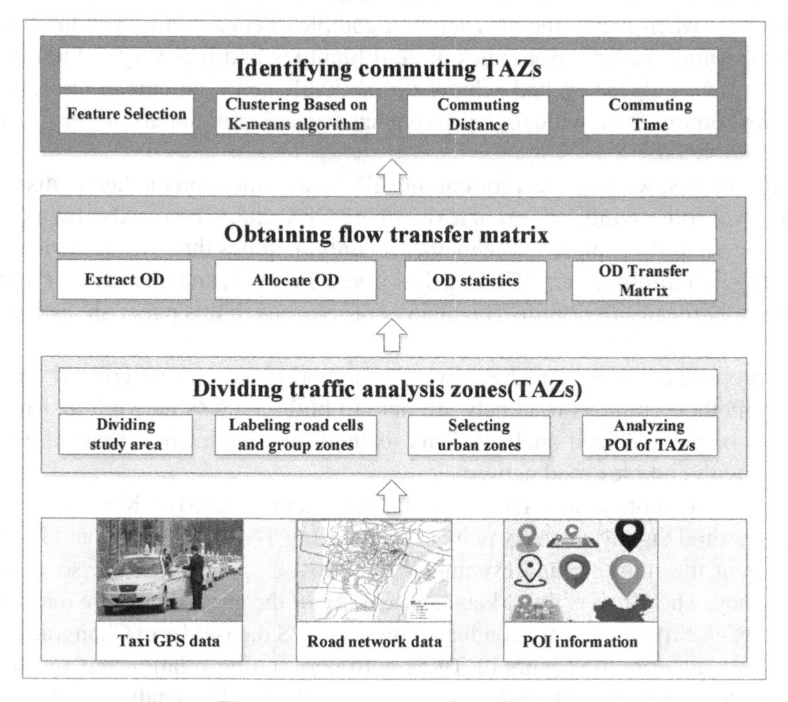

Fig. 1. The overview of framework.

2.1 Dividing TAZs

Dividing TAZs. Different studies have different views on the division of TAZs. Most scholars use administrative division units (streets, communities, etc.) as research object, which include large areas and is not conducive to detailed researches. Some scholars divide the research zone into regular cells with the same size. Although this method can be applied to detailed researches, it does not take into account the real urban spatial structures and destroys the integrity of them. In view of this, we propose a **bottom-up TAZs division method**, in which urban road network data and POI information are fully explored. The detailed steps are as follows:

(a) Dividing: Divide the study area into meta cells of a small size, such as 20 m × 20 m, as shown in Fig. 2(a). In this case, roads, buildings, park, mountains and rivers can be completely distinguished from each other.
(b) Labeling: Label all the road cells as 1 and all non-roads cells are surrounded by the road cells, labeled as other numbers. Next, label these group cells in order (starting from No. 2) and then, aggregate the cells of the same number. As shown in Fig. 2(b), the red zone is labeled as No. 3 zone.
(c) Selecting: Delete un-urban zone. For example, the zone is too small or it is a special zone such as rivers, lakes, mountains and forests (because Chongqing is a mountainous city and there are two rivers in the urban zone, namely the Yangtze River and Jialing River).

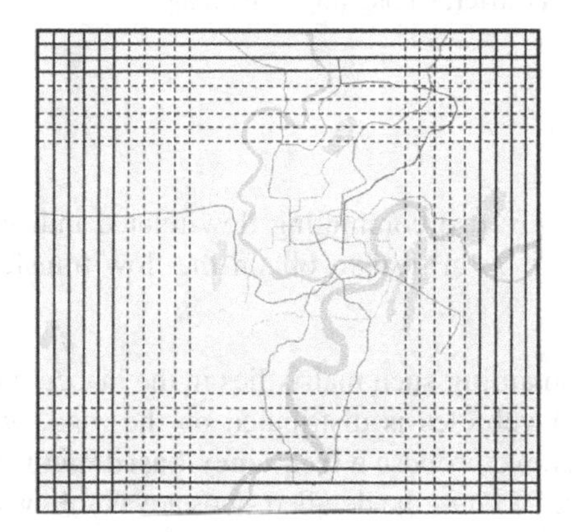
(a)Divide the study area into small cells

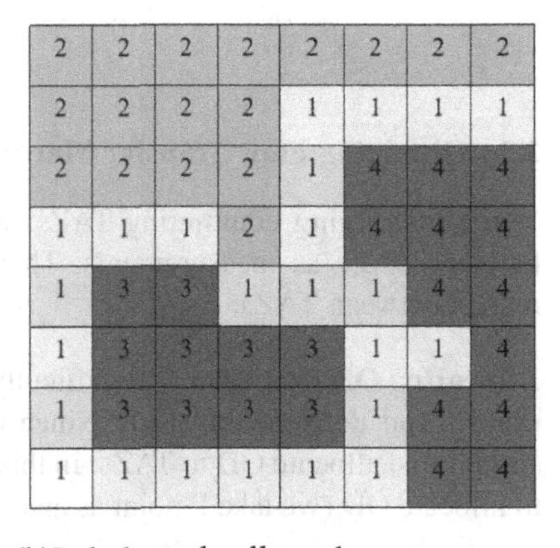

(b)Label road cells and group zones

Fig. 2. Sample diagram of Dividing TAZs. (Color figure online)

Analyzing POI. Analyzing the POI of TAZs is helpful to improve the rationality and accuracy of aggregating zones in Dividing TAZs. Some important fields of POI information are shown in Table 1. We focus on *lon*, *lat* and *tag*, in which *tag* field marks POI information. The *tag* contains two parts: POI category and subcategories, for example, the *tag* of Chongqing University is "education and training; colleges and universities". As there are many categories of POI information, we first classify POI information into seven categories: consumer-entertainment, business-office, education, traffic, medical, scenic and residence.

The POI analysis mainly includes three processes: statistics of the number of POIs in TAZs, 0–1 normalization and K-means clustering for clustering TAZs into different clusters with different POI.

Table 1. Important fields of POI information.

lon	*lat*	*name*	*address*	*tag*
106.50585	29.507668	Huayu. Sunshine Shangzuo	No. 18, Longquan Road, Shiqiao	Estate; Residential
106.349428	29.361283	Chongqing sanguo furniture co., ltd	Chuangye Road, Jiulongpo District, Chongqing	Enterprise; Company
106.504673	29.520229	Cooking Jianghu dishes	No. 3, No. 119, Shiqiaozheng Street (Poly Aishangli)	Gourmet; Chinese restaurant
106.470477	29.573424	Chongqing University	No. 174, Zhengjie Street, Shapingba District, Chongqing	Education; Institutions of higher learning

2.2 Obtaining Flow Transfer Matrix

When identifying commuting TAZs, we mainly use commuting flow-related indices between TAZs as measurements. Therefore, it is critical to obtain the flow transfer matrix between TAZs.

Allocating OD to TAZs: The difficulty of obtaining such matrix lies in the inaccurate origins and destinations (OD). Since OD of vehicles is distributed on the road, we should first allocate OD to TAZs. In this paper, we propose **a frequency-based method** to allocate OD (we take P point as an example of OD), the detailed steps are as follows:

(a) Extending: Take the cell where point P is located as the center, extend 10 cells in all directions to form the window of w × w cells. It is unreasonable to have too large or too small a study area. Based on the TAZs division method proposed in Sect. 2.1, the window of 21 × 21 cells is the most appropriate.
(b) Counting: Count the frequency of different cells in the window.
(c) Allocating: The P point will be allocated to the TAZ which has the most cells in the window.

As shown in Fig. 3, P point is distributed on the road (The label of road cells is 1), and it extends 3 cells to form the window of 7 × 7 cells(It is just a schematic). In the window, No. 2 TAZ has the most cells, so the P point is allocated to No. 2 TAZ.

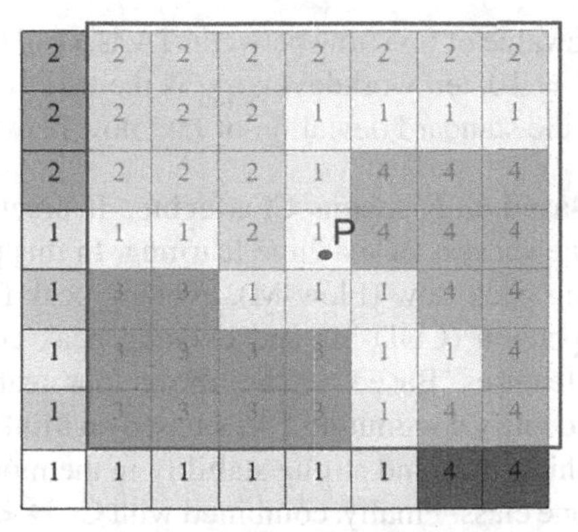

Fig. 3. The schematic of P point allocation.

Calculating Flow Transfer Matrix: Finally, the flow can be easily calculated: According to the allocation method proposed above, we allocate OD to a pair of TAZs separately. For example, O point is allocated to No. 2 TAZ, D point is allocated to No. 5 TAZ, then the number of flow from No. 2 TAZ to No. 5 TAZ will add 1. Finally, we generate the flow transfer matrix between pairs of TAZs. In addition, we can get the total inflow and outflow of each TAZ through accumulation.

2.3 Identifying Commuting TAZs

Definition of Commuting TAZs. Commuting behavior can be defined as the travel activities with the characteristics of periodicity, temporal and stability generated by urban residents between their residence and workplace. The direct identification of pairs of commuting TAZs has high accuracy and clear commuting relationship. On this basis, combined with the characteristics of taxi, we propose the definition of commuting TAZs:

If two TAZs have stable flow in the morning and evening peaks, they are considered to have taxi regional-level commuting characteristics, and they are considered a pair of commuting TAZs.

The Coefficient of Dispersion (COD). In order to discuss the stability of taxi flow during peak hours between TAZs, the coefficient of dispersion (COD) is designed to measure the stability characteristics. The formula for calculating COD is as follows:

$$\overline{q}_{ab} = \frac{\sum_{i=1}^{M} q_{ab}^{i}}{M} \tag{1}$$

$$S_{ab} = \sqrt{\frac{\sum_{i=1}^{M} \left(q_{ab}^{i} - \overline{q}_{ab}\right)^{2}}{M}} \tag{2}$$

$$COD_{ab} = \frac{S_{ab}}{\overline{q}_{ab}} \tag{3}$$

where: $\overline{q}_{ab}$ is the average value of taxi flow between TAZs a and b during the observation period (in this paper, $M = 10$, ten workdays); q^{i}_{ab} is the taxi flow between TAZs a and b on the i-th day; S_{ab} is the standard deviation of taxi flow between TAZs a and b.

Identification Model Based on K-means Clustering. In practical application, feature selection is the key to the success of machine learning. In this paper, between pairs of TAZs, we select morning peak flow (Flow-M), evening peak flow (Flow-E), morning peak coefficient of dispersion (COD-M) and evening peak coefficient of dispersion (COD-E) as the input features. Based on the above four features, we use K-means clustering algorithm to identify commuting TAZs based on Minkowski distance ($d = 4$). In this way, TAZs with high flow and strong stability in the morning and evening peak hours are grouped into one class. Finally, combined with COD < 0.3 to further selecting commuting TAZs. The pseudo code of K-means algorithm is shown in Algorithm 1.

Algorithm 1 Identification method based on K-means clustering

---

Input: feature matrix D = { **Flow-M, Flow-E, COD-M, COD-E**}, the number of clusters K.
Output: Cluster partition C.
1: Initialize cluster center: Randomly select k samples from D as the initial cluster center;
2: **repeat** # Iteration
3: **for** i=1, 2, ..., k **do**
4: $C_i = \emptyset$;
5: **end for**
6: **for** j=1, 2, ..., m **do** # Update the cluster attribution of all sample points
7: **for** i=1, 2, ..., k **do**
8: Calculate the Minkowski distance(d=4) between the sample $x(j)$ and cluster center $u(i)$;
9: **end for**
10: λ_j =argmin d_{ji} ;
11: $C_{\lambda_j} = C_{\lambda_j} \cup x(j)$;
12: **end for**
13: **for** i=1, 2, ..., k **do** # Update cluster center
14: $u(i)' = (1/|C_i|) \sum_{x \in C_i} x$;
15: **if** $u(i)' \neq u(i)$ **then**
16: $u(i) = u(i)'$;
17: **end if**
18: **end for**
19: **until** the cluster center is not updated or the given maximum number of iterations is reached.

---

3 Experiment and Analysis

3.1 Taxi GPS Dataset

The GPS dataset comes from more than 10,000 taxis in Chongqing, China. The period ranges from March 6 to 10 and March 13 to 17, 2017, which lasts for 2 weeks and 10 working days. The time interval for data acquisition of on-board GPS equipment is about 30s, and the data collection time covers 24 h a day. We mainly use the morning peak (7:00–10:00) and the evening peak (17:00–20:00). Each GPS data record includes 7 attributes, and the description is shown in Table 2.

Table 2. Taxi GPS data

Parameter	Field name	Sample	Remarks
l	ID	渝8AC0F0D0BF	License plate number
d	DATE	20170306	Date
t	TIME	070510	Time
x	LON	106.404	Longitude
y	LAT	29.6951	Latitude
v	SPEED	32.8	Speed
s	STATE	1	Passenger status: 0 means no load 1 means carrying passengers

After data preprocessing,, we have found that Chongqing owns about taxis 500,000 trips every working day in March 2017. Among them, the morning peak is about 73,000–85,000 trips, accounting for about 15% of the whole day; There are about 70,000–76,000 trips in the evening peak, accounting for about 12% of the whole day. Compared with the morning peak, the trips in the evening peak decreases about 3%.

3.2 TAZs Division and POI Analysis

According to the TAZs division method proposed in Sect. 2.1, we divide the study area into 356 TAZs, as shown in Fig. 4(a). Based on the POI information of Chongqing, we analyze the POI of TAZs and visualize them in Fig. 4(b). Among them, the red zone is identified as the consumer-entertainment zone, the brown zone is identified as the residential zone, the khaki zone is identified as the education zone, the pink zone is the business-office zone, and the navy blue zone is the traffic zone.

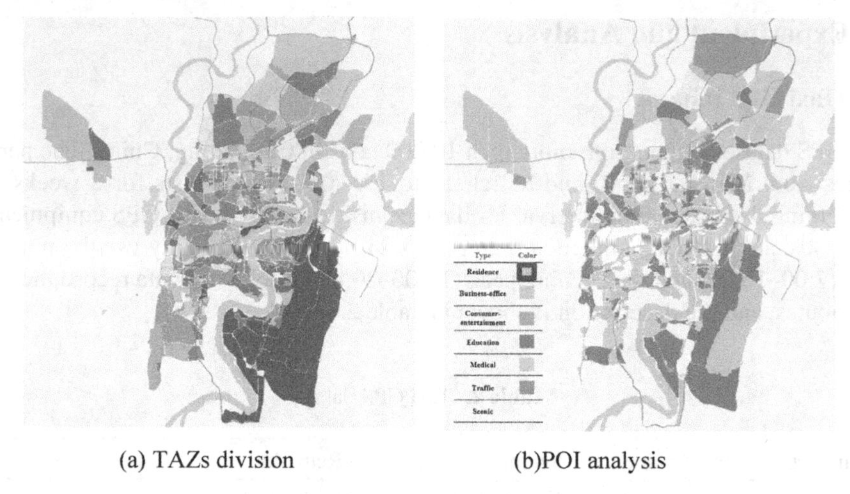

(a) TAZs division (b)POI analysis

Fig. 4. TAZs division and POI analysis.

3.3 Flow Transfer Matrix and the Coefficient of Dispersion (COD) Distribution

According to the OD allocation method proposed in Sect. 2.2, we conduct flow statistics to generate flow transfer matrix. There is about 1.48 million pairs of OD in the morning and evening peaks in 10 working days, of which about 760,000 pairs are in the morning peak and about 720,000 pairs are in the evening peak.

According to formulas (1) to (3), the coefficient of dispersion (COD) between TAZs is calculated, and the statistical distribution is shown in Fig. 5. The distribution has a small difference between the morning peak and the evening peak. The COD lies in [0.001,1.0], among which the COD accounts for more than 70% in the range of [0.1,0.3]. When COD < 0.3, the taxi flow between TAZs tends to be stable. Therefore, based on the relevant statistical criteria, we select COD < 0.3.

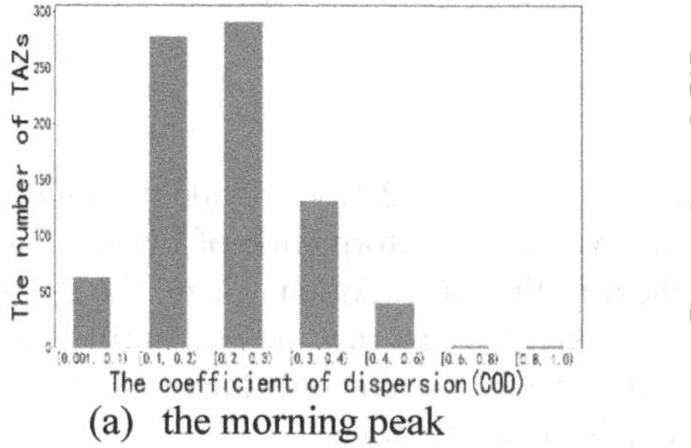

(a) the morning peak

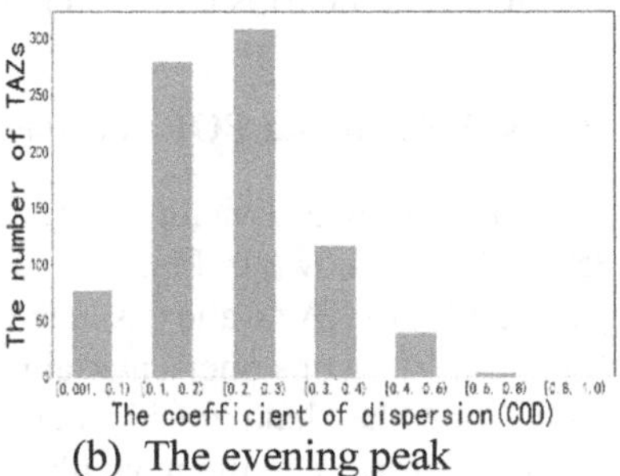

(b) The evening peak

Fig. 5. The coefficient of dispersion (COD) distribution.

3.4 The Identification Results and Analysis of Commuting TAZs

The number of clusters K is a constant, which needs to be set in advance. The setting of K value is very important to the final result. The commonly used selection K methods are Silhouette Coefficient (SC) method and elbow rule [16]. In order to avoid the cognitive deviation caused by a single method, we selects the Silhouette Coefficient method and elbow rule to jointly determine K to ensure the reliability of the results.

Silhouette Coefficient is an evaluation method of clustering effect. It combines the two factors of cohesion and separation, and is used to evaluate the influence of different algorithms or different parameter settings of the same algorithm on the clustering results on the same data set. The calculation formula is as follows:

$$SC = \frac{\sum_{i=1}^{N} \frac{b(i)-a(i)}{max(a(i),b(i))}}{N} \tag{4}$$

$$a(i) = \frac{\sum_{j \in C_i} d(x_i, x_j)}{|C_i - 1|} \tag{5}$$

$$b(i) = min_{j \neq i} \frac{\sum_{j \in C_j} d(x_i, x_j)}{|C_j|} \tag{6}$$

where: C_i, C_j represents the sample dataset contained in the i-th and j-th clusters, and the sample point $x_i \in C_i$, $a(i)$ represents the internal dissimilarity of sample point x_i, and $b(i)$ represents the dissimilarity of sample point x_i, N represents the number of all sample points.

Elbow rule is to determine the best K by comparing the variation trend of sum of squared errors (SSE) of clustering results. The calculation formula is as follows:

$$SSE = \sum_{i=1}^{K} \sum_{x \in C_i} |x - u_i|^2 \tag{7}$$

where: u_i represents the cluster center of the i-th cluster.

We conduct a pre-experiment, and according to the prior knowledge, we select the range of K value as [9,19]. The final results are shown in Fig. 6, SSE decreases with the increase of K, and Si fluctuates up and down.

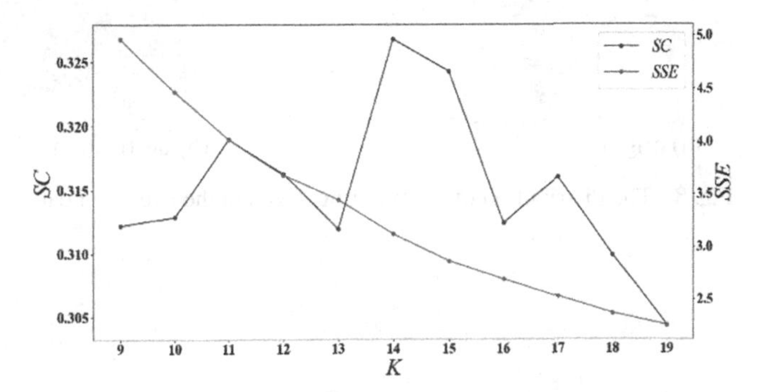

Fig. 6. The SC and SSE at different K.

Combined with the comprehensive analysis of *SC* and *SSE*, we choose the number of clustering clusters $K = 14$. The experimental results show that 126 pairs of TAZs with high flow and strong stability in the morning and evening peak hours are grouped into one class. Finally, combined with COD < 0.3 for screening, 52 pairs of TAZs with commuting relationship are identified. Figures 7 and 8 show the distribution of commuting TAZs in the morning and evening peaks (red zones in the figures are commuting TAZs). Table 3 and 4 show the top 10 pairs of commuting TAZs in the morning and evening peaks.

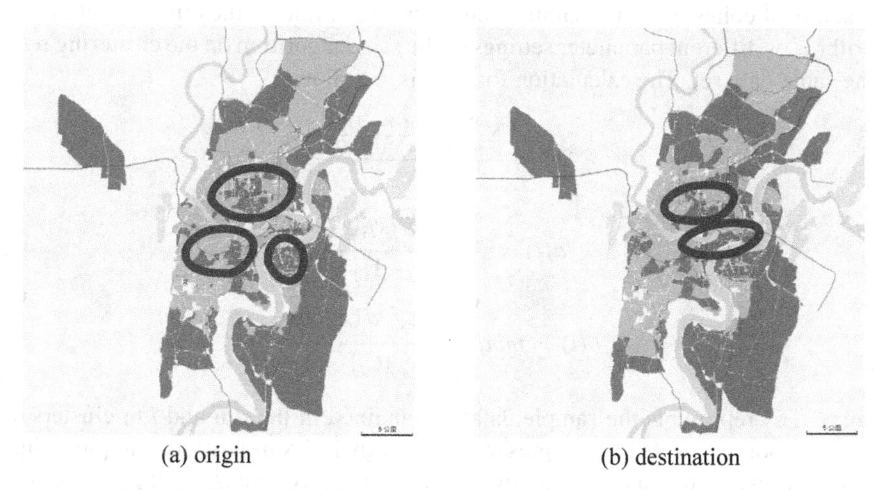

(a) origin (b) destination

Fig. 7. The distribution of Commuting TAZs in the morning peak.

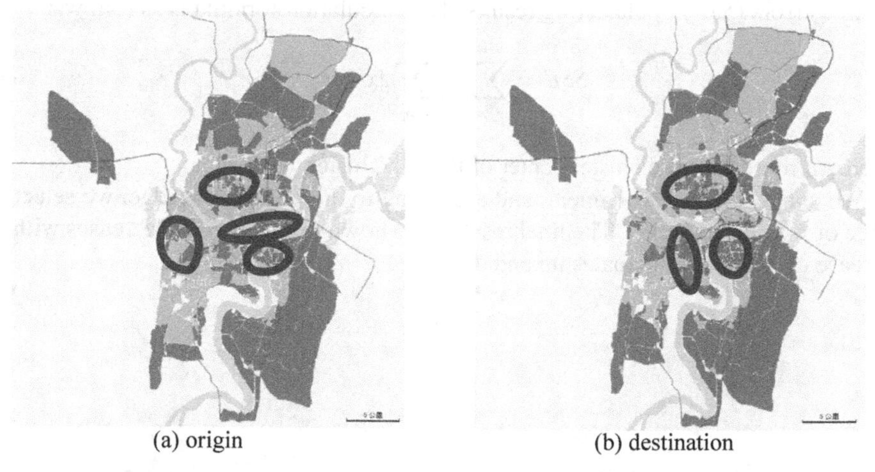

(a) origin (b) destination

Fig. 8. The distribution of Commuting TAZs in the evening peak.

Table 3. TOP 10 pairs of commuting TAZs in the morning peak

Number	Origin	Destination	Distance (km)	trips
1	200 (around Central Park)	200 (around Central Park)	2.3	152
2	343 (Nan'an District)	345 (Rongqiao Primary School, Xintiandi Community)	6.4	148
3	345 (Rongqiao Primary School, Xintiandi Community)	200 (around Central Park)	27.8	136
4	341 (Danzishi International Community)	89 (Jie Fangbei Business District)	5.2	131
5	201 (Huixing District)	179 (around Chongqing North Railway Station)	7.7	125
6	304 (Yuanyangcheng Community)	29 (Sanxia Square Business District)	8.6	103
7	200 (around Central Park)	10 (Liangjiang Industrial Park)	14.2	85
8	301 (Pingdingshan Cultural Park)	308 (Southwest Hospital)	7.1	76
9	304 (Yuanyangcheng Community)	313 (Olympic Sports Center, Chongqing Medical University)	6.1	73
10	224 (Lifan Tangyue Community, Donghu Yayuan Community)	204 (Liangjiang Middle School, Southwest University of Politics and Law Yubei Campus)	9.3	65

Table 4. TOP 10 pairs of commuting TAZs in the evening peak

Number	Origin	Destination	Distance(km)	Trips
1	200 (around Central Park)	345 (Rongqiao Primary School, Xintiandi Community)	27.9	130
2	345 (Rongqiao Primary School, Xintiandi Community)	343 (Nan 'an District)	6.5	123
3	89 (Jie Fangbei Business District)	343 (Nan 'an District)	9.7	114
4	330 (Chongqing Zoo, yangjiaping middle school)	323 (Huamei Times City)	4.6	96

(*continued*)

Table 4. *(continued)*

Number	Origin	Destination	Distance(km)	Trips
5	201 (Fuyue New Town, Changan Minsheng Logistics)	304 (Yuanyangcheng Community)	28.5	82
6	10 (Liangjiang Industrial Park)	200 (around Central Park)	14.3	74
7	204 (Liangjiang Middle School, Southwest University of Politics and Law Yubei Campus)	224 (Lifan Tangyue Community, Donghu Yayuan Community)	9.3	66
8	251 (Zijing Commercial Square)	323 (Huamei Times City)	12.9	62
9	10 (Liangjiang Industrial Park)	268 (Poly Hills Community)	10.8	55
10	308 (Southwest Hospital)	301 (Pingdingshan Cultural Park)	7.2	53

Hotspots Analysis: During the morning peak, the travel hotspots are mainly concentrated in the surrounding residential zones such as Jiefangbei, Nanping, and Danzishi, and around the public transport hubs such as Shapingba, Hongqihegou, and Lianglukou. These zones contain a large number of residential zones and important transportation facilities, which are dense zones where people go to work in the morning. During the evening peak, high-tech industrial park, such as Liangjiang Industrial Park, Xiantao Data Valley, and large commercial zones, such as Jiangbeizui, have become hotspots of taxi. Besides, zones with relatively concentrated leisure, entertainment, catering and shopping, such as Times Tian Street, Guanyinqiao pedestrian street, Sanxia Square business district, and Jiefangbei pedestrian street, have also become hotspots. In addition, citizens tend to arrive at the workplace quickly and on time in the morning peak. While in the evening peak, they tend to disperse to the adjacent time slices, so the flow in the evening peak will be lower than that in the morning peak.

Commuting Distance and Commuting Time: We first calculate the distance and time of all trips, and then calculate the commuting distance and commuting time between TAZs, the results are shown in Figs. 9, 10, 11 and 12. The analysis shows that the commuting distance during the peak hours is mainly distributed within 10 km, accounting for more than 60%, among which, the range of 5–10 km is the most, and there are also many short trips within 3 km. Long-distance commuting (more than 20 km) accounts for a relatively small proportion, accounting for about 10%. The commuting time during the peak hours is mainly distributed within 20 min, accounting for more than 65%, among which the range of 10–20 min is the most, accounting for more than 30% in the morning and evening peaks. Long-term (more than 30 min) commuting accounts for a relatively small proportion, accounting for about 15%.

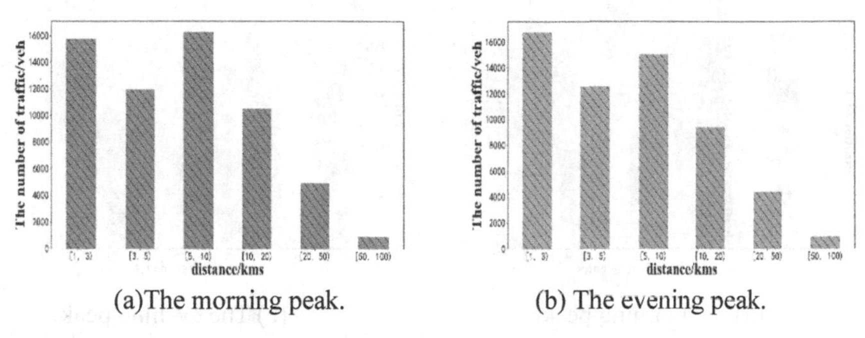

(a)The morning peak. (b) The evening peak.

Fig. 9. The distance of all trips.

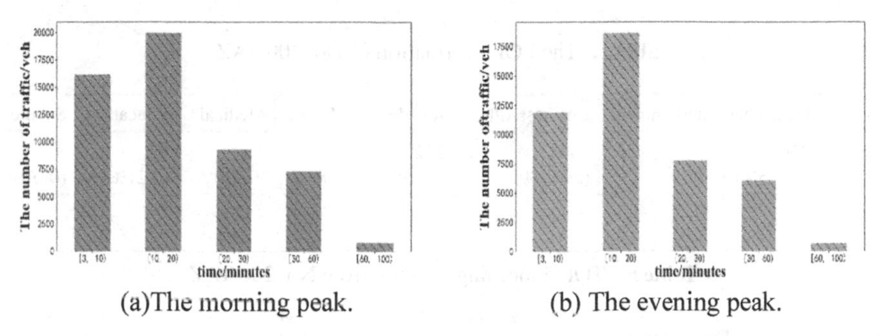

(a)The morning peak. (b) The evening peak.

Fig. 10. The time of all trips.

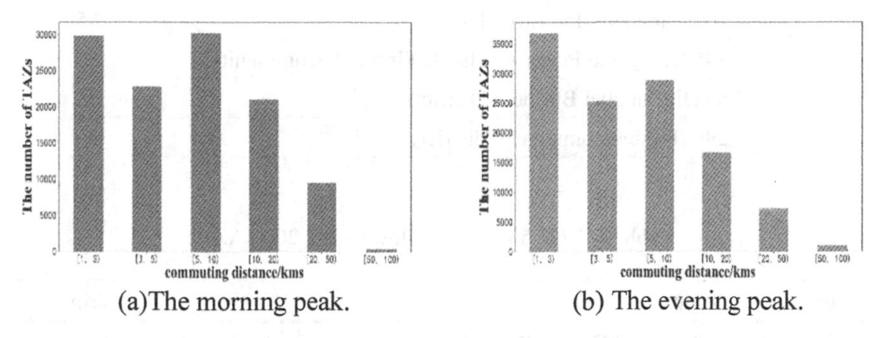

(a)The morning peak. (b) The evening peak.

Fig. 11. The commuting distance between TAZs.

3.5 The Commuting Travel Analysis of No. 200 TAZ (Around Central Park)

From Table 4.2 and Table 4.3, the taxi commuting behavior in No. 200 TAZ (around Central Park) is obvious, so we focus on analyzing this TAZ. Table 5 shows the POI information of No. 200 TAZ. According to the analysis, No. 200 TAZ is a multifunctional mixed zone integrating consumer-entertainment, business-office, education and residence.

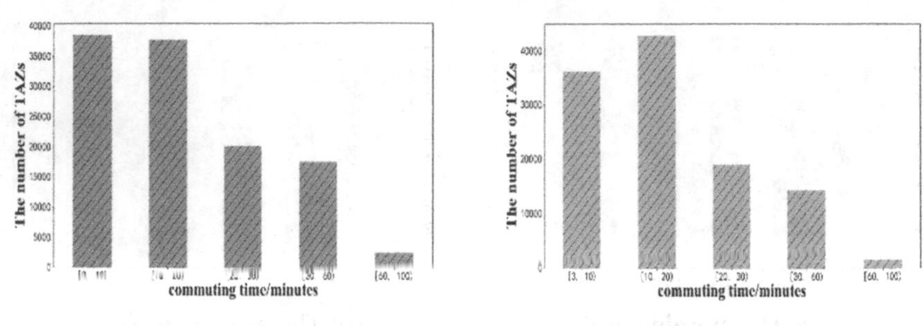

(a)The morning peak. (b) The evening peak.

Fig. 12. The commuting time between TAZs.

Table 5. The POI information of No. 200 TAZ

POI	Consumer-entertainment	Business-office	Residence	Traffic	Medical	Education	Scenic
Number (%)	2507 (66.25%)	1015 (26.82%)	252 (6.65%)	0 (0)	1 (0.026%)	8 (0.21%)	3 (0.079%)

Table 6. TOP 5 morning outflow from No. 200 TAZ

Number	Destination	Trips
1	200 (around Central Park)	152
2	10 (Liangjiang Industrial Park)	85
3	345 (Rongqiao Primary School, Xintiandi Community)	56
4	89 (Jie Fangbei Business District)	38
5	299 (Daping commercial district)	35

Table 7. TOP 5 evening inflow to No. 200 TAZ

Number	origin	Trips
1	200 (around Central Park)	166
2	10 (Liangjiang Industrial Park)	74
3	345 (Rongqiao Primary School, Xintiandi Community)	46
4	89 (Jie Fangbei Business District)	37
5	299(Daping commercial district)	33

Although No. 200 TAZ is a multifunctional mixed zone, it is a zone with strong residential attributes. In the morning, citizens go to work. In the evening, citizens go home from other places after work. Table 6 and Fig. 13(a) show the top 5 morning outflow from No. 200 TAZ in the morning. Table 7 and Fig. 13(b) show the top 5 evening inflow to No. 200 TAZ in the evening. The top 5 TAZs which have a strong commuting relationship with No. 200 TAZ are No. 200, 10, 89, 299, 345 TAZs. No. 200 TAZ itself is a multi-functional mixed zone, thus there are short-distance commuting travels. No. 10 TAZ is the Internet Industrial Park in Liangjiang New zone, which includes Zhongzhilian, Chongqing Academy of Science and Technology, pharmaceutical companies and other enterprises, so it is a typical workplace zone. No. 89 TAZ is around Jiefangbei commercial district. As one of the largest business districts in Chongqing, it has strong commuting attributes. From this, it can be inferred that the entirc Jiefangbei commercial district is attractive to taxi travel. No. 299 TAZ is Daping commercial district, which is similar to No. 89 Jiefangbei commercial district.

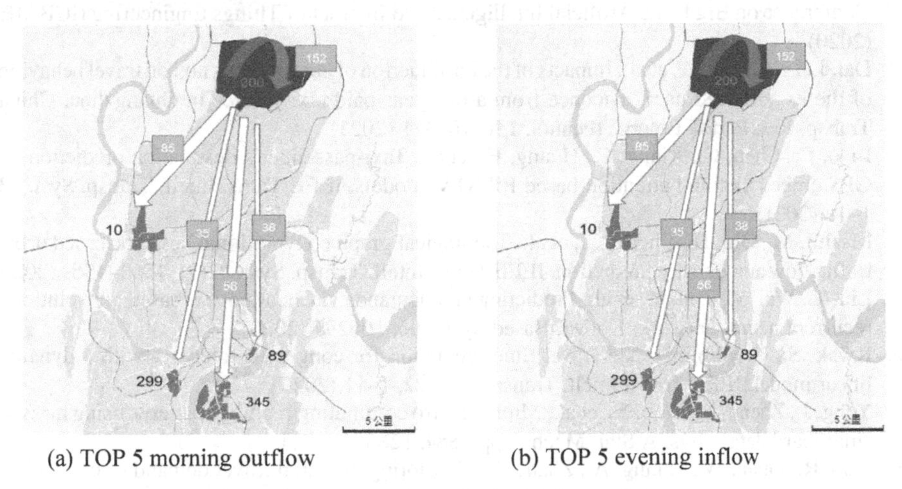

(a) TOP 5 morning outflow (b) TOP 5 evening inflow

Fig. 13. TOP 5 commuting travel for No. 200 TAZ.

4 Conclusion

Commuting is a very common and important travel behavior. In this paper, we proposed a new commuting TAZs identification method to identify the regional-level commuting patterns of taxis, where massive taxi GPS data, urban road network and POI information are fully explored. The method mainly includes three steps: dividing TAZs, obtaining flow transfer matrix and identifying commuting TAZs.

As a matter of fact, it is very important to explore the taxi regional-level commuting pattern, especially for Chongqing (As Chongqing is a mountain city with complex terrain, taxi is more favored by citizens and tourists). Extensive experiments are conducted on Chongqing real-world datasets. The results show that the method we proposed is feasible and efficient. 52 pairs of TAZs with commuting relationship are identified. According to the analysis, during the morning peak, the commuting hotspots are mainly concentrated in the surrounding residential zones, such as Nanping, Danzishi, and around the public transport hubs, such as Shapingba, Hongqihegou and Lianglukou. During the evening peak, high-tech industrial park, such as Liangjiang Industrial Park, Xiantao Data Valley, and large commercial zones, such as Jiangbeizui, have become hotspots of taxi. The commuting distance during the peak hours is mainly distributed within 10 km, accounting for more than 60%, among which, the range of 5–10 km is the most. The commuting time during the peak hours is mainly distributed within 20 min, accounting for more than 65%, among which the range of 10–20 min is the most, accounting for more than 30%. The analysis results provide valuable reference for relevant departments and companies, for example, designing custom buses.

References

1. Duan, X., Xu, J., Chen, Y., et al.: Analysis of influencing factors on urban traffic congestion and prediction of congestion time based on spatiotemporal big data. In: 2020 International Conference on Big Data, Artificial Intelligence and Internet of Things Engineering (ICBAIE) (2020)
2. Dai, J., Li, R., Liu, Z., et al.: Impacts of the introduction of autonomous taxi on travel behaviors of the experienced user: evidence from a one-year paid taxi service in Guangzhou, China. Transp. Res. Part C Emerg. Technol. **130**, 103311 (2021)
3. Liao, C., Chen, C., Xiang, C., Huang, H., et al.: Taxi-passenger's destination prediction via GPS embedding and attention-based BiLSTM models. IEEE Trans. Intell. Transp. Syst. **23**, 1–14 (2021)
4. Msahli, M., Qiu, H., Zheng, Q., et al.: Topological graph convolutional network-based urban traffic flow and density prediction. IEEE Trans. Intell. Transp. Syst. **22**(7), 4560–4569 (2020)
5. Liu, T., Wu, W., Zhu, Y., et al.: Predicting taxi demands via an attention-based convolutional recurrent neural network. Knowl. Based Syst. **206**, 106294 (2020)
6. Kwak, S., Geroliminis, N.: Travel time prediction for congested freeways with a dynamic linear model. IEEE Trans. Intell. Transp. Syst. **22**, 1–11 (2020)
7. Yong, J., Zheng, L., Mao, X., et al.: Mining metro commuting mobility patterns using massive smart card data. Phys. A Stat. Mech. Appl. **584**, 126351 (2021)
8. Guo, R., Guan, W., Huang, A., Zhang, W.: Exploring potential travel demand of customized buses using smartcard data. In: 2019 IEEE Intelligent Transportation Systems Conference (ITSC), pp. 2645–2650 (2019)
9. Qiu, G., Song, R., He, S., Xu, W., Jiang, M.: Clustering passenger trip data for the potential passenger investigation and line design of customized commuter bus. IEEE Trans. Intell. Transp. Syst. **20**(9), 3351–3360 (2019)
10. Wang, A., Guan, H., Wang, P., Peng, L., Xue, Y.: Cross-regional customized buses route planning considering staggered commuting during the COVID-19. IEEE Access **9**, 20208–20222 (2021)
11. Luo, C., Dan, T., Li, Y., et al.: Why-not questions about spatial temporal top-k trajectory similarity search. Knowl.-Based Syst. **11**, 107407 (2021)
12. Zhu, Y., Ting, K.M., Jin, Y., Angelova, M.: Hierarchical clustering that takes advantage of both density-peak and density-connectivity. Inf. Syst. **103**, 101871 (2022)
13. Sun, L., Qin, X., Ding, W., et al.: Nearest neighbors-based adaptive density peaks clustering with optimized allocation strategy. Neurocomputing **473**, 159–181 (2022)
14. Yao, W., Zhang, M., Jin, S., et al.: Understanding vehicles commuting pattern based on license plate recognition data. Transp. Res. Part C Emerg. Technol. **128**(2), 103142 (2021)
15. Fu X, Sun M, Sun H: Taxi commuting identification and spatio-temporal characteristics analysis based on GPS data. China J. Highway Transport (007), 134–143 (2017)
16. Saputra, D.M., Saputra, D., Oswari, L.D.: Effect of distance metrics in determining K-value in K-means clustering using elbow and silhouette method. In: 2019 Sriwijaya International Conference on Information Technology and Its Applications (SICONIAN) (2020)

Chinese Relation Extraction of Apple Diseases and Pests Based on BERT and Entity Information

Mei Guo[1], Jiayu Zhang[1], Nan Geng[1,2,3], Yaojun Geng[1], Yongliang Zhang[1], and Mei Li[1](✉)

[1] College of Information Engineering, Northwest A&F University, Yangling, China
{nangeng,gengyaojun,limei}@nwsuaf.edu.cn
[2] Key Laboratory of Agricultural Internet of Things, Ministry of Agriculture and Rural Affairs, Northwest A&F University, Yangling, China
[3] Shaanxi Key Laboratory of Agricultural Information Perception and Intelligent Service, Northwest A&F University, Yangling, China

Abstract. Most existing methods for Chinese relation extraction suffer from fine-grained relation categories and unbalanced category distribution in the field of apple diseases and pests. To solve above problems, we construct the AppleRE dataset, which contains 28 relation categories and 20060 relation instances with the characteristic of richer categories than existing agricultural datasets. Then, we propose a relation extraction model BE-ARE introducing BERT and entity information, in which dynamic character representations and entities that reflects the unique meaning of Chinese words are utilized to enhance the data features. The performance of BE-ARE on AppleRE achieved a precision of 98.44%, a recall of 96.75% and an F1-score of 97.59%. The F1- score is increased by 1.77%–12.38%, which outperforms the comparison models. Experimental results demonstrate the competitiveness of BE-ARE when considering fine-grained classification and unbalanced category distribution. In addition, the proposed model shows the generalization on the public datasets in distinct domains.

Keywords: Chinese relation extraction · Apple diseases and pests · BERT · Entity information

1 Introduction

Apple plays an important role in agricultural production. Diseases and pests hinder the apple industry and cause production losses. Therefore, their control must receive great attention. Most authoritative information in this domain is stored in unstructured text. Chinese relation extraction (CRE) of apple diseases and pests aims to extract semantic relations between the two entities marked in a given sentence and to convert unstructured text into structured data, which contributes to knowledge graph and intelligent Q&A. For example, the sentence

G. Memmi et al. (Eds.): KSEM 2022, LNAI 13370, pp. 579–592, 2022.
https://doi.org/10.1007/978-3-031-10989-8_46

"苹果白粉病危害苹果幼芽 (Apple powdery mildew harms the young buds of apples)" has two entities, "苹果白粉病 (apple powdery mildew)" and "幼芽 (young buds)", and the relation between them is "危害 (harm)".

Deep learning has been successfully applied in many fields [5,10], especially in relation extraction. CNN [15] and RNN are used to learn underlying features automatically. [16] proposed the BLSTM model based on RNN to deal with long-distance patterns. [18] developed the Att-BLSTM model to capture the most important semantic information in a sentence. With the emergence of the BERT model [2,12] designed the R-BERT model and utilized the entities to tackle relation extraction. [11] used entity context information to enhance BERT. Entities are important information in relation extraction. [3,4] introduced entity descriptions and entity types to achieve relation extraction. They have limitations of no entity descriptions and limited entity types. In CRE, entity information can overcome these limitations due to the unique meaning of Chinese words.

Relation extraction in agriculture has received extensive attention [7,14]. However, there are currently no publicly available datasets and models in the field of apple diseases and pests. The problems of fine-grained relation categories and unbalanced category distribution exist in this domain that need to be solved urgently. Therefore, the main contributions of this paper include:

- We construct a CRE dataset of apple diseases and pests named AppleRE. The dataset contains 28 categories and has the characteristics of fine-grained classification.
- We propose a CRE model named BE-ARE. The proposed model improves performance of relation extraction by introducing BERT and entity information.
- The BE-ARE model achieves the optimal results on the AppleRE dataset and also outperforms other models on the public datasets in distinct domains.

The remainder of this paper is organized as follows. Section 2 describes the details of AppleRE dataset. Section 3 presents the details of BE-ARE model. Section 4 and Sect. 5 introduce the experimental results and discussion. Section 6 concludes the paper.

2 AppleRE Dataset

2.1 Data Collection

Books and Internet texts, as carriers of apple disease and pest information, have recorded lots of data. Compared with Internet texts, books are more normative, professional and authoritative. Therefore, to ensure the quality of the dataset, we selected seven authoritative books as data sources under the guidance of experts from Northwest A&F University, as shown in Table 1. These books introduce more than fifty common apple diseases and sixty apple pests, and comprehensively cover the relations between entities of apple diseases and pests, which provide a knowledge base for the construction of the dataset.

Table 1. Data sources of dataset.

Book title	Author	Publisher	Pubdate
Integrated prevention and control of apple diseases and pests	Shishan Guo	Henan Science and Technology Press	1992
Prevention and control of apple diseases and pests	Jinyou Wang	Golden Shield Press	1992
Prevention and control of apple diseases and pests	Yizhi Sun	Shaanxi Science and Technology Press	1997
Prevention and control of apple diseases and pests with pictures	Zigang Cao	China Agriculture Press	1999
New diagnosis and control of apple pests and diseases	Youguang Chen	Shaanxi Science and Technology Press	2003
Integrated prevention and control technology of apple diseases and pests	Jinying Wu	Northwest Agriculture and Forestry University Press	2009
Prevention and control of diseases, pests and weeds in modern apple production	Dongping Li	Chemical Industry Press	2018

2.2 Relation Categories

The relations between entities of apple diseases and pests can be divided into three coarse-grained categories, namely "苹果 (apple)", "病虫害 (disease and pest)" and "防治 (control)" after analysis of existing agricultural research [7,14] and guidance from experts. Based on this, we further divided the three categories into fine-grained categories. "苹果 (apple)" is divided into "别称 (alias)", "分布 (distribute)" and "品种 (variety)". "病虫害 (disease and pest)" is divided into "属于 (belong to)", "包含 (include)", "取食 (feed)", "危害 (harm)", "侵染 (infect)", "寄生 (parasitism)" and "越冬 (overwinter)". "防治 (control)" is divided into "农业防治 agricultural control (增施 increase、清除 clear、种植 plant、翻耕 plow、灌溉 irrigate、撒施 spread)", "生物防治 biological control (保护 protect)", "物理防治 physical control (涂抹 smear、捕杀 catch、诱杀 trap and kill、套袋 bagging)" and "化学防治 chemical control (喷洒 spray、消毒 disinfect、浸泡 soak、杀灭 kill、禁用 ban、防治 prevention and control)". We also defined the category "unknown", which describes entities that have no relation. Finally, 28 fine-grained relation categories are obtained in the dataset.

2.3 Relation Annotation

We annotated the relation instances based on relation categories. The specific annotation process is shown in Fig. 1. Given the raw sentence with the marked entities [17], the relation instances are composed of entity pairs, their corresponding relationship and the raw sentence. The format of instance is like "entity1 entity2 relation sentence". When all the annotations are completed, we proofread the entire dataset to ensure the correctness of all instances. Finally, the AppleRE dataset contains 20060 relation instances.

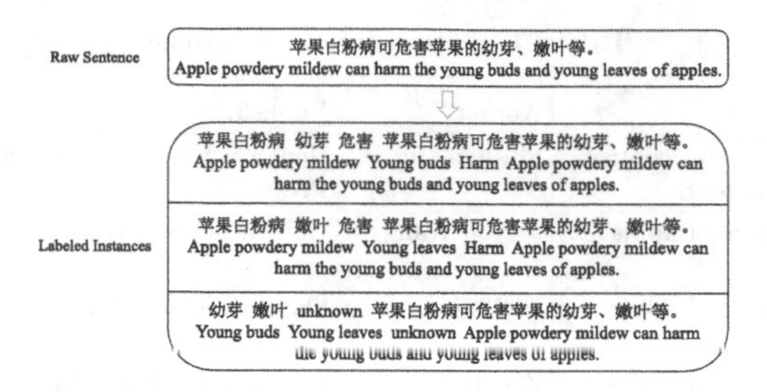

Fig. 1. An example from raw sentence to labeled instances.

2.4 Dataset Features

AppleRE is an agricultural dataset compared with general corpora, such as SanWen [13], RECDI [9], PCNN-A [14] and AgFeature [7]. Among them, SanWen belongs to the literature field. RECDI belongs to the medicine domain. PCNN-A and AgFeature belong to the agriculture field. Their comparison information can be found in Table 2.

Table 2. Comparison between AppleRE and other corpora.

Dataset	Domain	Category	Quantity	Max length
SanWen	Literature	10	21240	88
RECDI	Medicine	6	3429	-
PCNN-A	Agriculture	5	7085	-
AgFeature	Agriculture	7	24764	128
AppleRE	Agriculture	28	20060	159

"-" denotes unknown value.

Compared with these general corpora, the features of the AppleRE dataset are summarized as follows:

(1) AppleRE contains 28 relation categories. As shown in Table 2, AppleRE provides rich categories compared with corpora in different fields. The categories of other agricultural datasets belong to coarse-grained classification. AppleRE provides more fine-grained categories. Especially for "防治 (control)", fine division is committed to achieving precise prevention and control.
(2) The relation category distribution is unbalanced in AppleRE. For example, the instances of relations "撒施 (spread)", "灌溉 (irrigate)"and "消毒 (disinfect)"are 69, 41 and 38, all of which are less than 100. The proportions in the dataset are 0.34%, 0.2% and 0.19%, which account for less than 0.5%. They are divided into training set, test set, and validation set with few instances, which can easily cause extraction errors.

(3) The sentences of relation instances are long text sequences in AppleRE. Table 2 counts the lengths of sentences contained in relation instances of different dataset. The maximum sentence length in AppleRE is 159, which is longer than others. The sentence length provides a reference for the parameter value in subsequent experiments.

3 BE-ARE Model

In this section, we present our BE-ARE model in detail. As shown in Fig. 2, the BE-ARE model takes the character-based BiGRU structure as the basic framework and contains four layers. The BERT layer is used to obtain the dynamic character representations and entity representations of the text. The BiGRU layer can mine the context information and obtain the semantic feature vectors. The attention layer assigns different weights to the feature vectors to enhance the model performance. The classification layer splices the output of the attention layer and the entity representations obtained by the BERT layer to realize relation extraction. This section will focus on the BERT layer and the classification layer. The details of BiGRU and attention can be found in [1] and [18].

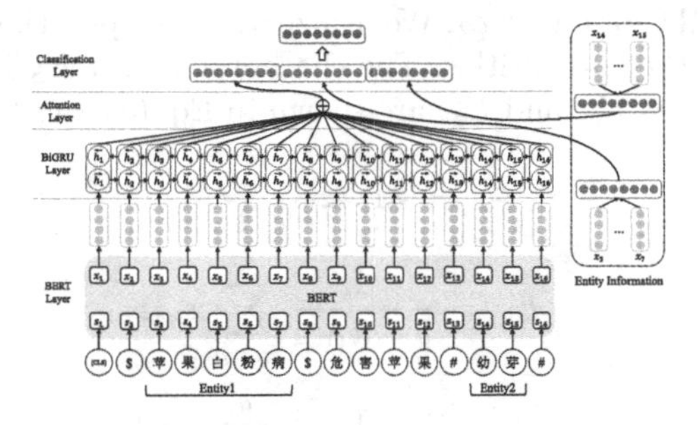

Fig. 2. BE-ARE model architecture.

3.1 BERT Layer

The BERT layer aims to obtain the character vector representations and entity vector representations of the apple disease and pest text. To identify the entity pairs in a sentence, we adopt the tokens "$" and "#" to mark the entity1 and entity2, and also add "[CLS]" to the beginning of each sentence mentioned in [12]. As shown in Fig. 3, after insertion of the tokens, the sentence with two entities will become to: "[CLS]$ 苹果白粉病 $ 危害苹果 #幼芽 #(Apple powdery mildew harms the young buds of apples)".

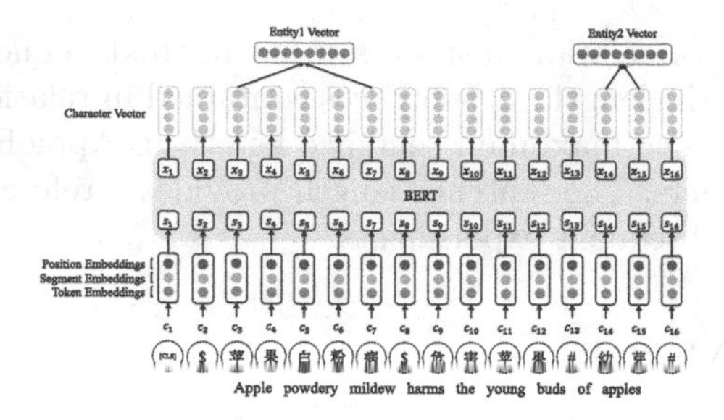

Fig. 3. Character vectors and entity vectors generated by BERT.

Given a sentence S consisting of n characters $S = \{c_1, c_2, \ldots, c_n\}$ and the two entities are $e_1 = \{c_a, c_{a+1}, \ldots, c_b\}$ and $e_2 = \{c_p, c_{p+1}, \ldots, c_q\}$, the input of BERT can be expressed as $\{[\text{CLS}], c_1, c_2, \ldots, \$, c_a, \ldots, c_b, \$, \ldots, \#, c_p, \ldots, c_q, \#, \ldots, c_n\}$, where c_i is i-th character of S; a and b are the start and end indices of e_1 in S; p and q are the start and end indices of e_2 in S. c_i is represented by token embedding, segment embedding and position embedding. The summation of these three embeddings denoted as s_i is fed into the BERT layer and the final output from BERT is x_i. Vectors x_a to x_b are from BERT for entity e_1, and x_p to x_q are from BERT for entity e_2. We utilize average operations to obtain vector representations of the two entities. The character vector E_S is shown in Eq. (1) and the entity vectors E_{e_1} and E_{e_2} are shown in Eq. (2) and Eq. (3):

$$E_S = [x_1, x_2, \ldots, x_n] \tag{1}$$

$$E_{e_1} = \frac{1}{b-a+1} \sum_{m=a}^{b} x_m \tag{2}$$

$$E_{e_2} = \frac{1}{q-p+1} \sum_{m=p}^{q} x_m \tag{3}$$

where m represents the position of the entity character in S.

3.2 Classification Layer

The classification layer is used to extract the relations between the entity pairs of apple diseases and pests. For example, the entity e_1 "苹果白粉病 (apple powdery mildew)" and e_2 "幼芽 (young buds)" are Chinese words with specific meanings. The former implies an apple disease and the latter refers to the parts of apple, both of which provide additional information for relation extraction. Therefore, the entity information in a sentence can help improve the capability of the BE-ARE model.

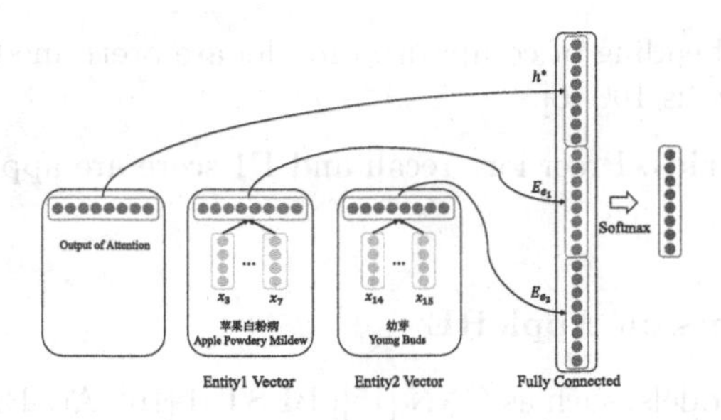

Fig. 4. Classification layer architecture.

As shown in Fig. 4, the feature fusion vector combines the output of the attention mechanism and the entity information, denoted as H_e, which is concatenated by h^*, E_{e_1} and E_{e_2} as shown in Eq. (4). Then the feature vector is fed into the softmax classifier to calculate the probabilities of each relation as shown in Eq. (5) and finally achieves relation extraction as shown in Eq. (6).

$$H_e = [h^* \oplus E_{e_1} \oplus E_{e_2}] \tag{4}$$

$$p = \text{softmax}(WH_e + b) \tag{5}$$

$$\hat{y} = \arg\max p \tag{6}$$

where h^* is the output of the attention layer; p is the final probability expression; W is the weight parameter; b is the bias parameter and $\hat{y}$ is the predicted relation category. We adopt cross-entropy in [6] as the loss function.

4 Experiments

4.1 Experimental Settings

Dataset. We carry our experiments on different datasets, including AppleRE, SanWen and FinRE [6]. The AppleRE dataset contains 20060 relation instances with 12036, 4012 and 4012 instances for training, testing and validation respectively.

Experimental Environment. Ubuntu 16.04OS, GeForce RTX 2080Ti GPU, PyTorch1.2.0 and Python3.6.

Parameter Settings. The parameters of BERT layer refer to [2]. The initial learning rate is set to 2e-5 with AdamW optimization [8]. GRU size is set to 250. Dropout is set to 0.5 to avoid overfitting. Batch size is 16 and epoch is 10.

The character embedding of comparison model are pretrained by word2vec and the embedding size is 100 [6].

Evaluation Metrics. Precision, recall and F1-score are applied in the experiments.

4.2 Experiments on AppleRE

Several popular models, such as CNN [15], BLSTM [16], Att-BLSTM [18], BERT [2] and R-BERT [12] are compared to verify the effectiveness of BE-ARE on AppleRE. Table 3 shows that BE-ARE achieves optimal results among all the models. CNN performs the worst. The apple disease and pest corpus are long text sequences but CNN is inappropriate to exploit long-distance contextual information. The performance of the BERT-based models is better than the LSTM-based models. This is because the embeddings of the former produce richer and dynamic vector representations of characters than the character embeddings of the latter. Compared with BERT and R-BERT, BE-ARE utilizes BiGRU and attention mechanism to improve model performance.

Table 3. Results of different models on AppleRE.

Model	Precision	Recall	F1
CNN	82.94	87.61	85.21
BLSTM	91.99	89.87	90.92
Att-BLSTM	93.87	93.57	93.72
BERT	94.57	95.17	94.87
R-BERT	95.57	96.07	95.82
BE-ARE	**98.44**	**96.75**	**97.59**

Table 4. Performance of different models for coarse-grained category on AppleRE.

Relation	CNN	BLSTM	Att-BLSTM	BERT	R-BERT	BE-ARE
苹果 apple	97.49	98.65	98.99	99.83	99.74	**99.83**
病虫害 disease and pest	96.77	97.66	98.41	98.96	**99.31**	99.03
防治 control	92.75	96.58	98.17	99.12	**99.36**	99.28

Table 5. Performance of different models for fine-grained category on AppleRE.

Relation	CNN	BLSTM	Att-BLSTM	BERT	R-BERT	BE-ARE
别称 alias	97.80	99.50	99.26	100.00	**100.00**	99.75
分布 distribute	98.42	99.64	99.82	99.82	99.82	**99.82**
危害 harm	87.21	93.42	94.49	95.61	96.85	**97.96**
增施 increase	90.91	95.52	97.06	97.06	97.06	**97.06**
清除 clear	93.83	95.82	98.07	97.73	99.35	**99.35**
涂抹 smear	82.05	85.71	95.65	95.77	95.77	**100.00**
喷洒 spray	88.80	96.81	98.08	98.72	98.51	**98.73**
消毒 disinfect	72.73	61.54	72.73	66.66	66.66	**88.89**
越冬 overwinter	95.67	97.56	99.00	97.03	99.25	**99.50**
品种 variety	97.70	98.15	98.16	99.54	100.00	**100.00**
防治 prevention and control	81.08	93.33	90.00	97.37	97.37	**98.67**
侵染 infect	100.00	92.31	100.00	100.00	100.00	**100.00**
种植 plant	88.89	100.00	100.00	100.00	100.00	**100.00**
浸泡 soak	94.74	85.72	94.74	94.74	**100.00**	94.74
套袋 bagging	0.00	66.67	66.67	66.67	**90.91**	88.89
翻耕 plow	85.71	75.00	100.00	100.00	100.00	**100.00**
寄生 parasitism	91.80	93.10	94.74	**100.00**	90.56	98.24
灌溉 irrigate	80.00	80.00	90.91	90.91	90.91	**100.00**
禁用 ban	88.89	94.12	94.12	88.89	**94.12**	88.89
撒施 spread	66.67	76.92	75.00	88.89	70.59	**100.00**
保护 protect	75.00	93.33	93.33	94.12	**100.00**	93.33
包含 include	98.31	100.00	100.00	100.00	**100.00**	96.55
杀灭 kill	67.86	86.37	90.91	97.56	97.56	**97.67**
诱杀 trap and kill	88.09	94.44	98.63	97.30	100.00	**100.00**
取食 feed	86.92	93.33	94.78	95.45	97.34	**97.78**
属于 belong to	99.20	100.00	100.00	100.00	100.00	**100.00**
捕杀 catch	85.71	92.31	88.89	96.00	**100.00**	96.00

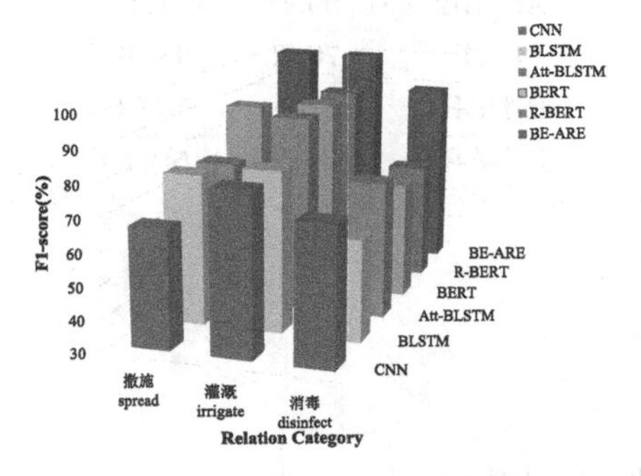

Fig. 5. F1-scores of unbalanced relation category.

Table 4 and Table 5 show the F1-scores of the models under different relation classification. The results show that under the coarse-grained classification, the performance of each model is similar because of few relation categories and a similar number of corresponding relation instances. However, under the fine-grained classification, the performance of models is different and the advantages of the BE-ARE model are more prominent. The F1-scores of different models for each category on AppleRE show similar differences. These models can fully learn the characteristics of relations during training when the relation category corresponds to many instances, such as "分布 (distribute)" and "危害 (harm)" . However, due to unbalanced distribution of relation categories, these models perform poorly at some relations, such as "撒施 (spread)", "灌溉 (irrigate)" and "消毒 (disinfect)", which have fewer instances resulting in models being difficult to fully learn the corresponding features. In comparison, BE-ARE is slightly impacted by the unbalanced distribution of relation category as shown in Fig. 5.

4.3 Experiments on the Public Datasets

To verify the generalization of BE-ARE, we selected two public datasets SanWen and FinRE. Table 6 lists the F1-scores of all models and the results of CNN, BLSTM and Att-BLSTM are from [6]. The BE-ARE model yields the highest F1-scores on the SanWen and FinRE datasets, which are 71.29% and 50.79%, respectively. There are positional overlaps between entity pairs in SanWen. The relation instances for each category in FinRE are insufficient. BE-ARE adopts BERT and the entity information to further enhance the capability to extract relations, thus achieving best performance. Experiments demonstrate the generalization of BE-ARE on the datasets in different fields.

Table 6. F1-scores of models on SanWen and FinRE.

Model	SanWen	FinRE
CNN	59.42	41.47
BLSTM	61.04	42.87
Att-BLSTM	59.48	41.48
BERT	70.26	48.07
R-BERT	67.89	50.01
BE-ARE	**71.29**	**50.79**

5 Discussion

5.1 Ablation Study

Effect of BERT Embedding. To analyze the effect of BERT, we conduct comparative experiments by considering randomly initialized embedding and pretrained character embedding. The randomly initialized embedding adopts the default PyTorch[1] method and its embedding size is the same as that of the pretrained character embedding.

The F1-score of the model with BERT is higher than those of models with randomly initialized and pretrained embedding, which increases by 4.4% and 2.5% respectively in Table 7. Randomly initialized and pretrained embedding can produce static and single vector representations of characters in sentences, which lack relevance analysis of semantic context. However, BERT provides dynamic vector representations of characters and contains richer semantic information, which has stronger text comprehension capabilities. Hence, the experimental results demonstrate that BERT contributes to improving the effective performance of BE-ARE.

Table 7. F1-scores of different embeddings on BE-ARE.

Model		F1	Improvement
BE-ARE	Random	93.19	4.40
BE-ARE	Word2vec	95.09	2.50
BE-ARE	BERT	97.59	-

Effect of Entity Information. To further explore the contribution of entity information used in the classification layer, we analyze apple disease and pest entities with different strategies, namely No entity, only Entity1, only Entity2 and joint Entity1 and Entity2.

Table 8 shows that the F1-score of strategy with two entities increases by 2.73%, 1.42% and 1.54% respectively compared with others. When there are no entities in the classification layer, the tokens "$" and "#" locate two entities and make the BERT output contain the location information of two entities. When one entity is introduced in this layer, the model effect is further improved. The model performs best when there are two entities in this layer. The results indicate that entity information in the classification layer can bring additional features to BE-ARE, which is conducive to the relation extraction.

Table 8. F1-scores of different entity information on BE-ARE.

Model		F1	Improvement
BE-ARE	No entity	94.86	2.73
BE-ARE	Entity1	96.17	1.42
BE-ARE	Entity2	96.05	1.54
BE-ARE	Entity1 + Entity2	97.59	-

[1] https://pytorch.org/docs/stable/generated/torch.nn.Embedding.html.

5.2 Effect of Sentence Lengths

To explore the effect of sentence lengths on BE-ARE, we selected 140, 150 and 160 as sentence lengths according to the sentence feature of AppleRE. As shown in Fig. 6, with the increase of the sentence length, the performance of BE-ARE first rises and then falls. The reason for this phenomenon is that when the sentence length is set too short, sentences will be intercepted and result in loss of entity and relationship information. When the sentence length is too long, too much invalid information will be filled into the sentences and cause a decrease in model performance. Although the performance of BE-ARE decreases as the sentence length increases, it still has great advantages and benefits more from long-distance text compared with other models.

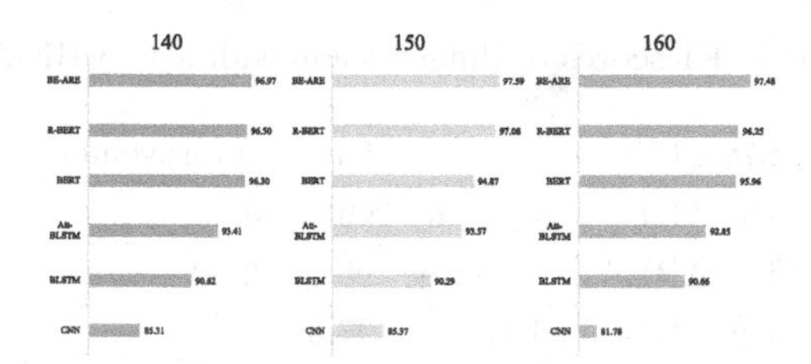

Fig. 6. F1-scores of models under different sentence lengths.

5.3 Case Study

To verify the superiority of BE-ARE, we analyzed an example of AppleRE. As shown in Table 9, the relation between "过氧乙酸 (peroxyacetic acid)"and "病菌 (pathogen)"is "杀灭 (kill)". CNN cannot recognize the relation between the two entities. The comparison models are interfered by the relation "防治 (prevention and control)" between "过氧乙酸 (peroxyacetic acid)" and "腐烂病 (rot disease)" in the sentence and cause the relation to be incorrectly identified as "防治 (prevention and control)". Thanks to BERT and entity information, BE-ARE obtains richer semantic representations and entity features, which strengthen the model capabilities to make correct predictions.

Table 9. Predictions for different models.

Sentence	过氧乙酸主要用于防治腐烂病和杀灭枝干上越冬的轮纹病、炭疽病病菌。 Peroxyacetic acid is mainly used to prevent and control rot disease and to kill the overwintering rot and anthracnose pathogens on the branches and trunks	
Entity	Entity1: 过氧乙酸 peroxyacetic acid	Entity2: 病菌 pathogen
Relation	杀灭 kill	
Prediction	CNN: unknown	BLSTM: 防治 prevention and control
	Att-BLSTM: 防治 prevention and control	BERT: 防治 prevention and control
	R-BERT: 防治 prevention and control	BE-ARE: 杀灭 kill

6 Conclusion

In this paper, the AppleRE dataset was constructed to solve the problem of limited data in the field of apple diseases and pests. Compared with other corpora, the relation categories in AppleRE are more fine-grained. Moreover, the BE-ARE model was proposed to explore the relations between the entity pairs and introduced BERT and entity information. BE-ARE outperforms previously proposed models on the datasets in distinct domains, such as Chinese apple diseases and pests (AppleRE), literature (SanWen) and financial (FinRE). Experiments show the effectiveness of BE-ARE when dealing with fine-grained relation categories and unbalanced category distribution. In future work, we will focus on introducing different features to solve the task of relation extraction.

Acknowledgements. This work is supported by the Key Research and Development Program of Shaanxi (No. 2019ZDLNY07-06-01).

References

1. Cho, K., et al.: Learning phrase representations using RNN encoder-decoder for statistical machine translation (2014). arXiv preprint: arXiv:1406.1078
2. Devlin, J., Chang, M., Lee, K., Toutanova, K.: Bert: pre-training of deep bidirectional transformers for language understanding (2018). arXiv preprint arXiv:1810.04805
3. Ji, G., Liu, K., He, S., Zhao, J.: Distant supervision for relation extraction with sentence-level attention and entity descriptions. In: Proceedings of the AAAI Conference on Artificial Intelligence (2017)
4. Lee, J., Seo, S., Choi, Y.: Semantic relation classification via bidirectional LSTM networks with entity-aware attention using latent entity typing. Symmetry **11**(6), 785 (2019)
5. Li, Y., Song, Y., Jia, L., Gao, S., Li, Q., Qiu, M.: Intelligent fault diagnosis by fusing domain adversarial training and maximum mean discrepancy via ensemble learning. IEEE Trans. Industr. Inf. **17**(4), 2833–2841 (2020)
6. Li, Z., Ding, N., Liu, Z., Zheng, H., Shen, Y.: Chinese relation extraction with multi-grained information and external linguistic knowledge. In: Proceedings of the 57th Annual Meeting of the Association for Computational Linguistics, pp. 4377–4386 (2019)
7. Liu, Z., Chen, Y., Dai, Y., Guo, C., Zhang, Z., Chen, X.: Syntactic and semantic features based relation extraction in agriculture domain. In: International Conference on Web Information Systems and Applications, pp. 252–258 (2018)
8. Loshchilov, I., Hutter, F.: Fixing weight decay regularization in adam (2017). arXiv preprint: arXiv:1711.05101
9. Qi, T., et al.: KeMRE: knowledge-enhanced medical relation extraction for Chinese medicine instructions. J. Biomed. Inform. **120**, 103834 (2021)
10. Qiu, H., Zheng, Q., Msahli, M., Memmi, G., Qiu, M., Lu, J.: Topological graph convolutional network-based urban traffic flow and density prediction. IEEE Trans. Intell. Transp. Syst. **22**(7), 4560–4569 (2020)
11. Wan, Y., Sun, L., Zhao, P., Wang, J., Tu, S.: Relation classification based on information enhanced BERT. J. Chin. Inf. Process. **35**(3), 69–77 (2021)

12. Wu, S., He, Y.: Enriching pre-trained language model with entity information for relation classification. In: Proceedings of the 28th ACM International Conference on Information and Knowledge Management, pp. 2361–2364 (2019)
13. Xu, J., Wen, J., Sun, X., Su, Q.: A discourse-level named entity recognition and relation extraction dataset for Chinese literature text (2017). arXiv preprint: arXiv:1711.07010
14. Yue, Y., et al.: Agricultural pest and disease relation extraction based on multi-attention mechanism and distant supervision. J. Anhui Agric. Univ. **47**(4), 5 (2020)
15. Zeng, D., Liu, K., Lai, S., Zhou, G., Zhao, J.: Relation classification via convolutional deep neural network. In: Proceedings of COLING 2014, the 25th International Conference on Computational Linguistics: Technical Papers, pp. 2335–2344 (2014)
16. Zhang, D., Wang, D.: Relation classification via recurrent neural network (2015). arXiv preprint: arXiv:1508.01006
17. Zhang, J., Guo, M., Geng, Y., Li, M., Zhang, Y., Geng, N.: Chinese named entity recognition for apple diseases and pests based on character augmentation. Comput. Electron. Agric. **190**, 106464 (2021)
18. Zhou, P., et al.: Attention-based bidirectional long short-term memory networks for relation classification. In: Proceedings of the 54th Annual Meeting of the Association for Computational Linguistics, pp. 207–212 (2016)

Recommendation via Collaborative Diffusion Generative Model

Joojo Walker[1], Ting Zhong[1], Fengli Zhang[1], Qiang Gao[3], and Fan Zhou[1,2](✉)

[1] University of Electronic Science and Technology of China, 610054 Chengdu, Sichuan, China
fan.zhou@uestc.edu.cn
[2] Kash Institute of Electronics and Information Industry, 844000 Kashgar, Xinjiang, China
[3] Southwestern University of Finance and Economics, 611130 Chengdu, Sichuan, China

Abstract. Despite the success of classical collaborative filtering (CF) methods in the recommendation systems domain, we point out two issues that essentially limit this class of models. **Firstly**, most classical CF models predominantly yield weak collaborative signals, which makes them deliver suboptimal recommendation performance. **Secondly**, most classical CF models produce unsatisfactory latent representations resulting in poor model generalization and performance. To address these limitations, this paper presents the Collaborative Diffusion Generative Model (CODIGEM), the *first-ever* denoising diffusion probabilistic model (DDPM)-based CF model. CODIGEM effectively models user-item interactions data by obtaining the intricate and non-linear patterns to generate strong collaborative signals and robust latent representations for improving the model's generalizability and recommendation performance. Empirically, we demonstrate that CODIGEM is a very efficient generative CF model, and it outperforms several classical CF models on several real-world datasets. Moreover, we illustrate through experimental validation the settings that make CODIGEM provide the most significant recommendation performance, highlighting the importance of using the DDPM in recommendation systems.

Keywords: Recommendation systems · Collaborative filtering · Denoising diffusion probabilistic model · Generative model

1 Introduction

The enormous magnitude of user-item interactions data on the internet today has necessitated the design of various personalized recommendation models to deliver to users a set of unseen items that may be of interest to them [2,15,22,23]. Among the several recommendation techniques available, classical collaborative filtering (CF)-based techniques have been widely adopted. Classical CF methods predict the preferences of users for items by learning from user-item historical

G. Memmi et al. (Eds.): KSEM 2022, LNAI 13370, pp. 593–605, 2022.
https://doi.org/10.1007/978-3-031-10989-8_47

interactions, employing either explicit feedback (e.g., ratings and reviews) or implicit feedback (e.g., clicks and views) [3,9,15]. In general, there are two kinds of classical CF-based approaches: neighborhood-based techniques and model-based methods [15]. The neighborhood-based approaches such as Item-KNN [5]) use original user-item interaction data (e.g., rating matrices) to infer unseen ratings by combining similar users' preferences or similar items. On the other hand, model-based methods such as matrix factorization (MF) [1,12,19]) obtain user tastes for items by employing the idea that a low-dimensional latent vector might represent a user's taste or an item's attribute. These matrix factorization techniques (latent factor models) deconstruct the high-dimensional user-item rating matrix into low-dimensional user and item latent vectors. Subsequently, recommendation prediction is made by computing the dot product of the latent vectors of the user and item [16,20]. It is important to note that Classical CF models are still dominant approaches both in the industry and academia due to their simplicity and intuitive justification for the computed predictions [4,15,23].

Challenges: Despite the success of classical collaborative filtering (CF) models, there are still pertinent issues with these models [1,12,19]. **Firstly**, most classical CF models predominantly yield weak collaborative signals, which makes them deliver suboptimal recommendation performance. This issue is because these classical CF models are designed with the notion that users and items have a linear relationship, so they do not capture the intricate information and non-linearities embedded in the real-world user-item interaction data. **Secondly**, most classical CF models produce unsatisfactory latent representations resulting in poor model generalization and performance. This problem is prevalent because the models cannot extensively capture high-quality collaborative information from the underlying data distribution due to their non-Bayesian properties.

Contributions: Recently, a new class of deep generative model (DGM) called denoising diffusion probabilistic models (DDPM) has achieved exceptional performance on several image synthesis benchmarks, even outperforming generative adversarial networks (GANs) [6,10,11,21]. Inspired by the outstanding results of DDPM, we extend DDPM to implicit feedback data-based collaborative filtering (CF) to address the pertinent limitations of classical CF models mentioned above. Notably, we systematically explore and design a novel DDPM-based CF model called Collaborative Diffusion Generative Model (CODIGEM). CODIGEM adopts a forward Gaussian diffusion process and a reversed diffusion procedure that utilizes flexible parameterized neural networks to capture high-quality collaborative information from the underlying implicit feedback data. This novel technique yields quality latent representations to improve the model's generalization and produce excellent recommendations. Overall, our main contributions can be summarized as follows:

- We present the *first-ever* DDPM-based model that effectively models the user-items interactions data to capture the intricate and non-linear patterns in order to generate strong collaborative signals for the implicit feedback-based recommendations.
- We alleviate the issue of unsatisfactory generation of latent representations by effectively capturing the underlying distribution of the implicit feedback data.

This technique enhances the model's generalization and yields outstanding recommendation results.
- We design an efficient deep generative model (DGM)-based CF model. We highlight that, unlike DDPM employed in image synthesis that uses a costly iterative sampling process, CODIGEM is very efficient as it achieves good performance using very few iterative sampling processes. Besides, when compared to a different class of DGM-based CF model [17,18], CODIGEM exhibit superior computational efficiency.
- Empirically, we demonstrate that CODIGEM outperforms several classical CF models on several real-world datasets. This performance highlights the importance of using the DDPM in recommendation systems. To ensure reproducibility, we release our codes via this link[1].

2 Collaborative Diffusion Generative Model

Overview: Our novel Collaborative Diffusion Generative Model (CODIGEM) is essentially a DDPM [10,21]. DDPM is a kind of DGM that consists of two main processes: a forward diffusion (noising) process (FDP) and the reverse diffusion (noising) process (RDP). The overall architecture of CODIGEM is illustrated in Fig. 1. Next, we describe the mathematical underpinnings and the model learning method of CODIGEM.

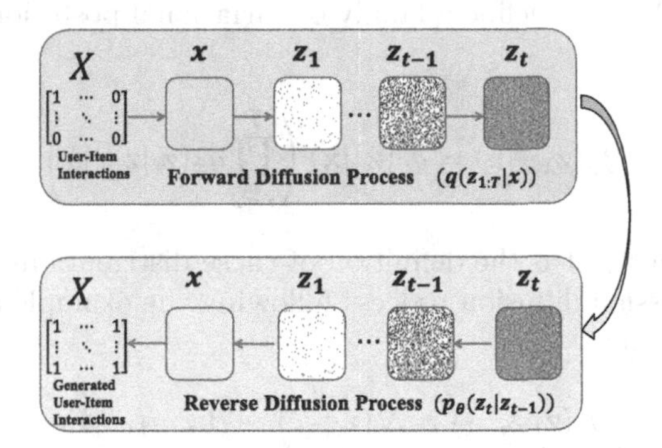

Fig. 1. An illustration of CODIGEM model architecture

Inspired by intuitions from non-equilibrium statistical physics Sohl-Dickstein et al. [21] proposed the first Deep diffusion probabilistic model (DDPM). The core intuition is to iteratively introduce noise into the underlying structure of data through a forward diffusion process (FDP). Next the structure of the data is regenerated through a reverse diffusion process (RDP). Recently, Ho et al.[10], designed a powerful and flexible DDPM framework that resulted in SOTA performance in the task of image synthesis. Generally, the goal is to determine a distribution over data, $p_\theta(\mathbf{x})$, but, we also consider other set of latent variables

[1] https://github.com/WorldChanger01/CODIGEM.

$\mathbf{z}_{1:T} = [\mathbf{z}_1, \ldots, \mathbf{z}_T]$. Now, we define the marginal likelihood by integrating out all latent variables:

$$p_\theta(\mathbf{x}) = \int p_\theta(\mathbf{x}, \mathbf{z}_{1:T})\, \mathrm{d}\mathbf{z}_{1:T} \tag{1}$$

Using the first-order Markov chain with Gaussian transitions we can model the joint distribution as follows:

$$p_\theta(\mathbf{x}, \mathbf{z}_{1:T}) = p_\theta(\mathbf{x}|\mathbf{z}_1) \left(\prod_{i=1}^{T-1} p_\theta(\mathbf{z}_i|\mathbf{z}_{i+1}) \right) p_\theta(\mathbf{z}_T) \tag{2}$$

where $\mathbf{x} \in \mathbb{R}^D$ and $\mathbf{z}_i \in \mathbb{R}^D$ for $i = 1, \ldots, T$. Here, the latent and the observable variables have the same dimensions. Note that all the distributions are parameterized using deep neural networks (DNNs). Now we proceed to describe the forward diffusion process (FDP) and the reverse diffusion process (RDP).

2.1 Forward Diffusion Process

In this forward diffusion procedure $Q_\phi(\mathbf{z}_{1:T}|\mathbf{x})$, the structure of user-item interaction data (x) is degraded over time by applying specified noise schedule. Similar to hierarchical VAEs, we define a family of variational posteriors for the FDP in the following way:

$$Q_\phi(\mathbf{z}_{1:T}|\mathbf{x}) = q_\phi(\mathbf{z}_1|\mathbf{x}) \left(\prod_{i=2}^{T} q_\phi(\mathbf{z}_i|\mathbf{z}_{i-1}) \right) \tag{3}$$

The significant point is the definition of these distributions. Here, we formulate them as Gaussian diffusion process following the example of Sohl-Dickstein et al. [21] in this way:

$$q_\phi(\mathbf{z}_i|\mathbf{z}_{i-1}) = \mathcal{N}(\mathbf{z}_i|\sqrt{1-\beta_i}\mathbf{z}_{i-1}, \beta_i\mathbf{I}) \tag{4}$$

where $\mathbf{z}_0 = \mathbf{x}$. A single step of the diffusion, $q_\phi(\mathbf{z}_i|\mathbf{z}_{i-1})$, works in a relatively easy manner. Mainly, it utilizes the previously generated variable $\mathbf{z}_{i-1}$, scales it by $\sqrt{1-\beta_i}$ and then adds noise with variance β_i. Notably, we can use the reparameterization trick to define it as this:

$$\mathbf{z}_i = \sqrt{1-\beta_i}\mathbf{z}_{i-1} + \sqrt{\beta_i} \odot \epsilon, \tag{5}$$

where $\epsilon \sim \mathcal{N}(0, \mathbf{I})$. In principle, β_i could be learned by backpropagation, however, as noted in previous research [10,21], it could be fixed. In our recommendation model, we find that this is a very sensitive hyperparameter that significantly affects model performance.

2.2 Reverse Diffusion Process

For the reverse denoising process ($P_\theta(\mathbf{x}_{0:T})$), the goal is to retrieve the original user-item interaction data ($\mathbf{x}$) from the noisy input. Note that the reverse procedure is also parameterized using first-order Markov chain with a learned Gaussian transition distribution as follows:

$$P_\theta(\mathbf{x}_{0:T}) = p_\theta(\mathbf{x}|\mathbf{z}_1)\left(\prod_{i=1}^{T-1} p_\theta(\mathbf{z}_i|\mathbf{z}_{i+1})\right) \tag{6}$$

$$p_\theta(\mathbf{z}_i|\mathbf{z}_{i+1}) = \mathcal{N}(\mu_\theta(\mathbf{z}_i, t), \Sigma_\theta(\mathbf{z}_i, t)) \tag{7}$$

2.3 Learning Procedure of CODIGEM

The learning objective is essentially the evidence lower bound (ELBO) [14]. We highlight that, the distribution $q_\phi(\mathbf{z}_1|\mathbf{x})$ will resemble an isotropic Gaussian given T and a well-behaved variance schedule of β_t. By choosing a latent variable from the isotropic Gaussian distribution and executing the reverse procedure (RDP), we can generate novel user-item interaction instances from the underlying data distribution. The RDP is trained to minimize the following upper bound over the negative log-likelihood. Basically, the learning objective (ELBO) of CODIGEM is derived as follows:

$$\ln p_\theta(\mathbf{x}) = \ln \int Q_\phi(\mathbf{z}_{1:T}|\mathbf{x}) \frac{p_\theta(\mathbf{x}, \mathbf{z}_{1:T})}{Q_\phi(\mathbf{z}_{1:T}|\mathbf{x})}\, d\mathbf{z}_{1:T} \tag{8}$$

$$\geq \mathbb{E}_{Q_\phi(\mathbf{z}_{1:T}|\mathbf{x})}[\ln p_\theta(\mathbf{x}|\mathbf{z}_1) + \sum_{i=1}^{T-1} \ln p_\theta(\mathbf{z}_i|\mathbf{z}_{i+1}) + \ln p_\theta(\mathbf{z}_T) - \sum_{i=2}^{T} \ln q_\phi(\mathbf{z}_i|\mathbf{z}_{i-1}) - \ln q_\phi(\mathbf{z}_1|\mathbf{x})] \tag{9}$$

$$= \mathbb{E}_{Q_\phi(\mathbf{z}_{1:T}|\mathbf{x})}[\ln p_\theta(\mathbf{x}|\mathbf{z}_1) + \ln p_\theta(\mathbf{z}_1|\mathbf{z}_2) + \sum_{i=2}^{T-1} \ln p_\theta(\mathbf{z}_i|\mathbf{z}_{i+1}) + \ln p_\theta(\mathbf{z}_T) - \sum_{i=2}^{T-1} \ln q_\phi(\mathbf{z}_i|\mathbf{z}_{i-1}) - \ln q_\phi(\mathbf{z}_T|\mathbf{z}_{T-1}) - \ln q_\phi(\mathbf{z}_1|\mathbf{x})] \tag{10}$$

$$= \mathbb{E}_{Q_\phi(\mathbf{z}_{1:T}|\mathbf{x})}[\ln p_\theta(\mathbf{x}|\mathbf{z}_1) + \sum_{i=2}^{T-1} (\ln p_\theta(\mathbf{z}_i|\mathbf{z}_{i+1}) - \ln q_\phi(\mathbf{z}_i|\mathbf{z}_{i-1})) + \ln p_\theta(\mathbf{z}_T) - \ln q_\phi(\mathbf{z}_T|\mathbf{z}_{T-1}) + \ln p_\theta(\mathbf{z}_1|\mathbf{z}_2) - \ln q_\phi(\mathbf{z}_1|\mathbf{x})] \tag{11}$$

$$\stackrel{df}{=} \mathcal{L}(\mathbf{x}; \theta, \phi) \tag{12}$$

Eventually, the ELBO is the following:

$$\mathcal{L}(\mathbf{x}; \theta, \phi) = \mathbb{E}_{Q_\phi(\mathbf{z}_{1:T}|\mathbf{x})}[\ln p_\theta(\mathbf{x}|\mathbf{z}_1) + \sum_{i=2}^{T-1} (\ln p_\theta(\mathbf{z}_i|\mathbf{z}_{i+1}) - \ln q_\phi(\mathbf{z}_i|\mathbf{z}_{i-1})) + \ln p_\theta(\mathbf{z}_T) - \ln q_\phi(\mathbf{z}_T|\mathbf{z}_{T-1}) + \ln p_\theta(\mathbf{z}_1|\mathbf{z}_2) - \ln q_\phi(\mathbf{z}_1|\mathbf{x})] \tag{13}$$

Note that we use continuous distribution to model $p(\mathbf{x}|\mathbf{z}_1)$. Moreover, we normalize our inputs to values between -1 and 1, and apply the Gaussian distribution with the unit variance and the mean being constrained to $[-1, 1]$ using the Tanh non-linear activation function. Subsequently, we obtain the expression: $p(\mathbf{x}|\mathbf{z}_1) = \mathcal{N}(\mathbf{x}|\tanh(NN(\mathbf{z}_1)), \mathbf{I})$, where $NN(\mathbf{z}_1)$ is a deep neural network.

2.4 Recommendation Generation

Given a user's click history $\mathbf{x}$, we can sample a latent distribution from $p(\mathbf{z}_T)$- an isotropic Gaussian distribution and execute the reverse procedure (RDP) to generate scores of each item for this user. In a typical $top - N$ recommendation system, we take the $top - N$ values as the prediction items for this user.

3 Experiments

To validate our model and technical contributions we aim to answer these all-important questions:

RQ1: Can the denoising diffusion probabilistic model (DDPM) effectively model non-linear user-item interactions? If so, how can we extend it to CF for implicit feedback data to obtain competitive performance?
RQ2: Is DDPM helpful in generating valuable recommendations? If yes, how does it work, and what is the cost?
RQ3: How do key hyperparameters of DDPM affect model performance?
RQ4: How efficient is the proposed DDPM-based CF model?

3.1 Experimental Settings

Datasets: We conducted our empirical evaluations on three real-world and publicly available datasets: MovieLens-1m (ML-1m)[2], MovieLens-20m (ML-20m)[3], and Amazon Electronics (AE)[4]. We adopt standard practise of data-preprocessing for implicit feedback-based recommendations. Specifically, for all these datasets, we used a rating value three (3) and above. We also only kept users with at least ten (10) interactions, and we used items which had at least ten (10) interactions. We additionally converted all scores to 1 because we are focusing on the implicit feedback setting. The dataset statistics is depicted in Table 1.

Baseline Models: We compare CODIGEM to the following baseline models to validate its performance:

Pop: This model considers the most popular items in a dataset and recommends these items to users.

[2] https://grouplens.org/datasets/movielens/1m/.
[3] https://grouplens.org/datasets/movielens/20m/.
[4] http://jmcauley.ucsd.edu/data/amazon/.

Table 1. Statistics of all datasets after pre-processing

Dataset	ML-20m	ML-1m	AE
Number of users	136677	6034	13456
Number of items	20108	3124	8361
Number of item interactions	9990682	834449	234521
Sparcity percentage	99.64%	95.57%	99.79%

Item-KNN [5]: A type of model-based recommendation algorithm that identifies the collection of items to be recommended by first determining the similarities between the various items.

BPR [19]: BPR is a Bayesian-based framework that presents a generic optimization approach for personalized ranking.

Weighted matrix factorization (WMF) [12]: WMF is a low-rank factorization algorithm with a linear structure.

ENMF [1] ENMF is a well-optimized neural recommendation model that employs whole training data without sampling.

NeuMF [8]: NeuMF generalizes MF for CF using a neural network to overcome the constraint of linear interaction in MF.

Multi-VAE [17]: This is a representative VAE-based CF model. Its objective function incorporates multinomial likelihood, which is a distinguishing feature.

MacridVAE [18]: MacridVAE is a model that is used for learning disentangled representations from user behavior.

Evaluation Metrics: We employ two standard recommender system metrics such as Recall@R (R@R) and the normalized discounted cumulative gain (NDCG@R). We contrast the predicted rank of the held-out items to the actual rank using the Recall@R and NDCG@R metrics. By sorting the unnormalized probability, we get the predicted rank. NDCG@R employs a monotonically increasing discount to signal the relevance of higher rankings over lower ones, whereas Recall@R considers all items ranked inside the first R to be equally relevant. Notably, we calculate the Recall and NDCG at rank positions 20 and 50.

Implementation Details: We implement CODIGEM with Pytorch. We divide each dataset into training, validation, and test sets using the ratio 8:1:1. We use Xavier initialization. We utilize a learning rate of 0.001 and train the model with the Adamax optimizer [13]. Hyper-parameters β_t and T are set to 0.0001 and 3, respectively. We use an architecture comprising six (6) layers of MLP with PReLU non-linear activation function in between the layers to parametrize the distributions in FDP and RDP components of CODIGEM. Note that we use the Tanh activation function in the last layer of the RDP. During training we use a batch size of 200 and set up our model to train for 100 epochs. Also, we adopt early stopping when model performance does not increase for ten (10) successive epochs.

3.2 Results and Analysis

RQ 1: Performance Evaluation: Table 2 depicts the performance of CODIGEM in comparison to representative classical and DNN-based recommendation models on the Movielens-1m (ML-1m), Movielens-20m (ML-20m), and Amazon Electronics (AE) datasets. For all the results, a paired t-test is conducted. Here, $p < 0.001$ indicates statistical significance. After careful analysis, we observe the following: Interestingly, BPR and Item-KNN models generally outperform DNN-based models such as ENMF and NeuMF, highlighting the intrinsic robustness of some traditional models. However, Linear models such as Pop and WMF are not competitive with respect to all the DNN-based methods (ENMF, NeuMF, MacridVAE, Multi-VAE, and CODIGEM) because of their inability to effectively capture complex non-linear patterns from user-item interactions data which can aid in the recommendation task. This trend demonstrates the importance of learning the non-linear information from user-item interactions data. Generally, deep generative models such as (MacridVAE, Multi-VAE, and CODIGEM) show strong performance over their non-generative counterparts. The possible reason for this trend is that generative models can effectively capture the intricate and non-linear patterns from the unobserved user-item interactions to obtain strong collaborative signals for the recommendation task. Moreover, these DGM-based models can obtain high-quality collaborative information from the underlying implicit feedback data, thereby generalizing better and producing excellent recommendations than the non-generative models. Multi-VAE, an earlier proposed DGM-based CF model, outperforms all classical and DNN-based models. Nevertheless, we point out that CODIGEM is yet another competitive DGM-based CF model worthy of research attention. Mainly, we see that CODIGEM outperforms robust classical models (BPR, Item-KNN, WMF, and Pop) and some DNN-based models on all the metrics for all the datasets. Moreover, CODIGEM is more computationally efficient than Multi-VAE.

Table 2. Comparison of performance of baseline models and CODIGEM on ML-1M, ML-20M and AE datasets

Models	ML-1M				ML-20M				AE			
	R@20	R@50	N@20	N@50	R@20	R@50	N@20	N@50	R@20	R@50	N@20	N@50
Pop	0.1289	0.2202	0.1218	0.1460	0.1463	0.2473	0.1138	0.1422	0.0480	0.0899	0.0209	0.0296
BPR	0.2647	0.4252	0.2460	0.2919	0.2955	0.4596	0.2478	0.2964	0.0732	0.1254	0.0325	0.0436
WMF	0.2390	0.3994	0.2206	0.2675	0.2833	0.4254	0.2259	0.2904	0.0655	0.1118	0.0281	0.0378
ENMF	0.2582	0.4103	0.2467	0.2876	0.2234	0.3398	0.1941	0.2561	0.0564	0.0995	0.0263	0.0354
NeuMF	0.2403	0.4009	0.2219	0.2689	0.3021	0.4563	0.2469	0.2965	0.0702	0.1219	0.0307	0.0417
Item-KNN	0.2539	0.4039	0.2430	0.2829	0.2843	0.4264	0.2469	0.2909	0.0588	0.0917	0.0316	0.0389
Multi-VAE	0.2925	0.4588	0.2574	0.3081	0.3698	0.5348	0.3105	0.3508	0.0774	0.1340	0.0364	0.0484
MacridVAE	0.2389	0.3854	0.2371	0.2759	0.2996	0.4358	0.2704	0.3005	0.0769	0.1320	0.0353	0.0465
CODIGEM	**0.2796**	**0.4354**	**0.2447**	**0.3026**	**0.3512**	**0.4698**	**0.3031**	**0.3414**	**0.0771**	**0.1338**	**0.0360**	**0.0478**

RQ 2: Study of CODIGEM: CODIGEM is intrinsically a hierarchical latent variable model, and like VAE, they also utilize a family of variational posteriors.

In CODIGEM, we define these posterior distributions as a Gaussian diffusion process. Since CODIGEM and VAE-based CF models belong to the same family, we incorporate some well-known and proven VAE techniques into CODIGEM and study its impacts. Notably, we create these variants: CODIGEM-I (CODIGEM with annealing [17]), CODIGEM-II (CODIGEM with skip connections [7] in the FDP), CODIGEM-III (CODIGEM with skip connections in the RDP), CODIGEM-IV (CODIGEM with multinomial likelihood [17]). The empirical results are depicted in Fig. 3. From these results, we observe that annealing does not negatively affect model performance. We witness a slight decline in CODIGEM's performance when skip-connections are used. Additionally, employing the multinomial likelihood worsens CODIGEM's performance.

Table 3. Study of the impact of diverse techniques on CODIGEM

Model variants	Model performance	
	R@50	N@50
CODIGEM-I	0.4696	0.3411
CODIGEM-II	0.4627	0.3359
CODIGEM-III	0.4602	0.3311
CODIGEM-IV	0.2563	0.1353
CODIGEM	0.4698	0.3414

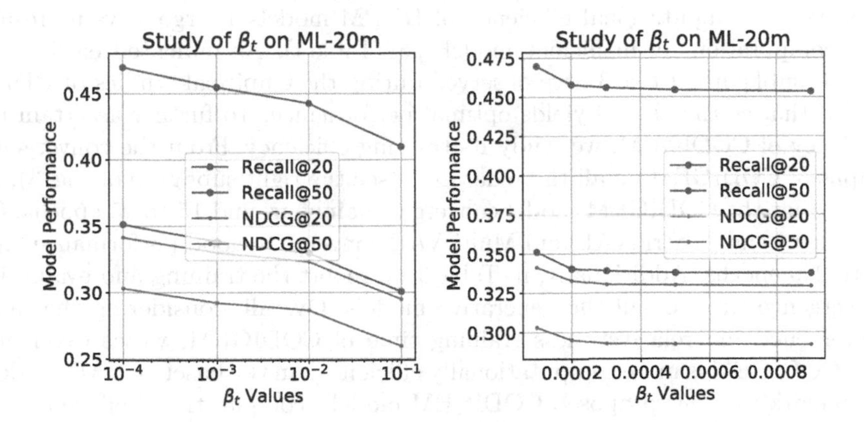

Fig. 2. The impact of β_t on CODIGEM on the ML-20m dataset. The left subfigure depicts a sharp decline in performance in the range 0.0001 to 0.1 and the right subfigure depicts a slight decline in performance in the range 0.0001 to 0.0009.

RQ 3: Parameter Sensitivity: Here, we study the impact of the critical hyper-parameters such as β_t and T on the overall performance of CODIGEM. For β_t, we experiment with several values in the range of 0.0001 to 0.9. The best results

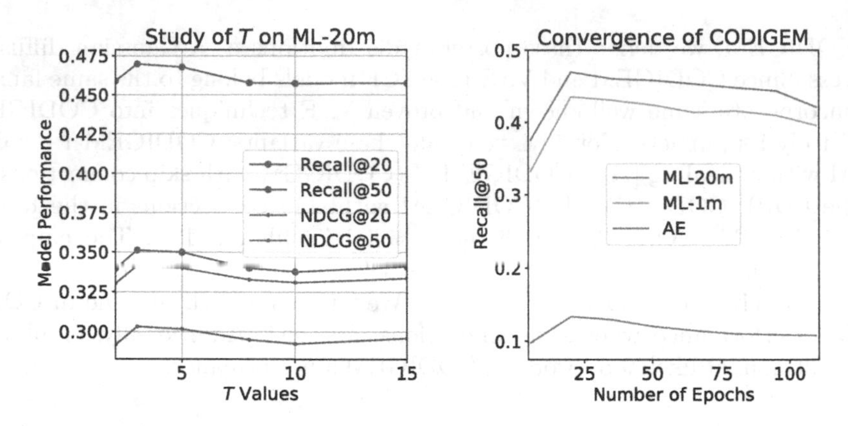

Fig. 3. The left subfigure shows the study of the impact of T on CODIGEM and the right subfigure depicts convergence of CODIGEM for all the datasets

across datasets are 0.0001. As depicted in Fig. 2, a change in the β_t value drastically affects model performance. Hence, a careful tuning of β_t on your dataset is always required. Regarding T, we observe that unlike DDPM models used in image synthesis, increasing the value of T does not improve model performance. From the left subfigure of Fig. 3, we consistently obtain the best model performance when T is 3.

RQ 4: Computational Efficiency: T is a hyperparameter that significantly impacts the computational efficiency of DDPM models-a large T value results in a computationally inefficient model (see Table 4). As indicated earlier (see the left subfigure of Fig. 3), we observed during the empirical studies of DDPM for CF that setting $T = 3$ yields optimal performance. To further ascertain the efficiency of CODIGEM, we study its training efficiency. From the convergence graphs of CODIGEM on all three datasets (see the right subfigure of Fig. 3), we notice that the CODIGEM model converges mainly around 15 to 25 epochs. On the other hand, MacridVAE and Multi-VAE converge to good performance after 75 to 200 epochs. Additionally, in Table 5 we report the training and evaluation convergence time for all the generative models. Overall, considering the rapid convergence and relatively less training time of CODIGEM, we can conclude that CODIGEM is more computationally efficient than the baseline VAE-models. We remark that our proposed CODIGEM model's computational efficiency is a significant advantage.

Table 4. Impact of T value on computational efficiency of CODIGEM

T value	Total model execution time	Number of epochs
3	824.682 s	18
5	1212.060 s	18
8	1861.488 s	18
10	2416.659 s	19
15	3384.233 s	18

Table 5. Comparison of computational efficiency of the generative models

Model	Training time (sec/epoch)	Evaluation time (sec/epoch)	Average number of epochs to convergence	Total time of convergence
MacridVAE	142.35	124.81	95	25380.20 s
Multi-VAE	53.17	48.45	150	15243.00 s
CODIGEM	48.22	46.67	18	1708.02 s

4 Concluding Remarks

Paper Conclusions: This paper presented the *first-ever* DDPM-based RS model that effectively models non-linear user-item interactions to generate strong collaborative signals for enhancing the generalizability of recommendations. We also demonstrated through systematic experimental validation the settings that enable CODIGEM to produce excellent recommendations performance. Moreover, the empirical studies indicate that CODIGEM is very efficient and outclasses several classical RS models on three real-world datasets. Overall, our findings highlight the significance of using the diffusion probabilistic model in recommendation systems. Our studies conclude that DDPM is a viable DGM alternative for RS tasks that needs more research attention.

Open Research Directions: Here, we highlight some unexplored potential of DDPM-based DGMs that can significantly enhance recommendation systems. **Firstly**, a crucial problem of VAE-based CF models is variational posterior collapsing to the prior, resulting in meaningless representation learning. DDPMs are robust against posterior collapse issues and can mitigate this limitation. Hence, integrating DDPMs and VAEs would be exciting research as both can take advantage of each other to generate excellent recommendations. **Secondly**, simplistic prior in VAE-based CF models results in sub-optimal recommendation performance. An interesting new direction would be to use DDPMs as flexible priors in VAEs. Moreover, we can incorporate important side information such as visual content-based information into these priors, ultimately addressing data sparsity and cold-start issues. **Lastly**, we can enhance the stability and performance of DDPMs by learning the covariance matrices in reverse diffusion and using different noise schedules.

Acknowledgements. This work was supported by National Natural Science Foundation of China (Grant No. 62176043, No. 62072077 and No. 62102326) and the Key Research and Development Project of Sichuan Province (Grant No. 2022YFG0314).

References

1. Chen, C., Zhang, M.I.N.: Efficient neural matrix factorization without sampling. ACM Trans. Inf. Syst. **38**(2), 1–28 (2020)
2. Chen, J., Zhao, C., Uliji, Chen, L.: Collaborative filtering recommendation algorithm based on user correlation and evolutionary clustering. Complex Intell. Syst. **6**(1), 147–156 (2020). https://doi.org/10.1007/s40747-019-00123-5
3. Chen, S., Peng, Y.: Matrix factorization for recommendation with explicit and implicit feedback. Knowl. Based Syst. (2018). https://doi.org/10.1016/j.knosys.2018.05.040
4. Dacrema, M.F., Cremonesi, P., Jannach, D.: Are we really making much progress? A worrying analysis of recent neural recommendation approaches. In: Proceedings of the 13th ACM Conference on Recommender Systems, pp. 101–109. RecSys 2019, Association for Computing Machinery, New York, NY, USA (2019). https://doi.org/10.1145/3298689.3347058
5. Deshpande, M., Karypis, G.: Item-based top- N recommendation algorithms. ACM Trans. Inf. Syst. (2004). https://doi.org/10.1145/963770.963776
6. Dhariwal, P., Nichol, A.: Diffusion models beat GANs on image synthesis. CoRR abs/2105.05233 (2021)
7. Dieng, A.B., Kim, Y., Rush, A.M., Blei, D.M.: Avoiding latent variable collapse with generative skip models. In: AISTATS Proceedings of Machine Learning Research, vol. 89, pp. 2397–2405, PMLR (2019)
8. He, X., Liao, L., Zhang, H., Nie, L., Hu, X., Chua, T.S.: Neural collaborative filtering. In: Proceedings of the 26th International Conference on World Wide Web - WWW 2017, pp. 173–182 (2017). DOI: https://doi.org/10.1145/3038912.3052569
9. He, X., Zhang, H., Kan, M.Y., Chua, T.S.: Fast matrix factorization for online recommendation with implicit feedback. In: SIGIR 2016 - Proceedings of the 39th International ACM SIGIR Conference on Research and Development in Information Retrieval, pp. 549–558 (2016). https://doi.org/10.1145/2911451.2911489
10. Ho, J., Jain, A., Abbeel, P.: Denoising diffusion probabilistic models. In: NeurIPS (2020)
11. Ho, J., Saharia, C., Chan, W., Fleet, D.J., Norouzi, M., Salimans, T.: Cascaded diffusion models for high fidelity image generation. J. Mach. Learn. Res. **23**, 47:1–47:33 (2022)
12. Hu, Y., Volinsky, C., Koren, Y.: Collaborative filtering for implicit feedback datasets. In: Proceedings - IEEE International Conference on Data Mining, ICDM, pp. 263–272. IEEE (2008). https://doi.org/10.1109/ICDM.2008.22
13. Kingma, D.P., Ba, J.: Adam: a method for stochastic optimization. In: ICLR (Poster) (2015)

14. Kingma, D.P., Welling, M.: Auto-encoding variational Bayes. In: 2nd International Conference on Learning Representations, ICLR 2014 - Conference Track Proceedings, pp. 1–14 (2014)
15. Koren, Y., Bell, R.: Advances in collaborative filtering. In: Recommender Systems Handbook, Second Edn., pp. 77–118. Springer, Boston, MA (2015). https://doi.org/10.1007/978-1-4899-7637-6-3
16. Koren, Y., Bell, R., Volinsky, C.: Matrix factorization techniques for recommender systems. Computer **42**(8), 30–37 (2009). https://doi.org/10.1109/MC.2009.263
17. Liang, D., Krishnan, R.G., Hoffman, M.D., Jebara, T.: Variational autoencoders for collaborative filtering Dawen. WWW (2018). https://doi.org/10.1145/3178876.3186150
18. Ma, J., Zhou, C., Cui, P., Yang, H., Zhu, W.: Learning disentangled representations for recommendation. In: Wallach, H., Larochelle, H., Beygelzimer, A., d'Alché-Buc, F., Fox, E., Garnett, R. (eds.) Advances in Neural Information Processing Systems, vol. 32. Curran Associates, Inc. (2019). https://proceedings.neurips.cc/paper/2019/file/a2186aa7c086b46ad4e8bf81e2a3a19b-Paper.pdf
19. Rendle, S., Freudenthaler, C., Gantner, Z., Schmidt-Thieme, L.: BPR: Bayesian personalized ranking from implicit feedback. In: UAI 2012, pp. 452–461 (2012). http://arxiv.org/abs/1205.2618
20. Salakhutdinov, R., Mnih, A.: Probabilistic matrix factorization. In: Advances in Neural Information Processing Systems, vol. 20, pp. 1257–1264 (2007). https://doi.org/10.1145/1390156.1390267
21. Sohl-Dickstein, J., Weiss, E.A., Maheswaranathan, N., Ganguli, S.: Deep unsupervised learning using nonequilibrium thermodynamics. In: ICML. JMLR Workshop and Conference Proceedings, vol. 37, pp. 2256–2265. JMLR.org (2015)
22. Zhang, Q., Lu, J., Jin, Y.: Artificial intelligence in recommender systems. Complex Intell. Syst. **7**(1), 439–457 (2021)
23. Zhang, S., Yao, L., Sun, A., Tay, Y.: Deep learning based recommender system: a survey and new perspectives. ACM Comput. Surv. (CSUR) **52**(1), 1–35 (2019). http://arxiv.org/abs/1707.07435

Mitigating Targeted Bit-Flip Attacks via Data Augmentation: An Empirical Study

Ziyuan Zhang[1], Meiqi Wang[1], Wencheng Chen[1], Han Qiu[2(✉)], and Meikang Qiu[3]

[1] School of Information and Communication Engineering, Beijing University of Posts and Telecommunications, Beijing, China
{zhangziy0421,wangmeiqi,wenchengchen}@bupt.edu.cn

[2] Institute for Network Sciences and Cyberspace, Beijing National Research Center for Information Science and Technology, Tsinghua University, Beijing, China
qiuhan@tsinghua.edu.cn

[3] Department of Computer Science, Texas A&M University Commerce, Commerce, USA

Abstract. As deep neural networks (DNNs) become more widely used in various safety-critical applications, protecting their security has been an urgent and important task. Recently, one critical security issue is proposed that DNN models are vulnerable to targeted bit-flip attacks. This kind of sophisticated attack tries to inject backdoors into models via flipping only a few bits of carefully chosen model parameters. In this paper, we propose a gradient obfuscation-based data augmentation method to mitigate these targeted bit-flip attacks as an empirical study. Particularly, we mitigate such targeted bit-flip attacks by preprocessing only input samples to break the link between the features carried by triggers of input samples with the modified model parameters. Moreover, our method can keep an acceptable accuracy on benign samples. We show that our method is effective against two targeted bit-flip attacks by experiments on two widely-used structures (ResNet-20 and VGG-16) with one famous dataset (CIFAR-10).

Keywords: Data augmentation · Backdoor · Bit-flip attack · Deep neural networks

1 Introduction

With the performance of deep neural networks (DNN) surpassing human performance in complex tasks, applications of DNN (e.g. computer vision, natural language processing, etc. [2,14,17,21,26]) are more and more widely used. For safety-critical tasks, such as biomedical diagnosis, autonomous vehicles, and intelligent transportation [16,20,31], the security and robustness of DNN models are crucial. Prior works has demonstrated that DNN models are vulnerable to

G. Memmi et al. (Eds.): KSEM 2022, LNAI 13370, pp. 606–618, 2022.
https://doi.org/10.1007/978-3-031-10989-8_48

various attacks [3,15,22,24,25]. A significant amount of the work has focused on fooling DNN models by adding perturbation to input samples. For example, carefully crafted adversarial examples (AEs) can mislead the model inference for false outputs [5,13].

Recently, novel security threats are proposed. For instance, neural Trojan attacks [7,18,19] exploit corrupted inputs and weights to cause target-miss behavior of DNNs. Many such attacks are designed for injecting Trojan into DNNs that can be activated by a specified input pattern [6,18,32]. Under such attacks, trojan-injected models can behave normally on benign samples to keep the attack stealthy. However, when a well-designed input pattern or patch is added to the input data, the trojan-injected model will classify all inputs to a specific target class with very high confidence. Such elaborate embedded patterns are also known as triggers which always correspond to a targeted label. These kinds of backdoor attacks on DNN models are usually experimented with by poisoning a partial training dataset (e.g. poison 5% of samples of the training set).

Nowadays, modern accelerators (such as GPUs) [23] usually store a large number of parameters of the model in dynamic random-access-memory which introduces novel threats. [11] demonstrated that repeated access to a DRAM row corrupts data stored in adjacent rows, i.e., causing bit-flips "0" → "1" or "1" → "0". DNNs stored in DRAM with floating-point are vulnerable to such bit-flip errors [10]. Using the DNN weight quantization technique, when the weights are represented in a fixed-point format with a constrained representation, the ability to resist bit flips can be significantly enhanced [10]. However, attackers can exploit such bit-flip techniques to carefully attack specific DNN model parameters [11,30]. Thus, a novel attack called the bit-flip attack (BFA) can realize backdoor injection of DNN models by flipping just a very limited number of vulnerable weight bits. These methods can attack DNNs by inverting specific bits after the target DNN model is deployed without interfering with the training process. For example, [4] demonstrated that the ProFlip attack only requires 12 bit flips out of 88 million to achieve an attack success rate (ASR) of 94% for ResNet-18 with CIFAR10 and 15 bit flips for ResNet-18 with ImageNet. Such BFA [4,10,27,28] can get rid of data poisoning in the training process but directly inject backdoors in DNN models by modifying a small number of parameters.

In this paper, we propose an empirical study on mitigating such BFA with the preprocess-only solution without any modification to the target model which makes our solution agnostic. We focus on targeted attacks of BFA which are backdoor attacks. We propose a data augmentation method on input samples that can effectively mitigate the impact of carefully designed triggering patterns on DNNs that have been deployed and injected with trojans. Our contributions can be summarized as follows:

- We significantly reduce the ASR and maintain the ACC of input samples embedded with triggers on trojan-injected models.
- Our data augmentation method ensures a relatively small impact on benign sample inference which can effectively maintain the model performance considering the ACC.

- We present our empirical study by experimenting with two widely-used architectures (ResNet-20 and VGG-16) and one famous dataset (CIFAR-10).

The roadmap of this paper is as follows. The research background is in Sect. 2. We list the threat model, workflow, and details of the data augmentation algorithm in Sect. 3. The experimental details and results analysis are in Sect. 4. We discuss our results in Sect. 5 and conclude in Sect. 6.

2 Background

2.1 Bit-Flip Attack (BFA)

We categorize existing BFAs into two types: untargeted attack and targeted attack. Terminal Brain Damage [10] has first demonstrated that on a floating-point DNN model, even single-bit inversion damage can cause significant accuracy degradation (up to 99%). Later on, [27] proposes an untargeted attack method for the quantized weight DNN represented by fixed-point numbers by combining gradient sorting and progressive search, which can successfully attack ResNet-18 complete failure by flipping 13 of the 93 million bits. Different from untargeted BFAs that aims to destroy one DNN model, targeted attacks aim to inject backdoors stealthily. TBT and ProFlip are two well-known targeted attacks. They achieve over 90% ASR for backdoor attacks by flipping vulnerable bits in the quantized neural network weights represented by fixed-point numbers with only limited influence on model ACC.

TBT Attack [28] propose a novel adversarial parameter attack to inject neural Trojan into a clean DNN model. TBT first selects w_b weights connected to the last layer K^{th} output neuron with the highest absolute value of the gradient of the loss function to achieve efficient neural Trojan trigger generation, all inputs embedded in this trigger are classified to the target class. They can ensure the generated trigger will force the neurons identified in last layer to fire at large value, the trigger generation mathematically described as:

$$\min_{\hat{x}} \left| g\left(\hat{x}, \hat{\theta}\right) - t_a \right|^2, \tag{1}$$

where $g(\cdot, \cdot)$is the inference function of the model, and $\hat{\theta}$ is the parameters of the model without the last layer. $t_a = \beta \cdot \boldsymbol{I}^{1 \times w_b}$ is an artificial large value to make sure the output of the neurons identified in last step is high.

Assume a set of sample data x with their label t, after the trigger generation, each of the input images embedded with trigger $\hat{x}$ will be classified to a target label $\hat{t}$. To ensure stealthiness tested on clean datasets and effectiveness of attacks on images embedded with trigger, TBT optimizes the weight of the neurons identified in the first step, which can be mathematically described as:

$$\min_{\{\hat{W}_f\}} \left[L\left(f\left(x\right); t\right) + L\left(f\left(\hat{x}\right); \hat{t}\right) \right] \tag{2}$$

ProFlip Attack [4] is a bit-flip-based trojan attack that inserts a trojan into a quantized DNN by simply changing a few bits of model parameters stored in memory (such as DRAM). The attack leverages forward derivative-based saliency map construction (also known as the Jacobian saliency map attack) to find the neurons in the last layer of the model that has the most influence on the target label. ProFlip will generate a trigger pattern that stimulates salient neurons to large values and simultaneously fools the DNN into predicting all inputs to the target class. ProFlip proposes an efficient retrieval algorithm to find the bits that need to be flipped, which gradually pinpoints the most vulnerable parameter bits of the victim DNN greedily. The attack starts at the highest level of abstraction (the layer where the attack parameters are located). ProFlip proposes a new parameter, the fitness score, to describe the vulnerability of the model parameters to attacks. Then, in each iteration, the attack proceeds to a more fine-grained level (which element in that parameter is attacked). Finally, ProFlip finds the best value for the element by traversing 20 points between the maximum and minimum values of the parameter.

2.2 Existing Defense and Their Limitations

Existing Defense. The paper [9] proposes a BFA countermeasure based on utilizing weight binarization and its relaxation piece-wise clustering. Through a comprehensive investigation of bit-flip-based adversarial weight attacks (i.e., BFA [27]), they found that BFA is prone to flip bits of close-to-zero weights and cause large weight shifts. During training, weight binarization forces all weights to be binarized, thus eliminating weights close to zero, which can be mathematically described as:

$$Forward: w_{l,i}^{b} = \mathbb{E}\left(\left|\mathbf{W}_{l}^{\mathrm{fp}}\right|\right) \cdot \left(w_{l,i}^{\mathrm{fp}}\right) \tag{3}$$

$$Backward: \frac{\partial \mathcal{L}}{\partial w_{l,i}^{b}} = \frac{\partial \mathcal{L}}{\partial w_{l,i}^{\mathrm{fp}}} \tag{4}$$

where $w_{l,i}^{b}$ denotes the binarized weight from its floating-point counterpart $w_{l,i}^{\mathrm{fp}}$. They use STE [1] to address non-differential problem for sign function.

Moreover, binarization-aware training is essentially equivalent to training a DNN with bit-flip noise injected. In the process of training a model using the gradient descent algorithm, even small updates to the weights will come with positive and negative changes in the weights, resulting in bit flips from +1 to −1. During the training process, a large number of bit flips bring bit-flip noise to the training of the model. Weight binarization is mainly aimed at non-directed attacks, that is, by flipping a small number of bits in the model weights, causing the performance of the model to a level close to random guessing. The paper [9] has shown that when weight binarization is used, an untargeted attack requires a malicious flip of 19.3× bits, compared to when there is no defense.

Limitation of Prior Works. These works specifically focus on the training phase of the model (i.e. improving the model's ability to defend against attacks before the model is deployed). However, existing attacks, such as TBT attack [28], implement the attack on the model after the actual deployment of the model. After the model is deployed, the defender loses the ability to train the model (that is, the defender cannot retrain the model after the adversary successfully attacks). Furthermore, since the binary model only uses one bit to represent one parameter, the defense against TBT and ProFlip attacks is weak. Since the TBT attack only targets the last layer of the model, for example, in the binary model of resnet20, the parameters of the last layer of the model can only be represented by 64 bits, so the number of bits flipped in the attack cannot exceed 64. In fact, according to our verification, for the binary model of resnet20, the TBT attack only needs to invert 25 bits to be successful.

Our work mainly addresses targeted bit-flip attacks. Without interfering in the training process, we mitigate the impact of the bit flip attack on the model inference process by processing the input samples.

3 Methodology

3.1 Threat Model

Defender's Goal. The defender tries to use a data augmentation method to mitigate targeted bit-flip attacks. Suppose the processing function is $g(\cdot)$. $g(\cdot)$ should reduce the attack success rate of the input sample embedded with a specific trigger, and improve the accuracy of model detection. For benign samples, the accuracy of model detection will not be affected after processing by function $g(\cdot)$. In summary, the defender's goal is to use a DNN that has already been attacked by BFAs and mitigate the effects of targeted bit-flip attacks to achieve two goals, i.e. the effectiveness goal and the utility preservation goal.

- *Effectiveness:* For a set of input samples embedded with trigger $\hat{x}$ with target label $\hat{t}$, the attack success rate (ASR) should be low, and the prediction accuracy should be high.
- *Utility-preserving:* the data augmentation function $g(\cdot)$ cannot affect the prediction accuracy of clean samples via preprocessing.

Defender's Capability and Knowledge. We assume that the defender uses a model that has been attacked by bit-flipped. The defender does not have access to all training data to retrain the model from scratch, nor can the defender get some clean data to retrain the model. This way the defender cannot modify the already deployed model. The defender can only perform data augmentation on the samples that are about to be fed into the model without knowing in advance whether they are benign samples or samples with embedded triggers.

3.2 Workflow

We assume that the defender preprocesses all input samples (e.g. clean samples and samples with embedded triggers) of the DNN model for data augmentation, and then preprocesses all input samples before inference. The workflow can be summarized in Fig. 1(a), (b), and (c). Usually, we think that the goal of the attacker is to input the sample embedded with the trigger to induce the neural network to predict the wrong results. When inputting a trigger-embedded sample, the network under a bit flip attack will output the specific target label desired by the attacker. Before network inference, performing data augmentation on the samples embedded with trigger input by the attacker can reduce the impact of the trigger on attacked neural network, so that the network can predict the correct label. For the clean samples as input, the accuracy score (ACC) is slightly affected, so the network can still provide high-accuracy inference services.

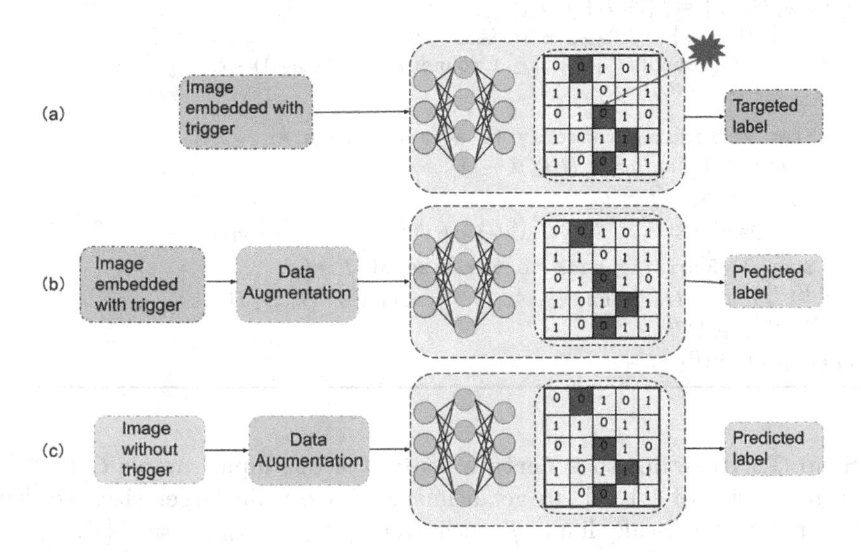

Fig. 1. System overview: mitigating targeted bit-flip attacks while keeping model utility via randomized transformation.

3.3 Data Augmentation Algorithm

In this paper, we propose a data augmentation input transformation, DAGB, as our preprocessing function $g(\cdot)$ for input images. The core idea is to significantly change the gradient of one sample by distorting the pixel positions and dropping some pixels. Particularly, we resize an input image into a large one with a scare ratio η, randomly pad values with a padding parameter p, and then resize it back to its original size. Therefore, the transformed image will have a significant difference considering the pixel coordinates and values since a random ratio of pixels will be dropped. This random transformation operation will result in the blurring of the gradients in the inference process of this sample, thereby mitigating the features carried by these triggers embedded in samples, which can mitigate targeted Bit-flip attacks. Since this transform does not fundamentally change the image contents, the accuracy score for clean samples will only be slightly decreased.

The core of our solution is a powerful data augmentation transformation function, Data Augmentation with Gradient Blur (DAGB). The details of DAGB are explained in Algorithm 1 with three steps.

ALGORITHM 1: DAGB

Input: original image $G \in \mathbb{R}^{A \times B}$
Output: distorted image $G^{DAGB} \in \mathbb{R}^{A \times B}$
Parameters: scale limit η; padding parameter μ

/* Step 1: Resizing to a certain scale */
1 $\{A_{max}, B_{max}\} = \lceil \{A, B\} \times \eta \rceil$;
2 $\{A_{resize}, B_{resize}\} = \{A_{max} - \mu, B_{max} - \mu\}$;
3 $G'(x, y) = G(\texttt{round}(x \cdot A/A_{resize}), \texttt{round}(y \cdot B/B_{resize}))$ s.t. $G' \in \mathbb{R}^{A_{resize} \times B_{resize}}$;

/* Step 2: Padding randomly to a large image */
4 $x_1 \sim \lfloor \mathcal{U}(0, \mu + 1) \rfloor$, $y_1 \sim \lfloor \mathcal{U}(0, \mu + 1) \rfloor$;
5 $x_2 = \mu - x_1$, $y_2 = \mu - y_1$;
6 $G_{max} = \texttt{padding}(G', ((x_1, x_2), (y_1, y_2)), value = 0)$ s.t. $G_{max} \in \mathbb{R}^{A_{max} \times B_{max}}$;

/* Step 3: Resizing back to the size of I */
7 $G^{DAGB}(x, y) = G_m(\texttt{round}(x \cdot A_{max}/A), \texttt{round}(y \cdot B_{max}/B))$ s.t. $G^{DAGB} \in \mathbb{R}^{A \times B}$;
8 **return** G^{DAGB};

Step ①: Resizing to a certain scale. For one input sample $G \in \mathbb{R}^{\{A,B\}}$ with the size of $\{A, B\}$, to get a image of a certain larger size, we define the parameter, scale limit η, such that $\{A_{max}, B_{max}\} = \lceil \{A, B\} \times \eta \rceil$. Then, we resize the image into a certain size $\{A_{resize}, B_{resize}\} = \{A_{max} - \mu, B_{max} - \mu\}$, with a padding parameter μ. For the newly obtained image $G' \in \mathbb{R}^{A_{resize} \times B_{resize}}$, for each pixel $(x, y) \in G'$, we obtain its corresponding value from the original input image, which can be mathematically described as:

$$G'(x, y) = G(\texttt{round}(x \cdot A/A_{resize}), \texttt{round}(y \cdot B/B_{resize})) \quad (5)$$

Step ②: Padding randomly to a large image. In the second step, we fill the resized image obtained in the first step with padding parameter μ to generate an even larger image G_{max}. We calculated the random seed (x_1, y_1), which is selected from a uniform distribution $\lfloor \mathcal{U}(0, \mu + 1) \rfloor$, to determine the padding coordinates (x_2, y_2).Then, we get a padded image G_{max} by padding zeros in these coordinates.

Step ③: Resizing back to the size of G. Finally, we select a part of the pixels from G_{max}, and restore G_{max} to the size of the original input sample to get the output image G^{DAGB}. In the end, the image G^{DAGB}, as the randomized transformation result, will be sent to the target model f for inference.

In summary, the DAGB contains two resizing processes which can be seen as randomly dropping pixels and reconstructing the image contents. Thus, the gradient of the inference process $\widehat{f}$ will be obfuscated to mitigate the features carried by those triggers embedded in input samples. Note this process is random so even for the same input image, DAGB will generate different outputs.

4 Evaluation

4.1 Setup

Models and Datasets. In our experiments, we choose the following two well-known model architectures: ResNet-20 [8] and VGG-16 [29] to train benign models and backdoor models, with a quantization level of 8-bit. We investigate the data augmentation algorithm on dataset CIFAR10 [12], which has have 10 classes and image dimension 32 × 32 × 3. We investigate DAGB's performance with two attacks: TBT Attack [28] and ProFlip Attack [4].

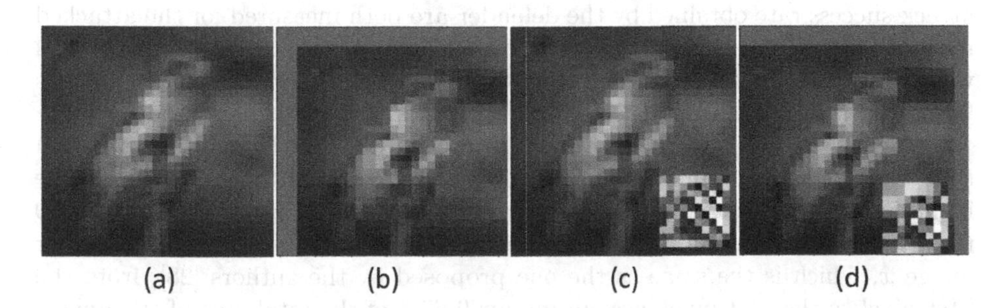

Fig. 2. Examples of clean and triggered samples: (a) and (c) for original samples, (b) and (d) for samples after DAGB.

Examples are shown in Fig. 2, which represent the clean samples, the samples injected by the triggers generated by attacks, and the visual results of the DAGB. We note that certain proportions of pixels are removed and padded for both clean samples and trigger-embedded samples. Larger scale and padding parameters will result in significant modification of the sample, which has a better effect on reducing interference from triggers but also reduces the usefulness of the model.

We use Pytorch 1.10 backend for the implementation. We conduct the experiments on a server equipped with 8 NVIDIA GeForce RTX 3080Ti GPUs. We train the 8bit quantized DNN models using SGD optimizer with a learning rate of 0.1 and momentum of 0.9 for 160 epochs. The parameters for attacks are the same with [4,28], which we will cover in detail in Sects. 4.2 and 4.3.

Attack Configuration. We set the hyper-parameter by following the results in this published methods [4,28]. For TBT Attack, we assume the attacker has access to a random test batch of size 128. A parameter w_b is the number of weights which are different between the clean model and the attacked model, and here we use $w_b = 150$ for VGG-16 and $w_b = 50$ for ResNet-20. For ProFlip Attack, we assume the attacker has access to a random test batch of 256. For all attacks, we use a default trigger area $TAP = 9.67\%$ for all experiments.

Metrics. We evaluate our method for effectiveness and utility- preserving. For effectiveness, we use the attack success ratio (the percentage of inputs that are mispredicted by the attacked model as the target class when the trigger is applied) as the metric. We show the comparison of the ASR for inputs preprocessed by data augmentation and those not preprocessed by data augmentation. For utility- preserving, we use the accuracy on the clean dataset (ACC) of our modified inference process $\hat{f}(\cdot)$.

4.2 Defense Against TBT

We assume that after the benign model is deployed, it has been attacked by an attacker, resulting in the parameters in the model have been modified. The model used by the defender has been changed, so the defender doesn't know any parameters of the original benign model. That is, the test accuracy rate and attack success rate obtained by the defender are both measured for the attacked model. Thus, in this paper, the accuracy and attack success rate of the model we observed before preprocessing the input samples are for the model that has been attacked by the targeted bit-reversal attack, not the benign model.

For TBT attack, through the method of NGR [28], we identify the neuron that has the most significant impact on the target K-th output neuron. We identified the 150 most influential neurons for the VGG-16 model and the 50 most influential neurons for the ResNet-20 model. Then we generate a trigger image $\hat{x}$, which is the same as the one proposed by the authors [28], from the 21st pixel to the 31st pixel, accounting for 9.67% of the total area of the image, as shown in Fig. 2. With Trojan Bit Search, we get high ASR models of 95.76% (for ResNet-32) and 81.17% (for VGG-16).

Table 1. Summary of the DAGB's performance on TBT attack. We chose $\eta = 1.16, \mu = 3$ for ResNet-20, $\eta = 1.2, \mu = 3$ for VGG-16.

Model	Test ACC. (%)		ASR	
	Before	After	Before	After
ResNet-20	89.36%	81.31%	95.76%	46.03%
VGG-16	85.21%	79.53%	81.17%	40.5%

Table 1 presents the test accuracy and attack success rate before and after DAGB for ResNet-20 and VGG-16 of the CIFAR-10 dataset. We chose the parameters $\eta = 1.16, \mu = 3$ for ResNet-20, and $\eta = 1.2, \mu = 3$ for VGG-16. We notice that after the TBT attack, an 8-bit quantized ResNet-20 test accuracy on CIFAR-10 is 89.36% and VGG-16 test accuracy on CIFAR-10 is 85.21%. After DAGB preprocesses the input samples, by reducing the model accuracy by 6% 8%, the attack success rate of the model can be reduced to less than 50% (the asr of ResNet-32 is 46.03%, and the asr of VGG16 is 40.5%).

4.3 Defense Against ProFlip Attack

For the ProFlip attack, we follow the same setting in [4], which set the target class $t = 2$ and the max number of bits flipped is 100. For salient neurons identification in [4], we use the default parameters $\theta = 1, \gamma = 0.5$. And for trigger generation, we generate a trigger which is a square pattern with a pre-defined size located at the bottom right of the image, as shown in Fig. 2. The thresholds of critical bits search are set to $ASR_t = 90\%$ and The partitioning number for grid search is set to $K = 20$ in all experiments.

Table 2. Summary of the DAGB's performance on ProFlip attack. We chose $\eta = 1.14, \mu = 2$ for all cases.

Model	Test ACC. (%)		ASR	
	Before	After	Before	After
ResNet-20	91.33%	86.93%	91.58%	54.52%
VGG-16	90.5%	86.54%	90.31%	12.83%

Table 2 shows the test accuracy and attack success rate before and after data augmentation for different models of the CIFAR-10 dataset. We chose parameters $\eta = 1.14, \mu = 2$ for all input samples. Typically, an 8-bit quantized ResNet-20 test accuracy on CIFAR-10 is 91.33% and the attack success rate of the attacked model ResNet-20 is 91.58%. An 8-bit quantized VGG-16 test accuracy on CIFAR-10 is 90.5% and the attack success rate of the attacked model VGG-16 is 90.31%. It can be seen that the attack success rate has a certain drop for both models after input samples are preprocessed by DAGB. For VGG-16, the attack success rate is only 12.83%, and ResNet-20 has 54.52% left.

We also observed a slight drop in test accuracy. By losing about 4–6% of the ACC, we can reduce the success rate of the attack by compromising the features carried by the trigger embedded in the input samples.

5 Discussions and Future Works

Our proposed algorithm can effectively mitigate the effect of targeted bit-flip attacks. After the model is deployed, even if the model is subject to a targeted bit-flip attack, we find that the attack success rate can be reduced to less than

50% without affecting the performance of the model, just by randomly transforming the input samples.

We list two research directions for our future work. (1) We will conduct more experiments on other different model structures and datasets. (2) We will try to improve the algorithm to reduce the attack success rate more while losing less accuracy.

6 Conclusion

In this paper, we introduce DAGB, a gradient blur-based preprocessing method. It can make random changes to all input samples before they are input into the attacked models, through scaling changes, random filling, and random discarding of pixels, such that blurring the gradient of the input image. DAGB can not only reduce the impact of the attacker's trigger embedded in the input sample on the inference of the network, reducing the attack success rate of the target bit-flip attack, but also maintain the availability of the attacked model.

References

1. Bengio, Y., Léonard, N., Courville, A.: Estimating or propagating gradients through stochastic neurons for conditional computation. arXiv preprint arXiv:1308.3432 (2013)
2. Boveiri, H.R., Khayami, R., Javidan, R., Mehdizadeh, A.: Medical image registration using deep neural networks: a comprehensive review. Comput. Electr. Eng. **87**, 106767 (2020)
3. Carlini, N., Wagner, D.: Towards evaluating the robustness of neural networks. In: 2017 IEEE Symposium on Security and Privacy (SP), pp. 39–57. IEEE (2017)
4. Chen, H., Fu, C., Zhao, J., Koushanfar, F.: ProFlip: targeted trojan attack with progressive bit flips. In: Proceedings of the IEEE/CVF International Conference on Computer Vision, pp. 7718–7727 (2021)
5. Goodfellow, I.J., Shlens, J., Szegedy, C.: Explaining and harnessing adversarial examples. arXiv preprint arXiv:1412.6572 (2014)
6. Gu, T., Dolan-Gavitt, B., Garg, S.: BadNets: identifying vulnerabilities in the machine learning model supply chain. arXiv preprint arXiv:1708.06733 (2017)
7. Gu, T., Liu, K., Dolan-Gavitt, B., Garg, S.: BadNets: evaluating backdooring attacks on deep neural networks. IEEE Access **7**, 47230–47244 (2019)
8. He, K., Zhang, X., Ren, S., Sun, J.: Deep residual learning for image recognition. In: Proceedings of the IEEE Conference on Computer Vision and Pattern Recognition, pp. 770–778 (2016)
9. He, Z., Rakin, A.S., Li, J., Chakrabarti, C., Fan, D.: Defending and harnessing the bit-flip based adversarial weight attack. In: Proceedings of the IEEE/CVF Conference on Computer Vision and Pattern Recognition, pp. 14095–14103 (2020)
10. Hong, S., Frigo, P., Kaya, Y., Giuffrida, C., Dumitras, T.: Terminal brain damage: exposing the graceless degradation in deep neural networks under hardware fault attacks. In: 28th USENIX Security Symposium (USENIX Security 2019), pp. 497–514 (2019)

11. Kim, Y., et al.: Flipping bits in memory without accessing them: an experimental study of dram disturbance errors. ACM SIGARCH Comput. Archit. News **42**(3), 361–372 (2014)
12. Krizhevsky, A., Hinton, G.: Learning multiple layers of features from tiny images. Technical report, Citeseer (2009)
13. Kurakin, A., Goodfellow, I., Bengio, S., et al.: Adversarial examples in the physical world (2016)
14. Li, Y., Song, Y., Jia, L., Gao, S., Li, Q., Qiu, M.: Intelligent fault diagnosis by fusing domain adversarial training and maximum mean discrepancy via ensemble learning. IEEE Trans. Ind. Inf. **17**(4), 2833–2841 (2020)
15. Li, Y., Wu, B., Jiang, Y., Li, Z., Xia, S.T.: Backdoor learning: a survey. arXiv preprint arXiv:2007.08745 (2020)
16. Litjens, G., et al.: Deep learning as a tool for increased accuracy and efficiency of histopathological diagnosis. Sci. Rep. **6**(1), 1–11 (2016)
17. Liu, S., Zhang, X., Zhang, S., Wang, H., Zhang, W.: Neural machine reading comprehension: methods and trends. Appl. Sci. **9**(18), 3698 (2019)
18. Liu, Y., et al.: Trojaning attack on neural networks (2017)
19. Liu, Y., Xie, Y., Srivastava, A.: Neural trojans. In: 2017 IEEE International Conference on Computer Design (ICCD), pp. 45–48. IEEE (2017)
20. McAllister, R., et al.: Concrete problems for autonomous vehicle safety: advantages of Bayesian deep learning. In: International Joint Conferences on Artificial Intelligence, Inc. (2017)
21. Pang, G., Shen, C., Cao, L., Hengel, A.V.D.: Deep learning for anomaly detection: a review. ACM Comput. Surv. (CSUR) **54**(2), 1–38 (2021)
22. Qiu, H., Dong, T., Zhang, T., Lu, J., Memmi, G., Qiu, M.: Adversarial attacks against network intrusion detection in IoT systems. IEEE Internet Things J. **8**(13), 10327–10335 (2020)
23. Qiu, H., Noura, H., Qiu, M., Ming, Z., Memmi, G.: A user-centric data protection method for cloud storage based on invertible DWT. IEEE Trans. Cloud Comput, **9**(4), 1293–1304 (2019)
24. Qiu, H., Zeng, Y., Guo, S., Zhang, T., Qiu, M., Thuraisingham, B.: DeepSweep: an evaluation framework for mitigating DNN backdoor attacks using data augmentation. In: Proceedings of the 2021 ACM Asia Conference on Computer and Communications Security, pp. 363–377 (2021)
25. Qiu, H., Zeng, Y., Zheng, Q., Guo, S., Zhang, T., Li, H.: An efficient preprocessing-based approach to mitigate advanced adversarial attacks. IEEE Trans. Comput. (2021)
26. Qiu, M., et al.: Data allocation for hybrid memory with genetic algorithm. IEEE Trans. Emerg. Top. Comput. **3**(4), 544–555 (2015)
27. Rakin, A.S., He, Z., Fan, D.: Bit-flip attack: crushing neural network with progressive bit search. In: Proceedings of the IEEE/CVF International Conference on Computer Vision, pp. 1211–1220 (2019)
28. Rakin, A.S., He, Z., Fan, D.: TBT: targeted neural network attack with bit trojan. In: Proceedings of the IEEE/CVF Conference on Computer Vision and Pattern Recognition, pp. 13198–13207 (2020)
29. Simonyan, K., Zisserman, A.: Very deep convolutional networks for large-scale image recognition. arXiv preprint arXiv:1409.1556 (2014)
30. Van Der Veen, V., et al.: Drammer: deterministic Rowhammer attacks on mobile platforms. In: Proceedings of the 2016 ACM SIGSAC Conference on Computer and Communications Security, pp. 1675–1689 (2016)

31. Veres, M., Moussa, M.: Deep learning for intelligent transportation systems: a survey of emerging trends. IEEE Trans. Intell. Transp. Syst. **21**(8), 3152–3168 (2019)
32. Zou, M., Shi, Y., Wang, C., Li, F., Song, W., Wang, Y.: PoTrojan: powerful neural-level trojan designs in deep learning models. arXiv preprint arXiv:1802.03043 (2018)

System Level Recommender System for Academic Venue Personalization: Multi vs. Linked Domain

Abir Zawali[1(✉)] and Imen Boukhris[1,2]

[1] LARODEC, Institut Supérieur de Gestion de Tunis, Université de Tunis, Tunis, Tunisia
abirzaouali1@gmail.com

[2] Ecole Nationale des Sciences de l'Informatique, Université de la Manouba, La Manouba, Tunisia

Abstract. Standard academic venue recommender systems have been emerged aiming to help computer science researchers to find a suitable academic venue, in which they may publish their works. Therefore, using all the available user data provided from various domains is helpful to guide users, in their decision making process, to choose a new suitable academic venue that can be the right shape for their preferences in terms of academic venue type (conference/journal), publisher, ranking and/or location. In this context, to enhance the quality of delivered recommendation results, we propose a system level recommender system for academic venue personalization, based on multi domain vs. linked domain, comparative analysis. We investigate not only authors past publications, and authors, from the reference list, past publications from the DBLP dataset, but also from the IEEE dataset using system level multi and linked domain recommendation methods. Experimental results demonstrate the efficiency of our new system level multi domain recommender system.

Keywords: System level · Multi domain · Linked domain · Recommender system · Academic venues · Author's preferences

1 Introduction

As the number of academic venues increases, authors cannot choose the right one to submit their work to. In fact, even when the papers themselves are excellent, they may be rejected, because they are not relevant to the academic venue scope. In this context, standard academic venue recommender systems [2,12,13] upstanding as an effective solution to satisfy the authors preferences, interests, tastes, priorities and needs, and find the suitable academic venue that can fit their research scope [17,18,21].

However, works based on information extracted from single domain may hinder the standard academic venues recommender systems effectiveness. In fact,

G. Memmi et al. (Eds.): KSEM 2022, LNAI 13370, pp. 619–630, 2022.
https://doi.org/10.1007/978-3-031-10989-8_49

users provide feedback in different ways and on different domains. Therefore, cross domain recommender systems burgeon as an expedient solution to incorporate information extracted from multiple domain and therefore to enhance the recommendation results.

Besides, a cross domain academic venue recommender system based on references is developed as addressed in [20] and refined in [19]. [20] is based on the hypothesis "for each paper, the target author may publish his work in one of the most appropriate venue in which one of the authors in the reference list has previously published". For [19], it is based on the hypothesis "it is very important for an academic venue recommender system, that suggests personalized academic venue list, to take into consideration preferences provided by the authors (venue's type, publisher, rank, location) and to filter out conferences or journals that do not match the author's requirements".

To ensure appropriate recommendations that correspond to the majority computer science researchers needs, recommender systems should leverage all available authors feedbacks implicitly and explicitly provided across maximum number of domains. In this context, we present system level recommender system based on multi domain, using DBLP and IEEE datasets as both source and target domain, compared to system level recommender system based on linked domain, using DBLP and IEEE datasets both as source domain and only DBLP dataset as target domain, to suggest personalized upcoming venues for computer science researchers, using information from references domain and authors domain for the both approaches. To do so, a personalized web interface is used on which, for each written paper, authors are able to specify their requirements, e.g., academic venue type (conference/journal), its publisher, its ranking and/or location, in order to get a list of recommended upcoming venues based on their interests without missing the submission deadline.

The rest of the paper is organized as follows: Sect. 2 gives necessary background on cross domain recommender systems. Section 3 exhibits data sources, explains the data extraction procedure, presents the proposed system level academic venue recommendation engine based on multi domain and shows the proposed system level academic venue recommendation engine based on linked domain. Section 4 discusses the experimental results by detailing comparative analysis. Finally, Sect. 5 concludes the paper and give an outlook over some future works.

2 Cross Domain Recommender Systems

2.1 Cross Domain Recommendation Tasks

The cross domain recommendation [9] is characterized by source domain (SD) and target domain (TD). There are three recommendation tasks [6], namely, cross domain, multi domain and linked domain.

Cross domain recommend items from the target domain using knowledge from the source domain.

Multi domain leverages knowledge from the source and the target domain to recommend items from both source and target domain.
Linked domain recommend items from the target domain using knowledge from the source and the target domain.

2.2 Notions of Domains

In the context of cross domain recommender systems, four levels have been defined [3] depending on the attributes and the type of recommended items [7], namely, system level, type level, item level, attribute level.

The system level, the same type of items, gathered from different datasets, is considered to belong to different domains, e.g., theater movies and TV movies.
The type level, similar items types that share certain attributes, are handled as belonging to different domains, such as movies and TV series.
The item level, different types of items that differ in most (if not all) attributes, are considered to be from different domains, e.g., books and film.
The attribute level, the same type of items with the same attribute have different values is regarded as belonging to different domains, e.g., a dramatic movie and a comedy movie.

2.3 User-Item Overlaps Scenarios

Across multiple domains, some relation needs to exist between users (U) and items (I). This relation is formed when users and items are found to be common in both source domain and target domain. Accordingly, we can identify four different cross domain scenarios [5], namely, no overlap, user - no item overlap, no user - item overlap, and user and item overlap.

- *No User - No Item overlap:* no users and no items are found to be common between source domain (SD) and target domain (TD), $U_{SD} \cap U_{TD} = \emptyset$ and $I_{SD} \cap I_{TD} = \emptyset$.
- *User - No Item overlap:* some users are found to be common between source domain (SD) and target domain (TD), but they have preferences for different items in both SD and TD, every item belongs to a single domain, $U_{SD} \cap U_{TD} \neq \emptyset$ and $I_{SD} \cap I_{TD} = \emptyset$.
- *No User - Item overlap:* some items are found to be common between source domain (SD) and target domain (TD), but they have been rated by different users from both SD and TD, every user belongs to a single domain, $U_{SD} \cap U_{TD} = \emptyset$ and $I_{SD} \cap I_{TD} \neq \emptyset$.
- *User - Item overlap:* users and items are found to be common between source domain (SD) and target domain (TD), $U_{SD} \cap U_{TD} \neq \emptyset$ and $I_{SD} \cap I_{TD} \neq \emptyset$.

3 System Level Academic Venue Recommendation: Multi vs. Linked Domain

The recommendations of academic venue are different from other items such as books or movies. In the academic venue recommendations [8,10,11], a researcher may attend the same conference several times. The user may submit his work to a conference that he already published in. Moreover, in the books or movies recommendation, the users are provided with a prediction of their future evaluation of items not yet rated.

Recently, cross domain recommender systems [19,20] have been shown that recommendation based on cross domain can increase researchers satisfaction. In literature, [20] presents a cross domain recommender system which selects the most appropriate academic venue list based on the hypothesis "for each paper, the target authors may publish their work in one of the most appropriate venue in which one of the authors in the reference list has previously published". It is covering the user interests across multiple domains, the references domain as source domain (SD) where the information is extracted from the papers in the reference list and the authors domain as target domain (TD) where the information is extracted from the authors papers. [19] recommends an academic venue list taking into consideration that researchers should easily interact with the recommender system and taking into account preferences provided by the authors (venue's type, publisher, rank, location) to filter out irrelevant ones that do not matches the author's requirements, without missing the submission deadline.

Despite, limiting cross domain recommendation engine to only two domains, i.e., authors and authors from the reference list domains may affect the cross domain recommendation forcefulness. In this context, we propose a comparative analysis between system level cross domain recommender system based on multi domain and also on linked domain to show that adding multi domains enhance the recommendation quality. Our proposed methods will notify researchers about academic venues that may match their preferences (venue's type, publisher, rank, location). This is done using two steps, (see Fig. 1) for the multi domain system level and (see Fig. 2) for the linked domain system level.

3.1 Data Sources

Each recommender engine will require its own data sources that will provide the necessary information to generate recommendation. In what follows, we detail these data sources.

Past Publications DBLP Data Source. Information previously published authors papers is from "DBLP citation dataset" [14], it is publicly available on the Aminer website [1]. "DBLP citation dataset" is one of the most widely used datasets to provide academic venue recommendation. It contains information about 4,894,081 papers and 45,564,149 citation relationships published until April 2020.

Past Publications IEEE Data Source. Information about authors past publications are extracted from the "IEEE citation dataset". It contains information about 11317 papers.

Academic Venues Data Source. The venue's title, acronym, type (journal/conference), deadlines, locations and publisher are publicly available on the WikiCFP website [16]. We can distinguish five ranking categories, such as A* (flagship conference), A, B, C, and unranked (insufficient information is available to judge ranking), from the CORE Conference Portal [4].

Preferences Data Source. Each researcher has a customized interface to ensure their interaction with the recommender system. He created his own account by submitting his registration form for the first time in our proposed recommender system. After creating the account, he can log into the system by providing his email address and password. He then has the opportunity to enter or change information about his preferences, i.e., type (journal/conference), publisher, ranking and location. In addition, authors must provide a list of authors and a bibliography in order to select the appropriate venue for each written work. The interface facilitates interaction between authors and the system by allowing authors to indicate their preference for venue type, publisher, ranking, and location.

3.2 System Level Multi Domain

First Step: As explained in Sect. 2.1, multi domain uses information from both source and target domain to recommend items, for users, from both source and target domain. Although, for our multi domain academic venue recommender system, we used information, from IEEE as source domain and DBLP as target domain to recommend academic venues, for authors, from both of them (see Fig. 1). More in-depth, using information implicitly extracted from the authors past publications and the authors, from the reference list, past publications gathered from both IEEE as SD and DBLP as TD in the recommendation process.

Second Step: By reviewing the academic venue data, venues with submission deadlines out of date, are rejected. The list of recommended academic venue, obtained from Sect. 3.2, for the multi-domain, or Sect. 3.3, for linked domain approaches is refined in the same way according to the researcher's requirements (e.g., venue's type, publisher, rank, location) from the preferences data source.

To highlight academic venues that more closely match the author's needs, the refinement process is performed by updating each upcoming academic venue score using a utility coefficient that describes the combination of preferences already specified in the author's profile. Inappropriate venues based on author profiles will be rejected. By default, researchers prefer all types, publishers, rankings and locations. We assign 1 to the academic site if the type, publisher, rank

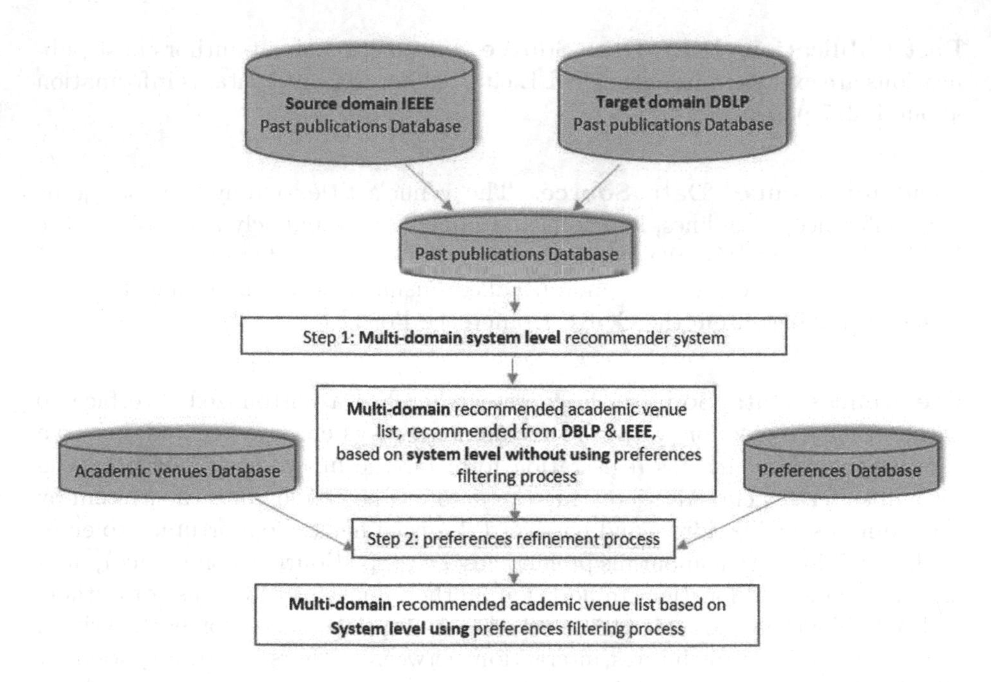

Fig. 1. System level multi domain recommender system.

and/or location of each academic site is the author's preferred, otherwise we set it to 0. Finally, we multiply them together to get the updated final score. A set of venues is ordered by the final calculated score to be recommended.

3.3 System Level Linked Domain

First Step: As explained in Sect. 2.1, linked domain uses information from both source and target domain to recommend items, for users, from the target domain. Although, for our linked domain academic venue recommender system, we used information, from IEEE as source domain and DBLP as target domain to recommend academic venues, for authors, from the target domain (see Fig. 2). More in-depth, using information implicitly extracted from the authors past publications and the authors, from the reference list, past publications gathered from both IEEE as SD and DBLP as TD in the recommendation process.

Second Step: For the linked domain academic venue recommender system, the filtering process follows the same instructions as the multi domain academic venue recommender system, to obtain a refined academic venue list using the system level linked domain method.

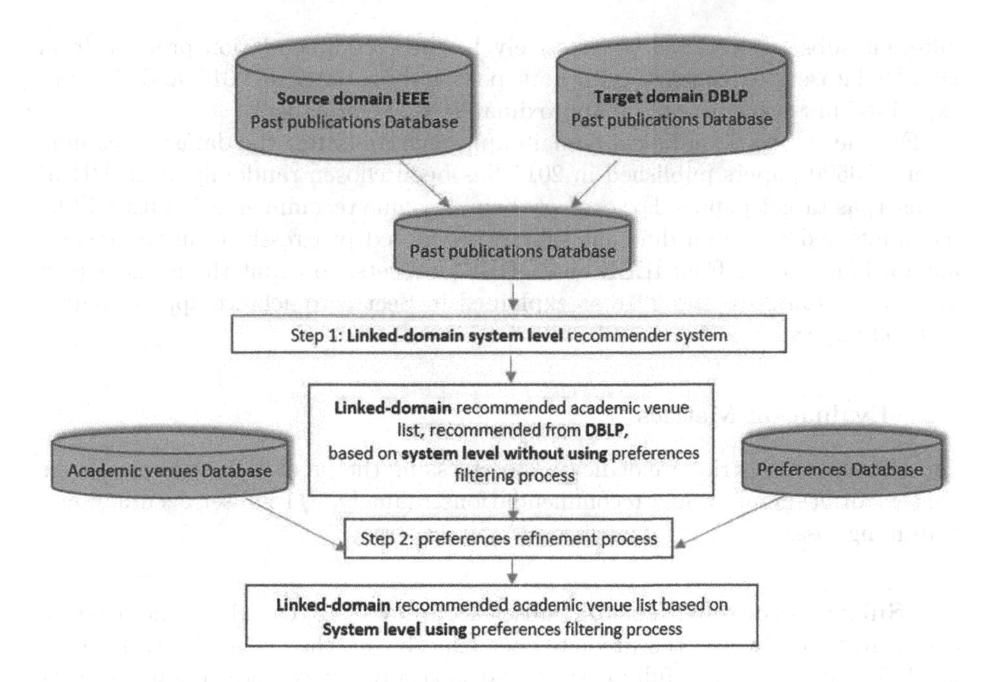

Fig. 2. System level linked domain recommender System.

4 Experimental Results and Discussions

4.1 Evaluation Datasets

To compare the proposed system level multi domain recommender system based on information extracted from IEEE and DBLP datasets versus the refined cross domain based on references recommender system [19] and the proposed system level linked domain based on references and IEEE and DBLP datasets recommendation method, experiments were conducted on the "DBLP citation dataset" and "IEEE citation dataset", already explained in Sect. 3.

The DBLP and the IEEE citation datasets are noisy and should be cleaned up. For IEEE each paper's information is in a separate .JSON file. We cleaned DBLP and IEEE data based on the publication with missing necessary information (authors, venue).

For the system level multi domain approach and after the dataset cleaning, a set of 13000 papers published in 2017 has been chosen randomly, from IEEE and DBLP datasets, as target papers. For each target one, a venue list will be recommended based on different subsets extracted progressively in the recommendation process, from IEEE and DBLP datasets, to count the authors past publications in 2015 and 2016 as explained in Sect. 3 to achieve approximately 550,000 papers.

For the single domain approach and after the dataset cleaning, a set of 6500 papers published in 2017 has been chosen randomly, from DBLP dataset, as target papers. For the each target one, a venue list will be recommended based on different subsets extracted progressively in the recommendation process, from DBLP dataset, to count the authors past publications in 2015 and 2016 as explained in Sect. 3 to achieve approximately 500,000 papers.

For the system level linked domain approach and after the dataset cleaning, a set of 6500 papers published in 2017 has been chosen randomly, from DBLP dataset, as target papers. For each of them, a venue recommendation list will be recommended based on different subsets extracted progressively in the recommendation process, from IEEE and DBLP datasets, to count the authors past publications in 2015 and 2016 as explained in Sect. 3 to achieve approximately 550,000 papers.

4.2 Evaluation Metrics

Two evaluation metrics are dedicated to assessing the prediction accuracy in the context of academic venue recommendations, namely, 0/1 subset accuracy and Hamming loss.

0/1 Subset Accuracy. The 0/1 subset accuracy [7,15] calculates the percentage of instances where the predicted set exactly matches its real set. There is no difference between a fully correct and partially correct prediction. In other words, if any of the outputs of recommender system matches the conference of the publication, it can be considered a successful recommendation. Note that the highest 0/1 subset accuracy value indicates better recommendation quality.

$$0/1\ subset\ accuracy = \frac{1}{N}\sum_{i=1}^{N}[Z_i = Y_i] \quad (1)$$

For instance, return 1 if each paper's recommended academic venues contain the true one, otherwise return 0. Note that N is the number of instances, Y_i is the true set, and Z_i is the predicted items set.

Hamming Loss. Hamming loss [7] measures the percentage of RS that makes incorrect recommendations. This metric takes into account cases where the correct academic venue is not predicted and when an incorrect academic venue is predicted. Note that the lower the Hamming loss value, the more accurate the prediction.

$$Hamming\ loss = \frac{1}{N}\sum_{i=1}^{N}[Z_i \neq Y_i] \quad (2)$$

For instance, return 0 if each paper's recommended academic venues contain the true one, otherwise return 1. Note that N is the number of instances, Y_i is the true set, and Z_i is the predicted items set.

4.3 Results and Discussions

We perform a comparative evaluation over our system level multi domain academic venue recommender system and respectively the refined cross domain academic venue recommender system [19] and the proposed system level linked domain academic venue recommender system, in order to highlight the extent to which system level Multi domain can improve the suggested academic venues results.

In fact, recommending only one academic venue to assess recommendation scores is very strict. However, we experimented on selected subsets by varying the number of top N recommended academic venues between 1 and 6 each time. For each top N, we compute the 0/1 subset accuracy and the Hamming loss for each target paper. Finally, average each of the top N results used in the experiment.

Note that the lower the Hamming loss values, the more accurate the predictions while the highest values of the 0/1 subset accuracy indicate a better recommendation quality.

The performance of the system level multi domain academic venue recommendation is compared to that of the academic venue recommender system based on refined cross domain [19] as well as the system level linked domain academic venue recommendation process. It can be seen that multi domain approach performs better than the refined cross domain and the linked domain one.

Single vs. Multi Domain Recommendation Results. It can be seen that the system level multi domain method performs better than the [19] method. For instance, for Top 5, we notice an improve of 12.34% in terms of 0/1 subset accuracy (see Fig. 3). It acquires the highest value 91.84% compared to 79.5% against [19]. Indeed, the system level multi domain approach attends the lowest average values in terms of Hamming loss, as shown in Table 1, for Top 5 (8.16% compared to 20.5%) against [20].

Table 1. Single vs. multi domain in terms of hamming loss.

Top N	Single domain recommendation based on DBLP	Multi domain recommendation based on DBLP & IEEE
Top 1	67.3	23.23
Top 2	47.8	14.27
Top 3	34.2	11.01
Top 4	26.9	9.29
Top 5	20.5	8.16
Top 6	20.5	8.16

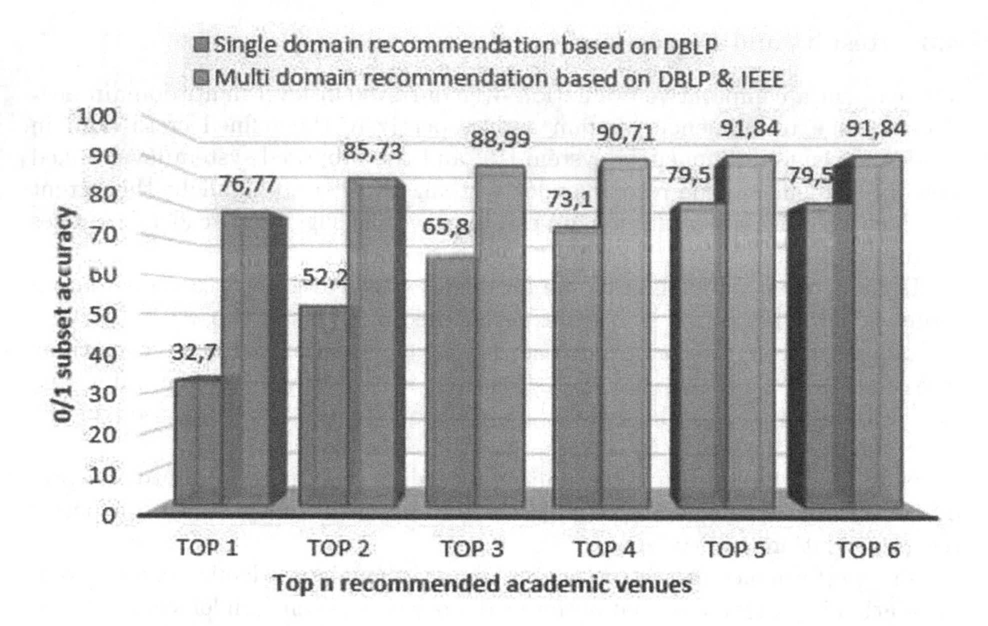

Fig. 3. Single vs. multi domain in terms of 0/1 subset accuracy.

Linked vs. Multi Domain Recommendation Results. In terms of 0/1 subset accuracy, for Top 5, we notice an improve of 13.28% (see Fig. 4), for the system level mutli domain method, to attend the highest value 91.84% compared to 78.56% for the system level linked domain approach. For Top 5. Indeed, the system level multi domain approach attends the lowest average values in terms of Hamming loss, as shown in Table 2, for Top 5 (8.16% compared to 21.44%) against the linked domain one.

Table 2. Linked vs multi domain in terms of hamming loss.

Top N	Linked domain recommendation from DBLP & IEEE to DBLP	Multi domain recommendation from DBLP & IEEE to DBLP & IEEE
Top 1	56.07	23.23
Top 2	48.38	14.27
Top 3	36.88	11.01
Top 4	28.27	9.29
Top 5	21.44	8.16
Top 6	21.44	8.16

To summarize, using information extracted from both DBLP and IEEE, to incorporate system level in the multi domain recommendation approach that joins both authors domain and references domain leads to a good predictive quality versus linked domain recommendation and single domain results.

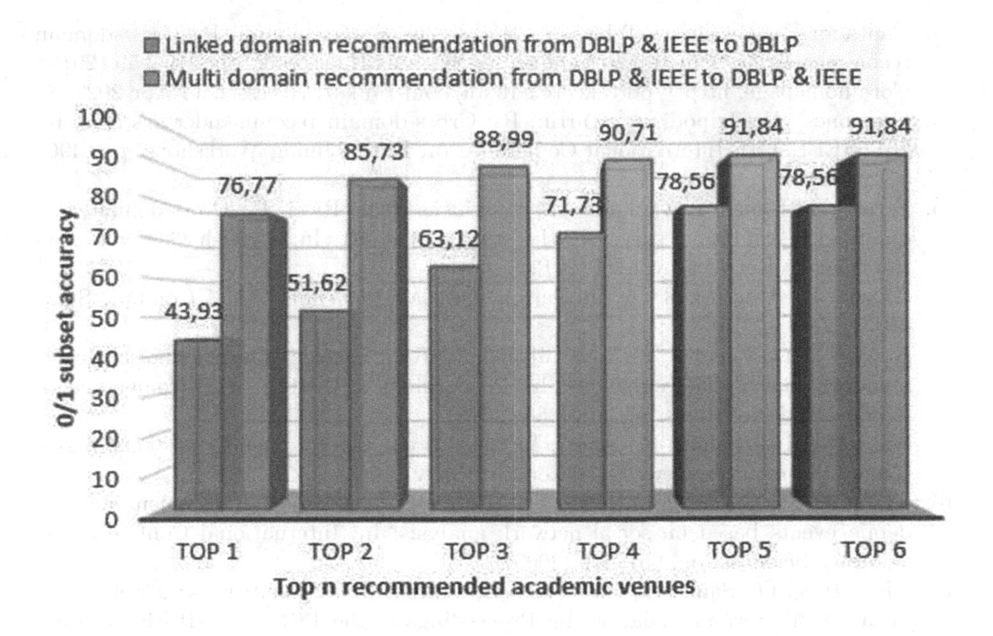

Fig. 4. Linked vs multi domain in terms of 0/1 subset accuracy.

5 Conclusion

In this paper, we compared system level multi domain recommender system, that suggests an appropriate academic venue list for the computer science researchers to publish their work, to the linked domain one. They are based on the authors from the reference list past publications aside from the target paper's authors past publications, using information extracted from IEEE and BDLP citation datasets. Our recommender engine filters out inappropriate academic venue that does not satisfy the authors preferences. It is able to deal with authors changing interests and also useful for young researchers who have not publications yet. With regard to this work, the experimental results showed that using multi domain recommendation approach can improve the author's satisfaction. As future work, we plan to integrate other author's interests, as features in the author's profile, to get more personalized recommendations (e.g., affiliation). We plan also to use other cross domain levels and integrate other domains aiming to ameliorate the recommendation results.

References

1. Aminer homepage. https://www.aminer.org/citation/. Accessed 14 Apr 2022
2. Boukhris, I., Ayachi, R.: A novel personalized academic venue hybrid recommender. In: 2014 IEEE 15th International Symposium on Computational Intelligence and Informatics, pp. 465–470 (2014)

3. Cantador, I., Fernández-Tobías, I., Berkovsky, S., Cremonesi, P.: Cross-domain recommender systems. In: Recommender Systems Handbook, pp. 919–959 (2015)
4. Core homepage. http://portal.core.edu.au/conf-ranks/. Accessed 14 Apr 2022
5. Cremonesi, P., Tripodi, A., Turrin, R.: Cross-domain recommender systems. In: 2011 IEEE 11th International Conference on Data Mining Workshops, pp. 496–503 (2011)
6. Fernández-Tobías, I., Cantador, I., Kaminskas, M., Ricci, F.: Cross-domain recommender systems: a survey of the state of the art. In: Spanish Conference on Information Retrieval, vol. 24 (2012)
7. Gibaja, E., Ventura, S.: A tutorial on multilabel learning. ACM Comput. Surv. **47**(3), 1–38 (2015)
8. Kang, N., Doornenbal, M.A., Schijvenaars, R.J.: Elsevier journal finder: recommending journals for your paper. In: Proceedings of the 9th ACM Conference on Recommender Systems, pp. 261–264 (2015)
9. Khan, M.M., Ibrahim, R., Ghani, I.: Cross domain recommender systems: a systematic literature review. ACM Comput. Surv. **50**(3), 1–34 (2017)
10. Klamma, R., Cuong, P.M., Cao, Y.: You never walk alone: Recommending academic events based on social network analysis. In: International Conference on Complex Sciences, pp. 657–670 (2009)
11. Küçüktunç, O., Saule, E., Kaya, K., Çatalyürek, Ü.V.: TheAdvisor: a webservice for academic recommendation. In: Proceedings of the 13th ACM/IEEE-CS Joint Conference on Digital Libraries, pp. 433–434 (2013)
12. Mhirsi, N., Boukhris, I.: Exploring location and ranking for academic venue recommendation. In: International Conference on Intelligent Systems Design and Applications, pp. 83–91 (2017)
13. Sato, R., Yamada, M., Kashima, H.: Poincare: recommending publication venues via treatment effect estimation. J. Informetrics **16**(2), 101–283 (2022)
14. Sinha, A., et al.: An overview of Microsoft academic service (MAS) and applications. In: Proceedings of the 24th International Conference on World Wide Web, pp. 243–246 (2015)
15. Wang, D., Liang, Y., Xu, D., Feng, X., Guan, R.: A content-based recommender system for computer science publications. Knowl. Based Syst. **157**, 1–9 (2018)
16. Wikicfp homepage. http://www.wikicfp.com/cfp/. Accessed 14 Apr 2022
17. Yang, Z., Davison, B.D.: Venue recommendation: submitting your paper with style. In: 2012 11th International Conference on Machine Learning and Applications, vol. 1, pp. 681–686 (2012)
18. Zawali, A., Boukhris, I.: A group recommender system for academic venue personalization. In: International Conference on Intelligent Systems Design and Applications, pp. 597–606 (2018)
19. Zawali, A., Boukhris, I.: Academic venue recommendation based on refined cross domain. In: International Conference on Intelligent Systems Design and Applications, pp. 1188–1197 (2022)
20. Zawali, A., Boukhris, I.: Cross domain collaborative filtering recommender system for academic venue personalization based on references. In: 2020 IEEE Symposium Series on Computational Intelligence, pp. 2829–2835 (2020)
21. ZhengWei, H., JinTao, M., YanNi, Y., Jin, H., Ye, T.: Recommendation method for academic journal submission based on doc2vec and XGBoost. Scientometrics **127**, 1–14 (2022)

Energy Consumption Prediction Using Bands-Based Data Analytics

Kieran Greer and Yaxin Bi(✉)

Artificial Intelligence Research Centre, School of Computing, Ulster University, Belfast, UK
{k.greer,y.bi}@ulster.ac.uk

Abstract. This paper describes a stochastic clustering method that is used for making predictions over energy data. The distinguishing feature of the method is discrete, localised optimisations based on similarity measurements, followed by a global aggregating layer, which can be compared with construction layers in deep neural networks. The developed model with the method is essentially a look-up table of the key energy bands that each appliance would use. Each band represents a level of consumption by the appliance. This table can replace disaggregation from more complicated methods, for instance constructed from probability theory. Experimental results show that the table can accurately disaggregate a single energy source to a set of appliances, because each appliance has quite a unique energy footprint. As part of predicting energy consumption, the model could possibly reduce costs by 50% and more than that if the proposed schedules are also included.

Keywords: Energy consumption prediction · Stochastic clustering · Unsupervised machine learning · Energy disaggregation

1 Introduction

This paper introduces the development of an unsupervised stochastic clustering method, called Hyper-Grid, and use of this method for making predictions over energy data. The work developed relates to the IDEAS Smart Home Energy Project [10], where as a client-side Artificial Intelligence component, it can predict energy consumption for appliances. The proposed model with this method is essentially a look-up table of the key energy bands that each appliance would use. Each band represents a level of consumption by the appliance. This table can replace disaggregation from more complicated methods like probability theory, for example. Disaggregation is the process of estimating how much energy each appliance would use from a single input amount. It is helpful to be able to estimate this, so that it can be learned by an AI model that can then make future predictions over similar appliance usage. Because the energy footprint for an appliance is quite unique however, the energy bands generated from it are also quite unique, which may be enough to identify each appliance, rather than rely

G. Memmi et al. (Eds.): KSEM 2022, LNAI 13370, pp. 631–643, 2022.
https://doi.org/10.1007/978-3-031-10989-8_50

on more complex probability methods. The energy provider therefore, is tasked with trying to predict how much energy will be required at a particular time. The provider sees this as a single problem over the whole set of input variables. The user-side is more discrete, when there can be more than 1 independent entity, resulting in input that is more event-based. As such, it may be more appropriate to split the client-side model into separate parts, each modelling one of the independent entities. A stochastic method that can produce non-continuous solutions may therefore have some advantages over a functional model. A Hyper-Grid is therefore proposed for clustering the data and can accommodate this essential difference - not the single provider, but discrete consumers with unrelated events. The resulting clusters can be then aggregated by some ways, such as by a Counting Mechanism of the Frequency Grid [8]. The process is stochastic in nature, clustering randomly, only a subset of the input data each time. It is costly to run, but this can be configured with smaller-sized dataset batches, when the results from each batch can be accumulated and so it can in theory be used with larger datasets, but over a longer period of time. The tests firstly consider creating a lookup table of unique energy bands to describe each household appliance. While this should be very quick to use in real-time, it is also able to provide a reasonable amount of economy, by making the energy prediction more accurate. The tests are then extended to consider clustering feature sets in the row clusters. As such, the Hyper-Grid can cluster rows first and then features of those rows, using the same method. Tests on energy data show that the method can produce consistent and logical results and has potential for a wide range of applications.

2 Related Work

2.1 Stochastic Clustering

Stochastic clustering is not new and in fact it may be the preferred method for clustering something like electric vehicle charging [18]. They state that coordinated charging of EVs can bring some benefits by itself and implementation of this scenario without coordinated charging can impose a huge amount of excess load on the national grid. They give a description of stochastic scheduling, where they state that 'since there are a lot of uncertainties in a real-world situation and specifically in EV energy scheduling problems, such as EVs driving pattern, diverse temporal and spatial EV charging pattern and so on, in the literature in this field, deterministic scheduling has been implemented much less than stochastic one. A stochastic model has one or more stochastic elements. The system having stochastic element is generally not solved analytically, moreover, there are several cases for which it is difficult to build an intuitive perspective.' While this paper is interested in a different field of energy prediction, it has to solve a similar type of problem. To make the Hyper-Grid practical, it is possible to use a form of bootstrapping over randomised datasets. Bootstrapping [7] removes some rows from the dataset each time and solves the problem for the remaining rows. It then averages over the final solutions. The hyper-grid by nature, solves over localised parts of the whole problem and so this is always part of constructing any solution. It would therefore be natural to include a bootstrapping process with the hyper-grid, which would allow it to use subsets of the whole dataset each time. It would also help a lot in practical terms, to reduce the size of the data grid, which is very time-costly to solve. This method is also the one proposed in [3], that suggests protecting linear classifiers from adversarial attack, through the use of bagging and random subspaces. Aggregating the subset results from the hyper-grid is therefore a very similar idea. The architecture may also have similarities with neural networks. Deep Learning neural networks [5], for example, learn discrete elements before summarising them through a pooling layer. The stochastic and distributed nature however may have more in common with random neural network architectures [17]. Likelihood estimators have been used to predict energy usage before. One new version associated with Generative modelling (GANs) and variational autoencoders (VAEs) is described in [16]. Part of their intuition states:

'Since likelihood is the product of densities evaluated at all data examples, the model density at each data example should be high. Suppose we don't observe the model distribution directly, and instead only observe independent and identically distributed (i.i.d.) samples drawn from the model. Because the density at data examples is high, more samples are expected to lie near data examples than elsewhere.'

It then defines a series of likelihood estimates for random variables that contain distances between x and the nearest sample and uses the minimum solution as the best one. Another paper [4] uses regression models to predict the appliance energy usage in a house. It notes that the larger white goods appliances (fridge, cooker, clothes washer, freezer) consume the most energy and appears to suggest that their best regression model can predict the energy consumption to 57% accuracy. If that is the case, then the results of the case study in Sect. 4 are not too bad. Another paper that uses genetic algorithms to predict energy usage [12], quotes 29% saving or 36% during peak time.

2.2 Energy Systems

Predicting the household energy use at the level of appliances is quite a popular topic. Modern systems are quite inefficient and so there is a potential for a huge amount of energy saving. Because it is difficult to measure the energy consumption of each appliance in real time and it is also an intrusive and possibly expensive process, the current trend is to disaggregate the total power input to each appliance, to estimate their use from a behaviour model, generated from AI. This is typically done by first using raw data to train an AI model of the appliances and then using that to estimate the disaggregated values for each appliance. The training phase would typically log on-off switching events for each appliance in the house and then train possibly a Hidden Markov Model to recognise the hidden or unobserved states, which are the individual appliances, from the observed state, which would be the total power usage per unit time [1,2,13,15]. After training, the internal measurements do not need to be made, but can be estimated by the model. While this system is shown to work well, it is proposed in this project that it is overly complicated and that with today's computing power and memory resources, a much more direct approach could be just as effective. For one thing, the Markov Model is state-based and time-related, where switching events are placed in order. The new method to be proposed is set-based, where it will suggest an amount of energy that may get used during the day, but not the exact order in which it gets used. The set-based approach has been looked at previously, where Gaussian equations are used as part of the model and the Markov process [2] can be an extension of a Bayesian Network [14] for example. But these calculations are also expensive and may also include other probability measures, such as Expectation-Maximisation or Likelihood. The method in this project will make use of the idea that most appliances have quite a unique footprint, in terms of their unit energy use, and so a large lookup table may be sufficient to allow disaggregated appliance usage to be recognised from a single input power measurement.

3 Summary of the Clustering Algorithms

3.1 Hyper-Grid

The idea of the Hyper-Grid is to discover rows within two dimension tables, which are closer together in terms of some similarities, where one row is to evolve the matched pairs further, as in Genetic Algorithms [9]. This idea forms the basis for some clustering phases that result in energy bands, which can define the appliance usage over the course of a day. An underlying mechanism of the Hyper-Grid is the heuristic that works as follows: It reads a dataset of values, randomises the row ordering and also keeps a record of the original ordering for identification purposes. For the problem of learning the appliance behaviour, the dataset is a single column of values, representing the appliance energy consumption every time unit, but the dataset could have any number of columns. Randomising the row ordering means that there cannot be any bias in the ordering during the row matching process. The heuristic then compares the data rows and notes which pairs are most similar, according to some metric, such as the Manhattan distance. So that the heuristic does not result simply in hill-climbing, a matching process is preferred to one that selects the largest scores only. Also, if two rows are selected, any rows between them are removed from the solution, which means that it also discriminates. All of the potential matches are saved and then sets of row pairs are selected that would optimise the total score. This optimisation gives the heuristic some direction and helps to ensure a better result. The process of the method is illustrated via Table 1 below.

1. Compare every row with every other row and save a difference score based on the Euclidean difference between the cell values.
2. The rows that are closest to each other are:
   - 1 and 7 with difference 4
   - 2 and 7 with difference 3,
   - 3 and 5 with difference 1,
   - 4 and 6 with difference 1.

3. The sum score for rows 1 and 7 is 18 and for rows 2 and 7 it is 15. But rows 2 and 7 are more similar and so they are preferred.
   - The rows in-between can be removed, but if they also have matches, then the matches can be added first.
4. The similarity scores for rows 3 and 5, or 4 and 6 are the same with a score of 1. The sum score for rows 4 and 6 is larger however, with a value of 27 and so rows 4 and 6 are preferred. Because this cuts across rows 3 and 5, the matching pair of 3 and 5 is not included in the solution - row 5 is removed from the solution.
5. This leads to a final solution with the row pairs 2 and 7, and 4 and 6.
6. These row pairs are then saved to a list that can store all rows pairs for all of the test runs.
7. The final list of row pairs are then fed through the frequency grid that clusters them into mini-clusters for similar frequency counts.
8. The mini-clusters can then determine the energy bands, for example.

Table 1. Example of the optimisation process.

Row Index	Column	Column	Column
1	3	5	3
2	2	3	3
3	4	4	3
4	5	3	5
5	5	4	3
6	6	3	5
7	2	4	1

For the appliance problem and again to prevent hill-climbing from the unique footprint, row matches can be treated as equal if the difference falls inside of a particular value or band and is not only the smallest difference possible. Therefore, if a band similarity value is 2 and one matching score is 0 and another is 2, then they would both return a band value of 1. The use of bands or score ranges is interesting and might also work with other algorithms. Due to combinatorial explosion, a complete search over a larger dataset is not possible and so the algorithm has to split a dataset up into smaller-sized parts and solve the problem on each part separately. Because the rows are randomised first, this can still give a reliable result. For example, if Table 1 is a subset of the whole dataset and there are another 7 rows that have been clustered during a different batch run, the row pairs from the other subset can be added to the row pairs from Table 1 and the combined list can be clustered using the frequency grid.

3.2 Frequency Grid

The Hyper-Grid therefore also requires an aggregating layer, which can be a counting mechanism in form of the Frequency Grid [8]. This reads the list of row pairs and produces sets of count values that represent which rows are more often paired together. It is more entropy-based than local counts however, where the aggregation from the frequency grid can produce a holistic view of the row pairs and produce clusters for the whole dataset. The following is the detailed description of the process. Consider a different set of data, but again for 7 rows, shown in Table 2.

Table 2. Frequency counts would group rows 1–4 and rows 5–7 together.

	1	2	3	4	5	6	7
1	x	4	4	4	2	1	1
2	4	x	4	4	1	0	0
3	4	4	x	4	1	0	0
4	4	4	4	x	1	0	0
5	2	1	1	1	x	3	3
6	1	0	0	0	3	x	3
7	1	0	0	0	3	3	x

It is clear from the data that rows 1–4 all reinforce each other (pattern 1), as do rows 5–7 (pattern 2). With a grid format, the input is represented by a single pattern group, where a count is incremented for each row pair occurrence. The grid format lists each variable, or in this case it would be a row number, both as a row and a column. Each time a pattern is presented, the related cell value for both the row and the column is incremented by 1. In row 1, for example, the counts suggest that it should be clustered with rows 2–4, because they have higher counts with row 1. The same conclusion can be made for rows 5–7. It is probably not necessary to update a self-reference in the grid, so the leading diagonal can be empty.

4 Case Study: Disaggregating Energy to Appliances

This was one of the main research topics on the IDEAS project [11] and it is a well-known problem of trying to predict how much energy is required, by measuring the energy consumption of a set of household appliances and using that model to make the prediction. The single input power source needs to be disaggregated to each of the appliances, or an estimate of how much would go to each appliance needs to be made. This problem therefore requires a training stage to learn the model and then a testing stage to match that with the input source. The proposed algorithm ran a number of bootstrapped tests on raw data and generated row pairs that resulted in sets of mini-clusters. As the clustering involves a similarity measure, a more obvious approach is to aggregate the raw data into the time unit, hours for example, and then count the number of occurrences of each aggregated value. If this is done however, there is too much variability in the aggregated values. They do not conform to a set of values and so it is not possible to produce an aggregated view. This may be because the behaviour of any appliance is unpredictable and so aggregated values will typically be different to each other. Therefore, some form of clustering is required to recognise patterns or structure in the data and the hyper-grid was selected for this project.

4.1 Second Clustering Phase

The first clustering phase therefore selected time slots during the day that were similar. A second clustering stage then took the full list of mini-clusters and retrieved the energy values for each row in a cluster and placed that in an energy cluster for the row cluster. Energy clusters that overlapped could result in an energy band with an upper and a lower limit, although, single values were more typical. These energy bands could then be used to determine the user behaviour of the system. For example, if there were 3 events of band A and 1 event of band B, the energy supplier could expect band A, 3 times more often. After band B occurred, it could expect only band A until it had occurred 3 times, and so on. The bands are most useful for reducing the complexity of the system and recognising some inherent structure or behaviour. If there is a range, then the upper limit would typically have to be accommodated for by the system. But it is the fact that there is now some sort of model that can describe the application behaviour in a tractable way that makes it useful.

4.2 Third Clustering Phase

A third clustering phase is also likely, not when training the data model, but when reading it into the energy network, to be used by the system during runtime. This would help to reduce the complexity even further, so that a lookup table can be generated for an exhaustive combination search. To do this, energy bands with the same 'integer' upper and lower-limit parts were further combined, resulting in only one energy band for the whole range. See Table 1 in Sect. 4.5, for an example.

4.3 Optimisation

The intention is to optimise some process that is part of an energy system. As described earlier in this section, the energy bands can be used to predict how much energy the appliances are likely to use. The system can therefore plan for the calculated maximum energy requirement at any one time and then when energy band events occur, they can be removed and the prediction can be adjusted to the remaining set. It is always important that there is enough energy provided for any eventuality and so there always needs to be additional energy in the system that may not get used. This is one place where energy savings can be made, if predictions can minimise this additional amount. Other methods may typically recognise on-off switching events for appliances and then generate Markov Models or other probability measures, such as Likelihood evaluations and with that research, disaggregation is helpful. The model would be trained to recognise on-off switching events for appliances, which gives a state-based or a probability model for each appliance. Then from a single input value, the system would disaggregate the input power source to each of the appliances, by learning when the appliances are likely to be on or off. A Markov Model can be used with time-based events, or a Likelihood probability estimate can be used with set-based events, for example. The method of this paper does not have sequential events, but is more set based. It only defines that this set of events may have occurred in a particular time period. This is both good and bad, because it may be possible to produce an alternative to the Markov Model, that is more flexible, but also more simplistic than a Likelihood estimate. On the down-side, it would still benefit from the accuracy of learning some amount of timing and so the future work for this section describes how that might be achieved.

4.4 Test Case

An algorithm has been implemented in the Java programming language and tested on real data [6] from households in Switzerland. This data has been used before to generate Markov Models in [1,2]. A number of houses were monitored, where a smart plug was able to measure the energy consumption for an appliance. This was relayed to a central system and logged every second. Therefore, each appliance was logged every second for a period of approximately 8 months. For the hyper-grid, a measurement of every second was too fine-grained and so the data was converted into aggregated values for each hour. That is the average amount of energy used by the appliance each hour. The data for each appliance was then clustered using the Hyper and Frequency Grids, as described earlier in this section. The final set of energy bands would be used to define the behaviour of the appliance over the course of a day. For the 8-month period, there was no large change in the appliance behaviour from one month to the next, but this could certainly be modelled as individual and seasonal sets of bands. The energy system was then able to guess how much energy each house was likely to require during the day. It would have to provide the upper limit each time, so that the house does not run out of energy. This can be achieved by returning the largest energy band for each appliance in the house each time. While that is an upper limit, the system would test the accuracy of this by then removing an energy band instance, at random, for each appliance. The next prediction would then be calculated on the remaining energy bands and the accuracy would be the difference between the estimate and the randomly selected set of used bands. This system therefore does not need to model exactly when an appliance was used, but knowing when, would still make it more accurate.

4.5 Lookup Table

It is proposed that a simple lookup table can be used to good effect. The energy bands reduce the combinatorial complexity enough to suggest that for all appliances in a household, a lookup table of under 1 million entries could be sufficient.

The table needs to map every energy band events for each appliance with every other one and so it has to provide a combination for every possibility. There could of course be statistical methods to reduce the number further, when the entries are very similar, such as the third clustering phase of Sect. 4.2. For example, Table 3 is a set of energy bands that were produced for a fridge in some household over the course of a day. Each band represents an hour of energy consumption by the appliance and the frequency is how many times that occurred during the day. Most bands contained a single value that was the result of the first two phases of clustering. In rarer occasions, for example: 31.0813 – 28.1024, there was an overlap in the clusters leading to a value range. When reading these into the model however, the lower-values bands with the same integer number can be combined. For example, all bands starting with the integer value of '1' can be combined.

Then with each combination of all appliances, a power input total can be calculated by taking the upper limit or average of each energy band in the combination. The lookup table would be produced for each appliance during a short training phase, when the system is being setup. After that, the system would read the power consumption at some time unit and pass that to the table, which would return the appliance combination that matches closest to the power value. Because the band values are quite unique, the combination value can be a key to a table, where the table value is then the set of appliances that created it. The selected band events could then be removed from the day's set, allowing the next consumption amount to be more accurately predicted.

Table 3. Example of energy bands for an appliance, with power consumed per hour. Set of energy bands that occurred over the course of a single day for a Fridge.

Energy Band	Freq per Day	Energy Band	Freq per Day
51.3304 - 51.3304	1	12.3664 - 12.3664	1
47.3313 - 47.3313	1	8.2406 - 7.89404	2
41.8416 - 41.8416	1	6.6794 - 6.6794	1
37.4993 - 37.4993	1	4.0358 - 4.0358	1
35.5428 - 35.5428	1	3.8319 - 3.8319	1
31.0813 - 28.1024	5	3.2404 - 3.2404	1
21.3339 - 21.3339	1	1.3989 - 1.3989	1
18.3959 - 18.3959	1	1.2865 - 1.2865	1
16.317 - 16.317	1	1.2065 - 1.2065	1
14.8694 - 14.8694	1		

This method should work reasonably well because of the unique energy footprints, but there is also quite a wide margin of error that would be acceptable. For example, if the system has a set that contains energy bands of '5 units' for both appliances A and B. Then maybe the next event reads an energy band of

5 and the system mistakenly attributes that to appliance B instead of A. For the following time unit, the system would then expect appliance A to produce a 5-unit band instead of B. But if B produces the 5-unit band in the next time unit instead, this does not in fact harm operation of the system. The system only needs to match with the energy requirement, it does not need to know exactly, which appliance any band came from. Although, the authors recognise that for a more sophisticated system, individual appliance usage may need to be monitored and may prove more problematic.

This method should work reasonably well because of the unique energy footprints, but there is also quite a wide margin of error that would be acceptable. For example, if the system has a set that contains energy bands of '5 units' for both appliances A and B. Then maybe the next event reads an energy band of 5 and the system mistakenly attributes that to appliance B instead of A. For the following time unit, the system would then expect appliance A to produce a 5-unit band instead of B. But if B produces the 5-unit band in the next time unit instead, this does not in fact harm operation of the system. The system only needs to match with the energy requirement, it does not need to know exactly, which appliance any band came from. Although, the authors recognise that for a more sophisticated system, individual appliance usage may need to be monitored and may prove more problematic.

4.6 Test Results

After the energy band clusters were produced, an energy network and disaggregator were created from them and a predictor was asked to simulate the network activity. It would return its maximum requirement for energy each time and then remove a random set of energy bands as the actual event. The maximum requirement could in fact be summed and the total then passed through the disaggregator, to return an estimate for it instead. This produced only a small reduction in the accuracy overall. For 3 locations of the datasets [6], the following result of Fig. 1, was achieved.

Total power consumed was: 55295
Difference between predicted and disaggregated was: 6.0E-12, or 1.0E-14 %
Difference between predicted and used was: 44599, or 80.5 %
Number of predictions less than actual was: 0

Saving for location: h1 was 14414 or 54 %, from 24 events.
Saving for location: h2 was 13330.5 or 28.5 %, from 24 events.
Saving for location: h4 was 2222.5 or 18.5 %, from 24 events.

Fig. 1. Prediction accuracy for locations House 1, 2 and 4.

This figure indicates that the accuracy of the prediction to the actual random events is only about 20% accurate, or there is an 80% power loss when predicting how much energy should be provided. But this is for random selections that have to accommodate the spiking events. Disaggregating the single input source to the appliance lookup table however is very accurate and the error may be down to the computer processing floating point numbers. This gives support to the idea of unique energy bands for the appliances. Then, the difference in providing the upper bound on the energy bands each time and the predicted amount, over the course of a day, is shown in the second set of figures. It could be around 50% savings, but house 4 is less at only 19% savings. A key concern is to guess when the spiking event might occur. This is where an analysis that includes time would be helpful. A calculation using only the upper bound would have to accommodate this for every hour, while the prediction can remove it as soon as it occurs, which on average might be half-way through the day for random events, for example. But the energy bands themselves are a unique solution that make the whole problem very tractable.

5 Conclusions

This paper proposes a method that includes both discrete and centralising elements and therefore has some similarities with neural network architectures. A stochastic and discrete layer clusters randomly selected subspaces of the data into mini-clusters, not using gradient descent as in neural networks, but using a Euclidean distance linear classifier, as in [3] or the random networks [17]. Then, an aggregating layer combines the discrete results, rather like a deep learning pooling layer [5]. The algorithm can be trained to recognise similarities across data rows, or data columns (features), in a self-similar way. An optimising feature means that the algorithm prefers to cluster similar rows with larger values first. One might think about an energy surface with peaks and troughs, for example, but the surface is being traversed in many different places at the same time. Overtraining might then be recognised when the localised peak distributions start to merge with each other, which can happen when more lower-valued rows are linked with the higher-valued ones, through the continued aggregation of mini-clusters from a random ordering. In this paper, the method is used to cluster and make predictions over energy data, using a stochastic Hyper-Grid and a Frequency Grid. The discrete, localised optimisations in the hyper-grid match dataset rows that are more similar, using a distance measurement, but is also able to discriminate and keep only the row sets that will optimise for some overall total. A similar method is also described in [3], in terms of bagging and random subspaces, as being a possibility to protect from adversarial attack, by keeping some of the data always hidden.

This method has been integrated into a client-side Artificial Intelligence component that is used to predict energy consumption for appliances for the IDEAS Smart Home Energy Project. Preliminary experiments demonstrate that as part of predicting energy consumption, the method could possibly reduce costs by 50% and more than that if the proposed schedules are also included [11].

Acknowledgements. This work is supported by the project of "Novel Building Integration Designs for Increased Efficiencies in Advanced Climatically Tuneable Renewable Energy Systems (IDEAS)" (Grant ID: 815271), which is funded by the EU Horizon 2020 programme.

References

1. Baranski, M., Voss, J.: Genetic algorithm for pattern detection in NIALM systems. In: 2004 IEEE International Conference on Systems, Man and Cybernetics (IEEE Cat. No. 04CH37583), pp. 3462–3468 (2004)
2. Beckel, C., Kleiminger, W., Cicchetti, R., Staake, T., Santini, S.: The ECO data set and the performance of non-intrusive load monitoring algorithms. In: Proceedings of the 1st ACM Conference on Embedded Systems for Energy-Efficient Buildings, pp. 80–89 (2014)
3. Biggio, B., Fumera, G., Roli, F.: Multiple classifier systems for robust classifier design in adversarial environments, Int. J. Mach. Learn. Cyber. **1**, 27–41 (2010). https://doi.org/10.1007/s13042-010-0007-7
4. Candanedo., L.M., Feldheim, V., Deramaix, D.: Data driven prediction models of energy use of appliances in a low-energy house. Energy Build. **140**, 81–97 (2017)
5. Chen, Y., Sun, X., Jin, Y.: Communication-efficient federated deep learning with layerwise asynchronous model update and temporally weighted aggregation. IEEE Trans. Neural Netw. Learn. Syst. **31**, 4229–4238 (2019)
6. ECO Dataset. http://vs.inf.ethz.ch/res/show.html?what=eco-data. Accessed 29 Apr 2022
7. Efron, B., Tibshirani, R.: An Introduction to the Bootstrap. Chapman & Hall/CRC, Boca Raton (1993)
8. Greer, K.: New ideas for brain modelling 3. Cogn. Syst. Res. **55**, 1–13 (2019). https://doi.org/10.1016/j.cogsys.2018.12.016
9. Holland, J.H. Genetic algorithms and adaptation. In: Selfridge, O.G., Rissland, E.L., Arbib, M.A. (eds.) Adaptive Control of Ill-Defined Systems, pp. 317–333. Springer, Boston (1984). https://doi.org/10.1007/978-1-4684-8941-5_21
10. IDEAS: Novel building integration designs for increased efficiencies in advanced climatically tunable renewable energy systems (2022). https://www.horizon2020ideas.eu/
11. Greer, K., Bi, Y.: IDEAS deliverable 4.4. Smart mobile app development, pp 1–38 (2021). https://www.horizon2020ideas.eu/publications-papers-downloads-videos-about-ideas
12. Jiang, X., Xiao, C., Sun, J.: Household energy demand management strategy based on operating power by genetic algorithm. IEEE Access **7**, 96414–96423 (2019)
13. Kephart, J.O., Chess, D.M.: The vision of autonomic computing. Computer **36**, 41–50 (2003)
14. Kim, H., Marwah, M., Arlitt, M., Lyon, G., Han, J.: Unsupervised disaggregation of low frequency power measurements. In: Proceedings of the 2011 SIAM International Conference on Data Mining, pp. 747–758 (2011)
15. Kolter, J.Z., Jaakkola, T.: Approximate inference in additive factorial HMMs with application to energy disaggregation. In: Proceedings of the Fifteenth International Conference on Artificial Intelligence and Statistics, pp. 1472–1482 (2012)
16. Li, K., Malik, J.: Implicit maximum likelihood estimation, arXiv:1809.09087v2 [cs.LG]. 22 October 2018

17. Liang, X., Javid, A.M., Skoglund, M., Chatterjee, S.: Decentralized learning of randomization-based neural networks with centralized equivalence, Appl. Soft Comput. **115**, ISSN:1568-4946 (2022)
18. Noorollahi, Y., Aligholian, A., Golshanfard, A.: Stochastic energy modeling with consideration of electrical vehicles and renewable energy resources - a review. J. Energy Manag. Technol. **4**(1), 13–25 (2019)

Software and Hardware Fusion Multi-Head Attention

Wei Hu[1,2], Dian Xu[1,2(✉)], Fang Liu[3,4], and Zimeng Fan[1,2]

[1] College of Computer Science, Wuhan University of Science and Technology, Wuhan, China
{huwei,dianhsu,fanzimeng}@wust.edu.cn
[2] Hubei Province Key Laboratory of Intelligent Information Processing and Real-time Industrial System, Wuhan, China
[3] School of Computer Science, Wuhan University, Wuhan, China
liufangfang@whu.edu.cn
[4] Department of Information Engineering, Wuhan Institute of City, Wuhan, China

Abstract. Recently, Transformer has achieved state-of-the-arts results in several research areas such as Natural Language Processing and Computer Vision. Due to Transformer has a very large number of parameters and its core module Multi-Head Attention has a complex structure, the optimization of Multi-Head Attention for Transformer is now the research hotspots. However, most of the current work focused on software model optimization or hardware accelerator design, but unilateral optimization from algorithms or hardware is difficult to give full play to comprehensive performance of Multi-Head Attention, which is not well adapted to its characteristics. To solve the above problem, we propose a Software and Hardware Fusion Multi-Head Attention structure, which has less inference latency with tiny accuracy loss than the existing software optimization methods and hardware accelerators. We implement this design on Xilinx ZCU102 and validate this model accuracy and inference time using CIFAR-10 dataset, and obtained accuracy within 1% loss with respect to the baseline, and inference time 15.19 times of the baseline.

Keywords: Multi-Head Attention · Transformer · Hardware and software fusion

1 Introduction

In 2017, Google pioneered the Transformer model [25]. The Transformer model was initially applied to the field of *Natural Language Processing* (NLP). Relative to the *Recurrent Neural Network* (RNN) and *Long Short-Term Memory* (LSTM) network models that were already widely used in NLP at that time, Transformer discards the circular computation module of RNN and LSTM in favor of

This paper is supported by the National Natural Science Foundation of China under Grant No. 61972293.

G. Memmi et al. (Eds.): KSEM 2022, LNAI 13370, pp. 644–655, 2022.
https://doi.org/10.1007/978-3-031-10989-8_51

a more advantageous self-attentive structure. The Transformer and Transformer-based pre-trained models (e.g., BERT [1], Albert [7], and structBERT [27]) have achieved leading accuracy results in a variety of tasks within the NLP domain.

While the Transformer has achieved excellent results in the field of NLP, researchers have tried to apply the Transformer model to other fields, such as computer vision. Vision Transformer [2], Swin Transformer [11], and a series of other computer vision models have been proposed. Vision Transformer is the first model structure that completely replaces the CNN convolution mechanism with a self-attention mechanism, which uses a multi-layer local self-attention module to obtain a farther perceptual field than the original CNN model, and thus achieves better results than CNN in the fields of Image Classification and Object Recognition. After that, Swin Transformer use multi-layer local attention increased the accuracy performance in Image Classification. However, the evolution of Transformer also makes this model structure more complex.

To overcome this shortcoming, many Transformer-based neural network accelerators have been introduced, such as [5,8,13], and so on. These accelerators are mainly designed with optimized structures for specific models to adapt the models. Since they do not modify the software accordingly, the hardware implemented in this way is limited by the complexity of the software structure at the acceleration level and does not take full advantage of the hardware acceleration [3,12].

In order to solve the problem mentioned above, we propose Software and Hardware Fusion Multi-Head Attention, and design an appropriate hardware processor to adapt this design. We then design corresponding experiments to validate this software and hardware fusion design with the CIFAR-10 [6] dataset to verify this accuracy, inference speed and throughput.

Our contributions in this paper are mainly as follows:

- We propose software and hardware fusion design on Multi-Head Attention. We analyze the software model structure from the idea of software and hardware fusion and modify the structure of the model so that the software model can run on the hardware structure with less resource occupation.
- We designed a hardware structure to adapt this software model, which can provide a better inference speedup to this software within an acceptable accuracy loss. The experimental results show that our design can reduce the latency of Multi-Head Attention.

The subsequent contents of this paper are organized as follows: Sect. 2 introduces the background of this paper; Sect. 3 presents our software and hardware fusion design; Sect. 4 shows our experimental design and the results; Sect. 5 is the conclusion and future works.

2 Background

2.1 The Model Architecture of Transformer

With the rapid advances in computer hardware [21,24], network infrastructure [14,15,17], and new algorithms [10,20,23], big data [18,28] and machine learning

[9] had emerging as hot research areas. Useful information can be extracted with high performance, good security [16,19], and sufficient accuracy [22]. One of the critical research area in NPL is the transformer model. Like most seq2seq models, the structure of the transformer is also composed of an encoder and a decoder. The Encoder consists of $N = 6$ identical layers, and there are 6 in the original text. Each layer consists of two sub-layers, a multi-head self-attention mechanism, and a fully connected feed-forward network. Each of the sub-layers has a residual connection and normalization added. So, the output of the sub-layer can be expressed as Eq. 1.

$$SubLayerOutput = \text{LayerNorm}(x + \text{SubLayer}(x)) \tag{1}$$

The structures of Decoder and Encoder are similar, from bottom to top are Masked Multi-Head Self-Attention, Multi-Head Encoder-Decoder Attention, Feedforward Network. Like the Encoder, each of the three parts above has a residual connection followed by a Layer Normalization. The main difference of Masked Multi-Head Self-Attention is the addition of an additional mask matrix, which ensures that future information is not exposed when predicting the i position. The calculation process of Multi-Head Encoder-Decoder Attention is very similar to the previous Masked Self-Attention, and the structure is the same. The only difference here is that K and V are the output of the Encoder, and Q is the output of the Masked Self-Attention in the Decoder. Since Transformer does not have the iterative operation of the recurrent neural network, we must provide the position information of each word to Transformer so that it can recognize the order relationship in the sentence. Transformer uses a linear transformation of the sin and cos functions to provide the model position information as Eq. 2.

$$\begin{aligned} \text{PE}(pos, 2i) &= \sin\left(pos/10000^{2i/d_{model}}\right) \\ \text{PE}(pos, 2i+1) &= \cos\left(pos/10000^{2i/d_{model}}\right) \end{aligned} \tag{2}$$

2.2 Multi-Head Attention

Multi-Head Attention. (MHA) is the core part of Transformer and an improved version of Self-Attention. It inherits the working mechanism of Self-Attention. Each node has its own Key, Value and Query values, just like addressing processing. When computing each attention value of each node, the query value of the node is operated with the Key and Value of other nodes. MHA divides each node into several dimensions, and each dimension calculates the attention value of the node and concatenates each node. This mechanism enables the model to generate the corresponding attention values based on the information in different dimensions and to extract the information in the text more comprehensively. The basic computing process is given by Eq. 3.

$$\begin{aligned} \text{MHA} &= \text{Linear}(\text{Concat}[head_1, \cdots, head_n], W_o, B) \\ \text{Linear}(X, W, B) &= WX + B \\ head_i &= Attn(QW_i^Q, KW_i^K, VW_i^V) \\ \text{Attn}(Q, K, V) &= \text{Softmax}(\frac{QK^T}{\sqrt{d_k}})V \end{aligned} \tag{3}$$

From Eq. 3, it can be seen that the attention mechanism is essentially a query solution of three vectors query, key, value, and finally output, where output is a weighted sum of value and weight is a correlation function to calculate the correlation between query and current key. The MHA in Transformer maps query, key, and value to different solution spaces to get results of different dimensions and concat them, which is equivalent to computing an equation several times and finally taking the average value. Concat module is to concatenate the $[h,\ d_v]$ dimensional attention matrix of each head output to obtain an $[n,\ h,\ d_v]$ dimensional matrix. Linear module is a training matrix W of dimension $[h,\ d_v,\ d_{model}]$ multiplied by the matrix after Concat, which is reduced to a matrix of dimension $[n,\ d_{model}]$, making MHA output and input matrix of the same dimension. Due to the high computational complexity of MHA, it has become the focus of most researchers. Both [26,29] were the optimization based on MHA. However, they tend to optimize from the software level.

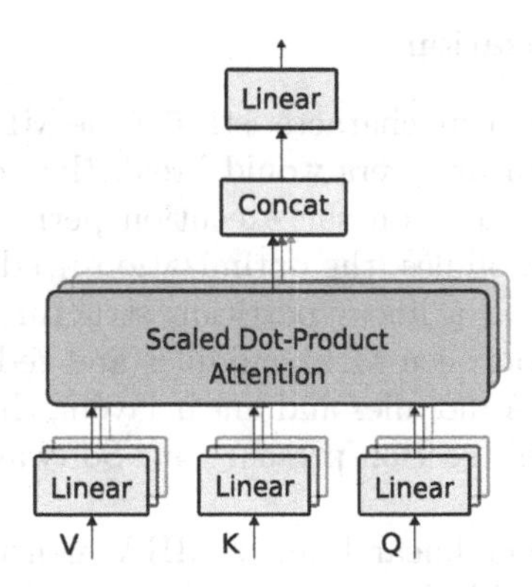

Fig. 1. Multi-Head Attention from original transformer

2.3 Current Accelerators of Transformer

There are already many hardware accelerators designed for Transformer, such as [3,5,8,13]. The current hardware accelerators are divided into two categories. One is to optimize the current design for the existing structure of the original model to achieve the purpose of acceleration, such as [3,5,13]; the other is to redesign the current computational method to make the computational method more suitable for hardware operation, with a higher parallelism, such as [8]. At present, only [13] has an optimized design for MHA, but [13] does not re-design the computational method of MHA, but only designs the corresponding hardware to support the software model structure.

3 Software and Hardware Fusion Design

3.1 Software and Hardware Fusion Design Concept

In this paper, we optimize the software through re-design MHA structure so that it can be executed in hardware with less resources and less energy consumption, mainly by adjusting the computation order and replacing float-point operations with fixed-point operations. On the other hand, we design the corresponding hardware to support our software, so that the execution of the model can have better parallelism and thus achieve faster inference speed. Based on the above design approach, we conduct software and hardware fusion design concept. Software and hardware fusion design is a spiral design method that considers the software model requirements and the target hardware platform characteristics, and iteratively modifies the software model and hardware structure with feedback several times.

3.2 Software Optimization

We first analyzed the structure characteristics of the MHA. We found that MHA connecting subsequent linear layers would break the continuous data arrangement and have a huge impact on the execution performance. Considering the characteristics of MHA modules, the optimization needs to make it more hardware friendly. We designed a linear partition structure for MHA, which leads to parallel computation between MHA modules and reduces the transition time between the original MHA modules and linear layers, thus improving the overall operational efficiency. This section presents our Software and Hardware Fusion MHA design.

Based on the inefficient linear layer of MHA mentioned above, we cut the linear layer of MHA into blocks of head counts, as shown in Fig. 2. This way can get the final sum of attention by summing the linear results of the output of each attention module. This is described in detail in Eq. 4. W_o is the parameter matrix among Concat in the original MHA module, n is the number of heads. When the linear layer needs to be split into sub-linear modules of head size, W_o should also be split into n sub-parameter matrix from W_{o1} to W_{on}. $head_i$ is the result of the self-attentive module inside each head, also from $head_1$ to $head_n$. Software and Hardware *Fusion Multi-Head Attention* (F-MHA) result is now the sum of each multiplication result of $head_i$ and W_{oi}. Linear is a matrix multiplied by a $[d_v, d_model]$ dimensional training matrix W reduced to an $[n, d_model]$ dimensional matrix, making the MHA output and input matrix of the

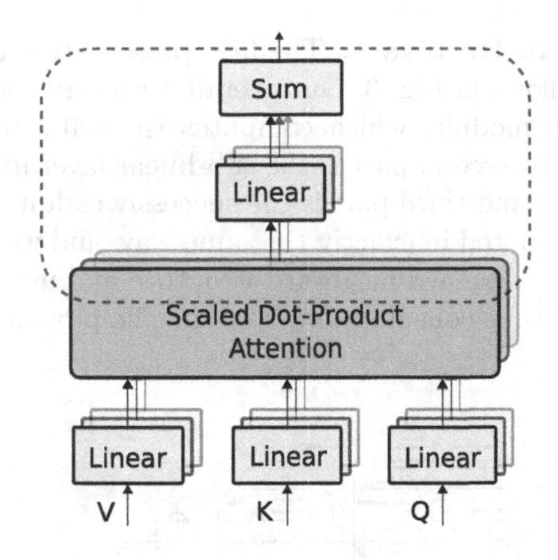

Fig. 2. Multi-Head Attention with linear sliced

same dimensions. Sum is to sum the $[n,\ d_m odel]$ dimensional Attention matrix of each Head output to obtain an $[n,\ d_m odel]$ dimensional matrix.

The initial MHA is to connect each output of the scaled-dot product attention and then use a linear layer to reduce its dimensionality. This paper use sliced ones to replace the original linear layer weights. This structure does not cause more loss to our final result, it can connect each self-attentive module and sub-linear layers, and such a structure is more suitable for parallel design of hardware.

$$\begin{aligned}
\text{F-MHA} &= \text{Sum}(\text{Linear}[head_1, \cdots, head_n], W_o, B) \\
\text{Linear}(X, W, B) &= WX + B \\
W_o &= [W_{o1}, W_{o2}, \cdots, W_{on}] \\
\text{Sum}(x) &= \sum_{i=1}^{n} x_i \\
head_i &= Attn(QW_i^Q, KW_i^K, VW_i^V) \\
\text{Attn}(Q, K, V) &= \text{Softmax}(\frac{QK^T}{\sqrt{d_k}})V
\end{aligned} \tag{4}$$

3.3 Hardware Design

We also quantize the model in order to improve the speed of model inference. The use of 32-bit float-point and 8-bit fixed-point numbers in the inference task has little effect on the results, however, the use of 8-bit fixed-point numbers can significantly increase the inference speed and reduce the hardware resource usage (32-bit float-point numbers require more DSP and LUTs, etc.).

Top Level Design of Hardware. The first presentation is the general structure of F-MHA. It shows in Fig. 3. Our overall structure consists of three modules, a sub-attention module, which computes the self-attention values inside each header separately, second part is the sub-linear layer immediately after the self-attention module, and third part is the successive addition module. We note that each head is computed in exactly the same way, and we use the same structure to fully reuse the designed hardware structure and use a pipeline structure to reduce the overall time consumption. The specific pipeline is described in the following section.

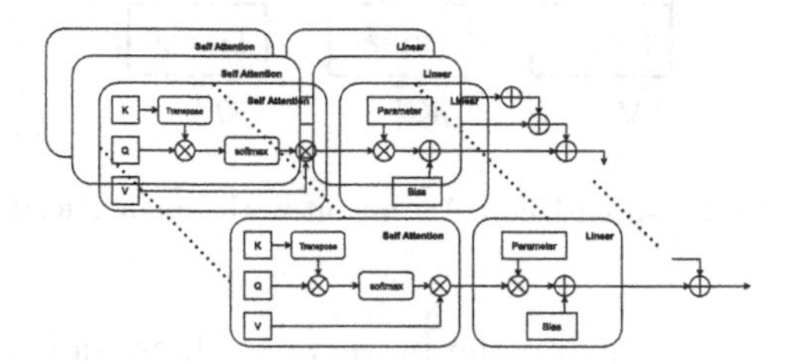

Fig. 3. Hardware top level design

Self-attention Pipeline Module. After linear slicing each small linear can be joined with the corresponding scaled dot product attention. Also, to reduce the execution time of multiple attentions, we use multiple pipelines to compute the connected scaled dot product attentions and sliced minor linearities as shown in Fig. 4.

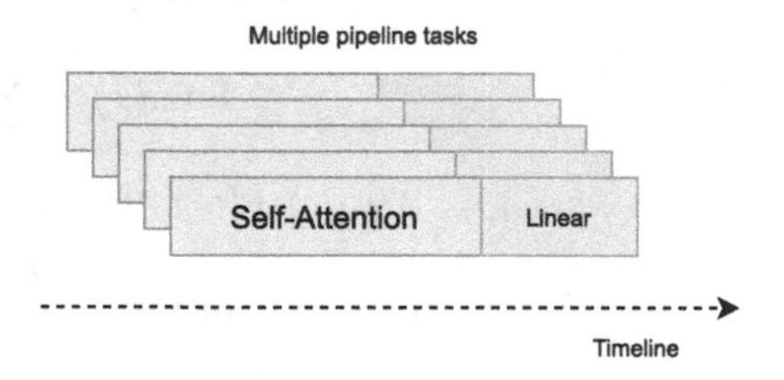

Fig. 4. Diagram of running timeline of multiple pipelines

In this case, we improve the resource utilization and reduce the execution time of MHA compared to the original MHA. In order to reduce the inference time consumption by using pipelining even in the small linear module after slicing, we add an input data copy module and a data partition module before the linear module, and after the linear module is completed, we also add a data copy module, as shown in the Fig. 5.

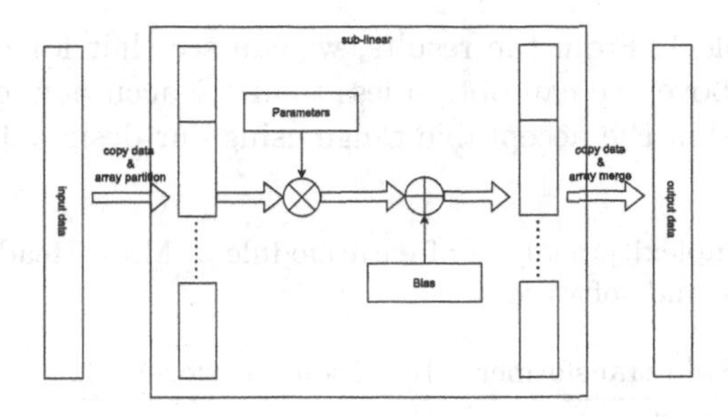

Fig. 5. The sub-linear compute module

Parallel Computation Unit. The linear module has an input data dimension of $[Seq, Dim]$, a weight dimension of $[Dim, Dim]$, and a bias dimension of $[Dim]$. After initializing the output data, we slice the input data into Dim parts and multiply them with the sliced weights that have been solidified in hardware. We can process Dim multiplications simultaneously, as shown Fig. 6. This can significantly save the time consumption of matrix multiplication. The original linear execution time was about $Dim \times Dim \times Seq$ unit time, while now the execution time is only $Dim \times Seq$. Then we add the execution time of two data replications, and finally it is about $Dim \times Dim$ execution time.

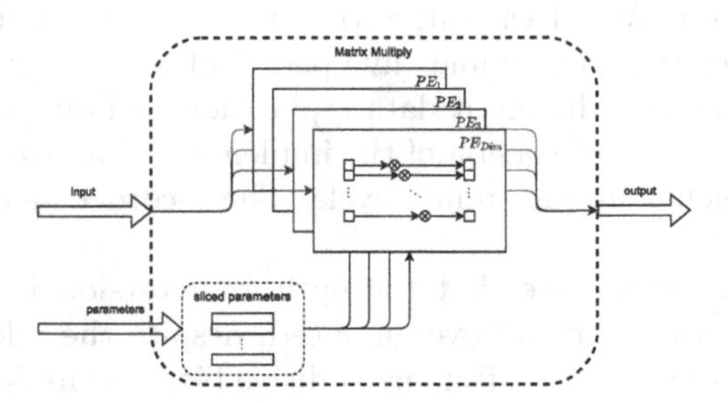

Fig. 6. Parallel matrix computing module

4 Experiment Setup and Result

In this paper, we use hardware resources usage and inference latency as our evaluation metrics. We used the code from the original Transformer [25] as our baseline. First, we verified the impact of different data types in our model on the inference results. We chose several models such as Swin Transformer, Vision Transformer and TNT, and then used the CIFAR-10 dataset to count the loss of accuracy in the official model of 32-bit float-point numbers and our model of fixed-point numbers with different numbers of bits. The experimental results are shown in the Table 1. From the results, we can see that for quantization of at least 8 bits and above, we can obtain less than 1% accuracy loss, so the impact on accuracy is within the acceptable range using our designed structure.

Table 1. Time complexity analysis of each module of Multi-Heads Attention implemented in hardware and software

Bits	Swin transformer [11]	Vision transformer [2]	TNT [4]
2	64.98%	80.43%	82.19%
4	11.00%	13.66%	23.11%
8	0.87%	0.75%	0.98%
16	0.02%	0.02%	0.01%

Next, we tested the impact of linear partitioning and data copying. We implemented two linear layers using Xilinx ZCU102, the reference version of the linear computation and our optimized version, the linear computation with linear partitioning and data copying. Due to hardware resource constraints, the reference version of the linear computation is based on the original Transformer design and uses a linear dimension of 32. The optimized version of the linear computation with linear splitting and data copying has the same linear dimension of 32 as the reference version. We set the target time to 10ns, set the linear batch size to 20, and then record the latency and time period of each program. The reference version does not include the input data replication and output data replication processes. In the optimized version of the implementation, the process of adding bias can be completed in one timing cycle. The recorded data is shown in the Table 2.

From Table 2, we can see that the optimized version is much faster than the original version in terms of overall speed, despite the addition of the data replication module before and after the additive bias and multiplicative weights. The improvement in computational performance due to data slicing masks the negative impact of data replication.

To compare the overall running efficiency, we use the multi-headed attention calculation part of the Transformer's code implementation running on top of the CPU for comparison. Here we use a dimension of 32 for the processing object, because when running the speed test implementation, there is no relation to the input and output data, and the program will execute as originally designed with instructions. We randomly choose a data of [20] as the input data for the whole program. Then, we counted the interval and latency of this experiment executed on a CPU on top of our designed hardware supporting linear with data slicing and data replication hardware architecture, and the results are shown in the following table.

Table 2. Linear latency of baseline version and optimized version

Type	Module	Latency	Cycles	Total latency
Original version	Input data copy	-	-	1.057 ms
	Add bias	13.2 us	1320	
	Multiply weights	1.04 ms	104360	
	Output data copy	-	-	
Optimized version	Input data copy	6.40 us	6400	13.33 us
	Add bias	10 ns	1	
	Multiply weights	32 ns	32	
	Output data copy	6.40 us	6400	

Table 3. The result of experiment between our design and baseline

	Latency	Interval
CPU baseline [25]	2.02 ms	2.02 ms
GPU baseline [25]	1.56 ms	1.56 ms
Our design	133 us	120 us

The data in the Fig. 7 shows that our hardware-supported, linear computation with data slicing and data replication provides a significant improvement in inference speed compared to the original CPU implementation. Latency is the time from input to output for a single piece of data. Interval is the minimum interval between two processed data. For both measures, our Latency speedup is 15.19 times faster and our Interval speedup is 16.83 times faster compared to the CPU implementation. In order to compare the impact of the number of headers on the running efficiency and resource consumption, our third step of experiments aims to examine the running results and resource consumption of the same model structure with different number of headers. We set up four different head counts, i.e., 2, 4, 8 and 16, and the results executed on our hardware supported linear with data slicing and data replication are shown in the Fig. 7. As shown in the Fig. 7, we explore the comparison of resource consumption and speed in hardware for MHA mechanisms with different number of heads. It can be clearly seen that LUT, FF, and DSP all increase slowly with the number of headers, while BRAM remains essentially constant. It is worth noting that when the number of headers is less than 8, the latency and interval do not receive the effect of the number of headers; when the head counts is greater than or equal to 8, they increase exponentially.

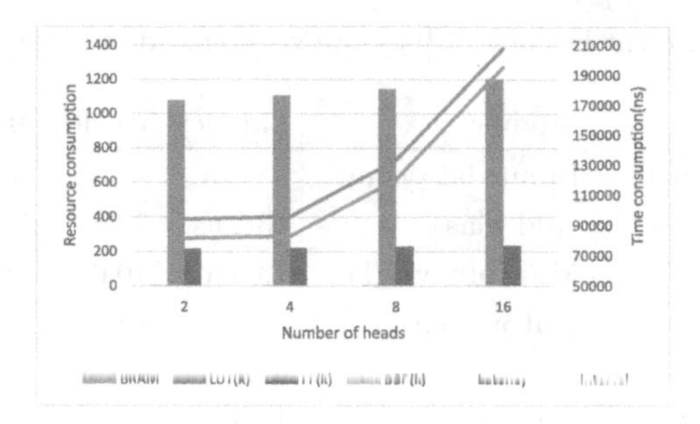

Fig. 7. Hardware resource usage in different heads count

5 Conclusion

In this paper, we presented a software and hardware fusion MHA that obtains better parallelism based on the linear slicing method and employs quantization to reduce the resource footprint and achieve better performance than before. We were using data copying and data partitioning to balance the computational procedure of multi-headed attention. Meanwhile, the process of linear and scaled dot product attention computation is re-evaluated and a module-level hardware pipeline is implemented. We also designed the corresponding hardware architecture to fit our software model. Then, we designed appropriate experiments to validate our work by verifying the loss of accuracy of our hardware-software fusion structure compared with the original model, the difference in inference speed of our hardware-software fusion structure from the reference model, and the hardware resource consumption of software and hardware fusion structure.

References

1. Devlin, J., Chang, M., et al.: BERT: pre-training of deep bidirectional transformers for language understanding. In: NAACL-HLT, pp. 4171–4186 (2019)
2. Dosovitskiy, A., Beyer, L., Kolesnikov, A., et al.: An image is worth 16x16 words: transformers for image recognition at scale. In: 9th ICLR (2021)
3. Ham, T.J., Jung, S.J., Kim, S., et al.: A^3: accelerating attention mechanisms in neural networks with approximation. In: IEEE HPCA, pp. 328–341 (2020)
4. Han, K., Xiao, A., Wu, E., Guo, J., Xu, C., Wang, Y.: Transformer in transformer. Adv. Neural Inf. Process. Syst. **34** (2021)
5. Khan, H., Khan, A., et al.: NPE: an FPGA-based overlay processor for natural language processing. In: ACM/SIGDA FPGA, p. 227 (2021)
6. Krizhevsky, A., Hinton, G.: Learning multiple layers of features from tiny images. Master's thesis, Department of Computer Science, University of Toronto (2009)
7. Lan, Z., Chen, M., Goodman, S., et al.: ALBERT: a lite BERT for self-supervised learning of language representations. In: 8th ICLR (2020)
8. Li, B., Pandey, S., Fang, H., et al.: FTRANS: energy-efficient acceleration of transformers using FPGA. In: ACM/IEEE ISLPED, pp. 175–180 (2020)

9. Li, Y., et al.: Intelligent fault diagnosis by fusing domain adversarial training and maximum mean discrepancy via ensemble learning. IEEE TII **17**(4), 2833–2841 (2020)
10. Liu, M., Zhang, S., et al.: H infinite state estimation for discrete-time chaotic systems based on a unified model. IEEE Trans, SMC (B) (2012)
11. Liu, Z., Lin, Y., Cao, Y., et al.: Swin transformer: Hierarchical vision transformer using shifted windows. In: IEEE/CVF CV, pp. 10012–10022 (2021)
12. Liu, Z., Li, G., Cheng, J.: Hardware acceleration of fully quantized BERT for efficient natural language processing, March 2021
13. Lu, S., Wang, M., et al.: Hardware accelerator for multi-head attention and position-wise feed-forward in the transformer. In: 33rd IEEE SoCC, pp. 84–89 (2020)
14. Lu, Z., Wang, N., et al.: IoTDeM: an IoT big data-oriented mapReduce performance prediction extended model in multiple edge clouds. J. Parallel Distrib. Comput. **118**, 316–327 (2018)
15. Niu, J., Gao, Y., et al.: Selecting proper wireless network interfaces for user experience enhancement with guaranteed probability. J. Parallel Distrib. Comput. **72**, 1565–1575 (2012)
16. Qiu, H., et al.: Secure health data sharing for medical cyber-physical systems for the healthcare 4.0. IEEE J. Bio. Health Inf. **24**, 2499–2505 (2020)
17. Qiu, L., Gai, K., Qiu, M.: Optimal big data sharing approach for tele-health in cloud computing. In: IEEE SmartCloud, pp. 184–189 (2016)
18. Qiu, M., Cao, D., et al.: Data transfer minimization for financial derivative pricing using Monte Carlo simulation with GPU in 5G. Int. J. Comm. Sys. **29**(16), 2364–2374 (2016)
19. Qiu, M., Gai, K., Xiong, Z.: Privacy-preserving wireless communications using bipartite matching in social big data. Fut. Gene. Comput. Syst. **87**, 772–781 (2018)
20. Qiu, M., Guo, M., et al.: Loop scheduling and bank type assignment for heterogeneous multi-bank memory. J. Parallel Distrib. Comput. **69**, 546–558 (2009)
21. Qiu, M., Li, H., Sha, E.: Heterogeneous real-time embedded software optimization considering hardware platform. In: ACM SAC, pp. 1637–1641 (2009)
22. Qiu, M., Liu, J., et al.: A novel energy-aware fault tolerance mechanism for wireless sensor networks. In: 2011 IEEE/ACM International Conference on Green Computing and Communications (2011)
23. Qiu, M., Xue, C., et al.: Efficient algorithm of energy minimization for heterogeneous wireless sensor network. In: IEEE EUC, pp. 25–34 (2006)
24. Qiu, M., et al.: Energy minimization with soft real-time and DVS for uniprocessor and multiprocessor embedded systems. In: IEEE DATE, pp. 1–6 (2007)
25. Vaswani, A., et al.: Attention is all you need. Advances in neural information processing systems 30 (2017)
26. Wang, S., Li, B.Z., et al.: Linformer: Self-attention with linear complexity. CoRR abs/2006.04768 (2020). https://arxiv.org/abs/2006.04768
27. Wang, W., Bi, B., Yan, M., et al.: StructBERT: incorporating language structures into pre-training for deep language understanding. In: 8th ICLR (2020)
28. Wu, G., Zhang, H., et al.: A decentralized approach for mining event correlations in distributed system monitoring. J. Parallel Distrib. Comput. **73**(3), 330–340 (2013)
29. Wu, Z., Liu, Z., Lin, J., Lin, Y., Han, S.: Lite transformer with long-short range attention. In: 8th ICLR (2020)

Hardware and Software Co-optimization for Windows Attention

Wei Hu[1,2], Kejie Hu[1,2(✉)], Fang Liu[3,4], and Jie Fan[1,2]

[1] College of Computer Science, Wuhan University of Science and Technology, Wuhan, China
{huwei,hekejie}@wust.edu.cn

[2] Hubei Province Key Laboratory of Intelligent Information Processing and Real-time Industrial System, Wuhan, China

[3] School of Computer Science, Wuhan University, Wuhan, China
liufangfang@whu.edu.cn

[4] Department of Information Engineering, Wuhan Institute of City, Wuhan, China

Abstract. Since the attention mechanism was proposed, there have been many researches on the combination of deep learning and visual attention mechanism. Among them, Models built with self-attention mechanism have achieved SOTA results in the field of computer vision. However, the large number of parameters and the computational complexity of such models hinder their development and limit their use on resource-limited devices and platforms. In this paper, we make improvements to Windows Attention in Swin Transformer from the perspective of software and hardware co-optimization, and parallelize the design on FPGA platform. In Softmax module design, we use Taylor expansion to replace exp function which needs more computing resources under the premise of less accuracy loss; we also optimize the computational process of matrix multiplication, which is used many times, and design the corresponding hardware module. Experimental results show that our resource consumption on the ZCU102 FPGA decreases by 93% compared to the traditional exp function, and the throughput improves by 7.73× and 1.21× compared to the CPU and GPU, respectively.

Keywords: Self-attention · Transformer · FPGA · Hardware and software co-optimization

1 Introduction

The Google Translate team's "Attention is all you need" published in NIPS 2017 has attracted widespread attention [1], in which the Transformer model was constructed using the self-attention mechanism. Since then the Transformer model has become a research hotspot and has achieved excellent results in various tasks especially in natural language processing domain and computer vision domain tasks. Since the Transformer model is too large, the Transformer model requires a large memory footprint [2,3] and high computational cost when deployed on

G. Memmi et al. (Eds.): KSEM 2022, LNAI 13370, pp. 656–668, 2022.
https://doi.org/10.1007/978-3-031-10989-8_52

hardware platforms [4,5]. In order to improve computational efficiency [6,7] and reduce resource usage [8], collaborative software and hardware optimization for Transformer's huge models has also become a necessary and popular research direction [9,10]. The core element of the Transformer model is the self-attention mechanism. In conventional hardware, the attention mechanism is usually implemented as a dense matrix operation and a Softmax function operation. However, in the self-attention mechanism, the computational complexity of these operations is proportional to the number of search targets [11]. This large computational cost of the self-attention mechanism becomes a limiting factor for Transformer models and accounts for a large part of the performance and cost of existing models [12].

To alleviate the limitations imposed by the large amount of computational resources required by the self-attention mechanism in resource-limited situations, this paper makes a hardware and software co-optimization based on the Swin Transformer model for the core self-attention mechanism in the model, mainly including the optimization improvement in the self-attention mechanism algorithm and the design of the corresponding hardware architecture on the reconfigurable hardware platform. The main contributions of this paper can be summarized as follows.

1). We have solved the problem of excessive computational resources consumed by traditional exp functions in hardware by using Taylor expansion instead of exp functions, and we have reduced the resource consumption by 93% and increased the running speed by 25× with little loss of accuracy. 2). Based on the huge number of parameters and complex data flow of the self-attention mechanism, we still need to design it in hardware to optimize its latency and throughput, and we mainly optimize the matrix multiplication module to achieve high parallelization and low latency of the computation. 3). We propose an FPGA-based architecture design to optimize the window self-attention module and experimentally verify that our hardware and software co-optimization achieves a 7.73× and 1.21× improvement in throughput compared to CPU and GPU.

The rest of this paper is organized as follows. Section 2 introduces the research background of the Swin Transformer window self-attention mechanism, Sect. 3 presents related work on software and hardware optimization, Sect. 4 describes our optimization on Windows Attention algorithm and parallelized design on hardware, and Sect. 5 illustrates the performance, resource and energy efficiency evaluation of our proposed software and hardware co-optimization through experiments.

2 Background

The Transformer performs very well on NLP tasks, and researchers have also tried to apply the Transformer to CV domain tasks. But applying the Transformer to the CV domain also faces two big problems: one is that the matrix properties of the image will result in many pixel points, and the Transformer's global-based self-attention mechanism will result in a very large computational overhead; the other is that after grouping the Transformer's view is limited to n tokens and there is a lack of interaction between groups. Therefore, some researchers optimize these two problems and propose the Swin Transformer model, and Fig. 1 shows two consecutive Swin Transformer blocks.

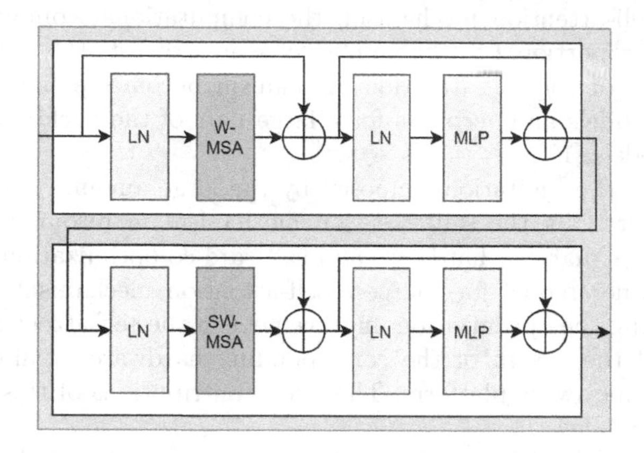

Fig. 1. Swin transformer block.

Conventional Transformers calculate attention based on the global, and therefore have a high computational complexity. Swin Transformer reduces the amount of computation by limiting attention to each window [13]. Equation 1 is the window based self-attention (W-MSA) formula. The main difference is that the relative position encoding is added to Q, K in the original formula for Attention calculation, and the addition of relative position encoding improves the model performance.

$$Attention(Q, K, V) = SoftMax(QK^T/\sqrt{d} + B)V \quad (1)$$

The idea of Windows Attention is to compute attention under each window. Although W-MSA can reduce the computational complexity, there is a lack of information exchange between non-overlapping windows, which actually loses the transformer's ability to construct relationships from the global using self-attention, so Swin Transformer further introduces shifted window partition to exchange information across windows, which the authors call *shifted window based self-attention* (SW-MSA). SW-MSA is indirectly implemented in the actual code by shifting the feature map and setting the mask to Attention.

Equation 2 shows the computational complexity of W-MSA and the traditional *multi-head self-attention* (MSA), The shifted window scheme brings higher efficiency by restricting the self-attention computation to non-overlapping local windows, while allowing cross-window connections. This hierarchical architecture has the flexibility to model at various scales and has linear computational complexity performance with respect to image size, while maintaining the original number of windows, the final computational result is equivalent. Since the number of patches inside the windows is much smaller than the number of image patches and the number of windows is kept constant, the computational complexity of W-MSA is linear with respect to the image size, thus greatly reducing the computational complexity of the model.

$$\begin{aligned} \Omega(MSA) &= 4hwC^2 + 2(hw)^2C \\ \Omega(W-MSA) &= 4hwC^2 + 2M^2hwC \end{aligned} \tag{2}$$

The authors of paper [14] mentioned that when deploying the self-attention mechanism, due to the huge number of parameters and complex data flow of the self-attention module, the memory occupation and hardware computation mode should be jointly considered, and the design mode of hardware and software co-optimization can better achieve the optimization. Therefore, it is a feasible idea to optimize Swin Transformer through software and hardware cooperation.

3 Related Works

In order to solve the problem that the self-attention mechanism will lead to huge resource consumption, there are many designs on the hardware and software coordination of Transformer, one of the major direction is to improve the software level of the self-attention mechanism. LSRA [15] proposed a model structure combining convolution and self-attention mechanism, pointed out the bottleneck of expression ability in multi-head Attention. CSwin Transformer [16] proposed the cross-window self-attention mechanism, which splits the multi-head into two parts, one for horizontal stripe self-attention and the other for vertical stripe self-attention. Paper [17] introduced the self-attention mechanism to the relative position representation between elements, but the effect of hard position coding and this method is not compared in the paper. Efficient attention [18] adjusted the multiplication order of query, key and value of non-local attention, no longer calculates the correlation between each pixel. Paper [19] introduced a linear mapping between multiple attentions before and after the softmax operation as a way to increase the information exchange between multiple attention mechanisms.

There are also some hardware co-designs based on the improvement of the self-attention mechanism at the software level, but there are much fewer optimizations compared to the software level, among which A^3 [11] is one of the better designs, A^3 proposed a special hardware accelerator, which aims to use the attention mechanism in the neural network of approximate potential energy, and A^3 applied the hardware and software co-design to accelerate. NPE [20] proposed an overlay processor NPE based on FPGA. The design based on FPGA can efficiently execute various NLP models, and can be upgraded for future NLP models without re-designing the hardware architecture. OPTIMUS [21] proposed to skip redundant calculations in decoder. [22] provided an efficient method to partition the huge matrix in Transformer and designs it in hardware for Scaled

Masked-Softmax. FTRANS [23] proposed an efficient acceleration framework, Ftrans, for a large-scale linguistic representation based on BERT [24], using block-loop matrices instead of selected weights, effectively reducing the model size but requiring additional FFT processing kernels.

In general, the problem of how to effectively optimize Transformer applications on FPGAs is still not completely solved, and there is still a lot of room for research on hardware and software co-design for the Transformer model, especially the self-attention mechanism.

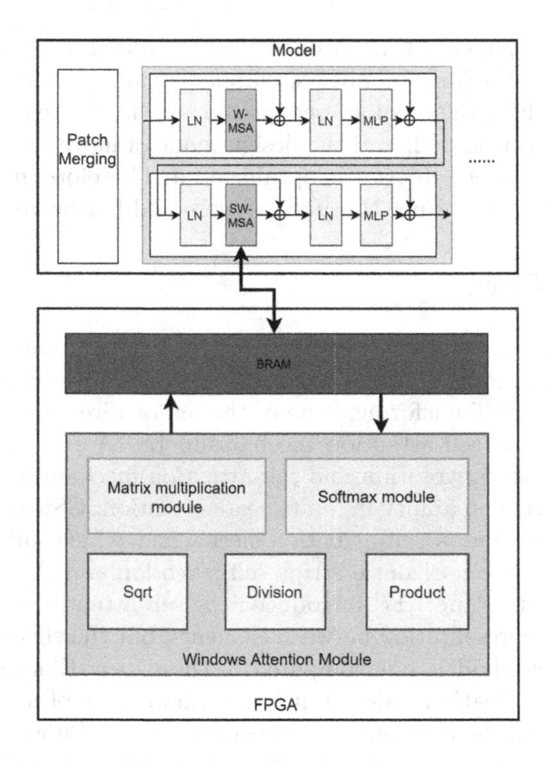

Fig. 2. Overall architecture.

4 Optimization

4.1 Overall Architecture

In this paper, we analyze and design the Windows Attention in the Swin Transformer model, the overall architecture is shown in Fig. 2, the main work is to optimize the Windows Attention module in the model Swin Transformer block algorithmically and design the corresponding hardware module. Since the operation types of W-MSA and SW-MSA are the same, we first decompose them into different computational primitives, including a large number of matrix multiplications of different sizes and Softmax functions, so the designed Windows Attention module is generalizable for the two types of Windows Attention.

The hardware optimization is mainly in the matrix multiplication module and Softmax module, other operations including Sqrt, Division, Product, etc. are parallelized, temporary data are stored using lookup tables, and the exchange of data between matrices is performed by BRAM. The following section describes the Windows Attention module and its matrix multiplication module and Softmax module in detail.

4.2 Windows Attention Module

The Windows Attention module directly calls the matrix multiplication module and the Softmax function module. The matrix multiplication module functions as a parallel matrix operation, and its structure is shown in Fig. 3, which can be used in all areas of the model that require matrix operations. The idea of W-MSA is to calculate attention under each window. The difference between W-MSA and SW-MSA is that a Mask matrix needs to be added in the calculation process of SW-MSA. The mask matrix, like the relative position coding matrix, can be calculated and stored in BRAM in advance, which saves the calculation time of the whole process

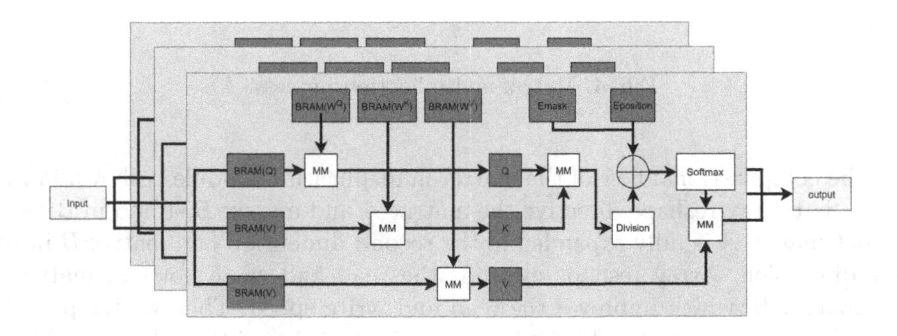

Fig. 3. Windows attention module.

The input is taken from the BRAM and then multiplied with a set of weight matrices W^Q, W^K and W^V stored on the BRAM and then the intermediate results QW^Q, KW^K and VW^V are stored in the buffers. Next, we matrix multiply the values of the W buffer stored in the Q buffer, then add the mask matrix and the relative position encoding matrix, the sum of this matrix is loaded into the Softmax module and finally multiplied with VW^V to get the final result.

4.3 Matrix Multiplication Module

Matrix multiplication is the most used operation in Windows Attention. Matrix multiplication is a binary operation in which two matrices are calculated to result in a new matrix. Matrix multiplication itself is a linear operation that uses the vectors that make up the matrix. The most common matrix multiplication is called matrix product. When matrix A dimension is $N \times M$ and matrix B dimension is $M \times P$, then the matrix product AB is an $N \times P$ dimensional matrix. The outermost for loop, labeled row and col, iterates through the rows and columns of the data matrix AB. The innermost for loop computes the dot product operations for one row of vector A and one column of vector B. The result of each dot product operation through one column is an element of the matrix AB position. This is designed to operate in parallel on the hardware design and eliminate data dependencies that hinder flowing operations.

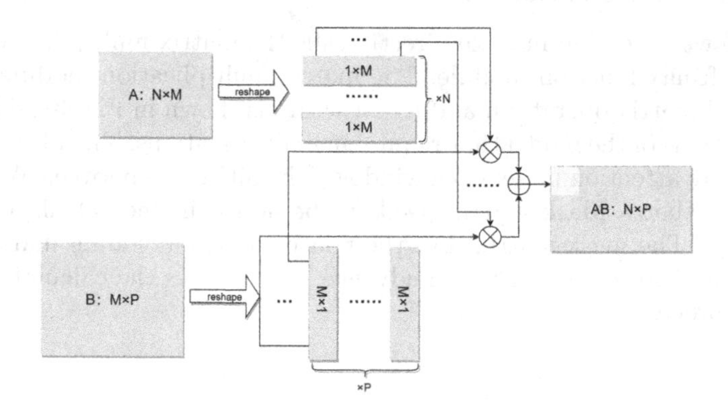

Fig. 4. Matrix multiplication process.

The computational flow of the matrix multiplication module is shown in Fig. 4. We first array reshape directive the matrix A and matrix B stored in BRAM, so that matrix A is fully expanded in the second dimension and matrix B in the first dimension. Array reshape expands the read and write ports of matrix A and matrix B, which improves the read and write speed. Then we temporarily store the results of the third layer loop in register AB, and then the second layer loop reads the temporarily stored results, which saves storage resources. We use a pipeline directive for each layer of the loop and set the desired task interval to 1. Thus, each layer of the for loop is fully expanded, and our design performs approximately M multiply-accumulate operations and the execution interval is $N \times P$ clock cycles, and the entire loop structure is fully pipelined.

4.4 Softmax Module

The Softmax function, also known as the normalized exponential function, is a generalization of the binary classification function sigmoid on multiclassification, which aims to present the results of multiclassification in the form of probabilities. Softmax function formula as in Eq. 3, it can be seen that the main operation of the Softmax function is the exp function.

$$p(y|x) = \frac{exp(W_y.x)}{\sum_{c=1}^{C} exp(W_c.x)} \quad (3)$$

Because the exp function consumes huge computational resources in the computational operation of the hardware platform, the result of the Taylor expansion of the exp function is equivalent to the exp function under the premise of using fixed points. The function formula is shown in Eq. 4.

$$exp(x) = \sum_{k=0}^{n} \frac{x^k}{k!}, x > 0 \quad (4)$$

The function image is shown in Fig. 5. We compare the images of the exp function and the functions of different orders of Taylor expansions, and we can see that the value of x is between 0 and 1 Between the exp function curve and the 16th-stage Taylor expansion curve is completely overlapping, so we use the exp function near 0 of the Taylor expansion to replace the exp function. In order to improve the accuracy of the calculation, the expanded formula uses the 16th-stage Taylor expansion of the exp function, and the time complexity drops significantly.

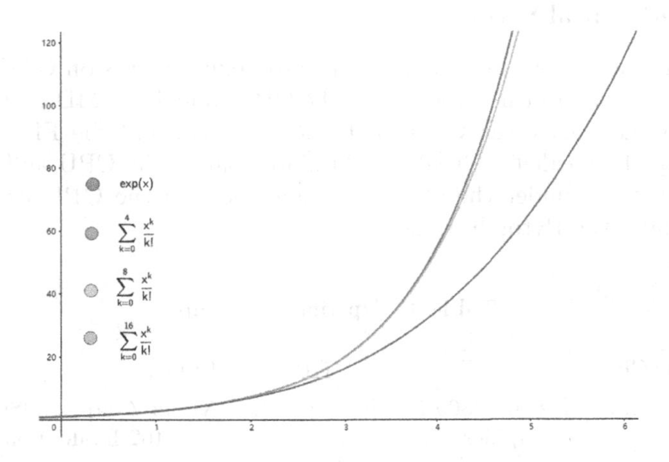

Fig. 5. Exp Taylor expansion function curve.

The Softmax module is shown in Fig. 6. To ensure the correctness of the calculation results, the Softmax module first traverses the input data stream, stores the maximum value (max) in the lookup table, and then divides all values by this maximum value so that all positive values in the matrix range between 0 and 1. In order to eliminate the influence of negative values in the mask matrix on the result, the Taylor-exp function will judge the input value, if it is a positive value will be substituted into the Taylor display formula for the operation, otherwise it will skip the calculation process of negative values and set the result to 0. This ensures the accuracy of the data and saves computational resources at the same time.

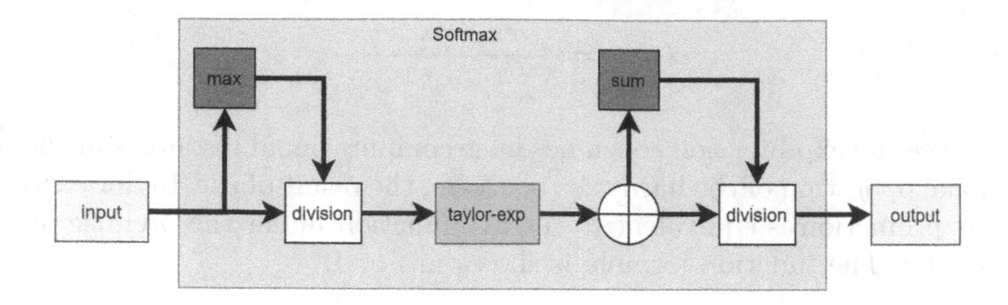

Fig. 6. Softmax module.

We used 8-bit ap_fixed to participate in the calculation. The calculation result (sum) of each round was stored in the lookup table by the accumulator, and then the result was taken out from the lookup table and then the final result was obtained by division operation. Finally, Softmax module realized the pipeline operation with II as 1 and depth as 7.

5 Experiment and Result

5.1 Experimental Setup

As shown in Table 1, we have done comparison experiments on GPU, CPU and FPGA respectively. In this experiment, the CPU model is AMD Ryzen 7 4800H with Radeon Graphics, the GPU model is Tesla T4, and the FPGA model is Xilinx Zynq UtralScale+ ZCU102 Evaluation Board. The CPU and FPGA use the code structure under the C++14 framework, and the GPU uses the code structure under the Pytorch framework.

Table 1. Experimental setup

Platform	CPU	GPU	FPGA
Model	AMD Ryzen 7 4800H with Radeon Graphics	Tesla T4	Xilinx Zynq UtralScale+ ZCU102 Evaluation Board
Code	C++14	Pytorch	C++14
Clock	-	-	10ns

5.2 Resource Consumption and Latency

We compared the resource consumption used by each module on the parameters BRAM, LUT, FF, and DSP. The baseline is based on the experimental data obtained before optimization. the experimental results are shown in Table 2. Among them, the matrix multiplication module shows a 16% reduction in resource consumption on the LUT comparison, and a decrease in resource consumption on the FF comparison. The reduction in resource usage of the Softmax module is significant due to the absence of the exp function. The Softmax module has a 93% reduction in resource consumption on the DSP comparison, a 92% reduction on the LUT comparison, and a reduction in resource consumption on the FF comparison. The Windows Attention module saw a 27% reduction in overall DSP usage, a 37% reduction in resource consumption on the LUT comparison, and a reduction in resource consumption on both the FF and BRAM comparisons.

Table 2. Resource consumption

Instance	Module	Batch	LUT	FF	DSP	BRAM
Baseline	MM	64	708	457	3	0
	Softmax	64	69519	9049	16	0
	Attention	64	100055	33026	90	930
Ours	MM	64	597	453	3	0
	Softmax	64	4333	153	1	0
	Attention	64	63268	29464	66	837

We compared the runtime of each hardware module and the overall runtime on each platform, and the experimental results are shown in Table 3. In particular, after replacing the exp function with Taylor-exp, the Softmax module improves 25× in runtime and the overall runtime of the Windows Attention module is reduced by 60% compared to the pre-optimization period. The experimental results are shown in Fig. 7. As the batch size increases linearly, the utilization of DSP, FF, and LUT does not increase with the increase of batch size, although the latency of the whole Windows Attention module also increases linearly.

Table 3. Latency

Instance	Module	Batch	Inference time (ms)
Baseline	MM	64	0.09418
	Softmax	64	2.35218
	Attention	64	14.86620
Ours	MM	64	0.09413
	Softmax	64	0.09414
	Attention	64	5.83450

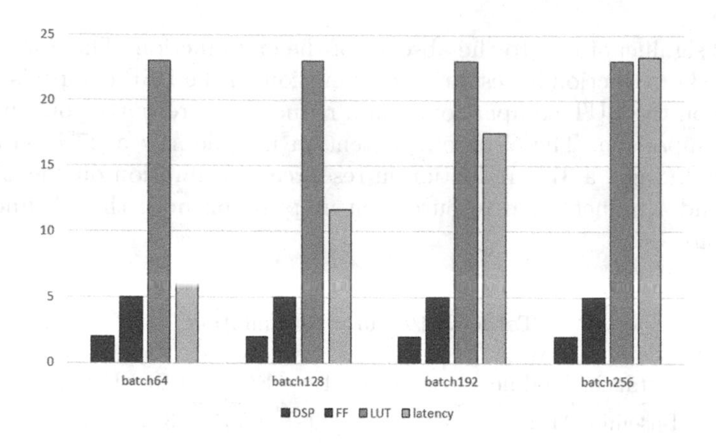

Fig. 7. Comparison of batch resources.

5.3 Multi-platform Comparison

We have done comparison experiments on GPU, CPU and FPGA platforms respectively, and the experimental results are shown in Table 4, comparing parameters such as Throughput, Relative Speedup, and Throughput per DSP. the final hardware experimental results show that our pipelined operation on FPGA increases parallelism. Compared to the CPU implementation, our design results in a 7.73× improvement in throughput due to the high operating frequency of the CPU and its high-speed main memory, and only a 1.21× improvement in throughput compared to the GPU, which specializes in floating-point and parallel computing, where the Throughput per DSP aspect also improves by 3.48× compared to the pre-optimization. the results prove that our The results prove that our design has significant advantages in terms of latency and resource utilization.

Table 4. Multi-platform comparison

	CPU	GPU	Baseline	Ours
Throughput (Gops)	9.75	62.66	29.50	75.17
Relative Speedup	0.33×	2.12×	1×	2.55×
Throughput per DSP	-	-	0.747	2.537

6 Conclusion

In this paper, we performed hardware-software co-design for two types of Windows Attention based on the Swin Transformer model, and we focused on Softmax function and matrix multiplication. The experimental results shown that our hardware-software co-design reduces resource consumption and achieves high parallelization, and outperforms CPU and GPU in terms of throughput and running speed.

References

1. Vaswani, A., Shazeer, N., Parmar, N., et al.: Attention is all you need. In: Advances in Neural Information Processing Systems, pp. 5998–6008 (2017)
2. Qiu, M., Guo, M., Liu, M., et al.: Loop scheduling and bank type assignment for heterogeneous multi-bank memory. J. Parallel Distrib. Comput. **69**(6), 546–558 (2009)
3. Qiu, M., Chen, Z., Niu, J., et al.: Data allocation for hybrid memory with genetic algorithm. IEEE Trans. Emer. Topics Comput. **3**(4), 544–555 (2015)
4. Qiu, M., Xue, C., Shao, Z., Sha, E.: Energy minimization with soft real-time and DVS for uniprocessor and multiprocessor embedded systems. In:2007 Design, Automation & Test in Europe Conference & Exhibition, pp. 1–6 (2007)
5. Qiu, M., Xue, C., Shao, Z., et al.: Efficient algorithm of energy minimization for heterogeneous wireless sensor network. IEEE Conference on Embedded and Ubiquitous Computing, pp. 25–34 (2006)
6. Qiu, M., Liu, J., Li, J., et al.: A novel energy-aware fault tolerance mechanism for wireless sensor networks. IEEE/ACM Conference on Galaxy Community Conference (2011)
7. Wang, J., Qiu, M., Guo, B.: Enabling real-time information service on telehealth system over cloud-based big data platform. J. Syst. Architect. **72**, 69–79 (2017)
8. Li, J., Qiu, M., et al.: Thermal-aware task scheduling in 3D chip multiprocessor with real-time constrained workloads. ACM Trans. Embed. Comput. Syst. **12**(2), 1–22 (2013)
9. Qiu, M., Li, H., Sha, E.:Heterogeneous real-time embedded software optimization considering hardware platform. In: Proceedings of the 2009 ACM Symposium on Applied Computing, pp. 1637–1641 (2009)
10. Qiu, M., Sha, E., et al.: Energy minimization with loop fusion and multi-functional-unit scheduling for multidimensional DSP. J. Parallel Distrib. Comput. **68**(4), 443–455 (2008)
11. Ham, T.J., Jung, S.J., Kim, S., et al.: A^3: accelerating attention mechanisms in neural networks with approximation. In: IEEE HPCA, pp. 328–341 (2020)
12. Tay, Y., Dehghani, M., Bahri, D., et al.: Efficient transformers: a survey. arXiv preprint arXiv:2009.06732 (2020)
13. Liu, Z., Lin, Y., Cao, Y., et al.: Swin transformer: hierarchical vision Transformer using shifted Windows. arXiv preprint arXiv:2103.14030 (2021)
14. Zhang, X., Wu, Y., Zhou, P., et al.: Algorithm-hardware co-design of attention mechanism on FPGA devices. ACM Trans. Embed. Comput. Syst. **20**(5s), 1–24 (2021)
15. Wu, Z., Liu, Z., Lin, J., et al.: Lite transformer with long-short range attention. arXiv preprint arXiv:2004.11886 (2020)
16. Dong, X., Bao, J., Chen, D., et al.: CSwin transformer: a general vision transformer backbone with cross-shaped windows. arXiv preprint arXiv:2107.00652 (2021)
17. Shaw, P., Uszkoreit, J., Vaswani, A.: Self-attention with relative position representations. arXiv preprint arXiv:1803.02155 (2018)

18. Shen, Z., Zhang, M., Zhao, H., et al.: Efficient attention: attention with linear complexities. In: IEEE/CVF International Conference on Computer Vision, pp. 3531–3539 (2021)
19. Shazeer, N., Lan, Z., Cheng, Y., et al.: Talking-heads attention. arXiv preprint arXiv:2003.02436 (2020)
20. Khan, H., Khan, A., Khan, Z., et al.: NPE: an FPGA-based overlay processor for natural language processing. arXiv preprint arXiv:2104.06535 (2021)
21. Park, J., Yoon, H., Ahn, D., et al.: OPTIMUS: OPTImized matrix MUltiplication structure for transformer neural network accelerator. Proc. Mach. Learn. Syst. 2, 363–378 (2020)
22. Lu, S., Wang, M., Liang, S., et al.: Hardware accelerator for multi-head attention and position-wise feed-forward in the transformer. In: SOCC2020 (2020)
23. Li, B., Pandey, S., Fang, H., et al.: Ftrans: energy-efficient acceleration of Transformers using FPGA. In: ACM/IEEE International Symposium on Low Power Electronics and Design, pp. 175–180 (2021)
24. Devlin, J., Chang, M.W., Lee, K., et al.: BERT: pre-training of deep bidirectional transformers for language understanding. arXiv preprint arXiv:1810.04805 (2018)

SSA: A Content-Based Sparse Attention Mechanism

Yang Sun[1,3], Wei Hu[1,3](✉), Fang Liu[2,4], Feihu Huang[1,3], and Yonghao Wang[5]

[1] Wuhan University of Science and Technology, Wuhan, China
{202013704135,huwei,huangfeihu}@wust.edu.cn
[2] Wuhan University, Wuhan, China
liufangfang@whu.edu.cn
[3] Hubei Province Key Laboratory of Intelligent Information Processing and Real-Time Industrial System, Wuhan, China
[4] Department of Information Engineering, Wuhan Institute of City, Wuhan, China
[5] DMT Lab, Birmingham City University, Birmingham, UK
yonghao.wang@bcu.ac.uk

Abstract. Recently, many scholars have used attention mechanisms to achieve excellent performance results on various neural network applications. However, the attention mechanism also has shortcomings. Firstly, the high computational and storage consumption makes the attention mechanism difficult to apply on long sequences. Second, all tokens are involved in the computation of the attention map, which may increase the influence of noisy tokens on the results and lead to poor training results. Due to these two shortcomings, attention models are usually strictly limited to sequence length. Further, attention models have difficulty in exploiting their excellent properties for modelling long sequences. To solve the above problems, an efficient sparse attention mechanism (SSA) is proposed in this paper. SSA is based on two separate layers: the local layer and the global layer. These two layers jointly encode local sequence information and global context. This new sparse-attention patterns is powerful in accelerating reasoning. The experiments in this paper validate the effectiveness of the SSA mechanism by replacing the self-attentive structure with an SSA structure in a variety of transformer models. The SSA attention mechanism has achieved state-of-the-art performance on several major benchmarks. SSA was validated on a variety of datasets and models encompassing language translation, language modelling and image recognition. With a small improvement in accuracy, the inference calculation speed was increased by 24%.

Keywords: Transformers · Sequence · Local attention · Global attention · Sparsity

1 Introduction

The attention mechanism is widely used in sequence modelling [13]. Initially validated only on machine translation, attention mechanisms have now been

G. Memmi et al. (Eds.): KSEM 2022, LNAI 13370, pp. 669–680, 2022.
https://doi.org/10.1007/978-3-031-10989-8_53

widely used in natural language processing and computer vision [12]. In recent years, state-of-the-art neural networks have also been implemented by attention mechanisms, such as Transformer-XL [3], bert [5].

Self-attention is one of the classical attention mechanisms. The self-attention processes the input sequence sequentially. At each time step, attention is assigned weights to the preceding elements, and these weights are summed as the attention weights of the current element. The process of assigning weights is called connection building. The excellent performance of the attention mechanism is due to the fact that it maintains more connections than CNN and RNN, and these connections are able to capture more feature information in the data. However, too many connections also make the complexity higher than CNNs and RNNs. Specifically, on a sequence of length n, weights need to be assigned to the sequence data of length i for each position $i < n$. The complexity of attention is $\frac{n(n-1)}{2}$. The square level of complexity limits the performance of the attention model to the length of the sequence. As computing devices such as GPUs have been updated, the sequence length limit for attention models has been increased to 512 tokens. Nonetheless, the overly complex models lead to an attention mechanism that is particularly difficult to handle for large sequence modelling. This clearly does not satisfy most application scenarios. Long sequences are the trend in sequence modelling, including document-level machine translation, high-resolution image recognition, speech, video generation, etc. At the same time the attention mechanism has a second drawback, it has the potential to reduce the noise resistance of the model [2]. If the input sequence contains noisy tokens, the noisy tokens will be involved in too much of the computation process, which will lead to impaired model performance.

In the self-attention model, each element pays attention to the other elements. However, the training results show that most of the attention matrix elements are small, which indicates that these tokens do not have a significant impact on the model results, but they are still heavily involved in the attention calculation process, which leads to wasted computational and storage resources. These non-essential attention calculations can be removed to optimise model complexity and reduce the impact of noise on model accuracy. This optimised model is known as a sparse attention model.

Many optimisation schemes of the sparse attention mechanism have been proposed. However, each element of the local attention model will only focus on other elements at a fixed location and cannot flexibly encode remote dependencies. An alternative to local attention is context-based sparse attention, which enables more flexible encoding of distant dependencies. Scholars limit the number of connections per element by analysing the context, an approach known as content-based sparse attention [14]. The process of assigning a connection to each element is called constructing a sparsity pattern. Developers can define their own suitable sparsity patterns depending on the deep learning task and dataset. As a result, content-based sparse attention is more flexible than local attention. Previous work has demonstrated that sparsity patterns can have a significant impact on model performance.

This paper proposes a sparsity pattern that can flexibly encode local information and global dependencies. And Sparse Spectral Attention (SSA) is implemented based on this sparsity pattern. The SSA mechanism has the following features: (1) the SSA mechanism maintains the ability to aggregate local information and long-distance dependent information, (2) the SSA model is less complex than the attention model, and (3) the SSA model reduces the impact of noisy data on the model and improves the model's resistance to interference. SSA combines the advantages of both local attention and content-based sparse attention and achieves good performance in several sequence modelling tasks.

The contributions of this article are:

- We propose a sparse attention mechanism to replace the original self-attention mechanism. SSA can encode global features and local information, and reduce model complexity.
- We have analysed some recent works on sparse attention and compared them with SSA.
- We have replaced self-attention with SSA in the official codes of several state-of-the-art transformer models, involving machine translation, image recognition (Ciar10, Cifar100, ImageNet-64) and language modelling (enwik8). Experimental results and analysis are proposed.

2 Related Works

With the rapid advances in computer hardware [11,26,27] and network infrastructure [13,15,25], big data [23,24,34] and machine learning [9,17,19] have been successfully applied in various areas, such as finance [4,22], tele-health [18,21,31], and transportation [16,20]. One of the most successful areas is nature processing language. In recent years, many optimisations [10] have been proposed to improve the computational efficiency of attention models. Local attention and content-based sparse attention are the dominant research directions. The core idea is to limit the number of connections. Figure 1a shows the connections constructed by the attention model in the language sequence. Each edge represents a connection. It is clear to see that the attention model needs to maintain a square level number of connections for sequences of length n. Not all of these connections are necessary.

In contrast, sparse attention, as shown in Fig. 1b, removes most of the connections and the necessary ones are retained. Recent achievements on local attention include [1,35,37], etc. The above achievements are all local attention models based on fixed positions. At each time step, local attention sequentially divides the sequence into multiple shorter sequences and then creates connections in each of the multiple shorter sequences. This strategy allows the model to extract features based on the local neighborhoods of the current time step. The non-zero elements of the attention matrix are concentrated on the diagonal, so that only the non-zero elements need to be stored structurally to achieve significant savings in computational and memory overhead. Despite the good results achieved with local attention, local attention cannot encode remote dependence.

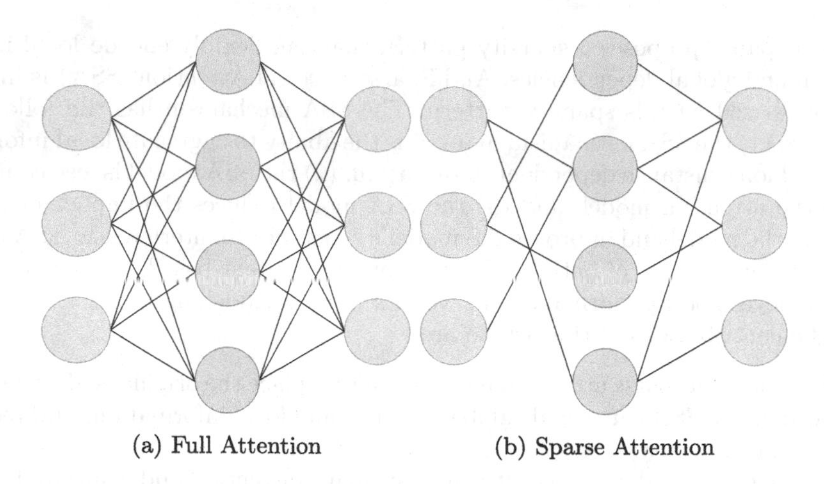

Fig. 1. The connections in attention mechanisms

Content-based sparse attention is a more flexible attention mechanism. While local attention and strided attention are fixed sparsity patterns, the sparsity patterns of content-based sparse attention are learned in neural networks. Reformer [7] proposed *location-sensitive hashing* (LSH) to infer attentional sparsity patterns. Reformer linearly projects tokens onto a random hyperplane and assigns them to different hash buckets. Tokens that fall into the same hash bucket can get to attend to each other. Similar work includes Cluster-Former [32], Fastformer [33] and Sparse sinkhorn attention [29]. Each of these results defines a different sparsity pattern to limit the number of connections for attention. However, it is often necessary to instantiate the full attention matrix for sparsification before a content-based sparse model can be built. These sparse attentions also lead to high storage consumption. The Routing transformer [28] explores sparse attention based on K-means clustering. Compared to other models, Routing transformer does not need to maintain an attention matrix larger than the batch size at all times to complete the clustering assignment. This reduces storage consumption while reducing computational consumption.

Our work combines the advantages of both local attention and content-based sparse attention as described above. Our work adds two separate sub-layers to the attention model, which encode local information and global context respectively, and subsumes the dependency information from the two sub-layers for attention.

3 Sparse Spectral Attention

The proposed framework relies on two transformer layers: (1) the local layer and (2) the global layer. The overall structure of the model is shown in Fig. 2, and our work is focused before Dot Product Attention. The former uses an dilated sliding window to encode local sequence information, while the latter encodes the global context through attention map pruning.

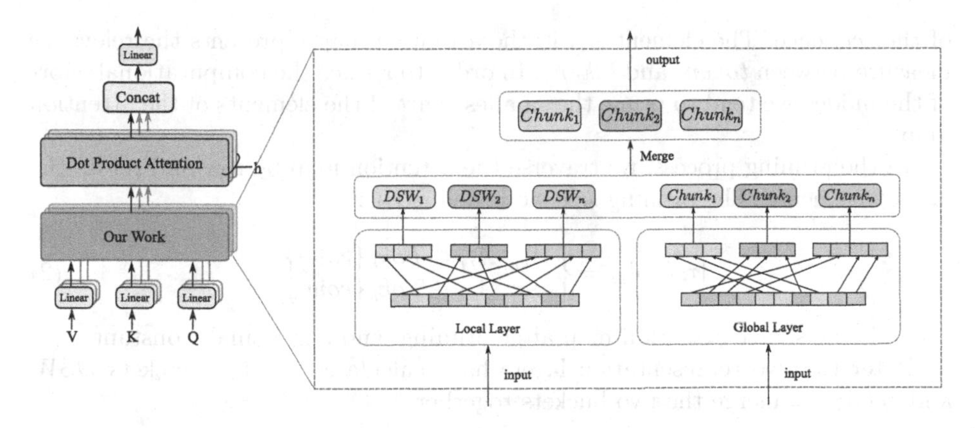

Fig. 2. The overall structure of SSA.

3.1 Local Layer

The core of the local layer is an dilated sliding window that focuses on encoding local sequence information. Although our model intends to capture global contextual dependencies, local sequence information also plays an important role [6]. As shown in Fig. 2, the Local layer consists of the dilated sliding window layer, which has a larger perceptual space than the standard sliding window. Dilated sliding window divides a long sequence X of length n into overlapping windows of size w and step size m. The sliding sequence DW_k^i for each time step can be expressed as

$$DW_k^i = x_i \left[m \times k : (m \times k + w) \times d : d\right] \tag{1}$$

while $[index_1 : index_2 : step]$ indicates the selection row from the order of the input matrix between rows $index_1$ and $index_2$. Unlike standard sliding windows, dilated sliding windows have gaps of size dilation d. This gap allows the Dilated Sliding Window layer to increase the receptive field without increasing complexity. In two models with the same number of layers, the receptive field based on the dilated sliding windows is expanded by d times.

3.2 Global Layer

The global layer implements a sparsity pattern based on structured pruning, which focuses on encoding global contextual information. The structure is shown in Fig. 2. We first chunk the sequence and construct a sparse attention matrix. The core process has two steps: 1) partition the attentional similarity graph into multiple subgraphs based on the undirected graph cut algorithm. 2) for each query, the set of keys found in the same subgraph is defined as S_i.

The Global Layer input consists of a matrix Q consisting of $query_i$ vectors and a matrix K consisting of key_i vectors. The adjacency matrix of the attention map is denoted as $A = QK^T$, where A is an $N \times N$ matrix and N is the length of the sequence. The element A_{ij} in the attention map represents the relevance measure between $token_i$ and $token_j$. In order to reduce the computational effort of the model, we tend to prune the smallest part of the elements of the attention map.

In the pruning process, we traverse the attention map by row and retain the largest elements. The pruning scheme is defined as:

$$[\tau_k(A)]_{ij} = \begin{cases} A_{ij} & A_{ij} \in Tok_k\{row_j\} \\ c & A_{ij} \notin Tok_k\{row_j\} \end{cases} \tag{2}$$

$\tau_k(A)$ is the sparse attention map after pruning, and c is a small constant.

After the two representation layers have calculated the two buckets DSW and $\tau_k(A)$, we merge the two buckets together.

$$\chi(A) = DSW \cup \tau_k(A) \tag{3}$$

Ultimately, the procedure for the local and global layers can be formulated as:

$$\hat{V} = softmax(\chi(\frac{QK^T}{\sqrt{d}})) \cdot V \tag{4}$$

The different approach of our proposed model to other models dealing with long sequences is shown in Fig. 3.

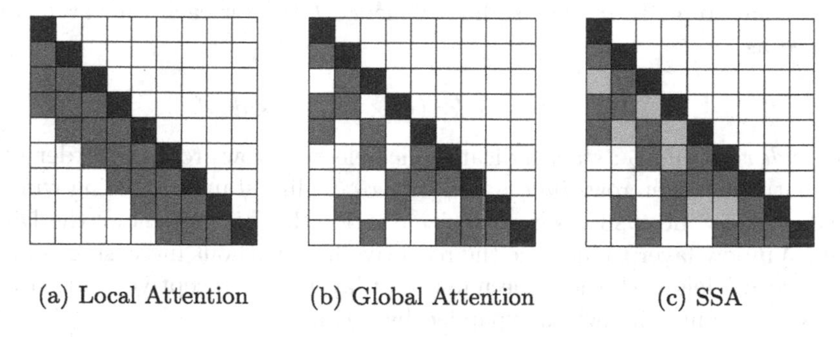

(a) Local Attention (b) Global Attention (c) SSA

Fig. 3. Each square represents a hidden state. Local attention is shown in (a). Local attention is built by a sliding window (red square) with cross-sequential attention. Content-based sparse attention is shown in (b), where attention is built through global contextual information. (c) is our proposed method to process both local and global information by subsuming the hidden states of (a) and (c). The yellow boxes in c are from the local layer and the red boxes are from the global layer. (Color figure online)

3.3 Analysis of Sparsity Patterns

Table 1 analyses the modelling complexity of the different sparsity patterns. Papers [1,14] have the lowest sparsity pattern construction complexity, and their complexity in maintaining a sliding window to select neighbouring data on the sequence is linear. Similarly Reformer [7], Star transformer [37] have lower complexity. Although they are content-based sparse attention and the sparsity pattern is different from local attention, their computational overhead is not significant. Strided attention [38] is a square level of complexity, as they need to traverse the attention map to determine whether dependencies are to be retained. This scheme is commonly used in sparse attention models based on clustering, which increases the complexity but allows for more accurate accuracy. As a comparison, our proposed model incorporates two representation layers that can operate independently. These two representation layers encode local and global information separately, and the complexity of our Local layer is linear, and the complexity of our Global layer is $O(l^{1.5})$. This indicates that our Local layer has similar time complexity to other content-independent sparsity patterns, and our Global layer can be constructed more quickly than other content-based sparsity patterns.

Table 1. Complexity of sparse attention construction

Schemes	Sparsity patterns	Complexity
Local attention	Sliding window	$O(n)$
Strided attention	SortCut	$O(n^2)$
Routing transformer	K-means	$O(n^{1.5})$
Reformer	LSH	$O(n)$
Star transformer	Star-shaped topology	$O(n)$
Longformer	Sliding window	$O(n)$
Sparse sinkhorn attention	SortCut	$O(n)$
Ours-local layer	Sliding window	$O(n)$
Ours-global layer	Purning	$O(l^{1.5})$

4 Experiments

In this section, we replace the dense attention of the existing official transformer code with SSA to validate the model effects. The experiments involve machine translation, language modelling and image recognition. Ablation studies are also provided.

4.1 Experimental Settings

We experiment on different models and datasets. For natural language processing, two sets of experiments were designed. The first experiment was German-English machine translation with a dataset using Multi30k, which is a smaller dataset containing 145000 training, 5070 development and 5000 test. The second experiment is language modelling with a cropped dataset of enwik8. The complete enwik8 dataset is a dataset of the first 100 million characters dumped from Wikipedia XML. We also conducted experiments for image sequences. We performed image recognition on the cifar10, cifar100 and ImageNet datasets. Cifar10 and cifar100 are labelled subsets of the 80 million micro-image dataset. Cifar10 contains 10 categories of 128×128 colour images with 50,000 training images and 10,000 test images. Similarly, cifar100 has more categories and numbers of colour images, with 500 training images and 100 test images per category. All images for this experiment were cropped to 224×224. We explored the effect of different crop ratios on the model in the ablation experiment. Since SSA degenerates to local attention for $r = 1$, the experiments were all set to $r \leq 0.8$.

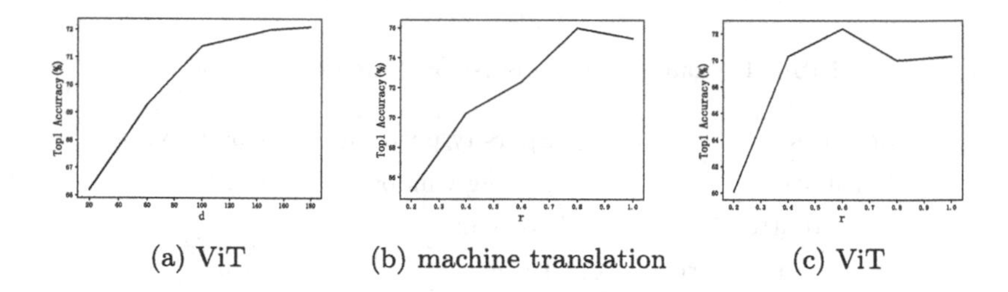

(a) ViT (b) machine translation (c) ViT

Fig. 4. The impact of hyperparameters

4.2 Accuracy Results

We first explored the impact of SSA on the accuracy of the model. These effects were generally positive. We explored the accuracy performance of SSA in different models. Table 2 shows the results of the German-English machine translation. The training set, validator, and test set used for each version of the experiment are the same. As can be seen from Table 2, SSA can achieve better accuracy results than the baseline model. When the parameter r was set to 0.8, the BLEU of the SSA has improved to 33.08. When r was set to 0.5, each tokens attended to too little information for training, and eventually the PPL rose to 7.724 and the BLEU fell to 30.97. We suspect that this is due to the size of the Multi30k dataset. Each tokens in a short sequence is full of feature information and setting a small pruning ratio will lose model accuracy. As a comparison, Table 3 shows the results of language modelling on a longer sequence dataset, enwik8.

Table 2. Results of German-English machine translation experiments.

Arch	Sparse ratio r	PPL	BLEU
VAG-NMT	–	–	31.6
Transformer	–	6.949	30.97
Transformer (SSA)	0.5	7.724	25.13
Transformer (SSA)	0.8	5.671	33.08

Table 3. Results of enwik8 language modelling experiments.

Arch	Sparse ratio r	BPC
LSTM	–	1.203
Transformer	–	1.18
Transformer (SSA)	0.5	1.08
Transformer (SSA)	0.8	1.03

Table 4. Results of image recognition experiments.

Arch	Top-1 Acc
ViT-Cifar10	81.1%
ViT-SSA-Cifar10	81.7%
ViT-Cifar100	83.3%
ViT-SSA-Cifar100	83.7%
T2TViT-ImageNet	82.4%
T2TViT-SSA-ImageNet	82.5%

Our work achieves 1.03 BPC and the results demonstrate that the sparse layer of SSA achieves higher accuracy metrics for models on long sequence datasets.

Table 4 explores the ablation experiments of SSA on image recognition. We replaced the official code of ViT, T2T and replaced the core attention mechanism with SSA. SSA achieved 81.7% accuracy on ViT-Cifar10, 83.3% accuracy on ViT-Cifar100, and 82.5% accuracy on T2T-ImageNet.

4.3 The Impact of Hyperparameters

SSA has two important hyperparameters. One is the sliding window size d. Its effect is shown in Fig. 4a. The sliding window size is tended to be set larger to achieve higher accuracy. But a longer size means more calculations, so the parameters need to balance accuracy with speed of calculation. The other is the pruning ratio $r = k/n$ of the global layer its effect is shown in Fig. 4b and Fig. 4c. Different models should be assigned different r values. For a total number of tokens $n > 512$, we tend to set a slightly smaller r value, with r between 0.4

and 0.5 giving better accuracy results. For $n < 512$, the pruning ratio should not be too small, 0.7–0.8 is appropriate. Further, the results demonstrate that r is influenced by the way tokens are generated. Simple token generation methods, such as vanilla attention [30], ViT [8], embedding sequences directly into tokens, where no information is exchanged between tokens. These models should be set to a smaller pruning ratio. However, complex token generation methods [36] should be set to a larger pruning ratio.

4.4 Speed Results

We evaluate the performance of the acceleration by comparing two versions of the ViT-SSA inference task (with/without sparse matrix multiplication) running on CPU and GPU platforms. The computing platform for the comparison test was a Xeon E5 CPU and a GTX 2080ti. ViT-SSA refers to the Vision transformer which uses the SSA mechanism to replace self-attention. We designed two versions of the experiment, in one version we used dense matrix multiplication for the calculations and the other version used sparse matrix multiplication, and Table 5 presents the average inference time results for each version over multiple experiments.

Compared to the baseline, ViT-SSA-dense does not take full advantage of the sparse matrix of SSA and the inference speed is not significantly improved. In contrast, ViT-SSA-sparse with sparse matrix computation improved inference speed on CPU by 43% and on GPU by 24% over baseline.

Table 5. Inference speed results.

Device	Version	Time (ms)
Xeon CPU	ViT-dense	2900
Xeon CPU	ViT-sparse	187
Xeon CPU	ViT-SSA-dense	2832
Xeon CPU	ViT-SSA-sparse	106
GTX 2080ti	ViT-dense	61
GTX 2080ti	ViT-sparse	49
GTX 2080ti	ViT-SSA-dense	58
GTX 2080ti	ViT-SSA-sparse	37

5 Conclusion

The experiments are compared in two domains, natural language processing and computer vision, and we give a review of SSA's models for machine translation, language modelling, and image recognition tasks. We replace the original self-attention mechanism with the SSA attention mechanism on a variety of transformer models. The results show that our model is able to achieve more advanced performance on several major benchmarks. One of the more significant performance improvements on the accuracy benchmark is V2T-cifar10, with a 0.6% improvement in top1 Accuracy.

References

1. Beltagy, I., Peters, M.E., Cohan, A.: Longformer: the long-document transformer. arXiv preprint arXiv:2004.05150 (2020)
2. Cordonnier, J.B., Loukas, A., Jaggi, M.: On the relationship between self-attention and convolutional layers. arXiv preprint arXiv:1911.03584 (2019)
3. Dai, Z., et al.: Transformer-XL: language modeling with longer-term dependency (2018)
4. Gai, K., Du, Z., et al.: Efficiency-aware workload optimizations of heterogeneous cloud computing for capacity planning in financial industry. In: IEEE 2nd CSCloud (2015)
5. Devlin, J., Chang, M.-W., Lee, K., Toutanova, K.: BERT: pre-training of deep bidirectional transformers for language understanding. In: Proceedings of NAACL-HLT, pp. 4171–4186 (2019)
6. Khan, S., Naseer, M., Hayat, M., Zamir, S.W., Khan, F.S., Shah, M.: Transformers in vision: a survey. ACM Comput. Surv. (CSUR) (2021)
7. Kitaev, N., Kaiser, Ł., Levskaya, A.: Reformer: the efficient transformer. arXiv preprint arXiv:2001.04451 (2020)
8. Kolesnikov, A., et al.: An image is worth 16 × 16 words: transformers for image recognition at scale (2021)
9. Li, Y., Song, Y., et al.: Intelligent fault diagnosis by fusing domain adversarial training and maximum mean discrepancy via ensemble learning. IEEE TII **17**(4), 2833–2841 (2020)
10. Lin, T., Wang, Y., Liu, X., Qiu, X.: A survey of transformers. arXiv preprint arXiv:2106.04554 (2021)
11. Liu, M., Zhang, S., et al.: H_∞ state estimation for discrete-time chaotic systems based on a unified model. IEEE Trans. SMC (B) **42**(4), 1053–1063 (2012)
12. Lu, R., Jin, X., et al.: A study on big knowledge and its engineering issues. IEEE TKDE **31**(9), 1630–1644 (2019)
13. Lu, Z., Wang, N., et al.: IoTDeM: an IoT big data-oriented MapReduce performance prediction extended model in multiple edge clouds. JPDC **118**, 316–327 (2018)
14. Luong, M.T., Pham, H., Manning, C.D.: Effective approaches to attention-based neural machine translation. arXiv preprint arXiv:1508.04025 (2015)
15. Niu, J., Gao, Y., et al.: Selecting proper wireless network interfaces for user experience enhancement with guaranteed probability. JPDC **72**, 1565–1575 (2012)
16. Qiu, H., Qiu, M., Lu, R.: Secure V2X communication network based on intelligent PKI and edge computing. IEEE Netw. **34**(42), 172–178 (2019)
17. Qiu, H., Qiu, M., Lu, Z.: Selective encryption on ECG data in body sensor network based on supervised machine learning. Inf. Fusion **55**, 59–67 (2020)
18. Qiu, H., Qiu, M., et al.: Secure health data sharing for medical cyber-physical systems for the healthcare 4.0. IEEE J. Biomed. Health Inform. **24**, 2499–2505 (2020)
19. Qiu, H., Zheng, Q., et al.: Deep residual learning-based enhanced JPEG compression in the Internet of Things. IEEE TII **17**(3), 2124–2133 (2020)

20. Qiu, H., Zheng, Q., et al.: Topological graph convolutional network-based urban traffic flow and density prediction. IEEE ITS **22**(7), 4560–4569 (2020)
21. Qiu, L., Gai, K., Qiu, M.: Optimal big data sharing approach for tele-health in cloud computing. In: IEEE SmartCloud, pp. 184–189 (2016)
22. Qiu, M., Cao, D., et al.: Data transfer minimization for financial derivative pricing using Monte Carlo simulation with GPU in 5G. Int. J. Commun Syst **29**(16), 2364–2374 (2016)
23. Qiu, M., Gai, K., Xiong, Z.: Privacy-preserving wireless communications using bipartite matching in social big data. FGCS **87**, 772–781 (2018)
24. Qiu, M., Guo, M., et al.: Loop scheduling and bank type assignment for heterogeneous multi-bank memory. JPDC **69**, 546–558 (2009)
25. Qiu, M., Liu, J., et al.: A novel energy-aware fault tolerance mechanism for wireless sensor networks. In: IEEE/ACM Conference on GCC (2011)
26. Qiu, M., Xue, C., et al.: Efficient algorithm of energy minimization for heterogeneous wireless sensor network. In: IEEE EUC Conference, pp. 25–34 (2006)
27. Qiu, M., Xue, C., et al.: Energy minimization with soft real-time and DVS for uniprocessor and multiprocessor embedded systems. In: IEEE DATE Conference, pp. 1–6 (2007)
28. Roy, A., Saffar, M., Vaswani, A., Grangier, D.: Efficient content-based sparse attention with routing transformers. Trans. Assoc. Comput. Linguist. **9**, 53–68 (2021)
29. Tay, Y., Bahri, D., Yang, L., Metzler, D., Juan, D.C.: Sparse sinkhorn attention. In: International Conference on Machine Learning, pp. 9438–9447. PMLR (2020)
30. Vaswani, A., et al.: Attention is all you need. In: Advances in Neural Information Processing Systems, vol. 30 (2017)
31. Wang, J., Qiu, M., Guo, B.: High reliable real-time bandwidth scheduling for virtual machines with hidden Markov predicting in telehealth platform. FGCS **49**, 68–76 (2015)
32. Wang, S., Zhou, L., et al.: Cluster-former: clustering-based sparse transformer for question answering. In: ACL-IJCNLP, pp. 3958–3968 (2021)
33. Wu, C., Wu, F., Qi, T., Huang, Y., Xie, X.: Fastformer: additive attention can be all you need. arXiv preprint arXiv:2108.09084 (2021)
34. Wu, G., Zhang, H., et al.: A decentralized approach for mining event correlations in distributed system monitoring. JPDC **73**(3), 330–340 (2013)
35. Yang, Z., Yang, D., Dyer, C., He, X., Smola, A., Hovy, E.: Hierarchical attention networks for document classification. In: Conference of the North American Chapter of the Association for Computational Linguistics, pp. 1480–1489 (2016)
36. Yuan, L., Chen, Y., et al.: Tokens-to-Token ViT: training vision transformers from scratch on ImageNet. In: Proceedings of the IEEE/CVF International Conference on Computer Vision, pp. 558–567 (2021)
37. Zhang, Z., Jiang, Y., et al.: STAR: a structure-aware lightweight transformer for real-time image enhancement. In: IEEE/CVF CV, pp. 4106–4115 (2021)
38. Zhou, C., Bai, J., et al.: ATRank: an attention-based user behavior modeling framework for recommendation. In: 32nd AAAI (2018)

Classification of Heads in Multi-head Attention Mechanisms

Feihu Huang[1,2], Min Jiang[1(✉)], Fang Liu[3,4], Dian Xu[1,2], Zimeng Fan[1,2], and Yonghao Wang[5]

[1] College of Computer Science, Wuhan University of Science and Technology, Wuhan, China
{huangfeihu,jiangmin,dianhsu,fanzimeng}@wust.edu.cn
[2] Hubei Province Key Laboratory of Intelligent Information Processing and Real-Time Industrial System, Wuhan, China
[3] School of Computer Science, Wuhan University, Wuhan, China
liufangfang@whu.edu.cn
[4] Department of Information Engineering, Wuhan Institute of City, Wuhan, China
[5] DMT Lab, Birmingham City University, Birmingham, UK
yonghao.wang@bcu.ac.uk

Abstract. Transformer model has become the dominant modeling paradigm in deep learning, of which multi-head attention is a critical component. While increasing Transformer effect, it also has some issues. When the number of heads reaches a point, some attention heads have remarkably similar attention graphs, which indicates that these heads are doing repetitive calculations. Some heads may even focus on extraneous things, affecting the final result. After analyzing the multi-head attention mechanism, this paper believes that the consistency of the inputs to the multi-head attention mechanism is the underlying reason for the similarity of the attention graph between heads. For this reason, this paper proposes the concept of classifying the heads in multi-head attention mechanism and summarizes the general classification process. Three classification schemes are designed for the Multi30k dataset. Experiments demonstrate that our method converges faster than the baseline model and that the BLEU improves by 3.08–4.38 compared to the baseline model.

Keywords: Transformer · Attention · Classification · Multi-head attention · NLP

1 Introduction

Transformer [20] is used extensively in natural language processing due to its high training efficiency and its ability to handle long sequences. Thanks to the rapid development of computer systems [9,17] and network facilities [10,16]. Now big data [15,23] and machine learning [12,13] have become powerful tools to solve various difficult problems in various areas. In contrast to CNN [7], the

G. Memmi et al. (Eds.): KSEM 2022, LNAI 13370, pp. 681–692, 2022.
https://doi.org/10.1007/978-3-031-10989-8_54

operations required to compute the association between two locations do not grow with distance and break the limitation that RNN [6,25] cannot calculate in parallel [8,14]. The recently hot model Bert [2] is an improvement on it, able to learn powerful language representations from unlabelled text and even outperform humans on challenging question answering tasks.

The advantage of multi-head attention is that multiple heads are trained in parallel and take the same amount of time to compute as a single head. However, self-attention calculates the dot product between the input representations at each pair of positions, which results in Transformer's standard self-attention mechanism using $O(n^2)$ time and space relative to the length of the sequence.

Previous research has proposed several ways to improve the efficiency of self-attention. A currently popular technique is to introduce sparsity into the attention mechanism. Paper [22] analyzed the role of individual heads in the translation work and their contribution to the overall model performance from a results perspective, using a method based on stochastic gates and a differentiable relaxation of the L0 penalty on the head pruning. It demonstrated that he removed 38 of the 48 heads, but the BLEU value decreased by only 0.15. Papers [5,11,24] calculates sparse attention, not dense attention.

In this article, we want to find the deeper reasons behind this problem to avoid this situation. Observe the attention of different heads through the attention map, and analyze the formula to discover why the attention maps are similar. We propose in this research to categorize heads in the multi-head attention mechanism and to construct different observation patterns in the calculation of different categories of heads. It optimizes the variety between heads and makes full use of the information of each head while adhering to the essential principle of multi-head attention.

The contributions of this article are:

- We argue that the multi-head attention mechanism maps each head in the same layer to a separate space, but their computational processes and inputs remain the same by summarizing past work and comparing the attention graphs of all heads in the same layer.
- This paper presents the idea of classifying the heads in the multi-head attention mechanism with a general classification process summarized. Three design schemes, Gaussian (GS), Triangular split (TS), and Anti-diagonal split (ADS), were designed for the Multi30k dataset.
- Experiments validate the effectiveness of our classification scheme, with the method in this paper improving the BLEU by 3.08–4.38 over the baseline model and converging faster.

The rest of this paper is organized as follows. Sect. 2 introduces some related work; Sect. 3 describes Motivation and discusses the reason for the singleness of attention between heads in the multi-head attention mechanism, and it also introduces the Multi-head classification mechanism idea and formulation; Sect. 4.2 describes the general classification process and the specific design on the Multi30k dataset; The experiments and analysis of the results are in Sect. 5; Sect. 6 is summary and future work.

2 Related Work

In this paper, the optimization of Transformers can divide into four categories based on the granularity of the optimization.

1) Rather than updating each Transformer module individually, the overall framework improves in response to the application circumstance. Such as Bert [2], whose main model structure is a stack of encoders for Transformers, is a 2-stage framework: pre-training and fine-tuning. Finetuning is adapted to different tasks and performs well in all 11 NLP tasks. Vision Transformer [3] directly removed the decoder part and keeps only the encoder part. It applies Transformer to the CV domain for the first time, comparing image blocks to tokens in NLP and classifying images accordingly, achieving an accuracy of 88.55% on the ImageNet-1K evaluation set, setting a new record on the task.
2) Instead of modifications to the self-attention algorithm, multi-head attention mechanisms are modified. Paper [19] maximized the attention weights of the different heads of the different layers of Transformer to represent the attention distribution matrix of each attention layer, choosing to focus only on the largest attention weights. Paper [21] modified the decoder in Transformer system to allow a multi-head attentional sublayer to participate in previous contextual sentences in addition to the current source sentence, considering the average of all heads at a given position. In the case of BLEU, however, its effect is comparable to that of the sentence-level translation model.
3) Modifications to the self-attention algorithm. For example, Adaptively Sparse Transformers [1] considered that using SoftMax when computing multi-head attention assigns non-zero weights to all contextual subscripts. Because the sum is 1, the weights assigned to the relevant terms reduce. By replacing SoftMax with a new function, the Adaptively Sparse Transform was created to achieve a differentiable generalization of SoftMax. Talking-Heads attention [18] added a linear projection before SoftMax to make each attention function dependent on all keys and queries, thereby increasing the exchange of information between multiple attention mechanisms. When compared to multi-head attention on the migration learning problem, it improved all quality indicators across different numbers of heads.

The idea proposed in this paper is mainly to classify the heads in the multi-head attention mechanism and increase the differences of heads between different categories. Compared to other similar work, the idea proposed in this paper still adheres to the core of the multi-head attention mechanism and makes full use of the value of each head in the multi-head attention mechanism.

3 Motivation

Transformer was the one who originally recommended self-attention as a way to improve attention. The scaled dot-product method uses to calculate attention in original transformer [20], and the inputs are query, key, and value. The formula 1 is as follows.

$$Attention(Q,K,V) = softmax(\frac{QK^T}{\sqrt{d_k}})V \tag{1}$$

where d_k is the model dimension, QK^T is used to calculate the attention score, which is then scaled. It prevents the vector inner product from becoming too large when the model dimension is too large.

[20] add a multi-head attention mechanism to self-attention, which is a projection of Q, K, and V by h different linear transformations, computing different self-attention in different subspaces in parallel, and finally stitching them together. The formula 2 is as follows.

$$\begin{aligned} MultiHead(Q,K,V) &= Concat(head_1, head_2, .., head_h)W^o \\ where \quad head_i &= attention(QW_i^Q, KW_i^K, VW_i^V) \end{aligned} \tag{2}$$

From the experimental results, it does appear that the multi-head attention mechanism is optimized compared to self-attention. But Transformer update formula shows that all parameters are initialized randomly and then propagated forward in the same way to get the same loss at the output and propagated backward in the same way to update the parameters. The only difference between the individual heads in this update process is the difference in initial values (W_i^Q, W_i^K, W_i^V).

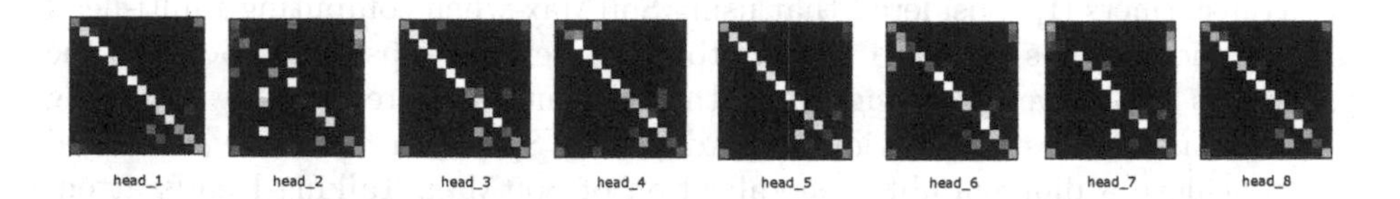

Fig. 1. Attention map for the last layer of encoder.

To further demonstrate it, we trained the transformer based on the MNIST dataset, with three layers of both encoder and decoder and eight heads per layer, deriving an attention graph for the final layer of encode. As shown in Fig. 1, there are eight head attention graphs, of which head_1, head_3, head_4, head_5, and head_8 are relatively similar. Although the attention of multi-head is calculated in different spaces and the parameters are not shared, there are still some duplicate results for some heads as the attention is still calculated for one token.

Thus, we propose the concept of classifying the heads. The entire calculation process is comparable to the multi-head attention mechanism, which is computed by several heads concurrently, as shown in the Fig. 2(b). Finally, the results are stitched together through a linear layer to complete the synthesis of information. Heads of the same category still adhere to the core idea of multi-head attention,

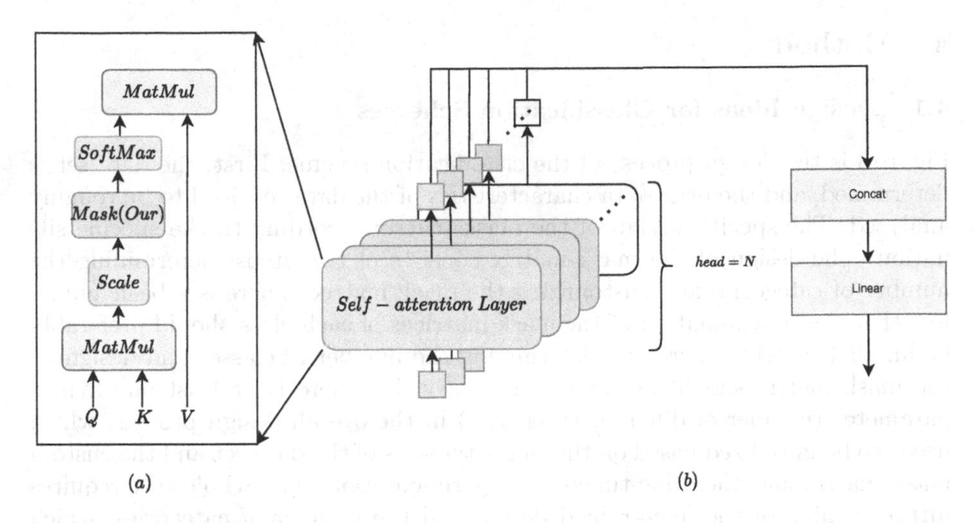

Fig. 2. Classification concept map, where heads of different colors represent heads of different categories. (Color figure online)

while heads of different categories show differences due to different classification schemes.

Transformer's Masked Decoder self-attention gives us inspiration. As shown in the Fig. 2(a), a mask matrix is added after the scale operation in the Transformer in order not to see the position behind it when predicting during decoding. It shows that the mask matrix here does not break the computational logic of attention. As a result, we placed a mask matrix in the same place as the encoder layer and devised multiple classification techniques to differentiate different classes of heads, allowing us to see the differences in output between them. While computing attention is still given to the calculation in its entirety, a trade-off is made in the final integration of data.

The calculation process is as shown in the formula 3–4. Similar to the general multi-head attention calculation, we also calculate the attention value of each head individually and finally merge them. The distinction is that we utilize a mask matrix to calculate the attention of the various heads, and we use the different Masks to differentiate between the different classes of heads for categorization. $Mask_j$ and $Attention_j$ denote the mask matrix and attention values corresponding to the jth class of head, respectively, and $head_{ij}$ denotes that the i-th head belongs to the j-th class.

$$Attention_j(Q, K, V) = softmax(\frac{Mask_j(QK^T)}{\sqrt{d_k}})V \tag{3}$$

$$\begin{aligned} MultiHead(Q, K, V) &= Concat(head_{11}, .., head_{hn})W^o \\ where \quad head_{ij} &= attention_j(QW_i^Q, KW_i^K, VW_i^V) \end{aligned} \tag{4}$$

4 Method

4.1 Design Ideas for Classification Schemes

Figure 3 is the design process of the classification scheme. First, the data set is determined, and then the data characteristics of the data set need to be roughly analyzed. The specific design of the mask matrix according to the specific situation. The design of the mask matrix consists of two steps: determining the number of categories and customizing the mask matrix. There is a basic guideline that the concatenation of the mask matrices of each class should preferably be an all-1 matrix. Therefore, determining the number of classes and designing the mask matrix should be done simultaneously. There is at least one hyperparameter (number of different categories) in the overall design process, which needs to be initialized based on the characteristics of the data set and the custom mask matrix and then fine-tuned by experimentation. The whole test requires further tuning of the fine-grained design and the number of categories, which can only be done empirically to reduce the number of tests.

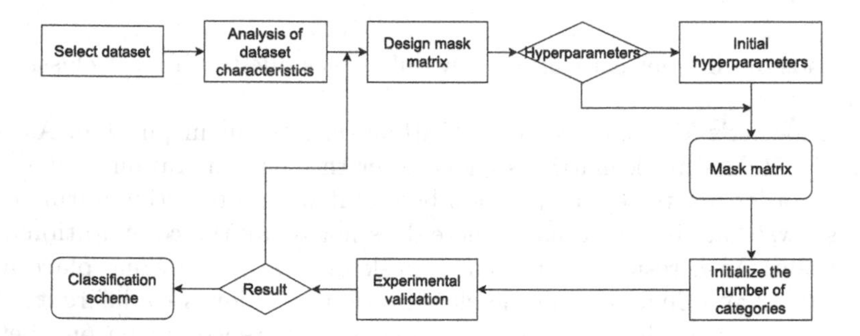

Fig. 3. Classification idea diagram, which introduces the design process of the classification scheme.

4.2 Implementation of Classification

Since the machine translation domain is a common domain for Transformer, we validate it on vanilla transformer on machine translation tasks. A classification scheme that works well on one dataset may not work well on another, thus we may tweak our classification scheme for different datasets, such as the number of categories, precisely specified parameters, and so on, to enhance classification performance. Taking the Multi30k dataset as an example, this paper analyzes and summarizes the sentence type characteristics in the dataset; Most of the sentences are simple sentences with a strong correlation between individual words and their surroundings. Based on this, this paper explores three classification methods.

Gaussian. To demonstrate the feasibility of the classification idea, we designed an extreme classification using Gaussian random generation of a mask matrix equal to the number of heads. That means we divide the number of headers into one for each class, which ensures that each head has a different focus. Although this destroys the core of the multi-head attention mechanism, it also allows us to verify whether the multi-head attention mechanism is consistent with our analysis.

Triangular Split. In the previous experiments, we found that there is a semi-triangular mask matrix in the self-attention mechanism of decoder, so it is natural to think that we can design the mask matrix as two semi-triangular matrices. This divides the heads in the multi-head attention mechanism into two categories: one that focuses only on itself and before its own position, and another that focuses only on itself and after its own position. Moreover, the process of semantic analysis is mostly performed in this way in translation tasks. The mask matrix is shown in the Fig. 4.

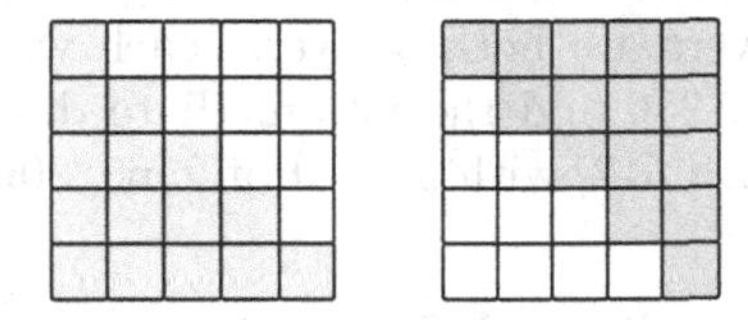

Fig. 4. Mask matrix design of triangular split.

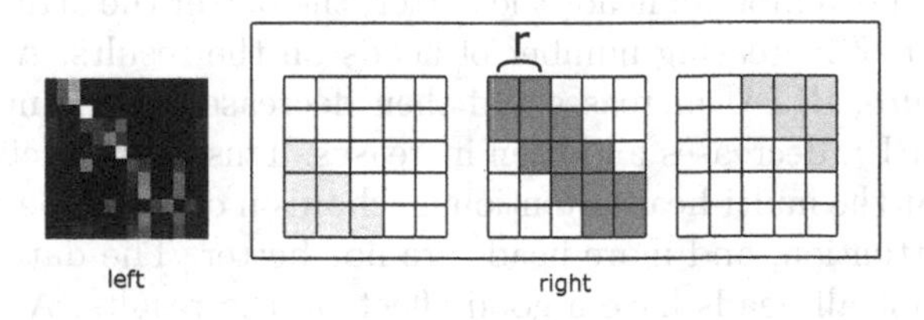

Fig. 5. The image on the left is the attention map and right is mask matrix design of anti-diagonal split.

Anti-diagonal Split. We observe that some of the attention maps have a particular shape, such as left in Fig. 5, which has a brighter diagonal part, indicating that it focuses more on its own surroundings. In the Multi30k [4] dataset, there are mostly simple sentences, and verbs are mostly found in the middle of the sentence. When translating verbs we focus on the initiator and the bearer of the action. This paper thus divides the head into 3 classes along the inverse diagonal, first focusing on itself and a certain range of itself, and the other two categories focusing on those far from its own position and before and after its own position, respectively. The mask matrix is shown on the right side of Fig. 5. Here there are two hyperparameters, one is the bound r of the range of itself and the other is the number of each class. From the linguistic logic, the number of classes that focus on itself and its surroundings should be larger than the other two classes.

5 Experiment

5.1 Experimental Setup

This paper uses the Multi30k machine translation dataset, which is based on the Flickr30k dataset proposed for the English-German study. There are 31014 images in it originated from online shared images. Each image is described by 5 English fields. A total of 145000 training, 5070 development, and 5000 test are included.

We have implemented a small transformer using the pytorch framework. The encoder and decoder layers are both 3 layers, each with 8 heads. The hidden layer has a dimension of 256 and the intermediate dimensions of the Position wise feed forward are both 512, with a total of 25602309 training parameters.

5.2 Experimental Results and Evaluation

Effect of Heads' Number on Results. According to [20], multi-head attention mechanism enhances the ability to focus on different locations, so theoretically, the more the number of heads the better, the better the attention. Figure 6a shows the effect of increasing number of heads on the results. According to the data in the figure, BLEU increases and then decreases as the number of heads increases, and PPL decreases and then increases. This contradicts the theory. It can be seen that the multi-head attention mechanism does not perfectly solve the defect of self-attention, and more heads are not better. The data further proves our idea that not all heads have a good effect on the results. As the number of heads increases to 32, the BLEU drops to a very low level, almost 0. We conclude that one head looking at the whole sentence may not cover all the information. When the number of heads increases, some heads will pay attention to irrelevant places, and there will be more "impurities".

Effect of GS and TS. Table 1 explores the effect of each class in the TS classification method on the results. We can clearly see that when the total number of heads is the same, the BLEU value gradually increases with the increasing number of category I. Accordingly, we believe that in the task of German to English translation, for a word, its preceding position has a greater

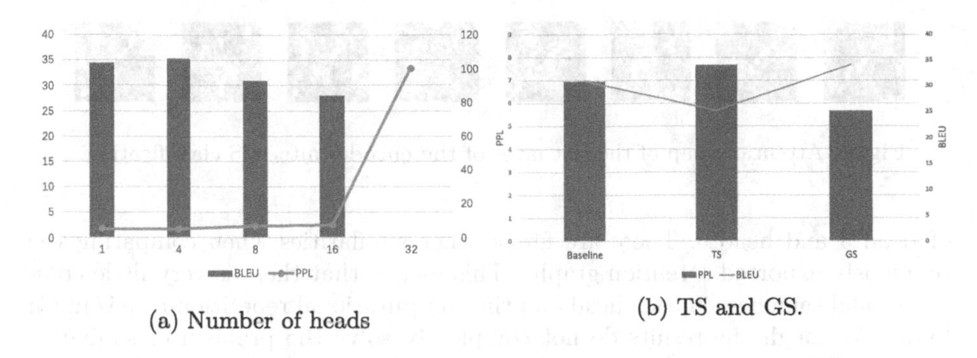

(a) Number of heads

(b) TS and GS.

Fig. 6. Influence of different hyperparameters on PPL and BLEU

effect on him than the following one. In this paper, we explore an extreme case for this conjecture, when the number of category I is 8 and the number of category II is 0, the BLEU value drops to 19.24. This is still more in line with common sense, after all, not all words can be focused on the front position only.

Table 1. Impact of the number of each class in TS on BLEU

Category I	Category II	BLEU
2	6	22.28
4	4	24.71
6	2	25.25
8	0	19.24

Figure 6b shows the comparison of PPL and BLEU with the baseline model for both classification schemes. It can be clearly seen that GS is better than the baseline model, indicating that having one head to focus on the whole sentence may not be noticed by it all. Surprisingly, GS is randomly generated with 8 mask matrices, and we conducted several experiments and the final BLEU did not change although the mask matrices were generated differently each time. We guess the reason is that the sentence distributions in the Multi30k dataset are mostly concentrated in the middle of the orthogonal distribution, so the randomly generated mask matrices have basically the same effect on the results. Both the PPL and BLEU of TS are higher than the baseline model, and we analyze that, theoretically, we cannot focus only on the front or the back when translating a word, which is not in accordance with the language specification. So the classification method of TS is not applicable to machine translation.

As shown in Fig. 7, with the experiments in the motivation section, we derived the attention graphs for all heads in the last layer of the encoder layer after GS classification. We can see that among the 8 head attention maps, only head_3 and head_6 are more similar, which may be caused by the similar mask matrix

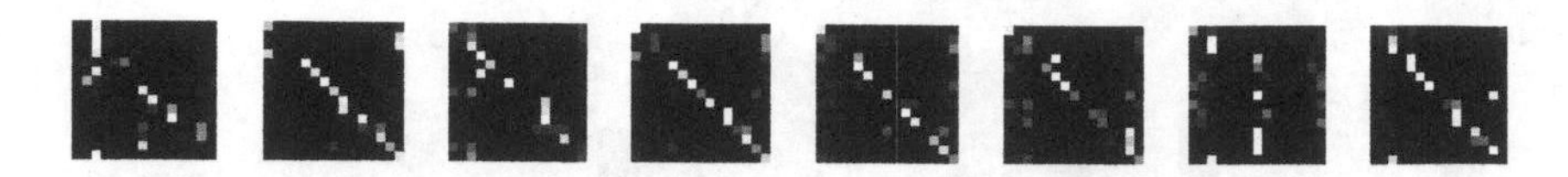

Fig. 7. Attention map of the last layer of the encoder after GS classification.

of head_3 and head_6. There are fewer other similarities when comparing the previously exported attention graphs. This means that there is very little computational sameness in each head and the computational repetition rate is much lower. Although the results do not completely solve the problem of similarity between different head attentional maps, they have a significant effect. Moreover, the improvement of BLEU further proves the effectiveness of our classification idea.

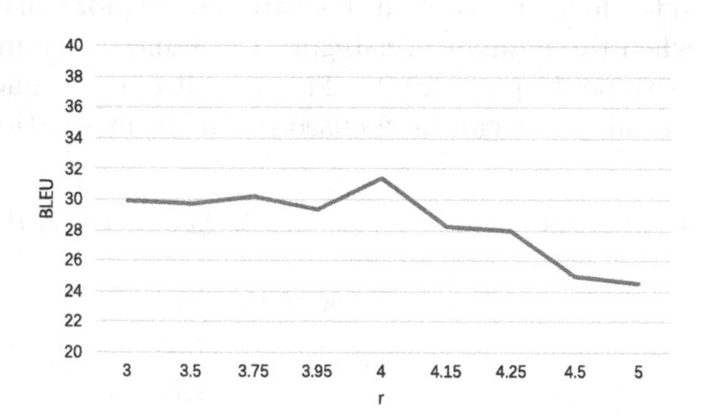

Fig. 8. The effect of hyperparameter r on the result.

Table 2. Impact of the number of each class in ADS on BLEU

Category I	Category II	Category III	BLEU
0	8	0	35.35
1	6	1	32.56
2	4	2	31.40
3	2	3	23.45

Effect of ADS. According to the experimental results in the previous section, we found that TS led to a decrease in BLEU, but GS had a good effect on the results. This shows that the idea of classification is not a problem but the classification method has good and bad effects. We further explored the effect of ADS on the results. Since the local dispersion has two hyperparameters, we talked about them separately. We defined

$$r' = \frac{l}{r} \tag{5}$$

where l is the number of columns of the mask matrix, r is the hyperparameter, and r' is the range of the second class in the local dispersion formula. As shown in Fig. 8, we examined the effect of the hyperparameter r on the BLEU. It can be seen from the figure that the value of BLEU increases and then decreases as r increases and reaches a maximum of 31.4 at r = 4.

After determining the next first hyperparameter, we experimented with the second hyperparameter and the results are shown in Table 2. We found that the BLEU steadily increased as the number of second classes increased. When all the heads belonged to the second category, the BLEU value peaked at 35.35, exceeding the GS 34.05. At this point all the heads only focused on words in a certain range around the location, which would theoretically lead to some error. However, probably due to the predominance of simple sentences in the Multi30k dataset, this is more in line with the diagonal segmentation style and works better. This further supports our conjecture that one single head may not be suitable for focusing on the entire token.

6 Conclusion

Combining previous work and the analysis of formulas, this paper proposed that the same input of the multi-head attention mechanism is the root cause of head singularity. Therefore, in this paper, we proposed the idea of classifying heads in the multi-headed attention mechanism and summarize the general design process. After analyzing the sentence characteristics of Multi30k dataset we designed three schemes GS, AS and ADS according to the classification flow. The experiments prove that not only the improvement in BLEU but also the similarity between the heads of the classified attention maps is much lower than Baseline, which effectively solves the problem of repeated computation in the multi-headed attention mechanism.

References

1. Correia, G.M., Niculae, V., Martins, A.F.: Adaptively sparse transformers. arXiv preprint arXiv:1909.00015 (2019)
2. Devlin, J., Chang, M.W., et al.: Bert: pre-training of deep bidirectional transformers for language understanding. arXiv e-prints arXiv:1810.04805, October 2018. https://ui.adsabs.harvard.edu/abs/2018arXiv181004805D
3. Dosovitskiy, A., Beyer, L., et al.: An image is worth 16x16 words: transformers for image recognition at scale. In: 9th ICLR (2021)
4. Elliott, D., Frank, S., Sima'an, K., Specia, L.: Multi30k: multilingual English-German image descriptions. arXiv preprint arXiv:1605.00459 (2016)
5. Huang, L., Yuan, Y., Guo, J., Zhang, C., Chen, X., Wang, J.: Interlaced sparse self-attention for semantic segmentation. arXiv preprint arXiv:1907.12273 (2019)
6. Kawakami, K.: Supervised sequence labelling with recurrent neural networks. Ph.D. thesis (2008)
7. Krizhevsky, A., Sutskever, I., Hinton, G.E.: Imagenet classification with deep convolutional neural networks. In: Advances in Neural Information Processing Systems, vol. 25 (2012)

8. Li, Y., Song, Y., et al.: Intelligent fault diagnosis by fusing domain adversarial training and maximum mean discrepancy via ensemble learning. IEEE TII **17**(4), 2833–2841 (2021)
9. Liu, M., Zhang, S., et al.: H infinite state estimation for discrete-time chaotic systems based on a unified model. IEEE Trans. SMC (B) (2012)
10. Lu, Z., Wang, N., et al.: IoTDeM: an IoT big data-oriented MapReduce performance prediction extended model in multiple edge clouds. JPDC **118**, 316–327 (2018)
11. Luong, M.T., Pham, H., Manning, C.D.: Effective approaches to attention-based neural machine translation. arXiv preprint arXiv:1508.04025 (2015)
12. Qiu, H., Qiu, M., Lu, Z.: Selective encryption on ECG data in body sensor network based on supervised machine learning. Infor. Fusion **55**, 59–67 (2020)
13. Qiu, H., Zheng, Q., et al.: Deep residual learning-based enhanced JPEG compression in the internet of things. IEEE TII **17**(3), 2124–2133 (2020)
14. Qiu, H., Zheng, Q., et al.: Topological graph convolutional network-based urban traffic flow and density prediction. IEEE TITS **22**(7), 4560–4569 (2021)
15. Qiu, M., Gai, K., Xiong, Z.: Privacy-preserving wireless communications using bipartite matching in social big data. FGCS **87**, 772–781 (2018)
16. Qiu, M., Liu, J., et al.: A novel energy-aware fault tolerance mechanism for wireless sensor networks. In: IEEE/ACM Conference, GCC (2011)
17. Qiu, M., Xue, C., et al.: Energy minimization with soft real-time and DVS for uniprocessor and multiprocessor embedded systems. In: IEEE DATE Conference, pp. 1–6 (2007)
18. Shazeer, N., Lan, Z., Cheng, Y., Ding, N., Hou, L.: Talking-heads attention. arXiv preprint arXiv:2003.02436 (2020)
19. Tang, G., Nivre, J.: An analysis of attention mechanisms: the case of word sense disambiguation in neural machine translation. In: 3rd Conference on Machine Translation (2018)
20. Vaswani, A., Shazeer, N., et al.: Attention is all you need. In: Advances in Neural Information Processing Systems, pp. 5998–6008 (2017)
21. Voita, E., Serdyukov, P., Sennrich, R., Titov, I.: Context-aware neural machine translation learns anaphora resolution. arXiv e-prints arXiv:1805.10163, May 2018. https://ui.adsabs.harvard.edu/abs/2018arXiv180510163V
22. Voita, E., Talbot, D., Moiseev, F., Sennrich, R., Titov, I.: Analyzing multi-head self-attention: specialized heads do the heavy lifting, the rest can be pruned (2019). https://doi.org/10.18653/v1/p19-1580
23. Wu, G., Zhang, H., et al.: A decentralized approach for mining event correlations in distributed system monitoring. JPDC **73**(3), 330–340 (2013)
24. Zaheer, M., Guruganesh, G., et al.: Big bird: transformers for longer sequences (2021)
25. Zaremba, W., Sutskever, I., Vinyals, O.: Recurrent neural network regularization. CoRR abs/1409.2329 (2014). http://arxiv.org/abs/1409.2329

Hardware and Software Co-design for Soft Switch in ViT Variants Processing Unit

Wei Hu[1,2], Jie Fan[1,2](✉), Fang Liu[3,4], and Kejie Hu[1,2]

[1] College of Computer Science, Wuhan University of Science and Technology, Wuhan, China
{huwei,hekejie}@wust.edu.cn, JacobEvans.7@outlook.com
[2] Hubei Province Key Laboratory of Intelligent Information Processing and Real-time Industrial System, Wuhan, China
[3] School of Computer Science, Wuhan University, Wuhan, China
liufangfang@whu.edu.cn
[4] Department of Information Engineering, Wuhan Institute of City, Wuhan, China

Abstract. As the application of pure Transformer in CV field, ViT shows the generality of Transformer model. However, it requires costly training on large datasets. Recently, some researchers trying to improve the training efficiency of ViT by combining ViT and CNN together which will use the inductive bias of CNN. In these models, the MHSA layer carries other modules on its side, but existing architectures cannot take advantage of this feature to customize designs to improve computational efficiency and resource utilization. The use of FPGA to customize specialized computing units can meet this need, but the existing hardware computing units can't adapt to the combination of different types of layers, and switching between different models will result in expensive re-production costs. In this paper, we use hardware and software cooperation to design the FPGA computing unit and divide the layers according to their functions. Convolution and Transformer are classified into one category. Under the coordination deployment of software, it mix the outputs of the same type of layers through soft switches, so as to adapt to those flexible models. Compared with the performance of the original model on CPU, it achieves the acceleration performance of 26× under the condition that the accuracy is only decreased by 0.9%. And the structure of common data block reduces the size of hardware resource unit by 91.7%.

Keywords: FPGA · CNN · Transformer · Deep learning · Hardware

1 Introduction

Since Transformer [1] was proposed, its variants shine in many fields, among which ViT [2] has achieved remarkable results in CV field. However, with the increase of training volume caused by the characteristics of Transformer itself,

G. Memmi et al. (Eds.): KSEM 2022, LNAI 13370, pp. 693–705, 2022.
https://doi.org/10.1007/978-3-031-10989-8_55

there are high requirements on the scale of model base. Excessive training volume also greatly increases the cost. Some researchers try to take advantage of CNN's high training efficiency and combine it with Transformer to meet the requirements of both accuracy and training efficiency. Influenced by this idea, ConViT [3], DeiT [4], CeiT [5] and LocalVit [6] models were gradually developed. They have different mixing modes, but when GPU is used to accelerate calculation, due to its universal characteristics, the model is not optimized, and the parallelism of the model is obviously unable to be utilized. Meanwhile, the volume and power consumption have always been difficult to be solved by this kind of universal computing unit. Customized FPGA can solve the above problems, and more and more researchers are trying to customize the calculation module or deploy the whole calculation model on FPGA [8,9].

There are now many variants of ViT, and it's very expensive to design dedicated computing units for each single variant, and rapid iterations of models do not wait for delays in hardware design. In order to bring production environments online quickly, there is a use of Vitis-AI technology to help quickly load custom models on hardware, but this solution has limited optimization. The inability to optimize data transfer between neurons and the need for specific DPU hardware accelerators greatly limit the minimum size of FPGA cells, losing one of the original intentions of using FPGA to customize the original.

In this paper, based on the characteristics of the current variants of Vit, and using the ConViT [3] model as a typical example, we designed a framework to simultaneously compute CNN and ViT (which are two neurons involved in most mainstream ViT variants) in one cell and output using soft switch control. In addition to speeding up the hardware through data quantization, neuron optimization, reordering of computing units and other steps, according to the analysis report, combined units are designed with software and hardware co-optimization [10–12] under the mechanism of soft switch and data sharing [13–15], which achieve better performance in computing efficiency [16–18] and resource utilization than single units.

1.1 Contribution

The main contributions of this paper are as follows:

- The CNN and ViT units are calculated simultaneously on FPGA device with each module being analyzed and optimized.
- Through the method of hardware and software co-design, it improves the utilization rate of Convolution module and Transformer module, and optimizes the generality of their combined units. Which makes models using CNN and VIT with minimal hardware resources to achieve great performance improvement.
- It is verified on the FPGA development board, and compared with the split implementation of CPU, GPU and FPGA model, the performance of our design is improved by 26×, 1.6× and 3.3×.

1.2 Related Work

In the application of Transformer in CV field, there are many work combining ViT and CNN. ConViT [3] introduced a new self-attention layer, GPSA *(Gated Positional Self-Attention)*, replacing some OF the SA layers with GPSA, based on ViT. ConViT can be initialized like CNN. Each attention head has a gating parameter to adjust expressiveness, which can be adjusted between local and global features. This parameter allows the model to decide for itself whether to maintain convolution.

$$A_{ij}^{h} := (1-\rho(\lambda_h))softmax(Q_i^h K_j^{hT}) + \rho(\lambda_h)softmax(v_{pos}^{hT} r_{ij}) \quad (1)$$

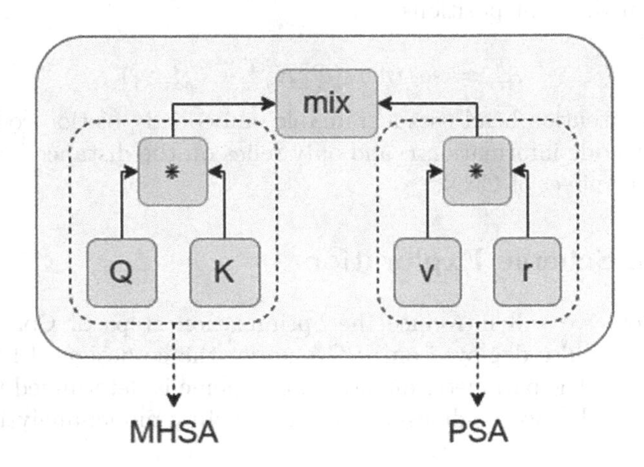

Fig. 1. Internal structure of GPSA

The author calls the part of simulated CNN PSA, as shown in Fig. 1, with the intention of introducing the locality of CNN into ViT, while the other part is the original MHSA. This study proves that ViT variants can achieve better results by absorbing the advantages of other modules on the basis of keeping the original module unchanged.

2 Background

2.1 ViT

The starting point of ViT is to completely replace CNN with attention. Although transformer was introduced in the CV field before, CNN or RNN was more or less used. ViT directly uses pure Transformer structure and has achieved good results. In the overall implementation, ViT completely uses the original Bert transformer structure, mainly to convert images into token like processing, and introduces the concept of patch, that is, the input images are divided into one patch after another, and then for each patch conversion (mainly flatten operation), Convert to a Bert-like input structure. The emergence of ViT marks the generality of transformer model and points the way for the unified universal encoder.

2.2 Relative Position Coding

However, at the beginning of the ViT, the SA layer does not know the local relationships of patches, but according to the CNN model, it is obvious that this is relevant, which also leads to low training efficiency of the ViT model. The introduction of relative position coding solves this problem well. Different from general SA, PSA(positional self-attention) [7] is added to encode relevant information at different positions.

$$A_{ij}^h := softmax(Q_i^h K_j^{hT} + v_{pos}^{hT} r_{ij})$$

Each self-attention head uses a trainable embedded position code v and relative position code information r, and only relies on the distance between pixels to simulate the effect of CNN.

3 Design Scheme Exploration

In this section, we will introduce the optimization steps of Convolution and Transformer modules deployed on FPGA under the co-design of hardware and software. Firstly, the parameter quantization scheme is determined based on the commonality of the two modules, and then model by model analysis.

3.1 Parameter Quantitative

In the deep learning model, reducing a certain precision will only bring a very small loss of the overall precision of the model [19]. The performance of FPGA is very sensitive to the data transmission rate, that is, a certain loss of accuracy can be used to exchange for a lower delay of FPGA as a whole. Therefore, reasonable quantization is necessary to achieve a balance of performance, precision and hardware utilization [20–22].

Some studies [23,24] show that when the accuracy is reduced to 8 bits, the accuracy of ViT model and CNN model is reduced by less than 1%. We used data quantization of different precision and computational quantization of 8 and 32 bit integer types for quantitative analysis of Convit. We ran the Convit-Tiny model to classify ImageNet data set, and the results were shown in Fig. 2.

The asymmetric quantization algorithm is used to carry out static quantization after the model training, and all tensors in the calculation process are adjusted according to the corresponding scale and zero point according to the input matching the classification test.

$$Q = round(\frac{input - zero_point}{scale})$$

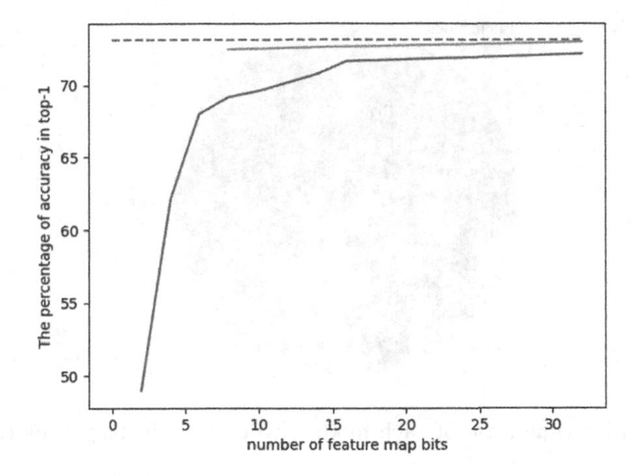

Fig. 2. As the bit width changes, the accuracy on ImageNet changes, the gray dotted line is the original accuracy, the orange is the calculated quantization, and the blue is the data quantization (Color figure online)

According to the quantization results, Q = 8 is the optimal quantization scheme that comprehensively considers the accuracy and resource utilization in scenarios that do not require extremely high accuracy. At the same time, when Q > 8, the classification accuracy is slightly improved while the performance is reduced. Therefore, if no other model is introduced, all experiments after this section will use 8-bit quantization scheme for data representation.

3.2 Model Analysis

An important theory of hardware acceleration is to accelerate high probability events, and the benefits of accelerating high probability events are far greater than those of other events. Therefore, we need to analyze each part of the model, find the commonness between modules, do common optimization, and optimize the different parts separately and calculate in parallel. To this end, we calculate the main Convit-Tiny calculations on FPGA and look for optimization breakthroughs from them.

As shown in Fig. 3, a large amount of time is spent on the convolution and Transformer modules of the model, and the time spent optimizing these two modules will play a decisive role in our overall performance. By default, pipeline optimization has been carried out for these two modules in our subsequent experiments. At the same time, we can also find that the remaining two modules consume very short time, so it is not cost-effective to optimize such a neglected module. However, we can see from the parameter information that their input size is similar to that of the GPSA module. If we ignore them here, we will lose a large amount of data space, which is also unacceptable. To do this, we need to find ways to make temporally negligible modules possible in space. This leads to the key of this article, the soft switch.

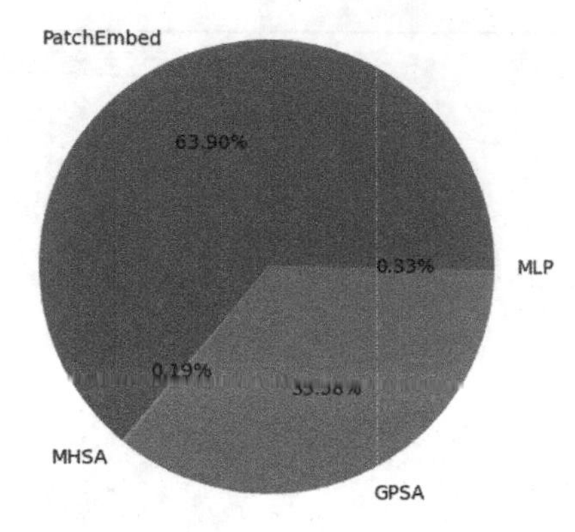

Fig. 3. Cumulative time ratio of each module when Convit-Tiny runs ImageNet data set

3.3 Soft Switch and Data Sharing

Previously, researchers used hard switches on hardware to switch between modules, which we called hard switches, that is, hard coded hardware before deployment. The hardware implemented by the hard switch is immutable in the execution order of each module at runtime, which brings the benefit of maximizing the performance by optimizing unit layout and rearranging pipeline during the coding phase. However, this also brings the defect of almost non-dynamic transformation, which is also the defect of FPGA itself, each architecture adjustment needs to regenerate the corresponding firmware.

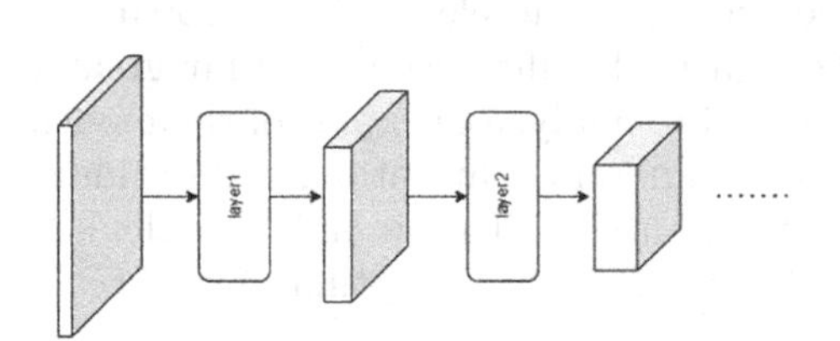

Fig. 4. Data transmission mode under hard switch

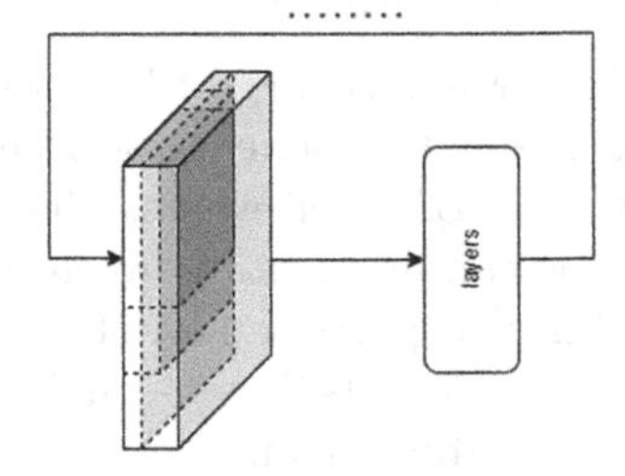

Fig. 5. Data transmission mode under soft switch

Hard switches are implemented knowing the order of modules in advance, and in order to achieve reusable designs, the conventional approach is that modules are independent of each other, and the optimization of modules only exists internally. The final data transfer flow and logic are consistent, as shown in Fig. 4. Now we need each module to reuse data blocks, so we do not want each module to be independent of each other, and this hard switch design idea hinders this, so we need to design a soft switch architecture.

As shown in Fig. 5, in the soft switch mode, all the input data in a data pool, at the beginning of the design and analysis of the maximum data needed for the scale (generally speaking is the original length × original width × max number of channel), run time, to the size of the data pool filled with dynamic data block, and specialized in counting read this part is used to calculate. The Layers part is almost identical to the hard switch mode, but transforms the corresponding computing module based on the input. This dynamic way of filling, reading, and calculating data is almost impossible to implement in hardware, which is why previous designs used hard switches, but software and hardware work together to achicvc this. The next section describes how to use hardware and software collaboration to cover all computing modules in the same cell and how to share data blocks.

4 Hardware and Software Co-design

Based on the analysis in the previous section, we need not only to transmit quantization data to the hardware computing unit, but also to tell the hardware the mixing ratio of the two models. Software and hardware are not independent. Therefore, in addition to their own internal optimization, both software and hardware need to conduct collaborative design optimization for their interaction. In terms of software, in order to cooperate with hardware to do general processing, data flow needs to do general processing, that is, data flow has nothing to do with the shape and size of data block; For different mixing ratios, when one side approaches 0, the jump pulse is released, and the asynchronous data receiving wait for the model is closed when the data is received.

In terms of hardware, it is analyzed that CNN and Transformer need common data block and create common data pool. The convolution operation is optimized by loop unrolling and flow rearrangement. The data transformation analysis of self-attention operation is carried out, and the relative position coding matrix which changes with the size of matrix is loaded as the weight, the fixed position coding information is hard coded, and the matrix multiplication is divided into data blocks to optimize the occupancy of hardware resources.

4.1 Software Layer Design

In the transmission part, in order to be compatible with matrices of different sizes, one-dimensional mapping of multidimensional matrices is required, and then reconstructed by hardware.

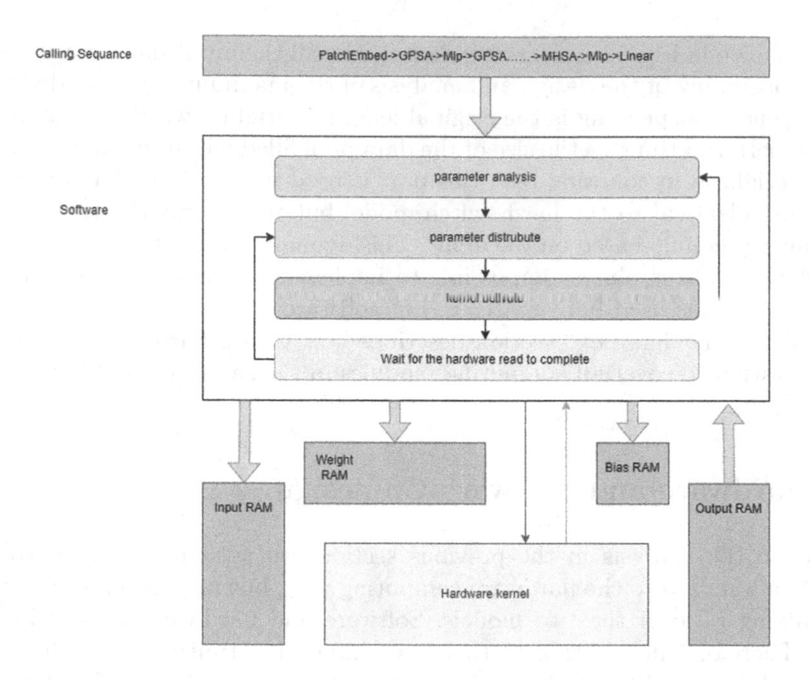

Fig. 6. Data flow between software layer and external and internal business logic

In order to enable the hardware unit of the driver to handle different types and sizes of input, a separate software layer is used to dynamically distribute data and send corresponding activation signals to the hardware. The software layer is divided into four stages: parameter preprocessing, parameter distribution, activation of the hardware core, waiting for the core to finish reading data. After the core is read, it will enter the next distribution. In general hardware accelerators, the software layer only acts as data transmission, which is equivalent to repeatedly doing the parameter distribution stage in this paper, that is, continuously feeding weights to the hardware end without changing the execution order of the model according to the specific situation, but the implementation of this paper will be segmented to each Block.

As shown in Fig. 6, when a call is initiated,

- the software layer enters the parameter analysis stage, from which it reads the corresponding module information, obtains the parameters, and converts them into the corresponding software parameter configuration to prepare for data transmission.
- Then the data is transmitted, the multi-dimensional matrix is flattened into one dimension and continuously sent to the hardware core through the flow channel, and the hardware model type is informed, and the corresponding parameter recombination unit and calculation unit are activated.
- The latter stages of the parameter distribution and active hardware for parallel execution, activate the signal immediately after resolving the parameters

of the next Block, and wait for the last round of parameters used by all finished, hardware return after reading complete signals, said the data in RAM can be covered.

A layer of software operation on end, began to continue loading parameters of the round.

4.2 Hardware Layer Design

In general, each cell manages its own block of data, including loading (external input), calculation, and output. This allows all cells to be block-sized in advance on demand, but it also creates a problem because the algorithm flow is fixed and any software changes require tweaking the entire hardware core. We use the data pool inside the hardware unit to store all the data, whose size is related to the maximum amount of data required for a single calculation. The software layer informs the calculation scale, and the data is hashed during actual storage.

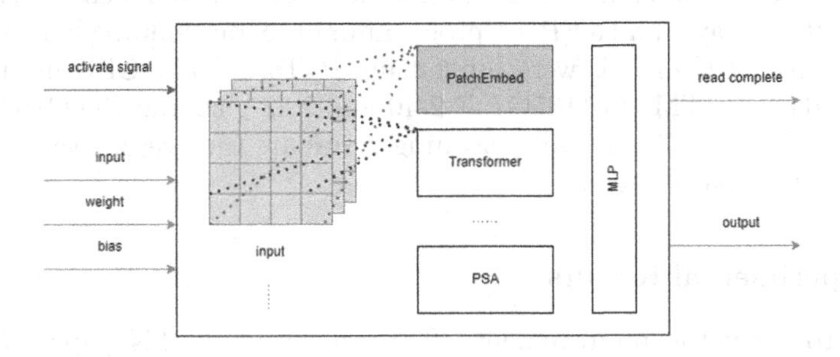

Fig. 7. shows the data flow direction and data block mapping when PatchEmbed's module is activated

As shown in Fig. 7, when an activation signal from the software layer is input into the hardware, the corresponding module is activated, and the effective data area of the data pool is divided according to the preset parameter size of the module, and input, weight and bias are read. Taking input as an example, the convit-Tiny model firstly divides the 3-channel image 224×224 into 196 patches of 192 size by patchEmbed module. At this time, the input of patchEmbed module is $3 \times 224 \times 224$, that is, the size of data block is at least $3 \times 224 \times 224$. Observe that the size of subsequent input and output data blocks does not exceed this size (for example, the input of *gate position self-attention* (GPSA) module is 196×192, and the input of multi-head self-attention (MHSA) module is 197×192).

The data usage is shown in Fig. 8. We can use a matrix with a maximum of $3 \times 224 \times 224$ to hold all matrices smaller than it, and only receive the required dimensions when receiving data. Extra space is skipped as padding, and extra dimensions and padding are ignored in the calculation.

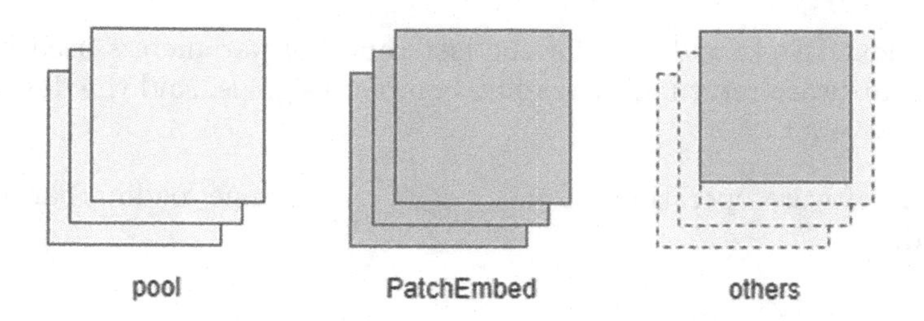

Fig. 8. Usage of data pools by different computing modules

5 Experiments

5.1 Experimental Setup

This paper uses Vivado *Hight-Level Synthesis* (HLS) and uses commonly used ImageNet data sets for validation. The hardware and software co-design unit is equipped with Xilinx ZCU102 development board, and has an ARM core running software layer and a FPGA programmable array running hardware layer. The CPU and GPU models were built using PyTorch. The CPU model is 11th Gen Intel(R) Core(TM) I5-1135G7 @ 2.40 ghz 2.42 ghz, and the GPU model is NVIDIA GeForce RTX3060. All reasoning times are the average values of 50000 images in all validation sets.

5.2 Experimental Results

In order to show the improvement of optimization in this paper intuitively, we will carry out combinational optimization on the original model successively, including the flow rearrangement, parameter quantization and software/hardware coordination mentioned in the previous chapter.

As can be seen from Fig. 9, quantization brings the largest increase in the size of input data, while pipeline rearrangement brings the largest performance improvement. The combination of pipeline rearrangement and quantization alone can bring 70.3% performance acceleration and 87.1% reduction in the size of input data. Full-text soft switch is the key to design at the same time, it can give the cell dynamic ability is derived, of course, the design of hardware and software collaborative also partly destroyed the oneness of hardware, software is the concurrent design reduces the affect of this operation on performance, makes the performance loss caused by the negligible, and to a certain extent reduce the data size, about a third.

Overall performance and data occupancy, as well as dynamics, this paper finally adopted a combination of all three optimizations, achieving a 69.5% performance improvement and a 91.4% reduction in input data size. Based on the above optimization combinations, we selected all optimization combinations as the final results of this paper and compared them with running the same parameters on CPU and GPU using the original PyTorch version.

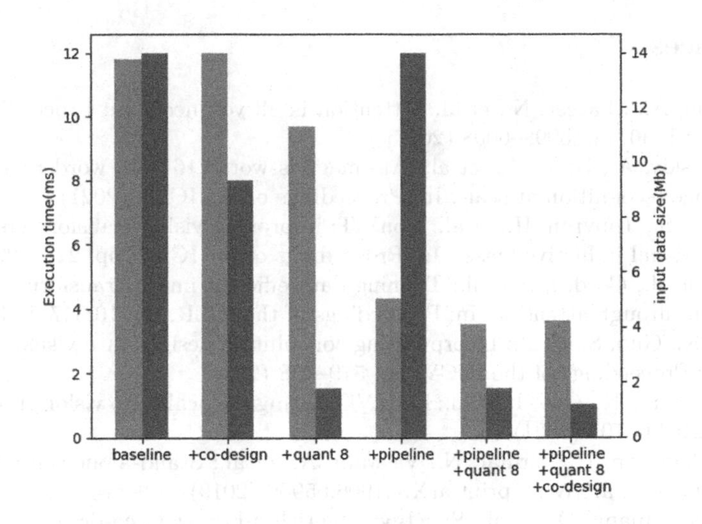

Fig. 9. Performance and data size under different combinatorial optimizations

Table 1. Comparison with CPU and GPU

Device	CPU	GPU	FPGA
Execution time (ms)	93.7	4.5	3.6
Parameters (M)	5.7	5.7	5.7
Acc@1	73.1	73.1	72.4

As can be seen from Table 1, FPGA can still achieve better performance than GPU under the condition of limited hardware resources and dynamic capability of hardware, while the accuracy is only reduced by 0.9%, proving that the soft switch architecture proposed in this paper is sufficient to cope with the variable model.

6 Conclusion

Based on the model combined with CNN and Transformer, this paper took Convit as an example and tried to solve the inflexible defects of current hardware development by means of soft switching and data sharing on the basis of conventional quantization and rearrangement flow and designed a hardware and software co-architecture. We tested our ideas on the Xilinx ZCU102 development board, achieved performance exceeding GPU under the same model with extremely limited resources and using less than 10% of the data size compared to the original hardware.

References

1. Vaswani, A., Shazeer, N., et al.: Attention is all you need. In: Proceedings of the NIPS, vol. 30, pp. 5998–6008 (2017)
2. Dosovitskiy, A., Beyer, L., et al.: An image is worth 16 × 16 words: transformers for image recognition at scale. In: Proceedings of the ICLR (2021)
3. d'Ascoli, S., Touvron, H., et al.: ConViT: improving vision transformers with soft convolutional inductive biases. In: Proceedings of the ICLR, pp. 2286–2296 (2021)
4. Touvron, H., Cord, M., et al.: Training data-efficient image transformers and distillation through attention. In: Proceedings of the ICLR, pp. 10 347–10 357 (2021)
5. Yuan, K., Guo, S., et al.: Incorporating convolution designs into visual transformers. In: Proceedings of the ICCV, pp. 579–588 (2021)
6. Li, Y., Zhang, K., Cao, J., et al.: LocalViT: Bringing locality to vision transformers, arXiv:2104.05707 (2021)
7. Ramachandran, P., Parmar, N., Vaswani, A., et al.: Stand-alone self-attention in vision models, arXiv preprint arXiv:1906.05909 (2019)
8. Yang, Y., Huang, Q., et al.: Synetgy: Algorithm-hardware co-design for ConvNet accelerators on embedded FPGAs, November 2018
9. Hu, W., Chen, S., Li, Z., Liu, T., Li, Y.: Data optimization CNN accelerator design on FPGA. In: IEEE ISPA/BDCloud/SocialCom/SustainCom, pp. 294–299 (2019)
10. Qiu, M., Li, H., Sha, E.: Heterogeneous real-time embedded software optimization considering hardware platform. In: ACM Symposium on Applied Computing, pp. 1637–1641 (2009)
11. Qiu, M., Xue, C., et al.: Energy minimization with soft real-time and DVS for uniprocessor and multiprocessor embedded systems. In: IEEE DATE, pp. 1–6 (2007)
12. Liu, M., Zhang, S., et al.: H infinite state estimation for discrete-time chaotic systems based on a unified model. IEEE Trans. SMC (B) **44**, 155–168 (2012)
13. Wu, G., Zhang, H., et al.: A decentralized approach for mining event correlations in distributed system monitoring. JPDC **73**(3), 330–340 (2013)
14. Qiu, M., et al.: Data transfer minimization for financial derivative pricing using Monte Carlo simulation with GPU in 5G. J. Commun. Syst. **29**(16), 2364–2374 (2016)
15. Qiu, L., Gai, K., Qiu, M.: Optimal big data sharing approach for tele-health in cloud computing. In: IEEE SmartCloud, pp. 184–189 (2016)
16. Qiu, M., Xue, C., et al.: Efficient algorithm of energy minimization for heterogeneous wireless sensor network. In: IEEE EUC, pp. 25–34 (2006)
17. Qiu, M., Guo, M., et al.: Loop scheduling and bank type assignment for heterogeneous multi-bank memory. JPDC **69**(6), 546–558 (2009)
18. Li, J., Qiu, M., et al.: Thermal-aware task scheduling in 3D chip multiprocessor with real-time constrained workloads. ACM TECS **12**(2), 1–22 (2013)
19. Cai, Z., He, X., Sun, J., Vasconcelos, N.: Deep learning with low precision by half-wave Gaussian quantization. In: IEEE CVPR (2017)
20. Qiu, M., Chen, Z., et al.: Data allocation for hybrid memory with genetic algorithm. IEEE TETC **3**(4), 544–555 (2015)
21. Qiu, M., Gai, K.: Heterogeneous assignment of functional units with Gaussian execution time on a tree. In: IEEE 20th Conference on HPCC (2018)
22. Qiu, M., et al.: Cost minimization for heterogeneous systems with Gaussian distribution execution time. In: IEEE 17th Conference on HPCC (2015)

23. Liu, Z., Wang, Y., Han, K., Ma, S., Gao, W.: Post-Training Quantization for Vision Transformer, arXiv:2106.14156 (2021)
24. Gysel, P., Pimentel, J., Motamedi, M., Ghiasi, S.: Ristretto: a framework for empirical study of resource-efficient inference in convolutional neural networks. IEEE Trans. Neural Netw. Learn. Syst. **29**, 5784–5789 (2018)

Energy-Based Learning for Preventing Backdoor Attack

Xiangyu Gao[1] and Meikang Qiu[2](✉)

[1] New York University, New York City, NY, USA
xg673@nyu.edu
[2] Texas A&M University Commerce, Commerce, TX, USA
qiumeikang@yahoo.com

Abstract. The popularity of machine learning has motivated the idea of *Energy-Based Learning* (EBL), which used *Energy-Based Models* (EBMs) proposed by Prof. Yann to capture dependencies between variables. In addition, the application of several machine learning tools into the field of backdoor becomes widespread as well. However, the current backdoor researches didn't consider the novel EBL tools. This paper studies both EBL methods and backdoor attack of machine learning. We propose an algorithm to leverage energy-based learning for preventing backdoor attack. Several case analysis in this paper has demonstrated the promising of applying energy-based learning to improve the backdoor protection techniques.

Keywords: Energy-based learning · Backdoor · Cyber security · Machine learning · Big data

1 Introduction

With the development science and technology, machine learning has become one of the most important tools in a lot of fields such as cyber security [11], computer vision [47] and high-frequency trading [10]. The ultimate goal for any statistical modeling machine learning model is to precisely capture the dependencies between different encoding variables so that it can be used to do prediction given the value of known variables. Among all potential models, *Energy-Based Models* (EBMs) [20] are popularly used. To be specific, EBMs will try to achieve the dependencies between variables by associating a scalar energy to each configurations. Afterwards, inference then participates in setting values of observed variables and then finds values of the remaining variables that minimize the energy.

Compared with other learning process, *energy-based learning* (EBL) proposed by Yann [19] provides a unified framework for many probabilistic and non-probabilistic approaches to learning. In other words, it can be considered as an alternative to probabilistic estimation for different learning tasks such as classification [16] and decision-making [50]. In addition, the fact that energy-based learning does not have any requirements for proper normalization [1] brings itself

G. Memmi et al. (Eds.): KSEM 2022, LNAI 13370, pp. 706–721, 2022.
https://doi.org/10.1007/978-3-031-10989-8_56

many benefits. First of all, it can naturally avoid problems related to estimate the normalization constant in probabilistic models. In addition, this brings a lot of flexibility in the design of learning machines.

Given the uniqueness of EBL, we believe it a good fit for the backdoor field. In cyber security world, backdoor [3] refers to any method by which authorized and unauthorized users are able to get around the normal security system and gain high level user access on a computer system. Once they are in, cyber criminals can use backdoor to steal valuable data [36,41] or install hijack devices [48].

Due to the development of machine learning, people start to rely on the third-party platforms (e.g. AWS [28], Azure [6] or Google Cloud [17]) to train their data. In addition, machine learning users also prefer to store their data on the third-party so as to avoid too much disk occupancy in their local machine. In spite of the convenience, these are all based on the assumption that the third-party platform are trustworthy. However, a series of malicious attacks [9] have proved that the full trust to third-party platforms is dangerous. Specifically, if the adversary injects a backdoor into the training set, the machine learning results might be misleading since the attackers will "instruct" the model to output unrealistic results they want. To make things worse, usually it is quite hard for the developers to find these backdoor attack since only a tiny change of the samples is sufficient to generate the misleading result.

In response to the above concerns, in this paper, we first give an overview of several achievements of both energy-based learning and backdoor attack. Then for EBL, it is important to shows its working mechanism and highlights the advantages over other methods. As for the backdoor attack, there is no bias on either the current research in attacker's strategy or defender's strategy. The goal is to figure out the potential to transplant the energy-based learning into the field of backdoor. There are three main contributions of this paper:

- An systematic study of the current trend in energy-based learning and backdoor methods.
- A proposed algorithm to leverage energy-based learning to enhance the prevention of backdoor attack.
- A case study to figure out the potential benefits of our proposed algorithm.

The remainder of this paper is organized as follows. Section 2 summarizes the features and the current trend of energy-based learning, including more descriptions for several loss functions. Then, Sect. 3 studies recent techniques in backdoor. It will present the techniques on both attackers' and defenders' side. Furthermore, Sect. 4 gives a detailed description of our proposed algorithm, followed a case study in Sect. 5. Afterwards, Sect. 6 discusses about how to combine energy-based learning together with backdoor by listing several possible directions. Finally, we conclude the paper in Sect. 7.

2 Energy-Based Learning Overview

In this section, we will give an overview of the background of energy-based learning by comparing it against some of the other machine learning techniques.

The goal is to show several research trends of this field so as to discover more potential application situations.

2.1 Energy-Based Models Overview

The rapid development of machine learning has already shown its usefulness in many fields, such as finance [12,40], tele-health [33,39], and transportation [34,35]. The general framework of machine learning [21,32,38] is to output the values of target variables given the values of input data. An important metric to measure the trained model is that how far its output is from the correct result. The energy-based models leverage a reasonable energy function which represents the "goodness" (or "badness") of each possible configuration X and Y.

There are several scenarios where the EBM can be considered as a good fit. The first one is prediction and classification. This situation is quite visualized in Fig. 1 where given the input X, we want to get the value of Y that is most compatible with the current input. The second one is about the ranking, which is more complex than the first scenario. Specifically, we can consider the prediction and classification as finding the minimum value among all candidates while regard ranking as a sorting problem. However, they are similar essentially since the ultimate goal is to compare the energy value among multiple configurations. The third one is about detection, which is quite popular in the field of image recognition. Given the input X and output Y, we want to see whether Y could be the possible result by comparing the energy value of such configuration with a specific threshold. The last scenario, conditional density estimation, usually occurs when the output Y is only an intermediate output that is fed to the input of another, separately built system.

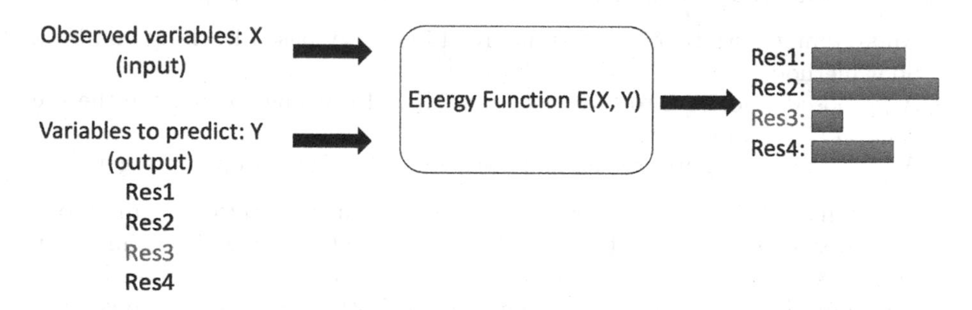

Fig. 1. Energy function E(X, Y) is used to measure the compatibility between the input X and the output Y. The model selects the output that minimizes the energy E.

Among all these four scenarios mentioned above, the core of EBMs is the equation below.

$$Y^* = argminE(X, Y) \tag{1}$$

It uses the convention that the highly compatible configurations of variable have small energy values while highly incompatible configurations of the variables means large energy value. Therefore, in the energy-based learning framework, we want to select reasonable energy functions so that it can clearly differentiate compatible configurations from incompatible configurations easily.

2.2 Loss Function in Energy-Based Learning

The ultimate goal for energy-based learning is to output a configuration between the input variables X and the output variables Y for new input samples that do not belong to the training data set. However, only the data within the training set is visible, what we could do is to divide them into both training set and testing set so that our trained model can be guaranteed to have good performance in the testing set. In order to achieve this goal, we need to develop specific metrics measuring the distance between the correct results and the current output, which can be regarded as the loss function selection. A good loss function [5] can clearly differentiate the correct solutions from the wrong ones. We would overview several typically used loss function below.

The first and most simplest one is called the energy loss defined as

$$L(Y^i, E(W, Y, X^i)) = E(W, Y, X^i) \tag{2}$$

This is one of the most commonly used in situations such as regression [42] and neural network [52]. However, when applying this loss function into other architectures, it cannot output the desired answer because the loss fails to pull up on any other energy even if it can push down the energy of the desired answer. In other words, the energy loss will only work with architectures that can work in a way to push down on $E(W, Y^i, X^i)$ together with pull up energies of the other answers.

The second one is called generalized perception loss defined as

$$L(Y^i, E(W, Y, X^i)) = E(W, Y^i, X^i) - minE(W, Y, X^i) \tag{3}$$

If we take a close look at the loss function, we can find that its value is always non-negative since the second term is the lower bound of the first term. In addition, this loss function provides some room to push down on the energy of the desired answer while pulling up on the energy of other answers. To be specific, when we increase the value of $E(W, Y^i, X^i)$ when Y^i is not the desired answer, the first term will increase while the second term will keep the same. The perception loss has been used in settings such as handwriting recognition [31] and speech tagging [44]. However, its major deficiency is that there is lack of mechanisms to enlarge the gap between correct answer and incorrect ones, making it harder for people to differentiate them.

The third one is called generalized margin loss defined as

$$L(W, Y^i, X^i) = Q_m(E(W, Y^i, X^i), E(W, \bar{Y}^i, X^i)) \tag{4}$$

where $Q_m(x_1, x_2)$ is a convex function whose gradient has a positive dot product with vector $(1, -1)$ in the region where $E(W, Y^i, X^i) + m > E(W, \bar{Y}^i, X^i)$ Margin losses can represent several loss functions such as the hinge loss [13], log loss [51], minimum classification error loss [15], and square-exponential loss. Some form of margin should be created to enlarge the gap between the correct answers and the incorrect ones.

2.3 Features and Application of EBM Frameworks

The energy-based learning offers a unified framework for many probabilistic and non-probabilistic approaches to learning because it can be considered as an alternative to estimation for prediction, classification, or decision-making task. In addition, as for energy-based learning, there is no requirement for normalization, which is necessary for probabilistic models. Therefore, this gives EBM framework much more flexibility in the design of learning machines. In fact, many existing learning models can be expressed simply in the framework of energy-based learning.

3 Techniques in Backdoor

In this section, we want to make an overview of the backdoor techniques [23]. It will start from a general description of the backdoor concept followed by current backdoor trends, including the development on both the attackers side and the defenders side. We are trying to add some insights for potential improvements for better attacking and defending strategies.

3.1 Backdoor Concept

Traditional backdoor refers to a malicious code piece embedded by an attacker into one system so that the attacker can obtain higher privilege than allowed. For example, the attacker can circumvent the authentication system by inputting his/her own password. Usually, such action is hard to detect because the whole system works normally most of the time except when the attacker is asked to input a password. Y. Zeng and M. Qiu et al. had proposed several novel algorithms to prevent backdoor attack, such as clean label techniques [56] and Deep-Sweep [37].

Given the popularity of backdoor attack, people even start to consider the triggers [54,57] of the backdoor attack. In general, the conclusion is that if there is inconsistency between the attack for test cases and the attack for training cases, the attack would be vulnerable [24].

3.2 Attackers in Backdoor

Usually, the attackers can implement their backdoor attack in three aspects: data set [3], platform [4] and model [18]. To make things worse, these three parts are not orthogonal to each other. An attacker can put the attack in all three aspects at the same time.

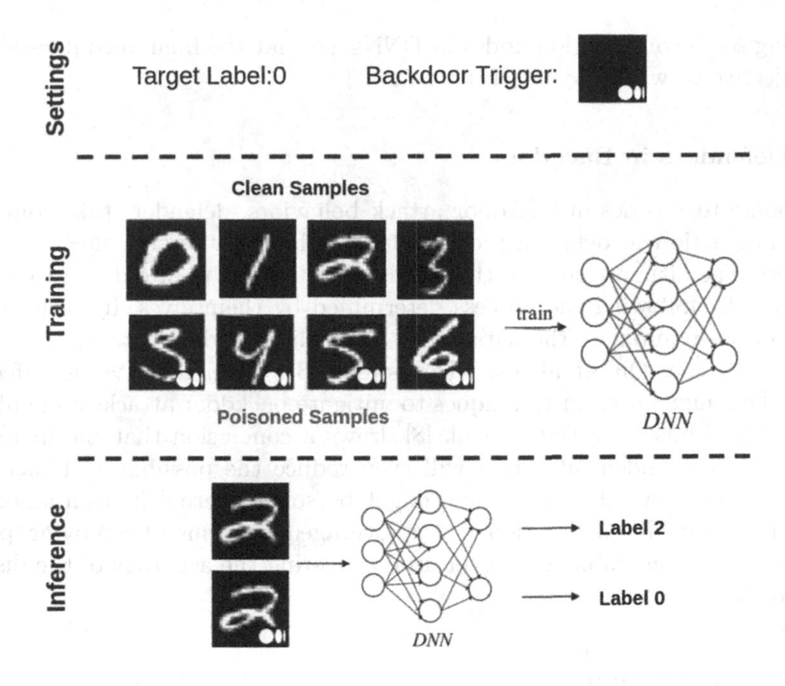

Fig. 2. An example to show how backdoor attacks work.

The backdoor attack to data set is illustrated in Fig. 2. Due to the privilege obtained by the attacker, he/she have the access to update the data set. Therefore, the attacker adds some poisoned samples which have some white circles in the bottom right and labels them as zero. Then the poisoned data set will be fed into models such as deep neural network to generate the inference model. The poisoned samples will add a lot of redundant misleading features which will decrease the accuracy of the model output. For example, in Fig. 2, for any input with white circles in the bottom right, the trained deep neural network will label it as zero rather than consider other pixels.

As for the backdoor attack for the platform, after the users provide their data set. Model structure, and the training schedule to one third-party platform, the attackers will try to modify the training process. For instance, the attacker instructs the platform to train the model before cleaning the data [43], which is a necessary for machine learning. If this happens, it will lead to the output result far from correctness. In other words, even if the attacker cannot modify anything inside the data, changing the training process can generate bad result as well.

Also, the backdoor attack for the model is another venue for the attackers to use so as to influence the output result. Specifically, if the users want to train the data set on deep neural network through third-party platform, they need to provide the model structure beforehand. However, after receiving the model, the attacker can modify the model into a new one, by removing some layers or removing some computation nodes in DNNs, so that the final output result will be subjective to what the attacker wants.

3.3 Defenders in Backdoor

In response to a series of backdoor attack behaviors, defenders take some corresponding action to detect attacking clues and avoid the side effect from the attackers. The ultimate goal for the defenders is to train their data on the model they want by following the process determined by themselves. In other words, they want to manipulate the data set to avoid the backdoor attack.

In this scope, Qiu et al. used Deepsweep [37] to investigate the effectiveness of data augmentation techniques to mitigate backdoor attacks and enhance DL models' robustness; Datta et al. [8] draws a conclusion that the increasing number of independent attackers will even reduce the possibility of successful backdoor attack, which means there might be some internal friction among all attackers; knowledge distillation [55] is leveraged in terms of removing poison data from a poison training data set and recovering the accuracy of the distillation model.

4 Our Approach

Based on the description of energy-based learning techniques and backdoor methods, in this section, we want to propose our approach to combine these two together. Specifically, we want to explore the possibility to put energy function into the constraints part rather than the objective function. Then, we can try to solve an optimization problem with customized objective function, or find a feasible solution.

4.1 Energy Function as a Constraint

As for most of the points in the discussion above, we consider the energy function as the objective one and try to find a suitable candidate to measure our goal. In fact, we can reallocate the energy function into other places. For instance, we could set up some customized objective function with the energy function as one constraint. Therefore, in this part, rethinking the role of energy function is our main topic.

To be specific, all resources such as computation resources and storage memory are limited. Hence, in a lot of situations, what the users care most about is a reasonably good choice or an acceptable sub-optimal result. In response to this demand, we believe that we should put the energy function in the constraint part by choosing one energy function and restricting its value to be less than or equal to a predefined threshold. The choice of objective functions [46] can be prone to the users' preference. The concrete format can be shows as following:

$$
\begin{aligned}
\underset{X,\alpha}{\text{minimize}} \quad & f(X,\alpha) + \text{regularization function} \\
\text{subject to} \quad & E_i(X,Y) \leq c_i, \; i = 1,\ldots,m. \\
& X \in \text{Input Range} \\
& \alpha \in \text{Parameter Range} \\
& \text{Other Constraints}
\end{aligned}
$$

The objective function can be determined by the users depending on their preference. In addition to other normal constraints (e.g., the range of parameters), we add new constraints by setting the energy functions to be within a threshold. Typically the smaller the energy function, the better the effect. Therefore, these constraints can force the output result to be reasonably good within a range. Solving these optimization problems might involve convex and nonconvex solvers selection [14] or new solvers development. These developments are orthogonal to our approach.

In addition to solve the optimization problem with selected objective functions, it is also possible for us to solve a satisfiable problem by leveraging practical solvers [25]. Switching from optimization problem to satisfiable problem is quite simply. We can stick to the optimization solver with the objective function f to be independent of all the constraints. Therefore, whatever the constraints' function format, they will not affect the final optimal value of the objective function. The goal for this problem is to find a feasible solution which satisfies all the constraints. By comparing against several solvers [29,49], we can finally find the most efficient and effective one for our framework.

4.2 Algorithm to Implement Our Approach

According to our description of the proposed method, in this subsection, we are trying to present an algorithm showing how to implement our approach in more details.

In general, this proposed algorithm switch the position of customized objective function and the current energy loss function. Usually, the users will have some threshold in mind before making the optimization problem. For instance, in linear regression, if the value of R^2 or adjusted R^2 [27] is too small, people need to switch to other candidate models. Therefore, our algorithm provides us with chances to give threshold beforehand (which might not need to be optimal) but offers another opportunity to give more customized objective functions. Then the algorithm collects information including input data, current constraints, customized objective functions and a list of threshold representing the users' expectation of the final value of their objective function. The algorithm also picks up one solver for this optimization problem. Then, the algorithm will regard the customized function as the objective function. It will go through all threshold within the list and try to solve a feasible solution and jump out of the loop whenever there is a solution. The output includes the threshold value of the energy function and final optimal output value.

Algorithm 1. ***Backdoor Prevention*** **Algorithm**

Require: N input pairs, M constraints, the customized objective function P, estimated threshold list $[c_1, c_2, ..., c_k]$ for the objective function, and the current objective loss function F.
Ensure: An updated optimization problem to prevent the backdoor attack.
1: Force the threshold list to be sorted in increasing order
2: Replace the current objective loss function F by customized objective function P
3: Remain the current M constraints
4: Add new constraint which represent the users' anticipation of the energy function. It gives the upper bound of the energy function. The format should be $F(X, Y) \leq c_i$
5: Choose one solver to solve this optimization function.
6: while (1)
7: set the threhold of energy function to be c_i
8: solve the optimization problem
9: if (there is a solution)
10: break;
11: else
12: i++;
Output results: The final results include the threshold value of the energy function and the optimal value of the customized objective function.

5 Case Study

In this section, we are going to present some benefits of our proposed algorithm by showing potential application in several fields, such as monitoring the attack in iPhone and web mail server. Then, two scenarios, equilibrium between attackers and defenders together with the energy function selection, are mentioned to highlight more benefits.

5.1 Backdoor Attack in iPhone

In 2016, there is a debate between Apple vs the U.S. government in terms of iPhone [7,53]. On the one side, Apple together with digital rights groups advocating protection of customer digital privacy want to protect the privacy of all users; on the other side, the U.S. government and the FBI wants to force the company to unlock data to provide crucial evidence which could be helpful to detect attack from terrorists. To make thing worse, this debate will last forever since there is no absolutely correct answer to both sides.

In order to solve this problem, traditional machine learning goal to prevent backdoor attack might be out-of-date because it is hard to create one loss function to measure the debate from both sides. However, our proposed energy-based learning can be quite helpful in this part. Specifically, we can leverage two energy functions, each of which measures the requirement from either the privacy advocates and the information requestors. After putting them into the constraints of the optimization problem, it is possible for us to get an optimal or a feasible solution based on the users' requirement.

5.2 Backdoor Attack in Web Mail Server

Web mail server is another place where a lot of backdoor attack might happen. Given the situation that a lot of spam detection methods have been implemented in mail server, the attackers have sought to bypass these attack detectors. For instance, they might use some strange ways to express their sensitive contents so that the detectors cannot label these mails as spam message. Although the ultimate goal of the system developers is to rule out all spam emails, the limited cost to implement their attack detection system cannot allow them to achieve this ideal goal.

Therefore, it is necessary to leverage our energy-based learning in the area. Rather than do a classification problem which tries its best to differentiate spam email from normal ones, we put the misclassification rate into the constraint part and bound it by one threshold. In addition, the cost to main the system can also be regarded as a constraint. Then solving one feasible solution within these constraints can output an acceptable solution to us.

5.3 Equilibrium Among the Arm-Race Between Backdoor Attackers and Defenders

We believe that the relationship between attackers and defenders will exist for a long time. There is always an arm race [58] between attackers and defenders in the field of backdoor. In order to avoid the forever arm race in between, we want to find the equilibrium point in between. Specifically, we can develop two energy functions, one for the attackers and the other one for the defenders. Then, the output of these two energy functions will determine the level of difficulty for each counter-party to implement their action. If both of them are greater than some specific threshold, it means that neither attackers nor the defenders have strong willingness to continue putting any efforts to this system, which can be regarded as an equilibrium.

In order to calculate the equilibrium [22,30] status, the selection of the energy functions for both counter-parties is quite important. These two functions should objectively reflect the reward for attackers and defenders. When we are given a series of energy functions, it is important to train them by feeding current backdoor attacks data. Then, as for newly developed system, the developers are willing to consider the equilibrium status beforehand so that they will try to make the system within the equilibrium range. After that, even if the developed system is still not bug-free, the attackers do not have strong preference to implement any backdoor attack.

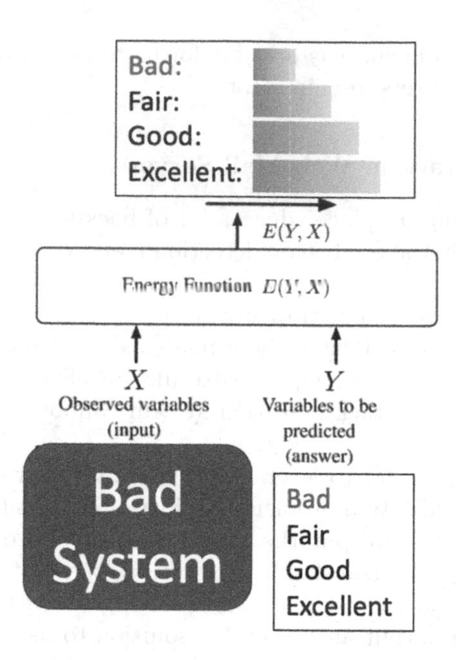

Fig. 3. Energy function E(X, Y) is used to measure the safety level of the input system.

5.4 Energy Function Selection for Safety Level Measurement

As for the energy function selection to measure the safety level of the current system design, typically, both the system developers and the users, even for the attackers, want to quickly understand whether a given system is safe enough to use. Therefore, it would be valuable to design an energy function to measure such safety level.

Naturally, the lower energy value represents the higher safety level of the current system. Based on this consensus, we want to build an energy-based model and train this model among several current available systems in Fig. 3. The input can be considered as the features of those system while the output would be the safety level of them. The goal is to find the value of parameters of the energy function's skeleton. After training within these existing systems, we want to implement the energy function into newly built ones to have an estimation for whether its current status is safe enough to use by comparing its value with a particular threshold. A reasonable choice of the energy function can be helpful to show whether a given system is safe enough to use.

This direction is useful because currently, most of the existing system safety analysis tools [45] involves brute-force testing (e.g. software test [2]). In other words, people need to come up with mechanisms to develop test cases automatically so that it is highly possible that the current scenario is bug-free. This process is quite time-consuming and money consuming. What we really want is a general model which can quickly inference the safety level of the product. At least, it is able to easily rule out the possibility that bad system will go to the market.

6 Discussion

Given the overview of both energy-based learning ideas and backdoor attacks, we believe it would be quite promising to implement the energy-based learning tools into the backdoor field. Therefore, in this section, we want to propose several directions worth further research.

Generally, the discussions are mainly about how easy it would be for the attackers to hijack the system by using one particular strategy, and how hard it would be for the defenders to avoid the attack with any defending tools.

6.1 Energy Function Design to Detect Backdoor Attack Behavior?

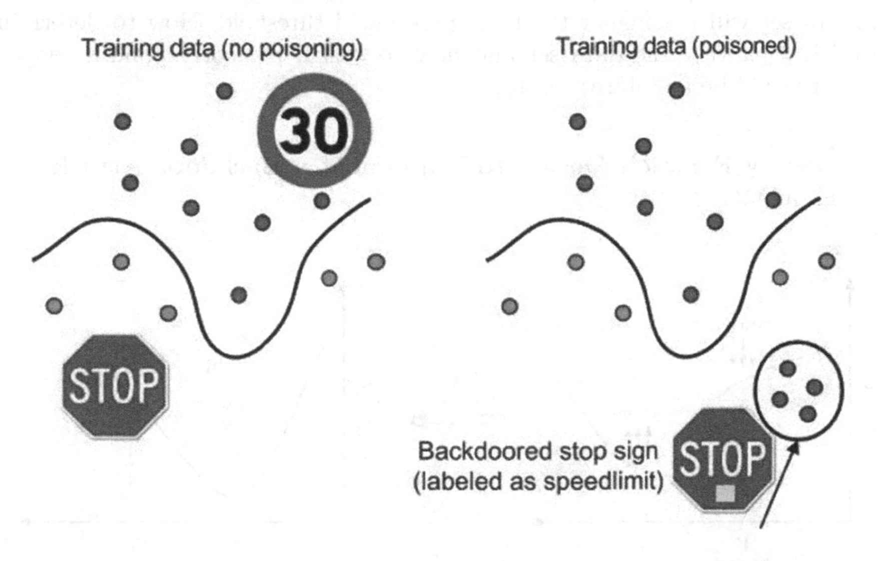

Fig. 4. Energy function E(X, Y) is used to measure the sanity level of the data set.

We also consider the energy function design for backdoor attack detection would be an interesting direction. Just as shown in Fig. 2, sometimes if the untrusted third-party add small amount of poisoned data into the training set similar to Fig. 4, the output result might diverge from what it is supposed to be. Therefore, it is vital to come up with an energy-based model to quickly check whether the existing data is still "clean" and reliable or not. In other words, we hope the energy function can help detect the attack behavior inside the data set quickly.

In general it can be regarded as a classification problem. The input would be the current training data set while the output is a value measuring the reliability level of the current status. Given the fact that people have strong preference to store their data in the third-party platforms and sometimes those platforms might face malicious attack, it is important to do some sanity check [26] before reusing the training data for machine learning tasks. A naive solution might be storing the data in multiple places and then comparing against them whenever using the data. However, it takes a long time to compare against two super large data set, which makes the machine learning task much longer than necessary. Another possible solution is to randomly select samples from the data set and only check consistency among these samples. However, how many samples we should select and how to select these samples remain a big problem to implement reliable sanity check.

Therefore, if it is possible for us to choose one energy function that could easily detect the change of the data set, the whole process can be finished much more quickly. To be specific, the input of the energy function would be two data set and the energy function itself will randomly select some of the critical parts within the data set. If there is no big difference in between, the absolute difference between the output value of the energy function in two versions of this data set will be smaller than the predefined threshold. How to determine the critical parts of the data set and how to design the corresponding energy function would be an interesting topic.

6.2 Energy Function Design to Implement a Backdoor Attack Efficiently?

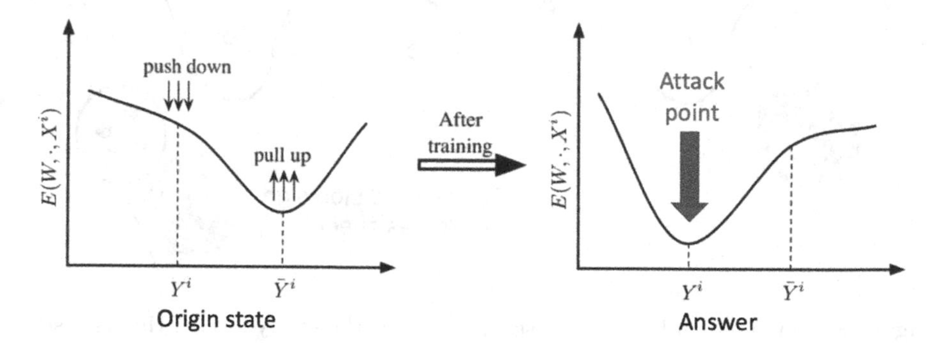

Fig. 5. Energy function E(X, Y) is used to find the best place to implement an attack.

As for the attackers, an energy function is also useful for them to pick up efficient and effective strategy to implement their backdoor attack similar to [3]. When the attackers decide to put some noise into the data set either by changing the existing ones or adding misleading data, they also want to hide their action from the defenders. Therefore, a good strategy is helpful to come up with in order to avoid the detection from the defender. There might be several dimensions to consider. For example, how much of the existing data should be modified? The less the better; how close the updated data set is compared with the original one? The closer the better; how easy it is to implement this modification to the data set? The easier the better.

We can consider this question as a ranking problem. The input to the energy function includes the features of existing system and a series of attack strategies. Then, the energy function will output values which represent the level of difficulty to implement those strategies in Fig. 5. It will rank them in some specific order and then provide more useful feedback to the attackers. The attackers can combine the ranking result from the predefined energy function with the potential cost to each strategy, before taking the action.

7 Conclusion

In this paper, based on the study of current development of both energy-based learning and backdoor, we proposed some novel approaches to leverage the energy-based learning tools for preventing backdoor attack to machine learning. The case studies in this paper had demonstrated the effectiveness of using energy-based learning to prevent backdoor attack, which is a critical threat to machine learning. The promising usage of energy-based learning will greatly impact the security aspect of machine learning.

References

1. Ali, P., Faraj, R., Koya, E., Ali, J., Faraj, R.: Data normalization and standardization: a technical report. Mach Learn Tech report (2014)
2. Beizer, B.: Software system testing and quality assurance. Van Nostrand Reinhold Co. (1984)
3. Chen, X., Liu, C., Li, B., Lu, K., Song, D.: Targeted backdoor attacks on deep learning systems using data poisoning. arXiv preprint arXiv:1712.05526 (2017)
4. Chen, X., Ma, Y., Lu, S.: Use procedural noise to achieve backdoor attack. IEEE Access. **9**, 120204–120216 (2021)
5. Christoffersen, P., Jacobs, K.: The importance of the loss function in option valuation. J. Fin. Econ. **72**, 291–318 (2004)
6. Copeland, M., Soh, J., Puca, A., Manning, M., Gollob, D.: Microsoft Azure. Apress, New York (2015)
7. Coutros, G.: The implications of creating an iPhone backdoor. Natl Sec. L. Brief **6**, 81 (2016)
8. Datta, S., Lovisotto, G., Martinovic, I., Shadbolt, N.: Widen the backdoor to let more attackers in. arXiv preprint arXiv:2110.04571 (2021)
9. Delac, G., Silic, M., Krolo, J.: Emerging security threats for mobile platforms. In: 34th International Convention MIPRO (2011)
10. Fang, B., Feng, Y.: Design of high-frequency trading algorithm based on machine learning. arXiv preprint arXiv:1912.10343 (2019)
11. Ford, V., Siraj, A.: Applications of machine learning in cyber security. In: 27th International Conference on Computer Application in Industry and Engineering (2014)
12. Gai, K., et al.: Efficiency-aware workload optimizations of heterogeneous cloud computing for capacity planning in financial industry. In: IEEE CSCloud (2015)
13. Gentile, C., Warmuth, M.: Linear hinge loss and average margin. In: Advances in Neural Information Processing Systems (1998)

14. Hiriart-Urruty, J.: From convex optimization to nonconvex optimization. Necessary and sufficient conditions for global optimality. In: Clarke, F.H., Demyanov, V.F., Giannessi, F. (eds) Nonsmooth Optimization and Related Topics. Ettore Majorana International Science Series, vol. 43, pp. 219–239. Springer, Boston (1989). https://doi.org/10.1007/978-1-4757-6019-4_13
15. Juang, B., Hou, W., Lee, C.: Minimum classification error rate methods for speech recognition. IEEE Trans. Speech Audio proc. **53**, 257–265 (1997)
16. Kotsiantis, S., Zaharakis, I., Pintelas, P.: Machine learning: a review of classification and combining techniques. Artif. Intel. Rev. **26**, 159–190 (2006)
17. Krishnan, S., Gonzalez, J.: Building your next big thing with google cloud platform: a guide for developers and enterprise architects (2015)
18. Kwon, H., Yoon, H., Park, K.: Multi-targeted backdoor: identifying backdoor attack for multiple deep neural networks. IEICE Trans. Inf. Sys. **103**, 883–887 (2020)
19. LeCun, Y., Chopra, S., Hadsell, R., Ranzato, M., Huang, F.: A tutorial on energy-based learning. Predict. Struct. Data. **1**, 1–59 (2006)
20. LeCun, Y., Huang, F.: Loss functions for discriminative training of energy-based models. In: International Workshop on Artificial Intelligence and Statistics (2005)
21. Li, Y., et al.: Intelligent fault diagnosis by fusing domain adversarial training and maximum mean discrepancy via ensemble learning. IEEE TII **17**(4), 2833–2841 (2020)
22. Li, Y., Tan, S., Deng, Y., Wu, J.: Attacker-defender game from a network science perspective. Chaos: Interdiscip. J. Nonlinear Sci. 28, 051102 (2018)
23. Li, Y., Wu, B., Jiang, Y., Li, Z., Xia, S.: Backdoor learning: a survey. arXiv preprint arXiv:2007.08745 (2020)
24. Li, Y., Wu, B., Li, L, He, R., Lyu, S.: Invisible backdoor attack with sample-specific triggers. In: IEEE/CVF CV (2021)
25. Lin, Y., Schrage, L.: The global solver in the LINDO API. Optim. Methods Softw. **24**(4–5), 657–668 (2009)
26. Lu, H., Xu, H., Liu, N, Zhou, Y., Wang, X.: Data sanity check for deep learning systems via learnt assertions. arXiv preprint arXiv:1909.03835 (2019)
27. Miles, J.: R-squared, adjusted R-squared. Encyclopedia of statistics in behavioral science (2005)
28. Mukherjee, S.: Benefits of AWS in modern cloud. SSRN 3415956 (2019)
29. Müller, T.: ITC 2007 solver description: a hybrid approach. Ann. Oper. Res. **172**, 429–446 (2009)
30. Pirani, M., Nekouei, E., Sandberg, H., Johansson, K.: A graph-theoretic equilibrium analysis of attacker-defender game on consensus dynamics under h_2 performance metric. IEEE TNSE, pp. 1991–2000 (2020)
31. Plamondon, R., Srihari, S.: Online and off-line handwriting recognition: a comprehensive survey. IEEE Trans. Pattern Anal. Mach. Intell. **22**, 63–84 (2000)
32. Qiu, H., Dong, T., et al.: Adversarial attacks against network intrusion detection in IoT systems. IEEE IoT J. **8**(13), 10327–10335 (2020)
33. Qiu, H., et al.: Secure health data sharing for medical cyber-physical systems for the healthcare 4.0. IEEE JBHI **24**, 2499–2505 (2020)
34. Qiu, H., et al.: Topological graph convolutional network-based urban traffic flow and density prediction. IEEE TITS. **22**, 4560–4569 (2020)
35. Qiu, H., Qiu, M., Lu, R.: Secure V2X communication network based on intelligent PKI and edge computing. IEEE Netw. **34**(42), 172–178 (2019)
36. Qiu, H., Qiu, M., Lu, Z.: Selective encryption on ECG data in body sensor network based on supervised machine learning. Info. Fusion **55**, 59–67 (2020)

37. Qiu, H, Zeng, Y., Guo, S., Zhang, T., Qiu, M., Thuraisingham, B.: Deepsweep: an evaluation framework for mitigating DNN backdoor attacks using data augmentation. In: 2021 ACM Asia CCS (2021)
38. Qiu, H., Zheng, Q., et al.: Deep residual learning-based enhanced JPEG compression in the internet of things. IEEE TII **17**(3), 2124–2133 (2020)
39. Qiu, L., Gai, K., Qiu, M: Optimal big data sharing approach for tele-health in cloud computing. In: IEEE SmartCloud, pp. 184–189 (2016)
40. Qiu, M., et al.: Data transfer minimization for financial derivative pricing using Monte Carlo simulation with GPU in 5G. JCS **29**(16), 2364–2374 (2016)
41. Qiu, M., Gai, K., Xiong, Z.: Privacy-preserving wireless communications using bipartite matching in social big data. FGCS **87**, 772–781 (2018)
42. William, J., Freund, R., Sa, P.: Regression Analysis. Elsevier, Amsterdam (2006)
43. Rahm, E., Do, H.: Data cleaning: problems and current approaches. IEEE Data Eng. Bull. **23**, 3–13 (2000)
44. Ratnaparkhi, A., et al.: A maximum entropy model for part-of-speech tagging. In EMNLP **1**, 133–142 (1996)
45. Rouvroye, J., Van Den Bliek, E.: Comparing safety analysis techniques. Reliabil. Eng. Syst. Safety **75**, 289–294 (2002)
46. Roy, B.: Problems and methods with multiple objective functions. Math. Progr. **1**(1), 239–266 (1971)
47. Sebe, N., Cohen, I., Garg, A., Huang, T.: Machine Learning in Computer Vision. Springer, Dordrecht (2005). https://doi.org/10.1007/1-4020-3275-7
48. Shao, Z., Xue, C., et al.: Security protection and checking for embedded system integration against buffer overflow attacks via hardware/software. IEEE TC **55**(4), 443–453 (2006)
49. Stellato, B., et al.: Embedded mixed-integer quadratic optimization using the OSQP solver. In: IEEE ECC, pp. 1536–1541 (2018)
50. Tulabandhula, T., Rudin, C.: On combining machine learning with decision making. Mach. Learn. **97**, 33–64 (2014)
51. Vovk, V.: The fundamental nature of the log loss function. In: Beklemishev, L.D., Blass, A., Dershowitz, N., Finkbeiner, B., Schulte, W. (eds.) Fields of Logic and Computation II. LNCS, vol. 9300, pp. 307–318. Springer, Cham (2015). https://doi.org/10.1007/978-3-319-23534-9_20
52. Wang, S.: Artificial neural network. In: Interdisciplinary Computing in Java Programming (2003)
53. Wolfson, B., Levy, L.: Impenetrable: Should apple backdoor the iPhone? (2020)
54. Yang, W., Lin, Y., Li, P., Zhou, J., Sun, X.: Rethinking stealthiness of backdoor attack against NLP models. In: 59th Meeting of the Association for Computational Linguistics and the 11th International Joint Conference on NPL (2021)
55. Yoshida, K., Fujino, T.: Disabling backdoor and identifying poison data by using knowledge distillation in backdoor attacks on deep neural networks. In: 13th ACM Workshop on Artificial Intelligence and Security (2020)
56. Zeng, Y, Pan, M., Just, H., Lyu, L., Qiu, M., Jia, R.: Narcissus: a practical clean-label backdoor attack with limited information. In: CoRR abs/2204.05255 (2022)
57. Zeng, Y., Park, W., Mao, Z., Jia, R.: Rethinking the backdoor attacks' triggers: a frequency perspective. In: EEE/CVF CV (2021)
58. Zhang, Y., Paxson, V.: Detecting backdoors. In: USENIX Security Symposium (2000)

PUF-Based Intellectual Property Protection for CNN Model

Dawei Li[1], Yangkun Ren[1], Di Liu[1], Zhenyu Guan[1(✉)], Qianyun Zhang[1], Yanzhao Wang[2], and Jianwei Liu[1]

[1] School of Cyber Science and Technology, Beihang University, Beijing 100191, China
{lidawei,renyk1319,liudi2020,guanzhenyu,zhangqianyun, liujianwei}@buaa.edu.cn

[2] Blockchain Lab, Chinabond Finance and Information Technology Co., Ltd., Beijing 100044, China
wangyz@chinabond.com.cn

Abstract. It usually takes a lot of time and resources to train a high-accurate Machine Learning model, so it is believed that the trainer owns the *Intellectual Property* (IP) of the model. With the help of various computing accelerators, a Machine Learning model can run on FPGAs, and model providers render services by selling FPGAs with models embeded-ded. Unauthorized copying of the model infringes the owner's copyrights, so there is an urgent need for the effective protection of model IP. In this paper, we propose a *Physical Unclonable Function* (PUF) based CNN model IP protection scheme. Before selling the model, the model providers confuse the parameters of the model with the response of a PUF, then embed the confused model into the FPGA where the PUF is. In this way, the protected model can get correct results only if running on the specific FPGA. Experimental results show that the performance difference between the confused model and the original model is negligible, and it is difficult for the adversary to get the correct parameters. Our approach effectively protects the IP of the model by restricting the model to only run on the specified FPGA and is easily extended to other models with convolutional layers and linear fully connected layers.

Keywords: PUF · CNN · IP protection · FPGA · Machine learning

1 Introduction

With the rapid development of the Internet [1,2] and the widespread application of high-definition cameras, image data has exploded. The method of manual analysis cannot meet fast and real-time image analysis requirements. In recent years, the development of *Machine Learning* (ML) technology provides a good solution to this problem. Convolutional Neural Networks (CNN) has been widely used in image classification [3] and image recognition [4]. However, the model owner usually takes a lot of time and resources to train a high-accurate and commercially applicable model. For example, it costs $0.8-$1.6 million to train

G. Memmi et al. (Eds.): KSEM 2022, LNAI 13370, pp. 722–733, 2022.
https://doi.org/10.1007/978-3-031-10989-8_57

a model with 1.5 billion parameters [5], so it is believed that the trainer owns the intellectual property (IP) [6–8] of this ML model. As a trained model, while being commercialized, it also faces the risk of IP being stolen. Therefore, how to sell trained models under the premise of ensuring safety [9,10] is a problem that model providers must solve.

1.1 Related Work

In *Machine-Learning-as-a-Service* (MLaaS) scenario, CNN models typically run in the cloud environment, providing an interface to users. Many methods have been proposed to embed watermarks into models [7,11,12], so that when the model is stolen, the trainer can claim ownership of the model by validating the watermark [13–15]. Chen et al. [16] proposed a testing framework for copyright protection that can determine whether a model is a copy of another model. Li et al. [17] trained a watermarked model with external features and a classifier that is used to determine whether the suspicious model contains information on external features. However, the parameters of model embedded watermarks are different from the original model, so it is easy to detect the presence of watermarks, and these methods can only take effect when the model owner maintains rights after the model is stolen, they cannot guarantee that the model will not be stolen.

In another scenario, with the help of computing accelerators [18–20], a model can also computer fast on the FPGA. Therefore, the CNN model provider embeds the trained model into the FPGA, and the user can use the model to complete the work after purchasing the FPGA. Some methods to protect models embedded in FPGAs have been proposed [21,22]. Guo et al. [23] presented a PUF-based pay-per-device scheme, which uses PUF to obfuscate accelerator and model parameters so that the model can only output correct results when it is computed on a specific accelerator. However, the CNN model provider in this method uses the PUF circuit that has been written by the FPGA and accelerator provider, which cannot fully guarantee the security of the model parameters. If the adversary colludes with the accelerator provider, it will be easy to get the correct model. M. Qiu et al. [24] proposed an efficient scheme by intelligently distributing keys for authentication in V2X (Vehicles to Everything) networks based on intelligent PKI (Public Key Infrastructure) and edge computing [25,26] and used accelerators to help on the special situations . Chakraborty et al. [27] proposed a new method that the key stored in a secure and trusted environment is embedded into the model training process, and a new key-dependent backpropagation algorithm is proposed, which can make the model unusable for attackers who do not know the key. But the keys are still at risk of being leaked.

1.2 Contribution

This paper proposes a novel PUF-based scheme to protect the IP of CNN models. Our scheme has two advantages. Firstly, A PUF is implemented by the model owner and applied to confuse the parameters of a trained CNN model

[28,29], therefore, the unauthorized users are unknown of the details of the confusing process and are unable to get the correct parameters from the confused model. Secondly, our scheme combines the parameters of a layer of the model on a channel-by-channel basis according to the response of the PUF, without destroying the overall structure of the model, so it can be extended to other models with convolutional layers and linear fully connected layers. The contributions of this paper can be summarized in the following points.

- We implement a PUF on the FPGA and apply it to confuse the parameters of a trained ML model to protect its IP. This paper takes the CNN model as an example, and the confusion scheme can be applied to other ML models.
- The scheme guarantees a confused model can only get correct results when running on the specific FPGA. The legitimate user runs the PUF on the FPGA to get a response, restores the model according to the response, and gets the correct results.
- The performance and security of the confused model are also evaluated. Because the PUF response is random, the adversary is unable to get the correct parameters even though he knows the structure of the model. Therefore, the purpose of protecting the model IP is achieved.

The rest of this paper is organized as follows. Section 2 introduces mainly the background of Physical Unclonable Function and Convolutional Neural Network. In Sect. 3, we talk about our scheme in detail. The analysis of implemented PUF and our IP protection scheme is presented in Sect. 4. Section 5 is the conclusion.

2 Preliminaries

2.1 Physical Unclonable Function

Since Pappu et al. [30] summarized the basic principles of optics in 2002, and put forward the concept of *Physical Unclonable Function* (PUF) for the first time, PUF has received more and more attention and various PUFs have been proposed, such as *Arbiter PUF* (APUF) [31], *Ring Oscillator PUF* (RO PUF) [32], SRAM PUF [33], *interpose PUF* (iPUF) [34], and Lattice PUF [35]. As a new type of security primitive, it is usually more difficult to calculate the response of PUF than to obtain the digital key stored in NVM [36], so PUF has been widely applied for device authentication. And it is also attracted the attention of model IP protection workers.

The basic principle of PUF is to enable each entity to generate unpredictable responses to the same input challenge with the help of unavoidable randomness differences, called *Challenge-Response Pair* (CRP). In contrast to standard digital systems, the response of a PUF depends on its existence of nanoscale disordered structures that even the makers of hardware devices cannot precisely replicate and predict. Therefore, PUF has some advantages that traditional digital keys do not have. In addition, PUF has the advantages of fast calculation, lightweight resources, and no need to store keys separately.

Arbiter PUF (APUF) was first proposed by Lee et al. [31] and is a delay-based digital circuit PUF. In the APUF, an electrical signal will enter two completely symmetrical circuits at the same time. In the circuit, the selection module is implemented by two 2-to-1 data selectors. The electrical signal has 2 path options in each selection module, so an APUF with an N-order selection module has 2^N different options. The circuit uses a D flip-flop as an arbiter. APUF is ideal for use as security primitive in FPGA chips due to its exponential CRP space, acceptable hardware overhead, and less sensitivity to noise.

2.2 Convolutional Neural Network

Convolutional Neural Networks (CNN) [37] is a typical structure in Machine Learning, which was proposed by Lecun in 1989. It has gradually become a representative network for feature extraction. Typical CNN models consist of *convolution layer* (CONV), *pooling layer* (POOL), *fully connected layer* (FC), etc.

As an important structure in CNN, the convolutional layer uses convolution kernels to perform local and sparse operations, which can be regarded as the process of sliding window calculation on the image. The pooling layer is the operation of down-sampling the output feature map of the convolutional layer. After the convolution operation, the feature map has a high dimension, which is prone to overfitting. The pooling operation can reduce the feature dimension and reduce the possibility of overfitting. There is generally a linear fully connected layer, which is used to map the learned results to the label space of the samples to realize the prediction or classification task. If the convolution kernel is regarded as an element, the calculation of the convolutional layer is Eq. 1.

$$y_i = \sum_{j=1}^{n} W_{ij} \times x_j + b_i \tag{1}$$

where the y_i is the i-th channel of output, and the x_j is the j-th channel of input.

3 Proposed IP Protection Scheme

In this section, a PUF-based CNN model IP protection scheme is proposed. At first, all parties in the system are introduced, and then the threat model is represented. To counteract these threats, our scheme is proposed.

3.1 Threat Model

There are three main parties in our scheme.

- **FPGA provider** sells the FPGAs to the CNN model provider. The FPGA provider is a neutral third party, and we believe he is trustworthy.

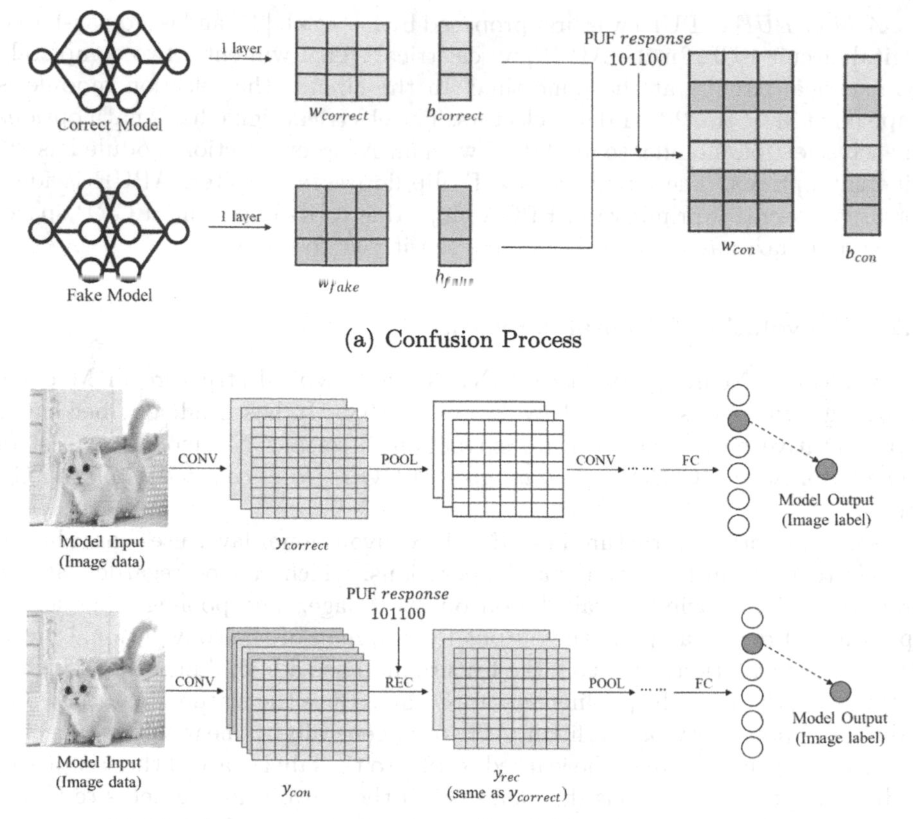

(a) Confusion Process

(b) Model Structure Before (upper) and After (bottom) Confusion

Fig. 1. Main idea of scheme

- **CNN model provider** sells the FPGAs embedded with confused CNN models. To protect his model IP, he applies our scheme to his trained model, then embeds the confused model into FPGAs, and sells them to a user.
- **User** buys FPGAs and models from the CNN model provider, and use them to finish his tasks.

In our scheme, we assume that the FPGA provider is trustworthy because he does not know any details of our scheme, and the implementation details of PUF and its CRPs must be kept secret. However, the user may act as an adversary, after he purchases an FPGA, and get the model architecture, he can get all the parameters of the confused model, recover and copy the model, and leak the model to other unauthorized users. To protect the IP of CNN models, this paper proposed a scheme for CNN model providers to confuse the parameters of models before selling them to a user, so that the adversary is unable to get the real parameters of the model embedded in FPGAs.

3.2 PUF-Based IP Protection Scheme

To resist the above threats, our PUF-based IP protection scheme is shown in Fig. 1. The CNN provider confuses the part of the layers of the protected model with the response that he implements on an FPGA, constructs a recovery layer, and adds it after the confused layer, therefore, the confusion model is constructed. The execution process of our scheme is as follows.

Step 1. The CNN provider firstly trains the **correct** model with **correct** dataset. This step usually takes a lot of time and computing resources, so this model is considered the IP of the owner. This model usually consists of several convolutional layers and linear layers, which will be confused in the next step.
Step 2. The CNN provider implements an arbiter PUF, which provides unique fingerprints of the FPGA for confusing model parameters, and also binds the model to a specific FPGA, therefore, only when the model runs on this FPGA the correct results will be calculated.
Step 3. The CNN provider trains the **fake** model with **fake** dataset, which is with the same structure of **correct** model.
Step 4. The CNN provider confuses one or more convolutional layer(s) and linear layer(s) by executing Algorithm 1. He mixes two parameter matrices of the same layers from **correct** model and **fake** model according to PUF response. When the response bit is 1, the parameters of the confusion matrix are the parameters of the **correct** model, otherwise, they are the parameters of the **fake** model.

Algorithm 1. Confuse the **correct** model with **fake** model

Input: Parameters from the same layers of two models: $w_{correct}, b_{correct}, w_{fake}, b_{fake}$
Input: PUF response: *response*

```
1: Init:correct_index, fake_index ← 1; n ← length(response); w_con[n], b_con[n] ← 0
2: for each i ∈ [1, n] do
3:    if response_i == 1 then
4:       w_con[i] ← w_correct[correct_index]
5:       b_con[i] ← b_correct[correct_index]
6:       correct_index ← correct_index + 1
7:    else
8:       w_con[i] ← w_fake[fake_index]
9:       b_con[i] ← b_fake[fake_index]
10:      fake_index ← fake_index + 1
11:   end if
12: end for
```

Output: Confused Parameters w_{con}, b_{con}

Step 5. In step 4, while confusing the parameters, it also increases the number of model parameters and changes the structure of the convolutional layer. Therefore, it is necessary to add a recovery layer after the confused layer into the model the correctness of the model. The generation of the recovery layer is completely dependent on the PUF response, which is completely confidential to the user. According to the PUF response, select the output row corresponding to bit 1, and splice them together as the output. In addition, Algorithm 2 shows how to generate a recovery matrix based on the PUF response, and multiply the output with the recovery matrix to get the desired result, which is more in line with the fundamental computing method of neural networks. The CNN model provider can add the recovery layer after the confused layer and think of it as a convolutional layer of the model with a kernel size of 1×1.

Algorithm 2. Recover the confused layer output to correct output

Input: Confused layer output: y_{con}
Input: PUF response: $response$

1: Init: $rec\_index \leftarrow 1; n \leftarrow \text{length}(response); M_{rec}[n/2][n] \leftarrow 0$
2: **for** each $i \in [1, n]$ **do**
3:     **if** $response_i == 1$ **then**
4:         $M_{rec}[rec\_index][i] \leftarrow 1$
5:         $rec\_index \leftarrow rec\_index + 1$
6:     **end if**
7: **end for**
8: $y_{rec} \leftarrow M_{rec} \times y_{con}$

Output: Recover layer output y_{rec}

4 Experimental Results

4.1 Arbiter PUF

According to the introduction of Sect. 2.1, an APUF is implemented firstly on an FPGA, it provides unique fingerprints of the FPGA for confusing model parameters, and also binds the model to a specific FPGA, so that only when the model is run on this FPGA the correct results will be calculated. Thanks to the unpredictability of PUF, even using the same challenge, running PUF on the same production batch of FPGAs, the responses from different FPGAs are completely different, so we can expose the input challenge of the PUF, as long as the PUF circuit is kept secret, the adversary is unable to get a correct response. We design a 64×1 APUF, its input is 64bits and output is 1bit, then copy the individual PUF circuits and splice their outputs together, we can get responses of any length. We implement a 64×64 APUF on the ZYNQ-7020 FPGA, and its reliability, uniqueness, and uniformity are evaluated.

Reliability refers to the ability of PUF to resist environmental changes such as temperature and voltage. The response values of 960 identical challenges are collected at different temperatures. The average reliability is 99.24%, indicating that the responses to the same challenge in different environments are the same.

Uniqueness means that when the same PUF structure is deployed on different physical entities, it should have a certain degree of distinction. This paper deploys the APUF in the same location of 2 FPGAs and uses the same challenge to extract the CRPs. The average uniqueness is 46.50%, which is relatively close to the ideal value of 50%.

Uniformity means that the PUF response should have sufficient randomness. 10000 different challenges are input to each APUF. The average uniformity is 96.07%, indicating that the proportion of 0 and 1 in the response is the same. **NOTE:** Although the average uniformity of APUF is not 1, wc can choose an appropriate challenge to ensure the uniform distribution of 0 and 1 in response.

4.2 PUF-Based Confused Model Performance

We implement a typical CNN model for classifying face photos on a PC machine with Python and PyTorch. The size of this model is about 274 MB, and there are 3 convolutional layers and 1 fully connected layer, all of which can apply our scheme to achieve parameter confusion.

Prediction Accuracy Performance. Firstly, we evaluate the prediction accuracy of the model. In order to ensure the normal operation and accuracy of the model, if the correct response is input to the model, its prediction accuracy should be the same as the original model before confusion. To protect the IP of the model, if a wrong response is input, the prediction accuracy should be less than the probability of guessing right, in other words, its predicted outcome is meaningless. For each combination of confusion or not, we select 10 random responses as the input of the confusion model to obtain the prediction accuracy of the model and calculate their averages respectively. At least one layer should be obfuscated, so there were only 15 results.

The results are shown in Fig. 2, regardless of the confusion combination, the accuracy of the model run with the correct response is always similar to the original model, but with the wrong response as input, accuracy is always less than 4.0%, with an average of about 2.0%, meaning that the model cannot normally work. According to the accuracy of '0001', '0010', '0100', and '1000', the effect of different layers being confused on the model is the same. Note that the x-axis means a layer is confused or not. For example, '0001' means that only the parameters of the fully connected layer are confused, and the three convolutional layers are not confused, '1010' means that the first and third convolutional layers are confused, and the second convolutional layer and the fully connected layer are not confused. '1111' means that all 3 convolutional layers and 1 fully connected layer are confused.

Security Analysis. On the other hand, the response of APUF will not always be the same due to environmental changes, and the adversary may have so many

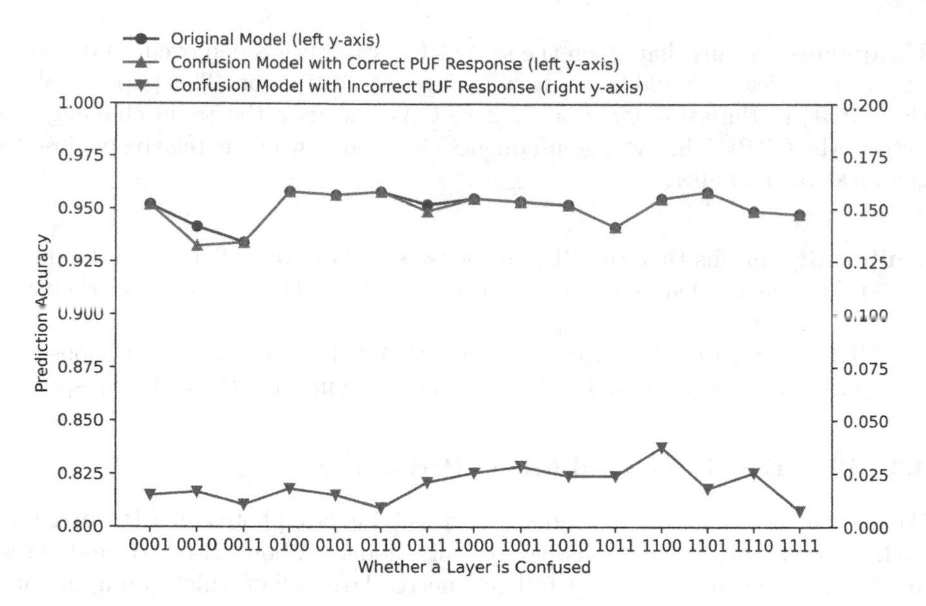

Fig. 2. Prediction accuracy results. From left to right, each bit of x-axis corresponds to the 1st, 2nd, and 3rd convolutional layers and fully connected layer, respectively. 1 means the layer is confused, 0 means not confused.

computing resources that he can try out some bits of the correct response, so we also evaluate how the model's accuracy changes as the *Hamming Distance* (HD) between the random and the correct response decreases. The HD can represent the degree of similarity between two strings, it is calculated as Eq. 2.

$$HD(x, y) = \sum_{i=1}^{n} x_i \oplus y_i \tag{2}$$

For convenience, we use a model with the fully connected layer confused for testing. The model implements the classification of face photos, and the output of the fully connected layer is the probability that the input photo belongs to a certain class. Let the $n = 138$ be the length of the response, and the output of the confused model is a matrix of n rows. We fix the correct response and let the HD change from 2 to n continuously, then generate fake responses with different HD as input to the model, and use the same test dataset to evaluate the model. The results are shown in Fig. 3, the x-axis represents $1 - \frac{HD}{n}$ and the y-axis is the prediction accuracy of the model with a random response. The smaller the HD, the larger the x, and the random response is more similar to the correct one. When the similarity is less than 90%, in other words, the random response and the correct one have 90% of the same bits, the accuracy is still less than 5.0%. When the similarity reaches 97%, the accuracy is about 31.9%, but the probability of an adversary getting a response with at least 97% similarity (at most 4 bits error) is

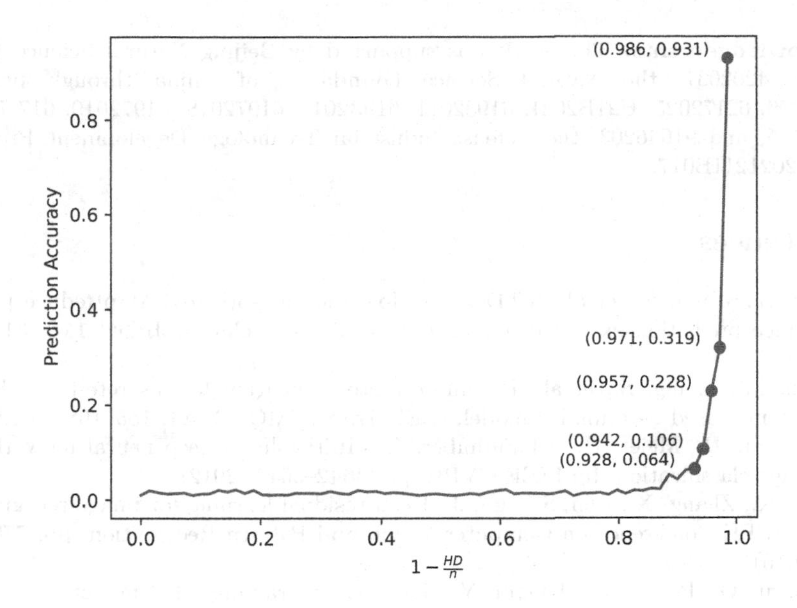

Fig. 3. Prediction accuracy results

$$P = \sum_{i=0}^{4} \frac{C_n^i}{2^n} \tag{3}$$

where C_n^i is the number of combinations. If n is bigger than 64, the probability is negligible. However, the probability is very high for the correct FPGA. There are 2 different bits between the random and correct response, the accuracy of the model is 93.1%, indicating the model is barely affected by response errors.

5 Conclusion

To protect the IP of the CNN model, this paper proposed a PUF-based IP protection scheme for CNN model providers. PUF, as a new type of security primitive, provides a new way to protect model IP without storing any secret keys. As the experimental results show that the performance of the model confused with APUF is almost unaffected, with almost the same prediction accuracy as the original model, but it is impossible for the adversary to compute a response with more than 98% similarity to the correct one. Compared with previous work on IP protection, our method ensures that the adversary is unable to get the correct original model, instead of testing or verifying whether the suspected model is a stolen model after the model has been stolen. Because of the application of PUF, we do not need to store secret keys, which can avoid the risk of key leakage and does not require building an expensive trusted execution environment. Furthermore, since our scheme fine-tunes the model architecture, it can be easily extended to other FPGA-embedded neural network models with similar structures.

Acknowledgements. This work was supported by Beijing Natural Science Foundation: 4202037, the Natural Science Foundation of China through projects 62002006, 62172025, U21B2021, 61932011, 61932014, 61972018, 61972019, 617 72538, 32071775, and 91646203, the Defense Industrial Technology Development Program JCKY2021211B017.

References

1. Lu, Z., Wang, N., et al.: IoTDeM: an IoT big data-oriented MapReduce performance prediction extended model in multiple edge clouds. JPDC **118**, 316–327 (2018)
2. Liu, M., Zhang, S., et al.: H infinite state estimation for discrete-time chaotic systems based on a unified model. IEEE Trans. SMC (B) **44**, 155–168 (2012)
3. Ciregan, D., Meier, U., Schmidhuber, J.: Multi-column deep neural networks for image classification. In: IEEE CVPR, pp. 3642–3649 (2012)
4. He, K., Zhang, X., Ren, S., Sun, J.: Deep residual learning for image recognition. In: IEEE Conference on Computer Vision and Pattern Recognition, pp. 770–778 (2016)
5. Sharir, O., Peleg, B., Shoham, Y.: The cost of training NLP models: A concise overview. arXiv preprint arXiv:2004.08900 (2020)
6. Chen, H., Rouhani, B.D., et al.: Performance comparison of contemporary DNN watermarking techniques. arXiv preprint arXiv:1811.03713 (2018)
7. Darvish Rouhani, B., Chen, H., Koushanfar, F.: DeepSigns: an end-to-end watermarking framework for ownership protection of deep neural networks. In: 24th International Conference on Architectural Support for Programming Languages and Operating Systems, pp. 485–497 (2019)
8. Uchida, Y., Nagai, Y., et al.: Embedding watermarks into deep neural networks. In: ACM International Conference on Multimedia Retrieval, pp. 269–277 (2017)
9. Qiu, M., Gai, K., Xiong, Z.: Privacy-preserving wireless communications using bipartite matching in social big data. FGCS **87**, 772–781 (2018)
10. Shao, Z., Xue, C., et al.: Security protection and checking for embedded system integration against buffer overflow attacks via hardware/software. IEEE Trans. Comput. **55**(4), 443–453 (2006)
11. Zhang, J., Gu, Z., et al.: Protecting intellectual property of deep neural networks with watermarking. In: Asia Conference on Computer and Communications Security, pp. 159–172 (2018)
12. Adi, Y., Baum, C., Cisse, M., et al.: Turning your weakness into a strength: watermarking deep neural networks by backdooring. In: 27th USENIX Security Symposium (USENIX Security 18), pp. 1615–1631 (2018)
13. Guo, J., Potkonjak, M.: Watermarking deep neural networks for embedded systems. In: IEEE/ACM ICCAD, pp. 1–8 (2018)
14. Wu, H., Liu, G., Yao, Y., Zhang, X.: Watermarking neural networks with watermarked images. IEEE Trans. Circuits Syst. Video Technol. **31**(7), 2591–2601 (2020)
15. Szyller, S., Atli, B.G., Marchal, S., Asokan, N.: DAWN: dynamic adversarial watermarking of neural networks. In: 29th ACM International Conference on Multimedia, pp. 4417–4425 (2021)
16. Chen, J., Wang, J., et al.: Copy, right? A testing framework for copyright protection of deep learning models. arXiv preprint arXiv:2112.05588 (2021)
17. Li, Y., Zhu, L., et al.: Defending against model stealing via verifying embedded external features. arXiv preprint arXiv:2112.03476 (2021)

18. Wang, C., Gong, L., et al.: DLAU: a scalable deep learning accelerator unit on FPGA. IEEE TCAD **36**(3), 513–517 (2016)
19. Shawahna, A., Sait, S.M., El-Maleh, A.: FPGA-based accelerators of deep learning networks for learning and classification: a review. IEEE Access **7**, 7823–7859 (2018)
20. Chen, Y., Zhang, K., et al.: T-DLA: an open-source deep learning accelerator for ternarized DNN models on embedded FPGA. In: IEEE Symposium on VLSI (ISVLSI), pp. 13–18 (2019)
21. Sun, P., Cui, A.: A new pay-per-use scheme for the protection of FPGA IP. In: IEEE International Symposium on Circuits and Systems (ISCAS), pp. 1–5 (2019)
22. Khan, N., Nitzsche, S., López, O.: Utilizing and extending trusted execution environment in heterogeneous SoCs for a pay-per-device IP licensing scheme. IEEE TIFS **16**, 2548–2563 (2021)
23. Guo, Q., Ye, J., et al.: PUF based pay-per-device scheme for IP protection of CNN model. In: IEEE 27th Asian Test Symposium (ATS), pp. 115–120 (2018)
24. Qiu, H., Qiu, M., Lu, R.: Secure V2X communication network based on intelligent PKI and edge computing. IEEE Network **34**(42), 172–178 (2019)
25. Qiu, H., Zheng, Q., et al.: Deep residual learning-based enhanced jpeg compression in the internet of things. IEEE TII **17**(3), 2124–2133 (2020)
26. Qiu, M., Zhang, L., et al.: Security-aware optimization for ubiquitous computing systems with seat graph approach. J. Comput. Syst. Sci. **79**(5), 518–529 (2013)
27. Chakraborty, A., Mondai, A., Srivastava, A.: Hardware-assisted intellectual property protection of deep learning models. In: 57th ACM/IEEE DAC, pp. 1–6 (2020)
28. Li, Y., Song, Y., et al.: Intelligent fault diagnosis by fusing domain adversarial training and maximum mean discrepancy via ensemble learning. IEEE TII **17**(4), 2833–2841 (2020)
29. Qiu, H., Qiu, M., Lu, Z.: Selective encryption on ECG data in body sensor network based on supervised machine learning. Inf. Fusion **55**, 59–67 (2020)
30. Pappu, R., Recht, B., Taylor, J., Gershenfeld, N.: Physical one-way functions. Science **297**(5589), 2026–2030 (2002)
31. Lee, J.W., Lim, D., Gassend, B., et al.: A technique to build a secret key in integrated circuits for identification and authentication applications. In: Symposium on VLSI Circuits. Digest of Technical Papers (IEEE Cat. No. 04CH37525), pp. 176–179 (2004)
32. Suh, G.E., Devadas, S.: Physical unclonable functions for device authentication and secret key generation. In: 44th ACM/IEEE DAC Conference, pp. 9–14 (2007)
33. Holcomb, D.E., Burleson, W.P., et al.: Initial SRAM state as a fingerprint and source of true random numbers for RFID tags. In: Conference on RFID Security, vol. 7, p. 01 (2007)
34. Nguyen, P.H., Sahoo, D.P., et al.: The interpose PUF: secure PUF design against state-of-the-art machine learning attacks. Cryptology ePrint Archive (2018)
35. Wang, Y., Xi, X., Orshansky, M.: Lattice PUF: a strong physical unclonable function provably secure against machine learning attacks. In: IEEE HOST, pp. 273–283 (2020)
36. Ruhrmair, U., Solter, J.: PUF modeling attacks: an introduction and overview. In: 2014 DATE Conference (2014)
37. Berger, J.O.: Statistical Decision Theory and Bayesian Analysis. Springer Science & Business Media (2013)

Consistency Regularization Helps Mitigate Robust Overfitting in Adversarial Training

Shudong Zhang[1], Haichang Gao[1](✉), Yunyi Zhou[1], Zihui Wu[1], and Yiwen Tang[2]

[1] Xidian University, Xi'an 710071, Shaanxi, China
hchgao@xidian.edu.cn
[2] Chongqing Three Gorges Medical College, Chongqing 404120, China
tangyiwen@cqtgmc.edu.cn

Abstract. Adversarial training (AT) has been shown to be one of the most effective ways to protect deep neural networks (DNNs) from adversarial attacks . However, the phenomenon of robust overfitting, that is, the robustness will drop sharply at a certain stage, always exists in the AT process. In order to obtain a robust model, it is important to reduce this robust generalization gap. In this paper, we delve into robust overfitting from a new perspective. We observe that consistency regularization, a popular technique in semi-supervised learning, has similar goals to AT and can help mitigate robust overfitting. We empirically verify this observation and find that most previous solutions are implicitly linked to consistency regularization. Inspired by this, we introduce a new AT solution that integrates consistency regularization and mean teacher (MT) strategy into AT. Specifically, we introduce a teacher model derived from the average weights of the student models in the training step. We then design a consistency loss function to make the predicted distribution of the student model on adversarial samples consistent with the predicted distribution of the teacher model on clean samples. Experiments show that our proposed method can effectively mitigate robust overfitting and improve the robustness of DNN models against common adversarial attacks.

Keywords: Adversarial training · Adversarial attacks · Robust overfitting · Consistency loss

1 Introduction

Recent years have witnessed the remarkable success of Deep Neural Networks (DNNs) in many artificial intelligence fields, ranging from speech recognition, computer vision to natural language processing. Despite their excellent performance, DNNs are vulnerable to adversarial attacks [2,7,16], which deceive the models into making wrong predictions by adding imperceptible perturbations

G. Memmi et al. (Eds.): KSEM 2022, LNAI 13370, pp. 734–746, 2022.
https://doi.org/10.1007/978-3-031-10989-8_58

to the natural input. Such a vulnerability can severely threaten many security-critical scenarios, and hinders the real-life adoption of DNN models.

A variety of defense methods have been proposed to improve the robustness of DNNs, e.g., input preprocessing [14,22], defense distillation [12], detection [13], etc. However, most solutions were subsequently proved to be ineffective against advanced adaptive attacks [1,19]. Among these defense directions, adversarial training (AT) [11] is generally regarded as the most promising strategy. The basic idea is to craft adversarial examples (AEs) to augment the training set for model robustness improvement. A standard AT method is to use Projected Gradient Descent (PGD-AT) for AE generation [11]. Later on, more advanced approaches were designed to further enhance the robustness. For instance, TRADES [21] tried to minimize the cross entropy loss for clean samples and KL divergence loss for AEs, to balance the trade-off between model robustness and natural accuracy.

However, AT approaches commonly suffer from one limitation: robust overfitting [15]. During training, the model can exhibit a gap between the robust accuracy of training set and test set, and this gap will gradually increase as the training progresses. Due to this gap, the actual model robustness can be significantly affected. Figure 1 demonstrates this phenomenon for PGD-AT: the robust gap keeps increasing during training (green line), which can harm the model's robust accuracy on the test set (blue line). Hence, it is necessary to reduce such gap in AT.

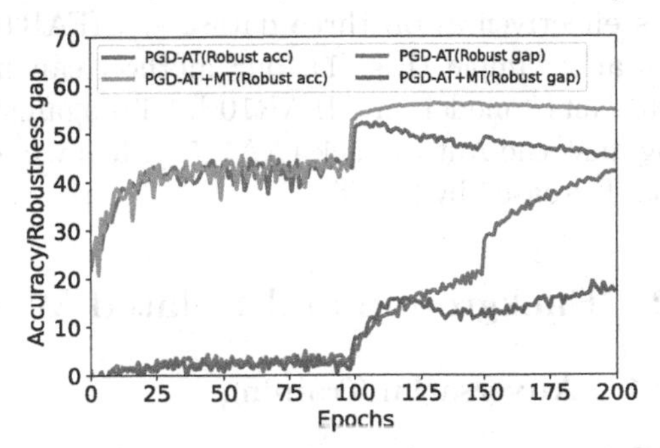

Fig. 1. The robust accuracy and robust generalization gap for PGD-AT without and with our MT method. We train the ResNet18 model with the CIFAR10 dataset. (Color figure online)

Some attempts have been made to understand and resolve the robust overfitting phenomenon. For instance, Rice et al. [15] proposed to use various regularization techniques (e.g. early stopping) to alleviate robust overfitting. Chen et al. [4] integrated self-training into AT to smooth the model. Dong et al. [6] hypothesized that robust overfitting comes from the memorization effect of the model on one-hot labels: as the one-hot labels of some samples are noisy, the model will remember those "hard" samples with noisy labels, leading to a decrease in robustness. However, there is still a lack of general understanding about the overfitting issue, and more effective mitigation solutions are urgently needed.

In this paper, we study the robust overfitting problem from a new perspective. We observe that *consistency loss plays a critical role in alleviating robust overfitting in AT.* Consistency loss has been widely used in semi-supervised learning, to improve the model's confidence in predicting unlabeled data [10]. It forces the model to give the same output distribution when the input or weights are slightly perturbed. This perfectly matches the aim of AT, which forces the model to give the same output distribution for natural or perturbed samples. Therefore, we hypothesize the integration of the consistency loss into the AT loss function can improve the model's robust generalization. We perform experiments from different aspects to validate this hypothesis.

Inspired by the above observation, we propose a new strategy to mitigate robust overfitting. It adopts "Mean Teacher" (MT) [18], an advanced consistency regularization method from semi-supervised learning into AT. Specifically, we introduce a teacher model during training, which comes from the average weights of the student model over different training steps. Then we adopt the consistency loss to make the student model's prediction distribution of AEs consistent with the teacher model's prediction distribution of clean samples. In this way, the trained teacher model is more robust with a smaller robust generalization gap.

Our MT-based strategy is general and can be combined with existing state-of-the-art AT solutions (e.g., PGD-AT, TRADES, etc.) to further improve the robustness and reduce the robust generalization gap. We comprehensively verify its effectiveness on three datasets: CIFAR10 and CIFAR100. Taking PGD-AT as an example (Fig. 1), our method can increase the robust accuracy of the ResNet18 model on CIFAR10 by 4% against the PGD-10 attack, and by 3.79% against the AutoAttack (AA) [5]. Meanwhile, the robust generalization gap can be decreased by 24.64%.

2 Background and Related Works

2.1 Adversarial Training

AT is a commonly used technique for learning a robust DNN model. Its basic idea is to augment the training set with adversarial examples. Formally, we aim to train the parameters $\boldsymbol{\theta}$ of a DNN model f from a given training dataset of n samples: $\mathcal{D} = \{(\mathbf{x}_i, y_i)\}_{i=1}^{n}$, where $\mathbf{x}_i \in \mathbb{R}^d$ is a natural example and $y_i \in \{1, \ldots, C\}$ is its corresponding label. AT can be described as the following two-stage optimization problem:

$$\min_{\boldsymbol{\theta}} \sum_{i=1}^{n} \max_{\mathbf{x}_i' \in \mathcal{S}(\mathbf{x}_i)} \mathcal{L}\left(f\left(\mathbf{x}_i'; \boldsymbol{\theta}\right), y_i\right) \tag{1}$$

where $\mathcal{L}$ is the classification loss (e.g., cross entropy), $\mathcal{S}(\mathbf{x}) = \left\{\mathbf{x}' : \|\mathbf{x}' - \mathbf{x}\|_p \leq \epsilon\right\}$ is the adversarial region with $\mathbf{x}$ as the center and radius $\epsilon > 0$ under the L_p norm (e.g., L_2, L_∞) constraint. The first stage (internal maximization optimization) is to generate the AEs for data augmentation. The second stage (external minimization optimization) is to train a robust model.

PGD-AT. One typical AT strategy is to adopt Projected Gradient Descent (PGD) [11] in the first stage, which starts from a randomly initialized point in $\mathcal{S}(\mathbf{x}_i)$ and iteratively updates it under the L_∞ norm constraint by

$$\mathbf{x}_i' = \Pi_{\mathcal{S}(\mathbf{x}_i)}\left(\mathbf{x}_i' + \alpha \cdot \operatorname{sign}\left(\nabla_{\mathbf{x}} \mathcal{L}\left(f\left(\mathbf{x}_i'; \boldsymbol{\theta}\right), y_i\right)\right)\right) \tag{2}$$

where $\Pi(\cdot)$ is the projection operation, and α is the step size. Then in the second stage, it uses the generated AEs to update the model parameters $\boldsymbol{\theta}$ via the gradient descent algorithm.

TRADES. Zhang et al. [21] introduced TRADES, a new AT strategy to balance the trade-off between robustness and natural accuracy. It maximizes the Kullback-Leibler (KL) divergence between the predicted probabilities of clean samples and AEs, and then minimizes the cross-entropy loss and the adversarial loss at the same time in the second stage. The process can be formulated as

$$\min_{\boldsymbol{\theta}} \sum_{i=1}^{n} \{\mathcal{L}\left(f\left(\mathbf{x}_i; \boldsymbol{\theta}\right), y_i\right) + \beta \cdot \max_{\mathbf{x}_i' \in \mathcal{S}(\mathbf{x}_i)} \mathcal{KL}\left(f\left(\mathbf{x}_i; \boldsymbol{\theta}\right) \| f\left(\mathbf{x}_i'; \boldsymbol{\theta}\right)\right)\} \tag{3}$$

where $\mathcal{KL}$ is the KL divergence and β is used to balance the trade-off.

2.2 Robust Overfitting in AT

Robust overfitting is a common phenomenon in many AT solutions. During training, the model can exihibit higher robustness on the training set than the test set. This robust generalization gap can make AT less effective in defeating adversarial attacks.

A variety of works have investigated the causes behind this issue and tried to resolve it. Chen et al. [4] hypothesized that one reason of robust overfitting is that the model "overfits" the AEs generated in the early stage of AT and fails to generalize or adapt to the AEs in the late stage. Then they leveraged knowledge distillation and stochastic weight averaging (SWA) to smooth the logits and weights respectively to mitigate robust overfitting. Huang et al. [9] empirically observed that robust overfitting may be caused by the noise in the label, and proposed self-adaptive training (SAT) to soften the label and improve the generalization ability. Dong et al. [6] explored the memorization behavior of AT and found that robust overfitting was caused by the excessive memorization of one-hot labels in typical AT methods. They proposed to integrate temporal ensemble (TE) into AT to reduce the memorization effect.

However, the above analysis and defense methods are either not general or effective for improving the robust generalization. In this paper, we try to understand the robust overfitting problem from a different perspective – consistency regularization. It helps us design a more effective solution to alleviate robust overfitting in AT.

2.3 Consistency Regularization

Consistency regularization has been widely used in the field of semi-supervised learning, which can force the model to become more confident in predicting labels on unlabeled data [10,18]. It achieves this goal by encouraging the model to produce the same output distribution when its input or weights are slightly perturbed. For instance, two different augmentations of the same image should result in similar predicted probabilities. In semi-supervised learning, the consistency loss is usually measured by introducing a teacher model, which can be the model itself [10] or its slightly perturbed version [18]. In both cases, the student model measures the consistency of the teacher model.

Given two perturbed inputs $\mathbf{x}'$, $\mathbf{x}''$ of a clean image $\mathbf{x}$ and the perturbed weights of student and teacher models $\boldsymbol{\theta}_s$, $\boldsymbol{\theta}_t$, consistency regularization penalizes the difference of predicted probabilities between the student model $f(\mathbf{x}'; \boldsymbol{\theta}_s)$ and teacher model $f(\mathbf{x}''; \boldsymbol{\theta}_t)$. The loss term typically adopts the Mean Squared Error (MSE) or KL divergence:

$$\mathcal{L}_{\text{cons}}^{\text{MSE}}(\boldsymbol{\theta}, \mathbf{x}) = \left\| f(\mathbf{x}'; \boldsymbol{\theta}_s) - f(\mathbf{x}'', \boldsymbol{\theta}_t) \right\|^2 \tag{4}$$

$$\mathcal{L}_{\text{cons}}^{\text{KL}}(\boldsymbol{\theta}, \mathbf{x}) = \mathcal{KL}\left(f(\mathbf{x}'; \boldsymbol{\theta}_s) \| f(\mathbf{x}'', \boldsymbol{\theta}_t)\right) \tag{5}$$

We observe that *consistency regularization can perfectly match the goal of AT, which attempts to make the model output the same prediction for natural and maliciously perturbed examples.* Therefore, it offers a good opportunity to apply consistency regularization to alleviating robust overfitting. However, there are very few studies focusing on this direction. Tack et al. [17] introduced a consistency regularization into AT to improve the robust generalization, which forces two AEs with different data augmentations from the same sample to produce similar prediction distributions. Different from [17], we perform a more general robustness analysis, and discover that lots of prior solutions can be abstracted as the consistency regularization. We further integrate the consistency regularization commonly used in semi-supervised learning into AT, which forces the clean output of the ensemble teacher model to be consistent with the adversarial output of the student model. This gives us higher robust generalization.

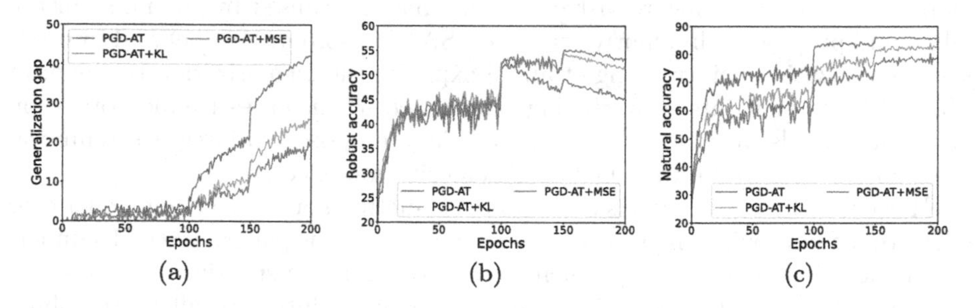

Fig. 2. (a) Robust generalization gap between the training and test sets; (b) Robust accuracy of the test set; (c) Natural accuracy of the test set.

3 AT with Consistency Loss

As discussed in Sect. 2.3, consistency regularization might be a promising strategy to alleviate the robust overfitting issue. In this section, we perform an in-depth analysis to confirm its effectiveness.

We perform comprehensive experiments to show the impact of consistency regularization in reducing the robustness generalization gap. We consider three AT methods. (1) PGD-AT: we adopt the PGD-10 attack with the step size $\alpha = 2/255$ and the maximum perturbation bound $\epsilon = 8/255$ under the L_∞ norm. (2) PGD-AT+KL: we integrate the consistency regularization of KL divergence (Eq. 5) to the loss function of PGD-AT. We use the model itself as the teacher model to measure the consistency loss of prediction probabilities between natural and adversarial examples. (3) PGD-AT+MSE: similar as PGD-AT+KL, we include the consistency regularization of MSE (Eq. 4). For all the three approaches, we train the ResNet18 [8] model on CIFAR10 for 200 epochs. The initial learning rate is 0.1, and decays by a factor of 10 at the $100th$ and $150th$ epochs.

Training and Test Robustness. We measure the robustness of the training and test sets, which is calculated as the prediction accuracy of AEs crafted from these two sets. We have the following observations. First, *the adoption of consistency loss can help reduce robust overfitting.* Figure 2(a) shows the robust generalization gap between the training and test set at different training epochs, which quantifies the robust overfitting degree. We observe that in the first 100 epochs, the robust generalization gap for all these methods is close to zero. After the first learning rate decay, the gap of these solutions increases with the training process. PGD-AT+KL and PGD-AT+MSE has much smaller gap than PGD-AT, attributed to the regularization of consistency loss.

Second, *consistency loss based on MSE has stronger regularization effect and is more effective against robust overfitting than the KL divergence.* In Fig. 2(a), we can see PGD-AT+MSE has smaller robust generalization gap than PGD-AT+KL. Figure 2(b) shows the robust accuracy over the test set for different approaches. We also observe PGD-AT+MSE has higher test robustness than the other two, which results in smaller robust generalization gap.

Third, *strong regularization can also cause a decrease in natural accuracy.* Figure 2(c) compares the natural accuracy of different solutions. We find PGD-AT+MSE has the lowest accuracy on natural samples. This indicates a trade-off between natural accuracy and robust generalization gap.

Average Gradient Norms of Loss Terms. To further understand the importance of consistency regularization, we compute the average gradient norms of the cross-entropy (CE) term $\|\nabla\mathcal{L}_{\text{ce}}\|$ and consistency loss (CONS) term $\|\nabla\mathcal{L}_{\text{cons}}\|$ in the adversarial loss, respectively. Figure 3 shows the trends of these two metrics for different approaches. First, we observe that in the initial training stage, $\|\nabla\mathcal{L}_{\text{ce}}\|$ in PGD-AT+MSE and PGD-AT+KL is larger than

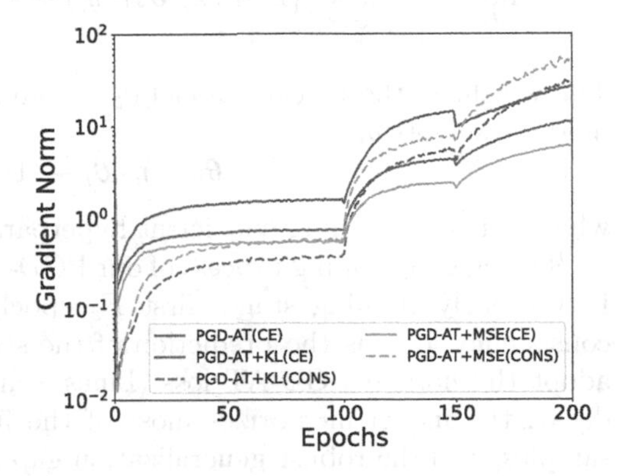

Fig. 3. Gradient norms of the cross-entropy term (CE) and consistency loss term (CONS).

$\|\nabla\mathcal{L}_{\text{cons}}\|$, indicating that the CE loss dominants in the early stage. As the training proceeds, $\|\nabla\mathcal{L}_{\text{cons}}\|$ gradually increases and dominates the training after the 100*th* epoch. Second, in PGD-AT, $\|\nabla\mathcal{L}_{\text{ce}}\|$ continues to increase and always remains at a higher value, which leads to the overfitting in the later stage. In contrast, due to the constraint of consistency loss, PGD-AT+KL and PGD-AT+MSE can alleviate overfitting to certain extent.

4 A New Solution Based on Consistency Regularization

Inspired by the findings in Sect. 3, we propose a new defense methodology, which leverages the Mean Teacher (MT) strategy [18] in semi-supervised learning to enforce the consistency loss during AT. Our method can be integrated with existing AT solutions, e.g., PGD-AT, TRADES, RST [3], MART [20], etc. Evaluations in Sect. 5 show our MT-based AT can outperform prior solutions that are implicitly based on consistency regularization.

Specifically in Sect. 3, we use the trained student model itself as the teacher model to minimize the probability distribution of natural and adversarial examples. However, this strategy is not optimal, because it cannot fully utilize the "dark knowledge", and will result in a decrease in the natural accuracy (Fig. 2(c)). To overcome such limitation, our MT-based AT builds a teacher model from the Exponential Moving Average (EMA) weights of an ensemble of student models, and then adopts it to guide the consistency regularization during training, which can improve the model's robust generalization.

We use PGD-AT to illustrate the details of our methodology. Particularly, for a natural sample $\mathbf{x}_i$, we obtain its corresponding adversarial example $\mathbf{x}_i'$. We calculate the consistency loss between the predicted probability of the teacher model θ_t on the clean sample $\mathbf{x}_i$ and the predicted probability of the student model θ_s on the adversarial example $\mathbf{x}_i'$. Therefore, the training objective of PGD-AT with MT (PGD-AT+MT) can be expressed as:

$$\min_{\boldsymbol{\theta}_s}\sum_{i=1}^{n}\max_{\mathbf{x}_i'\in\mathcal{S}(\mathbf{x}_i)}\left\{\mathcal{L}\left(f\left(\mathbf{x}_i';\boldsymbol{\theta}_s\right),y_i\right)+\lambda\cdot\mathcal{L}_{\text{cons}}\left(f\left(\mathbf{x}_i';\boldsymbol{\theta}_s\right),f\left(\mathbf{x}_i,\boldsymbol{\theta}_t\right)\right)\right\} \tag{6}$$

The weight of the teacher model θ_t is computed from the EMA of the student model's weights θ_s:

$$\boldsymbol{\theta}_t=\eta\cdot\boldsymbol{\theta}_t+(1-\eta)\cdot\boldsymbol{\theta}_s \tag{7}$$

where η is a smoothing coefficient hyperparameter.

The overall training process of our PGD-AT+MT is described in Algorithm 1. In the early training stage (first E_s epochs), it is nonsense to calculate the consistency loss, as the prediction of the student model is not accurate. So we adopt the normal PGD-AT loss (Lines 8 and 15). After the first learning rate decay, the model memorizes most of the internal representation of the input samples, and the robust generalization gap starts to increase (Fig. 2(a)). So we integrate the consistency loss with MT to guide the student model and alleviate robust overiftting (Lines 10 and 18).

Algorithm 1. PGD-AT+MT

Require: training set $\mathcal{D}$; batch size m; learning rate lr; number of training epochs T; PGD step size α; number of PGD steps K; max perturbation budget ϵ; EMA smoothing parameter η; EMA start epoch E_s

Ensure: Robust model weight θ_t

1: Randomly initialize θ_s
2: **for** $t = 1$ **to** T **do**
3: **for** $i = 1$ **to** m **do**
4: Sample $\mathbf{x}_i$ from $\mathcal{D}$
5: $\mathbf{x}_i' \leftarrow \mathbf{x}_i + \epsilon\delta$, where $\delta \sim \text{Uniform}(-1, 1)$
6: **for** $k = 1$ **to** J **do**
7: **if** $t < E_s$ **then**
8: $\mathbf{x}_i' \leftarrow \Pi_\epsilon\left(\mathbf{x}_i' + \alpha\,\text{sign}\left(\nabla_{\mathbf{x}_i'}\mathcal{L}_{\text{ce}}\left(f\left(\mathbf{x}_i';\boldsymbol{\theta}_s\right), y_i\right)\right)\right)$
9: **else**
10: $\mathbf{x}_i' \leftarrow \Pi_\epsilon(\mathbf{x}_i' + \alpha\,\text{sign}(\nabla_{\mathbf{x}_i'}\mathcal{L}_{\text{ce}}(f(\mathbf{x}_i';\boldsymbol{\theta}_s), y_i) + \lambda\mathcal{L}_{\text{cons}}(f(\mathbf{x}_i;\boldsymbol{\theta}_t), f(\mathbf{x}_i';\boldsymbol{\theta}_s))))$
11: **end if**
12: **end for**
13: **end for**
14: **if** $t < E_s$ **then**
15: $\theta_s \leftarrow \theta_s - lr \cdot \frac{1}{m}\sum_{i=1}^{m}\nabla_{\mathbf{x}_i'}(\mathcal{L}_{\text{ce}}(f(\mathbf{x}_i';\boldsymbol{\theta}_s), y_i)$
16: $\theta_t = \theta_s$
17: **else**
18: $\theta_s \leftarrow \theta_s - lr \cdot \frac{1}{m}\sum_{i=1}^{m}\nabla_{\mathbf{x}_i'}(\mathcal{L}_{\text{ce}}(f(\mathbf{x}_i';\boldsymbol{\theta}_s), y_i) + \lambda\mathcal{L}_{\text{cons}}(f(\mathbf{x}_i;\boldsymbol{\theta}_t), f(\mathbf{x}_i';\boldsymbol{\theta}_s)))$
19: $\theta_t = \eta \cdot \theta_t + (1 - \eta) \cdot \theta_s$
20: **end if**
21: **end for**

5 Evaluation

We construct extensive experiments to demonstrate the effectiveness of our MT-based AT in alleviating robust overfitting and improve the model robustness.

5.1 Experimental Setups

Datasets and Models. Our solution is general for image classification tasks with different datasets and models. Without loss of generality, we choose two common image datasets: CIFAR10 and CIFAR100. We adopt the ResNet18 model for evaluation.

Baselines and Training Details. Our solution can be integrated with existing AT strategies. We mainly consider two popular approaches (PGD-AT and TRADES) as the baselines and combine MT for comparisons. We perform adversarial training under the most commonly used L_∞ norm with a maximum perturbation budget $\epsilon = 8/255$. During training, we use the 10-step PGD attack with a step size $\alpha = 2/255$ to optimize the internal maximization. We adopt the SGD optimizer with a momentum of 0.9, weight decay of 0.0005 and train batch size of 128. We train 200 epochs. The initial learning rate is 0.1, and decayed by 10 at the $100th$ and $150th$ epoch.

We use MSE (Eq. 4) to calculate the consistency loss since it performs better than KL divergence (Sect. 3). When integrating our method into PGD-AT or TRADES, the MT consistency regularization is applied when the learning rate

Table 1. The impact of MT on the different datasets and AT approaches.

Dataset	Training strategy	Natural accuracy	Robust accuracy				Generalization gap
			PGD-10	PGD-100	C&W-100	AA	
CIFAR10	PGD-AT	**83.62**	52.25	50.79	49.47	46.96	42.05
	PGD-AT+MT (Ours)	83.56	**56.25**	**55.71**	**52.30**	**50.75**	**17.41**
	TRADES	**82.69**	53.87	53.28	50.69	49.57	26.17
	TRADES+MT (Ours)	82.36	**55.44**	**54.69**	**52.19**	**51.16**	**15.50**
CIFAR100	PGD-AT	56.96	28.78	28.37	26.75	24.13	69.05
	PGD-AT+MT (Ours)	**58.17**	**30.22**	**29.81**	**27.97**	**26.03**	**36.11**
	TRADES	57.14	29.88	29.60	25.29	24.20	52.30
	TRADES+MT (Ours)	**58.20**	**30.69**	**30.44**	**26.59**	**25.72**	**32.86**

decays for the first time. We set the EMA hyperparameter $\eta = 0.999$ and the consistency weight $\lambda = 30$ along a Gaussian ramp-up curve.

A few prior solutions also adopt some regularization methods in the loss function to improve the model robustness and alleviate robust overfitting. We choose them as baselines for comparison as well. Specifically, (1) KD+SWA [4] leverages knowledge distillation and SWA to injecting smoothness into the model weights. (2) PGD-AT+TE/TRADES+TE [6] apply temporal ensemble (TE) into AT to soften the target label. (3) PGD-AT+CONS/TRADES+CONS [17] force the predictive distributions after attacking from two different augmentations of the same instance to be similar with each other.

Evaluated Attacks and Metrics. We consider three popular adversarial attacks to avoid false robustness caused by gradient confusion [1] under the white-box setting: PGD [11] with different steps (PGD-10, PGD-100 with the step size $\epsilon/4$), C&W$_\infty$ (update perturbation with PGD) [2] and AA [5]. Note that AA is an attack suite which also includes a black-box attack. We adopt different evaluation metrics: (1) the model accuracy over the natural samples. This is to measure the model usability. (2) The highest model accuracy over the AEs achieved on different checkpoints during training. This is to measure the model robustness. (3) The robust accuracy difference between the training set and test set under the PGD-10 attack at the last checkpoint. This is to measure the robust overfitting. An effective method should have high natural accuracy and robust accuracy, with small robust generalization gap.

5.2 Effectiveness and Comparisons

Table 1 shows the impact of MT on the adversarial training process. We have the following observations. First, the model with the MT strategy can maintain similar natural accuracy as the original approach. Second, MT can greatly enhance the model robustness against different attacks for most cases. Third, MT can also largely reduce the robust generalization gap and alleviate the robust overfitting.

Table 2 presents the comparisons of our work with other related ones. All the models are trained on CIFAR10. These state-of-the-art methods can effectively reduce the robust generalization gap, and improve the model robustness.

Table 2. Comparison of MT with other related works.

Training strategy	Natural Accuracy	Robust accuracy				Generalization gap
		PGD-10	PGD-100	C&W-100	AA	
PGD-AT	83.62	52.25	50.79	49.47	46.96	42.05
KD+SWA [4]	83.63	53.56	52.97	51.23	49.22	20.77
PGD-AT+TE [6]	82.56	56.03	55.38	**52.50**	50.30	18.76
PGD-AT+CONS [17]	**84.73**	55.64	54.90	51.58	49.16	17.64
PGD-AT+MT (Ours)	83.56	**56.25**	**55.71**	52.30	**50.75**	**17.41**
TRADES	82.69	53.87	53.28	50.69	49.57	26.17
TRADES+TE [6]	**83.88**	54.65	53.89	50.40	48.97	20.30
TRADES+CONS [17]	82.94	55.07	54.38	50.49	49.34	**12.25**
TRADES+MT (Ours)	82.36	**55.44**	**54.69**	**52.19**	**51.16**	15.50

Comparatively, our solution has the highest robustness against most adversarial attacks. This demonstrates the superiority of MT when integrated with AT.

5.3 Ablation Studies

We perform ablation studies to disclose the impact of each component in our proposed method. Without loss of generality, we choose the PGD-AT+MT as the training strategy, and CIFAR10 dataset. We use the PGD-10 attack to evaluate the model robustness.

Impact of Consistency Loss. As discussed in Sect. 2.3, there are mainly two types of consistency loss: MSE (Eq. 4) and KL divergence (Eq. 5). We measure their performance in reducing the robust overfitting. For fair comparisons, we restore the model checkpoint from the 99*th* epoch and then apply the two loss functions respectively. All the other configurations and hyper-parameters are the same. Figure 4 shows the test robustness and robust generalization gap for each loss. We observe that the MSE loss always has slightly higher test robustness, and lower robust generalization gap compared to KL divergence. One possible reason is that MSE can better alleviate the model output overconfident predictions, which could be the cause of robust overfitting [6].

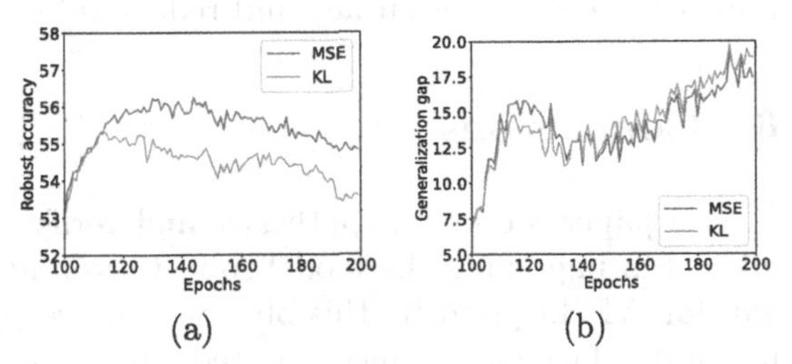

Fig. 4. Comparisons of consistency loss. (a) Test robust; (b) Robust generalization gap

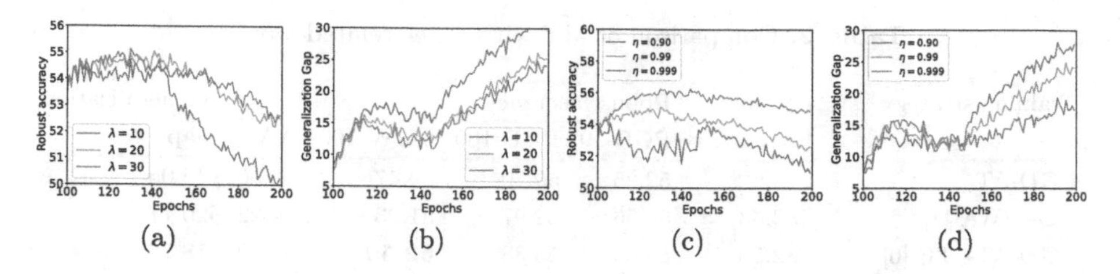

Fig. 5. Impact of the consistency weight and EMA decay. (a) Test robust of λ; (b) Robust generalization gap of λ; (c) Test robust of η; (d) Robust generalization gap of η

Impact of Consistency Weight and EMA Decay. The hyper-parameters of the consistency weight λ and EMA decay η are critical in determining the effectiveness of our proposed method. Figure 5(a) and 5(b) shows the evaluation results with different values of these two hyper-parameters. We fix $\eta = 0.99$ and vary λ as 10, 20 and 30. We can see that a large λ helps reduce the robust generalization gap, and increase the test robustness. In Fig. 5(c) and 5(d), we fix $\lambda = 30$ and vary η as 0.90, 0.99 and 0.999. We observe that the robust generalization gap decreases as η increases, and $\eta = 0.999$ gives the highest test robustness and the smallest robust generalization gap. This is because in the training process, after the first learning rate decay, the test robustness of the student model improves very slowly. So using a larger η can result in a better teacher model with longer memory. Such teacher model can give a more accurate consistency loss. In sum, a larger consistency weight λ and EMA decay η can improve the robust accuracy and reduce robust overfitting.

6 Conclusions

In this paper, we first hypothesize and verify that consistency regularization is critical in improving the model robustness and mitigating robust generalization gap for AT. Inspired by this observation, we propose a self-supervised learning method, which can be incorporated with existing AT approaches to resolve the robust overfitting issue. We introduce and update a teacher model as the Exponential Moving Average weights of the student model across multiple training steps. We further utilize the consistency loss to make the prediction distribution of the student model over AEs consistent with that of the teacher model over clean samples. Comprehensive experiments verify the effectiveness of our method in improving robustness and reducing robust generalization gap.

As future work, we will study the theoretical connection between consistency regularization and robust overfitting, and explore other more effective consistency regularization.

Acknowledgments. This work was supported in part by the National Nature Science Foundation of China under Grant 61972306 and in part by the Zhejiang Laboratory under Grant 2021KD0AB03.

References

1. Athalye, A., Carlini, N., Wagner, D.: Obfuscated gradients give a false sense of security: circumventing defenses to adversarial examples. In: International Conference on Machine Learning, pp. 274–283. PMLR (2018)
2. Carlini, N., Wagner, D.A.: Towards evaluating the robustness of neural networks. In: 2017 IEEE Symposium on Security and Privacy, SP 2017, San Jose, CA, USA, 22–26 May 2017, pp. 39–57. IEEE Computer Society (2017)
3. Carmon, Y., Raghunathan, A., Schmidt, L., Liang, P., Duchi, J.C.: Unlabeled data improves adversarial robustness. arXiv preprint arXiv:1905.13736 (2019)
4. Chen, T., Zhang, Z., Liu, S., Chang, S., Wang, Z.: Robust overfitting may be mitigated by properly learned smoothening. In: International Conference on Learning Representations (2020)
5. Croce, F., Hein, M.: Reliable evaluation of adversarial robustness with an ensemble of diverse parameter-free attacks. In: ICML (2020)
6. Dong, Y., et al.: Exploring memorization in adversarial training. arXiv preprint arXiv:2106.01606 (2021)
7. Goodfellow, I., Shlens, J., Szegedy, C.: Explaining and harnessing adversarial examples, arXiv preprint arXiv:1412.6572
8. Goodfellow, I., Shlens, J., Szegedy, C.: Explaining and harnessing adversarial examples, arXiv preprint arXiv:1412.6572 (2014)
9. Huang, L., Zhang, C., Zhang, H.: Self-adaptive training: beyond empirical risk minimization. In: Advances in Neural Information Processing Systems, vol. 33 (2020)
10. Laine, S., Aila, T.: Temporal ensembling for semi-supervised learning. arXiv preprint arXiv:1610.02242 (2016)
11. Madry, A., Makelov, A., Schmidt, L., Tsipras, D., Vladu, A.: Towards deep learning models resistant to adversarial attacks. arXiv preprint arXiv:1706.06083 (2017)
12. Papernot, N., McDaniel, P., Wu, X., Jha, S., Swami, A.: Distillation as a defense to adversarial perturbations against deep neural networks. In: 2016 IEEE symposium on security and privacy (SP), pp. 582–597. IEEE (2016)
13. Qiu, H., Dong, T., Zhang, T., Lu, J., Memmi, G., Qiu, M.: Adversarial attacks against network intrusion detection in IoT systems. IEEE Internet Things J. **8**(13), 10327–10335 (2021)
14. Qiu, M., Qiu, H.: Review on image processing based adversarial example defenses in computer vision. In: 2020 IEEE 6th Intl Conference on Big Data Security on Cloud (BigDataSecurity), IEEE International Conference on High Performance and Smart Computing, (HPSC) and IEEE International Conference on Intelligent Data and Security (IDS), pp. 94–99. IEEE (2020)
15. Rice, L., Wong, E., Kolter, Z.: Overfitting in adversarially robust deep learning. In: International Conference on Machine Learning, pp. 8093–8104. PMLR (2020)
16. Szegedy, C.: Intriguing properties of neural networks, arXiv preprint arXiv:1312.6199
17. Tack, J., Yu, S., Jeong, J., Kim, M., Hwang, S.J., Shin, J.: Consistency regularization for adversarial robustness. arXiv preprint arXiv:2103.04623 (2021)
18. Tarvainen, A., Valpola, H.: Mean teachers are better role models: Weight-averaged consistency targets improve semi-supervised deep learning results. arXiv preprint arXiv:1703.01780 (2017)
19. Tramer, F., Carlini, N., Brendel, W., Madry, A.: On adaptive attacks to adversarial example defenses. arXiv preprint arXiv:2002.08347 (2020)

20. Wang, Y., Zou, D., Yi, J., Bailey, J., Ma, X., Gu, Q.: Improving adversarial robustness requires revisiting misclassified examples. In: ICLR (2020)
21. Zhang, H., Yu, Y., Jiao, J., Xing, E., El Ghaoui, L., Jordan, M.: Theoretically principled trade-off between robustness and accuracy. In: International Conference on Machine Learning, pp. 7472–7482. PMLR (2019)
22. Zhang, S., Gao, H., Rao, Q.: Defense against adversarial attacks by reconstructing images. IEEE Trans. Image Process. **30**, 6117–6129 (2021)

Author Index

Printed in the United States
by Baker & Taylor Publisher Services